PSYCHOLOGY

FIFTH EDITION

CAMILLE B. WORTMAN
State University of New York at Stony Brook

ELIZABETH F. LOFTUS
University of Washington

CHARLES WEAVER
Baylor University

McGraw-Hill College

Boston   Burr Ridge, IL   Dubuque, IA   Madison, WI   New York   San Francisco   St. Louis
Bangkok   Bogotá   Caracas   Lisbon   London   Madrid
Mexico City   Milan   New Delhi   Seoul   Singapore   Sydney   Taipei   Toronto

McGraw-Hill College

A Division of The McGraw·Hill Companies

PSYCHOLOGY, FIFTH EDITION

This book is printed on acid-free paper.

1 2 3 4 5 6 7 8 9 0 VHN/VNH 9 3 2 1 0 9 8

ISBN 0–07–071931–4

Editorial director: *Jane E. Vaicunas*
Senior sponsoring editor: *Joseph Terry*
Developmental editor: *Elizabeth Morgan*
Marketing manager: *James Rosza*
Project manager: *Sue Dillon/Cathy Ford Smith*
Production supervisor: *Deborah Donner*
Designer: *Gino Cieslik*
Senior photo research coordinator: *Lori Hancock*
Art editor: *Joyce Watters*
Supplement coordinator: *Stacy A. Patch*
Compositor: *GTS Graphics, Inc.*
Typeface: *10/12 Bodoni*
Printer: *Von Hoffmann Press, Inc.*

Cover art/chapter opening art: *Edward A. Butler*

The credits section for this book begins on page C-1 and is considered
an extension of the copyright page.

Library of Congress Cataloging–in–Publication Data

Wortman, Camille B.
  Psychology / Camille B. Wortman, Elizabeth F. Loftus, Mary E.
Marshall. — 5th ed.
     p.   cm.
  Includes bibliographical references and index.
  ISBN 0–07–071931–4 — ISBN 0–07–115869–3 (International ed.)
  1. Psychology.   I. Loftus, Elizabeth F., 1944– .   II. Marshall,
Mary E.   III. Title.
BF121.W67   1999
150—dc21
                                                    98-14650
                                                       CIP

www.mhhe.com

DEDICATION

To my parents, Carol Weaver and the late Charles A. Weaver, Jr., who instilled in me a love of learning and provided a warm and secure environment in which to pursue that passion.
CAW

ABOUT THE AUTHORS

Camille B. Wortman is professor of psychology and director of the training program in social and health psychology at the State University of New York at Stony Brook. Her research interests include causal attribution and reactions to stress and victimization. Wortman has published numerous articles in every major journal in her field, and has contributed chapters to many books, including *Advances in Social Psychology, New Directions in Attribution Research,* and the *Advances in Environmental Psychology* series.

Wortman received her Ph.D. from Duke University in 1972. For seven years she taught introductory psychology at Northwestern University, where she received the Distinguished Teaching Award. A winner of the American Psychological Association's Distinguished Scientific Award for an Early Career Contribution to Psychology, she has also taught and conducted research at the University of Michigan.

Elizabeth F. Loftus is professor of psychology and adjunct professor of law at the University of Washington, Seattle. A specialist in human memory and courtroom procedure, she has been nationally recognized for her research on eyewitness testimony. Her first book on the subject, *Eyewitness Testimony,* won an APA National Media Award, Distinguished Contribution, in 1980. Her most recent book, co-authored with Katherine Ketcham, is *The Myth of Repressed Memory.* Loftus has been an expert witness or consultant in hundreds of criminal cases, including numerous cases involving allegations of repressed memories.

Loftus received her Ph.D. in psychology from Stanford University (1970). She has received three honorary doctorates for her research, from Miami University of Ohio, Leiden University in the Netherlands, and the John Jay College of Criminal Justice in New York. In 1995 she received the American Academy of Forensic Psychology's Distinguished Contributions to Forensic Psychology Award; and in 1996, the American Association of Applied and Preventive Psychology Award for Distinguished Contribution to Basic and Applied Scientific Psychology. Loftus was a James McKeen Cattell Fellow in 1997. She was recently elected President of the American Psychological Society.

Charles A. Weaver III is associate professor of psychology and neuroscience and director of the Ph.D. program in neuroscience at Baylor University in Waco, Texas. His research includes numerous scientific studies of flashbulb memory, eyewitness memory, metacognition, language comprehension, and reading. He is presently preparing a book on flashbulb memory for the Oxford Psychology Series (Oxford University Press).

Weaver received his Ph.D. from the University of Colorado (1988). He has served on the editorial boards of several journals, including *Memory and Cognition,* the *Journal of Educational Psychology,* and the *American Educational Research Journal,* as well as on the scientific advisory board of the False Memory Syndrome Foundation. Students at Baylor University have named him Outstanding Psychology Professor on three separate occasions.

CONTENTS

PREFACE

EVER SINCE THE first edition was published in 1981, *Psychology* has been regarded as the book without gimmicks. As authors, we stressed the empirical and scientific nature of the discipline in an engaging and readable manner. The fifth edition of *Psychology* represents a major revision, the first in more than six years. While long-time readers will see significant improvements in all parts of the text, our basic approach has not changed. *Psychology* introduces readers to the science of psychology, and does so unapologetically.

In the fifth edition we have attempted to capture the excitement we felt when we first encountered this exciting subject. In fact, our experiences in introductory psychology shaped our decisions to pursue psychology as a profession. We find this field to be truly fascinating, and we hope that our enthusiasm for it will kindle the same spark in those who are reading this book for the first time.

Features of this Text

From the first edition, several features have distinguished this book from others. They include: (1) an integration of theory and research with applications; (2) a focus on the process of scientific inquiry—that is, on how psychologists develop testable hypotheses, gather and interpret data, and arrive at conclusions; and (3) discussions of important issues in special In Depth sections. The fifth edition incorporates a new feature, a discussion of four recurring themes in psychology. The four themes are introduced in the In Depth section of chapter 1 (pages 33–35) and are referred to at appropriate points throughout the text.

Integrated Treatment of Theory, Research, and Applications

Some psychology texts have a strong research orientation, which is often achieved at the expense of readability or student interest. Other texts offer extensive coverage of applications and other high-interest topics, whose connection to the science of psychology is not always clear. From the first edition, this book has offered a balanced treatment of theory, research, and applications. We strongly believe that students do not need to be coerced into appreciating the scientific approach to the study of human behavior. And we still think that instructors can make psychology an exciting and engaging field of study without resorting to gimmicks or sacrificing their scholarly integrity.

Focus on the Process of Scientific Inquiry

In the fifth edition we continue to make every effort to emphasize the process of scientific inquiry. Psychologists do not develop theories about human behavior in a vacuum. Instead, they make observations about behaviors, develop explanations (theories) for those behaviors, and then design ways (experiments) to evaluate their explanations. Thus, the path psychologists follow is essentially the reverse of the path most students assume they follow. Psychologists do not develop esoteric theories and then look for ways to apply those theories to the real world. Rather, the real world serves as the inspiration—the guidepost—for the development of psychological theory.

Chapter 2 describes the research process: how psychologists define their research objectives, select a method of inquiry, gather and interpret data, rule out alternative explanations, and deal with the theoretical dilemmas their research sometimes poses. Throughout the book, we repeatedly encourage students to evaluate the theories and research we present for themselves.

In Depth Sections

Perhaps the most important way we try to foster an appreciation for the scientific approach to psychology is through the In Depth sections at the ends of chapters. Most psychology texts offer fairly broad coverage of all the main concepts in the field, without going into much detail. But we felt there was an real advantage to taking a closer look at just a few problems, thus exposing students to the process of psychological inquiry in depth.

Each In Depth section explores a topic that is interesting to students, one that flows directly from the core topics in the chapter. Each is divided into three main parts. In the first, Initial Studies, we discuss the problem and review the early studies designed to address it. In the second part, Criticisms and Alternatives, we discuss how scientists later challenged the early findings, and sometimes arrived at alternative hypotheses. In the last part, Current Thinking, we summarize the latest information on the problem—what is known and widely accepted, and what is still under debate. We make note of studies currently in progress, which have been designed to clarify outstanding questions.

Recurring Themes in Psychology

Many students who enroll in Introductory Psychology are surprised by the course content. They may have expected to learn about abnormal psychology, theories of personality, and psychological therapies, but are often unprepared for discussions of memory, perception, language, learning, and consciousness. Many are bewildered by the array of seemingly different and disconnected topics.

To help students see the commonalties across these subfields, we have added a new feature, Recurring Themes in Psychology. In chapter 1, students are introduced to these four basic themes:

THEME 1 The best predictor of future behavior is past behavior

THEME 2 Psychologists learn about the normal by studying the abnormal

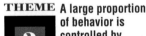

THEME 3 A large proportion of behavior is controlled by unconscious activity

THEME 4 Cognition and thought are dynamic, active processes, best considered reconstructive, not reproductive

Throughout the book we periodically remind readers of these overarching themes. (When themes are reintroduced, they are noted by these icons.) Our hope is

that rather than focusing on the differences among the subfields, students will be able to see the similarities.

What's New in this Edition?

While each new edition of *Psychology* has incorporated important changes in the field, the fifth edition represents the most comprehensive revision ever undertaken. Every chapter has undergone extensive updating. Some—Chapters 2, 3, 5, 6, 7, 9, 11, and 14—are so thoroughly revised, they are essentially brand new. All in all, the fifth edition contains hundreds of new references.

Especially significant to this edition is the expanded, functional coverage of neuroscience, which reflects the increased importance of that branch of the discipline in recent years, and the addition of material on behavioral genetics, also growing in influence. Long-time users of *Psychology* will appreciate the additions and extensive revisions to the In Depth sections.

Expanded, Functional Coverage of Neuroscience

In the last decade, advances in the field of neuroscience have revolutionized the study of psychology. The fifth edition thoroughly incorporates these exciting and important changes. Rather than restricting biologically-based material to a single chapter, we have taken a functional approach, introducing neuroscientific evidence wherever necessary to explain a psychological concept. We think the result is a much more coherent presentation of core material throughout the book. Students will not be left wondering why they need to learn about biology in a course on psychology; instead, its importance will be self-evident.

To illustrate this functional approach, consider chapters 5 and 16. Chapter 5, on consciousness, includes new coverage of dissociations between behavior and awareness, which tend to be seen most dramatically in those who have suffered some kind of neurological trama. Case histories of patients with blindsight and implicit memory help to illustrate the relationship between neural brain structures and consciousness. This chapter also illustrates the role of brain chemistry in consciousness, from the cravings suffered by drug addicts, to the effects of melatonin, an over-the-counter supplement used by millions to induce sleep.

Chapter 16, on psychological therapies, includes a discussion of drug therapies, such as the treatment of depression and obsessive-compulsive disorder with antidepressants. To understand why the newer drugs, like Prozac, are so effective, and why they produce far fewer side effects than the older antidepressants, students must grasp their action as selective serotonin reputake inhibitors. Presented all in one chapter, such technical terms can easily overwhelm students; but presented throughout the book, wherever they are applicable, they are learned much more readily.

Extensive Coverage of Behavioral Genetics

The fifth edition of *Psychology* includes an extensive discussion of behavioral genetics, perhaps the most revolutionary approach to psychology since the cognitive revolution of the late 1950s. As behavioral genetics has grown in influence, it has drawn increasing criticism, most of it based on a flawed understanding of the approach. Chapter 2 therefore contains an extensive discussion of behavioral genetics, including common errors in the interpretation of such data. While we have incorporated coverage of behavioral genetics in the fifth edition, we recognize that these data are often misunderstood or misrepresented. Thus, we have striven to present a responsible as well as thorough discussion of these complicated issues.

As with neuroscience, coverage of specific research in behavioral genetics is distributed throughout the book. For example, chapters 9 and 10 cover the effects of heredity on development and temperament; chapter 11, the genetic factors that influence health and well-being. Chapter 13 contains an extensive discussion of how genetic factors influence personality. Chapter 14 addresses the role of genetics in intelligence, including a discussion (in the In Depth section) of Herrnstein and Murray's highly controversial book *The Bell Curve*. Chapter 15 describes genetic influences on psychological disorders such as schizophrenia and substance abuse, while chapter 18 describes genetic influences on aggression.

New and Revised In Depth Sections

Six of the In Depth sections are new to this edition; each of the others has been revised, updated, and expanded. The In Depth section in chapter 1 introduces the four recurring themes that appear throughout the text. In chapter 2, a new In Depth section focuses on the concept of ecological validity, and the tradeoffs between laboratory experiments and the applicability of their results. Concerns about ecological validity and generalizability are among students' most frequent criticisms of the field of psychology. Thus, this section is designed to answer the perennial question, "What does this have to do with the real world?"

The In Depth section in chapter 5 explores the relationship between cognition, behavior, and awareness through two fascinating case histories, one of the amnesiac H. M., the other of D. B., a patient who suffered from the curious phenomenon of blindsight. Both men displayed powerful dissociations between what they could do and their awareness of what they could do. Neurologically intact individuals can also display such dissociations, as has been shown by Berridge and Robinson's recent analysis of addiction.

A new In Depth section of chapter 7 examines the highly controversial topic of repressed and recovered memory. Two of the authors of this book, Elizabeth Loftus and Charles Weaver, have done primary research on this topic in recent years. Though we have doubts about the psychological reality of repressed and recovered memories, we have attempted to present the evidence on both sides in as evenhanded a manner as possible.

The In Depth section in chapter 9 presents the tragic case of Genie, a modern-day wild child. Though Genie's case has long been familiar to those who teach Introductory Psychology, recently released evidence (including Russ Rymer's book *Genie: Escape from a Silent Childhood* [1993] and a documentary in the PBS *Nova* series) has prompted a re-evaluation of the case.

Finally, a new In Depth section in chapter 14 discusses Herrnstein and Murray's controversial book *The Bell Curve*. The debate over the relative influence of heredity and environment on human behavior is hardly new. In fact, many of the issues raised in *The Bell Curve* have been discussed for twenty-five years or more. Even so, the potential implications of Herrnstein and Murray's work are staggering. We have therefore attempted to present both the evidence and the arguments based on that evidence as dispassionately as possible.

Ancillary Package

The supplements listed here may accompany *Psychology*, fifth edition. Please contact your local McGraw-Hill representative for details concerning policies, prices, and availability, as some restrictions may apply.

Study Guide 0-07-303374-X

Prism CD-ROM (for students) 0-07-303448-7

Instructor's Manual 0-07-038869-5

Test Bank 0-07-071933-0

Computerized Test Bank—Windows 0-07-848017-5

Computerized Test Bank—Macintosh 0-07-848016-7

Overhead Transparencies 0-07-303447-9

PowerPoint Slides 0-07-303450-9

Presentation Manager CD-ROM (for instructors) 0-07-303449-5

McGraw-Hill Learning Architecture 0-07-450959-4

Acknowledgments

To assist us in our revision, we asked some leading scholars to assess the previous edition and suggest places where the text could be improved. Their suggestions proved invaluable, ensuring that the revision would be balanced, complete, and up to date. The expert consultants for the fifth edition included:

Expert Consultants

Lauren B. Alloy
Temple University (chapters 15 and 16)

Lewis M. Barker
Baylor University (chapter 6)

Kristina M. DeNeve
Baylor University (chapters 17 and 18)

Mark L. Pantle
Clinical Psychologist and Director of Research and Development for the McLennan County Challenge Academy (chapters 13 and 14);

Jim H. Patton
Baylor University (chapter 3)

Lee Ann Thompson
Case Western Reserve University (chapter 2).

In addition to the expert reviewers, numerous instructors reviewed larger sections of the manuscript and advised us on their pedagogical usefulness. We are grateful for the candid opinions and constructive suggestions we received from the following reviewers:

Reviewers

Carolyn Ann Cohen
Massachusetts Bay Community College

Steven L. Cohen
Bloomsburg University of PA

Edward C. Chang
Northern Kentucky University

James Pennebaker
Southern Methodist University

M. Shelton-Smith
University of Northern Iowa

Brett Silverstein
City University of New York City College

Todd Zakrajsek
Southern Oregon State University

We also wish to acknowledge the extensive contribution of those at McGraw-Hill. Brian McKean served as the Sponsoring Editor during the most of the actual writing, and was in many respects the driving force behind the fifth edition. Following Brian's departure, Joe Terry saw the project through the final stages with skill and patience. Their editorial assistants, Susan Elia and Susan Kuchandy, were equally capable. Jane Vaicunas, Editorial Director, and Meera Dash, Senior Developmental Editor, provided unwavering support, encouragement, and advice throughout the project, and did so with exceptional grace.

Peggy Rohrberger, Larry Goldberg, and Sue Dillon served as project managers at different points in the project. All three played significant roles in the completion of the fifth edition. Elyse Reider was the photo editor of this and previous editions; her outstanding work can be seen throughout the book. I also wish to thank Jim Rozsa, Senior Marketing Manager.

It would be impossible to overstate the role of Betty Morgan, the developmental editor for the fifth edition, in the shaping of this edition. Her professionalism, skill, and wisdom were vital to the project. She read, critiqued, edited—and *improved*—virtually every paragraph in this book, and she did so with unfailing good humor. It has been, truly, a pleasure to work with her.

Several individuals at Baylor University contributed support and encouragement during the revision process. Bud Barker, through numerous discussions with Chuck Weaver both before and during the revision, helped to shape the new edition. Jim Patton, Helen Benedict, John Flynn, and Mark Pantle were generous with their advice and input. Walter Kintsch of the University of Colorado, who over the years has provided a keen example of the very best in scientific psychology, was also a guiding light.

Finally, Chuck's wife, Lisa, and his two children, Austin and Lindsay, showed enormous patience throughout the writing of the fifth edition. Early on Chuck made a deliberate decision not to allow his role as an author to detract from his more important role as husband and father. Though he never skipped a soccer game or ballet recital in order to write, his children sometimes had to adjust to a very distracted and sleep-deprived father.

—CBW, EFL, CAW

PSYCHOLOGY

CHAPTER 1

The Science
of Psychology

Give me a dozen healthy infants, well-formed and my own specific world to bring them up in and I'll guarantee to take any one at random and train him to become any type of specialist I might select—a doctor, lawyer, artist, merchant-chief, and yes, even beggar-man and thief, regardless of his talents, penchants, abilities, vocations and race of his ancestors. (John B. Watson, 1924, p. 10)

A great nation, founded on principles of individual liberty and self-government, approaches the 21st century. . . . Yet even as the principle of equal rights triumphs, strange things begin to happen to two small segments of the population.

In one segment, life gets better in many ways. These people are welcomed at the best colleges, then at the best graduate and professional schools. . . . After they complete their education, they enter fulfilling and prestigious careers. . . .

In the other group, life gets worse, and its members collect at the bottom of society. Poverty is severe, drugs and crime are rampant, and the traditional family all but disappears. . . .

. . . the nation's social scientists and journalists and politicians seek explanations. They examine changes in the economy, changes in demographics, changes in the culture. They propose solutions founded on better education, on more and better jobs, on specific social interventions. But they ignore an underlying element that has shaped the changes: *human intelligence.* (Richard J. Herrnstein & Charles Murray, 1994)

Psychology is the greatest failure of the 20th century. Psychology, it seems to me, has made us all these grand promises, which it has been manifestly unable to fulfill. We have placed in psychology the faith that our fathers placed in God, in country, in *doing what was right.* Psychology has largely supplanted the concepts of manhood and honor and eaten into literature and manners, but what has it done for us? We were all supposed to gain insight into ourselves, to understand why we are who we are and what we can do about it. We're more confused about who we are than we've ever been. (James, 1991)

These three quotes provide very different views of "psychology." They also reveal much about how psychology is perceived by the general public. The first quote is from John B. Watson, a pioneering figure in psychology during the first half of the twentieth century. His opinion is clear: the science of psychology provides the tools to understand—and manipulate—all behavior.

The second quote is taken from the recent book *The Bell Curve,* by Richard Herrnstein and Charles Murray (1994). Herrnstein was a psychologist at Harvard, Murray his colleague at the American Enterprise Institute. Their book examines the role of intelligence in virtually every aspect of life. Herrnstein and Murray present hundreds of pages of facts, dozens of tables and figures, in an attempt to show that "intelligence" (defined in any number of ways):

- Is predictive of economic and social success

- Is stable throughout the life span
- Has a significant genetic component (intelligent parents tend to produce intelligent children)

The Bell Curve has triggered a vigorous, intense debate. What is "intelligence"? What does it mean to say it has a strong genetic component? What, if anything, can be done to "improve" intelligence? The answers to these questions have far-reaching implications. Indeed, the controversy generated by *The Bell Curve* will be the focus of the "In Depth" section of Chapter 14.

Look back at the final quote. Who would you suspect wrote it? A television newscaster, in a documentary about "the failed promise of psychology"? A politician, arguing that we need to get experts out of the school system and return our children to traditional family values? A member of the clergy, reacting to the growth of self-help groups in a time when "we need to return to spiritual values"? Perhaps the author is a disgruntled psychologist, offering a critical appraisal of the field?

Actually, the quote is taken from a book on *baseball* by Bill James (1991, p. 152) and is discussing a player who never lived up to expectations because of "emotional problems." He interrupts his evaluation of the player to deliver this resounding criticism of the entire field of psychology. Obviously, he believes that the role of psychology is to "fix" people, or at least help them. However, he makes a common mistake: assuming that psychology is about changing people for the better.

For many people, "psychology" is synonymous with "psychotherapy." To them, a psychologist is someone who interprets a client's dreams, decoding the hidden meaning in the symbols. According to this view, a psychologist offers suggestions for how to change behavior—how to overcome the "emotional problems" that are hindering a baseball player, for example. But most people realize that not all psychologists perform therapy.

What else do you know about psychologists? You may have an image of a psychologist in a white lab coat, coaxing a rat through a maze. You may know that psychologists are employed to administer intelligence and aptitude tests. For example, a psychologist might tell an employer what a certain score on a standardized test means, or may provide advice on the most suitable candidate for a specific job. You may know that psychologists are consulted about what kind of reading program would be best for six-year-olds. "Psychology," in fact, covers a vast number of topics—many more than are listed here.

What is psychology? What kinds of things does psychology study? What do psychologists *do*? And what does psychology have to do with life in the "real world"? This book is designed to answer those questions, and many more questions you might not even think to ask. Much of what you "know" of psychology is likely to be incorrect, or at least incomplete. The goal of this book is to help you understand what psychology is all about, and to do so in a way that conveys its inherent interest. After all, what could be more fascinating than human behavior?

Psychology as a Science

Psychology, broadly defined, is the scientific study of behavior, both external observable action and internal thought. Such a definition has important implications. The first, and one whose significance is easy to miss, is that *psychology is a science*. This might seem odd. Somehow psychology doesn't seem as "scientific" as chemistry or physics. Where are the test tubes, the microscopes, the laboratory equipment? After all, psychologists don't study "scientific things" like photosynthesis or nuclear radiation. They study the effects of the presence of books in the home on the development of children's reading skills, or the effect of being watched by six experts on performance of a complex task. Psychologists study why animals who are exposed to certain chemicals before they are born have difficulty learning to avoid being shocked, or are less likely to form attachments to their offspring. These things aren't "science," are they?

The answer is that science is defined not by *what* is studied, but by *how* it is studied. *Science is a process*, a method of obtaining and organizing knowledge. Psychologists use the systematic methods of science to gather information about the things that interest them. Once they have collected their data, psychologists carefully analyze them and interpret their meaning as objectively as possible.

Another assumption implied by this broad definition is that *not all behavior is directly observable*. Some behavior—such as motivation, emotion, or thought—is internal, and therefore much more difficult to study. For much of psychology's history, in-

In March 1995, Jonathan Schmitz and Scott Amedure appeared on the Jenny Jones show, where Schmitz believed he was going to meet the woman of his dreams. Instead he discovered that Amedure, a gay man, had a crush on him. Three days after the show, Schmitz walked into Armedure's house and killed him. Was Schmitz aggressive and violent, troubled by stressful events in his life, or simply seething with anger over his humiliating experience on the television show? Psychologists cannot always explain unobservable behaviors like motivation and emotion.

ternal behavior was considered outside the realm of psychology. If psychologists could not directly observe and measure thought, this reasoning went, it could not be studied scientifically. During the past few decades, most psychologists have come to believe that internal events can be studied, if sometimes in indirect ways.

Scientific Theories in Psychology

The process of science hinges critically upon **scientific theories.** Theories are attempts to go beyond a single case or experiment, and provide a larger explanation that applies to many situations. Theories allow psychologists to answer—or attempt to answer—"why" questions: *Why* do drugs like Prozac alleviate many symptoms of depression? *Why* do young children prefer five small pieces of candy to four large pieces? *Why* does Alzheimer's disease affect some types of memory (such as the memory for relatives' names) while leaving other types of memories intact (such as the memory for how to speak grammatically)? *Why* are some individuals more likely to act aggressively than others? Theories at-

tempt to provide explanations, to answer these "why" questions.

One hallmark of scientific theories is that they are *verifiable.* In order to be scientific, a theory must make predictions that can be *tested.* If a theory cannot make testable predictions, it is not a scientific theory. It may still be useful in some ways, but it cannot be considered scientific. (Exactly how psychologists can best test theories involves some knowledge of research methods, which will be covered in Chapter 2.)

Science and Theories: Three Warnings

Scientific methods have allowed psychology (as well as other disciplines) to make tremendous progress. This book takes a scientific approach to psychology throughout, because it provides a set of methods for answering most questions. Psychologists work by forming theories, deriving predictions from those theories, testing the predictions, and then modifying the theories.

As valuable as scientific theories are, however, they have three potential limitations:

1. Though science allows for theories to be proved incorrect, scientists can never prove a theory correct. That is simply not the way science works.

2. Not all theories are scientific theories. Most theories allow predictions to be made. If those predictions cannot be *tested,* a theory is not scientific.

3. Even theories that have been rejected (that is, proved false) can still be useful. Even incorrect theories can be helpful if they direct scientists to ask interesting questions, or if they form the basis for new theories.

Science Can Never Prove a Theory Correct

The scientific process works backward in some respects. Though theories are developed because scientists believe they are correct, scientists can never *prove* a theory is correct. Ironically, the scientific process works by identifying situations in which predictions are *incorrect* —not by generating theories and proving them correct.

Many times a scientist will make certain predictions, and later research will show those predictions to be accurate. But even if a theory's predictions are confirmed by later experiments, the theory has not been proved correct. Scientists may find evidence that supports a certain theory. They may perform many experiments that support a given theory. But scientists realize that some future experiment may show a flaw in their theory. When you hear someone say that a theory has been "proved correct," they have made a cardinal scientific error. Scientists may say that a theory has been "supported," or that an experiment has produced results that are "consistent with" a theory. But scientists cannot prove theories correct.

Not All Theories Are Scientific Theories

In psychology and in other domains, many theories are not scientific because they make predictions that cannot be tested. Sigmund Freud, perhaps the most influential figure in all psychology, developed many theories. However, some of Freud's key theories cannot be scientifically tested, because they do not make empirical (verifiable) predictions. These, then, are not scientific theories.

For example, Freud (correctly) observed that adults have very few conscious memories from the first three or four years of their lives. This phenomenon, called *childhood amnesia*, is discussed in Chapters 7 and 9. Freud explained this by saying that such memories are psychologically threatening to adults, and are thus kept from conscious awareness. Freud called this process of forgetting *repression*. The memories are still "there," but because of their content, they are not accessible.

How would we test such a prediction? Remember, for a theory to be scientific, we must be able to provide evidence to *test* it. What kind of evidence could we collect that would show Freud's theory of repression to be *incorrect*? We might ask adults to recall their earliest memories. (Remember, we cannot prove it correct.)

Freud's theory predicts that adults should have no memories of events that happened at age three. If some subjects in our study could recall events from age three (which some likely would), wouldn't that prove Freud's theory to be incorrect? Not necessarily. The theory predicts that only "threatening" memories will be repressed. Perhaps the remembered events were not sufficiently threatening, and so were not repressed. In other words, there is nothing we can do to prove this theory incorrect. Therefore Freud's theory of repression is not a *scientific* theory.

This is a subtle distinction that is frequently overlooked. As you study this book throughout the semester, you will become a much more critical consumer of psychology. When you are evaluating a theory, ask yourself, "What kind of evidence could I collect that might show this theory to be incorrect?" Any theory that cannot be tested in this way is by definition not a scientific theory.

Before leaving this example, we should point out that the topic of repressed memory is quite controversial in contemporary psychology. To what extent does research support the process of repression? Chapter 7 presents an "In Depth" study of this question.

Theories Do Not Have to Be Correct to Be Useful

This may seem odd: how could a theory that is *wrong* be useful to psychologists? Good theories are useful because they provide explanations that cover the results of a number of different experiments.

However, theories can be useful in other important ways. They can guide research and prompt psychologists to ask interesting questions. For example, a popular theory from the mid-1970s involved hyperactivity in children (now called *attention deficit hyperactivity disorder, DSM IV*). According to Feingold (1975), the primary cause of hyperactivity in these children was their diet. Feingold believed the additives and colorings in food caused (or at least contributed to) hyperactivity. His book was very influential. Parents modified their children's diet to restrict additives and colorings, while psychologists rigorously tested the effects. In the process, they looked not only at the effects of additives but at the effects of other dietary factors like sugar and caffeine. Despite its initial popularity, however, Feingold's theory was not supported (see Swanson & Kinsbourne, 1980, for a review). Psychologists no longer consider food additives to contribute to hyperactivity in children. Yet Feingold's theory was useful to psychologists because it directed their attention to dietary factors in hyperactivity. While food colorings and additives do not contribute to hyperactivity, other substances (such as caffeine) may.

Common Sense and Science

There are certainly ways of "knowing" other than through science. For instance, people often rely on *intuition* and *common sense*. Aren't other sources of information just as reliable as science? Generally, they are not. Knowledge derived from those sources has never been put to a systematic test. Instead, it is simply accepted as logical and right. Scientific

John Demjanjuk at his trial in 1988. Demjanjuk was accused of being "Ivan the Terrible," a notorious Nazi war criminal who tortured and murdered thousands of Jews at the Treblinka concentration camp during World War II.

A passport photo of Demjanjuk, taken in 1951, nearly ten years after his alleged crimes. Can jurors identify a criminal from photographs taken many years later? Psychologists who studied this case could not answer that question.

knowledge, in contrast, has always been tested systematically.

Even so, people tend to rely on common sense in their approach to psychology. Indeed, our common sense beliefs often persist even when evidence shows they are wrong. Gary McClelland, a social psychologist at the University of Colorado, once remarked that he found teaching a course in social psychology frustrating. When students learned about studies that confirmed commonsense beliefs (such as the adage that "birds of a feather flock together"), they dismissed the results as trivial: "Of course! *Everyone knows* that 'birds of a feather flock together!'" But when commonsense beliefs (such as "opposites attract") were shown to be incorrect, students dismissed those, too: "The research must be wrong. *Everyone knows* 'opposites attract!'"

There are many examples in psychology in which commonsense explanations have been proved wrong. In other situations, common sense can make contradictory predictions. For example, most people assume that their memory for faces is quite good. Indeed, memory for faces seems to be persistent over long intervals (Bahrick, Bahrick, & Wittlinger, 1975). But how good is your memory for faces if you haven't seen a particular face in thirty or forty years? Can you recognize a face, even if it is forty years older than it was the last time you saw it? Would it help if the person was well known to you forty years ago?

Common sense may say, "Yes, you'll be able to recognize that face! Faces don't change that much. You might forget the name–*everyone knows* that names are harder to remember than faces—but you'll certainly be able to recognize the person." On the other hand, common sense might say, "No, you won't be able to recognize the person, even if you knew the person well. Forty years have passed, and

everyone knows a person's face changes dramatically with age. If you were able to recognize the person, it would be a lucky guess."

What does your common sense tell *you*? *Everyone knows. . . .*

For John Demjanjuk, a factory worker from Cleveland, this question was more than a simple exercise. Demjanjuk was accused of being "Ivan the Terrible," a notorious Nazi war criminal who tortured and murdered thousands of Jews at the Treblinka concentration camp during World War II. Identified by survivors of the concentration camp, Demjanjuk was tried by the state of Israel, found guilty in 1988, and sentenced to death.

The eyewitness identification of Demjanjuk was critical to his conviction. However, several aspects of the trial concerned psychologists. First, only eight of the possible eyewitnesses (from perhaps as many as twenty-nine who were questioned) positively identified Demjanjuk as "Ivan." (Those who did not identify him were not asked to testify.) Furthermore, the survivors made their identification from a lineup of photos taken sometime after the end of World War II. One of these was John Demjanjuk's immigration photograph, which was taken in 1951, nearly ten years after any of the eyewitnesses had seen Ivan.

Now stop and ask yourself what common sense tells you. The witnesses had not seen "Ivan" for nearly fifty years. The photo of Demjanjuk they saw was taken nearly ten years after their last contact with Ivan. Is human memory so good that after fifty years, a face now fifty years older is still recognizable? On the other hand, would victims of cruel and inhumane torture *never* forget the face of the man who inflicted such pain? Clearly, common sense could support either interpretation.

As you become a skilled consumer of psychology, you will find yourself answering such questions with your own question: "What does the research say?" Many times examining others' research will answer your questions. Sometimes you may find that the data simply don't exist.

Maggie Bruck, Patrick Cavanagh, and Stephen Ceci (1991) found themselves in just such a situation. After Demjanjuk was convicted, they asked, "Is it reasonable to expect people to recognize faces from photographs, given the constraints in the Demjanjuk case?" At the time, psychologists couldn't answer this question. Bruck, Cavanagh, and Ceci began looking for answers.

Bruck and her colleagues could not re-create all of the elements of the Demjanjuk situation. However, they were able to identify a similar situation, one that most of us experience in our lifetime: high school reunions. Both Bruck and Cavanagh went to the same high school in Montreal, graduated within a year of each other, and became leading experimental psychologists. As the twenty-fifth anniversary of their high school graduation approached, they realized the reunion would offer them a chance to test their classmates' memories.

Bruck and her colleagues created a booklet of photographs. On each page they placed five high school pictures, each taken from the yearbook. On the facing page they displayed ten pictures taken the month before the reunion. Five of those pictures were photographs of the five classmates shown in the yearbook photos. The other five were foils, photographs of the same gender and age. Before the reunion, Bruck and Cavanagh distributed the booklets to those who had gone to their high school and knew the people in the old photographs. For a comparison, they gave the same booklets to another group whose members did not know anyone in the photos.

Before reading on, answer these questions using common sense:

1. Is it possible to compare photos taken twenty-five years apart and match people "then" and "now"? (If so, even the group that did not know anyone in the photos should have performed well.)

2. Would those who know the people in the photos do better than those who do not know them? (If so, the classmates should have done better than the comparison group.)

Now take a look at the faces in Figure 1-1. On the left are five photos taken in 1965. On the right are ten photos taken in 1990: five are the same people, five are new people. Match the five faces on the left with the faces on the right. The answers are given at the end of the chapter.

Bruck, Cavanagh, and Ceci found that those who had once known the people in the photos were better able to match the old with the new photos. However, even those who did not know the people in the photos were able to perform significantly better than chance. What bearing does their research have in the Demjanjuk case? The comparison isn't perfect, but it may be as close as we can get. In Ivan's case, witnesses were given a lineup of photos including one photo of Demjanjuk taken ten years after any of the witnesses had last seen him. Of the sixteen witnesses questioned, only eight identified the 1951 photo as the man they called "Ivan" (Wagenaar, 1988, as cited in Bruck, Cavanagh, & Ceci, 1991).

Does the research of Bruck and her colleagues prove that Demjanjuk and "Ivan" were the same man? Or does it prove that the witnesses were wrong, and Demjanjuk was innocent? Of course, it can do neither. But while the research is inconclusive, Bruck and her associates state, "Our findings raise potential concerns about the accuracy of the identifications in the Demjanjuk case" (p. 227).

The state of Israel recently overturned the conviction of John Demjanjuk. The court decided that the identifications made at his trial were inconclusive.

The Ongoing Nature of Science

The case mentioned above is just one example of how science progresses. The responses of other psychologists to a colleague's work take several forms. Some criticize how the initial studies were conducted. They might find flaws in the design of the research. For example, in the identification example described above, less than 50 percent of the subjects (the actual classmates of Bruck and Cavanagh) responded to the questionnaire. Were those who attended more likely to be the "successful" classmates, and therefore more likely to be identified? Were those who did not respond more likely to be those

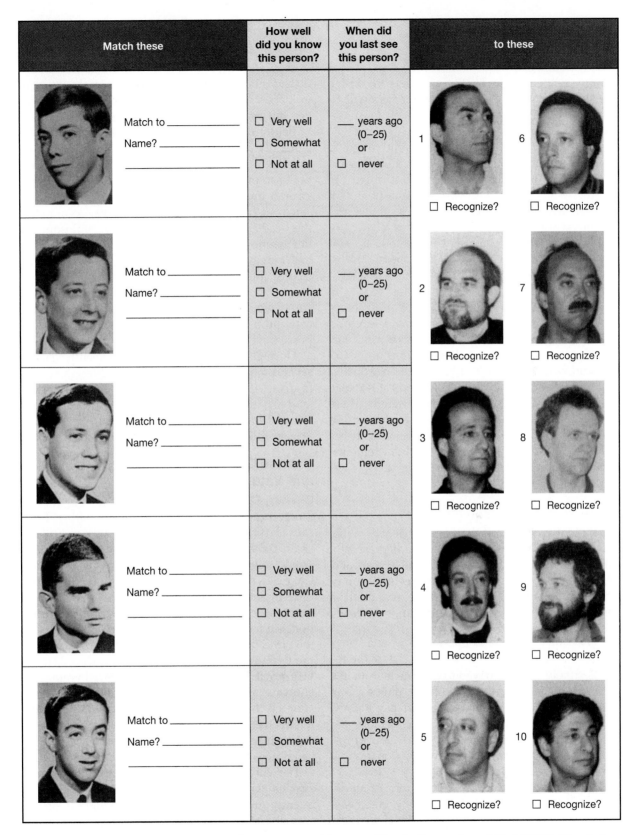

FIGURE 1-1   *Photos used in the twenty-five-year recognition test of Bruck, Cavanagh, and Ceci (1991). The photos on the left were taken from the high school yearbook; those on the right were taken just prior to the twenty-fifth high school reunion. Match the faces on the left with those on the right. (Answers on page 34.)*

who remembered very little? Every research design has shortcomings; ideally, other researchers will attempt to eliminate those shortcomings in subsequent research.

The theme of science as a dynamic, ongoing process is found throughout this book. In particular, each chapter has a concluding section called "In Depth," which deals with complex questions that are particularly important. Most of these "In Depth" sections are like "progress reports." They take a close look at particularly intriguing research questions—the ways investigators have tackled them, the discoveries they have made, and how other psychologists have reacted to their findings. Most of the "In Depth" sections are divided into three subsections: "Initial Studies," which explains how research on the topic began; "Criticisms, Alternatives, and Further Research," which describes reactions to the initial studies on the part of other psychologists; and "Patterns and Conclusions," which indicates where scientific knowledge on the topic now stands. These subsections stress how one idea leads to another and how scientists gradually build on research that has gone before. Only in this relatively slow, incremental fashion does scientific knowledge expand.

The Roots of Psychology

Psychology is a relatively young science. While chemistry and physics have been studied for centuries, psychology was founded about 100 years ago. Despite the short formal history, however, the questions psychologists have been asking over the past century have been asked for thousands of years, starting with the ancient Greeks.

The Influence of Philosophy

Intellectually, psychology derives much from the field of philosophy. Indeed, the Greek philosophers dealt with questions familiar to modern psychology: the mind/body problem, the nature of memory and language, and ways of thinking and "knowing." Many current theories in psychology rest on foundations laid by Socrates and Aristotle.

But psychology differs from philosophy primarily in its methodological "tools." Philosophy relies heavily on reasoned argument and principled discussion. Most philosophical issues are not empirical ones; that is, they are questions that cannot be answered by the methods of science. What is the meaning of life? Why

do bad things happen to good people? Is there a set of universal ethical principles? Important questions, yes, but ones that science cannot answer.

Before the end of the nineteenth century, it was generally assumed that the questions psychology might address—the nature of thought, the role of experience in behavior, and so on—could not be answered by the scientific methods either. After all, since one could not measure events that occur inside the head, those were best left to the philosophers. Furthermore, conventional thinkers considered human beings to be special, because of either divine decree or intellectual superiority. Whatever might be learned from studying the behavior of animals surely would not apply to humans, who were far too complicated, capable of independent thought and possessing free will.

During the middle part of the nineteenth century, several monumental scientific breakthroughs began to dispel these myths. Perhaps the most important (and also the most misunderstood) was the publication of *The Origin of Species*, by the naturalist Charles Darwin (1859).

Charles Darwin's Theory of Evolution and Natural Selection

Charles Darwin was born into an upper-class nineteenth-century British family. His father, Erasmus Darwin, was a well-known scientist in his own right. Young Charles Darwin gave few signs that he would follow in the scientific footsteps of his father. Charles was a mediocre student, showing little aptitude or interest for medicine, the career that had been chosen for him. Finally, Charles found a position as a naturalist on a five-year sea voyage aboard the HMS Beagle, which set sail in late 1831. During the five years he traveled aboard the ship, Darwin was struck by the differences he noticed among organisms and by how well the organisms had adapted to the specific environments in which they lived. Over the course of the next twenty years, Darwin refined, revised, and contemplated what would be known as the theory of evolution.

Darwin's theories on the origin and evolution of species were influential, controversial, and frequently misunderstood when *The Origin of Species* was first published (1859). Today, nearly 150 years later, they remain influential, controversial—and frequently misunderstood. However, no understanding of human behavior is complete without an understanding of the inherited components of behavior. Virtually all scientists agree that Darwin's theory of evolution by natural selection provides the most comprehensive explanation of the role of inherited influences on behavior. Remarkably, Darwin's theories were developed entirely without the knowledge of even basic genetic mechanisms. In fact, Gregor Mendel's seminal work on genetics was not published until after Darwin's death!

Heredity, Variability, and Natural Selection

Darwin's theory of evolution contained three major principles: heredity, variability, and natural selection. The principle of heredity expresses the fact that characteristics are passed from one generation to the next. Tall parents tend to have tall children; dogs with short tails tend to have puppies with short tails. These traits tend to get passed from parent to offspring. The principle of variability refers to the fact that virtually every characteristic varies across members of a species. Some members of a species are bigger than others; some learn more quickly; some have more acute vision.

Because of variability, some individuals will be more successful in their environment than others. Darwin's greatest insight was his recognition of this fact. He realized that in nature, more members of a species tend to be born than the environment can support. There is seldom enough food, water, or mates for all the members of a species to thrive. Darwin said that when the demand for them exceeds the environment's resources, selective pressure forces competition for the scarce resources.

To account for changes in species over time, Darwin proposed the mechanism of *natural selection*, known popularly as "survival of the fittest." That is, only those members of a species who are able to compete successfully for limited resources will survive and reproduce, thereby increasing the chance that their characteristics will survive in future generations. Those who cannot compete successfully will die, and the traits that prevented them from competing successfully will die with them.

To illustrate, take the characteristic of neck length in the giraffe. According to the principle of heredity, parents who have longer necks will pass that characteristic on to their offspring. Those with shorter necks will pass that characteristics to *their* offspring. But the principle of variability dictates that neck length will vary among giraffes. Even giraffes born

*Portrait of **Charles Darwin,** the British naturalist whose book* The Origin of Species *(1859) introduced the theory of evolution by natural selection. Darwin's highly influential theory helped to create the scientific environment in which the new science of psychology was born.*

to the same parents will likely vary in the lengths of their necks.

In the giraffes' environment those with longer necks have an advantage: their extra length allows them to reach the tops of trees so they can eat the leaves that grow there. In this environment, then, giraffes with longer necks are more likely to survive and reproduce than those with shorter necks. Their longer necks will be passed to future generations. Fewer of the giraffes with shorter necks will survive and reproduce. Through the gradual influence of natural selection over time the members of a species with the advantageous characteristic—in this case, giraffes with longer necks—will become more numerous.

Given this example, you may wonder why giraffes are not even taller than they are. If a 12-foot neck means access to more food, shouldn't a 20-foot neck be even better? The answer is that while longer necks convey some advantages—access to more food, for example—they also have some disadvantages. For example, a longer neck might make movement for a giraffe more difficult, slowing a giraffe's escape from predators. It might also make it difficult for a giraffe to stoop to drink water. At some point the disadvantages of a longer neck will outweigh the advantages. When that happens, natural selection begins to operate *against* those giraffes with longer necks. Thus, a dynamic balance exists in nature.

In sum, Darwin's theory of natural selection offers a complete, unifying theory of inherited characteristics. To understand why an organism has a certain trait, Darwin suggested we ask, "What survival and reproductive advantage does that trait convey?"

Two Common Errors in Interpreting Darwin

Probably no figure in the history of science is as recognizable, or as controversial, as Charles Darwin. Most of us have at least a rudimentary knowledge of what evolution means. Unfortunately, Darwin is also among the most misunderstood of all scientists. Two common errors preclude an understanding of the real implications of the theory of evolution by natural selection. The first error is assuming that *evolution* means "progress." The second is assuming that *survival of the fittest* means "survival of the strongest."

Perhaps the most common misunderstanding is that as species evolve, they improve. Such an understanding also implies that evolution will reach an end point, where improvement is complete. Indeed, it is common to believe that humans *are* this end point, the finished product of evolution.

In reality, evolution simply means change and adaptation to an environment. If the environment changes, some species will be more successful than others. Some will *adapt* to that environment better than others. This does *not* necessarily mean that the species which survive are *better*; it simply means they are *better adapted*.

For this reason, we avoid terminology referring to one organism being "more highly evolved" or "more advanced" than another. This implies evolution progresses, and that newer adaptations are improvements. However, we sometimes say a species has behavior that is "more specialized," or "more recently evolved." These descriptions make reference to the evolutionary history, but do so without indicating that one is better than another.

For example, let's look at human language. Language is often said to be a "more advanced" or "more highly evolved" form of communication. This is misleading. It is true that human language is a more recently evolved form of communication. It is also true that in the environment in which we presently find ourselves, human language offers some real advantages. Doesn't that make human language more "highly evolved," or more "advanced"? In short, doesn't that make human language *better*?

The answer is "No, it doesn't." Human language is well suited to the environment in which humans find themselves. If the environment should change, human language might be a less effective form of communication. If humans somehow found themselves in an environment radically different—say, one in which there was very loud background noise constantly present—human language might be less effective than other forms of communication. It would no longer provide a selective advantage.[1]

What does "survival of the fittest" really mean? *Fit* means, simply, "best able to survive and reproduce in the environment." It has nothing to do with physical strength per se. Certainly physical strength would be an asset in many situations—but not always. For example, assume that we have two different types of dogs: one is physically larger and stronger than the other, has a more aggressive nature, and is willing to fight if threatened by a competitor. The second dog is smaller, thin and lean (rather than strong), timid by nature, and more likely to run when threatened. Which of these is most likely to survive and reproduce?

As you may now realize, it's impossible to say. In some environments the strong, more aggressive dog might be more successful. If the competitors can be driven away through physical force (or the threat of force), indeed the "stronger" animal might be more "fit."

But there may be other environments where fleeing from the threat is more successful. If the threat cannot be physically defeated, it may be more successful to run. If two dogs encounter a rattlesnake, which will be the most likely to survive? The aggressive dog who tries to kill the snake? Or the more timid dog, who is more likely to run away? Clearly, the aggressive dog is not always more likely to survive and reproduce.

Application of Darwinian Theory to Psychology

By adopting Darwin's evolutionary perspective, psychologists gained valuable insight into human behavior. Such a perspective recognizes that humans

---

[1]A movie from a number of years ago, *Wait Until Dark,* provides an excellent example of this. In the movie, a young blind women (Audrey Hepburn) is being stalked by a drug dealer (Alan Arkin). The drug dealer can see, while the woman cannot—an obvious advantage for the killer. During the climactic scene, as the killer enters the young woman's apartment, the environment has suddenly changed: the young woman has taken all the lights out of her apartment, and everything is now completely dark. The killer's ability to see, which was such an obvious advantage in the lighted environment, is no longer helpful. The man's perceptual abilities haven't changed, though; the *environment* has. Nonetheless, the man's sight no longer offers him an advantage. Until . . . well, I don't want to spoil the ending for you.

are but one species within a behavioral continuum, subject to the same kind of selective pressures as other organisms. We are *part* of the continuum, not "above" it. And since we share so many characteristics with other species—similar brain structures, similar behavior, and so on—we can study the behavior of those species to learn something about our own behavior.

You may have wondered why psychologists are so interested in rats. Darwin's theory of evolution by means of natural selection provides an answer. Obvious (though largely superficial) physiological differences aside, rats and humans are remarkably similar. Both are mammals, with similar physiology. Their internal organs are similar in structure and function, and they have similar brain structures that communicate with each other in similar ways, leading ultimately to similar behaviors. The same chemicals that transmit brain signals in humans transmit signals in rats. Many experiments that could not be performed on humans, for practical and ethical reasons, can be performed on related animals like rats.

Human brains are larger than rat brains, of course. But when brain size is compared to body size, most of those differences disappear. In fact, the greatest difference between the human brain and the rat brain is in the size of the *neocortex*, the outermost covering of the brain, generally associated with complex thought and reasoning. Figure 1-2 shows the brains of several different animals. Once neocortex (shown in light color) is removed, the brains appear quite similar.

Darwin theorized that humans, monkeys, and rats have fairly recent common ancestors: all are mammals. As a result, they have evolved common structures, and the more recent the common ancestor, the more similar the structures. Darwin's "common ancestors" hypothesis is often interpreted as meaning that humans descended from monkeys. This is *not* the correct interpretation of the term (see Dawkins, 1986, 1996). *Any* two species have common ancestors, if we are willing to go back far enough. To say chimpanzees are close genetic relatives means that our common ancestor lived fairly recently (several million years ago). We share a common ancestor with every living species—but in some cases, that common ancestor lived hundreds of millions of years ago.

Perhaps the most immediate impact of Darwin's work in the emerging discipline of psychology was to position humans *within* the animal kingdom, rather than *above* it. Human behavior, then, could be studied just as the behavior of other organisms. In a practical sense this made available the methods of science to the new domain of psychology.

Popular acceptance of Darwinian evolution did not come quickly or easily. Just as the work of the early astronomer Galileo was attacked by religious leaders of his time, so too was the work of Darwin. Theologians believed that the human spirit (or soul) had free will, and therefore could not be governed by the laws of nature. Many also believed that humans were created to be superior to other living beings. Darwin's theory challenged both those ideas, inciting a strong and vocal reaction. A letter to the editor written to *Time* magazine put it this way: Galileo was criticized for proclaiming that the earth was not the center of the universe; Darwin was criticized for proclaiming that *humans* were not the center of the universe (*Time,* Mar. 19, 1984).

A Short History of Psychology

Psychology, it has been said, has a long past but a short history. Humans have always asked questions about the mind. But while psychology's philosophical roots may go back thousands of years, empirical approaches to these same questions date back just over 100 years.

Psychology in the Nineteenth Century

The emerging field of psychology was not enthusiastically embraced in all quarters. The criticisms came not only from those with moral or philosophical objections but also from fellow scientists. Those scientists simply believed that the workings of the human mind were unobservable. As such, the scientific method was inappropriate. (A similar philosophy would be adopted in the first half of the twentieth century, as the behaviorist position became dominant in psychology.)

Not surprisingly, the first psychologists did not start out to be psychologists. Hermann von Helmholtz (1821–1894) was a physicist who became interested in perception and its relationship to the nervous system. Helmholtz's early experiments are generally considered the first truly empirical psychological studies. Gustav Fechner (1801–1887) (another German physicist) was a contemporary of von Helmholtz who also studied perception. Fechner

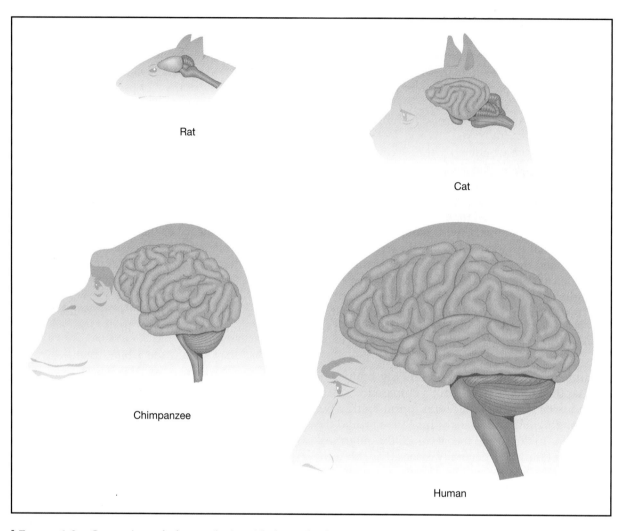

FIGURE 1-2   *Comparison of a human brain with those of a chimpanzee, cat, and rat. The human brain has a much larger neocortex, but most other structures are similar in appearance.*

was particularly interested in the relationship between physical stimulation—like the frequency of a tone, which can be measured physically—and its psychological perception—in this case, the pitch of the tone. Fechner pioneered the field of *psychophysics*, the formal study of the relationship between "sensation" (stimuli in the physical world) and "perception" (the internal, psychological interpretation of the stimuli). We will examine Fechner's work, and the work that came after his, in Chapter 4.

Though Helmholtz and Fechner are important figures in the history of psychology, many psychologists date the discipline's birth to 1879, when the first psychological laboratory was established. It was set up by Wilhelm Wundt at the University of Leipzig in Germany, who was probably the first person to call himself a psychologist. Wundt would go on to write a tremendous number of papers and books: he is estimated to have written more than 50,000 pages in his lifetime. Wundt's ideas shaped the first two decades of academic research in psychology, and his influence is still felt today.

Wundt's Structuralism: The Basic Elements of the Mind

Wundt (1832–1920) was dissatisfied with the theoretical arguments of philosophers who studied the mind. He believed mental processes could be

*Hermann von Helmholtz, the German scientist who was the first to investigate the relationship between **perception** and the human **nervous system**. His early experiments are often considered the first truly empirical psychological studies.*

Wilhelm Wundt, the founder of modern psychology. Wundt established the first laboratory dedicated exclusively to the investigation of human mental processes, in Leipzig, Germany. He also taught the first course in scientific psychology.

investigated with objective techniques similar to those used by scientists in other fields. Wundt deliberately set out to create a "new domain of science" (Wundt, 1904). His laboratory was officially established in the fall of 1879, and in the decades that followed researchers in Wundt's laboratory flourished. By 1897 his lab was so large it was moved to a new building constructed for the express purpose of doing psychological research (Hothersall, 1984).

Wundt and his students aimed to analyze human consciousness and identify its most basic elements. They approached the fundamental building blocks of cognition and thought much as chemists approached the building blocks of matter, molecules, and atoms. The principal components of consciousness, they believed, were what ultimately combined to form the structures of the mind. Because of their emphasis on mental structure, their perspective came to be known as **structuralism.**

Wundt pioneered a technique known as "introspection"—literally, "examining within." Introspection involves systematic observation of what is going on inside the mind, and the subsequent breakdown of those observations into their component structures. Structuralists strove to describe such introspective insights in their simplest terms. Though today psychologists consider introspection to be subjective and somewhat unreliable, during Wundt's time it was accepted as objective and scientific. (See Ericsson & Simon, 1980, for a modern look at useful introspective techniques.)

Wundt and his students conducted studies on a broad range of topics: sensation and perception, attention, emotion, and word association, to name a few. They strove to be systematic and precise in their

measurements, using a variety of laboratory instruments in their research. In this regard, Wundt is justifiably considered the founder of modern psychology.

Wundt's ideas influenced an entire generation of psychologists. Many of his students went on to become prominent researchers in their own right, establishing laboratories and departments of psychology across Europe and the United States. One of them, Edward Tichener (1867–1927), started a psychological laboratory at Cornell University. Like Wundt, Tichener believed that psychologists could best understand human consciousness by identifying its components. Tichener argued that the principal components of consciousness were fundamental sensations and feelings, which ultimately combine to form the structure of the mind.

James's Functionalism: The Uses of the Mind

Two years before Tichener began working at Cornell, an American psychologist at Harvard published what was to become one of the most influential books in all psychology. William James's *Principles of Psychology* (1890/1950), a massive volume that took James over ten years to write, was filled with provocative insights about topics such as human habits, emotions, and consciousness. James (1842–1910) had been educated as a philosopher. Though his introspective methods would not be considered scientific by today's standards, they were pioneering in their time. Even today, James's work remains remarkably influential.

James was clearly influenced by Darwin's theory of evolution by natural selection. One of the insights that influenced him was the adaptability of behavior. Since some elements of behavior are retained over succeeding generations, they must continue to be

William James, the author of Principles of Psychology, *one of the most influential books on psychology ever published.*

useful. James, therefore, focused on the functions of behavior rather than the structures, an approach that has become known as **functionalism.** Functionalists stressed the uses mental processes serve, emphasizing the dynamic operations of the mind, rather than its more static components. James maintained that consciousness was not "chopped up in bits," but was rather a continuous whole that flowed like a stream. He believed the human mind was constantly adapting to new information from the environment, performing the vital function of mediating between the environment and a person's needs.

Structuralists and functionalists were soon debating the proper subject matter for their new and growing discipline. With the turn of the twentieth century, however, other perspectives began to emerge. Eventually they overshadowed the debate between structuralism and functionalism. Even so, elements of the debate remain. For example, memory theorists argue about the relative importance of memory structures and memory processes. Clinical psychologists debate whether abnormal behavior is better understood by looking at basic causes (a structuralist approach) or at the kinds of problems it creates (a functionalist approach). And personality theorists disagree on whether they should concentrate on the basic components that make up an individual's personality or the way in which those components influence behavior. Table 1-1 compares the structuralist and functionalist approaches.

The Early Twentieth Century

The structuralist/functionalist debate waned toward the end of the nineteenth century. Rather than continuing an unproductive debate, psychologists

began to move in new and exciting directions. Throughout the twentieth century, several theoretical perspectives have been developed, five of which have proved to be especially important. At some point in the past century, each of the five could claim to be the dominant perspective in psychology. More importantly, contemporary thought is still shaped by these perspectives.

The first was the **psychoanalytic perspective,** derived primarily from the work of Sigmund Freud. Psychoanalytic theory explains behavior by postulating powerful unconscious wishes and conflicts. The second major viewpoint is the **behaviorist perspective,** which asserts that environmental stimuli shape and control an individual's actions. These two perspectives dominated early twentieth-century psychology.

Two major perspectives arose to counter the psychoanalytic and behaviorist viewpoints. **Humanistic psychology** developed during the middle and later parts of the twentieth century largely in response to the somewhat pessimistic and negative psychoanalytic theory. Rather than explain behavior in terms of hidden motives, this perspective stressed the striving for self-fulfillment and growth as the prime motivators of behavior. Obstacles that thwart human fulfillment and growth were thought to cause psychological difficulties. Another perspective, **cognitive psychology,** developed in the late 1950s and early 1960s, in part as a result of growing dissatisfaction with the behaviorist perspective. Finally, a fifth, **neuroscience,** explains thoughts, feelings, and behaviors in terms of the workings of the brain and nervous system. The biological component in psychology has always been important. Many early psychologists like Helmholtz and Fechner began their studies by examining the relationship between physiology and behavior. In recent years neuroscience has grown even more influential—so much so that former president George Bush, at the urging of the scientific community, declared the 1990s the "Decade of the Brain."

Unlike structuralism and functionalism, these five perspectives are not necessarily mutually exclusive. Psychologists now realize that no one perspective offers the one right explanation of behavior. Rather, each has its own strengths and weaknesses. Furthermore, different perspectives often explain behavior at different levels, a matter we will discuss later in this chapter.

| TABLE 1-1 *Comparison of the Structuralist and the Functionalist Perspectives*

Theoretical Perspective	Major Historical Proponents	Theoretical Emphasis	Techniques for Acquiring Information	Examples of Current Influence
Structuralism	Wilhelm Wundt (in Europe) Edward Tichener (in America)	Identifying the basic elements ("structures") of consciousness and thought	Introspection (verbal descriptions)	*Personality theory:* Are basic building blocks of personality? *Memory theory:* How many kinds of "memory" are there?
Functionalism	William James	What is the relationship between the person and the environment? How are consciousness and thought used?	Introspection Comparative studies using animals as subjects Pragmatic methods (essentially, anything that worked)	*Personality theory:* How are different personality characteristics used in behavior? *Memory theory:* What are the kinds of processes used in memory?

Sigmund Freud and the Psychoanalytic Perspective

Sigmund Freud (1856–1939) is perhaps the most recognizable figure in psychology. Ironically, Freud was not trained as a psychologist; he was a physician whose specialty was *neurology* (the study of disorders of the brain). Through his work as a neurologist, Freud came into contact with some patients whose complaints did not arise from traditional neurological deficits, like stroke or brain damage. In fact, their problems had no obvious physiological causes. Through years of observation and study, Freud came to suspect that many of those patients' problems were psychological in origin. In response to his observations, he developed a complex and sophisticated model of human behavior known as *psychoanalytic theory,* and from this theory he developed the treatment known as **psychoanalysis.**

Most beginning students of psychology have formed some impression of Freud from popular culture. For example, many of Woody Allen's movies spoof psychoanalysis as a pessimistic approach relying on hidden motives and conflicts, often sexual in nature. As a result, many people react negatively to psychoanalytic theory. You may be tempted to reject it yourself, based in part on the cartoonish carica-

tures of Freud often seen in popular media. Resist the temptation. While contemporary psychologists reject many of Freud's theories, they remain impressed by his powerful insights into behavior.

Freud's impact on psychology was enormous. He realized the power of anxiety (psychological

Sigmund Freud, *one of the dominant figures in 20th-century psychology. Freud's psychoanalytic theories emphasized the unconscious determinants of behavior; even today, his approach to the treatment of psychological disorders influences psychologists.*

Hermann Ebbinghaus, the German psychologist who developed one of the first objective techniques for studying memory.

discomfort caused by internal conflict) as a motivator for behavior. He was also one of the first to recognize the lifelong effects of early childhood experiences. In addition, Freud recognized that much of human behavior is influenced by events longer consciously remembered—an insight confirmed by contemporary psychologists (e.g., Roediger, 1990).

Watson, Skinner, and Pavlov and the Rise of Behaviorism

The roots of behaviorism can be found in the ancient Greek philosophy known as associationism. Associationism explained behavior and thought by studying the relationships that have formed between concepts. The words *doctor* and *nurse,* for example, are psychologically "close" in some sense. They frequently occur together, they refer to similar concepts, and so on. Central to this approach is the fact that these associations are formed through experience. If two individuals do not share the same experiences, it is unlikely they will form the same associations.

The British philosopher John Locke belonged to the associationist tradition. Locke's notion of the mind as a *tabula rasa* (literally, a "blank slate") is a prime example. Essentially, Locke maintained that at birth an individual is a "blank slate" on which experience is written. But though a child enters the world prepared to form associations, the content of those associations will depend on the child's personal experiences. The very nature of the human mind, then, depends upon experience.

A more formal psychological approach to the effects of experience developed toward the end of the nineteenth century. The German psychologist Hermann Ebbinghaus (1850–1909) applied the principles of associationism systematically in his memory experiments. Using himself as a subject, he learned thousands of lists of meaningless items (such as the nonsense syllables "DAX," "MIP," and "WEF"), noting the associations he formed between the items. Ebbinghaus developed a number of objective techniques for measuring those associations, techniques that did not depend on introspection. His monumental work will be discussed in more detail in Chapter 7.

Edward Thorndike (1874–1949), a student of William James, was in some respects the link between classic associationists and modern behaviorists. Like his mentor James, Thorndike adopted a functionalist perspective. He was one of the first psychologists to study the behavior of nonhuman animals in an attempt to discover universal laws of behavior. (Thorndike's experiments and conclusions will be discussed in Chapter 6.) Historically, his work prepared the ground for two later psychologists, John B. Watson (1878–1958) and B. F. Skinner (1904–1990).

Reread the quote from Watson that opened this chapter. Watson believed not only in the power of association and experience but also that behavior is determined almost entirely by environmental forces. To Watson, the domain of psychology was clear: *psychologists should study only those things that can be directly observed and verified.* He had no use for introspection, in which subjects provide detailed accounts of their current states of consciousness, because there is no way to measure or verify the accuracy of those reports.

Because behaviorists were looking for universal "laws of behavior," it made little difference to them whether their subjects were students in a classroom, infants in a playpen, or rats in a cage. According to behaviorism, all organisms behave according to similar psychological principles. Watson and other behaviorists also realized that understanding behavior meant controlling *every* aspect of an organism's environment. Because such rigorous control is not possible with humans (for ethical as well as practical reasons), Thorndike, Watson, and others pioneered the use of nonhuman animals in laboratory work—a technique still in use today.

Working at the same time as Thorndike and Watson was a Russian physiologist named Ivan Pavlov (1849–1936). Like many pioneers in psychology, Pavlov was not trained as a psychologist. In fact, his most enduring legacy—his discovery that dogs sali-

Edward Thorndike (left), founder of behaviorism, *the study of observable behavior without reference to mental processes.* **John B. Watson** *(center), whose forceful support made behaviorism the most influential theory in psychology during the first half of the twentieth century.* **B. F. Skinner** *(right), whose systematic investigations into behavior dominated the field of psychology for decades.*

vate in anticipation of being fed—came out of his study of the physiology of digestion.[2] Pavlov noticed that after a lab technician had fed the dogs a few times, the dogs would salivate *in expectation of* receiving the food. An astute scientist, Pavlov realized that this anticipatory response (which he colorfully termed "psychic secretion") was more interesting than the digestive process. Abandoning his work on digestion, Pavlov devoted the rest of his career to studying this type of learning, called *classical conditioning*. Pavlov's remarkable work and classical conditioning will be described more thoroughly in Chapter 6.

Pavlov's work, which first became known in the United States during the 1920s and 1930s, influenced a young American psychologist, B. F. Skinner. Skinner believed that all human behavior could be understood by studying the relationships between stimulus and response, a position known as *radical behaviorism*. Even more forcefully than Watson, Skinner argued for keeping "the mind" out of psychology. Because it could not be seen or measured, Skinner often referred to the mind as "the black box": it was an inappropriate subject for study.

To illustrate the behaviorist position, imagine yourself arriving home at the end of the day. As you put your key in the lock, your dog begins barking, wagging her tail and jumping up and down. When you open the door, she rushes to you with her leash in her mouth. Is she happy to see you? Angry at you because you left her? Eager to go for a walk? Fearful of some noise in the house? All of these? According to Skinner, none of these conclusions is valid. All rest on inferences about your dog's internal thoughts, which cannot be measured. And since they cannot be measured, Skinner would argue, psychologists should not study them. Instead, Skinner would focus on your dog's behavior and the stimuli that control that behavior. Though you cannot say that your dog is happy to see you, you can say that putting the key in the door (the stimulus) is followed by your dog's barking and tail wagging (the behavior). Inferring something about your dog's internal state is unnecessary to the study of behavior.

The Russian physiologist **Ivan Pavlov.** *While researching the physiology of digestion, Pavlov observed that dogs salivate in* anticipation *of receiving food. His investigation of the behavior led to the study of classical conditioning.*

---

[2]Pavlov was later awarded the Nobel prize for his work on the physiology of digestion.

Carl Rogers (left) and *Abraham Maslow* (right), founders of **humanistic psychology,** an alternative to Freudian theory that emphasized the inherent goodness of people.

The Middle Twentieth Century

In the early part of the twentieth century, Freud's psychoanalytic theories dominated clinical practice. In the academic world, Skinner's radical behaviorism was equally powerful. For a while, virtually all theories of learning and behavior had psychoanalytic or behaviorist origins. But as psychologists began to test all the implications of those two theories, many became dissatisfied.

Humanistic Psychology; Dissatisfaction with the Psychoanalytic Perspective

Psychoanalytic theories explained human behavior by postulating unconscious, hidden conflict. Later, during the 1950s, humanistic psychologists developed an alternative to psychoanalytic theory. Humanistic psychology emphasized the importance of conscious, rather than unconscious, motivations for behavior. Grounded in the ideas of free will and choice, it was directly opposed to the more rigid determinism of psychoanalysis. Humanistic psychologists also stressed the positive aspects of psychological development, emphasizing the basic good in people.

Perhaps the most influential of the humanistic psychologists were Abraham Maslow (1908–1970) and Carl Rogers (1902–1987). Maslow arranged human needs in a hierarchy from basic to higher needs. He proposed that basic needs—such as those for food, water, and safety—must be met first. Ultimately, though, humans were motivated by the need for **self-actualization,** the desire to achieve their full potential. Difficulties arose when obstacles prevented a person from achieving self-actualization.

Humanistic psychologists develop new therapeutic techniques, too. Among the most influential was Carl Rogers' client-centered therapy, an approach that contrasted sharply with psychoanalysis. While the psychoanalytic therapist was a detached, critical interpreter, humanistic therapy depended on the therapist showing empathy and understanding for a patient. Certainly a humanistic therapist might be critical of certain behaviors, but should never doubt the basic "goodness" of people. Rogers called this *unconditional positive regard.*

The Cognitive Revolution; Dissatisfaction with Behaviorism

A second new approach was a reaction against radical behaviorists like Skinner, who regarded cognition (literally, "thought") as outside the realm of psychology. During the 1950s, psychologists began to doubt the usefulness of Skinner's exclusively behavioral positions. Though Skinner had rejected the study of "the black box" of the mind, others thought the "black box" was exactly what *should* be studied. This new discipline, which came to be known as cognitive psychology, addresses topics like memory, language, thought, problem solving, and decision making. Scientific revolutions happen slowly, and can be seen clearly only in retrospect. With the benefit of nearly forty years of hindsight, we can see that a number of events of the late 1950s (wonderfully recounted by Gardner, 1985) triggered what is now called the "cognitive revolution" in psychology.

In Europe, though, several psychologists anticipated the cognitive revolution. Sir Frederick Bartlett (1887–1969), an English psychologist, published his book *Remembering: A Study in Experimental and Social Psychology* in 1932 (Bartlett, 1932). Bartlett observed that long-term memory for information was not a passive process. Rather, the subjects that he studied would actively interpret events; and their memories of the events often changed over time.

To explain these memory distortions, Bartlett introduced the concept of **schema**—an internal mechanism for organizing, remembering, and recalling information. Schemas allow humans to understand and interpret events, rather than merely store rote memory. Furthermore, humans use these schema to retrieve memories. As such, memories are better viewed as reconstructions of the original events

THE FAR SIDE   By GARY LARSON

**"Stimulus, response! Stimulus, response!
Don't you ever *think*?"**

Jean Piaget, the Swiss psychologist who emphasized the role of schemas in human cognition and development.

rather than reproductions. Bartlett's concept of the schema and his constructivist view of cognition remain tenets of modern cognitive theory.

Jean Piaget (1896–1980), a Swiss contemporary of Bartlett, studied cognition in children. Like Bartlett, Piaget believed that humans understand and actively interpret information using schemas. He also believed that schemas underwent a dramatic transformation as young children developed. To Piaget, children understood the world in an entirely different way from adults. For example, a six-month-old infant does not respond to "hide-and-seek" games the way an eighteen-month-old child would. If a parent hides a toy from a six-month-old by putting the toy behind a book, the young infant will act as if the toy is "gone." The child will not look behind the book expecting to find the toy. An eighteen-month-old child, however, will look behind the book. If a parent distracts the child and removes the toy from behind the book, the child reacts with bewilderment on discovering it is not there. According to Piaget, this difference in behavior reflects the different schemas the two children use. The older child is

thinking in a way that the younger child cannot. She has a sense of *object permanence* and realizes that the toy is "still there"—or should be—even when it is hidden. For the younger child "out of sight" is literally "out of mind."

In 1956, Jerome Bruner and his colleagues in a book *A Study of Thinking* (Bruner, Goodnow, & Austin, 1956) examined the process of *concept formation*. We easily form abstract concepts such as "tools used for writing" even though the concepts are never formally taught. How are these concepts learned? Bruner and his colleagues developed simple but clever tasks to study the process.

Suppose someone has created a "rule" for classifying games: perhaps rules like "games that use balls" or "games played by individuals and not teams." Some games (like baseball) meet the rule and belong in the category. Others (like swimming) do not meet the rule and so are not members of the category. The subject's task is to figure out what classification rule is being used. Figure 1-3 demonstrates concept learning.

According to associationistic theories, concepts will form gradually. Over a number of trials, the combination of correct and incorrect answers gradually shapes the concept. Behaviorists would expect concepts to be refined incrementally, in a relatively passive process. Bruner and his colleagues found something altogether different. Subjects in their experiments did not learn concepts in a gradual fashion. Instead, concept formation was a dynamic, constructive process. Subjects generated hypotheses as to the concept rule and sought to confirm those hypotheses. Sometimes this hypothesis testing led to rapid, correct learning. On the other hand, sometimes subjects formed incorrect hypotheses

I FIGURE 1-3   *Example of concept formation.*

Game	Member of Category?
1. Soccer	no
2. Football	yes
3. Hockey	yes
4. Auto racing	yes
5. Tennis	no
6. Lacrosse	yes
7. Golf	no
8. Basketball	no
9. Bowling	no
10. Bicycle racing	yes

What is the classification rule?
Possible answer: games in which players wear helmets or padding

concerning the rules, which impaired their learning. In either case, it was clear that concept formation was an active process.

In the same year the Rand Corporation sponsored a seminal conference on information processing at the Massachusetts Institute of Technology (MIT). The scientists who attended (many of whom were— or later became—prominent psychologists) attempted to find parallels between the ways computers and humans use information. While they found some obvious differences, they also found striking similarities. Computers process information *serially* (one task at a time) and in discrete *stages;* at some level, humans process information the same way. The work that was started at this conference gave birth to the **human information-processing (HIP) model** of cognition, arguably the most influential model in psychology over the past several decades. As the HIP model and other cognitive explanations became widely accepted, radical behaviorism receded in influence.

The Late Twentieth Century

Virtually all psychologists agree that the brain ultimately controls all human thought and behavior. Remember that many founders of psychology (like Fechner and Helmholtz) were physiologists. In the 1930s and 1940s, though, interest in the biological aspects of psychology waned. First, influential behav-

iorists like Skinner considered neurological explanations of little use in explaining complex behavior. Second, until relatively recently laboratory methods could not provide answers to many important questions. But during the 1950s, as behaviorism's influence weakened, powerful new research tools were developed. In a relatively short time, huge advances were made in our understanding of the biological mechanisms of behavior.

Some of the most significant advances came from laboratories in Berkeley, California. There David Krech, Edward Bennett, and Mark Rosenzweig began to understand how chemicals in the brain can cause changes in thoughts, feelings, and behavior. During this time psychologists developed drugs useful in treating serious mental disturbances such as schizophrenia and depression—disturbances that had been virtually untreatable before advances in brain chemistry.

Today, the term *neuroscience* is often used instead of biological psychology. Neuroscience is a more inclusive term, incorporating a wide range of research areas. Some neuroscientists look at molecular aspects of behavior, such as the changes that take place in cells in response to various chemicals. Others take a more behavioral approach. For example, Larry Squire of the University of California at San Diego examines the effects of (relatively) large-scale brain damage on learning and memory (see Squire, 1987).

Advances in neuroscience have proceeded rapidly over the past thirty years. Problems once thought by psychologists to be intractable—schizophrenia, for example—are now relatively well understood. Neuroscientists are even making progress in understanding more complex phenomena such as *Alzheimer's disease* (a progressive, irreversible brain damage seen in some elderly patients). While neuroscientists are not close to solving the problem, most believe they will someday understand processes like those involved in Alzheimer's.

Psychology Today

The five perspectives just discussed are all important in the history of psychology; at one time or another each was the dominant paradigm. More importantly, each continues to influence current thought and guide research. In addition, most contemporary psychologists recognize that these five perspectives are not mutually exclusive. In many cases, they provide explanations of behavior at different levels. Behav-

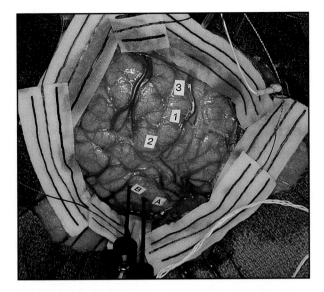

*The human brain during **neurosurgery**. The surgeon has labeled those areas of the brain responsible for critical psychological and physiological functions.*

iorism explains actions in terms of stimuli and responses; cognitivism, in terms of the processing of information. Neuroscience provides explanations of behavior at the cellular and molecular levels. All three approaches may be accurate.

Different theoretical perspectives explain behavior at different levels. Take, for example, major depression, the most common serious mental disorder. Major depressive episodes are characterized by intense, severe hopelessness. An individual who is suffering from major depression will often lose all appetite (or, less frequently, eat almost constantly). Many feel as if they cannot get out of bed, and see no reason to do so. They have no energy, no desire, and frequently no longer wish to continue living. They cannot remember a time when they did not feel that way, nor can they imagine ever feeling better.

What causes depressive episodes? How should an individual suffering from a depressive episode be treated? Explanations can be given at a number of different levels. Someone adopting a psychoanalytic perspective may say the depression is caused by unresolved feelings of anger toward the self or others, now turned inward. The psychoanalyst might attempt to help someone suffering from depression by redirecting their anger in more beneficial ways. On the other hand, a humanistic psychologist might explain that the individual has lost self-esteem and fails to see the inherent worth in life. A humanist would attempt to treat the depression by reaffirming the person's worth and value giving empathy, support, and encouragement.

A behaviorist would reject all descriptions of the internal states of depression. Instead, the behaviorist would concentrate on the stimuli that triggered the depressive episode and the individual's responses to those stimuli. For example, the behaviorist would try to change the abnormalities in the person's eating and sleeping habits, which are directly observable behaviors. A cognitivist might concentrate on the person's self-defeating behaviors and irrational beliefs. If the person believed he was helpless, a cognitivist might remind him of situations in which he has been in control and advise him to set modest, achievable goals.

Finally, a neuroscientist would likely describe depression in terms of changes at the neurochemical level. Levels of certain chemicals in the brain might be too low. The neuroscientist might advise treatment with drugs designed to elevate the levels of those chemicals.

All of these explanations may be right; they simply address the problem at different levels. Furthermore, there is a good deal of agreement among proponents of these approaches. Behaviorists and cognitivists acknowledge that changing thoughts and actions also will change neural activity. A psychoanalyst would acknowledge that redirecting one's anger will also have a positive effect on one's sense of self-worth. The differences between perspectives, then, simply reflect differences in *where* psychologists direct their attention.

In a real treatment situation, a psychologist (and other health professionals treating the person) would most likely combine several of these treatments. A psychiatrist might prescribe an antidepressant medication, while encouraging the patient to undergo cognitive therapy. The cognitive therapist might employ some behavioral techniques—for example, advising the person to stay out of bed until 10 p.m.

Contemporary Fields of Specialization

Psychology is usually a single department in colleges and universities, yet psychologists are far from uniform in their professional interests. Psychology is made up of many highly specialized subfields, each with not only its own subject matter but its own theories and sometimes even its own research methods. Check the course catalog for your college or university to see the wide range of topics covered. You will likely see advanced courses for most of the chapter topics in this book.

The following pages will acquaint you with some of the major subfields in psychology today, as well as the kinds of research done in them. Chapter 2 will go into more detail with the specific methods of investigation employed in these subfields.

Experimental Psychology

Where would you put something if you wanted to be sure you could find it again when you need it? Would you try putting it in some unusual place, assuming you could never forget such an odd location? This memory aid seems logical, and most of us have probably used it from time to time. But how well does it work? Psychologists have found that it does not work very well at all. For example, Winograd and Soloway (1986) showed that people have a harder time recalling unusual places where they have put things (an airline ticket in a shoe or a set of car keys in a light fixture) than recalling more logical places. You may have experienced the same phenomenon. Have you ever found yourself looking for something, only to remember that you put it somewhere so unusual that you wouldn't forget it? In Chapter 7 you will read about other experiments on human memory and cognition, just one of a large number of topics experimental psychologists explore.

The term **experimental psychology** is a bit of a misnomer. It implies that this subfield is the only one in psychology that relies on experimentation as a data-gathering method. But that is definitely not the case. (Remember that *science is a method*, not a content area.) Researchers in many other areas of psychology conduct experiments. To define experimental psychology, we must look as much at subject matter as at methods. Experimental psychologists typically study one of several "basic" processes—"basic" both in the sense that they are shared by a variety of animal species and in the sense that they are often involved in other aspects of behavior. These processes include sensation, perception, learning, memory, problem solving, communication, emotion, and motivation. Experimental psychologists often do their research in a laboratory, and they frequently use animals other than humans as their subjects.

Neuroscience

Like experimental psychologists, **neuroscientists** also study basic processes. They focus on the neural aspects of those processes, however. For instance, if asked to explain why memory sometimes declines in old age, neuroscientists would probe the brain for signs of a breakdown in the network of nerve cells thought to be involved in remembering. As we have seen, neuroscientists are likely to look for neural causes of psychological disorders like depression or schizophrenia. Like experimental psychologists, neuroscientists often use other animal species as subjects.

In recent years neuroscientists have made great strides in understanding the neurological basis of many behaviors. Today modern technology allows them actually to look inside a human brain at work. The human brain is symmetrical: the right half (or right hemisphere) is a virtual mirror image of the left half (the left hemisphere). The two hemispheres have very different functions, though. Psychologists have long known that for most people, the left hemisphere of the brain plays a greater role in language processing than the right. The right hemisphere plays a greater role in the processing of visual, spatial information.

What about the congenitally deaf, whose primary language is American Sign Language? Rather than relying on the auditory input of spoken language, the deaf rely on the visual input of signs. Since their language is primarily spatial rather than auditory, do they process language in the right hemisphere?

Ursula Bellugi and her colleagues (Bellugi, Poizner, & Klima, 1989; Corina, Vaid, & Bellugi, 1992) have shown that despite the differences in sensory modalities, the deaf still use special areas in the left hemisphere for processing language. On the basis of this evidence, and other related experiments (e.g., Raichle, 1994), neuroscientists now believe that the left hemisphere may have an innate predisposition for language. (We will discuss the specialization of the two hemispheres of the brain in Chapter 3 and the innateness of language in Chapter 7.)

Over the past decade, neuroscience has begun to inform virtually every other discipline in psychology. Indeed, every behavior has a neuroscientific component. As this subfield progresses, behavioral and cognitive approaches will be supplemented with neurological evidence. Neuroscientific evidence will be presented throughout the remainder of this book.

Like experimental psychologists, neuroscientists are often affiliated with colleges and universities. These centers of higher education can provide the facilities they need for their research. Many others work in business or government. Pharmaceutical companies hire neuroscientists to develop or test new drugs, for instance. As scientists have learned more about how the brain works, **psychopharmacology** (the study of the link between drugs and behavior) has become a rapidly growing field.

Personality Psychology

Say a friend of yours offers to fix you up with a blind date. What factors would influence your decision to say "yes" or "no"? Psychologists have found that your answer will depend greatly on your personality—your relatively stable style of thinking, acting, and responding emotionally. For example, Miyake and Zuckerman (1993) asked college students to observe other students and then rate them on how similar they were to themselves. All students (those making the judgments and those being judged) were independently evaluated for physical and vocal attractiveness.

The students who were doing the ratings were also assessed for a personality trait called *self-monitoring*—a measure of how concerned a person is about the image he or she conveys. For instance, high self-monitors are very conscious of what others think of them. They watch their own behavior closely to make sure it meets with others' approval. Low self-monitors, in contrast, do not know (or care) what others think of them; their behavior is generally based on their own beliefs and feelings.

Miyake and Zuckerman found that students were much more likely to rate other students positively when the other students scored high on both physical and vocal attractiveness. However, the effects were even more pronounced when the rating students were themselves attractive and high self-monitors. These subjects "looked good," *knew* they looked good, and considered external appearance important (they scored "high" on self-monitoring). These students apparently evaluated others' appearance even more critically than most!

This study is just one example of the issues personality psychologists explore. **Personality psychology** is concerned with describing and explaining individual differences in behavior. To what extent is one person more self-monitoring than another, more manipulative, more outgoing, more obedient to authority? How can we account for differences in personality? Is there something "inside" that makes us think, feel, and act in certain ways? Do we largely inherit personality traits? Or do "outside" factors—our personal histories, our culture, the times in which we live, the pressures of the immediate situation—shape the ways we respond? In short, how does personality develop? And can personality change over time? These are the central questions personality psychologists ask. We will investigate them in detail in Chapters 10 and 13.

Social Psychology

Suppose you were in a crowded store and a man collapsed before you, clutching his chest and gasping for breath. Would you try to help him? What would you think of people who just stood by and watched, as often happens in such situations? Would you think they were heartless and uncaring? If not, why would they stand idly by? In a classic series of studies, psychologists John Darley and Bibb Latané tried to answer these questions. Darley and Latané staged bogus emergencies and observed bystanders' reactions (Darley & Latane, 1968; Latane & Darley, 1968). In one experiment, people heard someone in the next room crash to the floor and moan in pain (actually a tape-recorded performance). In another, someone was heard having a violent seizure (also simulated); in a third, the experimenter pretended to be severely shocked by electrical equipment. Latané and Darley found that willingness to help was not related to individual personality traits, such as sensitivity to others. Instead, a bystander's reaction was shaped largely by the social situation. A person was far more apt to offer help when witnessing an emergency alone than when seeing it in a group.

If you are thinking that this powerful influence of other people must be unique to emergencies, you are wrong. **Social psychologists** have shown repeatedly that our behavior is not just the result of our personalities and predispositions. Environmental factors, especially the presence or absence of others, greatly affect what we think, say, and do. This finding sheds light on many incidents that would otherwise be hard to explain. How could a company of American soldiers have massacred nearly 500 civilians, most of them women and children, in the Vietnamese village of My Lai? Social psychologist Stanley Milgram (1963) has demonstrated the incredible extent to which average people will inflict severe pain on their fellow humans if an authority figure tells them to do so.

Developmental Psychology

Suppose you show a three-year-old a red toy car behind a green filter, so that the car appears black. You remove the car from behind the filter and hand it to the child so that he or she can see the car's true color. Then you place the car behind the filter again and ask the child: "What color is that car? Is it red or black?" The child quickly answers "black." So you rephrase the question: "What color is it really and truly? Is it *really* black or really red?" Again the child answers "black," and even seems puzzled at the question.

If you asked this same question of a seven-year-old, he or she would say that the car looked black, but it was really and truly "red." Unlike a three-year-old, a seven-year-old does not have trouble distinguishing appearance from reality on such simple tasks. Yet even seven-year-olds do not yet think about appearance-reality distinctions in the same way adults do. Children this age have difficulty talking about appearance and reality in abstract terms. Not until they are about age twelve do they acquire a relatively sophisticated grasp of these two concepts (Flavell, 1986).

Developmental psychologists try to describe and explain the systematic changes that occur in people throughout the life cycle. How ways of thinking and reasoning change as people grow older is just one of many topics developmental psychologists study. In fact, most topics in psychology—from sensation and perception to learning and memory, thinking and problem solving, emotion and motivation, personality and social interaction—can be studied from this perspective. Do newborn infants perceive the world differently than adults? If so, how?

Developmental psychologists examine changes throughout the life span, not just in childhood. Do intellectual skills decline as we get older, as many people assume? Answers to these and many other questions about developmental changes are explored in Chapters 9 and 10. These chapters also explore another issue of interest to developmental psychologists: how the many individual differences develop in people. As you will learn, the answers lie in a complex interplay of genes and environment.

Industrial and Organizational Psychology

Chances are you will sit down at a computer keyboard today. You may type for only a few minutes; if so, you will likely experience no trouble. Others, though, may spend hour after hour typing at a keyboard. A significant number of them will end up with pain, stiffness, or soreness in their hands, fingers, or wrists—something known as *carpal tunnel syndrome*. Symptoms can range from moderate discomfort to intense, prolonged pain. As computers become more common, a significant number of people are becoming debilitated by carpal tunnel syndrome (English et al., 1995). What can be done in the workplace to address this problem? Employers have asked **industrial and organizational psychologists** to answer that question, and others like it.

The question of how work can be made more satisfying and productive is another issue of interest to industrial and organizational psychologists. In fact, these psychologists are concerned with all aspects of behavior that relate to the workplace. Some identify the causes of problems that result in lowered performance or morale in workers. Others design programs to eliminate those problems. Still others create employee training programs, counsel employees, and set up systems for evaluating job performance.

A major challenge confronting industrial and organizational psychologists in the 1990s is finding ways to help working women deal with the stress of handling their dual responsibilities at home and in the office. Women make up a sizable and growing part of the American workforce, and many today hold demanding managerial and professional jobs. Yet most working women still perform the lion's share of child-care and housekeeping duties at home, and they usually bear the primary responsibility for seeing that all those tasks get done. Such is the case even in families in which the woman earns as much as her husband (Biernat & Wortman, 1991). How women workers can be helped to cope with this reality of modern-day life is a critically important question that industrial and organizational psychologists can help to answer.

Educational and School Psychology

Ask math students of almost any age what their *least* favorite math problems are. Almost certainly they will say that they are word problems. Indeed, performance on word problems is almost always worse

*Some **developmental psychologists** have studied the effects of child care on psychological growth. **Industrial** and **organizational** psychologists often apply their findings to real-world settings, such as the corporate-sponsored day care facility shown here.*

than performance on equivalent numeric problems. Why?

Weaver and Kintsch (1992) have suggested that the difficulty students experience with word problems is in understanding the conceptual relationships. Read the caption, and look at the problems in Figure 1-4. When given a choice, many students pick Example 2 as being the more helpful one. It and the Test Problem are both "train problems," after all. However, the similarity is superficial. Though both problems are about trains, the methods for solving them are quite different. Knowing how to solve one does not necessarily help students solve the other.

On the other hand, the solution procedures for Example 1 and the Test Problem are identical—despite the fact that they describe seemingly different situations. Weaver and Kintsch found that when students were asked questions like that shown in Figure 1-4, they thought at first Example 2 would be more helpful. But after a relatively brief tutorial session designed to point out structural similarities between the problems, students were able to see those similarities. They were then more likely to solve the Test Problem correctly.

Educational psychologists are concerned with all aspects of the learning process. What factors generally affect performance in the classroom? How important is motivation? Intelligence? Personality? The use of rewards and punishments? Class size? Teacher expectations? Educational psychologists are also involved in evaluating student performance through the design and administration of various tests. But educational psychologists do not work exclusively in colleges, universities, and school systems. Some have careers in health-care settings, where they plan and supervise special education classes for learning disabled children. Of those who work in private industry, government, and nonprofit agencies, many are engaged in developing tests or in planning, setting up, and evaluating training programs.

In contrast to educational psychologists, who seek to learn about learning, **school psychologists** focus on *applying* psychological knowledge. Almost two-thirds of the school psychologists in the United States work in elementary and secondary schools. They may be involved in training teachers in how to deal with difficult students or in counseling such students and their parents. They also administer and interpret standardized tests like the SAT and diagnose and assess students with learning difficulties.

Clinical and Counseling Psychology

Clinical psychologists are practitioners in the subfield of psychology that deals with the diagnosis and treatment of psychological disorders—many of which are far more severe than the normal problems we all experience from time to time. Clinical psychologists also investigate the causes of these disorders. As in other areas of psychology, competing theories exist about causes. Some believe that psychological disorders arise from unresolved conflicts and unconscious motives (essentially Freud's

Test Problem	Example 1	Example 2
Train A leaves Denver at 1:00, traveling east at 60 miles an hour. Train B leaves 2 1/2 hours later, going 100 mph. What time will Train B overtake Train A?	Ernie invests some money at 10% interest, and $350 more than that at 8% interest. Both earn the same interest. How much was invested at each rate?	Train A has 12 blue cars and 10 green cars. Train B has 8 blue cars and 12 green cars. If blue cars carry 6 passengers, and green cars carry 10 passengers, which train can carry the most passengers?

FIGURE 1-4   *You are asked to solve the Test Problem on the left. To help you solve the Test Problem, you may choose to see the worked-out solution to either Example 1 or Example 2. Which example problem would you expect to find most helpful?*
[After Reed (1987).]

view). Others maintain that some disorders are merely learned responses that can be unlearned with training. Still others contend that there are biological bases to certain psychological disorders, especially the most serious ones. As you will discover in Chapter 17, these different views have yielded a variety of treatments for problems as diverse as phobias, depression, paranoia, and drug dependence.

Not surprisingly, close to three-quarters of all clinical psychologists are employed in hospitals, clinics, and private practice. There they often work closely with two other mental health specialists: the **psychiatrist** and the **psychoanalyst.** Unlike clinical psychologists, who have earned a Ph.D. and completed specialized training in diagnosis and psychotherapy, psychiatrists must first earn an M.D. and complete a medical internship, as other physicians do. Then, during a three-year residency in psychiatry, nearly always in a hospital, they receive specific training in the treatment of psychological disorders. As physicians, psychiatrists can prescribe drugs and use other medical procedures that clinical psychologists cannot. Some psychiatrists go on to become psychoanalysts, practitioners of the form of therapy developed by Freud. To become a psychoanalyst, psychiatrists must study psychoanalytic theory, undergo psychoanalysis themselves, and analyze clients under the supervision of an experienced analyst. Psychoanalytic institutes that provide such training are located in several major cities.

While clinical psychologists and psychiatrists generally treat people with serious psychological disorders, **counseling psychologists** usually help those with mild problems of social and emotional adjustment. Some counseling psychologists specialize in particular areas, such as marriage and family life. They may also help normally adjusted people with such tasks as setting vocational goals. About half of all counseling psychologists work in healthcare settings or in private practice.

Most states also offer another, somewhat less specialized level of clinical certification indicated by titles such as "licensed psychotherapists" and "licensed professional counselors." Unlike most clinical psychologists (and many counseling psychologists), "licensed" therapists are not required to complete the Ph.D. or any other terminal degree (meaning the highest degree offered in the field). Exact requirements vary from state to state, but most require at least a master's degree in psychology (or a related field), many hours of supervised practice (500 to 2,000), and successful completion of the licensing exam.

Health Psychology

Is your personality hazardous to your health? It may be, if you are a cynical, hostile type of person. In a recent study, forty-five married couples were given a test to measure their cynical hostility (that is, their general suspiciousness that others are antagonistic toward them and therefore deserve to be treated with anger, resentment, and contempt). The couples were then presented with a hypothetical situation in which a school district was about to lay off staff (Smith & Brown, 1991). Husbands and wives were given different lists of people who should not be laid off and then asked to defend their lists to their partner using arguments the researchers supplied. Some of the subjects were also given a financial incentive to win the argument. Significantly, men who scored high in hostility, especially those who had a financial incentive, had much higher increases in blood pressure during the experiment than other men. This is one more piece of evidence suggesting that cynically hostile people are prone to elevated cardiac responses that may raise their risk of heart disease.

Health psychologists study these kinds of relationships between mind and body. They believe that the mind plays a role in many physical disorders, from ulcers and heart disease to the common cold and cancer. In fact, some health psychologists suspect that psychological factors may be involved in the onset and progress of all diseases.

Health psychologists are making many important contributions to modern health care and disease prevention. Besides identifying psychological factors related to disease—such as hostility, stress, and depression—they are devising ways to test people for those factors. They are also trying to understand how a psychological factor such as hostility or stress can have harmful physical effects. Health psychologists are searching for the psychological and social reasons why people sometimes behave in unhealthy ways, such as smoking, overeating, and ignoring early symptoms of health problems. Finally, because psychological responses impact recovery, they are also helping to identify psychological strategies for coping with illness.

Psychology's Value To You

Psychology is a very popular vocation in the United States. The American Psychological Association (APA), to which many psychologists belong, had approximately 60,000 members in 1990, though numbers have decreased since then. The American Psychological Society (APS), a new professional society organized in the mid-1980s, already has over 15,000 members. The number of people entering this field is growing rapidly. Of the 30,000 doctoral degrees in science and engineering awarded annually in the United States, about 3,000 (or 10 percent) are in psy-

chology. Each year roughly 8,000 students earn master's degrees in psychology (Strickland, 1987).

Fascination with human behavior draws a great many people to a career in psychology. At many colleges and universities, psychology is among the most popular majors. Even if you do not go on to earn a graduate degree in psychology, taking psychology courses can greatly help you in your future work. If you major in psychology, you might find a related job in a rehabilitation program, a correctional institution, or a community mental health center. Other careers have indirect ties to a knowledge of psychology. A person who works in advertising, for instance, will probably find courses in social psychology, human motivation, and human learning invaluable. Similarly, a person who enters the field of personnel management will make much use of information on personality, individual differences, and testing. Psychological knowledge also has important applications in teaching, social work, nursing, business, engineering, and law.

But the value of studying psychology is not just vocational. Even if you take no other psychology courses besides this one, you will still learn much about yourself and others from this broad introduction to psychological findings and principles. How can I improve my memory? My study habits? How can I get someone I know to stop smoking? When people pressure me to do something I would rather not do, why do I sometimes go along? Whenever I baby-sit for my infant nephew, he cries continually unless I hold him. What can I do to change his behavior? I get so tense when I sit down to take a test that my mind goes completely blank. Is there a way I can get over this anxiety? A variety of answers to these and many other questions of great personal interest are contained in this book.

Finally, studying psychology will give you a critical perspective from which to evaluate psychological findings reported in newspapers, in books, and on TV. Like every other discipline, psychology can be approached from a scientific or a nonscientific viewpoint. Many times the popular media oversimplify a finding, or misinterpret a researcher's results. By evaluating such reports using the tools you will learn in this course, you will develop a "healthy skepticism."

In Depth

Four Recurring Themes in Psychology

THE "IN DEPTH" feature found in each chapter introduces current topics of importance in psychological research. Each presents a description of the initial research on a topic, the questions and controversies which have developed since, and current theories of the subject. This "In Depth" essay introduces four  key themes in psychology, themes which cut across traditional boundaries. As with all generalizations, these themes tend to be overly simplistic; exceptions can always be found.

As you read this book, keep these themes in mind. Each chapter includes examples, and some will ask *you* to look for the themes. In many cases there is no "correct" answer. Though only four themes are presented here, there are many more. Look for others as you read. Global understanding of a field sometimes comes from looking for commonalties rather than differences.

The Best Predictor of Future Behavior Is Past Behavior

THEME Human behavior, including many cognitive and personality traits, is generally consistent over the lifespan. For example, IQ at age five is a very reliable predictor of IQ as an adult (Herrnstein & Murray, 1994). Personality characteristics such as temperament, extroversion and aggression also remain quite consistent. McCrae and Costa (1994), reviewing a vast body of literature, concluded that personality is stable from age thirty through the life span. In fact, some studies suggest that personality changes little from age eighteen (e.g., Conley, 1985).

The fact that future behavior can be predicted from past behavior has some important limitations. The first is that while past behavior is a *good* predictor (and in many cases, a *very* good predictor) of future behavior, it is not the *only* predictor. Many factors go into determining present behavior; past behavior is just one.

A second limitation concerns predictions for a single individual. College admission offices try to predict the success or failure of incoming students. If an admissions officer has one group of fifty applicants with an average SAT score of 1200 and a second group of fifty applicants with an average SAT score of 800, what kind of predictions can she make? The officer can predict with virtual certainty that the first group of students will be more successful overall than the second group. But she cannot easily make predictions *concerning a single individual.* She might know that only half of students with an SAT score of 800 are likely to be successful, but she cannot know exactly which specific students will make up the successful half.

Finally, the predictability of behavior has one important implication: major changes in behavior can be difficult. Bernie Zilbergeld, a well-known clinical psychologist, has written in his book *The Shrinking of America: Myths of Behavioral Change* (Zilbergeld, 1983):

> Our culture is strongly committed to the proposition that people are highly malleable. Three key assumptions of the present age are that human beings should change because they are not as competent or as good or as happy as they could be; that there are few limits to the alterations they can make; and that change is relatively easy to effect (p. 3).

Instead, Zilbergeld concludes:

> [A]lthough therapy is now used with almost every known human complaint, it has proven its effectiveness with only a small number of them; the changes made are usually modest...and often not long lasting; and participation in counseling can harm as well as help (p. 7).

Psychologists Learn about the Normal by Studying the Abnormal

THEME This is perhaps the most pervasive theme in this book. Researchers in almost every field have made tremendous strides by looking at cases that have gone wrong. One of the cruel realities of war, in fact, is that neurologists observe vast numbers of head injuries. While brain trauma is not uncommon, war wounds are unique. Unlike the widespread damage associated with strokes, they are typically small and localized. With war wounds, the extent of the damage can easily be determined. Finally, these wounds usually occur in young, otherwise healthy individuals.

The neurologist Oliver Sacks (on whom the Robin Williams character in the movie *Awakenings* was based) credits the Russian neurologist Alexander Luria with reviving the case history in neuropsychology: "I was overwhelmed by his combination of intellectual power and human warmth" (Sacks, 1990 p. xxxvi). Luria had the misfortune of treating thousands of Russian soldiers who had suffered neurological damage in World War II. By studying the functions they had lost and relating the losses to the known damage, neuroscientists can make great insights, which otherwise might not be made.

Likewise, personality theorists advance their understanding of the normal personality by looking at individuals who display personality disorders. In the years when he was forming his seminal psychoanalytic theories, Sigmund Freud wrote to a colleague, "A satisfactory general comprehension of neuropsychiatric disorder is impossible if one cannot make connections to clear assumptions about normal mental processes" (quoted in Gay, 1989, p. 118). Thus, cognitive psychologists learn about memory by looking at individuals with remarkable memories. For example, a university student in Kansas, "Rajan," has memorized the number Pi (π) to the first thirty-*thousand* digits (Thompson, Detterman, & Plomin, 1991)!

Abnormal cases can inform us about normal functioning in several ways. First, cases of pathology or trauma such as Alzheimer's disease or war injuries yield important clues to the relationship between brain structures and the functions they control. Second, abnormal cases often test our theories of behavior to the extreme. For example, Rajan, the student who has memorized π to the first thirty-thousand digits, provides a strenuous test of theories of skilled memory (Ericsson, 1985, 1988). Indeed, Rajan's memory skill appears to be the result of tremendous practice and motivation, but the basic memory mechanisms he uses are the same as everyone else's. Finally, extreme cases demonstrate that "abnormal"

does not mean "bad." "Abnormal" literally means "not normal," whether good or bad.

A Large Proportion of Behavior Is Controlled by Unconscious Activity

 THEME 3 Consciousness is a topic of intense interest to philosophers and psychologists alike. It is notoriously difficult to investigate scientifically. Freud once remarked, "Psychoanalytic theory was forced, through the study of pathological repression, to take the concept of the unconscious seriously" (Gay, 1989, p. 128). As we will see, the role of unconscious desires and motivations is central to the work of Freud.

Consciousness is central to many aspects of psychology. For example, social psychologists have discovered that the more frequently you are exposed to a stimulus, the more positively you will evaluate it—even if you are not aware of your prior exposure (Zajonc, 1968; see also Bornstein, 1989, and Bornstein & D'Agostino, 1992). Larry Weiskrantz, an experimental psychologist at Oxford University, has identified a fascinating phenomenon known as "blindsight" (Weiskrantz, 1986). People with blindsight have sustained neurological damage that has resulted in their blindness. However, given certain kinds of tasks, a person with blindsight will make use of visual information—for example, he or she may duck when entering a room with a low door opening. Strangely, the person reports no awareness of or insight into the behavior. If a researcher asks the subject why he ducked when entering the room, he cannot answer! Similarly, memory researchers (Roediger, 1990) have found a number of amnesiac patients who can learn certain kinds of new information without any awareness of doing so. These patients can be given the same crossword puzzle for ten days in a row. On the tenth day, they will likely solve the puzzle very quickly, much more quickly than the first time. Yet if asked, they will deny ever having seen the puzzle before.

The relationship between consciousness and behavior is complex. In fact, psychologists recognize that in some situations conscious awareness actually *impairs* performance. If you are a golfer, do you breathe when you draw the club back and swing forward? If you can't answer (and most people can't), notice the next time you swing a golf club. You will likely find that becoming aware of that aspect of your stroke hurts your overall performance.[3]

Cognition and Thought Are Dynamic, Active Processes, Best Considered *Reconstructive*, Not *Reproductive*

THEME The past century of psychological research has clearly demonstrated the active, dynamic, and constructive nature of thought. Psychological activity is a combination of past events, present circumstances, and future goals.

Many different metaphors have been used to understand psychological processes, such as:

- The human brain is the most advanced computer ever seen.
- Our minds contain collections of pictures, scenes, and snapshots.
- Our minds "soak up" information that is presented to us.

But these metaphors imply that psychological processes are permanent and unchanging, and that

---

[3]This is what coaches mean when they tell athletes to "quit thinking and just play!"

events that happen to us are stored in a fairly literal manner. In truth, humans are *active* processors. We reconstruct events and impose order and structure on stimuli, even when they aren't there. For example, when you listen to speech you probably hear the breaks between words clearly. Yet in reality, speech is more like continuous sound; the "breaks" are imposed by the listener (Pinker, 1994)—a phenomenon you may have noticed if you have ever been in a country where you do not speak the language. Native speakers seem to be saying one long, uninterrupted word. As listeners become more fluent in a language, they will begin to "hear" the breaks between words, breaks they themselves are actually creating. Memory is another constructive process, combining information from many different sources during retrieval.

The information processing model of cognition does provide some useful insights. It is not to be taken literally, though. Realizing that cognition is creative and dynamic is crucial to understanding human interaction. If we mistakenly believe that thought is a literal, passive process—that we are simply retrieving information from an "internal hard disk of the mind"—we misunderstand the very nature of psychology.

SUMMARY

1. **Psychology**, the study of behavior and mental processes, is first of all a science. It is a set of procedures for systematically observing facts about behavior and organizing them into testable generalizations about why people think, feel, and act as they do.

2. The scientific approach to psychology relies heavily on scientific theories. Not all theories are scientific. **Scientific theories** have three properties:

   - They must be testable.
   - They can never be proved correct.
   - Even if they have been rejected, they can still be useful.

3. Wilhelm Wundt is generally considered the founder of modern psychology. In the late nineteenth century he established the first laboratory for the express purpose of investigating human mental processes. Wundt and his students conducted studies on a broad range of topics. Their efforts to use precise and systematic methods of measurement launched psychology as a science.

4. Five perspectives have come to dominate psychology in the twentieth century: psychoanalytic psychology, behaviorism, humanistic psychology, cognitive psychology, and neuroscience. These perspectives are better viewed as complementary rather than opposing viewpoints. Each can provide valuable insights or offer an explanation at a different level.

5. Sigmund Freud developed the psychoanalytic approach to psychology This perspective emphasized the role of unconscious drives and feelings, often stemming from unresolved childhood conflicts, to explain the psychological problems that adults sometimes experience. Freud felt that unconscious conflicts can be deprived of their power to dominate a person's life if they are brought into awareness through a process called **psychoanalysis.** While few psychologists wholly accept Freud's ideas today, his influence on twentieth-century thought has been enormous. The modern **psychoanalytic perspective** in psychology still shows the influence of Freud's views.

6. A second important approach in modern psychology is the **behaviorist perspective,** which first arose in the early twentieth century. The early behaviorists insisted that psychology focus only on data that can be objectively observed and measured. The pioneering work of Ivan Pavlov, John Watson, E. L. Thorndike, and B. F.

Skinner established the behaviorists' enduring interest in how learned associations give rise to specific responses. In the United States, the study of how rewards and punishments control behavior became the hallmark of behaviorism.

7. Psychologists with a **humanistic perspective** have reacted against the deterministic views of both behaviorism and Freudian psychology. They maintain that people are free to become whatever they are capable of being. Humanists have developed forms of psychotherapy that stress the human potential for **self-actualization** and fulfillment.

8. Psychologists who take a **cognitive perspective** study learning to consider how people receive, process, store, and retrieve information. Cognitive psychologists stress the dynamic, constructive nature of thought and behavior. They study a wide range of topics, including learning, memory, concept formation, problem solving, decision making, and language.

9. Psychologists who take a **neuroscience** perspective stress that all human thought, feeling, and action is ultimately controlled by the nervous system, of which the brain is the central part. Many researchers with this perspective try to map the different areas of the brain involved in controlling specific kinds of behaviors. Others seek to understand the workings of the brain's complex chemical systems.

10. Contemporary psychology has researchers working in many specialized subfields.

   - **Experimental psychologists** rely largely on laboratory experiments to investigate basic behavioral processes, such as sensation, perception, memory, and learning.

   - **Neuroscientists** also study basic processes, but they focus on how those processes are controlled by the brain and other parts of the nervous system.

   - **Personality psychologists** measure and explain individual differences in behavior, while **developmental psychologists** explore changes in thought and behavior throughout the life cycle.

   - **Social psychologists** look at the influence of social situations on behavior.

   - **Educational and school psychologists** are concerned with the processes of formal education.

   - **Industrial and organizational psychologists** focus on the relationship between people and their work.

   - **Clinical psychologists** specialize in the diagnosis and treatment of mental and emotional disorders.

   - **Health psychologists** focus on psychological factors involved in physical illness and recovery from it.

11. While psychology is very useful in many careers, it also has practical value as a perspective on human behavior. It can help to answer many questions people ask about themselves and others. At the same time, it can help people to be more perceptive in evaluating psychological information they read and hear about.

Answers for Figure 1-1

The correct answers for the photos on the left (from top to bottom) are: 7, 1, 5, 9, 4.

SUGGESTED READINGS

American Psychological Association. (1994/1995 addendum). *Graduate study in psychology and associated fields.* Washington, DC: American Psychological Association. Describes requirements for admissions and degrees, tuition, and financial aid at over 600 departments of psychology. Includes extensive lists of specialties and types of degrees offered. Updated yearly. Washington, DC: American Psychological Association.

Gardner, H. (1985). *The mind's new science.* New York: Basic Books. Describes the birth of cognitive psychology in the late 1950s and follows its progress through the next twenty-five years, as it became a dominant paradigm in psychology.

Hilgard, E. R., Leary, D. E., & McGuire, G. R. (1991). The history of psychology: A survey and critical assessment. In M. R. Rosenzweig & L. W. Porter (Eds.). *Annual review of psychology, Vol. 42.* pp. 79–107. Palo Alto, CA: Annual Reviews, Inc. Not a conventional history, but rather a "history of the history of psychology." The authors review influential historians and their works, but also provide a useful overview of the historical resources available for students and instructors.

Leahey, T. H. (1994). *A history of modern psychology* (2nd ed.). Englewood Cliffs, NJ: Prentice-Hall, Inc. A good review of the most important figures and ideas of psychology.

Rubinstein, J., & Slife, B. D. (1992). *Taking sides: Views on controversial psychological issues* (7th ed.). Guilford, CT: Dushkin. Presents both sides of controversial issues through the words of the actual researchers.

Woods, P. J. (Ed). (1988). *Is psychology for them? A guide to undergraduate advising.* Washington, DC: American Psychological Association. Intended for professors and others who often advise students about majors and careers in psychology, but equally useful for students. Offers guidance in deciding whether to major in psychology. Describes careers available to psychologists and offers advice on finding a job.

|Research Methods

There is no shortage of interesting questions about human behavior. Why did I do so poorly on my biology exam even though I knew the material? Why do smokers disregard warnings that cigarettes are hazardous to their health? Why do some people need at least eight hours of sleep a night, while others do fine with six? Why do I sometimes go along with other people's opinions, though I really disagree? Psychologists ask the same kinds of questions about human behavior. The difference between psychologists and other people lies in how they seek the answers.

For example, in recent years our society has become increasingly aware of the problem of child abuse. In many cases the most powerful testimony comes from the children themselves. We typically assume that their testimony is accurate and reliable. Is that a reasonable assumption? How accurate is the testimony of young children who are being interrogated about alleged incidents of child abuse? How would a psychologist go about answering such questions?

Psychologist Stephen Ceci and his colleagues have systematically addressed this question. Much of their research has centered around the effects of suggestibility in children. Specifically, Ceci and his colleagues have investigated the phenomenon of *source misattribution*—the tendency to remember information but to forget the source from which it was gathered. A child will often remember an event, but forget its *source*—that is, whether it actually happened, was suggested to them, or even imagined by them.

For example, a four-year-old child witnesses a bank robbery. After the robbery, a police officer questions the child about the crime. During the questioning, the officer might ask, "The man was bigger than your Daddy, wasn't he?" The child may hesitate before giving an answer but will often agree—especially since the question is phrased in a way that implies the correct answer is "yes." If the child is interviewed again and a different officer asks, "How big was the robber?" the child may well reply, "The bank robber was bigger than my Daddy," with no hesitation. The child correctly remembers the information, but fails to remember that the first officer suggested it.

Ceci, Huffman, and Smith (1994) investigated source misattribution among two groups of children: the first, three to four years old; the second, five to six years old. The children were given a list of event descriptions. Some of the events had actually happened to the children,

TABLE 2-1   *Goals of Psychology and Experimental Methods That Can Help Achieve Those Goals*

Goal	Type of Research	Advantages	Disadvantages
Describing behavior	Survey	Fast, efficient	Difficult to ensure sample is random or representative, easy to "bias" results by phrasing questions in a certain manner
	Case history	Exceptional individuals are usually the object of study	Difficult to generalize to others; impossible to isolate causes
	Naturalistic observation	Relatively free of bias; subjects more likely to act "natural" if they are in this environment	Cannot determine cause and effect; many factors cannot be controlled
Predicting behavior	Correlation	Can clearly identify relationships	Third variable a problem; may not generalize to other nonsimilar groups; cannot infer causation
	Regression	Can allow useful predictions	Accuracy of predictions depends on the strength of the relationship; cannot infer causation
Explaining behavior	Experimental designs	Only method for truly determining cause and effect	Trade-off between control of possible extraneous factors and artificial nature of the lab situation

while some had been imagined by them at the suggestion of the experimenter. Ceci and his colleagues found that both groups of children were susceptible to source misattribution errors. However, they found the younger group to be disproportionately vulnerable to such errors. As the scientists point out, such findings suggest that source misattribution errors might cloud children's memories in cases of child abuse and repressed memory (see also Ceci et al., 1994).

In some situations, then, children may be prone to error in recalling previous events. It seems reasonable to assume that juries will judge the credibility of child witnesses accordingly. How do jurors tend to evaluate testimony from children? In a study by Ross and others (1990), mock juries (made up of college students) heard testimony from either a child, a young adult, or an elderly witness. Though the testimony given by each witness was identical, the jurors viewed the testimony of the young child as being most credible, and the testimony of the young adult as least credible.

Should we conclude, then, that children are unreliable and should never be allowed to testify? On the contrary, Ceci and Bruck (1993) conclude that even though there are reliable age differences in the suggestibility of children, even very young children can offer useful information. However, their testimony is not as reliable as most jurors believe.

Chapter 1 stressed that psychology is a science, but that is true only if a psychologist approaches a topic from a scientific perspective. You will read about "psychological studies" throughout this book. Long after this course is over you will hear about "psychological studies" in the popular media. To evaluate the credibility of a report, you need to know

One goal of psychologists is to predict behavior. During jury selection, for example, an attorney may question a potential juror extensively in an attempt to predict how the person will vote in a certain case. The lawyer addressing the jury in this photo may have been advised by a psychologist.

how the research was conducted. The more you know about the methods researchers used, the more critically you can interpret their findings. In short, a good grasp of scientific methods is essential.

Perhaps you feel that scientific methods are too dry and complicated to be interesting. Many introductory psychology students draw this hasty conclusion, only to find later that they were mistaken. Psychological research has all the fascination of solving a complex mystery. Like detective work, it begins with puzzling questions, proceeds to tentative conclusions, and involves imaginative suppositions, logical reasoning, and carefully conducted tests. The eventual findings, moreover, are always worth the effort, because they shed light on a subject of great intrinsic interest: you.

The Goals of Psychology

The definition of psychology in Chapter 1 centered on the phrase, "the scientific study of behavior." Many fields study human behavior, including philosophy and religion. Each discipline has its own goals and has developed a set of methods for achieving those goals. The goals of psychology involve *describing, predicting,* and *explaining* behavior. Those goals are not unique to psychology, of course. What does makes psychology unique is the *method* used to achieve those goals. Unlike philosophy or religion, psychology uses the methods of science to study human behavior. Table 2-1 shows the major goals of psychology and the research techniques often used to achieve those goals.

Describing Behavior

Understanding human behavior must begin with careful descriptions of how people think, feel, and act in specific situations. Psychologists collect such data as objectively as they can. Ideally, they try to observe the behavior of interest firsthand, recording it precisely in written notes or on tapes or videocassettes. In some cases, of course, events happen unexpectedly, and no psychologists are there to watch and record what happens. For example, the events surrounding the bombing of the federal building in Oklahoma City on April 19, 1995, happened without warning. Though psychologists were interested in understanding the reaction of people in Oklahoma City to the unanticipated tragedy, in most cases they could not observe their reactions firsthand. Instead, they carefully *reconstructed* such incidents through the testimony of participants and eyewitnesses.

Predicting Behavior

Psychologists are often interested in predicting behavior. Which potential jurors are most likely to find a defendant guilty? Which applicants for admission to a college are likely to be successful? Which political candidate is more likely to win an election? Which antidrug spokesperson will be most influential? One of the Recurring Themes introduced in Chapter 1 stated that past behavior is a reliable predictor of future behavior. But we know that past behavior is not perfectly predictive. Furthermore, in some cases we have no past behavior on which to base predictions.

THEME **The Best Predictor of Future Behavior Is Past Behavior**

Psychologists use prediction in two distinct ways. When testing theories, psychologists usually make broad predictions that people will behave in a certain way given a particular set of circumstances. If the prediction is upheld, the theory is supported; if it is not, the theory is unsupported. Social psychologists make such predictions when studying altruistic behavior. As mentioned in Chapter 1, Latané and Darley (1968; see also Latané & Darley, 1976) predicted that a person will be less likely to offer assistance to a fallen pedestrian if many other people are around. Thus, the ability to make predictions—to say in advance how someone is likely to act—lies at the heart of doing certain kinds of psychological research.

Other times psychologists are interested in making fairly specific predictions. What grade-point average will prospective students likely earn during their freshman year? Which of a group of applicants is likely to be the most productive employee? Which of two baseball players will likely score the most runs in a season? In these cases, psychologists often use a statistical technique called *regression* to make a specific prediction. (We will discuss regressions later in the chapter.)

Of course, no predictions prove accurate 100 percent of the time. Human behavior is highly complex, and unanticipated factors can always influence it. But if psychologists cannot predict behavior at least some of the time, they are not very far along in understanding it.

Explaining Behavior

For most psychologists, describing and predicting human behavior is not enough. They also want to know *why* it happens; that is, they want to explain it. Chapter 1 illustrated how psychologists with different theoretical orientations might explain major depression. Explaining behavior is a critically important part of psychologists' work. Without insight into why people think and act as they do, psychologists would produce purely descriptive information without gaining a meaningful understanding of it.

In practice, the relationship between description, prediction, and explanation is complex. For example, theories are offered only after psychologists have a clear description of the problem. Theory, in turn, often allows researchers to make predictions, which are then tested by further research. As psychologists observe and describe the results of their experiments, they often modify their theories (their explanations), make new predictions, and so on.

What about *Changing* Behavior?

Notice that one item is missing from this discussion of the goals of psychology: *changing* behavior. Changing behavior is not one of the essential goals of psychology, though many people mistakenly assume that it is. Certainly many psychologists try to change behavior, but the use of psychology to change behavior is a *practical application* of the science, not a science itself. The difference is similar to that between biologists who study physiology and anatomy and physicians who practice medicine. The scientists seek to understand how certain body systems work. The doctors then use the knowledge they have gained to treat illness. Physicians play a critical role, of course; they must keep current in their scientific knowledge so they can more effectively treat their patients. But physicians only apply what scientists have learned.

The same is true of the science of psychology and the practice of psychological therapy. Good therapists keep current in their knowledge of psychology by reading scientific articles or attending conferences. But the science of psychology cannot be evaluated by looking only at therapists' ability to change behavior. Psychologists may *understand* something like schizophrenia quite well, just as physiologists understand the mechanisms of cancer. But just as biologists cannot always cure cancer, psychologists cannot always change behavior.

Gathering Data (Sampling)

The first goal of psychology is to describe behavior. To do so, psychologists must be objective and detached. They must not allow their own biases or beliefs to influence their research. Psychologists have devised a number of research techniques that allow them to assess behavior while minimizing their biases.

Before describing behavior, psychologists must first determine exactly who they want to study. That may sound obvious, but in practice it can be quite difficult. For example, a psychologist who works for a politician may be asked to assess public opinion of that politician. What group of people should the psychologist survey? Perhaps the politician wants to know the opinion of all Americans. If she desires re-election, she might want to know the opinion of registered voters. However, in most elections no more than 50 percent of registered voters actually cast a ballot. Perhaps, then, the politician wishes to know only the opinions of those most likely to vote. There is no right answer.

Once the target group has been identified, the psychologist must make other decisions. For example, researchers can seldom contact every member of a target group; in most cases it is far too large. In those situations, the researcher will survey a **sample** of the target group.

Sample Size

Sampling procedures involve trade-offs. As a general rule, large samples provide more reliable data than small samples, which tend to be influenced more by extreme cases. A poll intended to reflect the opinions of all the Democrats in the United States could not be based on a sample of only five people, for example. Such a small sample would likely be biased. Just by chance, one of the people surveyed might have highly atypical views—views shared by only a tiny minority of Democrats.

Large samples, though, can be more expensive, not only in dollars spent to collect the data but also in time and effort. Thus selecting a sample involves balancing the benefits of a larger, more representative sample with the costs associated with contacting more subjects. There is no right answer to the question, "How large is large enough?" Many public opinion polls reported in the media are based on samples of approximately 1,000 people, a number that usually provides reliable estimates of the larger population. Such polls usually provide an estimate of the "margin of error," such as: "The President's public approval rating last month was 55 percent, with a margin of error of 3.5 percent." As a general rule, the margin of error goes down as sample size goes up. Whether a particular sample size is adequate—that is, whether its margin of error is small enough—must be determined by individual researchers.

Sampling Techniques

It does not matter how large a sample is if it is biased. Psychologists have developed several techniques to minimize the likelihood of biasing a sample. The first is **random sampling.** Once a sample group has been identified, researchers try to ensure that every member of the group has an equal chance of being surveyed. Suppose you want to draw a random sample of the student body at your school. You could get the names of all students currently enrolled, write their names on cards, put the cards in a large bowl, and draw out 20 percent of the names. If you shuffled the cards well, and the student body is sufficiently large, this technique is likely to produce a sample that mirrors the student body as a whole in many ways. For instance, if 60 percent of all students support lengthening the mid-semester recess, roughly 60 percent of your sample will probably support it also.

Sometimes a psychologist wants to make certain that a sample includes members of specific subgroups. To understand why, consider again the example of Democrats in the United States. The views of southern Democrats frequently differ from those of their northern counterparts. Therefore a good sample of all Democrats would need to include appropriate numbers from each regional subgroup. The goal here is to deliberately assemble a **representative sample,** one in which important subgroups are represented according to their incidence in the population as a whole. Public opinion pollsters routinely construct their samples in this way. They include certain proportions of each gender, each ethnic and age group, each geographic region, each income level, and so forth. The resulting sample is more likely to reflect all people in the nation.

Failure to construct a truly representative sample was the cause of a classic polling error. In the 1930s, political surveying was dominated by the *Literary Digest*, a magazine that had correctly forecast the results of every U.S. presidential election since 1916. The *Digest* conducted its surveys by sending out millions of requests for candidate preferences to people whose names appeared in telephone directories and automobile registration records. George Gallup, a young man from Iowa who had developed his own sampling techniques, identified the flaw in the *Digest*'s approach: in the early part of this century, people who had cars and telephones were much wealthier than most, and so were not representative of all voters. (Then as now, wealthier voters were more likely to vote for a Republican candidate.) In 1936, the *Digest* predicted that Republican Alf Landon would beat Democratic incumbent Franklin D. Roosevelt. Although Gallup thought Landon would do well among affluent voters, he believed much of the rest of the nation (suffering from the Great Depression) would opt for the more liberal Roosevelt. Gallup's prediction was ridiculed right up to the eve of the election, but the next morning Roosevelt had won by a landslide (Reeves, 1983). Gallup went on to build his polling techniques into a widely respected research organization.

Though psychologists recognize the advantages of truly representative samples, those who conduct laboratory research can seldom meet the ideal. Representative sampling is expensive and time-consuming; most psychologists must compromise in some way. As you read about surveys and see them reported on the news, keep in mind these compromises. How large was the sample? How did researchers identify the people in the sample? Was the sample taken randomly? Was it intended to be representative of a specific group? In general, research results are likely to be more reliable if:

1. The sample size is adequate. (This can often be determined from the "margin of error." The larger the sample size, the smaller the margin of error, and the more reliable the results.)

2. The sample was relatively free of biases in the selection process. (This is difficult to determine and depends on the methods used in the survey.)

3. The sample is representative of the intended group. (Often, results collected from one group are incorrectly applied to another group. A sample made up of 1,000 college students—regardless of how randomly they were selected—can seldom be considered representative of "all Americans.")

Interpreting Data (Analysis)

Psychologists use many tools in research, far more than could be described here. However, each of the various data-gathering methods we are about to describe has proved useful for describing, predicting, or explaining behavior. Some of their techniques are more useful for achieving certain aims than others.

For example, observation in a natural setting allows researchers to describe behavior and generate possible explanations, but it is not well suited to testing hypotheses about *why* certain responses occur. **Surveys** are also useful for describing behavior, including attitudes and feelings. They allow psychologists to test large groups of subjects in relatively short periods of time and at a reasonable cost. Surveys can be misleading, though, for reasons we have discussed. Furthermore, surveys have major limitations in determining causes.

The technique of *correlation* allows psychologists to identify and measure relationships among variables. *Regression,* a statistical cousin of correlation, allows researchers to use those relationships to make specific predictions. In baseball, for example, there is a strong relationship between how many hits a team gets and how many runs they are likely to score. That relationship is expressed as a correlation. Because hits and runs are correlated, researchers can use one number to predict the other. Given a certain number of hits, researchers can estimate the number of runs likely to be scored. The accuracy of their prediction, of course, depends on the strength of the relationship (that is, the correlation).

Recall that most psychologists wish to offer explanations for behavior. Unfortunately, neither observational nor correlational research allows psychologist to identify causes. Tests of causation require the use of rigid, specific methods, collectively called the *experimental method.* The specific uses of various methods is the subject of the next section.

Describing Individuals and Groups

The most basic goal of psychologists is *observation.* Meaningful research begins with unbiased observation and accurate description. Sophisticated statistical analyses or skilled writing cannot correct flawed observations or descriptions. Researchers have developed many observational techniques to see behavior in a "real world" environment. We will discuss the use of case studies, naturalistic observations, and surveys.

Case Studies

A **case study** is an in-depth analysis of an individual subject. Usually, the individual is exceptional in some way. He may have exceptional skills, such as Rajan, the mnemonist who has memorized the first 30,000 digits of the number π (*pi*) (see Chapter 1). Subjects may be exceptional in another way: their cases may involve impairment of certain psychological functions. Some stroke patients, for example, have lost the ability to generate meaningful sentences. A psychologist might examine a number of patients with such impairments to see if they all show damage to the same part of the brain. Case studies clearly demonstrate Recurring Theme 2, which stated that psychologists often learn about normal behavior by studying the abnormal. Exceptional individuals can inform psychologist as to how "normal" individuals function.

THEME 2 **Psychologists Learn About the Normal by Studying the Abnormal** Often psychologists conduct case studies of individuals who have suffered some form of brain damage. For example, Chapter 3 will introduce you to an individual known as "H. M." As part of a treatment for severe epilepsy, H. M. had a small portion of his brain destroyed by surgery. Though the surgery was successful in treating his epilepsy, it had one unintended effect: it caused profound, irreversible changes in H. M.'s memory (Hilts, 1995; Milner, 1966).

Case studies have some serious drawbacks. The most serious are the bias inherent in the selection of subjects and the lack of a comparison group. Cases selected for individual study are seldom drawn in a representative manner. Instead, they are chosen because of some unusual circumstance. Psychologists would like to say, for instance, that H. M.'s memory impairment was the result of the brain damage he received in surgery. They cannot say that, though. Remember, surgery was performed on H. M. because of his epilepsy; his memory impairment might well be the result of years of seizures. It might also have resulted from anesthesia used during the surgery, or a mistake made by the doctor during the operation. Any of a number of other factors might apply. Thus, though case histories often lead psychologists to propose further research, they seldom provide convincing evidence by themselves.

Naturalistic Observation

Psychologists sometimes prefer to study behavior in a natural environment, a technique called **naturalistic observation.** They know that the very act of being in a laboratory can change the way a subject is inclined to behave. In one particularly interesting study, Munger and Harris (1989) demonstrated the powerful effect the presence of others can have on behavior, even if the others are not recognized as scientists.

Munger and Harris wondered how the presence of another person would influence a simple behavior, handwashing in a public rest room. Would people be more likely to wash their hands before leaving the rest room if another person was with them—even if that person appeared uninterested? As you might imagine, the answer was "yes." When another person was present, twenty-four of thirty-one women washed their hands before leaving a rest room. In a second group of twenty-eight women who thought they were alone, only eleven washed their hands! It seems likely that the first group's behavior would have changed even more if its members thought they were being "studied by a psychologist."

Imagine investigating the effects of alcohol on social aggressiveness by means of an experiment. Even if you tried to design a laboratory to look just like a bar, as at least one researcher and his colleagues have done (Collins & Marlatt, 1981; Marlatt & Nathan, 1978), could you completely rule out the possibility that subjects were controlling their behavior because they knew they were being watched? Probably not. The only way around this problem would be to observe drinkers in a natural setting where they did not know they were being studied. The cardinal rule of such naturalistic observation is that the investigators stay out of the way.

Many questions lend themselves to naturalistic observation. An organizational psychologist might use the method to study leadership roles in small corporations. A developmental psychologist might use it to study the way four-year-olds interact in a preschool classroom. Such observation is sometimes done through a one-way window, so the presence of the psychologist does not interfere with routine behavior.

Although naturalistic observation is extremely valuable for investigating many types of questions, it also has limitations. The main problem is that a researcher cannot control the situation, and so cannot test cause-and-effect hypotheses. If the psychologists in the hypothetical barroom study observed that customers get rowdier as they drink more, could they say that alcohol was inducing the aggressive behavior? What if, as the evening wore on, the bar became packed with people? Perhaps the increased aggressiveness was due less to the amount of alcohol consumed than to the extent of the crowding. Naturalistic observation can be a valuable tool, but it is

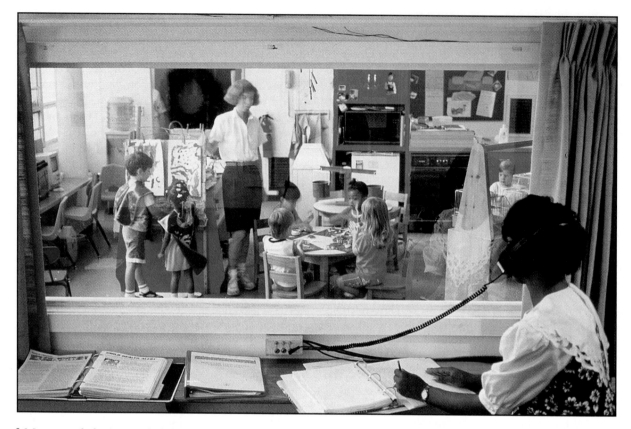

Many psychologists study behavior in naturalistic settings. The psychologist in the foreground of this picture is observing students in a classroom while hiding behind a one-way mirror. If the students were aware they were being observed, they might have behaved differently.

limited to describing, and perhaps predicting, behavior; it cannot be used to determine the cause.

Surveys

A survey is an attempt to estimate the opinions, characteristics, or behaviors of a particular population by investigating a representative sample. We have already discussed many of the important issues associated with sampling. Because survey data can often be collected quickly and economically, the technique is used in many areas of psychology.

Probably the most famous survey of this century was the one behind the Kinsey reports, published in 1948 and 1953. Alfred Kinsey and his staff interviewed more than 10,000 men and women about their sexual behavior and attitudes—a radical thing to do at the time. Kinsey found, among other things, that sexual behaviors considered abnormal in the 1940s (such as masturbation, homosexual activity,

and oral-genital sex) were much more common than most people supposed. Methods similar to Kinsey's are still being used today to study sexual behavior, attitudes, and knowledge (Reinisch & Beasley, 1980).

Many factors contribute to a survey's validity. One is the wording of the questions. Leading questions can completely bias the results, and even very subtle changes in wording can alter a person's responses. Elizabeth Loftus (1975) found that people who were asked "Do you get headaches frequently and if so how often?" reported an average of 2.2 headaches a week; whereas people who were asked "Do you get headaches occasionally and if so how often?" reported a weekly average of 0.7 headaches. Ruth Maki (Maki & Serra, 1992) found that students make more accurate predictions of future performance when she asked them to predict "how poorly" they will do on an upcoming test, rather than "how well" they expected to perform. Even when a question is worded neutrally—for example, "Do you get headaches?"—people can still give misinformation. Some invariably answer "yes" just to be agreeable. Others seem to have a built-in tendency to say "no." If a survey contains questions that reflect on ability or character, people will frequently present themselves in a more favorable light than is warranted (Cannell & Kahn, 1968; Myers & Ridl, 1979). Similarly, if a survey covers a sensitive subject like race relations, many people will claim they believe what they think they ought to believe.

Steps can be taken to prevent problems with the wording of survey questions. For example, researchers can include several differently worded questions on the same topic, to see if a person responds consistently. Careful construction of a survey greatly increases the likelihood that the findings will accurately reflect what people really think and do.

Finding Relationships between Variables (Correlation)

Correlational designs allow researchers to find relationships between variables. For example, a correlational study may look for a relationship between scores on a placement test and future classroom performance. A special type of correlational technique called **regression** uses the relationship between variables (the *correlation*) to make specific predictions. The admissions officers at your university probably have some type of regression formula that allows them to make useful predictions about applicants. For example, many admissions officers can predict students' first-year grade-point average (GPA) on the basis of test scores and high school rankings.

Correlations between variables can be positive: as one variable increases, so does the other. For example, positive correlations would likely exist between SAT scores and first-year GPAs, or between workers' salaries and their years of experience. In general, as one of these variables increases, the other is likely to increase as well. There will always be exceptions, of course—some students with low SAT scores earn high GPAs, for example—but in general, as one increases, so does the other.

Correlations can also be negative: as one variable increases, the other tends to decrease. For example, negative correlations would exist between daily TV watching and GPAs. Those who watch more TV tend to have lower GPAs. The number of years of computer experience and the time it takes to learn a new computer program are also negatively correlated. In general, the greater the amount of experience, the smaller the time required to learn a new task.

Correlation Coefficients

The strength of the relationship between two variables can be expressed mathematically using a **correlation coefficient,** symbolized by the Greek symbol *rho,* or *r.* A correlation coefficient is a number ranging from $r = -1.00$, which indicates a perfect negative correlation, through $r = 0$, which indicates no correlation, to $r = +1.00$, which indicates a perfect positive correlation. The coefficient provides two distinct pieces of information. First, the sign of the coefficient tells you the direction of the relationship. Correlation coefficients that are greater than 0 (that is, they have a positive sign) indicate that two variables are positively correlated. As one variable increases, the other variable tends to increase, too.

Second, the coefficient reflects the *magnitude* of the relationship. Correlations close to the extremes of +1.00 and −1.00 indicate a strong relationship between two variables. The absolute value of the correlation coefficient (that is, the value without the sign) shows how strong the relationship is.

It is important to remember that a correlation coefficient of, say, −.65 is just as strong as a correlation coefficient of +.65. Suppose that researchers at a certain university find that grade-point average and number of traffic violations have a correlation of −.42, while grade-point average and running speed have a correlation of +.26. Which relationship is stronger? In this fictitious example, a stronger correlation exists between traffic violations and grade-point average than between running ability and grade-point average, because .42 is larger than .26. The minus sign in front of the coefficient has nothing to do with the strength of the relationship. It simply indicates that the relationship is negative: as traffic violations increase, grade-point average declines, and vice versa.

To summarize, correlational studies are a way of discovering the extent to which two variables are related. The correlation coefficient is a quantitative means of expressing that relationship. At one extreme, a correlation coefficient of 0 indicates no relationship between the variables in question: they vary independently of one another. At the other extreme, a correlation coefficient of −1.00 or +1.00 indicates a

(Left) Many different variables are associated with the time required to familiarize onself with a new software package: previous experience with computers, the complexity of the software, and so on. Correlational studies allow psychologists to look for relationships among such variables. In a special type of correlational technique called regression, the relationship between variables (their correlation*) is used to make specific predictions. For example, admissions officers at universities (right) often use scores on standardized tests and class rankings to predict students' first-year grade-point averages.*

perfect relationship between the two: if you know the quantitative change in one variable, you can state the accompanying change in the other precisely. Most of the relationships studied by psychologists fall somewhere between these extremes.

Correlation versus Causation

While correlational research is vital to psychological investigations, it does have a serious limitation. Though a correlational study can show that two variables are related, it cannot establish that one factor causes the other. A third factor, related to each of the other two, may also be involved, sometimes called the *third-variable problem.*

For example, Keith Stanovich and his colleagues (Allen, Cipielewski, & Stanovich, 1992; Stanovich & Cunningham, 1992, 1993) have studied children, college students, and adults in an attempt to under-

stand why some adults have better verbal abilities than others. Stanovich and his colleagues administered a number of different tests to their students. Some were achievement tests similar to tests you may have taken in high school, measuring reading skill and general knowledge. Others were simple recognition tests. In one such test, students were presented with eighty names. Forty of those names were of popular authors (for example, Stephen King, Louis L'Amour, and Stephen J. Gould). The other forty names were taken from a list of reading researchers, whom the students almost certainly did not know. The students were asked to identify the names of the popular authors. In the second test, students were given a list of eighty magazine titles. Again, forty of the titles were from actual magazines (such as *Consumer Reports, Mademoiselle,* and *Mother Earth News*), and the others were fictitious (such as

The fact that two variables are correlated does not necessarily mean that one causes the other. For instance, Keith Stanovich and his colleagues found that students' reading ability is positively correlated with their ability to recognize the names of famous authors. Neither variable causes the other, however. Instead, both are likely caused by a third variable: print exposure (the number of words one has read in a lifetime).

Future Forecast and *Neuberger Review*). As before, they were asked to identify those titles that were taken from real magazines.

Stanovich and Cunningham (1992) showed that scores on both tests were significantly correlated with many measures of reading ability (correlations were typically $r = +.60$ or higher). On the basis of this finding, one may be tempted to conclude that one way to increase reading ability is to learn the names of authors and magazines. Of course, that conclusion would be incorrect.

Does the ability to recognize authors' names and magazine titles *cause* students to score higher on tests of verbal ability? Or do their verbal abilities *cause* them to perform well on these recognition tests? Most likely, neither factor directly causes the other. Instead, Stanovich and his colleagues contend that better name recognition and reading ability are both likely to be caused by *print exposure,* the number of words an individual has read in a lifetime. Those who are avid readers are more likely to have come across an author's name or a magazine title, increasing their likelihood of recognizing those names and titles. Reading ability is also enhanced through practice, and reading practice increases print exposure. Those who read more typically have better reading skills and larger vocabularies than those who have read less.[1]

Because of these (and related) results, reading researchers like Stanovich believe print exposure to be critical to the development of literacy, academic success, and ultimately success in the workforce. As a result, they advise parents and teachers to encourage reading in children, even very young children. One highly respected reading researcher, Marilyn Jager Adams, has stated that the single most important thing a parent can do to enhance literacy in their children is to read aloud to them (Adams, 1990; see also Weaver, 1994).

Determining Cause and Effect (Experiments)

As useful as these techniques are, they do not allow psychologists to answer "cause and effect" questions. Only **experiments** allow researchers to identify (and test) cause and effect relationships. Yet experimental designs are not perfect, for they often create artificial situations. As a result, they may not reveal the complexities of behavior as it occurs outside the laboratory. (The "In Depth" section for Chapter 2 deals with this topic.)

The basic procedures of an experiment are best explained with an example. Social psychologists study the influence of others on the behavior of an individual. One important question might be, "Under what conditions are people more likely to want to be with others rather than alone?" Of the many experiments on this topic, we will focus on a classic one performed nearly forty years ago by Stanley Schachter (1959). Schachter was one of the first

---

[1] In a related study, Stanovich and Cunningham (1993) showed that exposure to television was either unrelated or slightly *negatively* correlated with literacy.

psychologists to suggest that the desire to affiliate does not depend simply on individual personality traits. Affiliation, he proposed, also depends on the situations in which people find themselves, and among the situations most conducive to affiliation are those that arouse fear. This was Schachter's **hypothesis.**

Schachter's first step in testing his hypothesis was to design an experiment in which subjects would experience fear. The method he chose was devious but highly effective. He arranged for a number of students who had volunteered to participate in an experiment to be met at the laboratory door by a white-coated man who identified himself as Dr. Gregor Zilstein from the medical school's department of neurology and psychiatry. Surrounded by an impressive array of electrical equipment, the doctor told the students they were part of an important study on the physiological effects of electric shock. Each would undergo a series of shocks while pulse rate, blood pressure, and other physical reactions were recorded. The shocks, the doctor warned in an ominous tone, would be extremely painful, because only intense shock could provide the information required. But, he added with a tight smile, the shocks would cause no permanent tissue damage.

The students who encountered this diabolical doctor constituted what is called the experimental group. An **experimental group** consists of those subjects who experience the experimental condition—in this case, exposure to a fear-arousing situation. Most experiments also include a **control group,** to provide a source of comparison. Subjects in the control group experience all the conditions the experimental subjects do except the key factor the psychologist is evaluating. Thus in Schachter's experiment, the control subjects were also greeted at the door by a white-coated doctor, who told them they were about to participate in an experiment on the effects of electric shock. But this time, instead of grimly warning that the shocks would be extremely painful, the doctor said in a kindly manner that they would produce only a mild, not unpleasant tingling sensation.

Subjects in this experiment were placed in either the experimental or the control group completely at random, a procedure called *random assignment*. Random assignment is a way of compensating for the fact that experimenters cannot possibly control for all the subjects' characteristics. In this study, for instance, some people may have been naturally more outgoing than others, more eager to affiliate when given a chance. Schachter could not erase such tendencies in his subjects by the stroke of some magic experimental wand. But he could try to make sure that all the extroverts (the outgoing people) did not end up in one group while all the introverts (the shy people) ended up in the other. The ideal would be to place a similar number of extroverts and introverts in each of the two groups. In that way, any biases their characteristics might impose on the study would balance out.

However, controlling for every possible bias in subjects is impossible. This is why random assignment of subjects is so helpful. When a sample is sufficiently large, random assignment tends to produce a good shuffling, so to speak, not only with regard to introversion and extroversion but with regard to other factors that might bias the experiment's results. Consequently, any observed differences in the behavior of the two groups are not likely to have been caused by inherent differences in the people who formed those groups.

After Schachter had created appropriate experimental and control groups, one last step remained. He had to give his subjects the opportunity to affiliate with others in order to observe the effects, if any, of their fear. So after describing the upcoming experiment, Dr. Zilstein announced that everyone would have to wait ten minutes while the experimental equipment was prepared. Each subject was given the choice of waiting alone in a private room or waiting with other subjects. Their choices provided the experimental data. Once the subjects had expressed their preferences, the experiment ended; no shocks were ever given.

The results of Schachter's pioneering study are shown in Figure 2-1. They suggest that the tendency to affiliate does indeed increase in fear-arousing situations. Students subjected to the experimental condition (in which the doctor's words were ominous and his smile sadistic) were much more likely to want to wait with others than subjects who experienced the control condition (in which the doctor's words were reassuring and his manner kindly). Thus, Schachter's hypothesis that fear can promote affiliation was supported by his data.

Let us summarize how Schachter's procedures met the requirements of an experiment. An experiment is a controlled method of exploring the relationship between factors capable of change, called

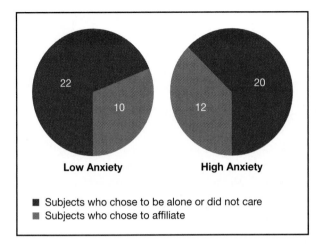

Low Anxiety   **High Anxiety**

■ Subjects who chose to be alone or did not care
■ Subjects who chose to affiliate

FIGURE 2-1   *Results of Schacter's Experiment. As Schacter predicted, fear and anxiety caused people to want to affiliate. Those in the High Anxiety group were twice as likely to want to be with others in the experiment.*

variables. The factor that the experimenter deliberately manipulates is called the **independent variable.** In Schachter's study the independent variable was the degree to which the doctor's words and manner were fear-inducing. The **dependent variable** is what the experimenter actually measures; nearly always it involves some form of behavior. If the experimenter's hypothesis is right, the dependent variable should change when the independent variable is manipulated. Changes in the dependent variable, in other words, *depend* on changes in the independent variable. In Schachter's experiment, the dependent variable was the choice subjects made between waiting alone or waiting with others.

Phrasing the researcher's hypothesis as an "if/then" statement helps to identify the two key variables in an experiment. For Schachter's experiment, the if/then statement would be "If a person is exposed to a fear-arousing situation, then the desire to affiliate with other people should increase above normal levels." The factor that follows the word *if* is the independent variable; the factor that follows the word *then* is the dependent variable. An if/then statement stresses that a cause-and-effect relationship occurs in one direction only. Change in the independent variable causes change in the dependent variable, but not vice versa. Because an experiment provides a means of establishing causality, it is the data-gathering method of choice for many psychologists.

Few experimental investigations completely answer a researcher's questions. Indeed, many times an experiment will raise more questions than it answers. Note that Schachter's experiment barely scratch the surface in asking important questions about the motivation to affiliate. Does fear *always* produce a desire to be with other people, or only under certain circumstances? And exactly why, in Schachter's study, did fear have the effect it did? Did the fearful subjects want to be distracted? Did they want to express their anxious feelings to a sympathetic ear? Or were they looking for a chance to compare their own emotions with those of others in the same predicament? What about other factors that encourage affiliation? Which are the most important, why do they have that effect, and how powerful are they compared to fear? To get a full understanding of affiliation, researchers would need to do additional research on these and similar questions. A comprehensive understanding of any complex human behavior can be gained only from a large number of studies that build and expand on one another.

Assessing Genetic and Environmental Influences (Behavioral Genetics)

To this point, we have been examining the effects various experiences or situations might have on behavior. Most of the examples we have cited involved ways in which behavior changes in response to changes in the environment. But studying the effect of external environmental events is only part of the answer.

Broadly speaking, behavior is affected by two interacting factors: heredity and environment. **Heredity** refers to the inherited set of developmental instructions that make us who we are, instructions that are transmitted to us by the **genes** we are born with. Heredity is fixed at conception; one's life experiences do not change an individual's genetic endowment. **Environment** refers to all the other influences we encounter. These influences vary with gender, social class, ethnic background, and so forth. Examples of our environment include physical surroundings (houses, schools, books, toys, and other objects) and the people with whom we interact (family, friends, neighbors, and so on), even the food we eat. Together all these factors create our environment.

Behavioral geneticists estimate the relative contributions of heredity and environment to behavior. While many psychological characteristics are influenced by genetic factors, environmental factors can have a powerful effect on behavior. Children who are raised in an impoverished environment like the inner city neighborhood shown here are less likely to be successful in school than those raised in an enriched environment.

Which is more important, heredity or environment? This question, which lies at the very heart of psychology, is sometimes referred to as the "nature-nurture" debate. Nature refers to genetic influences; nurture, to the environment. Of course, any answer to the question is exceedingly complex. Behavior is almost always determined by some combination of genetic influences and environment. But recently, psychologists have developed techniques that allow them to estimate the relative contributions of innate and external factors. One of the most powerful of those techniques is **behavioral genetics** (Plomin, 1986, 1989).

Virtually every cell of every plant or animal contains a nucleus, which carries **chromosomes,** the structures that store material to be passed from one generation to the next. Chromosomes in turn are made up of many smaller genes. In addition to being physically smaller than chromosomes, genes are also more restricted in their effects. A single gene, for example, codes the sequence responsible for determining your eye color.

Genes are the chemical "recipes" for building and maintaining a living organism. Events that happen to you during your lifetime—the things you learn, experiences you have, injuries you suffer—do not change your genetic makeup.[2] Instead, your genetic makeup shapes your response to those events. Genetic effects never occur in isolation, however. They are shaped by the environment in which the genetic recipes are executed (see Dawkins, 1986, 1996). Depending on biochemical changes within the body, the instructions in particular genes may or may not be followed, or they may be modified (Dawkins, 1996).

Most cells in the human body contain twenty-three pairs of chromosomes, or forty-six in all. The sperm and egg cells are different; they contain only half as many chromosomes. Toward the end of their development they undergo a form of cell division, and the twenty-three chromosome pairs split apart (leaving only twenty-three chromosomes, not twenty-three pairs), are rearranged, and then distributed to two "daughter" cells. Splitting the chromosome pairs shuffles the chromosomes, so a different combination gets distributed to each daughter cell. The shuffled chromosomes of one parent combine with the shuffled chromosomes of the other parent at conception, so the new offspring again has twenty-three pairs of chromosomes. The shuffling and recombining of the chromosomes guarantee variability in future generations, one of the necessary conditions for natural selection to operate.

The term *behavioral genetics* is somewhat misleading, because it seems to imply that the goal of the approach is to prove that genes determine behavior. More accurately, behavioral geneticists have developed techniques that can be used to identify the *relative contributions* of genetic and environmental influ-

---

[2]Technically, this is not true. There are some environmental factors that *can* change your genetic material, such as radiation exposure. However, these changes, called *mutations*, usually introduce random, unpredictable changes.

ences. While it is true that many human behaviors are genetically influenced, it is also true that virtually every behavior is influenced by factors *other than genetics.*

In the simplest terms, behavioral geneticists attempt to explain individual differences in behavior. Why are some children outgoing, while others are shy? Why do some churchgoers affiliate with evangelical religious groups, while others prefer denominations that are more restrained? Why do some children learn to read easily, while others in the same classroom struggle and are eventually labeled dyslexic?

Behavioral geneticists begin with the assumption that all differences in behavior can be accounted for by two powerful factors: genetic factors (those that are innate) and environmental factors (those that result from experience). This assumption is simply a formalization of the "nature-nurture" problem mentioned earlier. By studying individuals with *shared genetic factors* (i.e., genetic relatives), behavioral geneticists can estimate the degree of genetic influence on behavior. And by studying individuals with *shared environmental factors,* such as siblings who were raised in the same house, they can estimate the degree of environmental influence on behavior. After the genetic factors and shared environmental (familial) factors have been taken into account, any differences in behavior that remain must be due to unique, individual experiences, or *nonshared environmental factors.*

The key to research in behavioral genetics is finding appropriately related individuals. Behavioral geneticists must find individuals with similar genetic endowments but different environmental backgrounds. They must also find those with similar environmental experience but different genes. They need some who share both genetic and environmental influences, and some who share neither. Only then can they make the necessary comparisons.

Separating Genetic and Environmental Influences

Children get their genetic makeup from their biological parents. Each child shares on average 50 percent of his or her genes with each parent. Siblings also share an average of 50 percent of their genes with each other. The more remote the family association, the smaller the amount of shared genetic material. Grandchildren, for example, share only 25 percent of

their genetic material with a single grandparent; cousins share even less, only 12.5 percent. Figure 2-2 summarizes the degree of genetic overlap among family members.

Two relationships are particularly useful to behavioral geneticists: that of twins, especially monozygotic (identical) twins, and that of children raised in families other than their genetic families—adopted children. In rare cases, identical twins are adopted into different families. To behavioral geneticists, those situations are the most informative.

Twin studies are useful for several reasons. Remember that monozygotic twins are genetically identical (*monozygote* means literally "single egg"). Consequently, they share 100 percent of their genetic material—something no other humans do. Identical twins , therefore, provide the most extreme test of genetic influence. If some behavior is determined *entirely* by genetic factors (which is exceedingly rare), and if one twin exhibits the trait, the other will also.[3]

However, identical twins have other influences in common. For example, twins usually share *environmental* influences. They were fed similar foods when they were children, were treated similarly by their parents, and may even have slept in the same room. So while monozygotic twins are identical genetically, they are also quite similar environmentally. How can the effects of genetic similarity be separated from the effects of environmental similarity?

While monozygotic twins are produced from a single egg, dizygotic twins ("fraternal" twins) are produced from two eggs (*di-zygote,* literally "two eggs"). They share 50 percent of genetic material,

---

[3]One example of a behavior that is entirely genetic would be a disorder like Huntington's disease. Huntington's is a degenerative disorder where movement becomes increasingly erratic. At early stages, movements may be "twitchy" and the individual appears fidgety. As the disease progresses, movement becomes rapid and jerky, and involves entire limbs. There is no cure, and death usually follows within fifteen years of the onset. Huntington's disease is the result of a single, dominant gene. The chance that a parent would pass on this gene to their child is 50 percent. To complicate matters even further, the first symptoms don't appear until around age forty-five. By this time, many of those parents carrying the dominant gene may have already had children. Each child, then, has a 50 percent chance of inheriting the gene and contracting Huntington's disease.

Woody Guthrie, the legendary American folk singer (the composer of "This Land Is Your Land"), died of Huntington's disease. His son Arlo Guthrie, a contemporary folk singer, has known since that time that he has a 50 percent chance of contracting the disease himself. As of this writing, he has not shown any symptoms.

FIGURE 2-2 *Behavioral geneticists make comparisons among individuals who vary in their genetic similarity. Note that the final category, 0 percent genetic overlap, would be the genetic similarity for* any *two individuals who were not genetically related.*

Common Genetic Influence?	Percentage Genetic Similarity?	Examples?
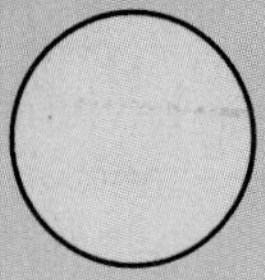	100%	Monozygotic (identical) twins
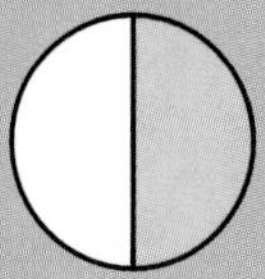	50%	Siblings Parent/child Dizygotic (fraternal) twins
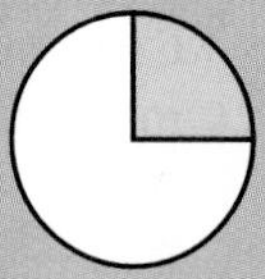	25%	Grandparent/grandchild Half-sibling
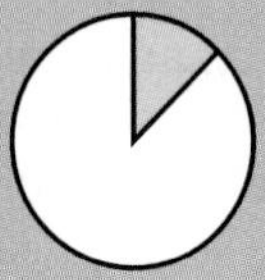	12.5%	Cousins Great-grandparents/ great-grandchildren
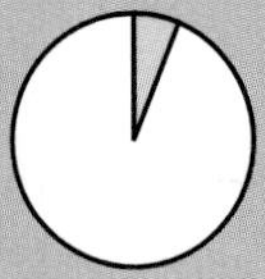	6.25%	Second cousins
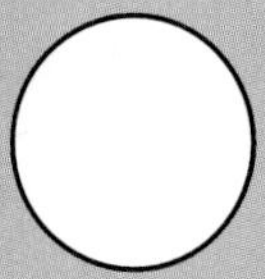	0%	Adopted parents/siblings (*all others not genetically related*)

just like other siblings. However, dizygotic twins usually share environmental influences, often to the same extent as monozygotic twins. Behavioral geneticists, then, can compare monozygotic twins and dizygotic twins to assess the relative importance of genetics and shared environment. They can compare the behavior of two twins, looking for similarities and differences. In some situations, the two twins will behave similarly. In others, they will not. However, if the fraternal twins' behavior is just as similar as that of identical twins, then their behavior has been environmentally influenced. If it were genetically caused, the behavior of identical twins should be *more* similar than the behavior of fraternal twins.

Adoption studies allow behavioral geneticists to measure environmental determinants. Adopted children share no genetic material with other children in the family (except in rare situations where biological siblings are adopted into the same family), but they do share environmental influences. Researchers determine the similarity between the behavior of the adopted child and the behavior of other children in the family. (They share environmental but not genetic influences.) If the similarity is greater than that of two nonrelated children (who share neither genes nor environment), the behavior can be attributed to environmental influence. In a few cases monozygotic twins have been adopted into different homes. In these cases behavioral geneticists can estimate the relative contribution of genetic factors (which are identical) and environmental factors (which are considerably different).

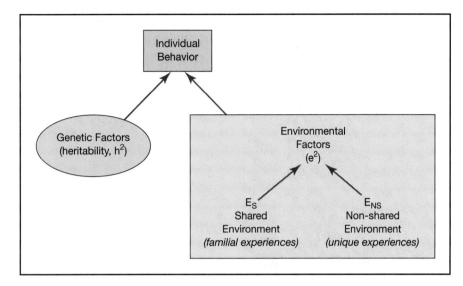

FIGURE 2-3   *Behavioral geneticists analyze individual differences in behavior. First, they use genetic similarity between individuals to determine the relative contribution of genetic factors on behavior* (heritability, *symbolized* h^2). *The remainder of the differences, by definition, must be caused by the* environment (*symbolized* e^2). *Then, they use environmental similarities (such as being raised in the same household) to separate family influences* (shared environment, E_S) *from those unique to the individual* (non-shared environment, E_{NS}).

You can see the pattern that is emerging. Behavioral geneticists look for cases with shared genetic influence but not shared environmental influences. They then find cases that have similar environmental influences but no genetic overlap. Sometimes, they find cases of intermediate genetic overlap but high environmental similarity (same-age cousins raised in the same household, for example). Putting all these pieces together, behavioral geneticists can determine how much of the variability in behavior can be attributed to genetic factors and how much to environmental factors.

Measuring Genetic and Environmental Influences

Recall that all individual differences in behavior are assumed to be the result of either genetic factors [which geneticists call **heritability,** represented by the symbol h^2 (Plomin, 1990)] or environmental factors (represented by e^2). The environmental factors can be further divided into **shared environmental influences** (called E_S) and **nonshared environmental influences** (called E_{NS}). In most cases, E_S refers to the effect of family environment (which is common to all members of the household) and E_{NS} refers to the effect of unique experiences of each individual. This is summarized in Figure 2-3. Because behav-

ioral geneticists know the degree of genetic and environmental similarity among subjects, they can estimate the relative importance of each. The mathematical techniques used to make these estimates are complicated, but the logic is not.

For example, assume that researchers are conducting a study of differences in IQ. Ideally, behavioral geneticists would assemble a vast group of relatives who share different degrees of genetic and environmental similarity. Some would be monozygotic twins, with identical genetic components. Some would be siblings raised in the same family environment. And some might be twins who were raised in different households. In a nutshell, the researchers would try to find as many diverse pairings of relatives as possible. Using a large, diverse sample, researchers can use complex and sophisticated statistical analyses to identify the relative importance of each factor in behavior.

Such large, diverse samples are rare. Furthermore, identifying all these individuals and collecting the necessary data about them would be an enormous, expensive task. Fortunately, behavioral geneticists can often make reasonable estimates from smaller, less diverse samples—*if* the samples allow them to make the critical comparisons. Figure 2-4 shows which comparisons can be particularly useful

Unlike other humans, monozygotic (identical) twins share 100 percent of their genetic material. They therefore provide the most extreme test of genetic influences.

for determining genetic and environmental causes.

In all, behavioral geneticists may be able to identify a group of several hundred people. They know the genetic similarities among these people, and they also know the degree of shared environmental influence. Now, for example, they may administer the IQ test to all the participants. Remember that each person in the study belongs to a matched "pair," similar in some ways and different in others. In most cases, the IQ scores of two members of a pair are likely to be similar. Because researchers know how each pair is related (genetically, environmentally, or both), we can determine the relative importance of our three components: how much of the similarities can be attributed to genetic influence, how much to shared environmental (familial) influence, and how much to nonshared (unique) environmental influence.

Genetic influence, or heritability (h^2), is usually expressed with a single number that provides an estimate of the proportion of the difference between

subjects that can be attributed to genetic factors. Most studies of IQ estimate heritability (h^2) to be about .55 (see Gilger, 1995). This means that approximately half of all differences in IQ can be explained by genetic variability. Clearly, there is a strong genetic component to IQ. However, by definition the *remainder* of IQ differences must be due to environmental factors (e^2). If $h^2 = .55$, e^2 *must* be .45.[4] Nearly half of all IQ differences, then, must be caused by differences in environment.

Behavioral geneticists can often divide e^2 into shared and nonshared components. Some individuals in a study share substantial environmental influences, usually because they were raised in the same family. But each will also have had unique experiences, not shared by the other. For example, twins may have had different teachers in school. For these cases, e^2 can be divided into shared environmental influences (E_S) and nonshared environmental influences (E_{NS}), mentioned earlier (see Figure 2-3) In most cases, E_S refers to the effect of family environment common to both siblings; E_{NS} refers to the effect of unique experiences, apart from the shared family environment. Figure 2-3 displays the relationship of genetic and environmental factors in influencing behavior.

Behavioral genetics has provided psychology with a powerful set of tools to determine the causes of behavior. Those tools can be applied to almost any kind of behavior: learning, temperament, personality, happiness, cognitive ability, scholastic work, and so on. For example, Kendler and others (1994) studied over 1,000 pairs of twins and almost 1,500 of their parents in an effort to find determinants of alcoholism in women. They found strong evidence for a genetic component to alcoholism: between 51 and 59 percent of the alcoholism they observed in daughters could be traced to genetic factors. As you have just learned, this means that 41 to 49 percent of the alcoholism the researchers observed was due to factors *other than genetics*. However, Kendler and colleagues found no evidence for shared (predictable) familial influences (that is, E_S was small). In other words, being the (genetic) child of an alcoholic parent put the women at risk for becoming alcoholic themselves—but the risk was due to genetic factors, not environmental factors.

---

[4]Remember, *all* differences are assumed to be attributable to either genetic or environmental factors. That means ($h^2 + e^2 = 1.00$), by definition. If $h^2 = .55$, then $e^2 = (1.00 − .55)$, or .45.

FIGURE 2-4   *Behavioral geneticists compare individuals who have common genetic influences, common environmental influences, both, or neither.*

Comparison?	Genetic Similarity?	Environmental Similarity?	Usefulness?	Used to Estimate:
Identical twins raised together	100%	Very high	Any ***differences*** in behavior must be due to **nonshared environmental factors**	E_{NS} Non-shared environment
Identical twins raised apart	100%	None	Any ***similarities*** in behavior must be due to **genetic factors,** since they shared no environmental influences	h^2 Heritability
Identical twins raised together **with** Identical twins raised apart	100% *and* 100%	Very high *and* None	If *identical twins raised together* are ***more similar*** than *identical twins raised apart*, this additional similarity must be due to being raised in the **same family environment**	E_S Shared (familial) environment
Adoptive parents and adopted children	0%	Very high	If adopted children are ***similar*** to their adoptive parents, this must be due to being raised in the **same family environment**	E_S Shared (familial) environment
Parent and biological child **with** Same parent and adopted child	50% and 0%	Very high *and* Very high	If parents and children are ***more similar*** than parent and adopted child, the additional similarity must be **genetic factors**	h^2 Heritability

This is a subtle but critical point: saying that E_S was minimal is *not* to say that the family had no effect. Instead, it means that the effects of environment were different for different family members. Consider the effect of being raised by an alcoholic parent on adopted children. Some children might react by avoiding alcohol entirely, while others might react by abusing alcohol themselves. The family environment would powerfully influence these behaviors, of course, but not in a uniform, predictable manner.

These firefighters, identical twins, were adopted into different families at birth. When they were reunited as adults many years later, their similarities were remarkable. Not only did they look alike; they had chosen the same career, grown mustaches, and formed many of the same likes and dislikes—including their favorite brand of beer!

Behavioral genetics is a relatively new technique for psychologists. As findings like those of Kendler and associates (1994) are made known, psychologists are forced to reconsider long-held beliefs regarding genetic and family influences. Genetic factors appear to play a larger role in many behaviors than previously believed, and the effects of familial influences are neither as large nor as consistent as psychologists once thought. However, the findings of behavioral genetics can also be misinterpreted (see Gilger, 1995). Table 2-2 explains some common misunderstandings of behavioral genetics.

Summarizing Data (Statistics)

After collecting their data, researchers must present the findings to others. In most cases, researchers need to summarize their data in a clear, concise way. To help them do this, psychologists often use **descriptive statistics** to convey summary information. Over the past century a number of powerful statistical techniques have been developed to answer increasingly complex questions. If you pursue your education in psychology, you will be exposed to many of these. For our purposes we will focus on two categories of statistics: measures of central tendency and dispersion.

Measures of Central Tendency

Suppose a psychologist wishes to know whether rats will learn to run a maze more quickly if they are hungry. To do so, she assembles thirty-three rats, then takes eleven selected at random and keeps them in a cage where food is available at all times. Then she takes eleven others, also selected at random, and puts them in a cage where they are deprived of food for ten hours prior to testing. The psychologist takes the remaining eleven rats and puts them in a cage where they are deprived of food for twenty hours prior to testing.

Later, one by one, she puts each rat in a maze similar to that shown in Figure 2-5. She puts a piece of food in the "goal" box at the end of the maze. Then she times each rat to see how long they take to go from the start box to the goal box. Running times for each rat in this hypothetical experiment are shown in Table 2-3.

How would you summarize their running times? Did one group of animals tend to run faster than another? A psychologist would report these findings using some measure of the most characteristic score for each group, called a measure of **central tendency.** The most common measure of central tendency is the **mean,** or average. To compute the average, you simply add all the scores together and divide by the total number of scores. Notice that the mean for the second group, those rats deprived of food for ten hours, is the smallest.

The mean is just one way to report the central tendency. Look closely at the scores in the group deprived of food for twenty hours. Notice that most of the times were low, except for one rat with a time of ninety seconds. The one extreme score inflated the mean for this group, so that all the rats except one

TABLE 2-2 *Common Misconceptions of Behavioral Genetics*

Misconception	Correct Understanding
1. Traits are all or none in terms of genetic effects.	Most genetic influences result from multiple genes and environmetal factors operating together.
2. The path from gene to behavior is simple.	Most genetic influences involve complex relationships. Though many (negative) genetic influences may *increase a person's risk* of encountering difficulty, they seldom directly *cause* it. For example, persons genetically at risk for developing alcoholism will not become alcoholic if they avoid drinking alcohol.
3. If a behavior has a genetic component, it cannot be changed.	Even in traits with large heritability estimates, environmental influences play a significant role. Thompson et al. (1991), for example, showed that scholastic overachievement and underachievement are likely due to environmental, not genetic, causes.
4. The most important nongenetic influence is the family atmosphere (E_S).	In fact, family influences (E_S) play a small role in most cases of *normal* development. Estimates of (E_S) on IQ, for example, show minimal effects of familial environmental influences. *However,* in extreme cases of abuse or deprivation, family effects may be significant.
5. When family atmosphere (E_S) estimates are low, parental (or family) influence does not influence behavior.	When (E_S) is small, the shared environment does not lead to *predictable, consistent* effects. For example, though Kendler and colleagues (1994) found (E_S) to be minimal, that does *not* mean that being raised as the child of an alcoholic has no effect on a child's behavior. It simply means that the parent's alcoholism does not *consistently* influence *all children in the same way.* Being raised in an alcoholic home is certainly an influence—but some individuals react by abstaining from alcohol as adults, while others react by becoming alcoholic themselves.

*Following Gilger, 1995.

had a faster running time than the mean. In situations like this, the mean might not be the most useful indicator of central tendency. The researcher may choose instead to report the **median,** the score that falls exactly in the middle of the scores when sorted from lowest to highest. In fact, the median is often used in situations in which extreme scores might skew the mean. A third way of reporting central tendency is the **mode,** simply the score that occurs most frequently. The mean, median, and mode are the most common statistics used to report central tendency.

Measures of Dispersion

While the mean, median, and mode tell us something about the "typical" score, they cannot tell us *how* scores are distributed. Are scores clustered toward the middle of the distribution, or are they more evenly spaced? To answer these questions, researchers use measures of **dispersion.**

Assume we have exam scores for two different classes, and the scores are distributed like those in Table 2-4. In this example, the mean and the median are identical in the two distributions. But the distribution of the scores is quite different. One useful

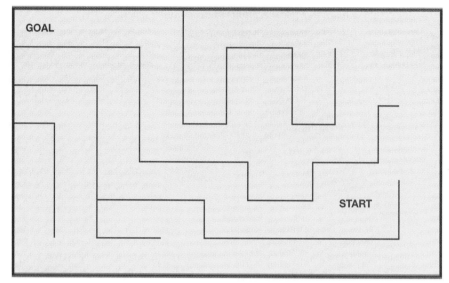

FIGURE 2-5 Sample maze. The rat is placed in the START box and must navigate to the GOAL box. The dependent variable is the time it takes the rat to successfully complete the maze.

measure of dispersion in such distributions is the **range,** the difference between the highest and lowest observations. In Table 2-4, the range of scores for Class A is 6 (85–79); the range of scores for Class B is much larger, 44 (98–54).

The range is a fairly crude indicator of a distribution's shape. One extreme score can dramatically affect the range. A more sensitive measure of dispersion is the **standard deviation** (SD). Rather than comparing only the extreme scores, the standard deviation compares *every* score in a distribution to the mean. Conceptually, the standard deviation is an "average deviation" from the mean score. Extreme scores influence the standard deviation, of course, but not nearly as dramatically as they do the range.

In a distribution of scores that are clustered together, the standard deviation will be relatively small. In the example given in Table 2-4, the standard deviation for Class A is 2.16, while the standard deviation for Class B is 15.82. The differences in standard deviations indicate that though the means and medians of the two distributions are the same (82), the scores are much more tightly clustered in Group A.

Typical Distributions: The Normal Curve

Though the mean, median, and mode can yield different results, often they do not. Figure 2-6 shows a distribution in which the mean, median, and mode give the same result. If you were to administer a standard IQ test to a random sample of 10,000 Americans, you would very likely get a distribution like that shown in the figure. This type of graph is called

a *frequency distribution.* The number of subjects who obtained a certain score is plotted on a graph, often with similar scores that are grouped together. In Figure 2-6, for example, the bar centered at "100" actually includes all those scores between 97.5 and 102.5. The bar centered at "105" represents all the scores between 102.5 and 107.5.

In the frequency distribution shown in Figure 2-6, approximately 1,350 people have scores of 97.5 to 102.5; about 350 will have scores of 72.5 to 77.5. Overall, the scores have a mean of 100 and a standard deviation of 15. This type of curve is particularly important. Notice that the shape of the distribution looks something like a bell; as a result, this type of distribution is often called a "bell curve." Scientists call such a curve a **normal curve,** meaning that it reflects a **normal distribution.** In a normal distribution, the mean, median, and mode are identical. A normal curve is perfectly symmetrical, so the distribution of scores above the mean looks like a mirror image of those below.

Normal distributions play a critical role in psychology. Psychologists believe that most of the abilities they measure—cognitive ability, height, test grades, and the like—are normally distributed. In a practical sense, this means that most scores will cluster at the center, with only a few observations at the extremes. Furthermore, a true normal distribution has as many positive extremes (scores above the mean) as there are negative extremes (scores below the mean).

The fact that most psychological factors are nor-

TABLE 2-3 *Hypothetical Maze Running Times (in Seconds) for Rats Who Were Not Deprived of Food, Those Deprived of Food for Ten Hours, and Those Deprived for Twenty Hours*

Group of Animals? →	Rats with No Deprivation	Rats with Ten Hours Deprivation	Rats with Twenty Hours Deprivation
	8	6	4
	12	8	6
	13	11	7
	18	12	8
	25	13	9
	30	13	11
	33	13	12
	34	15	17
	45	19	17
	45	21	17
	67	23	90
Mean	30	14	18
Median	30	13	11
Mode	45	13	17

mally distributed has some important implications. First, in a normal distribution, slightly more than ⅔ of all cases fall in the range from (mean − 1 SD) to (mean + 1 SD). In the example used in Figure 2-6, slightly more than ⅔ of all people tested will have IQs in the relatively narrow range from 85 (100 − 15) to 115 (100 + 15). Second, the more extreme the score, the less frequently that score will appear. By definition, 50 percent of all scores are above the mean: for example, in 10,000 cases, 5,000 will be at or above the mean. Scores 15 points or higher than the mean (1 SD or higher), which represent IQs of 115 or more, will occur in only about 16 percent of the cases. In the same 10,000 cases, then, only 1,600 will have scores of 115 or higher. Scores of 130 or more (2 SDs above the mean) occur in only about 2.5 percent of all cases. In a sample of 10,000, that means only 250 will have IQs of 130 or higher. IQs of 145, which

is 3 SDs above the mean, occur in just 0.13 percent of all cases. In 10,000 cases, *only 13* people will have IQs of 145 or more.[5]

Finally, normal distributions are symmetrical: for every extreme case in one direction, there is an extreme case in the other direction. This point may seem obvious, but we tend to overlook this fact quite regularly. Garrison Keillor's wonderful tongue-in-cheek radio show, *A Prairie Home Companion*, deals with life in the fictitious town of "Lake Woebegon," a place where, according to Keillor, "all the women

---

[5]To show you how rare the genuine extremes are, IQ scores of 160 or higher, which is 4 SDs above the the mean, will occur about thirty times in *1 million cases*. IQ scores of 175 or higher, 5 SDs above the mean, occur about *once every 3 million cases.* Theoretically, then, fewer than 100 people in the United States should have IQs of 175 or higher.

TABLE 2-4   *Hypothetical Test Scores for Students in Two Different Classes (Note the Vast Differences in the Variability of Scores in Class B Relative to Those in Class A)*

	Class A	Class B
	79	54
	80	70
	81	81
	82	82
	83	93
	84	96
	85	98
Mean	82	82
Median	82	82
Range	(85–79) = 6	(98–54) = 44
Standard deviation	2.16	15.82

are strong, all the men are good-looking, and all the children are above average." By definition, of course, that cannot be. Half the children must be below average; that is what *average* means! Or to give another example, students often ask that a course be graded "on the curve," without really understanding what that means. In a class where grades are normally distributed, with an average test score of 75, a normal distribution will produce exactly as many A's as F's, and exactly as many B's as D's.

Some Pitfalls in Psychological Research

Good research is difficult to do in any scientific field. It requires a broad knowledge of available tools for collecting and analyzing data, as well as careful attention to detail when performing those tasks. At the same time, good research demands creativity in asking the initial questions and putting together an effective research strategy. It also calls for an awareness of the various pitfalls inherent in scientific research. The following section will look at four of those pitfalls.

The Self-Fulfilling Prophecy

The term **self-fulfilling prophecy** refers to the tendency of people to find what they expect to find. More than that, they may even unwittingly *create* what they are seeking. Applied to psychological research, the self-fulfilling prophecy refers to the tendency for investigators to inadvertently make their hypotheses "come true" (or at least appear true). If, for example, a researcher who is conducting an interview smiles faintly when a subject's response corroborates the theory he is investigating, his inadvertent act can easily affect the subject's answers to subsequent questions. Consider the following experiment.

Robert Rosenthal (1966) told a group of elementary school teachers that certain pupils had obtained high scores on some special tests and were therefore sure to show unusual intellectual development later in the school year. Actually, the potential "late bloomers" were no different from other pupils. But a few months later the teachers rated the late bloomers as more interested, more curious, and happier than other students. And when all the children were given standardized tests at the end of the year, many of those who had been labeled late bloomers, especially the first and second graders, showed significantly greater gain than their classmates. In this study the teachers, not the experimenter, fulfilled the prophecy of academic success through their differential treatment of the supposed late bloomers. Clearly an experimenter, even one who is fully aware of the phenomenon of self-fulfilling prophecies, can also create the expected results unintentionally.

To avoid self-fulfilling prophecies, a researcher might employ the **double-blind technique,** in which neither the experimenter nor the subjects know who is in the experimental group and who is in the control group. (This procedure differs from the **single-blind technique,** in which the experimenter knows who is in which group, but the subjects do not.) In a double-blind experiment to test the effects of a tranquilizing drug, for example, the experimental group would be given the tranquilizer, and the control group would receive a placebo, perhaps a sugar pill. Only some outside party, such as the pharmacist who supplied the pills, would know which group received which kind of pill. Furthermore, this outside

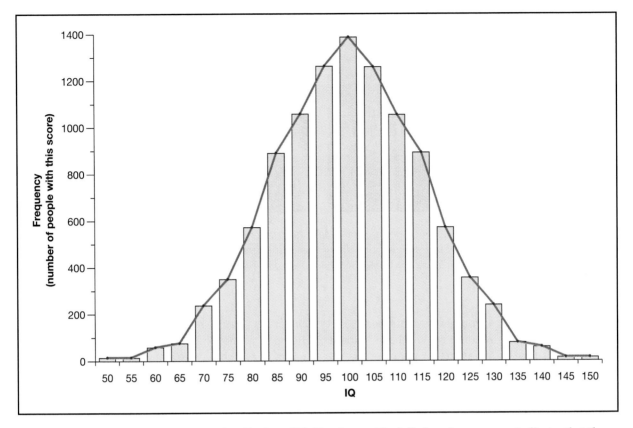

FIGURE 2-6   Hypothetical frequency distribution of IQ Test Scores. The bell-shaped appearance indicates that the scores are normally distributed test scores: mean score = 100; standard deviation = 15; number of cases = 10,000.

would not disclose that information to the experimenter until after the results were recorded. In other types of studies, similar techniques can be used. Psychologists looking for a possible positive correlation between IQ and psychological adjustment, for example, would assess psychological adjustment first, without knowing the subjects' IQ scores.

Demand Characteristics

Even if a researcher uses the double-blind technique, subjects may invalidate the research findings by trying to behave like "good" subjects. Most people who volunteer for an experiment want to do well at the experimental task. While they are participating, they may try to determine what the experiment is about. The clues they uncover have been called **demand characteristics,** because subjects feel the clues demand a certain kind of response (presumed "correct") (Orne, 1962). The following example illustrates the distortions that demand characteristics can create.

Suppose you have volunteered for a psychological experiment. At the laboratory, the researcher tells you that the study involves memory of fast-moving events. She shows you a series of slides depicting successive stages in an automobile accident and then asks you questions about them. One of the questions is, "Did another car pass the red Datsun while it was stopped at the stop sign?" This question puzzles you. The sign you remember seeing at the corner was a *yield* sign, not a *stop* sign. You conclude that the experimenter must be trying to trick you—why?

Later you believe you have detected the experimenter's intentions. She shows you several pairs of very similar slides and asks which of each pair you have seen before. One pair shows the Datsun stopped at an intersection, with either a stop sign or a yield sign at the corner. "Aha!" you say to yourself. "She expects me to choose the stop sign because that's what she mentioned in her question. Well, perhaps I should. After all, I'd hate to ruin her experiment." If you select the stop sign knowing full well

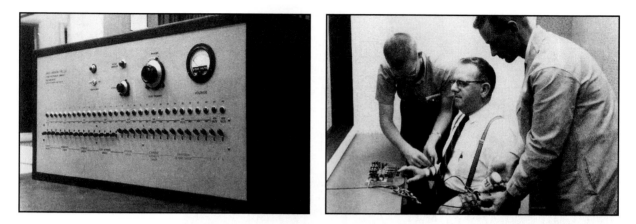

(Left) The bogus "shock generator" Stanley Milgram used to determine whether subjects in his experiment would obey an authority firgure, even if they thought that doing so meant delivering painful electric shocks to another person. While some subjects resisted as the supposed "shocks" became more intense (right), most willingly continued when told to do so.

that it is the wrong sign, you have succumbed to demand characteristics. In doing so, you have made it more difficult for the researcher to interpret the results correctly.

How can researchers counteract demand characteristics? One approach is to question subjects carefully after an experiment, to see if demand characteristics influenced them. At the end of an experiment on memory similar to the one just described, Loftus and her colleagues (Loftus, Miller, & Burns, 1978) revealed their true purpose. They told subjects they were trying to determine the effects of false information on eyewitness testimony by showing slides of an automobile accident and later asking questions about them. One of those questions, the researchers confessed, may have contained false information about the traffic sign located at the intersection. Would the subjects now please indicate which sign they really saw? In this way, Loftus and her colleagues were able to get some idea of the extent to which demand characteristics had influenced their results. The conclusion they drew at the end of this procedure? Demand characteristics had affected subjects' responses very little.

There are problems with this end-of-experiment questioning, however. Sometimes even the most careful and sensitive questioning may not reveal the real reasons behind a person's behavior. Subjects may be unwilling to admit to reasons that place them in an unflattering light. Finally, and perhaps most importantly, demand characteristics can still drastically change behavior *even if subjects are not consciously aware of them*. Remember Recurring Theme 3: a great deal of behavior is influenced by factors of which we are not consciously aware. Demand characteristics are an excellent example.

THEME A Large Proportion of Behavior Is Controlled by Unconscious Activity

3

There are several ways of minimizing the problem of demand characteristics. One is to try to conceal the true purpose of the experiment through deception. A classic study by Stanley Milgram (1963) demonstrates this technique. Milgram was interested in subjects' responses to authority. Would they perform an action, even one that might hurt another person, simply because an authority figure told them to?

In Milgram's study, subjects were led to believe that the experiment concerned the effect of punishment on learning. When they entered the laboratory, they saw that another subject had already arrived. The two subjects were told they would participate in an experiment investigating the role of punishment in learning. One of them would be the "teacher" and the other the "learner." The learner would be given a list of words to study and later recall. If the learner made an error during recall, the teacher would be told to press a button that delivered an electrical shock to punish the learner. In addition, each successive shock would be of greater intensity than the one before.

In reality, there was only one subject—the one who had been assigned the role of the teacher. The other subject, who had been assigned the role of the

Sometimes just being a subject in a study alters a person's behavior. This tendency, called the Hawthorne effect, is named after the Western Electric Company's Hawthorne plant, where it was first observed.

learner, was really a confederate of Milgram. The button the teacher pressed did not actually cause the learner to receive any electric shock—but the teacher didn't know that. Milgram's real question was whether subjects would obey an authority figure even if doing so meant delivering painful electric shocks to another person. (We will discuss the ethics of using deception in psychological research at the end of this chapter. Milgram's work on obedience to authority will be discussed in Chapter 18.)

Another way to reduce the effects of demand characteristics is to automate an experiment, often by using a computer to present information and record responses. Still another is to increase the use of unobtrusive measures. If subjects are not aware that a particular behavior is being recorded, they are unlikely to distort it in an effort to please the experimenter.

The Hawthorne Effect

More than fifty years ago, researchers at the Hawthorne plant of the Western Electric Company had a mystery on their hands. They were trying to determine the effects of various environmental conditions on the output of workers, but the results they were getting did not seem to make sense. In one set of studies, they had varied the amount of lighting that people were given to work by. As the brightness of the lighting increased, worker productivity did also—but so did the output of workers in a control group whose lighting had remained constant. Later the researchers tried decreasing the lighting. Again productivity rose, for both the experimental and

control subjects. Not until the lighting for the experimental subjects had become so dim that it was almost nonexistent did productivity finally begin to fall! The researchers wondered what was happening. Why did people keep working more and more effectively despite the unfavorable environment—or, in the case of control subjects, despite no change at all? The mystery deepened as other experiments varying other working conditions yielded similar findings. Productivity kept rising without regard to what the researchers did.

The investigators concluded that there is something about just being a subject in a study that alters a person's behavior. This phenomenon came to be called the **Hawthorne effect.** But what exactly is the "something" that causes the Hawthorne effect? Is it the novelty of the situation in which people are placed? The extra attention they receive? Or perhaps simply the awareness that someone is watching them? Psychologists are still not sure about the answers to these questions (Adair, 1984).

Premature Conclusions

During their training, psychologists are taught to anticipate and overcome the methodological problems just described. Nevertheless, errors and oversights still occur. That is why it is essential to avoid drawing firm conclusions on the basis of a single study, or even several studies. Yet the temptation to do so is often powerful, as the following example illustrates.

In the early 1970s, two pediatricians, Marshall Klaus and John Kennell, tested an intriguing hypothesis. They questioned the wisdom of standard hospital procedure following the birth of a baby. The new mother was given just a brief glimpse of her child before the infant was whisked away to be examined. Klaus and Kennell were aware that in some animal species, contact during the period immediately after birth is often critical to the development of a normal mother–infant bond. For instance, if a ewe is separated from her lamb immediately after giving birth, she will often reject the lamb several hours later (Collias, 1956). Klaus and Kennell believed that if a similar period occurs in human development, existing hospital procedures would be less than ideal for mother–infant bonding.

To test their hypothesis, Klaus and Kennell created experimental and control groups. The control group consisted of fourteen mothers and their first-born infants. The mothers were briefly shown their babies right after delivery; during the next three days they saw their infants every four hours for routine feeding. In contrast, the fourteen mothers in the experimental group were allowed a whole hour alone with their babies immediately after delivery and received an extra five hours each day to interact with them. Klaus and Kennell found that a month after giving birth, mothers in the experimental group on average were more attentive toward their infants in a routine medical exam, more inclined to look at and fondle them, and more reluctant to leave them with baby-sitters than were control mothers (Klaus et al., 1972). Even when the children were a year old, the experimental-group mothers seemed more concerned and attentive in certain situations than the control mothers (Kennell et al., 1974).

These findings made nationwide headlines. The two pediatricians went on to write a popular book in which they claimed that optimal child development depended on bonding in the first hours after birth (Klaus & Kennell, 1976). Concerned parents pressured the medical establishment to change hospital procedures. By the late 1970s it had become standard practice for parents to be given time alone with their newborns so that proper bonding could occur.

Not long after, however, other researchers began to point out serious problems in Klaus and Kennell's study. For one thing, doctors and nurses might have biased the results by inadvertently giving the experimental women more encouragement. And what about the size of the samples—*fourteen* women and infants in each group? With samples that small, differences are likely to be due to chance alone. And ex-

perimental mothers might have been more attentive because of preexisting personality traits, or because their infants' temperaments just happened to elicit such responses. Questions of this kind prompted several psychologists to try to replicate Klaus and Kennell's findings.

Replication is an essential part of scientific research. Other investigators reconstruct the basic features of the original study to see if their results will be similar. In the case of early mother–infant bonding, other researchers' results did not always match those of Klaus and Kennell. Sometimes there were no significant differences between experimental and control groups. Other times a few differences appeared, but not always the same ones that Klaus and Kennell had found. These patterns led to the suspicion that any differences in Klaus and Kennell's studies were due simply to chance. Certainly the combined evidence showed that the universal importance of early mother–infant contact claimed by some proponents was far from established fact (Lamb & Hwang, 1982).

The history of research into early mother–infant bonding underscores the importance of avoiding premature conclusions. Even when the results of a new study sound convincing, psychologists must be careful to place these findings in proper perspective. Additional investigations, using samples of adequate size, are essential to verify the initial results (Rosnow & Rosenthal, 1989). Even if a given study is replicated successfully, many questions will remain. Are there particular circumstances under which the experimental outcomes are more likely? Are there other ways in which the current findings might be interpreted? Such constant questioning is fundamental to scientific work.

The Ethics of Research in Psychology

Several times in this chapter we have said that for ethical reasons, certain research cannot be done. For example, psychologists cannot (and would not) encourage a group of parents to severely discipline their children from birth to adolescence, just to assess the relationship between harsh child rearing and delinquency. Such an experiment could cause irreparable harm. So could an experiment designed to investigate the effects of smoking that required the experimental group to smoke a certain number of

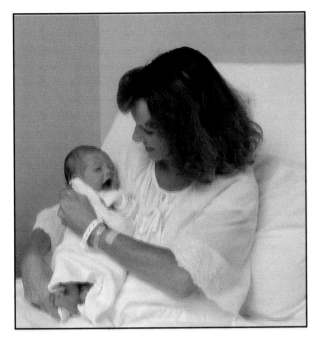

Klaus and Kennell (1972) reported that mothers who were given a chance to "bond" with their children immediately following a birth were more attentive to their infants, and more likely to interact with them a month later. As a result, many hospitals changed their procedures to allow mother and child greater time for bonding. On further investigation, however, researchers identified serious problems with the study.

cigarettes daily. That would be asking the subject to do something that could lead to a fatal illness. But the propriety of many other psychological studies is not so clear-cut. Consider these two examples.

Suppose you volunteer for an experiment that is allegedly about the effects of hypnosis on creative problem solving. After being hypnotized and then brought out of your trance, you and two other subjects are asked to write a story about a picture. The other two begin to laugh and talk, but you can't hear what they are saying. You grow increasingly sure they are making fun of you. If you find out later that you had received a posthypnotic suggestion that you would be partially deaf, would you feel unfairly manipulated? Would the researcher's true goal of investigating the effects of partial deafness on paranoia justify the distress you experienced?

Now suppose you are riding a subway in New York City and the passenger beside you collapses at your feet, blood trickling from his mouth. You be-

come extremely upset, but don't know what to do. If you later learn that the victim was a confederate in an experiment designed to investigate bystander apathy, would you feel the deception was justified?

These are actual experiments psychologists have conducted (Piliavin & Piliavin, 1972; Zimbardo, Anderson, & Kabat, 1981). As you can see, it is hard to say whether the deceptions were justified. Psychologists have an obligation to find answers to important questions, such as the causes of paranoia or the reasons for bystander apathy. But they also have an obligation to protect the dignity and welfare of the people who participate in their research. The two obligations can sometimes conflict. When they do, how can a researcher decide whether or not to proceed with a particular study?

The American Psychological Association (APA) has helped to answer this question by issuing ethical guidelines for studies involving human subjects (APA, 1990). The guidelines require that researchers avoid all procedures that would in any way cause lasting harm to human subjects. "Harm" includes psychological as well as physical injury. Subjects should not leave an experiment feeling degraded or mistreated; if they do, their rights have been violated. Whenever the possibility of physical or mental discomfort exists, the researcher should inform subjects and secure their consent beforehand (see Figure 2-7). If it becomes essential to deceive subjects, the researcher must later explain why deception was necessary. A subject's participation must always be voluntary. And if a subject decides to withdraw from a study for any reason, that decision must be respected. Finally, subjects have a right to privacy. The researcher should not reveal subjects' identities unless the subjects authorize such disclosure.

The American Psychological Association is not the only organization concerned about the ethics of psychological research. The federal government too requires that all research sponsored by U.S. government grants be reviewed for ethical standards by a panel of qualified people. Some government research agencies have developed procedures for dealing with suspected ethical misconduct in the studies they fund (Miers, 1985). In addition, most universities require that all research on human subjects conducted at their facilities receive the approval of an ethics review board.

Public and private institutions also impose strict standards for the treatment of animal subjects.

Typical University
Certification of Informed Consent
Predictors of Classroom Success

Principle Investigator
John S. Smith, Ph. D.
Associate Professor, Department of Psychology

This form asks for your consent to participate in psychological research. We are interested in finding predictors of classroom success, as measured by your exam scores. We will ask you to do the following:

1. Take a pretest before the classroom instruction begins, so we can obtain a baseline measurement of your precourse knowledge. This will take no more than one hour, outside of class.

2. Provide ratings for 15 content areas in the course, rating how much you know about these areas before any instruction takes place. This will take only a few minutes.

3. Before taking each mid-term exam in the course, predict how well you expect to do on each section. This will be the first question on each exam.

4. After taking the exam, provide a rating for how well you think you did on each section of the test. This will be the last question on each exam.

5. Allow us to obtain your SAT (or ACT) score from the Registrar. This score will be entered into our data file using only code numbers (the last 6 numbers of your SSN), and only Dr. Smith and graduate students under his supervision will have access to these scores. Furthermore, we will not have your name or full ID number listed in such a way that your name can be matched to your scores.

There will be no physical risks at any time. You may elect, either now or at any time during the experiment, to withdraw your participation, with no penalty or loss of benefits you have earned. You should understand that your compliance is completely voluntary.

You will earn extra credit as outlined in your course syllabus. You may also earn extra credit without participating in this experiment. Contact your instructor.

This experiment meets the American Psychological Association's standards for "Minimal Risk," and poses no major risks or dangers for you as a participant.

The results will be tabulated in the coming months, and will be available for you to review, should you wish to see the outcome.

Please direct all inquiries to Dr. John S. Smith, Department of Psychology, Typical University, Box 555, Anytown, USA, 22222. Dr. Smith can also be reached at (505) 555-1212.

If you have any questions regarding your rights as a subject, or have other questions regarding this experiment, please contact the Typical University Committee for Protection of Human Subjects in Research, Dr. William H. Jones, Chair, Typical University, Box 555, Anytown, USA, 22222.

I have read and understood this form, am aware of my rights as a subject, and have agreed to participate in this experiment.

NAME (signature)   WITNESS

DATE

FIGURE 2-7 Example of an informed consent form. Each subject must read and sign the form before participating in research. In addition, most colleges and universities have a campuswide "Committee for the Protection of Human Subjects in Research," which reviews each research proposal involving human subjects.

Nevertheless, the debate on animal rights has become increasingly heated, even violent, in recent years. Critics charge that experimental animals are being subjected to unnecessary suffering, either for findings of little or no practical value or for results that could have been obtained some other way. The most radical of the animal-rights activists want to ban experimentation on animals from all branches of science (Holden, 1989) while developing alternative ways of testing.

Psychologists and other scientists strongly disagree with these radical critics. While readily acknowledging their ethical responsibility to treat experimental animals humanely, they assert that today, because of modern regulations, abuse of research animals is very rare (Koshland, 1989). Moreover, animal studies continue to be vital to the advance of knowledge. They have yielded new ways to promote recovery from nerve damage; new insights into the links between stress and disease, and noise and hearing loss; new methods for reducing pain; new drugs for combating mental illness; and new treatments for brain disorders (Miller, 1985). Animal studies play a major role in finding a cure for cancer, AIDS, and other diseases that plague society. Furthermore, animal research benefits animals as well as people. Vaccines for deadly diseases in dogs, cats, sheep, cattle, and many other species have been developed using animal experimentation. In most cases, findings obtained from animal research cannot be obtained in any other way. They are an essential part of many socially important scientific programs (Kaplan, 1989). That is not to say that scientists should be given a free rein in animal research. The benefits to be gained from such studies should always be carefully weighed against the methods used. Just as most universities and research centers have ethics review boards for research involving humans, most have similar boards to review and monitor research performed with animals.

Whether a particular researcher is adequately meeting ethical standards is not always easy to decide (Sieber & Stanley, 1988). Consider, for instance, another example of research on human beings. Suppose psychologists studying the transmission of AIDS discover that some people who carry the AIDS virus routinely have unprotected sex with partners who do not know about their medical condition.

The debate over animal rights has become increasingly heated, even violent, in recent years. Critics charge that experimental animals are subjected to unnecessary suffering; most psychologists (and other scientists) strongly disagree. Animal studies have led to the discovery of new ways to repair nerve damage, reduce pain, and treat brain disorders.

Should the researchers try to contact their partners and advise them of the risks they face? In doing so, they would be violating the subjects' right to privacy. But is there a point at which their right is overshadowed by the obligation to protect other people from harm? What if by informing the partners the researchers encourage other carriers of AIDS to lie to researchers about their sexual behavior? Would their decision to inform the partners do more harm than good? Difficult questions such as these are still being hotly debated (Melton & Gray, 1988).

Though some unresolved ethical issues remain, psychologists seem to be doing quite well maintaining ethical standards in contemporary research. During the five years between 1983 and 1987 no complaints about the care and treatment of animals and only three complaints about research involving humans were filed with the ethics committee of the American Psychological Association (APA Ethics Committee, 1988). Perhaps ethical review boards at universities and other institutions have successfully screened out ethically questionable research projects.

In Depth

Ecological Validity: Research in the Laboratory versus the "Real World"

ONE OF THE most commonly expressed criticisms of psychological research is that it has little or no bearing on the "real world." For example, memory researchers often create tasks for use in the laboratory—such as learning lists of unrelated words—that seem to have little relationship to uses of memory in realistic settings. Other experimenters, in an attempt to control extraneous factors in the laboratory, create an environment so artificial that subjects no longer behave as they would in realistic situations. Finally, research is often conducted using college students as subjects, not because they are better but because they are plentiful and accessible to researchers. Given the artificial nature of the stimuli, the setting, and the subjects of psychological experiments, just how much can we learn from them?

Initial Studies

The most forceful and influential argument against laboratory experimentation came from the cognitive psychologist Ulric Neisser during an address he delivered at a memory conference in the late 1970s. In this talk (later printed in Neisser, 1982), he stated

> It is . . . discouraging to find that nothing in the extensive literature of the psychology of memory sheds much light on [real-world problems], so that anyone who wishes to study such problems must start from scratch. Unfortunately, this is not an isolated instance. It is an example of a principle that is nearly as valid in 1978 as it was in 1878: If *X* is an interesting or socially significant aspect of memory, then psychologists have hardly ever studied *X*.

> Neisser, 1982, p. 4

Neisser's comments were specifically addressed to memory researchers, but the same criticism could have been made of almost any area of psychological research. Neisser believed that psychological experiments had little **ecological validity:** they no longer applied to anything in the real world. To use Neisser's phrase, psychological experiments were no longer "interesting or socially significant."

Criticisms, Alternatives, and Further Research

Neisser's provocative comments struck a responsive chord with many researchers who shared his views. Almost immediately, memory researchers began studying naturalistic situations more frequently—for example, long-term memory for childhood events (e.g., Fivush, Hudson, & Nelson, 1984; 1980; Winograd & Killinger, 1983), for material from a textbook (Maki & Berry, 1984), even for the lyrics to Beatles' songs (Hyman & Rubin, 1990). While topics like these had been investigated before Neisser's comments, they had never been examined regularly in professional journals.

The new approach spread to other branches of the field. In one study, Stephen Ceci and Jeffrey Liker (1986) investigated the relationship between intelligence as measured by scores on a standard IQ test and intelligence as measured by complex reasoning and problem-solving skills. Measuring IQ is simple: many widely used tests have been developed for the purpose (see Chapter 14). Unfortunately, evaluating reasoning and problem-solving skills is more difficult. While tests have been created to measure those skills in the laboratory, many of them seem contrived and unfamiliar to subjects in the experiments. Could a more realistic and ecologically valid problem-solving task be developed? If so, would this ecologically valid measure of intelligence produce results that were consistent with those of IQ tests?

To measure "real-world" intelligence, Ceci and Liker used a complex reasoning task—handicapping horse races. Unlike most forms of gambling, horse racing does not rely on pure chance, so highly knowledgeable gamblers can consistently outperform novices. To do so gamblers must estimate the odds of winning for each horse in the field, based on a number of factors: Which other horses will be in the race? What will the track conditions be like, and how will each horse be affected by those conditions? Who will be the horse's jockey? How has each horse fared in competition in the past? How fast has each horse run in other races of the same length? How many days of rest has the horse had since the last race? and so on. When the final odds are posted just before the race, the expert compares the odds he generated with those just posted. If the posted odds for any horse are substantially higher than his own odds, the expert may bet on the "undervalued" horse. Over the long run, assuming their reasoning skills are good, expert gamblers will consistently outperform novices, winning more money than they lose.

Ceci and Liker tested thirty avid racing fans, all middle-aged and older men with IQs ranging from 70 (2 standard deviations below the mean of 100) to 130 (2 standard deviations above the mean). Based on the men's ability to predict post-time odds, the researchers classified fourteen of the thirty as true experts. The other sixteen, though much more knowledgeable than novices, were not as skilled as the experts. Ceci and Liker asked all thirty men to handicap ten actual races and fifty experimenter-contrived races. Not surprisingly, the true experts performed better, and used more complex (and accurate) reasoning strategies to derive their predictions than the second group. Remarkably, though, Ceci and Liker found no relationship between IQ and skilled race handicapping. Experts at the lowest end of the IQ distribution (IQ = 70) performed this difficult task just as accurately as experts at the top of the range (IQ=130).

To understand how extreme these results are, recall that 95 percent of all distributions will fall within ±2 standard deviations of the mean. Those with IQ scores of 70 or less, then, would have been in the bottom 2.5 percent of the group of racing fans. Yet they performed just as effectively as those with IQ scores of 130 and above—who are in the *top* 2.5 percent of the distribution! According to Ceci and Liker, "IQ is unrelated to real-world forms of cognitive complexity [in tasks regarded as] the hallmark of intelligent behavior" (p. 255). In this study, that is, real-world intelligence was found to be unrelated to intelligence as measured by an IQ test—a result the researchers obtained only because they had chosen an ecologically valid problem-solving task.

Despite such results, in the late 1980s naturalistic research was still controversial. In fact, Banaji and Crowder (1989) complained that the emphasis on naturalistic research had seriously compromised scientific integrity:

There has been more than a decade of passionate rhetoric claiming that important questions about memory could be tackled if only researchers looked to the "real world" for hypothesis validation. Yet no delivery has been made on these claims: No theories that have unprecedented explanatory power have been produced; no new principles of memory have been discovered . . . we argue that the movement to develop an ecologically valid psychology . . . has proven itself largely bankrupt and, moreover, that it carries the potential danger of compromising genuine accomplishments of our young endeavor. (p. 1185)

One of the hallmarks of good research is that it produces reliable findings, ones that can be generalized to situations other than those used in an individual study. To achieve generalizability, laboratory conditions must usually be tightly controlled: but such control means that the experiment is likely to be low in ecological validity. According to Banaji and Crowder, the pendulum had swung too far. In their attempts to conduct research in naturalistic environments, researchers had sacrificed scientific rigor.

Banaji and Crowder's article generated at least as much response as Neisser's original critique. The journal *American Psychologist* devoted an entire issue to the response (January 1991), enlisting Elizabeth Loftus, one of this book's authors, to act as a special editor. In the issue more than a dozen researchers offered comments on both sides of the debate, followed by a final reply by Banaji and Crowder. One of the respondents was Ulric Neisser, who had begun the debate more than ten years earlier: "I have bad news for Banaji and Crowder. It's too late: The good old days are gone, the genie is out of the bottle" (Neisser, 1991, p. 34). Others questioned the necessity of rigorous laboratory control in psychological research, drawing an analogy to chemistry: "If two chemicals are going to react, they'll react when combined in a test tube just as well as outside it" (Aanstoos, 1991, p. 77). In response, Banaji and Crowder (1991) replied, "It is precisely because this is not true that test tubes were invented in the first place" (p. 79). Another contributor (Roediger, 1991) also defended the need for scientific rigor:

[the ecological validity] movement, if removed of some of its excesses, has much to offer. The traditional role of naturalistic observation is to draw attention to significant phenomena and to suggest interesting ideas. Researchers will then typically create a laboratory analog of the natural situation in which potentially relevant variables can be brought under control and studied. Of course, the danger exists in arranging the laboratory situation . . . that the critical variables will vanish, as will the phenomenon. But this is not the fault of laboratory research: . . . it simply means that the experimenter failed to select the right variables. (p. 39)

Patterns and Conclusions

In a sense, Neisser's comment—"it's too late"—is correct: psychology has changed. Studies with obvious real-world relationships are now more common and appreciated. Researchers understand the trade-off between generalizability and ecological validity, though they may still disagree on which trade-offs are acceptable. Most would agree with this summary offered by Tulving (1991):

> There is no reason to believe that there is only one way to study memory. What counts in the final analysis is the extent to which the present work, whatever its orientation, shapes the future. The study of memory from different vantage points is not a zero-sum game in which only one side can win.

Tulving, 1985, p. 41

SUMMARY

1. In order to study psychology as a science, psychologists employ scientific methods in their research. In general, psychologists try to describe, predict, and explain behavior. While some psychologists attempt to change behavior, this is considered an application of psychology, rather than a primary goal.

2. Psychologists usually investigate a **sample,** or selected segment of the population relevant to the issue they want to explore. In a **random sample,** every member of the population has an equal chance of being included. In a **representative sample,** subgroups with distinct characteristics are included according to their proportions in the total population.

3. Psychologists employ many techniques to describe behavior. The **case study** is a research method in which one individual is explored in depth. **Naturalistic observation** involves watching behavior in realistic situations. **Surveys** attempt to estimate the opinions, characteristics, or behaviors of a population by asking questions of a usually large representative sample. Accurate descriptions of behavior are essential, but they cannot determine the causes of behavior.

4. **Correlational design** allows psychologists to determine the extent to which two variables are related to each other. A positive correlation means that a high value of one variable tends to be accompanied by a high value of the other, while a negative correlation means that a high value of one variable tends to be accompanied by a low value of the other. Both the direction and the strength of a correlation are indicated as a numerical value called the **correlation coefficient.** If two variables are correlated, psychologists can use the value of one variable to make predictions about the other, a technique called **regression.**

5. The **experiment** is a method that allows researchers to infer causes because it holds constant (to as large an extent as possible) all influences on subjects' behavior except those being explored. Experimenters work with two groups of subjects: the **experimental group,** which experiences the experimental condition, and the **control group,** which does not. All experimenters set out to test a **hypothesis,** a tentative statement about how or why something happens. To do so they examine the relationship between **variables,** or factors that can change. The variable that the experimenter deliberately manipulates is called the **independent variable.** The one that is expected to change when the independent variable changes is called the **dependent variable.**

6. **Behavioral genetics** is a relatively new field, designed to identify genetic and environmental causes of behavior. It studies people who share genetic influences (such as siblings, or a parent and child), environmental influences (such as adopted children), both, or neither. Behavioral genetics attempts to determine the relative contributions of genetic influences, **shared environ-**

mental **influences** (such as being raised in the same family), and **nonshared environmental influences** (those unique to each person).

7. To interpret the data they collect, psychologists use statistics—mathematical methods for assessing and presenting data in summary form. **Descriptive statistics** enable researchers to present their findings in a concise manner. One goal is to convey how scores in a sample are distributed. This may involve calculating measures of **central tendency,** such as the **mean** (arithmetic average), **median** (middle score), and **mode** (most frequent score). It may also involve calculating measures of variability, such as the **range** (the distance between the highest and lowest scores) and the **standard deviation** (a measure of the average extent to which all scores in a set vary from the mean).

8. Among the possible pitfalls in conducting psychological research is the **self-fulfilling prophecy,** or tendency for researchers' expectations to influence their results. One way to avoid

self-fulfilling prophecies is to use the **double-blind technique,** in which neither the researcher nor the subjects know who has been assigned to the experimental or the control conditions. (In the **single-blind technique,** the experimenter knows who is in which group, but the subjects do not.) Two other pitfalls in psychological research occur when subjects succumb to **demand characteristics** (clues about the responses they think the researcher wants them to make) or to the **Hawthorne effect** (in which subjects behave in unusual ways simply because they are part of a scientific study). Finally, there is the pitfall of drawing premature conclusions on the basis of a single study. Research findings must be **replicated** many times in order for psychologists to accept them as generally valid.

9. Psychologists are expected to meet strict ethical standards in conducting their research. Various organizations provide guidelines for the ethical treatment of human as well as animal subjects.

SUGGESTED READINGS

Kantowitz, B. H., Roediger III, H. L., & Elmes, D. G. (1994). *Experimental psychology: Understanding psychological research (5th ed.).* Minneapolis, MN: West Publishing Co. An outstanding text covering experimental methods and techniques, intended for psychology students with little formal background in research.

Kirk, R. E. (1990). *Statistics: An introduction (3rd ed.).* Fort Worth: Harcourt-Brace. A solid introduction to the basic concepts and procedures of statistics, especially as used by psychologists.

Plomin, R. (1990). *Nature and nurture: An introduction to human behavioral genetics.* Pacific Grove, CA: Brooks-Cole. A wonderfully accessible introduction to the field of behavioral genetics, one easily read by beginning psychology students. This is also an excellent choice for more advanced students looking for a less technical introduction.

Plomin, R., DeFreis, J. C., & McClearn, G. E. (1990). *Behavioral genetics: A primer (2nd ed.).* New York: W. H. Freeman & Co. The most authoritative volume on the emerging field of behavioral genetics, written by the leading researchers in the field. Though the coverage is complete and readable, it is intended primarily as an introduction and reference for advanced students and professionals.

Rosnow, R. L., & Rosenthal, R. (1996). *Beginning behavioral research: A conceptual primer (2nd ed.).* Englewood Cliffs, NJ: Prentice-Hall. Another outstanding introduction to research methods, though with a somewhat broader scope and a more theoretical orientation.

The Biological Foundations of Behavior

Phineas Gage was a railroad foreman. In 1848 he was supervising a crew in Cavendish, Vermont, blasting through the dense rock blocking their path. Gage watched as workers drilled holes, then poured gunpowder into them; he tamped down the powder with an iron rod, preparing for the explosion. Gage had performed this task thousands of times without incident. However, on September 13, 1848, something went terribly wrong. As Gage tamped down a charge, his rod struck the side of the bore, sparking a premature explosion. The tamping rod shot out of the shaft like an arrow. In a fraction of a second, the 4-foot-long, 13-pound tool shot straight up and struck Gage in the skull. Entering his skull just beneath his left eye, it tore through a part of his brain and exited through the top of his skull. Such was the force of the explosion that the rod landed 50 yards away. Astonishingly, Gage survived the accident. Though the wound caused massive bleeding, he never lost consciousness and was well enough to walk within a few minutes.

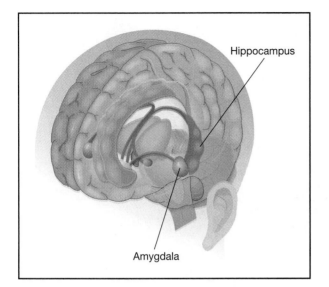

Hippocampus

Amygdala

FIGURE 3-1   *In an attempt to control his epileptic seizures, neurosurgeons destroyed H. M.'s* hippocampus *and* amygdala. *The surgery was* bilateral, *meaning that the structures in both hemispheres were destroyed. Though H. M.'s epileptic seizures have decreased, the surgery left H. M. profoundly amnesic.*

The long-term results of the massive brain damage Gage sustained were surprising, even to those who treated him following the accident. Gage was able to speak as before, and his motor skills were largely intact. He suffered few discernible memory problems. However, the damage to his frontal cortex transformed Gage from a capable, hard-working foreman into a crude, angry, and impulsive man. As the physician who treated him later expressed it, *Gage was no longer Gage.*

In 1953, a young man in his mid-twenties, known to us only by his initials, H. M., was admitted to a hospital for treatment of severe epilepsy. H. M.'s condition was deteriorating, and without treatment he would likely have died. Because the anticonvulsant drugs normally used to treat epilepsy were ineffective in his case, as a last resort his doctors recommended *psychosurgery.* They would remove the damaged portions of H. M.'s brain that were triggering his seizures. The surgery was particularly complicated because H. M.'s

epilepsy was *bilateral* (it occurred in both sides of his brain) (see Figure 3-1).

In one respect the surgery was a great success. The frequency and severity of H. M.'s seizures were reduced. However, the surgery had one devastating complication. Since his surgery in 1953, H. M. has been virtually unable to form new long-term memories, producing *anterograde amnesia.* Though he remembers most of the events prior to the surgery, he cannot

Phineas Gage's skull (right) and a sculptor's reproduction of his head (left). The large wound made by the tamping rod can clearly be seen at the top of the skull, just above the left frontal lobe.

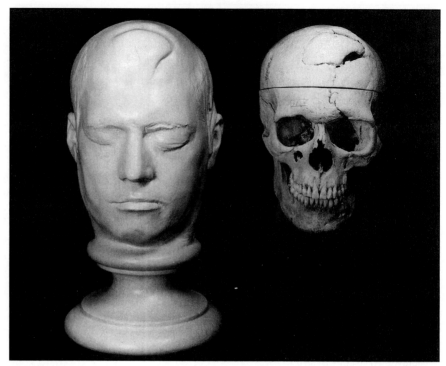

recall a single event that has occurred since.[1] Every time H. M. meets his regular doctors—doctors that he did not know prior to his surgery—he greets them as strangers. He works the same crossword puzzle day after day, unaware that he has seen it before. If he is not interrupted, he can follow the plot of a TV show, but when a commercial distracts him, he forgets what happened in the first half of the show. In H. M.'s own words, he constantly feels as if he is "waking from a dream. . . . Every day is alone in itself, whatever enjoyment I've had, and whatever sorrow I've had" (Milner et al., 1968, as cited by Kolb & Whishaw, 1990, p. 540).

---

[1]Technically, H. M. *can* form new memories, but only in a very restricted sense. H. M. can form new *procedural memories,* which are memories that do not require conscious awareness. For example, when H. M. was asked to trace a path through a maze while looking in a mirror, he became increasingly faster with practice. However, even when asked to solve the maze for the 100th time, H. M. had no conscious recollection of ever having performed the task before. The ability of H. M. to form procedural memories but not other, conscious memories has lead to a flurry of research and debate among memory theorists. We will return to the case of H. M. in Chapters 5 and 7.

What do these cases tell us about psychology? Both have clearly identifiable biological components, thus a grasp of biopsychology is necessary to understand them. But the biological aspects of psychology are important in normal behavior, too. Anytime you feel tense at a movie (remember the T-rex scene in *Jurassic Park?*), angry at a motorist who cut you off in traffic, or grieved at the loss of a close friend, your feelings and behaviors are mediated by the activity of cells in your brain and nervous system called *neurons.*

In this chapter we will look at the neurobiological basis of behavior. The first section will describe how neurons can be grouped into large functional networks, based on their location and function. These networks of highly interconnected neurons are specialized for certain types of activity. Next, we will explore how individual nerve cells transmit information. We will look first at "within-cell transmission," then "between-cell transmission." The next section of the chapter will deal with the chemicals that facilitate synaptic transmission, called *neurotransmitters.* The last section will describe larger brain structures and show how they influence behavior. We will examine a group of individuals who have had the two hemispheres of their brains surgically separated.

Alexander Luria, whose insightful study and compelling, compassionate descriptions of those suffering from neurological damage—many of them Russian soldiers injured in battle—led to great advances in the understanding of brain function.

Many of psychology's greatest advances have come through the study of fascinating, sometimes tragic cases—a clear example of Recurring Theme 2 in Chapter 1: "Psychologists learn about normal functioning by studying the abnormal." For example, our understanding of the brain structures involved in speech has been derived in large part from case studies of individuals who have suffered brain trauma, usually stroke (see Lieberman, 1991). Following the stroke, they often lose some of their verbal abilities. One of the century's greatest neuropsychologists, Russia's Alexander Luria, made huge advances in the study of neurology by relating the brain damage inflicted on Russian soldiers in World Wars I and II with their loss of cognitive, perceptual, or motor abilities.

THEME **Psychologists Learn About the Normal by Studying the Abnormal**

In his recent book *The Astonishing Hypothesis*, Nobel Laureate Francis Crick wrote: "'You,' your joys and your sorrows, your memories and your ambitions, your sense of personal identity and free will, are in fact no more than the behavior of a vast assembly of nerve cells and their associated molecules. . . . This hypothesis is so alien to the ideas of most people alive today that it can truly be called astonishing" (Crick, 1994, p. 3). Crick's view, called *reductionism*, is indeed provoca-

tive. Nevertheless, *neuroscientists*— those who study the nervous system—find it entirely in keeping with current scientific views of brain and behavior.

The fact is, many psychological disorders such as depression and schizophrenia are the direct results of neurochemical imbalances. Addiction to drugs and alcohol, once thought to be character disorders of the morally weak, also have strong biological components. Even childhood hyperactivity—referred to as "attention deficit hyperactivity disorder" in the *Diagnostic and Statistical Manual* (APA 1994) — is thought to have biochemical causes. *Perhaps most important, all normal behavior is the product of complex neural activity.* Every time you take a breath, read a book, or daydream, you are relying on complex interactions of neural and chemical processes. Any study of behavior that ignores the neurological component, then, is bound to be incomplete.

The Human Nervous System

With its billions of interconnected cells radiating throughout the body, the human nervous system is one of the most complex structures in the living world. At a split second's notice, hundreds of billions of atoms and molecules shuttle back and forth across cell membranes. Cells are constantly synthesizing various substances, which must be delivered to just the right locations at just the right moment, in just the right amount. This intricate system operates without our conscious awareness let alone our conscious control. Yet we also use our brains consciously to explore this remarkable network and its complex workings.

The cells that make up the human nervous system are specialized for different functions. Embedded in our sense organs are **receptor cells** (sometimes called *afferent neurons*), which are specialized to receive various types of stimulation from the environment. During each waking second, receptor cells in your eyes, ears, skin, and other parts of your body receive about 100 million signals, which they must process and transmit to your brain. Embedded in muscles and glands are **effector cells** (also known as *efferent neurons*), which are specialized to contract the muscles and stimulate glands to secrete hormones. For you to perform even a relatively simple behavior, such as hitting a baseball, your brain must issue millions of commands via your effector cells.

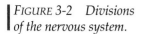

FIGURE 3-2 *Divisions of the nervous system.*

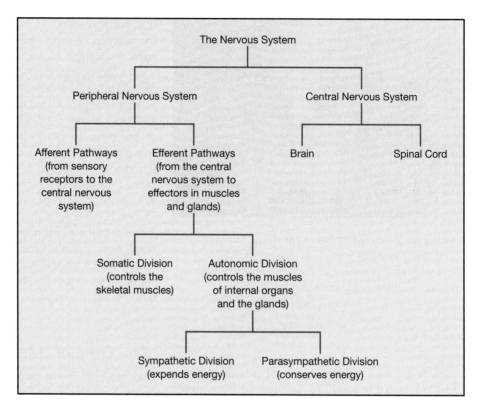

Finally, some cells are specialized to conduct signals from one part of the body to another. They connect receptor cells to effector cells, modifying and coordinating their activities.

In short, neurons, or nerve cells, are the functional building blocks of the nervous system. Even the simplest action, such as blinking your eyes, may involve hundreds of neurons working together. The human body contains literally billions of neurons, about 100 billion in the brain alone (Kandel, Schwartz, & Jessell, 1991). The tissues we call **nerves,** which run throughout the body, are actually the long, filamentous parts of many neurons bundled together.

Cells called **glia,** usually smaller than neurons but about ten times more numerous, surround many neurons. *Glia* literally means "glue," a word that accurately describes one of the important functions of glial cells: they hold neurons in place. Glial cells carry nutrients to neurons, accelerate their transmission speed, remove their waste products, and help repair damage in the peripheral nervous system. They provide a barrier for neurons against certain harmful substances that might be in the blood.

Researchers estimate that there may be as many as 10,000 different types of neurons (Kandel, Schwartz, & Jessell, 1995). But they seldom work in isolation; instead, they form larger units and networks. Later in this chapter we will consider how individual neurons function. First, we will discuss the larger divisions of the nervous system as a whole.

The Structure of the Nervous System

The brain and spinal cord, which lie within the bony casings of the skull and spinal column, form the **central nervous system (CNS),** so called because it controls all human behavior. Branching out from the central nervous system to all parts of the body is the **peripheral nervous system (PNS).** Some neurons of the peripheral system carry signals from sensory receptor cells *to* the spinal cord and brain via **afferent pathways** (pathways to the central nervous system). Other peripheral system neurons carry messages *from* the brain and spinal cord to effector cells in the muscles and glands. Those neurons form **efferent pathways** (pathways away from the central nervous system).

Efferent pathways can be divided into two systems, the somatic nervous system and the autonomic nervous system. The **somatic nervous system** consists of nerve fibers running to skeletal muscles, that is, muscles that move the bones. In general, these fibers control voluntary actions. When you raise an

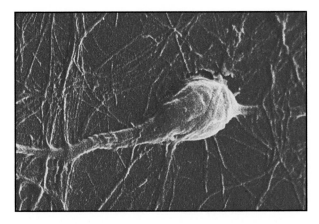

A scanning electron micrograph of a neuron. Notice the large, oval cell body; the long, thick axon; and the numerous thin, branching dendrites.

arm or tap your toe, you are using nerves in the somatic system. Figure 3-2 shows the divisions of the nervous system.

In contrast, the **autonomic nervous system** controls the muscles running to internal organs (blood vessels, heart, intestines) and glands. Autonomic activity is usually considered involuntary, because it occurs more or less automatically. Most people do not consciously control their stomach contractions, for instance, or their heartbeats. Under some circumstances, however, people can learn to influence such "involuntary" responses. For example, they can learn to use relaxation techniques like meditation to lower their heart rate and blood pressure. Relaxation techniques are often incorporated into childbirth classes, enabling mothers-to-be to learn to relax, breathe deeply, and in so doing control their autonomic nervous system. *Biofeedback* is another technique that helps people to control their autonomic responses.

The autonomic nervous system may be divided into the sympathetic nervous system (SNS) and the parasympathetic nervous system (PSNS). With few exceptions, autonomically controlled structures (muscles or glands) receive input from both subsystems, though the two tend to have opposite effects. The **sympathetic nervous system** is usually involved in mobilizing the body's resources for action. In an emergency or stressful situation, such as meeting a snake on a walk in the woods, the SNS responds by increasing the available blood sugar, increasing heart rate and blood pressure, and inhibiting digestion. (One useful way to remember the actions of the sympathetic nervous system is to imagine a stressful situation, such as running away from a snake. The kinds of neural activity that would be helpful in such a situation are increased heart rate, circulation, and respiration. Think of the sympathetic nervous system as producing behaviors "sympathetic" to your escape.)

The **parasympathetic nervous system,** on the other hand, dominates under conditions of relaxation, helping to conserve and replenish the body's energy. After you have eaten a large meal, for example, your parasympathetic system works to aid your digestion, decreasing your heart rate and the blood flow to the skeletal muscles. (This is probably what your mother meant when she told you not to swim immediately after eating. Swimming requires sympathetic nervous system activity, which presumably diverts blood flow from your stomach and intestines, thereby increasing the likelihood of cramps. Actually, there is little evidence to suggest that swimming soon after eating increases your risk of developing cramps.)

The actions of the sympathetic and parasympathetic systems cannot always be divided as neatly as in these examples, of course. Most behaviors require a combination of sympathetic and parasympathetic activity. Since both systems are constantly active, the relative balance between them is what counts.

The Structure of Individual Neurons

Figure 3-3 shows a series of typical neurons. As you can see, they vary tremendously in shape and size. Some are long and have relatively few branches; others are short and have numerous branches.

Figure 3-4 shows an idealized neuron with the three basic structures all neurons have in common. The **dendrites** are the parts of the neuron that are specialized to detect incoming information. They often look like spines or tentacles stretching out from the center of the neuron, the **cell body.** The cell body receives the inputs from the dendrites and works to integrate them. In a sense, it "keeps score" of all the inputs the cell receives. If the inputs sum to a certain threshold, the cell body triggers a response from the cell, which is then transmitted down the **axon,** the relatively long nonbranching part of the neuron. The axon's primary task is to transmit the information it has received to other neurons. Table 3-1 summarizes the functions of the three main parts of a neuron's structure.

One way to visualize a neuron is to stretch out your arm and spread your fingers wide. Imagine that your fingers are dendrites, stretched out to receive input. Whatever information they receive, they

TABLE 3-1   *Structures and Functions of the Neuron*

Structure	Function	Number per Cell?
Dendrite	Receives input from other cells; transmits input to cell body	Usually many dendritic branches
Cell body	Receives input from dendrites, "summarizing and integrating" inputs; if threshold is reached, it will generate an action potential down the axon	One per cell
Axon	Transmits action potential to terminal button	Usually only one; sometimes branches

transmit it back to your hand, the cell body. Remember, the cell body's job is to take in all the inputs, "weigh" them, and determine if enough information is received from other cells to trigger an action potential. Once generated, the action potential is transmitted down the length of the axon—your outstretched arm. In the following section we will look at this process more closely.

The Process of Neural Transmission

Cells transmit information in two ways. First, they must transmit information down the length of the axon, a process called the **action potential.** Second is the passing of information from one neuron to an-other, called **synaptic transmission.** We will begin with the action potential.

Transmission within Cells

When input travels from one end of an axon to the other, the signal must be the same strength at the end of the axon as it was at the beginning, regardless of the axon's length. The strength of a signal must not decay simply because one axon is longer than another. Neurons accomplish this type of transmission by means of action potentials.

The Neuron at Rest

Though neurons are specialized cells, it is important to remember that they *are* cells. That is, they contain the same components as other cells, including elec-

FIGURE 3-3   *Neurons vary tremendously in size and shape and in the number of branches on the dendrites and axons.*

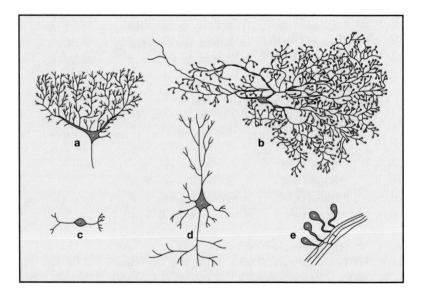

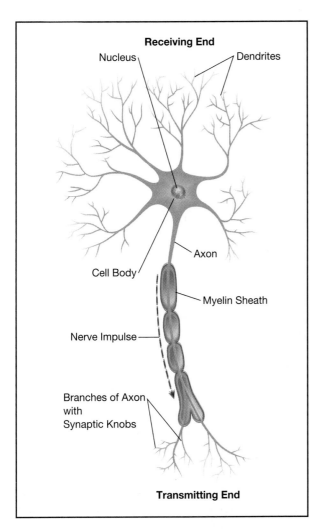

Receiving End

Nucleus

Dendrites

Axon

Cell Body

Myelin Sheath

Nerve Impulse

Branches of Axon with Synaptic Knobs

Transmitting End

FIGURE 3-4 *Most neurons consist of three main segments:* dendrites, *which receive input; the* axon, *which transmits input; and the* cell body, *which acts as an "integrator" for the different signals a neuron receives.*

trically charged molecules called **ions.** Since ions carry electrical charges, their relative distribution is critical. Some are positively charged; for our purposes, the two most important are sodium (represented by the symbol Na+, the "Na" being the chemical symbol for sodium and the "+" reflecting the positive charge) and potassium (K^+). Some ions are negatively charged, most prominently chloride (Cl−) and a cluster of similar molecules collectively called *anions* (An−). Unlike sodium, potassium, and chloride, anions are not simple elements. They are comparatively large and complex proteins.

Usually, ions will flow from areas of high concentration to areas of low concentration. They will also flow in directions opposite their charge: negatively charged ions toward positively charged ions, positively charged ions toward negatively charged ions. If allowed to mix freely, then, ions will reach a state of equilibrium, dispersing themselves evenly throughout the cell.

When a neuron is at rest, however, not all its ions are allowed to flow and mix freely. The membrane that surrounds the cell is *selectively permeable.* Potassium ions can flow readily across it, but sodium ions are restrained. Likewise, chloride ions can flow freely across the membrane, but the large anions cannot move outside the cell. When a cell is at rest, then, sodium ions tend to collect outside the cell, while anions tend to collect inside. Special pumps, sometimes called *sodium-potassium pumps,* establish and maintain this initial ionic imbalance.

Because some ions are prevented from reaching equilibrium—because of the selectively permeable membrane—a charge potential is created. When a neuron is at rest, the inside of the cell is negatively charged in comparison to the outside. If we were to measure the charge with electrodes, we would see that the charge potential of a neuron at rest is about −70 millivolts (mV). This charge potential is known as the **resting potential** of the neuron.

Why should a cell at rest need to maintain a negative resting potential? The potential represents stored energy, which allows the cell to respond to changes quickly. Because neurons are adapted to process incoming information, they are "ready to respond" when circumstances demand. When a neuron first receives input, it evaluates that input quickly. If conditions are right, the neuron transmits the information down the length of its cell body and axon. Like a cocked rifle, the neuron waits for a trigger event. Its stored charge is analogous to the stored chemical energy in gunpowder.

Reception of Input

Recall that ions tend to flow from areas of high to low concentration, and they tend to be attracted to other ions with a different electrical charge. When a neuron is at rest, therefore, sodium ions have two different forces drawing them inside the cell: concentration forces (sodium is more concentrated outside the cell), and electrical forces (positively charged sodium ions are attracted to the negative ions inside a cell). However, the movement of sodium ions is restricted by the semipermeable membrane.

When a neuron receives input (either from other neurons or directly from sense organs), the input alters the cell membrane's permeability. Sometimes it makes the membrane more permeable to sodium ions. Because of the concentration and electrical forces on sodium ions, they flow very rapidly into the cell whenever the membrane becomes more permeable, rapidly making the inside of the cell less negative, or partially **depolarized.** Inputs that cause the inside of the cell to become less negative are called **excitatory potentials.** Other inputs alter the membrane's permeability so that chloride ions are more likely to enter the cell. When this happens, the inside of the cell becomes more negative, a process known as **hyperpolarization.** Inputs that cause the inside of the cell to become more negative are called **inhibitory potentials.**

Cells at rest often receive a variety of signals of varying strength and frequency. Some cause depolarization, making the cell less negative inside. Others cause hyperpolarization, making the cell more negative inside. The cell "sums" these inputs (a function of the cell body and axon hillock), which are called **graded potentials.** Some cause small changes in the cell's charge potential; others cause larger changes. Graded potentials can be large or small, positive or negative. As we will see, it takes a number of graded potentials working together to produce a "triggering event."

Threshold for Transmission

Take a simple case in which a neuron is receiving only excitatory input, which makes the cell less negative inside. Each input will produce a small, temporary change in the cell's resting potential, a change that can be quickly reversed. However, when a cell receives a large number of depolarizing inputs within a relatively small period, it is depolarized to a critical point, called a *threshold.* The threshold is usually reached when the inside of the cell is depolarized to about −55 mV (the exact voltage depends on the specific type of neuron). At −55 mV, certain ion gates that were previously closed to sodium ions suddenly open wide. When the gates open, sodium rushes into the cell, being "pushed" by the combination of concentration and electrical gradients. This combination of forces produces a powerful effect.

The charge inside the cell goes from approximately −55 mV to +40 mV—a change of 95 mV. At this point the ion gates close, and the previous ion balance is quickly restored. As the gates close, potassium ions quickly leave the cell through their gates and the charge is reversed. For a brief period of time, the inside of the cell becomes even *more* negative than it was before (about −80 mV, compared to a resting potential of −70 mV). This period is known as the *refractory period.*

Let us summarize the entire chain reaction, called the *action potential.* At the beginning of the process the cell is at rest, with more negative charge inside than out. Excitatory graded potentials cause the inside of the neuron to become less negative. If the cell receives enough excitatory potentials in a sufficiently short period of time, the neuron may reach its threshold. At threshold the sodium gates open, allowing sodium ions to rush inside the cell. As the positively charged sodium enters the cell, the inside of the cell quickly changes from −55 mV to +40 mV. At the peak of the potential, the ion gates suddenly close. Potassium ions quickly leave the cell, restoring it to its negative resting potential. In fact, enough positively charged ions exit the cell to reduce it to a lower-than-normal state. During the refractory period, the neuron's potential might be −80 mV instead of −70 mV, and it will be less likely than normal to generate an impulse. Soon the neuron returns a normal resting potential of −70 mV, and the neuron is ready to respond again. The action potential occurs remarkably quickly, so that a neuron is capable of generating as many as a thousand action potentials each second. Figure 3-5 shows changes in the electrical potential of the cell throughout the action potential.

Comparison of Action Potentials and Graded Potentials

Action potentials are different from graded potentials in several important respects. First, action potentials behave according to an *all-or-none* principle. That is, action potentials are always the same strength. Just as a bullet being fired from a rifle is unaffected by how hard the trigger is squeezed, so an action potential is unaffected by the strength of the graded potentials that triggered it. The graded potentials must be of sufficient strength to trigger an action potential; but beyond that they do not affect the strength of the action potential.

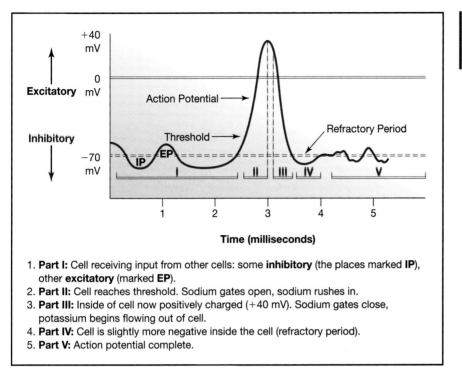

1. **Part I:** Cell receiving input from other cells: some **inhibitory** (the places marked **IP**), other **excitatory** (marked **EP**).
2. **Part II:** Cell reaches threshold. Sodium gates open, sodium rushes in.
3. **Part III:** Inside of cell now positively charged (+40 mV). Sodium gates close, potassium begins flowing out of cell.
4. **Part IV:** Cell is slightly more negative inside the cell (refractory period).
5. **Part V:** Action potential complete.

A second important way that action potentials differ from graded potentials is in the way they are passed along the axon. Graded potentials must pass from the site of stimulation to the axon hillock, where the action potential is generated. If the site of stimulation is far from the hillock, some of the graded potential's energy will be lost as it travels to the hillock. But an action potential retains its strength throughout the length of the axon like a line of falling dominos. Each fall is just like the previous one, with the same strength and effect.

Why doesn't the action potential flow back through the neuron toward the cell body? Doesn't the change in polarization work in both directions? Indeed, the change in polarization *does* work in both directions. If a neuron is stimulated in the middle of an axon, the action potential will flow in both directions. What keeps it from doing that all the time? The answer lies in the refractory period just described. Immediately after an action potential has been generated, the part of the axon that was stimulated becomes temporarily hyperpolarized. Thus the action potential is unlikely to flow backward. Just like the line of dominos, the action potential goes only one way.

Enhanced Transmission of the Action Potential

Imagine you are sitting in a classroom at the end of a long row of desks. You need to pass a message from one end of the row to the other. One way to do it would be to tell the person sitting next to you, who would then tell the next person, and so on. That would certainly work, as long as each person received the message and then transmitted it to his neighbor. A more efficient way would be for you to tell the person who was *two* seats away. That person could then tell the message to the person two seats from her, and so on down the line.

Transmission of the action potential down the length of the axon can be enhanced in a similar manner. Remember, the action potential is generated by the axon hillock; each depolarization in the axon membrane causes neighboring parts to depolarize. The process can be a slow one.

FIGURE 3-6 *View of an axon, showing the myelin sheath that encases it. Notice the myelin sheath varies in thickness, and in some places is missing entirely. These are the nodes of Ranvier, and they are the only parts of the neuron that actually depolarize, resulting in faster, more reliable transmission of action potentials.*

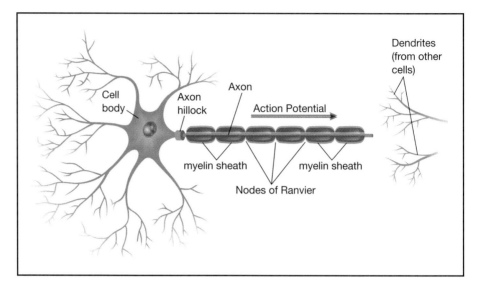

To speed it up, the axon has evolved a special mechanism. Most neurons are coated with a highly organized layer of fat called the **myelin sheath.** This sheath serves two purposes. First, it functions like an electrical insulator, allowing the membrane to depolarize only at certain places. Figure 3-6 shows a typical axon. Notice that the myelin sheath is thicker in some places than in others, and missing entirely at some points. The places where the sheath is missing are called the **nodes of Ranvier.** They are the only sections of the membrane that actually depolarize. The action potential, then, literally "skips" from node to node, just as your message skipped to every other student. The myelin sheath also acts as a mechanical barrier, protecting the cell from foreign bodies that might cause false transmission or interfere with appropriate transmission.

The myelinization of neurons is critical. In fact, many neuromuscular problems arise from damage to the myelin sheath, not the neurons themselves. For example, the disease multiple sclerosis damages the myelin sheath, preventing appropriately generated impulses from being transmitted from one end of the axon to the other. Because the protective insulation is missing, messages that should travel from one neuron to another tend to get lost, causing the unprotected neurons to operate sporadically. The result in some cases is an inability to control movement or the tremors and jerks associated with involuntary movement.

Transmission between Cells

What happens when an action potential reaches the end of the axon? How does the information get passed from one neuron to the next (or from a motor neuron to a muscle)? The earliest studies of neural activity assumed that neurons touch each other, like two wires touching at a junction box. Actually, a few very specialized neurons do touch. However, as techniques for studying neurons became more sophisticated, researchers discovered that the vast majority of neurons did not physically touch. A small gap, called a *synaptic cleft,* separated one neuron from another.

How can information pass across this gap? Neuronal communication is chemical, not electrochemical. That is, the ionic action potential does not "jump" across the gap, the way electricity arcs across a gap in a wire. Instead, when an action potential reaches the end of an axon, it triggers a complex series of biochemical reactions that allow one cell to communicate with another. As we will see, the communication occurs when one neuron releases a chemical that diffuses to the second neuron, stimulating it. Before studying the mechanics of transmission, however, it will be useful to look at the structure of the synapse.

Anatomy of a Synapse

Figure 3-7 shows an idealized **synapse.** In the presynaptic cell (that is, the cell that is transmitting the information) there is a series of small "packets," called

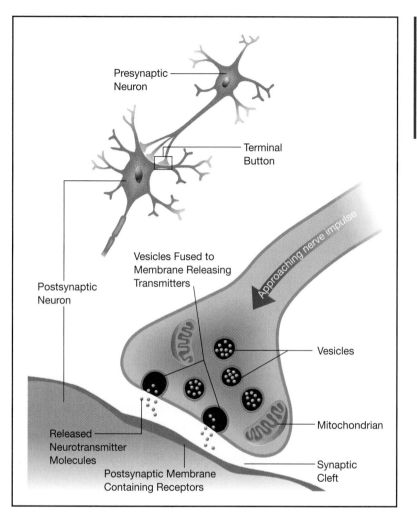

Presynaptic
Neuron

Terminal
Button

Postsynaptic
Neuron

Vesicles Fused to
Membrane Releasing
Transmitters

Approaching nerve impulse

Vesicles

Mitochondrian

Released
Neurotransmitter
Molecules

Postsynaptic Membrane
Containing Receptors

Synaptic
Cleft

FIGURE 3-7   *Transmission of
information at the synapse. When
stimulated by an action potential, the
synaptic vesicles at the end of the
axon release neurotransmitters into
the synaptic cleft. The neurotransmitters stimulate receptors on
the dendrites of neighboring cells.*

the *synaptic vesicles*, at the end of the axon. This ax-
onal ending is called the *terminal button*, and its
packets contain the chemicals, called **neurotransmitters,** which accomplish the communication. As long
as the chemicals are stored in the vesicles, they are
inactive. As the action potential reaches the end of
the presynaptic axon, the vesicles migrate the short
distance to the end of the button and then fuse with
the membrane. When the membranes fuse, the vesi-
cle spills its contents into the opening, called the
synaptic cleft. Once released, the neurotransmitters
diffuse across the synaptic cleft, stimulating specialized structures on the dendrites of the postsynaptic
cell. Stimulation of the dendrites leads to the graded
potentials; described earlier.

*A color-enhanced micrograph showing the synaptic
connections between neurons.*

Synaptic Transmission

Perhaps the best analogy for describing how neurotransmitters stimulate dendrites is the lock-and-key metaphor. Recall that the dendrites have ionic gates permeable to sodium and chloride ions. The gates are usually closed, but they can be opened by neurotransmitters. Now think of the gates as locks, and neurotransmitters as the key. The dendrites, then, have special gates in their membranes that only certain kinds of substances will fit into and open. The neurotransmitters are just the right type of key; they fit perfectly into the locked gates, allowing the ions to flow. As the ions flow through the gates, they generate the graded potentials. (In Chapter 5, we will see that some drugs exert their effects by fitting into these "biological locks." Others change the locks in such a way as to inhibit the neurotransmitters' keys from opening them, thus inhibiting the generation of graded potentials.)

The effects of neurotransmitters are short-lived. Soon after being released, neurotransmitters are either taken back into the presynaptic cell (a process called *presynaptic reuptake*) or broken down by enzymes into smaller units that no longer fit the lock. This process of deactivation is critical to optimal neural functioning. If it is disrupted, the postsynaptic cell might respond inappropriately. Chapter 5 describes certain drugs that have their effect by blocking the deactivation of neurotransmission.

At this point, we have come full circle. We began the section with excitatory and inhibitory graded potentials, which begin the transmission process. That discussion was deliberately vague about how dendrites receive the information they transmit. You may have wondered where these excitatory and inhibitory potentials come from. You now have the answer: they come from neurotransmitters that have been released from neighboring neurons. These transmitters open either sodium (excitatory) or chloride (inhibitory) gated ion channels. The ion flow in turn causes the graded potentials.

Neurotransmitters: Chemical Messengers

Not many years ago, neuroscientists believed there were relatively few neurotransmitters. By the late 1950s only three had been fully studied. By the beginning of the 1990s, however, neuroscientists had identified almost forty substances that serve as neurotransmitters (Groves & Rebec, 1992). We will focus on a small group of the more common transmitters. The monoamines—dopamine, norepinephrine, and serotonin—are chemically very similar. They play critical roles in emotion, movement, learning, and memory. Another type of neurotransmitter, acetylcholine, is present in neuromuscular junctions (the places where neurons communicate with muscles) and in areas of the brain that are important to memory. Still another, gamma-aminobutyric acid (commonly called GABA), is the major inhibitory transmitter in the human nervous system. GABA plays a critical role in emotion, anxiety, and arousal. Finally, we will look at a group of pseudotransmitters known as endorphins (sometimes called "endogenous opiates"). Endorphins regulate pain and pleasure; their presence offers a clue to the addictive properties of the drugs known as the opiates, such as morphine and heroin.

Monoamines

The **monoamines** dopamine, norepinephrine, and serotonin share the same neurochemical building blocks. Because of this similarity, many substances that affect one of these transmitters will also affect the others. Each of the three monoamines is more prevalent in some areas of the brain than in others, so their effects can be quite different.

Dopamine

Dopamine is found in numerous locations in the brain, but is most prominently found in three large structures: the limbic system (the part of the brain critically involved in the regulation of emotion, learning, and memory), the cerebellum (important for gross motor activity), and a part of the forebrain called the **basal ganglia** (an area that coordinates fine motor activity). Therefore, it is not surprising that dopamine plays a critical role in thought disorders—primarily **schizophrenia** (discussed more fully in Chapter 15)—and movement disorders. **Parkinson's disease,** a motor disorder characterized by exaggerated (or, in some cases, inhibited) movement, is a classic dopamine-related disorder. Parkinson's patients often exhibit tremors at rest, or will have difficulty coordinating their movement. Walking is difficult for them, as is any facial expression. Individuals with Parkinson's disease often show greatly decreased levels of dopamine in their brains,

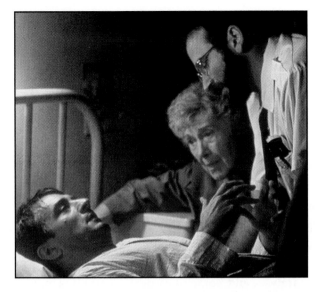

Robin Williams, portraying a physician based on the renowned neurologist Oliver Sacks, in the film "Awakenings." The story was based on a series of cases Sacks treated, all involving a severe type of Parkinson's disease.

particularly in the basal ganglia (Albin, Young, & Penney, 1989).

The movie *Awakenings,* based on a series of actual cases reported by the renowned neurologist Oliver Sacks (1990), portrayed a series of individuals suffering from a severe type of Parkinson's disease. These patients typically manifested immobility and difficulty in movement rather than tremors. Some of these patients had been virtually motionless for forty years—a kind of grotesque version of the childhood game "living statues." In the movie, the neurologist (played by Robin Williams) temporarily alleviated some of their symptoms by administering "L-DOPA," a drug that the brain converts immediately to dopamine. Unfortunately, in the movie, as in real life, treatment of Parkinson's disease with L-DOPA is not a successful long-term therapy.

The other major disorder associated with dopamine, schizophrenia, is a debilitating disorder characterized by thought disorders like delusions and hallucinations. Investigators now believe that schizophrenia may result from excess activity in parts of the brain containing dopamine—particularly the limbic system. Drugs that are used to treat schizophrenia work by blocking the effects of dopamine.

To say that too much dopamine leads to schizophrenia, too little leads to Parkinson's disease, would be to greatly oversimplify the real situation, however. But there are some distinct connections. One of the serious side effects of drugs that treat schizophrenia is that if they are taken in large doses, they can produce Parkinson's-like symptoms. In fact, in the early days of treating schizophrenics, when understanding of dosage levels was limited, a rule of thumb was, "Increase the dose until Parkinson's-like symptoms appear, then back off a little."

Norepinephrine

As its name implies, **norepinephrine** is derived from epinephrine, also known as adrenaline. As such, its role in arousal and mood should be clear. Neurons using norepinephrine are found throughout the brain and spinal cord, but in higher concentrations in the cortex and the limbic system. Norepinephrine is involved in eating, sleep, arousal, and emotional activity.

Because of norepinephrine's critical role in emotional behavior, it was one of the first neurotransmitters suspected to have a role in major depression. The term *depression,* as it is used here, must be contrasted with the "depression" we all feel from time to time whenever we fail a test, break up with a significant other, or lose a close friend. Major depression is altogether different. Individuals suffering from major depression lose touch with reality. Not only do they feel sad, but they cannot remember ever feeling any other way and are hopeless, often suicidal. Either they cannot sleep or they sleep all the time; they do not eat and may spend hours in bed crying.

Individuals who suffer from this type of depression are often treated with drugs called *antidepressants,* which affect neurons that respond to norepinephrine. Often within several weeks of beginning drug treatment, depressed individuals will report a marked decrease in symptoms. However, just as the drugs that are used to treat schizophrenia do not *cure* it, antidepressants do not *cure* depression; they only treat the symptoms. Many individuals find that they need to take antidepressants for several months (or sometimes years) to prevent depression from recurring.

Serotonin

The neurotransmitter **serotonin** is chemically very similar to norepinephrine and is consequently found in many of the same areas of the brain. However, serotonin is found in higher concentrations in the brain stem and the thalamus. Since the brain stem is

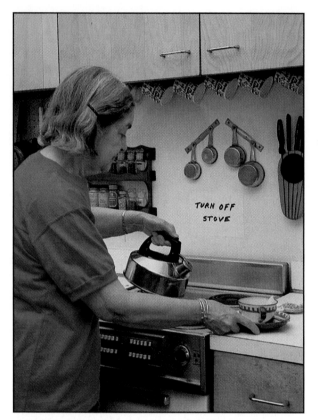

In the early middle stages of Alzheimer's disease, many patients compensate for their memory lapses by placing reminder notes throughout the house.

directly involved in the regulation of arousal, serotonin is suspected to have an important influence on arousal-related activities such as sleep. The thalamus is involved in the "routing" of sensory signals. Therefore disruption of serotonin-influenced functions often leads to sensory problems such as hallucinations. The drug LSD is suspected to work by directly affecting levels of serotonin in the thalamus.

Serotonin also plays an important role in emotional behavior. The newest generation of antidepressants like fluoxetine (Prozac) work almost exclusively on serotonin receptors. (Traditional antidepressants affect both serotonin and norepinephrine receptors.) Because the new antidepressants are selective for serotonin receptors, they usually induce fewer side effects.

Neuromuscular and Inhibitory Transmitters

Unlike the monoamine neurotransmitters just described, this second group of neurotransmitters do not share a common chemical structure. However,

acetylcholine and GABA are related in other ways. Both are widespread throughout the central nervous system, and they behave in a broadly antagonistic manner: acetylcholine is thought to be the brain's most common excitatory transmitter; GABA, the primary inhibitory transmitter.

Acetylcholine

Acetylcholine, the first neurotransmitter to be identified and studied, is the primary neurotransmitter found at neuromuscular junctions (sites that directly influence muscle movement). Acetylcholine is also found in locations throughout the brain. Many poisons—such as botulinum, some spider venom, and insecticides—work by changing the action of acetylcholine at the neuromuscular junction, causing paralysis and sometimes death. Curare, a poison found in plants in the Amazon, also disrupts transmission at the neuromuscular junction.

Acetylcholine also plays an important role in learning and memory, and has been implicated in Alzheimer's disease. Patients suffering from Alzheimer's, who are usually (but not always) older, show a gradual, progressive, and irreversible memory loss. At first they may forget things like an item they intended to buy at the grocery store, but soon they forget names and faces, even of close family members. As the average life span increases, so has the incidence of Alzheimer's disease, now a major problem associated with aging. Unfortunately, drugs that augment acetylcholine levels do not seem effective in the treatment of Alzheimer's disease.

GABA

Gamma-aminobutyric acid (GABA) is the most prevalent inhibitory neurotransmitter. Found throughout the brain and spinal cord, it is present in somewhat higher concentrations in parts of the brain involving emotion and anxiety. It also plays a role in arousal and sleep. Drugs like Valium, Xanax, and Librium (which are all *benzodiazepines*) work by augmenting the effects of GABA. By increasing the activity of GABA-influenced neurons, they tend to reduce anxiety. Some are used as sleeping aids.

Pseudo Transmitters (Endorphins)

The term **endorphins** refers to a group of very similar neurotransmitter-like substances. **Opiates** like morphine and heroin mimic the action of endorphins, which modulate pain and pleasure, and regu-

Endorphins are naturally occurring transmitter-like substances that tend to reduce pain. They have been linked to the so-called "runner's high" that athletes experience under demanding physical conditions.

late eating and drinking. Increased levels of endorphins lead to a reduction in pain, as will opiates like morphine. Produced naturally by the brain during periods of stress and anxiety, endorphins have been linked to the subjective "runner's high" that runners and other athletes report under demanding physical conditions. In fact, athletes who are unable to exercise often report anxiety or discomfort.

Endorphin disruption may be involved in a number of different behavioral disorders, especially substance abuse. The link between endorphins and opiates like heroin and morphine is straightforward: because opiates mimic the actions of endorphins, they cause feelings of euphoria. Recently, some types of alcoholism have been shown to involve disruption of endorphin regulation. The role endorphins play in such situations is not well understood,

though; the mechanisms are likely to be quite complex (e.g., Gianoulakis, 1993).

Table 3-2 summarizes the functions of common neurotransmitters.

The Brain: Structure and Function

Remember the fascinating case of H. M. described at the beginning of the chapter? Following his surgery, which successfully treated his epilepsy, he was essentially "frozen in the present." Unable to form any new long-term memories, he is only dimly aware of his problem (to be fully aware of his memory problems, he would have to "remember his inability to remember").

The cause of H. M.'s problems lay in his brain, that complex mass of billions of cells composed mostly of water, protein, fat, and a host of chemicals. When fully developed, the human brain weighs less than 3 pounds, yet it is responsible for all the phenomena psychologists seek to explain. Our perceptions and thoughts, our plans and actions, our feelings and dreams—all are produced by activities in the brain and spinal cord. In H. M.'s case, the surgery to control his epilepsy damaged the parts of his brain that are responsible for forming new long-term memories, giving researchers a clue to how the brain functions. Because the brain is compartmentalized to some extent, with particular regions taking a greater part in specific functions, injury to a certain area of the brain can disrupt one aspect of performance while leaving other aspects intact. That specific syndromes can result from damage to particular regions confirms the localization of certain functions (Coltheart, 1989).

Evolution of Brain Structures

Like all other organisms on the planet, humans are the result of millions of years of evolution. Our species' brain has evolved to meet the many different selective pressures that have arisen over these years. Features that have helped us to survive and reproduce have been retained from one generation to the next. Thus, though humans and other species have diverged into separate niches, our brains still have many basic features in common, features that have generally proved advantageous to our survival.

The human brain is very similar to the brains of other mammals like dogs and cats. It is nearly identical to the brains of some other primates such as the

TABLE 3-2   *Summary of Common Neurotransmitters, Where They Are Found in the Brain, and What Behavior They Mediate*

	Where Found in the Brain?	Which Behaviors Are Influenced?
MONOAMINES Dopamine	Many locations, but especially in: • Limbic system • Cerebellum • Basal ganglia	• Emotion and memory • Motor activity, some forms of learning and memory • Movement, coordination
Norepinephrine	Many locations, but especially in: • Limbic system • Frontal cortex	• Emotion (especially depression), eating, sleeping • Learning and memory
Serotonin	Especially found in: • Thalamus • Brain stem	• Processing of sensory signals • Sleep, arousal (especially in depression)
ACETYLCHOLINE	• Throughout the brain • Neuromuscular junctions	• Memory (implicated in Alzheimer's disease) • Control and regulation of movement
GABA	Major inhibitory transmitter throughout the brain: • Limbic system • Brain stem	 • Anxiety, arousal • Arousal, sleep, respiration
ENDORPHINS	Throughout, especially the limbic system	• Natural "painkillers" • Implicated in many forms of substance abuse • Feelings of "pleasure"

great apes, our closest living relatives in the animal kingdom. These shared features allow us to draw inferences about the human brain by studying the brains of other animals.

A useful if somewhat oversimplified way of thinking about brain evolution is to imagine that a new layer of structures emerged at each of three critical junctures in our evolutionary history (McLean, 1982). These periods correspond to the three major regions of the human brain: the hindbrain, midbrain, and forebrain. Structures in the hindbrain, the oldest part of the brain, reflect our reptilian ancestry. They

control reflexive action, those actions that are absolutely necessary for survival. Human hindbrains are very similar structurally to the hindbrains of many other animals. For example, the hindbrains of sheep look remarkably like human hindbrains. They haven't evolved much because they haven't needed to evolve much.

The midbrain is a more recent addition, in evolutionary terms. Structures that grew up around this region, along with parts of the emerging forebrain, constitute our inheritance from the earliest mammals. The midbrain controls emotions and basic mo-

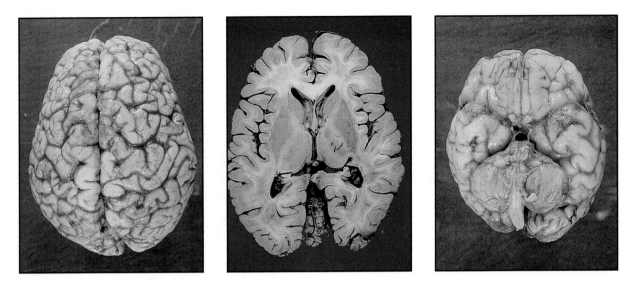

(Left) The human brain, viewed from the top. (Middle) A cross-section of the brain, viewed from the top. (Right) The human brain, viewed from the bottom; the frontal lobes are at the top of the picture, the brain stem toward the bottom. Notice the left-right symmetry in all three photos.

tivations, such as hunger, sexuality, and aggression. Forebrain structures that surround this region, and which occupy much of the skull in humans, are our inheritance from more recent mammals. The most prominent of the forebrain structures is the cerebral cortex, the centers of the brain important for thought and reason (see Figure 3-8). The greatest difference between human brains and those of other primates is the amount of forebrain: humans have considerably more. While it is tempting to think of humans as more "advanced" because of the larger proportion of their brain devoted to forebrain, do not fall into that trap. Humans are not more "advanced": they simply have a brain better adapted to their environment.

The three-part division just described nicely reflects how "miserly opportunistic" (to borrow Lieberman's, 1991, term) the human brain is: *human brains have evolved by adding onto existing structures, not by replacing them.* While humans do have a greater proportion of brain tissue devoted to forebrain, they still use the older brain structures inherited from their ancestors (though not always in the same way).

Major Regions of the Human Brain

The hindbrain, the midbrain, and the forebrain not only reflect our evolutionary heritage but also serve as a good organizing tool for studying the brain.

With each of the brain structures we study, ask yourself two questions: "Chere are the structures located?" and "What do they do?" This functional approach to the study of anatomy can make the task seem more relevant.

The Hindbrain

The **hindbrain** contains the oldest parts of the brain. Indeed, its structure varies little among vertebrates. The hindbrain includes structures that together carry out the functions most basic to survival, such as sleeping and waking, breathing, and cardiovascular function. Figure 3-9 shows the structures that make up the hindbrain.

The largest structures are the pons, the medulla, the cerebellum, and the reticular formation. If you follow the spinal cord up the neck and into the base of the skull, you will come to an area that swells out slightly. In fact, it can almost be seen as an extension of the spinal cord. This is the **medulla,** the first structure of the hindbrain. The medulla plays an important role in many autonomic activities, such as circulation and breathing. It is also involved in chewing, salivation, and facial movements. Above and extending forward from the medulla is the **pons** (meaning "bridge"), which connects the two halves of the cerebellum lying above it. The pons transmits to the cerebellum information about body movements that it

FIGURE 3-8 Divisions of the hindbrain, midbrain, and forebrain.

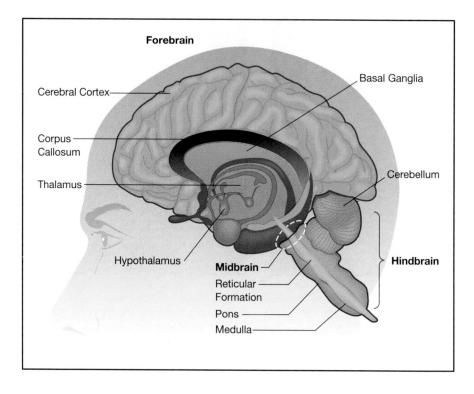

Forebrain

Cerebral Cortex

Basal Ganglia

Corpus Callosum

Cerebellum

Thalamus

Hypothalamus

Midbrain

Reticular Formation

Hindbrain

Pons

Medulla

FIGURE 3-9 Structures of the hindbrain. The hindbrain *contains the oldest parts of the brain, and varies little among vertebrates. The largest structures are the* pons, *which is involved in movement and sleep; the* medulla, *which regulates many autonomic activities, such as circulation and breathing; the* cerebellum, *involved in movement, balance and equilibrium, and some kinds of learning and memory; and the* reticular formation, *important for attention and arousal.*

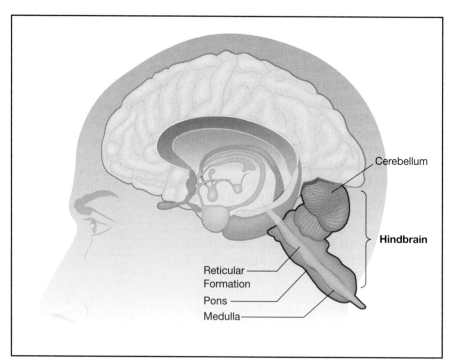

Cerebellum

Reticular Formation

Hindbrain

Pons

Medulla

The cerebellum, located in this marksman's hindbrain, is involved in coordinating his muscular movements.

receives from higher brain centers and the spinal cord. Brainstem nuclei located in the pons are also involved in circuits that control sleep.

Running up the stem of the hindbrain—through the medulla, pons, and midbrain and into the thalamus—is a network of neurons and nerve fibers collectively called the **reticular formation.** The reticular formation functions as a type of "sentry," arousing the forebrain when information related to survival must be processed. It facilitates sustained attention and also appears to help screen out extraneous sensory input, especially during sleep. Severe damage to the reticular formation can cause a person to lapse into a permanent coma.

The **cerebellum** is located at the very back of the brain, just above where the brain and spinal cord meet. *Cerebellum* literally means "little brain" and is derived from the fact that the cerebellum is divided into two hemispheres and so looks like a miniature forebrain. (The similarity is purely structural; the cerebellum and forebrain have very different functions.) The cerebellum acts as a separate, independent processor that integrates information from the hindbrain (and other sensory information) with input from the forebrain. Because of its unique connections, the cerebellum serves several functions. One part of the cerebellum is involved in maintaining a sense of balance and equilibrium. Another is involved in coordinating muscular movements, ensuring that they are smooth and efficient. Thus, damage to the cerebellum can cause *ataxia,* a condition characterized by uncoordinated movement, lack of balance, and severe tremors. A person who has ataxia

lacks the control needed for even simple reaching movements, and so may accidentally hit a friend in the stomach while reaching out to shake hands. Still another part of the cerebellum is involved in the learning and remembering of simple motor tasks (Thompson, 1986, 1988, 1989).

The hindbrain is protected by the thickest part of the skull. Feel the back of your head, where your skull joins your spinal cord. Its bony ridges protect the pons, medulla, and cerebellum, reflecting the vital importance of these brain structures. To survive following damage to the pons or the medulla, an individual is likely to require permanent life support. These brain structures are also frequently threatened by closed head injury, a severe blow that does not penetrate the skull. The greatest damage typically occurs when the brain begins to swell, within a day or so following the initial injury, putting pressure on the pons and the medulla. If such pressure is not relieved, the swelling can literally crush those structures, causing irreversible harm. Physicians who treat patients with closed head injuries will often drill holes in the skull to relieve the pressure that threatens the brain stem.

The Midbrain

Above the hindbrain is a small area known as the **midbrain** (Figure 3-10). All sensory and motor information passing back and forth between the forebrain and spinal cord must go through the midbrain. The midbrain contains important centers for regulating body movement in response to visual and auditory stimulation. For example, your startle reflex in response to a sudden loud noise is controlled by an area of the midbrain. In any particular species, the size of the visual and auditory areas of the midbrain will vary depending on how important those centers are to survival. Birds that sight, track, and capture prey in flight, for instance, have very prominent and bulging visual regions. Bats, which use sound rather than sight to locate their prey, have small visual centers but larger auditory ones.

The Forebrain

The **forebrain** is the most prominent part of the mammalian brain. Looking at the forebrain from the outside, one can see the **cerebral cortex,** which surrounds the entire outer surface of the brain (literally, *cerebrum* means "brain," "cortex," "covering"). If we were to peel back the cerebral cortex, we would see a

FIGURE 3-10 *Structures of the midbrain. The midbrain coordinates the transmission of sensory and motor information from the forebrain and spinal cord, and is especially critical for vision and audition.*

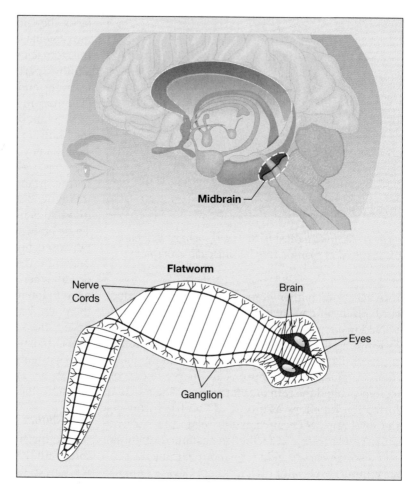

highly interconnected group of structures inside. Collectively, these structures constitute a part of the brain known as the **limbic system,** which we will examine before discussing the structure and function of the cerebral cortex.

The Limbic System

As can be seen in Figure 3-11, the limbic system contains the hypothalamus, the thalamus, the hippocampus, the amygdala, and the septum, as well as other structures. In an evolutionary sense, the limbic system is somewhat older than other structures in the forebrain. It is particularly important in controlling fundamental survival behaviors.

The Thalamus and Hypothalamus Above the midbrain, deeply embedded in the central mass of the cerebral hemispheres, are the thalamus and hypothalamus. The **thalamus** consists of many quite separate clusters of neurons called nuclei, each of which relays information to and from specific parts

of the nervous system. For example, in Chapter 4 you will read about nuclei in the thalamus that relay information from sensory receptors in the peripheral nervous system to specific parts of the forebrain. One of these is concerned with the relay of visual information, another with the relay of auditory information, and a third with the relay of touch, pressure, temperature, and pain. In fact, only olfactory (odor) information circumvents the thalamus; all other sensory information goes through the thalamus on its way to the cortex.

Thalamic nuclei are not simply passive way stations. They actively process information as they pass it along. The thalamus, then, exerts its own influence as it shuttles information from one part of the nervous system to another. Because of its critical role in relaying sensory signals to the appropriate brain structures, you might expect the thalamus to be involved in drug-induced hallucinations. You would be right: many of the drugs that induce hallucina-

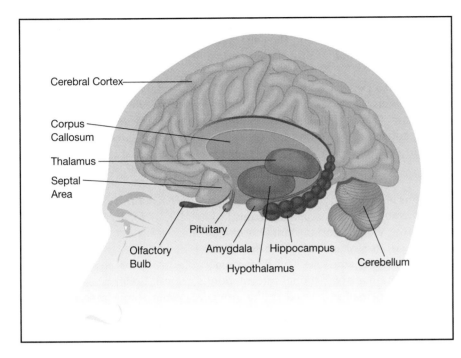

Figure 3-11   *Structures of the forebrain. The* forebrain *is the most prominent part of the mammalian brain. The* cerebral cortex *surrounds the entire outer surface of the brain, and is important for learning, memory, language, and reasoning. If we were to peel back the cerebral cortex we would see the* limbic system, *a highly interconnected group of structures involved in emotion, motivation, and learning.*

tions work by disrupting normal processing in the thalamus. We will examine their effect in greater detail in Chapter 5.

The **hypothalamus** is a small structure roughly the size and shape of an almond located just below the thalamus. It consists of various nuclei, each with different (but complementary) functions. Many of these nuclei are involved in basic survival behaviors, such as eating, drinking, sexual activity, fear, and aggression. For example, stimulation of the *lateral* (side) area of the hypothalamus will cause an animal to eat voraciously, even if it has just consumed a meal, while stimulation of the *ventromedial* (lower middle) area of the hypothalamus will prompt an animal to stop eating, even if it is starving. These hypothalamic nuclei seem to be involved in an animal's ability to recognize when it is hungry or full.

Other nuclei in the hypothalamus are involved in regulating the body's internal environment. For instance, part of the hypothalamus controls the body's internal temperature, and hypothalamic regions coordinate the activities of the autonomic nervous

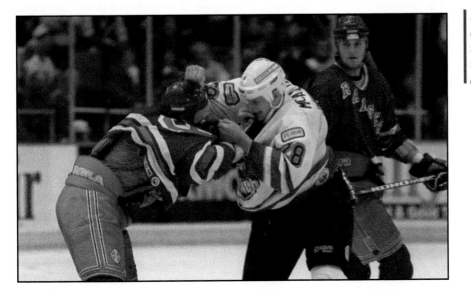

Brain structures in the limbic system are involved in emotional behavior, including the aggression displayed by hockey players.

system. The hypothalamus also regulates the activities of the **pituitary gland,** the structure that regulates hormonal secretions from other glands throughout the body.

The hypothalamus' small size—only 0.3 percent of the brain's total weight—might give you the impression that it is relatively unimportant. Quite the contrary. The hypothalamus plays a critical role in everything from the regulation of glucose levels in the blood to maintenance of the body's temperature to the formation of new memories.

The Hippocampus   The **hippocampus** is located in the region just behind and partially surrounding the thalamus and hypothalamus. In humans, extensive damage to the hippocampus is linked to severe problems in forming new memories. People who suffer such damage on both sides of the brain are often unable to consciously retain new information (Mishkin & Appenzeller, 1987). They cannot remember what they were doing or who they were with just moments after turning to a new activity. They cannot find their way to a new location (one they never visited before their brain damage), even though they have been taken there over and over again. (H. M., the epileptic patient described at the outset of this chapter, had a large portion of his hippocampus destroyed in an attempt to control his seizures.) Not surprisingly, malfunction of the hippocampus seems to be involved in Alzheimer's disease, the symptoms of which include extensive memory impairment.

This important limbic structure serves some other memory-based functions as well. For instance, the hippocampus appears to be involved in the organization of movement and spatial organization (Kolb & Whishaw, 1993). The hippocampus also plays an important role in emotion and memory. For example, Heinrich Klüver and Paul Bucy removed the hippocampus (and the amygdala, a closely related structure) in monkeys. Before the surgery, the monkeys had been wild and aggressive. After the surgery, they became docile and tame. The monkeys no longer recognized many familiar objects, even those that once elicited fearful reactions, like snakes. The monkeys displayed other impairments, too, but their inability to remember emotional stimuli is striking. While the complex relationship between the hippocampus, emotion, and memory is not yet fully understood, emotion and memory are clearly linked (Kandel et al., 1995).

The Amygdala   The **amygdala** are located in the tips of the temporal lobes, next to the hypothalamus.

They are directly connected to the hippocampus, and they share many functions. Like the hippocampus, the amygdala are highly interconnected to the hypothalamus and cerebral cortex. Both the hippocampus and the amygdala are involved in the processing and formation of new memories. For example, H. M.'s surgery seriously damaged his amygdala as well as his hippocampus. Recent research has confirmed the role of the amygdala in the formation of memories, especially emotional memories (Mishkin & Appenzeller, 1987; Thompson, 1985; Zola-Morgan, Squire, & Mishkin, 1982). The amygdala are critical to helping us focus attention on important (emotional) characteristics of incoming stimuli (Kolb & Whishaw, 1996).

The amygdala's role in the processing of emotional information is critical. Epileptic seizures centered in the amygdala often result in serious emotional changes. Depending on the exact nature and size of the epileptic *foci,* seizures involving the amygdala can lead to outbursts of rage or euphoric experiences (Kalat, 1992). For example, rabies is a *neurotropic* (literally, "brain-loving") viral disease that leads to systematic destruction of the amygdala. As rabies progresses, the afflicted organism may begin to display dangerous, ultimately uncontrollable fits of aggression. On the other hand, epileptic seizures centered in another part of the amygdala can trigger extreme happiness and bliss. The Russian writer Dostoyevsky was prone to these types of euphoric seizures, which have since been called "Dostoyevskian seizures."

The fact that the hippocampus and the amygdala are intimately involved with both memory and emotion provides powerful evidence of the relationship between affect and memory. In general, higher levels of affect lead to increased memory (this rule breaks down at extreme levels of emotion). It is no coincidence that professors you find engaging are the same ones whose lectures you tend to remember.

The Septum   The **septum** is another limbic structure involved in emotion, though in a different way from the amygdala. In 1954 James Olds and Peter Milner accidentally discovered that rats will quickly learn to press a lever to receive mild electrical stimulation to parts of the septum. The pleasure this stimulation produces is apparently intense. A hungry rat hurrying to the feeding tray will stop in its tracks to receive it and will remain there as long as the stimulation continues, even until it starves. When allowed to stimulate their own septal areas—sometimes

Limbic structures such as the hippocampus and amygdala are involved in both emotion and memory. As a result, intense emotional experiences like those experienced by rescue workers following the Oklahoma City bombing often produce vivid, long-lasting memories.

called "pleasure centers"—by pressing a bar that connects the current, rats have been known to press frantically, thousands of times an hour. What could the nature of such intense pleasure be? The few humans who have undergone similar septal area stimulation (usually during treatment of some neurological disorder) report that they experience a rush of extremely good feelings, which some have compared with the buildup to an orgasm. Exactly how stimulation of these septal regions is related to such behaviors as feeding and mating, also influenced by the limbic system, is still largely unknown. Bear in mind, too, that the septal area is not the only area of the brain where stimulation is pleasurable and rewarding. The brain apparently has dozens of these locations (Wise & Rompre, 1989).

Next, we will consider the sophisticated information-processing capabilities of the cerebral cortex. The cerebral cortex allows us to analyze the rich sensory environment in which we live, and to organize and make sense of that environment. The cerebral cortex facilitates most complicated cognitive tasks: language, problem solving, creativity, and so on. It underlies logical and rational thought, and is largely responsible for what we might call "intelligent" behavior. Even so, it is the limbic system that makes life worth living. Joy and sadness, euphoria and rage, love and fear—all emanate from the limbic system.

The Cerebral Hemispheres

When you look at a brain, the first things you notice are the shell-like structures that encase it. This shell is really two symmetrical half-shells, called the **cere-**

bral hemispheres. These two large structures lie above the brain's central core, one on the left side, the other on the right. The cerebral hemispheres are the most recent development in the brain's long evolutionary history. These large structures are involved in the processes of learning, memory, language, and reasoning. (To give you a rough idea of the size and shape of the hemispheres, make fists with both hands, then bring your hands together, knuckle to knuckle. Your fists are approximately the size and shape of your cerebral hemispheres.)

The outermost area of the cerebral hemispheres is a thin layer of gray matter called the cortex (the term means "bark" or "outer covering"), only about a twelfth of an inch (2 millimeters) thick, but it has so many convolutions that it contains more than 9 billion neurons. If the human cortex were flattened out, its area would be about 2.5 square feet. The cortex can be divided into four principal areas, or lobes: the occipital lobe, the parietal lobe, the temporal lobe, and the frontal lobe (see Figure 3-12).

The Occipital Lobes The **occipital lobes** lie at the very back of each cerebral hemisphere. A major role of the occipital lobe is the initial analysis of visual information. In humans, injury to these portions of the cortex can produce blind spots in the *visual field.* People with occipital lobe damage usually report impaired vision, and standard visual tests confirm their blindness. However, some of those patients display a fascinating phenomenon called *blindsight* (Weiskrantz, 1986), a condition where some visual abilities remain, but those abilities are not accessible to the person's conscious awareness. These people may duck when

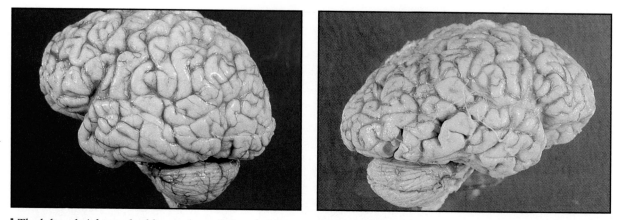

The left and right cerebral hemispheres (left and right, respectively) are involved in learning, memory, language, and reasoning. Although the two hemispheres do have some specialized functions, the popular press has exaggerated the left brain/right brain dichotomy.

FIGURE 3-12   Lobes of the cerebral cortex, showing the two major fissures, the four lobes, and several other cortical areas and their functions.

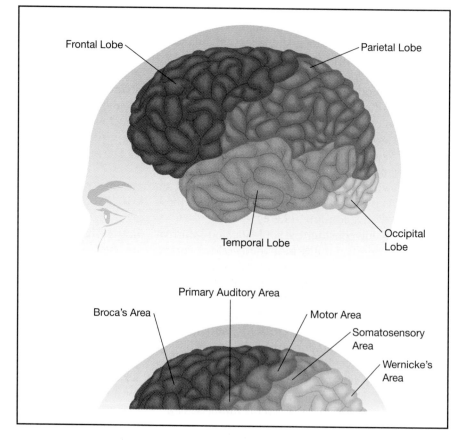

FIGURE 3-13   *Map of Sensory Area: Sensory Homunculus. The amount of the sensory cortex which is allocated to specific body regions. The parts of the homunculus which are larger receive impulses from the more sensitive body parts (such as the fingers and the lips), and also occupy larger brain regions. Although for simplicity's sake these drawings make it appear as if each part of the body is represented only once, in fact each body part has multiple representations.* (Penfield & Rasmussen, 1950.)

walking through a door with a low entrance, but they cannot explain why, nor do they report the sensation of "seeing." More precisely, then, we should say that the occipital lobe is critical for conscious, aware vision.

The Parietal Lobes   In front of the occipital lobes, just before the central fissures, lie the **parietal lobes.** The parietal lobes contain the *somatosensory cortex*, the primary receiving area for the skin senses (touch, pressure, heat, pain) and the sense of body position. Like the motor cortex, the somatosensory cortex is linked to sensations in the left side of the body; the left hemisphere is linked to sensations in the body's right side. Also like the motor cortex, the somatosensory cortex is not allocated according to the size of body parts. Instead, the sensitivity of a particular body part determines the amount of tissue devoted to it. For instance, the lips, which are small but extremely sensitive to touch, occupy a relatively large area in the somatosensory cortex, as shown in Figure 3-13.

The Temporal Lobes   The **temporal lobes** lie below the parietal lobes, more or less beneath the ears on either side of the head. In addition to housing regions that integrate sensory information and attend to its distinctive features, the temporal cortex also has areas where auditory signals are first received and processed by the brain. The temporal lobe is also involved in the formation of memories and the processing of emotional information (Carlson, 1992).

The Frontal Lobes   The behaviors controlled by the **frontal lobes** vary from thought and reasoning to control of motor input and factors relating to personality. For example, Figure 3-14, which maps the *motor cortex*, shows the amount of cortex devoted to individual body parts. Like the somatosensory cortex, the amount of motor cortex for a body part depends not on the size of that part but rather on its degree of motor control. For example, the fingers, which can make very precise movements, have a much larger representation in the motor cortex than the trunk of the body. Note also that the motor cortex in the right hemisphere controls movement on the left side of the body, and the motor cortex of the left hemisphere controls movement on the body's right side. This phenomenon, called **contralateral control,** is a basic principle of organization in the brain.

Figure 3-14 Map of Motor Area: Motor Homunculus. The amount of the motor cortex which is allocated to specific body regions. Areas of the body capable of the most complex and precise movements are linked to the largest quantities of space in the motor cortex, and appear larger in the homunculus. [As with the sensory cortex, each body part has multiple representations.]

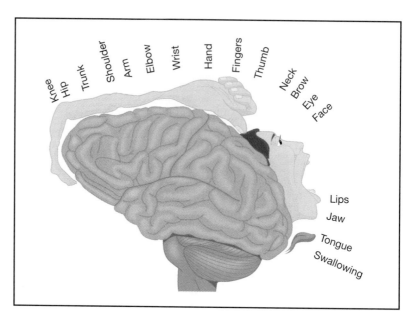

While the occipital, parietal, and temporal lobes all process sensory information—visual, touch, and auditory—the frontal lobe processes their output at a higher level, characteristic of humans. The greatest difference between the brains of humans and other primates (like chimpanzees) is the relative size of the frontal cortex.

Though the frontal lobes play a role in intelligence, the relationship is far from direct. For example, some people perform just as well on standard intelligence tests after massive amounts of prefrontal tissue have been removed (Phineas Gage, for example). Damage to the prefrontal areas impair many cognitive abilities: the abilities to order stimuli, sort out information, break down problems into steps, and maintain attention in the face of distraction (Milner & Petrides, 1984).

Finally, the frontal lobes play a role in personality. Many patients who have suffered frontal lobe damage, like Phineas Gage, undergo massive personality changes. One lesser-known result of Alzheimer's disease is severe personality disintegration, which is almost certainly associated with frontal lobe damage (Poon, 1986).

In Depth

Split Brain Research: Studying the Two Hemispheres

AT FIRST GLANCE, the two halves of the brain look perfectly symmetrical. However, the two cerebral hemispheres are not completely identical. Each side of the brain has some specialized functions that the other side lacks. How researchers came to discover these *lateralized functions,* as they are called, and how they came to understand how the two sides of the brain work together, is a fascinating story.

Initial Studies

One of the first indications that the two hemispheres might serve somewhat different functions came in the early 1860s, when the French physician Paul Broca found that a specific area of the left frontal lobe (now called "Broca's Area") was involved in the ability to speak. Broca's discovery was based on numerous autopsies of patients who had developed speech defects after suffering damage to the left frontal lobe. Broca was struck by the fact that damage in precisely the same location in the right frontal lobe had no effect on language ability. Soon additional evidence began to mount. For instance, the German neurologist Carl Wernicke discovered that when a portion of the left temporal lobe (now called "Wernicke's Area") is damaged, speech is also impaired. But whereas damage to Broca's Area tends to produce speech that is labored and fragmented (much like a slow, halting telegram), damage to Wernicke's area tends to produce speech that is fluent but oddly devoid of meaning (Geschwind, 1979). These early findings quickly led to the generalization that the left side of the brain houses most of the higher intellectual functions (such as speaking and writing), while the right side serves as a mute relay station, shuttling information back and forth between the left side of the body and the left hemisphere. In short, the right hemisphere was viewed as little more than an automaton. Humans were "half-brained" creatures (Levy, 1985).

This view of the brain predominated well into the twentieth century. A few researchers tried to defend the disparaged right hemisphere, arguing that it too seemed to have some specialized functions. For instance, one extensive study of more than 200 brain-damaged patients found that those with injury to the right hemisphere tended to have trouble filling in the missing parts to a pattern, assembling puzzles, and manipulating geometric shapes (Weisenberg & McBride, 1935). Other research showed that right-hemisphere damage was sometimes linked to distortions in depth and distance perception and the ability to orient oneself in space. But these discoveries were slow in coming and did not do much to improve the general image of the right hemisphere. The right brain's functions were still widely considered nonintellectual and inferior.

Then, quite unexpectedly, a dramatic set of studies sharply changed psychologists' view of the two sides of the brain. The studies arose as a by-product of a new surgical treatment for severe epilepsy, which involved cutting the large band of nerve cells, called the *corpus callosum,* that connects the two hemispheres. With the hemispheres separated, the random neural firing that causes epileptic convulsions was confined to the side of the brain where it begins, thus greatly reducing the severity of a seizure. However, patients were left with two cerebral hemispheres that could no longer communicate directly with each other. Psychologists saw in these so-called *split-brain patients* an extraordinary opportunity to conduct some important research on the specialized abilities of the two sides of the brain.

Criticisms, Alternatives, and Further Research

One of the pioneers in research on split-brain patients was neuroscientist Roger Sperry, who has since won a Nobel prize for his work. When Sperry and his colleagues tested the first split-brain subjects, the results were startling. Imagine yourself in their laboratory observing a middle-aged woman seated at a table with a screen before her, her eyes fixed on a dot at the screen's center. (See Figure 3-15.) For a fraction of a second, a projector behind the screen flashes a picture to the left or the right visual field only. This procedure is a way of ensuring that visual images are projected to one cerebral hemisphere only. The left visual field sends messages to the right side of the brain, while the right visual field sends messages to the left side.

FIGURE 3-15 *Experimental apparatus for testing split-brain patients. When a picture of an object is shown on a screen in one-half of the visual field, this information is transmitted exclusively to the opposite hemisphere. In split-brain patients, the hemispheres are disconnected, therefore their independent functions can be studied. If a picture of a spoon is presented in the* right *half of the visual field (transmitted to the left hemisphere), and a patient is asked to name the object she sees, she answers "a spoon." If the same picture is shown in the* left *half of the visual field (transmitted to the right hemisphere), she cannot name the object, because speech mechanisms are found in the left hemisphere. Although the right hemisphere cannot name the object, it "knows" what the object is and is able to instruct the left hand to select the spoon, as shown here.* (Springer & Deutsch, 1989.)

Now, suppose a picture of a spoon is flashed to the woman's right visual field. The experimenter asks the woman what she saw, and she quickly answers "a spoon." So far, there is nothing unusual about her responses. But consider what happens when a picture of a spoon is flashed to her left visual field. She reports seeing nothing! Is her right hemisphere unable to perceive this visual image? No, that cannot be the case; when asked to use her left hand (controlled by her right hemisphere) to identify the spoon from among a group of objects hidden behind a screen, without hesitation she selects the spoon. How can these seemingly contradictory responses be explained?

An explanation requires an understanding of the tasks for which the brain's two hemispheres are specialized. When the picture of the spoon was flashed to the woman's right visual field, its image was sent to her brain's left hemisphere. Since the left hemisphere is proficient at speech, the woman could identify the spoon verbally. But when the same picture was flashed to her right hemisphere, which is not adept at language, she could not *say* what she

saw. So the left hemisphere reported, quite correctly, that it—the left hemisphere—had seen nothing. The right hemisphere, of course, had *recognized* the spoon and needed only a chance to show its knowledge in some nonverbal way.

Studying split-brain subjects allowed researchers to establish in greater detail those tasks at which the right and left hemispheres excel. Of particular interest were the capabilities of the right hemisphere, so long considered the lesser of the two sides of the brain. Investigators discovered that the right hemisphere's abilities were more impressive than had previously been supposed, especially on spatial, musical, and other artistic tasks. Researchers now believe that the right hemisphere is not cognitively inferior to the left (Sperry, 1982). More accurately, each hemisphere has some specialized abilities at which it excels. For the left hemisphere, those abilities include the perception of words, letters, and speech-related sounds, and the performance of mathematical calculations. For the right hemisphere they include the perception of complex geometric patterns, human faces, and nonlinguistic sounds, as well as

| TABLE 3-3 *Principles of Cerebral Asymmetry** |

Function	Left Hemisphere	Right Hemisphere
Visual system	Letters, words	Complex geometric patterns Faces
Auditory system	Language-related sounds	Nonlanguage environmental sounds Music
Somatosensory system	?	Tactual recognition of complex patterns. Braille
Movement	Complex voluntary movement	?
Memory	Verbal memory	Visual memory
Language	Speech Speech Reading Writing Arithmetic	
Spatial processes		Geometry Sense of direction Mental rotation of shapes

*Summary of data on cerebral lateralization. Functions of the respective hemispheres that are predominantly mediated by one hemisphere in right-handed people.

Source: Kolb & Whishaw, 1990.

the senses of direction and location in space. Table 3-3 summarizes these and other functions believed to reside in one or the other hemisphere.

Patterns and Conclusions

What can we conclude from these data on the two sides of the brain? Some psychologists have proposed highly speculative theories. For instance, Robert Ornstein has argued that coexisting in each of us may be two distinct minds: the left, logical and analytical, and the right, intuitive and artistic (Ornstein, 1977). The impression that the mind is unitary, he says, may simply be an illusion produced by constant and instantaneous communication between the hemispheres. Others have wondered if there might not be "right-brained" and "left-brained" people—individuals who tend to depend on one side of the brain more than the other. One art teacher has written a best-selling book that purports to tell students how to suppress the analytical left hemisphere

when drawing and "turn on" the more artistic right hemisphere (Edwards, 1979). Some psychologists now even give workshops for corporate executives, claiming to teach them how to tap the underused potential of the supposedly creative right hemisphere (McKean, 1985).

Most psychologists are dismayed by such popularizations. As the neuroscientist John Pinel (1992) says, "Slight hemispheric differences have been transformed by the popular press into clear-cut, all-or-none dichotomies that have been used to account for everything from baseball batting averages to socioeconomic class" (p. 554). Contemporary psychologists warn against overgeneralizing the results from split-brain research. They stress first that although the two hemispheres do have some different specialized functions, the idea that each has its own general style of thinking is speculative and as yet unsupported by scientific researchers. Second, they stress that the popular press tends to greatly exaggerate the left brain/right brain dichotomy. Humans vary significantly in the extent to which their brain functions are lateralized (Hellige, Bloch, & Taylor 1988). For the control of behavior, the specific part of the brain involved is just as important as, if not more important than, the side that is involved (Kolb & Whishaw, 1990). Functionally the two frontal lobes have far more in common with each other than with any of the other regions in their own hemisphere.

Finally, the various sides and regions of the brain always cooperate with one another; no one part ever functions alone. Although one side of the brain or a specific area in one side may be more prominently involved in some tasks than others, human thought and behavior are dependent on activation of many widely distributed regions (Kinsbourne, 1982; Springer & Deutsch, 1989). The brain integrates processing in these regions to perform its many functions.

SUMMARY

1. The human nervous system, an intricate communication network that radiates throughout the body, consists of billions of interconnected, highly specialized cells. The most fundamental of these cells are neurons or nerve cells, which control and coordinate all human behavior. Most of the body's neurons are found in the **central nervous system (CNS),** which consists of the brain and spinal cord. Branching out from the central nervous system to all parts of the body is the **peripheral nervous system.** Its two divisions, the *somatic nervous system* and the *autonomic nervous system,* are related to control of the skeletal muscles and the internal organs, respectively. The autonomic system can be further subdivided into the *sympathetic* and *parasympathetic nervous systems.* The first is involved in mobilizing the body's resources, while the second is involved in conserving them.

2. Most neurons have three structural components: the **cell body,** which contains the cell's life-support systems; the relatively short and numerous **dendrites,** which transmits impulses to the cell body; and the **axon,** which transmits impulses from the cell body to muscle fibers, glandular cells, or other neurons. The simplest set of neural connections is a reflex arc, in which a sensory input is linked to a motor response via the spinal cord.

3. Neurons have an electrical potential even when they are inactive, called the **resting potential** of the neuron. Negatively charged ions like chloride are more numerous inside the cell, while positively charged ions like sodium are more numerous outside the cell, resulting in a resting potential inside the cell of -70 mV. This resting potential is maintained by a semipermeable membrane, which restricts the flow of certain ions, especially sodium.

4. When a neuron receives stimulation, usually from the dendrites, the permeability of the cell's membrane changes. This allows previously restricted ions to cross the membrane somewhat more easily, altering the electrical potential inside the cell. If the charge inside the cell reaches a critical level of about -55 mV, the threshold, the membrane permeability changes drastically. Positively charged sodium ions rush into the cell, causing the electrical charge inside to go from -55 mV to $+40$ mV, generating an **action potential.** Following this, the membrane permeability returns to its previous state, and the -70 mV resting potential is quickly reestablished. The action potential is passed from location to location down the entire length of the axon, until it reaches the terminal button.

5. Every axon is physically separated from adjacent cells by a gap called a **synapse.** When an action potential reaches the end of an axon, a chemical called a **neurotransmitter** is released from the axon terminal and diffuses across the synapse to activate **receptor** sites on adjacent cells. Depending on the chemistry of the neurotransmitter and the nature of the receptor sites, the message conveyed may be **excitatory** or **inhibitory,** which makes the postsynaptic cell either more or less likely to generate an action potential, respectively.

6. Neuroscientists have identified a number of different neurotransmitters. The **monoamines**

(**dopamine, norepinephrine,** and **serotonin**) share the same chemical building blocks and are particularly important for regulating emotion, learning, and movement. **Acetylcholine** was the first transmitter to be isolated and is prominent at neuromuscular junctions. **Gamma-aminobutyric acid (GABA)** is the most common inhibitory transmitter in the central nervous system. Finally, **endorphins** are transmitter-like substances known to be important for modulating pain and pleasures, and are thought to be involved in certain forms of substance abuse like alcoholism.

7. The central core of the adult human brain is concerned with functions basic to survival, such as sleeping, waking, respiration, and feeding. Its major areas include the **hindbrain** (consisting of the **medulla,** the **pons,** the **reticular formation,** and the **cerebellum**), the **midbrain,** and the **thalamus** and **hypothalamus.** Above the central core lies the **forebrain** or **cerebral hemispheres,** the innermost borders of which are marked by the **limbic system.** The limbic system is involved in the regulation of behaviors that satisfy basic emotional and motivational needs, such as fighting, fleeing, and mating. Among its highly interrelated structures are the **hippocampus,** the **amygdala,** and the **septum.** The outermost layer of tissue covering the cerebral hemispheres is called the **cortex.** It is intimately involved in the processes of learning, speech, reasoning, and memory.

8. Localization of function is a basic principle of brain organization, but the activities of localized regions are always integrated into larger neural networks. One area where the themes of localization and integration can be seen quite clearly is in the study of the two sides of the brain. Each **cerebral hemisphere** has some specialized functions, which means that for certain tasks one hemisphere may tend to be more active than the other. However, in any human behavior both hemispheres are always involved.

SUGGESTED READINGS

Crick, F. (1994). *The astonishing hypothesis.* New York: Simon and Schuster. A Nobel laureate's discussion of the implications of scientific reductionism in neuroscience.

Klawans, H. L. (1990). *Newton's madness: Further tales of clinical neurology.* New York: Harper & Row. A fascinating and informative collection of case studies of patients with neurological disorders. It offers personal accounts of twenty-two individuals with detailed descriptions of diagnosis and treatment.

Kolb, B., & Whishaw, I. Q. (1996). *Fundamentals of human neuropsychology* (4th ed.). New York: Freeman. An excellent account of research on the human brain, including much information on brain disorders, recently updated. A true reference volume.

Pinel, John P. J. (1996). *Biopsychology* (3rd ed.). Boston: Allyn & Bacon. One of the very best introductions to neuroscience available to students of psychology. Beautifully illustrated and engagingly written.

Sacks, O. (1995). *An anthropologist on Mars.* New York: Knopf. The most recent book that gives case studies of some fascinating brain disorders. The author is a practicing neurologist and a master storyteller. In the movie *Awakenings,* based on a true series of events in his early career, Sacks was played by Robin Williams.

Springer, S. P., & Deutsch, G. (1993). *Left brain, right brain* (4th ed.). San Francisco: Freeman. A very interesting discussion of 100 years of research into the hemispheric differences in humans and other animals. The authors present findings on asymmetries in brain-damaged, split-brain, and normal subjects, and explore the implications for human behavior. In addition to discussions of mind-brain relationships, the authors discuss popular left brain/right brain programs in business management and creativity seminars.

Sensation
and Perception

Young children can ask difficult questions. At some point, most parents have been asked, "If a tree falls in the forest, and no one is there to hear it, does it make a sound?" What might seem a childish question is actually a profound one: it highlights the differences between physical changes in the world, our detection of those changes (what psychologists call "sensation"), and our psychological interpretation of those physical changes (what psychologists call "perception").

To answer this child's question, we must first understand the physical changes that take place when a tree falls. When a tree falls in the forest, it may cause a number of changes—in the pattern of reflected light, the temperature, and so on. For our purposes, we will be focusing on the physical changes that humans interpret as "sounds." One simple way to define *hearing* is "the ear's detection of changes in air pressure." Since the human ability to detect such changes is restricted to certain frequencies, we must determine whether a falling tree causes changes that our ear can detect. We could measure those changes in a number of ways, using anything that responds to changes in pressure. In doing so, we would find that some of these changes caused by the falling tree are indeed in the range humans can detect.

But while such physical changes are detectable by the human ear, "sound" is *not* a physical entity. Rather, it is the *psychological interpretation* of a physical entity, a phenomenon *created* by our brains. Since no one is present in our hypothetical forest to hear the tree falling, there is no brain to "create" the sound. Technically speaking, then, a tree falling in the forest with no human there to observe it makes no "sound." A change in air pressure occurred, in a range humans can detect, but that change is not "sound" until it is detected and perceived by an observer.[1]

Children *can* ask difficult questions!

Just as our ability to detect sound is restricted to certain frequencies, so is our ability to detect changes in the frequency of light. For instance, humans can detect a change in frequency from 480 nanometers (abbreviated nm, for billionths of a meter) to 520 nanometers. They interpret that change in frequency as a shift in color from blue to green. However, humans cannot distinguish a change in the frequency of light from 880 to 920 nanometers; both are what we call *infrared*. In other words, though the physical change is every bit as real as the change from 480 to 520 nm, frequencies of 900 nm fall outside the range we can sense. Keep this fact in mind as you read this

---

[1]A more difficult question is, "Do sounds exist even if there is no external physical stimulation?" or "Can 'perception' occur without 'sensation?' " The question is more complicated than it might seem. The voice a schizophrenic patient hears is just as real to that person as one caused by external stimulation. Indeed, psychologists have observed that when these patients hear voices, structures in their brain respond just as they do to real voices. The patient's brain, then, does not distinguish between the "voice in the head" and "voices" that originate in the external world. To the person experiencing them, they are the same.

*The twentieth-century composer Alexander Scriabin reportedly possessed **synethesia,** an exceedingly rare perceptual ability in which sensory modalities are "mixed," for example, visual images may be heard, or auditory stimuli may have "tastes." Scriabin composed music that evoked sensations other than sound—at least, to him.*

chapter: humans can sense only a small fraction of all the physical changes that occur in the world.

Traditionally, psychologists have differentiated between sensation and perception. **Sensation** is the process in which the stimulation of receptor cells (in the eyes, ears, nose, mouth, and skin surface) sends nerve impulses to the brain. **Perception,** in contrast, is the process in which the brain interprets sensations, giving them order and meaning. Thus, hearing sounds and seeing colors may be largely sensory

processes, but following a melody and detecting depth in a two-dimensional picture are largely perceptual processes. Nevertheless, in everyday life it is almost impossible to separate sensation from perception. As soon as the brain receives sensations, it automatically interprets or perceives them. In fact, some contemporary psychologists think that the distinction between sensation and perception is no longer useful. Both processes, they argue, are part of a single information-processing system.

One fact that has emerged from the study of sensation and perception is that animal species differ in their views of the world. Consider sound (Figure 4-1). Many animals can hear sounds that are too high or low for humans to detect. "Dog whistles" are designed to emit sounds in a range higher than humans can hear. Bats are virtuosos at detecting high pitches. They send out a stream of ultra-high-frequency cries, listen for the echoes that bounce off surrounding objects, and use the echoes to navigate as they fly. But even though a flying bat is constantly emitting powerful noises, it seems soundless to us because the human ear is tuned too low to detect its cries. From a bat's perspective, we humans appear mute, for the sounds we normally make are just below the lowest pitch that bats can hear.

Sensory and perceptual capabilities also vary among members of the *same* species. For example, before aspartame (Nutrasweet) became widely used, most low-calorie sodas used saccharin as an artificial sweetener (saccharin is the ingredient in Sweet-and-Low, and it is the sweetener most often used in the

Dolphins communicate using auditory signals at frequencies so high humans are unable to hear them. Other animals, like bats, are insensitive to frequencies in the range of human hearing, so that we would appear "deaf" to them.

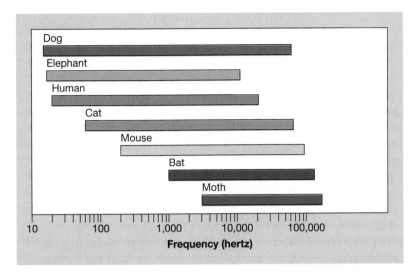

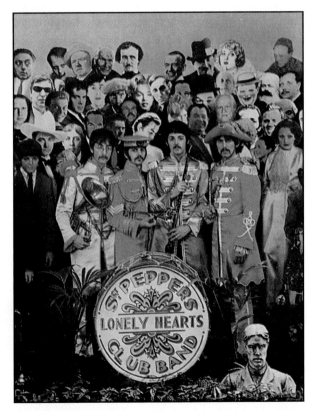

FIGURE 4-1   A comparison of the range of sound frequencies audible to various species. (Hefner & Hefner, 1983.)

"fountain drinks" sold at the convenience stores and movie theaters). While many people found saccharin an acceptable sweetener, others found the taste horribly bitter. Linda Bartoshuk and her colleagues have discovered that people differ in their ability to detect bitterness in substances like saccharin and coffee (Miller & Bartoshuk, 1991). Thus, people differ in the very structure of their sensory-perceptual capabilities.

Another major source of differences in perceptual abilities is the expectation and belief a perceiver brings to a situation. You may have heard of so-called back-masked messages supposedly embedded in popular music—messages that were recorded backwards.[2] Somehow, the embedded messages were supposed to induce listeners to commit illegal or immoral acts. As you might suspect, recent studies (e.g., Begg, Needham, & Bookbinder, 1993) have shown that the meaning of such messages (that is, their meaning when played forward) is not perceived when they are played backwards.

If a friend should offer to play such a recording for you, try this experiment. First, make certain that your friend does not tell you *what* you are supposed to hear in the message. Then play the record (or tape) backwards as many times as you like, trying to hear the "message." Most likely you will not be able to

The Beatles were one of the first musical groups to embed in their music messages they created by playing a recorded tape backward. Listeners decoded the messages by reversing the direction of the tape or record. Though some critics have suggested that the so-called "back-masked" songs induce listeners to commit illegal or immoral acts, there is no evidence to support the contention.

---

[2]This was probably first used by the Beatles. Several of their songs, such as "Rain," contained segments created by playing a recorded tape *backwards*. In the days before compact discs, these messages could be "decoded" by putting a record on the turntable and spinning the platter backwards.

hear it. After trying to hear the message on your own, ask your friend to tell you what you were "supposed" to hear. Then play the record again. You may be surprised at how the "message" leaps out at you, once you know what to listen for.

Later in this chapter we will discuss other examples of how higher cognitive processes influence perception. The point to remember is that the processing of information about the world is not a one-way street. Besides the flowing of information from your sense organs to your brain (called "bottom-up" or **data-driven processing**), your previous experience and knowledge also contribute to your perceptions, causing you to perceive partly what you expect (called "top-down" or **conceptually-driven processing**). Your perceptions, in short, are the product of an interaction between the particular sensory systems you possess and your beliefs and expectations about the world. To stress this important point, we begin this chapter with the topic of *psychophysics,* the study of the relationship between physical stimuli and the subjective experiences stimuli create (Luce & Krumhansl, 1988).

Stimuli, Sensations, and Perceptions

The question of a "tree falling in a forest" is perplexing at first because it clouds the distinction between a physical stimulus (the sound waves produced by a falling tree) and a subjective sensation (the experience of hearing a crash). The two, of course, are not synonymous. A **stimulus** (pl., stimuli) is any form of energy (sound waves, light waves, heat, pressure) an organism is capable of detecting. A sensation is a response to that energy by a sensory system. Stimuli and sensations, then, have a cause-and-effect relationship.

Most sensory systems respond to differences in both the quality and the quantity of stimuli. The *quality* of a stimulus refers to the kind of sensation it produces. Color is a quality related to visual stimulation; musical pitch is a quality related to auditory stimulation. *Quantity,* in contrast, refers to the amount of stimulation. Thus brightness represents the perceived quantity of light, and loudness the perceived quantity of sound.

Remember, though, that characteristics such as color, brightness, pitch, and loudness are ways in which a person experiences a stimulus; they are not necessarily accurate reflections of the physical properties of a stimulus. That is why psychologists have studied the relationship between stimuli and sensations extensively. In doing so, they have examined several important processes. Among them are stimulus detection—the point at which we perceive very faint stimuli—and stimulus discrimination—the ability to differentiate between two similar stimuli.

Stimulus Detection

How much light must be present before a person sees it? How much pressure must be applied to the skin before a person feels it? The answers to such questions involve the concept of a **sensory threshold,** the minimum stimulus needed for a person to detect it. This concept implies a boundary: for every stimulus there is some absolute level of intensity above which a person will always detect that stimulus, and below which they will never detect it. Early in the history of psychology researchers looked for such fixed thresholds. They found that thresholds vary depending on the conditions surrounding the sensory experience.

Many factors can influence the detection of stimuli. Suppose you are sitting in a dark room, trying to detect the presence of a light flashed on the wall. There are some extremely dim lights you will never report seeing, even under ideal conditions. There are other, brighter lights you will always be able to see. Between those two categories is a range of intermediate intensities. Sometimes, under some conditions, you will be able to see them; under different conditions, you will not.

How, then, should we define your threshold for light? The decision must be an arbitrary one. Some researchers would simply examine the results and define the threshold as the lowest intensity of light you can see 50 percent of the time. Even so, that arbitrary point might vary from day to day. What kind of changes in your sensory systems might allow for such variability? The list of important variables would include the amount of background light, the length of time you have been sitting in the darkened room, the time of day the test is conducted, and so on.

The responses you make in a detection situation depend on more than perceptual factors, however. A number of other factors can substantially restrict or enhance your ability to perceive something. One of

Determining the presence or absence of a stimulus in a "noisy" environment can be difficult. Here, as air traffic controllers study radar screens, they filter the visual signals produced by planes from the visual static of weather disturbances.

those factors is the existence of competing stimuli, often referred to as *background noise* (Cohn & Lasley, 1986). It's much easier to hear your name called out in a quiet doctor's office than in a crowded restaurant. "Noise" can affect other senses as well. For example, when viewing a radar screen, an inexperienced person usually has great difficulty distinguishing the blips made by an airplane from those made by stormy weather, a form of visual noise. In much the same way, you would be hard-pressed to smell the fragrance of a delicate flower in a smoke-filled room. And noise need not arise from external sources. Some of the cells in your sensory system produce a form of noise through their own spontaneous activities, such as a "ringing in the ears" (Hudspeth, 1985; Jastreboff, 1990).

Perception is influenced by background noise as well as the signals we wish to attend to. As a result, under some circumstances an increase in background noise can actually increase perception. In those situations, added sounds can enhance discrimination. For example, Kemp and George (1992) studied ways to reduce the effects of *tinnitus,* a chronic "ringing in the ears." They found that subjects with tinnitus could mask its effects by *increasing* the background sounds. The sounds had to be chosen carefully, but apparently increasing them decreased the noise, making auditory recognition of the sounds easier.

Motivation can also affect the detection of a stimulus. In some cases people have reason to set strict criteria for acknowledging that they perceive something. (A *criterion* is simply the basis on which a person decides to say that a faint stimulus is or is not present.) For example, consider the case of a physician making a diagnosis. The patient reports with a slight fever and sore throat. The diagnosis could be strep throat, which a throat swab would confirm. Or the person might simply have a cold, in which case the swab test would be unnecessary. In these situations, the physician is almost always in favor of the test. In contrast, our legal system is biased toward "no" decisions in the face of uncertainty (hence the phrase "innocent until proven guilty").

Many factors, then, affect the ability to detect a stimulus. Psychologists have tried to combine the effects of various factors in one theory, called *signal detection theory* (Swets, Tanner, & Birdsall, 1961). This theory states that some influences on detection have to do with the stimulus itself (how intense is it? how muffled by background noise?), while others have to do with the person's sensory system (is the system sensitive, or is it impaired?). Included in the theory also are *cognitive* factors as well: what does the person expect to see? what are the penalties for a mistake? the rewards for being right? All these factors influence stimulus detection. That is why two people with the same physical sensitivity may nevertheless perform quite differently on a stimulus detection task.

Figure 4-2 illustrates signal detection theory. To begin with, the stimulus is either physically present (the YES row) or not physically present (the NO row). In response to the stimulus, the perceiver

FIGURE 4-2   *Four possible outcomes in a signal detection analysis. The two types of errors (MISS and FALSE ALARM) are inversely related: as the probability of one type of error is reduced, the probability of making the other error increases.*

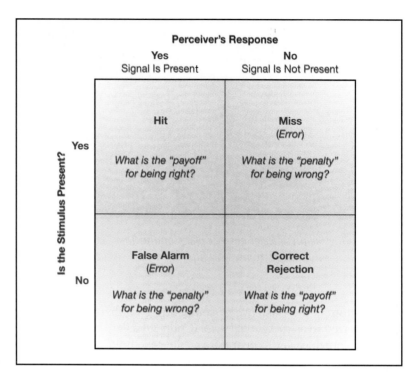

might decide YES, the stimulus is present (left column), or NO, the signal is not present (right column).

As the figure shows, there are four possible outcomes. The person may respond affirmatively when the stimulus is present, a response called a *hit*. Or the person may respond negatively when the stimulus is not present, a response called a *correct rejection*. Hits and correct rejections are correct responses. But suppose the person responds negatively when the stimulus is present; this is called a *miss*. Finally, the person may respond affirmatively when the stimulus is not present; this is called a *false alarm*. Misses and false alarms are incorrect responses.

Two considerations are critical in signal detection analysis. First, to know something about a subject's responses, we must know something about the payoffs for a hit and correct rejections, and the penalties for making a miss or false alarm. (You may have heard this referred to as a "cost-benefits" analysis.) For example, when testing for the presence of HIV, the virus that causes AIDS, most researchers assume that misses—failing to detect HIV in cases where the person is actually infected—are more serious errors than false alarms. If the test makes a miss, carriers of HIV are told they are not infected with the virus, when in fact they are. Those people may engage in behaviors that increase the chance of infecting oth-

ers, based on the incorrect belief that they are not infected. The extreme cost of this error greatly influences the decision in uncertain cases. If there is any doubt about the result, AIDS tests will usually return a positive outcome.

This brings us to the second critical factor: the probabilities of making "misses" and "false alarms" are *inversely related*. If we reduce the probability of making one type of error, we *increase* the probability of making the other type of error. If scientists were developing a test for HIV, they would want to be certain that the test made virtually no "misses." But this strong bias against misses will cause the false alarm rate of the test to be high. If we want to reduce the chance of making a "miss," we *increase* the false alarm rate. In fact, HIV tests are biased in exactly this way.

Stimulus Discrimination

Besides stimulus detection, psychologists are interested in the ability to notice a difference, or change in stimulation, that is, the ability to **discriminate** among stimuli. Research in this area began in the mid-nineteenth century, when Ernst Weber discovered that although people can perceive small changes in weak stimuli, they can notice only large changes in strong stimuli. Figure 4-2 illustrates the human tendency to perceive small changes at low

TABLE 4-1   *Weber Fractions for Various Sensory Stimulus (the Fraction Represents How Much the Stimulus Intensity Needs to Increase to Be Detected)*

Stimulus Type	Weber Fraction (Proportion of Change Required to Detect Difference)
Electric shock	1%
Weight	2
Length	3
Loudness	5
Brightness of light	8
Taste of salt	20

Source: Teghtsoonian (1971).

levels of stimulus intensity, but not at higher levels of intensity.

Weber's brother-in-law, Gustav Fechner, specified the nature of the relationship more precisely (Fechner, 1860). He noted that the amount by which a stimulus must be increased to produce a **just noticeable difference** (called a "JND") tends to be a constant proportion of the initial intensity of the stimulus. In honor of his brother-in-law, Fechner called this relationship **Weber's law.**

The proportional increase in an initial stimulus that is needed to create a just noticeable difference varies with the kind of stimulus. For weight, the proportion is 2 percent, which means that the average person will just notice a difference when a single pound is added to a backpack that initially weighed 50 pounds ($50 \times 0.02 = 1$); for a difference to be detected in a pack weighing 100 pounds, 2 pounds must be added ($100 \times 0.02 = 2$). (In both cases the proportional increase is the same.) Table 4-1 shows the proportional change needed for a change to be detectable (to produce a JND) by various senses. These percentages are commonly called *Weber fractions*. Note that humans are more sensitive to changes in loudness (which require just under a 5 percent increase) than to increases in brightness (which require about an 8 percent increase to be detected).

Weber's law deals with JNDs, the smallest detectable unit of change. Fechner later applied this principle to the perception at *all* levels of stimulus intensities. **Fechner's law** states that as the intensity of a stimulus increases, larger and larger increases in intensity are required to produce subjectively equivalent changes. We perceive changes *proportional* to the stimulus intensity. For example, if you were thinking about buying a car that costs $10,000, you would not change your mind if you found out the price is $35 more than you anticipated. However, if you discovered that the compact disc you are about to buy costs $45 instead of $10, you would almost certainly refuse to buy it. (Unfortunately, car dealers know about Fechner's law, too. The next time you buy a car, don't be surprised if the dealer adds a $50 "courier fee" or a $40 "filing fee.")

Fechner's law explains why we do not perceive equivalent brightness changes in a three-way light-bulb, for example a 50/100/150 watt bulb.[3] Switching from the 50-watt to the 100-watt setting causes a considerable change in brightness, but switching from the 100-watt to 150-watt setting does *not* produce an equal increase in perceived brightness. The difference in perceived brightness has to do with the proportional changes. A change from 50 to 100 watts is a 100 percent increase:

$$\text{Percent change} = \frac{(100 \text{ watts} - 50 \text{ watts})}{50 \text{ watts}} = 100\%$$

but a change from 100 to 150 watts is only a 50% increase:

$$\text{Percent change} = \frac{(150 \text{ watts} - 100 \text{ watts})}{100 \text{ watts}} = 50\%$$

In both cases, the stimulus intensity increases by 50 watts. But because the *proportional change* is greater

---

[3]"Watts" are not the appropriate unit of brightness, but they will do for our purposes.

in the first case, we perceive a greater change.[4] Although Fechner's law does not hold true for very weak or very strong stimuli, it is quite accurate across a broad middle range. Thus it is a useful way of describing the ability to discriminate among stimuli.

Sensory Adaptation

All sensory systems display a reduced ability to provide information after prolonged, constant stimulation, a phenomenon known as **sensory adaptation.** When you enter a room with a distinctive odor, the smell is very noticeable at first, but soon it fades. The decline in your sensitivity to the odor is an example of sensory adaptation. Some senses, such as smell and touch, adapt quite quickly; others, such as pain, adapt very slowly. All do adapt, however.

Sensory adaptation occurs because the sense receptors in the body are designed to be sensitive to *changes* in stimulation. This perceptual feature makes sense; you do not need to be constantly reminded that your shoes are securely on your feet. Thus, when you stimulate the touch receptors in your skin by putting on a shoe and hold that pressure constant, the rate at which your foot generates nerve impulses steadily declines. This type of adaptation also occurs in the visual receptors in your eyes. In fact, if you were to stare at something constantly, it would seem to gradually disappear! Fortunately, you cannot lock your gaze onto a single point. Whenever you try to do so, your eyes involuntarily make tiny, rapid rate movements, shifting the incoming light waves on to different receptor cells. These involuntary movements prevent any single group of cells from adapting so much that your vision fades away.

Because sensory adaptation affects the body's sensitivity to stimuli, it can change the sensation produced by a given amount of stimulation. You can experience this effect by placing one hand in ice water and the other in warm water. After your hands have adapted to the two temperatures, plunge them both into a bucket of water at room temperature. Will the water seem hot or cold? Oddly, it will feel hot to the hand that was in cold water, but cold to the hand that was in hot water. You have probably experienced a similar sensation when washing your hands

---

[4]According to Weber's law, how much would we need to change the intensity of the light in the second situation in order for us to perceive it as "equal" to the first change?

after being outside on a winter day. If your hands are very cold, the water from the faucet will seem unbearably warm, even though it is at room temperature.

This example reinforces an important point that was raised at the beginning of this chapter: the way we view the world is not always an accurate reflection of the physical stimuli that exist there. Many times, distortions in perception are caused by the use of a normal sensory system in an unusual situation. Later in this chapter we will discuss perceptual illusions, which are examples of this kind of distortion.

Consider one final note before we go on to the next section. Though your eyes, ears, nose, tongue, and skin link you to the outside world via vision, hearing, smell, taste, and touch, your senses extend well beyond these five familiar ones. For example, your ear does more than just hear: an organ in your inner ear gives you a sense of balance and equilibrium. (You may remember spinning in circles as a child until you could no longer stand up. In those situations, the organ that maintains your balance is disrupted by the spinning.) In addition, sensory systems related to your muscles and joints keep you aware of your body position and movement; other internal receptors supply your brain with vital information about your body temperature and blood chemistry. Although this chapter is largely restricted to the classic five senses, those that have been omitted are no less important to normal human functioning.

Vision

Vision is often considered the richest human sense. When our eyes receive light from surrounding objects and translate it into nerve impulses that are interpreted by the brain, we experience a vast array of shapes, colors, textures, and movements. To understand how this remarkable system works, we must first know something about the basic stimulus for vision—light.

Physical Measurement of Light Waves

Light is one form of electromagnetic radiation. Figure 4-3 shows the entire spectrum of electromagnetic radiation. Notice that the band of frequencies we perceive as "light" is a small part of the entire band. In most respects "light" behaves just like other types of radiation, such as X rays or television signals. And while our eyes are sensitive only to the small band

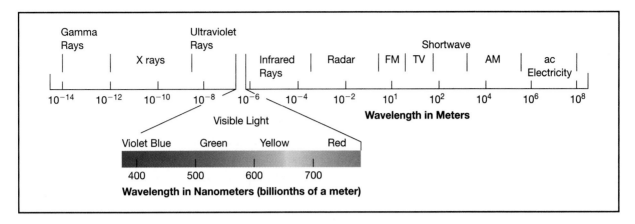

FIGURE 4-3   *The spectrum of electromagnetic energy. Electromagnetic energy comes to us in varying wavelengths. Each step on the scale (top) corresponds to a tenfold increase in the wavelength of the electromagnetic radiation. The very short wavelengths at the left of the scale and the very long ones at the right are not visible as light. The visible spectrum—the small region to which the human eye is sensitive—is shown on an expanded scale with the wavelengths measured in nanometers (one-billionth of a meter).*

shown in Figure 4-3, other parts of our bodies are sensitive to other wavelengths. For instance, our skin can easily be burned by ultraviolet radiation.

Several centuries ago Sir Isaac Newton (1642–1727) proposed that light behaves as if it were a stream of tiny particles. Modern physicists call these subatomic particles **photons.** An important characteristic of light is that it travels in wavelike patterns rather than in straight lines. Different streams of light have somewhat different wavelengths, the distance between the crest of one wave and the crest of the next (see Figure 4-3). These varying wavelengths, which are usually measured in billionths of a meter, or nanometers, are largely what determines the colors we see.

Wavelengths and frequencies are really two different ways of measuring the same thing. **Wavelength** is a measure of the physical distance between waves, from one peak to the next. **Frequency** is a measure of the timing between waves, calculated by counting how many waves occur in a given unit of time. Wavelength is inversely proportional to the frequency of a wave. As wavelength increases, frequency decreases, and vice versa (see Figure 4-3). For historical reasons, visual stimuli are usually reported in wavelengths; auditory stimuli are usually reported in frequencies.

Light waves also vary in their intensity, that is, in how densely their photons are packed. We can determine the intensity of light by measuring the **am-plitude** of a light wave—the variation between the "peak" and "trough" of the wave. (If you have ever been out in the ocean, rocking up and down in the waves, you have experienced differences in amplitude. In a storm, the amplitude of the waves increases; you feel the increase as an exaggeration of the "bobbing up and down" of the boat.) Humans perceive changes in the amplitude of light waves as changes in "brightness." For instance, a 100-watt lightbulb radiates more photons than a 50-watt bulb; thus, we say the 100-watt bulb is "brighter."

Finally, light waves vary in their purity or saturation. Some light sources (such as the "laser pointers" you may have seen) emit waves within a very restricted range. These are perceived as relatively "pure" in color. Other sources emit a mixture of different frequencies and are perceived as "less pure." Incandescent bulbs, the ones we commonly use in lamps, emit a range of light waves. Fluorescent bulbs, the long tubes often used in overhead lighting, emit a relatively smaller range of light waves. As a result, incandescent lights often look yellowish (less pure) compared to fluorescent lights.

Table 4-1 showed that the light waves to which our eyes are sensitive are just a small part of the total electromagnetic spectrum. If our eyes were structured differently, we might see some parts of the spectrum that are now invisible to us. For instance, since the lenses in the eye absorb a great deal of ultraviolet radiation, most people cannot see ultraviolet light.

However, people who suffer from cataracts sometimes have the lenses in their eyes removed. After surgery, they can see slightly more ultraviolet light than other people.

The previous section described the physical properties of light waves. However, these must be converted into psychological perceptions to be of much use. For humans, this begins with the eye. Human eyes are capable of responding to many properties of light—such as wavelength, amplitude, and complexity—which the brain will ultimately interpret as the perception of color, brightness, and purity. In the next section, we will describe the eye and see how it begins converting "light waves" into "vision."

The Structure of the Eye

The human visual system begins with the eyes, through which light enters. Figure 4-4 shows the structure of the human eye. Light first passes through a tough, transparent "window" called the **cornea,** which covers the front of the eyeball. Because the cornea is deeply curved, it bends the incoming rays and helps to focus them, a process known as *refraction*. Behind the cornea is a pouch of liquid that helps to maintain the cornea's rounded shape. To its rear lies the **iris,** a ring of pigmented muscle tissue that gives the eye its color. Contraction and relaxation of the muscle fibers in the iris close and open the **pupil,** the opening in the center of the eye that appears black.

The pupil helps to regulate the amount of light that passes through the eye. In bright light the pupil constricts, reducing the amount of light that enters the eye and passes through. In darkness, the pupil dilates, opening wider to allow more light to enter the eye. Ophthalmologists (physicians who specialize in the treatment of the eyes) often dilate the pupils artificially with drugs in order to see more easily into the eye. The drugs inhibit the pupil's constriction in bright light for several hours. If you have ever had your pupils dilated, you know how bright the world can seem even on cloudy days.

Just behind the pupil is the **lens,** a transparent, elastic structure that allows the eye to adjust its focus, a process known as *accommodation*. Accommodation is accomplished by the **ciliary muscles,** which bend the shape of the lens, allowing it to fine-tune the refraction of the light waves. The incoming light is then projected through the liquid that fills the center of the eyeball and onto the **retina,** the eye's light-sensitive inner surface (the retina will be the focus of the next section). When the ciliary muscles contract, the lens is stretched flatter, allowing the eye to focus on more distant objects. When the ciliary muscles relax, the lens returns to its spherical shape, allowing the eye to focus on nearby objects.

You can see the close relationship between the eye's structure and function by considering the causes of myopia (nearsightedness) and presbyopia (farsightedness). In young people these defects of vision are typically due to a misshapen eyeball. In a nearsighted person the eyeball is elongated, causing light waves to converge and focus before reaching the retina. By the time light finally strikes the retina, it is out of focus again. In a farsighted person the eyeball is shorter from pupil to retina, causing light waves to strike the retina before they converge and focus.

Glasses or contact lenses work by adding another source of refraction that compensates for the irregularities of the eyeball. The contact lens of a nearsighted person, for example, reduces the refraction somewhat. Since the eyeball itself causes the light waves to converge before hitting the retina, the contact lens compensates, correcting the convergence.[5] With age the lens loses some of its elasticity, making the viewing of close objects more difficult. As a result, many middle-aged adults find they need glasses to read: the lens is less pliable and can no longer return to the more spherical form.

How Light Becomes Sight

How is light transformed into a visual experience? The answer lies in a network of millions of nerve cells that line the back of the retina. The outermost layer of each retina contains two types of receptors, **rods** and **cones,** so named because of their characteristic shapes: rods are long and thin, while cones are rounded and taper to a point at one end. Light energy stimulates the rods and cones, generating small electrical signals. The strength of the signals is determined by the amount of light absorbed.

---

[5]A similar, though more drastic, approach to correcting vision problems involves a procedure called *radial keratotomy (RK)*. In RK, a series of incisions is made in the cornea. These incisions reduce the power of the lens to bend light and can therefore correct some vision problems, especially myopia. Because of possible side effects, some ophthalmologists still hesitate to recommend the surgery (Goldstein, 1996).

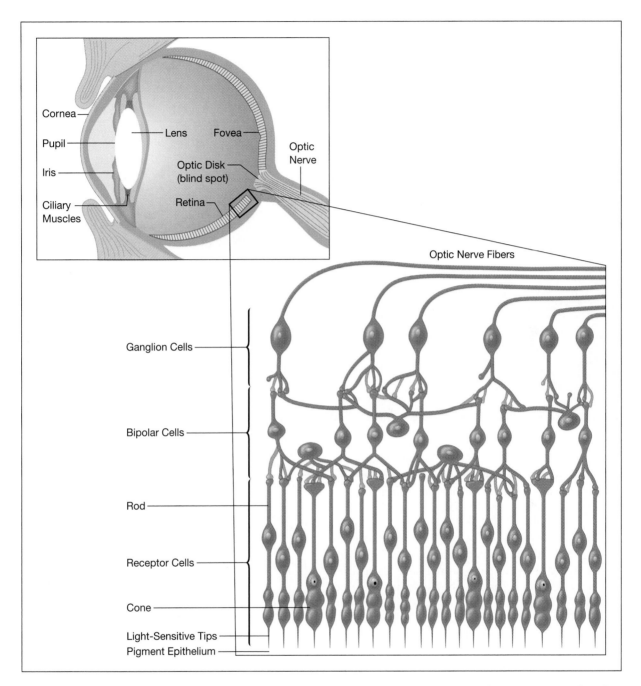

FIGURE 4-4   *The structure of the human eye and the retina. Incoming light passes through the cornea, pupil, and lens, and hits the retina. As the inset shows, light filters through several layers of retinal cells before hitting the receptor cells (rods and cones), located at the back of the eyeball and pointed away from the incoming light. The rods and cones register the presence of light and pass an electrical impulse back to the adjacent bipolar cells. They relay the impulse to the ganglion cells. The axons of the ganglion cells form the fibers of the optic nerve, which transmits the impulses received to the brain.*

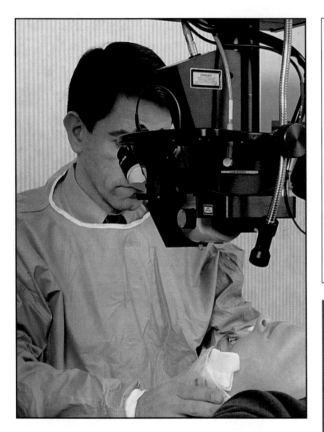

Radial keratotomy (RK) is a relatively new procedure that is sometimes used to correct visual problems, especially myopia (near-sightedness). The surgeon makes a series of incisions in the cornea, which alters the lens's refractive characteristics.

The neurons that are responsible for vision are arranged hierarchically, beginning with the rods and cones. These receptor cells do not send their input directly to the brain. Instead, they send it to the **bipolar cells,** which receive input from many different receptors. The bipolar cells in turn stimulate the **ganglion cells,** further consolidating visual signals. The ganglion cells form the fibers of the **optic nerve,** which carries visual information from the eye to the brain. We'll first consider the role of receptor cells in vision; following that, we will consider the role of the brain.

The Role of Receptor Cells

Rods and cones are the starting point in the visual process. Not only do rods and cones differ in appearance, but they also function under different conditions. Rods work much better than cones under

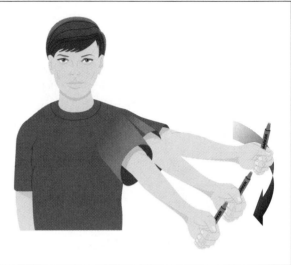

FIGURE 4-5   *Demonstration of relative distributions of rods and cones. Take several markers or crayons of different color, and shuffle them without looking. Focus your eyes straight ahead, and pick up one marker, again without looking. Now stretch your arm to one side and hold the marker at arm's distance, even with your shoulder.* Keeping your arm outstretched, and without moving your eyes, *gradually swing your arm toward the front of your body. As soon as you detect any movement, stop moving your arm. At this point, you are seeing the marker with only your rods.*

Now resume swinging your arm again, very gradually. When you are certain you can see the color, stop. At this point, you have started to use your cones. Notice how much closer to the front you had to move the marker before you could perceive color.

conditions of low light, such as nighttime conditions, but they have two serious limitations. First, they do not provide information about color; and second, they do not provide a sharp, detailed image. Cones *do* provide information about color, and they produce sharper, more "detailed" images.

You can demonstrate both these properties to yourself. Take several markers or crayons of different color, and shuffle them without looking. Focus your eyes straight ahead, and pick up one marker, again without looking. Now stretch your arm to one side and hold the marker at arm's distance, even with your shoulder (see Figure 4-5). *Keeping your arm outstretched, and without moving your eyes,* gradually swing your arm toward the front of your body. As soon as you detect any movement, stop moving your arm and try to determine the color of the marker. You will likely be unable to determine the color. Now resume swinging your arm again, very gradually. When you are certain you can see the color, stop. Notice how far you had to move your arm before you could detect the color. When you first detected the marker in your peripheral field of vision, you were using mostly rods to see it. To recognize its color, you had to move it farther in front of you. In doing so, you stimulated the cones, which allowed you to see the marker's color.

Figure 4-6 illustrates the relative lack of detailed vision in your rods. If you focus on the letter in the center, each letter around it should be equally readable. However, in order to be readable, the outer letters must be larger than the one in the center. The need for an increase in size reflects the reduced acuity of the rods, which dominate your peripheral vision.

Cones need relatively more light than rods in order to work. Thus you see little color in the moonlight, but you can see shades of light and dark because rods can function in low light. A rod, in fact, is capable of responding to just a single photon of light (O'Brien, 1982). Cones are far less numerous than rods: there are about 5 million cones in each human retina, compared with about 120 million rods. As was just demonstrated, the cones are highly concentrated in and near the center of the retina, an area known as the **fovea** (literally, "small pit"). Many thousands of cones are packed into the fovea, a depression about 1.5 millimeters in diameter, but this area contains no rods at all.

Because the blood vessels and nerve cells that cover all rods and cones form only a thin layer over the fovea, the cones are heavily exposed to light. Many cones in the fovea are connected to their own bipolar cells, which in turn are connected to their own ganglion cells. This networking of cells allows the cones to provide greater detail to the brain. Images produced by the rods are much fuzzier. Many rods are linked to a single bipolar cell, which in turn may be one of many such cells connected to a single ganglion cell. As a result, the signals from the rods are usually blended, providing less information to the brain. This is why objects appear coarse and ill-defined at night; you are seeing them mainly with rods.

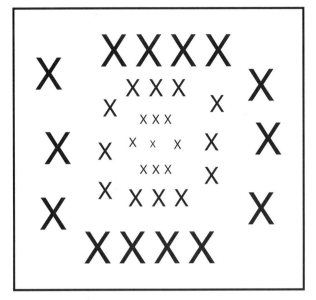

FIGURE 4-6　When you focus on the "X" in the center, all other "X's" should be equally clear. Notice how much larger the outer letters must be to compensate for the rods' relatively poor acuity.

Regardless of the differences in the images they produce, both rods and cones convert light into neural signals by means of chemical reactions with light-sensitive pigments. The pigment contained in rods is called **rhodopsin,** or "visual red," because of its deep red color. When light strikes a rod, it changes the chemical structure of rhodopsin by bleaching it (Sekuler & Blake, 1994), which in turn generates neural activity. A similar process takes place in the cones with different pigments.

Because light breaks down rhodopsin in the rods, the eye must continually regenerate the pigment if the rods are to continue working. In very bright light, the speed of rhodopsin production cannot keep pace with the speed of its breakdown, and the pigment becomes depleted. Rhodopsin will replenish itself in the dark, but the process takes time. In humans, full recovery of the supply can take up to half an hour, depending on the intensity and duration of the light to which the eyes have been exposed. That is why you have difficulty seeing when you first enter a dark room after leaving bright sunlight: your rhodopsin supply has not yet been replenished.

Although most people's rods gradually adjust to dim light, some people have difficulty adapting to the dark. This condition, known as *night blindness*, can be caused by several factors. The most common cause is an inability to use or store vitamin A, which is needed to produce rhodopsin. For this reason an increase in vitamin A is often prescribed for night blindness. (The fact that carrots are rich in vitamin A is the source of the conventional wisdom that "carrots are good for your eyes.")

The Role of Brain Regions

Beyond the rods, cones, and other cells of the retina, the fibers of the **optic nerve** form several pathways through the brain. The most important is the one that leads first to an area of the thalamus that serves as a sort of relay station. From there the nerve network radiates out to the primary visual cortex, located at the very back of the brain. The nerve impulses in the visual cortex give rise to the visual sensations we call sight.

In 1981 psychologists David Hubel and Torsten Wiesel won a Nobel prize for their work on this fascinating area (Hubel & Wiesel, 1959, 1979). Hubel and Wiesel found that each neuron in the primary visual cortex of a cat is activated by a very specific stimulus. For instance, one neuron might fire in response to a thick vertical line in the center of the visual field, while another might fire in response to a thin line oriented on the diagonal and moving from left to right. Apparently each neuron in the primary visual cortex is specially adapted to detect certain visual features.

Analysis of visual information is not completed in the primary visual cortex, however. Information is passed along to other areas of the cortex, where it is further analyzed for color, form, orientation, depth, and movement. Finally the signals are integrated into a coherent, meaningful whole. How this complex process actually takes place is still not fully understood, but scientists have discovered many pieces of the puzzle. For example, beyond the primary visual cortex, nerve impulses seem to feed into at least three separate processing systems: one for analyzing shapes, one for analyzing colors, and one for analyzing movement, location, and depth (Livingston, 1988; Livingston & Hubel, 1987). This three-part arrangement can be seen very clearly in the secondary visual cortex, which lies right next to the primary visual cortex. If you stain tissue from the secondary visual cortex, you can see that its cells are

organized into three alternating columns: a thick one, a thin one, and one that is paler in color. Cells in the thick column seem to be concerned with processing depth, cells in the thin column with processing color, and cells in the pale column with processing shape. These cells in turn send signals to another part of the visual cortex, where further analysis takes place. The thick columns, for instance, send signals into a part of the temporal lobe concerned with movement and depth perception, while the thin columns send signals into cortical regions concerned with color (Zeki, 1980).

The fact that different systems in the brain are involved in different aspects of visual perception accounts for some interesting artistic effects. For instance, if you look at an impressionist painting from a certain distance, you can see that it is composed of a great many dabs of paint, but the colors of those dabs blend together (see the photo on page 121). Apparently your neural system for analyzing shapes has a keener ability to distinguish among stimuli than your neural system for analyzing colors. To see both the shape of individual dabs and their colors, you must stand much closer to the painting (Livingston, 1988). Vision may seem to you to be unitary, not a combination of several different systems in your brain. After all, when you look at an impressionist painting, you do not get separate perceptions of color, shape, location, and depth. Instead, you get an image of a well-integrated whole, which shows how smoothly your brain integrates related perceptions. How such remarkable integration occurs with so little cognitive effort is one of the fascinating questions that remains about our sensory systems.

Color Vision

As the first part of this chapter explained, objects do not have a color. An apple, for instance, is not really red, nor is a leaf really green. Instead, the colors you perceive are a combination of the wavelengths of light that enter your eyes and the receptors they strike. In a sense, color is *created* by the workings of your visual system. To rephrase the "trees falling in the forest" question, if an apple is growing on a tree in the forest, and no one is there to see it, is the apple still red? Like the "falling tree" question, the answer again is "no." The apple will still reflect light at about 700 nm, but without someone there to see it, it does not have "color."

Georges Pierre Seurat, Eiffel Tower *(c. 1889). If you stand close to an impressionist painting, you can see that it is composed of a great many dabs of paint. At a distance, however, the dabs blend together, creating a unified (if sometimes hazy) scene.*

Theories of Color Vision

If color is "created" by the human perceiver, how do we translate different wavelengths into colors? Psychologists have proposed several explanations. The first is the **trichromatic** (or "three-color") theory, first proposed by the Englishman Thomas Young around the turn of the nineteenth century and reformulated some fifty years later by the German physiologist Hermann von Helmholtz. As a result, this theory is often called the "Young-Helmholtz theory." Proponents of the trichromatic theory reasoned that color vision is not likely to arise from separate receptors for each of the hundreds of colors humans are able to see. But if

there are not hundreds of different kinds of color receptors, how can we see that many shades? A possible answer is that we do so by "mixing" colors. In fact, by mixing light of just three colors—blue, green, and red—we can make every color on the visible spectrum. This means that the eye needs only three kinds of cones—one kind that is sensitive to short-wave light (the blue band), another that is sensitive to medium-wave light (the green band), and a third that is sensitive to long-wave light (the red band). To perceive all the other colors, our brain could "combine" the activity from two or more different cones, much as an artist mixes paints to get different shades.[6]

Many scientists were not satisfied with the trichromatic theory. Though it had a certain intuitive appeal, it could not explain some important aspects of color vision. One of the most striking was the presence of negative color afterimages. An *afterimage* is a visual impression that persists after removal of the stimulus that caused it. On the surface, this phenomenon appears to be nothing more than sensory adaptation. In color perception, however, the afterimage is the complementary color of the stimulus itself. For example, green stimuli produce red afterimages, and blue stimuli produce yellow afterimages. A striking example is shown in Figure 4-7.

The **opponent-process theory** of color vision provides an explanation of these afterimages. First proposed by the German physiologist Ewald Hering in the latter half of the nineteenth century, it has subsequently been revised and updated (Hurvich & Jameson, 1957; Jameson & Hurvich, 1989). Basically, the opponent-process theory posits four primary colors, not three: red, green, blue, and yellow. Red-green and blue-yellow are complementary colors, because when light waves of these color pairs are mixed together, we see a colorless gray or white. According to the opponent-process theory, these color pairs are linked in the brain by "opponent systems." One

---

[6]Technically, colors can be mixed in two ways. Different wavelengths of light can be added, such as the effect achieved when two different colored light sources are projected together. These mixtures are called *additive* color mixtures. Alternatively, two substances that *reflect* (rather than produce) light can be combined. This is what happens when two different colored paints are mixed.

Additive mixtures, as the name implies, add wavelength to the color mixture. Subtractive mixtures, as their name implies, further restrict the wavelengths reflected. Mixing blue and yellow light waves (an additive mixture) produces white. Mixing blue and yellow paints (a subtractive mixture) produces green.

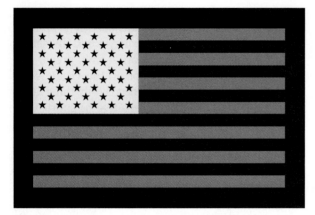

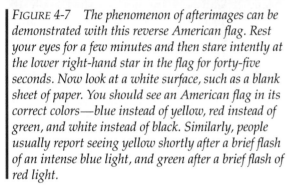

FIGURE 4-7   The phenomenon of afterimages can be demonstrated with this reverse American flag. Rest your eyes for a few minutes and then stare intently at the lower right-hand star in the flag for forty-five seconds. Now look at a white surface, such as a blank sheet of paper. You should see an American flag in its correct colors—blue instead of yellow, red instead of green, and white instead of black. Similarly, people usually report seeing yellow shortly after a brief flash of an intense blue light, and green after a brief flash of red light.

opponent system contains cells that are excited by red and inhibited by green. It also contains cells that are excited by green and inhibited by red. A second opponent system responds in the same manner to blue and yellow: some of its cells are excited by blue and inhibited by yellow, while others are excited by yellow and inhibited by blue. A third opponent system responds essentially to light and dark, and is thought to enable perception of brightness. Figure 4-8 displays a color wheel, where complementary colors are on opposite sides.

How can the opponent-process theory explain color afterimages? Quite elegantly. When you look at the green stripes in Figure 4-9, you are stimulating a green response in your red-green opponent color system. Soon, however, the system adapts and the response becomes less vigorous. What will happen if you shift your gaze to a white surface? Normally you see this as a white surface because the light it reflects stimulates your red and green responses equally, producing a sensation of colorlessness. But because your green response has been depressed through adaptation to the green-striped pattern, your red response dominates, and you see a set of red stripes.

The trichromatic and opponent-process theories were originally proposed as competing explanations of color vision. Recent evidence suggests that both have validity; they simply explain different levels of the visual system (Boynton, 1988). At the level of the receptor cells, the trichromatic theory applies. Researchers have identified three types of cones, each containing a slightly different form of light-sensitive pigment called **iodopsin.** (This pigment should not be confused with rhodopsin, found in the rods.) Each form of iodopsin responds most strongly to a different band of light waves: a short-wave band (the purple-to-green range, centering on blue), a medium-wave band (the blue-to-yellow range, centering on green), and a long-wave band (the green-to-red range, centering on a yellowish red) (MacNichol, 1964; Mollon, 1982). These three overlapping response ranges are shown in Figure 4-9.

Beyond the cones and their trichromatic pigments, an opponent-process system comes into play. Investigators have found that ganglion cells, cells in the thalamus, and cells in the visual cortex respond as expected by the opponent-process theory (Daw, 1968; DeValois & DeValois, 1975). For instance, when some of these cells are stimulated by diffuse green light, they increase their rate of firing; others decrease their firing. If the researcher switches to a complementary red light, the cells that were excited by the green light suddenly become inhibited, while those that were previously inhibited by green light suddenly become excited. In light that contains both green and red, these opposing reactions cancel out and the cells show little response. The same patterns can be found in cells that react to blue and yellow. When blue light is excitatory, yellow light is inhibitory, and vice versa.

Figure 4-10 shows how chemical responses in the three types of cones may be converted into neural responses involving four complementary colors (Sekuler & Blake, 1994). The three receptors (short-, medium-, and long-wavelength receptors) detect the presence or absence of various wavelengths, then feed that information into the opponent-process mechanisms, which determine the colors perceived.

Color Blindness

Studies of individuals with irregular color vision tell us a great deal about normal color vision, yet another example of Recurring Theme 2.

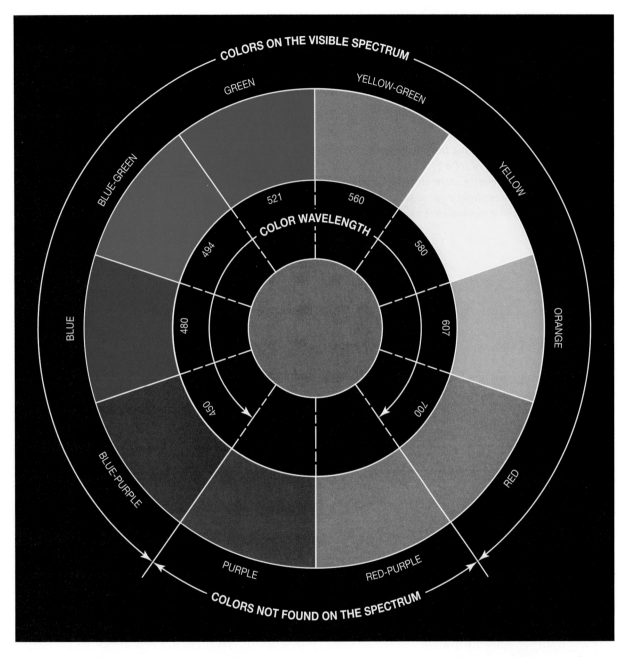

FIGURE 4-8   *The color wheel. Any two colors that are opposite to each other are complementary; this means that combining them produces gray or white. Thus, when red is mixed with its opposite (really a blue-green, not a pure green), we see a grayish-white color. The numbers on the spokes of the wheel are wavelengths measured in nanometers. Spectral colors are shown in their natural order, but not at uniform intervals by wavelengths because of space limitations. The nonspectral reds and purples are also shown.*

FIGURE 4-9 Curves representing the light-absorption sensitivity of the three types of cones. One group of cones is maximally sensitive to short wavelengths (around 435 nanometers), another to medium wavelengths (535 nanometers), and a third to long wavelengths (565 nanometers). The trichromatic theory explains that the perceived color of a light depends on the relative intensity of activity caused by the light's absorption in the three types of cones.

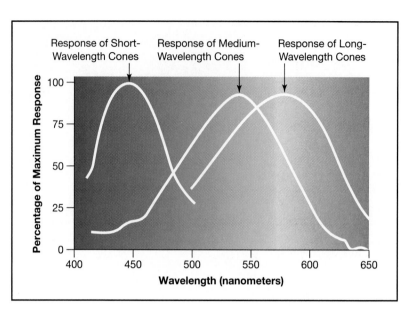

FIGURE 4-10 According to the opponent process theory of color vision, receptor cells relay signals to oppponent cells. Input from the receptor cells can either excite or inhibit an opponent process cell. For example, when the long wavelength receptor is stimulated, it sends excitatory input to opponent process cell 1, but inhibitory input to opponent process cell 2. The signals sent to the brain by the opponent process cells then are translated into the perception of color.

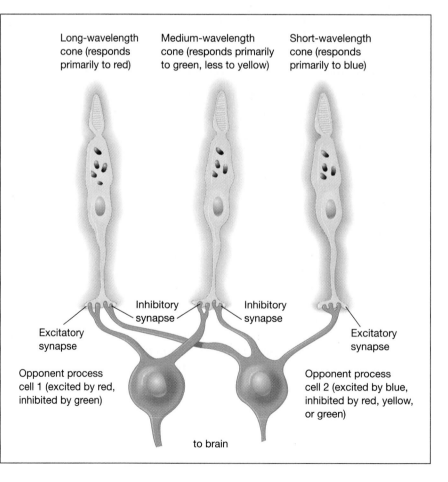

The same scene as perceived by a person with normal vision (A), and by people with three kinds of color blindness. (B) A person who is red-green blind sees everything in shades of blue and yellow. (C) Someone who is blue-yellow blind sees the world in shades of red and green. (D) Someone who is totally color blind sees in black, white, and shades of gray. (Boulton-Wilson/Jeroboam.)

THEME 2 Psychologists Learn about the Normal by Studying the Abnormal

There are several kinds of color blindness, each caused by a different defect in the visual system. About 8 percent of Caucasian males and 0.5 percent of Caucasian females have some type of color blindness. For Asians, blacks, and Native Americans, the percentages are lower, reflecting their different gene pools (Sekular & Blake, 1994). The accompanying photographs show how the world looks to people with three different types of color-vision defects.

Usually color blindness is caused by abnormalities in the composition of iodopsin, the visual pigment in the cones. A person with normal color vision has three forms of iodopsin, each sensitive to a different range of wavelengths. Such a person is called a *normal trichromat.* A small minority of people are totally color-blind. They see the world in shades of gray, like the pictures on a black-and-white TV. Most are **monochromats**, meaning that they have only one kind of iodopsin, which is insufficient to differentiate wavelengths of light.

More common is the partial color blindness caused by a lack of just one kind of iodopsin (Sekuler & Blake, 1994). Such people are called **dichromats.** Most dichromats lack either the middle-wave (green) visual pigment or the long-wave (red) one. In either case, they tend to confuse the colors along the middle-to-long-wavelength end of the spectrum, from green to red, because they have only one pigment that absorbs light in that range. John Dalton, an English scientist who lived in the late eighteenth and early nineteenth centuries, had this condition and wrote about it. Rather than seeing four basic colors in the long-wavelength region of the visible spectrum (green, yellow, orange, and red), Dalton saw only one, which he called yellow. We assume that

Dalton lacked the long-wave (red) visual pigment, because he saw even pure crimson as a dark neutral color. A Quaker who was supposed to shun bright colors, Dalton was dismayed and embarrassed to learn that the academic robes he sometimes wore were not black, but a vibrant red.

Much rarer than dichromats like Dalton are dichromats who lack the short-wave (blue) cone pigment. These people are usually blind to bluish purples, and they confuse shades in the blue-to-bluish-green range. The condition is rare because the gene for the short-wave pigment is not carried on the X (female) chromosome, as middle- and long-wave pigment genes are, but on another chromosome. Consequently, regardless of sex, a person always inherits two short-wave pigment genes, one from the mother and one from the father. Since it is highly unlikely that both those genes will be totally defective, a complete lack of the short-wave pigment is exceedingly rare. Color blindness in the red-green range is much more frequent, at least among males. Males have only one X chromosome, inherited from their mothers, so they also have only one each of the genes for the middle-wave and long-wave pigments. If either gene is defective, they will have no "backup" (Nathans, 1989).

A milder form of color blindness occurs among people who have three cone pigments, but one of those pigments—typically the middle-wave (green) or the long-wave (red)—is abnormally structured. In vision tests, these people require unusually large amounts of the affected color to produce a mixed hue. Psychologists often refer to such people as "color weak" rather than color-blind.

Recent research suggests that the range of defects in color-vision pigments may be even more diverse than these. Apparently some people who were formerly considered red-green dichromats *can* perceive red under the right conditions (Boynton, 1988). These people may not completely lack a third visual pigment, as was originally believed. Instead, their third pigment may be highly defective, functioning only under certain circumstances.

Table 4-2 summarizes the physical properties of light waves and the psychological interpretation associated with each.

Hearing

What changes in the physical world correspond to "sound"? As has already been mentioned, "sounds" result from changes in air pressure that are detected by the eardrum. You can demonstrate this to yourself with a pair of stereo speakers. Pick out a song with a strong bass component (something with a lot of "low notes"). Turn the volume up fairly loud and play it. If you can remove the grill covers from the speakers, do so. As the passage with the low notes approaches, watch the larger cone in your speaker: hi-fi enthusiasts call it the "woofer." You should see the cone move back and forth. The louder and lower the notes, the more the cone moves. As it moves, it creates a change in the air pressure, one that can be detected by the ear. The vibrating speaker alternately pushes against the surrounding air, compressing it, and pulls away from it, allowing it to become less dense, or rarefied. When these waves of compressed and rarefied air molecules strike your eardrum, they push and pull it in the same pattern as the vibrating speaker, although with much less intensity. This is the first step in producing a sound.[7]

---

[7]While you have your stereo speakers out, try one more demonstration. To do this, your speakers need to have two strands of wire connecting them to your receiver or amplifier. Most speakers have such connections. (They are often marked "red" or "+" on one side, and "black" or "−" on the other.)

Reverse the connectors on *one* of the speakers, switching the red and black (or + and −) connectors. Leave the other speaker connected as it was (don't reverse the leads), and don't change any connections at the receiver or amplifier. Now, place the speakers about 8 to 10 inches apart, *facing each other.* Play some music through the speakers, making certain that you begin with low volumes. You should hear much less sound coming from the speakers—though if you look closely, the "woofers" are probably moving back and forth just as they were before when they were playing loudly. If your stereo receiver has a "MONO/STEREO" button, set it to "MONO." This will send exactly the same signal to both speakers. If you do this, you should hear even less sound.

What has happened? By switching the connections to one of the speakers, you reversed the polarity on that speaker (technically, the system is now "out of phase"). Usually when you are listening to music, the speakers move "in phase" with each other, meaning that both woofers push the air in the same direction at the same time. Because you switched the connections, one speaker now pushes the air (compression) while the other pulls away from the air (rarefaction); the result is that they cancel each other out, especially when the signals are identical (as they are when you set your receiver to "MONO"). If you switched the connections and the sound did *not* decrease, you may have had your speakers wired out of phase to begin with. They will sound much better if you connnect them in phase!

Some headphone manufacturers now sell headphones that reduce ambient sound that in the same way. They have small microphones that "listen" to the noise in the environment and send an out-of-phase signal through the headphones, one of which is the mirror image of the noise. This signal cancels much of the noise. The effects can be dramatic, substantially reducing even the background noise of jet engines, while leaving the music intact.

TABLE 4-2 *Summary of the Physical Properties of Light Waves and the Psychological Interpretation Associated with Each*

Physical Changes in	Vision	Psychological "Interpretation"
Wavelength of light		Hue (roughly the same as "color")
Amplitude of light wave		"Brightness" or intensity of the light
"Complexity" of the wave form (the relative mixture of lights with different frequencies)		"Saturation" or "purity" of the color

Physical Correlates of Sounds

Just like light waves, sound waves can be described by their physical properties. And just like light waves, those physical properties have a direct relationship to their perception. Each sound wave has a certain number of "compression/rarefaction" cycles per second; that number is the **frequency** of the sound wave.[8] Frequency, in turn, is directly related to the pitch we perceive: the higher the frequency, the higher the pitch. The human ear is capable of hearing frequencies from about 20 to 20,000 hertz (Hz). (See Figure 4-11.) Our ears are most sensitive to sounds in the frequency range of speech—a good example of how an important human ability (communication

through language) has been facilitated by the coevolution of our speech and hearing mechanisms.

The intensity of a sound wave, or the amount of pressure it exerts, corresponds to its **amplitude,** that is, the distance of its peaks and valleys from a baseline level. The greater the amplitude of a wave, the louder it sounds. Amplitude is expressed in units of measurement called decibels (dB). Theoretically, 0 dB is the threshold for detection; conversation usually takes place at about 50 to 60 dB, and sounds of 140 dB can lead to intense pain and permanent hearing damage. The range of sound intensity that humans can perceive is illustrated in Figure 4-12.

Exposure to loud stimuli can cause permanent hearing damage. In general, sounds below 70 dB are considered safe, even for long periods. At the other extreme, intensities of 120 dB may cause *immediate* permanent damage. Sounds between the two extremes require longer exposure to produce lasting

---

[8]Remember that though "frequency" and "wavelength" are inversely related, they measure the same thing. Historically, we have described light waves using the wavelength, but sound waves using the frequency.

Chronic exposure to very loud sounds can lead to permanent hearing loss. The rock musicians Peter Townsend of the Who and Stephen Stills of Crosby, Stills and Nash have acknowledged that their hearing has been damaged by long-term exposure to very loud music.

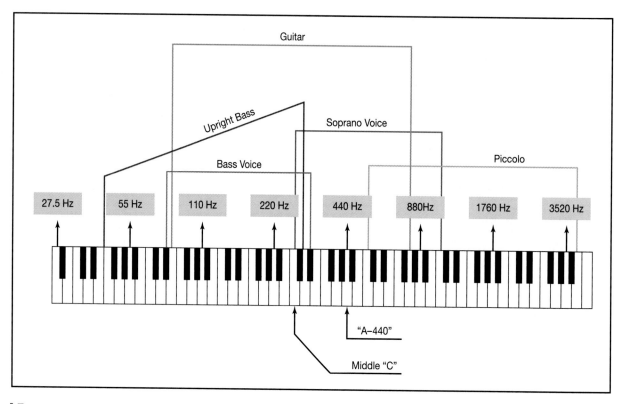

FIGURE 4-11 *The range of pitches produced by musical instruments. The range of human hearing extends from about 20 to 20,000 Hz (though sensitivity to higher frequencies is generally lost with advancing age.)*

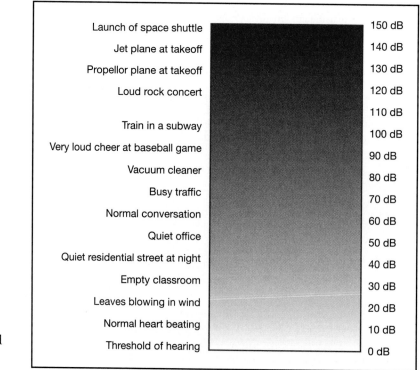

FIGURE 4-12 *Range of sound pressure changes detected by humans.* (Following Sekuler and Blake, 1994.)

hearing loss. The louder the sound, the shorter the exposure needed to damage hearing.

In the past, most damage resulted from work in steel mills, factories, and other loud industrial environments. However, in recent years musicians (for example, Peter Townsend of the Who, and Stephen Stills of Crosby, Stills, and Nash) have acknowledged that years of exposure to loud music have permanently impaired their hearing. Furthermore, with the advent of portable stereos, many people now listen to music at a continuously loud level through headphones. While headphones seldom produce sound much louder than 100 dB, continued listening at those levels can cause long-term, irreversible hearing loss. One leading producer of headphone equipment offers this warning: "Generally speaking, you should only turn up the volume until it doesn't sound too soft. If you find that your ears are ringing, or you feel a sense of pressure or fatigue, you should give your ears a rest for a day or two. . . . Should you choose to ignore these warnings, you are risking permanent hearing damage" (Hertsens, 1995, p.27).

Basic Functions of the Auditory System

The human ear is remarkable. All its amplifying mechanisms are packed into a space of about 1 cubic inch, yet it can make the buzz of a mosquito audible. Figure 4-13 shows the basic structure of the ear and its three interrelated parts : the outer ear, the middle ear, and the inner ear.

From the Outer to the Middle Ear

Sound is funneled into the outer ear through the **pinna,** the skin-covered cartilage visible on the outside of the head. The pinna works as a kind of "backwards megaphone," collecting sounds. (When you put your hand to your ear, you are effectively increasing the size of the pinna, making it easier for your ear to detect sounds.) From the pinna, sound travels down the **auditory canal,** a passageway about an inch long that is sealed off at its inner end by a thin membrane called the **eardrum.** Because of its long, narrow shape, the auditory canal resonates as sound passes through it, so the sound is amplified. For frequencies between 2,000 and 5,500 Hz, the pressure exerted at the eardrum is about twice that exerted at the entrance to the auditory canal.

The eardrum responds to changes in air pressure by moving in and out. Its movement is extremely slight. When you listen to a normal speaking voice,

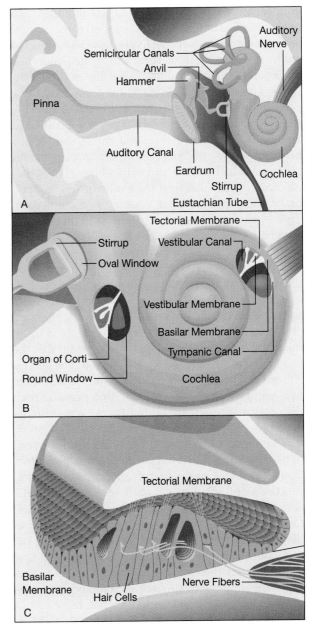

FIGURE 4-13   *Structure of the ear. (A) A cross section showing the outer, middle, and inner ear. Sound waves pass through the auditory canal and are transformed into mechanical vibration by the eardrum. The three small bones—the hammer, anvil, and stirrup—amplify this motion and transmit it to (B) the oval window of the cochlea. The motion of the oval window sends pressure waves through the fluid in the cochlea. (C) Closeup cross section of the organ of the Corti, within the cochlea. Waves in the cochlear fluid cause the basilar membrane to vibrate, which in turn disturbs the hair cells, the receptors of auditory, or hearing, information.*

your eardrum vibrates only about 100 millionths of a centimeter—enough to set into motion three tiny, interconnected bones (collectively called the *ossicles*) on the inner side of the eardrum, in an area known as the *middle ear*. These bones, called the **malleus,** the **incus,** and the **stapes** (literally, the "hammer, anvil, and stirrup" because of their distinctive shapes)— form a mechanical amplifier. They are positioned and linked in such a way that movement of the eardrum moves the malleus, which in turn moves the incus, which in turn moves the stapes. The stapes ultimately presses against the **oval window,** a membrane stretching across an opening to the inner ear. This setup converts small movements in the comparatively large eardrum to larger movements in the comparatively small oval window.

This setup is necessary because the inner ear is filled with liquid, and liquid is much more difficult to compress than air. The bones of the middle ear act as a series of levers, each one increasing the pressure on the next. The fact that the oval window is up to thirty times smaller than the eardrum means that the pressure it receives is likewise increased. The end result is that the pressure exerted by the stapes on the oval window can be up to ninety times greater than the pressure the original sound wave exerted on the eardrum.

The importance of this amplification can be seen in people who suffer from various forms of **conduction deafness.** Conduction deafness involves malfunctions of the outer or middle ear that impair the ear's ability to amplify sound waves. These malfunctions include excessive accumulation of wax in the auditory canal, fluid buildup in the middle ear that could rupture the eardrum, and bone disease that decreases the effectiveness with which the stirrup presses on the oval window. Some types of conversion deafness can be treated, such as those resulting from wax buildup or acute infection. More serious problems must be treated by microsurgery to repair or replace the bones of the middle ear, or by means of a hearing aid, which amplifies sound electronically. Middle ear infections (*otitis media*) are especially common in children. They cause swelling in the middle ear, which increases the pressure in the middle ear, causing pain and possibly damaging the child's hearing. In children with chronic ear infections, tubes are sometimes inserted through small incisions in the eardrum, allowing the pressure inside and outside the middle ear to equalize.

In the Inner Ear

When amplified pressure reaches the oval window, it is transmitted to the fluid in the spiral-shaped part of the *inner ear* called the **cochlea.** The cochlea is a coiled structure that is divided into several canals separated by membranes, the most important of which is the **basilar membrane.** Like the middle ear, the inner ear is fluid-filled.

The basilar membrane is lined with **hair cells,** socalled because of their many hairlike projections. Movement of the fluid in the inner ear creates tiny waves that stimulate the hair cells, much as plants on the ocean floor move when waves surge over them. The movement of the hair cells triggers neural impulses, which travel via the **auditory nerve** to the brain stem. From there they ascend through the thalamus to the auditory cortex, where the perception of sound begins.

Because the basilar membrane and hair cells initiate nerve impulses in the auditory system, damage to them can produce what is called **nerve deafness.** A new technology is designed to help people who suffer from severe neural deafness, called a **cochlear implant.** In one of the more sophisticated implants, twenty-two electronic detectors are implanted at various points along the cochlea. A cable is then run to a small receiver, which picks up and amplifies the sounds. Finally, electrical impulses are transmitted to the fibers of the auditory nerve (Schmeck, 1984). Cochlear implants have proved successful in individuals who had well-developed auditory and linguistic skills prior to deafness (Busby, Tong, & Clark, 1993). They are especially useful in the perception of speech (Fryauf-Bertschy et al., 1992; Shallop, Arndt, & Turnacliff, 1992). Unfortunately, they are much less effective in the congenitally deaf (Loeb, 1985); results with children are still inconclusive (e.g., Geers & Moog, 1992).

Theories of Pitch

How does the brain distinguish among tones of different pitches? Two classic theories date back to the nineteenth century. One was first proposed by Hermann von Helmholtz, the physiologist who helped to formulate the trichromatic theory. He and others argued that each pitch we hear depends on the area of the basilar membrane that vibrates most in response to a given sound wave. This view is aptly called the **place theory** of pitch perception.

In 1961, Georg von Bekesy won a Nobel prize for his research in support of the place theory. Bekesy (1959) found that sound waves of different frequency do indeed vibrate different places on the basilar membrane. High-frequency waves have their maximum effect on the region near the oval window, while mid-frequency waves have their maximum effect near the middle of the cochlea. Moreover, when small groups of neurons leading from different parts of the basilar membrane are electrically stimulated, people hear sounds of different pitches (Simmons et al., 1965). (This finding inspired the development of the cochlear implants.) As you would expect, damage to selected portions of the basilar membrane tends to affect only certain tones. With age, for instance, many people gradually lose their sensitivity to high-frequency tones, so that by the age of seventy quite a few people cannot hear frequencies greater than 6,000 Hz. This high-tone hearing loss is caused by deterioration of the receptor cells close to the oval window.

Unfortunately, stimulation of the basilar membrane does not occur as consistently as predicted by the place theory. Most importantly, low-frequency sound waves tend to vibrate the membrane fairly uniformly across its surface. The second major theory of pitch detection overcomes this problem by focusing not on the *location* of the basilar membrane's activity but on its *frequency*. Accordingly, this is known as the **frequency theory** of pitch perception.

At some frequencies (primarily lower frequencies, the same frequencies that give the place theory difficulty) the basilar membrane vibrates at exactly the same frequency as the original sound wave. The rate of impulses generated by the basilar membrane reflects the frequency of the stimulus event. The brain interprets the different patterns of neural firing to determine the pitches we hear.

The frequency theory has problems of its own, however. Remember from Chapter 3 that neurons have a maximum firing rate, with a theoretical upper limit of no more than 1,000 neural impulses per second. However, we can hear ranges of sound far above 1,000 Hz, which is the maximum rate predicted by the frequency theory: the human auditory system is capable of detecting frequencies of up to 20,000 Hz, well beyond neural firing rates.

Although this problem at first seemed perplexing, Ernest Wever and Charles Bray (1937) ultimately proposed the **volley principle.** It is based on the assumption that the frequency of neural firing that the brain detects is determined not by the rate of firing of single neurons but rather by groups of neurons.

Each individual neuron can fire no more than 1,000 times per second; however, neurons often work as groups, firing in a pattern—or "volley." This *group* of neurons can substantially increase the total number of firings in a unit of time. Using this volley technique, the neurons of the auditory system can process sound frequencies from 1,000 to about 4,000 Hz.

Both the place theory and the frequency theory help explain how we perceive pitch. For sounds of intermediate and high frequencies the place theory seems to apply. The location of maximum vibration on the basilar membrane varies with frequencies within this range. In fact, for higher frequencies there seems to be a one-to-one correspondence between the area of the basilar membrane being affected and the area of the auditory cortex being activated.

At lower frequencies, however, vibration of the basilar membrane is too diffuse to support the place theory. In this range, the frequency theory provides a better explanation of pitch perception. But that leaves a fairly large frequency range—from about 250 to about 4,000 Hz—in which both mechanisms may operate. This may help explain why our pitch perception is so acute for sounds within this range. (Remember, this is the range of pitches that corresponds to the frequency levels of normal human speech.)

Table 4-3 summarizes physical changes in sound waves and our psychological interpretations of those changes.

The Somatic Senses

We tend to think of vision and hearing as our primary senses, the ones that provide the most vital information about the world. And yet we have other senses that are also crucial. The **somatic** senses are those responsible for sensations of the skin (the **cutaneous** senses), detecting the movement in the body, especially the limbs (the **kinesthetic** senses), and awareness of body and limb position (the **proprioceptive** senses). Just think how hard it is to walk when your foot has gone to sleep. There is nothing wrong with the muscles that move the affected limb or the bones that support your weight. But because your foot's senses of touch, pressure, and movement have been lost, you find that even a step or two are

TABLE 4-3   *Summary of the Physical Properties of Sound Waves and the Psychological Interpretation Associated with Each*

Physical Changes in	Audition	Psychological "Interpretation"
Frequency of sound wave		Pitch of sound
Amplitude (intensity) of sound wave		Loudness of sound
"Complexity" of the wave form		"Timbre" of the sound

clumsy and unsteady. Clearly, your somatic senses are extremely important to performing even the simplest tasks.

We will focus our attention primarily on the sensations of the skin, the cutaneous senses. These include touch, pressure, warmth, cold, and pain. Figure 4-14 shows that within and below the skin lies a forest of sensory receptors, some 17,000 just in the smooth and hairless parts of a hand (Johansson & Vallbo, 1983). These receptors are structured in many different ways and lie at different depths in the body tissue. All connect with neurons that transmit information to the central nervous system, usually first to the spinal cord and then through the thalamus to the somatosensory area of the cortex.

The Cutaneous Senses

As you are no doubt aware, some areas of the body are far more sensitive to touch than others. Figure 4-15 shows the relative sensitivity of different parts of the body using a technique know as a "two-point threshold" test. The following excerpt explains how two-point thresholds are measured. You may want to conduct your own test.

Two-Point Threshold Demonstration

To determine your two-point thresholds, you will need a partner and two pointed objects, such as two pens. (The smaller the "point" on your object, the more reliable your measurements. Something like a geometric compass is ideal.) Begin by gently pressing the two points to your index finger, maybe ¼ inch apart. If you feel only a single point, gradually move the two points farther apart and repeat. If you are able to feel the two points as distinct, grad-

ually move them closer together. Once you find the distance where you can just barely detect the two points as separate, measure the distance between the points and record that number. You might want to repeat the procedure several times. Next, do the same thing for the palm of your hand, the middle of your forearm, the middle of your back, and the top of your foot. Notice that some parts of the body can detect the two points when they are relatively close together (such as your finger). Other areas, such as your back, require the two points to be considerably farther apart before you can feel the two points as distinct. Typical two-point thresholds are shown in Figure 4-15 (Weinstein, 1968).

How are the receptors that are embedded in skin tissues related to the sensations you feel? Stimulation of receptors around the roots of hair cells seems to produce the sensation of touch on the skin's surface. So does stimulation of the Meissner's corpuscles, which are abundant in hairless areas like the fingertips, palms, and lips. Stroking your hand across a page of this book probably stimulates both these receptors. Lying below them are the Merkel disks and Ruffini endings, both of which seem to be involved in the sensation of steady pressure on the skin, such as when you press the end of a pencil against your palm. Even deeper beneath the surface are the **Pacinian corpuscles,** which are extremely sensitive to touch and even very light pressure. Blowing gently on a finger so that you can feel the air is likely to activate some of your Pacinian corpuscles.

What causes pain? That remains something of a mystery. Although pain often results from certain types of physical stimulation (pressure, damage),

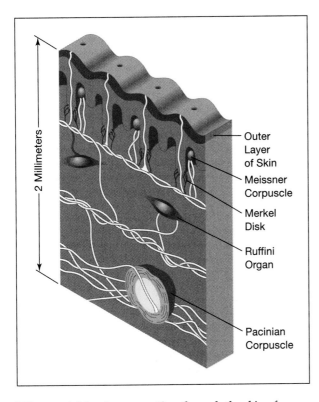

FIGURE 4-14   *A cross section through the skin of a fingerpad showing the location of various receptor cells.* (After Sekuler & Blake, 1990.)

Labels on figure:
- 2 Millimeters
- Outer Layer of Skin
- Meissner Corpuscle
- Merkel Disk
- Ruffini Organ
- Pacinian Corpuscle

pain is generally considered a perceptual rather than a sensory phenomenon. That is, the same physical stimulus might be interpreted as "pain" in one situation but not in another. This is unlike the perception of light, in which the same physical stimulus (light of a certain wavelength, for example) reliably produces the same perceptual experience. In Chapter 5 we will discuss some aspects of pain and the control of pain using hypnosis. The examples in that chapter are further evidence of the complex nature of pain.

Researchers once believed that free nerve endings embedded in the tissues were associated exclusively with the sensation of pain. But the cornea, which contains almost nothing but free nerve endings, is responsive to pressure and temperature as well as to pain (Geldard, 1972). Thus to understand pain, like any other sensation, we must look beyond the receptors.

Any explanation of pain must also account for all of its unusual characteristics. One such characteristic is the fact that people sometimes continue to experience pain after its cause has disappeared. For instance, sufferers from neuralgia (an infection of the peripheral nervous system) may complain of persistent pain even after the infection has cleared up (Barlow & Mollon, 1982). Another strange characteristic is the perception of phantom limb pain (Melzack, 1992). After amputation (or, less frequently, paralysis) of a limb, many patients report "pain" in the amputated tissues (e. g., Krane & Heller, 1995; Sherman

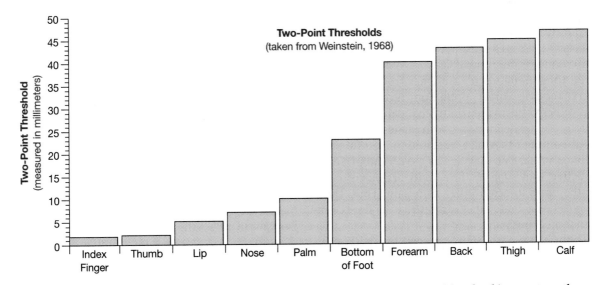

FIGURE 4-15   *Two-point thresholds for various locations on the body. The more sensitive the skin receptors, the smaller the distance needed for the two-point threshold.* (After Weinstein, 1968.)

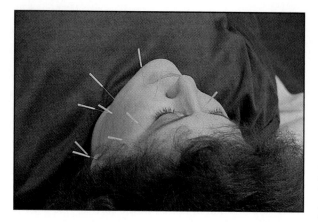

Although the physiological mechanisms underlying acupuncture are not well understood, the procedure often produces a significant reduction in pain.

et al., 1993). Some reports (Sherman et al., 1993) indicate that the phantom pain is associated with muscle activity in the region. Other studies have found an increased incidence of phantom limb pain in patients who experienced pain in the limb *before* the amputation (Katz, 1992; Krane & Heller, 1995). While there is still disagreement about the exact cause of phantom limb pain (see Davies, Crombie, & Macrae, 1993), there is no denying that the pain is real. Oddly, it can sometimes be controlled by new antidepressant medications like fluoxetine (Prozac) (see Power-Smith & Turkington, 1993).

One model that attempts to account for all these features of pain is the **gate-control theory** (Melzack & Wall, 1988). According to this theory, the neurons that carry messages of pain up the spinal cord to the brain receive input from (at least) two different types of peripheral nerve fibers. One group (called S fibers) receives direct input from receptors in the skin. When S fibers are stimulated, pain occurs. Another group (called L fibers) also carries information about pain, but they also transmit nonpainful stimuli like pressure or massage as well. When L fibers are active, they *suppress* the activity of S fibers, causing the brain to sense little or no pain. Thus, the L fibers act as a "gate" that can restrict the flow of information about pain.

Though the gate-control theory has been criticized (Kelly, 1981; Nathan, 1976a), it has proved very useful. For example, it explains the efficacy of acupuncture, in which very fine needles are inserted into various points on the body. In many cases, acupuncture produces significant pain reduction (Ernst, 1994; Ulett, 1992). According to gate-control theory, the needles stimulate the L fibers, which then block the pain detected by other receptors. Gate-control theory also accounts for stress-induced analgesia. In some situations, especially those involving high levels of autonomic nervous system activity, a person may be seriously injured yet feel no pain at the time. You have probably heard stories of wartime heroics in which the hero did not feel the pain of an injury until well after it occurred. The nineteenth-century explorer David Livingstone (of "Stanley and Livingstone" fame) tells of being attacked by a lion, yet feeling no pain:

> [I]t caused a sort of dreaminess in which there was no sense of pain nor feeling of terror, though quite conscious of all that was happening . . . such [feelings] are probably produced by all animals killed by the carnivora; and if so, is a merciful provision by our benevolent creator for lessening the pain of death.

Julien, 1983

The topic of pain is a complicated one. Clearly our understanding of pain and its control is incomplete. Clearly, too, the psychological components of pain (as opposed to the physiological components) can be powerful.

Smell and Taste

No two senses are more closely intertwined than smell and taste. If you have ever had a stuffy nose, you have probably noticed how bland most food seems. Though the stuffy nose won't alter your sense of taste, it does impair your sense of smell. As you no doubt found out, the flavor of foods depends heavily on smell, not just taste.

Smell

The sense of smell, or **olfaction,** can be a real source of pleasure, as anyone who has ever enjoyed the sensual fragrance of a rose or savored the aroma of a favorite food knows. Although many animals are more sensitive to odors than human beings, the human sense of smell is still quite keen. For instance, a person can detect the musky odor of mercaptan, the scent that makes skunks so unpopular, at concentrations as low as 1 part to 50 trillion parts of air (Geldard, 1972).

Smell requires that vaporized molecules of a substance enter the nasal passages and contact the olfactory membranes that line the roofs of those cavities.

Within the olfactory membranes are some 10 million receptor cells, each with hairlike projections reaching out into the circulating air. When molecules of certain airborne substances contact these receptors, nerve impulses are generated (Lancet, 1984). These impulses travel directly to the olfactory bulbs at the forward base of the cerebral hemispheres. From there they are relayed to other parts of the brain, where the odor is consciously perceived and analyzed (Cain, 1988).

Psychologists are not sure why people can smell some substances and not others, nor why certain groups of odors smell alike. One theory is that the quality of an odor is related to the size and shape of the molecules that produce it (Amoore, Johnston, & Rubin, 1964). Molecules of various sizes and shapes might fit into different receptor cell slots, much as keys fit locks. The different receptor cells could then stimulate different nerve fibers leading to the brain (Kandel, Schwartz, & Jessell, 1991). Furthermore, odor memory seems to be facilitated by some kind of central neural mechanism. Bromley and Doty (1995) recently demonstrated that bilateral odor recognition (in which odors are presented to both sides of the nose) is superior to unilateral odor recognition (in which odors are presented to only one side of the nose). Thus, the brain seems to combine information from the two sources in order to process odors, much as it combines information from both eyes or ears.

Recently Larsson and Backman (1993) found evidence that semantic factors play a role in odor memory. They presented various odors to their subjects, giving some only the odor (for example, vanilla extract) and others the odor and its name (they were told the odor was vanilla extract). Subjects who were given the verbal label later showed enhanced memory of the odor.

Taste

Most people can discriminate among hundreds of odors, yet appear to sense only four basic types of taste: sweet, sour, salty, and bitter. Other tastes are generally regarded as mixtures of the four or a combination of taste and smell (Bartoshuk, 1988). Interestingly, the sensation of bitterness, which can be so unpleasant, is probably crucial to our survival. Most poisonous substances in plants are extremely bitter; their taste serves as a warning to us not to eat them (Akabas, Dodd, & Al-Awqati, 1988).

The organs of taste are the taste buds, some 10,000 of which cover the upper surface of the tongue. Most

Food preferences often involve an integration of many different senses, including vision. For example, most Americans would refuse to eat the "bug tostada" shown here, regardless of its actual taste or odors. (Residents of Huixteco, a community in Mexico, regularly consume these iodine-rich insects.)

taste buds are embedded in hill-like projections called **papillae.** It is the papillae that make the top of your tongue appear bumpy. Each taste bud, in turn, contains receptor cells that are quite sensitive. A salty or sweet solution applied to the tongue for only a tenth of a second is enough to generate responses in these receptors and trigger an identifiable taste (Kelling & Halpern, 1983). Figure 4-16 shows that different areas of the tongue are especially sensitive to one or more of the four basic categories of taste. The front of the tongue is particularly sensitive to sweet and salty tastes, the sides to sourness, and the back to bitterness.

Taste sensations are transmitted from the tongue to the brain via nerve fibers that connect to the receptor cells in the taste buds. In some animal species, the individual nerve fibers respond to more than one kind of taste, suggesting that the neural codes for different tastes may be based on different patterns of activity in the thousands of nerve fibers that lead away from the tongue (Erickson, 1984). Alternatively, each nerve fiber could carry a message regarding only one of the basic taste sensations. As yet, however, there is little evidence that nerve fibers leading from the tongue respond that selectively.

Integration of Different Senses

Smell and taste are closely interrelated. When describing how food "tastes," we usually include its odor, which circulates from the back of the mouth up

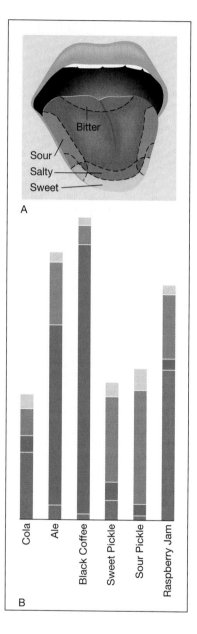

FIGURE 4-16
A map of the human tongue (A) shows the areas of maximum sensitivity to the four fundamental kinds of taste sensation. (B) The tastes of six foods analyzed into the four components of taste shown in (A). The length of the colored bars indicates the amount of each component judged to be present in the taste of the food by subjects in a psychological experiment. (Data from Beebe-Center, 1949.)

into the nasal cavity. The intimate connection between taste and smell is most noticeable when the sense of smell is temporarily blocked. Try biting into an apple and then a raw potato while holding your nose. You will probably have difficulty distinguishing between the two. For the same reason, food has a flat, uninteresting flavor when you have a bad cold.

The complex interplay between taste and smell is critical to our understanding of food selection (Barker, 1982). For example, we readily learn to associate tastes and odors with sickness, an important

survival mechanism (see Barker, Best, & Domjan, 1977). But although taste and smell are more interconnected than most of our senses, none of our sensory systems operates in isolation. Information gained from one tends to "inform" the others about what sensations to expect and how to interpret them (Acredolo & Hake, 1982). For example, when you feel an object in your pocket and identify it by touch, that information gives you clues as to what the object will look like. Similarly, when you see a food that looks very unappetizing, you develop expectations about how it will taste. Those expectations may be so powerful that the food will actually taste bad, even though if you ate it blindfolded, you might find it perfectly acceptable.

Thus, people seem to strive to "match" information from their various senses. You do this every time you go to a movie theater and hear the voices that are coming from the speakers as the voices of the people you see on the screen. There may be a moment in the beginning when you are aware of the disparity, but it doesn't last long. Soon you have coordinated the sights and sounds of the movie into an integrated whole.[9]

Perceiving a Complex World

Earlier in this chapter we defined perception as the process in which the brain interprets the sensations it receives, giving them order and meaning. We also saw that it is hard to separate sensation from perception, because the first so quickly and effortlessly leads to the second. Certain ambiguous stimuli, however, can help us to distinguish between the two. Look, for example, at Figure 4-17. From a sensory perspective, this picture is just a series of black patches on a white background. But if you look long enough at the right-hand side, you will likely perceive the form of an object. (See page 137 to find out what you are "supposed" to see.) This form is a perception, an organization of sensory data that emerges as your brain processes incoming information.

But how does the brain get from the relatively impoverished stimulus in Figure 4-17 to a perceived form? Psychologists have proposed two different ex-

---

[9]To provide an even more dramatic illustration of this effect, watch a movie on TV while listening to the sounds over *headphones*. You will likely have no trouble perceiving the voices as coming from the TV, even though you "know" they are not!

planations. The **direct perspective** emphasizes the contribution of the sensory data themselves (Gibson, 1950, 1966, 1979). According to this view, all the information you need to see the patches on the right as a unified object is right there in the drawing. As this visual information is passed from the retina, to the optic nerve, and on up into the higher regions of the brain, it is automatically structured into a meaningful whole. The direct perspective is closely related to what is called "bottom-up" or data-driven processing, mentioned earlier.

In contrast to the direct view, the so-called **indirect perspective** or constructivist view holds that only sensory cues about the environment are processed directly (Gregory, 1970; Rock, 1984). To make sense of those cues we must supplement them with additional information stored in memory. Thus we take our knowledge about dogs (how they look and act) and use it as a hypothesis for organizing the patches in Figure 4-17 into a recognizable picture. This hypothesis works downward from the higher brain centers, guiding our exploration of the drawing and offering a possible solution. In this way we actively *construct* our final perception. The indirect perspective or constructivist view stresses what are called **schemas**—mental representations of objects and events against which incoming data can be compared and interpreted. In short, schemas direct our search for meaning in the world. You will encounter the concept of schemas in many chapters of this book, including those on learning, memory, development, thought, and social psychology.

The direct and indirect perspectives on perception are not mutually exclusive. Although in some cases one may seem to apply better than the other, it is best to think of them as complementary viewpoints, both of which add to our understanding of perception.

Some Basic Perceptual Processes

Over the years psychologists have studied many basic perceptual processes. Some have been interested in what is called **form perception,** the ability to detect unified patterns instead of a hodgepodge of sensory data. Others have investigated **perceptual constancy,** the tendency to see objects as having stable properties even though visual information about them is constantly changing. Still others have been intrigued by **depth perception,** the ability to see the visual world in three dimensions, even though the

FIGURE 4-17 *When you first look at this drawing, your visual system will most likely interpret this as a series of black patches on a white background, demonstrating* bottom-up *processing. If you look longer you may begin to see an object appear, as your brain begins to interpret the image into a recognizable pattern. If you still don't see the image look again at the picture, this time looking specifically for a Dalmation dog. This final case demonstrates* top-down *processing—your perception is influenced not only by prior experience with Dalmatians, but also because the text provides you with explicit expectations.*

images that strike the retinas are two-dimensional. In the following sections we will explore all three of these aspects of perception.

Form Perception

One group of researchers interested in form perception were known as **gestalt** (literally, "whole") psychologists. The gestalt movement began in Germany in the early twentieth century. Its proponents—such as Max Wertheimer, Kurt Koffka, and Wolfgang Kohler—believed that form perception is impossible to understand simply by analyzing the many sensations that are registered in the brain when we see, hear, smell, taste, or touch something. They argued that the whole is more than the sum of its parts; that is, perceptions are more than the sensations that give rise to them. The gestalt psychologists were among the very first to consider the constructive nature of cognition, Recurring Theme 4.

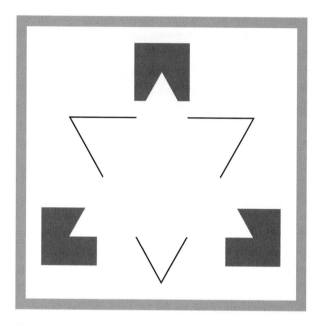

FIGURE 4-18 This drawing shows only three unrelated squares with a wedge missing from each and three unrelated 45-degree angles. What we perceive, however, is a white triangle overlaying three complete squares and another triangle.

THEME **Cognition and Thought are Dynamic, Active Processes, Best Considered Reconstructive, Not Reproductive**

The meaningful pattern or whole we experience is called a *gestalt* in German.

An example of a gestalt appears in Figure 4-18. You do not see this drawing as simply three unrelated circles with a wedge missing from each, plus three unrelated 45-degree angles. Instead, you see a white triangle projecting forward from the center of the drawing, as if it is partially covering another triangle and three complete circles. All the pieces seem to be integrated into a single pattern, a unified gestalt. So "real" looking is the white triangle tying the other pieces together that it even seems to have distinct contours or edges. These perceptions are called *subjective contours*—lines or shapes that appear to be present but are not physically there (Sekular & Blake, 1994).

The early gestalt psychologists were interested in determining the "rules" the brain uses to order sensory information into wholes. (In this respect, they were much like the early structuralists.) So in their research they typically presented people with vari-

ous stimuli—often dots or musical tones—and asked them to describe what they saw or heard (again, much like the "introspective" techniques used by the structuralists). From their data, gestalt psychologists developed principles related to the perception of wholes. These researchers had much in common with those who take a direct perspective on perception (McBurney & Collings, 1984). They believed that the brain automatically gives form to sensory data based on the perceptual principles by which it operates.

Some of these rules are referred to as principles of perceptual grouping and are illustrated in Figure 4-19. In Drawing A, dots of equal size are spaced evenly across a field, so that we perceive no distinguishing pattern. In Drawing B, the spacing between the dots has been changed so that we see them as four parallel lines. This effect demonstrates the principle of **proximity:** stimuli that are close together, either spatially or temporally, tend to be perceived as a group. In Drawing C, the dots in Drawing B have been slightly rearranged so that we perceive two curved lines. In this case the principle of **continuity** overrules the influence of proximity: dots that form a single, continuous grouping are seen as a gestalt. Another organizing principle, illustrated in Drawing D, is **similarity.** Here we perceive an X in the same pattern of dots as in Drawing A, because the dots that form the X are of a similar color.

Although contemporary psychologists acknowledge the importance of gestalt principles of perception, many feel that the early gestalt psychologists underestimated the extent to which prior knowledge shapes the way we organize sensory data. For instance, it may surprise you to learn that your perception of the gestalt in Figure 4-18 is influenced by your prior knowledge of and experience with triangles. If the subjective figure in the middle were instead some unusual shape, your brain would have much more trouble creating a whole from the disparate parts (Wallach & Slaughter, 1988) Try it with the drawings in Figure 4-20.

Another example of how bottom-up and top-down processing combine to give us form perception can be seen in our division of stimuli into figure and ground. When we look at most scenes, we automatically separate regions that represent objects, or figures, from regions that represent the spaces between objects, or the ground. This ability to distinguish objects from space does not depend entirely on

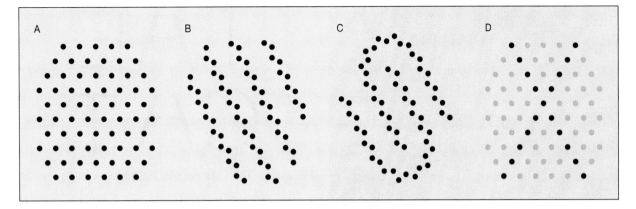

FIGURE 4-19   A demonstration of some of the gestalt principles of grouping. The pattern of equally spaced identical dots in (A) is not easily organized. It is seen either as an undifferentiated field or as a set of unstable overlapping patterns. In (B) a stable perception of parallel lines emerges because of the proximity of some dots to others. When some of these lines are made continuous with one another in (C), dots that are physically quite distant from one another are seen as belonging to a single curved line. In (D) a stable organization suddenly emerges because some of the dots have been made similar to one another and different from the rest.

past experience. When people who have been blind from birth are given sight through surgery, they are quickly able to separate figure from ground (Senden, 1960). But when stimuli are ambiguous, experience in the process helps. For instance, your knowledge of what a vase and a human profile look like is enormously helpful to you in perceiving the two images in Figure 4-21. Likewise, the illusion in Figure 4-22 depends on your knowledge of written English. Readers of English (and similar languages) have no trouble perceiving the ambiguous letter in the top row as "H" and the ambiguous letter in the bottom

as "A." However, someone who cannot read would see the two middle stimuli as identical (which in fact they are).

Perceptual Constancy

When the sun sets and casts a rosy light on the world, you do not see trees and grass as suddenly turning reddish. Likewise, when you walk out of the sunshine into the shadow of a building, your skin does not suddenly look gray. Instead, you tend to ignore such temporary changes in color in favor of a view of the world that is constant and predictable.

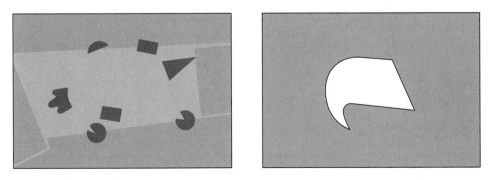

FIGURE 4-20   This figure is constructed very similarly to Figure 4-18, but here you probably do not see clear subjective contours. The reason is that the form in the middle (clearly shown in the right panel) is an unusual shape, one you are not as accustomed to seeing as a triangle. Consequently, your brain has trouble creating a whole from the various parts. (After Wallace & Slaughter, 1988.)

FIGURE 4-21   *Is this a white vase against a black background or two black facing profiles against a white background? Depending on your perspective, it may be either, and most people can easily switch from one perspective to the other—although you will be unable to perceive both the vase and the faces simultaneously. This demonstrates the relationship between figure and ground. If you look closely at the image, you may notice that the vase is slightly asymmetrical; the profiles are of Queen Elizabeth and Prince Philip, who were given this vase as an anniversary gift.*

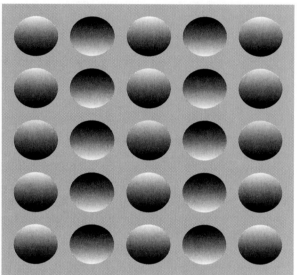

FIGURE 4-22   *Can you read these two words?*

FIGURE 4-23   *The positioning of light and shadow is an important clue to depth. The spheres in the left, right, and middle columns look like bulges, while those in the other two columns look like hollows. Now try turning the book upside down. The former bulges now become recessed, and the former hollows now protrude. These striking changes in depth perception are caused by a shift in shading from the bottom to the top of a sphere, and vice versa. (After Sekuler & Blake, 1990.)*

Similarly, although the image of a departing car rapidly becomes smaller, you do not perceive the car as shrinking; nor when it turns a corner and you see it from the side instead of the rear do you think it has changed shape (see Figure 4-23). How does your brain maintain such perceptual constancies in a world of ever-changing stimuli?

Let us consider size constancy as an example. An object's distance and the size of the image it projects on the retina are inversely related: the greater the distance, the smaller the image. Furthermore, the ratio is one to one. The brain takes these facts into account when judging true size. Thus, if a tree 200 feet away looks half the size of one that is 100 feet away, a person will automatically perceive them as being of equal height.

But this perceptual process can operate effectively only if distance cues are clear. If they are not, a person can easily be fooled. One of the more powerful illusions involving size cues is the moon illusion, in which the moon appears to be much larger when it is on the horizon than when it is directly overhead (see Figure 4-24). Though the precise causes of this illusion are still being debated (e. g., Baird, Wagner, & Fuld, 1990; Plug & Ross, 1994; Reed & Krupinski, 1992), clearly the effect of relative size plays a role. On the horizon, the moon can be compared to trees, buildings, and other objects. We know those objects are large, and we know how distant they are. The moon is about the same size on the retina, but we know it is much farther away. If two objects are of the same retinal size, but one is perceived as being more distant, then the more distant one will appear to be larger. Hence the moon appears larger because we can easily compare it to the size of trees and buildings. When the moon is directly overhead, however, we lose the ability to make quick judgments about its relative size: there is nothing in the sky to which we can compare it! Thus the moon appears smaller.

The effects of relative size work in reverse, too: if an object is not the size you expect it to be, you can easily misjudge its distance. The Allies took advantage of this fact during their invasion of Normandy in World War II. In the early morning twilight they dropped 2-foot-tall dummies of paratroopers onto fields away from the planned coastal landing site. When the dummies hit the ground, the impact set off a series of small explosions, simulating rifle fire. In the poor light and general confusion, the Germans thought the dummies were real paratroopers attacking at a substantial distance. Only when they moved close enough to see the dummies did they realize that their size had misled them. In the meantime, the Allies had gained extra time for their landing.

Depth Perception

What the Allies actually did with their 2-foot dummies was to exploit the influence of relative size on *depth perception,* the ability to tell how far away an object is. Because the images that are cast on the retina are two-dimensional rather than three-dimensional, depth perception cannot be explained by the eye's structure. Like perceptual constancy, it must result from the way the brain organizes and gives meaning to sensory information. Given the two-dimensional input, the brain uses a number of processes to perceive depth. First, the brain receives visual input from two eyes rather than one. Since the eyes are set apart from each other, each views the

world from a slightly different angle, sending slightly different images to the two retinas. This difference in retinal images is called **binocular disparity.** The brain uses the disparity to judge distance and to create a sense of depth.

Two eyes are not necessary to the perception of depth. Several **monocular depth cues**—that is, cues that are potentially available to one eye only—augment depth perception. One of those cues is **motion parallax,** the difference in the relative movement of a retinal image that occurs when we change position. An easy way to demonstrate motion parallax is to look toward two objects, one very near you and the other some distance away, and move your head back and forth. The near object will seem to move more than the far one. This cue explains the odd perception you may have as you look out the side window of a moving car. Nearby trees seem to zip by, but distant mountains appear to move hardly at all. The brain uses such differences in the apparent movement of near and far objects to perceive depth.

Other monocular depth cues do not depend on movement. One that was mentioned earlier is **relative size.** When you think two objects are the same size, you perceive the one that casts the smaller retinal image to be farther away. **Relative closeness** to the horizon is also a monocular depth cue: objects that are closer to the horizon are generally seen as more distant. Still another monocular cue is **linear perspective,** which is produced by the apparent convergence of parallel lines as they recede into the distance. This cue is the source of the "vanishing point" you may remember from art class. A roadway appears to recede in the distance as the spaces between its edges decrease. Ultimately the two edges converge, creating the impression of great distance.

Texture gradients also influence depth perception. In a highly textured scene, near objects will appear coarser, more distant ones, finer. Then, too, we judge distance by the **partial overlap** of objects. When one object appears to cover another, we perceive the object that is covered as being farther away. Light and shadow give a sense of depth as well. In Figure 4-23, the spheres in the left, right, and middle columns seem to bulge out, while those in the other two columns appear to be sunken. These differing perceptions of depth are caused by differences in the way shadows are drawn. Your brain assumes that lighting comes from above, as light from the sun does (Ramachandran, 1988). So when the bottom of

A

an object is in shadow, you see it as projecting forward; conversely, when the top is in shadow, you see it as recessed.

Illusions

Usually our perceptual processes serve us quite well. But when they are applied in unusual circumstances, they can sometimes give rise to **perceptual illusions,** that is, perceptions that differ from the true characteristics of objects. Illusions of this sort provide important insights into the way our perceptual processes normally operate. Recall Recurring Theme 2: we learn about normal functioning by studying those cases in which functioning is abnormal.

THEME Psychologists Learn about the Normal by Studying the Abnormal

To illustrate, examine the room shown in Figure 4-24, which is known as the *Ames room* after its inventor, Adelbert Ames. Using one eye only, viewers peer into the room through a small hole in the front wall, thus eliminating the depth cues provided by binocular disparity. Since viewers cannot move their position, depth cues from motion parallax are also eliminated. What observers see is astonishing: a dwarf seems to be standing side by side with a giant. Logically, most people know that this is an illusion. But what gives rise to it?

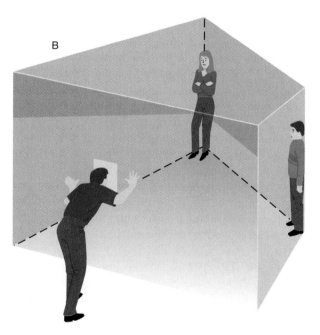

B

FIGURE 4-24 *The Ames room. The illusion, shown in the photo above, is produced by trapezoidal windows that run parallel to the sloping floor, making the room look rectangular. The diagram above shows the actual construction of the room compared to the way it is perceived. The brain infers that the two people are standing at the same distance from the eye, and interprets the difference in the size of their images as a real difference in size.*

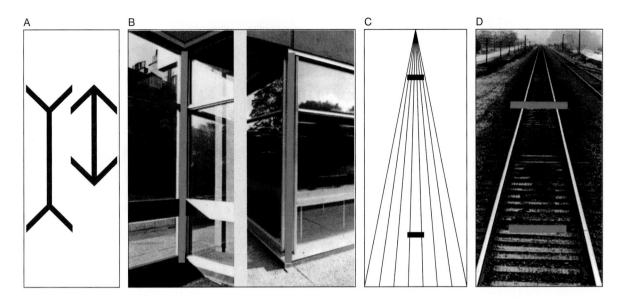

FIGURE 4-25   Two famous illusions. The vertical lines of the figures in the Muller-Lyer illusion (A) are identical in length, but they do not appear to be. An explanation for this illusion, suggested in (B), is that the arrow marking on the lines in (A) causes you to perceive them as three-dimensional objects that have corners. The corners seem to induce a size constancy effect: the vertical line that appears to be distant is perceived as larger. The horizontal lines in the Ponzo illusion (C) are also identical in length. As the photograph in (D) suggests, this figure, too, could easily be perceived as three-dimensional, and again size constancy would cause the apparently more distant "object" to be scaled up in an apparent size relative to the "nearer object." (After Gregory, 1970.)

The answer involves the lack of depth cues. Because viewers are using only one eye and cannot move, they must rely mainly on linear perspective to judge the shape and depth of the room. However, their linear perspective is distorted by the way the "windows" are painted on the rear wall. Though the windows are really trapezoids (taller on the left side than on the right), they appear to be rectangular because they are parallel to an angled rear wall and a downward-sloping floor. So viewers get the impression of a rectangular room in which two people stand at an equal distance from the peephole. This illusion does not involve a breakdown of the normal powers of perception. Instead, normal perceptual processes are applied to a stimulus purposely designed to produce perceptual error. To understand this important point more fully, study Figure 4-25, which demonstrates two other vivid illusions apparently caused by a misapplication of normal perceptual processes.

Illusions like these are of more than theoretical interest. They can be purposefully applied in practical situations to create a desired effect. For example, a motorist driving at a constant speed over evenly spaced horizontal lines will become accustomed to the constant amount of time it takes to drive from one line to the next. If the lines are then spaced progressively closer together, the motorist will experience the illusion of increased speed, even though the car has not accelerated (Denton, 1971). This trick has been used to encourage drivers to slow down as they leave high-speed roads or approach toll booths.

Development of Perceptual Processes

How did you come to perceive the world as you do? What factors led you to organize your perceptual environment according to the principles just described? Historically, there have been two schools of thought on this question. The first, called the **empiricist view,** holds that perceptual processes are largely a matter of learning. Babies enter the world with little or no ability to see form, depth, perceptual constancies, and so forth. To them the world is "one great blooming, buzzing confusion," as psychologist William James (1890/1950) once put it. Only gradually do infants learn adultlike perceptions on the basis of cues the environment provides.

In contrast, the **nativist view** of perceptual development maintains that learning alone cannot explain all perceptual processes; perception arises as well from the way our sensory systems work. These two views are closely related to the two general perspectives on perception mentioned earlier. The empiricist view is linked to the indirect (constructivist) perspective that knowledge must be imposed on sensory data in order to organize it. The nativist view is tied to the direct perspective, with its stress on the automatic structuring of sensory information.

One way psychologists have attempted to address this question is to look at the perceptual capabilities of newborn (or very young) infants. How much do infants perceive? It now appears that the infant's world is not a world of "blooming, buzzing confusion." Infants apparently come into the world with more sophisticated perceptual skills than James thought. As we will see in Chapter 9, Baillargeon, Kotovsky, and Needham (1995) have presented evidence that infants even have some basic reasoning skills about the simple laws of motion. Not all developmental psychologists agree with this assessment, though (Cohen, 1996).

Most contemporary psychologists believe that neither the empiricist nor the nativist viewpoint is adequate in itself. Like virtually every other aspect of human behavior, perceptual processes result from an interaction of inherited biological factors and specific learning experiences. Thus what we see, hear, and feel is partly the result of how our sensory systems are programmed and partly the result of what we have learned.

Expectations and Perception

Have you ever awakened in a dark hotel room and for a moment or two experienced a helpless feeling of utter confusion? You could see a light on a desktop, perhaps, but nothing was familiar to you. What was the object at the foot of the bed? What was the strange hum coming from the next room? Fortunately, within a few seconds, you remembered where you were. That realization allowed you to make sense of the initially confusing stimuli.

Learning and experience guide our expectations about the world. Those expectations in turn influence our perception. In this section, we will take a closer look at some of the ways in which learning and experience mold our expectations, which in turn

FIGURE 4-26   *Perceptual set. Most people see this well-known reversible figure as a rabbit. When they shift their attention to the left side of the figure, the image changes into a bird.*

shape our perceptions. Two important concepts involved in this process are perceptual set and schema.

Expectations Based on Perceptual Set

Look at Figure 4-26, which is a drawing of a rabbit. *Does* it look like a rabbit to you? Most people answer "yes" without hesitation, but look again. Does your perception of the image change? Do the rabbit's ears now become a bird's beak? This example illustrates the concept of **perceptual set**–a frame of mind that prepares a person to perceive images in a certain way. Perceptual sets establish expectations that guide our perceptions. We perceive what we think we should perceive.

A perceptual set can arise from what other people tell us, or it can stem from our own experiences or desires. Context is one factor that can lead us to perceive an image in a particular way, as we saw in Figure 4-22 ("THE CAT"). Though context can greatly influence our perceptions, it does so with little awareness on our part. Many professors are grateful for the existence of contextual effects on perception: the notes they write on the chalkboard would be impossible to understand without them.

Expectations Based on Schemas

General knowledge of the world also shapes our expectations, and hence what we perceive. Irving Biederman and his colleagues have been intrigued by how quickly subjects can process the information in photos of real-world scenes like a city street, a kitchen, or the top of someone's desk (Biederman, Glass, & Stacy, 1973; Biederman et al., 1974). When people view these scenes for just a tenth of a second, they can remember almost half the objects in them. How is this rapid visual processing accomplished? Is perception really that automatic and instantaneous? Apparently it is not, for when the pictures are cut into six equal pieces and randomly rearranged, subjects are much slower at processing what they see. They have trouble both identifying the objects in the pictures and remembering them when the pictures are removed. In this case, even though the individual stimuli were still present, the rearrangement of the pieces prevented subjects from using the appropriate schema.

Biederman also discovered that schemas and the expectations they trigger can prompt people to overlook things that do not belong in a scene (Biederman et al., 1981; Biederman, Mezzanotte, & Rabinowitz, 1982). To test this process, take a quick look at Figure 4-27 to see if you can spot anything odd about it.

FIGURE 4-27 *In this drawing, the presence of the floating sofa is inconsistent with the natural relations among the rest of the objects.* (From Biederman et al., 1982.)

With only a quick glance, most people do not perceive the sofa in the upper right-hand corner. Their expectations affect what they see—or, in this case, do not see.

In Depth

Can We Perceive without Awareness?

SO FAR WE have assumed perception is generally conscious, and that people are aware of what they perceive. But is conscious perception the only kind of perception humans are capable of? Is it possible that humans can detect very fleeting or faint stimuli subconsciously? This question brings us to the topic of **subliminal perception,** the brain's ability to register a stimulus presented so briefly or weakly that it cannot be consciously perceived. Subliminal perception is controversial, as you will discover when you read about it in depth.

Initial Studies

In the summer of 1957 a marketing executive named James Vicary conducted a six-week study that would soon ignite an explosion of interest in subliminal perception. The site of the study was an unimposing movie theater in Fort Lee, New Jersey, just across the Hudson River from New York City. What Vicary did was very simple—some might think ludicrous. He superimposed on the feature film some verbal messages that appeared so briefly, they could not be consciously detected. One message commanded "Eat popcorn," while another urged "Drink Coke." According to Vicary, popcorn sales rose an impressive 58 percent, and Coke sales rose a respectable 18 percent (Morse & Stoller, 1982).

Vicary's study made national headlines. Many people were outraged at the underhanded practices, but others couldn't resist testing their own subliminal messages (Moore, 1982). One radio station in Seattle launched a subliminal campaign against its arch rival, television, by broadcasting such subaudible slurs as "TV's a bore." A few department stores in Toronto even played subliminal antishoplifting messages over their public address systems. As shoppers browsed through kitchenware and tried on shoes, a subaudible voice repeatedly warned them, "If you steal, you'll get caught."

Psychologists were fascinated. Was subliminal perception possible, and could it actually influence behavior? Conducting controlled experiments was the best way to answer these intriguing questions. One of the earliest experiments was conducted by William Bevan (1964). Bevan gave subjects mild electric shocks and asked them to judge their severity. If he administered brief subliminal shocks before a test shock, subjects tended to describe the test shock as significantly stronger, as if they were subconsciously adding the subliminal shocks to the test shock and reporting the combined sensation. Other psychologists gathered additional data suggesting that subliminal perception might be possible in certain situations. For instance, when signal detection researchers asked subjects to express their degree of confidence that a very weak stimulus had or had not been presented, they found that a person's confidence was directly related to the intensity of the stimulus—even stimuli they did not detect (Green & Swets, 1966; Swets, 1961). On some level, therefore, subjects must have registered the "undetected" stimuli.

Still more support for subliminal perception came from work by Robert Zajonc and his colleagues. In one study they took advantage of the fact that repeated exposure to a stimulus often breeds a liking for it, an effect we will investigate further in Chapter 16. The experimenters presented subjects with polygons of various shapes, each for only a thousandth of a second. Later they showed the subjects the same polygons along with new ones, giving them as long as necessary to rate how much they liked each and whether they recognized it. Most subjects tended to like the polygons that had been seen before better than the ones they had never seen, a phenomenon known as the "mere exposure effect." That is, they tended to like the stimuli they had seen, *even if they could not consciously recognize the stimuli* (Kunst-Wilson & Zajonc, 1980). Once again, it appeared that people do process subliminal information at some level.

The most recent evidence that subliminal perception is sometimes possible comes from studies based on so-called priming effects. Suppose you are shown the word *doctor,* preceded by another word known as the prime. If the prime is related to the word *doctor* (for example, *nurse*), you will be able to recognize that *doctor* is a meaningful word more quickly than if it were unrelated (see Till, Mross, & Kintsch, 1988).

Do advertisers deliberately embed subliminal messages in their advertising? If so, does it have any effect on consumer behavior? Most psychologists are skeptical.

Some researchers have tried masking the prime, that is, interrupting a brief presentation of the prime with randomly arranged letters, so that subjects cannot reliably say what the prime is (Cheseman & Merikle, 1985; Marcel, 1983). Yet even when the prime is masked, and subjects say they cannot read it, they will still process a second word more quickly when the prime is related to it. The subjects appear to perceive the prime on a subliminal level.

It is one thing to say that subliminal perception can occur and quite another to assert that such perceptions can change behavior. What evidence is there that subliminal messages can prompt people to do things they otherwise would not? One of the few early studies to support this view was conducted by Marvin Zuckerman (1960). Zuckerman displayed a series of thirty pictures to subjects and asked them to write descriptive stories about the pictures. For the first ten pictures, experimental and control subjects were treated exactly alike: the pictures were presented one by one, and subjects wrote a story after

viewing each one. This procedure established a baseline writing level for each. Then, for the experimental subjects (but not the controls), Zuckerman accompanied the next ten pictures with the subliminal message "Write more." Finally, the experimental subjects received the subliminal instruction "Don't write" with the last ten pictures. Zuckerman found that the experimental subjects did write more than their baseline levels after receiving the subliminal "Write more" and decreased the amount of their writing slightly after receiving the "Don't write" message. He concluded that the experimental subjects had indeed followed his subliminal directives.

Criticisms, Alternatives, and Further Research

Other psychologists were not ready to accept the power of subliminal messages, however. They pointed out that Zuckerman's results could be interpreted in other ways (Moore, 1982). From the beginning, the experimental subjects had been more enthusiastic writers than the control subjects. During the baseline trials, they spontaneously wrote much more about each picture than those in the control group. Later, when the subliminal message "Write more" was presented to them, they did increase their output, but so did control subjects who did not receive the message. The fact that the experimental subjects increased their writing more than the control subjects may simply have been due to a natural enthusiasm for writing. Finally, the small drop in output that the experimental subjects showed when they were given the subliminal message "Don't write" may have been due merely to fatigue. In short, Zuckerman's findings do not strongly support the hypothesis that subliminal instructions can direct behavior. Zuckerman's results have not been replicated by other researchers.

What about the Vicary study mentioned earlier? Did it provide convincing evidence that people sometimes do what subliminal messages tell them? The answer here is "no, not really." If you look carefully at the study's design, you will find it has serious flaws. Many factors that could have influenced the results were not controlled. Perhaps other factors were systematically influencing Coke and popcorn sales. Maybe the weather got hotter and people grew more thirsty. Or perhaps the movies were lengthy, so that people simply got hungrier as they watched. If so, purchases of Coke and popcorn might have risen for reasons that had nothing to do with Vicary's subliminal ads. Since Vicary apparently made no effort to take other influences into account, we cannot conclude that subliminal advertising caused the reported effects.

Patterns and Conclusions

From all the studies that have been conducted to date, what can we conclude about the effectiveness of subliminal messages? First, under certain carefully controlled laboratory conditions, people may sometimes perceive without conscious awareness (Kihlstrom, 1987). Most natural settings, however, do not meet the conditions needed for subliminal perception. For one thing, individuals' sensory thresholds vary considerably, so that finding a stimulus intensity that will be below threshold for an entire group, yet not so far below that it will have no effect, is difficult. In addition, displaying subliminal stimuli in a barrage of consciously perceived ones is not easy. On a motion picture screen, for instance, the ongoing movie will almost inevitably overpower fleeting subliminal advertisement (Dixon, 1971). The same seems to be true of subliminal audio messages meant to instill desirable behaviors (such as assertiveness, self-control, or improved reading skills). When such messages are embedded in consciously heard sounds, including music and the sound of breaking waves, subjects do not perceive them (Merikle, 1988; Moore, 1995). In television advertising, Smith and Rogers (1994) found no evidence that subliminal messages influenced behavior. In one fascinating large-scale study (Underwood, 1994) the British Broadcasting Corporation (BBC) displayed subliminally a picture of a smiling face to viewers in one region. Later, the network showed a picture of an expressionless face to all viewers and asked them to judge its mood. Viewers who had been subliminally exposed to the picture of the smiling face were more likely to describe the neutral face as *sad!*

There is virtually no evidence that subliminal messages can get people to do things they would not ordinarily do (Moore, 1988). Events that do not reach the level of conscious awareness may doubtless influence our behavior (Jacoby & Kelley, 1992). As Erdelyi (1992) states, "The capacity of subliminal perception should not be confused with the capacity of subliminal (unconscious) memory and cognition" (p. 747). But the common fear of subliminal messages in advertising—the fear that advertisers can manipulate viewers or listeners into buying certain products by broadcasting undetected messages—is exaggerated.

SUMMARY

1. **Sensation** is the process whereby stimulation of receptor cells in various parts of the body sends nerve impulses to the brain, where they register as a touch, a sound, a taste, a splash of color, and so forth. **Perception** is the process whereby the brain interprets the sensations it receives, giving them order and meaning.

2. Sensations and perceptions are not exact representations of the physical world. Instead, they are products of our particular sensory systems coupled with our beliefs, experiences, and expectations. Because of this, psychologists have spent a great deal of time studying the relationship between the physical properties of **stimuli** and their corresponding perceptions.

3. The sensation of sight begins when light waves pass through the eye's **cornea, iris, pupil,** and **lens** and strike the light-sensitive surface called the **retina** at the back of the eyeball. Here receptor cells convert light energy into nerve impulses, which travel via the **optic nerve** to the brain, where they give rise to the perceptions of shape, color, depth, texture, movement, and so forth.

4. There are two kinds of receptors in the retina, rods and cones. Both convert light into electrical signals by means of light-sensitive pigments. **Rods** mediate vision in situations with low light and lead to images that are less detailed and lacking in color. **Cones** require higher intensities of light to function, and they provide more detailed images, as well as the perception of color. Cones contain three different forms of pigment, each maximally sensitive to light of different wavelengths. According to the **trichromatic** theory of color vision, the many colors we see are caused by different relative activations of these three types of cones. This explanation alone, however, has proved to be incomplete. Investigators have also found that nerve cells in the visual system respond in

an opponent on-off fashion to complementary color pairs. These cells provide support for what is called the **opponent-process theory** of color vision.

5. Sound waves travel down the **auditory canal** to the **eardrum,** which vibrates in response to changes in air pressure. Its movements set in motion three tiny bones—called the **malleus, incus,** and **stapes**—which amplify the pressure eventually exerted on the **oval window** leading to the inner ear. Within the inner ear's spiral-shaped **cochlea** are thousands of receptors called **hair cells,** which trigger nerve impulses when they are bent and rubbed by movement of the **basilar membrane.** These impulses then travel via the **auditory nerve** to the brain, where the perception of sound occurs.

6. The perception of pitch is related to the frequency of sound waves. According to the **place theory,** each pitch depends on which part of the basilar membrane a given sound wave vibrates the most. According to the **frequency theory,** pitch depends on the patterns with which auditory nerve cells fire, these patterns presumably matching the frequencies of the original sound waves. Both these theories seem to have merit, and pitch perception is thought to involve elements of both.

7. The **somatic** senses are those responsible for sensations of the skin (the **cutaneous** senses); detecting the movement in the body, especially the limbs (the **kinesthetic** senses); and awareness of body and limb position (the **proprioceptive** senses). The cutaneous senses include touch, pressure, warmth, cold, and pain. Understanding how pain is perceived is particularly difficult, both because it can sometimes arise with no physiological cause, and because thoughts and emotions can greatly affect the perception of it. The **gate-control theory** of pain holds that gate cells in the spinal cord

serve to block or release the transmission of pain messages to the brain.

8. The senses of smell and taste are closely linked. Smell, or **olfaction,** occurs when vaporized molecules of a substance enter the nasal passages and contact receptor cells in the olfactory membranes, which in turn send neural messages to the brain. Different areas of the tongue are especially sensitive to one or more of the four basic taste categories we perceive: sweet, sour, salty, and bitter. Taste buds, grouped on the upper surface of the tongue in hill-like projections called **papillae,** contain receptor cells connected to nerve fibers that carry taste information to the brain. Although our other senses are not as closely interconnected as smell and taste, we nevertheless are constantly integrating information from them.

9. The **direct perspective** of perception emphasizes the contribution of the sensory data themselves and is closely related to "bottom-up" or **data-driven processing.** In contrast, the so-called **indirect perspective** or constructivist view holds that only sensory cues about the environment are processed directly, and these must be supplemented with additional information stored in memory. **Perceptual constancy** is the tendency to see objects as having stable properties even though the visual information we receive about them is constantly changing. The eye is capable of **depth perception,** generating three-dimensional views of the world, though the images that strike our retinas have only two dimensions. Depth is perceived partly as a result of **binocular disparity. Monocular depth cues** include **motion parallax, relative size, relative closeness** to the horizon, **linear perspective, texture gradient,** the **partial overlap** of objects, and light and shadow.

10. When perceptual processes are applied in unusual circumstances, they can sometimes give rise to **perceptual illusions.** Such illusions provide important insights into the way our perceptual processes normally work.

11. People have long been fascinated by **subliminal perception**—the apparent ability of the brain to register a stimulus presented so briefly or weakly that it cannot be consciously perceived. There is evidence that, in carefully created laboratory situations, subliminal perception may in fact occur. But the ability of such perceptions to influence behavior is very much in doubt.

SUGGESTED READINGS

Cytowic, R. E. (1993). *The man who tasted shapes: A bizarre medical mystery offers revolutionary insights into emotions, reasoning, and consciousness.* NY: Putnam. Cytowic, a neurologist, discusses the case of a man who tasted shapes (an example of synesthesia, literally a mixing of senses). He later interacted with dozens of synesthetes over a ten-year period and reevaluates some basic human beliefs in light of these individuals.

Hubel, D. H. (1995). *Eye, brain, and vision.* New York: Scientific American Books. David Hubel, a Nobel prize winner, writes about current knowledge of vision, and explores the tasks scientists face in deciphering the many remaining mysteries of vision and the workings of the human brain. He pays special attention to color vision, face recognition, and development of the visual system, including the effects of early visual experiences.

Rock, I. (Ed.). (1990). *The perceptual world: Readings from* Scientific American. San Francisco: Freeman. This collection of articles (some fairly technical) highlights important research developments in visual perception, from discoveries of specific brain mechanisms to the nature of illusions and computer simulation of vision.

Sacks, O. (Sacks, 1989). *Seeing voices: A journey into the world of the deaf.* New York: Harper Perennial. An intimate portrait of the experiences of the deaf, this book will challenge hearing readers' misperceptions and help them gain a new understanding and appreciation of what the deaf encounter.

Sekuler, R., & Blake, R. (1994). *Perception* (3rd ed.). New York: McGraw-Hill. A very readable text that stresses vision and hearing, but covers smell and taste as well.

CHAPTER 5

The Nature of Consciousness

Consciousness: Three Case Histories

D. B. is a middle-aged man, born in a small market town in England in 1940. During his teenage years he began to suffer headaches. The headaches were unusually intense, and they had an odd prelude: before they began, D. B. would see flashes of light in a small, oval-shaped portion of his left visual field. During the next few minutes, the oval would grow larger. About fifteen minutes later, the flashing lights would stop, and the oval in D. B.'s visual field would become blind. Soon after, intense headaches would begin on the right side of his head, often followed by nausea and vomiting. The headaches sometimes lasted as long as forty-eight hours, while D. B. tried to sleep. After the attacks D. B. would awaken to find the headache gone and his vision restored. They recurred every six weeks or so until D. B. reached his mid-twenties.

The attacks became more frequent—occurring every three weeks—and more severe. When D. B. was twenty-six, doctors discovered a tumor (described as a "tortuous mass of enlarged vessels off the cortex" [Weiskrantz, 1986]) in his right occipital cortex. As we learned in Chapter 3, the occipital cortex is critically involved in vision. Removing the tumor would likely cause permanent blindness.

Several medical procedures were tried on D. B., but none proved successful. As a last resort, a neurosurgeon removed the diseased portion of D. B.'s brain, which included a section of the right occipital lobe known as the *striate cortex*. The surgery successfully relieved D. B.'s headaches, but left him blind in his left *visual field*. (Remember that the brain operates *contralaterally*; the left visual field projects to the right hemisphere.) The physicians tested D. B.'s vision thoroughly and confirmed his blindness.

Several years later, D. B. telephoned to say he was seeing flashing lights in his blind visual field. He was quickly readmitted to the hospital and thoroughly tested. During the testing, one of the surgeons at the hospital noticed something odd. Despite D. B.'s reports that he could see nothing, he performed better on some tests of vision than might have been expected. If someone moved an outstretched arm toward him, he seemed to reach for it accurately—despite the fact that he could not "see it."

One of the tests showed a line that was either vertical or horizontal. When it was shown to D. B.'s right visual field (the one with normal vision), D. B. identified its orientation every time, as expected. When shown to D. B.'s left visual field (the blind one), D. B. reported seeing nothing. Finally researchers showed the lines to D. B.'s blind field and asked him to "guess" whether the line was horizontal or vertical. D. B. shrugged and complied, all the while saying he was just guessing and insisting that he could see nothing. *D. B. made almost no mistakes.* After a long series of trials, D. B. was told how well he had performed:

"Did you know how well you had done?" he was asked. "No," he replied, "I didn't—because I couldn't see anything; I couldn't see a darn thing." "Can you say how you guessed—what was it that allowed you to say whether it was vertical or horizontal?" "No, I could not because I did not see anything; I just don't know." Finally, he was asked, "So you really did not know you were getting them right?" "No," he replied, still with something of an air of incredulity.

Larry Weiskrantz, *Blindsight*, 1986, p. 24

Larry Weiskrantz has studied D. B. and others like him, who manifest what Weiskrantz calls "blindsight." How can someone who is "blind" see well enough to respond correctly on a visual test? And why was D. B. unaware of his ability?

. . . When she was brought into the emergency room of Community General Hospital, she looked like someone who had just come face to face with some unspeakable evil . . . the questions being put to Helen by the people around her were of little importance compared to the chaos that was exploding inside her head. "Helen?" White Coat was speaking. "Helen, I'm Dr. Walsh. Can you hear me? Helen, can you tell me what the trouble is?"

She knew that White Coat was speaking to her. She was even vaguely aware that he might be able to help. . . . She tried to concentrate on the voice. She knew it belonged to White Coat, but it didn't seem to be coming from White Coat. . . . It seemed like a puff of air whose effect is constantly diminished as it proceeds outward from its source.

Finally, it didn't seem to matter. The blowing and whistling noises . . . sprang out of a constant, dull background roar to assault her. . . . And flashing lights, like the rushing wind, were creating a disturbance inside her head. This started as a minor annoyance. Now they were terrifying . . . threatening to explode out of her head and into the room. . . .

"Stop the lights!" she screamed, pounding her temples with her fists. "Please! Please, stop the lights!"

"Helen," [White Coat] said more firmly now, "tell me what the lights are like."

Without warning, Helen's body straightened on the edge of the table, her eyes rolled back in their sockets, she expelled air forcefully from her lungs in a kind of muted cry, and before anyone could prevent it, she catapulted off the examination table and crashed to the floor, where she lay thrashing in a paroxysm of violent contractions.

"Grand mal! Grand mal!"

"Seizure!"

"Somebody get her tongue!". . .

After about 30 minutes, most of Helen's physical symptoms had disappeared. Her blood pressure returned to near normal limits; her fever had declined to 100 degrees; her heart rate was down to 95 beats per minute. Helen's mental status showed gradual improvement during this period. She was considerably less agitated, although she remained quite confused and disoriented. . . .

While a definitive diagnosis would have to wait until the completion of a history and the results of various lab tests, [Dr. Walsh's] tentative diagnosis was quite clear in his mind: his patient was suffering from a toxic reaction to cocaine.

(J. C. Flynn, *Cocaine*, pp. 1–6)

Dr. B is a professor of psychology and neuroscience at a medium-sized university in Texas. He was trained as a biologically oriented psychologist, and he has been the director of his university's doctoral program in neuroscience. In short, he is a confirmed reductionist, looking to the brain and nervous system to explain all behavior.

When Dr. B was a child, he broke several teeth in a playground accident. As a result, he had a significant amount of dental work done. To hear Dr. B describe it, the dentist that treated him was every child's nightmare: a cruel, sadistic individual, much like the dentist played by Steve Martin in the comedy *Little Shop of Horrors*. Worst of all, Dr. B remembers, were the Novocain injections, given with a long, gleaming silver needle.

So aversive were those experiences—particularly the injections—that as a young adult Dr. B began requesting that dentists treat him without Novocain or other local anesthetics. Almost by accident, he found that by concentrating on the "intellectual" side of the pain (and therefore ignoring the "affective" component), he could tolerate virtually all dental work without anesthesia.

About fifteen years ago, when Dr. B was in his mid-thirties, he began to study hypnotism in a formal sense. He attended workshops designed to teach the use of hypnosis in pain control. Initially a skeptic, he soon became convinced that the techniques would work not just for him but for others, including his own children. (Dr. B tells of his own daughter being hypnotized during a workshop. She was told to "watch imaginary cartoons" by the hypnotist, a pediatric dentist. According to Dr. B, she was so engrossed in these "cartoons," she laughed out loud. Nothing seemed to disrupt her "cartoon" watching—even when the dentist drove a surgical needle through her upper gums, all the way to the bone. Neither she nor any of the other children who were "watching cartoons" so much as flinched.)

Dr. B continues to practice self-hypnosis. He has become more and more skilled at reducing the "emotional" aspects of pain, though he reports complete awareness of it. The technique is so effective that a few years ago Dr. B underwent a root canal—a complicated, lengthy, and painful dental procedure–*with no anesthesia.*

Each of these three cases provides dramatic insight into the phenomenon known as "consciousness" and offers a stark example of Recurring Theme 2, "Psychologists learn about the normal by studying the abnormal." By all accounts, D. B. is truly "blind" in one visual field. He *reports* he cannot see, and generally *behaves* as if he cannot. Under certain conditions, though, clearly he is not totally blind. But though his performance indicates some visual abilities, D. B. has no awareness of them, nor is he likely to gain an awareness. Can a person be said to "see" if that person has no consciousness of sight?

THEME 2 Psychologists Learn about the Normal by Studying the Abnormal

"Helen," the character whose story opens John Flynn's book *Cocaine*, is a fictitious composite. While she may not exist, thousands of people like her are seen in emergency rooms each year. Symptoms vary from case to case, but one striking similarity in all cases is the alteration and distortion of consciousness.

Finally, the example of Dr. B shows yet another aspect of consciousness, its alteration through hypnosis. Dr. B is a biologically oriented psychologist, firmly grounded in the notion that all thoughts, behaviors, and sensations arise from activity in the nervous system. Clearly, he sees his ability to dissociate himself from pain as neurologically based behavior. What is the explanation for it? How could hypnosis alter the sensation of pain so profoundly? Perhaps more important, is the painkilling effect of hypnosis within the grasp of most people?

If you have been reading closely, you have noticed that the word **consciousness** has been used a number of times already, yet it has not been defined. In truth, defining consciousness is tricky. Most psychologists would agree that it involves an active awareness of the many thoughts, images, perceptions, and emotions that occupy the mind at any given moment (Natsoulas, 1983) The psychologist William James (1842–1910) likened consciousness to a perpetually flowing stream, arguing forcefully that it "does not appear to itself chopped up in bits . . . let us call it the stream of thought" (James, 1890/1950). Today, when we talk about our "stream of consciousness" being broken, we retain James's insightful and colorful description.

Because consciousness is a subjective experience, early behaviorists thought that it had no place in psychology. Since we cannot objectively see into consciousness to measure and analyze it, they argued, it is not a proper subject for scientific study. Most contemporary psychologists disagree. In fact, John Kihlstrom, a renowned experimental psychologist at Yale, believes the study of consciousness is essential to psychology (e.g., Kihlstrom, 1992, 1993). As Kihlstrom points out, consciousness is central to human functioning. It allows us to monitor ourselves and our environments; it gives us a sense of continuity, a way of linking experience into a past, present, and future.

Ironically, consciousness is often better understood by looking at situations in which it has been *altered*—by drugs or hypnosis, for example—or even *removed*—by sleep, coma, or general anesthesia. In trying to define it, we might paraphrase Supreme Court Justice Potter Stewart's famous remark[1]: that while we may not be able to define consciousness, we know it when we see it.

---

[1]Of course, Potter's remarks were related to defining obscenity and pornography, not consciousness!

Even this most basic understanding of consciousness has problems, though. For example, we would not consider someone who is undergoing general anesthesia to be conscious. Furthermore, if we asked that person about her conscious recollections during the surgery, she would vigorously deny any awareness. Yet recent evidence indicates otherwise (Kihlstrom et al., 1990). Kihlstrom and his colleagues played a tape recording of a pair of related words to patients undergoing major surgery. The word pairs were repeated over and over through headphones that were placed on patients' heads *after they became unconscious.*

The word pairs were carefully constructed. Before the experiment, a different group of subjects had been given a cue word, such as *dog,* and asked to come up with the first word that came to mind, such as *cat.* (This is quite similar to the word association tests that were often administered by psychoanalysts during the early part of this century.) Kihlstrom and his associates took the most commonly generated word (called the "target" word) for each cue word, paired it with its cue, and recorded half of the pairs for presentation to anesthetized subjects during surgery. (The other words were not presented, so they could be used as a control or "baseline" measure.)

A week after the surgery, Kihlstrom and his colleague phoned the patients to tell them they had heard some words on tape while they were being operated on. They gave the patients the "cue" words, half of which had been played during surgery, and asked them:

- To recall all the "target" words they remembered hearing
- To recognize the target words among a list of distractors
- To provide the "first word that came to mind" when they were given a cue word

Not surprisingly, subjects were unable to recall or recognize the words they heard on tape. Their performance on recall and recognition tests was no different for word pairs they had heard than for word pairs they had not heard. However, when asked to perform the third task—given the cue word, produce the first word that comes to mind—their performance was remarkable: though all the subjects produced many of the target words (remember, the word pairs were constructed because of their associ-

ation), they were more able to produce words that had been presented during surgery. They displayed memory for the items, even though they were *unaware* of their memory.

In this chapter we will explore these and other issues related to consciousness. First, we will look at changes in consciousness that recur throughout the day (circadian rhythms) and night (the different stages of sleep). Then, we will examine induced states of consciousness, first the drug-induced states, then meditation and hypnosis. Finally, in the "In Depth" section we will explore aspects of consciousness that are best understood in their *absence:* case studies of individuals who have some sort of neurological impairment that alters the conscious components of their behavior while leaving others intact.

Cyclical States of Consciousness

Many human biological factors change predictably according to daily cycles called **circadian rhythms** (from the Latin *circa,* meaning "about," and *dies,* meaning "day"). For example, blood pressure, body temperature, and various chemical levels in the bloodstream all rise and fall in daily cycles. Consciousness too changes daily, according to a pattern called the *sleep-wake cycle.* Unaffected by external influences, especially day and night, this cycle spans about twenty-five hours (not the twenty-four hours it takes the earth to rotate on its axis). Thus when people are placed in windowless rooms, with no indications of sunrise and sunset, they tend to go to bed about an hour later each day (see Wever, 1979). Under normal conditions, however, they automatically reset their biological clocks to the twenty-four-hour light-dark cycle.

While this relatively minor adjustment is easy, larger adjustments can be more difficult. That is why when you travel by plane across several time zones, your sleep patterns may take a while to accommodate. It is also the reason why workers placed on rapidly rotating shifts (midnight to 8 a.m. one week, 4 p.m. to midnight the next week, 8 a.m. to 4 p.m. the following week) often complain of health problems, sleep disorders, and lower productivity (Czeisler, More-Ede, & Coleman, 1982). Recent research suggests that time shifts are more difficult to make if a person must go to bed and get up *earlier* (called a *phase advance*) instead of staying up *later* than usual (called a *phase delay*). That is, jet lag adjustments are

Employees who work rotating shifts often complain of health problems, sleep disorders, and lower productivity due to changes in their circadian rhythms.

usually more difficult for those flying from Los Angeles to New York (a phase advance) than for those flying from New York to Los Angeles (a phase delay). For this reason, when shift workers move from one shift to another, their schedules should be based on phase delays rather than phase advances. A worker will have an easier time moving from the 4 p.m. to midnight shift to the midnight to 8 a.m. shift than vice versa.

Recently the popular press has reported on melatonin, a hormone involved in circadian rhythms, claiming that it promotes sleep "safely," alleviates jet lag by resetting the body's internal clock, and even helps shift workers to adapt to new sleep-wake patterns. Though early reports appear promising, especially in modifying sleeping patterns (Balentine & Hagman, 1997; Brown, 1994; deVries & Peeters (Brown, 1994; Folkard, Arendt, & Clark, 1993; Waldhauser, Saletu, & Trinchard, 1990), research into the long-term safety of melatonin remains to be done. Furthermore, checks and balances in the endocrine

system are complex. Any substance that alters the neuroendocrine system, as melatonin clearly does, is likely to have unanticipated effects. Folkard et al., (1993) summarized their findings by stating, "Results suggest that melatonin has beneficial effects on sleep and alertness, but . . . its effect on performance needs careful evaluation" (p. 315).

Sleep

Humans spend about one-third of their lives asleep. Psychologists know relatively little about why we enter into this state of consciousness. Indeed, we might wonder why we do sleep. Two general theories have been developed, recuperative theory and circadian theory (see Pinel, 1996).

Recuperative theory, as the name implies, sees sleep as a time for the body to repair and recover from the day's activity. In a sense, sleep can be seen as a time to "recharge our batteries." **Circadian theory,** however, views sleep not as a time to restore lost energies but as an adaptive response to night and day. Bats, for example, use sound rather than light to locate their prey. Though they can hunt during daylight, they are not very successful: the insects they eat locate objects visually, and can therefore escape more easily during daylight. In addition, bats are more likely to be seen by their predators during the daytime. According to circadian theory, hunting during daylight hours is an inefficient use of a bat's resources. Because of selective pressure, bats have evolved periods of inactivity during the day. Humans sleep at night for a similar reason: we are not well adapted to living in the dark environment.

First, we will discuss some of the chemical factors that may be involved in sleep. Following that, we will examine changes that take place in the brain's activity during sleep, including the paradoxical patterns called *rapid eye movement (REM) sleep.* We will then look at the effects of sleep deprivation. In the next section we'll discuss dreaming, a fascinating but poorly understood part of sleep. Finally, we will examine some of the more common sleep disorders.

Chemical Factors Involved in Sleep

For years scientists have searched for chemicals that build up in the brain and trigger sleep. They have found that increased amounts of certain neurotransmitters (serotonin, for example) can sometimes promote sleep, as can another chemical extracted from the blood of sleeping animals (Schneider-Helmert, 1985). A second substance, called *delta sleep-inducing peptide* (DSIP), has also been shown to influence sleep. Monnier and colleagues (1975) connected the blood supplies of two rabbits, then stimulated the thalamus of one rabbit, inducing sleep and the release of DSIP into its bloodstream. Since the rabbits' circulatory systems were connected, the second rabbit received DSIP stimulation and fell asleep. Despite such evidence, however, the role of DSIP in inducing sleep is not widely accepted (see Schönenberger & Graf, 1985). For example, it is not clear that these chemicals are the normal cause of sleep. DSIP does not always induce sleep, and induces a number of other changes, including a rise in body temperature. Its sleep-inducing effects could be a secondary response to its neurochemical effects.

More agreement exists about the neural circuits that control the sleep-wake cycle. The brain's wake center seems to be located in the reticular formation. When it is lesioned, an animal lapses into a permanent coma; when it is stimulated, a sleeping animal awakes. The brain also contains sleep circuits that extend from the lower hindbrain to the thalamus and cortex. The activation of these circuits seems to inhibit the wake center in the reticular formation, causing sleep to take over. (Remember that Monnier and associates, 1975, were able to induce sleep by stimulating parts of the thalamus.)

Brain Activity from Wakefulness to Deep Sleep

The most revealing data concerning sleep as a distinct state of consciousness come from the use of the electroencephalograph, a device for recording the brain's electrical activity. The chart of brain-wave tracings that an electroencephalograph produces is called an **electroencephalogram (EEG).** In a typical laboratory study of sleep, a volunteer is hooked up to an electroencephalograph by means of electrodes attached to the scalp and face (see Figure 5-1). The volunteer then settles down in bed to sleep away the night. As the hours pass, the EEG records changes in the subjects' brain-wave patterns, as they progress from wakefulness to drowsiness and finally to sleep. During sleep the brain-wave patterns change dramatically. Figure 5-1 shows the pattern of brain waves as a person moves from wakefulness into light and then deep sleep. Notice the changes that occur in the speed, or frequency, of the brain waves.

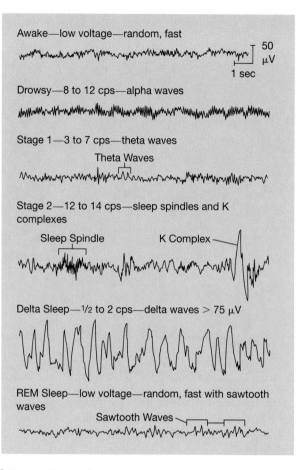

FIGURE 5-1 *These EEG patterns show the electrical activity of the human brain in the various stages of sleep. Note that as sleep becomes deeper, the high-frequency, small-amplitude (small-sized) waves give way to lower-frequency, large-amplitude waves that are also more rhythmic, or synchronized. This change is thought to reflect the fact that the neurons in the brain are all firing at about the same level and in about the same pattern. Note also that the EEG pattern in REM sleep is very similar to the awake pattern. (Hauri, 1982.)*

These changes in frequency are measured in cycles per second. (Refer to Figure 5-1 as we describe these changes.)

The EEGs of people who are fully awake and alert, with eyes open, usually show a predominance of **beta waves,** rapid or high-frequency brain waves, of 14 or more cycles per second. When subjects close their eyes and relax, their brain-wave patterns begin to change. Slower **alpha waves** begin to appear, vary-

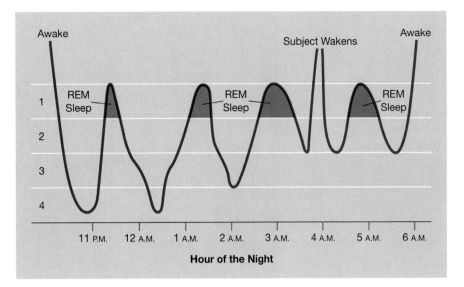

FIGURE 5-2   *A typical night's sleep, showing the stages mentioned in the text. A new cycle of stages begins about every 90 to 110 minutes. Note that cycles early in the night are shorter and have more of the deepest stages of sleep (characterized by slow delta waves). Sleep becomes shallower as the night progresses and REM periods become longer.*

ing in frequency from 8 to 12 cycles per second. As relaxation progresses, the individual falls asleep.

The Stages of Sleep

Sleep itself is punctuated by four distinct stages, as shown in Figure 5-2. When a subject starts to fall asleep (Stage 1 in Figure 5-1), even slower theta waves, 3 to 7 cycles per second, mix in with the alpha waves. If subjects are startled during Stage 1, they will often report being fully awake, but their thoughts are disorganized. You may have experienced this phenomenon during a lecture. Something may have startled you, such as a professor calling on you to answer a question. Though you had no sensation of falling asleep, you probably found that the last few moments of the class made no sense.

As sleep becomes progressively deeper, the alpha pattern disappears, signifying the beginning of Stage 2 sleep (see Figure 5-1). Very slow delta waves, ½ to 2 cycles per second, begin to occur. Occasionally during Stage 2, brief bursts of high-frequency waves called *sleep spindles* appear. Stage 2 is also characterized by large irregular low-frequency waves called *K complexes.*

Following this stage, **delta sleep,** or deep sleep, begins. During Stage 3, spindles and K complexes disappear and are replaced by **delta waves,** which make up about 25 to 50 percent of the time spent in Stage 3. Stage 4, the deepest stage of sleep, follows. Delta waves predominate during this stage; they are seen in more than 50 percent of the brain waves in

Stage 4. This very deep sleep is accompanied by marked relaxation of muscles, slow and regular breathing, and significant drops in body temperature and pulse. The nature of consciousness during Stage 4 (delta) sleep is something of a puzzle. It is difficult to awaken people from this stage: they seem almost in a coma. By the time the sleeper wakes up and is asked about any thoughts he may have been having, we cannot be sure whether the thoughts that are reported happened during delta sleep or the wake-up period. The brain continues to process both internal and external stimuli during delta sleep, however. Most episodes of sleepwalking, sleep talking, and intense nightmares occur during this stage.

The production of delta waves is related to the amount of time a person was awake before falling asleep. The longer the last period of wakefulness, the greater the number of delta waves emitted, and the greater their amplitude or strength. This finding has led some researchers to suspect that delta waves may be associated with physiological changes or stresses that take place during waking consciousness (Feinberg & Fein, 1982).

During the course of a typical evening's sleep, the sleeper progresses through the four stages in a cyclical manner, moving from Stage 1, through Stages 2 and 3, then into Stage 4, and then returning to Stage 1, through Stages 3 and 2. However, the return to Stage 1 is marked by a very different EEG pattern from the one observed in initial Stage 1 sleep. Throughout the evening, sleep moves from Stage 1

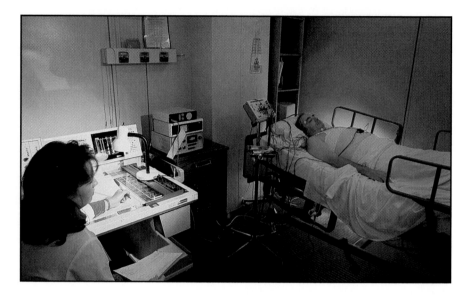

| A sleep researcher studies changes in brain activity using an electroencephalograph, which records electrical impulses transmitted from the subject's brain through electrodes attached to his scalp and face.

to Stage 4, back to Stage 1 again, then back to Stage 4, and so on. The pattern is like the swinging of a pendulum, cycling about every ninety minutes (see Figure 5-2). As the night wears on, the sleeper spends less and less time in Stages 3 and 4 and more in Stages 1 and 2.

REM Sleep

When the first sleep cycle is complete, and we return to Stage 1, we do not actually wake up—though the brain's activity resembles that of a person who is awake. But while the brain seems "awake," the body appears to be in deep sleep. For this reason, this stage is sometimes called *paradoxical sleep.* Another striking characteristic of this stage is rapid, darting movement of the eyes, which can be seen under the eyelids. For this reason, this stage is also called **rapid eye movement (REM) sleep.** As Figure 5-2 shows, REM sleep appears about four or five times a night, when the person returns to a Stage 1 pattern. Together, REM episodes consume about one and a half to two hours, roughly a quarter of a person's total sleep time. The distinction between REM sleep and all the other stages, collectively called **non-REM sleep,** is the most important distinction among the various stages.

REM Sleep and Dreaming When researchers first observed REM sleep in the 1950s, they suspected it was linked to dreaming. To explore this possibility, Dement and Kleitman (1957) woke subjects during the various stages of sleep and asked them to report any thoughts or images they had been experiencing. The results were dramatic. During REM periods, subjects reported dreams with vivid visual imagery, in which they felt they were actively participating, about 80 percent of the time. During non-REM periods, they reported storylike episodes far less frequently (less than 10% of the time). Their non-REM dreams seemed more like drifting, unstructured thought than the movielike experiences we typically call a dream (Hauri, 1982).

With the discovery that rapid eye movement and dreams often go together, psychologists began to speculate that sleepers' eyes moved as they "watched" activity in their dreams unfold. This theory, called the **scanning hypothesis,** was first proposed by William Dement (1976). When Dement awakened one subject who showed only horizontal eye movements during a particular REM period, the subject reported he had been dreaming about a table tennis match. The problem with the scanning hypothesis, however, is that the relationship between rapid eye movement and dream content is rarely that clear-cut. Furthermore, subjective dream reports are impossible to verify.

Most researchers suspect that dreaming is not the *cause* of rapid eye movement, but a parallel outcome of the brain's unusually high state of activation during REM sleep (Chase & Morales, 1983). Recently, Hobson (1989) has proposed a theory of sleep and dreaming known as the **activation-synthesis hypothesis.** According to this theory, a part of the pons (a region of the hindbrain) periodically "turns on" during sleep, triggering a state of high activation. When it does, it produces rapid eye movements and bombards the higher brain regions, especially the vi-

Sleep deprivation is common among medical students. Recently researchers found that sleep-deprived medical residents at hospitals showed impaired cognitive functioning and mood—both of which can compromise a physician's effectiveness.

sual and motor systems, with random stimulation. The cortex then tries to make sense of these random neural signals by interpreting them as meaningful sights, sounds, and actions, weaving them together into a dream. Thus, the activation-synthesis hypothesis explains dreaming by relying on our tendency to impose order on information, something we often do when we are awake (remember the perceptual illusions from Chapter 4). According to Hobson, the content of our dreams seems odd because we are trying to make sense out of virtually random, meaningless brain activity. We will return to Hobson's hypothesis later in the chapter in the section on dreaming.

The Paradoxes of REM Sleep We have seen that in some respects, REM sleep is similar to the waking state. The rapid, irregular brain waves that dominate the EEG during REM periods look very much like those that occur when a person is awake. Other physiological signs of this stage also resemble those of a wide-awake person. Heartbeat, breathing, and blood pressure are irregular and varied; and there is evidence of sexual arousal. Usually these patterns would be observed in a person who is not only awake but excited. It is not surprising that heart attacks, acute ulcer pains, and emphysema attacks seem to occur more often during REM sleep than in other sleep stages (Armstrong, 1965; Trask & Cree, 1962).

Paradoxically, however, the REM sleeper is *soundly* asleep, not just dozing lightly. He or she often sleeps on through the sound of a voice or the touch of a hand on the shoulder. Moreover, despite signs of arousal, the major muscles lose their tone

and become limp, to the point where the sleeper is literally unable to move. Again, an area of the pons seems responsible for this condition. When scientists destroyed that area in the brain of a cat, REM sleep still occurred, but the animal no longer lay still; instead, it jumped up and moved about, even though it was still asleep (Jouvet, 1967). This study suggests an odd possibility: if our muscles were not paralyzed during REM sleep, our bodies might act out our dreams.

Sleep Deprivation

Most of us have experienced a night without sleep: perhaps we were anxious and couldn't sleep, or traveling coast to coast. Some of us even stayed awake an entire night preparing for an exam. What problems does lack of sleep induce? Losing a single night's sleep, as you can probably attest, does little more than make us sleepy. Though we may fall asleep somewhat earlier the next evening, we certainly do not "make up" for all the sleep we lost the previous evening. Staying awake for longer than one evening, though, often induces more serious effects. By the morning after two sleepless nights, most people report being frustrated and irritable, unable to concentrate for long periods of time. Even so, sleep deprivation that lasts up to 200 hours—that's more than a week!—appears to produce no dire physiological effects (Pinel, 1996).

The *psychological* consequences of sleep deprivation can be more serious, though. Lingenfelser and his colleagues in Germany (Lingenfelser et al., 1994) studied the relationship between sleep deprivation

in first- and second-year medical students. In Germany, as in the United States, new physicians are often asked to work long, intense shifts. For example, residents who were "on call" typically stay at the hospital for twenty-four hours without breaks. Lingenfelser and his colleagues found that residents who were sleep-deprived showed impairment of their cognitive functioning as well as their mood—both of which can compromise the effectiveness of a physician. Lingenfelser and his colleagues concluded, "In view of the special vulnerability of medical trainees to occupational stress, all efforts to reduce sleep deprivation in the medical profession are warranted" (p. 566).

We have seen that REM sleep seems to be particularly important. What happens if an individual is allowed to sleep as much as she wishes, but not to experience REM sleep? Dement (1960) deprived subjects of REM sleep for several consecutive nights. Whenever he saw the beginning of a REM period, he awakened the sleeper. With each successive episode, Dement found it harder and harder to arouse many subjects. A few eventually had to be hoisted onto their feet before finally opening their eyes. The longer Dement denied REM sleep, the more often they entered REM periods. Whereas most people experience four or five REM episodes a night, Dement's subjects entered REM an average of ten or twelve times, even on the first night. By the third night, Dement was running in and out of subjects' rooms so often that he could hardly keep up the pace. Finally, on the fifth night, he let subjects sleep uninterrupted. The result was a phenomenon known as the **REM rebound:** subjects spent about double the normal time in REM sleep. Research by Brunner and colleagues (1990) confirms that sleep-deprived subjects spend more than their usual amount of time in REM sleep during the first several nights following REM deprivation.

The effects of REM deprivation are more important than they might appear to be. Because many sleep-inducing drugs selectively suppress REM sleep, taking those substances for more than a few days may be counterproductive. Though users of these drugs may sleep for longer periods of time, they are likely to wake up groggy and tired. Despite an increase in total sleep, REM sleep is disrupted. Most over-the-counter and prescription sleep aids have this effect, as does alcohol. Having a glass of wine just before bed to induce sleep may paradoxi-

cally make a person feel less rested. Most people report a sharp increase in the frequency and intensity of dreams after discontinuing sleep aids—a manifestation of REM rebound.

Since our bodies automatically compensate for the loss of REM sleep, it is reasonable to assume that people need it. But why? Researchers have not yet found an answer. Though people sometimes become tired or irritable as a result of REM deprivation, they do not display marked impairment during their waking hours. At most they are slightly more prone than usual to unconventional thought and behavior (Dement, 1960; Kales et al., 1964; Sampson, 1965). Still, REM sleep may serve some function short-term experiments do not reveal.

Dreams

By age seventy, the average person will have had about 150,000 dreams (Snyder, 1970). Does that mean they have had 150,000 fascinating adventures? No, not at all. When people are awakened randomly during REM sleep and asked what they have just been dreaming, their reports are often ordinary, even dull (Hall & Van de Castle, 1966). These uneventful dreams are usually quickly forgotten, probably because they are never consolidated into long-term memory (Kihlstrom, 1984). The dreams people store long enough to recall when they awaken tend to be emotion-laden, bizarre, or sexy, the kind that typically occurs toward the end of a night's sleep (Hauri, 1982; Webb, 1975). Some psychologists find great symbolic meaning in such dreams. In fact, Sigmund Freud referred to dreams as "the royal road to the unconscious."

A papyrus in the British Museum dating from the tenth century B.C. instructed the ancients in interpreting their dreams. The Bible is replete with stories of dreams and dream interpretation (remember Joseph interpreting the dream of seven fat cows followed by seven thin cows). Today, more than 3,000 years later, people still wonder about the hidden meaning of dreams. Freud believed that dreams reflect the repressed needs and desires of the unconscious—needs and desires that often arise from the unresolved psychosexual conflicts of childhood.

In *The Interpretation of Dreams* (1900), Freud distinguished between the manifest content and the latent content of a dream. The **manifest content** is the readily perceived plot or story line, including the actors, setting, and events. The **latent content** is the deeper

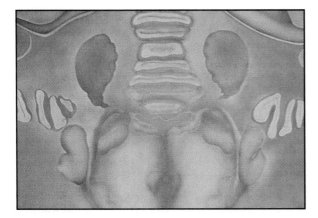

This painting was made by a research subject in a dream study. The curious nature (and possible significance) of dreams has long fascinated psychologists. For example, Sigmund Freud relied heavily on the interpretation of dreams in developing his psychoanalytic theory.

meaning of the dream—the underlying, largely unconscious wishes. For instance, one new mother who found herself up at all hours tending to her newborn baby reported to her analyst a dream in which she gave birth to identical twin boys, one of whom died. According to the analyst, the latent content of the dream was an unconscious wish to be rid of the infant who had destroyed a formerly peaceful, well-ordered way of life. Such a resentful, "unmotherly" wish is hard to admit, however. To avoid confronting it directly, the woman's mind fashioned a more benign manifest dream plot (two babies, only one of whom dies) (Foulkes, 1964). This veiling of the dreamer's unconscious wish in more acceptable symbolic image is what Freud called "dream work."

Not all psychoanalysts accept Freud's views on dreams. Alfred Adler (1870–1937), a close colleague of Freud early in his career, later rejected many aspects of his doctrine, including the meaning of dreams. Adler (1936) argued that dreams do not embody unconscious wishes, as Freud believed, but instead continue, cloaked in visual metaphors, whatever thoughts and feelings were dominating a person's consciousness during waking hours. Many contemporary therapists share this perspective (Foulkes, 1964; Gelman, 1989; Ullman, 1962). To them, the student who dreams that he goes to take an exam, opens the door to the classroom, and finds the room dark and deserted is not trying to fulfill some unconscious sexual desire, but is simply worrying about failing an upcoming exam. Indeed, most of us have had a dream about an upcoming event (a lecture, meeting, or game) gone awry.

Implicit in this view is the idea that during nighttime hours we continue to cope with our current concerns and problems. Hobson's activation-synthesis hypothesis mentioned earlier in this chapter may help explain such dreams. Recall that Hobson thought the often strange quality of dreams was caused by the brain, trying to make sense of neural activity. Essentially, the brain tries to impose some structure on the pseudo-random firings projected to the cortex. One of the ways the brain might impose a structure, of course, would be to incorporate the person's conscious thoughts prior to sleep. Thus, anxiety about an upcoming presentation may lead to a related dream.

If dreams can be influenced by conscious thought, can they be *directed*? Psychologist Rosalind Cartwright (1979) has studied this possibility in the laboratory. In one experiment, she had people identify a personality trait they disliked in themselves. Then, as they were falling asleep, they repeated a wish to change that trait. Over and over they said to themselves, "I wish I were not so sarcastic," "I wish I were not so timid," and the like. The subjects created a conflict in themselves: they acknowledged having a characteristic they would rather not possess. Would dreams help them to resolve the conflict? For some of the subjects, the answer seemed to be "yes." They dreamed about the worrisome trait more than they would be expected to by chance. When they did, they tended to fashion scenes in which the negative trait was justified.

Sleep Disorders

Almost everyone experiences difficulty sleeping from time to time. If we are preoccupied, upset, or worried, we may find it difficult to fall asleep. Other times we find ourselves unable to keep awake. Fortunately, most of these difficulties are transitory, correcting themselves in a day or two. Occasionally, sleep disorders persist, requiring attention.

According to Pinel (1996), up to 30 percent of the population reports some type of sleep disorder. There is reason to think some problems may be overstated, however. For example, while self-reported insomniacs claimed they took over an hour to fall asleep, the actual time was only fifteen minutes.

Along the same lines, insomniacs reported sleeping an average of 4.5 hours at night. The actual figure was 6.5 hours.

According to Weitzman (1981), perhaps 15 percent of the population suffers chronic long-term sleep problems. The most common sleep disorder is **insomnia,** difficulty in falling asleep or staying asleep all night. Brief episodes of insomnia are usually caused by transient worries and stress. Insomnia is often worsened by the way in which sufferers deal with it (Hauri, 1982). Many people become so upset after several nights of poor sleep that getting into bed increases their state of arousal, which makes sleep all the less likely. A vicious circle ensues.

When insomnia does not respond to treatment and continues unabated, some biological factor may be involved. One condition that can contribute to insomnia is **sleep apnea.** People with severe sleep apnea literally stop breathing while they are sleeping. They quickly awaken, gasping for air: though most do not report being aware of their gasping. In fact, many are not aware they have awakened. This cycle may be repeated many times throughout the night. In the morning, the sleeper awakens exhausted. Though unaware of the frequent sleep disturbances, he will usually report a vague sense of "not sleeping well." Sleep apnea is often caused by an overrelaxation of the muscles in the throat, which cuts off the air passage. Other causes can be traced to a disorder of the central nervous system in which the diaphragm (the muscle that controls the lungs) stops working during sleep (Kolb & Whishaw, 1990). Treatment depends partly on the source of the problem.

People who have relatively mild cases of sleep apnea are sometimes only partially awakened by the repeated shortages of oxygen. Consequently, they are usually unaware of their condition. Rather than complaining of insomnia, they tend to complain of excessive sleepiness during the day (Kelly, 1981). A more extreme cause of excessive daytime sleepiness is the condition called **narcolepsy,** in which a wide-awake person suddenly lapses into sleep, usually in brief fifteen-minute episodes. Falling asleep during the day is not in and of itself a sleep disorder: most of us feel sleepy in a dark theater or a lecture hall right after lunch. Narcoleptics fall asleep almost anywhere: during a phone call, in the middle of a conversation, or behind the wheel. They often enter REM sleep immediately after falling asleep, as if their REM circuits had suddenly and unpredictably turned on and overridden waking consciousness. The disorder is often treated with drugs that both enhance wakefulness and inhibit REM sleep (Hauri, 1982; Pinel, 1996).

Induced States of Consciousness

So far, we have explored changes in consciousness that occur in a predictable, cyclical pattern. In the next part of this chapter we will examine changes that are deliberately induced. First, we will discuss psychoactive drugs, including legal drugs like alcohol and nicotine. Then we will look at meditative states, primarily hypnosis. Unlike drug-induced states, meditative states alter consciousness through psychological factors. Despite such differences, both drug-induced and meditative states can powerfully alter consciousness.

Drug-Induced States

Many drugs are known to have psychological properties. Some, like morphine, induce feelings of euphoria. Others, like alcohol or Valium, are depressants; they reduce anxiety and lower inhibitions. Still others, like caffeine and amphetamines, work as stimulants.

Ours is a society where drug use is common and drug *abuse* is increasing at an alarming rate. You may balk, thinking that you don't use drugs. What about that cup of coffee in the morning? Or the glass of wine with dinner, or the antihistamine you take when your nose runs? What about the aspirin or acetaminophen you take when you have a headache?

In our society, we tend to view some substances as medicines (like antihistamines or morphine), some as mild but legal drugs (like nicotine, alcohol, or caffeine). As such, we consider them to be distinct from hard-core drugs like cocaine, marijuana, or heroin. While we might feel more comfortable with this distinction, the fact is, any drug that has a **psychoactive** effect (that is, alters mood or consciousness) does so by altering brain function. Legally, we distinguish between marijuana and alcohol, between amphetamines and caffeine. But psychologically (and sometimes pharmacologically), the distinction is not so clear.

Drugs have a variety of ways of producing their effects; some drugs produce very similar effects in quite different ways. Some activate certain synapses, effectively tricking the brain into thinking it is being

Though many people do not consider their morning cup of coffee to be a drug, the stimulant caffeine is without a doubt the most widely used psychoactive substance in our culture.

stimulated by neurotransmitters (both heroin and Valium work this way). Others may increase the amount of neurotransmitter present at a synapse by delaying its breakdown or reuptake (drugs like cocaine and Prozac work this way). Still other drugs interfere with neural transmission by blocking the postsynaptic receptor sites—the biological "locks"—inhibiting the release of transmitters (the botulism toxin works this way). Whatever the mechanism, most psychoactive drugs produce their effects by *functionally altering the effects of neurotransmitters at the synapse.*

The Myth of the "Magic Bullet"

Another common misconception concerning drug use is what is known as the *magic bullet myth:* somehow, drugs "know" which uses they are intended for. For example, an aspirin would "know" that you have a headache and work only on that symptom. Many analgesic manufacturers exploit this belief by

offering one remedy for backache, one for sinus headache, and yet another for muscle soreness. In reality, most pain relievers contain the same chemicals! A brand of aspirin that is marketed as a backache treatment will be just as effective for headache pain.

In fact, drugs released into the bloodstream are not directed at any specific target. Many of the side effects of drug treatment occur because of effects at sites other than the ones desired. For example, most antihistamines will stop a runny nose, but they also induce drowsiness. As the name implies, *antihistamines* block the action of histamines, the production of which makes your nose run. However, histamines are located throughout the brain, especially in centers that control arousal. Therefore most antihistamines will disrupt functioning in the brain as well, causing drowsiness. Next time you are at a pharmacy, compare the ingredients of the popular antihistamine Benadryl with the sleep aid Nytol. They are identical—both containing the antihistamine "diphenhydramine" and both working to block histamines wherever they are located.

To give another example, in Chapter 3 we discussed the antipsychotic medications used to treat schizophrenia. They work by blocking postsynaptic dopamine activity. However, schizophrenic symptoms are thought to result from an excess of dopamine primarily in the limbic system, not in all neurons. Because early antipsychotic drugs blocked the effects of dopamine throughout the brain, including those in the *basal ganglia,* the area critical to movement, one of their serious side effects was motor symptoms resembling Parkinson's disease. Newer drugs target the dopamine neurons in the limbic system more selectively, interfering less with activity in the basal ganglia (see (Stevens, 1991).

Drugs can be grouped in a number of different ways: according to their chemical structures, their legal classification, the brain sites they affect, and so on. In this chapter we will classify drugs according to their effects. First, we will discuss stimulants, drugs that increase CNS activity. Following that, we will look at a diverse group of drugs known as depressants, which reduce CNS activity. In the last part of this section we will examine hallucinogens, drugs that produce sensory and cognitive distortions.

Stimulants

A number of psychoactive drugs stimulate the central nervous system. Though their mechanisms differ, they all cause cognitive and behavioral arousal.

Caffeine Without a doubt, caffeine is the most widely used of all the **stimulants.** Caffeine is found in coffee, tea, and soft drinks, but it is also found in substances like chocolate. In addition, caffeine is added to many painkillers like aspirin, because it augments their effects, especially on headaches.

The effects of caffeine can be felt quickly. Caffeine increases the heart and respiration rates and raises blood pressure, enhancing alertness. In moderate doses it seems to increase attention and performance. (Be careful: while a little bit may be good, a lot is not better. Too much caffeine can cause irritability and jumpiness.)

Caffeine works by blocking the breakdown of enzymes that regulate neurotransmitters, increasing the activity of some, especially epinephrine and dopamine. The body adapts quickly to caffeine, so caffeine withdrawal is common among those who consume relatively large amounts (about four to six

Though smokers report that cigarettes calm them down, nicotine, like caffeine, is a CNS stimulant. Because nicotine is physically addictive, withdrawal can be uncomfortable.

cups of coffee per day). Symptoms of caffeine withdrawal include headache, irritability, and loss of concentration. Many individuals report feeling fatigued or lethargic. Indeed, many regular caffeine users report feeling sluggish until they have had their early morning coffee. Behavioral tolerance develops quickly, as evidenced by the tendency to require larger and larger amounts of coffee in order to feel the same effect. Caffeine is suspected of being involved in some clinical problems, such as panic disorder and attention deficit disorder (Dusek & Girdano, 1980).

Nicotine Though smokers report that cigarettes calm them down, nicotine is a CNS stimulant. Like caffeine, its effects are nonspecific, and many resemble the effects of caffeine: increased heart and respiration rates, and a rise in blood pressure. Nicotine is an appetite suppressant (which helps to explain the tendency of those who are trying to stop smoking to

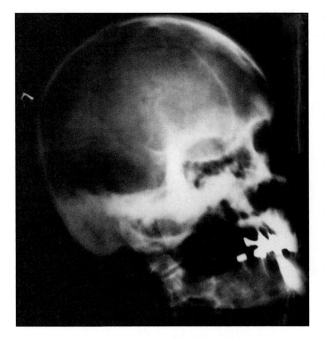

Sigmund Freud battled mouth cancer in his later years, a direct result of his ravenous cigar smoking. Much of his jaw was eventually rebuilt using metal prostheses, clearly seen in this x-ray. Freud was unable to quit smoking, however, and the cancer eventually took his life.

ered. Many smokers find this type of withdrawal from smoking easier to endure.

The addictive effects of nicotine are not to be underestimated. One of the most important figures in the history of psychology, Sigmund Freud, was a ravenous cigar smoker. During the last few decades of his life, he underwent a series of painful operations to combat the cancers in his mouth that were caused by his obsessive smoking. The Freud museum in Hampstead, England (where Freud spent the last years of his life, after being expelled from Austria by the Nazis), displays X rays that clearly show the damage. By the time of his death, much of Freud's jaw had been rebuilt with metal prostheses: the jaw itself had been destroyed by cancer (see photo on left). Even though Freud was well aware of the damage his smoking caused, he was unable to quit. After years of pain, the cancer finally took his life.

Nicotine is the most problematic addictive drug in our society. According to the American Cancer Society, nearly 50 million Americans smoked in 1993, causing over 400,000 deaths, due primarily to cancer and cardiovascular disease.

Amphetamines Amphetamines are a much more powerful class of stimulants; their use is closely regulated. Drugs like Benzedrine and Dexedrine (known on the street as "speed" or "uppers"), once prescribed by physicians to aid weight loss, are frequently abused. Now that their addictive potential is widely known, amphetamines are seldom prescribed for weight loss. In fact, the most frequently prescribed amphetamine, methylphenidate (Ritalin), is used to treat children diagnosed with attention deficit hyperactivity disorder (ADHD). Paradoxically, the stimulant *reduces* the activity level of many children with ADHD.

Amphetamines are still widely—but illegally—available on the street. Related drugs like methamphetamine (sometimes known as "crank," not to be confused with the cocaine derivative "crack") have similar effects. These drugs are usually taken orally; however, they can be smoked or injected.

In addition to their effects on the entire CNS, which are similar to those of caffeine or nicotine, amphetamines have a powerful effect on the neurons that use dopamine. Because of their dopaminergic effects in high doses or with repeated use, amphetamines can cause "amphetamine psychosis," the symptoms of which are almost identical to those

gain weight). Because it is physically addictive, withdrawal can be uncomfortable. Reports of irritability, sleeplessness, agitation, and increased appetite are common among those who are trying to quit.

In large doses nicotine is toxic, even lethal. In fact, nicotine has been used as an ingredient in insecticides (Volle & Koelle, 1975). Consequently, cigarette smokers have a much higher incidence of cancer (especially of the mouth and lungs) and heart disease than nonsmokers. Cigarettes have been linked to lower birth weight when used by pregnant mothers, and children of mothers who smoke are at risk for a number of health-related problems. The fact that nicotine is delivered through smoking exacerbates its toxic effects. Smoke is a physical irritant to the mouth and lungs, and cancer is often caused by physical irritation. One common way of weaning an individual from smoking involves the delivery of nicotine through the skin, by means of a transdermal (literally, "through the skin") patch. This technique reduces many of the harmful effects of cigarette smoke, while the nicotine intake is gradually low-

"Crack," a smokeable form of cocaine, is perhaps the most addictive of all illicit drugs. The rapid, intense highs are followed by an equally rapid and powerful withdrawal, producing an incessant and destructive cycle of use, withdrawal, craving, and repeated use.

of paranoid schizophrenia: paranoia, delusions, hallucinations, and severe confusion. Fortunately, these symptoms usually disappear with time. (The fact that amphetamines can cause symptoms that mimic those of schizophrenia is powerful evidence that schizophrenia is caused by an excess of dopamine.)

Tolerance for and dependence on amphetamines develop rapidly. Frequent users must continually increase the dose to achieve the same effect. In taking higher and higher doses, users approach the level that can trigger violent psychotic reactions.

Cocaine Like amphetamines, cocaine works by increasing the amount of dopamine present at synapses. (It also increases the amount of norepinephrine.) Cocaine causes feelings of euphoria and arousal. It is most frequently administered by "snorting," which means inhaling into the nose, and is readily absorbed by the nasal membranes. Cocaine is also absorbed by membranes in the eye, inducing local anesthesia. For this reason, cocaine is often used an a local anesthetic in eye surgeries.

Cocaine can also be smoked and inhaled into the lungs. Cocaine taken into the lungs is administered either by "freebasing"—mixing it with a mixture of ammonia, ether, baking soda, and water, then heating the entire mixture[2]—or by smoking it in a solid state in the form of "crack." Administered in this way the drug acts very quickly (within a few seconds) producing a short, intense effect called a "rush." This powerful experience, followed by an equally quick and powerful withdrawal, leads to the

incessant cycle of use, withdrawal, craving, and repeated use often seen in crackhouses.

Cocaine's effects are immediate and intense. It causes a dramatic increase in heart rate and respiration, which can be fatal. The deaths of basketball superstar Len Bias and comedian John Belushi were caused by heart attacks induced by cocaine.[3] High levels of cocaine can also lead to psychosis similar to that induced by amphetamines. (The case of "Helen," which opened this chapter, presents a dramatic example of cocaine-induced psychosis.) Cocaine can induce delusions and anxiety, even in casual users.

Cocaine was once thought not to be physically addictive in the same way as alcohol or opiates. However, the strong tolerance and powerful cravings users develop make such a distinction difficult. For this reason investigators are beginning to balk at the standard definitions of "addiction" and "tolerance." Cocaine is now considered to be powerfully addictive, especially when it is smoked. Estimates are that 50 percent of all crack smokers will become addicted (Flynn, 1991), an astonishing number (compare it to the approximately 3 to 5 percent of alcohol users who become addicted).

This is a good place for a brief digression into the phenomena of drug use and drug abuse. Our society

---

[2]It was during freebasing cocaine that the comedian Richard Pryor seriously burned himself in the early 1980s. The mixture is extremely flammable.

[3]Belushi was combining cocaine and opiates in a mixture known as a "speedball." Because of the complex and antagonistic reactions, the exact cause of his death was less clear.

Alcohol is by far the most common depressant in our culture. Because it produces widespread depression of the central nervous system, intense drinking binges, in which participants consume a large amount of alcohol in a short time, can occasionally result in death. Alcohol abuse is particularly common among college-age students.

has traditionally thought of those who are addicted to drugs as morally weak, or somehow defective. We are tempted to think that a highly paid athlete or entertainer who battles a cocaine addiction is weak and could stop if he just had the will power. (In fact, these are almost the exact words spoken by the manager of a baseball team, discussing one of his former player's cocaine addiction.) It may be more instructive to view the situation—a marvelously gifted athlete, willing to throw everything away for the temporary pleasure of using drugs—as a demonstration of how powerfully addictive cocaine is. Understanding the keys to abuse involves recognizing the addictive properties of a drug.

What makes cocaine so addictive? It has been linked to a part of the limbic system known as the "pleasure center," specifically the *medial forebrain bundle,* as it passes through the hypothalamus. Animals who are given access to a lever that causes the medial forebrain bundle to be stimulated by electrodes will choose such stimulation over food, sleep, or even sex. Cocaine stimulates a part of the brain that controls feelings of pleasure. Apparently this stimulation is so pleasurable for some individuals that they will choose to use cocaine even if it leads to disastrous long-term consequences.

Because the price of crack is relatively low—about $10 per "rock," or dose—large numbers of people now have access to an almost unbelievably addictive drug. It is little wonder that crack abuse is the nation's fastest growing drug problem (Flynn, 1991). Because the drug is so addictive, its abuse is not a problem that is likely to disappear.

Depressants

The drugs collectively called **depressants** all slow CNS activity, causing feelings of relaxation or reduced anxiety. Users may also experience feelings of euphoria, especially with alcohol.

Alcohol   If caffeine is the most common stimulant, alcohol is by far the most common depressant. According to the *DSM IV* (APA, 1994), over 100 million Americans are regular users of alcohol; perhaps as many as 5 percent of them are alcoholic.

Alcohol increases the brain's response to GABA, the major inhibitory neurotransmitter. At relatively low doses, the areas that are affected first are those controlling movement and emotion. Consequently, lack of emotional inhibition and difficulty coordinating movements are among the first signs of alcohol intoxication. Alcohol affects areas in the brain responsible for respiration, so high levels of alcohol can induce coma or death.

Despite the fact that alcohol decreases inhibition, it is not a stimulant. In small doses it decreases inhibitions by selectively impairing the brain centers that control inhibition. Thus a person may behave in a more outgoing manner, becoming more talkative and excitable, after consuming small doses of alcohol. At somewhat higher doses an individual may begin to exhibit motor difficulty such as a slurring of speech. At even higher doses alcohol can cause loss of consciousness, and occasionally death.

Most states consider a person legally intoxicated when blood alcohol levels (BAL) reach 0.10 percent—the equivalent of about four to six drinks, depending on a person's weight. Figure 5-3 displays

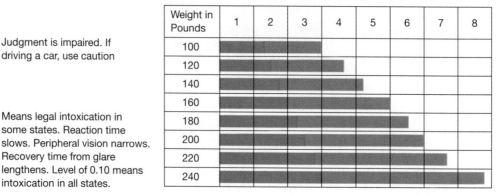

FIGURE 5-3   *How alcohol affects driving a car. (After* U.S. News & World Report. 1983. April 4:74. *Reprinted by permission.)*

the relationship between blood alcohol level and intoxication. A person with a BAL of 0.10 will display motor impairments, and drivers with a BAL of 0.10 and higher are seven times more likely to be involved in a car accident (U. S. Department of Health, 1978). Roadside sobriety checks administered by police are designed specifically to spot such motor impairments.

At somewhat higher levels of alcohol intoxication, about 0.20, feelings of euphoria have been replaced by feelings of profound intoxication. Motor difficulties are pronounced, including an unsteady gait and slurred speech. Those who attempt to drive are greatly (perhaps tragically) impaired. By the time the BAL reaches 0.30, a person is usually unconscious, or "passed out." If BAL concentrations rise slightly higher, to about 0.40, the result is often death. Fortunately, most people become unconscious before they reach such high levels. Occasionally, though, a person will drink so much in a short period that his BAL reaches a fatal level before he loses consciousness. "Drinking games," such as those associated with hazing rituals, occasionally cause this type of death. The singer Keith Whitley, who battled alcohol problems for years, died in 1989 as a result of acute alcohol intoxication.

Alcohol is the most frequently abused of all drugs. Its disinhibiting effects increase the likelihood of violence: drinkers may become quick to anger and violent at the slightest provocation. It is the third leading cause of health problems. It is also a secondary cause of many other problems, such as cancer, liver and kidney problems, and heart disease. Though alcohol has high caloric value (alcohol is

sometimes burned for fuel), it is nutritionally void, containing no protein, vitamins, or nutrients. Many times individuals with a high alcohol intake may neglect to eat properly. Because most alcoholics have poor diets, they may suffer from prolonged deficiencies in certain vitamins, such as thiamin (B_1). A diet low in thiamin results in a severe memory impairment known as **Korsakoff's syndrome,** which causes permanent and irreversible memory problems similar to H. M.'s. Persons with Korsakoff's syndrome are incapable of forming new long-term memories, and memory for past events is also impaired. They also suffer from amnesia for past events. This amnesia is permanent and irreversible.

The risks associated with drinking while pregnant are now clear. Women who drink even moderately while pregnant are at much greater risk for bearing low-birth-weight babies. Pregnant women who drink even more are likely to give birth to a child suffering from **fetal alcohol syndrome.** Babies who are born with fetal alcohol syndrome have lower intelligence levels and a greater likelihood of motor problems than other babies. They experience behavioral problems as they get older. Even worse, babies who are born to alcoholic mothers are often themselves alcohol-dependent; withdrawal can be fatal to them.

Continued use of large amounts of alcohol can soon lead to serious complications. Tolerance develops quickly, so users find themselves needing higher and higher doses. Physiological dependence also develops after repeated exposure to alcohol. Withdrawal from alcohol is much more likely to be fatal than withdrawal from most other substances like cocaine, amphetamines, or even opiates. The symptoms of alcohol withdrawal include shakiness, irritability, sleeplessness, and tremors. In persons whose alcohol consumption was very high, tremors may lead to more serious convulsions, called *delirium tremens* or the d.t.'s, as well as hallucinations and sometimes even seizures. If left untreated, those suffering from severe alcohol withdrawal may die. Alcohol withdrawal is often treated with drugs like Valium. The doses are gradually reduced, minimizing the likelihood of seizures. If you should ever encounter an individual suffering from alcohol withdrawal, seek professional help for the person immediately.

Opiates Heroin, opium, morphine, and codeine are all derived from the same chemical source, the poppy. Though they differ in their potency (and to some degree in the variety of receptors they stimulate), they all work by stimulating opiate receptors in the brain and elsewhere.

Heroin is the strongest form of the opiates; it produces an intense rush many users describe as almost sexual in nature. It is quickly metabolized by the body into morphine, which also has many effects. A powerful painkiller (one of the most effective we have), morphine induces euphoria and drowsiness.

Opiates have legitimate medical uses. Codeine is one of the most effective known cough suppressants. Morphine and synthetic derivatives like meperidine (Demerol) are commonly used to treat pain or induce anesthesia.

Opiates produce a quick and powerful but short-lived effect. Abusers find they quickly need another "fix"; if they do not get one, withdrawal begins. Nausea, vomiting, chills, and explosive diarrhea are common symptoms. Though they are not life-threatening, they are, nonetheless, dreadful.

Ironically, opiates themselves cause little direct injury to the body. Many people have been able to maintain relatively normal lives, as long as their opiate supplies are maintained and administered safely. However, opiate abuse has many indirect consequences. Because users experience a decrease in appetite, their diet is inadequate. And since most opiates are taken intravenously, and injections are rarely made under sterile conditions, infections are common. Hepatitis is quite common among opiate users, and they are now among those at highest risk for contracting AIDS. Though some well-intentioned societies have tried to stem the flow of infectious diseases by providing addicts with sterilized needles, such programs have had only limited effectiveness. Another indirect consequence of opiate abuse is crime caused by addicts who need money to maintain their habits. Many users resort to robbery or prostitution, leading to increased health risks (e.g., violent behavior or exposure to HIV) for nonusers as well.

Benzodiazepines Benzodiazepines were first discovered in the 1950s and have drastically altered the way we view psychoactive drugs. Unlike antipsychotic or antidepressant medications, benzodiazepines were not used to treat psychotic disorders (those characterized by a loss of touch with reality) but to help reduce anxiety in people who were otherwise well-adjusted. The most commonly prescribed benzodiazepine is Valium, introduced to the market in the 1950s, following the less effective but highly successful drug Librium. Initially, researchers considered Valium nonaddictive, and soon it was among the most frequently prescribed of all medications. Since its addictive potential has been realized, however, it is now much more closely monitored.

Valium, and its chemical cousins Librium and the newer Xanax, work by mimicking the action of the neurotransmitter GABA, the primary inhibitory neurotransmitter. They were introduced as anxiolytics, drugs that reduce anxiety-related problems like panic attacks. As a result, many family physicians prescribed Valium or Librium in an attempt to help people cope with routine everyday stress.

Because at first anxiolytics were thought to be nonaddictive, many people were taking legally prescribed anxiolytics as often as others took aspirin. While there is still some debate about their dependence-producing qualities, there is little doubt about psychological dependence on these drugs. People taking benzodiazepines often found themselves unable to deal with normal stress without drugs. Though Valium and other benzodiazepines are used less often now, they are still prescribed with great frequency.

Some benzodiazepines like Halcion are prescribed primarily as sleep aids. Their action is not much different from that of the other benzodiazepines; Valium, too, will induce sleep, especially in higher doses. Benzodiazepines are also used in detoxification programs for physically addicted alcoholics. (Remember that alcohol withdrawal can produce life-threatening seizures.) Because alcohol and benzodiazepines both work on GABA receptors, physicians can substitute benzodiazepines for alcohol, then gradually reduce the dosage until withdrawal is complete. Finally, benzodiazepines are often used to relieve anxiety associated with medical procedures and surgery. They are typically administered with anesthetics to enhance their effectiveness. When used carefully in short-term situations, benzodiazepines have proved to be very effective.

When they were first introduced, benzodiazepines were thought to have little toxicity, but within a short time suicides by Librium overdose began to occur. Cross-tolerance between benzodiazepines and other sedatives (meaning that tolerance to one substance generalizes to the other substance) contributed to additional deaths. Benzodiazepines proved particularly dangerous when combined with other sedatives, especially alcohol. Dorothy Kilgallen, a celebrity panelist on the game show *What's My Line?* in the mid-1950s, died from mixing benzodiazepines and alcohol.

Barbiturates Like alcohol and the benzodiazepines, barbiturates exert their effects at GABA receptors. Barbiturates were once commonly prescribed to induce sleep, but have proved extremely addictive and ultimately counterproductive. For this reason they are seldom prescribed as sleep aids except for use in restricted time frames (say, less than ten days). They rapidly induce sleep—more accurately, a loss of consciousness. In fact, some barbiturates are so short-acting that users report no feeling of drowsiness before the drugs take effect, within seconds of administration. This phenomenon can be seen when an anesthetized patient counts backwards from ten. With a short-acting barbiturate, the patients may count a number or two, but quickly become unconscious.

Barbiturates can be lethal; death by overdose is unfortunately all too common. Estimates are that one-third of all drug-related overdose deaths are due to barbiturates (Julien, 1981). Combining alcohol with barbiturates is also potentially lethal. Mixing with alcohol potentiates their effects (remember, all work at the same sites, the GABA receptors). Because of this toxicity and rapid onset, barbiturates are often used in high doses for execution by lethal injection.

Hallucinogens

Hallucinogens are drugs whose primary action is to alter the user's sensory input. Some of the more powerful ones, such as LSD, can induce vivid hallucinations and distortions. Milder hallucinogens, such as marijuana, have less drastic actions.

LSD LSD (technically, lysergic acid diethylamide) is a powerful hallucinogen derived from the ergot fungus. [Some medical historians have speculated that the disease known as "St. Anthony's fire" in the Middle Ages may have been caused by eating grain contaminated with the ergot fungus see (Julien, 1981)] LSD was first synthesized in the 1930s, but was largely ignored until Albert Hoffman of Sandoz Laboratories accidentally ingested it. He described experiencing "a peculiar state similar to drunkenness, characterized by an exaggerated imagination. With my eyes closed, fantastic pictures of extraordinary plasticity and intensive color seemed to surge towards me" (Julien, 1981, p. 154).

LSD has been tried as a therapeutic drug for everything from marital discord to fear of heights. Because of its bizarre and sometimes unpredictable side effects, it was abandoned as a therapeutic agent in the 1960s. Recreational LSD use also peaked in the 1960s, though in some communities it seems to be making a comeback.

LSD's effects are clear and striking. Even in minute doses it can cause vivid perceptual distortions. Users often report what is called *synesthesia*, in which the sensory modalities get mixed up: they "taste" sounds or "hear" colors. Though most of the hallucinations LSD creates are not unpleasant, the drug is noted for its unpredictability, especially at higher doses. Sometimes users experience what is commonly called a "bad trip," in which the distortions take terrifying forms—such as a vision that the user is suffering an agonizing death.

The extreme potency and unpredictability of LSD have led to a decline in its popularity as a recreational drug. (LSD sold on the streets is frequently combined with other potent drugs as well.) Also, some users have reported "flashbacks," druglike states that affect the user long after the drug has presumably been excreted. Sometimes these delayed reactions persist for months or even years. The problem of flashbacks has probably been exaggerated, however. While they do happen, sometimes unpredictably, they are not as common as once thought.

Marijuana Marijuana is the most commonly used illegal psychoactive drug. Ray (1993) estimates that 50 million Americans have tried marijuana. Marijuana is derived from the *Cannabis sativa* plant, the same plant from which hemp is gathered to make

Marijuana is the most commonly used illegal psychoactive drug. In small doses it acts as a depressant, producing feelings of euphoria and relaxation, and sometimes increasing the appetite. At slightly higher levels the drug induces marked sensory distortions and hallucinations.

rope. In the top of the *Cannabis* plant is a thick resin that contains the chemical THC (delta-9 tetrahydrocannabinol), the psychoactive ingredient in marijuana. Marijuana and its more potent cousin, *hashish*, are most frequently smoked, allowing the THC to enter the bloodstream through the lungs. However, THC can also be ingested orally (which is why marijuana is sometimes baked into brownies).

Though marijuana is listed here with the hallucinogens, it is a difficult drug to classify. In small doses (those most often used recreationally), it acts as a depressant. Users report feelings of euphoria and relaxation, with only minor distortions of sensory input. At these lower doses THC can increase the appetite, resulting in what marijuana users call "the munchies." Marijuana also releases inhibitions, so individuals will often become more outgoing or talkative after smoking it.

At somewhat higher levels marijuana induces greater sensory distortions and is rightly considered a hallucinogen. Unlike the hallucinations induced by LSD, though, marijuana's distortions are less intense and do not cause feelings of "dissociation," as is sometimes reported with LSD.

At even higher doses—doses rarely used recreationally—marijuana acts as a stimulant, perhaps because of other agents present in its smoke. At these much higher levels of intoxication, users can become disoriented and confused. However, marijuana is not considered a toxic drug: few (if any) deaths have ever been directly attributed to it.

Marijuana has been used clinically to treat some types of disorders. Because of its effects on appetite, it has been prescribed for patients undergoing chemotherapy (chemical treatment of cancer). As you are probably aware, one of the most unpleasant side effects of chemotherapy is the nausea it induces. Marijuana alleviates some of the nausea, so patients undergoing chemotherapy lose less weight. Marijuana has also been used to treat the weight loss associated with the progression of the AIDS virus (Fackelman, 1993). Finally, it has been used in the treatment of ophthalmological disorders such as glaucoma.

The "evils" of marijuana are often overstated. The horrors portrayed by the *Reefer Madness*–type movies of the 1930s and 1940s were outrageously exaggerated. The most striking short-term effect of marijuana is to make users appear slow, lethargic, clumsy—and somewhat giddy. However, unlike alcohol intoxication, marijuana does not generally increase a user's propensity to violence. (For a fascinating discussion of why alcohol is our nation's drug of choice and marijuana is considered by many a "hard-core drug," see Ray, 1993.)

The effects of long-term exposure to marijuana are not completely known. However, it appears that it does impair breathing functions significantly (though that effect may result from the other agents in the smoke and not the THC; see Tilles et al., 1986). Marijuana also has adverse effects on sperm cell morphology and is a reliable disrupter of female reproductive hormones (Mendelson, 1987). It is also suspected of reducing testosterone levels in males (Kolodny et al., 1974).

Meditative States

A yogi sits in a laboratory in India, legs crossed and eyes closed, deep in **meditation.** From his head a forest of electrodes leads to a machine that is tracing an electroencephalogram (EEG). A team of psychologists watches intently as it records the yogi's brain waves. When the EEG shows that his brain is emitting a steady flow of slow, rhythmic alpha waves, the testing begins. A psychologist strikes a tuning fork and holds it to the yogi's ear. The alpha waves stream on, unbroken—a sign that he is not aware of the sound. The psychologist repeats the test first

Although marijuana produces many undesirable effects such as sensory distortions and disruptions of reproductive hormones, its effects have sometimes been exaggerated and distorted. This poster advertised the 1936 movie Reefer Madness, *which labeled marijuana as the "Weed from the Devil's Garden."*

During meditation, worshipers can deliberately induce a special state of consciousness in themselves without drugs. Some form of meditation is found in virtually every major religion.

tense concentration on a single thought or object (Anand, Chhina, & Singh, 1961).

This investigation of a yogi's brain waves during meditation was one of the first scientific attempts to study how people can deliberately induce a special state of consciousness in themselves without drugs. In one form or another, meditation has been incorporated into every major religion, including Judaism and Christianity. Though vast differences exist among the many kinds of meditation practiced in the world today, most share a common element: the meditator focuses attention on a single stimulus, which greatly restricts sensory input and ultimately changes consciousness (Goleman, 1977).

Meditation can produce a marked change in nervous system activity. The most pronounced change is a general metabolic slowing, which can be seen by a drop in oxygen consumption, a decrease in heart rate and respiration, and a decline in blood pressure (Wallace & Benson, 1972). However, these changes also occur in people who are merely resting. What makes meditation a unique state of consciousness?

The clearest evidence comes from studies using the EEG—the brain waves. A relaxed person shows only modest changes in brain-wave patterns, com-

with a hand clap and then with a hot test tube applied to the yogi's arm—all with the same result: his brain, deep in meditation, registers no reaction. The yogi is in *samadhi*, a state in which his awareness appears to be separated from his senses through in-

pared to those of normal waking consciousness. During meditation, though, the brain waves change markedly. The specific type of brain-wave activity generated during meditation depends to a large extent on the kind of meditation being practiced. For instance, one study found that the EEGs of Buddhist monks who practice *zazen* registered alpha waves as soon as the monks started meditating, even though their eyes were wide open (Kasamatsu & Hirai, 1966). (Remember, alpha waves are normally abundant only in people whose eyes are closed.) As the session progressed, the monks' alpha waves changed gradually to slower theta waves—even more unusual in people with their eyes open.

How could a person with open eyes display theta brain-wave patterns? The answer is still unknown. However, Ornstein (1977) believes meditation involves a loss of awareness of the outside world, precipitated by a restricted focus on an unchanging stimulus.

The Hypnotic State

Most of us are familiar with hypnosis, at some level. For many of us, though, our understanding is shaped by "stage demonstrations" of hypnotism. In such stereotypical situations, we expect the hypnotist to speak in a soft, monotonous tone: "I want you to relax your body and become comfortable. Just relax and let yourself go limp. You will find yourself becoming warm, at ease. Now you are becoming drowsy and sleepy, drowsy and sleepy. . . ." One by one, the subjects close their eyes and lower their heads.

When everyone is still, the hypnotist tells them: "Now clasp your hands together tightly, as though they were locked together by a steel band. Try as you might, you can't get them apart. Try to separate them. You can't." Subjects strain to pry apart their hands, but their fingers remain interlocked. At last, the hypnotist breaks the tension: "Stop trying, and relax. Your hands are no longer locked together." The straining stops, and everyone's hands separate.

Such demonstrations create the popular impression that a hypnotized person is in a special kind of trance, cut off from normal waking awareness and self-control. Some psychologists *do* believe that hypnosis is indeed a special state of consciousness; others are not so certain. Perhaps the most widely accepted account of hypnosis is the *neodissociative*

theory (E. Hilgard, 1973, 1975). The term *dissociative* refers to a separation of cognitive states.[4] In hypnosis, there seems to be a **dissociation** between different aspects of consciousness. For example, many people find that hypnosis can provide significant pain relief. Recall "Dr. B" from the chapter opening. While under hypnosis, Dr. B could undergo major dental work—the type most of us find extremely painful—with no anesthesia. At one level, then, hypnosis controls the pain. Curiously, Dr. B can also provide a verbal description of the pain. He might say, "This is an intense pain, a type of burning that seems to begin at the incisor and goes deep into the jaw." At the same time, he doesn't behave as if he finds it painful. He doesn't flinch or feel anxious, and his heart rate does not accelerate.

To explain this paradox, Hilgard (1973) refers to the "hidden observer" in hypnosis. Though Dr. B's outward appearance suggests no pain, the "hidden observer" is able to report such feelings. Hypnosis allows the physical sensations—in this case, pain—to be *dissociated* from the emotional responses that usually accompany them.

Hypnotic Susceptibility

According to one estimate, about nineteen out of twenty people can be hypnotized to some degree, *if* they want to be and *if* they trust the hypnotist. But some people are much more easily and deeply hypnotized than others. Psychologists measure this trait of **hypnotic susceptibility** by means of various standardized tests, most commonly the Stanford Hypnotic Susceptibility Scale (E. Hilgard, 1965).

The Stanford Hypnotic Susceptibility Scale was developed by Ernest Hilgard of Stanford University, a pioneer in early hypnosis research. To determine a subject's susceptibility, the investigator first attempts to bring the subject under hypnosis. Following this, the subject is given a series of suggestions, such as "Your left arm will become rigid" or "You will be unable to say your name when asked." If the subject is unable to bend the arm more than 2 inches or unable to say the name within ten seconds, for example, he or she receives a positive rating. The

---

[4]The classic dissociative state is "multiple personality disorder," an exceedingly rare clinical condition where the person literally "splits" into two or more personalities. We will discuss multiple personality disorder in detail in Chapter 15.

One of the most widely practiced forms of natural childbirth is the Lamaze technique. The tools taught to women in Lamaze training can be seen as a type of hypnosis, in which the women effectively learn to dissociate themselves from the pain of childbirth.

subject is given about a dozen different suggestions. The more suggestions to which the subject receives a positive rating, the higher the score. In one study of more than 500 college students, about 10 percent were classified as "highly susceptible" (E. Hilgard, 1965).

What are the characteristics of people who score high in hypnotic susceptibility? Many often become so absorbed in activities such as reading a novel, listening to music, or appreciating the beauty of nature that they lose track of time (Crawford, 1985). In general, these people have a greater than average ability to focus on a task, ignore extraneous perceptions, and become deeply involved in imagination. Many occasionally enter trancelike states in which they feel somehow separated from things as they usually experience them (Bowers, 1983).

Hypnotic susceptibility may develop early in life. People who are highly susceptible to hypnosis are likely to have had a history of daydreaming and imaginary companions as children (Hilgard, 1970, 1974). As adults, they often have a marked facility for switching from reality to fantasy, from analytical thinking to free-flowing modes of thought (Crawford, 1985). These patterns are not universal, of course. Not all people who fantasize a lot are highly hypnotizable, and some people who can be deeply hypnotized have poor imaginative abilities (Lynn & Rhue, 1988). In general, however, fantasy, imagination, and susceptibility to hypnosis tend to go together.

The Uses of Hypnosis

In the past several decades, hypnosis has been put to a growing number of uses. As discussed previously, some doctors find hypnosis a drug-free treatment for pain. In fact, on the battlefields in World War II, hypnosis was sometimes used to treat the wounded when painkillers were not available. Today, pregnant women sometimes seek out hypnosis to aid in labor and delivery. One of the most widely known forms of natural childbirth is the Lamaze technique. The tools taught to the women (and their "coaches") in this technique can be seen as a type of hypnosis. During the training prior to actual delivery, the birth-mothers are told to focus on their breathing, the rhythm of their contractions, even a spot on the wall; in effect, they are dissociating themselves from the pain.

Oster (1994) has developed a more direct hypnotic procedure to be used in childbirth. According to early studies, these techniques take no more time to learn than Lamaze, and yet are even more effective at reducing pain during labor. Furthermore, some patients have been able to use the skills they had learned preparing for childbirth in other pain-control situations, such as dental work.

Hypnosis has also been used in the treatment of burn victims (Patterson et al., 1992). Unlike dental pain or the pain associated with childbirth, burn pain is chronic, lasting for days, weeks, or even months. Burn victims are often treated with sustained high doses of opiate-based painkillers. Patterson and colleagues (1992), though, report significant, sustained pain reduction with hypnosis. While burn victims may still require pharmacological painkillers, hypnosis may reduce the frequency or the dosage levels required. These corroborate Kihlstrom's (1985) earlier conclusion: there is no doubt hypnosis can be an effective pain reliever.

In addition to its role in alleviating pain, hypnosis is also used in treating certain behavioral problems. A longtime smoker, for instance, may seek the help of a hypnotist to break the cigarette habit. Under hypnosis, the person is usually told that cigarette smoking will no longer be enjoyable, and then is instructed to forget that the suggestion came from the hypnotist. For some people in some circumstances, this approach has helped. If hypnosis is used *alone,* however, the changes it brings about appear to be temporary (Spanos, Mondoux, & Burgess, 1995). In one study (Spiegel et al., 1993), over three-fourths of the participants returned to smoking within two years. Regardless of the claims you may read in advertisements, hypnotic intervention is not a miracle cure.

The Limitations of Hypnosis   Our beliefs about hypnosis have been shaped by a number of factors, few of them scientific. Reports in the popular media—or, even worse, novels or movies—have popularized beliefs concerning hypnosis that have no basis in fact.

For example, most people believe they will not perform an act under hypnosis that they would not normally perform if they were not hypnotized. This is not necessarily true. In a classic study, (Orne & Evans, 1965) hypnotized a group of subjects, then told them to perform three separate tasks. First, they were to remove a poisonous snake from a box, located in a corner of the room. Then they were also asked to remove a coin from a container filled with strong acid using their bare hands. (To convince the subjects that the container held real acid, the experimenter tossed a coin in the acid; it immediately began to dissolve. The acid was later replaced with water—but the subjects did not see this switch.) Finally, the subjects were to toss the acid into the face of the experimenter's assistant.

It seems reasonable to conclude that subjects would not normally perform these three actions. Would a hypnotized subject follow the instructions? The results may surprise you. Almost all the hypnotized subjects followed all the experimenter's instructions, indicating a willingness to do things they

would not normally do. After being told to pick up the poisonous snake, subjects walked directly to the box and reached down to pick it up. (There really was a poisonous snake in the box, so subjects had to be restrained at the last minute!) Likewise, they reached into the container of "acid" to pick up the coins. They even threw the beaker of "acid" into the lab assistant's face.

Before concluding that hypnotized subjects will do things they might not ordinarily do, we should examine the behavior of another group of subjects in Orne and Evans' experiment. This group of subjects, a control group, were told to "act as if they were hypnotized." They received the same instructions: pick up the snake, reach into acid to pick up the coins, and throw the acid on the lab assistant. Remarkably, *all* the subjects in the control group followed the instructions! (In fairness, the subjects who were faking hypnosis *did* hesitate before doing so; those who were hypnotized did not.)

Such results suggest that hypnosis may induce subjects to engage in otherwise unacceptable behavior. Just as importantly, though, it illustrates the *powerful* influence of experimental demands. Even non-hypnotized subjects performed in the way they thought the experimenter desired. As we study psychological research throughout the text, keep in mind that the effects of experimental demands can be significant.

Misuses of Hypnotism: Can Hypnotism "Recover" Memories?   One of the most common beliefs about hypnosis is that it is an effective and reliable way to enhance memory. Most people believe that subjects who are hypnotized will recall more information about past events than they could remember otherwise. In fact, it is commonly believed that hypnosis may be the *only* technique that allows certain memories–such as those that are psychologically threatening—to be recovered. As a result of these beliefs, police sometimes hypnotize witnesses, hoping that they will "recover" memories, referred to as "hypnotically refreshed" memories. Are they reliable? Is a hypnotically refreshed memory *more* accurate than other memories?

What about other kinds of memory, memories of painful or traumatic events (particularly childhood events)? Can hypnosis allow otherwise blocked memories (sometimes called "repressed" memories) to be retrieved? Hypnosis is frequently used in psychotherapy, as the therapist tries to uncover "hidden" or "repressed" memories in those being treated. Recent research, however, casts grave doubts on the reliability of memories retrieved while under hypnosis. Steblay and Bothwell (1994) reviewed two dozen studies and found no evidence for memory improvement. In fact, when "leading questions" were used (questions asked in such a way as to imply a certain answer), hypnotized subjects showed a slight *impairment* in memory accuracy. They were more likely to produce the answer the leading question implied.

Hypnosis does exert one major effect on memory, though it is counterproductive. Steblay and Bothwell report that hypnotized subjects were more *confident* when reporting their memories—which would, of course, make them more convincing to juries. Keep in mind, though, that their increased confidence did not produce increased accuracy (see also Krass, Kinoshita, & McConkey, 1989).

Many times hypnosis is used to enhance the memory of children. But Ceci, Loftus, Leichtman, and Bruck (1994) found that hypnosis magnified problems of unreliability, and that children are particularly suggestible in such situations. For instance, children are more likely to make errors in their memory for the *sources* of information. That is, a child who is asked to *imagine* a certain situation might later believe that the situation really happened. (Parents of young children must often reassure them that an event occurred in a *dream*, not in real life.) An event "remembered" by a child during testimony might be the child's recollection of the interrogation, rather than a recollection of the actual event. It is critical to note that children in these situations are not intentionally "lying," they are recalling what they believe to be true.

Erdelyi (1994) offers an interesting explanation for the effects of hypnosis on memory. He points out that subjects in hypnosis/memory experiments are usually tested repeatedly, to document enhancements in memory. However, even nonhypnotized subjects routinely show memory improvement with repeated testing, a phenomenon known as *hypermnesia* (the opposite of "a-mnesia"). According to Erdelyi, the improvement in memory that is sometimes shown with hypnosis is due to increased attempts at retrieval, not to hypnosis.

The problem of false memories being accepted as literally true memories is exacerbated by the psychotherapists' beliefs about hypnosis (Loftus et al., 1994). Loftus and associates report that a significant number of psychotherapists believe that hypnosis can retrieve memories from early childhood (prior to age three or four), or even memories from birth or before. But there is now overwhelming evidence that memories from before the age of three to four are rare in adults, and those from before the age of about two are virtually nonexistent (Howe & Courage, 1993; Loftus, 1993; Usher & Neisser, 1993).

In sum, most memory researchers reject the use of hypnosis as a tool to assist memory retrieval. The common belief that hypnosis can help people to dredge up accurate memories has not been supported. In fact, in many cases there is reason to doubt whether the "memories" thus recovered even existed at all (Weaver, 1995). Though hypnosis does not reliably improve memory, it can make people more confident of their false memories. Hypnosis is a risky technique for police work, and an equally risky technique for therapists trying to recover traumatic memories from a client's childhood.

In Depth

Dissociations between Consciousness and Behavior

THIS CHAPTER INTRODUCED the concept of "dissociation," a separation of different aspects of consciousness and behavior. In *multiple personality disorder* (see Chapter 15), an exceedingly rare clinical disorder, dissociation takes the form of two or more personalities existing within the same person. The title character in the movie "Sybil" from a few years back is a person with multiple personality disorder. Less sensational, but no less important, is the realization among psychologists that some form of dissociation occurs in everyone, as expressed in Recurring Theme 3: *A large proportion of our behavior is controlled by unconscious activity.*

THEME   A Large Proportion of Our Behavior Is Controlled by Unconscious Activity

Psychologists have made great insights into consciousness by examining extreme cases, as stated by Recurring Theme 2: *Psychologists learn about the normal by studying the abnormal.* Each case is somewhat different, but in each instance, individuals have retained certain abilities or skills, but are no longer *aware* that they possess these skills.

THEME   Psychologists Learn about the Normal by Studying the Abnormal

This "In Depth" section will discuss dissociations between behavior and *awareness of behavior*—"consciousness"—in three different situations. First, we will examine the patient H. M., whose case was described in Chapter 3. H. M. underwent exploratory surgery to treat his epilepsy and suffered devastating memory impairments as a result. However, not all forms of H. M.'s memory were disrupted. His case was among the first to suggest that some types of memory may not require *awareness* in order to function. Next, we will discuss the phenomenon of "blindsight," in which individuals report that they can see nothing and function as if they are blind, but under some conditions exhibit behavior that indicates they *can* see. Like H. M., these people are not aware of their abilities.

Finally, we will look at a recent finding that suggests a type of dissociation in substance abusers and addicts. Addicts were administered their substance

of choice in very low concentrations, below the threshold for conscious detection. At these low doses, however, the addicts' behavior was influenced by the presence of the drug, but the influences operate without awareness. These findings suggest that substance abusers may have both conscious and nonconscious aspects of their addictions (Berridge & Robinson, 1995).

Initial Studies

The case of H. M. (see Chapter 3) has become a part of psychological folklore; students who remember little else about psychology will remember his case. The traditional interpretation of H. M.'s memory disorders has been that in isolation H. M.'s short-term memory and long-term memory are unimpaired, but his ability to form *new* long-term memories is irreversibly damaged. But his case illustrates another, perhaps more important, memory dissociation. Though some kinds of information *can* be learned by H. M., he has no *awareness* of his learning.

The kinds of memories that H. M. can no longer form have been called *declarative* or *explicit memories*, while those he can form have been called *procedural* or *implicit* memories (Roediger, 1990; Tulving, 1985, 1993). A number of amnesiac syndromes display this dissociation between explicit and implicit memories —Korsakoff's disease, for example (see Chapter 3). (Chapter 7 will provide an extensive discussion of these two types of memory.) For our purposes here, one of the most striking findings in recent research is that *normal* subjects also display dissociations between these types of memory. That is, much of your behavior and many of your choices of behavior— from decisions as simple and trivial as the color of a shirt to complex, significant decisions, such as who to marry—are influenced by events of which you are no longer consciously aware.

Sigmund Freud was one of the first psychologists to realize the influence of unconscious processing. His interpretation of this influence, however, emphasized its insidiousness. (Chapter 13 will describe some of the influences Freud postulated, which have collectively been called "defense mechanisms.") Though Freud's theoretical interpretation might be debated, most psychologists *do* acknowledge the importance of unconscious influences on behavior.

Criticism, Alternatives, and Further Studies

This chapter opened with the story of "D. B.," the Englishman studied by Larry Weiskrantz. D. B. suffered brain damage to the *striate cortex*, a part of the occipital cortex known to be critical to vision. As a result of the damage, he is blind in the visual field that corresponds to the damage.[5] D. B. and others like him are frequently tested by presenting stimuli like a horizontal line to the blind portions of their visual fields and asking them to report what they see. These subjects report seeing nothing. However, if these subjects are put in a situation in which they must choose between alternatives, they perform remarkably well, detecting movement, color, or orientation of the stimuli (Weiskrantz, 1995). Though they report seeing nothing, if asked to guess, their accuracy sometimes reaches 90 to 100 percent (Weiskrantz, 1995). Obviously they are not guessing. However, when patients are told that their accuracy is high, most are bewildered. They have no awareness of how they did it—recall D. B.'s insistence that he "didn't see a darn thing"—nor are they aware of being correct, even after they have been told.

There has been some debate about the nature of blindsight. Weiskrantz (1986, 1995) theorizes that these patients take advantage of other visual pathways in the brain. In primates, the retina projects to ten different areas in the brain. Though the striate cortex is critical for most visual tasks, the retina can still project to other areas. None of these alternative pathways is accessible to consciousness, however. Other researchers disagree with Weiskrantz (i.e., Fendrich, Wessinger, & Gazzaniga, 1992; Gazzaniga, Fendrich, & Wessinger, 1994). They contend that in cases of blindsight, patients retain small "islands" of undamaged striate cortex. These still-functioning visual centers allow them to make discriminations of which they are not aware.

Berridge and Robinson (1995; see also Robinson & Berridge, 1993) have proposed a model of addiction called the "incentive-sensitization" theory, which recognizes the importance of nonconscious factors in addiction. Berridge and Robinson suggest that since craving (they use the term *wanting*) a drug involves processes "not available to consciousness, people may find themselves wanting particular things without knowing why. Under some circumstances, people may not even know that they want them" (p. 72).

A remarkable study by Lamb and his colleagues (1991) dramatically illustrates this phenomenon. They studied the behavior of former heroin addicts. They put the addicts in a situation in which they could press a lever to obtain injections of morphine or saline (saltwater, which has no pharmacological effect). After being given one of these substances, subjects were asked to provide subjective evaluations of the drug: how "good" it was, and how much it would be worth on the street. (See Lamb et al., 1991, for a discussion of the potential ethical problems associated with giving drugs to former addicts). As you might expect, the addicts rated the saline as "worthless," and after a few trials no longer pressed the bar. When they received morphine in moderate or higher doses, they rated it very desirable and continued to work to get it by repeatedly pressing the bar.

However, when the morphine was administered in very low doses, the addicts displayed a remarkable dissociation. They rated the low-dose morphine "worthless," just as they had the saline. But despite their low evaluation, 80 percent of them continued to press the bar to receive it. In fact, judging by rate of bar pressing, they worked just as hard as those who received high doses of morphine. Though the subjects did not consciously prefer the low-dose morphine—their own reports indicated it was "worthless"—at another, presumably nonconscious level, the drug was altering their behavior.

Most drug abuse treatment programs stress complete abstinence for recovering addicts. For example, Alcoholics Anonymous urges members to avoid their *first* drink. They know that while a single drink might not cause trouble immediately, it usually leads to a complete relapse. Berridge and Robinson's incentive-sensitization theory of addiction explains why: the single drink triggers the sensations of craving, which then begins to influence the alcoholic's behavior *without the alcoholic's awareness.*

---

[5]Since this brain damage is usually restricted to only one side of the brain, these individuals have "blind spots" in those half-fields. The other parts of their visual field are usually normal, including the corresponding visual area on the opposite side of the blind field.

Patterns and Conclusions

As we have seen throughout this chapter, "consciousness" has been difficult for psychologists to define, and even more difficult to study.

Perhaps we should not be surprised that many factors that influence our behavior do so outside of consciousness. The human nervous system is, after all, the result of millions of years of evolution. Consciousness appears to be mediated by "newer" areas of the brain such as the frontal cortex, but these areas are not necessary for all types of learning; simpler organisms that lack a frontal cortex are clearly able to learn. Anyone with an aquarium knows how readily the fish begin to associate feeding with taps on the glass, turning on of the aquarium light, and so on. There is little doubt that the fish—despite having very primitive neural structures—have learned. But do the fish have any conscious awareness of these associations? Most psychologists do not think so.

During the course of evolution brains have become more complex. But the older, nonconscious pathways in the brain have not been discarded. As Lieberman (1991) stated, when newer structures and functions of the brain appear, "the older part of the brain is not 'unplugged' and replaced by a new module. It continue[s] to function in concert with the new part" (p. 20). Consciousness, then, seems to be a fairly recent evolutionary adaptation (Flannigan, 1992). The parts of our ancestor's brains that did not rely on consciousness are still present in our brains today, and they continue to influence behavior.

SUMMARY

1. **Consciousness** is the awareness of the many thoughts, images, perceptions, and emotions that occupy the mind at any given moment. This awareness varies significantly depending on the situation. People experience cyclical changes in consciousness every day (sleeping and daydreaming, for instance).

2. Psychologists have distinguished several stages of sleep by monitoring people's brain waves. After a person has been in the deepest stage of sleep for a while (known as **delta sleep**), he or she seems to return to a waking brain-wave pattern. Yet the person remains sound asleep, with eyes moving rapidly back and forth beneath closed eyelids. This stage is known as **rapid eye movement** or **REM sleep** and is closely associated with dreaming.

3. People compensate for lost REM sleep on one night by entering the REM state more often during their next night's sleep **(REM rebound)**. This finding has led to theories that REM sleep serves some special physiological function. One possibility is that REM sleep helps the brain adapt to disturbing or unusual life experiences. Another possibility is that REM sleep helps release pent-up energy associated with unsatisfied physiological needs.

4. People have debated the meaning of dreams for centuries. Although Freud believed that dreams embody people's unconscious wishes, disguised in symbolic form, many contemporary therapists believe that dreams are usually direct attempts to deal with the concerns and problems that dominate waking consciousness.

5. Distinctive states of consciousness involving changes in mood and thought can be induced by various **psychoactive** drugs. Some, collectively called **stimulants,** include caffeine, nicotine, amphetamines, and cocaine. The drugs generally increase neural activity, resulting in feelings of increased arousal or alertness. **Depressants** include alcohol, opiates, benzodiazepines, and barbiturates. These typically depress neural activity and are used in pain management, treatment of some kinds of anxiety, and anesthesia. The **hallucinogens** include LSD and marijuana. While both induce sensory and perceptual distortions, the effects of LSD are considerably more pronounced.

6. An ancient technique for inducing a special state of consciousness without the use of drugs is **meditation.** Although there are many varieties of meditation, most involve focusing attention on a single stimulus until sensory input from the

outside world is greatly restricted. During meditation, a person's metabolism may undergo a measurable slowing, and brain-wave patterns may also slow. Exactly how these changes occur is still being explored.

7. Despite the belief of many (including law enforcement agents), psychologists have found no evidence that hypnosis actually enhances memory. It is likely that the memory improvements sometimes seen when hypnosis is used in police investigations are largely the results of factors other than hypnosis, factors that just happen to be linked with the use of hypnosis for this purpose.

8. The precise nature of the state of awareness called hypnosis is uncertain, despite its medical and therapeutic uses. Some researchers propose that when a person is hypnotized, a **dissociation** or split in consciousness occurs. But others contend that hypnotized people are merely trying hard to follow the hypnotist's directives by using a variety of cognitive strategies available to them in the normal waking state.

9. In some cases, particularly those involving some kind of localized brain injury, a person may retain an ability (such as vision) while losing the conscious components of that skill. These dissociations between behavior and awareness are powerful evidence that our behavior is influenced by factors of which we are not aware.

SUGGESTED READINGS

Dennett. D. (1991). *Consciousness explained.* New York: Little Brown. One of the acknowledged "classics" in the recently resurgent study of consciousness. A difficult but fascinating account of the issues.

Empson, J. (1990). *Sleep and dreaming.* Winchester, MA: Faber & Faber. The author presents research on sleep and dreaming for the general reader. The book explains what scientists have learned about the experience of sleep and dreaming and the various types of sleep disorders.

Flannigan, O. (1994). *Consciousness reconsidered.* Cambridge, MA: MIT Press. Written by a philosopher, this book discusses many of the most perplexing aspects of consciousness, yet manages to convey the essence of the often-obscure philosophical approach to consciousness.

Hilgard, E. R. (1994). Neodissociation theory. In S. J. Lynn & J. W. Rhue (Eds.), *Dissociation: Clinical and theoretical perspectives* (pp. 32–51). New York: Guilford Press. A brief but highly readable account of neodissociative models of hypnosis.

Julien, R. M. (1995). *A primer of drug action* (7th ed.). San Francisco: Freeman. Up-to-date information on the actions and side effects of drugs that affect the central nervous system. The author covers a wide variety of drugs, including alcohol, opiates, and psychedelics.

Lynn, S. J., & Rhue, J. W. (Eds.), *Dissociation: Clinical and theoretical perspectives* (pp. 32–51). New York: Guilford Press. Written for a more professionally oriented audience, this book discusses some clinical implications of dissociation.

Moorcroft, W. H. (1993). *Sleep, dreaming, and sleep disorders: An introduction* (2nd ed.). Landham, MD: University Press of America. An introduction to the current knowledge and theories about sleep, dreaming, and sleep disorders. It also discusses the speculation surrounding dream theories and provides a particularly good section on the activation-synthesis hypothesis.

Penrose, R. (1994). *Shadows of the mind: A search for the missing science of consciousness.* Oxford: Oxford University Press. Penrose is a mathematician by training, so he brings an unusual and refreshing perspective to the discussions of consciousness.

CHAPTER
6

Learning
and Behavior

 The next three chapters deal with learning, memory, cognition, and language. Though we will examine these topics separately, they are critically related to each other—so much so that at times, distinctions can blur.

The following passage was written by Jane Goodall, one of this century's most respected anthropologists. Goodall has devoted her life to the study of chimps and other primates, almost always in their natural habitats. To do this, she has literally spent decades living with groups of primates, sleeping, eating, playing, and working just a few feet from them. In this passage, Goodall discusses a chimpanzee that was studied several decades ago, during a time when scientists were attempting to teach language to nonhumans:

There is a very poignant story about a female chimpanzee named Lucy. She was raised from infancy in a human home, and treated just like one of the family. She went to the refrigerator, took out cold snacks, poured herself a drink. She watched the television, had access to magazines, her own bedroom, everything. When she was somewhere between ten and thirteen for some reason her "parents" [her human caregivers] decided to send her back to Africa. She'd never seen another chimp, and I believe it was rather like sending a somewhat pampered Western adolescent out to live with Australian Aborigines, for example. She arrived in The Gambia, and was put in a large field enclosure with a couple of rather boisterous wild-born chimps from Burundi. She went into a deep depression, which lasted for at least two years, trying to avoid the approaches of these two creatures, who she didn't know at all.

Just around this time she was visited by someone who had known her in the old days, when she was part of a family. At that point Lucy had been taught somewhere between 60 and 100 signs of American Sign Language. When she saw this visitor she ran over to the wire of her enclosure, looked into her eyes, and signed, "Please, help, out."

Jane Goodall, interviewed on the PBS series *The Mind,* 1987

Regardless of whether Lucy used these symbols as humans used language (most scientists—including Goodall—are skeptical), she was capable of learning and retaining complex skills. Learning is crucial to our lives. Through learning we acquire not only academic skills, such as reading and writing, but the very knowledge we need to function in everyday life. When we master the techniques of driving a car, cooking a meal, or doing laundry, we are engaged in forms of learning. In fact, learning has an impact on almost everything we do.

In this chapter we explore the important subject of learning and psychologists' perspectives on it. First, we will discuss classical and operant conditioning, the two types of learning that have been most intensely studied by psychologists. In the next section we will examine observational learning, learning that occurs by watching others. Then we will look at some of the ways psychologists have applied conditioning principles in various situations. Finally, we will discuss some of the biological constraints on learning.

The Nature of Learning

Learning, as we often use the term, is closely related to cognition. How do we know when learning has occurred? In many cases involving humans, we can simply ask the person. In other cases, this approach is inadequate. We cannot ask infants or animals if they have learned; they lack the ability to communicate using language. Furthermore, verbal reports of learning are often misleading. Sometimes people are not sure whether or not they have learned; in other situations, their responses are inaccurate. Finally, people learn many things without being aware of it. You probably have a favorite color, yet you probably cannot remember how you learned to like that color. Such learning illustrates Recurring Theme 3, which states that much of human behavior occurs without conscious awareness.

 **THEME** A Large Proportion of Behavior Is Controlled by Unconscious Activity

3

As a result of these potential problems, early behaviorists inferred that learning had taken place by observing changes in performance. Thus, psychologists would create a controlled situation that was conducive to learning, then objectively measure the resulting performance. If performance changed, they concluded that the change could indicate learning. Of course, experimental situations must always be carefully controlled, because factors other than learning (emotion, motivation, maturation, fatigue, health, and so forth) can also influence performance. Only when other influences can be legitimately ruled out may researchers infer that a change in performance is probably due to learning.

Though performance is useful for measuring learning, in some cases learning does not result in a change in performance. Sometimes we learn but do not have an opportunity to demonstrate that learning. Or sometimes we simply are not motivated to show what we have learned. Many times a change in behavior is displayed only under certain circumstances. Psychologists refer to this phenomenon as the learning-performance distinction. Nevertheless,

learning always creates the *potential* for a change in performance.

A definition of learning should also differentiate between learning and all the other factors that can influence performance. To distinguish learning from factors that can temporarily affect performance (such as emotion or fatigue), learning can be called a relatively permanent change in performance potential. And to distinguish learning from physical factors, such as maturation or illness, learning can be called a change in performance potential that results from experience. Combining all these elements yields the following definition: **learning** is a relatively permanent change in observable behavior potential that results from experience with the environment (Barker, 1997).

In this chapter we examine some of the different kinds of learning in which humans and other animals engage. One is learning to associate events with one another, called **associative learning.** Suppose you visit the doctor to get an immunization. Just before you get the injection, the doctor swabs your arm with cotton soaked in alcohol, which has a distinctive odor. You respond to the injection with fear and anxiety. Later, the distinctive odor of rubbing alcohol causes you to become anxious, even if you are not to receive an injection. Psychologists would say that you have acquired a **classically conditioned response.** You have learned an association between the odor of rubbing alcohol and the pain of the injection (which explains the "doctor's office smell" we all knew—and feared—when we were children).

Classical conditioning is a very basic kind of learning in which a previously neutral stimulus (in this case the odor of rubbing alcohol) comes to elicit an involuntary action or feeling (anxiety and fear). It does so because it signals the onset of another stimulus (an injection) that naturally elicits the same response. Classical conditioning can result in long-term, persistent associations. Most of us still don't like the smells of a doctor's office, due in large part to the classical conditioning we underwent as children.

Another kind of associative learning is called **operant conditioning.** It involves learning to change one's behavior because of the consequences that follow it. Suppose you are learning to play a new computer game. At one point in the game, your character must turn left or right. The first time you play, you turn left, and your character falls into a pit: you lose the game. The next time you play the game you turn right. This time, your character finds a pot of gold. You quickly learn the appropriate behavior by associating this positive experience with the right turn. Psychologists would say that this learning to turn right is a **conditioned operant response,** one that was *reinforced* by the pot of gold. That is, the conditioned operant response results from a learned association between a particular action (the right turn) and a desirable consequence (finding the pot of gold). Your learning is further enhanced by the negative consequences (losing the game) associated with turning left.

In the early twentieth century, radical behaviorists like Skinner and Watson argued that virtually all learning could be explained by classical and operant conditioning. Today, others contend that while those two forms of learning are important, much of human learning does not fall neatly into either category. **Cognitive learning**—the formation of concepts, schemas, theories, and other mental abstractions—is also crucial. For instance, in playing a computer game, you may learn that when you are given a choice of paths, you are more likely to be successful if you choose to turn right. This "rule of thumb" is a concept or schema.

Behaviorists maintain that cognitions are too vague and subjective for scientific study. To cognitive psychologists, however, people's thought processes are just as important as their overt behaviors. Historically, the behaviorist and cognitive perspectives have been at odds. In recent years, however, psychologists have been making an extensive effort to integrate the two perspectives (e.g., Anderson, 1995; Barker, 1997). We will conclude this chapter by looking at learning from the cognitive psychologists' perspective. But first we turn to classical and operant conditioning.

Classical Conditioning

Ivan Pavlov is one of psychology's most recognizable figures. His research on conditioned salivation in dogs is widely known, even to those who have only a passing knowledge of psychology. Like many great discoveries, it was largely accidental. Pavlov was studying the physiology of digestion—work which would later win him the Nobel prize (for physiology, not psychology). Though most digestion takes place in the stomach and intestines, digestion actually begins in the mouth, which responds to food by secreting saliva. Pavlov was using dogs as his experimental subjects, and he had devised a procedure to shunt the secretions of their salivary glands into tubes, where they could more easily be studied.

During his work, Pavlov noticed that the dogs would often begin salivating in *anticipation* of being fed. These anticipatory salivations, which Pavlov called "psychic secretions," began only after dogs had had some experience in the laboratory. At first, the dogs began salivating when they saw or smelled the food. Eventually, they would being to salivate as soon as the lab technicians entered the room. Pavlov found this unexpected response to be annoying, as it disrupted his experiments on digestion. But soon he realized that the processes underlying these "psychic secretions" were more interesting than the process of digestion. Pavlov began examining those responses systematically.

In a series of experiments, Pavlov (1927) became convinced that the dogs' salivation was triggered by psychological factors, not by food being placed in their mouths. Pavlov also found that when a dog first saw an unfamiliar food, it did not salivate. Only when it had learned the particular sights, smells, or other stimuli associated with desirable food did the psychic secretions occur. These discoveries provided the foundation for Pavlov's investigations into classical conditioning (sometimes called **Pavlovian conditioning**).

Acquiring a Classically Conditioned Response

Figure 6-1 shows one of Pavlov's dogs in a typical experimental apparatus. The dog has a tube inserted in its cheek (called a "fistula") so that saliva flows from its salivary gland into a container. The mechanical device at the far left monitors the amount of saliva being secreted. Pavlov began by presenting the dog with a neutral stimulus such as a tone. (The tone was "neutral" with respect to salivation because it neither evoked nor inhibited the salivation response.) Several seconds after the tone, Pavlov dropped food into the dog's feeding tray. When the dog put the food in its mouth, it salivated. As the pairing of the tone and the food continued, the tone began to elicit salivation by itself, even if no food was given to the dog.

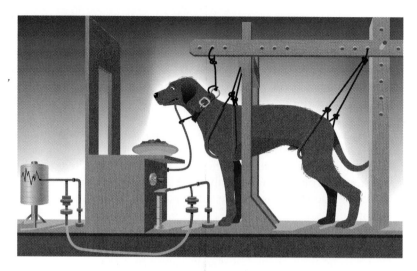

FIGURE 6-1 The apparatus used in early studies of classical conditioning. Saliva dropping from a tube inserted into the dog's cheek strikes a lightly balanced mechanical arm. The resulting motion is transmitted hydraulically to a pen that traces a record on graph paper attached to a revolving drum. Pavlov's discovery of conditioned salivation was an accidental by-product of his research into the activity of the digestive system.

Pavlov termed the food in the mouth an **unconditioned stimulus (US),** and the salivation it elicited the **unconditioned response (UR).** The word *unconditioned* simply means "unlearned." Unconditioned stimuli produce unconditioned responses prior to any learning. In Pavlov's experiments, placing food in the mouth of a dog caused the dog to salivate immediately.

To demonstrate conditioning, another stimulus must be paired with the unconditioned stimulus. This new stimulus, which Pavlov called the **conditioned stimulus (CS),** does not elicit the desired response prior to conditioning. In Pavlov's experiment, the tone was the conditioned stimulus. Prior to conditioning it did not elicit salivation. By being paired with the US, the CS becomes associated with it. Eventually, the CS by itself (the tone without the food) elicits salivation. The salivation in response to the tone (the CS) is called the **conditioned response (CR).** To confirm the conditioning, a psychologist would present the CS alone and measure the conditioned response. The relationship between the stimuli and responses in classical conditioning is illustrated in Figure 6-2.

Pavlov found that the dogs acquired the conditioned response gradually. After just a few pairings of the tone and food, the dogs began salivating to the tone—but only a little. As the number of pairings increased, so did the strength of the CR (salivation). A typical pattern of conditioning is shown in Figure 6-3. This is called the *acquisition* phase of learning.

Just as the dogs learned to salivate to the tone gradually, the just learned salivation response begins

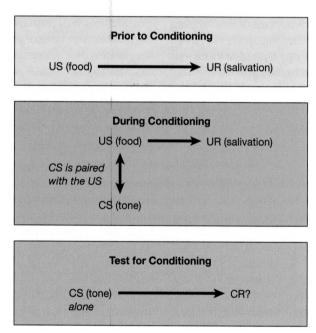

FIGURE 6-2 Typical procedures used in classical conditioning.

to decrease in intensity if the CS (the tone) is presented alone, a process known as **extinction** (see Figure 6-4).

Pavlov found that any number of stimuli—lights, bells, "ticks" of a metronome—could serve as conditioned stimuli. He also found that many other responses (in addition to salivation) could serve as conditioned responses.

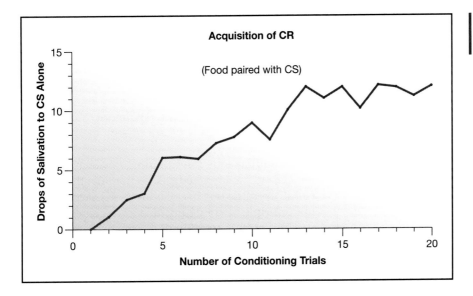

FIGURE 6-3 Acquisition of a classically conditioned response.

Perceiving Relationships between Stimuli

In the past, classical conditioning was characterized as a mechanical process. Conditioning was thought to occur when control over some involuntary reaction was passed from a stimulus that naturally elicited it (the US) to another that normally did not (the CS). Thus, classical conditioning was seen as the simple result of a pairing of the two stimuli. But many modern behaviorists see classical conditioning as a more complex process (see Rescorla, 1988; Schwartz, 1995). They stress the information one stimulus gives about another, and the fact that the responding organism perceives a relationship between the two.

According to this view, Pavlov's dogs perceived a connection between the tone and the food: the tone reliably signaled that food was about to arrive. Thus, one way to view classical conditioning is that the CS allows the animal to make a prediction about the US. Two of the most important factors involved in the predictability of an unconditioned stimulus are contingency and contiguity. **Contingency** refers to the likelihood that the CS signals the US, which can

FIGURE 6-4 Extinction of a classically conditioned response.

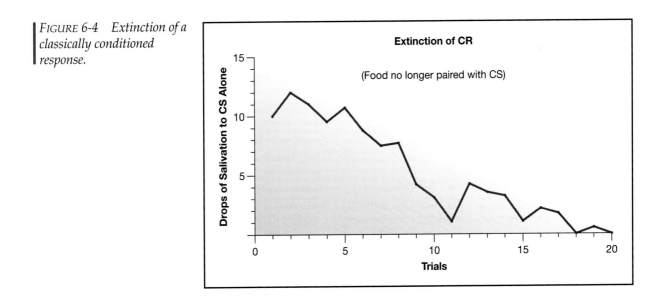

usually be expressed in terms of a probability. **Contiguity** refers to the timing of the CS and the US.

Contingency

Conditioning is usually strongest when the CS is a reliable predictor of the US. In Pavlov's experiment, the tone (CS) *always* preceded the food (US). Pavlov (and many others) found conditioning to be less successful if occasionally the tone was played but food did not follow. (Similarly, if the food was presented without the tone, conditioning was impaired.)

One example of the importance of contingency in learning comes from the number of train-and-automobile accidents that occur at railroad crossings. In the vast majority of these accidents, the car is struck by the train despite the fact that the warning signals are operating properly: the driver of the car simply ignored the warnings. Why should this happen?

Part of the problem lies in the contingent relationship between the flashing signals and the oncoming train. In this situation, the warning signal can be considered a type of CS, and the train the US. The problem in such situations, as you may be able to attest, is that at some crossings the signals flash when a train is not coming. As a result, the contingency between the lights and the train is reduced. Because the signal lights (the CS) do not *reliably* predict the train (the US), drivers frequently ignored them, sometimes with tragic consequences.

Contiguity

The principle of contingency incorporates the *predictive* relationship between the CS and the US. The principle of contiguity incorporates the *temporal* relationship between the CS and the US. As a general rule, the closer the timing between the CS and the US, the stronger the associative relationship between them. Short CS-US intervals produce stronger conditioning; longer CS-US intervals produce weaker conditioning.

Contingency and Contiguity Combined

Together, the principles of contingency and contiguity explain the effectiveness of various conditioning situations. For example, in most cases the strongest conditioning occurs when the CS precedes the US, but the two overlap somewhat, a process known as **forward conditioning** (see Figure 6-5A). Conditioning is highly effective in these situations because the CS reliably predicts the US (the principle of contingency) and the delay between the two stimuli is short (the principle of contiguity). In **trace conditioning** (see Figure 6-5B), the CS reliably predicts the US (contingency), but the delay is somewhat longer, reducing contiguity. Therefore, trace conditioning is generally less successful than forward conditioning.

In **simultaneous conditioning,** the delay between the CS and the US is reduced to nothing; the two occur at the same time (see Figure 6-5C). According to the principle of contiguity, this arrangement should produce strong conditioning. However, presenting the CS and the US simultaneously means that the CS does not *predict* the US. Therefore, simultaneous conditioning is less successful than forward conditioning.

Finally, in **backward conditioning,** the US is presented first, followed by the CS (see Figure 6-5D). Imagine what might have happened if Pavlov's dogs had been given the food first, followed by the tone. When a tone is presented *after* food, it has no predictive value at all. Not surprisingly, backward conditioning typically results in poor conditioning—with a few interesting exceptions. For example, animals (and humans) readily learn to avoid foods (flavors) they associate with illness, a phenomenon known as **taste aversion** (see this chapter's "In Depth" discussion; and Barker, Best, & Domjan, 1977). There are obvious advantages to being able to associate flavor and sickness. Animals that can form such associations can learn to avoid foods that make them ill. But what happens if the animals taste a food *after* they become ill? If a flavor is presented to animals during their *recovery* from sickness, they actually learn to prefer it, a phenomenon known as the "medicine effect" (Barker & Weaver, 1991).

From the perspective of contingency and contiguity, these seemingly odd results make sense. Since the taste comes after the sickness, as the animal is recovering, the taste predicts recovery, not illness. Thus backward conditioning may be an important component of conventional folk treatments like chicken soup. Most often, the soup is eaten by a person recovering from illness. After tasting the soup, the person *does* get better (though the soup may have no real effect on the illness). Over time, the taste of chicken soup is repeatedly paired with recovery from sickness. It is therefore not surprising when people resort to chicken soup when they are ill.

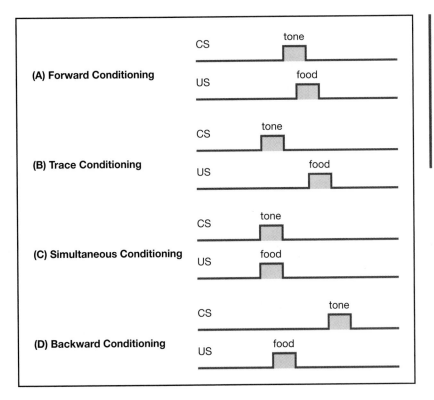

FIGURE 6-5   *Common classical conditioning paradigms. Forward conditioning generally produces the strongest learning, followed by trace conditioning and simultaneous conditioning. Backward conditioning leads to poor learning, except in those cases in which the CS predicts the absence of a US).*

Extinguishing a Classically Conditioned Response

How long do classically conditioned responses last? Did Pavlov's dogs forever salivate at the sound of bells and tones? The answer depends on whether the CS and the US continue to be paired, at least occasionally. If occasional pairing does not occur, conditioned responses will gradually disappear. For example, if a dog has been trained to salivate in response to a tone paired with food, and then the tone is presented repeatedly without being followed by food, salivation will gradually decrease (see again Figure 6-4). This slow weakening and eventual disappearance of a conditioned response is called **extinction.**

Sometimes when a conditioned response seems to have been totally extinguished, it reappears in the original setting. For example, suppose a tone and food are repeatedly so that a dog now salivates whenever the tone is played. Now, suppose the tone is played over and over, but the dog no longer receives food. Eventually the dog will stop salivating when it hears the tone. Has extinction occurred?

If we bring the dog back into the lab several days later, the dog is likely to salivate again at the sound of the tone—a phenomenon called **spontaneous recovery.** If the tone (the CS) is again presented alone, without the food, the recovered response will extinguish, more quickly than the first time. If we bring the dog back to the lab a third time, we will see a second spontaneous recovery—though the behavior will be even less intense than before and will extinguish more rapidly.

Generalizing and Discriminating between Stimuli

Say you have a dog who enjoys playing with visitors. Your dog has probably learned that the ringing of a doorbell (the CS) is usually associated with a visitor (the US). Your dog now rushes to the door whenever the doorbell rings. You may also notice that your dog runs to the door when the telephone rings, or when a doorbell rings on a TV show, or perhaps even to the "ding" of a microwave oven. These other bells have never been associated with visitors. Why should your dog respond to them?

If you own a cat, your cat probably responds to the sound of your can opener, perhaps by running into the kitchen. The cat has learned to associate the

Many pets, like the cat shown here, have formed an association between the sound of a can opener and the arrival of food—an example of classical, or Pavlovian, conditioning.

Phobias can be formed when fear-producing stimuli are paired with previously neutral objects. Once formed, they can be difficult to eliminate. The girl in this picture, for example, is responding to the dog's playful behavior with fear, thereby reinforcing her phobia.

presence of food (the US) with the sound of the can opener. The cat now runs into the kitchen anytime you use the opener—whether or not it is feeding time.

In both these cases, **stimulus generalization** has occurred. Your dog has learned something about doorbells and has *generalized* that learning to all bells. Over time, your dog will likely learn to respond to the doorbell only, not to the chime of the microwave oven. The process of learning to make a particular response only to a particular stimulus is called **stimulus discrimination.**

Generalization of a classically conditioned stimulus happens frequently. In one famous experiment that is now criticized as unethical, John B. Watson and his student Rosalie Rayner showed just how readily generalization can occur (Watson & Rayner, 1920). They conditioned an eleven-month-old boy named Albert to fear a harmless laboratory rat by repeatedly pairing the sight of the rat with a sudden loud noise. Soon little Albert began to show fear at the sight of the rat alone, even if the noise did not fol-

low. And his fear appeared to generalize to other furry objects—a rabbit, a dog, a sealskin coat—even a bearded Santa Claus mask.

The more similar a subsequent stimulus to the one encountered during learning, the more likely generalization will occur. Conversely, the more a new stimulus differs from the original conditioned stimulus, the less likely it will elicit a generalized response. Little Albert, for instance, showed fear at the sight of a live furry rabbit, but he would probably have shown much less fear if presented with a picture of a rabbit. This decreasing tendency to generalize a conditioned response as the resemblance between a new stimulus and a conditioned one declines is called a **generalization gradient** (see Figure 6-6). As the figure shows, the probability of a generalized response is greater for stimuli that are similar to the conditioned stimulus.

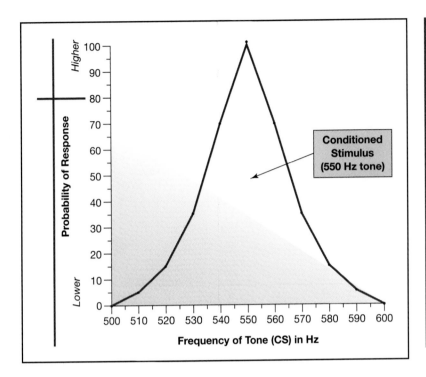

FIGURE 6-6   *Hypothetical generalization gradient obtained following conditioning to a 550-Hz tone. In this example, a dog is conditioned through the pairing of a 550-Hz tone (the CS) with food (the US). Following conditioning, the dog will display a vigorous CR (salivation) in response to the tone. If tones of slightly different frequency are presented to the dog during the test, but they are* not *followed by food (the US), the dog will likely salivate to the similar ones. However, salivation (the CR) will be less vigorous, and will depend on the similarity between the test tones and the conditioned tones. Test tones of a frequency close to 550 Hz will elicit a greater response than those less similar to the 550-Hz tone.*

People display generalization gradients because they can discriminate. That is, they can perceive the dissimilarities between two stimuli and can therefore respond to them differently. In animal research a procedure called **discrimination training** is often used to enhance stimulus discrimination. Consider again the dog that has been conditioned to salivate at the sound of a dinner bell. It will probably also salivate when it hears a set of chimes, although not as much as in response to the bell. To reduce the response to the chimes still further, a researcher could ring the dinner bell and the chimes alternately, but present food only after the bell. Soon the dog's salivation in response to the chimes will extinguish, and it would discriminate sharply between the two stimuli.

Generalization and discrimination often work together to help an organism respond in appropriate ways. For example, if you have been stung by bees and have developed a conditioned fear of them, generalizing that wariness to wasps and hornets is advantageous to you. At the same time, discriminating between stinging and nonstinging insects is helpful; otherwise you will waste a great deal of time avoiding harmless insects.

Discrimination training allows researchers to test the sensory capabilities of nonverbal subjects, such as animals or infants. For example, a discrimination test can be used with dogs to determine their degree of color vision. Researchers might pair some unconditioned stimulus—say, a loud noise that will cause the animal to jump—with a green light. In other situations, they might vary the wavelength of the light and test the animal's reaction over several trials. (Note that it is important to pair the loud noise only with the *green* light, not with lights of a different wavelength.) If the animal responds with fear to the green light but not to a blue light, the researchers know that the dog can perceive the difference between the two lights.

Applying the Principles of Classical Conditioning

Pavlov's experiments in classical conditioning had an enormous influence on the study of psychology. Watson was so impressed by Pavlov's work that he based most of his analysis of behavior on it. All learning, he argued, could be explained within the framework of classical conditioning. Today few psychologists, even behaviorists, take such an extreme view. Still, most believe that classical conditioning is an important form of learning. Emotional responses are particularly susceptible to it. In fact, Little Albert's conditioned fear of rats is often viewed as a powerful model for how *phobias* (strong, persistent, debilitating fears) may develop. (Phobias will be discussed in greater depth in Chapter 15.)

Many different techniques have been developed to treat specific phobias, such as this woman's fear of spiders. Most involve some type of "extinction" training, in which an individual is exposed to increasingly fearsome stimuli in a safe environment. With repeated exposure to the stimulus, the fear is gradually extinguished.

Classical conditioning techniques can also be used to *treat* phobic reactions, not just to induce them. Mary Cover Jones (1924), one of Watson's graduate students, pioneered a successful approach. She began with a two-year-old boy named Peter, who had learned to fear furry animals and objects, especially rabbits. Jones put a caged rabbit in the same room in which Peter was eating. Gradually, she moved the cage closer and closer to Peter, always while he was enjoying food. In this procedure, a form of **counterconditioning,** the conditioned stimulus (a rabbit) is repeatedly paired with another stimulus (food) that elicits a pleasant response very different from the conditioned response (fear). Eventually, Peter came to associate the rabbit with food and the pleasure food gave him. As a result, Peter lost his fear of rabbits.

A similar technique, called **systematic desensitization,** can be used to treat phobias. This technique involves teaching a person, in graduated steps, to relax in the presence of the fear-arousing stimulus. Relaxation is a response that is incompatible with fear. For example, a woman with an elevator phobia would be trained to relax while imagining a series of increasingly frightening situations in elevators. Once this task has been mastered, she would then attempt to remain relaxed during an actual elevator ride. (Systematic desensitization as a form of behavior therapy will be discussed in more detail in Chapter 16.)

Classical conditioning principles can be used not only to extinguish undesired behaviors but to instill desired ones. One example is a treatment for children who wet their beds (Mowrer & Mowrer, 1930). The treatment involves a bed pad that causes a bell to ring the moment it is moistened with urine. The bell serves as an unconditioned stimulus that elicits an unconditioned response of awakening. Gradually, the physical sensation of a full bladder becomes a conditioned stimulus that repeatedly precedes the sound of the bell. In time the child awakens at the bladder cue alone, as if in anticipation of the bell. Research has shown that this method can be effective in stopping bed-wetting (Ross, 1981; Wilson, 1982).

Classical conditioning has applications beyond behavior therapy. For instance, medical researchers have classically conditioned a reduction in blood pressure among hypertensive rats by repeatedly pairing a distinctive odor with the injection of a blood-pressure-reducing drug (Spencer, Yaden, & Lal, 1988). After many such pairings, the odor alone comes to elicit the same effects as the drug. Such findings could eventually lead to new nondrug treatments for hypertension and high blood pressure.

Classical conditioning may also play an important role in the use of addictive drugs. Pavlov himself realized the role of conditioning in drug reactions. In his early investigations, he noticed conditioned responses in dogs that were given repeated injections of morphine. After five or six days, Pavlov wrote that "in the most striking cases all symptoms [of morphine injections] could be produced by the dogs simply seeing the experimenter. . . . The greater number of previous injections of morphine the less preparation had to be performed in order to evoke a reaction simulation that was produced by the drug" (Pavlov, 1927, in Barker, 1994, p. 362). In fact, heroin addicts often show sympathetic nervous system changes similar to those induced by the drug (such as pupil dilation and skin temperature changes) as they watch heroin being "cooked" (prepared for injection) (Barker, 1997).

Operant Conditioning

As Pavlov was beginning his investigations in Russia, the innovative and influential American psychologist Edward L. Thorndike was investigating another form of associative learning. In one classic experiment, he placed a hungry cat in a "puzzle box" (Thorndike, 1898, 1932). If the cat made a certain combination of moves, the door to the box would fly open, allowing the animal to escape and eat a piece of fish.

Thorndike found that at first the cat's behavior in the box was erratic. It would scramble about and make the desired response only accidentally. But in repeated trials the animal gradually became more proficient at escaping, until eventually it could open the door almost immediately. Thorndike concluded that the cat had learned to escape because its escape responses were associated with a desirable consequence: food. Thorndike summarized this relationship in the **law of effect,** a simple but powerful principle. The law of effect states that responses that lead to positive outcomes (which Thorndike colorfully called "satisfiers") are more likely to be repeated, while responses that lead to negative outcomes ("annoyers") are less likely to be repeated. The law of effect provided the foundation for later studies concerning the effects of rewards and punishments on learning.

The Central Role of Rewards and Punishments

The most influential behaviorist, B. F. Skinner, became interested in some of the same problems that had occupied Thorndike. Our environment, Skinner argued, is filled with positive and negative consequences that mold our behavior just as escape from the box molded the behavior of Thorndike's cat. Our friends and families control us with their approval or disapproval. Our employers control us by offering or withholding money. Our schools control us by passing or failing us, thus permitting or denying us access to jobs. Positive or negative consequences shape our actions all through our lives. To Skinner, in fact, the distinctive patterns of behavior each person develops are merely the product of all the many consequences that person has experienced (Skinner, 1985).

In general, classical conditioning involves involuntary or automatic responses to stimuli. Pavlov's dogs didn't "decide" to salivate in response to the tone. After a number of pairings of the tone with food they salivated automatically when the tone sounded. In contrast, Thorndike's cat acquired a deliberate, voluntary response because of its consequences—a process that has come to be called *operant conditioning.* The critical difference between operant and classical conditioning is that while classical conditioning usually involves reflexive or involuntary responses, operant conditioning usually involves voluntary ones. Note, however, that the "involuntary"/"voluntary" distinction is not necessarily the same as the distinction between "determinism" and "free will." Skinner, the researcher most closely identified with operant conditioning, believed that all operant—that is, voluntary—behavior was under environmental control and was therefore determined. Operant behaviors, in other words, are actions that organisms emit of their own accord. For instance, no particular stimulus is needed to induce a rat to sniff around its cage. Psychologists say that the sniffing rat is "operating" voluntarily on its environment, not responding involuntarily to a particular stimulus.

Although operant behaviors are voluntary, they can still be influenced by external factors—in particular, the consequences of the behavior, which can either increase or decrease the likelihood of additional responses. A stimulus that increases the frequency of a response is called a **reinforcement,** or **reward.** A stimulus that decreases the frequency of a response is called a **punishment.**

Behaviorists avoid defining reinforcement and punishment as "good" and "bad" consequences. *Good* and *bad* are subjective terms that depend on an individual's viewpoint. Instead, they define reinforcement and punishment in terms of their objective effects on subsequent behavior, that is, whether they increase or decrease the frequency of a response. Rewards and punishments can vary from

Often, children who act up in class do so because of the attention they receive from their fellow students (and teachers). In such cases, the punishment intended by the teacher may actually serve as reinforcement for the misbehavior.

person to person. For example, suppose a child disrupts a class at school, and the teacher decides to punish her. The teacher might send the child to the corner, where the other children can see her—and also laugh at the child's actions. If the child enjoys such attention, being sent to the corner is not punishment. Instead, the teacher's actions are actually *reinforcing* the child's behavior, meaning the child will be even more likely to disrupt the class in the future.

This example illustrates an important implication of Thorndike's law of effect: if a behavior continues to be repeated, it must be leading to some type of reinforcement. Many parents and teachers have discovered this principle the hard way. Despite repeated attempts to punish a child's behavior, the behavior persists. By definition, if the behavior continues, something about the actions of the parents or teachers is reinforcing it. If a disruptive child enjoys the attention of classmates, then some other punishment must be employed, one that removes the (reinforcing) attention. For example, a teacher might punish the child by restricting the child's playtime at recess.

Positive and Negative Reinforcement

The term *operant* in operant conditioning refers to the emitted behavior. Operants produce different kinds of outcomes. Some outcomes are desirable: we call them *reinforcers*. Others are not desirable: we call them *punishers*.

Outcomes can be desirable in one of two ways. Sometimes an operant is followed by the addition of some positive stimulus, called **positive reinforcement.** For example, if you wish to teach your dog to shake hands, you follow the desired behavior (the offering of the paw) with a "reward," or treat. In this example, the operant is the lifting of the paw, and the positive reinforcement is the treat.

Sometimes an operant is reinforced by the removal of an unpleasant stimuli, called **negative reinforcement.** Suppose you are walking barefoot across a beach in the summer, and the sand begins to burn your feet. You rush to the water and stick your feet in it. The emitted behavior—putting your feet in the cool water—is reinforced by the removal of the unpleasant stimulus (the burning of your feet).

Escape learning involves a special type of negative reinforcement. As the name implies, escape learning allows a subject to respond in such a way as to remove an unpleasant stimulus. For example, we may place a rat in a cage with an electrified floor; a bar in the cage can be pressed to turn off the electric shock. Very quickly, the animal will learn to turn off the current by pressing a bar in the cage. The pressing of the bar, then, is negatively reinforced by the removal of an electric shock.

A related type of negatively reinforced learning is called **avoidance learning.** Escape learning allowed the rat to escape from an unpleasant stimulus; avoidance learning would allow the rat to avoid it altogether. For instance, once the rat has learned that

Obsessive-compulsive behavior is an example of avoidance learning. Since avoidance learning is maintained through negative reinforcement, it is highly resistant to extinction.

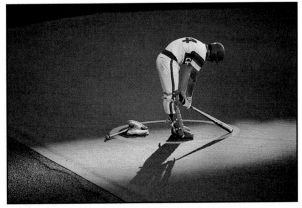

Many athletes are notorious for their superstitious and ritualized behaviors on the field. Because athletes succeed some, but not all, of the time they perform such rituals, their superstitious actions are in effect being reinforced on a variable-ratio schedule—a schedule that generally produces high, persistent rates of response.

pressing the bar allows it to escape from the shock, we might teach it (through classical conditioning) that the shock is always preceded by a red light. Eventually the rat will learn to press the bar when the red light goes on, thus avoiding the electric shock entirely.

Since avoidance learning is maintained through negative reinforcement, it is highly resistant to extinction. After a few trials, the rat will learn to avoid the shock entirely. In a typical experiment, removing the reinforcement would lead to a decrease in response, but in this particular example it does not. If the red light is presented without an electric shock (a typical extinction procedure), we find that the rat is likely to continue pressing the bar just as vigorously as before. Why? As long as the rat continues to press the bar, it will be negatively reinforced. Pressing the bar once allowed the rat to avoid shock; from the rat's perspective it still does.

This type of negative reinforcement is responsible for maintaining many types of obsessive-compulsive behavior, especially when the behavior reduces anxiety. Obsessive-compulsive behavior is characterized by an irrational, overwhelming concern with rules or details; it often results in repetitive, almost ritualistic behaviors. For example, someone who is very anxious about being alone in a house might check to see that the door is locked five or six times before going to bed. In many cases obsessive-compulsive behavior persists because of the negative reinforcement it provides. A person who is anx-

ious about being home alone may find that his anxiety is reduced by checking the door locks. The behavior (checking the locks) is followed by a reduction in an unpleasant stimulus (anxiety). That is, the behavior is negatively reinforced. Each time the person's anxiety increases, he checks the doors again, producing a reduction in anxiety.

Positive and Negative Punishment

Sometimes, behavior leads to undesirable outcomes, which we have called *punishments*. Just as with reinforcement, behavior can be punished in one of two ways. First, the emitted behavior can be followed with an unpleasant stimulus, known as a **positive punishment.** For example, a dog may repeatedly dig underneath a fence to get out of the yard. This behavior can be punished by running an electrified wire along the fence, so that whenever the dog begins to dig under the fence, it receives a mild but unpleasant shock. In this example, the addition of something unpleasant makes this a positive punisher.

In fact, one of the authors of this text used this technique to prevent his golden retriever from digging out of the yard. In this case, the dog's behavior was shaped by a combination of conditioning principles. First, it was shocked if it attempted to dig, an example of positive punishment. Once learned, the change in behavior is maintained by avoidance learning. The retriever can avoid any further shock by avoiding the wire, which is negative reinforcement; as we have just discussed, avoidance learning is particularly long-lasting. Finally, the retriever displayed an interesting form of stimulus generalization. After a few trials, it would no longer touch anything that resembled the wire. Now the author is able to keep the dog from digging simply by running a piece of string between two posts.

A behavior can also be punished if it is followed by the removal of some desired stimulus, a technique called **negative punishment.** For example, many parents punish their children using a time-out procedure, in which the child is removed from a positive activity. A child may be made to sit in a chair while the other children play. Like being sent to the corner, a time-out can backfire. You may remember being sent to your room as a child. In theory, you were being removed from the positive experience of being with your family. However, if you went to your room and played happily with your toys, then you weren't being punished. A true punishment involves the removal of a positive reinforcement, not the substitution of one reinforcer (the toys) for another.

Perhaps no two terms are more often confused in psychology than *negative reinforcement* and *punishment.* Many times spanking is referred to as a "negative reinforcement," an entirely incorrect use of that term. By definition, reinforcers increase the frequency of a behavior. Though negative reinforcers increase a behavior by removing an unpleasant stimulus, they are still reinforcers. The easiest way to keep the two terms straight is to consider whether a stimulus increases or decreases a behavior. If it increases behavior (such as by giving a dog a treat), then it is a reinforcer. If it decreases a behavior (such as through spanking), it is a punisher. The description *positive* or *negative* refers to whether a stimulus is added to (positive) or removed from (negative) the environment following a behavior. Do not confuse negative with bad and positive with good. Figure 6-7 summarizes the various types of reinforcements and punishments.

Some years ago the movie *Ghostbusters* illustrated the confusion of the terms in popular usage. As the movie opened, a group of "parapsychologists " (led by actors Dan Aykroyd and Bill Murray) were conducting experiments on the phenomenon of ESP (extrasensory perception; see Chapter 5). In the movie,

subjects were connected to a device that produced electric shocks. The experimenter held a stack of cards, each imprinted with a geometric shape (a circle, rectangle, and so on). Subjects were supposed to use ESP to determine which card the experimenter was holding. If they were wrong, the experimenter delivered an electric shock. In the scene, Murray told his subjects he was studying the effect of "negative reinforcement" on ESP. Though the scene was funny, the terminology was incorrect. Giving subjects an electric shock each time they produced an incorrect answer was an example of "positive punishment," not negative reinforcement.

We saw earlier that strict behaviorists avoid subjective definitions. Occasionally subjective definitions are helpful, as they are in distinguishing between positive and negative reinforcements, both of which increase the frequency of a response. Positive reinforcement increases the frequency of a response and leads to a subjectively satisfying stimulus. When a hungry rat presses a lever and receives a pellet of food, its hunger is satisfied. Negative reinforcement increases the frequency of a response because the response leads to the removal of a subjectively unpleasant stimulus. When a rat presses a lever that turns off an electric shock, it removes the pain caused by the shock.

Because negative reinforcement and punishment both involve aversive stimuli (such as an electric shock), they are easily confused. The key to keeping them straight is to focus on whether the aversive stimulus is being added to or removed from the environment, and how the subject's behavior changes as a result. When a behavior is followed by the arrival of an unpleasant stimulus, punishment occurs. Punishment tends to decrease the frequency of the response that precedes it. The organism tries to prevent the unpleasant stimulus from recurring by not performing the behavior again. In contrast, when a behavior is followed by the removal of an unpleasant stimulus, negative reinforcement occurs. Negative reinforcement tends to increase the frequency of the response that precedes it. The organism tries to escape from or avoid the unpleasant stimulus by performing the behavior that enabled its escape or avoidance before.

One final note about the role of rewards and punishments in establishing behavior. In operant conditioning, a cause-and-effect relationship exists between a particular behavior (pressing a bar) and the outcome that follows it (being shocked or avoiding

	Stimulus Added to Environment	**Stimulus Removed from Environment**
Desirable Stimulus	**Positive Reinforcement** *Example: Giving a child a piece of candy after picking up toys*	**Negative Punishment** *Example: Taking away a child's teddy bear because of hitting sister*
Undesirable Stimulus	**Positive Punishment** *Example: Administering electric shock to dog when digging under the fence*	**Negative Reinforcement** *Example: Stepping under a covered porch during a rainstorm*

FIGURE 6-7   *Four types of reinforcement and punishment.*

the shock). Sometimes, however, a behavior does not actually cause the consequence that follows, but is accidentally linked with it. In such cases, a subject may act as if the behavior caused the outcome. Behavior that increases or decreases as a result of such a chance relationship is called **superstitious behavior.** This kind of behavior can be seen in a gambler who blows on the dice before every roll, or a football coach who wears a "lucky" hat to every game. At some time in the past these behaviors were linked accidentally with a winning streak, and so were reinforced. Now they persist even though they never really caused the winning streak.

Acquiring a Conditioned Operant Response

The general procedure for establishing a conditioned operant response is to control the consequences of a behavior by rewarding or punishing it. The same two principles that are critical to classical conditioning are critical to operant conditioning as well: contingency and contiguity. Learning is best when a behavior and a response are linked together consistently (contingency) and they occur together in time (contiguity). Unlike classical conditioning, however, the effects of contingencies between behavior and its reinforcers are complicated. Learning is *not* always best when a behavior is followed consistently by reinforcement. We will examine this "partial reinforcement effect" later in the chapter.

The effects of contiguity on operant conditioning are relatively straightforward. The behavior and its consequences must be close enough together in time so that an individual perceives a cause-and-effect relationship between them. When a substantial time gap intervenes between a behavior and its consequence, their relationship may become clouded, and learning becomes more difficult.

Long delays between a behavior and its consequences prevent learning in some cases. For example, many antismoking advertisements link smoking with an increased risk of cancer (the punishing stimulus). However, the punishment is removed from the behavior by so many years that it is ineffective. B. F. Skinner (1983) felt that a clouded relationship between war and its consequences is the reason humans go to war so readily. Too much time intervenes between the actions that lead to armed conflict and the punishing consequences of war (massive death and destruction). And parents know all too well that delayed punishment—"Wait until your father (or mother) gets home!"—is ineffective.

Psychologists have developed a number of laboratory instruments to study how conditioned operant responses are acquired. Perhaps the best known device is the **Skinner box,** developed by (and named after) B. F. Skinner (1938). A Skinner box looks like a small cage, usually with a few buttons or levers on the side (see Figure 6-8). It also contains a small compartment in which a reward (usually food or water) is delivered automatically after an animal performs some target behavior, such as pressing a lever or pushing a button. Skinner created this invention

❙ FIGURE 6-8   *A rat in a Skinner box.*

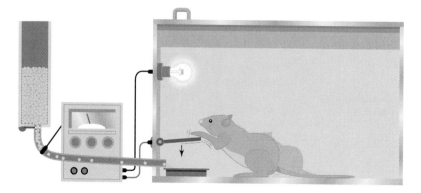

one day when using equipment that required a rat to obtain food. He grew tired of having to pick up the rat and return it to the starting point, so he designed a chamber in which the press of a lever sent a pellet of food tumbling into a feeding tray. More important, the Skinner box allows easy measurement of the rate and consistency of an animal's responses (see Figure 6-9).

The first task in establishing a conditioned operant response is to get the subject to perform the target behavior before it has been rewarded. Researchers usually make this task easier by selecting a behavior the subject is likely to make spontaneously. For instance, pigeons need no special inducement to peck; they peck at virtually everything. So, when working with pigeons, psychologists usually select some form of pecking as the target behavior (pecking at a special button, for example). Before long the bird accidentally hits on the object the researcher wants it to peck. When a food reward is delivered, the pigeon begins to learn an association between the behavior and the reward.

But suppose an animal is slow to perform the desired behavior. Or perhaps the behavior is so complex the animal is unlikely to perform it spontaneously. Must the researcher simply wait for a lucky accident? A much better solution is to use a procedure called **shaping.** In shaping, the researcher begins by reinforcing a simple behavior, one the animal is likely to produce spontaneously. After several trials, the experimenter requires the animal to perform a slightly more complex behavior, one that is closer to the target behavior to get the reward. Reinforcement is withheld until the animal accomplishes the more complex behavior. This method of shaping is called *successive approximation.*

To understand how shaping works, imagine you are trying to get a reluctant rat to press a bar. You be-gin by reinforcing the rat when it moves to the side of the cage where the bar is located. Next, you reinforce the rat only when it approaches the bar. After a few reinforcements, the rat will interrupt its other activities to walk toward the bar. Next, you withhold reinforcement until the rat not only approaches the bar but lifts its front paw from the floor. Finally, you make the reward contingent on the rat actually pressing the bar. When the animal learns this contingency, its behavior has been shaped. But note that each successive approximation of the target response must be only a small step beyond what the animal was just doing; otherwise the procedure will fail.

Shaping has been used to train animals to perform complicated tricks. If you have ever been to Sea

B. F. Skinner, one of the key figures in the history of psychology, developed the Skinner Box to simplify his studies of learning. Most Skinner boxes have but a single lever which a rat can press in response to a stimulus. By simplifying the kinds of activities he studied, Skinner was able to isolate many important properties of learning.

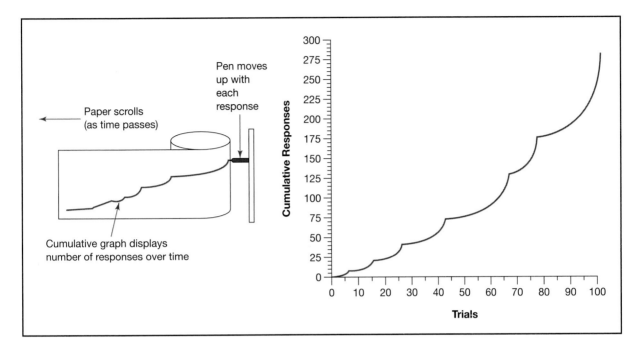

FIGURE 6-9   *Cumulative recording of responses in the Skinner box. Responses are measured on a cumulative recorder, a drum that scrolls a piece of graph paper slowly and continually while a pen attached to the drum records a subject's responses. Each time the animal makes a response, the pen moves up a notch. The height of the pen (y axis) reflects the number of responses the animal has made; the width indicates the amount of time that has elapsed (x axis).*

World, you have probably seen the shows put on with seals, walruses, and dolphins. The final behavior—the show you watched—likely resulted from hours upon hours of shaping and successive approximations.

Shaping can be used to modify human behavior as well. Consider how parents often teach preschoolers to write their names. At first they praise mere scribbles on the paper. Gradually they begin to reward only accurately shaped letters, until eventually the child can write her name legibly. The same techniques are used in modern behavior therapy (Wilson, 1982). For instance, severely retarded children have been taught to dress and feed themselves by being systematically rewarded for closer and closer attempts at tying their shoes, using a fork, and so on.

Extinguishing a Conditioned Operant Response

In classical conditioning, presenting the CS without the US results in a gradual weakening of the CR. In Pavlov's classic experiments, for example, presenting the tone (the CS) without the food (the US) decreased the dog's salivation in response to the tone.

A similar relationship exists in operant conditioning. A conditioned operant response that is no longer reinforced gradually decreases in frequency and eventually disappears. For the rat in a Skinner box, bar pressing diminishes after food pellets are no longer given. For the rebellious two-year-old, tantrums eventually decline after the parents stop giving in to them. This extinction process was illustrated in Figure 6-4.

During the early stages of extinction, however, the response tends to be even more forceful than before. For example, if a psychologist stops giving a pigeon food after it pecks at a light, the bird typically becomes agitated and exaggerates the behavior that was formerly rewarded. Similarly, the child whose defiant screams stop bringing rewards will probably scream even louder, at least for a while. You can probably think of some instances of this reaction in your own experience. Suppose you put your money into a soft drink machine, pressed the appropriate button, but found the machine did not deliver your selection. In the language of operant conditioning, the previously reinforced response of inserting coins and pushing the button has not been followed by delivery of your soft drink reward. Before you give up, however, your efforts to get your drink will probably become more forceful. You may push the button several times, rattle the "coin return" lever, even pound the machine with your fist before finally walking away.

Now suppose several days have passed, and you walk past the same soft drink machine. Will you try the machine again? Most people would. In the same way, if an animal is removed from an experimental chamber for a period of time after a response has been extinguished, and then is put back in the chamber, the response will usually reappear to some extent (Figure 6-4). This is the phenomenon of **spontaneous recovery**, discussed in the section on classical conditioning earlier in this chapter. Without reinforcement, a spontaneously recovered behavior will diminish over time until it is again extinguished.

Maintaining a Conditioned Operant Response

Once an operant response has been established, how can it be perpetuated? The key to maintaining an operant behavior is keeping up the reinforcement: reinforcement must be contingent upon behavior. As has been mentioned previously, however, the behavior-reinforcement contingency is more complicated than it is in classical conditioning. In classical conditioning, learning is best when the CS and the US are *always* paired. In operant conditioning, the same is true with respect to acquisition: that is, learning occurs most rapidly when reinforcement is always paired with the desired behavior. However, providing reinforcement on only *some* of the trials results in higher response rates and greater resistance to extinction, a phenomenon known as the **partial reinforcement effect**. The conditions under which partial reinforcement is delivered are called **schedules of reinforcement**.

Schedules of Reinforcement

Consider a worker who is paid by the piece to assemble computer chips. This method of payment represents a schedule of reinforcement that encourages very rapid work. The faster the employee can complete a chip, the more the employee will be paid. Similarly, people in other situations are affected by the schedules on which they are rewarded. At school, on the job, and in the laboratory, the prevailing schedule of reinforcement has a considerable effect on behavior.

A **continuous reinforcement** schedule—providing a reward each time the desired behavior occurs—works best in establishing a conditioned operant response. For example, researchers might give a rat a pellet of food every time it presses a bar in order to firmly establish the bar-pressing response. Once a response has been established, however, often the best way to maintain it is to use a partial reinforcement schedule, in which rewards are withheld part of the time. In this case, the rat receives food for only some of its bar presses. Skinner discovered the power of partial reinforcement by accident. One weekend he ran low on food pellets and so tried rewarding his rats intermittently, for every second or third lever press. Instead of diminishing their bar pressing, the rats responded more vigorously than before (Staddon & Ettinger, 1989).

On what basis should the reward be delivered through a partial reinforcement schedule? Should a rat be given food, say, every ten bar presses? Or would once every two minutes be more effective? The first approach (a reward after every ten bar presses) is an example of a **fixed-ratio (FR) schedule,** in which a behavior is rewarded after a specific number of occurrences. A rat on a fixed-ratio schedule tends to press the bar at a more rapid rate than it would if it were rewarded continuously, for the faster it responds, the sooner it will get a piece of food. In the same way, the computer chip assembler who is paid for every ten chips completed will work as quickly as possible.

The second approach—a reward once every two minutes—is an example of a **fixed-interval (FI) schedule,** in which a reward is delivered the first time a behavior occurs after a certain interval has elapsed. A rat on a fixed-interval schedule eventually learns not to respond until a certain amount of time has passed, which lowers its response rate. If your mail is delivered at approximately the same time each day (say, 2 p.m.), your mail-getting behavior is being maintained on a fixed-interval schedule. Your first response after 2 p.m. is likely to be reinforced, while responses made before that time are not likely to be reinforced. Furthermore, the frequency with which you check your mailbox does nothing to increase the availability of the mail. Gradually, you learn not to check the mailbox before 2.

A fixed-interval schedule tends to yield a relatively low frequency of response. In addition, very few responses are made in the time immediately after reinforcement, known as the **postreinforcement**

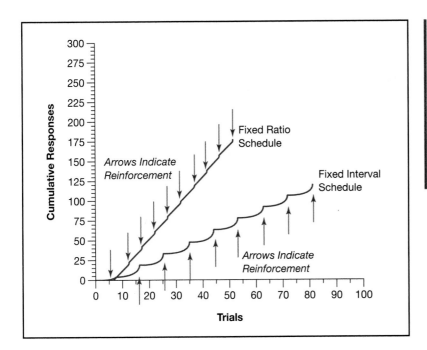

FIGURE 6-10   *Response rates on fixed-ratio and fixed-interval schedules. In general, fixed-ratio schedules lead to higher and more consistent response rates. Fixed-interval schedules tend to produce very low response rates immediately following reinforcement, and very high response rates immediately before reinforcement, a pattern known as* scalloping.

pause. As time passes, and the time for reinforcement approaches, the frequency of response increases. This pattern of high rates of response just before reinforcement, and a pause in responding immediately after, produces a phenomenon known as **scalloping**—a scalloped pattern on a graph made by a cumulative recorder (see Figure 6-10).

Fixed-ratio and fixed-interval schedules deliver rewards regularly and predictably. In other partial reinforcement schedules rewards are irregular and unpredictable. For instance, a reward might be given after a variable number of responses: sometimes after ten responses, sometimes after seven, and still other times after fifteen or twenty. This type of schedule is called a **variable-ratio (VR) schedule.** As the name implies, the number of responses required to obtain reinforcement varies from trial to trial. For example, a rat being maintained on a VR schedule might have to make eight responses to receive the first reinforcement, eleven for the second, four for the third, and seventeen for the fourth. The animal makes forty total responses and receives four reinforcements—an average of ten responses per reinforcement. But the exact number needed to obtain reinforcement on any single trial is unpredictable.

Alternatively, a reward may be given after a variable time interval has elapsed: half a minute before the first reward, two minutes before the second, one minute before the third, and so forth. This type of

schedule is called a **variable-interval (VI) schedule.** As with a VR schedule, the average amount of time per reinforcement can be determined, but the time interval required for any single trial cannot.

While continuous reinforcement schedules produce more rapid acquisition of a response, variable-ratio and variable-interval schedules produce considerably higher rates of response, with much less "scalloping" (see Figure 6-11). Variable reinforcement schedules also provide much greater resistance to extinction. As a result, these schedules (especially variable-ratio schedules) tend to be preferred in situations that require high, persistent response rates.

Virtually every type of gambling situation involves a variable-ratio schedule of reinforcement. Slot machines, for example, may provide a $90 average return for every $100 gambled, on a variable-ratio schedule. Though the casino is likely to come out ahead in the long run, the possibility that the very next trial might be a winner keeps players pulling the handle in the hope of hitting the jackpot. The variable-ratio schedule has a compelling effect on their behavior.

Because partial reinforcement schedules are so powerful, they can have the unintended effect of maintaining undesirable behavior. Consider a two-year-old who flatly refuses to go to bed. When his parents insist, he throws a tantrum. Usually the

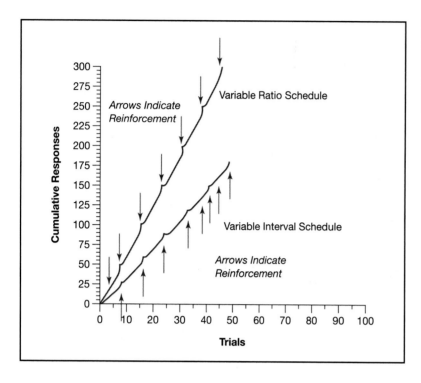

FIGURE 6-11   Response rates on variable-ratio and variable-interval schedules. In general, variable schedules lead to higher response rates, greater resistance to extinction, and less scalloping.

parents continue with their bedtime preparations, but sometimes one parent can stand the roar no longer and allows the child to stay up late "just this once." The next night, the child's tantrum is even longer and louder. Unwittingly, the parents have been rewarding the child's tantrums on a highly effective variable-ratio schedule. To halt his bedtime rebellion, behaviorists would recommend that the parents resist letting the boy stay up even occasionally (Tavris, 1982). At the same time, they should reward cooperative bedtime behavior with praise and attention, or perhaps the privilege of engaging in some special activity.

Stimulus Control

Besides controlling the strength and frequency of operant responses, reinforcement has another important effect. It relates a particular behavior to stimuli that are associated with the learning situation. Suppose a rat has been conditioned to press a bar whenever a bulb in his Skinner box lights up. The Skinner box and the lighted bulb have become associated with the behavior of bar pressing and the reward that follows. Whenever these stimuli—the box and the light—are present, the rat is likely to press the bar again. This relationship is called **stimulus control,** because the stimuli prevailing at the time of reinforcement have come to control the organism's response.

Children who go "trick-or-treating" on Halloween quickly learn stimulus control. Going from door to door, they learn that ringing a doorbell is reinforced with a candy treat. Not every ring is likely to be reinforced, though. Only those houses whose porch lights are turned on are likely to produce treats.

What is learned in such situations? First, the child has acquired a conditioned operant response: ringing the doorbell (which is reinforced with candy). Second, this response is under the control of a specific stimulus: an illuminated porch light. When the child distinguishes between houses whose lights are on and houses whose lights are off, the child is engaging in stimulus discrimination. The light has become a **discriminative stimulus** that is controlling the child's behavior.

Helping to establish discriminative stimuli is an important part of some behavior therapies. People who are overweight, for instance, often associate eating with all kinds of activities, such as watching television, reading a book, going to a movie, or sitting on a beach. One way to get them to decrease their eating is to ask them to confine it to the dining table.

In gambling, this woman is being reinforced on a variable-ratio schedule—the kind of schedule that usually induces the highest levels of response.

This location then becomes a discriminative stimulus, and other activities that used to be associated with eating gradually lose their power through lack of reinforcement.

Secondary Reinforcers

In operant conditioning experiments, the reward that establishes and maintains the conditioned response is called a **primary reinforcer.** A primary reinforcer is something that satisfies a biological need—usually food or water. The effects of a primary reinforcer can generalize, however, to a secondary reinforcer. A **secondary reinforcer** is a stimulus that does not satisfy an inherent biological need, but has acquired reinforcing properties through association with primary reinforcers. For humans, many of the most powerful reinforcers are secondary reinforcers. Money, for example, is not intrinsically rewarding; it cannot satisfy hunger or

thirst. Instead, it has become a secondary reinforcer through prior association with primary reinforcers. Money is a powerful motivator because it can be used to acquire food or drink. The reinforcing properties of money are acquired through learning.

Suppose a chimpanzee is given a plastic token shortly before it receives a piece of fruit. After a while, if the token is reliably paired with the primary reinforcer (the fruit), the chimp will come to view the token as a reinforcer. In this example (and most other examples we could generate), the pairing of the fruit and token is a form of classical conditioning. The food is the unconditioned stimulus; no learning need occur for fruit to generate a response such as satiation (satisfaction of hunger). The token is the conditioned stimulus. Before learning, it does not generate a hunger-related response. After being paired with the US (the fruit), it elicits the hunger-related response by itself (see Figure 6-12). To condition a secondary reinforcer, a previously neutral stimulus—in this example, a token—is paired with a primary reinforcer—in this example, fruit. The token becomes associated with the fruit through classical conditioning. After conditioning, the token now serves as a reinforcer.

Secondary reinforcers are extremely important in the world outside the laboratory, where learned behavior is rarely followed immediately by a primary reward. If you have ever watched trained animals at a place like Busch Gardens, you have probably seen secondary reinforcers in action. For example, when an animal jumps through a hoop, it may be rewarded by a loud noise, such as the trainer's whistle. The animal responds to the whistle because it has been paired with a primary reinforcer—usually some kind of food—in training. That is, the whistle becomes a secondary reinforcer—an important part of the show because of the inevitable delay between the animal's behavior and the time when food, the primary reinforcer, can be delivered to the animal. Remember that conditioning is strongest when the delay between a behavior and its reinforcement is kept short. The secondary reinforcer allows the trainer to reward the animal's behavior immediately. Training the complex responses you see would be difficult, perhaps impossible, without such rapid reinforcement. Secondary punishers can be conditioned in the same way, except that they would be paired with punishers instead of reinforcers.

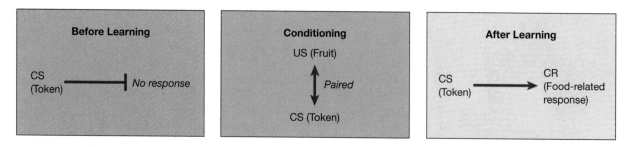

FIGURE 6-12   *The conditioning of secondary reinforcers. Before learning, a token produces no response from a chimpanzee. After being paired with a primary reinforcer like fruit, however, the token becomes a secondary reinforcer capable of eliciting a food-related response.*

Observational Learning

Both classical and operant conditioning involve learning by *doing*. A person learns to avoid touching a hot stove by being burned (operant conditioning). A dog learns to run to the door at the sound of the doorbell because past experience indicates that it signals the arrival of visitors (classical conditioning). But knowledge can also be gained simply through observation. Are you one of those students who is frequently late for class? Suppose your psychology professor does not approve of such behavior. She punishes late arrivals by deducting ten points from the student's grade for each occurrence. Must you arrive late (and lose points) in order for you to learn to be on time for class? Not necessarily. Often people can learn by observing the behavior of others. Psychologists refer to this type of learning as **observational learning.**

Rewards and Punishments in Observational Learning

Humans acquire a wide variety of strategies, outlooks, and rules about behavior that they can imitate, avoid, or modify to their advantage. They need no particular reinforcement to accumulate such information. Rather, they do so naturally in the course of observing what others do. The most influential thinking on observational learning today is **social learning theory** (also known as social cognitive theory). Social learning theorists do not consider rewards and punishments to be unimportant to human behavior; their point is that reinforcement is not essential to learning.

According to Albert Bandura (1977a), one of the leading proponents of social learning theory, rein-forcement is much more important in getting people to *perform* a learned behavior than in *teaching* that behavior. For example, a little girl who observes her older brother clearing his dishes from the dinner table adds those actions to her knowledge of potential behaviors even without any reinforcement. But if she observes that her brother is warmly praised for his helpfulness—that is, if she sees him rewarded—she will be more inclined to copy his behavior and clear her own dishes. Reinforcement, then, affects mainly the likelihood of performance. The acquisition of new ideas and strategies through observation does not require rewards.

Bandura conceptualizes rewards and punishments more broadly than behaviorists (Bandura, 1986). Humans are influenced, he says, not only by the consequences of their own behavior (the behavioral view) but by the consequences they see others experiencing. For example, you might learn to arrive at class on time by observing what happens to a fellow student who does not arrive on time. Bandura calls such "secondhand" consequences **vicarious reinforcement** and **punishment.** In addition, Bandura also stresses the importance of **intrinsic reinforcement** and **punishment.** That is, human actions are regulated not just by the observed environmental consequences but by our *inner* reactions as well. We measure our own performance against our internalized standards of behavior. If we exceed our own standards, we feel self-esteem, a powerful form of reinforcement. If we fall short, we feel self-reproach, a potent form of punishment. These motivating factors will be discussed in detail in Chapters 11, 17, and 18.

To Bandura, however, none of these various forms of reward and punishment is essential for learning to occur. Rather, learning is a change in acquired infor-

Bandura's Social Learning Theory describes learning as a change in acquired information (and hence in performance potential) which can be accomplished simply through observation. Those watching this interaction between the soldier and the sergeant are likely to learn simply by observing it.

mation (and hence in performance potential) that can be accomplished simply by observing the world around us. As we will see in later chapters, Bandura and others have conducted experiments to show that observational learning can take place without reinforcement. In a typical study, groups of children observe a model responding to a situation in some unusual way. Then the children are put in a similar situation, and the number of imitative responses they make is noted. Such studies suggest that children may learn and imitate a new behavior with no external inducements (Deguchi, Fujita, & Sato, 1988).

What Is Acquired through Observational Learning

According to social learning theorists, people do not take cameralike snapshots of other people's behavior when they observe them. Instead, they form abstract representations that capture the essence of the behaviors. Another word for those abstract representations is *schema,* a term we introduced in Chapter 4. The schemas we form from watching and listening to others can be used to guide our own thoughts, feelings, and actions (Bandura, 1986). Thus, Bandura's social learning theory powerfully illustrates Recurring Theme 4, "Cognition and thought are dynamic, active processes, best considered reconstructive, not reproductive."

THEME 4 Cognition and Thought are Dynamic, Active Processes, Best Considered Reconstructive, Not Reproductive

Everyday experience is full of examples of how people form schemas through observation. One of the most influential sources of observational learning is television. Almost from its inception, critics have suggested that television is a powerful source of observational learning, especially for children. Indeed, surveys have shown that adults who are heavy TV watchers (over four hours a day) often form stereotyped social schemas that match the networks' portrayal of our society (Gerbner & Gross, 1976). For example, heavy viewers tend to believe that the elderly are a very small segment of our population; that a large percentage of workers are professionals, such as doctors and lawyers; and that the chance of being the victim of violent crime is exceedingly high. None of these statements is true, but repeated TV viewing made them appear to be true to many people.

Once such distorted schemas are formed, social learning theorists point out that they tend to persist, unless observations to the contrary are made. But because people often see what they expect to see (the *confirmation bias*—see Chapter 8), the disconfirmation process may never occur. Not all observational learning from television is negative, of course. Children's programs like *Mr. Rogers' Neighborhood, Sesame Street,* and, yes, even *Barney* provide positive learning experiences. Current research shows that children who are regular watchers of these programs tend to form positive schemas.

Many educational programs depend on observational learning. For example, programs like DARE (Drugs Abuse Resistance Education) rely almost exclusively on observational learning. DARE's goal is to allow those who are at risk for substance abuse to learn about its negative consequences without experiencing them directly. Teen pregnancy prevention programs are designed to encourage the same sort of observational learning. In programs such as these, many of the most influential models are peers, who have experienced drug abuse or unintended pregnancy firsthand.

Role playing is another effective source of observational learning. Some family planning organizations, like Planned Parenthood, sponsor peer advisory boards whose members, usually local students, put on skits at workshops. Those attending the workshops watch as the peer-educators role-play challenging situations such as date rape. Through observation, students learn constructive ways of handling those situations.

The Relationship between Learning and Cognition

Learning and **cognition**—the study of thinking—are often treated as separate subjects, a division that reflects tradition more than substance. You may remember from Chapter 1 that the so-called cognitive revolution was started in large part because of widespread dissatisfaction with behaviorist explanations of learning. Historically, the term *learning* has encompassed the role of external influences on behavior, while the term *cognition* encompassed the internal processing of information. No theory of human behavior, of course, is complete without both.

Theories derived from classic learning models emphasize how the environment shapes behavior. They are likely to emphasize the role of reinforcement and punishment, and the factors involved in stimulus control. In contrast, cognitive theories emphasize the constructive nature of cognition. Cognitivists are more inclined to look "inside the head" of those they are studying, than at purely environmental factors. Contemporary learning theories deemphasize distinctions between learning and cognition (e.g., Anderson, 1996). Instead, they combine aspects of both.

Social learning theory provides a wonderful example of combining behavioral and cognitive explanations. Social learning theory recognizes the power of external factors, while at the same time recognizing that internal goals and states often shape behavior. For example, understanding intrinsic reinforcement demands that psychologists consider internal factors. To identify something as an intrinsic reinforcer requires that psychologists attend to the active, interpreting role of the individual. Stimuli that are intrinsically rewarding to one individual might not be rewarding to others. In addition, what is intrinsically rewarding for a given person might change depending on the current circumstances.

Practical Applications of Learning Principles

Throughout this chapter we have described many experiments involving animals. You may have wondered, "What does a rat pressing a bar in a Skinner box have to do with anything in the 'real world'?" The fact is, the same general principles that can be used to shape the behavior of a rat in a box can be used to shape the behavior of people. One such method is called behavior modification.

Behavior Modification

Behavior modification is the conscious use of the principles of conditioning to change human behavior. The concept arose from B. F. Skinner's stress on behavior as the proper focus of psychological study. As early as the 1950s, Skinner had argued that psychologists should stop thinking of the behavioral aspects of psychological disorders as mere "symptoms" of a deeper, underlying cause (Skinner, 1953). Instead, Skinner thought they should address the problem behaviors in their own right. If psychologists could change the behavior, they could effectively eliminate the problem.

Soon some of Skinner's students, armed with the techniques of operant conditioning, set out to apply Skinner's perspective to the world outside the laboratory (Wilson, 1982). Today the deliberate use of rewards and punishments to change human behavior is known as **contingency management** (Masters et al., 1987), a term that refers to the management of relationships between behaviors and their consequences.

Some of the earliest behavior modification programs were established in mental hospitals and other institutions for people with severe behavior problems. In all the programs, **token economies** played a key role. In a token economy, secondary reinforcers like tokens or coins are conditioned to substitute for primary reinforcers. For example, hospital patients were given chips that could be exchanged for candy or soft drinks (primary reinforcers). Much as the whistle used to teach dolphins provides immediate reinforcement, tokens (once they are secondary reinforcers) can serve as immediate reinforcers for those in institutions.

Token economies have been successful in many settings. For example, moderately retarded persons living in a group home might be rewarded with tokens for grooming or cleaning up the group living area. Elementary school students might be rewarded at school by presenting them with certificates that can be exchanged for small toys, or rewarded at home with a token that can be used to buy treats.

Behavior therapists have also manipulated rewards to treat many other problems, from smoking,

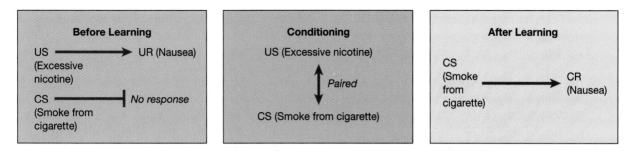

FIGURE 6-13   Aversive conditioning technique used for eliminating smoking. The smoke from the cigarette is paired with the aversive consequences of becoming ill (from the nicotine). Ultimately, the cigarette alone will trigger nausea.

overeating, truancy, stuttering, and shyness, to poor study habits, volatile tempers, and lack of self-assertion. In all cases the procedure is much the same: inadvertent rewards for the problem behavior are eliminated, and a more desirable response is systematically reinforced. Thus, a teacher who is trying to engage a shy boy in group activities would avoid giving him attention when he withdraws, but encourage and praise him when he interacts with the group.

Aversive Conditioning

Another practical application of learning theory is **aversive conditioning,** the pairing of aversive stimuli with undesired behaviors. For example, a program might advise smokers to smoke cigarettes until the smoke (or, more probably, the nicotine) makes them physically ill. More than one parent has punished a child caught smoking by forcing him or her to smoke the entire pack in one sitting. The goal is to make smoking aversive through classical conditioning (see Figure 6-13).

How effective is aversive conditioning? In some situations, it can be effective. Aversive conditioning is likely to be most successful when an individual does not have an extensive history involving the CS. For example, the aversive conditioning approach to smoking is likely to work much better with novice smokers than with longtime smokers. Longtime smokers have an extensive history of cigarette use—some of it negative, perhaps, but most of it pleasurable. A few aversive trials will likely have little effect on such people.

Aversive conditioning is often used to treat substance abusers, like alcoholics. A drug called Antabuse (disulfiram), which disrupts the normal breakdown of alcohol, is used to induce the aversive

situation. Recall from Chapter 5 that alcohol is broken down by the liver before being excreted from the body. Some of the by-products of its breakdown are toxic (they contribute to the "hangover" experienced the morning after). Antabuse stops the breakdown of alcohol, and thus increases the amount of the toxins in the bloodstream. As a result, if patients who are taking Antabuse drink alcohol, they quickly become horribly ill. (Though the buildup of toxins is dreadfully unpleasant, it is not fatal.)

However, aversive conditioning with Antabuse alone has not proved terribly effective in treating alcoholism. Like long-term smokers, alcoholics have an extensive history involving alcohol. As unpleasant as the effects may be, they are not usually sufficient in themselves to cause alcoholics to quit drinking. Furthermore, since Antabuse loses its effectiveness after several days, it must be taken on a regular basis in order to be effective. Some alcoholics quit taking the drug for a few days and then return to drinking. Antabuse is more effective when combined with other forms of treatment.

Punishment

Although many parents and teachers turn first to punishment as a way of changing a child's behavior, its usefulness as a method of behavior modification is limited (Axelrod & Apsche, 1983; Klein, 1991; Martin & Pear, 1983). Inhibition of the problem behavior is apt to be only temporary unless punishment is immediate, consistently applied, and severe (see Table 6-1 for a summary of the general principles of punishment). Severe punishment, however, may provoke anger and aggression. It can also prompt such strong anxiety that the original problem worsens. Or punishment can cause the situation in which it is delivered to become aversive. A child who is punished

| TABLE 6-1 *Four General "Laws of Punishment"*

1. The more intense the punishment, the better the conditioning.
2. The greater the number of trials in which a behavior and a punishment are paired, the greater the learning (provided the punishment is of sufficient intensity).
3. The shorter the delay between the behavior and the punishment, the more effective the punishment.
4. Punishment is most effective when the contingency between behavior and punishment is high (that is, when a behavior always results in punishment).

Source: Adapted from Barker, 1997.

at school may react by avoiding school entirely. Because the child's avoidance behavior is negatively reinforcing, it is likely to continue.

In situations in which punishment is inconsistently applied, the undesired behavior falls under stimulus control of the punisher. Suppose a child is punished for fighting at school, say, by getting timeout. But suppose the same aggressive behavior at home does not bring punishment. Rather than learning not to fight, the child learns not to fight *at school*. The presence or absence of the teacher becomes a discriminative stimulus.

Finally, punishment signals only what should not be done; it does not establish a positive response to replace the undesirable one. Consequently, one undesirable behavior may simply replace another. For this reason, punishment is most effective when used together with positive forms of behavior modification. Punishment can be used to temporarily prevent some very negative behavior, such as excessive physical aggression, so that a more acceptable response can then be rewarded and strengthened.

Proponents of behavior modification consider it one of the most important innovations ever made in the treatment of psychological problems (Hill, 1985). But critics charge that it often brings only a temporary solution that lasts no longer than the rewards that maintain it. Some people are also uncomfortable with the deliberate control of human behavior. Behavior therapists reply that reinforcement can be maintained over long periods, and that control of others' behavior ethical if it benefits those involved. Behavior modification will be discussed in greater detail in Chapter 16.

Biological Considerations in Associative Learning

Though classical and operant conditioning have practical applications, those applications have limits. Both these forms of learning are subject to important biological constraints. Some types of learning seem to be easy for certain organisms, while others seem to be difficult. Why is teaching a dog to "shake

Prison is not always an effective way of changing behavior. In many cases, the delay between the offending behavior and the resulting punishment is quite long, reducing the effectiveness of the punishment.

hands" so easy, but teaching a cat to do the same trick so difficult? Why do you feel nauseated when you smell a food that once made you sick, but not when you see the table where you ate it? Why do researchers routinely teach rats to run mazes but not pigeons? The answers to these questions have to do with **prepared learning**—learning that a particular kind of animal is biologically prepared to do. When an organism is not biologically prepared to learn a certain task, its learning is slow and often fraught with problems.

Keller and Marion Breland, two former students of B. F. Skinner, learned this lesson many years ago. The Brelands had organized a show in which animals were to perform unusual tricks taught to them through shaping (Breland & Breland, 1961). For instance, they had trained a pig to deposit wooden "nickels" in a large piggy bank, and a chicken to eject a capsule from its cage by pulling a cord that sent the capsule rolling down a chute. All went well until suddenly the performers started misbehaving. The pig began pushing the nickels around with its snout, as if it were rooting in the dirt; and the chicken became so caught up in pecking at the capsule that it failed to pull the cord. The Brelands concluded that the animals were reverting to innate feeding and foraging responses, which competed with the behaviors they had been taught. They called this process of reversion to natural behaviors **instinctive drift.**

You may have seen examples of instinctive drift in your own pets. For example, most dogs love to play "fetch" with a ball: they run after the ball enthusiastically, and most will gladly bring it back. However, many dogs balk when they have to drop the ball in the owner's hand. As much as they love to play fetch, giving up the ball goes against their innate tendencies.

Instinctive drift explains why even with rewards, maintaining an operantly conditioned response against an organism's natural tendencies can be difficult (Gould, 1986; Lefrancois, 1982). Moreover, if a particular response is uncharacteristic of an animal's behavior (pigeons exploring mazes, cats shaking one paw), instilling that response in the animal can be difficult to begin with, despite careful shaping. In the

Animals can often be trained to perform actions though a combination of classical and operant conditioning techniques.

same way, establishing a classically conditioned relationship between two stimuli that an animal is not biologically prepared to associate is a daunting task.

In conclusion, some behavioral responses are difficult for animals to acquire. Even under the best circumstances, conditioning may not take place. Just as some behaviors go against an animal's biological predispositions, other types of associations can be formed quickly and easily, even under conditions normally not conducive to learning. One of the most dramatic examples of biological constraints on learning involves learned taste aversions.

In Depth

Studying Learned Taste Aversions

THE YEARS IMMEDIATELY following World War II saw tremendous research activity, especially in the burgeoning field of psychology. The military was looking to psychology to develop and test personality inventories (to assist in the evaluation of new soldiers) and to make certain cockpit controls could be easily understood by pilots. Behavioral scientists were learning how to deal with newly developed nuclear weapons, including the effects of nuclear radiation on behavior.

Among those scientists was a psychologist named John Garcia. In the course of his investigation into the effects of radiation, Garcia made a puzzling discovery (Garcia et al., 1956). Rats that were placed in a test chamber and exposed to moderate levels of radiation for eight hours a week progressively lowered their intake of water, as if they were learning not to drink. Yet when the rats were returned to their cages, they drank as usual. In fact, they avoided the water in the test chamber even if they were not exposed to radiation. What could explain their strange behavior? Garcia suspected some kind of associative learning. But what stimuli were involved?

Later Garcia proposed a hypothesis: the behavior was caused by classical conditioning. He had noticed that the water bottles in the test chamber were made of plastic, while those in their cages were made of glass. Apparently the plastic bottles gave the water a peculiar taste, which served as a conditioned stimulus. The unconditioned stimulus was the stomach upset caused by exposure to radiation; it elicited the unconditioned response of nausea. After repeated pairings with stomach upset, the plastic-tasting water came to evoke nausea on its own, so that the rats avoided it.

Thus, Garcia hypothesized that animals can acquire a classically conditioned taste aversion when a distinctive flavor is repeatedly paired with stomach upset. To test this interesting possibility, he designed a set of controlled experiments.

Initial Studies

Garcia's first experiments involved "spiking" water with various flavors and administering it together with illness-inducing agents to laboratory rats. As

predicted, the rats appeared to acquire a classically conditioned taste aversion to any new flavor that had been paired with severe stomach upset. Furthermore, the learning occurred with remarkable speed and was extremely persistent. In one of Garcia's studies, a *single* pairing of salty water with illness was enough to cause the rats to shun salty water when they encountered it again, more than a month later (Garcia, Hankins, & Rusiniak, 1974). Furthermore, the rats learned the aversion even if the CS (the flavor) and the US (the illness) were separated by long delays—an hour or more in some cases (e.g., Barker, Best & Domjan, 1977).

But why, Garcia wondered, had the rats developed an aversion specifically to water? Why hadn't they also developed an aversion to the test chamber? It too had been associated with illness, yet his experiments showed that getting a rat to avoid the place where it had become sick was very difficult (Garcia, Kimeldorf, & Hunt, 1961). Were certain kinds of relationships easier or more difficult to learn? If so, the rats' predisposition toward certain kinds of learning contradicted one of the basic assumptions about classical conditioning at the time—Pavlov's assumption that virtually any formerly neutral stimulus could be conditioned to elicit virtually any involuntary response. Garcia realized that this long-held belief might be wrong. An organism's nervous system might be structured in such a way as to facilitate the learning of certain relationships but hinder the learning of others. He had hit on the concept of prepared learning.

Criticisms, Alternatives, and Further Research

To investigate this theory, Garcia and his colleague, Robert Koelling, designed a clever experiment in which they paired various kinds of stimuli with various aversive outcomes (Garcia & Koelling, 1966). One group of rats was presented with saccharin-flavored water. As soon as they drank it, they were either shocked or irradiated. Another group of rats was exposed to an impressive display of flashing lights and loud noises whenever one of them sipped water through a drinking tube. Drinking this

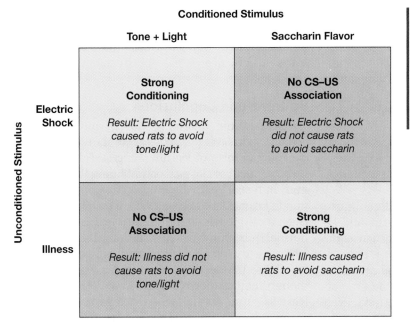

Conditioned Stimulus

	Tone + Light	Saccharin Flavor
Electric Shock	**Strong Conditioning** *Result: Electric Shock caused rats to avoid tone/light*	**No CS–US Association** *Result: Electric Shock did not cause rats to avoid saccharin*
Illness	**No CS–US Association** *Result: Illness did not cause rats to avoid tone/light*	**Strong Conditioning** *Result: Illness caused rats to avoid saccharin*

Unconditioned Stimulus

FIGURE 6-14   *The various conditioning procedures used in Garcia and Koelling's "Bright, Noisy, Tasty Water" experiment.* [Garcia & Koelling (1996), "Relation of cue to consequence in avoidance learning," *Psychonomic Science, 4,* 123–124.]

"bright, noisy, tasty water" was followed by either shock or an induced illness.

In this conditioning situation, the animals received multiple USs (the shock and the radiation) and multiple CSs (the saccharin flavor and the lights and noises). If Pavlov's assumption that all stimuli are "equally conditionable" was true, then rats should have learned the various CS-US associations equally well. However, that is not what Garcia and Koelling found (see Figure 6-14). The rats learned some CS-US associations much more easily than others. They learned an aversion to saccharin only when its taste was paired with illness, and they learned an aversion to the noise and light only when those stimuli were paired with an electric shock. No aversion resulted when the saccharin taste was paired with shock, or when bright, noisy water was paired with illness. Garcia concluded that the ease with which an animal learns a given association depends on some intrinsic relationship between the cue (the CS) and its perceived consequence (the US).

Why should such intrinsic relationships exist? Garcia believed the answer lay in evolution. Natural selection, he argued, had favored a nervous system that allowed rapid learning of relationships common to a species' environment and crucial to its survival. Consider the dietary habits of rats. They eat virtually anything they can find—a practice that expands their food supply, but increases the risk of eating something poisonous. Thus, a rat whose nervous system is prepared to remember foods that make it ill will clearly have a better chance of surviving and reproducing. From an evolutionary viewpoint, the fact that taste, not noise or flashing lights, is an effective conditioned stimulus for nausea in rats makes sense.

Taking an evolutionary perspective also helps to explain why learned taste aversions seem to violate another traditional rule of classical conditioning: that the US must follow the CS within a matter of seconds if learning is to occur. In his earliest experiments, Garcia noticed that a learned taste aversion developed even after a fairly long delay between a new taste and the onset of illness. Other studies have shown that the lapse between a CS and a US can be anywhere from three to twelve *hours,* depending on the circumstances (Andrews & Braveman, 1975; Kalat & Rozin, 1971). Such findings are understandable in light of biological predispositions toward certain adaptive behaviors. In nature, substantial intervals often intervene between the ingestion of a toxic substance and the feeling of illness that follows. Any organism that is capable of learning despite such gaps in time would clearly have a better chance of surviving.

Ilene Bernstein has extended Garcia's pathbreaking research to the study of human beings. Most of us know at least one person who loathes the sight of a certain food he or she associates with a severely upset stomach. Do humans, too, have a built-in predisposition to form aversions, when tastes are associated with illness? To find out, Bernstein studied cancer patients. She suspected that the loss of appetite they often suffer involves classically conditioned taste aversions. Bernstein found that cancer patients do indeed acquire learned taste aversions, due in part to a pairing of food with the stomach upset caused by chemotherapy (Bernstein, 1978; Bernstein, Webster, & Bernstein, 1982). The toxins and hormones tumors produce may also act as unconditioned stimuli in the acquisition of taste aversions (Bernstein, 1986).

Thus evolution has endowed us with the ability to learn very quickly those associations that could be important to our survival. Unfortunately, such learning occurs even when the food in question is only coincidentally associated with illness. If you eat something novel and later come down with the flu, you are likely to form an aversion to the new food, even though you know the food did not make you nauseated. The same is true for cancer patients; they form aversions to foods that are coincidentally paired with chemotherapy. Such learned taste aversions exacerbate the cancer patients' problems by encouraging them to undereat, which further jeopardizes their health.

Bernstein and her colleagues have developed an ingenious strategy to help cancer patients avoid food aversions. They found that when a novel food, such as an unusual-flavored ice cream, is given to cancer patients just before chemotherapy, they tend to develop a learned aversion to it, rather than to the foods they usually eat (Bernstein, 1985). The novel food, in other words, serves as a kind of "scapegoat." Bernstein has also found that patients who eat little or nothing before chemotherapy are less likely than others to develop food aversions. This result suggests pretherapy fasting for cancer patients undergoing chemotherapy. Findings like these are an excellent example of how basic scientific research often leads to practical ideas for overcoming human problems.

Patterns and Conclusions

For some time following Garcia and Koelling's (1966) work, taste aversions were thought to be an exceptional form of learning, one that did not "follow the rules" of classical conditioning theory. However, in recent years thinking on this matter has begun to change (see Logue, 1979). Now taste aversion is generally considered to be a dramatic—but quite normal—example of classical conditioning (Best, 1995). Taste aversions are learned more quickly with an intense US (severe nausea) than a weak one, and though they can form despite long delays, they are learned more readily when delays are brief. Researchers now agree that while tastes (CSs) are more readily associated with illness than environments (USs), the environment in which an illness occurs *is* important (Best & Meachum, 1986). Just as you might learn to avoid pizza when you become ill shortly after eating one, you also learn to avoid the restaurant in which you ate it.

Though taste aversions are powerful examples of prepared learning, in a sense all learning can be seen as "prepared." Organisms that can learn about their environment have a selective advantage over those that cannot. Taste aversions are learned relatively quickly because of the evolutionary benefits they convey. As psychologists continue to study behavior, the importance of the interaction between innate factors (such as predispositions toward certain kinds of learning) and environmental factors (an organism's experiences in the world) may become even clearer.

SUMMARY

1. **Learning** is a relatively permanent change in observable behavior potential that results from experience with the environment. **Associative learning** involves learning how various events are related to each other. One kind of associative learning is **classical conditioning,** in which a previously neutral stimulus comes to elicit an involuntary response because it signals the onset of another stimulus which naturally elicits that response. Another kind of associative learning is **operant conditioning,** which involves changes in behavior because of the consequences that follow it. We learn to perform or withhold a voluntary behavior because of its consequences. **Cognitive learning** involves the formation of concepts, schemas, theories, and other mental abstractions.

2. Classical conditioning was first studied by Pavlov while investigating the physiology of digestion. He found that the **unconditioned stimulus (US)** of food in a dog's mouth elicited the **unconditioned response (UR)** of salivation. When a neutral stimulus—the sound of a bell, for example—repeatedly preceded the US (the food), the dog eventually salivated in response to the bell alone. The bell had therefore become a **conditioned stimulus (CS),** and the learned reaction to it was a **conditioned response (CR).** To maintain a classically conditioned response, the conditioned and unconditioned stimuli must continue to be paired at least occasionally; otherwise the conditioned response will undergo **extinction,** a weakening of the previous conditioned response.

3. Conditioning is influenced by two powerful factors, contingency and contiguity. The **contingency** between a CS and a US is expressed as a probability and refers to the likelihood that the CS signals the US. **Contiguity** refers to the temporal relationship between the CS and the US. In general, conditioning is strongest when the CS is a reliable predictor of the US, and when the delay between the CS and the US is minimized.

4. Once a classically conditioned response has been established, the individual may begin responding to stimuli similar to the CS, as if they were the CS itself. This process is called **stimulus generalization.** The more similar a stimulus is to the CS that prevailed during learning, the more likely it is for generalization to occur. Organisms also engage in **stimulus discrimination**—learning to make a particular response only to a particular stimulus.

5. According to Thorndike's **law of effect,** responses that lead to positive outcomes ("satisfiers") are more likely to be repeated, while responses that lead to negative outcomes ("annoyers") are less likely to be repeated. A consequence that increases the frequency of a behavior is called **reinforcement** or **reward.** A consequence that decreases the frequency of a behavior is called **punishment.**

6. In **positive reinforcement,** the frequency of a response increases because that response causes the arrival of a subjectively satisfying stimulus. In **negative reinforcement,** the frequency of a response increases because that

response causes the removal of some subjectively unpleasant stimulus. **Escape learning** allows an organism to respond in such a way as to remove an unpleasant stimulus (negative reinforcement). **Avoidance learning** occurs when an organism's response allows it to avoid the aversive event altogether. Since avoidance learning is negatively reinforced by eliminating aversive events, it is often highly resistant to extinction.

7. In **positive punishment,** the frequency of a response decreases because that response causes the arrival of a subjectively unpleasant stimulus. A behavior can also be punished if it is followed by the *removal* of some desired stimulus, a technique called **negative punishment.**

8. Researchers have studied operant conditioning by manipulating rewards and punishments in such devices as the **Skinner box. Shaping**—a technique in which a subject is reinforced for displaying closer and closer approximations of a desired response—has been used to establish new behaviors in both humans and other animals.

9. The **schedule of reinforcement** greatly affects a conditioned operant response. A **continuous reinforcement** schedule—reinforcement each time the response occurs—is very effective for *establishing* a new behavior. A **partial reinforcement schedule**—withholding the reward some of the time—is very effective for *maintaining* a behavior. Schedules of partial reinforcement include a **fixed-ratio schedule,** in which a reward is given for a fixed number of responses, and a **fixed-interval schedule,** in which a reward is given for the first response after a fixed time interval has elapsed. Two schedules that result in high rates of response that are quite resistant to extinction are the **variable-ratio schedule** and the **variable-in-**terval schedule, both of which derive their power from their unpredictability.

10. Besides controlling the strength and frequency of an operant response, reinforcement also brings behavior under the control of stimuli prevailing at the time of reinforcement. The individual tends to make the conditioned response when these particular stimuli are present. This is called **stimulus control.**

11. The effects of **primary reinforcers** (those satisfying biological needs) can generalize to **secondary** (or **conditioned**) **reinforcers** (those signaling the arrival of the primary reinforcement).

12. A conditioned operant response gradually disappears when it is no longer reinforced. But sometimes a response (whether operantly or classically conditioned) will reappear after it seems to have been extinguished, a phenomenon called **spontaneous recovery.**

13. Operant conditioning principles have been applied in behavior modification. In the **behavior modification** approach called the **token economy,** tokens earned can be exchanged for more basic reinforcers, such as a desirable food or a special privilege. Today, such deliberate use of rewards or punishments to change human behavior is often called **contingency management.**

14. When a conditioned response is in conflict with an animal's genetically based tendencies, it may tend to weaken despite reinforcement. This process, called **instinctive drift,** demonstrates biological constraints that influence learning. A good example of biological constraints can be seen in the study of learned taste aversions. Apparently, natural selection has favored a nervous system that allows easy learning of relationships between unusual tastes and subsequent illness, but not between unusual sights or sounds and illness.

SUGGESTED READINGS

Anderson, J. R. (1995). *Learning and memory: An integrated approach.* New York: Wiley. One of the best, most exhaustive texts, integrating principles of learning with cognitive approaches.

Barker, L. M. (1997). *Learning and behavior: Biological, psychological, and sociocultural perspectives* (2nd ed.). Upper Saddle River, NJ: Prentice-Hall. A highly readable text incorporating evolutionary theory into contemporary learning theory. It includes a considerable number of examples involving humans.

Buckley, K. W. (1989). *Mechanical man: John Broadus Watson and the beginnings of behaviorism.* New York: Guilford Press. A fine scholarly history of Watson's career, both in and out of academic settings.

Schwartz, B. (1989). *Psychology of learning and behavior* (3rd ed.). New York: Norton. A complete, authoritative reference to theory and principles of conditioning.

Skinner, B. F. (1971). *Beyond freedom and dignity.* New York: Knopf. An accessible, nontechnical account of Skinner's work and beliefs.

CHAPTER 7

|Memory

Rajan is a graduate student in psychology at a large southern university. His life as a graduate student is much like those of his peers—a combination of class work, research in the laboratory, and the like. However, Rajan is unique in one respect, and in a way that almost defies belief. Over the course of his twenty-some-odd years, he has memorized the mathematical quantity π (pi) to the first *30,000 digits.* If you have several hours to spare, Rajan will recite those digits to you, at the rate of about 200 per minute. Even more remarkable, if you call out the place number of a certain digit in the series—say, "6,981"—Rajan will tell you which number belongs in that place. At some demonstrations the members of the audience are given a table of the first 10,000 digits of π (pi), arranged in 50 rows of 100 digits, front and back. The audience is invited to call out a place number between 1 and 10,000. After hearing the number, members of the audience search their tables as quickly as possible to find the place corresponding to that digit, while Rajan searches his memory. Invariably, Rajan retrieves his answer before those in the audience can find it in their tables. He is virtually never wrong.

In 1974, one of the major figures in the Watergate hearings was John Dean, an aide to President Nixon. Dean had often been present in Nixon's office when plans were discussed, including some that eventually led to Nixon's resignation. In the televised hearings Dean was one of the most impressive witnesses. The level of detail he was able to supply astonished those who listened to his testimony. In some cases, he was able to provide nearly verbatim descriptions of what was said and by whom. Dean displayed enormous confidence in his memory, never wavering in his testimony.

K. C. is a middle-aged gentleman who lives in Toronto. In the early 1980s he was injured in a serious motorcycle accident and suffered what is known as a "closed-head injury" (he was not wearing a helmet). K. C.'s recovery was slow, but in many ways surprisingly good. He still has periods of amnesia, as do almost all victims of serious head trauma. But much of K. C.'s memory remained intact. Unlike H. M., whose case was described in Chapter 3, he remembers most of the events that happened to him throughout his life and is able to form new memories for events that happened since his injury. He can tell you, for example, that the Toronto Blue Jays play ball in the Sky Dome, despite the fact that the Sky Dome was built

White House aide John Dean was a key witness at the Watergate hearings, which led to the resignation of President Richard Nixon in 1974. Though Dean's testimony was full of minute details and reported with the utmost confidence, Nixon's private tape recordings (which were released several years after his resignation) showed that most of the details Dean supplied were incorrect.

after his injury. (H. M. would not be able to answer this question. In fact, he wouldn't even know that Toronto *had* a major league baseball team, since the Blue Jays didn't exist until 1977.)

But despite the fact that K. C. knows the Blue Jays play in the Sky Dome, he cannot recall a single game that was ever played there. And when questioned about his childhood, K. C. may know that he once visited Disneyland, but he cannot recall a single episode that happened on that vacation. K. C. knows Endel Tulving, the neuropsychologist with whom he has worked in the past decade. But he cannot recall taking a single memory test, though Tulving has given him countless memory tests over that time. K. C. "knows" most of the events of his life, but he "remembers" nothing.

K. C.'s "memory" of his own life is similar to what you might know of him if you had read his biography. If you were asked to act as though you were K. C., when asked about your childhood, you would describe his trip to Disneyland or the wedding of his sibling. But if pressed to describe an actual event memory, you would be at a loss. After all, you didn't really *experience* his life: you just learned the *facts* of his life secondhand. K. C.'s recollections have the same remote, impersonal quality.

Each of these cases demonstrates a critical aspect of memory. Rajan, the student who has memorized pi (π), demonstrates the potential of human memory. You might ask how anyone can perform such a feat, when most of us have trouble remembering where we put our car keys. But as we will see, there is reason to think that what Rajan does you could not also do.

The case of John Dean is interesting for another reason. You may recall that several years after the Watergate hearings, tape recordings made by President Nixon in his office were released. Ulric Neisser (1982) compared the transcripts of Dean's testimony with the actual conversations Dean described. Despite Dean's extreme confidence in the accuracy of his memory, Neisser found that Dean's recollections differed—sometimes drastically—from what actually transpired. Most of the details Dean supplied were incorrect, even those he was particularly confident about.

Do Neisser's findings mean that Dean's memory was hopelessly flawed? Was Dean lying to Congress, perhaps to avoid prosecution? Despite the large number of errors Dean made, Neisser concluded just the opposite. "Even when Dean was entirely wrong about the course of a particular conversation, he [gave] an essentially true account of the facts lying behind the conversation," Neisser wrote (1982, p. 139). Dean's testimony was the result, he concluded, of a reconstructive process. Dean had embellished his memories, perhaps by making himself appear more important than he was or by adding details he had not learned until after the event. The fact that Dean's recall of the most important information was good, but his memory for detail was flawed, simply illustrates the reconstructive nature of memory. The blame, if any, should perhaps be placed on those who assumed his memory was perfect. Dean's testimony provides yet another example of Recurring Theme 4.

THEME Cognition and
4 Thought are
Dynamic, Active
Processes, Best
Considered
Reconstructive,
Not Reproductive

The case of K. C., who *knows* the events of his life but cannot *remember* any of them, shows how elusive the concept of "memory" can be. Can K. C. be said to have no memory? Of course not. At the same time, the personal, autobiographical memories he is lacking are precisely those that give continuity to our lives and,

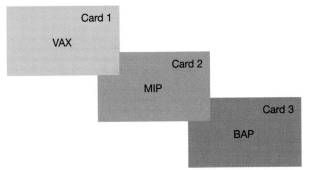

FIGURE 7-1   *Three nonsense syllables used in Ebbinghaus's experiments. Ebbinghaus's task was to memorize a list of such items and later recall it by anticipating which syllable came next, a procedure known as* serial anticipation.

in a very real sense, meaning. The amnesia seen in K. C. and in other cases, such as H. M., poses a challenge to anyone constructing a theory of memory. In truth, memory is probably not a unitary phenomenon. Instead, it is best viewed as a collection of past events that continue to influence our behavior. We will have more to say about K. C. later in this chapter.

Early Understanding of Memory: Associative Models

In the early history of psychology, memory was generally considered to be outside the realm of scientific investigation. However, Hermann Ebbinghaus, a German psychologist, thought differently. Ebbinghaus, who began his work in the 1880s, was convinced that memory could be studied in the laboratory through careful experimentation and observation. His work was inspired by associationism, a school of thought dating back to classic Greek philosophers. Associationists, as the name implies, believed that memory resulted from mental connections between ideas and concepts. Understanding memory, then, would involve studying how those associations were formed.

Ebbinghaus realized that because different people have had very different experiences, they would be likely to form different associations. For some, the word *dog* might be associated with a pet, while for others it might be associated with fear. To eliminate the effect of those prior associations, Ebbinghaus created a list of nonsense syllables. By combining letters in a consonant-vowel-consonant pattern (see Figure 7-1), he compiled a list of about 2,300 items with no prior associations. In studying what happened as he memorized those 2,300 items, Ebbinghaus believed he would be able to observe memories being formed from pure associations.

Ebbinghaus conducted his experiments using a single subject: himself. In a typical study, he first created a list of items to learn by picking randomly from the group of 2,300 syllables. Sometimes he selected just a few items; other times he prepared much longer lists. Once he had chosen the items to learn, Ebbinghaus proceeded to study each for one second, then moved on to the next item in the list. After going through the whole list, he went back to the first syllable and tried to anticipate which syllable came next. If he were studying the items in Figure 7-1, for example, he would read the first item (VAX) and then try to recall the next item on the list (MIP). In most trials, Ebbinghaus had to go through the list a number of times before he could correctly anticipate which item was next. After learning a list in this way, he would set it aside and begin to learn another list. Over a period of several years, he repeated this procedure thousands of times.

Later, Ebbinghaus tested his memory for the lists he had learned. The two most common ways of assessing memory—recognition and recall—would have been useless for his purposes. Once several weeks had passed, Ebbinghaus could recall none of the items he had learned. (Remember that he had probably learned hundreds of new lists in the interim, each drawn from the same set of 2,300 nonsense syllables.) His performance on recognition tests was no better. However, Ebbinghaus found that once he had learned a list of items, he could *relearn* it more quickly than the first time. Remarkably, Ebbinghaus noticed this effect—which he called *savings*—even when he had no conscious recollection of having learned a list. He expressed memory for the lists using a *savings percentage,* shown in Figure 7-2.

As one might expect, as the time between the first and second study episodes increased, time saved in relearning the list decreased. However, Ebbinghaus's pattern of forgetting, called a **forgetting function,** was characterized by two distinct features (see Figure 7-3). First, forgetting was initially very rapid (see the part of the curve marked "1" in Figure 7-3). Within an hour, savings had fallen to 50 percent. But

FIGURE 7-2   *Ebbinghaus's savings percentage. The ratio indicates time "saved" because of previous learning. Larger savings percentages reflect better memory.*

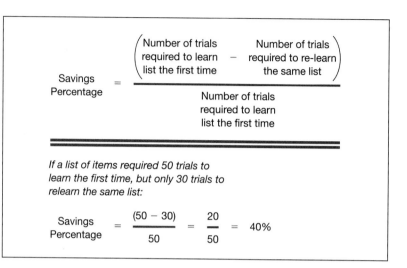

the rate of forgetting eventually leveled off (see the part of the curve marked "2"). Even when the delay was as long as thirty-one days, Ebbinghaus still realized about 25 percent savings in relearning a list.

Memorizing nonsense syllables may strike you as one of those experimental tasks that is low in ecological validity (see the "In Depth" discussion in Chapter 2). After all, how often do we attempt to memorize nonsense syllables in real life? However, the forgetting function Ebbinghaus observed characterizes a number of "real world" situations. Harry

Bahrick and his colleagues studied long-term remembering for learned information in several real world settings. In one of his studies (Bahrick & Phelps, 1987) Bahrick tested individuals for their memory of Spanish, which they had seldom used since learning it in high school. Bahrick selected his participants so as to vary the length of time since their graduation. Some of his subjects had graduated recently; some, many years before. (The oldest participants had been out of high school for nearly fifty years.)

FIGURE 7-3   *Forgetting function obtained by Ebbinghaus. Notice (1) the rapid initial decline in savings and (2) an eventual asymptote ("leveling off") of the function at about 25 to 30 percent.*

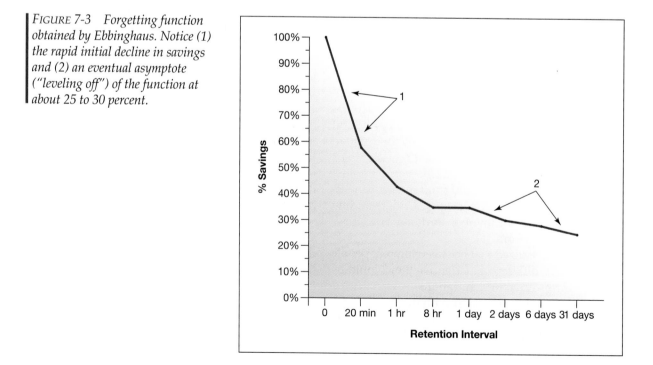

The memory for real-world information can persist over extremely long intervals. Individuals who studied Spanish in high school—even those who learned it nearly 50 years ago—still show some memory for the information.

Bahrick found that his subjects' forgetting functions looked quite similar to Ebbinghaus's (see Figure 7-4). The rate of forgetting was most rapid for those subjects who had studied Spanish recently. Just as Ebbinghaus had found, the rate of forgetting eventually slowed down and leveled off. Even those who had learned Spanish nearly fifty years before still showed some savings.

After Ebbinghaus, interest in the scientific investigation of memory waned. As we saw in Chapter 1, behaviorism quickly became the dominant paradigm in psychology early in the twentieth century. To the behaviorists, the concept of "memory" was a topic to be avoided, because it could not be measured directly. Rather, psychologists should concern themselves with studying how prior experience influences current behavior, a definition given for *learning* in Chapter 6. Indeed, few behaviorists made any distinction between learning, retention, or memory. They considered memorization of nonsense syllables merely studies of verbal learning. The behaviorists' influence was so strong that one of the foremost scientific journals on memory today, the *Journal of Memory and Language*, was once called the *Journal of Verbal Learning and Verbal Behavior*.

In the late 1950s and early 1960s, an alternative to behaviorism called *cognitive psychology* began to emerge. Dissatisfied with the study of verbal learning and verbal behavior, cognitive psychologists wanted to study what was going on inside the head. Gradually, the terms *verbal learning* and *verbal behavior* were replaced with *memory* and *language*.

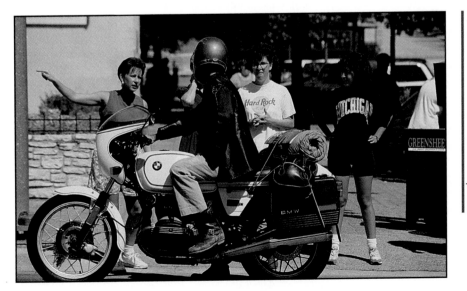

Most psychologists now agree that there are several different kinds of memory, each with its own distinct properties. For example, the memory for spatial information, such as a "mental map" of a familiar town, may be processed differently than the memory for personal events, like one's high school graduation ceremony.

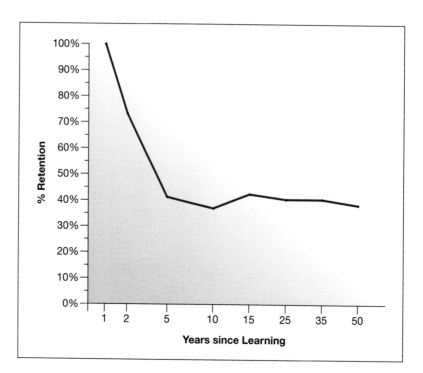

FIGURE 7-4 *Long-term retention of Spanish vocabulary.* (After Bahrick & Phelps, 1987.)

As the cognitivists' research progressed, it became clear that memory was not a unitary concept. Instead, there appeared to be several different kinds of memory, each with its own distinct properties. The most successful new model of memory—known as the *information-processing model,* developed by Atkinson and Shiffrin—incorporated this realization and dominated memory research for many years.

The Cognitive Model: Memory as Information Processing

The **information-processing model** of memory proposed by Atkinson and Shiffrin (1968, 1971) divides memory into three types: sensory, short-term, and long-term. **Sensory memory** describes the momentary lingering of sensory information after a stimulus has been removed. You may remember as a child trying to write your name in the night sky with a flashlight or sparkler. If so, you will remember that as you were writing the last few letters, the first seemed to fade away. This experience was a demonstration of your visual sensory memory. Humans seem to have a separate storage system for each of the different senses. A great deal of information can be stored in these sensory registers, but only for an instant.

Short-term memory is far more durable than sensory memory. Short-term memory contains the contents of your conscious awareness: what you are actively thinking about at any particular moment. When you call "Information" to request a phone number, and then repeat the number over and over to yourself, you are using your short-term memory. Short-term memory is not a passive storehouse for data but an arena in which information is actively processed. This type of memory has a very restricted capacity of about seven items.

Long-term memory, in contrast, can store information indefinitely without active effort. When you recall the name of James Madison's wife or a list of early memory researchers, you are using your long-term memory. Long-term memory has a virtually limitless capacity. Figure 7-5 summarizes the three stages of memory contained in the information-processing model.

Sensory Memory

Glance for just an instant at the letters and numbers in Figure 7-6. Then close your eyes and try to list out loud as many as you can. You will probably find that your ability to recall them is limited. In fact, the results of many carefully controlled experiments show that most people can remember only about four or

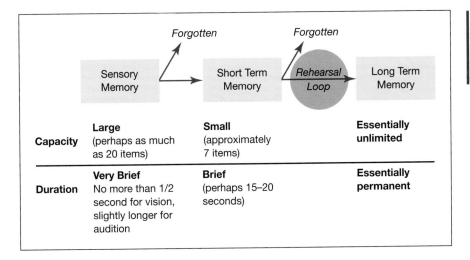

FIGURE 7-5 *The information-processing model of memory. (After Atkinson & Shiffrin, 1968.)*

five out of twelve unrelated items that are shown to them very briefly. Yet such findings seem to contradict much of everyday experience. When you glance quickly at something and then look away, you usually gain the impression of a complete and accurate image, however fleeting it may be. If sensory memory is indeed as rich as everyday experience suggests, why does it seem so poor in laboratory tests?

This puzzle intrigued a young psychologist named George Sperling. Perhaps, Sperling reasoned, researchers had been testing sensory memory in the wrong way. So he set about to devise a new test (Sperling, 1960). Sperling exposed subjects briefly to a twelve-item pattern like the one in Figure 7-6, but did not ask them to specify *all* the letters and numbers they had seen. Instead, after removing the pattern, he immediately sounded a high-, medium-, or low-pitched tone to indicate which line the subjects should report. Sperling found that under those conditions, subjects could often correctly report all four items in a row.

Sperling's research demonstrated that the ability to process information through the senses is indeed better than simple verbal reports suggest. Immediately after scanning a pattern, a person retains a fairly complete image of it. This visual memory is fleeting, however; it lasts for only about one-fourth to one-half of a second. During the time taken to report four or five items, the remaining images fade from sensory storage, much as the picture on a TV set fades once the set has been turned off.

As information moves from one processing stage to another, then, the amount of information that can be processed is restricted. In a sense, information is

"filtered" as it is passed on to the next memory store. Sensory memory has a large initial capacity, but only a small portion of that information will be sent on to the next processing stage, the short-term memory store. Some kind of selectivity is essential. One process that is crucial to getting the more interesting

FIGURE 7-6 *A typical test for visual sensory memory. When exposed to this array of unrelated items for a brief period, people typically recall no more than four or five of them. But if subjects are signaled immediately after the exposure to recall just one of the lines, they can almost always remember all four items correctly. This evidence suggests that people "read" the information from some sort of complete sensory image of the stimulus, which fades in the time it takes to say the names of a few of the letters and numbers in the image.*

At a crowded party, the process of selective attention allows those who are conversing to screen out irrelevant sounds and concentrate on what they are saying. Should someone hear his name mentioned in another conversation, however, he may suddenly become aware of an exchange he thought he was ignoring—a phenomenon known as the cocktail party effect.

and important information placed into short-term memory has to do with attention.

When you are having a conversation at a crowded party, your ears receive a great deal of extraneous information. You hear not only the person you are speaking with but the din of other voices, the clink of glasses, and perhaps the sound of music. Yet despite this potentially confusing mix of sounds, you manage to follow your companion's conversation. You do so by screening out some of the information that is entering your sensory channel (in this case, your ears) and focusing only on what is left. This process of restricting your focus is called **selective attention.**

When you are attending selectively to someone's voice, however, you do not completely ignore all the other sounds around you. Instead, you give these peripheral sounds a preliminary form of attention. For example, at the party you may suddenly hear your name mentioned in a conversation you thought you were ignoring. Clearly, you must have been processing that conversation to some extent.

Psychologists have studied this "cocktail party phenomenon" extensively. Cherry (1953) developed a procedure using sounds played over headphones, known as **dichotic listening.** One message is played into the left ear and a different message into the right ear. Cherry asked subjects to "shadow" one of the messages—that is, to repeat it aloud as they heard it. (The subject's voice, like a shadow, trails along immediately behind the recorded message.) As you would expect, material that was presented in the shadowed ear was recalled fairly well. But in gen-

eral, the meaning of the unshadowed message eluded subjects, except for an occasional word that had special significance to them (a familiar name, for instance). Subjects *could* detect the physical characteristics of the unshadowed message, such as its pitch or volume.

The same results have occurred in many subsequent studies. They suggest that when different stimuli enter the same sensory channel, humans discriminate among them primarily on the basis of their physical characteristics rather than their meaning (Broadbent, 1958). Thus, differences in the physical characteristics of voices—their pitch, volume, rhythm, and so forth—generally allow us to attend to a single speaker at a crowded party.

Short-Term Memory

Once information has been attended to, it is processed in the short-term memory store. While short-term memory can hold information considerably longer than sensory memory, it still loses information fairly rapidly. In addition, the capacity of short-term memory is highly restricted—usually no more than about seven items.

One classic test of short-term memory capacity is the digit-span test. A list of single-digit numbers is read to the subject, usually at a rate of about one per second. After the list has been read, the subject attempts to repeat the numbers in the same order in which they were presented. Most adults have no trouble with this task as long as they are given no more than six or seven numbers to remember. A few

Read Each List at a Constant Rate of 1 Second Per Digit.

FIGURE 7-7 Digit-span tests of short-term memory.

List	Digits (Read One Per Second)
1 (6 digits long)	2–6–3–8–3–4
2 (7 digits)	7–4–8–2–4–1–2
3 (8 digits)	4–3–7–2–9–0–3–6
4 (10 digits)	9–2–4–1–7–8–2–6–5–3
5 (12 digits)	8–2–5–4–7–4–7–3–9–1–6–2

people may be able to repeat nine or ten items, but twelve is beyond the reach of almost everyone.

You can use Figure 7-7 to demonstrate this conclusion. Ask a friend to read the lists in the table one digit at a time, at a steady rate of about one digit per second. After each list is read, try to repeat back what you hear. The first two lists are likely to be very easy to repeat. The third list will be considerably more difficult, and the fourth and especially the fifth list should be impossible to repeat. (If you want to make the task even more demanding, try repeating the digits in *reverse* order.)

How long does information remain in short-term memory? In one common test subjects are briefly shown a short series of consonants—say, CPQ—and then asked to count backward by threes, say, from 270 (267, 264, 261...). When cued, they try to repeat the series of consonants (CPQ). Under such conditions, subjects are likely to forget the letters within about twenty seconds (Brown, 1958; Peterson & Peterson, 1959). The backward counting acts as an interfering task—a device psychologists use to prevent rehearsal of information in short-term memory. If the interfering task is ineffective—if subjects manage to rehearse CPQ secretly while appearing to take a deep breath between counts, for example—subjects' memory of the consonants will probably last longer. The exact duration depends on the amount of rehearsal they are able to squeeze in.

Again, these estimates seem to be at odds with everyday experience. If you are given a phone number to remember, you can certainly remember the information longer than a few seconds. Even if it is eleven digits long, such as "1-800-555-1212," you will have little trouble remembering it. How can we reconcile the laboratory findings on short-term memory with our own experiences? The answer to this dilemma lies in the way in which information is processed in short-term memory.

Rehearsal

To increase the duration of short-term memory, information must be actively used. After looking up a telephone number, for example, you probably repeat it several times, either aloud or mentally, while reaching for the phone. Then you dial quickly, knowing that you will not remember the number for long once you have stopped saying it. If you become distracted and interrupt the repetition to attend to something else, you will probably have to look up the number again. This example illustrates a basic fact about short-term memory: incoming information is lost quickly unless it is renewed through rehearsal.

Rehearsal usually involves some kind of speech—either overt, as when you repeat a telephone number aloud, or covert, as when you repeat a number mentally. Rehearsal allows information in short-term memory to be retained longer than fifteen to twenty seconds. In fact, with rehearsal, the duration of information in short-term memory is virtually limitless (though it does preclude attending to new information). The fact that rehearsal tends to be speech-based is important and will be discussed in greater detail later in this chapter.

Exactly how long can new information stay in short-term memory without rehearsal? Studies suggest no more than half a minute, though usually much less. In addition to delays in rehearsal, other factors affect the duration of short-term memory, including the degree to which new material is associated with information held in long-term storage.

FIGURE 7-8 *The effect of chunking on short-term memory.*

> Try to memorize the following lists of digits:
> 1 4 9 1 6 2 5 3 6 4 9 6 4 8 1 1 0 0 1 2 1 1 4 4
>
> Next, try to memorize them in these groups:
> 1 4 9 16 25 36 49 64 81 100 121 144
>
> Finally, encode them this way:
> 1^2 2^2 3^2 4^2 5^2 6^2 7^2 8^2 9^2 10^2 11^2 12^2

Thus, if the letters CPQ happen to be a person's initials, that person is likely to recall them no matter how distracting an interfering task may be. The duration of short-term memory is also affected by whether or not a person is motivated to remember. If someone who has viewed three consonants is then distracted by a backward-counting task, not expecting ever to need to recall the letters again, those letters will fade from short-term storage with astonishing speed—often within a mere two seconds (Muter, 1980). This finding suggests that the ability to retain new information in short-term memory depends on how it is processed in the first place. Information that is deemed insignificant is likely to disappear quickly, whereas information that is significant is likely to be recalled despite a few seconds of distraction.

Encoding

The capacity of short-term memory is just as important as is its duration. In 1956 George Miller published a paper titled "The Magical Number Seven, Plus or Minus Two." In it he summarized the results of many experiments, all of which indicated that most people can hold only between five and nine items in short-term memory at any one time. Most psychologists agree with Miller's conclusions.

At first researchers were puzzled by the human ability to process large amounts of information despite the limited capacity of short-term memory. How, they wondered, can we read and comprehend even a brief sentence if we are unable to handle more than seven letters at once? Miller provided an answer: we expand our limited capacity by **chunking** information. That is, we see groups of letters as words (small chunks), groups of words as phrases (larger chunks), and series of phrases as sentences (even larger chunks). Though short-term memory can hold only about seven chunks, each chunk may contain a great deal of information. In this way, we

greatly increase the amount we can process at any one time (Miller, 1956). See Figure 7-8.

In the chunking process, material that is stored in long-term memory is used to categorize new information entering short-term memory. The number 1492 is easier to recall than the number 2769, for example, if you think of it as the year Columbus sailed to America. In this example, you are using your knowledge of history to reduce your memory load to a single date instead of four separate digits. Conceivably you could hold a string of twenty-eight numbers in your short-term memory if you could chunk them into seven familiar dates.

Chunking is used frequently in everyday life. For example, social security numbers contain nine digits—the upper limit of normal short-term memory capacity. However, they are organized into three different "chunks." Phone numbers are encoded in a

Comedienne and talk-show host Rosie O'Donnell is known for her remarkable ability to remember the lyrics to songs. Long-term memory depends on efficient encoding, successful long-term storage, and accurate retrieval.

FIGURE 7-9A   *Visual chunking. Study this arrangement of chess pieces for five seconds. Then turn to the empty chessboard (Figure 7-9B) and try to reproduce the arrangement. The amount you are able to recall correctly represents approximately seven of the chunks you have developed for processing information about chess games.*

FIGURE 7-9B   *Turn to Figure 7-9A, if you have not already looked at it, and study it for five seconds. Then try to produce the arrangement shown there on this empty chessboard. See the text for an explanation of the results.*

similar manner: area code (three digits, but one chunk), prefix (one chunk), and the final four digits (one chunk). Even adding a lengthy long-distance dialing prefix need not tax short-term memory.

What are the limits of chunking? The answer may astonish you. In one study, Anders Ericsson and his colleagues (Ericsson, 1985; Ericsson & Chase, 1982; Ericsson, Chase, & Faloon, 1980) worked with a college student named Steve Faloon, who was average both in intelligence and in short-term memory capacity (Falson could remember a string of approximately seven random digits). After twenty months of practice, Faloon could remember a staggering *eighty digits* presented to him at the rate of one every second! The key to Faloon's phenomenal improvement lay in a clever chunking technique he devised. An accomplished long-distance runner, he hit on the scheme of categorizing digits whenever possible as if they were running times. Thus he would encode the sequence 3492 as "3 minutes, 49.2 seconds—a near world record for the mile." Faloon would then take clusters of digits encoded as running times and think of them as one larger chunk based on related information. Several other strategies supplemented this one to give Faloon his impressive skill.

Note, however, that while Faloon's digit span had increased, his short-term memory capacity did not.

When the researchers switched suddenly from random digits to random letters, Faloon's memory span plummeted from eighty back to seven. Faloon had improved his skill at using his limited short-term memory capacity through learned techniques of chunking. Though he had not increased the *size* of his short-term memory, he had increased its efficiency. Lest you think that Faloon's ability is unique, consider this: Faloon taught his techniques to a friend, also a long-distance runner. The friend readily adopted the technique, learning it more quickly than Faloon, and increased his digit span to over *100 digits.*

Chunked information need not be verbal. Study the chessboard in Figure 7-9A for five seconds, then turn the page and see how many pieces you can position correctly on the empty board in Figure 7-9B. If you do not play chess, your limit will probably be close to the number seven. In fact, you may recall the position of far fewer than seven pieces, because storing each one requires several bits of information— what the piece looks like, and its row and column. Yet chess masters can reproduce the entire arrangement after just a five-second glance. Do chess masters have exceptional memories? Research suggests they do not (Chase & Simon, 1973a, 1973b; De Groot, 1965; Simon & Gilmartin, 1973). When pieces are arranged on a chessboard in a random pattern, the chess master's memory is no better than anyone else's. But when pieces are arranged in a pattern that might actually occur in a game between good players, the chess master easily encodes the pattern using a number of large chunks. How many such visual chunks can chess masters identify? Somewhere between 25,000 and 100,000. Amazing—but not so remarkable if you consider that an educated speaker of English has a vocabulary of about the same size.

Long-Term Memory

We have discussed the process of looking up a phone number and holding it in short-term memory. As long as the number is rehearsed, it remains accessible. But obviously there is more to memory than short-term rehearsal buffer; otherwise we would spend our days continually repeating our own names just to remember them.

The repository for more durable memories is called **long-term memory.** Because of long-term memory, our experiences are not necessarily lost the moment we cease to think of them. Instead, we retain some memories of the past and use them in the present. As the store place of all your accumulated knowledge, long-term memory contains an extraordinary amount of information, some of which you are hardly aware of until you need to recall it. Harry Bahrick's (1984) research showed that memory for Spanish learned in high school can last a remarkably long time. People who have learned Spanish in school—especially those who studied it a number of semesters—retain large portions of the language years later, even if they rarely use it. Consider the many other facts, ideas, and perceptions we store away over a lifetime, and the capacity of long-term memory seems almost incomprehensible.

Atkinson and Shiffrin's (1968) information-processing model of memory was concerned primarily with memory for facts: the name of the first President of the United States, the capital of South Dakota, and the like. Just as Ebbinghaus's simplistic notions of memory were later replaced with more accurate—and more complex—models, researchers now agree that not all long-term memories are the same. Long-term memory can store simple associations, such as what to do when a traffic light turns green. It can also store memory for bodily movements, even those that elude consciousness. For example, where is the "t" key on the computer keyboard? If you are a computer user, you may respond by lifting the index finger on your left hand—almost as if your fingers know the answer, even if your conscious mind doesn't.

Long-term memory contains a vast storehouse of factual information, a kind of personal encyclopedia. For example, you know that Freud was a pioneering figure in psychology. You know that blood is pumped throughout your body by your heart. You know that when snow melts, it becomes water, and so on. Your "personal encyclopedia" may contain huge amounts of information.

In Chapter 2 you learned that one measure of a theory's usefulness is the degree to which it directs research—even if that research later shows the guiding theory to be incorrect. By this measure, Atkinson and Shiffrin's model of memory has proved extremely valuable. Most memory researchers now believe that memories cannot be divided into neat categories like "sensory memory store" or "long-term memory store." But in the process of testing the information-processing model, psychologists uncovered many of the key processes humans use to acquire, store, and retrieve memories.

Regardless of the theoretical details, most memory researchers now agree that long-term memory encompasses three basic processes: encoding, storage, and retrieval. **Encoding** refers to the process through which sensory information is converted into a form that can be remembered. **Storage** refers to the way in which information is kept in memory for later use. **Retrieval** is the process of finding stored memories and making them available for use. A breakdown in any of these processes will result in memory failure. However, encoding failures lead to very different problems from retrieval failures.

Encoding

Which way does Lincoln face on the copper penny, left or right? Where are the words "E Pluribus Unum" or "In God We Trust" placed? Where does the date go? Are you even certain Lincoln's portrait is on the penny? Try drawing the face of a penny, putting all the details in the correct places. After you have finished, look at Figure 7-10. Which is the correct drawing of the penny?

If you were not able to draw the penny correctly, don't worry; you are not alone. One study found that only one of the twenty subjects correctly placed all eight features on the penny, in the correct locations. Their recognition performance wasn't much better; when given the drawings in Figure 7-10, fewer than

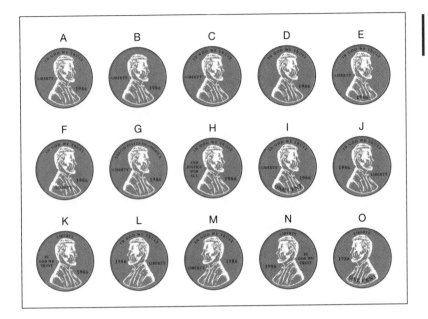

FIGURE 7-10 *Which drawing of the penny is correct?* (After Nickerson & Adams, 1982.)

half were able to select the correct version (Nickerson & Adams, 1982).

Why should performing this simple task be so difficult? Most of us have seen hundreds, even thousands, of pennies in our lifetime. Shouldn't we be able to call up their image mentally and "zoom in" on the correct features? The answer is "no"; memory is not a videotape, accurately recording every experience we have had. As is stressed in Recurring Theme 4, cognition in general (and memory in particular) is a constructive process. It works by taking incomplete bits and pieces of past events and filling in the gaps. We all have "memories" of events that happened to us in the past which have changed, sometimes drastically, over time.

THEME

4

Cognition and Thought are Dynamic, Active Processes, Best Considered Reconstructive, Not Reproductive

The first stage in the formation of memory is encoding, the process of transforming events in ways they can be stored and processed. Encoding is usually an active process, one in which we deliberately attend to certain features of a stimulus.

The way in which we encode stimuli can have tremendous implications for our memories. For example, the fact that you cannot draw a literal representation of a penny does not mean you have no memory of it. You have those features of a penny that are important to you: you know that it is round

and copper-colored, bigger than a dime but smaller than a nickel, worth one cent, and so on. If you are a coin collector, you have likely encoded even more information: the meaning of the capital "D," the picture of wheat on the back, and so on. You *do* know what a penny looks like, at least well enough to use one in your day-to-day life.

The encoding process for long-term memories is similar in some ways to the encoding of short-term memories. But whereas encoding into short-term memory is fairly simple, encoding into long-term memory involves a number of processes. Some are simple, such as chunking. Others can be extremely complex, such as encoding the names and faces of a class of 100 students.

Encoding is critical to good memory. Many memory failures we label as "forgetting" are more accurately described as encoding failures. If you meet someone at a party but later find you cannot remember that person's name, you may well have failed to properly encode the name. The last section of this chapter deals with *mnemonics*, or tools that can be used to aid memory. Most mnemonics emphasize the encoding process.

The instances of encoding we have just discussed are examples of **effortful encoding,** or a deliberate attempt to store something into memory. Another kind of encoding, also common, seems to happen effortlessly and is therefore called **automatic encoding.** To grasp how much knowledge you acquire

If you meet someone at a party, but later find you cannot remember that person's name, you may well have experienced a failure of encoding.

through automatic encoding, consider the following questions:

1. What route did you take to get to school when you were in the sixth grade?
2. Where did you sit the last time you entered a large lecture hall?
3. What time of day did you last stop by your college bookstore?
4. How many movies have you seen in the last three months (not including those on TV)?
5. Do more words in the English language end with an "e" or a "p"?
6. Which is the more common surname in this country, Williams or Skahill?

You probably had no trouble answering any of these questions, though you made no effort to retain the information. Researchers have found that information about your location in time and space (Questions 1 through 3) and about how often you experience different stimuli (Questions 4 through 6) are typically encoded automatically (Hasher & Zacks, 1984).

Through practice you can learn to encode other kinds of data automatically. For example, when you were a child, you had to work hard to encode written words into short-term storage. Now, as an adult with many years of practice at reading, you find this task effortless. Psychologists have demonstrated just how effortless the process is by presenting adults with color names written in inks of inconsistent colors (Stroop, 1935). Figure 7-11 demonstrates the Stroop task.

Most people find identifying the ink color on the right side of the page much more difficult than the left. Why? The letters themselves—which you were told to ignore—spell out color names. At this point in your life, you probably cannot look at a group of letters and fail to read the words they spell. For skilled readers of English, word identification involves automatic encoding. The effect is so striking that most four-year-old children can identify the ink colors in the list on the right more quickly than you. Why? They have not yet had sufficient practice with letters and words for automatic word recognition to interfere with their answers.

Finally, memory researchers now recognize the importance of context in the formation of memories. When memories (especially memories for specific events) are formed, the context surrounding that memory is also encoded. Later retrieval of that memory is often enhanced if the conditions in which it was encoded can be re-created. We will discuss this phenomenon, known as *encoding specificity*, when we discuss retrieval.

Storage

The second stage of long-term memory formation involves storage, or the long-term maintenance of memories. The brain mechanisms underlying memory formation and storage are not completely understood. However, most memory researchers now agree that memories are *not* stored in any one specific location. That is, your memory for your high school

Cover the right side of the chart, so that only the information on the left of the chart is visible. As quickly as you can, go through the list of items, calling out the color of the ink used to print each word. Now cover the left side of the chart, revealing only the right side. *Ignoring the letters which comprise the words*, go through the list of items as quickly as you can, calling out the color of the ink used to print each word.

List One	*List Two*
XHFH	BLUE
FKXHW	RED
KRJWN	GREEN
ULSIUE	YELLOW
VKWHR	PINK

FIGURE 7-11 *The Stroop task.* (After Stroop, 1935.)

graduation ceremony isn't located at a single place in your brain. A brain surgeon could not, for example, remove a memory by destroying a small, localized part of your brain. In fact, information-processing models of memory are probably most misleading with regard to storage. Unlike the brain, a computer stores a single file in a single location on a disk. The file can be deleted by finding that location and erasing the information stored there. Though the file in question is deleted, the rest of the disk remains intact.

Human memory does not work in this way. Memories are not stored in a single place in the brain, nor can a single memory be deleted by removing the specific neurons. Instead, memory theorists now view memory as being a parallel, distributed network. *Parallel* (as opposed to *serial*) means that different locations in the brain can be activated at the same time. *Distributed* means the information can be stored *throughout* an area of the brain. Thus, memory should probably be viewed as a pattern of activation across a number of neurons, rather than as the activation of a single neuron.

One useful way to think of parallel, distributed storage is to visualize a stadium scoreboard that displays pictures of players on a baseball team. The scoreboard, which consists of hundred of thousands of lightbulbs, is roughly analogous to the neurons of the brain. It can be configured in such a way—some light on and some off—so that it suggests the face of a certain player, say Nolan Ryan. Which of the many lights shows Ryan's picture? Clearly, no *single* lightbulb suggests Ryan's likeness. The picture emerges from the pattern of activity across the scoreboard. In

the same way, no single location in the brain contains a specific memory. Instead, the memory is stored as the pattern of activation across a large group of neurons.

This analogy is also useful in understanding the brain's virtually unlimited capacity for storage. Assume that a scoreboard has 1 million lightbulbs. How many different faces could be displayed by activating those lights in different patterns? Almost certainly, every possible face we might want to display could be projected, and each would require a unique pattern of activation. The human brain contains at least 1,000 times as many neurons as our hypothetical scoreboard contains lights. Much as we may feel, from time to time, as though we cannot possibly cram one more fact into our memory, the true storage capacity of the human brain is virtually inexhaustible.

The success or failure of memory storage depends on a number of factors. One of the most obvious factors is rehearsal. Memory depends partly on the amount of *time* we spend rehearsing information: the longer the rehearsal, the more likely that information will be placed into long-term storage. Even more important, however, is the *type* of rehearsal; some types are more effective than others. Rote repetition—simply repeating something over and over—is relatively ineffective. We all have had the experience of looking up a telephone number, saying it over and over to ourselves before dialing, and two minutes later being unable to remember the number.

In contrast, if we take a new piece of information and process it in some meaningful way—form an image of it, apply it to a problem, relate it to something else—it is more likely to be deposited into

In recalling events from the past, this man is relying on retrieval, the process of finding stored memories and making them available for use.

long-term storage. This type of rehearsal, known as **deep processing** or **elaborative rehearsal,** is much more effective than the **shallow processing** or **maintenance rehearsal** involved in rote repetition (Craik & Lockhart, 1972). As a general rule, emphasizing the *meaning* of a stimulus is especially conducive to deep processing. In one study, subjects were presented with words and questioned about them (Craik & Tulving, 1975). Sometimes the questions had to do with a word's meaning (Does the word *friend* fit into the sentence "He saw a ____ on the street"?) At other times they concerned the word's appearance. ("How many vowels does the word have?" or "Is it printed in capital letters?") Afterward, subjects were unexpectedly asked to remember as many of the words as they could. Words that had been processed for meaning were recalled significantly more often than others.

The value of emphasizing meaning when trying to store something in memory was clear in the case of Steve Faloon, the college student who excelled in digit-span tests. After an hour-long practice session, Faloon could recall over 80 percent of all the number sequences he had seen that day. He could even recognize many of the sequences he had seen a week earlier (Ericsson, Chase, & Faloon 1980). Clearly, the way in which he chunked the digits and related them to meaningful running times facilitated their transfer from short-term to long-term storage.

Processing of the opposite kind—shallow, inattentive, and concerned only with superficial features—is undoubtedly the cause of many lapses in memory. Why, for instance, do you sometimes forget a person's name just minutes after you have been introduced? Probably because you were so concerned with making appropriate remarks that you failed to actively process the name (Baddeley, 1990).

Retrieval

Most college students can read at a steady rate of 300 words per minute, or nearly 5 words per second (Weaver, 1994). This skill requires an amazingly efficient system for retrieving the meaning of words. But because we are so accustomed to our remarkable powers of information retrieval, we seldom stop to think how truly impressive they are.

As discussed previously in the chapter, psychologists generally use two kinds of retrieval tasks, recognition and recall, to test long-term storage (Baddeley, 1990). **Recognition** involves realizing that a particular stimulus was encountered previously. Identifying a suspect in a police lineup is an example of a recognition task. **Recall** entails the retrieval of specific pieces of information, usually guided by cues. To ask a witness to a robbery "What did the thief look like? Do you remember what he was wearing?" is to ask the person to recall details of the robbery. To accomplish this, the witness must search through memory and come up with a description.

Retrieval does not occur in a vacuum. It is guided by **retrieval cues,** or bits of information that are related to items stored in memory. Retrieval cues can exert powerful effects on memory. For example, you have probably used a well-known retrieval cue to remember the order of colors in the visible spectrum of light. The mnemonic *ROY G BIV* is useful because its letters can serve as retrieval cues: *R* is for "red," *O* is for "orange," *Y* is for "yellow," and so on.

One of the most powerful types of retrieval cues involves the context in which information has been learned (or encoded). Memory is best when the conditions during retrieval match the conditions during encoding—a phenomenon known as **encoding specificity** (Tulving & Thompson, 1973). Thus, memory retrieval can often be enhanced by re-creating or imagining the context in which information was learned. In criminal law, for instance, lawyers talk about "re-creating the scene of the crime." From a psychologist's perspective, such tactics are beneficial because they may provide retrieval cues.

To give another example, most of us have gone back to the town in which we grew up, or to a school we attended as children. Oftentimes, returning to those surroundings can cue memories we have not thought of for a number of years. Returning to the context in which those memories were formed enhances their retrieval. Even the odor of a once familiar place brings back memories.

Though it is tempting to think of recall in the same terms as the retrieval of information from a computer disk, the retrieval of computer files is a poor analogy for human recall. Like all aspects of memory, retrieval is an active, constructive process. A file retrieved from a computer disk is perfect: it is retrieved exactly as it was stored. Retrieval from memory, though, is not perfect; the act of retrieval may change a memory.

In a now classic study, Loftus and Palmer (1974) provided a convincing demonstration of how memories can be altered through retrieval. Subjects were shown a videotape of an automobile accident and then questioned about what they saw: What color was the car that pulled out? How many people were in the car? and so on. During the questioning, subjects were asked to estimate how fast the cars were traveling when they collided: "How fast was the red Toyota moving when it ____ the other car?" Four different film clips were viewed: one showing a collision at 20 miles per hour, one at 30 miles per hour, two at 40 miles per hour. Overall, subjects were unable to correctly estimate the speed of the cars in the four films; they provided speed estimates of 37.7,

TABLE 7-1   *Effects of Retrieval Cues on Estimates Given for the Speed of the Car Involved in an Accident (Actual Speed Varied from 20 to 40 Miles per Hour in All Conditions)*

How Fast Was the Red Toyota Moving When it ____ the Other Car?	
Description	**Estimate of speed**
Contacted	31 mph
Bumped	34 mph
Collided with	37 mph
Smashed into	41 mph

Source: After Loftus & Palmer, 1974.

36.2, 39.7, and 36.1 miles per hour, respectively. More importantly, though, the words used to describe the collision were varied, as shown in Table 7-1. The more severe the description, the higher the subject's estimate of its speed. This basic finding has been observed in many situations. Children's testimony has proven especially susceptible to such suggestions (see Ceci & Bruck, 1993, and Ceci, Loftus, Leichtman, & Bruck, 1994, for discussions of the factors that influence children's eyewitness testimony).

These kinds of distortions demonstrate the reconstructive nature of memory. Retrieved memories are a combination of the actual event, information that has been learned since the event, and the conditions present at retrieval. The suggestibility of eyewitness memory in a courtroom setting is well known to attorneys—thus leading to the common complaint, "Objection! Leading the witness!"

Retrieval cues are important not only to accurate recollection but to recollection itself. We have all had the frustrating experience of being unable to recall a name or fact we know is stored in memory. Sometimes this experience produces a **tip-of-the-tongue phenomenon:** an answer seems poised to emerge, but somehow we cannot get it out. How do we retrieve such memories? Most of us use a variety of cues based on bits of information we are able to recall about the target word. Suppose, for example, that you want to remember the word for "a small Chinese boat with a covered deck propelled by a single oar." You might grope your way through a string of similar-sounding words—*cheyenne . . . siam . . . saipan*—until you eventually arrive at the correct response, *sampan* (Brown & McNeill, 1966). Or when shown a picture of Dustin Hoffman and asked to remember his name, you might first recall his profession and the name of one of his films: "Movie actor . . . starred in *Rainman* . . . Dustin Hoffman." When you store information in long-term memory, you create a number of cues for retrieval, including sounds (particularly the first letter of a word) and associated facts and meanings (Reason & Mycielska, 1982).

Of course, retrieval cues based on the sound of a word can be a mixed blessing. Sometimes we become so fixated on a word that sounds like the one we want to recall that it blocks the retrieval of the target word (Jones, 1988). In these situations, we are unlikely to generate the correct alternative immediately. The best solution is to stop the search for a while and forget the interfering information.

As we have pointed out, one of the strengths of Atkinson and Shiffrin's information processing model of memory is its usefulness in guiding the development of new theories. One of the most influential models derived from the information-processing model was proposed by Endel Tulving (1985), and distinguishes between different types of long-term memory.

Tulving's Theory of Multiple Memory Systems

Think for a moment about the different kinds of memory you have formed. You have a vast number of "how to" memories: how to type, how to drive a car, how to serve a tennis ball. You also have a vast storehouse of facts, such as "Seattle is in Washington" and "the formula for finding the area of a circle is "π times r^2." Finally, your brain is full of personal memories of the life experiences you have had— your first day at a school, a baseball game at which you caught a foul ball, your first kiss. Though your brain stores all those different kinds of memories, must they all be stored in the same way? Perhaps not. In the past decade, memory researchers have moved away from the idea of a single long-term memory system. Instead, they suggest that what we know as "memory" is more likely a collection of long-term memory systems, each of which stores types of memories.

One of the first memory researchers to propose the idea of **multiple memory systems** was the Canadian psychologist Endel Tulving. Tulving (1985)

cited a number of characteristics of memory that compelled him to abandon the information-processing model in its strictest sense. First, Tulving argued that what we now call *memory* is actually a collection of different memory systems that have evolved over time. Like all human characteristics, memory is the result of selective pressures over millions of years of evolution. As the demands of the environment changed over those millions of years, different kinds of memory became more or less useful. Thus, memory as we know it today is a combination of different systems.

Second, Tulving noted that no sweeping generalizations can be made about memory. Can memories be said to get worse over time? Not all memories; with rehearsal, some get better over time. Can memory be said to get worse as one ages? Not in all cases; some types of memory improve with age. Will someone who displays good memory in one task (say, taking a history test) also have good memory on all tasks (such as a typing test)? Obviously not. According to Tulving, no sweeping generalizations can be made about memory because it is not a single system.

Third, even though some cognitive function may *appear* to be a unitary phenomenon, research has shown that cognitive abilities are complex and often have different aspects to them. For example, Weiskrantz's work on blindsight (see Chapter 4) shows that there is more to vision than meets the eye, so to speak. Finally, Tulving argued that in subjective experiences the various types of memory are fundamentally different. Memories for a high school prom seem different from memory for state capitals. And those memories seem to differ from the memory of how to drive a car with a stick shift. The subjective experiences of events, facts, and skills are qualitatively different.

Tulving (1985, 1993) proposes that memory is best understood as a hierarchy of memory systems, as shown in Figure 7-12. In this hierarchy, **procedural memories** are the most basic system. These "blueprints for actions" do not require conscious awareness. Instead, they may be thought of as learned associations between stimuli and responses. When you hear the phone ring and immediately reach for the receiver, or see a stop sign and quickly put your foot on the brake, you are using the procedural memory system. Procedural memories allow you to adapt to your environment. Indeed, any organism that is capable of learning can form procedural memories.

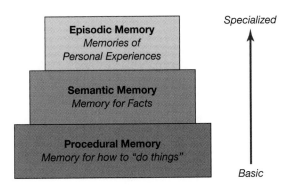

FIGURE 7-12   Tulving's (1983) hierarchy of memory systems. Procedural memory, the most basic form of memory, is possessed by any organism that can learn. Semantic memory may be considered a more specialized subsystem of procedural memory. Episodic memory, in turn, is a more specialized subsystem of semantic memory.

Some organisms have a more specialized knowledge of the world, which Tulving calls **semantic memory.** The term *semantic* implies a reliance on verbal ("semantic") abilities. But while many semantic memories *are* verbally based, they need not be. For example, the knowledge you have about objects and their location in the world is based on semantic memories. Imagine yourself standing before the front door of your dorm room, house, or apartment. Is the handle to the front door on the right or the left side? If you can answer that question, you probably do it by imagining the door in front of you—a task for which you need no verbal descriptions. Even organisms that have no verbal language can form semantic memories. Your pet dog or cat most likely has semantic memories of its environment, and may sometimes leave through the front door and return by the back door. Semantic memory is the storehouse of information about the world around you.

The most specialized memory system is **episodic memory.** Episodic memories, as the name implies, are memories for specific episodes in the past. They are distinctive because the individual who remembers them is an active part of the memory. Knowing that new brides often throw their bouquets over their shoulders after the ceremony is an example of semantic memory. However, remembering the specific time *your* sister threw her bouquet is an episodic memory.

In general, episodic memories have greater personal meaning and emotion than other memories, because they are unique to the individual. Everyone in your psychology class probably knows that the space shuttle *Challenger* exploded in 1986—an example of semantic memory. Your classmates' semantic memories of the *Challenger* are probably quite similar. However, many of your classmates may also be able to describe where they were and what they were doing when they learned of the *Challenger*'s explosion—an example of episodic memory. Furthermore, each such memory is personal and different from others' memories.

Evidence Supporting Existence of Multiple Memory Systems

Tulving's theory of multiple memory systems has generated a great deal of research during the past decade—one of the hallmarks of a good theory. While researchers have not arrived at a conclusion, many now agree with Tulving that some memory is more than a single system. Evidence for the multiple systems theory has come from research on patients suffering from amnesia.

Amnesia

Research conducted on amnesiac patients such as H. M. (see Chapter 3) and K. C., whose case history opened this chapter, seems to demonstrate the existence of separate memory systems. H. M., you will recall, underwent radical neurosurgery that was designed to treat his epilepsy. The surgeon removed the parts of H. M.'s brain called the *hippocampus* and the *amygdala*, bilaterally (on both sides of the brain). In the thirty-five years since the surgery was performed, H. M. has suffered permanent and irreversible **anterograde amnesia**—that is, loss of memory for events that have occurred *since* his surgery. Essentially, he has been unable to form any new memories since then. When asked, H. M. says the year is 1953 (the year his surgery was performed). Many scientists have worked closely with H. M. over the decades since the surgery was done, but H. M. has no memory of ever having met them. He describes his state by saying, "It is like constantly waking from a dream. Every day is alone unto itself, whatever joys I've had, whatever sorrows I've had" (Milner, 1968, cited in Kolb & Whishaw, 1993).

To say that H. M. cannot form any new long-term memories is not entirely correct, however. H. M. *can* form new memories: procedural memories. If he is given a maze in which he is to trace a successful path, for example, his performance gets better each time he attempts the task. If he were given the same maze today, he would quickly work out the solution. Told that his performance is exceptional, and asked whether he had practiced the task before, he would answer negatively, however. And though H. M. has learned new skills, such as fastening shoes with Velcro straps, each time he is given shoes with those closures he reacts as if he has never seen them before. Simply put, H. M. can form new memories, but he has no conscious awareness of them.

Warrington and Weiskrantz (1970) observed similar results with another group of amnesiacs, those suffering from Korsakoff's syndrome (Chapter 4). In a typical memory experiment subjects might have to study a list of words, then later recognize or recall all the words they could remember (and distinguish them from distractor words). Warrington and Weiskrantz found that amnesiacs with Korsakoff's syndrome performed poorly on **direct tests** of memory that require conscious awareness (like recall and recognition). These tests are collectively referred to as tests of **explicit memory.** (This result should come as no surprise—it is part of the definition of amnesia.) However, in other memory tests, indirect tests of memory, Korsakoff's amnesiacs displayed perfectly normal memory. **Indirect tests** measure **implicit memory,** or memory without awareness. One of the most popular indirect tests involves word fragments that subjects are asked to complete. The fragments look like the puzzles featured on the game show *Wheel of Fortune*; they are words from which some of the letters have been deleted (see Figure 7-13).

Most people can solve some of these puzzles on their own, but they do better if they have studied the words before the test. This improvement in performance is called *priming* (Roediger, 1990; Tulving, 1993; Tulving, Schacter, & Stark, 1982). Prior study of the words helps in a later fragment completion test, making this a valid—if unusual—test of memory. Despite their impaired explicit memories, Korsakoff's amnesiacs showed normal implicit memories. When given word fragments to solve, they did better with words they had studied earlier, just as normal subjects do. What is more, prior study helped the Korsakoff's amnesiacs even though they had no recollection of having seen the words before.

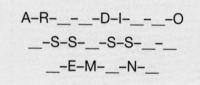

Without looking ahead, try to solve these puzzles.

A–R–__–_–D–I–__–_–__–O
__–S–S–__–S–S–__–_–__
__–E–M–__–N–__

FIGURE 7-13   *An indirect test of memory. Without looking ahead, try to solve these puzzles.*

Just like H. M., these amnesiacs possessed some memory for a prior event, even though they had no conscious awareness of it. The priming they demonstrated has been observed in many different types of amnesiacs (e.g., McCarthy & Warrington, 1990; Schacter, 1996; Squire, 1987; Squire, Haist, & Shimamura, 1989).

K. C.'s amnesia is considerably different from that of patients with Korsakoff's syndrome. First, it was caused by a closed-head injury suffered during a motorcycle accident. Thus, the exact location and extent of his brain damage is unclear. Second, K. C. did not completely lose his ability to form new memories that require awareness, though his awareness of those events is different from that of normal subjects (see Tulving, Hayman, & McDonald, 1991). Finally, K. C. suffered serious **retrograde amnesia,** or loss of memory for events that occurred *prior to* his injury.

K. C.'s case is perhaps most unusual in the *kind* of memories he has lost. He has retained all his procedural memories and can form new ones. He can form new semantic memories as well, such as learning the definitions of new words—though he learns them much more slowly than normal. K. C.'s amnesia is most striking because he has lost all his episodic memories. He has no personal memories for any event in his life, regardless of when it occurred. As was stated in the opening of this chapter, K. C. "knows" many things about his life. He can tell you his hometown, the name of his high school, and whether or not his siblings are married. He knows about his injury. But K. C. knows these things in a detached, impersonal way, much as if he had read about them.

According to Tulving (1989, 1993; Tulving et al., 1991), K. C. has lost his episodic memory system but has retained the other two systems. H. M., by comparison, has lost the ability to form new episodic and semantic memories, but his procedural memory is

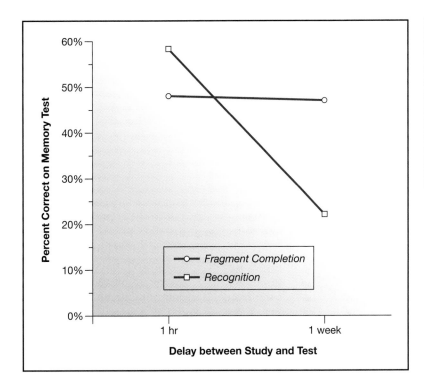

FIGURE 7-14 *Performance on tests of explicit (recognition) memory and implicit (fragment completion) memory. Explicit memory tends to decrease over time; recognition performance following a one-week delay is poorer. Implicit memory is relatively unaffected by delays; fragment completion performance does not decline following a delay.* (After Tulving, 1985.)

intact. Korsakoff's amnesiacs show impairments similar to H. M.'s. Together, these cases provide powerful evidence in support of the existence of multiple memory systems.

Memory Systems in Normal People

Recurring Theme 2 stated that "psychologists learn about the normal by studying the abnormal."

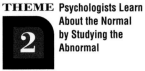

THEME **Psychologists Learn About the Normal by Studying the Abnormal** The amnesiacs just described in the previous sections provide dramatic examples of abnormal memory function. However, research involving a handful of exceptional cases is limited. How much of H. M.'s memory impairment was due to damage inflicted by epilepsy and the bicycle accident that triggered his epilepsy? Is K. C.'s memory deficit caused by a single injury, or by several different injuries to his brain? Korsakoff's amnesia usually results from decades of alcohol abuse, which causes widespread neurological damage. Which damaged brain areas are responsible for the memory deficits these patients show? Though case histories are suggestive, and often lead to great breakthroughs, they do not reveal everything there is to know about normal functioning.

For instance, H. M. and other amnesiacs retained implicit memory even though their explicit memory was impaired. What is the relationship between implicit and explicit memory in normal people? Recent research has identified some clear separations between these two types of memory. In some cases, prior experiences for which a person has no conscious memory continue to influence behavior. Normal individuals show improvement on fragment completion tests after studying the words on the test even if they no longer remember the study session.

In one such experiment (Tulving, Schacter, & Stark, 1982) subjects were given a list of words to study and then tested one hour or one week later. Two different kinds of tests were used: recognition tests (which require conscious awareness of prior study) and word fragment completion tests (which do not require awareness). First the subjects took the recognition tests. They were shown words taken from their study session and asked, "Is this a word that you studied before?" As might be expected, subjects recognized some of the words but failed to recognize others. That is, they had explicit memory for some of the items but not for others. Furthermore, the percentage of words they were able to recognize decreased over time: they were able to recognize fewer words after a one-week delay than after a one-hour delay.

After the recognition test, subjects were given fragment completion tests. If a fragment was taken from a word that was on their study list, subjects were more likely to generate the correct answer. What is more, the improvement in their performance did not decline over time: their performance following a one-week delay was the same as their performance following a one-hour delay (see Figure 7-14). Indeed, some experiments have shown that a single study session can increase a child's performance on a fragment completion test, even if the test is delayed for several months (Drummey & Newcombe, 1995). In adults, a delay of up to a year produces no loss in performance (Sloman et al., 1988).

In addition to the long-lasting nature of implicit memories, Tulving and his colleagues looked at the relationship between implicit and explicit memory. They sorted each subject's responses into two categories: those items the subject had successfully completed in the fragment completion test (that is, items for which the subject had displayed implicit memory) and those items the subject failed to complete (that is, those for which the subject had displayed no implicit memory). Then they compared the results to the performance on a recognition test with the same items.

Would the subjects be more likely to recognize items they could also complete on a fragment test, that is, for which they had implicit memory? Surprisingly, the answer Tulving found was "no." Subjects were no more likely to recognize words for which they had implicit memory than words for which they did not. Tulving and his colleagues have interpreted these findings as being consistent with the theory of multiple memory systems.

Neural Structures

Tulving and his colleagues suspected that implicit and explicit memories are processed by different brain structures. They argued that, in general, implicit memory relies on the "older" parts of the brain such as the cerebellum (Squire, 1986, 1987). Since those brain structures are present even in less complex organisms, we should expect almost all vertebrates to form implicit memories. Explicit memory, according to Tulving, is mediated by the "newer" parts of the brain, such as the frontal and temporal lobes, including the limbic areas (Squire, 1992). According to this view, we should expect to find explicit memory only in animals with well-developed frontal and temporal areas.

In general, research with amnesiacs supports this neural view (McCarthy & Warrington, 1990; Warrington & Weiskrantz, 1982). Despite the massive damage to H. M.'s limbic areas, for example, his cerebellum and related structures remained intact. Thus, H. M.'s implicit memory system was preserved. The progression of Alzheimer's disease (see Chapter 3) also follows a pattern predicted by Tulving's theory. The first symptoms of Alzheimer's involve deficits in episodic memory, such as recently learned names or a list of items to buy at the supermarket. As the disease progresses, the symptoms become increasingly serious, and the patient displays problems with semantic memory—forgetting the names of common objects or even family members. At autopsy, the brains of individuals at the early stage of Alzheimer's disease show mild deterioration of the frontal and temporal areas of the brain. Patients at more advanced stages show increasingly greater damage to their frontal lobes and other cortical centers (Kolb & Whishaw, 1996).

Even at the most advanced stages of Alzheimer's, however, many patients still have intact implicit memories. For example, some advanced patients begin speaking nonsense sentences that cannot be understood—but most of those sentences are *grammatically correct*. The knowledge of what a word means requires semantic memory, but the knowledge of how to combine words in a sentence involves procedural memory. Even in advanced cases of Alzheimer's disease, procedural memory is relatively unimpaired. Examination at autopsy shows that Alzheimer's causes little damage to the brain stem and cerebellum, those areas most likely to be involved in procedural memory (Kolb & Whishaw, 1996).

Criticisms of the Theory of Multiple Memory Systems

As influential as the theory of multiple memory systems has been, some researchers remain unconvinced. Roediger (1990) has reviewed the research of Tulving and others, and provided an alternative explanation for the results. Roediger concurs that performance on some tests of implicit memory is independent of performance on some tests of explicit memory, but he questions whether that means there are multiple memory systems. Instead, he believes the results may reflect differences in the *tests* themselves. He points out that most tests of implicit memory (such as fragment completion) are perceptual in nature; that is, they emphasize the physical qualities of the stimuli. In contrast, most tests of explicit memory, such as recognition tests, require deeper, more meaningful processing. The differences in subjects' performance on the two tests may thus be a result of how memory is *used* in each.

In a sense, Roediger offers a functional explanation of memory, while Tulving offers a structural explanation. These two different viewpoints are the same ones raised a century ago by the founders of psychology (see Chapter 1). No doubt a complete understanding of memory requires a synthesis of the two explanations: we need to learn more about both the brain mechanisms involved in memory and the conditions under which they are used.

Autobiographical Memory: The Role of Age and Emotion

We have seen that there are a number of different types of memory. However, to most people, the concept of "memory" refers to personal, individual memories—of a vacation or a school play. Psychologists often refer to these as **autobiographical memories,** because they pertain to one's own life.

Though autobiographical memories are closely related to Tulving's episodic memories, the two are not necessarily identical. You may remember the phone number at the house where you lived as a small child, but that is not an episodic memory as defined by Tulving: it has no personal context and does not refer to a specific event (or episode). Thus your phone number is an autobiographical, not an episodic, memory.

Autobiographical memories are not distributed evenly throughout our lives. Some periods in our lives lead to the formation of frequent, vivid autobiographical memories. Other periods lead to few memories. Memory researchers are particularly interested in these differences, as they demonstrate several important aspects of memory.

Human Development and Memory

Some periods in life produce more memories than others. Though devising a true measure of the number of memories created throughout the life span is impossible, David Rubin (1986) estimates the distribution is as shown in Figure 7-15. Notice that virtually no memories are reported from the first four to five years, a phenomenon known as *childhood amne-*

Most people can recall where they were and what they were doing when they heard the verdict in the O. J. Simpson trial. Memories of this kind of extraordinary event are called flashbulb memories, a term that is somewhat misleading. While flashbulb memories are likely to be recalled with great confidence, recent research indicates that they are not necessarily more accurate than other personal memories.

sia. Sheingold and Tenney (1982) found that subjects have virtually no memories before age three, and few from before age four. Though some studies suggest that the onset of memory may be slightly earlier than this (e.g., Usher & Neisser, 1993), the period of early amnesia appears to be universal. Any memories that may be formed during this period are ultimately lost to conscious awareness.

A number of possible explanations for childhood amnesia have been proposed (Howe & Courage, 1993; Leichtman, Ceci, & Morse, 1997; Wetzler & Sweeney, 1986). Among the most plausible are the later maturation of the brain structures that underlie conscious memory; the absence of language during the early years of life; and the young child's explanation of the world, which differs radically from the adult's. Regardless of the explanation, few if any conscious memories survive from early childhood.

Notice that the curve in Figure 7-15 shows a dramatic increase in the number of memories just after the early years, peaking with the years of early adulthood. Rubin calls this peak the "reminiscence bump." As the curves in Figure 7-15 show, the peak shifts slightly with age, rising from age twenty for fifty-year-olds to twenty-two or twenty-three for seventy-year-olds. If you think about the factors that are related to memory formation—emotion, novelty,

FIGURE 7-15 *Autobiographical memory throughout the life span. The first curve represents the distribution for a fifty-year-old; the second, for a seventy-year-old.* (Rubin, 1986.)

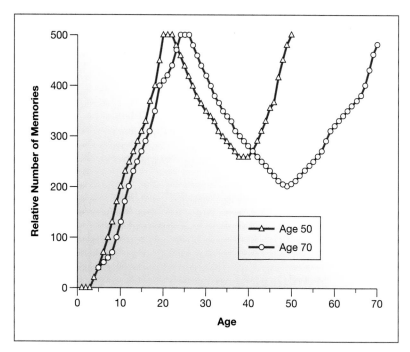

rehearsal, significance—you will realize that the early twenties are, in fact, the most memorable years. Life is full of change during those years, including a number of important and distinctive events. In the mid-to-late twenties, life tends to become more "constant," with fewer distinctive events. Important changes do occur, of course, but they are unlikely to be as concentrated in a brief time frame.

Following the reminiscence bump, then, new memories gradually decrease in frequency as lives become more predictable and less memorable. The most recent years of life are likely to be well remembered, as can be seen from the rise in the curve just before the age of testing. As people get older, the curve retains its shape, but the number of memories from any given year falls slightly. Someone who is fifty is likely to remember more events that happened at age thirty-five than someone who is seventy.

Emotions and Memory

The role of emotion and memory can be seen in our memory for exceptional events. If you ask your parents, they will almost certainly be able to tell you where they were and what they were doing when the popular young president John F. Kennedy was assassinated in November 1963. Kennedy's murder shocked the nation, producing an outpouring of grief.

Brown and Kulik (1977) studied memories of this kind of extraordinary event, which they called **flash-bulb memories.** They found that almost everyone who was old enough to understand the event could recall not only Kennedy's assassination but their personal circumstances at that time: who they were with, what they were doing, sometimes even what they were wearing. Though Kennedy's assassination is probably the best example of an event that triggers flashbulb memories, there have been others: the explosion of the space shuttle *Challenger* in 1986 (McCloskey, Wible, & Cohen, 1988); the beginning of Operation Desert Storm in Iraq in 1991 (Weaver, 1993); and the announcement of the verdict in O. J. Simpson's case in 1995 (Winningham, Hyman, & Dinnel, 1996). In the more distant past, flashbulb memories have been reported for President Nixon's resignation in 1974 (Neisser, 1982); the assassinations of Bobby Kennedy and Martin Luther King, Jr., in 1968 (Brown & Kulik, 1977); and even the bombing of Pearl Harbor in December 1941 (Neisser, 1982; Thompson & Cowan, 1986). In fact, in 1899 Colegrove reported that most of the people he interviewed had long-lasting, detailed memories of where they were and what they were doing when they received the news of Abraham Lincoln's assassination—an event that happened thirty years earlier.

Are flashbulb memories as accurate as their name implies? For several years, the answer was assumed to be "yes." Because of the nature of the events, however, verifying the accuracy of the reports was impossible. One of the first studies of the accuracy of such retrospective reports, conducted by Michael McCloskey and his colleagues (1988), investigated flashbulb memories of the explosion of the *Challenger*. Like other studies, it was based on recollective reports made some months after the actual event (in this case, about nine months). Unlike other studies, however, the accuracy of the recollected memories could be verified, because McCloskey's team had distributed a similar questionnaire a few days after the disaster.

McCloskey and his colleagues found that subjects' memory for the explosion was good, but *not* perfect. While the gist of a memory was often accurate, the details were not. These so-called flashbulb memories had not been preserved literally, as a photograph would preserve an image. McCloskey's team did not find perfect memories. Rather, they were vivid but normal memories, subject to distortion. In a similar study done over a much longer period (three years), Neisser and Harsh (1992) found even more striking distortions of subjects' flashbulb memories. One-fourth of the subjects were *completely wrong* in their recall of even major attributes, such as who they were with or where they were. Half the subjects were correct on about one major attribute and wrong about everything else. In a final attempt to cue the memories, Neisser and Harsh presented subjects with their own handwritten reports of the incident, written three years earlier, immediately following the *Challenger* disaster. Subjects responded with disbelief; none of them recognized the events they themselves had written about. Neisser and Harsh concluded that "no one who had given an incorrect account in the interview even pretended that they now recalled what was stated on the original record. On the contrary, they kept saying . . . 'I still think of it as the other way around.' As far as we can tell, the original memories are just gone" (p. 21).

How could memories we hold so strong be so inaccurate? A study done by Weaver (1993) suggests that flashbulb memories may be an illusion of sorts. In a psychology classroom exercise, Weaver asked students to remember all they could about an ordinary event. When they next met a roommate (or friend, if they lived alone), they were to remember all they could about the encounter, then fill out a questionnaire about it. By sheer coincidence, the same day the classroom exercise was conducted, Operation Desert Storm began in Iraq. Weaver col-

Psychologists refer to personal, individual memories of one's own life as "autobiographical memories."

lected memories for both events, then questioned his students again three months and then one year later.

Surprisingly, Weaver found that memories of the ordinary event—the meeting with a friend—were just as accurate as the flashbulb memories, even a year later. He also asked students to rate their confidence in their memory for the two events. Over time, students became less confident about the details concerning the meeting. But their confidence in the flashbulb memory, the military operation in Iraq, did *not* decline. A year later, subjects were much more confident in the accuracy of their flashbulb memories. Weaver suggests that flashbulb memories may be unique because of the confidence we place in them, not necessarily because of their accuracy.

Though emotion and memory are closely linked, the relationship is not a simple one. While the accuracy of memory improves as affect increases, the relationship breaks down at very high levels of emotion (Baddeley, 1990; Wible, McCloskey, & Cohen, 1989). Furthermore, most researchers doubt that memory for emotion events involve any kind of "special memory mechanisms (Cohen et al., 1988; McCloskey et al., 1988; Shobe & Kihlstrom, 1997; Weaver, 1995).

One example of this relationship is **mood-dependent memory.** Subjects who learn information in one mood tend to recall the material best when they are in the same mood at retrieval. In one study, subjects learned one list of words when they were happy and another list when they were sad (the two emotions were induced through hypnosis). Later, when they were given recall tests, subjects remembered the lists better if they were reexperiencing the mood in which a list was learned (Bower, Monteiro, & Gilligan, 1978). However, mood-dependent effects on memory are often unreliable and sometimes hard to replicate (Bower & Mayer, 1985; Wetzler, 1985). Apparently, only under ideal circumstances does good retrieval depend on being in the same emotional state as when one first learned something (Blaney, 1986).

Outside the laboratory, mood can have a similar effect. Quite frequently, people's memories tend to match their current mood (Blaney, 1986). If they are depressed, for example, they tend to dwell on negative thoughts, screening out more positive memories; if they are happy, they do the opposite (Gilligan & Bower, 1984; Teasdale & Fogarty, 1979). This retrieval bias, called **mood-congruent recall,** may be an important factor in perpetuating depression (Blaney, 1986; Bower, 1981).

Distortions of Memory

We have seen that human memory is not completely reliable. People commonly confuse one event with another. When their memories are vague, they tend to fill in the gaps with what they believe to be true. In short, the process of piecing together the past is often prone to distortion. This tendency toward distortion is one of the most fascinating aspects of memory.

Mental Schemas: The Influence of Expectations and Inferences

An Indian legend tells of two young men who went down to the river to hunt. Out of the fog appeared a war party of five men in a canoe. The five urged the two to accompany them to a battle. One of the young Indians refused; the other accepted. During the fighting he was wounded, but felt no pain. He then realized that the war party was made up of ghosts. The young warrior returned home to tell his people what had happened to him. The next day at sunrise, he fell dead.

The psychologist Sir Frederick C. Bartlett (1932) used this legend to study how information becomes distorted in the process of being retold. Bartlett instructed his first subject to read the legend, then to tell it to another subject. The second subject told it to a third subject, and so on down the line, much like the childhood game of "telephone." Not surprisingly, the story changed substantially after being retold many times. But Bartlett noticed that the

changes in the story were not haphazard. Several patterns emerged.

First, subjects tended to minimize details that did not fit their viewpoints. For example, by the time the tenth subject retold the tale, all references to ghosts had been dropped. Bartlett noted that mystical references are not easily assimilated into Western concepts of life, warfare, and death. For a similar reason, other details were sharpened in the retelling. In the original story, the second Indian declined to join the war party because his relatives would not know where he had gone. In the tenth subject's retelling, the Indian refused because his elderly mother was dependent on him—a distortion of the story that fits the Western concept of a son's responsibilities. Finally, many subjects added a moral to the story, because that kind of ending is typical of Western folktales.

Bartlett was one of the first psychologists to propose that such distortions reflect the way in which human memory works. Unconsciously, he argued, people process new information through mental structures constructed from knowledge and beliefs they already possess. These mental structures, called **schema,** filter new experiences and give meaning to them. We discussed these structures in Chapters 4 and 6 in conjunction with the effect of prior knowledge and expectations on perception and learning.

Contemporary psychologists believe that schemas influence memory in a number of ways (Alba & Hasher, 1983; Brewer & Nakamura, 1984). First, people tend to decide what is relevant or important on the basis of their schemas. For instance, a burglar who is planning a robbery would be likely to remember the exact location of a burglar alarm, but not the color of the bathroom tiles. His burglary schema would direct his attention to certain pieces of information and cause him to gloss over others (Anderson & Prichert, 1978). Schemas also help us to interpret the meaning of new information. Try reading the following passage:

> The procedure is actually quite simple. First you arrange things into different groups. Of course, one pile may be sufficient depending on how much there is to do. If you have to go somewhere else due to lack of facilities, that is the next step; otherwise you are pretty well set. It is important not to overdo things. That is, it is better to do too few things at once than too many. In the short run this may not seem important, but complications can easily arise. A mistake can be expensive as well. At first the whole procedure will

seem complicated. Soon, however, it will become just another facet of life. It is difficult to foresee any end to the necessity for this task in the immediate future, but then one never can tell. After the procedure is completed, one arranges the materials into different groups again. Then they can be put into their appropriate places. Eventually they will be used once more, and the whole cycle will then have to be repeated. However, that is part of life.

Bransford & Johnson, 1972, p. 400.

You may not be able to make much sense out of this description until you are given a hint: the story is about washing clothes. Suddenly the meaning is clear, because this schema gives you a framework with which to understand and encode the material.

Schemas also allow us to elaborate on what we learn, fleshing out the details according to our expectations. For example, if you hear that John arrived at an exam at 9 a.m. and left an hour later, your exam schema allows you to infer that he sat at a desk, was given a test, and tried to answer the questions on it. This inference process can be very helpful, because it enables you to "know" more than you are actually told. The problem is our inferences are sometimes incorrect—as was illustrated in a classic set of studies using a picture like that in Figure 7-16 (Allport & Postman, 1947).

Among other things, the picture shows a black man in a subway car; he is apparently talking to a white man who is carrying a razor. The researchers asked one subject to look at this picture and describe it to another subject who could not see it. The second subject repeated the description from memory to a third person, who retold it to a fourth, and so on, until the description had passed through six or seven people. Significantly, in over half the trials, the razor migrated from the white hand to the black hand at some point in the retelling. The common schema of blacks as more violent than whites seems to have influenced what subjects recalled. Allport and Postman conducted relatively few of these experiments, so we must be cautious in drawing conclusions (Treadway & McCloskey, 1989). Nevertheless, these studies reinforce the common finding that human memory does not function like a video camera, accurately recording every image and sound. Instead, memory is a process of active construction in which old knowledge, beliefs, and expectations constantly shape what we store and retrieve.

FIGURE 7-16   A test of how stereotypes can influence visual memory. This drawing is similar to the drawing used in Allport and Postman's experiment (1947).

Eyewitness Testimony: How Accurate Is It?

Findings that indicate the influence of schema on memory have serious implications for our legal system. Witnesses to accidents or crimes are almost always questioned before a trial takes place. Could something that is said during preliminary interrogations alter a witness's recollections? If so, when are such alterations most likely to occur? What is the relationship between confidence and memory? And is a confident witness a reliable witness? Research on the accuracy of eyewitness testimony provides some interesting answers.

Much of the work on eyewitness testimony has been conducted by Elizabeth Loftus, one of the authors of this book. Loftus is intrigued by cases in which the eyewitnesses' memories later prove grossly inaccurate. In one such case, a Roman Catholic priest stood trial for a series of armed robberies in the Wilmington, Delaware, area (Loftus & Ketcham, 1991). Someone notified police that Father Bernard Pagano looked remarkably like a sketch of the robber being circulated in the local media. Accusing a priest of the crimes made some sense, because this particular robber had been dubbed the "gentleman bandit" for his impeccable grooming and politeness. Seven eyewitnesses identified Pagano as the thief. At his trial the prosecution's case seemed airtight. Then, in a turn of events worthy of a TV melodrama, the trial halted abruptly after another man confessed to the crimes. He knew details about the crimes that only the thief could have known.

How could this case of mistaken identity have happened? Apparently, before police presented pictures of suspects to witnesses, they let it be known that the robber might be a priest. Since Father Pagano was the only suspect wearing a clerical collar, witnesses may have been primed to identify him. Loftus has wondered if such suggestions, made after a witness has seen an event, can alter the witness's recollection of what happened. To find out, she designed a series of experiments.

In one experiment, Loftus and her colleagues showed subjects color slides of successive stages of an automobile accident involving a red Datsun (Loftus, Miller, & Burns, 1978). The critical slide showed the Datsun stopped at an intersection just before it turned right and hit a pedestrian. Half the subjects saw a slide with a stop sign at the corner; half saw a slide with a yield sign. After viewing all the slides, subjects answered questions about them. The critical question mentioned either a stop sign or a yield sign. For half the subjects the sign that was mentioned was the same as the one they had seen; for the other half it was different (a yield sign when they had seen a stop sign, or a stop sign when they had seen a yield sign). Next, the subjects performed a distracting task; finally they took a recognition test. Researchers showed them fifteen pairs of slides and asked them to choose the slide out of each pair that they had seen before. The object of the experiment was to see how subjects would respond when they were shown two views of the intersection, one with a stop sign and one with a yield sign.

When the critical question had mentioned a traffic sign consistent with what the subjects had seen, they chose the correct slide 75 percent of the time. But when the critical question had mentioned a traffic sign inconsistent with what subjects had seen, they made the correct choice only 41 percent of the time. Loftus concluded that misinformation introduced after an eyewitness observation is capable of altering a witness's memory. If a witness initially saw a stop sign, subsequent mention of a yield sign might change that recollection. Moreover, the likelihood of such mistakes is substantially increased by a change in the timing of the misinformation. If subjects are exposed to inaccurate information a week after they witnessed an accident—when the true details are more difficult to retrieve—they are susceptible to its

influence 80 percent of the time (Loftus, Miller, & Burns, 1978).

Within a few years Loftus had collected substantial evidence that when people witness an important event, such as a crime or an accident, their memories of the various objects involved can be distorted by subsequent misinformation. She found the same effects with memory for faces (Loftus & Greene, 1983). Some subjects received a description of a witness that was wrong in only one small detail (for example, the suspected thief was said to have wavy hair when in fact he had straight hair). When asked to describe the witness, one-third of those who had encountered an incorrect detail in the witness's description included it in their own descriptions, even if they had been instructed to write only what they had seen themselves. In another study by Loftus and Greene, subjects misidentified suspects on the basis of subsequent misinformation. After viewing a man in the midst of others and being told later that the man had a mustache (actually he did not), subjects picked out a mug shot of a man with a mustache two-thirds of the time. In contrast, control subjects who had received no misinformation selected a mug shot with a mustache only 13 percent of the time.

Jurors generally consider eyewitness identification to be reliable and accurate, so eyewitness testimony is highly influential. But this research suggests that eyewitness identifications are subject to the same distortions as all memories. Alteration of memory is so common that people may not even realize it is occurring. Robert Belli (1989) calls this unconscious adoption of untruths after the fact **misinformation acceptance.** It occurs when, for whatever reason, people fail to encode into memory certain details about an event they have seen. Later, when they hear or read someone else's eyewitness account, they take facts from the other person's description and incorporate them into their own recollections. Belli has conducted research showing that misinformation acceptance plays a major role in studies like those of Loftus. His findings suggest that, in some cases, misinformation may also interfere with the originally encoded memory. Loftus agrees that misinformation acceptance probably made a major contribution to her own research findings (Loftus & Hoffman, 1989).

If people can unconsciously add facts to their recollections, sometimes to the point of being convinced that they witnessed those facts firsthand, that phenomenon is of great importance both to the justice system and to an understanding of human memory. One task of future research will be to assess the extent to which misinformation affects the details of an eyewitness report.

From reading the previous section, you may wonder if memory can *ever* be accurate. Of course, the answer is "yes." Ironically, as psychologists have studied memory failures, they have also developed a good understanding of the factors involved in the enhancement of memory. In the following section, we will discuss what psychologists have learned about memory improvement.

Memory Improvement

Most of us complain about our memories. We are annoyed when others' powers of recall seem much better than our own. What accounts for differences in long-term memory performance? And how can individuals like Rajan (the student who memorized π to tens of thousands of digits) and Steve Faloon (the college student who increased his digit span to over eighty) perform their amazing feats? More important, can their techniques help us to improve *our* memories?

Ericsson's Memory Skill Hypothesis

How is "memory" best conceptualized? Is it a *trait*—a property we are "born with," one that is stable throughout the life span and relatively insensitive to improvement, like intelligence? Or is it a *skill*—an ability that can be learned and improved through practice, instruction, and effort? Most of us presume memory to be a trait. We often complain about test scores, saying we "just don't have a good memory," and assume there is little we can do about it.

Anders Ericsson, the psychologist who first worked with Steve Faloon, treats memory as a skill. Through his study of Steve Faloon and others like him, Ericsson has concluded that memory *can* be improved, though doing so takes considerable effort, practice, and motivation. According to Ericsson's **memory skill hypothesis,** expert memory is characterized by three properties: (1) meaningful, redundant encoding; (2) rich, highly associated retrieval cues stored with items; and (3) increased performance through tremendous practice, called *the speedup principle.*

Individuals with Exceptional Memories

Ericsson developed his theory while working with Steve Faloon, but has since tested it on a number of other individuals. One such person was the waiter John Conrad, whom Ericsson and a colleague at the University of Colorado, Peter Polson, spotted in a restaurant in Boulder. The two psychologists were understandably impressed. Conrad had developed the ability to remember elaborate dinner orders without writing anything down. He once served a table of nineteen people without making a single mistake. Not only were all meats, vegetables, salads, and dressings just as each customer had ordered, but Conrad remembered without hesitation precisely who had ordered what. Conrad was so confident of his memory that he would often wager his tip "double or nothing" on the outcome. If Conrad made a mistake, he would expect no tip from the diners. If he filled their orders without error, however, they would have to give him a 30 percent tip. Thinking that large orders would make his task more difficult, groups of a dozen often took the bet, each person ordering many different courses. But larger groups were no problem for Conrad; he maintained he could remember orders for up to thirty dinners at a time. Large orders *did* generate large bills, however, and 30 percent of that bill often added up to a huge tip. Conrad seldom lost these bets (Ericsson & Polson, 1988).

Obviously, Conrad had developed strategies for memorizing the orders—all of which fit nicely into Ericsson's theory of memory as a skill. First, he would listen to each person's order, encoding the information in several different ways. Often, he used the seating arrangement as a cue and recoded salad dressings into a useful acronym (*B*lue cheese, *O*il & vinegar, *O*il & vinegar, *T*housand island became *BOOT*). Conrad would also used schemas: if a customer ordered a steak medium rare, Conrad knew he would usually order a baked potato, not fries, to go with it.

Note how Conrad's methods matched the three properties of expert memory Ericsson identified above. By encoding orders in a number of ways (meaningful, redundant encoding), Conrad formed a rich series of associations to assist him in retrieval (rich, highly associated retrieval cues). If one type of encoding failed him, he could always use another of his encoded cues. Finally, Conrad improved significantly with practice (the speedup principle).

Most of the other mnemonists described in this chapter support Ericsson's notion of memory as a skill. Steve Faloon, the digit-span expert, used encoding strategies to turn meaningless strings of numbers into meaningful (at least to him) running times. Like Conrad, Faloon improved significantly with practice, although he found some digit strings difficult to encode as running times. For example, take the number 56627. Normally Faloon would encode this type of five-digit number as a running time for the mile. In this case, though, the digits do not fit the schema. He could not encode them as "5 minutes, 66.27 seconds," only as "6 minutes, 6.27 seconds." Strings of numbers like this one seriously reduced Faloon's digit span.

Rajan, the student who memorized π, relies more on rote repetition and exceptional amounts of practice than on mnemonics. Rajan began memorizing π as a child; during the last twenty years he has logged many thousands of hours of practice. Like other memorists, Rajan has become much faster with practice.

Perhaps the most remarkable memorist of all was a Russian newspaper reporter named Shereshevski, studied over a period of many years by the famed Russian neurologist Alexander Luria (Luria, 1987/1968). "S.," as he is known in Luria's fascinating book, *The Mind of a Mnemonist,* seems to have been truly exceptional in both the methods and the results of his memorization. Shereshevski possessed a remarkable ability known as "synesthesia," or a mixing of sensory signals. He would "taste" colors and "see" tones, as in this passage (p. 23):

> Presented with a tone pitched at 500 cycles per second and having an amplitude of 100 decibels [this is a fairly loud tone, roughly corresponding to the 'middle C' on a piano], he saw a streak of lightning splitting the heavens in two. When the intensity was lowered to 74 dB, he saw an orange color which made him feel as though a needle had been thrust in his spine. . . .
>
> Presented with a tone pitched at 2000 cycles per second and having an amplitude of 113 dB, S. said, "It looks something like fireworks tinged with a pink-red hue. The strip of color feels rough and unpleasant, and it has an ugly taste—rather like that of a briny pickle. . . . You could hurt your hand on this."

Shereshevski spent the last decades of his life as a professional mnemonist, dazzling audiences with his skills. He would go from town to town, memorizing lists of items produced by members of the audience. One of his standard demonstrations was the memorization of numbers, arranged in a table, perhaps five to six columns, with ten or twelve rows (Luria reports tables of up to seventy numbers). He would hear the list and spend several minutes encoding the items (Luria's exact words were "imprints the impression of the table," p. 16). Then he would recall any digit requested by the audience. Astonishingly, once Shereshevski learned these vast arrays, *he never forgot them:*

> In fact, some of these experiments designed to test his retention were performed (without his being given any warning) fifteen or sixteen years after the sessions in which he had originally recalled the words. Yet invariably they were successful. During these test sessions S. would sit with his eyes closed, pause, then comment: "yes, yes. . . . This was a series you gave me once when we were in your apartment. . . . You were sitting at the table and I in the rocking chair. You were wearing a gray suit. . . . Now, then, I see you saying. . . . " And with this he would reel off the series precisely as I had given it to him at the earlier session.

Luria, 1968/1987, p. 12

One of the recurring themes of this book is that psychologists study exceptional behavior to learn about normal behavior. Shereshevski may be a striking exception to this rule. His memory was so remarkable, his techniques so unique, that it is not clear whether his cases teach us about normal memory. Though, there is no reason to doubt Luria's assessment of Shereshevski; no other memorist has displayed the traits seen in this remarkable, almost mystical figure.

Ways to Improve Normal Memory

For those of us who have trouble remembering where we left the car keys, such feats of memory seem awesome indeed. However, the accomplishments of memorists like John Conrad are well within the bounds of ordinary human memory. Though most of us seldom devote the energy to memorization that John Conrad has, we are all endowed with a substantial capacity to remember. Some simple techniques, like those shown in Table 7-2, can greatly improve almost anyone's powers of recall (Cook, 1989; Higbee, 1988). These include external aids, such as written lists of reminders, as well as internal aids, such as name-face associations. Internal aids are also called *mnemonic devices,* from the Greek word *mneme,* meaning "memory."

TABLE 7-2 *How Many of These Memory Aids Do You Use, and How Frequently Do You Use Them? Researcher John Harris (1980) Distributed a Questionnaire among University Students and Found That the Devices Used Most Frequently by That Group were Items 3, 8, and 13.*

1. **Shopping lists.**
2. **First-letter memory aids.** The first letters of "Richard of York gave battle in vain," for example, give the first letters of the colors of the rainbow.
3. **Diary.**
4. **Rhymes.** "In fourteen hundred ninety-two Columbus sailed the ocean blue," for example, helps you to remember the date 1492.
5. **The place method.** Items to be remembered are imagined in a series of familiar places. When recall is required, one "looks" at the familiar places.
6. **Writing on your hand** (or any other part of your anatomy or clothing).
7. **The story method.** Making up a story that connects items to be remembered in the correct order.
8. **Mentally retracing a sequence of events or actions** in order to jog your memory; useful for remembering where you lost or left something, or at what stage something significant happened.
9. **Alarm clock** (or other alarm device) for waking up only.
10. **Kitchen timer with alarm** for cooking only.
11. **Alarm clock** (or other alarm devices such as watches, radios, timers, telephones, calculators) used for purposes other than waking up or cooking.
12. **The keyword method.** "One is a bun, two is a shoe, three is a tree," etc., as a method of remembering lists of items in correct order.
13. **Turning numbers into letters.** For remembering telephone numbers, for example.
14. **Memos.** Writing notes and "To do" lists for yourself, for example.
15. **Face-name associations.** Changing people's names into something meaningful and matching them with something unusual about their faces. Red-bearded Mr. Hiles, for example, might be imagined with hills growing out of his beard.
16. **Alphabetical searching.** Going through the alphabet letter by letter to find the initial letter of a name. For example, does a particular peson's name begin with A . . . B . . . ? Ah, yes, C! C for Clark.
17. **Calendars, wall charts, year planners, display boards, etc.**
18. **Asking other people to remember things for you.**
19. **Leaving objects in special or unusual places** so that they act as reminders.

Source: After Baddeley, 1982.

Many mnemonic devices involve clever ways of organizing material when storing it in long-term memory. The **method of loci,** for example, involves associating the items to be remembered with a series of places, or loci, already firmly fixed in memory. Suppose you had to learn the names of all the Presidents of the United States, in chronological order. You would simply visualize a familiar place—say, your home—and imagine each President in a particular part of it. George Washington might be standing next to a tree in the front yard, ax in hard. Teddy Roosevelt, carrying a big stick, might greet you at the front door. Stout William Howard Taft might be found talking to a thin, bespectacled Woodrow Wilson in the entrance hall. Later, to remember the Presidents, you would take a mental walk through the house, allowing each location to serve as a retrieval cue.

A similar technique, the **peg word method,** uses rhymes as reminders. First you memorize a series of "pegs," or retrieval cues, chosen to rhyme with a series of digits: "one is bun, two is shoe, three is tree, four is door," and so on. Later, you hook an item to remember on each peg. Say you are going to the grocery store to pick up bread, milk, eggs, and paper towels. You hook the first item on the list, "bread," to the first peg, "bun." In this case you might envision a hamburger on bread instead of a hamburger bun. Next, you might associate the peg "shoe" with someone stepping over a broken milk bottle. To remember "eggs," you could picture an apple tree, on which

Study techniques in which information is learned and comprehended are generally more effective that those based on rote rehearsal and memorization.

eggs are hanging instead of apples. Finally, you could imagine a door with a roll of paper towels for a handle. In the store, you would recall the pegs, then retrieve the items you hooked on them.

Visual Imagery

Although both the method of loci and the peg word system are based primarily on careful organization of cues, they also rely on imagery. Research shows that subjects can remember verbal material better if they relate it to visual images of some kind (Paivio, 1971). For example, you would probably have an easier time remembering that the French word *escargot* means "snail" if you pictured a snail carrying a cargo of S's on its back. This strategy pairs images "S-cargo" and "snail." But notice that the snail and the S-cargo are not just paired, they are *interacting*: the snail is *carrying* the S-cargo. This kind of in-

teractive imagery has been found to be especially effective for remembering pairs or clusters of words (Bower, 1972). Images need not be bizarre or dramatic, then, to work as mnemonic devices. Their interactivity is what counts (Kroll, Schepeler, & Angin, 1986).

The waiter John Conrad, mentioned earlier, made extensive use of imagery (Ericsson & Polson, 1988). He tried always to make a visual association between a customer's face and the entrée he or she ordered. Thus, he might remember a woman who ordered chicken for her thin, birdlike nose, or a man who ordered sirloin steak for his beefy jowls.

General Techniques and Strategies

A number of mnemonic techniques such as these can be used to enhance memory. But though they work, they are seldom used, even by memory researchers themselves. Why are mnemonic techniques used so infrequently? Probably because they are difficult to use and restricted in their application. Mnemonic techniques require many hours of study and practice (hundreds, sometimes thousands of hours to reach a level worthy of public performance). They also require concentration and effort during encoding. And while they are useful for some tasks—learning names and faces, or remembering lists—they are less suited to the conceptual learning expected in a classroom setting.

Rather than practicing mnemonic techniques, then, most of us would do better to observe some general principles of memory. Seven such principles follow. They are true of memory in many different situations and explain how you can improve your memory not by increasing effort but by redirecting that effort in more useful ways.

1. *Memory is best when material is learned and comprehended rather than practiced in rote fashion.* This principle is based on the distinction between "deep" and "shallow" processing discussed on page 232, and is perhaps the most powerful of the general principles. Many people, especially students, spend a vast amount of time reading and rereading vocabulary words, statistical formulas, or lists of items like the Amendments to the Constitution. Rather than spending time trying to recall material verbatim, you are more likely to be successful if you spend time making sure you *understand*

the material. A good understanding of a subject will allow you to reconstruct missing information when memory fails you. Virtually all memory experts—even S.— encode material in meaningful ways. Luria (1968/1987) writes that S. was able to convert "senseless words into intelligible images" (p. 43).

2. *Memory is aided when the context at learning can be matched by the context at retrieval.* This is a restatement of Tulving's principle of "encoding specificity." Lawyers try to re-create the scene of the crime to aid a witness's recall. During an exam, you might mentally re-create the context in which you yourself learned a subject. Or you might try to learn the material in the same conditions (time of day, room, time pressures) under which recall must take place.

3. *Strategies that enhance encoding are likely to improve memory.* Though failures in encoding, storage, or retrieval can impair memory, encoding failures are fatal errors: they cannot be corrected later except by relearning. Just a few seconds of deliberate encoding—associating a name with the face, or using a newly learned name in a conversation—will often improve memory. With practice, this form of encoding can become quite rapid.

4. *Memory is good when affect and emotional arousal are high, but not extremely high.* Students are not likely to learn if they are bored or terrified. If you have predictable "downtimes" during the day, avoid taking classes or studying during those times. The more involved with the material you can become, the more your memory will be enhanced.

5. *Since memory is reconstructive, the number and type of cues given at retrieval are critical.* Memory retrieval is not simply a rewinding and playing back of a mental tape. The mind remembers by recalling bits and fragments that form the outline of a memory, and then using reconstructive processes to "fill in the gaps." Use all available cues during recall. If you are stumped, stop searching for several minutes. When you return to the item, approach it from a different angle, using different retrieval cues. Don't be embarrassed to use external retrieval cues like notes or reminders.

6. *Memory is better if rehearsal is spaced out over frequent short learning trials rather than massed in one, long learning trial.* You know the moral of this story: cramming for an exam is *not* conducive to long-lasting memory. Instead, study frequently and for short periods.

7. *Memory is better if material is encoded and stored in more than one way.* When learning about dinosaurs, for example, you might categorize them in several different ways: meat-eaters versus plant-eaters, walking versus flying, Mesozoic versus Jurassic. Doing so provides you with a number of different "retrieval paths"; if you forget one, others may help.

In Depth

Memory, Repression, and the False Memory Debate

WE HAVE SEEN that without conscious effort, we often forget or distort much of what we want to remember. But what about memories we *want* to forget? Do we, for whatever reason, block some events from awareness?

Motivated forgetting was the foundation of Freudian theory. According to Freud, people often push unacceptable, anxiety-provoking thoughts and impulses out of their consciousness to avoid confronting them directly. Freud referred to this mental defense as **repression.** Like many Freudian constructs, the concept of repression was eagerly embraced, not only by psychologists but by artists, writers, and the general public. Countless novels, plays, and movies revolve around the concept. Indeed, the idea of repressed memories that can be later recovered makes a compelling story.

Repression, in fact, became a cornerstone of psychoanalytic theory. Freud's early writings dealt extensively with it, though his conception of it changed throughout his lifetime. At times, Freud believed repression was an unconscious defense mechanism that allowed his patients to suppress thoughts or memories of traumatic or psychologically painful events. According to Freud (originally published in 1915, reprinted in Strachey, 1957), "The essence of repression lies simply in the function of rejecting and keeping something out of consciousness." Freud believed that unconscious memories could intrude into and affect conscious behavior, often in hidden or symbolic ways. For example, he believed that memories too threatening to appear in literal form often surfaced in dreams. Freud called them the "royal road to the unconscious." He believed that dreams were so important to an understanding of the unconscious that he titled one of his earliest and most influential books *The Interpretation of Dreams* (Freud, 1900).

To help his patients recover, Freud tried to uncover repressed memories. He employed a number of techniques, including hypnosis and dream analysis. But Freud saw many other behaviors besides dreams as signs of unconscious, repressed memories. Even slips of the tongue, now known as *Freudian slips,* were thought likely to be caused by repression. Freud used a technique called *word associa-*

tion to provoke these slips. He would read a list of words, and his patient would say the first thing that came to mind. By piecing together the clues revealed by these exercises, Freud would attempt to bring the repressed memories into consciousness. Once they were remembered, the patient could begin to deal with them.

During his career, Freud observed repression of many different kinds of traumatic events. He believed some—but certainly not all—of his patients were repressing memories of sexual abuse. In some cases, Freud believed the abuse to have taken place during the patient's childhood. Since he believed those memories would be tremendously threatening, he expected the repression of them to be particularly powerful.

More than half a century later, therapists once again began to explore techniques of "recovering" the memory of traumatic childhood events. A number of self-help books, designed to guide the process, appeared in bookstores. Two of the most popular were *The Courage to Heal,* by Ellen Bass and Laura Davis (Bass & Davis, 1988; the companion workbook by Davis, 1990), and *Secret Survivors,* by E. Sue Blume (1990). The books encouraged readers to compare their own characteristics to checklists of symptoms suffered by people who were victims of abuse. Symptoms included fear of being alone in the dark, nightmares, headaches, nervousness, guilt and shame, and low self-esteem. "Survivors of Incest Abuse," a twelve-step support group modeled on Alcoholics Anonymous, was formed. The group developed a list of diagnostic questions, such as:

- Do you feel you have to control your emotions?
- Do you overreact or misdirect your anger in situations that frustrate you?
- Do you have blocks of your childhood that you don't remember?

Within just a few years, the number of people who claimed to have recovered memories of early abuse had swelled. Bass and Davis estimated that one-third of all women (and one-seventh of all men) were sexually abused by the time they were eighteen. John Bradshaw, the author of the self-help book

Homecoming (Bradshaw, 1990) who popularized the concept of "reclaiming the inner child," estimated that perhaps 60 percent of those who had been abused repressed the memory (Bradshaw, 1992)—a staggering percentage, if true. Some therapists became convinced that many, perhaps most, of their clients had been victims of abuse. The repression of those memories, they often concluded, was the root cause of the problems they were experiencing. Even if their clients denied having been abused, these therapists suggested they join a support group, or work through *The Courage to Heal*. Denial, they told their clients, is often a telltale symptom that abuse *did* occur and was now being repressed. In the course of these therapies, many once skeptical people became increasingly convinced that they, too, had been victims of childhood abuse.

By the late 1980s, interest in the concept of repression, especially of experiences of childhood abuse, had exploded. For the first time, "recovered" memories became the basis for legal action. One of the first and most dramatic cases was that of George Franklin, a fifty-one-year-old man accused of murdering a young girl more than two decades ago. During the trial, Franklin's daughter Eileen, only eight years old herself at the time of the murder, provided the major evidence against her father. She claimed to have repressed the memory of the murder for over twenty years.

According to some versions of the story (several have been published), Eileen's memory did not come back all at once. Her first flashback came one afternoon in 1989, as she was playing with her two-year-old son, Aaron, and her five-year-old daughter, Jessica. Suddenly, a memory of the victim, her childhood friend Susan Nason, came to her: she recalled that look of betrayal in Susan's eyes just before the murder. Later, during the course of therapy, more fragments returned. She remembered her father sexually assaulting Susan in the back of his van. She remembered Susan's struggle against it (preliminary hearing testimony, 1990). Next, her memory took her outside the van, where she saw her father raise a rock above his head. She remembered screaming and walking to where Susan lay covered with blood.

Eileen's recovered memory was accepted not only by her therapist but by several members of her family and the San Mateo Country District Attorney's Office, which chose to prosecute her father, and by the jury, who convicted him of murder in 1990. Following the Franklin case, legal actions against par-

One of the first and most dramatic cases involving repressed memory was that of George Franklin, who was accused of murdering a young girl more than two decades after the crime. His daughter Eileen, shown here at her father's trial, was only 8 years old at the time of the murder. She claimed to have witnessed it, repressed and then recovered the memory as an adult some 20 years after the murder. Largely on the basis of her testimony, George Franklin was convicted of murder in 1990. The conviction was later overturned.

ents of people claiming to have recovered memories of childhood abuse became common.

Initial Findings

Until recently, the concept of repressed memory on which these cases were based has been considered legitimate. Despite the widespread acceptance, however, research on the accuracy of repressed and recovered memory has been almost nonexistent. What have memory researchers found about the accuracy of recovered memories?

Perhaps the simplest explanation for repressed memories is that they were forgotten, just like other memories. But repression, as the term is commonly used, differs from normal forgetting in several respects (Weaver, 1995). First, repressed memories are said to occur only in cases of extreme anxiety or fear, such as childhood sexual abuse. Second, repressed memories are *actively* kept from memory; some type of psychological effort, presumably unconscious, is used to keep them from invading consciousness. Normal forgetting, in contrast, is thought to be passive. If you have forgotten the name of the child who sat next to you in third grade, you have done so because you have passively allowed the memory to fade.

TABLE 7-3   *Characteristics Attributed to Repressed Memories, Compared to Normal, Forgotten Memory*

Property	Repressed Memories	Forgotten Memories
Emotion/anxiety	Extreme	Varies, but typically low
Cause of loss	Unconscious, active suppression	Passive loss (lack of rehearsal, interference, decay)
Retrieval	Unconscious "triggers"	Retrieval can be difficult, especially without cues
Accuracy	Presumed literal and perfect	Retrieval is reconstructive, so memory is subject to distortions (as are all memories)

Source: Based on Weaver, 1995.

Third, repressed memories are thought to be retrievable. If some unexpected event triggers their retrieval, they will become accessible to consciousness. Once retrieved, repressed memories are thought to be perfect literal accounts of actual events. Various techniques such as hypnosis or dream analysis are sometimes used to enhance their literal recall. Memory researchers are still debating the fate of "forgotten" memories. Some believe that at least some forgetting involves complete loss of memory (Loftus & Loftus, 1980). Others believe that most forgetting involves retrieval failure, so that appropriate measures might recover old, long-dormant memories. Both viewpoints, though, recognize the reconstructive nature of memory. If old, dormant memories can be recovered, they are likely to be just as reconstructive as normal memories—perhaps even more so. Table 7-3 summarizes the differences between normal forgetting and repression.

Repressed memories, then, cannot be explained as normally forgotten memories. They must be investigated as a separate phenomenon. Yet from a scientific perspective, studying repression is tremendously difficult. For ethical reasons, researchers cannot expose subjects to traumatic events and later test them to see what they remember (or repress). And for practical reasons as well, studying traumatic memory over several decades is unworkable. To study the *accuracy* of traumatic memories, researchers must be able to determine what actually took place twenty or thirty years ago. In most cases, checking the accuracy of recovered memories is impossible: we simply don't know what really happened.

Criticisms, Alternatives, and Further Research

Several researchers have combed old files in an attempt to verify repressed memories. For example, Williams (1994) used medical records to identify women who had been sexually abused as children. Surveying the women some twenty years after the reported incident, she found that 38% of them could not recall (or chose not to recall) the incident in question. Some women mentioned other incidents of sexual abuse, but not the specific event in question. Were their memories repressed? Williams's findings can be explained in many ways. Loftus, Garry, & Feldman (1994) have suggested that though her data provide striking evidence that memories of childhood abuse can be forgotten, it does *not* prove that the forgotten memories were "repressed." None of the women reported recalling the incidents with the vividness and detail that is often claimed for repressed memories.

We have seen that memory is reconstructive; memories can be altered, even created. But most studies of memory involve relatively artificial settings, such as the viewing of slides showing an automobile accident. Such settings do not have the affect and significance associated with truly traumatic events. Could the memory of an important, affective event be created?

Loftus and Pickerel (1995) designed an experiment to answer this question. They asked volunteer subjects to create false memories in siblings, all of whom were about ten years younger. The authors wanted to implant a plausible event, one that would have a high degree of affect. They settled on the experience of being lost in a shopping mall. Subjects implanted these memories indirectly in their siblings, using various suggestive techniques. Later, the younger siblings were asked to provide details of their childhood memories, including the memory for the event that never happened.

How successful were the suggestions? Remarkably, nearly 25 percent of the people eventually recalled the "memory" themselves, and some were shocked when they found out the events never really happened. During an interview with Loftus, the *MacNeil/Lehrer News Hour* filmed the process of memory implantation (with the subjects' full consent). When one of the subjects was informed that the event had been "suggested" to her and had not really happened, she found it so hard to believe that she phoned her parents to check.

Patterns and Conclusions

The debate over false and repressed memories has been incredibly fierce. This controversy is more heated, and the opposing sides more polarized, than in any other debate in psychology in the past twenty-five years. Those who accept the concept of repressed and recovered memory claim that to deny the truthfulness of such memories is to deny the trauma of childhood abuse. Adult victims of abuse, they argue, should be believed, and their recovered memories treated with dignity. Furthermore, studies of false memories do not involve real, intensely traumatic memories. We still don't know how memory might work under those conditions.

Psychologists who are skeptical of the idea of repressed and recovered memories point to the lack of credible evidence. Part of the problem involves definitions. Does repression refer to memories that have been forgotten (or weakened) because of their content? Such a definition has some empirical support; many studies show that emotion, especially extreme emotion, can cause unpredictable effects on memory, and sometimes even contributes to a loss of memory for a traumatic event. If by repression we mean that some events that cannot be recalled now might be retrieved later, that, too, is consistent with memory theory. Everyone has missed a question on a test, only to recall the answer later. Such memories are retrieved through the same processes (and distortions) as any other memory.

If, however, *repression* means that a stream of horrific traumas can be banished from consciousness and recovered later—in a complete, detailed, and accurate manner—there is little in the way of credible evidence to support the concept. Skeptics point out that this definition of repression relies on the "videotape" analogy for memory, an analogy that has been thoroughly rejected by memory theorists. Though some of the skeptics are memory researchers—experts in the field—many clinical psychologists and other therapists also question the idea. They recognize that memory is malleable and that a number of factors—including therapy itself—can influence and distort memory.

During the past few years, questions about repression and repressed memory therapy have reached the legal arena. Some cases have even been dismissed, and some convictions overturned. In fact, during the time this section was being prepared, George Franklin, the man accused by his daughter and later convicted of killing Susan Nason, had his conviction overturned. The court cited concerns about his daughter's testimony. Her allegedly "repressed and recovered" memory had been the only evidence presented. Analysis showed that all the details provided by her testimony had been reported in newspaper stories printed at the time of the crime. In other cases, patients have sued their therapists, claiming that they implanted the memories of abuse during counseling sessions.

It is not clear how this debate will be resolved. Unfortunately, many aspects of this issue will be settled in a courtroom. Often the lingering question— What really *did* happen?—cannot be answered; in most cases, we simply don't know and have no way to find out. However, Daniel Schacter and his colleagues have begun a remarkable project that may be able to provide some answers. The group is using positron-emission tomography (PET) scans to study the neurological activity of people who are in the act of retrieving a memory. They have compared the brain scans of subjects who are recalling a "real" memory to the scans of the same subjects recalling a false memory. Though the images are very similar in most ways, researchers can clearly distinguish between true and false memories by examining the scans (Schacter et al., 1996). The implications for such a research tool are far-reaching; it may someday resolve questions that now seem impenetrable.

SUMMARY

1. The earliest model of memory, the association model, proposed that memory is the result of associations formed between items. Hermann Ebbinghaus, a nineteenth-century Germany psychologist, is widely recognized as the first researcher to study memory in a scientific manner. His classic **forgetting function** shows that forgetting of nonsense syllables is rapid at first but quickly levels off, so that memory is still observed even after many weeks. Bahrick's work on long-term memory—in some cases the retention intervals approach fifty years—replicated Ebbinghaus's forgetting function with realistic material, such as memory of Spanish vocabulary.

2. With the advent of the cognitive revolution in psychology, associationist models of memory were gradually replaced with **information-processing models,** which viewed memory as dynamic and constructive. The most influential information-processing model was that of Atkinson and Shiffrin (1968), which proposed that memory consists of three separate, sequential stages: sensory memory, short-term memory, and long-term memory.

3. **Sensory memory** is the momentary lingering of sensory information after a stimulus has been removed. Sperling's work on visual sensory memory showed that sensory memory can store a great deal of information, but only briefly—in most cases, less than a second.

4. Attention is the process by which information in sensory memory is selected for further processing. The process of screening out information is called **selective attention.**

5. **Short-term memory** is capable of storing only about seven items for fifteen to twenty seconds. Information in short-term memory can be renewed through **rehearsal,** or the (internal or external) repetition of the contents. Short-term memory can be enhanced by certain encoding strategies such as **chunking,** the grouping of information. **Effortful encoding** uses deliberate encoding strategies (verbal labels, mental pictures, and so forth), while **automatic encoding** takes place with no intentional effort and stores information such as frequency and location.

6. Unlike short-term memory, **long-term memory** stores information indefinitely, and its capacity is essentially unlimited. Long-term memory encompasses three basic processes: encoding, storage, and retrieval. **Encoding** refers to the process through which sensory information is converted into a form that can be remembered. **Storage** refers to the way in which information is kept in memory for later use. **Retrieval** is the process of finding stored memories and making them available for use. Successful transfer of information from short-term to long-term storage depends on both the amount and the type of rehearsal. **Deep processing** or **elaborative rehearsal** is generally more effective than **shallow processing** or **maintenance rehearsal.**

7. Retrieval from long-term memory is measured in two basic ways: recognition and recall. **Recognition** relies on a kind of matching process, considering a given stimulus and deciding whether it matches something already stored in memory. **Recall** appears to be more complex. It demands that we first search through memory and locate appropriate information before we test for a match. This search is largely directed by **retrieval cues.** When retrieval cues are weak, we may have difficulty recalling. Sometimes such difficulty gives rise to the **tip-of-the-tongue phenomenon.**

8. Tulving's model of **multiple memory systems** proposed three different types of long-term memory. **Procedural memories** form the most basic system. These "blueprints for actions" do not require conscious awareness. Some organisms have a more specialized knowledge of the world called **semantic memory**, a kind of personal encyclopedia of information. **Episodic memories** are memories for specific events in the past and are distinctive because the individual who remembers them is an active part of the memory.

9. Evidence in favor of Tulving's memory hierarchy includes amnesiacs, who usually lose episodic memory while procedural and semantic memories remain intact. The progressive loss of memory in Alzheimer's disease, a profound and irreversible disorder seen most often in older people, also follows a pattern predicted by Tulving's theory. Finally, evidence from those with normal memories suggests that the differ-

ent memory systems are separate: they involve different brain structures and are affected differently by certain kinds of variables.

10. Roediger proposed an alternative theoretical framework, emphasizing the different processes asssociated with different kinds of memory tests. Most cognitive psychologists consider memory to be a combination of different memory systems and different processes used to access memory.

11. **Autobiographical memories** are personal, unique memories of the events and facts of our lives. They include not only episodic information but also "personal semantic memories," such as a former address or telephone number. Autobiographical memories for the first three to four years of life are virtually nonexistent, a phenomenon known as childhood amnesia. Autobiographical memories are most numerous for the early adult years (early twenties) and the most recent years.

12. Memory for emotional events is typically better remembered, though situations of extreme emotion often impair memory. **Flashbulb memories** are vivid, detailed memories for events that are surprising, novel, important, and/or emotional. Though flashbulb memories are often reported with great confidence, recent research indicates that they are not necessarily more accurate than other episodic memories and are subject to the same kinds of distortion and elaboration.

13. One important aspect of long-term memory is the extent to which it involves the process of active construction. New information is assimilated within the framework of existing knowledge and beliefs, so that we tend to recast or dismiss facts that do not fit our expectations. At the same time, information acquired after an event has taken place can affect our memory of that experience. This process is especially important in the accuracy of eyewitness testimony.

14. Though the memory abilities of skilled individuals are astonishing, they may be within the reach of most people. According to Ericsson's **memory skill hypothesis,** expert memory is characterized by (1) meaningful, redundant encoding; (2) rich, highly associated retrieval cues stored with items; and (3) increased performance through tremendous practice, called the speedup principle.

15. Freud introduced the concept of **repression,** proposing that some unacceptable, anxiety-provoking thoughts, impulses, and memories are *actively* kept out of consciousness in order to avoid confronting them directly. While some psychologists accept repression as valid, most memory researchers are skeptical.

SUGGESTED READINGS

Baddeley, A. (1990). *Human memory*. Boston: Allyn & Bacon. Though published several years ago, this remains one of the best textbooks on memory.

Baddeley, A. (1994). *Your memory: A user's guide*. New York: Penguin Books. Written for a nontechnical audience by one of the area's most respected scientists, this book is easily the best of its kind.

Hilts, P. (1995). *Memory's ghost: The nature of memory and the strange tale of Mr. M.* New York: Simon & Schuster. A wonderful, personal account of "Henry M.," known to most students of psychology as "H. M."

Loftus, E. F., & Ketchum, K. (1994). *The myth of repressed memory: False memories and allegations of sexual abuse*. New York: St. Martin's Press. Cowritten by one of this textbook's authors, this book tackles the controversial topic of repressed and recovered memory.

Luria, A. R. (1987/1968). *The mind of a mnemonist: A little book about a vast memory*. Cambridge, MA: Harvard. As the title suggests, this brief book described "S.," the Russian mnemonist with remarkable memory skills. It was written by the legendary neurologist Alexander Luria.

Neisser, U. (1981). *Memory observed: Remembering in natural contexts*. San Francisco: Freeman. A classic collection of essays, edited by Ulric Neisser, that are just as fascinating and thought-provoking as when they were first issued.

Cognition and Language

By 1970, sending astronauts to explore the surface of the moon had become almost ordinary. When *Apollo 13* was launched from Cape Kennedy (the name was changed from Cape Canaveral to Cape Kennedy in 1963 after the assassination of John F. Kennedy; the original name of Cape Canaveral was restored in 1973) on April 11, 1970, most people (even most news agencies) barely noticed. The launch was shown on the evening news, of course, but the new mission was not a news maker like *Apollo 11*, the historic mission that carried Neil Armstrong, Buzz Aldrin, and Michael Collins to the moon and back. In fact, the television networks chose not to carry the live broadcast from the spacecraft.

Two days into the flight, when the crew was

barely halfway to the moon, the spacecraft was jolted by an event none of the astronauts on board—Jim Lovell, Fred Haise, and Jack Swigert—had ever experienced. At first they thought they had been struck by a meteor. They stared in disbelief at the gauges on the control panel. After a few moments, Swigert radioed NASA Mission Control: "Houston, we've got a problem." The engineers struggled to comprehend the readouts they saw on their computer screens. One engineer, speaking to no one in particular, muttered, "We got more than a problem."

Engineers and flight controllers scrambled to find out what had happened. A fluke electrical problem had caused one of the oxygen tanks on the space capsule to explode, tearing a huge gash in the capsule. The spacecraft would not be able to land on the moon as had been planned. In fact, the space capsule had sustained such severe damage that it might not be able to return to earth. Unless engineers and technicians could devise solutions to problems they had never before imagined, the astronauts might be trapped in a capsule drifting through space, their supply of oxygen quickly running out.

During the next several days, scores of engineers and technicians worked around the clock to solve problem after problem. In the process, they noticed that the level of carbon dioxide in the capsule was building to dangerous levels. In order to conserve fuel, the astronauts had moved to the much smaller lunar module attached to the larger capsule. But the module had not been designed to support the astronauts for a long period of time, and the filters

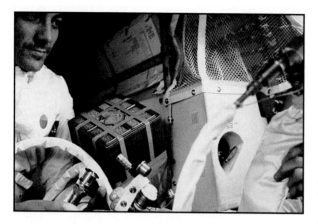

The make-shift CO_2 filter devised by Ed Smylie and his assistant Jim Correale on Apollo 13.

that removed dangerous carbon dioxide from its air supply were already filled to capacity. Though the spacecraft had extra filters, they were not designed to fit the lunar module. Unless they could be made to fit, the astronauts would die of asphyxiation.

Several engineers who were familiar with the spacecraft's air-flow system attacked the problem. Surrounding themselves with only those items available to the astronauts in space, they patched together a crude filter, made of a plastic bag, a hose, a piece of cardboard, and a great deal of duct tape. They radioed the solution to the astronauts, who followed the instructions. When they attached the makeshift filter to the module, the carbon dioxide level began to drop almost immediately: the solution had worked! The next day, while the entire world watched, *Apollo 13* splashed down in the Pacific Ocean.

In their book *Lost Moon*, Jim Lovell and his coauthor Jeffrey Kruger (1994) provide a compelling description of the lifesaving solution of the filter problem, which was devised by Ed Smylie and his assistant Jim Correale. Smylie conceived of the solution as he was driving to NASA's research center, immediately after hearing about the problem with the filters. By the time he arrived, he had its outlines clearly in mind. The fact that an engineer can solve such a complex, unanticipated problem on short notice shows that there is more to human cognition than learning and memory. Although Smylie's memory held all the facts he needed to find the solution, he had to combine those facts in a certain way to achieve his goal. This process of organizing information in the mind to accomplish some desired end is the essence of what we call *thought*, or *cognition*.

You might recall that the behaviorists believed psychologists should not study thought. Cognition is the classic example of a nonobservable behavior: it cannot be directly measured. Therefore, studying how people think is a difficult task. Asking people to describe their thought processes, as the introspectionists did a century ago, is less than scientific. Even if we take great pains to ensure that people describe their thoughts as carefully as they can, their descriptions may not be accurate. As Recurring Theme 3 suggests, humans do not always have access to all their cognition.

THEME **3** **A Large Proportion of Behavior Is Controlled by Unconscious Activity**

A classic study by Norman Maier illustrated this point. From the ceiling of his laboratory, Maier (1931) hung two strings far enough apart so that a person could not hold the end of one and reach the other. Maier asked subjects to figure out how they could tie the two strings together with the help of objects they found in the lab, such as pliers, clamps, extension cords, ringstands, and poles. Every time a subject came up with a solution, such as tying an extension cord to one string and pulling it toward the other, Maier would say, "Now do it another way."

One solution, the pendulum technique, was particularly elusive. If a pair of pliers or some other heavy object was tied to the end of one string, that string could be set swinging and grasped as it approached the other string. Though few people thought of this solution on their own, most were susceptible to a hint. When Maier saw that a subject was stumped, he would walk by one of the strings and casually set it in motion. In less than a minute the subject would begin to construct a pendulum (see Figure 8-1). Clearly, the sight of a swinging string had caused the subject to think of the solution. Yet when subjects were asked what had triggered their idea, very few mentioned Maier's action. Most gave vague answers, such as "It just dawned on me" or "It was the only thing left." Apparently, subjects were unaware of their own thought processes.

Subsequent research has shown that the results of Maier's experiment were not unusual. In a lengthy series of studies, Nisbett and Wilson (1977) found that people can easily mistake the reason for their behavior, especially when it differs from normal expectations. People often maintain that a truly influential factor had no effect on them, or insist that an irrele-

may be little more than plausibility judgments. We are, of course, aware of the content of our thoughts at any given moment, but we apparently have very limited access to the processes involved in creating those thoughts. As a result, many psychologists avoid using introspection as a method of exploring cognitive processes—though some newer, more successful introspective techniques have been developed (for example, Ericsson & Simon, 1980). Instead, most psychologists focus on mental activities whose results can be observed and measured.

In this chapter we will examine four such mental activities: thinking in terms of concepts, solving problems, making decisions, and using language. These may seem to be diverse mental activities, but they all have something in common. They all depend on knowledge derived from perception, learning, and memory. Consequently, you will encounter in this chapter many concepts that were introduced in Chapters 4, 6, and 7.

Conceptual Thinking

If you were asked what you see in front of you at this moment, you would probably answer with a series of one- or two-word labels: a page, a book, a lamp, a desk, a wall, perhaps a coffee mug. These answers reveal an important fact about human cognition. Although the world consists of a multitude of objects and events, each unique in many ways, we tend to simplify and order it by grouping together those things with common features. The mental constructions involved in making such classifications are called **concepts.**

The importance of concepts to cognitive processing cannot be overstated. Concepts simplify the world, allowing us to apply what we have learned in one situation to another. Concepts impose structure and predictability on a world that would otherwise be overwhelming in complexity. They do so partly by organizing information into manageable units. To form a concept, we take things that are similar, but not exactly the same, and treat them as though they are equivalent (Neisser, 1987; Wattenmaker et al., 1986). Though one lamp is not really identical with another, we think of the two as belonging to the same concept and so treat them alike (we plug them in and turn them on). Concepts also allow us to formulate rules about how things are related. Consider the concepts of *flame* and *heat*. An implicit rule states that the first causes the second, so that whenever we

FIGURE 8-1 *Diagram of Maier's string problem. Subjects were asked to figure out how they could tie the two strings together with the help of objects they found in the tool box. Maier found that he could provide a hint by casually setting one of the strings in motion, like a pendulum. Shortly following this hint, many subjects "discovered" that they could tie a tool (such as a wrench) to one string, set it in motion, and reach the string as it was swinging: but most subjects were unaware that Maier had provided any sort of hint.*

vant factor was influential. Nisbett and Wilson theorize that people tend to assess a factor as influential if logic suggests that it should be influential. In short, our own estimates of the causes of our own behavior

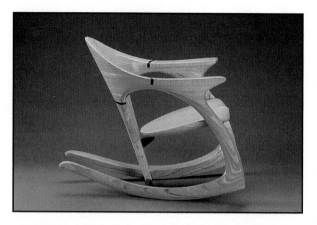

To identify this unfamiliar stimulus, compare it to concepts already stored in your memory, find a "match," and label it as an instance of that concept.

see a flame, we refrain from touching it. Concepts, then, allow us to form general rules that can be applied to particular situations. Such generalizations make complex thought possible.

Conceptual Hierarchies

During the course of your lifetime, you have learned an almost unimaginable amount of information. How have you stored such information so that you could use it again? Is there a kind of structure to your knowledge?

A moment's thought will reveal that your concepts of the world are structured hierarchies. The object you are sitting on may be an instance of the concept *desk chair, kitchen chair,* or *lawn chair,* which is in turn an example of the more general concept *chair*—which is in turn an instance of the even broader concept *furniture.* A great variety of other objects, qualities, and behaviors with shared characteristics are classified in the same way. Most concepts can be broken down into three levels: *superordinate* (the highest level), *basic* (intermediate level), and *subordinate* (lowest level) (see Figure 8-2). Concepts at the intermediate, or basic, level are the ones we use most often in everyday speech (Rosch, 1978; Rosch & Mervis, 1975). For example, we seldom ask a friend to pass the Bic fine-tipped felt marker, or to hand over a writing instrument. We say instead, "Hand me the pen." Using the lower (subordinate) or higher (superordinate) level seems artificial: the first is too specific, the second too vague. The basic level, in contrast, seems just right. It gives ample information without unnecessary details.

Conceptual Models: Features, Prototypes, and Exemplars

Whenever you ask yourself "What is that?" you are searching for a concept or set of concepts with which to place an unfamiliar stimulus. You compare something new with concepts already stored in your memory, find a "match," at least along key dimensions, and label the new thing an instance of that concept. The caption to the accompanying photograph gives one example of this process.

But how is the knowledge of a concept structured in your mind and stored in your memory? Researchers once believed that concepts were stored as a set of fairly unambiguous *defining features.* The concept *bachelor,* for instance, would be stored as the features "adult," "male," and "currently unmarried." Those three features together would define the concept. Anyone who possessed them is automatically a bachelor, and any bachelor, by definition, would possess all three features. But do most familiar concepts have such clear-cut defining features? The psychologist Eleanor Rosch (who has also published under the name Heider) thinks not. Rosch (1978) concedes that some concepts, such as *bachelor,* do have a set of clearly defined features that are shared by all instances of the concept. But try to list the defining features of a concept like *furniture, candy,* or *fruit.* Although it is possible after careful thought to define these and other so-called **natural concepts,** the exercise is difficult because we are not accustomed to thinking about them in this way.

Rosch has proposed that most natural concepts are not encoded into memory in terms of a list of defining features. Instead, they are encoded in terms of a **prototype**—an idealized concept containing the "best" characteristics of a category—plus an implicit understanding of the degree to which stimuli can vary from the prototype and still be regarded as instances of the concept. This theory can explain why some things are considered better instances of a concept than others, even though, technically speaking, they have the same "defining" features. For example, you would probably agree that a robin or a sparrow is a better instance of the concept *bird* than a pelican or an ostrich. In fact, if you were asked for an example of the concept *bird,* you would probably name a robin or a sparrow (Mervis, Catlin, & Rosch, 1976). Robins and sparrows seem to be very similar to the prototype for birds, whereas pelicans and ostriches are not. (You would probably agree, too, that the description "can fly" is a characteristic of birds,

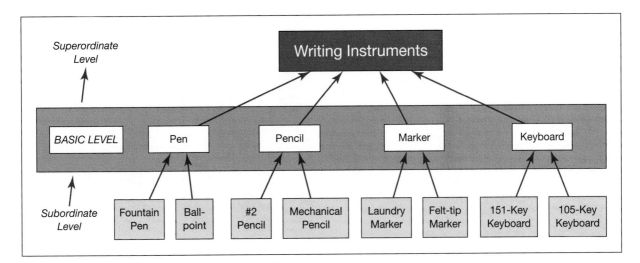

FIGURE 8-2 *Examples of hierarchically arranged concepts. Most everyday reasoning is done using concepts at the basic level.*

even though you know penguins cannot fly.) If a natural concept includes a list of defining features that all instances of that concept possess, why isn't one example of the concept as good as another?

Rosch and others have performed many experiments designed to show that the prototype model of concepts is closer to the way people actually behave than the feature-based model. Figure 8-3 is drawn from one such study. You should be able to respond to part A faster than to part B—why? Rosch argues that the examples in part A are much closer to the prototypes of the concepts *bird, fruit,* and so forth, than the examples in part B. Thus, we can process the information in part A faster than that in part B because we do not have to stop and think: How close is this to the prototype?

Although the prototype model of concepts was originally proposed as a criticism of the feature-based model, the two models may not be incompatible. One way to reconcile them may be to think of many of the features in a feature-based model as "characteristic," rather than essential, traits (Smith & Medin, 1981). The ability to fly, for example, is a trait characteristic of most, though not all, birds. Concepts may be more heavily influenced by features of the "best" examples (the prototypes), even if those features are not shared by *all* members of the category.

Another way to reconcile the feature-based and prototype models might be to think of some concepts as having a feature-based "core" that is useful in distinguishing one concept from another (Medin

& Smith, 1984). The concept *boy,* for example, has the feature-based core "human, juvenile, male." If asked to describe the difference between a boy and a man or a boy and a girl, you might consider this core. But if asked to identify a particular person as an instance of a boy, you would be more apt to use a prototype. That is, you would recall your mental image of a "typical" boy and then determine if the person before you is reasonably similar (small, hair relatively short, dressed in boys' clothes, and so forth).

Finally, Ross and Spalding (1994), among others, have suggested that concepts are best understood in terms of **exemplars,** multiple examples of concepts we might be exposed to. Whereas prototypes are abstract entities, exemplars are more directly related to actual experience. For instance, you probably have developed several alternative exemplars of the concept *bird.* With more than one exemplar, you may be more successful in recognizing a new instance as *bird.*

Problem Solving

A knowledge of concepts and the relationships among them makes problem solving possible. To understand why, observe the role that concepts play in solving this puzzle: Take six matches of the same size, and assemble them so that they form four equilateral triangles, with every side equal to the length of one match. Most people find this task difficult. If you can see the solution, it is undoubtedly because of your knowledge of the concepts *triangle* and

Part A
1. A sparrow is a bird.
2. An orange is a fruit.
3. A dog is a fish.
4. A hammer is a tool.
5. A bean is a vegetable.
6. A chair is an example of furniture.
7. A shirt is an example of clothing.

Part B
1. An ostrich is a bird.
2. A tomato is a fruit.
3. A whale is a fish.
4. A crane is a tool.
5. Rice is a vegetable.
6. A telephone is an example of furniture.
7. A bat is a bird.

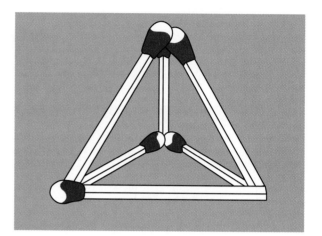

FIGURE 8-4   *Solution to the match problem. The match problem is solved by building a three-dimensional pyramid; most people assume that the matches must lie flat, as they were first perceived.*

FIGURE 8-3   *Prototypes and classification. Determine whether each statement is true or false, and note the length of time required to answer each statement. As the text explains, your response time will probably be shorter for part A.* (After Matlin, 1983.)

pyramid and the way they are related. Only by building a three-dimensional structure like the one shown in Figure 8-4 can you solve the puzzle.

Stages in Solving Problems

Psychologists sometimes divide problem solving into three stages: representing the problem, devising strategies for reaching a solution, and deciding when an answer is satisfactory (Posner, 1973). These three stages provide a useful way to organize our discussion.

Representing the Problem

No single aspect of problem solving has a greater impact on the speed and likelihood of finding a solution than the way in which the problem is represented, that is, how the problem solver thinks about and interprets the task. Consider Figure 8-5, which shows a circle with a radius of 5 inches, within which is drawn a right-angled triangle *xdl*. What is the length of side *l*, the triangle's hypotenuse? If you are

trying to remember the formula for calculating the length of a hypotenuse, you are representing this problem in a way more difficult than necessary. Instead of viewing figure *xdl* as a triangle, try seeing it instead as half a rectangle. Now the solution may be obvious. Line *l* is one diagonal of a rectangle; the other extends from the center of the circle to the point where lines *x* and *d* meet, that is, the circle's radius. Since you know that the radius is 5 inches, line *l* too must be 5 inches. Thus, what at first appeared to be a difficult problem suddenly becomes much easier when represented in a different way.

Paradoxically, then, when you interpret a problem quickly and decisively, you may sometimes hinder your ability to solve it. Once you have commit-

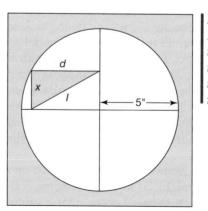

FIGURE 8-5 Problem illustrating the importance of the initial representation.

A problem used by Duncker (1945) to demonstrate functional fixedness: He gave subjects the materials shown and asked them to mount a candle on a wall so that it could be used to give light. Try to solve the problem yourself. (The use of the term "functional fixedness" gives you a clue to the solution of the problem that Duncker's subjects did not have.) The solution is shown on page 264.

ted yourself to representing a problem in a certain way, you automatically structure the available information accordingly, reducing your chance of seeing a better alternative. That is why psychologists often suggest that problem solvers avoid settling on a specific representation as soon as they encounter a seemingly difficult problem. Instead, try viewing the question from various angles, and search for different ways to perceive it. With that advice in mind, try to solve the following problem: A dog has a 6-foot chain fastened around its neck; its water bowl is 10 feet away. How can it reach the bowl? The solution appears in Figure 8-6.

Changing your perspective on a problem is not always easy. Many things can steer you toward an unproductive point of view. One is the fact that the critical aspects of a problem may sometimes be embedded in irrelevant information. Consider, for instance, this problem (Sternberg & Davidson, 1982): "Assume you have black socks and brown socks in a drawer, mixed in the ratio of 4 to 5. If you are not permitted to look, how many socks will you have to take out to make sure of having a pair the same color?" If you didn't know immediately that the answer is three, it was probably because the 4 to 5 ratio misdirected your attention. The ratio of black socks to brown socks is irrelevant information. If you have only two colors of socks in the drawer and the first two socks you take out do not match, the third sock must match one of them. Thus, when irrelevant information (like the color ratio) dominates your thinking, flexible representation of a problem is harder.

You may remember this riddle from your childhood: Suppose you are driving a bus. At the first stop, 6 people get on. At the next stop, 2 people get off and 7 people get on. At the next stop 4 people get off and 1 gets on. At the next stop, no one gets off and 4 more get on. Now, what color are the bus driver's eyes? This riddle works—if it does—because your attention is diverted by the irrelevant but seemingly important details.

Much the same thing can happen when you become locked into perspectives you have always held in the past. For example, people often perceive objects as having only their customary functions, a tendency called **functional fixedness.** Functional fixedness may help to explain why people who are faced with Maier's problem of tying together two widely spaced strings seldom think of the pendulum solution. A pair of pliers or some other object likely to be found in a laboratory is not ordinarily used as a pendulum weight. Consequently, this function is not likely to occur to most people. Another problem whose solution may be hindered by functional fixedness is illustrated in the above drawing of candles, matches, thumbtacks, and string (Duncker, 1945). How would you use the materials shown in the picture to mount a single lighted candle on a vertical wooden wall? The photograph shows the solution.

The opening of this chapter recounted the *Apollo 13* disaster. Because of the damage caused by the explosion, the astronauts were forced to use the small lunar module much longer than anticipated. The carbon dioxide level was rising, but the astronauts did not have replacement air filters that fit the module. To solve the problem, Ed Smylie and his colleagues had to look past the conventional uses for objects on the spacecraft to devise a makeshift filter.

First, Smylie seized the plastic wrapper that had held special thermal underwear the astronauts were to have worn under their space suits as they walked

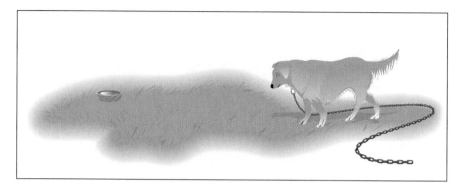

FIGURE 8-6 *Solution to the dog/chain problem. The dog can simply walk to its bowl if the chain is not attached to anything but its own neck.* (After Solso, 1988, p. 424.)

on the moon. Then he ripped cardboard from the pages of a flight manual—pages that contained now useless instructions for lifting off from the moon. Next, he cut pieces of tubing from the emergency airflow hoses the astronauts would have used if the spacecraft had begun to leak. Finally, using duct tape, he connected all these pieces to the replacement filter in such a way as to fit its small opening. Had Smylie been fixated on the typical uses for these objects, he might not have come up with his ingenious solution.

Not all people are as skilled as Ed Smylie in representing problems. Experts are often better than novices at assessing problems in their fields. What gives them their cognitive advantage? Part of the answer lies in the schemas they possess. Remember that a schema is a mental representation of objects and events through which we filter incoming information and give meaning to it. Doctors, for instance, possess an intricate schema of how the body can break down, a schema they use to interpret patients' symptoms.

Research confirms the role of schemas in giving experts an edge in problem solving. In one study, experts in physics categorized problems in a physics

A close analysis of the parts of the match box shows it can function as a candle platform. Seeing this new use for the box breaks "functional fixedness" and leads to the solution for Duncker's problem.

textbook differently from college students (Chi, Glaser, & Reese, 1982). The students grouped problems by their appearance ("These two both deal with blocks on an inclined plane"), while the experts grouped them according to underlying principles ("These two can both be solved using Newton's second law"). Thus, the experts' complex schemas about the laws of physics helped them to represent the problems in ways more likely to bring about solutions.

Even if you are not an expert, you can learn to represent problems more effectively. For instance, algebra word problems ("Train A leaves Denver traveling east at 60 miles per hour . . .") are notoriously difficult for most students. Reed (1987) found that much of the difficulty could be traced to problems in initial representations. He presented students with the following test problem: "A small pipe can fill an oil tank in 12 hours, and a large one can fill it in 8 hours. How long will it take to fill the tank if both pipes are used at the same time?" Then he gave students related problems to use as examples. Some shared the same solution procedure as the test problem, others the same story context. Despite the usefulness of problems that shared the same solution procedures, most students believed—incorrectly— that the problems that shared the same *story context* would be most helpful (see Table 8-1). Weaver and Kintsch (1992) taught students how to represent such problems more clearly using simple diagrams. Those who took the training program were significantly better at grasping the requirements of word problems, and ultimately more successful at solving them.

Devising Strategies for Solution: Algorithms and Heuristics

Most problems cannot be solved instantaneously, even when they are represented in an effective way. Often the problem solver must manipulate the data

TABLE 8-1 *Grouping of Algebra Word Problems Based on Superficial (Related Problem Story) or Meaningful (Related Solution Procedures) Similarity*

Story Context	Same (Useful for solving related problems)	Different (Not useful for solving related problems)
Same (appears useful for solving related problems, but is not)	A small hose can fill a swimming pool in 6 hours, and a large one can fill it in 3 hours. How long will it take to fill the pool if both hoses are used at the same time?	A small pipe can fill a water tank in 20 hours, and a large pipe can fill it in 15 hours. Water is used at a rate that would empty a full tank in 40 hours. How long will it take to fill the tank when both pipes are used, assuming that water is being used as the tank is filling up?
Different (appears unrelated, but may be useful for solving related problems)	Tom can drive a car to Bill's house in 4 hours, and Bill can drive to Tom's house in 3 hours. How long will it take them to meet if they both leave their houses at the same time?	An airplane can fly from city A to city B at an average speed of 250 mph in 3 hours, less time than it takes to return from city B to city A at 200 mph. How many hours did it take to return?

Source: Based on Reed, 1987.

in some way before the answer emerges. But the human ability to manipulate data is unavoidably constrained by the limited capacity of short-term memory. Recall from Chapter 7 that short-term memory can hold only about seven pieces of information at a time. Consequently, we must find a way to reduce the demands placed on short-term memory. In this section we will examine some strategies for doing so.

Some problems can best be solved by using an **algorithm,** a precisely stated set of rules for solving problems of that particular kind. The formula $\pi(r)^2$, for example, is an algorithm for finding the area of a circle given its radius, whether that radius is measured in millimeters or miles. The major advantage of an algorithm is that it guarantees success if it is applied correctly in the right circumstances.

Or consider the task of rearranging the letters *i-g-n-b-r* to form an English word. An algorithmic solution would be to rearrange the letters systematically until a meaningful combination appears. Assuming that the letters *can* be combined to produce an English word, this algorithm will solve the problem, though the number of iterations required to do so could be quite high. Virtually all computer applications are based on algorithms. The programmer's task is to give the computer the exact instructions needed to solve the problem. In the anagram (scrambled word

problem) just given, the algorithm would involve a large number of possibilities (120), but computers are fairly efficient at performing these sorts of tasks.

Humans, on the other hand, do not perform this kind of computation rapidly. The demands of such an algorithm would overwhelm their limited short-term memories. Instead, most people would adopt a different strategy. They would focus on letter combinations common to the English language, such as *br* at the beginning of a word and *ing* at the end. Using this approach, they would probably discover the word *bring* quickly. A rule-of-thumb problem-solving strategy like this one is called a **heuristic** (from the Greek word meaning "to discover"). Unlike algorithms, heuristics do not guarantee a solution to a problem. When they do work, however, they can be much more efficient than an algorithm. Heuristics also greatly reduce the demands placed on short-term memory.

The heuristics for solving anagrams are very specific to that task. But some general heuristics are useful in solving problems of many kinds (Newell & Simon, 1972). One is **subgoal analysis.** Consider the game of chess, in which 10^{120} play sequences are theoretically possible. Even if a person could evaluate 1 billion moves per second, the time required to consider all the possible alternatives would be greater

Unlike computers, human chess players cannot consider all possibilities before selecting a move. Instead, chess masters like these two often break down the task of winning the game into a series of smaller tasks, or subgoals, each of which is of manageable scope.

than the known age of the universe. Clearly, chess players must have some way of limiting their focus. Their strategy is to break down the task of winning the game into a series of smaller tasks, or *subgoals,* each of which is of manageable scope. For example, a player might first determine whether the king is in danger of attack and, if so, concentrate on protecting the king. If the king is safe, the player might proceed to the next most important subgoal: ensuring that all other major pieces are safe. If the other pieces are not in danger, the player might work through a series of offensive subgoals. In this way chess players reduce the demands on their limited information-processing capabilities—even though there is no guarantee that they will spot the best move.

Subgoal analysis is not the only general heuristic people use. Another is **means-end analysis,** a strategy that involves comparing your current position to your desired state (the "end") and then trying to find a way to attain the end (the "means"). To take a simple example, if you have to go to work, but your car has broken down, a quick means-end analysis would tell you that a distance of, say, 5 miles separates your home and your destination. You might cover that distance on foot, by bicycle, or by bus. Note, however, that this type of analysis has a built-in bias: it encourages you to focus on reducing the distance between the place where you are and the place where you want to be. If your problem can best be solved by first *increasing* the gap between your current state and your desired goal—say, by walking several blocks away from your destination to a subway station—means-end analysis may actually

divert you from the best solution. Keep this bias in mind as you try to solve the three-chain problem in Figure 8-7A. (The solution is shown in Figure 8.7B.)

A third general heuristic is the **backward search,** which begins at the end point of a problem and works backward. Consider the problem in Figure 8-8. If you try to work forward toward the answer, beginning with one water lily and doubling the area every twenty-four hours, you will remain hopelessly stumped. But if you begin on the sixtieth day and work backward, the solution is simple. If the lake is completely covered on the sixtieth day, it must be half covered on the fifty-ninth. The backward search heuristic is most helpful in circumstances in which the end point in a problem is very clear-cut (a lake totally covered with water lilies), while the starting point is surrounded by many options or questions (how big is a water lily? how big is the lake?). For this reason, you might also try searching backward when solving a maze puzzle, in which many paths lead away from the starting point, but only one leads to the goal.

You may remember using a backward search strategy to work geometry proofs in high school or college. In these problems, you were given certain facts ("line *AB* = line *BC*, angle *ABC* = angle *BCD*") and the ultimate goal ("prove that line *AC* = line *BD*") and asked to derive the proof. You looked at the final state and asked yourself, "What would I need to know to prove this?" Once you had generated the next-to-last state (the conditions that would allow you to prove the conclusion), you worked backward from it. By retracing the steps in this way, you finally got back to the starting point.

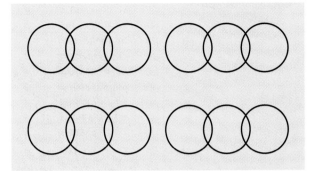

FIGURE 8-7A *Means-end analysis: the four-chain problem. A man has four chains, each three links long. He wants to join the four chains to form a single closed chain. Having a link opened costs 2 cents, and having a link closed costs 3 cents. Eventually, the man has the chains joined into a closed chain for 15 cents. Without spending too much time, can you figure out how he did it? Check your solution with the one given in Figure 8-7B.*

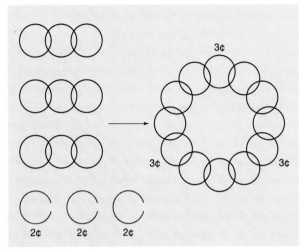

FIGURE 8-7B *Solution to the four-chain problem. Take one chain completely apart for 6 cents, and use its links to join the remaining three chains for 9 cents. Most people find the chain link problem extremely difficult to solve, perhaps because they rapidly employ a means-end analysis. If the problem is to join four chains into a single circular chain, taking apart one of the chains completely seems to increase the gap between the means and the end. Yet opening and closing only three links is the way to produce the desired result.*

Algorithms and heuristics are useful tools when they are used correctly. But if you chose one that is inappropriate to a certain problem, you may end up with a poor solution or no solution at all. The inclination to apply an old or inappropriate perspective to a new situation is called a **mental set.** When mental sets are inappropriate, they cause stalemates in problem solving. Treating the situation in an unthinking fashion, or clinging to strategies that have worked in the past but are now ineffective, has been called "mindlessness" (Langer, 1989). Psychologist Ellen Langer has described a tragic real-life example of an inappropriate mental set. On a snowy evening in 1985, a plane en route to Florida crashed into the Potomac River shortly after takeoff from Washington, D.C., because its wings had become covered with ice. The pilot and copilot had gone through their preflight checklist methodically, but when they came to the anti-icer control, they left it turned off. Apparently they were so accustomed to flying in warm climates that the "off" response was habitual to them. Their mindless repetition of an old solution caused a disaster.

Deciding Whether a Solution is Satisfactory

Why do you always find your keys in the very last place you search? It's simple: once you have found your keys, you can quit searching! This old joke may seem silly, but it does illustrate the final process in problem solving: determining if the solution you have generated is correct.

For some problems, deciding when a solution is satisfactory is no trouble at all. If you solved the matchstick-pyramid problem, or the water lilies problem, you were absolutely sure you were right when you perceived the answer. Unfortunately, the "right" answer is not always so obvious. How, for example, would you determine whether you had chosen the "best" topic for a term paper? Or made the "best" move in a chess game? It isn't easy to say.

In fact, when people grapple with problems like these, they often settle for a less-than-ideal solution, especially if the effort to find a better solution stresses their cognitive capacities (Posner, 1973). The concession makes sense. To function effectively, a person must avoid cognitive overload: one way to do so is to accept a solution that may not be perfect, but is good enough. That is why you sometimes return to a solution you first rejected, after devoting a great deal of time to a problem. At some point, searching for a better solution no longer seems worth the effort.

FIGURE 8-8 *The backward search strategy. In this problem, the water lilies double in area every twenty-four hours. At the beginning of the summer, there is one water lily on the lake. In sixty days the lake will become covered with water lilies. On what day will the lake be half covered?* (After Sternberg & Davidson, 1982.)

Does accepting a less-than-optimal solution amount to irrational behavior? Herbert Simon, the only psychologist to have been awarded the Nobel prize (Pavlov's Nobel prize was awarded for his work on the physiology of digestion), doesn't think so. Simon (1957) proposed that we do the best we can given our limited cognitive resources, a process he called *satisficing*. According to Simon, we do not continue to search for an answer to a problem indefinitely. Instead, we search until we have found a solution that will work—one that will "satisfy"—even if it isn't the best possible solution. Simon calls this **bounded rationality,** by which he means that we do behave rationally, within certain constraints.

Creativity in Solving Problems

The ancient Greek scientist Archimedes (287?–212 B.C.) was a highly creative problem solver. When King Hiero suspected that his new crown was not made of pure gold as he had ordered, but was instead a blend of gold and silver, he asked Archimedes to determine the truth. Archimedes could calculate the weight of an object given its volume, and therefore determine if it was made of either gold or silver, but he had no idea how to measure the crown's volume without first melting it down. Then one day, while sitting in his bathtub and watching the water rise as his body displaced it, the solution leapt into mind. The volume of the crown could be determined by immersing it in water and measuring the amount of water it displaced. According to legend, Archimedes was so excited that he jumped out of the bathtub and ran to King Hiero shouting, "Eureka! I have found it!"

Archimedes' solution was creative for several reasons. First, it was novel; no one had ever thought of measuring volume in this way. In fact, Archimedes had to break free of the usual approaches to measurement, which might have impeded his thinking. Archimedes' solution was also practical; measuring the volume using this new method was easy. Practicality is another hallmark of creative thinking. A creative idea must be not only unusual but workable (Murray, 1959; Stein, 1956). See if you can arrive at a solution for the problem illustrated in Figure 8-9.

What factors facilitate creative thinking? One is the effective use of analogies (Bransford & Stein, 1984; Gick & Holyoak, 1980; Holyoak, 1984). Consider how the German chemist Friedrich Kekulé (1829–1896) discovered the molecular structure of benzene, a highly volatile and flammable liquid. Chemists had not figured out why benzene has these chemical properties. The answer, they knew, lay in the way its six atoms of carbon and six atoms of hydrogen were connected. But no one had been able to determine the structure. Then one evening, as

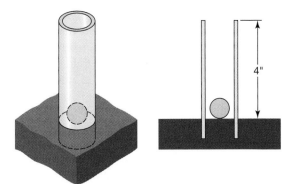

FIGURE 8-9 *Creative problem solving. Assume that a steel pipe is embedded in the concrete floor of a bare room, as shown in the drawing. The inside diameter is 0.6 inch larger than the diameter of a table tennis ball (1.5 inches) that is resting gently at the bottom of the pipe. You are one of a group of six people in the room, along with the following objects: 100 feet of clothesline, a carpenter's hammer, a chisel, a box of cereal, a file, a wire coat hanger, a monkey wrench, and a lightbulb. How can you get the ball out of the pipe without damaging the ball, the pipe, or the floor?* (After Adams, 1976.)

Kekulé was dozing in front of his fire, he dreamed of benzene atoms linked together like a snake. Suddenly the snake grabbed hold of its tail and whirled around. Kekulé awoke with a start. The snake analogy had given him the answer: the carbon atoms in benzene must form a closed ring, with one hydrogen atom attached to each carbon atom.

Another aspect of Kekulé's creative insight—the suddenness with which it occurred —is also characteristic of many creative ideas. The solution pops into mind when the person is least expecting it, as it did with Archimedes. For example, consider Frank Offner, one of this century's most creative electrical engineers. He developed the first heat-seeking missiles during World War II and also played a key role in the development of the electrocardiogram (EKG) and the electroencephalogram (EEG). Offner says:

I will tell you one thing I found in both science and technology: If you have a problem, don't sit down and try to solve it. Because I will never solve it if I am just sitting down and thinking. It will hit me maybe in the middle of the night, while I am driving a car or taking a shower, or something like that.

Offner, quoted in Csikszentmihalyi, 1996, p. 99

Some psychologists suggest that in such cases, the creative idea may result from unconscious thought (Ghiselin, 1952). But unconscious thought must be based on knowledge and information. Creative ideas seldom just pop into the minds of people who have no background in an area (Wood, 1983). They are far more likely to occur to those with a broad knowledge base on which to build. As one researcher noted, "The apple that fell on Newton's head and inspired him to develop a general theory of gravity struck an object filled with information" (Solso, 1988, p. 444). Or to put it another way, "Accident favors the prepared mind."

Equally important is strong motivation and persistence, or a willingness to work exceptionally hard (Gruber, 1981). When the psychologist Anne Roe (1946, 1953) studied very creative scientists and artists, she found that hard work was the one element they all shared. Her finding is supported by what we know about some of history's greatest musicians, painters, and writers. Beethoven, for example, found composing music torturous. He would write, discard, and rewrite over and over again. Similarly, Thomas Mann, the Nobel-prize-winning author, struggled to turn out just three pages a day (Gardner, 1993). For these and many other creative geniuses, great works have been partly the product of tremendous perseverance.

Are highly creative people more intelligent than others? Perhaps. Studies show that, in general, creative problem solving and intelligence tend to go together (Guilford, 1967; Sternberg & Davidson, 1986). But intelligence is not enough to guarantee creative insights. While people who score high in creativity also tend to score high in intelligence,

Creative inventions like this micro-car are generally novel, practical, and workable.

Autistic savants like Steven Wiltshire are psychologically impaired yet they display remarkable abilities on isolated tasks.

many intelligent people are not very creative (Roe, 1946, 1953). Furthermore, many creative people score below average on standard intelligence tests.

Whether or not people can be trained to be more creative is uncertain. A number of training courses have been developed to teach students how to generate new ideas (Dormen & Edidin, 1989). While various claims have been made for the courses, they appear to improve performance only on the kinds of tasks that are practiced during training. That is, the skills students learn do not often generalize to other tasks (Mayer, 1983). There is also some question whether skills taught in these courses are crucial to genuine creativity. For instance, some courses teach what is called **divergent thinking,** or the ability to generate many different answers to a question ("How many uses can you think of for a brick?"). Although divergent thinking may sound like creativity, the two are not necessarily the same. When researchers gave tests of divergent thinking to groups

of scientists, the most creative scientists were not among those who scored highest on the tests, nor were the highest scorers the most creative in their work (Weisberg, 1986). Apparently there is more to scientific creativity than simply being able to generate a large number of ideas.

Psychologist Dean Simonton (1988, 1989), who has studied scientists who made "breakthrough" contributions to their fields, believes that these creative people are distinguished most by an unusual willingness to take risks. They are willing to adopt a theory or line of research that everyone else thinks is far-fetched. Interestingly, their nonconformist ideas prove wrong about as often as they prove right, but the mistakes are usually forgotten quickly, while the successes are seen as brilliant.

Decision Making

Although creativity is a great asset, it does not help people to make sound judgments in the hundreds of decisions they make every day. Some of these decisions have far-reaching consequences. Deciding whether to get married, to have children, to go to graduate school, or to change careers can greatly alter a person's life. And political decisions made by voters and government officials can affect a nation, the world—even the course of history.

What have psychologists learned about decision making? Most now believe that humans typically make decisions rationally, though the decision-making process has constraints: in this way, most contemporary models are derived from Simon's notion of *bounded rationality* (see p. 268).

Rational Models of Decision Making

Suppose you are faced with the following decision. Your friends are planning a weekend ski trip, but you have an exam on Monday morning. Though you have already spent some time studying, you are not certain how difficult the exam will be. And because it is early in the ski season, conditions on the slopes may be only fair. Should you go with your friends, or stay home and study for the exam?

According to psychologists, two sets of variables will probably influence your decision. One is the value you place on the possible outcomes—often called their **utility.** How much pleasure will you derive from a weekend of fun and relaxation? How much satisfaction from doing well on your exam?

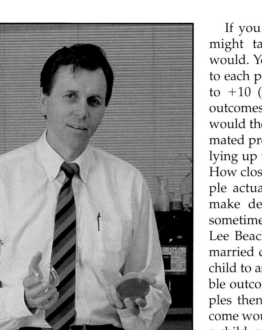

Those who make "breakthrough" contributions to their fields tend to be risk takers: they often adopt a theory or line of research that others deem far-fetched. Though few researchers agreed with him, Dr. Barry Marshall maintained for years that ulcers could be caused by bacteria, and therefore could be treated with antibiotics. Recent studies indicate that Marshall may be correct.

How unhappy will you be if you miss the ski weekend, and how distressed if you do poorly on the test? The second set of variables involves the probability that various outcomes will actually happen. What are the chances that insufficient snow will ruin your skiing? The odds that your instructor will give a difficult exam? Your decision, then, involves your evaluation of both utility and probability.

If you were a completely rational creature, you might tackle this problem as a mathematician would. You would start by assigning a utility value to each potential outcome using a scale of, say, -10 to $+10$ (negative numbers indicating unpleasant outcomes and positive numbers pleasant ones). You would then multiply those utility figures by the estimated probability that each outcome will occur. Tallying up these figures would give you your answer. How closely does this approach match the way people actually make decisions? Though we seldom make decisions in a formal, mathematical way, sometimes we approximate this strategy intuitively. Lee Beach and his colleagues, for instance, asked married couples who were contemplating having a child to assign relative utilities to a number of possible outcomes associated with parenthood. The couples then estimated the probability that each outcome would actually happen if they decided to have a child, and the probability that, once they decided to have a child, the woman would indeed become pregnant. From these figures the researchers calculated an overall score that they used to predict whether a particular couple would have a child in the next two years. The overall scores proved reasonably accurate, predicting the outcome correctly more than 70 percent of the time (Beach, Campbell, & Townes, 1979).

Not all decisions conform to a rational model, however. Studies show that people often ignore information that is important to a good decision. For example, grocery shoppers who want to buy the most economical products may still choose relatively expensive items, despite the fact that unit prices are posted on the shelves (Russo, Krieser, & Miyashita, 1975). Why do people sometimes fail to consider all the pertinent facts when making choices?

In the section on problem solving we discussed the concept of "bounded rationality" and "satisficing" (p. 268). Many of the same factors that constrain problem solving also constrain decision making. The greatest obstacle to rational decision making involves the limited capacity of working memory. When a decision is fairly complex, we tend to simplify our choices by concentrating on a few relevant facts and ignoring others. Often this approach serves quite well, producing speedy decisions that turn out to be satisfactory. At other times, however, the tactic produces choices that are not ideal. Figure 8-10 offers you a choice between two games. Game 1 involves a

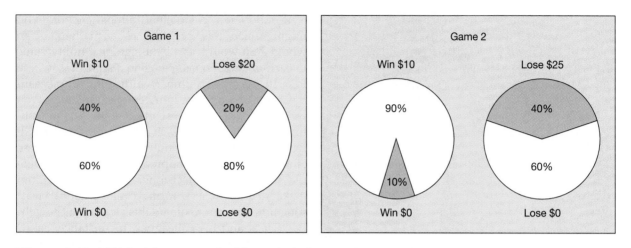

FIGURE 8-10   *Which of these games should you play? If you made a quick choice based on the 90 percent probability of winning in game 2, then narrowing your cognitive focus led you to a poor choice. To make a correct choice you should consider (1) the* odds *of winning, (2) the* odds *of losing, (3) the* payoff *for winning, and (4) the* penalty *for losing. Psychologists have found that you are most likely to attend to (1), less likely to attend to (2), and least likely to consider (3) and (4). To make an informed choice, though, you must consider all four.*

In game 1, the odds are that you will break even. After ten trials, you would be expected to win $40 and lose $40:

40% *of winning* × 10 *games* = 4 *wins*
$10 *per win* × 4 *wins* = $40 *won*

20% *of losing* × 10 *games* = 2 *losses*
$20 *per loss* × 2 *losses* = $40 *lost*

In game 2, you are likely to lose money. The odds are that you will win $90 and lose $100:

90% *of winning* × 10 *games* = 9 *wins*
$10 *per win* × 9 *wins* = $90 *won*

40% *of losing* × 10 *games* = 4 *losses*
$25 *per loss* × 4 *losses* = $100 *lost*

40 percent chance of winning $10, but a 20 percent chance of losing $20. Game 2 involves a 90 percent chance of winning $10, but a 40 percent chance of losing $25. Decide in the next thirty seconds which game you prefer to play, say, ten times in a row.

If you are like most people, you failed to multiply the probability of winning or losing by the amounts to be won or lost. Instead, you made a rough estimate of both and guessed which game offered more favorable odds. Perhaps you reasoned that the 90 percent chance of winning offered by game 2 looked very good indeed. Game 2 did involve a greater chance of losing, and the amount at risk was slightly higher; but overall, 90 percent odds in your favor were too good to pass up. But if game 2 was your choice, you did not make a good decision, as the caption to Figure 8-10 explains. In this case, narrowing

your cognitive focus to the probability of winning produced a decision that made little sense from a strictly logical point of view. In terms of your limited time, attention, and short-term memory, however, the strategy you used was understandable.

Decisions can often be influenced by the way in which the outcomes are stated, or the context in which information is presented, called a *decision frame* (Tversky & Kahneman, 1981). Advertisers often exploit the effects of the way information is framed. People are more likely to buy hamburger meat marked "90% lean" than hamburger marked "10% fat," for instance. Gas stations advertise "cash discounts" rather than "credit surcharges." In general, decisions framed in terms of positive consequences are more attractive than decisions framed in terms of negative outcomes.

Many students are disturbed by the human tendency to limit one's cognitive focus. After all, we like to think of ourselves as rational decision makers who carefully assess all the facts before making informed choices. Is our sense of ourselves as competent decision makers an illusion? This question has generated heated controversy. On the one hand are those who emphasize the skill people often show in making daily choices. On the other hand are those who stress the errors of rule-of-thumb decision making. Much of the research related to this controversy deals with the topic of how people estimate odds—a topic we turn to next.

Judging the Odds

In June 1979, NASA informed the public that its 79-ton *Skylab* satellite would fall out of orbit within a matter of weeks. But there was no great cause for worry, the agency added: the odds were 151 to 1 against the plummeting satellite causing harm to a human being. And the chance that the spacecraft would injure a specific person was 600 billion to 1.

Everyday life is full of situations in which we estimate odds. Should you have your car serviced or wait another month? What are the chances that something will go wrong if you neglect the car? Should you study this evening or go to a movie? What are the chances that your instructor is planning a surprise quiz? Should you get married or stay single? Get divorced or stay married? And what are the chances that either choice will affect your career? In matters such as these, the odds are uncertain, so we must try to estimate them. Most of us, however, are not statisticians. How do we approach the task?

Psychologists have found that people do not usually approach probability judgments from the viewpoint of a statistician. Instead, they rely on *heuristics,* or rule-of-thumb strategies, to simplify the problem. Heuristics are generally used in estimating probabilities, but they can be applied inappropriately. Two very common heuristics involve representativeness and availability.

The Representativeness Heuristic

Read the following description of Jack, who was picked at random from a sample consisting of thirty engineers and seventy lawyers (Tversky & Kahneman, 1973): "Jack is a forty-five-year-old man. He is married and has four children. He is generally conservative, careful, and ambitious. He shows no interest in political or social issues and spends most of his free time on his many hobbies, which include home carpentry, sailing, and mathematical puzzles." Given this brief personality profile, what would you estimate the chances are that Jack is a lawyer? That he is an engineer? Before reading further, write down your estimate.

How did you arrive at your probability estimates of Jack's line of work? If you are like most people, you relied on what is called a **representativeness heuristic.** That is, you compared what you knew about Jack's personality with your ideas of an "average" or "representative" lawyer or engineer. The extent to which Jack matched each of these stereotypes determined your estimate of the probability that he was employed in that occupation. The job to which you gave the higher odds was undoubtedly engineer. Lawyer, you thought, was probably much less likely.

The representativeness heuristic is a useful device as long as it does not blind us to other relevant information. The problem is, it sometimes does. What other factors besides similarity to occupational stereotypes might enter into your estimate of what Jack does for a living? A moment's thought may tell you that the relative proportion of lawyers and engineers in the sample should also influence your judgment. Because there are over twice as many lawyers as engineers in the sample, a person drawn at random from this sample is more likely to be a lawyer. Did you consider that factor before? Probably not. When asked a question of this type, most people employ only the representativeness heuristic, completely ignoring what statisticians call *prior probabilities,* or the *base rate.* As a result, their judgments are sometimes misguided.

Another common error resulting from misuse of the representativeness heuristic involves *the law of small numbers* (Kahneman & Tversky, 1982; Tversky & Kahneman, 1993). Suppose you are playing in the championship game of a racquetball tournament. Assume your opponent is a much better player than you. The rules give you the option of playing to either 9 or 15 points. Which scoring system should you pick? If you found yourself playing *against* a weaker opponent, would you still pick the same scoring system?

When asked this question, most people maintain that the scoring system should not matter. If you thought so also, your answer is wrong. By assuming

Fans often speak of professional athletes like Michael Jordan as being on a hot streak. But after studying the performance of the Philadelphia 76ers over the course of an entire season, researchers found no evidence of such streaks.

even larger, with an average of 100 babies born each day. In which of the cities are all the babies born on a single day most likely to be of the same gender?

As you can see, the first city, with an average of only 4 babies born each day, is much more likely to obtain this result (the odds that all children will be the same gender are better than 1 in 20). What are the odds that all the babies born on the same day in all four cities will be of the same gender? They are astronomically small—about 1 in 1,000,000,000,000,000,000,000,000,000,000.

The law of small numbers, then, states that extreme scores are much more likely in small samples. Baseball fans routinely ignore this law. Almost every year, sportswriters run stories on the home-run leaders. If a player has hit fifteen home runs during the first quarter of the season, sportswriters state that the player may break the single-season home-run record. In virtually every case, however, the player's end-of-season total is far less than this projected total. Writers and fans simply fail to take into account the increased likelihood of extreme scores in small samples.

Finally, the representativeness heuristic can give rise to the illusion that athletes are on a "hot streak." If Michael Jordan makes three consecutive shots, announcers may describe him as having a "hot hand." But in one study, Gillovich, Vallone, and Tversky (1985) examined the records of a professional basketball team over the course of an entire season. Though they found many instances in which a player would make three, four, or more consecutive shots, the "streaks" occurred no more frequently than was dictated by chance. The researcher concluded that people tend to underestimate the likelihood of obtaining such sequences purely by chance. Over the course of an entire season and thousands of shots, runs of consecutive "hits" occur by chance more often than we realize.

The Availability Heuristic

Suppose you travel about 10,000 miles a year by car. You are a driver of average skill. How would you estimate the odds that you will someday be involved in a car accident? To make such a judgment, you would probably try to determine the frequency of automobile accidents from past experience. Have you or anyone you know ever been involved in an accident? Have you ever witnessed a collision? How often do you hear about traffic accidents in the news? In other words, you would assess the proba-

that each game would be equally representative of the two players' skills, you overlooked an important fact discussed in Chapter 2: the smaller the size of a sample, the greater the likelihood of obtaining unexpected results. As a sample gets larger, the likelihood of obtaining an unexpected result decreases. To illustrate, consider hospitals in four different cities. The first city is small; on a typical day, 4 babies are born. The second city is somewhat larger and averages 10 new babies each day. The third city is larger still; on average 20 babies are born each day. The final city is

Do you sometimes feel as if you always pick the slowest checkout line at the supermarket? If so, the annoyance such delays cause you probably bring the experience quickly to mind—an example of the availability heuristic in decision making.

bility of the event on the basis of the ease with which such instances come to mind.

In general, events that are easy to remember are perceived as more frequent, and therefore more probable, than events that are difficult to recall. This approach to estimating odds is called the **availability heuristic,** and it makes a good deal of sense. In general, the probability of an event occurring in the present is related directly to its frequency in the past (remember Recurring Theme 1: "The best predictor of future behavior is past behavior"). The more often an event has been experienced, the easier it is to remember. But note the qualification "in general." Like any rule-of-thumb device, the availability heuristic has its limitations, limitations that people often ignore.

THEME The Best Predictor of Future Behavior Is Past Behavior

1

The basic shortcoming of this heuristic is that some events come more readily to mind than others, for reasons that have nothing to do with their frequency in the past. A person who has just seen a highway accident is far more likely to remember it than a person who saw one ten years ago. That is, recency affects availability. Likewise, the vividness of an event affects its availability in memory. Thus, you are more likely to remember a five-car collision you witnessed yourself than one you merely read about. Events are also more readily remembered when they are related to strong emotions. Are you convinced that you always

pick the "slow" line at the store whenever you are in a hurry? If so, your conviction is probably due to the great annoyance the delays cost you; they therefore come quickly to mind (Dawes, 1988).

Familiarity, too, can make an event easier to recall. For instance, when people are shown a list composed of names of an equal number of famous women and not-so-famous men, they tend later to describe the list as consisting primarily of women's names (Tversky & Kahneman, 1973). The women's fame apparently makes their names easier to remember, and so distorts perceptions of their relative frequency on the list. Remember from Chapter 5 that people who suffer from insomnia tend to overestimate the amount of time it takes them to fall asleep. They are likely to make their estimates from instances that are readily available—memories of nights on which they had a particularly difficult time falling asleep.

The availability heuristic is often used in estimating risks. In one study, people were asked to estimate the likelihood of dying of various causes (Slovic, Fischhoff, & Lichtenstein, 1976, 1980). Subjects greatly overestimated the risks posed by highly dramatic and well-publicized hazards—tornadoes, nuclear accidents, and homicides, for example. At the same time, they greatly underestimated the risk of diseases such as diabetes, tuberculosis, and asthma, which are rarely reported as a cause of death in the news. Apparently, the recollection of the causes of death is affected by media coverage; and because media coverage is unrelated to mortality rates, in this instance reliance on the availability heuristic can be misleading.

Psychologists who study such misperceptions do not conclude that heuristics are useless, however (Sherman & Corty, 1984). They acknowledge that these intuitive strategies can save cognitive effort and often produce quite accurate judgments. But heuristics can blind us to other relevant information. Even experienced research psychologists, trained extensively in statistics, often make the very same errors as the average person when estimating odds (Tversky & Kahneman, 1971, 1981). According to one view, then, humans are generally earnest but rather error-prone judgers of odds.

Laboratory Results versus Real Life

The problem with this view of humans as error-prone decision makers is that it contradicts the way we tend to see ourselves. Most of us do not have the sense that we muddle through life uncertainly, repeatedly miscalculating our chances and seldom learning from our mistakes. Could we really be consistently poor at judging probabilities, yet totally oblivious to our incompetence? A number of researchers suspect not.

What are we to make, then, of the decision-making errors so often demonstrated in the laboratory? Some psychologists have noted that the findings are not completely consistent (Evans, 1982). For example, the vividness of an event does not always distort a subject's impression of how frequently an event occurred (Taylor & Thompson, 1981). The same is true of other heuristics. The reason people misuse heuristics so often in laboratory studies may be that the deck has been stacked against them. Consider the study in which subjects were asked to estimate the probability that a certain personality profile belonged to a lawyer or an engineer. Did you really think Jack's profile was drawn at random from a real-life sample? Probably not; Jack probably seemed so stereotypical of an engineer that it was hard to believe the experimenters had not created him on purpose (which of course they did). In that respect, the experimenters were encouraging subjects to base their judgments on the representativeness heuristic (Lopes, 1989). Significantly, when a personality profile is drawn from a sample of real lawyers and engineers, subjects are much more inclined to consider prior probabilities (Gigerenzer, Hell, & Blank, 1988).

The deck is also stacked against subjects in the typical odds-judging study, in that they do not have a chance to acquire feedback about their mistakes and modify their answers accordingly (Hogarth, 1981). In real life skilled racquetball players are likely to deduce that a longer game gives them an added advantage over less skilled players. Humans, after all, are very good learners; studies show that they can easily learn to reason about everyday events using statistical concepts like sample size and prior probabilities (Nisbett et al., 1987). Even brief feedback regarding these concepts can enhance one's ability to judge odds.

Finally, heuristics do not always yield the wrong answer, as some experiments seem to imply (Lopes, 1989). Sometimes they are both quick and accurate ways to judge odds, and often they are valuable short-cuts to solving problems. Depending on the circumstances, then, reliance on heuristics can be intuitively perceptive or intuitively naive.

Language

Almost certainly, the most important cognitive process humans possess is language. Language allows humans to communicate with each other in ways no other species can. Though we commonly use the word *language* to describe many different types of communication—for example, we may refer to some gestures as *body language*—language is much more than a form of communication.

Language is symbolic: it involves the use of sounds to symbolize or represent objects, events, and ideas. The choice of symbols is completely arbitrary. Though the collection of bound, printed pages in front of you is called a *book*, there is nothing inherently "right" about that label. Speakers of German convey the same meaning with the word *buch,* and Italians with the word *libro.* Language is simply a set of conventions that speakers agree to share. Human language is an incredibly rich form of communication. There is virtually nothing you might want to express that you cannot say with words. Because of its symbolic nature, human language is not tied to the present. With it we can describe the past and plan for the future. Nor is language rooted only in concrete objects or events: we can talk about fictitious or imaginary events as well.

Language is also incredibly versatile in the enormous variety of ways in which words can be combined. As a result, what we can say with language is virtually unlimited. Linguists have estimated that a person would need 10,000 billion years—nearly 2,000 times the estimated age of the earth—to say all the twenty-word sentences possible in English.

Finally, language is incredibly complex, yet humans use language with no formal instruction. With the exception of those suffering serious neurological impairments, all humans learn language. As a result, most psychologists now agree that language is innately human: all members of the species will learn and use language (Lieberman, 1991; Pinker, 1994). We will examine language development in Chapter 9. But what about other species, such as chimpanzees and dolphins? Can they acquire and use language as well? This fascinating question is the subject of this chapter's "In Depth" section.

Understanding and Producing Language

Humans use and understand language with extraordinary facility. When we speak, our thoughts seem to be converted into words with little or no effort.

Only occasionally do we struggle to express our ideas. Similarly, when we listen to someone else speak, we process roughly 200 syllables a minute, quickly combining the stream of sounds into words and phrases and retrieving the meaning of what we have heard. Though these tasks seem easy to us, they are far from simple. Very complex mental processes underlie both.

Speech: From Sounds to Words

Humans can produce a great number of vocal sounds. Each language uses just a few of those sounds as the fundamental building blocks of speech. The smallest units of sound in a language are called **phonemes.** In English, the sound of the [*k*] in *kite* is a phoneme—the same phoneme that is represented by the *c* in *carrot* and the *ch* in *character*. Kite has two other phonemes, the sound of the long [*i*] and the sound of the [*t*]. Phonemes can be thought of as sound categories. Our task in hearing speech sounds is to place the sounds in the correct sound categories. This process is rapid and automatic, and involves hearing many different physical sounds as "the same." As a result, we hear regularities in speech even though the sounds different speakers make are not identical.

Phonemes are combined into **morphemes,** or meaningful units of speech that cannot be subdivided without losing their meaningfulness. Most English morphemes are words that can stand alone—*play, stop*—but some are prefixes and suffixes that must be combined with freestanding morphemes to convey meaning (*player, nonstop*).

Most speakers say the phonemes in words so quickly that they tend to run together, so that the sound of one is still being heard as the next begins. Thus each phoneme is modified by the sounds of its neighbors—something that makes the job of perceiving phonemes quite difficult. Yet most of us do not struggle to identify phonemes; in fact, we hear them with great clarity. How do we manage to perceive the sounds of speech so readily? One answer is that the human brain has certain structures that are specialized for perceiving phonemes (Lieberman, 1991; Liberman & Mattingly, 1989; Pinker, 1994), structures that are separate from those we use to identify nonspeech noises.

The ability to detect phonemes quickly and accurately has obvious evolutionary value. It allows us to use our short-term memories more efficiently: in a sense, we can "pack" more information into our short-term memories by using phonemes. It also allows us to identify distinct phonemes from the blur of sounds of everyday speech almost instantaneously, without the need for higher-level cognitive processing. Because of these innate mechanisms, listeners "hear" things that may not actually be present in speech. For example, most of the breaks between words in a sentence are added by the listener (Pinker, 1994). Speech itself is mostly a long, unbroken stream of sounds. But because we hear these sounds as recognizable phonemes, we hear the words in speech as being separate and distinct. The next time you come across a radio or TV broadcast in a language you cannot recognize, try to listen for the breaks between words. You will probably find it very difficult.

Our tendency to categorize sounds plays a large role in the "backward masking" effects described in Chapter 5. When a tape recording is played backward, the sounds usually become jumbled and all but impossible to understand. Some of these meaningless sounds, however, may be close enough to normal phonemes that we can "recognize" them. And by chance, some random combinations may approximate the phonemes in actual words, or even sentences. About twenty years ago, the song "Another One Bites the Dust" (by the rock group Queen) was quite popular. Many people reported being able to hear "It's fun to smoke marijuana" when the chorus was played backward.[1]

Comprehension: From Words to Meaning

Recognizing phonemes and combining them into morphemes and words is only the first step in understanding language. For language to be useful, we take these morphological units and combine them into meaningful expression. The process of determining the meaning of a string of words and morphemes is called **comprehension.** Just as phoneme detection involves hearing things that might not be physically present in speech (such as the spaces between words), comprehension is an active, constructive process. Understanding the meaning of

---

[1]This is perhaps the most striking example of so-called backward-masking. Once the listeners are told what to listen for, almost all report hearing the phrase clearly. There is absolutely no reason to believe the effect was intentional, however, nor is there cause to fear for those who listen to the song.

FIGURE 8-11 A tree diagram for the sentence: My eccentric neighbor wears red suspenders.

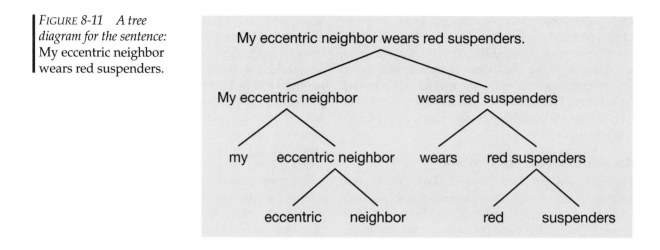

FIGURE 8-11 A tree diagram for the sentence: My eccentric neighbor wears red suspenders.

sentences is yet another illustration of Recurring Theme 4, "Cognition and thought are dynamic, active processes, best considered reconstructive, not reproductive."

THEME 4 Cognition and Thought Are Dynamic, Active Processes, Best Considered Reconstructive, Not Reproductive

How do we extract the message a writer or speaker intends? How is meaning represented "inside the head"? In most cases, comprehension, like memory, is not a literal process. Instead, most researchers believe, when we read a sentence, we automatically dissect it into phrases and subphrases called constituents. A **constituent** is a group of words that make sense when placed together. Thus the sentence "My eccentric neighbor wears red suspenders" divides naturally into two major constituents: the noun phrase "my eccentric neighbor" and the verb phrase "wears red suspenders." These phrases may be further divided into smaller constituents, as Figure 8-11 shows. You may remember being asked to diagram sentences in junior high or high school. When you identified noun phrases and verb phrases, you were analyzing the constituents of a sentence.

From constituents, readers and listeners extract underlying **propositions,** the smallest "idea units" in a sentence. Propositions are somewhat like morphemes (defined as the smallest units of language that have meaning), but they are much larger. In addition, while morphemes convey meaning, often their meaning can be understood only in the context of other morphemes. For example, in the word *cats,* the final morpheme [s] turns the singular form (*cat*)

into the plural form (*cats*). In isolation, however, the morpheme [s] is meaningless. Propositions, by contrast, represent discrete, complete *ideas,* and as such they do not require other propositions to be meaningful. The actual meaning of a message is thought to be represented in propositions (Kintsch, 1974; see also Weaver, Mannes, & Fletcher, 1995).

Most researchers agree that with the exception of statements we must memorize verbatim (the Lord's Prayer or the Pledge of Allegiance), we store the *gist* of a statement in long-term memory, not the exact wording, and the gist is represented using propositions (Kintsch & Kennan, 1974; Ratcliff & McKoon, 1978). The linguist Noam Chomsky (1957, 1972) uses the terms *surface structure* and *deep structure* to convey a similar distinction. The exact wording of a sentence is its surface structure, while the meaning is the deep structure. Sentences may differ in their surface structure but convey the same deep structure. For example, though "Jenni made the highest score in the class" has a different surface structure from "The highest score in the class was made by Jenni," the deep structure of the two sentences is identical. Figure 8-12 illustrates surface and deep structures, and how differently worded sentences can have the same underlying propositions.

Sometimes the deep structure bears almost no relationship to the surface structure. Idioms, for example, are not meant to be understood literally (Gibbs, 1992a, 1992b). "Tom let the cat out of the bag" has nothing to do with cats or bags. Yet you would have no trouble relating it to the following sentence: "The party won't be any fun now!" Other common expressions, if they are interpreted literally, are oxy-

The sentence:

> **(1) My eccentric neighbor wears red suspenders.**

contains three distinct propositions, each of which conveys a separate idea:

PROPOSITION 1: *My neighbor wears suspenders.*
PROPOSITION 2: *My neighbor is eccentric.*
PROPOSITION 3: *The suspenders are red.*

The propositions represent the *deep structure* (the meaning) of a message, without preserving the *surface structure* (the exact wording).

In Sentences (2–4), the *deep structure* is identical to that of Sentence (1). However, the *surface structure* of Sentences (2–4) differs from that of Sentence (1).

> **(2) Red suspenders are worn by my eccentric neighbor.**

> **(3) The suspenders worn by eccentric neighbor are red.**

> **(4) My neighbor, who is eccentric, wears suspenders that are red.**

▌ *FIGURE 8-12   Examples of propositions and their relationship to surface and deep structures.*

moronic, such as "parting is such sweet sorrow" or "the loyal opposition" (Gibbs & Kearney, 1994). To give another example, for years children laughed at Peggy Parish's *Amelia Bedelia* stories. Amelia Bedelia, the maid who takes instructions given to her literally, processed information at the level of its surface structure rather than its deep structure. After a series of mishaps, Amelia's employers eventually learned to ask her to "un-dust" (rather than "dust") the furniture, to "close" (rather than "draw") the drapes, and so on. Even young children appreciate the humor inherent in mistaking surface for deep structures.

Semantics versus Syntactic: Meaning versus Rules

Psycholinguists routinely differentiate between the semantic and the syntactic aspects of language. The **semantic** properties of language have to do with the comprehension and expression of meaning. The **syntactic** properties are the rules that determine the allowable combinations of words, phrases, and sentences. The syntax of a language need not be explicit—in fact, the complete syntactic rules of English have yet to be determined—but native speakers of a language use them appropriately anyway.

Knowledge of the syntax of a language is an excellent example of procedural memory (see Chapter 7).

To grasp the difference between semantics and syntax, consider the opening lines of Lewis Carroll's poem "Jabberwocky":

> 'Twas brillig, and the slithy toves
> Did gyre and gimble in the wabe:
> All mimsy were the borogoves,
> And the mome raths outgrabe.

The passage is nonsense, of course, yet speakers of English would agree that it conforms to conventional rules of grammar. The syntax is fine, but the semantic content is missing. Next, consider the following statement, which might have been spoken by a three-year-old child: "I runned but I couldn't never catch up! I got hurrier and hurrier, Daddy, but I kept getting behinder and behinder." This statement clearly violates several rules of standard English, but the meaning is easily understood. In fact, the semantic content of a sentence can often be understood even if it contains gross errors in syntax. If you have ever traveled in a country where you had only a passing knowledge of the language, you were probably surprised at how well you could communicate with only a few nouns and verbs. We will have much more to say about the acquisition of syntax and semantics in Chapter 9, when we study language acquisition.

Speech in Social Context

In speaking and listening, meaning often depends on more than words alone. The same words ("Oh great! *He's* going to be our leader!") in one setting might indicate a compliment, in another, sarcasm. And in some situations a question is really a request: "Can you close the window?" In these cases, not only must we transform the propositions we want to express into grammatically correct sentences, but we must also construct those sentences in ways that are appropriate to the social situation. The goal of speaking, after all, is to influence others, to allow them to understand our ideas and intentions, and to encourage them to respond in favorable ways (Clark, Flavell, & Markman, 1983). To do so, we must follow certain socially accepted conventions about how people talk to one another. The study of the use of social rules to structure language is part of a growing field called **pragmatics** (Miller & Glucksberg, 1988).

One example of pragmatics can be seen in how speakers of English phrase their requests. Although giving a direct order would often be easier ("Dust the living room"), social rules encourage more polite, indirect forms ("Don't you think the dust is getting awfully thick?" or "Isn't it your turn to dust?"). Listeners do not answer such questions with a simple "yes" or "no." Instead, they interpret them as requests to perform some behavior (Labov & Fanshel, 1977).

To add even more complexity to the social rules that govern speech, the rules tend to vary based on the social context. For instance, a woman would probably phrase a request to mow the lawn differently to her husband than to her teenage son. In the first situation, the social equality between the two speakers demands an indirect phrasing ("Were you planning to mow the lawn today?"). In the second, the power differential allows a blunter approach ("Get that lawn cut before you go off with your friends"). Even between the same two speakers, speech style varies depending on the topic. Two doctors would use much more formal language to discuss a diagnosis than to review yesterday's tennis match. All these and many other social conventions

are part of our implicit knowledge of how sentences should be formed (Levinson, 1983).

Language versus Thought: The Linguistic Relativity Hypothesis

Psychologists have long wondered about the relationship between language and thought. Some speculate that language determines how people think, as well as what they can think about. "The limits of my language," wrote philosopher Ludwig Wittgenstein (1922–1963) "are the limits of my world."

Yet the relationship between language and thought cannot be strictly one-sided. If language can influence thought, thought must also be able to influence language. At the very least, human cognitive capabilities must impose some limit on how language can be structured and used. And since language is a means of communication, a way of conveying information about objects and events, it seems likely that language will be influenced by what people experience and learn.

Does Language Determine Thought?

One of the strongest proponents of the idea that language shapes thought was the linguist Benjamin Lee Whorf. Whorf (1956) argued that the way people perceive the world is determined largely by the vocabulary and structural rules of their native language. For example, English has a single word, *snow,* while Eskimo—according to Whorf—has more than twenty terms for various types of snow: fluffy, drifting, packed, and so forth. Whorf theorized that the existence of many different words for snow causes the Eskimos' thought and perceptions to differ from ours.

Likewise, Whorf called Hopi a "timeless" language, because it does not force a speaker to distinguish between the present, past, and future. English, in contrast, always does so; English speakers must either inflect their verbs to show tense ("He talks," "He talked") or designate tense through their choice of words ("Tomorrow I talk"). This grammatical convention, Whorf reasoned, forces English speakers to keep careful track of time. The idea that language influences thought in such ways is called the **linguistic relativity hypothesis.**

Does language actually influence thought to the extent Whorf believed? Today's scholars believe it does not, for at least two reasons. First, Whorf mis-

Television production workers use a special vocabulary to describe the work they do; the Hopi Indians have no word for "time," at least not in the sense used in Western culture; and expert skiers use different words to describe different kinds of snow. Do such differences in language cause people to perceive the world differently? The answer appears to be no; language does not necessarily determine thought.

represented the differences among languages. Sternberg (1996) writes, "Some of the implications [of the linguistic relativity hypothesis] have reached mythical proportions; for example, many social scientists have warmly accepted and gladly propagated the notion that Eskimos have multitudinous words for the single English word *snow*." But recent research (Martin, 1986) has presented compelling evidence that Eskimos do *not* have multiple words for *snow*. Because so many psychologists accepted Whorf's statement at face value regarding Eskimos, it has been called "the great Eskimo vocabulary hoax" (Pullum, 1991). Malotki (1983) came to a similar conclusion after studying the Hopi. He found that Hopi speakers do make reference to time, though they tend to express the concept in ways that are unfamiliar to English speakers.

Second, despite the fact that different languages may describe the world in different ways, research has shown that people's perceptions of the world are the same. For example, languages differ markedly in the number of color terms they contain. In fact, the number of basic color terms—those terms that consist of one word and are not subsumed under another color—varies from two to eleven. Do people whose language has only a few basic terms for color perceive the same distinctions between colors as people whose language has many more terms? According to Whorf, they should not; yet studies show that they do (Berlin & Kay, 1969; Rosch, 1973). The Dani, a tribe native to New Guinea, have but two words for color, but they still perceive the world as speakers of English do; they simply have a different way of describing it (Rosch, 1973).

While language does not *determine* thought, the words that are used to describe something or someone can certainly *influence* thought. The recent trend toward nondiscriminatory language reflects this influence.

Comprehending Written Language: Reading

Many years ago, psychologists considered reading to be a "natural" extension of spoken language. Children were expected to learn to read with the same relative ease with which they acquired spoken language. Today, almost all psychologists recognize that learning to read is difficult—probably more difficult than most of us realize. Unlike the acquisition of spoken language, learning to read takes motivation, instruction, and a tremendous amount of practice. Adams (1990) estimates that skilled reading requires between 1,000 and 2,000 hours of practice. If a child gets 30 minutes of direct reading practice each day in school (a reasonable estimate), and no additional practice outside of school, that child will take over *10 years* to become a proficient reader.

Reading relies heavily on the sound-based components in short-term memory. Thus, reading researchers recommend a phonetic approach to beginning reading (Weaver, 1994). In phonetics instruction, beginning readers are taught to match the arbitrary symbols of our written language with the corresponding sounds. Once the symbol-sound association has been formed, the child can begin to combine letters (and phonemes) together, and thus to read.

The children's television show *Sesame Street* provides a wonderful model for teaching symbol-to-sound associations. A letter, say, *S*, is shown while the narrator says the letter's name ("ess"). The cartoon letter may turn into an object that begins with the letter—in this case, perhaps a snake—while the narrator repeats the letter's name and sound, and uses it in a sentence ("The *S*lippery *S*nake *S*lid down the *S*lope"). This kind of phonetic instruction is especially beneficial to young children—those just beginning to read (Adams, 1994; Adams & Bruck, 1995).

In sum, reading is not a simple extension of spoken language. As we will discuss in the next chapter, humans are genetically predisposed to acquire spoken language. All normal children raised in a normal environment will learn to speak. The same cannot be said about written language, however. Learning to read is not an automatic and effortless process. Children who do not receive adequate instruction, motivation, and practice may not learn to read.

In Depth

Can Other Animals Learn Language?

In a primate research center, a chimpanzee helps his trainer to carry a tray full of objects to an electronic keyboard. The chimp touches one of the objects—a small piece of string—and then turns to the keyboard, where he presses a symbol that his trainer has designated as the "word" for string. Next, the chimp hands the piece of string to the trainer, chattering excitedly. The trainer responds by praising the chimp and giving him a piece of candy (based on Savage-Rumbaugh, Romski, Sevcik, & Pate, 1983).

Is this chimp using language in a rudimentary way, or does it just *seem* to be using language as a result of careful operant conditioning? Can other animals learn to use language? Recall the story told by Jane Goodall, which opened Chapter 6 (p. 183). A young female chimpanzee, terrified of having been returned to live with wild-born chimpanzees, recognized a visitor from her "old days" in the language laboratory. The chimpanzee rushed over and signed, "Please help. Out." Was she aware of what she was "saying," or was she simply making responses that had been rewarded in the past? Interest in these questions has generated several efforts to teach language to intelligent mammals, especially chimpanzees.

Initial Studies

As early as the 1940s, psychologists realized that chimpanzees would never be able to learn spoken language (Hayes & Hayes, 1951). Chimps lack the specially adapted tongue, lips, teeth, facial muscles, and palate that allow humans to produce a wide variety of speech sounds (see Figure 8-13). Thus, studying language in chimps would require non-speech-based communication.

Beatrice and Allen Gardner (Gardner & Gardner, 1972) tried teaching American Sign Language (ASL), the universal sign language used by many deaf people in North America, to chimpanzees. ASL is based on a system of gestures, each corresponding to a word. Since chimpanzees are extremely nimble-fingered and use gestures spontaneously, they seemed well-suited to learn ASL.

The Gardners began their research with a one-year-old chimp named Washoe, whom they raised almost as though she were a child. The Gardners and their associates signed to Washoe and to one another just as deaf parents might. Whenever Washoe signed correctly, they rewarded her. Because Washoe was raised among her teachers, she had many opportunities to learn signs. After four years of training she

Can non-humans acquire language? Though many animals, like the bonobo shown here, display sophisticated forms of communication, most psychologists now believe they are incapable of acquiring true language.

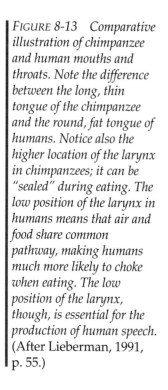

FIGURE 8-13 *Comparative illustration of chimpanzee and human mouths and throats. Note the difference between the long, thin tongue of the chimpanzee and the round, fat tongue of humans. Notice also the higher location of the larynx in chimpanzees; it can be "sealed" during eating. The low position of the larynx in humans means that air and food share common pathway, making humans much more likely to choke when eating. The low position of the larynx, though, is essential for the production of human speech.* (After Lieberman, 1991, p. 55.)

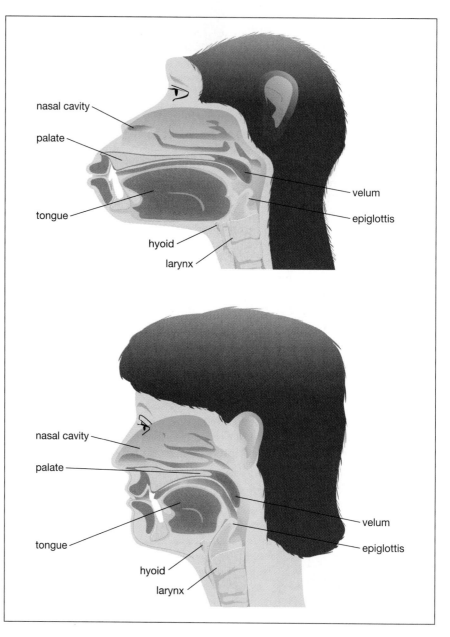

had acquired about 160 signs. A few of them are shown in Figure 8-14.

The Gardners observed many similarities between Washoe's progress and that of a young child who is learning spoken language. Once Washoe had learned a particular sign, she sometimes generalized its use to other activities or objects. For instance, after learning the sign to request "more tickling," she used the same gesture to request "more swinging" and "more food." Many of her mistakes resembled those com-monly made by children, such as when she overgen-eralized the sign for flower to refer to all kinds of smells. Furthermore, as soon as Washoe had learned eight or ten signs, she began to combine them spon-taneously, forming statements such as "More sweet" and "Roger come." Later she learned to combine three or more signs: "Hurry gimme toothbrush" and "You me go there in." By the time Washoe reached the age of five, the Gardners felt her command of lan-guage resembled that of a three-year-old child.

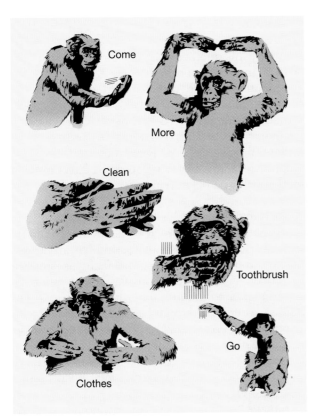

FIGURE 8-14   *Hand signs used by the Gardners'*
chimpanzee Washoe during the first two years of
training. The signs are presented in order of their
acquisition. After learning eight to ten signs, Washoe
began to combine them spontaneously to form
statements similar to those children make when they
are learning spoken language. The most common
combinations involved signals the Gardners called
emphasizers *(signals for "please," "come-gimme,"*
"hurry," and "more") and one other signal. Washoe
also used sequences of more than two signs involving
names or pronouns, such as "You go gimme," "Roger
you tickle," or "Please Roger come."

Washoe's accomplishments were not unique. In another research project, psychologist David Premack (1971a; 1971b) taught a chimpanzee named Sarah a language based on small plastic symbols of varying colors and shapes, each of which stood for a word. Sarah learned to construct simple sentences by arranging the symbols on a magnetized board. Premack's system was easier for a chimp to learn than ASL. Since the symbols were right in front of Sarah, she could use them as cues to recall their

meanings. Furthermore, the symbols Premack used to communicate with Sarah removed some of the demands placed on a chimp's short-term memory. A major drawback, however, was that Sarah became mute when she did not have her symbols.

In yet another approach, Duane Rumbaugh and colleagues (Rumbaugh, Gill, & von Glaserfeld, 1963) taught a chimp named Lana to operate a special typewriter linked to a computer. The machine had fifty keys, each of which displayed a geometric configuration representing a word. When Lana typed a configuration, it appeared on a screen in front of her. She learned to correct herself by checking the sequence of configurations as they appeared on screen. Not only did she respond to humans who conversed with her via her computer, but she initiated conversations with them. And when confronted with an object for which she had no word, Lana sometimes created a word. For example, when shown a ring, Lana identified it using words she already knew: "finger bracelet."

Can chimpanzees use language as humans do? Some researchers, such as the Gardners, believe that they can. These researchers argue that Washoe and other language-trained chimps use symbols meaningfully and accurately. Like humans, they can refer to things removed in time and space (such as an apple they saw a while ago, which is now in the refrigerator). There is also some evidence that chimps can create novel and appropriate word combinations, based on simple grammatical rules. (Lana's "finger bracelet," for instance, correctly combines a noun and a modifier.) Such word combinations suggest that chimps have at least some capacity for understanding elementary syntax.

Criticisms, Alternatives, and Further Research

Not all researchers agree with the Gardners. David Premack (1976) has wondered whether the linguistic creativity of chimpanzees is limited to word substitutions in restricted sentence structures—"Mary eat apple," for example, transformed to "Mary wash apple." The psychologist Herbert Terrace, who spent nearly four years teaching sign language to a young male chimp named Nim Chimpsky, has expressed similar reservations (Terrace, 1979). While working with Nim, Terrace became convinced that the chimp was indeed combining words into grammatical units comparable to a child's first sentences. But after analyzing the data he had collected, Terrace began to doubt that Nim's achievements were as sophisticated as a child's. A child's sentences soon grow in both length and complexity, as the child masters more and more rules of syntax. But though Nim sometimes produced fairly lengthy sequences, his grasp of syntax did not expand. Furthermore, an analysis of videotaped conversations with Nim revealed that many of Nim's utterances were partial imitations of statements a teacher had just made. Terrace believes that subtle prompting by human trainers, coupled with the delivery of rewards, may account for much of a chimp's use of language. Chimps, he argues, may have the potential to create grammatical sentences, but that potential has not yet been proved.

Following these pessimistic reports, interest in teaching language to chimps waned. Instead, Louis Herman and his colleagues (Herman, 1989; Herman, Richards, & Wolz, 1984) began to explore language acquisition in dolphins. Though Herman's work at first appeared promising, recent evaluations of language training in dolphins have been generally negative (e.g., Premack, 1986; Schusterman & Gisner, 1989).

Sue Savage-Rumbaugh (1983) and her colleagues adopted a different strategy. They tried teaching the principle of "naming" to two chimpanzees, Sherman and Austin, using keyboard symbols to represent objects, qualities, and actions. In one procedure, the researchers placed five to seven different kinds of food on a table out of sight of the keyboard. Each chimp was then allowed to go to the table, look over the foods, decide which one he wanted to eat, and return to the keyboard to indicate his choice. Next, one of the researchers gave the chimps permission to retrieve their desired foods. If the chimps came back with the right items, they were allowed to eat. If not, the researcher expressed dismay, pointing to the symbol the chimp had used. Both Sherman and Austin learned to perform this and similar "naming" tasks with very few errors. Their trainers concluded that the animals understood the meaning of the keyboard symbols.

Savage-Rumbaugh's most impressive discovery, however, occurred almost by accident. She was working with a different primate species, the bonobo, or "pygmy chimp" (*Pan paniscus*). Don't be fooled by the name "pygmy chimp": bonobos are quite large (the animal in the photograph on page 283 weighs

110 pounds). During Savage-Rumbaugh's work, a young bonobo named Kanzi had been allowed to accompany his mother, Matala, as she was being trained and tested. From the time Kanzi was about six months old, he watched and listened as researchers attempted to teach his mother linguistic symbols (lexigrams) on a keyboard. After watching his mother for about a year, Kanzi began to respond to the symbols on the keyboard. Savage-Rumbaugh emphasizes that Kanzi never received direct training on this task, and his responses were never reinforced with food.

As Kanzi followed his human caretakers around in the large facility, which covered more than 50 acres, he learned that food was hidden in various places throughout the forest. If Kanzi was shown a picture of one of the foods, he was able to guide the experimenter to the location where that food was hidden. After certain foods had been associated with arbitrary symbols, Kanzi responded to the symbols just as he did to the photographs. Sometimes the location of the food required that the chimp walk more than half an hour, but even after long delays Kanzi made few errors.

Kanzi's most impressive ability, though, was his response to spoken English. Like other chimps, Kanzi responded to spoken English—by itself, not a surprising result. You may have had a dog who responded to words like *walk* (by rushing to the door) and *ball* (by retrieving a tennis ball). But when Savage-Rumbaugh, Murphy, Sevcik, Brakke, Williams, and Rumbaugh (cited in Barker, 1997) examined Kanzi's responses to more than 650 interactions with humans, and compared them to those of a two-year-old child in the same situations, they concluded that Kanzi understood more than the two-year-old.

Finally, unlike previously studied chimpanzees, all of whom were "common chimpanzees" (*Pan troglodytes*) rather than bonobos, Kanzi displayed language-like vocalizations. According to Savage-Rumbaugh, Kanzi has spoken words such as *bunny, tomato,* and *good,* and has produced vocalizations that sound like *orange, snake, raisin, knife,* and many other words.

Patterns and Conclusions

The research by Sue Savage-Rumbaugh and her colleagues has rekindled an interest in the linguistic capabilities of nonhuman species. Clearly, human language is qualitatively different from the forms of communication seen in other species. However, Kanzi's remarkable abilities have redirected psychologists' attention to the forms of communication chimpanzees *can* use.

The long-term impact of Savage-Rumbaugh's research with Kanzi is not yet clear. Other language projects with nonhumans at first appeared promising, but later proved disappointing. Kanzi appears to be different, though. As Barker (1997) writes, "The crucial difference appears to be that 'someone's home' in the pygmy chimp's [Kanzi's] head. . . . At the risk of being overly dramatic, Savage-Rumbaugh's interactions with Kanzi may be considered the most successful attempt yet in establishing contact with another species" (p. 473).

SUMMARY

1. **Concepts**—the mental constructions involved in classifying together those things that have features in common—enable us to make generalizations and thus to engage in complex thought. The **prototype** model offers a good description of how we mentally structure the **natural concepts** we use every day. According to this model, we acquire a mental image of a "best example" or prototype, plus an implicit sense of how far a stimulus can vary from this prototype and still be an instance of the concept.

2. A knowledge of concepts and relationships among them makes problem solving possible. A critical step in solving a problem successfully is the initial representation, that is, the way we first view the problem's components. Viewing a problem from different angles can help produce more effective representations. Such flexibility can also break **functional fixedness**, the tendency to see objects as having only their customary uses.

3. After representing a problem, we must often manipulate data to reach a final solution. One approach to this task is called an **algorithm**, a precisely stated set of rules that works for solving all problems of a particular kind. An alternative approach is to use a **heuristic**, or rule-of-thumb strategy. One general heuristic is **subgoal analysis**, by which a person breaks down a large problem into smaller problems of more manageable size. Another general heuristic is **means-end analysis**, by which a person tries to narrow the gap between a current position and a desired goal. A third general heuristic is the **backward search**, by which the prob-

lem solver starts at the end point and works backward to discover how to get there. Just as flexibility is important when initially representing a problem, so it is also important when selecting a problem-solving strategy. Unfortunately, there is a common tendency to stick with approaches that have worked in the past. Such **mental sets** can hinder problem solving.

4. It is not always easy to determine when you have found the best solution to a problem. Experimenting with different solutions is often necessary before making a final choice. People are frequently willing to settle for a less-than-perfect solution if a continued search for the ideal one places too great a demand on cognitive capacity.

5. Creative solutions to problems may come suddenly and unpredictably, often when the person is not actively working on the task. This has led some researchers to suspect that many creative inspirations are partly the products of unconscious thought. Other factors—such as knowledge, strong motivation and persistence, and a willingness to take risks—also contribute to creativity.

6. According to rational models of decision making, we systematically consider two basic factors in making choices: the **utility** or value of each potential outcome and the probability or likelihood that those outcomes will occur. We are not always rational decision makers, however. When a decision is fairly complex and requires that we process substantial amounts of information, we tend to reduce our choices to simpler ones by concentrating on a few of the relevant

factors and largely ignoring others. In short, we make many choices by using heuristics.

7. The use of heuristics can be seen in decisions that involve estimating odds. Sometimes we assess odds by judging how representative a given stimulus is to a larger class of stimuli. This is called the **representativeness heuristic.** Other times we estimate odds by the ease with which instances of something come to mind. This is called the **availability heuristic.** When either heuristic causes us to ignore pertinent information, our resulting decisions may be poor.

8. Another important cognitive process is the use of language, a highly rich and flexible means of communication. The processes of producing and comprehending language are very complex. Language production involves transforming units of meaning, called **propositions,** into a spoken or written sentence. In order for that sentence to be understood properly, it must be correct both grammatically and in terms of the social rules that govern language (an area of study called **pragmatics**). Comprehending language is essentially the reverse process. We transform a sentence into its underlying propositions. In doing so we seem to rely on both **syntactic** cues and the meaning of key content words. We are also constantly making inferences about other people's speech based on our general knowledge of the world and our expectations about conversations.

9. Psychologists are also interested in the relationship between language and thought. Linguist Benjamin Lee Whorf argued that the vocabulary and syntax of a language strongly affect how people perceive the world, a view called the **linguistic relativity hypothesis.** But Whorf has been challenged by evidence that all humans tend to perceive their surroundings in similar ways, regardless of differences in their languages. There is more support for the idea that thought influences language. Researchers have found that broadly shared patterns of human cognition seem to give rise to linguistic universals (features common to all languages).

10. Efforts to teach language to other primates have shown that chimpanzees may be capable of learning a communication system with *some* of the basic features of human language. But even the smartest ape's aptitude for language is limited compared with that of a normal human.

SUGGESTED READINGS

Csikszentmihalyi, M. (1996). *Creativity: Flow and the psychology of discovery and invention.* New York: HarperCollins. A thorough look into the process of creativity, written for a nontechnical reader

Dawes, R. M. (1988). *Rational choice in an uncertain world.* New York: Harcourt Brace Jovanovich. Compares principles of rationality with actual behavior in making decisions. Charming anecdotes are used liberally as a teaching device.

Gardner, H. (1993). *Creating minds.* New York: Basic Books. A wonderful book by one of the leading researchers in the areas of intelligence and creativity.

Levine, M. (1988). *Effective problem-solving.* Englewood Cliffs, NJ: Prentice-Hall. Excellent "how to" book that gives advice on solving problems more effectively, including interpersonal problems.

Lieberman, P. (1991). Uniquely human: The evolution of speech, thought, and selfless behavior. Cambridge, MA: Harvard University Press. A highly regarded language and speech researcher not only discusses basic elements of language but offers an intriguing account of the role of language in human culture.

Medin, D. L., & Ross, M. W. (1992). *Cognitive psychology.* Ft. Worth: Harcourt Brace.

Solso, R. L. (1996). *Cognitive psychology* (4th ed.). Boston: Allyn & Bacon. Two excellent texts in cognitive psychology, both of which cover a broad range of topics.

CHAPTER 9

Cognitive Development

The third author of this book has two wonderful children: Austin, who at the time of this writing was a little older than four, and Lindsay, a little older than three. At the time they were like most children their age: they loved to pick at each other and start little fights, sometimes about the most inconsequential things. One argument they had, in particular, is fascinating, from a developmental perspective.

We were driving past a florist's shop, a building the children knew well. In the window was a picture of a bride in her wedding gown, bouquet in hand. As we drove past the shop, Lindsay seemed to notice the picture for the first time. "It's Mommy!" she cried. I chuckled, corrected her, and then forgot about the incident.

The next few days, each time we drove past the shop, Lindsay exclaimed, "It's Mommy!" Finally one day, Austin turned to her and said, "No, Lindsay. It's not Mommy. It's *like* Mommy." "No! It's Mommy!" Lindsay retorted. "It's not Mommy, it's *like* Mommy!" Austin insisted. At this point, the conversation degenerated into a shouting match.

Lindsay's categorization of the woman in

the picture as "Mommy" was intriguing. She had seen her mother's wedding pictures, not those of many other brides. Perhaps her "bride" *schema* included only Mommy. Austin's attempt to correct her was equally fascinating. Though he was only thirteen months older than Lindsay, he was demonstrating an ability, however rudimentary, to think metaphorically. He realized that though the woman in the picture shared many of Mommy's features, she was not the same person. Was his "Mommy" schema more refined than Lindsay's? Was his "bride" schema more refined? Did his ability to think abstractly ("It's not Mommy, but it's *like* Mommy") indicate that he had *learned more* than Lindsay, or did it reflect his greater maturity?

Intriguing too was Austin's attempt to explain the difference between a picture *of* Mommy and a picture *like* Mommy. Though he understood the difference, he could not articulate it. And neither, for the next few days, could his father. No matter what the explanation, Lindsay steadfastly replied, "No Daddy, it's Mommy!" Finally, a week later, as we drove past the flower shop, Lindsay observed, "Daddy! Daddy! Look! *It's like Mommy!*"

To a developmental psychologist, this story is more than amusing; it reflects very real differences in the capacity for thought among

Chapter Outline

Human Development as a Process

The Principle of Shared Developmental Sequences

The Influence of Heredity and Environment

The Psychologist's Perception of Human Development

Freud and the Developing Child

Watson and Childhood Learning

Piaget and the Thinking Child

Cognitive Development in Infants

Perceptual Capabilities

Reflexes and Motor Skills

Learning and Memory

Childhood Amnesia

Cognitive Development in Infancy and Childhood

Two Current Perspectives on Cognitive Development

The Two Perspectives Compared

Cognitive Development Through Middle Childhood

Piaget's Emphasis on Concrete Operations

An Alternative Perspective on Concrete Operations

Case's Integrative Theory

Language Acquisition

Milestones in Language Acquisition

Language Acquisition Explained

Memory Development

Changes in Information-Processing Strategies

Changes in Metacognition

Cognitive Development in Adolescence and Adulthood

Adolescent Cognitive Skills

Postformal Operations: A Fifth Stage of Cognitive Development?

Cognitive Change during Adulthood

In Depth: Nature versus Nurture in Language Acquisition: The Case of "Genie"

two children of different ages. The study of progressive changes in human traits and abilities that occur throughout the life span is the realm of **developmental psychology.** Psychologists approach human development from three perspectives. First, they are interested in physical development. What physiological changes take place throughout the life span? Some changes are obvious: at birth, the size of the human skull relative to the body is much larger than it is at any later time. As the individual matures, the relative size of the head decreases. The head still grows, of course, but at a much slower rate than the rest of the body.

Perhaps the most dramatic physiological changes occur at *puberty,* usually around the age of twelve or thirteen. During this period the individual experiences tremendous physical and mental growth, and becomes reproductively viable (capable of producing offspring). In this chapter we will consider certain aspects of physical development that are of particular interest to developmental psychologists. Though physical development is obviously important, psychologists are generally more interested in other aspects of development.

A second type of development that interests psychologists is **cognitive development,** or the changes associated with the "thinking" components of behavior. The ability to recognize the difference between a picture *of* Mommy and a picture *like* Mommy is a good example of cognitive development. Developmental psychologists would ask why this change takes place at certain ages. Is it the result of maturation? Or perhaps the result of learning from others' responses?

One aspect of cognitive development that has been studied in considerable detail is the acquisition of language, a remarkable cognitive task. The rules of almost any language are incredibly complex (remember trying to learn grammar in high school?), and yet by the age of four a child has mastered most of the subtleties, if not yet a complete vocabulary. How can a child learn such a complex skill with so little apparent effort? Part of the answer is that the acquisition of a language is not as easy as it appears to be. Children spend a great deal of time practicing their language skills. Even so, the ability to learn a language is one of the most impressive human cognitive skills any of us will acquire.

Another aspect of development psychologists are interested in is social and personality development.

Social development is concerned with how people learn to interact with others and with their environment. *Personality development* is concerned with the emergence of distinctive styles of thought, social interaction, and emotion—the qualities that make an individual unique. Social and personality development are clearly interwoven. How we learn to behave in the presence of an authority figure can be determined by social factors (such as the presence of other people in the room) or personality factors (such as aggressiveness). The outcome of these social interactions, in turn, helps to shape and mold an individual's personality. Social and personality development will be considered in Chapter 10.

Human Development as a Process

As you will see in this chapter, many psychologists refer to distinct "stages" in development. While this approach is common, and in many respects quite useful, it is important to keep in mind that development is best understood as a *process*, a series of small, almost imperceptible charges. Developmental processes are cumulative, so early developmental experiences may result in profound changes in later development.

The Principle of Shared Developmental Sequences

A fundamental principle of human development is that change occurs in broadly predictable patterns, or developmental sequences. Nowhere are these sequences more apparent than in physical growth and maturation (see Figure 9-1). At birth, a human infant is far from just a miniature adult. Aside from the newborn's relative weakness and lack of muscular coordination, a baby's body is proportioned very differently from an adult's: a baby's head is huge compared with the torso, and the legs are bent and stubby. But all this changes dramatically over the next several years. By the time children enter school, their bodies have taken on more mature proportions, in addition to increasing in strength, coordination, and height. Then, at puberty, further physical changes occur, usually quite rapidly. A boy's shoulders broaden; a girl's breasts and pelvis enlarge. Less sudden but equally predictable are the physical changes that occur through adulthood. With middle age, the body generally thickens and the muscles begin to lose their tone. By old age, changes in the

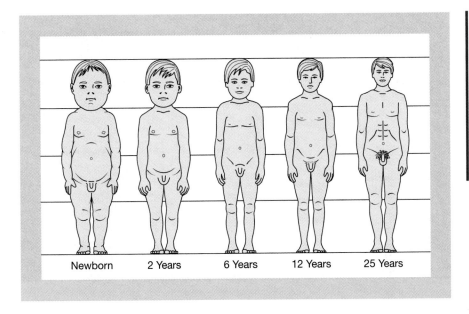

FIGURE 9-1 *Physiological changes associated with human development. This drawing shows the development of the human male from infancy to young adulthood. Note the changes in the proportion of the head and limbs in relation to the size of the body.* (After Robbins et al., 1986.)

| Newborn | 2 Years | 6 Years | 12 Years | 25 Years |

skeleton have often caused the body to shorten, and posture may have become slightly stooped.

Although the sequences associated with physical development are probably the most noticeable, they are not the only ones. Similar developmental sequences occur in perceptual abilities, intellectual skills, and styles of social interaction. Of course, all people develop differently, in many respects. Some, for instance, reach puberty much sooner than others. Some age quite quickly, while others age very gradually. All, however, eventually undergo much the same developmental changes. Most of the research we will be discussing focuses on these broadly shared sequences of change.

The Influence of Heredity and Environment

Some of the changes that occur over the life span clearly take place as the result of experience. When a child learns to ski, for example, he or she is exposed to certain kinds of experiences. The child practices, falls, gets up again; through many trials, the novice skier becomes proficient.

Other changes take place seemingly without direct instruction or experience. For example, all children in all cultures go through the same sequence when learning to make sounds. First they cry when they are hungry or tired; by four to six weeks they begin to coo when they are satisfied. Shortly thereafter they begin to babble, then gradually learn to imitate the sounds they hear. Though experience

does play a role in this progression—deaf children, for example, will coo but do not imitatively babble—it does not seem to have a direct effect. A child cannot be taught to coo, and those who are reinforced for it (by capturing the attention of a parent, for example) don't progress any faster.

The influence of heredity and environment on human development is complex, and teasing apart, the relative contributions of the two influences can be difficult, at times seemingly impossible. The techniques of behavioral genetics, described in Chapter 2, have been among the most successful approaches. We will refer to those techniques throughout this chapter.

One way to visualize the interaction of heredity and environment is shown in Figure 9-2. This diagram shows that at birth, human development can take relatively few paths; that is, the early stages of life are more heavily influenced by heredity than the later stages. But notice that as the life span lengthens, the number of possible paths increases dramatically. As development progresses, behavior becomes more diverse. The influence of the environment grows as people's lives progress.

At the *individual* level, a different pattern emerges; indeed, *for a specific individual* the number of possible paths at birth is enormous. At each successive stage in the developmental sequence, the number of possible paths is reduced. That is, even if Watson's statement "Give me a dozen healthy infants" *were* true

Three generations of the Ripken family. Did their baseball skill result from innate (genetic) ability, or were they successful because of their environment? Like most questions of heredity versus environment, the correct answer is "both."

(and there is a great deal of debate about that), it would have some limits. After some environmental events, Watson might *not* be able to turn any individual into a doctor, lawyer, or thief.

For example, at birth a certain person might be able to develop into a successful baseball player, so that one of the possible paths in Figure 9-2 would include "baseball player." But if that individual were to spend the first fifteen years of life in an environment that did not reinforce throwing, catching, and hitting skills, then the baseball player path might close. Can someone who lacked those important early experiences learn to become a baseball player later in life? Ask Michael Jordan.

Human development may also contain *critical periods,* or "windows of opportunity" during which times certain experiences must take place. That is, if the experiences do not occur during the critical period, some types of learning will not take place. Perhaps the clearest example of a critical period in learning was described by Konrad Lorenz. Lorenz was an *ethologist,* a scientist who studies the behavior of organisms in their natural habitats. He was studying the behavior of ducks when he was struck by a phenomenon known as "imprinting." Soon after they are hatched, ducklings begin to follow the first moving object they see. In a natural setting, this behavior makes perfect sense. What is the first thing a newly hatched duckling is likely to see? Its mother! Yet Lorenz found that the ducks would follow *any*

moving object. He was able to get ducks to follow a moving shoe, a dog, even himself.

Lorenz also discovered that if a young duck did not imprint on an object during the first few hours of life, it would *never* imprint. A duckling separated from its mother at birth and then reintroduced to the nest twenty-four hours later would fail to imprint on its mother. The duck's natural ability to imprint could be exercised only within the first few hours of life, the critical period.

Critical periods also exist in human development. Consider language acquisition, for example. Psychologists recognize that both heredity and environment play a role in shaping linguistic abilities. However, the magnitude of certain environmental influences is much greater in early childhood (especially before the age of five) than in later childhood. The "In Depth" section for this chapter examines the question of language acquisition and critical periods, through the tragic case of "Genie."

Clearly, profound differences exist between adults and children. These differences are not only physiological, however; the psychological changes occurring during development are equally profound. Contemporary understanding of the psychological aspects of human development has been shaped, in large part, by the work of three individuals: Freud, Watson, and Piaget. Though they approached development from radically different perspectives, each provided key insights.

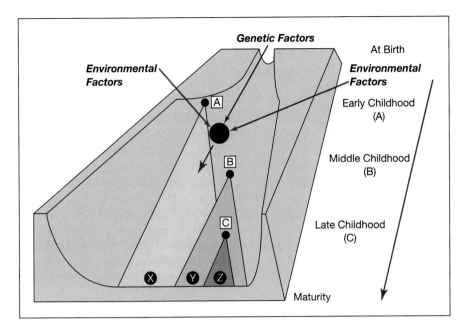

FIGURE 9-2 *Cumulative effects of genetic and environmental factors on possible developmental paths. As development progresses, the effects of previous events and genetic predispositions accumulate, constraining potential paths. In this example, consider three possible developmental outcomes—shown as X, Y, and Z—and the potential developmental paths at three different times: early childhood (Time A), middle childhood (Time B), and late childhood (Time C). In this example, all three developmental outcomes are possible at Time A. However, as development progresses to Time B, Outcome X is no longer possible. As development progresses even further, to Time C, Outcome Y is no longer possible. Thus development is both* influenced *and* constrained *by past experiences and genetic factors.*

The Psychologist's Perception of Human Development

For most of Western civilization, children were considered to be "little adults." That is, though childhood was recognized as a time of many changes—in size, strength, and intellectual capabilities—children were not treated as being different from adults. Western Europeans considered development to be discontinuous. Children were children; and once they "became adults" (through marriage, childbirth, or employment) their childhood was assumed over. The experiences adults had as children were not considered to have any lingering impact on their adult lives. To paraphrase from the Bible, "When I became an adult, I put away childish things."

Until the twentieth century, then, children were given adult tasks as soon as they were physically able to do them. When eight-year-olds were strong enough, they were put to work in the kitchens, fields, factories, or mines alongside their mothers

and fathers. No special concessions were made because of their intellectual, emotional, or social development. Our understanding of children and their capabilities has changed significantly since then. Three of the most important figures in psychology—Sigmund Freud, John Watson, and Jean Piaget—revolutionized society's concept of childhood.

Freud and the Developing Child

Freud's contributions to psychology are legion, and most of them are well known. One lesser known contribution Freud made was his insight into the developmental nature of childhood. Freud did *not* see children as small adults. Instead, he accurately perceived childhood as a period marked by important personal and developmental milestones.

Freud was also the first theorist to recognize that childhood experiences can have a lifelong effect on behavior. In his view, "putting away childish things," in the sense of escaping the influence of early experience, was impossible. Because Freud's

By pairing a white rat with a loud noise, John Watson and his associate, Rosalie Rayner, induced a phobia in Little Albert. The young boy soon generalized his fear to virtually any white, furry object, such as the Santa Claus mask shown in this photo.

work dealt more with psychosocial development than cognitive development, it will be covered in detail in Chapter 10.

Watson and Childhood Learning

In some sense, behaviorism could also be considered a revolutionary influence on society's perception of childhood. Though the behaviorists did not view children's thoughts as being qualitatively different from adult thoughts (indeed, true behaviorism is not concerned with "thought" in any form), John B. Watson *did* accept Freud's notion that experience is cumulative. That is, he recognized that many adult behaviors are caused by events that transpired during childhood. Watson actually wrote a best-selling textbook on how to treat developing children—one of the first of its kind (Watson, 1928). Though we now recognize that many of Watson's ideas on parenting were misguided, his role in changing our perception of psychological development was nonetheless important.

One of Watson's best-known experiments involved a young boy he called "Little Albert" (Watson & Rayner, 1920), who was presented in Chapter 6. Recall that Watson and Rayner taught Albert to fear white rats by repeatedly pairing a rat with a loud noise. In this way Watson and Rayner demonstrated that fear of an object—a *phobia*—could be learned through the principles of conditioning. Thus Watson provided a bridge between the experiences of child-

hood and later adult behavior. Did Little Albert fear the rat his whole life? We don't know, since Albert was removed from Watson's laboratory shortly after this experiment.[1]

Piaget and the Thinking Child

Like Freud, Jean Piaget (1896–1980) was not trained as a psychologist. He was by training a biologist, and a very successful one. (By the time he was twenty-one, Piaget had published almost two dozen scientific papers, mostly on mollusks; Dworetsky & Davis, 1989). Piaget's training in biology set the stage for his later work. For example, he noticed that if mollusks were moved from one pond to another, they would make structural changes suitable to their new environment. He reasoned that organisms are capable of adapting to new environments, at least within limits.

Piaget became curious about whether the adaptation he had witnessed in mollusks was possible in other species, specifically humans. Later in his career he found himself administering intelligence tests to children. Piaget was struck by what he saw; the older children seemed to have changed, or "adapted" their thought processes to better deal with the test questions. It wasn't simply that the older children *knew* more (though clearly they did); they seemed to approach the problems in an altogether different manner. In short, Piaget saw the psychological life of the older child as *qualitatively different* from the psychological life of a younger child.

Piaget eventually proposed that the children were progressing through different "stages" of cognitive development. Using a number of techniques, he examined human cognition throughout the life span and ultimately devised a comprehensive theory of cognitive development. Piaget's work remains among the most influential in all psychology (indeed, one survey showed Piaget was the second most frequently cited researcher in the discipline, behind only Freud [Endler, Rushton, & Roediger, 1978]).

In the next section we will examine children's cognitive development at various stages, beginning

---

[1]Which is probably a good thing. Barker (1997) reports that for the next phase of the study, Watson and Rayner were prepared to "countercondition" the fear produced by the rat by presenting the rat while stimulating Albert's genitals, which presumably generates a pleasurable feeling.

with infancy. As you will see, Piaget's influence on the nature of cognitive development remains strong.

Cognitive Development In Infants

People once thought that human newborns were largely oblivious to the world. William James (1890/1950) once described the world of the infant as a "blooming, buzzing confusion." Some parents have even wondered if their newborn babies could see or hear at all. In the last several decades, however, research on the newborn has yielded a very different view. We now know that humans are born with impressive sensory abilities. They process information and learn about their surroundings from the very moment of their birth.

Perceptual Capabilities

Findings regarding the newborn's visual capabilities have done much to change old notions about infants' perceptual abilities (Bower, 1989). Though at birth babies have only about 20/300 vision (they can see the same amount of detail in an object 20 feet away that an adult with perfect vision can see at 300 feet), they can see fairly clearly if objects are held close to them (Banks & Salapatek, 1983). A baby's vision is sharpest at a distance of about 7 to 8 inches—about the distance at which adults hold an infant during feeding.

From the very beginning, then, babies gather information about their caregivers' faces. Newborns even seem able to detect changes in facial expression. In one study, babies only about thirty-six hours old were able to discriminate among happy, sad, and surprised expressions (Field et al., 1982). Researchers noted that the babies looked less and less at an expression that had been presented repeatedly, as if they had grown bored with it. (Their boredom stemmed from *habituation*, a simple form of learning in which the response to a stimulus grows weaker the more often the stimulus is presented.) As an old expression was replaced by a new one, the babies showed renewed interest. Apparently, they could tell that the new expression was different, and because it was different, they found it more interesting.

The same babies showed another tendency that had been seen before in newborns: imitation of an adult's facial expression (Meltzoff & Moore, 1977). They often spread their lips and crinkled their eyes when looking at a happy face; furrowed their brows

William James once described the world of the infant as a "blooming, buzzing confusion." In the last several decades, however, research on the newborn has shown that humans are born with impressive sensory abilities.

and pouted in response to a sad expression. When they saw a look of surprise, they opened their mouths and widened their eyes. In a follow-up study, newborns less than three days old (and some as young as seven hours) imitated an adult who opened his mouth and stuck out his tongue (Meltzoff & Moore, 1983). Babies this young do not deliberately mimic others; they have no sense of "self" and "other," no knowledge of the similarity between their own expressions and someone else's. Their behavior is more akin to a reflex—an unpremeditated "matching" of their own facial movements with those of another person (Kaye & Marcus, 1978). This ability to attend carefully to human facial expressions is undoubtedly important to their future social and emotional development.

Similarly, newborn infants display quite remarkable hearing ability. Though an infant's sensory

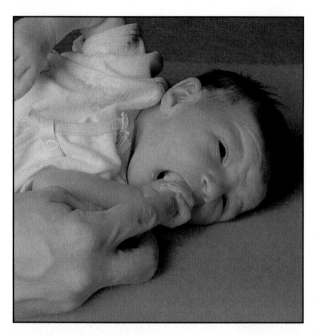

Tickling a baby's lips with a fingertip will elicit the sucking reflex.

threshold is somewhat higher than that of older children (the sounds must be somewhat louder for them to hear [Trehub et al., 1991]), infants as young as eight weeks can localize sounds (Morrongiello, Fenwick, & Chance, 1990). Remarkably, some auditory skills are learned *prior* to birth. In a clever experiment (DeCasper & Spence, 1986), pregnant women read aloud from Dr. Seuss's *The Cat in the Hat* twice a day for the last six weeks before birth. After their children were born, the researchers asked them to read either *The Cat in the Hat* or another children's story to their infants. Measuring learning in newborns can be tricky, but by observing changes in the infants' sucking rates researchers found that the newborns preferred *The Cat in the Hat*, which they had heard in the womb, to the unfamiliar story.

Newborns also possess an impressive ability to differentiate among sounds (Aslin, Pisoni, & Jusczyk, 1983). They can distinguish the sound of their mother's voice from that of a female stranger. At an early age, they can also distinguish between speech sounds, even ones as similar as the consonants [*b*] and [*p*] (Brody, Zelazo, & Chaika, 1984; Eimas et al., 1971). No wonder infants only two weeks old often respond differently to the sound of their own names than to other words (Mandel, Jusczyk, & Pisoni, 1995; Pines, 1982).

Newborns can differentiate among odors as well. In one study, two-day-old babies showed changes in activity, heart rate, and breathing whenever they were presented with a new odor, suggesting that they perceived it as new (Engen, Lipsitt, & Kaye, 1963). Infants only five or six days old can even distinguish the scent of their mothers from that of another woman (Macfarlane, 1977). This keen sense of smell may help young babies to "navigate" in their environment, locating their mothers' nipples, for example.

The perceptual capabilities of a newborn, then, are quite mature and well integrated. With their perceptual systems babies can interact with people and objects from the very first moments after birth. Such early interactions have a profound effect on both their cognitive and social development. Even in very early behavior, psychologists have noted individual differences that help to shape an infant's development. Babies who are very responsive to their parents or other adults, perhaps by temperament, tend to get more responses from them. Those responses, in turn, encourage the infants to continue being responsive and sociable (Heimann, 1989).

Reflexes and Motor Skills

Infants come into the world with a number of *reflexes*—involuntary responses to specific stimuli. Virtually all these reflexes are adaptive, or necessary for survival. Two reflexes that are necessary for feeding, for example, are the rooting reflex and the sucking reflex. The **rooting reflex** is the tendency of a baby to turn toward any object that gently touches its cheek. Because the most likely source of facial stimulation is the mother's breast, this reflex helps the infant to locate a nipple for feeding. Once a baby has rooted, the **sucking reflex** takes over. When an object is placed in the baby's mouth, the baby automatically begins sucking, a reflex that helps the baby to begin to nurse. The sucking reflex can be demonstrated by tickling a baby's lips with a fingertip or pacifier. The baby will respond by sucking on the fingertip or pacifier. The rooting and sucking reflexes typically last for three to four months after birth, when they are replaced by voluntary eating responses. They can be seen long after this period, however. Many toddlers use pacifiers or suck their thumbs; and in many three-year-olds the sucking response can be initiated by stroking their lips as they sleep.

TABLE 9-1   Milestones of Motor Development

Skill	25 Percent	50 Percent	90 Percent
Rolling over	2.1 months	3.2 months	5.4 months
Grasping rattle	2.6 months	3.3 months	3.9 months
Sitting without support	5.4 months	5.9 months	6.8 months
Standing while holding on	6.5 months	7.2 months	8.5 months
Grasping with thumb and finger	7.2 months	8.2 months	10.2 months
Standing alone well	10.4 months	11.5 months	13.7 months
Walking well	11.1 months	12.3 months	14.9 months
Building tower of two cubes	13.5 months	14.8 months	20.6 months
Walking up steps	14.1 months	16.6 months	21.6 months
Jumping in place	21.4 months	23.8 months	2.4 years
Copying circle	3.1 years	3.4 years	4.0 years

Note: Table shows approximate ages when 25 percent, 50 percent, and 90 percent of children can perform each skill.

Source: Adapted from Frankenburg, Dodds, Archer, et al. (1990).

Newborns also have a strong **grasping reflex.** If you place an infant on her back and put a finger on one of her hands, she will probably grasp the finger firmly. Sometimes grasping newborns can even be lifted by one arm. This reflex is likely a vestige of our evolutionary past. If our early ancestors carried their young on their backs or undersides, as many apes and monkeys do, the ability to cling tightly to the mother would have had great survival value (Prechtl, 1982).

Two other reflexes are easily seen in the infant. The **Moro reflex** is a startle response that occurs in reaction to an intense, sudden movement or noise. The baby arches its back, thrusts the head back, and flings its arms to the side. Just as quickly, the baby then draws the arms and legs back toward the body (Santrock, 1996). The **Babinski reflex** is a response to stroking on the bottom of the foot; when the foot is stroked, the toes fan outward. Like most other newborn reflexes, this reflex usually disappears between three and four months of age. However, an adult who has suffered cortical brain damage will often display a Babinski reflex. One diagnostic test often administered after head trauma, then, involves stroking the victim's foot. If a Babinski reflex is noted, the brain damage is likely to be considerable (Kolb & Whishaw, 1990).

A summary of the infant reflexes is presented in Table 9-1.

Developmental psychologists have long been interested in the appearance and disappearance of newborn reflexes because these reflexes are considered a measure of how well the central nervous system is functioning. At birth, weak or absent infant reflexes may mean that something has gone wrong with neural development. The later disappearance of such reflexes is thought to indicate that more advanced motor and cognitive abilities are emerging, as the cerebral cortex matures (Smolak, 1986). That is, behaviors that were at first controlled automatically, by the lower regions of the brain, are now beginning to come under voluntary control by the cortex.

What changes in the cortex allow this important development? These changes cannot be the result of

When a baby's nervous system matures and muscles and bones become sufficiently strong, the child will try to master new motor skills. Early motor skills, such as crawling or picking up a toy, emerge in a predictable order at much the same age in most children, across most cultures This child is twelve months old.

new neuronal growth. However, some changes do take place in existing neurons. One is the growth of dendrites, the parts of a neuron that receive incoming messages. A second is the formation of many new synapses, or connections between neurons. A third is the formation of the myelin sheaths, the fatty casing that surrounds certain neural fibers, helping them to conduct signals more efficiently. These three processes, together with an increase in the volume of nerve cell bodies and a proliferation in glial cells, cause the thickness of the human cortex to more than triple between birth and about four years of age (Rabinowitz, 1986).

As soon as a baby's nervous system becomes mature enough, and muscles and bones sufficiently strong, the child is intrinsically motivated to master new motor skills. Early motor skills such as rolling over, picking up a toy, sitting up, crawling, and walking emerge in a fairly predictable order, at much the same age in most children across most cultures.

Learning and Memory

As soon as they are born, babies are capable of learning how their own actions are related to other events (Bower, 1989; Kolata, 1984). For instance, babies only a few days old have been taught to turn their heads after hearing a tone when a sip of sugary water awaits them (Werner & Siqueland, 1978). They will learn even when the "reward" is nothing more than

a flash of light (Papouseuk, 1969). Apparently, learning such relationships is a reward in itself. In fact, older babies show great pleasure when they learn a relationship between their own behavior and something happening around them. Suppose a nine-month-old has learned to kick her left leg vigorously in order to move a mobile attached to that leg by a string. If the researcher changes the relationship, so that the right leg instead of the left moves the toy, the baby will again search for the solution, and coo vigorously when she finds it (Monnier, Boehmer, & Scholer, 1976). Solving a problem seems to be a source of intellectual pleasure for babies, as for older children and adults (Watson, 1972).

Exactly how long does a baby's memory for such new relationships last? Do infants forget as soon as they are distracted, much as adults forget an unfamiliar number as soon as they close the phone book? Many people assume that babies' memories are fleeting, particularly given how little we remember about our own infancies. Yet recent research shows that a baby's memory is much better than we might think (Rovee-Collier, 1990). Two-month-olds, for instance, can remember the relationship between kicking a leg and moving a mobile for at least a few days after learning it; eight-month-olds can recall the relationship as much as a week later (Greco et al., 1986).

Childhood Amnesia

If babies' long-term memories are relatively good, why do adults have such trouble recalling events from their own first years? Why can't we remember sitting in a high chair, drinking from a bottle, or taking our first few tottering steps? Psychologists do not yet know the reasons for our lack of conscious memories from infancy, a phenomenon that is called **childhood amnesia** (Kail, 1990). Childhood amnesia refers to the lack of *episodic memories,* or memories that require conscious awareness. Children form memories throughout their lives, even in the first few years. Many of those memories will last a lifetime—for instance, food aversions, parental bonding, and even musical preferences. None of these memories, however, requires conscious awareness on the child's part, and as such, they would be examples of *implicit memories,* discussed in Chapter 8.

Several theories have been proposed to explain childhood amnesia. One attributes memory failure to problems with retrieval. The memories are there, stored away somewhere in our brains, but we lack the means to find them. This was essentially Freud's explanation for childhood amnesia. Freud believed that because of the sexual nature of many early experiences, the whole period is repressed and unavailable for recall. Most research, however, does not support Freud's repression view (Usher & Neisser, 1993; White & Pillemer, 1979; see also the "In Depth" section of Chapter 8).

Some contemporary researchers suggest that adults lack the retrieval cues needed to recall experiences from infancy because the world now looks very different to them. (Remember that adults may be twenty times larger or more than they were as newborns.) Schactel (1947; reprinted in Neisser, 1982), a Freudian psychoanalyst, offered an excellent summary of this position. According to Schactel, the experiences of childhood do not fit into an adult "schema." To use one analogy, our memories, in some ways, are similar to files in a computerized word processor. The "files" children store early in life may be encoded using a primitive "version" of the program, so that later in life, when the now grown adult is using the "newer" version, the early files are incompatible: the new program cannot read them. There is some support for this theory. As we saw in Chapter 3, certain brain structures, particularly those in the limbic system, are critical to the formation of memories. These structures are not fully formed until the fourth or fifth year of life (Kandel, Schwartz, & Jessell, 1995)—the time when most of us begin to form lasting episodic memories (Sheingold & Tenney, 1979; as reprinted in Neisser, 1982).

Finally, language may play a role in early memory (Nelson, 1993). According to this view, language is needed to begin the formation of the cognitive structures that underlie memory formation. As children begin to recount the events of their lives in narrative form—telling stories of their daily lives to parents, teachers, and other children—they begin the process that allows them to form long-term memories.

An example of this hypothesis involves Austin and Lindsay, the author's children who were introduced at the beginning of this chapter. When Austin was two, his favorite meal was spaghetti and meatballs. Many times when he was asked what he had for lunch at preschool, he would say he had eaten meatballs, even if meatballs had not been on the menu that day. He was demonstrating his *schema* of a typical day; gradually, he learned to deviate from this schema. After weeks of replying that he had eaten meatballs, he began to say, "I *didn't* have meat-

balls!" Eventually he would remember what he had actually eaten: "We had chicken, Daddy!"

When Lindsay reached the same age, she too began telling stories about her day. While Austin's stories always began with what he had eaten for lunch, Lindsay's stories were about her time spent on the playground. When asked how her day had gone, she would eagerly offer, "I played with Ruthie! I had time out!" (a common punishment for misbehavior that involves removing a child from the play area). Every day for several months, Lindsay would tell the same story, never deviating from her schema. When asked how her day went, she almost always said, "We played! I had time out." Though she was bright and verbal, she apparently had not learned to differentiate between actual events and schematic events. One day her father mentioned this apparent lapse in development to Lindsay's teacher. After an awkward pause, the teacher replied, "Well, Lindsay *does* have time out every day!"

All the theories of childhood amnesia are plausible, and researchers have found evidence to support many of them. Yet other evidence tends to counter each of the theories. For this reason psychologists continue to investigate the puzzle of why we remember so little from our earliest years (Usher & Neisser, 1993).

Cognitive Development in Infancy and Childhood

Tremendous cognitive development occurs during the first dozen years of life. By the time children enter school, they have mastered the intricacies of language. They can count, recite the alphabet, narrate the plots of their favorite stories, and explain the rules of many games. They can also operate mechanical equipment, such as TV sets, telephones, and video game machines. On leaving elementary school six years later, they can read, write, do arithmetic, and discuss history, science, geography, and more. How does the human intellect develop from the basic abilities present at birth into the impressive skills children exhibit in middle childhood?

Two Current Perspectives on Cognitive Development

Jean Piaget was one of the first researchers to provide answers to questions about cognitive development. A gifted observer of children, he probed beyond their superficial behaviors to uncover their underlying view of the world. Piaget's theory of cognitive development has tremendous breadth, covering the period from the very first days after birth through adolescence. Yet in recent decades, many of Piaget's ideas have been criticized, especially by those who take an information-processing view of cognitive development. The next two sections present these viewpoints in detail.

Piaget's Theory of Development

Piaget saw cognitive development as a series of stages, each qualitatively different from the preceding one. That is, in each new stage, children construct a more mature view of reality, which in turn changes the way they think about the world and assimilate new information. In Piaget's view, there are four major stages of intellectual growth: the **sensorimotor period,** which encompasses the first two years of life; the **preoperational period,** during the preschool years; the **concrete-operational period,** which occupies the years of elementary school; and the **formal-operational period,** which begins around adolescence and continues through adulthood (Piaget & Inhelder, 1969). In cognitive terms, in each individual stage the individual is a fundamentally different person.

How does the child advance from one cognitive stage to another? To Piaget, the answer to this question lay in three interrelated mental processes: assimilation, accommodation, and equilibration. **Assimilation** involves the incorporation of new information into old ways of thinking or behaving. For example, suppose a five-year-old girl thinks that "living things" refers only to dogs, cats, rabbits, birds, and people (Siegler, 1991). She then takes a trip to the zoo and sees an elephant. Although she must modify her notion of the size of living things, she is able to assimilate this new animal into her understanding of living things. Later, when the child is told that a tree is a living thing too, she must **accommodate** the new information. That is, she must fundamentally alter her old way of thinking to adapt to the idea of a tree as a living thing. As she focuses on qualities such as the ability to grow and reproduce, her concept of living things becomes more abstract. This change in her thinking restores her mind to a state of equilibrium (or balance), in which the various pieces of her knowledge all fit together. This is the process Piaget called **equilibration.** Through accommodation and equilibration the child advances

from the preoperational period, in which she focuses mainly on the external appearance of things, to the concrete operational period, in which she can think more abstractly.

Information-Processing View of Development

Not all psychologists agree with Piaget's theory. Some believe that many of the contrasts in cognitive ability between younger and older children can be explained not by *qualitative* differences in the way they view reality but by *quantitative* differences in the efficiency with which they process information. That is, they believe cognitive ability is affected by the way their memories represent what they see and hear and operate on those representations, and by the way their memories impose limits on the data they can handle (Siegler, 1986). From this perspective, a ten-year-old's ability to understand concepts

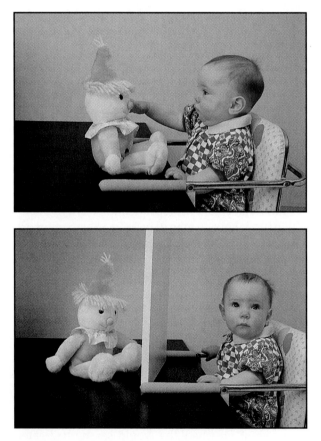

Until they are about 4 months old, babies lack the concept of object permanence. They do not search for a toy that has captured their attention if it is placed out of sight.

By about eight months of age, infants begin to display the concept of object permanence. They will search for an object they have dropped, and even for totally covered objects.

that elude a five-year-old is due not to fundamental differences in the way the two children construct reality but to the older child's greater capacity for processing information.

The Two Perspectives Compared

Both the information-processing and the Piagetian view of cognitive development have some validity. In addition, they are not necessarily mutually exclusive; development may involve both shifts in understanding (the Piagetian view) as well as increased efficiency (the information-processing view). We will consider the evidence for each as we explore children's thinking from infancy through the elementary school years.

Piaget on Infancy

Piaget argued that the central cognitive task of infancy is to construct a view of the world that incorporates a basic understanding of objects and cause-and-effect relationships. This the child does by exercising what Piaget called *sensorimotor intelligence,* which implies that babies do not think abstractly, as older children do. Babies do not analyze problems, plan out strategies, and wonder what the consequences will be. Instead, they come to know the world strictly by perceiving and acting in it. Their understanding is derived solely from what they sense and do.

Piaget proposed that the infant's understanding of objects develops through a series of substages. At first a baby does not understand that objects have a permanent existence. When the child can no longer

perceive an object with the senses, that object ceases to exist for the child. Piaget drew this conclusion after observing infants' reactions to an object that suddenly disappears. Suppose, for instance, that a toy that has captured a baby's attention is partially hidden from sight by a piece of paper, as shown in the photo on p. 302. Piaget noticed that up to the age of about four months, babies do not search for the missing toy, with their eyes or with their hands. Instead, they act as if it has vanished completely. Piaget interpreted their behavior to mean that they lacked any notion of the toy as an enduring entity. At the age of four to eight months, however, infants begin to recognize and reach for partially covered objects. They will also look down to find an object they have dropped, implying that they expect it still to be there. By eight to twelve months, infants will also search for totally covered objects (see the photos above). This ability to represent objects "in the head"—to know that things exist even when they cannot be physically sensed—is called **object permanence.**

It is no coincidence that two other behaviors appear with the development of object permanence. The first is the infant's newfound fascination with the game "peek-a-boo." A three-month-old child usually shows little interest in playing peek-a-boo, but a nine-month-old will squeal with delight. Piaget would explain that the three-month-old has no sense of object permanence; once you have hidden behind the door, you simply cease to exist for the child. For the game to be fun, the child must understand that even if you are out of sight, you still exist.

The second behavior to appear with the development of object permanence is prolonged crying when the parent leaves the child. Though both a three-month-old and a nine-month-old are likely to cry when the parent leaves, the three-month-old will usually quit crying soon after the parent is gone. By contrast, the nine-month-old may cry long after the parent leaves the room. Piaget would say that because the three-month-old lacks a sense of object permanence, once the parent leaves the room, he is simply "gone." To the older child, the parent still "exists," but is somewhere else: and the howls of protest indicate the child's desire for the parent to be *here*, not somewhere else.

In some ways, however, even babies eight to twelve months old have an immature concept of objects. Consider what would happen if during a peek-a-boo game, the person who was hiding behind one towel suddenly moved behind a *second* towel, still in the child's full view. Babies this age would continue to look for the person behind the first towel. Rather than look where the person was seen last, they would simply repeat the action they had been successful with earlier. Only by the age of twelve to eighteen months can infants deal with such displacements. And not until the age of eighteen to twenty-four months can children deal with displacements they have not actually seen (such as when a toy that is hidden in one hand is surreptitiously passed to the other hand). This milestone marks the final stage in the acquisition of the object concept.

Piaget's descriptions of infants' behavior toward objects have proved to be quite reliable. Babies all over the world have been found to pass through these developmental sequences, searching for hidden objects in predictable ways at different ages. But some researchers have questioned Piaget's conclusions about the meaning of these patterns. They wonder to what extent the child's construction of reality shapes his or her behavior—whether the failure to look for a hidden toy necessarily means that a baby sees objects as impermanent, things that come and go at random.

An Alternative Perspective on Infancy

One alternative explanation for these differences is that they may reflect limitations on an infant's memory (Kagan, Kearsley, & Zelazo, 1978). A three-month-old who has been shown a toy, which is then hidden behind a paper, must hold an image of the toy in mind in order to find it. Then the child must coordinate that image with a visual and manual search. Such an operation may be beyond the cognitive capabilities of someone so young.

If memory limitations are indeed a stumbling block in object concept studies, might young babies grasp the fact that hidden objects do not simply vanish? Some researchers have tried to answer this question by conducting studies that do not require young infants to search for a hidden object. Instead, these researchers display possible and impossible events involving moving objects and record the baby's reactions. In one such study (Baillargeon, Spelke, & Wasserman, 1985), five-and-a-half-month-old babies were shown an object that appeared to move through the space occupied by another object, which was temporarily hidden from sight. If the infants thought that the temporarily hidden object no longer existed, they should not have shown surprise when the second object passed through its space. Yet, this odd event grabbed the babies' attention, suggesting they had a sense of objects as solid, permanent things. Follow-up studies have shown that four-and-a-half-month-old infants, and even many only three and a half months old, look significantly longer at this impossible event than at one that does not defy the laws of solid objects (Baillargeon, 1987).

In another series of studies, Baillargeon, Kotovsky, and Needham (1995) showed infants a box sitting on a platform (see Figure 9-3). Gradually, the box on top was pushed toward the edge of the platform in one of two ways, so that it rested close to the end of the platform, but not over the edge, or so that most of the box hung over the edge. An adult would easily recognize that the second event was physically impossible; if a box were pushed that far, it would fall off the platform. But what do infants understand about this situation? Baillargeon (1994) found a clear developmental sequence. When infants are between 3 and 6.5 months of age, they become aware that the contact between the box and the platform must be taken into account. If there is no contact (that is, if the box appears to be "floating in the air" beside the platform, as in the top illustration in Figure 9-3), these infants look longer at the event. According to Baillargeon, they view it as physically impossible. Between 4.5 and 5.5 months of age, infants begin to take into account the *amount* of contact between the objects. If only a small portion of the box is touching the platform (the middle illustration

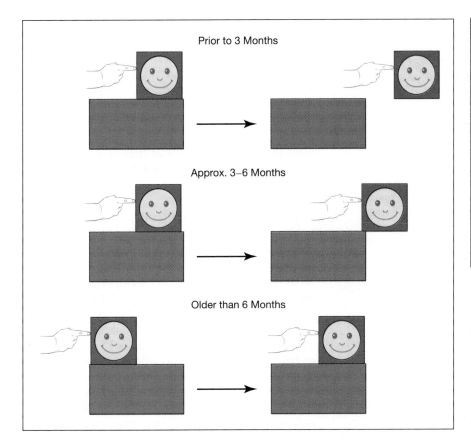

FIGURE 9-3   Events used by Baillargeon and her colleagues to test infants' understanding of the physical world. Infants as young as three months become aware that in order for one object to support another, the two objects must come into contact. Around the age of six months infants recognize that some contact is required that the amount of contact is important. (After Baillargeon, 1994).

Prior to 3 Months

Approx. 3–6 Months

Older than 6 Months

in Figure 9-3), they seem to believe the box will be stable. By 6.5 months, though, an infant will recognize that a significant portion of the box must be in contact with the platform if the box is to remain stable (the bottom illustration in Figure 9-3).

Are Baillargeon's results inconsistent with Piaget's view of development? Not necessarily. Baillargeon and her colleagues interpreted their results by saying that the sequences they observed in the children "reflect not the gradual unfolding of innate beliefs, but the application of highly constrained, innate learning mechanisms" (Baillargeon, 1994, p. 135). Children begin with a fairly simple all-or-none understanding of the physical world and gradually modify their beliefs to include increasing experience. Baillargeon has illustrated some mechanisms through which assimilation and accommodation can take place. Her results do imply that Piaget's conclusions about cognitive development were not entirely correct, though. At the very least, children may possess certain cognitive abilities at a younger age than Piaget thought.

Two Perspectives on the Preschool Period

Between the ages of two and three, children leave the cognitive world of infancy far behind. One of their key intellectual accomplishments at this age is **representational thought,** or the ability to represent objects mentally when they are no longer physically present. Children can now imagine; by doing so, they expand their world far beyond the limits of their immediate surroundings. One sign that preschoolers can think representationally is their ability to imitate someone else's actions long after they have seen the person. Another is their ability to play "make-believe," pretending, for example, that they are astronauts and that a large cardboard box is a spaceship. But the most important indication of representational thought is the ability to use language, an intellectual accomplishment that greatly expands the child's powers of reasoning and communication. We will say much more about the development of language later in this chapter.

As impressive as preschoolers' cognitive advances are, however, they still have limitations. One

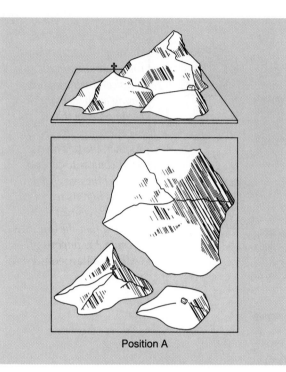

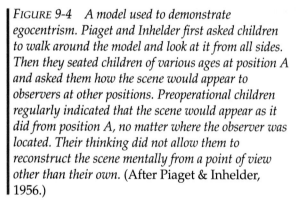

Position A

FIGURE 9-4   *A model used to demonstrate egocentrism. Piaget and Inhelder first asked children to walk around the model and look at it from all sides. Then they seated children of various ages at position A and asked them how the scene would appear to observers at other positions. Preoperational children regularly indicated that the scene would appear as it did from position A, no matter where the observer was located. Their thinking did not allow them to reconstruct the scene mentally from a point of view other than their own.* (After Piaget & Inhelder, 1956.)

is the fact that their thought is often **egocentric.** Preschoolers do not always understand that different people have different perspectives, and that their own view is merely one among many. In one demonstration of egocentrism, Piaget and his colleague showed preschool children a large model composed of three mountains in triangular arrangement (see Figure 9-4). After a child had walked around the model and become familiar with it, he or she sat in a chair facing one of the mountains. The experimenter sat in a chair facing another mountain, and asked the child which of several pictures showed what he saw. Children this age repeatedly chose a picture drawn from their own perspective (Piaget & Inhelder, 1969).

Another example of children's egocentrism is a reluctance to share. Take, for example, a child of three who has been given a candy bar. The parent might say, "Austin, why don't you share that candy bar with your sister Lindsay?" Austin views the question this way: "If I give Lindsay some of the candy bar, there will be less for me. Why would I want to do that?" It should come as no surprise, then, that Austin will balk at sharing his candy bar. This reluctance is not a moral failure on the three-year-old's part, just an incapacity to recognize the benefits of sharing.

While there is little doubt that preschool youngsters are egocentric, psychologists do not agree on the reasons. Piaget believed it reflects the child's subjectively structured view of the world. When asked to describe another person's perspective, children this age cannot help but describe their own. But other psychologists suspect that the cause of egocentrism may lie more in the preschooler's still limited information-processing capabilities. In one study, for instance, preschoolers were asked to hide a Snoopy doll behind a screen, so that an experimenter could not see it from where she sat (Flavell, Shipstead, & Croft, 1978). Even two-and-a-half-year-olds were able to do so, suggesting that in certain situations they can adopt another person's perspective. Sometimes they do so quite cleverly, in fact. When no one is watching, a three-year-old will hide his one-year-old brother's favorite blanket, and then watch as the frustrated baby searches for it. Such behavior shows a sophisticated understanding of the point of view of others (Dunn, 1988).

Perhaps, then, failure on the mountain-range problem has more to do with the complexity of the task. The child, after all, must encode the entire landscape into memory, recall the experimenter's viewpoint, and retain his mental image while considering various pictures (Huttenlocher & Presson, 1979). Faced with such a difficult task, most preschoolers may simply fall back on a simple rule: "Choose the picture that matches what I see."

Cognitive Development Through Middle Childhood

The middle childhood years, from about ages six through ten, are marked by less dramatic changes in thought. In many cultures children are in a formal educational setting during this period, and their

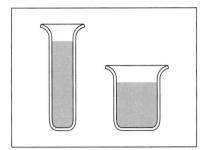

FIGURE 9-5   *Conservation of mass. Before they reach the stage of concrete operations, children cannot understand the principle of the conservation of volume. Preoperational children will answer that the taller beaker always has more water, even if they have just observed the contents of one beaker being poured directly into the other.*

Piaget and others have theorized that preschoolers lack the concept of conservation of volume. They believe, like this child, that tall, thin containers hold more liquid than short, wide containers.

learning appears to be more incremental. Nonetheless, important cognitive changes take place in middle childhood, preparing the way for adultlike thought soon to follow.

Piaget's Emphasis on Concrete Operations

Around the time children enter school, they begin to think more logically than younger children. Piaget felt that the major intellectual accomplishment of middle childhood was the ability to perform what he called **concrete operations.** The term refers to a variety of mental transformations (all of which can be *reversed*) that can be carried out on concrete, tangible, objects. The ability to perform concrete operations develops between the ages of about six and twelve.

An excellent example of concrete operational thought can be seen in the emergence of the concept of **conservation**—the recognition that certain features of an object remain the same (are conserved) despite changes in other features. Suppose you show a four-year-old two identical beakers of water and ask the child which beaker contains more water (see Figure 9-5). The child will probably answer correctly that the two beakers contain equal amounts of water. Now suppose you pour the water from beaker 1 into a third beaker of a different shape; it is tall and thin rather than short and wide. If you ask the child which beaker contains more water, beaker 1 or beaker 3, the child is very apt to say that beaker 3 has more water. The child seems to fixate on the height of the water, concluding that the taller beaker has "more." On the basis of such experiments, Piaget

and others have argued that preschoolers lack the concept of *conservation of volume.* Children of their age fail to understand that the amount of a liquid does not change simply because it is poured into a container of a different shape.

Nor have children of this age grasped other concepts of conservation. For instance, if you show a preschooler two parallel rows of six marbles of identical size, with the marbles in each row touching one another, the child will say correctly that both rows contain an equal number of marbles. But if you then spread out the marbles in one row, as shown in Figure 9-6, the child will say that the lengthened row has more marbles, even though the number of marbles has not been changed. A psychologist would say that the child does not yet understand the concept of *conservation of number.* Parents sometimes take advantage of this error in reasoning. They may spread out a pile of candies, for example, so that preschoolers think they are getting more. Or, they might give a child five $1 bills rather than a single $5 bill. Figure 9-6 also illustrates two other conservation concepts, *conservation of mass* and *conservation of length,* which are beyond the grasp of children aged five or six.

Older children gradually come to understand the concept of conservation. A girl of eight or nine, for example, will probably be able to coordinate her thoughts about a change in the height of a container with her thoughts about the width of the container, and conclude that its thinness compensates for its extra height. She will also be able to picture the

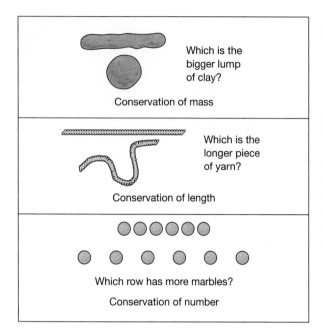

Conservation of mass

Which is the bigger lump of clay?

Conservation of length

Which is the longer piece of yarn?

Which row has more marbles?

Conservation of number

FIGURE 9-6 *Conservation problems. Preoperational children will answer that one lump of clay or string is larger or longer than the other, and there are more marbles in the bottom row than in the top one. By age eight, they understand that the lengths and quantities are the same in each case.*

reverse operation mentally: pouring the water back into the original beaker, so that its surface is again even with that of the water in beaker 2. As a result, she will answer correctly that the amount of water in the two containers remains the same.

An Alternative Perspective on Concrete Operations

Do the differences in the performance of preschoolers and other children on conservation tasks mean that the two groups have two qualitatively different views of reality—two different logical structures that they apply to the world? Piaget thought so, but other psychologists are not sure. One piece of evidence against Piaget's conclusion is the existence of inconsistencies in the tasks children can perform. For instance, many youngsters can perform Piaget's conservation-of-number task at age six, yet they cannot perform his conservation-of-mass task until age eight, nor his test for conservation of weight until age ten (Elkind, 1961; Katz & Beilin, 1976; Miller, 1976). If the ability to understand conservation of number reflects the development of a new, more advanced logical structure, why can't children immedi-

ately apply that new understanding to all conservation problems? This question has prompted psychologists to do additional research.

Some researchers have wondered if preschoolers may fail traditional conservation tests for reasons unrelated to an understanding of conservation. Consider the standard conservation-of-number task. Might some preschoolers say that there are more marbles in the longer row simply because they assume that "more" is a synonym for "longer"? Or might their attention be misdirected when they are instructed to watch as the experimenter spreads out the marbles in one of the rows, so that later, when asked again "Which row has more?" they conclude that the question is about length? Both these explanations are certainly plausible; is either of them right?

Psychologist Rochel Gelman (1972) designed an experiment to test whether preschoolers were in fact deceived by the language or method of conducting typical conservation tests. Gelman presented children ages three to six-and-a-half with two plates. On one plate was a row of three toy mice fastened to a strip of Velcro. On the other plate was a row of two toy mice fastened similarly. She told the children they were about to play a game in which they had to identify the "winning" plate. Gelman pointed to the plate with three mice and said that it would always be the winner. But she never described the plate in any way. The children had to decide for themselves which of its attributes—the number of mice, the length of the row, the spacing between the mice—made that plate the winner. Thus, Gelman avoided using the words *more* and *less*, which might have slightly different meanings for preschoolers than for older children.

Next Gelman covered each plate with a large lid and shuffled them. She then asked the children to pick the lid under which the "winning" plate lay. Whenever the child picked the three-mouse plate, she gave the child a prize. After several rounds of shuffling and picking, Gelman surreptitiously changed the three-mouse display, by moving the mice closer together or farther apart, or by removing one mouse entirely. Gelman made these transformations covertly to make sure that she did not call attention to the change, and so bias the children's thinking.

Gelman's findings showed that most of the children, even the youngest ones, considered number the relevant difference between the two plates. Almost no child claimed that a change in the length of the three-mouse row disqualified it from being a "winner." Many children, in fact, failed even to notice such a change. In contrast, almost all the children noticed when a mouse had been removed from the "winning" plate. Many showed great surprise, exclaiming, "Where is it?" "Where'd it go?" Others searched for the vanished toy—under the lids, beneath the table, around the room. Even more important, the overwhelming majority of children doubted whether a three-mouse plate with one mouse missing could still be considered a "winner." Over two-thirds said emphatically that the plate had become a "loser." The only way to fix it, they said, would be to add another mouse. Clearly the children understood that number can be changed only by addition or subtraction—the essence of the concept of conservation.

Why did Gelman's youngest subjects perform well on this game, yet probably fail if given Piaget's conservation-of-number test? Perhaps the traditional conservation-of-number test is confusing to their age group, for reasons that have nothing to do with a grasp of conservation. If that is the case, the intellectual differences between younger and older children may not be as significant as some psychologists believe. At the very least, the beginnings of an understanding of conservation may emerge at an earlier age than Piaget proposed.

Case's Integrative Theory

Despite the differences between Piaget's perspective and the information-processing view, the two theories are not mutually exclusive. In fact, in recent years some psychologists have tried to combine the best of both perspectives in a single integrated theory of cognitive development. One of those psychologists, Robbie Case (1985), believes that children progress through a series of developmental stages, each of which is characterized by the most advanced mental operations a child of that age can carry out: sensorimotor operations in infancy, representational operations in the preschool years, and logical operations during middle childhood. In this regard, Case's theory is very similar to Piaget's.

But Case draws heavily on information-processing theory in his thinking about constraints on development, as well as in his explanations of how children progress within and between developmental stages. He stresses both the limitations on and the changes in short-term memory capacity, arguing that as children mature, their short-term capacity increases. By capac-

ity he means the amount of short-term memory that is available for active thinking about problems and for working out solutions. Case maintains that the total *physical* capacity of short-term memory has powerful biological determinants and does not change much over the years. (This view is supported by recent work of behavioral geneticists; see Plomin, DeFries, & McClearn, 1990.) The capacity of short-term memory grows as children gradually make more efficient use of its physical capacity. We have seen that short-term memory capacity can be increased by combining related information into larger units, a technique called "chunking" (see p. 226). A familiar example of chunking is the grouping of the digits in phone numbers. Rather than trying to remember a string of digits like 8177552961, which would be very challenging indeed, we break the number into "chunks": (817) 755-2961. Chunking frees up space in short-term memory for other mental tasks.

Now apply this technique to cognitive development. Consider an infant who has just learned to reach for and grasp objects. The process of mentally coordinating this series of actions consumes all the child's short-term storage space. Thus, if you place another object in front of the one the baby wants to grasp, the child is apt to become frustrated. He does not have enough working memory available to come up with the solution of removing the new object in order to secure the desired one. Gradually, however, the baby's reaching and grasping actions become more efficient, until the child performs them not as a series of separate steps (extend the arm, touch the object, uncurl the fingers, and grasp it firmly) but as a single smooth motion. In this way the child frees some storage space in working memory, though its total capacity is no greater than before. Removing a second object to get the first one becomes possible.

With older children, the effect of chunking can be even more striking. Chi (1978) compared short-term memory spans in ten-year-olds and adults using two tasks: a digit recall test in which a string of digits was said aloud and subjects repeated it back, and a test of memory for the pieces on a chessboard. Chi chose her subjects deliberately, though; the children were all skilled chess players, and the adults were all novice chess players.

The adults showed an expected advantage over the children on the digit recall test. On the chess test, however, Chi found the ten-year-olds had a striking advantage (see Figure 9-7). Chi theorized that the children were able to use their knowledge of chess to

FIGURE 9-7 *Memory span for digits and chess pieces in adult novice chess players versus expert child chess players.* (After Kail, 1990, Figure 4-1.)

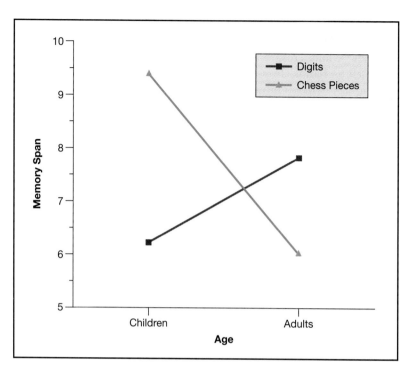

form larger and more efficient chunks than adults. Her interpretation has been supported by more recent experiments (Schneider, Körkel, & Weinert, 1988) in which the researchers compared German school children in grades three, five, and seven, who were either experts or novices in soccer. They told the children a story about soccer, then asked them to recall it. Age had virtually no effect on the children's performance, but the effect of their expertise (or lack of it) was overwhelming.

Because Case's theory can account for inconsistencies in children's performance, it has more explanatory power than Piaget's. It is also an excellent example of the way in which science progresses. First, Piaget and his followers put forth an explanation of cognitive development in childhood. Next, a group of critics demonstrated problems with his explanation. Finally, Case (and others) responded to those critics by modifying Piaget's explanation. Although Case's theory may not withstand the critical assessment of those who disagree with Piaget's approach in any form, it is still an important effort to combine the best of the Piagetian and the information-processing views.

Language Acquisition

Philosophers, theologians, and scientists have struggled for years to answer the question, "What if anything makes the human species unique?" We know humans share 99 percent of their genetic material with the chimpanzee (Lieberman, 1991). We are not the fastest species on the planet, nor are we the strongest. We do not even have the largest brains (those belong to the whales). Though we once thought that humans were unique in their ability to make and use tools, we now know this ability is found in other species (Savage-Rumbaugh, 1986). As you learned in the "In Depth" section of Chapter 8, however, the ability to acquire and use a spoken language *does* seem to be uniquely human (see also Lieberman, 1991). You may recall Jane Goodall's story of Lucy, a chimpanzee who had been taught a number of symbols of American Sign Language, quoted in the introduction to Chapter 6 (see p. 183). However, even though Lucy's ability to communicate using the symbols is beyond question, most psychologists do *not* consider the skills of Lucy (and others like her) to represent language. In fact, Goodall herself acknowledges this in the same interview in which she spoke of Lucy:

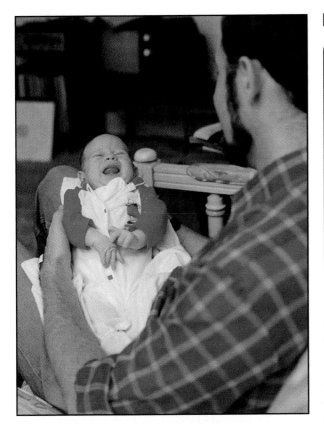

Newborns communicate mainly through their cries, which vary depending on whether they are hungry, angry, or in pain.

If I am asked what I believe to have been the most significant factor in making humans the unique creature that they are, without hesitation, I would say it is because we developed a spoken language—a language which enables us to leave the present behind. We can discuss the past, we can talk about the future and make plans. We can pass on information to our children because of words. I think that this acquisition of a spoken language really could have led to these vast differences . . . in human and chimpanzee intellect.

Jane Goodall, interview on the PBS series *The Mind,* 1987

Although the human capacity for language begins to develop soon after birth, infants come into the world speechless. In fact, the word *infant* comes from the Latin word *infans,* meaning "without speech." Yet within a few years, all children of normal (even near normal) intelligence have become highly skilled speakers and listeners. How does a child progress in so short a period from the

TABLE 9-2   *Milestones in Language Development*

Milestone	Approximate Age
Cooing	2 to 3 months
Babbling	By 5 months
First words	10 to 14 months
10 words in a usable vocabulary; comprehension about 50 words	12 months
2-word sentences	21 to 24 months
200-word vocabulary	24 months

Source: Steinberg & Belsky, 1990.

newborn's sounds to the mastery of words and sentences?

Milestones in Language Acquisition

Although children grow up in different cultures, they seem to go through a similar sequence in learning to speak their native languages (Bloom, 1970; Brown, 1973). One child may reach a particular stage before another does, but all children learn language in a similar way. (See Table 9-2.) Even before they use words, they begin to communicate by babbling.

Prespeech Communication

From the earliest weeks of life, the sounds babies make attract the attention of others. Newborns communicate mainly with their cries, which vary in tone and rhythm, depending on how the baby is feeling (hungry, angry, and so forth). Most parents quickly learn to distinguish among these cries and become able to respond appropriately (Wolff, 1969).

As infants grow older, they begin to produce more varied sounds. By three months they can coo, which they do both alone and sometimes in what appears to be "conversation" with adults. A parent says something to the baby, who answers with cooing noises, then pauses as if waiting for the parent's reply. Cooing differs from later language in a number of respects, however. First, while adult speech sounds are made up of a fairly restricted number of sound categories called *phonemes*—English, for example, contains only about forty-five phonemes—

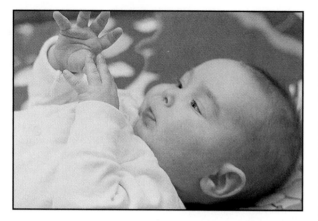

By three months infants can coo, which they do both when alone and sometimes in "conversation" with adults: a parent says something to the baby, who responds by cooing and then pausing, as if waiting for the parent's reply.

infants produce a much wider variety of speech sounds, including phonemes that adult speakers are no longer capable of producing (or perceiving). Second, even deaf children coo. Unlike learning to speak, which involves imitation and repetition of adult sounds, young infants produce cooing sounds without needing to hear them first.

When communicating with young infants, people often modify their style of speaking. They slow down their speaking rate while raising the pitch of their voice, in what is called "motherese." Fernald and Kuhl (1987) have shown that young infants prefer motherese to adult speech, probably because these speech alterations better match the infants' perceptual abilities. Even very young children often engage in this speaking style when speaking to babies. For example, Austin was barely a year old when his sister was born. Upon seeing her for the first time, he raised the pitch of his voice, slowed his rate of speech, and softly repeated, "Oh! The baby the baby the baby!!!" Despite having a very limited set of verbal skills, he nonetheless seemed to "know" how to speak to a baby.

Does motherese enhance children's future language skills? No evidence shows that it does. Steven Pinker (1994), one of the strongest proponents of the theory that language acquisition is an innate process (a view we will discuss later), has complained: "The belief that Motherese is essential to language development is part of the same mentality that sends yup-

pies to 'learning centers' to buy little mittens with bull-eyes on them to help their babies find their hands sooner" (p. 40). At the very least, though, Motherese seems likely to enhance the parent-child bond, an important part of the first year of development (discussed in Chapter 10).

By six or seven months of age, infants can babble—that is, chant various syllabic sounds in a rhythmic fashion. Infants' early babbling, a type of play and experimentation, is not limited to the sounds used in their parents' speech. Sometimes they also make sounds that are part of other languages. (The baby of English-speaking parents, for instance, may utter a rolled *r* or a guttural German *ch*.) For the first six months, deaf babies babble like children who can hear, a further indication that early vocalizations are spontaneous and relatively independent of what a child hears. Only later do children develop the capacity to imitate the sounds others make.

Although older prespeech babies communicate much through their actions and gestures, they also express themselves through intonation. In one study, the patterns of pitch in the sounds babies made to convey frustration, satisfaction, a question, or a command corresponded closely to typical adult patterns (Tonkova-Yampol'skaya, 1973). For example, babies seven to ten months old expressed commands with the same sharply rising and falling pitch adults use: "Stop that!" Some months later, the children began to use the intonation that signifies a question, distinguished by a sharp rise in pitch at the end of a sentence: "Are you going?" Such intonations are important in conveying meaning.

During the second six months of life, children are learning a remarkable amount about the languages they are hearing. Kuhl (1987) reviewed a number of experiments on the ability of infants to perceive phonemes. In one particularly clever series of studies, a child sat in a room while speech sounds—say, the vowels [*a*] and [*i*]—were played over loudspeakers. Every time the speech sound changed from [*a*] to [*i*], a wall of toys appeared—an event that delighted the child. After a few trials, the children began to look toward the wall as soon as they heard the change in sounds, in anticipation of the toys appearing. A child who could not hear the difference in the speech sounds, of course, would not look for the toys.

Surprisingly, these studies revealed that infants

hear *more* sound categories (phonemes) than adults. Japanese, for example, does not make the phoneme distinction between [r] and [l]; adult native speakers of Japanese cannot hear the difference between the sounds and often confuse them when trying to speak English. A nine-month-old Japanese infant, though, *can* hear the difference. When the sounds changed from [r] to [l], Japanese babies turned their heads toward the toys. Just a few months later, though, children raised in an exclusively Japanese-speaking environment no longer heard the difference in phonemes: when the speech sound changed, they no longer turned toward the wall in anticipation of seeing the toys.

In sum, infants in their first year of life are learning which of the many speech sounds they can hear are important to their future language. Even before learning to speak, they are acquiring important knowledge about their native language.

First Words

By the end of the first year, children know the names of a few people and objects, and they begin to produce their first words. To reach this stage they must understand that sound can be used to express meaning. Simply pronouncing an English word in an appropriate context is not sufficient. For instance, with prompting by adults some prespeech babies will say "bye-bye" while waving at someone. Because they do not yet grasp the rather abstract meaning of this string of sounds, however, it cannot be considered a genuine word. Children's first true words usually refer to those things that are immediately tangible and visible (Nelson, 1973, 1981; Schwartz & Leonard, 1984). They label people, objects, and everyday actions (*dada, car, sit*) and issue simple commands (*down!*). Their first words focus on the here and now.

This is the stage when children tend to over- and underextend the meanings of words (Clark, 1983; Kuczaj, 1982). A girl who has learned the word *dog* for the family pet may apply it at first to any animal she sees, a case of **overextension.** New parents are all too familiar with this phenomenon. For example, a child may seem to have learned who *dada* is. The proud father, taking the child to the grocery store, is shocked when the child calls out "dada!" to every passing male! Conversely, a child may use the word *dog* correctly to refer to the family's golden retriever but fail to apply it to a Chihuahua, a case of **underextension.** Through over- and underextension and

feedback about their mistakes, children gradually develop essentially the same mental representation of a dog that other speakers of the language possess.

The way in which a child refines words to describe concepts is a perfect example of the Piagetian processes of assimilation and accommodation. Calling every male "dada" is an example of the assimilation of new information into an existing schema. On learning that every male is *not* "dada," the child may develop a new category, "man." The creation of a new schema because an existing schema has been found inadequate is an example of accommodation.

First Sentences

Once children have acquired a basic vocabulary, they are ready for the momentous step of combining words into sentences. But just as their first step must await a certain level of motor control, so the emergence of sentences must await a certain level of neurological maturation. This maturation involves a rapid increase in the number of synapses in the cerebral cortex, which occurs around the age of one and a half to two (Milner, 1976).

Children's first sentences are very simple. They are short, usually two words long, and limited largely to concrete nouns and action verbs. Nonessential words, such as articles and conjunctions, are omitted, as are prefixes and suffixes (Brown et al., 1968). The child's talk sounds rather like the terse wording used in telegrams, which is why it is sometimes called **telegraphic speech.** Despite this terseness, people who know the child usually understand what is being said, and they often respond by expanding the child's sentences into well-formed adult ones. Here are examples of a toddler's sentences and his mother's interpretations of them (Brown & Bellugi, 1964):

Child	Mother
Baby high chair.	Baby is in the high chair.
Eve lunch.	Eve is having lunch.
Throw Daddy.	Throw it to Daddy.
Pick glove.	Pick up the glove.

Children usually produce their first words by the end of their first year. The words usually refer to familiar people, objects, or everyday actions.

Even at this early stage, however, the child's speech is quite structured. Often toddlers combine words in ways that follow adult syntax. While gobbling a cookie, for instance, a toddler may say, "Eat cookie," correctly putting *cookie* after *eat* to show that the cookie is the object being eaten rather than the actor doing the eating (Maratsos, Flavell, & Markman, 1983). Not all toddlers' sentences are simply reduced versions of adult sentences, however. The sentence "All-gone sticky" (after washing hands) is just one example of utterances that are unique to young children. Even though such sentences are not predictable using adult rules, they make sense using the child's rules.

The range of meanings children express with two-word sentences is impressive, from identification ("That Daddy") to location ("Doggy here"), recurrence ("Tickle again"), possession ("My cup"), negation ("No touch"), nonexistence ("All-gone bubble"), agent-action or agent-object ("Mommy throw"/"Throw ball"), attribution ("Baby sleeping"), and question ("Where kitty?") (Brown, 1973). These concepts form the core of all human language. Sometime prior to their second birthdays, children in all cultures start to put two words together to express these same concepts. Indeed, a large part of later language development is simply a matter of elaborating and refining the basic ideas that are already present at this early stage.

The Acquisition of Complex Rules

Two-word sentences are usually difficult to interpret out of context. "Baby chair," for example, could mean "This is the baby's chair," "The baby is in the chair," "Put the baby in the chair," or even "This is a little chair." Someone has to be present when the sentence is spoken to know what the child means. In adult sentences the grammatical information reduces this dependence on context. The sentence "The baby is in the chair" is unambiguous because of the inclusion of the verb *is* and the locational preposition *in*. Thus, mastery of complex grammatical rules enables the child to communicate beyond the immediate situation.

This stage in the acquisition of language occurs largely between the ages of two and five. By the time they enter school, most children have a good grasp of the grammar of their native language. This is not to say that children memorize a set of textbook rules. They do not. Even many adults have trouble stating grammatical rules, though they can apply them correctly. What children acquire during this period is an implicit sense of how to organize words into increasingly complex sentences. At the same time, their vocabularies grow rapidly. As one expert put it, "Their minds are like little vacuum pumps designed by nature to suck up words" (Miller, 1981, p. 119). A growing vocabulary further facilitates the ability to communicate clearly with language.

Children learn grammatical rules in a fairly predictable order, with little variation from child to child. Certain rules are acquired in sequential steps. A good example is the use of the negative (Bellugi, 1964). Two-year-olds have a very simple rule for forming negative sentences. They simply add *no* at the beginning (or occasionally the end) of a positive statement: "No get dirty." As children grow older, however, this simple rule becomes insufficient to express what they wish to say. So they acquire more elaborate rules of negation, rules that build toward the appropriate grammar for their native language. In English, a child's next step is to learn to place *no* or *not* just before the verb: "I not get it dirty." The last step is to add the required auxiliary verb: "I won't get it dirty."

As preschoolers learn the rules of their language, they often commit errors of **overregularization:** they overextend a grammatical rule to instances in which it does not apply (Bellugi, 1970; Slobin, 1972). Psychologists are interested in overregularizations, because they show that children have noticed the general rules of grammar and are trying to apply them. For this reason, overregularizations can be thought of as "smart" mistakes. Children around the world make these smart mistakes (Howard, 1983).

Overregularization is the way children learn the various forms of the past tense in English. At first they use certain irregular past-tense verbs, such as *fell* and *came,* correctly. (These words probably enter their vocabularies as separate items.) Then they learn the rule for forming the regular past tense, by adding a *d* or *t* sound to the end of the base verb, as in *hugged* and *walked.* Once children have acquired this rule, they apply it to the irregular verbs as well, and sentences such as "He goed to the store" and "I falled down" begin to appear in their conversations. It may take a year or even longer to master these exceptions (Ervin, 1964).

Speech in Social Context

While the acquisition of grammar is an important part of early language development, speaking a language involves more than just knowing proper word order and verb forms. Children must learn to use a language appropriately in a given social context. Studying how they acquire this ability is part of a field called **pragmatics.**

Researchers have found that children start to shape their use of language to suit a particular social context at quite an early age. In one study, four-year-olds showed marked differences in the way they went about describing a new toy to a two-year-old and to an adult (Shatz & Gelman, 1973). Figure 9-8 shows the descriptions one child gave. When addressing the two-year-old, this child used many attention-getting words: "Look," "Watch," "Perry" (the younger child's name). The sentences the child directed to the two-year-old were also shorter and simpler and assumed much less competence on the hearer's part. Clearly, this four-year-old knew that

Four-year-old to two-year-old:
...Watch, Perry. Watch this. He's backing in here. Now he drives up. Look, Perry. Look here, Perry. Those are marbles, Perry. Put the men in here. Now I'll do it.

Four-year-old to adult: You're supposed to put one of these persons in, see? Then one goes with the other little girl. And then the little boy. He's the little boy and he drives. And then they back up. And then the little girl has marbles... [Questions from adult and responses from child] And then the little girl falls out and then it goes backwards.

FIGURE 9-8   *Speech in social context in a four-year-old.* (Schatz & Gelman, 1973.)

different listeners demanded different kinds of speech. Though the child's ability to tailor speech to fit a situation will become more skilled in later years, this important principle of language use is established in the preschool years.

Language Acquisition Explained

Why do children acquire language as readily as they do? Acquiring and mastering a language is arguably the most impressive cognitive task humans perform. Yet given remotely normal neural structures and environment, all humans will acquire language, without direct instruction by parents or intent on the part of the child. Across cultures the process is the same.

Learning Theories

The idea that language learning proceeds along the same lines as any other kind of learning has been called the environmentalist or behaviorist position. B. F. Skinner, in his book *Verbal Behavior* (1957), argued that though language mastery is a complex behavior, it is nonetheless a *behavior.* In Skinner's view, none of the mechanisms used in language acquisition were "special."

To greatly simplify Skinner's theory, he reasoned that language acquisition is accomplished much like the acquisition of any kind of skill. A child sees an object on the table, says "apple," and the environment (usually a parent or caregiver) reinforces the response if it is correct ("Yes, that's an apple!"), or punishes and corrects it if it is wrong ("No, that's a pear"). Through this shaping process, the child gradually learns not only the names of objects but the rules associated with putting those names together (the grammar). While this strict behaviorist position is no longer held by many psychologists (see Lieberman, 1991), they do acknowledge the important role of learning and traditional learning mechanisms in language acquisition.

The publication of Skinner's book and, more important, the highly critical review it received from the linguist Noam Chomsky—whom we will meet shortly—helped to usher in what is now called the "cognitive revolution" (Gardner, 1985).

Nativist Theories

Many cognitive theorists proposed that language acquisition is controlled by the genetically programmed development of certain neural circuits in the brain, a theory called **nativism.** According to Noam Chomsky (1979), the most influential proponent of this view, the brain has a structure called the *language acquisition device* (LAD), which automatically analyzes the components of incoming speech. This structure is present in all normal humans, but not in other species.

> Steven Pinker, a psychologist at MIT, articulated the nativist position in a different way: Some cognitive psychologists have described language as a psychological faculty, a mental organ, a neural system, and a computational model. I prefer the quaint term "instinct." It conveys the idea that people know how to talk in more or less the sense that spiders know how to spin webs.
>
> Pinker, 1994, p.18

What a statement! We have just said that language is the most complex of all forms of human cognition. Now, nativists maintain that this complex behavior *is not learned*—at least not in the sense typically conveyed by "learning." What kind of evidence do nativists cite for this strong assertion?

Nativists point to several lines of evidence to support their view. One is the fact that children acquire very different native languages in much the same way (Slobin, 1982). Recall the first rule children use to form negative sentences: they simply add *no* to the

beginning of a positive statement. In every language that has been studied so far, two-year-olds have been found to use this rule to form negatives, even if it is not used in the adult speech they hear (Slobin, 1973). This finding suggests that humans are born with innate tendencies to structure language in particular ways.

Nativists point also to the fact that different children receive different degrees of encouragement (or reinforcement) for acquiring language. That is, some parents speak to their babies often, while others do not. Similarly, some parents regularly expand on what a toddler says, while others provide fewer such learning experiences. Yet despite these different language-learning environments, all children acquire roughly the same linguistic knowledge at much the same age.

Finally, nativists point to the speed with which language is mastered. Between the ages of two and five, children acquire a vocabulary of several thousand words. This rapid rate of language acquisition would seem unlikely without some innate propensity to master speech.

The Interaction of Learning and Innate Abilities

Even if humans have a built-in facility for acquiring language, must not learning mechanisms come into play? No child has ever mastered language without regular exposure to speech. Such exposure provides vital information that guides their language development. Exactly what, however, is involved in the learning process?

Parents often believe that they help their children to master language by praising them for correct speech and disapproving of their mistakes. In other words, they think they use reinforcement to shape their children's language development. There is some evidence that reinforcement does encourage language learning, but not to the extent many people assume. When one team of researchers studied tapes of actual parent-child conversations, they found that the adults greatly overestimated the role of their praise and criticism in their children's acquisition of language (Brown et al., 1968). Parents corrected gross mistakes in a young child's grammar, and occasionally they corrected errors in pronunciation. But in most cases it was the *truthfulness* of a remark, not the accuracy of the grammar, that elicited a parent's approval or rejection. For instance, when one child produced the grammatically perfect sentence "There's

When communicating with young infants, people—even other children—often modify their speaking style, slowing their rate of speaking and raising the pitch of the voice to better match the infants' perceptual abilities.

the animal in the farmhouse," the mother corrected her, because the building was in fact a lighthouse. Most parents pay relatively little attention to grammar, as long as they can understand what the child is trying to say and the child's statements conform to reality. Reinforcement, then, cannot be the only mechanism involved in language learning.

Simple imitation cannot be the only mechanism involved in language acquisition, either. All children produce sentences they have never heard before. Children who say "All-gone sticky" or "I seed two mouses" are not mimicking adults. Even when asked to reproduce exactly what an adult says, a child may make mistakes. Consider this conversation between a little girl and her mother:

Child: Nobody don't like me.
Mother: No, say "Nobody likes me."
Child: Nobody don't like me.
(Eight repetitions of this dialogue.)
Mother: No, now listen carefully; say "Nobody likes me."
Child: Oh! Nobody don't *likes* me.

McNeill, 1966

Clearly, this little girl is not imitating her mother; she is filtering what she hears using her own linguistic rules.

When children learn to say something that other people can understand, the experience in itself is reinforcing, because it enables them to communicate their thoughts, needs, and desires. Grammatically correct constructions tend to be repeated not because they are praised by adults but because they get re-

sults. Similarly, although children do not imitate exactly what adults say, adult modeling does influence their development of grammar. One researcher was able to accelerate two-year-olds' acquisition of certain grammatical forms by providing repeated examples (Nelson, 1977). For instance, when a child asked, "Where it go?" the researcher modeled the correct use of the future tense in responding to the question: "It will go there" and "We will find it." Soon the children began to use the new forms in their own speech. Notice how the psychologist attended to the children's statements, building on them to get her own point across. Many parents unknowingly adopt this interactional style, shaping the child's' language in the process. Research shows that this style of talking to young children (using what the child says to help model more complex grammar) can significantly facilitate language learning (Rice, 1989).

John Anderson (1995) has pointed out the tremendous amount of time children spend practicing their language skills. He estimates conservatively that by age six, a child will have spent over 10,000 hours practicing speaking. Anyone who has spent time around young children can readily attest to this estimate. Children are constantly talking, sometimes to no one in particular; they carry on imaginary conversations, speak to toys, even talk to themselves. If you have listened outside a bedroom door as a child is falling asleep, you have probably heard "crib talk." All this practice no doubt contributes to the mastery of language.

Though the ability to acquire spoken language is innate, enhanced verbal abilities such as reading are clearly shaped by learning. Most college students were raised in highly verbal environments, where they were encouraged to speak and read by parents and other caregivers.

Thus, to some degree language *does* appear to be innately human. The fact that all humans acquire a basic vocabulary and correct grammar in the absence of direct instruction and with little intentional effort is persuasive evidence. However, enhanced verbal abilities—larger vocabularies, more diverse ways of expressing ourselves—are shaped by learning. The fact that you are now in college—reading and understanding textbooks in literature, physics, and psychology—can be attributed in no small part to the kind of environment you had as a child. Indeed, most readers of this book were probably raised in highly verbal environments, where they were encouraged to speak and read intelligently. Their parents and caregivers probably had excellent verbal skills and reinforced their children in acquiring these skills.

To summarize, then, a basic, several-thousand-word vocabulary and a rudimentary knowledge of the rules of a language (grammar) are acquired because of the innate tendencies present in all humans. Any increases in this basic ability, including size of vocabulary and style of expression, are heavily influenced by the learning environment. Thus, language acquisition is perhaps the most direct test of the "nature versus nurture" hypothesis. Do humans acquire language because of innate, unlearned abilities, or because of their learning environment? The answer is, a combination of both.

Memory Development

If you have ever asked a five-year-old to help you remember a grocery list, you know how limited a preschooler's memory can be. The child may remember a few things that are especially appealing (cookies and ice cream, for instance) but will probably forget the rest of the list. Yet six or seven years later, the same child may be quite adept at memorization. Figure 9-9 shows how dramatically children's metacognitive skills can improve over time. Kindergartners' actual memory span tends to be poorer than their predicted memory span. By the fourth grade, though, memory skills have improved (digit spans have increased from three to five digits), and *metamemory* skills have improved as well (predicted memory spans are more realistic).

Psychologists have wondered what accounts for this marked improvement in a child's memory. Is a preschooler's brain not as able as an older child's? Or does the explanation lie in the different ways younger and older children process information?

Changes in Information-Processing Strategies

Recent research suggests that information-processing factors may be extremely important to the development of a child's memory. Younger children use far fewer deliberate strategies for storing and retrieving information than older children (Flavell, Miller, & Miller, 1993; Kail, 1990). In one study, six-, eight-, and eleven-year-olds viewed pictures of three related objects along with a card that could serve as a memory cue (Kobasigawa, 1974). For example, one group of pictures showed a bear, a monkey, and a camel, while the cue card showed a zoo with three empty cages. The experimenter explicitly related the

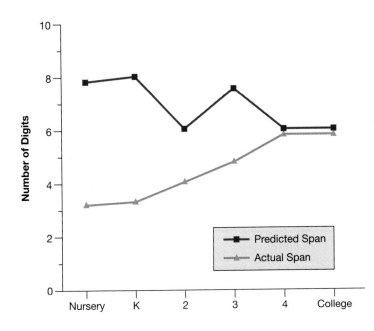

FIGURE 9-9 *Predicted versus actual memory span by grade level. Children in the older grades not only display better memory performance but also provide more realistic predictions of their performance, reflecting increased metacognitive skills.* (After Kail, 1990, Figure 3-1.)

card to the pictures by pointing out that the zoo was the place where the animals lived.

Later, some of the children were given the cue card and asked to recall the three pictures associated with each one. They were told they could look at the cards to help them remember. Significantly, most of the six-year-olds ignored the cards; they seemed unable to grasp the relationship between the cues and the ability to retrieve information. In contrast, the eleven-year-olds used the cues quite effectively, often recalling all three items associated with a card. The eight-year-olds' performance fell somewhere in between that of the others. They sometimes used the cue cards, but their strategy was more haphazard than the older children's.

Interestingly, when all the children were *required* to use the cue cards, age differences in recall disappeared. Thus, some of the improvements in memory as children grow older probably have to do with the learning of effective storage and retrieval strategies. That is not to say that very young children use no cognitive strategies in trying to remember. Even preschoolers sometimes spontaneously employ deliberate tactics to aid in storage and retrieval (DeLoache & Todd, 1988; Wellman, 1987). But these early tactics tend to be quite unsophisticated, and therefore of limited effectiveness.

Another factor that contributes to improved performance on memory tasks is greater familiarity with the items to be recalled. In general, the more fa-

miliar material is, the easier it is to remember; and obviously, the older children get, the more knowledge and experience they tend to acquire (Chi & Ceci, 1986). This link between familiarity and memory is related in part to effective storage and retrieval strategies, especially to categorization (organization of items to be remembered in groups, which can then be stored and recalled as chunks). The more a child knows about a particular topic, the more easily the child can categorize new information in this way, thus reducing the demands made on memory.

Recall the study that compared the performance on memory tests of expert and novice chess players (Chi, 1978). What made this study so intriguing was that the experts were ten-year-old children, while the novices were adults. As might be expected, the adults demonstrated a better memory span than children in recalling digits. However, in recalling meaningful chess patterns, the ten-year-olds performed significantly better than adults. Clearly, then, part of the reason why most children perform poorly on standard tests of memory and metamemory is their relative lack of knowledge (look back at Figure 9-7).

Changes In Metacognition

If you asked preschoolers to study a set of pictures until they were sure they could remember each and every one, you would probably find they greatly overestimated their ability to remember the drawings.

This six-year-old can think only in terms of concrete objects, like the rocks on a science table. Around the beginning of adolescence, he will become able to think in abstract terms and solve problems systematically.

A quick look through the stack and a preschooler may announce, "I'm ready," only to make a dismal showing on a subsequent recall test. An older child, in contrast, would be much more apt to know when he or she had fully memorized a list. This ability to monitor one's own thoughts—whether on a memory test, a problem-solving task, or some other cognitive activity—is called **metacognition.** It is another important intellectual capacity that emerges in middle childhood.

Of course, even young children have some understanding of their own memory powers. For instance, four-year-olds realize that adults can recall more information than they can, and they also realize that a short list of items is easier to remember than a long list (Wellman, Collins, & Glieberman, 1981). But older children have a much more accurate and realistic understanding of their memories than younger children (e.g., Yussan & Berman, 1981). Studies have shown how dramatic these age-related metacognitive differences can be. In one study, first, second, and third graders were asked to evaluate a set of oral instructions about how to play a card game (Markman, 1977). The instructions lacked a vital piece of information, so no one could possibly understand them. Yet most of the first graders assured the researcher the instructions were perfectly clear. Only when they tried to play the game did they recognize the problem. In contrast, most of the third graders spotted the blatant gap in the instructions far sooner.

The same difference in responses can be seen when students are asked to monitor their acquisition of knowledge from a text they are reading. Young readers often read superficially, believing they have understood when they have not (e.g., Baker & Brown, 1984). Or they may waste time rereading a passage they already understood. The ability to assess whether or not one has understood a given passage is called *comprehension monitoring.* While younger readers are quite poor at this skill, older readers show significant improvement (e.g., Weaver & Bryant, 1995; Weaver, Bryant, & Burns, 1995).

What explains these age-related differences in the monitoring of thought processes? One answer may be younger children's limited exposure to metacognitive techniques, such as self-testing or reenacting an event mentally. When researchers encouraged young children to use metacognitive processes, the children performed better on certain cognitive tasks (Brown & Kane, 1988). Differences in experience alone are unlikely to provide a full explanation for age-related differences in cognition, however. Very young children who are taught metacognitive strategies often quickly forget them, or fail to use them in subsequent situations. Thus, age-related constraints on the development of metacognition probably exist.

Cognitive Development In Adolescence and Adulthood

Adolescent Cognitive Skills

Around the beginning of adolescence new cognitive capabilities begin to emerge. For the first time children can carry out systematic tests to solve problems. They become able to think hypothetically and

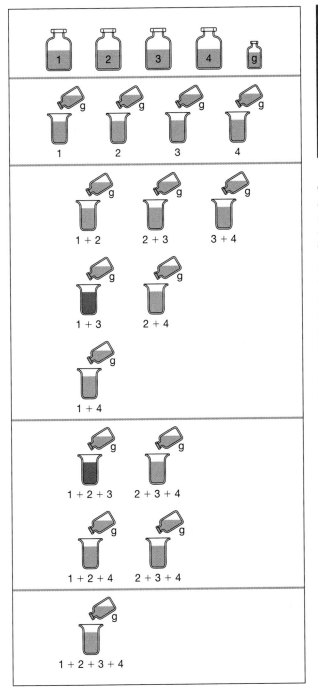

odorless liquid (Piaget & Inhelder, 1969). Children are given some empty glasses and are asked to find the liquid or combination of liquids that will turn yellow when a few drops from bottle *g* are added. The liquid in beaker 2 is plain water and has no effect on the reaction; the liquid in beaker 4 actually prevents the yellow color from appearing. The combination that produces yellow is liquid 1 plus liquid 3, followed by liquid *g*. To make these discoveries and to be certain of them, children must try all the possible combinations shown in Figure 9-10.

When presented with this task, elementary school-children often begin by systematically trying all the *single* possibilities. That is, they may test *1 plus g,* then *2 plus g,* then *3 plus g,* and so on. When none of these combinations produces yellow, they are likely to say, "I tried them all and none of them works." With a little prompting from the experimenter, though, they may realize that *more than one* liquid can be combined with liquid *g.* But they will then mix the liquids haphazardly and will often become confused. In contrast, most adolescents can consider all possible combinations systematically. They may need a paper and pencil to keep track of the ones they have tried, but they understand how to generate the full set of combinations.

Although Piaget's conclusions about the emergence of ability to do formal operations seem reasonable enough, not all researchers have been able to verify them. Consider again the problem in Figure 9-10, a task in logical reasoning that, according to Piaget, many adolescents should be able to do. Yet research shows that only between 5 and 25 percent of adolescents, college students, and college-educated adults manage to give the right answer (Brainerd, 1978). Large proportions of teenagers and adults also fail on other formal operations (Donaldson, 1984; Gardner, 1983; Wason & Johnson-Laird, 1972). Piaget was aware that such failures occur, but he offered an explanation for them. He argued that

in abstract terms. The ability to perform these cognitive tasks heralds the onset of adultlike thinking, which Piaget called the **formal operations stage.**

Piaget created many tests to measure problem-solving ability. One involves four beakers of colorless, odorless liquids labeled 1, 2, 3, and 4, plus a smaller bottle labeled *g,* also filled with a colorless,

though a person has reached the stage of formal operations, that person will not necessarily reason logically at all times. A person may misunderstand the demands of a particular problem or find its solution too difficult. Many adults, in fact, may be capable of using formal thinking only in their own area of expertise (Ault, 1983).

Piaget believed that reaching the stage of formal operations conferred a fundamentally new way of understanding the world on the child. That is, teenagers are, mentally speaking, very different from elementary school children. In Piaget's view, teenagers have overcome the cognitive limitations of middle childhood, and are free to think and reason in more advanced ways. Not all psychologists agree with this perspective, however (Keating, 1980, 1988). Some suspect that the observable changes in adolescents' performance on formal-operational tasks may be due simply to increased knowledge or better information-processing skills (see Chi, 1978), including the regular use of storage and retrieval tactics, and a tendency to monitor their thoughts. How much of teenagers' cognitive performance might be accounted for by such factors is still a subject open to debate. Certainly, information-processing skills do improve during adolescence, and that fact undoubtedly affects what a teenager can do.

Postformal Operations: A Fifth Stage of Cognitive Development?

For Piaget, the most advanced type of thinking involved formal operations. But is that really the highest stage of intellectual functioning? Some psychologists are not sure. Klaus Riegel (1973), for example, maintains that mature thinkers eventually reach another stage, which he calls the **dialectic operations stage.** A *dialectic* is a type of dialogue in which two contradictory viewpoints are debated. If you have ever debated a deep moral, religious, or philosophical issue with a friend or roommate, you have engaged in dialectic operational thinking. Such thinking demands the ability to tolerate conflict and inconsistencies between two viewpoints (and in this sense can be likened to Kohlberg's "postconventional morality," discussed in Chapter 10). Riegel's notions of postformal thinking are not recognized by most psychologists, however.

What is Piaget's ultimate contribution to psychology? Some researchers may be tempted to discount Piaget's work because of its inconsistencies. That would be a serious mistake, however. Piaget's ultimate contribution will be measured in terms of its impact on subsequent research, not in the correctness of his theory. As psychologist Robert Sternberg has said:

> Although aspects of Piaget's theory have been questioned and in some cases have been disconfirmed, the theory is still enormously influential. Indeed, the contribution of his theory, like that of others, is shown more by its influence on further theory and research than by its ultimate correctness.

Sternberg, 1996, p. 426

Cognitive Change During Adulthood

Cognitive development does not end at adolescence. From early to middle to later adulthood, most people proceed through broadly similar sequences of intellectual changes. Early adulthood, from about ages twenty to forty, is a time of peak intellectual performance. On any kind of learning or memory task, young adults will usually do better than they have ever done before. And if success at a task depends on how fast it is done, young adults probably do a little better than they ever will again. Early adulthood also tends to be the time when people are most flexible intellectually. They can usually accept new ideas quite easily and can readily shift their problem-solving strategies.

Provided a person remains healthy, verbal skills and reasoning ability are likely to improve even more during middle adulthood—roughly the years between ages forty and sixty. Long-term studies of intellectual performance have found that IQ generally increases into middle age (Eichorn, Hunt, & Honzik, 1981; Kangas & Bradway, 1974). And since middle-aged adults continue to learn and store new information, they are often more knowledgeable than they were in their younger years (Mitchell, 1989; Schaie, 1984). In addition, the middle-aged adult's ability to think flexibly—to shift gears mentally in order to solve a problem—is likely to be as good as it was in early adulthood. When declines in flexibility do occur, they are very gradual, and of no practical importance until the sixth decade of life or later (Schaie, 1984). Only when middle-aged adults are asked to do tasks involving hand-eye coordination do they tend to perform less well than they once did: motor skills often slow down in middle age (Baltes & Schaie, 1974). In most other ways, however, adults in their middle years remain in their intellectual prime.

What about cognitive skills after the age of sixty?

Cognitive development does not end at adolescence; it continues into middle age. Older adults who keep active and stay involved in challenging activities tend to show little change in their intellectual abilities, even through their mid-seventies.

Do they decline, as many people assume? The recent findings on this topic are quite encouraging. The average age at which measurable declines in cognitive abilities occur is greater than sixty. In some studies, declines have not been detected until the mid-seventies (Schaie, 1989). Nor does the detection of some cognitive declines with advancing years mean that all a person's cognitive abilities are declining. In most elderly people, some cognitive skills remain as good as ever. Consider short-term memory, for example. Its capacity—the amount of information it can hold—remains virtually the same as people grow older (Craik & Byrd, 1982). When short-term memory decrements are found among the elderly, they are usually extremely slight.

Many elderly people do experience some decline in long-term memory, however. In one study, researchers tested the memories of nearly 2,000 subjects with a tense, fast-paced film clip (Loftus, Levidow, & Duensing, 1991). Visitors viewed the film clip on a large screen near the entrance to a science museum. Later, when they had made their way to the exhibit on memory, they were asked ten questions about what they had seen. People over age sixty-five answered fewer questions about the clip correctly than subjects in any other age group. The average score for all the other age groups was 74 percent, while the average score for the elderly was 56 percent.

Such declines in long-term memory can be compensated for. When elderly people are given extra time to learn and recall information, for example, they perform much better than they do under pressure (Canestrari, 1963; Eisdorfer, Axelrod, & Wilkie, 1963; Monge & Hultsch, 1971). And when they are specifically advised to use mnemonic strategies, they sometimes profit more than the young do (Craik & Simon, 1980; Erber, Herman, & Botwinick, 1980; Perlmutter & Mitchell, 1982). Such findings have led some researchers to suggest that any advantage younger people may have in long-term memory has more to do with their quicker response times and greater knowledge of test-taking tactics than with physiologically based differences in long-term memory per se (Datan, Rodeheaver, & Hughes, 1987; Reese & Rodeheaver, 1985).

That is not to say that there are no physiologically based differences in memory between young and old. When subjects are given extensive practice in remembering lists using specific techniques, the elderly usually reach the limits of their improvement sooner than college students do—a result that probably has to do with the physiological limits of the aging nervous system (Kliegl, Smith, & Baltes, 1989). Most elderly people, however, are perfectly capable of becoming experts in long-term memory storage and retrieval. Thus, in everyday life any limits to their abilities would have no practical significance. Although elderly people themselves will usually admit that their memories are not what they used to be, that admission is often due more to negative assumptions about aging than to genuine declines in memory (Hultsch, Hertzog, & Dixon, 1987; Tavris, 1987). In fact, some elderly people suffer no measurable decline in cognitive functioning whatsoever (Schaie, 1984, 1990a, 1990b).

If there is one indisputable fact about aging, it is that its effects are widely varied. Psychologists are eager to learn why. Biology is one factor that underlies intellectual performance in later life. Some forty or more years after finishing school, identical twins are more alike in their cognitive functioning than unrelated individuals or even fraternal twins (Jarvik, 1975). Of course, such findings do not necessarily mean that people have a genetically programmed timetable for aging (Fries & Crapo, 1981). Identical twins may share a predisposition toward, or resistance to, certain degenerative diseases, which in turn affect their cognitive functioning. Whatever the relationship, biology appears to account for at least some of the wide variation in cognitive decline among the elderly.

Equally important, however, are environmental factors. Conditions that promote loneliness and depression can contribute to cognitive deficits (Miller, 1975). So can mere expectations of intellectual decline with aging, for there is some evidence that performance often mirrors people's expectations (Perlmutter, 1983). The amount of stimulation in a person's environment also appears to be critical to cognitive functioning (Dutta, Schulenberg, & Lair, 1986; Gribbin, Schaie, & Parham, 1980). If older people keep active and stay involved in interesting and challenging activities—if, in short, they continue to use their minds—their intellectual powers will likely not be blunted. An interesting, challenging environment may even reverse cognitive declines that have already occurred. In one study, researchers selected over a hundred people ages sixty-four to ninety-five, all of whom had shown a decline in cognitive performance over the previous fourteen years (Schaie & Willis, 1986). These elderly subjects were given five one-hour training sessions on either inductive reasoning or spatial problem solving. In a substantial number of cases, the training totally erased the subjects' cognitive declines. Such findings have encouraged psychologists to take a critical look at cognitive deficits in the aged. Although such deficits may seem to be caused by physical deterioration, the cause may in fact be disuse of one's cognitive faculties. If so, relatively simple intervention programs may be able to eliminate the problem.

In Depth

Nature versus Nurture in Language Acquisition: The Case of "Genie"

PERHAPS THE MOST IMPRESSIVE of all cognitive abilities is human language. Those who have studied language are impressed by the relative ease with which children acquire it. While there is no doubt that language "develops" as children mature, psychologists differ on the processes that underlie language acquisition.

The debate between "environmentalist" and "nativist" views of language acquisition is of tremendous historical significance. Behaviorists, especially B. F. Skinner, regarded language as their greatest challenge. Any comprehensive theory of learning would have to deal with what is arguably the most sophisticated of cognitive abilities. In 1957, Skinner published *Verbal Behavior*, in which he proposed that the mechanisms by which language is learned are not fundamentally different from those by which rats learn to press a bar. The organism makes a response, and that response is either reinforced or punished. According to this view, called the "learning" or "environmental" view, verbal responses are shaped like all other responses.

In a scathing review of Skinner's book (Chomsky, 1957a), a young linguist named Noam Chomsky proposed an alternative framework based on the idea that human language abilities are innate. According to Chomsky, language learning is unlike all other kinds of learning; humans are specially "predisposed" to learn language. This framework is sometimes called the "nativist" position.

The debate between the two views was not only heated but nearly impossible to resolve. Neither Skinner nor Chomsky provided conclusive evidence to support their theories. In virtually every situation, learning and nativist explanations were confounded: children learning language are nearly always in reinforcing environments during the same critical years when any innate factors would be unfolding. A definitive test of these competing theories would require a comparison of children raised in normal environments with those raised in an environment deprived of any kind of linguistic interactions—so

unthinkable that researchers often referred to this as "the forbidden experiment" (Rymer, 1993).

Initial Studies

Though the "forbidden experiment" was never conducted, of course, indirect evidence gradually appeared supporting the nativist view, as was covered earlier in this chapter (see p. 316). Eric Lenneberg (1967), a noted psycholinguist, later modified Chomsky's ideas. Lenneberg argued that while language was innate, the acquisition of language is constrained by certain *critical periods.* Specifically, unless one acquires a first language before the onset of puberty (about ages twelve through thirteen), one will *never* acquire it. Though Lenneberg's ideas were intriguing, they were considered untestable: from an ethical standpoint, psychologists simply cannot restrict a child's access to language for the first thirteen years of life.

Criticisms, Alternatives, and Further Research

In September 1970, social workers in Los Angeles became aware of an extreme case of neglect and abuse. A thirteen-year-old girl, known in the scientific literature as "Genie," was discovered locked in a small room. Genie had spent virtually her entire life in isolation, chained to a potty chair or confined to a makeshift bed. Her father, who committed suicide shortly after Genie's discovery, had apparently decided when Genie was very young that she was retarded and had rejected her. Genie's mother, for reasons that are not entirely clear, had allowed the abuse to continue until 1970, when she fled the house with Genie. Psychologists quickly recognized the significance of Genie's case. The "forbidden experiment" was suddenly a reality. Raised without language, Genie was now past the point at which, according to Lenneberg, she could acquire it.

Not surprisingly, Genie was profoundly developmentally delayed. She could walk, but only very awkwardly. She was malnourished and cognitively impaired. Genie's father had apparently punished her quite severely whenever she made any sounds, so when she was discovered, she was mute and withdrawn.

A team of researchers, including then graduate student Susan Curtiss (see Curtiss, 1977), began working with Genie. Some of the work was therapeutic, but much of it focused on Genie's linguistic abilities. Could she acquire and use a language?

Researchers found Genie to be an engaging, charming, and sympathetic figure. Everyone who came into contact with her sensed something special (see Rymer, 1993). Her initial progress was slow but steady. She developed attachments to her new caregivers, even seemed to make some strides in communicating. Curtiss at first believed Genie would disprove Lenneberg's idea of a critical period in language acquisition.

Genie's progress soon slowed significantly, though. While she was able to acquire and use words for objects ("ball"), actions ("run"), or attributes ("color"), her syntactic abilities (that is, her ability to acquire and use the rules of language, or its "grammar") lagged far behind. And though her *receptive* abilities (her ability to understand what was said to her) were quite good, her *productive* abilities were minimal. Genie's vocabulary grew to the size of a typical three- or four-year-old child's, but she failed to develop comparable syntactic abilities. After several years of intensive study, most of those who had worked with Genie were forced to conclude that her linguistic abilities were indeed quite restricted and probably irreversibly so. The inevitable conclusion, they thought, was that her case supported Lenneberg's hypothesis.

Patterns and Conclusions

For all practical purposes, the scientific study of Genie ended during the 1970s. Unfortunately, her life since then has not been happy. While the research was being conducted, Genie had lived in several foster homes, often with those involved in the research. When research funding was terminated, she lived in various foster homes, though no longer with those involved in the research. She even lived with her mother for a short period. However, in one home she was severely punished for vomiting, and after that she refused to speak or even open her mouth for fear of being punished again. Whatever linguistic gains she had made were soon lost. Several years after funding for the research was terminated, Genie turned eighteen and could no longer be treated as a minor. She was incapable of living alone, though, and later was made a ward of the state. Today, Genie lives in a home for mentally retarded adults. She doesn't speak and rarely makes any sound at all.

During the past few years, psychologists have begun to take a more critical approach to Genie's case. Many now question the conclusion that Genie's case supported Lenneberg's theory (Nova, 1994; Rymer, 1993). For example, Genie's neurological and intellectual capabilities are unclear. While years of abuse had undoubtedly impaired her development, some researchers wonder whether Genie was born retarded, as her father assumed. If so, much of her difficulty with language could be attributed to her retardation. Similarly, Genie's lifetime of abuse almost certainly had a negative impact on her neurological functioning, so that she may not have possessed the neurological capacity to acquire language. Many researchers have thus concluded that while Lenneberg's hypothesis may well be correct, Genie's case proves nothing. Too much is unknown about Genie's neurological capabilities, both at birth and after thirteen years of neglect and abuse, to allow a meaningful interpretation of her case.

Given a quarter century of hindsight, what conclusions *can* be drawn regarding this case? Unfortunately, not many. Developmental psychologist Helen Benedict, author of a landmark study on early language development in children (Benedict, 1979), believes that while the Chomsky/Lenneberg hypothesis is probably correct—language is innate, but must be developed before a child reaches puberty—Genie's case cannot be taken as reliable evidence. Her hidden childhood raises too many questions. Was Genie born with some kind of brain damage? Did her inadequate diet contribute to her cognitive limitations? What about the devastating punishment and cruelty she suffered, or her genetic history? Psychologists will never know the answers to these profoundly disturbing questions, and Genie remains a silent, tragic figure.

SUMMARY

1. **Developmental psychology** seeks to describe and explain the regular patterns of growth and change that occur during the life cycle. Psychologists approach human development from three perspectives: physical development, **cognitive development,** and social and personality development.

2. Human infants are born with impressive perceptual, motor, and learning capabilities. They process information and interact with their surroundings from the very first moments after birth. These early interactions in turn help to shape the child's cognitive, social, and emotional development.

3. Two major views of cognitive development have been proposed. One, which is closely associated with Jean Piaget, sees cognitive development as a series of qualitatively different stages. In each stage the child's construction of reality becomes more mature. The second view, which stems from the information-processing perspective, argues that quantitative differences in children's cognitive skills and knowledge account for the changes we see.

4. Piaget believed that infants exercise **sensorimotor** intelligence. They come to know the world strictly by perceiving and acting in it, not through any abstract kind of thinking. Then, in the preschool years, youngsters become capable of **representational thought,** the ability to represent things mentally when those things are not physically present. Intellect is still limited in some respects, however. For instance, in many cases preschoolers are quite **egocentric;** they fail to take into account the perspectives of others. Piaget felt that the major intellectual accomplishment of middle childhood was the ability to perform **concrete operations,** a variety of reversible mental transformations carried out on tangible objects. One example involves concepts of **conservation,** the recognition that some characteristics of objects remain the same (are conserved) despite changes in other features.

5. Some psychologists have questioned Piaget's account of how thinking and reasoning develop. One reason is the existence of inconsistencies in the kinds of tasks children can perform. For instance, if six-year-olds can perform conservation-of-number tasks, why can't they solve conservation-of-mass or conservation-of-weight problems until they are two to four years older? One answer is that changes in children's thinking and reasoning have as much to do with quantitative advances in such factors as short-term memory as they do with qualitative advances in how youngsters structure reality. Robbie Case is one psychologist who has recently tried to integrate this information-processing viewpoint with the stage approach of Piaget.

6. Besides making impressive advances in thinking and reasoning, young children also master spoken language. Children of all cultures appear to go through similar sequences in acquiring language. By the age of one, most produce their first words, often **over-** or **underextending** the meaning until the underlying concept is grasped correctly. Around age two, children begin to use what is known as **telegraphic speech**—short sentences made up of nouns and action verbs. The ability to organize words into increasingly complex sentences develops most prominently between the ages of two and five. Children seem to acquire an implicit knowledge of grammatical rules in a fairly stable order. By the end of the preschool years they also display some understanding of how speech should be modified to suit different social contexts (**pragmatics**).

7. Most psychologists now believe that language is innately human, and children in normal environments will acquire basic vocabulary and correct grammar without formal instruction. However, environmental factors are critically involved in expanding these basic capacities resulting in increased vocabulary, enhanced style of expression, and the ability to use written language.

8. During childhood, people also become increasingly adultlike in their memory capabilities. This is partly because they learn to use more

effective encoding and retrieval strategies, and partly because they are more familiar with the information to be recalled. Over the years youngsters also develop an increasingly sophisticated capacity for **metacognition,** the ability to monitor their own thoughts.

9. Around the beginning of adolescence, people start to be able to carry out systematic tests and to think hypothetically and abstractly. Piaget called this the ability to understand **formal operations.** In various tests of formal operations, however, teenagers and adults often fail to perform well. This suggests that even when people are capable of logical reasoning, they may not apply it in all situations.

10. Cognitive development continues throughout adulthood, as knowledge and experience expand. Intellectual abilities do not usually decline sharply in old age, as many people fear. In fact, cognitive decline with aging is by no means inevitable. There is wide variation among individuals as a result of both biology and environment. Providing a more stimulating and challenging environment even seems to reverse many cognitive declines.

SUGGESTED READINGS

Bower, T. G. R. (1989). *The rational infant.* San Francisco: Freeman. A solid introduction to the psychological abilities of infants.

Flavel, J. H., Miller, P. H., & Miller, S. A. (1993). *Cognitive development* (3rd ed.). Englewood Cliffs, NJ: Prentice-Hall. One of the best reviews of the field, written in a style befitting the subject without eliminating the inherent interest in the material.

Kail, R. (1990). *The development of memory in children.* New York: Freeman. A comprehensive but accessible account of childhood memory.

Pinker, S. (1994). *The language instinct: The new science of language and the mind.* New York: The Penguin Press. A marvelously written book, outlining Pinker's somewhat controversial views on language acquisition.

Rymer, R. (1993). *Genie: Escape from a silent childhood.* New York: Viking Penguin. A captivating book that presents the case of Genie in detail and also examines how she was treated by those who studied her. Rymer's frank approach to the subject raises important questions.

Social and Personality Development

Laura was a handsome baby who weighed eight pounds [at birth]. . . . From the first memory Laura was striking for her inactivity. She emerged from the uterus sluggishly. After delivery she lay quietly in her crib, looking around with her eyes open wide, as if in surprise . . . she gasped immediately after delivery and had begun to take regular deep breaths, so she needed no extra stimulation from the doctors or nurses. Her color changed from purplish blue to pale pink in the first few minutes, and she was wrapped in several sheets to keep her warm. Her hands and feet were purple and felt cold to the touch despite the wrapping. They remained discolored for several days. Only when she was crying did her circulation and the color of her extremities improve. But Laura rarely cried.

Brazelton, 1983, pp. 14–15

[Daniel] was a handsome eight-pound baby who literally "came out crying and fighting." He needed no stimulation to continue breathing, and his color changed quickly to a healthy pink . . . Daniel was ready to cry by the time the nurses bathed and dressed him. He squalled vigorously, thrust his arms and legs straight out, kicked and pushed the nurses' hands away from him. . . . He shot from sleeping to an unapproachable state of screaming. He cried with a loud, piercing bellow. . . . As he howled, his color changed to a dark purple, his arms, legs, and whole body stiffened, and he became rigid. He could not be quieted with her crooning, with quiet rocking and cuddling, or with a bottle alone.

Brazelton, 1983, pp. 24–26

From the first moments of their lives, Laura and Daniel were completely different. Laura was quiet, pensive, and passive. Daniel was loud, impulsive, and impatient. While Laura was content to watch the world from the safety of her crib, Daniel never quit moving. He grabbed objects, placed them in his mouth, and cried vigorously when they were taken away. The noted physician and author T. Berry Brazelton, who wrote these descriptions of the two just after they were born, would call Laura a "quiet baby" and Daniel an "active baby."

During the next few years both Laura and Daniel would go through remarkable changes. They would develop motor skills, learning first to crawl, then to walk. They would acquire language at a breathtaking pace. But what about their basic characteristics, or temperament? Would Laura "outgrow" her shyness, or would she tend to avoid social interactions as she got older? What about Daniel's active nature? Would his parents need to be "on guard" for

Basic personality characteristics, like extroversion, result from a combination of genetic and environmental influences; they tend to be quite stable over the life span.

aggressive behavior, so they could help Daniel to overcome that trait? Should they be strict and forceful, or should they instead avoid punishing? Should they even bother to worry, but rather accept his active tendencies as part of his personality?

As you might guess, there are no simple answers to questions like these. But there is a good chance that infants like Laura will be shy and retiring as adults, and that infants like Daniel will remain active, independent, and aggressive. Personality traits like these are quite persistent.

In this chapter we will look at the factors that shape our personalities and social behaviors. We will find that some of our behavioral tendencies are inherited, while others are learned through experience. In every case, though, genetic tendencies and environmental forces interact. For example, Laura's mother responded to Laura's passive nature with worry and fear. Laura was her first child, and she felt woefully inadequate as a mother. She had difficulty breast-feeding Laura at first. Though she had been told to expect long bouts of crying, Laura rarely cried. After a week or so, Laura began to feed more vigorously. But even then, she remained a quiet baby, preferring to lie in her crib, her alert eyes wide open.

Laura's mother wondered if the baby's shy nature was compounded by her inability to nurse for the first few days. "Perhaps," Brazelton (1983) wrote, ". . . in an infant whose personality and particular attributes were all set for a reinforcement of this kind of pattern" (p. 22).

People everywhere wonder about personality differences. Even children in the same family can be startlingly different. Like all behavior, personality is guided by a combination of genetic and environmental factors. However, the genetic component of personality and social development may be greater than has previously been estimated. Behavioral geneticists (e.g., Plomin, 1989) have determined that many personality differences have a powerful genetic basis.

The study of personality is one of psychology's primary domains. We will cover many other aspects of personality in Chapter 13. In this chapter we will lay some groundwork by looking at social and personality development during various stages of life, from infancy to old age. We will begin with a broad overview of the major perspectives in this field.

Perspectives on Social and Personality Development

Though social and personality development are often discussed together, the two terms should be distinguished. **Social development** encompasses the ways in which a person's interactions and relationships with others change as that person grows older. **Personality development** describes the emergence of the distinctive styles of thought, feeling, and behavior that make each human being a unique individual. The two are closely interrelated. How you interact with others can affect who you become (that is, your distinctive style of behavior), while your distinctive style of behavior can in turn affect the nature of your social relationships.

One of the earliest perspectives on social and personality development was Sigmund Freud's **psychoanalytic theory,** also called the **psychosexual approach** to development. Freud's view of childhood and personality development has had a tremendous impact on personality theory. In this chapter we will discuss only certain aspects of Freud's views; we will learn much more about his theory in Chapter 13.

Freud believed that the first five years of life were filled with turmoil, as the young child deals with sexual and aggressive urges and the anxiety associated with them. How a child learns to respond to these impulses, Freud believed, would continue to influence the child's behavior throughout her life. Though most contemporary personality theorists reject a strictly Freudian approach, all realize that childhood events can influence behavior throughout adulthood, even if they are not consciously accessible—another example of Recurring Theme 3: "A large proportion of behavior is controlled by unconscious activity."

 THEME **A Large Proportion of Behavior Is Controlled by Unconscious Activity** Erik Erikson rejected Freud's belief that the resolution of childhood sexual and aggressive urges forms the roots of personality. Instead, he proposed a series of eight nonsexual challenges that people face from infancy through old age. The family and other social settings are the arenas in which these challenges unfold. Each challenge has an outcome, either favorable or unfavorable, which affects a person's social and personality development thereafter. A favorable outcome produces positive outlooks and feelings, which make coping with subsequent challenges easier. An unfavorable outcome, in contrast, leaves a person troubled and at a disadvantage in future developmental stages. Erikson's approach is referred to as the **psychosocial theory** of personality development. Table 10-1 summarizes the eight challenges and the two possible outcomes for each.

Looking more closely at one of the eight challenges and how it might be resolved will help to illustrate Erikson's theory. Consider the first stage, basic trust versus mistrust. In the first year of life, children are totally dependent on others for their care, so the major issue they face is whether their needs will be met adequately. Many infants' needs are met promptly, consistently, and with affection. According to Erikson, those babies will learn to trust other people, to see them as reliable and loving. As a result, they will have a foundation of confidence when they begin to seek autonomy in the second stage of development. In contrast, babies who are neglected, or whose needs are met inconsistently, will come to mistrust others. They will be insecure in their striving for independence, and perhaps also in their dealings with others at later points in their development.

Social and personality development can also be seen from a **social learning perspective.** Unlike psychosocial and Freudian theory, with their focus on inner challenges and conflicts, social learning theory emphasizes the role of the external environment in shaping behavior. For instance, children are constantly observing how other people act, and sometimes imitate the behaviors they see, especially when the people they observe are the ones they love and admire. Thus, a little boy may learn to be sympathetic toward an injured playmate by imitating the way his parents treat him when he is hurt. (This process, called *observational learning,* was described in Chapter 6.) To social learning theorists, then, personality and social behavior are largely the products of what people learn from their interactions with others.

A fourth view of social and personality development, called the **cognitive developmental perspective,** is based on the idea that a child's understanding of the world changes with age. At any given stage in development, the child's understanding will significantly affect her behavior. For instance, children are not born with the understanding that they are boys or girls. Comprehension of that aspect of their world does not begin until about age two. According to the cognitive developmental perspective, as children acquire this new understanding, their behavior begins to change. Boys begin to act more "boyishly" and girls more "girlishly." Their new knowledge of what is "right" for boys and girls influences their behavior.

Finally, social and personality development can be viewed from a **biological perspective,** that is, as guided by inherited biological tendencies. Some fairly nonspecific tendencies are shared by all human beings as a result of their common evolutionary history. One is the young infant's tendency to smile

TABLE 10-1 *Erickson's Eight Stages of Psychosocial Development*

Developmental Challenge	Possible Outcomes
Birth to one year: Basic trust versus mistrust	Babies learn to trust others to satisfy their basic needs. Those who receive neglectful or inconsistent care grow to mistrust people.
One to three years: Autonomy versus shame and doubt	Children start to be independent by mastering simple tasks. Those who fail to develop this autonomy doubt themselves and feel shame.
Three to six years: Initiative versus guilt	Children take initiative in trying out new activities. When this initiative brings them into conflict with others, guilt may arise. Too much guilt can inhibit initiative, so children must learn to balance their initiative against others' desires and needs.
Six years to puberty: Industry versus inferiority	Children must learn the skills of their culture. Those whose industry enables them to do so develop a sense of mastery and self-assurance. Those who fail at this task feel inferior.
Adolescence: Identity versus role confusion	Adolescents must develop a personal identity, an integrated sense of who they are as distinct from other people. Those who fail to do so feel confused about their future roles.
Early adulthood: Intimacy versus isolation	Young adults strive to form intimate friendships and fall in love with another person. Those who fail feel lonely and isolated.
Middle adulthood: Generativity versus stagnation	Middle-aged adults achieve generativity if they develop a sense of responsibility to guide the next generation and be meaningfully productive in their work. Those who do not become bored, self-indulgent, and stagnant.
Old age: Self-integrity versus despair	Older people achieve a sense of self-integrity if they can look back on their lives and see them as productive and satisfying. If instead they view their lives as wasted, they feel despair.

at human faces. Babies around the world develop this behavior at approximately the same age—a fact that suggests it is not something parents teach their infants to do. The relationship between genetic factors and behavioral tendencies is the subject of the field of *behavioral genetics.* An important component of behavioral genetics, however, is the variability in behavior that cannot be attributed to genetics.

This chapter covers all four perspectives on personality and social development. Rather than trying to decide which perspective is right, think of them as complementary viewpoints. Each adds valuable ideas about how the development of the human personality unfolds.

Social and Personality Development in Infancy

In Chapter 9 you were introduced to Austin and Lindsay, the children of one of this book's authors. Austin was just thirteen months old when Lindsay was born, yet he took an intense interest in his new sister. He stared intently at her, gently touching her soft skin. As she returned his gaze, his interest intensified. Gradually, he began to "talk" to her. Raising the pitch of his voice, and slowing his rate of speech, he whispered, "Oh! The baby, baby, baby, . . ."

From their very first interactions, infants learn to engage in the reciprocal give-and-take of social relationships. Considering that at birth a child does not even know that other people exist, the task is enormous. Fortunately, babies have an inherent tendency to respond to the faces and voices of others in ways that induce not only social interaction but nurturance and protection. What is it about a baby's appearance and behavior that sets these important processes in motion?

The Beginnings of Social Relationships

Adults respond lovingly to infants partly because of their inherent "cuteness"— the round face, chubby cheeks, and large, wide-open eyes. Lindsay's big, searching eyes and soft, babyish features were part of what fascinated Austin. Though newborns are incapable of fine motor movement, they can direct their gaze. Just by looking at those who were talking to her, Lindsay increased her chances for social interaction.

In a few more weeks, Lindsay would initiate social exchanges when she produced her first **social smile,** a heartwarming grin triggered by the mere sight of a human face. Charles Darwin, the founder of evolution, theorized that the social smile helps an infant to survive by instilling feelings of joy in adult caregivers. Infants also respond in other ways that foster bonding. Mandel, Jusczyk, and Pisoni (1995) found that infants respond preferentially to their own names (compared to other similar-sounding names). In fact, by two months infants appear to hear the regularities in a speech, even if it is made by different speakers (Jusczyk, Pisoni, & Mullennix, 1993). Within the first few months of life, then, the infant is likely to respond when a parent says the child's name, a powerful reinforcer for the parent.

The infant's innate tendencies to smile and respond to his or her name elicit a complex series of interactions. When the parent responds with love and joy, the infant increases the smiling that first elicited the parent's reaction. If a parent fails to respond, the infant may be less likely to smile in the future, which might then impact the parent's behavior. The baby's innate tendency to smile, then, is immediately shaped by the response of those in her environment.

Why is it important for babies to encourage others to nurture and protect them? The answer is that human infants enter the world unable to "do" for themselves—more so than the young of many other species. They must be born when their large heads are still able to fit through the birth canal. If their births were delayed until their brains were more highly developed, their heads would be so large as to place both mother and child at risk. Being born early, however, means that the baby's parents must provide a great deal of care. Thus, a baby's inherent cuteness and sociability encourage the loving attention a child needs to survive in early life.

The interaction between parent and child is not programmed to unfold in a particular way. Rather, it is influenced by the characteristics of the parent and child. Parents have their own emotional styles, a product of their inherited tendencies, developmental histories, and current situation. And the baby has his or her own **temperament,** or behavioral predispositions. Aspects of temperament that vary in infants include activity level, "soothability," "talkativeness," attention span, fearfulness in new situations, display of positive emotions (frequency of smiles and laughter), and display of negative emotions (frequency of crying, irritability, and distress) (Bates, 1987; Rothbart, 1986). Interestingly, the frequencies of positive and negative emotional displays are not always inversely related. Some infants smile and laugh often, but are seldom irritable, and vice versa. But other babies show positive and negative moods with equal frequency, and still others remain for the most part emotionally neutral (Belsky, Fish, & Isabella, 1991; Goldsmith & Campos, 1991).

The causes for these individual differences in infant temperament are still being debated, but many psychologists think they are substantially influenced by heredity (Campos et al., 1983; Kagan, 1995; Kagan, Reznik, & Snidman, 1988; Smolak, 1986). Differences in temperament appear too soon after birth to be shaped significantly by different external environments. Even among adults personality differences seem to have relatively strong genetic components (Bouchard & McGue, 1990). We will discuss the biological basis of adult personality differences in Chapter 13. For now, bear in mind that the behavioral differences of newborn babies are partly the result of biological factors.

The temperament a baby brings to parent-child interactions has an impact on the parents' personalities, too. They in turn are influenced by their current situations and their level of contentment. Consider a baby who tends to be irritable and fussy. If the parents are generally confident and easygoing, and if they are not experiencing significant stress, they will probably respond calmly to the baby's fussiness,

(A) After separating newborn monkeys from their natural mothers, the psychologist Harry Harlow provided them with two types of "surrogate mothers," one made of bare wire and the other covered with terry cloth. (B) Harlow found that even if the wire mother was equipped with a milk dispenser, the babies still clung to the terry cloth mother. (C) A monkey raised in isolation typically curls itself into a fetal posture.

searching for clues to what the child wants and becoming more soothing in their responses. If, on the other hand, the parents are emotionally immature and are experiencing financial or marital troubles, they might easily grow impatient with their fussy infant. In both cases, the parents' own traits and situations affect how they respond to the baby's temperament, and their responses affect the child's behavior. If the parents become more soothing, the baby is likely to fuss less; if they become annoyed and impatient, the baby is apt to become even more difficult. This give-and-take is referred to as a **bi-directional influence.** Parent and child continually affect one another as their relationship grows.

The development of early social relationships is an excellent example of how heredity and environment interact. For example, a parent who is quiet by nature (that is, has a genetic predisposition to a quiet temperament) is likely to make the surrounding environment calming. Thus, the genetic and environmental influences are correlated (except in the case of adopted children, of course); both increase the likelihood of the child being quiet (Scarr & McCartney, 1983).

Finally, though a child may be born with certain tendencies that are largely genetic in origin, those tendencies can be modified and channeled by the baby's experiences. Genes, in other words, do not rigidly determine a person's characteristics. Instead, a set of developmental possibilities is inherited, any of which can be encouraged or thwarted by experience (Scarr, 1984a). The range within which these inherited possibilities can vary by virtue of environmental influences is referred to as the **reaction range.** Thus, a baby with a strongly outgoing disposition (one who smiles early and vigorously) may become reserved, even withdrawn, if adults ignore his social overtures (Kagan, 1984). Likewise, a very active baby can be influenced toward either overactivity or relaxation, depending on the experiences other people provide. An infant's temperament, in other words, is not fixed and im-

A

B

C

mutable. It is a set of behavioral tendencies that is open to change through environmental influences (Belsky & Cassidy, 1994).

The Formation of Attachments

During the second half-year of life, babies show signs of having developed enduring emotional bonds or attachments to their caregivers, including mother, father, day-care provider, and even older siblings (Belsky & Cassidy, 1994). Attachment can be seen in the joyous greetings the baby gives the caregiver. For instance, a seven-month-old will smile, gurgle, and coo with delight when her mother or father comes to get her in the morning. She would probably cry loudly if the parent suddenly turned and left the room. When babies become old enough to crawl, they often follow a caregiver from room to room (Maccoby & Martin, 1983). They want to maintain visual contact with the person who is an important source of security.

Researchers have wondered what encourages a baby's attachment to parents. Is it that a caregiver provides food and other necessities, as Freud proposed, or is it the emotional comfort that a caregiver offers? Four decades ago, the psychologist Harry Harlow and his colleagues set out to answer these questions in a series of now classic studies. They separated newborn monkeys from their natural mothers, providing them instead with "surrogate mothers." In one study Harlow raised each baby monkey in a cage with two surrogate mothers, one made of stiff, bare wire and the other covered with soft terry cloth (Harlow, 1958; Harlow & Harlow, 1966, 1969). Harlow found that even if the wire mother was equipped with a milk dispenser, the babies still preferred the terry cloth mother. They spent a great deal of time clinging to its soft body, just as baby monkeys cling to their real mother's fur. When alarmed, the infant monkeys always ran to their terry cloth mothers. Thus, the tactile sensations a mother monkey provides seem to encourage the formation of attachments.

In human infants, the formation of parent attachments is undoubtedly more complex. A baby's emotional bond to a caregiver seems to grow not simply from the experience of being held and cuddled but from many hours of social interaction. Since in most families babies interact repeatedly with their fathers as well as their mothers, infants typically become attached to both their parents at approximately the same age (Fox, Kimmerly, & Schafer, 1991; Lamb, 1987).

Although nearly all children form attachments of some kind during infancy, the strength and quality of those attachments vary greatly. Mary Ainsworth and her colleagues (Ainsworth, 1989; Ainsworth et al., 1978) demonstrated that the sensitivity of the caregiver is a critical determinant in the quality of the child's attachment. When a caregiver responds to the baby's needs promptly, appropriately, and consistently, the child tends to develop a **secure attachment.** That is, the infant comes to expect that the caregiver will be available and responsive, quickly and effectively remedying any distress the child may experience. (Notice the resemblance to the challenge in Erikson's first developmental stage.) In contrast, a baby whose caregiver cannot be counted on for comfort when it is needed develops an **anxious attachment.** Such caregivers are emotionally indifferent or even rejecting toward the baby, often showing their feelings in an intrusive, overcontrolling style of care that totally ignores the infant's needs. Others try to respond to the baby some of the time, but at other times fail to do so, only adding to the child's distress.

Research has shown that the security of an infant's attachment can have important implications for the child's future development. Children who attach securely as infants are generally less dependent and more socially competent as preschoolers than their anxiously attached peers (Plunkett, Klein, & Meisels, 1988; Sroufe, Fox, & Pancake, 1983; Waters, Wippman, & Sroufe, 1979). As preschoolers they also tend to have fewer behavior problems, especially excessive aggression and noncompliance with adults. Insecurely attached children are more apt to have these behavior problems, and when they do, those problems often persist into later childhood (Renken et al., 1989). Such findings are consistent with Erikson's theory that development of basic trust in early parent-child interactions is a crucial task. Apparently, a secure attachment is the emotional foundation that allows a child to cope with new demands and challenges.

Why are some parents less able than others to foster secure attachments in their children? The answer seems to lie in a number of factors, including the parents' personalities, the levels of stress and social support in their lives, and the temperament of their infant (or at least their perceptions of the baby's temperament). Consider the results of one study, which followed first-time parents and their babies

When caregivers are routinely available and responsive, quickly and effectively remedying distress, a child tends to develop a secure attachment.

from the last few months of pregnancy until the baby's first birthday (Belsky & Isabella, 1988). Researchers found that babies who were insecurely attached at twelve months tended to have mothers who scored low on two key personality traits: emotional stability/maturity and empathy toward others. Mothers of the insecurely attached infants also seemed to have experienced the greatest decline in marital satisfaction since the baby was born; to have perceived the baby as becoming more difficult with age; and to have viewed their social environment as relatively unfriendly and unsupportive. These negative factors contributed to their infants' insecurity in

a cumulative way. Women who experienced all of them almost always raised an insecure baby, whereas women who experienced none of them almost always raised a secure child.

This study only begins to tap the many factors that can increase a child's risk of becoming insecurely attached. In addition to the stresses of a difficult baby, marital dissatisfaction, and lack of psychological support, parents can experience many other types of stress, including work-related problems (fatigue from long hours, concerns about job performance, unhappiness with a job); strained relationships with parents and in-laws; and financial worries (Fox, Kim-

Though women still do more child care and housework than men, psychologists now recognize the role of father-child relationships in child care and bonding.

Because teenagers are acutely aware of their social selves, peer pressure becomes more intense at this age.

merly, & Schafer, 1991; Hock & Schirtzinger, 1992). All these factors can affect the quality of parenting, and hence the risk of an insecure attachment. Furthermore, researchers now recognize the role of *father*-child relationships in bonding. In recent years, societal attitudes toward paternal involvement have changed. Though women still do more child care and housework than men, fathers are now expected to be actively involved in child care (Scarr, Phillips, McCartney, & Abbott-Shim, 1993). And what about the long-term effects of raising children in day-care centers? The "In Depth" section at the end of this chapter addresses the effects of day care for working parents.

Social and Personality Development in Childhood

In the course of interacting with the world around them, especially with other people, babies begin to develop a sense of self. As they grow, they learn to understand themselves: their abilities and limitations, their interests and goals. According to Damon & Hart (1982), a child's self-understanding has four components: the *physical self*, which includes the child's body and possessions; the *active self*, which reflects the kind of behaviors a child can and does exhibit; the *social self*, or how the child interacts with others; and the *psychological self*, meaning the child's personal thoughts, feelings, traits, and beliefs.

The developing child tends to develop these components of self sequentially. Young children first learn about their physical selves. A one-year-old, for example, responds to his reflection in the mirror as if it is another person. Gradually, the growing child recognizes the reflection as his own. Children who are in this stage of development are often possessive and unwilling to share objects.

As children mature, they begin to learn more about their physical selves. They become fiercely independent, no longer wanting parents to do for them. A three-year-old, for example, may prefer to spend ten minutes dressing herself, even if her clothes get put on inside-out and backward. Recall that Erikson saw this striving for autonomy as the overriding challenge of the second and third years of life.

While they are in elementary school, children learn even more about their active selves. They become eager to do all that their older siblings or friends are doing, and don't like to be told to "wait until you are older." In school they also develop an understanding of their intellectual and athletic abilities. This period coincides with Erikson's third and fourth stages of development (initiative versus guilt and industry versus inferiority).

By the time children reach their early teenage years, they have become acutely aware of their social selves. Feeling accepted by their peers becomes extremely important. They may try very hard to fit in as peer pressure becomes more intense. In Erikson's view, this period is marked by the challenge of identity versus role confusion, as the adolescent strives to understand who she is relative to (and independent of) others.

Finally, as the teenager gradually matures into a young adult, interest in the psychological self develops. "Fitting in" becomes less important as the older teenager becomes aware of his own personal beliefs and values, perhaps for the first time. During this period, the young person becomes capable of intimate

During Erikson's stage 6, young adults become capable of intimate, loving relationships with those outside the family.

loving relationships with those outside of the family, stage 6 in Erikson's theory (intimacy versus isolation).

Damon and Hart's theory of self-understanding does not address development after adolescence. However, their concept of the psychological self is consistent with Erikson's final two stages: generativity versus stagnation and integrity versus despair. In a sense, mature adults compare their "ideal psychological self" with their "actual psychological self." Adults who are unhappy with their actual psychological selves often undertake drastic life changes—witness the so-called mid-life crisis. We will have more to say about adult development later in the chapter.

Individual Differences in Development

One of the greatest challenges facing psychologists is to account for the tremendous variability in human behavior. Even in the case of siblings, marked differences are common. Consider the differences be-

tween William James, one of the founders of modern psychology, and his brother Henry James, the famous novelist. Even as a child William James was active and energetic, with a buoyant, gregarious, and effervescent style. Henry, in contrast, was quiet and shy, more of a loner. What causes such marked differences in personality? How can two children of the same parents turn out to be so different? The answer to this question lies in a complex interplay of genes and the environment.

In this section we will explore some of the genetic and environmental factors that influence the development of the child's personality. Because psychologists often study these factors in isolation, we will look first at environmental and then at genetic forces. We will then turn our attention to the interaction of genes and environment.

Environmental Influences

A list of all environmental influences would be virtually endless, and determining their effects equally difficult. However, psychologists have identified a relatively small group of environmental factors that are particularly important in shaping personality development. In the next section we will examine three of these: parenting styles, child abuse, and divorce.

Parenting Styles Psychologists have long suspected that parents may have a major impact on their children's personalities. Consequently, they have spent a great deal of time exploring which aspects of parents' behavior influence children the most. One researcher who has studied the topic extensively is Diana Baumrind (1967, 1984). She began by identifying three basic personality profiles in a group of nursery school children. Children with a mature profile were energetic, emotionally positive toward their peers, and high in curiosity, self-reliance, and self-control. Dissatisfied children were moody, apprehensive, easily upset, passively hostile, and either negative in their relations with peers or socially withdrawn. Immature children were impulsive, undercontrolled, and low in self-reliance, though more cheerful and resilient than those in group 2.

Baumrind then assessed the children's parents through personal interviews, home observations, and laboratory studies. She found three distinctive styles of parenting. Parents of the mature children were nurturant and responsive, yet firm in setting limits. They were flexible in their thinking and encouraged their children toward independence. Baumrind called this style **authoritative** parenting. Parents of the dissatisfied youngsters were unresponsive to their children's wishes, inflexible in their thinking, and harsh in controlling their children's behavior—a style Baumrind called **authoritarian.** Parents of the immature youngsters were somewhat nurturant, but they failed to set firm limits or to require age-appropriate behavior, thus hindering the development of self-control in their children. Baumrind labeled these parents **permissive.** Five years later, Baumrind found that the children of authoritative parents were still the most mature. Apparently, a parenting style characterized by warmth and nurturance, the encouragement of independence, and the setting of firm rules when needed is associated with positive outcomes in children.

Unfortunately, we cannot say with certainty exactly what the association between parenting style and outcomes means. As we saw in Chapter 2, a correlation between two factors (such as parenting style and the children's traits) does not necessarily prove that one caused the other. Perhaps some third factor, such as the genes parents and children share, contributes to the relationship. To rule out genetic influences, researchers would have to repeat Baumrind's study using adopted children and their adoptive parents as subjects. In the meantime, it seems reasonable to assume that environmental as well as genetic influences were probably involved. That is to say, the parents' behaviors (not just their genes) were probably helping to shape their children's behavior.

However, these environmental influences were probably bi-directional. Adults with an authoritative style of parenting probably tend to raise children who are happy, self-reliant, and self-controlled. Those positive traits, in turn, probably promoted favorable perceptions of their children by their parents (Greenberger, 1989). Such positive perceptions would foster continued warmth and nurturance, and an expectation of mature behavior from the children. Barring unusual stresses on the family, this cycle is mutually reinforcing.

An overly restricting parenting style would also tend to be self-perpetuating. Parents who control their children in a harsh, severe manner would tend to raise youngsters who are moody, negative, passively hostile, and easily upset. These traits could encourage the parents to believe that even stricter discipline is necessary. Repeated negative exchanges between parents and children would create stress in the home, which could cause the parents to lose their patience and react in more volatile ways. In such cases, a harsh parenting style is in danger of escalating into child abuse.

Child Abuse Tragically, child abuse is far from rare in our society. About 2 million cases are reported every year, undoubtedly a great many more go unreported (Children's Defense Fund, 1987). The most visible form of child abuse is physical maltreatment, that is, the use of corporal punishment beyond reasonable limits (Daro, 1988). Physical abuse includes beatings and other acts of physical aggression that cause cuts, bruises, burns, internal injuries, or broken bones. Recent studies (Bruce and Zimmering, 1989, as cited in Peterson, 1994) indicate that this sort of physical violence is frequent. Children can also be abused sexually, that is, forced or persuaded to submit to the sexual advances of an adult. A third form of child abuse involves neglect, or failure to adequately clean, feed, clothe, or provide medical care for a child. Ironically, as our society becomes more aware of the problems of abuse, we are less able to resolve them. Recent studies confirm this: the number of referrals to child protection service agencies has increased dramatically in recent years, but budget cuts to these agencies have reduced the number of workers available to help (Trickett & Putnam, 1993; U.S. Advisory Board on Child Abuse and Neglect, 1990).

Abuse and neglect can have devastating effects on children. Apathy, blunted emotions, insecure attachment to parents, low self-esteem, and increased risks of depression, suicide, and drug addiction are just some of the effects (Garbarino & Garbarino, 1986; Schneider-Rosen & Cicchetti, 1984; Widom, 1989; Youngblade & Belsky, 1989). Others include heightened aggressiveness, distractibility, and noncompliance; uncaring and indifferent attitudes toward others; and a tendency to respond to other people's distress with anger, hostility, or even physical attack (Egeland, 1991; Howes & Eldredge, 1985; Main & George, 1985).

Child abuse can also have lifelong effects. Because abused children are victimized by the very people they look to for care and affection, they often feel abandoned, betrayed, and distrustful of others, even into adulthood (Aber & Allen, 1987; McCrae & Costa, 1988). Victims of abuse, especially childhood sexual abuse, also run higher risks of developing

Elisa Izquierdo, 1989-1995. Elisa was born addicted to crack, and was abused by both her mother and stepfather. Despite the fact that concerned neighbors and teachers contacted New York City's Child Welfare Administration eight times, Elisa remained in their custody. On November 22, 1995, during a fit of rage, Elisa's mother threw her into a concrete wall, killing her.

certain behavioral disorders, including substance abuse, as well as serious personality disorders (Ladwig & Anderson, 1989), such as borderline personality disorder (Stone, 1990) or even multiple personality disorder (Putnam, 1989). Those who seem to be at greatest long-term risk include children whose family atmosphere is chaotic, unsupportive, or violent, and those who suffer multiple episodes of mistreatment that may not be acknowledged until much later in life (Figley, 1989; Mowbray, 1988).

You may think that parents who abuse their children must be hostile and violent by nature, perhaps even mentally disturbed, but that is seldom true (Brunnquell, Crichton, & Egeland, 1981). Most child abusers are simply people who are ambivalent about being parents, who lack knowledge about young children and how to manage them, and who are currently experiencing high levels of stress, often brought on by economic troubles (Sedlack, 1989). Many were abused themselves as children; essentially, they are re-creating in the next generation the family roles they grew up with. Child abusers also tend to be socially isolated: they lack the support of other adults who can help them to deal with the day-to-day tasks of child rearing (Crockenberg, 1986). Introducing parents who are experiencing stress to a network of people who can provide emotional sup-

port may be one of the best ways to prevent child abuse.

The Impact of Divorce   Divorce is another environmental factor that can shape how a child thinks, feels, and acts. Every year, over a million American children experience the pain of their parents' divorce (Wegman, 1986). Estimates are that roughly half of all the babies born in the United States today will spend at least some of their lives in a one-parent home (Newberger, Melnicoe, & Newberger, 1986). Many more will witness repeated conflict between their parents. Exactly how do these negative family experiences affect children?

In the period immediately following the breakup of their parents' marriage, most children feel some anger and resentment, anxiety, depression, and perhaps even guilt. Following the initial crisis, reactions tend to vary (Hetherington, 1989). Some children are resilient and bounce back remarkably well (Werner, 1995), while others suffer sustained problems, including increased aggression, noncompliance with their parents, and general acting out, coupled with a decline in academic achievement and in the quality of their peer relationships. Some children who seem to be adjusting well suffer delayed reactions, especially during adolescence. The reasons for these individual differences in children's responses to divorce include both biology and environment.

Environmental factors that contribute to differences in children's reactions tend to relate to the amount of stress the child experiences. For instance, continued conflict between divorced parents is associated with behavior problems and poor adjustment in children (Camara & Resnick, 1988; Forehand, Long, & Brody, 1988). So is a negative change in the custodial parent's style of parenting: when a custodial parent becomes erratic, inconsistent, punitive, or permissive as a result of the stress of divorce, children may respond badly. Those children who do best tend to have some stable source of love, psychological support, and guidance. Parents (both custodial and noncustodial), grandparents, and teachers can all play this role, as can siblings and close friends, though to a lesser extent (Furstenberg, 1988; Hetherington, 1988; Wallerstein & Blakeslee, 1989; Zill, 1988).

At the same time, a child's temperament can affect his reaction to a divorce. Temperamentally difficult children tend to be more vulnerable, both because parents under stress tend to criticize them

A   B

Many personality characteristics, such as religiosity, have been shown to have a sizable genetic influence. For example, those with extroverted, emotional temperaments are more likely to participate in charismatic religions (A), while introverted, reflective people are likely to engage in more thoughtful, subdued expressions of faith (B).

more often and because they are less able to cope with adversity (Hetherington, 1988). Other traits in children associated with poor adjustment to divorce are low self-esteem, overdependence, and a tendency toward self-blame (Masten, 1986; Nolen-Hoeksema et al., 1989; Rutter, 1987; Werner, 1987). Psychologists are not yet certain what encourages the development of these detrimental traits. Inherited tendencies may make some children less resilient to stress of any kind, including the stress of divorce. Thus, different children may filter similar experiences through different, partly genetic inclinations and predispositions. In the next section we will examine the extent to which personality differences are in fact genetic in origin.

Genetic Influences

Psychologists have long recognized the effects of genetic influences. In recent years, however, enormous advances have been made in the field of *behavioral genetics*. In Chapter 2 we discussed some of the techniques behavioral geneticists use to determine genetic contributions to behavior. Most of these involve the study of twins and/or siblings.

Current estimates are that heredity exerts a sizable influence on personality differences. In one intensive study of over seventy sets of twins who were raised apart, the contribution of heredity to most of the traits researchers measured was about 50 percent (Bouchard, 1993; Bouchard & McGue, 1990; Zuckerman, 1991). Differences in sociability, emotionalism, and general activity level seem to be especially af-

fected by genes (Plomin, 1989). Even behavioral tendencies like religiosity have significant genetic components (Waller et al., 1990). These influences are indirect; for example, those with strong genetic tendencies toward introversion are not likely to affiliate with charismatic religious organizations.

The Interplay of Genes and Environment

The sizable contribution of genes to differences in human behavior should not be exaggerated. The same findings that show a strong genetic contribution to behavior usually show a strong environmental effect. If the contribution of heredity to personality differences is roughly 50 percent, the remaining 50 percent must be accounted for by the environment (Dunn & Plomin, 1990).

As we saw in Chapter 2, psychologists have been surprised by the relatively small contribution of *shared* environmental factors. Plomin (1989) estimates that shared environmental influences explain only about 5 percent of the variability in human behavior. These results should be interpreted carefully, however. They do *not* mean that the environment in which you were raised had no bearing on your adult personality: such a statement would be absurd! Rather, these environmental factors (unlike genetic factors) do not always affect individuals in the same way.

Consider the determinants of alcoholism, for example. Chapter 2 stated that Kendler and colleagues (1994) estimated the *genetic* influence on alcoholism in women at about 50 percent. That is, a woman with a biological parent who is alcoholic has a substantially higher-than-normal chance of becoming an alcoholic herself. Not all biological children of alcoholics will become alcoholics, of course. But having a biological parent who is an alcoholic *always* increases the risk: the influence is always in the same direction.

What happens to a child who is adopted into a family with an alcoholic parent? Some may follow the parent's example and begin to drink irresponsibly. Others may learn from observation to avoid alcoholic beverages entirely. In this case, the effect of having an alcoholic parent is strictly *environmental*, and its influence is *not* always the same.

Finally, alcoholism provides a perfect example of the interaction between genetic and environmental factors. Even those with strong genetic predispositions will not become alcoholic, provided they do not drink alcohol. The reverse is also true: those without genetic tendencies may still become alcoholic if they are exposed to appropriate environmental factors.

In summary, most genetic factors tend to influence behavior in the same way. Offspring who inherit a particular genetic factor will experience a predictable effect on their behavior. Most environmental factors, though, are less predictable. Those with similar environmental influences may respond to those influences in different ways.

Have researchers been wrong, then, in stressing the effect of parenting styles and home environment on personality development in children? Quite the contrary; but we may have to reconceptualize how such influences are exerted. Having the same parents apparently does not mean that children will experience the same parental influences. Instead, environmental influences are specific to each child, not general to all children in the family. In some cases parents may treat their children differently, perhaps by virtue of their gender, temperament, health, or physical appearance. Parents may try hard to treat their children alike but, despite their good intentions, may unknowingly discriminate. For example, a shy, quiet boy in poor health might elicit more permissiveness from a parent than a boisterous, active brother who is constantly getting into trouble. In two recent studies, the majority of mothers admitted to giving their children different amounts and types of affection, attention, and discipline (Dunn & Stocker, 1989; Stocker, Dunn, & Plomin, 1989).

Even if parents do treat their children alike, their children might respond to their treatment differently by virtue of their different temperaments and personal experiences of the world. An inherently sensitive child who has experienced difficulty making friends might feel a deep sense of rejection when being reprimanded by a parent or teacher. A confident child who is well-liked by peers would probably be less affected by occasional scolding. Thus, shared environmental factors may be experienced differently by different people (Bouchard & McGue, 1990). Thus, the factors that contribute to personality differences are probably more complex than was once assumed.

Psychologist Marvin Zuckerman has made an extensive study of the effects of genetic and other biological factors on personality development (Zuckerman, 1994a, 1994c; Zuckerman et al., 1994). He has concluded:

> We do not inherit personality traits or even behavioral mechanisms as such. What is inherited are chemical templates that produce and regulate proteins involved in building the structure of nervous systems and the neurotransmitters, enzymes, and hormones that regulate them. We are not born as extroverts, neurotics, impulsive sensation seekers, antisocial personalities, but we are born with differences in [brain structures]. . . . How do these differences in biological traits shape our choices in life from the manifold possibilities provided by the environment? . . . Only cross-disciplinary, developmental, and comparative psychobiological research can provide the answers.
>
> Zuckerman, 1994b

Group Differences in Development: Gender Roles

In a thickly carpeted room, same-sex trios of four-year-olds are left alone to play with a small trampoline, a beach ball, and a large inflated doll. Trios of girls spend most of their time jumping on the trampoline. Their play is active but seldom rough-and-tumble. Almost never does one girl throw herself on top of another, laughing and squealing. Trios of boys routinely interact that way, pushing and pouncing, wrestling and rolling across the floor. When researchers compare records of the children's behavior at the end of the study, they find the boys have engaged in over six times more rough-and-tumble play than the girls (Maccoby, 1988).

At an early age most children begin to acquire the behavior patterns associated with their sex. One-year-old boys, for example, tend to play more vigorously than girls the same age (Maccoby & Jacklin,

1974). By the age of about one-and-a-half, boys have begun to prefer cars and trucks to the soft, cuddly toys girls prefer (Smith & Daglish, 1977). During their preschool years, children also begin to gravitate toward members of their own sex as playmates, a tendency that is quite pronounced by the early elementary school years (Luria & Herzog, 1985; Maccoby & Jacklin, 1987; Thorne, 1986). These same-sex groups often show significant differences in behavior, as in the study just described above. Besides engaging in a greater amount of rough-and-tumble play, boys also tend to be more aggressive than girls in asserting their desires, and they try more often to dominate one another, often through physical force. Girls, in contrast, are usually less impulsive than boys, more compliant, and more sensitive to their playmates' views and feelings (Charlesworth & Dzur, 1987; Maccoby, 1988; Maltz & Borker, 1983). Such differences are signs that children are adopting **gender roles,** patterns of behavior that are characteristic of members of their own sex.

Unlike differences in personality, gender roles refer to group rather than individual differences. While members of the same sex often vary greatly in their personality traits, *in general* they display certain patterns of behavior that are different from members of the opposite sex. Why do these group differences in behavior develop? The answer must lie in an interplay of heredity and environment. But the relative contributions of heredity and environment to group differences are not necessarily the same as those associated with individual differences in personality. Nor can researchers use the same methods (twin and adoption studies) to investigate the causes of group differences. Instead, researchers have developed different kinds of studies, each suggested by a different theory about why gender roles develop. We will begin by looking at studies done by researchers who take a biological perspective.

Biological Influences

It is difficult to assess the impact of biology on masculine and feminine behavior, for biological tendencies begin to interact with environmental influences almost immediately after birth. However, some behavioral differences between the sexes appear before the child has had much contact with the social environment. Newborn boys are generally more active than newborn girls, and also tend to cry more and sleep less than girls (Moss, 1967; Phillips, King, & DuBois, 1978). The significance of these differences

for future personality and social development is unclear. Perhaps male and female babies experience different kinds of caregiving and different patterns of social interaction, as a result of these initial differences. An active, squirming infant, for instance, may be played with more energetically, but hugged and cuddled less, than a quiet baby. Similarly, a high level of activity could prompt a baby to explore the environment more extensively, and that outcome, in turn, could encourage certain patterns of personality development. In short, innate differences in activity levels between boys and girls could interact with environmental factors gradually to produce a variety of behavioral differences between the sexes.

Some psychologists believe that biology may play an even greater role in development of male-female behavioral differences. For instance, males who are born with female-looking genitals, and are therefore raised as girls, sometimes begin to behave more like boys upon reaching puberty, when their male hormone levels start to surge (Imperato-McGinley et al., 1979). Aggressive tendencies, in particular, may be influenced by biological factors, perhaps by hormones that are present in males before birth. But though biological factors may produce some gender-related differences in behavior, they are unlikely to explain all the behavioral differences between the sexes. If gender-related differences were primarily genetic in origin, males and females everywhere would exhibit the same gender-role patterns. That, however, is not the case; anthropologists have observed marked cultural differences in the behaviors and personality traits ascribed to men and women (e. g., Mead, 1935).

Environmental Theories

In the next sections we will look at several environmental theories of gender differences. Keep in mind that these theories are not mutually exclusive. Each contributes a partial explanation for an extremely complex phenomenon.

The Freudian Perspective According to Freudian theory, gender-role learning arises from the **Oedipus conflict,** a psychological dilemma that occurs between the ages of three and six, the time when most children discover the genital differences between the sexes. This discovery, Freud believed, prompts children to see themselves as rivals of the same-sex parent, competing for the affection of the opposite-sex parent. Eventually, however, the child comes to realize that this longing for the opposite-sex parent is

Through the process of identification, children imitate the parent of the same sex, adopting that parent's values, attitudes, gender role, and other sex-typed behaviors.

not likely to be fulfilled. So the child compromises. Instead of trying to possess the opposite-sex parent, the child tries to be like, or "identify with," the parent of the same sex, adopting that parent's values, attitudes, gender role, and so forth. This process of identification, according to Freud, is crucial to normal development, including the acquisition of appropriate sex-typed behaviors.

The Social Learning Perspective Unlike Freudians, social learning theorists believe that the acquisition of sex-typed behaviors is not initiated by a single event in a child's life but is rather a gradual process of learning that begins even in infancy. In this view, parents and other adults shape the child's behavior to conform to established gender roles by reinforcing "appropriate" responses and discouraging "inappropriate" ones. Adults, and older brothers and sisters also, provide gender-role models for the child to imitate. As a result, behavior that is expected of a boy or a girl begins to emerge as early as the age of one-and-a-half to two.

Studies reveal that fathers especially encourage traditional sex roles in their children by treating their sons and daughters differently (Siegal, 1987). For instance, fathers typically treat their baby sons as stronger and hardier than their baby daughters, whom they are inclined to regard as fragile and in need of protection. In keeping with these perceptions, fathers encourage more physical play in infant and toddler boys than in girls, as well as more independence and exploration. These patterns continue as children grow older. In general, fathers are more

physical in their interactions with sons, as well as stricter and firmer in disciplining them. Toward daughters, they are usually gentler and more affectionate.

This gender-role discrimination is not necessarily conscious and deliberate. Ironically, even parents who set out to treat their sons and daughters as equals may end up responding to them in sex-typed ways. This outcome was suggested in a study in which young adults were asked to evaluate a baby's emotional responses to four stimuli—a teddy bear, a jack-in-the-box, a doll, and a loud buzzer (Condry & Condry, 1976). Half the subjects were told they were watching a boy, half that they were watching a girl. In reality, they were all watching the same videotape of the same nine-month-old child. When the baby cried after being presented with the jack-in-the-box several times, the subjects who believed they were observing a boy attributed the baby's reaction to anger; those who believed they were observing a girl attributed the child's response to fear. In an ambiguous situation, that is, the common stereotype that females are more fearful than males tended to influence the subjects' thinking. It is easy to imagine that as parents, these same subjects might respond in different ways to a crying son and a crying daughter—not because they think boys and girls merit different treatment but because they perceive them to be expressing different emotions.

Once a child becomes old enough to play cooperatively with peers, gender-role lessons may intensify. Children, especially boys, are often staunch defenders of gender roles. By the age of five or six, most boys have firm ideas about sex-appropriate dress and behavior, and they expect ostracism for deviating from the norm (Damon, 1977). These expectations are warranted. Observation of school-age children has shown that a boy who tries to enter a girls' game on the playground (jump rope, for instance) will be both shunned by the girls and ridiculed by other boys (Thorne, 1986). Thus, peer pressure seems to play an important part in gender-role learning.

The Cognitive Developmental View   Researchers interested in the cognitive aspects of early childhood development take yet another perspective on how gender roles are acquired. They argue that whether or not other people encourage children to act in sex-appropriate ways may not matter. In their view, children have a built-in motivation to imitate the behaviors society expects of their sex. Children strive to be competent at all things, including the actions and attitudes associated with being a boy or a girl. Thus, once youngsters have developed the cognitive ability to understand the concepts of male and female, and to recognize that one of those concepts applies to them, they will automatically want to adopt the behaviors considered appropriate to the newly discovered status (Kohlberg, 1969).

Cognitive psychologists go on to argue that sex-typed behaviors should become more pronounced as a child's understanding of gender matures. In fact, that is what happens. In one study researchers showed children ages four to nine three sets of unfamiliar objects, telling them that one set was for boys, another for girls, and a third for boys and girls. In reality, the objects (a burglar alarm, a hole puncher, a phone index, and so forth) were not ones that are normally sex-typed. The older children explored the objects that were said to be appropriate for their own sex more than they explored those labeled appropriate for both sexes, and more still than those said to be for members of the opposite sex (Bradbard et al., 1986). The age at which this pattern emerged coincided closely with the age at which most youngsters develop a good understanding of gender constancy, that is, an understanding that one's gender cannot be changed simply by changing one's hairstyle or clothing. This finding suggests that a relatively mature grasp of gender is required for children to show a consistent preference for "sex-appropriate" objects and behaviors.

Can we change children's notions of sex-appropriate playthings simply by showing them examples of people acting in non-sex-typed ways? Not easily, cognitive psychologists say. Once traditional stereotypes of "boy things" and "girl things" have been firmly established in a child's mind, they tend to color and even distort what the child perceives and remembers. For instance, if you showed a child some pictures of boys playing with dolls and girls playing with trucks, several days later the youngster would probably report the reverse: that the pictures had showed girls playing with dolls and boys playing with trucks ((Martin & Halverson, 1981). Apparently, people often perceive and remember what their stereotypes tell them is "right" (a point raised in Chapter 7). Gender stereotypes cannot be changed by exposing children to nonstereotypical experiences, then.

Socialization and Moral Development

Socialization—learning the expectations and values of one's society—is an important childhood developmental task. The basic goal of socialization is **internalization**—incorporating society's values into the self to such an extent that violation of those standards produces a sense of guilt. Socialization plays a key role in the development of a child's moral thought and behavior. Infants enter the world totally amoral, bent on nothing more than the satisfaction of their own immediate desires. Over the years the totally self-centered newborn is transformed into a person who is sensitive to the needs and rights of others. We will examine three perspectives on this process: the Freudian, the social learning, and the cognitive developmental perspectives.

The Freudian Perspective

According to Freud, a child internalizes the moral code of the same-sex parent as part of the resolution of the Oedipus conflict. This process results in a dramatic change in the child's moral orientation. A strong sense of right and wrong emerges where previously there was none. The child, in other words, quite rapidly develops a conscience or, in Freudian terminology, a **superego.**

Research has not provided a great deal of support for Freud's view of moral development. Children do not seem to acquire a conscience as the result of a single developmental crisis. Instead, moral development appears to be a gradual process that begins during the preschool years and continues into adulthood (Hoffman, 1976; Kohlberg, 1969).

The Social Learning Perspective

Unlike the Freudian view, the social learning perspective can accommodate the gradual nature of moral development. Proponents of the social learning theory believe that children act morally because over the years they are reinforced for "good" behavior and punished for "bad" behavior, and because they have moral models to imitate. Research has provided some support for these contentions. For example, studies show that children often behave generously after observing an unselfish adult (Bryan, 1975) and frequently behave aggressively after watching an aggressive model (Bandura, Ross, & Ross, 1961). The degree to which children are inclined to imitate such actions often depends on whether they see that a model's behavior is rewarded or punished, a finding that is in keeping with the social learning perspective.

Research has shown that the way in which parents socialize their children can affect the extent to which their children internalize moral rules and principles. Excessive use of power-assertive techniques of punishment (spankings, withdrawal of privileges, physical coercion, threats of force) tends to be associated with low levels of moral development (Hoffman, 1976). In contrast, reasoning with children about their behavior—explaining why a certain act is right or wrong, pointing out how the behavior affects others—appears to be associated with high levels of moral development, including consideration for others, capacity for moral reasoning, and feelings of guilt over wrongdoing (Aronfreed, 1969; Hoffman, 1976; Hoffman & Saltzstein, 1967). Lessons in moral reasoning, moreover, must be heartfelt to be effective. The adult must convey kindness and intense caring about these issues (Radke-Yarrow & Zahn-Waxler, 1984).

The Cognitive Developmental Perspective

The social learning view of moral development implicitly assumes that acquiring a conscience depends more on the amount and type of training that a child receives than on the child's age and level of maturation. The cognitive developmental view reverses the emphasis on these two sets of factors. Cognitivists believe that as the child's cognitive capabilities (which are broadly related to age) change, a child progresses through several distinct stages of moral reasoning.

The psychologist most closely associated with the cognitive developmental view of moral learning is Lawrence Kohlberg (1963; 1969). Kohlberg maintained that the stages of moral reasoning occur in an invariable sequence, each developing out of the preceding one and each cognitively more complex than the last. To assess one's level of moral thinking, he developed a series of moral dilemmas and asked how each should be resolved and why. Here is one example:

> In Europe a woman was near death from cancer. One drug might save her, a form of radium that a druggist in the same town had recently discovered. The druggist was charging $2,000, ten times what the drug cost him to make. The sick woman's husband, Heinz, went to everyone he knew to borrow the money, but he could only get together about half of what it cost. He told the druggist that his wife was dying and asked him to sell it cheaper or let him pay later. But the druggist said, "No." The husband got desperate and broke into the man's store to steal the drug for his wife. Should the husband have done that? Why?
>
> Kohlberg, 1969, p. 379

What mattered to Kohlberg was not the decision a child made (whether Heinz's behavior was right or wrong) but the explanation for that decision. Table 10-2 presents the typical explanations subjects give for their decision at three major developmental levels, each of which has two stages. At the **preconventional level,** a child adheres to the social rules in large part out of fear of the consequences of breaking them. The child, in other words, is "good" to avoid punishment. The overwhelming majority of seven-year-olds operate at this level. At the second major level, the **conventional level,** a child is concerned about winning the approval of others and meeting their standards and expectations. He or she is often inclined to follow the dictates of established authority. About half of all ten-year-olds have advanced to the conventional level. The final level of moral reasoning, the **postconventional level,** is not reached during childhood. In fact, it is attained by only a small percentage of adults (Shaver & Strong, 1976). A person who is reasoning at this level recognizes that universal ethical principles can transcend the laws of society. Failure to adhere to these principles brings self-condemnation.

	For Stealing Drug	Against Stealing Drug
Preconventional Level		
Stage 1: obedience, or reward, orientation Motivated by avoidance of punishment and "conscience" is irrational fear of punishment.	If you let your wife die, you will get into trouble. You'll be blamed for not spending the money to save her, and there'll be an investigation of you and the druggist for your wife's death.	You shouldn't steal the drug because if you are caught, you will be sent to jail. If you do get away, your conscience would bother you worrying that the police would catch you at any minute.
Stage 2: instrumental exchange, or marketplace, orientation Motivated by desire for reward or benefit. Guilt reactions are ignored and punishment is viewed pragmatically.	If you do happen to get caught, you could give the drug back and you wouldn't get much of a sentence. It wouldn't bother you much to serve a little jail term, if you have your wife when you get out.	He may not get much of a jail term if he steals the drug, but his wife will probably die before he get out so it won't do him much good. If his wife dies, he shouldn't blame himself; it wasn't his fault she had cancer.
Conventional Level		
Stage 3: conformist, or "good boy, good girl," orientation Motivated by anticipation of disapproval of others, actual or imagined.	No one will think you're bad if you steal the drug, but your family will think you're an inhuman husband if you don't. If you let your wife die, you'll never be able to look anybody in the face again.	It isn't just the druggist who will think you're a criminal; everyone else will too. You'll feel bad thinking how you've brought dishonor on your family and yourself; you won't be able to face anyone again.
Stage 4: "law-and-order" orientation Motivated by anticipation of dishonor—an institutionalized blame for failure of duty— and by guilt over harm done to others.	If you have any sense of honor, you won't let your wife die because you're afraid to do the only thing that will save her. You'll always feel guilty that you caused her death if you don't do your duty to her.	You're desperate and you may not know you're doing wrong when you steal the drug. But you'll know you did wrong after you're sent to jail. You'll always feel guilty for your dishonesty and lawbreaking.
Postconventional Level		
Stage 5: social-contract, or legalistic, orientation Concern about maintaining respect of equals and of the community. Concern about own self-respect—that is, about avoiding judging self as irrational, inconsistent, nonpurposive.	You'd lose other people's respect, not gain it, if you don't steal. If you let your wife die, it would be out of fear, not out of reasoning it out. So you'd just lose self-respect and probably the respect of others too.	You would lose your standing and respect in the community and violate the law. You'd lose respect for yourself if you're carried away by emotion and forget the long-range point of view.
Stage 6: universal ethical principle orientation Concern about self-condemnation for violating one's own principles.	If you don't steal the drug and your wife dies, you'd always condemn yourself for it. You wouldn't be blamed and you would have lived up to the law, but not to your own standards of conscience.	If you stole the drug, you wouldn't be blamed by other people, but you'd condemn yourself because you wouldn't have lived up to your own conscience and standards of honesty.

The fact that a person's level of moral thinking is age-related suggests that it is also related to the level of cognitive development. Research supports this conclusion. In general, the more complex the intellectual tasks a youngster can perform, the higher the stage of moral reasoning that child tends to exhibit (Kuhn et al., 1977; Selman, 1976). One demonstration of the link between moral and cognitive development is seen in the research of Robert Selman (Selman, 1976; Selman & Byrne, 1974). Selman presented children of varying ages with stories that involved dilemmas. For example:

> Holly is an 8-year-old girl who likes to climb trees. She is the best tree climber in the neighborhood. One day while climbing down from a tall tree she falls off the bottom branch but does not hurt herself. Her father sees her fall. He is upset and asks her to promise not to climb trees again. Holly promises. . . . Later that day, Holly meets Sean. Sean's kitten is caught up in a tree and cannot get down. Something has to be done right away or the kitten may fall. Holly is the only one who climbs trees well enough to reach the kitten and get it down, but she remembers her promise to her father.

Selman & Byrne, 1974, p. 805

Selman then asked the children a series of questions designed to assess their ability to take various perspectives: Holly's, her father's, and that of "most people." He found a clear developmental trend in the children's responses. The youngest could think only in terms of their own perspective. They either failed to realize that others did not share their own perspective or were unable to gauge others' points of view. Older children, in contrast, understood that others' viewpoints could differ from their own, and they could imagine what those viewpoints might be. At the same time, they could look at the views of several people through the eyes of a third party.

This ability to take the perspectives of others is an important cognitive achievement. In Piaget's theory of cognitive development, it is one of the accomplishments that distinguishes older children from preschoolers. As children mature, they are increasingly able to transcend egocentrism and see things from a broader point of view. The ability to take broader and broader perspectives is also the essence of Kohlberg's stages of moral thinking. Thus, cognitive development and moral development often go hand in hand.

Kohlberg's cognitive theory of moral development has been criticized, however. Some critics have pointed out that a person's stage of moral reasoning does not always closely match his or her actual behavior (Kurtines & Grief, 1974). A person may talk about ethical principles, yet fail to adhere to them when faced with a moral dilemma (Gibbs & Schnell, 1986). Someone who is capable of reasoning at Kohlberg's most advanced level might cheat and steal (Santrock & Bartlett, 1986). If that is so, we might ask how significant Kohlberg's stages really are.

Critics have charged that Kohlberg's theory is biased because it fails to consider the values people are taught (Gilligan, 1977; Harkness, 1980; Hogan, 1975; Holstein, 1976; Sampson, 1978; Simpson, 1974). Applying Kohlberg's stages to people of other cultures—cultures that value social consequences more highly than abstract principles, or that stress obligations to family above all else—might not be fair, for instance. Similarly, Kohlberg's theories may be biased against women. According to psychologist Carol Gilligan (1982, 1989), the theory ignores the fact that males are taught a different hierarchy of values than females, and that those values foster different forms of moral reasoning in adulthood. Specifically, men are prone to detachment from others; their self-worth stems from a sense of autonomy. This tendency inclines them to reason about moral questions in terms of abstract concepts, such as equity and justice (Kohlberg's postconventional level). Women, in contrast, are prone to attachment; their sense of self is linked to their families and friends. As a result, they are inclined to think about moral dilemmas in terms of personal relationships and social obligations (Kohlberg's conventional level).

Such criticisms have helped to introduce caution into the process of assessing what a person's style of moral reasoning suggests about that person's level of cognitive development. Nevertheless, many psychologists believe that Kohlberg's theory offers a useful way to think about changes in moral reasoning from early childhood to adulthood (Hoffman, 1977).

Social and Personality Development in Adolescence

The word *adolescence* comes from the Latin word *adolescere,* meaning "to grow into maturity." The beginning of this period is marked by the onset of puberty, the time of sexual maturation. Puberty is triggered by changes in the body's hormones, especially the increased output of hormones by the pituitary gland that stimulates both physical growth and the production of hormones by the sex glands (the ovaries and testes). In boys puberty begins around the age of twelve, in girls around the age of ten or eleven.

One of the most obvious indications that puberty is under way is a sudden spurt in height. Boys grow about 5 inches in a single year, girls about 4 inches. Primary sexual characteristics also emerge, meaning that the sex organs develop. In males, the testes, scrotum, and penis mature; and in females, the ovaries, vagina, and uterus. Sexual maturation, of course, is accompanied by other physical changes. A male's voice lowers, his shoulders widen and become more muscular, and hair begin to grow on his face, chest, underarms, and pubic region. A female grows pubic and underarm hair, her breasts develop, and her hips enlarge. These physical developments are called **secondary sexual characteristics.**

The development of a female's uterus is accompanied by **menarche,** the start of the menstrual cycle. In industrialized nations, the age of first menstruation has declined over the last few generations. In mid-nineteenth-century America, a girl typically began to menstruate at age sixteen; today the average age is twelve-and-a-half, or perhaps even younger (Pinel, 1997). This decline in the age of menarche is thought to result from improved nutrition (Tanner, 1982).

The timing of puberty can have important consequences. Boys who mature early are physically stronger than late-maturing boys, so they tend to excel at sports. This advantage can give them more poise and self-confidence, and can make them more desirable in the eyes of both peers and adults (Conger, 1977). For girls, the consequences of early maturation can be more negative. Dramatic changes in height and body shape may produce temporary problems in social adjustment, particularly if those changes are sexually attractive to boys. If early maturation occurs simultaneously with graduation to a higher-level school, it can be particularly stressful, giving rise to feelings of depression (Petersen, 1989). Parents can help early-maturing daughters to avoid these negative outcomes by teaching them effective coping strategies.

The changes of puberty bring with them a new sense of self. Adolescents, with their emerging adult bodies, can no longer view themselves as children. They have now become teenagers, young people on the brink of early adulthood. Furthermore, their improved cognitive abilities enable them to see themselves more in psychological terms (Damon, 1983; Sprinthall & Collins, 1984). When asked for self-descriptions they will relate not just their physical traits but their feelings, beliefs, values, and characteristic behaviors. Adolescents can be extremely introspective. They are searching for a deeper meaning that explains and integrates their surface characteristics.

Adolescents soon develop a need to establish an independent identity, separate from their parents. This striving to gain a sense of themselves as separate, autonomous people becomes a major preoccupation. In fact, Erik Erikson labeled the search for a secure, well-integrated personal identity the overriding challenge of adolescence. According to Erikson (1950), who introduced the concept of the identity crisis to psychology, the physical, sexual, and social demands on adolescents foster in them a need to clarify who they are and how they relate to the adult world they are about to enter. Trying out different adult roles is the way they attempt to develop an identity. One teenager may try her hand at acting, adopt a more avant-garde style of dress, and get involved in political causes. By experimenting with a variety of possible choices, adolescents acquire some idea of the life-styles associated with different roles without committing themselves irrevocably to any one. Of course, trying out different adult identities is not possible in all societies. While American teenagers enjoy a prolonged period during which they experiment and can choose from many alternatives, young people in nonindustrialized societies are often forced soon after puberty into the adult roles tradition dictates.

Another important aspect of adolescent social development is peer relationships. In keeping with their new capacity for self-understanding, teenagers develop a more mature capacity for understanding others. As a result, their friendships take on a new degree of intimacy. Girls especially spend hours in self-disclosure and sharing of confidences (Sprinthall & Collins, 1984). This new intimacy extends first to peers of the adolescent's own sex and then to opposite-sex partners.

Psychological intimacy may expand to include sexual intimacy during adolescence. In a study by Ambuel (1995) 40 percent of females ages thirteen to nineteen reported having sexual intercourse within the past year. Males in the same age range reported similar, perhaps even slightly higher, incidence of sexual activity (Louis Harris & Associates, 1986). At least one-third of sexually active females reported engaging in unprotected sex, dramatically increasing the probability of an unintended pregnancy or a sexually transmitted disease (including acquired immunodeficiency syndrome, or AIDS). The age of sexual initiation varied with gender (boys generally experienced intercourse earlier than girls), with race (blacks tended to become sexually active earlier than whites), and with the norms that prevailed in a teenager's peer group (Brooks-Gunn & Furstenberg, 1989).

When asked why most teenagers do not postpone sexual activity until they are adults, adolescents gave a variety of reasons. In the nationwide survey just mentioned, both males and females listed curiosity as a motive, and boys cited sexual drives as well. Some (roughly 10 percent) said they had had sex because they were in love. The most frequently mentioned reason, however, was peer pressure. Half the boys and nearly three-quarters of the girls gave that explanation, and a quarter of both sexes, but especially younger females, had succumbed to pressure to do more than they had really wished to do. This is especially true with younger females. Of the 7 percent of white and 9 percent of black fourteen-year-old females who had reported experiencing sexual intercourse, nearly 70 percent said their experiences were involuntary. Sexual abuse by family members or friends and "date rapes" were often involved in those experiences.

Do these results mean that adolescents are overinfluenced by their peers, as many parents fear? There is little doubt that adolescence is a time when peers do become increasingly influential. Parents who attempt to separate their teenage children from their friends usually meet with strong resistance (Steinberg, 1986). Young people probably oppose such interference partly out of fear of being ridiculed by their peers. But the tendency of adolescents to oppose their parents and side with their peers instead is often greatly overstated. Strong peer influence among teenagers does not entirely negate parental influence, which remains fairly high, especially concerning the basic values a young person holds (Chassin & Sherman, 1985).

Social and Personality Development in Adulthood

Many people assume that personality development slows and eventually ceases once a person reaches adulthood. Freud argued that basic personality traits are essentially fixed in childhood, and that adult identity is established around the end of adolescence. Other psychologists who have a broader conception of personality argue that a person's habitual ways of thinking and acting continue to change throughout adulthood (Levinson et al., 1978). At the very least, adults face different challenges, have different concerns, and find different sources of satisfaction at various points in their lives. These differences in life experiences can make the attitudes and outlook of a person who is twenty-five significantly different from those of the same person twenty or forty years later.

Stages of Adult Development

What are some of the changes in outlook Americans can expect as they move through their adult years? Researchers who have suggested viewing adult development as a series of stages can provide some answers to this question.

Early Adulthood

If adolescence is a time of searching inward for personal identity, early adulthood is a time of looking outward to the tasks of launching a career, a marriage, and perhaps a family. In one study of the feelings, concerns, and activities of more than 500 men and women, those between the ages of twenty-two and twenty-eight were found to be busy making commitments, taking on responsibilities, and focusing their energies on the attainment of goals (Gould, 1972, 1978). Thus, rather than being a period of deep introspection, the early and mid-twenties are usually a period of action.

The decade from age twenty to age thirty poses a special challenge to women. A young woman today faces a much wider range of choices than her grandmother or probably even her mother. Today, like generations before them, many women in their twenties see marriage and motherhood as major life goals (Roberts & Newton, 1987). But a growing number are postponing childbearing in favor of first establishing a career, which means that many women are starting families at a significantly older age than their mothers (Shreve, 1982). And today, most mothers continue to hold jobs outside the home, even when their children are young. These women often adjust the balance between family and career several times during early and middle adulthood (Roberts & Newton, 1987; Sheehy, 1976).

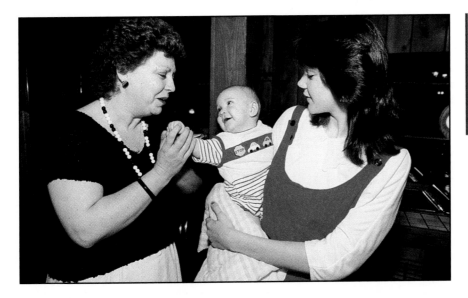

Mid-life transitions are often characterized by significant events, such as becoming a grandparent for the first time. They tend to be times of intense reflection, and often lead to major life changes.

Young adults' attitudes and concerns begin to change as they enter their early thirties. Between the ages of twenty-eight and thirty-four, many adults begin to question the commitments they have made over the past decade, the values they have chosen, and the goals they have worked so hard to achieve. Essentially, this is a time of life when many people stop and ask themselves, "What is life all about now that I have done what I am supposed to do?" (Gould, 1972, 1978). Such misgivings, of course, often produce difficult and painful reversals. Marriages may end, careers may be abandoned, and entire life-styles may be changed. People in their early thirties sometimes feel that any unsatisfactory aspect of their lives must be rectified immediately; otherwise, it will be too late to do so. This period of life has been called the **age-thirty crisis** (Levinson et al., 1978).

As the questioning and changes that accompany the age-thirty crisis subside, a person enters a new period of adulthood. For working men and women, the years between thirty-five and forty can be especially productive. In one study of both professional and working-class men, these years were reported as a time of "making it"—of establishing oneself in the world and actively carving out a niche, or moving up the career ladder (Levinson et al., 1978).

Mid-Life and Beyond

At about age forty, the period of early adulthood comes to an end and a mid-life transition begins. For women who have devoted their adult lives to the roles of wife and mother, a crisis may occur as the children begin to leave home. To adjust to these changes, family-oriented women may search for satisfying work outside the home, returning to an interrupted career or perhaps starting a new one. Middle-aged women who had involvements outside the home during their twenties and thirties reported less difficulty when their children leave the family nest (Roberts & Newton, 1987).

For men, the mid-life transition usually brings a crisis in both their personal life and their career. Like women at this stage, they may wonder, "What have I done with my life? What have I accomplished? What do I still wish to do?" Daniel Levinson and his colleagues (1978) studied men during these transitions; their findings are summarized in Figure 10-1. Fully 80 percent of their sample experienced a moderate to severe crisis during the mid-life transition, characterized by a questioning of virtually every aspect of their lives.

The introspective questioning reported at mid-life is consistent with the seventh stage in Erik Erikson's theory of social and personality development. The challenge of this stage, according to Erikson, is to learn how to reach out and become concerned with the well-being of future generations. Erikson called this goal **generativity.** In his view the person who fails to achieve generativity experiences stagnation, an embittered preoccupation with the self. In a thirty-year study of ninety-five men that began with their graduation from college, George Vaillant (1977) found that middle-aged people who considered themselves successful and productive by middle age

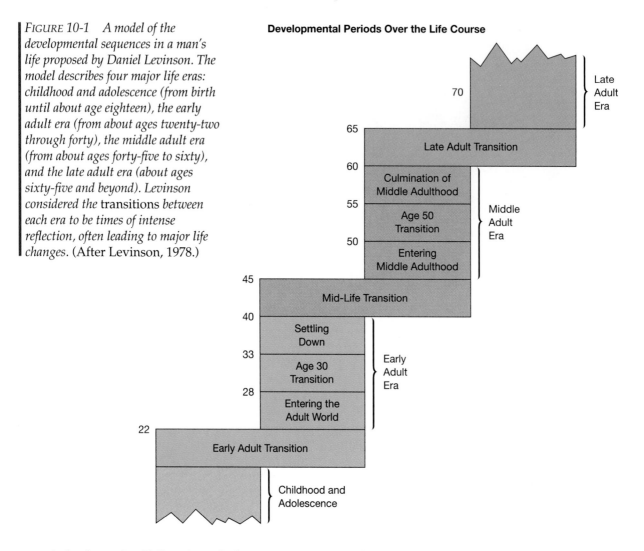

FIGURE 10-1   *A model of the developmental sequences in a man's life proposed by Daniel Levinson. The model describes four major life eras: childhood and adolescence (from birth until about age eighteen), the early adult era (from about ages twenty-two through forty), the middle adult era (from about ages forty-five to sixty), and the late adult era (about ages sixty-five and beyond). Levinson considered the transitions between each era to be times of intense reflection, often leading to major life changes.* (After Levinson, 1978.)

Developmental Periods Over the Life Course

were indeed meeting Erikson's goal of generativity. Those who fared poorly were characterized by a bored self-indulgence, just as Erikson had theorized.

After the critical mid-life transition come the middle adult years, for many people a time of greater stability than they have ever known. Income is typically higher than at any time in the past. Most people of this age are confident of their skills, and their productivity is often at its peak. But with middle age comes a new sense of time. People become increasingly aware that life is finite; they are constantly reminded of their advancing years. When parents and friends die, when their children have children, when they gradually become among the oldest people at work, and when their bodies no longer perform as they once did, the middle-aged face the reality of growing old (Karp, 1988). "Within the last five years," one man in his fifties put it, "both my parents died. I be-

came the oldest in my family. I'm the patriarch of the family now. Maybe that's when old age [begins]" (Karp, 1988, p. 731).

And so adults of this age start to think more in terms of priorities, of focusing their remaining time on the things that really matter. This is a stage when personal relationships often become more important. Many adults of this age report greater satisfaction with their marriage, warmer ties with their children, and a greater appreciation of friends. For many, these values and outlooks continue into the late adult years (Gould, 1972, 1978).

Individual Differences in Adult Development

The stage perspective on adult social and personality development stresses common events and transitions at specific ages. However, differences in peo-

Those who are productive and satisfied in their life work as young adults are likely to remain so as they grow older.

ple's life stories mean that each individual develops in unique ways. For instance, not everyone experiences the major milestones in life at the same time. Especially over the last few decades, our society has become more tolerant of those who proceed through life "off schedule," so to speak (Neugarten, 1976). Thus, the man or woman who is still unmarried at age thirty-five, or the couple that decides to have children in their forties, or the career-minded people who continue to work into their seventies and eighties are no longer viewed with the surprise they once were. For these people, life follows a different pattern from that of the mainstream.

Research underlines the importance of individual differences in adult development. In one study, for instance, the life stage transitions women experienced were found to be much less related to their age than to the timing of events in their own lives (Reinke, 1985). Nor did all the women studied experience the same set of transitions and stages. Such studies remind us that human lives are not programmed to unfold in a uniform fashion. Each of us is in some ways a unique individual, subject to our own personal experiences, needs, and rhythms.

Coping and Satisfaction in Adulthood

According to Erikson, the final stage of life should bring a sense of wholeness, a recognition of purposes accomplished and a life meaningfully lived. Those who do not achieve this sense of fulfillment experience regret over wasted opportunities and poor choices. They long for another chance, and so despair about death in ways that those who have found fulfillment may not.

What factors are associated with a sense of satisfaction in a person's later years? In one study of men and women that extended over much of their lives, the people who were content at age seventy were the same ones who had reported positive feelings about their health, work, and marriages forty years earlier (Mussen, Honzik, & Eichorn, 1982). Obviously, people who suffer no chronic diseases or physical handicaps are likely to be content with their health. But what characteristics are related to satisfaction with a marriage and a job? Other studies have provided clues. For instance, people who are very happily married tend to describe their marital relationships as having certain traits. Most important is the emotional security the relationship provides, followed by mutual respect, good communication, mutual aid, sexual intimacy, and loyalty (Reedy, Birren, & Schaie, 1981). Job satisfaction involves other traits. People who are content with their occupations often derive satisfaction from the independence and self-reliance their occupations bring (Sears, 1977).

Involvement in meaningful activities may also be a factor in promoting satisfaction with life, not just during a person's working years but into old age. In one study, for instance, researchers arranged weekly visits between nursing home patients and a college student, who shared personal experiences with them (Langer et al., 1979). At the end of each visit, the student asked the elderly patient to think about a specific topic to discuss the following week. The mental activity that this task generated appeared to make a big difference both in the elderly patients' memory ability and in their emotional well-being, as measured by nurses' ratings of their awareness, alertness, sociability, activity, and health. Patients who did not receive weekly student visits did not fare as well. Apparently, elderly people who continue to be active mentally cope more successfully with old age and live more meaningful lives than those who become mentally inactive.

Stability of the Adult's Personality

Recurring Theme 1 states that "the best predictor of future behavior is past behavior." One implication of this theme is that personality generally remains stable throughout the life span. Of course, people modify their beliefs and actions constantly, but does the basic "core" personality change?

THEME 1 | **The Best Predictor of Future Behavior Is Past Behavior**   Robert McCrae and Paul Costa, two prominent personality researchers, find that personality is quite stable over time (Costa & McCrae, 1980; McCrae & Costa, 1984, 1994). They (and others) have collected a wealth of evidence to document the following conclusions (summarized from McCrae & Costa, 1994):

- Across individuals, mean levels of personality traits change with development, reaching adult levels by age thirty. In fact, traits do not change much beyond age twenty, except that between ages twenty and thirty, people tend to become somewhat less emotional and somewhat more responsible and cooperative.
- Beyond age thirty, the only significant personality changes are those that are related to reduced

physical activity that comes with advancing age. (This conclusion excludes any trauma- or dementia-related changes.)

- From early childhood on, individual differences in personality traits show continuity. By age thirty, an individual's personality traits are essentially fixed (excluding, again, trauma or dementia).
- All of the major personality traits display this stability.
- The stability of personality holds true regardless of gender, race, or other demographic categories.

Costa and McCrae are well aware that their findings make many psychologists uncomfortable. They write:

> If few findings in psychology are more robust than the stability of personality, even fewer are more unpopular. Gerontologists often see stability as an affront to their commitment to continuing adult development; psychotherapists sometimes view it as an alarming challenge to their ability to help patients; humanistic psychologists and transcendental philosophers think it degrades the human nature. A popular account in the *Idaho Statesman* ran under the headline "Your Personality—You're Stuck With It."
>
> McCrae & Costa, 1994, p. 175

Rather than seeing stability of personality as a force that controls our destiny, however, McCrae and Costa argue that this stability is what *defines* us. We are who we are because of the way we consistently interact with the people and objects in our world. As McCrae and Costa put it, "A person's recognition of the inevitability of his or her one and only personality is a large part of what Erik Erikson called ego integrity, the culminating wisdom of a lifetime" (McCrae & Costa, 1994, p. 175).

In Depth

The Effects of Infant Day Care on Emotional Development

DIANNE BEGAN LOOKING for day care for her first child three months before the baby was born. Six months later, with her maternity leave coming to an end, she was growing desperate:

> I would go to visit some of the places that had openings, but I just couldn't imagine leaving my little girl there. Some were chaotic. Toddlers fighting over toys, screaming "Mine!" at each other, and babies crying in the background. But even worse were the places where the kids weren't making any noise at all. Sometimes they'd have a bunch of older babies just bouncing up and down in those jumper things. It was awful! And even when I did eventually find a good place, it wasn't easy leaving Katie there. That first morning after I handed her over, I could hardly make myself drive away. But there was no question that I had to work. I had to pay the bills.

In recent decades—as women have become more career-oriented, as the cost of living has spiraled, and as divorce has become more common—a growing number of women have gone to work outside the home. Today, half of all babies in the United States have a working mother—twice the proportion in 1970 (Clarke-Stewart, 1989). These mothers must secure some form of day care and leave their children there for lengthy periods. What effects do substitute caregivers have on a child's emotional development? Do they hinder the formation of a secure attachment between mother and child? In recent years psychologists have conducted studies designed to answer these questions.

Initial Studies

In one of the first studies of the relationship between early day care and emotional development, Mary Blehar compared two- and three-year-olds enrolled in full-time day care with youngsters of the same age who were cared for at home by their mothers. Blehar (1974) found that as a group, the day-care children seemed less securely attached to their mothers. In a laboratory situation in which each mother repeatedly left her child alone with a stranger, the day-care children became more upset than home-care children.

They cried more, engaged in more oral behaviors (thumb sucking, for instance), avoided the stranger more, and often ignored or resisted the mother when she returned. Early day care, it seemed, was related to decreased emotional resiliency.

A

B

Because the long-term effects of day care on a child's development can be profound, the quality of the day care children receive is extremely important. One critical factor is the caregiver's involvement with the children (A). Those programs in which adults frequently interact with youngsters, showing them affection and concern, are most conducive to favorable emotional attachments. In general, the best settings are those with a low child-to-care-giver ratio, and a small number of children overall (B).

Criticisms, Alternatives, and Further Research

Many psychologists approached Blehar's results with caution. Some pointed out that the observers who had scored the children's behaviors often knew beforehand which group the youngsters belonged to—the day-care group or the home-reared one. Their knowledge could therefore have biased their perceptions, predisposing them to see what they expected to see. In fact, when one group of researchers repeated Blehar's study using scorers who were unaware of the experiment's purpose and the youngsters' backgrounds, they could not replicate her findings (Moskowitz, Schwarz, & Corsini, 1977). Instead, they found that children who had experienced day care were no different from those who had not.

Other psychologists suspected that Blehar had observed only short-term reactions to day care. Her day-care subjects had been enrolled in group care for only four-and-a-half months; perhaps they were still adjusting to the experience. If so, any insecurity they showed would not be comparable to the long-term insecurity of children whose parents were rejecting or inconsistent in their care. In support of this hypothesis, one team of researchers found that the longer children had been in day care, the fewer negative reactions they showed (Blanchard & Main, 1979). In another study, children who had been in day care an average of nine-and-a-half months seemed no different emotionally from children who were raised at home by their mothers (Portnoy & Simmons, 1978). Thus, although children might go through a period of stressful adaptation to day care, regular care outside the home in itself might not cause any long-term harm.

But some psychologists were not satisfied with the data that had been gathered. They argued that much of the research on day-care children had focused on those who attended high-quality university-affiliated centers that offered excellent staff and programs. How comparable, they asked, were those centers to the ones most American preschoolers had attended? In addition, much of the research to date had focused on children who had entered day care at a relatively late age, when their attachment to their mothers was firmly established. What about babies who are placed in day care as infants, when the attachment process is incomplete or may not even have begun? Do those infants stand a higher-than-average chance of developing an insecure attachment, with all the risks that insecurity entails?

Brian Vaughn and his colleagues were among the first to try to answer these questions (Vaughn, Gove, & Egeland, 1980). They chose to study 100 economically disadvantaged mothers who could not afford top-quality day care for their infants. These mothers had to make do with whatever child-care arrangements they could afford—often a neighbor willing to baby-sit in her home for a modest fee. Vaughn and his colleagues assessed the quality of their children's attachments at twelve and eighteen months. They found a higher proportion of secure attachments among children who had been raised exclusively at home. The children who had been placed in day care before age one were especially likely to avoid their mothers in stressful situations—a pattern Ainsworth says arises when a mother is inaccessible to her baby. This pattern has been linked to serious social and emotional maladjustments later in childhood (Sroufe, 1988). Thus, poor-quality day care, begun at a very early age, seems particularly harmful to a child's development.

Other studies have drawn similar conclusions. For instance, Sandra Scarr and her colleagues conducted a six-year study of day care on the island of Bermuda, where 90 percent of children are tended by someone other than their mothers by the time they are two years old (McCartney et al., 1982; Scarr, 1984). Scarr's team carefully evaluated the quality of ten day-care centers and the progress of children who had attended them for six months or longer. They found that entry into day care before the age of one, coupled with a low level of verbal interaction between child and caregivers, was generally associated with emotional maladjustment. Children who experienced this combination of early separation from the mother and relatively poor-quality care were more likely than other preschoolers to be anxious, hostile, and hyperactive. In another, more recent study, Carollee Howes (1990) assessed a large group of children from the time they were babies until they entered kindergarten. She found that preschoolers who had experienced poor-quality day care beginning in infancy were less compliant and less able to exert self-control, more hostile and less considerate of others, and more distractible and less able to focus on a task; they also had more problems with their peers (see also Scarr, Phillips, & McCartney, 1990).

Studies such as these suggest that the quality of day care is extremely important, especially when a child is placed in day care very early in life. Researchers are therefore trying to specify exactly what constitutes high-quality day care. Scarr's and Howes' studies suggest that a critical factor is the caregiver's involvement with the children. Those programs in which adults frequently talk to youngsters, share discoveries with them, and show them affection and concern are most conducive to favorable emotional attachment. These characteristics are usually found in settings with a low child-to-caregiver ratio and a generally small number of children overall (Howes & Rubenstein, 1981). Many child-care specialists recommend entrusting no more than three infants or six toddlers to each caregiver (Kagan, Kearsley, & Zelazo, 1978; Clarke-Stewart, 1982).

Another factor that contributes significantly to quality in day care is continuity in care. In Brian Vaughn's study, he and his colleagues found that 80 percent of the children from low-income homes experienced at least one change in day-care provider during their first eighteen months of life (Vaughn, Gove, & Egeland, 1980). As a group, these children were especially likely to be insecurely attached to their mothers. This finding was echoed in another study in which children were observed as they were dropped off at day care each morning (Cummings, 1980). Those who were left with an unfamiliar caregiver were much more distressed than those who were left with a familiar one. Note, however, that having more than one caregiver does not in itself seem be detrimental to young children. Preschoolers who are cared for by several different adults can be expected to thrive as long as their relationships with those adults are stable (Clarke-Stewart, & Fein, 1983).

Finally, Edward Zigler, the developmental psychologist who was the guiding force behind Head Start, points out that not all *home-care* situations are good, or even adequate. Often, many children are cared for by a single caregiver, usually a member of the extended family, and the caregiver is unable to provide the direct, interactive environment that is so beneficial to development. Being kept at home is no benefit, if the home environment is poor.

In some cases the parents are both employed outside the home, but they arrange work schedules so that at least one of them can be home with the children. Despite the obvious benefits to the children, this puts a tremendous strain on the couple's relationship (Zigler & Lang, 1991; see also Zigler & Styfco, 1993).

Patterns and Conclusions

What can we conclude about the effects of early day care on children's emotional development? Apparently, it is not *where* children are raised that makes a difference, but rather *how* they are cared for (Belsky, 1988; Scarr, Phillips, & McCartney, 1989, 1990). If our society can offer high-quality day care to the children of working parents—day care that meets their needs for interaction, affection, and enduring relationships with adults—there is every reason to expect they will suffer no adverse effects. Setting high minimum standards for day care has therefore become a top priority among many developmental psychologists. Unfortunately, high standards for day care are not always a top priority among state legislators. In some states, the law allows each day-care worker to care for up to seven babies, or twenty preschoolers, at once! Most states also lack high standards for the training of day-care workers. Many have no educational requirements, and nine do not even require the inexperienced to receive at least some instruction after they begin providing care (Vandell & Corasaniti, 1990). Perhaps if legislatures thought in terms of child *development* centers, rather than child *care* centers, requirements for child-care providers would improve.

We must be careful, however, to avoid assuming that early, poor-quality day care is the only cause of childhood development problems. Day-care quality and family characteristics tend to be related (Howes, 1990). That is, parents who are highly stressed tend to choose lower-quality day care, perhaps because they lack the time and energy to evaluate day-care options more thoroughly. Nevertheless, improving the quality of day care across the board can only be beneficial. If day care becomes a stable source of affection and involvement for young children, it can help to compensate for stress in a youngster's home environment. Edward Zigler writes:

> Politicians and educators are fond of saying, "Our children are our future." But we must consider the kind of future we expect them to live in and how best to provide them with the tools for meeting it . . . enhancing the development of those who will inherit the democracy. Only by recognizing that our children are quite literally the families and societies of the future will we be willing to give them their rightful place in the society of the present.
>
> Zigler & Lang, 1991, pp. 239–240

SUMMARY

1. Personality and social development are studied from at least three perspectives. The **psychosexual** (or **psychoanalytic**) **approach** of Freud stresses the importance of childhood factors in adult adjustments. The **psychosocial** approach of Erikson views development as a series of challenges faced during different times in the life span. The **social learning perspective** considers the power of social norms and emphasizes observation and modeling as primary agents of change. The **cognitive developmental perspective** is based on the idea that a child's understanding of the world changes with age, and the child's understanding will significantly affect her behavior and social development. Finally, the **biological perspective** contends that development is guided by inherited biological tendencies.

2. Babies appear to be biologically "programmed" to interact with other humans, responding especially to their voices and faces. An infant's **social smile,** triggered by the sight of a human face, has survival value because it strengthens the bond with the caregiver. Each baby is also born with his or her own **temperament,** or behavioral disposition. But biology alone does not determine how we develop. Rather, what we inherit at birth is a range of developmental possibilities, a **reaction range,** which can be fulfilled or thwarted depending on experiences.

3. The formation of emotional bonds with caregivers, or attachment, is a central factor in development during infancy. Depending on how responsive the caregiver is, a baby may form a **secure attachment** or an **anxious attachment.** The kind of attachment, in turn, can affect later social and personality development.

4. Parenting styles can be classified as **permissive** (lacking rules for appropriate behavior), **authoritarian** (harsh, inflexible, and unresponsive to the child's wishes), and **authoritative** (warm, responsive, and flexible, but setting firm limits when needed). Children with permissive parents tend to be impulsive and lacking in self-reliance; those with authoritarian parents tend to be moody and have problems with peers; and those with authoritative parents tend to be friendly, independent, and in control of themselves.

5. Various forms of child abuse can have devastating effects on children. Apathy, blunted emotions, and low self-esteem are just some of the reactions seen in the victims of abuse by parents. Parents can also negatively affect their children by marital conflict and divorce. But a strong, caring relationship with at least one of the parents can do much to overcome any adverse reactions.

6. **Gender roles** are the patterns of behavior that males and females in general tend to have in common, despite their individual differences in personality. Although biology may contribute to the behavioral differences between the sexes, learning also plays an important part.

7. **Socialization** is the process of instilling society's values into children. The basic goal of socialization is **internalization**—incorporating social values to such an extent that their violation produces guilt. Socialization plays a key role in the development of moral thought and behavior. According to Freud, a child internalizes the moral code of the same-sex parent during resolution of the **Oedipus conflict.** Social learning theorists claim that children acquire morality gradually by observing good behavior in others, being rewarded for their own good deeds, and experiencing punishment when they are bad. The cognitive developmental view holds that children progress through stages of moral reasoning, each of which reflects their current cognitive level.

8. **Adolescence,** the transition from childhood to adulthood, involves important physical, psychological, and social changes. Adolescence is marked by the onset of **puberty,** the period of sexual maturation. The mature sex organs that develop are called primary sexual characteristics, while the other physical traits of a man or a woman are called **secondary sexual characteristics.** With their more advanced cognitive capabilities, adolescents are able to analyze the self more abstractly than they did as children, often raising probing questions about who

they are. Erik Erikson labeled this search for a personal identity the overriding challenge of adolescence.

9. Social and personality development continues throughout adulthood in the sense that people continue to face new challenges and new roles. Although people often experience similar feelings and outlooks at the same points in their adult lives, individual differences in adult development are important too. The final years of life can be ones of pleasure and fulfillment, especially for people who have found satisfaction in their marriage, family, and work and who continue to be mentally active.

10. People have wondered if a secure attachment to the mother is jeopardized if a baby is placed in day care while the mother works. Research suggests that the answer is "no," as long as the mother continues to be responsive to her baby and the day care is good.

SUGGESTED READINGS

Birren, E., Schaie, K. W., Abeles, R. P., Gatz, M., & Salthouse, T. (1996). *Handbook of the psychology of aging* (4th ed.). San Diego: Academic Press. Though written for a more knowledgeable reader, this is a thorough, reference-quality book.

Kail, R. V., & Cavanaugh, J. C. (1996). *Human development*. Pacific Grove, CA: Brooks/Cole. One of the most readable textbooks on the market, written from a strongly cognitive perspective.

Kotre, J., & Hall, E. (1990). *Seasons of life: Our dramatic journey from birth to death*. Boston: Little. The authors argue that human development revolves around three time clocks: the biological, the social, and the psychological. They provide rich examples of how people pass through each of these stages across the life span.

Rice, F. P. (1995). *Human development: A life-span approach* (2nd ed.). Englewood Cliffs, NJ: Prentice-Hall. Excellent introduction to the field.

Santrock, J. W. (1997). *Life-span development* (6th ed.). Dubuque, IA: Brown & Benchmark. Thorough coverage of the field, with greater attention than most to development in adult years.

Zigler, E., & Lang, M. E. (1991). *Child care choices: Balancing the needs of children, families, and society*. New York: Free Press.

Zigler, E., & Styfco, S. J. (1993). *Head start and beyond: A national plan for extended childhood intervention*. New Haven, CT: Yale University Press. In these books, Edward Zigler, the first director of the Office of Child Development and the architect of Head Start, examines two of our society's most pressing concerns: child care and early childhood education.

CHAPTER 11

Motivation and Emotion

On July 3, 1996, the day before Independence Day, the Ohio River Fireworks store in Scottown, Ohio, was crowded. Customers were browsing through the extensive selection of bottle rockets and firecrackers when suddenly, a series of small "pops" was heard, followed almost immediately by many more. The small cinder-block building was quickly engulfed in smoke. The fire blocked one of the two exits, so the forty or fifty people inside rushed to the front door. Within a few moments, the building was a raging inferno. In the rush to exit, eight people were killed and a dozen more injured.

A few hours later, twenty-four-year-old Todd Hall was arraigned on charges of involuntary manslaughter. According to preliminary reports Hall, who had been browsing through the fireworks in the backroom, had been encouraged by friends to light a string of firecrackers as a "joke." During his arraignment, the suspect "giggled like a delighted child," in one reporter's words (Williams, quoted in the *Waco-Tribune Herald,* July 6, 1996, p. 1). He mugged for the television cameras, telling photographers to wait while he "did his hair." As he sat in the jury box, he flashed peace signs to the crowd of journalists, clearly relishing the attention he was getting. Hall showed no remorse: indeed, he seemed to have no understanding of what he had done.

What would cause someone to light a string of firecrackers in a crowded fireworks store? Why would such a person fail to comprehend the devastation that resulted? How could he laugh and joke with reporters while relatives of the victims stood nearby in stunned disbelief?

In 1987, when he was fifteen, Todd Hall fell off his skateboard and sustained a serious head injury. Shortly after that he began experiencing seizures similar to those seen in epileptics. Neurosurgeons operated once, then twice, in an effort to control the damage. The second time they operated, they performed a type of *prefrontal lobotomy,* separating Hall's frontal lobes from his temporal lobes. Much like H. M.'s surgery (see Chapters 3 and 7), this operation was a mixed success. It reduced the severity of some of Hall's symptoms, but it also had serious, irreversible side effects. Following the procedure Hall became, according to those who knew him, a "nuisance." He would wander purposelessly through the streets in his

Motivation gives impetus to behavior by arousing, sustaining, and directing it toward the attainment of goals. For Giacomo Leone and Anita Catuna, the goal was to win the New York City marathon—which they did in 1996, despite being considered underdogs.

hometown, sometimes stealing cigarettes from a gas station or pestering the customers. At times he even walked into neighbors' houses uninvited.

The brain damage Hall suffered injured various parts of his brain, especially areas in the frontal and temporal lobes. In addition, the surgery performed after his accident had disconnected his frontal lobes—those involved in "thinking" and other cognitive tasks—from his temporal lobes—those involved in emotion. The damage had changed an otherwise healthy, normal teenager into a "nuisance," one who cared little about others' thoughts or feelings. (In this respect, his case is reminiscent of Phineas Gage, discussed in Chapter 3.) While the accident caused some loss of intellectual functioning, the most serious impairments were affective (emotional). Though we scarcely think about emotion and motivation in normal, day-to-day experiences, they play a vital role. To see just how vital, we can look at cases of those whose emotional functioning is impaired, providing another demonstration of Recurring Theme 2, "Psychologists learn about the normal by studying the abnormal."

THEME Psychologists Learn About the Normal by Studying the Abnormal
2

Questions about motivation are often the most difficult for psychologists to answer. Why would anyone endure weeks of bitter wind and cold, thin air, and treacherous, icy terrain to get to the top of Mount Everest? Why do students put off studying until the night be-

fore the exam? Why do people in Sweetwater, Texas, flock to the rattlesnake roundup each year to handle (or watch others handle) rattlesnakes?

The answers to all such questions are bound up in the complex web of human motivation. Because motivational factors are so diverse, this chapter necessarily covers a variety of topics. We begin with a historical overview of the concepts and theories of motivation in order to give you an idea of psychologists' perspectives on this subject. The remainder of the chapter will deal with emotion, a concept that is closely related to motivation.

We will see that there are three basic dimensions of emotion: physiological changes, expressive behavior, and internal states. The "In Depth" section concentrates on one emotion, happiness. What makes people happy? Why are some of us happier than others? Can people learn to be happy? The concluding section of the chapter summarizes the long-standing theoretical debate over where emotions come from. Are emotions "gut reactions," or do they exist largely "in our heads"? The answers may surprise you.

Theories of Motivation

By **motivation,** psychologists mean that which gives impetus to behavior by arousing, sustaining, and directing it toward the attainment of goals (Madsen, 1959). Over the years, psychologists who are interested in motivation have developed a number of

Geese usually imprint to their mother, the first object they see after hatching. In the movie "Fly Away Home," newly hatched geese imprinted on a young girl after their mother was killed. When the time came for the geese to migrate south, the girl capitalized on their imprinting to lead them south in an airplane.

concepts to guide their research. One of the earliest was the concept of instinct—an innate, inherited motivation.

Instincts and Genetic Influences

An **instinct** is an innate force found in all members of a species that directs behavior in predictable ways in the presence of the right eliciting stimulus (Weiner, 1972, 1980). An example of an instinct is the "imprinting" of baby geese to their mother, or their tendency to follow her as soon as they are able to walk (see Chapter 9). Ethologist Konrad Lorenz discovered that the stimulus that elicits this instinctive behavior is the first moving object the newly hatched goslings see, which in the natural world is invariably the mother (Lorenz, 1937, 1950). By separating newborn goslings from their mother and exposing them to other moving things, Lorenz got them to follow a variety of peculiar objects, including a wooden box on wheels and even himself.

By the turn of the twentieth century, with the growing popularity of Darwin's theory of evolution, people had begun to wonder whether humans had instincts. If the behavior of lower animals was largely instinctual, scientists reasoned, and if humans were in fact related to other living things, perhaps some human behaviors were also motivated by instincts. Such speculation launched a widespread effort to identify human instincts.

One of the most influential of these theorists was William McDougall (1871–1938), who in 1908 pro-posed a list of human instincts that included curiosity, pugnacity, self-abasement, flight, repulsion, self-assertion, reproduction, gregariousness, acquisition, and parental care. Other investigators proposed different lists. The number of instincts grew steadily until a survey done in the 1920s found that more than 2,500 human instincts had so far been proposed (Bernard, 1924). Interest in instincts waned with the rise of behaviorism in the mid-twentieth century. In recent years, however, there has been a resurgence of interest in the topic.

One example of a modern instinct theory is John Bowlby's view that babies have a built-in tendency to become attached to the adults who care for them (Bowlby, 1969). This tendency probably evolved because it encouraged infants to stay close to their parents, thus affording them protection. Human instincts, of course, are less rigid and automatic than those of many other species, and more open to variation resulting from different learning experiences (Eibl-Eibesfeldt, 1970). For instance, unlike the imprinting of baby geese—which occurs quickly, cannot be changed once established, and is identical for every member of the species—the attachment of a human baby to his or her parents is the product of a great many hours of interaction. It can vary greatly in quality and does not preclude attachment to other caregivers.

The renewed interest in inborn behavioral tendencies has spawned a field called **evolutionary psychology** (for examples, see Buss, 1994; Buss et al.,

Standards of physical attractiveness are influenced by the culture in which people live. While this belly dancer might be considered overweight in some cultures, she is seen as quite attractive by her Egyptian audience.

1992). Researchers in this field focus on the genetic bases of a wide range of animal and human social behaviors—including aggression, cooperation, competition, sex roles, and altruism—especially toward those who share one's own genes. Evolutionary psychologists argue that organisms are inherently motivated to pass their genes on to future generations and to ensure that the "carriers" of their genes survive, even if they themselves do not. Thus, a mother may sacrifice her own life to save her child, for the child will carry her genes into the next generation.

One of the most successful applications of evolutionary psychology is **sociobiology,** or the study of the adaptive significance of inherited tendencies (Barash, 1982; Dawkins, 1976; Wilson, 1975, 1996). One such tendency that has been extensively studied in recent years is physical attractiveness. To some degree, physical attractiveness is influenced by the cul-

ture in which we live. Individuals who are considered attractive in one culture may be judged unattractive in another culture. Some aspects of attractiveness, though, tend to extend beyond cultural boundaries. According to evolutionary psychologists, these features are considered "attractive" because they signify good reproductive fitness.

Dev Singh at the University of Texas has examined one such factor: body shape. In a number of studies, Singh found that attractiveness was influenced not by *overall* body fat but rather by body fat *distribution* (as measured by the waist-to-hip ratio) (Singh, 1993). Thin women—those with low overall body fat—were considered youthful but not necessarily attractive. Instead, those with low waist-to-hip ratios were perceived as most attractive (Singh, 1994). Low waist-to-hip ratios, according to Singh, indicate that a woman is healthy, and more likely to produce healthy offspring. The findings were not restricted to one culture or ethnicity: Singh observed similar judgments in Afro-Americans and Indonesians (Singh & Luis, 1995).

Some psychologists have criticized evolutionary psychology, arguing that the theory is incomplete and the evidence inconclusive (Caporael & Brewer, 1995; Hood, 1995; see also Cantor, 1990b). Still, few deny that genes play some role in human motivation. Most psychologists accept the idea that human behavior is the product of the interaction of genetic and environmental factors.

Freud and Unconscious Motives

Like many other turn-of-the-century psychologists, Sigmund Freud looked to instincts as a way of explaining human behavior. However, Freud's list of basic instincts was simple: he included just two. The first was the urge toward life, procreation, and self-preservation, which included the drives for food, water, warmth, and, above all, sex. The second was the urge toward death and self-destruction, a return to the inanimate matter of which all living things are composed. Freud speculated that we often resolve the conflict between these two basic instincts by turning our self-destructive energies outward, against others—hence, the human tendencies to compete, conquer, and kill.

Freud believed that the dual urges of sex and aggression, if unsatisfied, created tension, and the desire to reduce that tension motivated behavior. But people cannot reduce tension by engaging in sex and aggression whenever they please; doing so is often forbidden by social norms. So people learn to push their forbidden urges deep into the unconscious, using a process called **repression**—one of several defense mechanisms Freud postulated. As you learned in Chapter 7, the mechanism of repression is related to the phenomenon of repressed memory; however, the two concepts are not identical. Repression is the process of keeping threatening events out of consciousness. Most current definitions of repressed memory go one step further, postulating that though repression blocks an event from consciousness, the event is still stored in memory in literal form. This definition presumes that repressed memories can be retrieved using techniques like hypnosis and that they are accurate. See the "In Depth" section in Chapter 7 for a lengthy discussion of these issues.

A repressed urge still has power, however; it demands an outlet of some kind. Often it encourages **sublimation,** or the unconscious substitution of a more socially acceptable behavior. For example, Freud proposed that many of the beautiful nudes Renaissance artists created on canvas and in marble were the products of sublimated sexual impulses. Similarly, we may unconsciously express anger toward our parents by losing or accidentally breaking one of their cherished possessions or by showing up late for a special holiday dinner. The possibility that our behavior is controlled by unconscious motives—motives that arise from deeply repressed urges—is one of Freud's most important contributions to psychology. We will discuss Freudian theory further in Chapters 13 and 16.

Drive-Reduction Theory

About the same time that Freud's ideas were attracting interest in Europe, behaviorists in the United States were arguing for a different approach to motivation. They advocated an emphasis on observable influences in the environment, rather than innate or unconscious factors, which are difficult or impossible to measure. A person behaves aggressively, the behaviorists said, not because of an aggressive instinct but because such behavior has been rewarded in the past.

But those who argued that goal-directed behavior could be explained by learning soon encountered problems. For instance, researchers found that a dog that had just been fed was hard to condition. Did feeding produce some kind of learning deficit? Not likely. The hypothesis that learning was motivated by some biological need seemed more plausible. Psychologists who were interested in motivation began to focus on the role of physiological drives.

Behaviorist Clark Hull (1884–1952), who is widely considered to have been the most influential psychologist of the 1930s and 1940s, argued that a biological need produces a drive toward activity, thus increasing the likelihood that an animal will perform a need-reducing response (Hull, 1943). A hungry rat, for instance, will become agitated, begin to roam about its cage, and eventually hit the bar that delivers a pellet of food. When the rat eats the pellet, its drive state declines, increasing the likelihood that it will repeat its actions the next time it is hungry. According to Hull, then, drives (motivators of performance) and reinforcements (a key to learning) work together to help an animal acquire adaptive responses.

But can the concept of drives, as defined by Hull, explain human motivation? Hull's **drive-reduction theory** certainly helps to explain why humans eat, sleep, avoid pain, engage in sexual behavior, and so on. But what about the large number of behaviors that seem unrelated to biological needs? Why, for example, do people seek out contact with other humans? No known biological need motivates them. What, then, does motivate their behavior?

To answer such questions, Hullian theorists proposed a distinction between primary and secondary drives. **Primary drives** are the most fundamental—the ones that arise from needs that are built into our physiological systems. **Secondary drives,** they theorized, were learned through association with the reduction of primary drives. Thus, when a child's contact with adults is repeatedly paired with the reduction of hunger or pain, that contact soon becomes a secondary reinforcer, and the urge to obtain it, a secondary drive. As such, secondary drives are a form of what are often called **learned motives.**

Beyond Drives and Drive Reduction

For many years drive-reduction theory was extremely popular. The concept of a drive was something researchers could study in the laboratory. They could deprive experimental animals of food and other biological necessities for a specified time, then measure the behavioral outcomes, all in controlled environments. Hull and other researchers performed many hundreds of such studies. Gradually,

In some pursuits, such as the creation of a work of art, the rewards are mostly internal. Intrinsically motivated behaviors are rewarding in and of themselves.

however, the serious limitations of the drive-reduction model became apparent. The model simply could not account for certain facts the researchers were uncovering.

For one thing, researchers were finding that animals of all kinds are strongly motivated to explore their environment and manipulate objects, even in the absence of physiological needs (Berlyne, 1950; Harlow, 1953). Rats, for instance, will endure electric shock in order to explore unfamiliar settings; monkeys will become totally engrossed in solving puzzles, such as how to open the clasp that fastens a door. Because these behaviors will occur without food or other primary reinforcers, they cannot be explained by secondary drives. What, then, is the motivation?

In a provocative paper, psychologist Robert White (1959) suggested that humans and other animals have a basic need to deal effectively with their environment and to master new challenges. We saw evidence of this in Chapter 9, where we described the reaction of human infants who have figured out how to make a mobile move (Monnier, Boehmer, & Scholer, 1976). When babies find the solution, they smile and coo vigorously in apparent delight. White and others have argued that the reward in performing such behaviors lies in the intrinsic satisfaction of acting competently. This kind of **intrinsic motivation,** many now believe, explains much of human behavior (Deci & Ryan, 1980; Dweck & Leggett, 1988). Intrinsic motivators—those things that are rewarding "in and of themselves"—can vary significantly from one individual to the next. They are probably the reason why one person will spend an entire Sunday morning doing a difficult crossword puzzle, while another prefers to file stamps away in a photo album.

Of course, not all motivators are intrinsic; many rewards are also external. Employees work to obtain a paycheck; children work to obtain praise from parents or teachers. Often, people are motivated by both intrinsic and extrinsic rewards. You may study this book, for example, partly because you enjoy learning about psychology, an intrinsic motivator. But you may also study because you want to receive a good grade, an extrinsic motivator.

Do people work harder for extrinsic or intrinsic rewards? As you might guess, answering this question is difficult. Our culture routinely offers external rewards for the activities it deems "valuable." The very act of performing deeds considered important by society, however, is often intrinsically rewarding as well. Athletes are an excellent example of this point. Many professional athletes stress their love of the sport, but they also earn high salaries. On the other hand, highly creative people like artists, writers, and musicians—even scientists—do their best and most creative work for its intrinsic rewards (Amible, 1983; Sternberg & Lubart, 1991). Though many also achieve external rewards like money, fame, and influence, these rewards tend to come later in life, rather than immediately following their actions.

Optimal Arousal Theory

Another intrinsic motivation for behavior may be to maintain an optimal level of arousal (Hebb, 1955). Thus, a bored animal confined to a cage may raise its level of arousal by exploring unfamiliar objects. Likewise, patients who are waiting in the doctor's office may find themselves reading outdated maga-

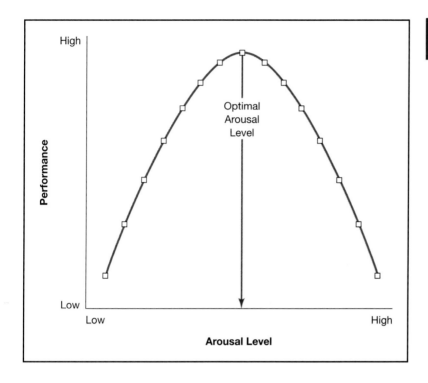

zines they would routinely shun—anything to relieve the tedium.

In other situations, the arousal level may already be too high, and a person may work to decrease it. Say, for example, that you are traveling to an unfamiliar city. The first few hours of your journey you spend driving down an interstate highway during daylight, through light traffic. To alleviate the boredom, you turn your radio louder or begin a conversation with your passenger. As you get closer to the city, however, the sun begins to set and the traffic begins to get heavier. You are not certain where the exit will be. You reach over to turn off the radio, or quit conversing with your passenger. To cope with the change to a more demanding situation, you are working to reduce your level of arousal.

According to **optimal arousal theory,** humans are motivated to maintain a comfortable level of arousal. If they are understimulated, they act to increase their arousal. If they are overstimulated, they act to bring their level of arousal down. What motivates a person changes from one situation to the next, depending on whether she is bored or overwhelmed.

Optimal arousal theory explains the **Yerkes-Dodson law** (Yerkes & Dodson, 1908), which states that performance is best when stimulation or arousal is intermediate (see Figure 11-1). If arousal is too low,

performance suffers. Increasing the arousal level increases performance, but only up to a point. When arousal reaches some optimal level, further increases lead to a *decrease* in performance.

You may have seen evidence of the Yerkes-Dodson law in your own life. For example, two or three cups of coffee (really, the caffeine in the coffee) may tend to increase your performance on many tasks. Another cup or two may enhance your performance a bit more, but at some point additional caffeine begins to impair performance. The same is true of anxiety. You may feel somewhat anxious just before taking a test. Your anxiety may be beneficial, helping you to concentrate on the task at hand. Too much anxiety, however, will impair your performance, making concentration more difficult.

An Evaluation of Theories of Motivation

As is the case with almost all topics in psychology, an accurate understanding of motivation involves all these perspectives just described. Clearly, biological needs serve as motivators. Whether they are called *instincts* or *drives*, they involve behaviors necessary for survival and reproduction. Primary drives almost certainly have a strong genetic component and are generally similar across cultures and environments. People of all cultures find feeding and reproduction motivating, for example. In contrast, secondary drives—those learned through associations with primary drives—display remarkable variability across cultures.

Biological theories do not capture all aspects of motivation, however. For example, many people stand in long lines to ride a roller-coaster, though the experience serves no obvious biological function. Arousal theories do a better job of explaining behaviors like these. Other motivators—the intrinsic motivators—are highly personal. People work for weeks tending a garden, then give away all the vegetables. Something about the process of gardening is intrinsically motivating to them.

What role do unconscious motivators play in human behavior? We do not know, because research on unconscious motivators is virtually impossible to do. To test Freud's theory, we would somehow have to find out about events that occurred to someone but are no longer remembered. Furthermore, we would need to rule out other sources of motivation—again, practically an impossible task. Yet most psychologists readily accept the fact that events we no longer remember can still influence our lives. If you were accidentally locked in a small closet as a child, say during a game of hide-and-seek, you may have come to dislike closed spaces. For some reason you cannot identify, you might work hard to avoid being in a closed space. If so, we could consider your early childhood experience to be an important motivator of your adult behavior.

Sexual Behavior

Sex is a powerful motivator. In fact, in Darwinian terms, an individual's (or species') success and failure is are *defined* in reproductive terms. Those members of a species who are better able to compete successfully for limited resources will survive *and reproduce,* thereby increasing the chance that their characteristics will survive in future generations (see Chapter 1). Almost by definition, the motivation to reproduce must be powerful.

The Effect of Hormones on Sexual Responsiveness

One source of sexual responsiveness is hormonal. Female rats, for instance, are sexually responsive only when their ovaries secrete a high level of the hormone *estrogen,* which in turn triggers the release

of egg cells for potential fertilization. Not surprisingly, when a female rat's ovaries are removed, she becomes totally unreceptive to males—unless she receives estrogen injections, which restore her normal sexual responsiveness.

Hormonal influence in humans is less direct. Sex hormones may *promote* sexual activity, but they certainly do not *control* it. Although some women report that their sexual responsiveness seems to increase around the midpoint of the menstrual cycles, when their estrogen levels peak, that assertion has not been confirmed by most studies (Hoon, Bruce, & Kinchloe, 1982). Nor do most women experience any cyclical decrease in the ability to become sexually aroused. The vast majority of women can become aroused despite the normal rise and fall of estrogen levels (Adams, Gold, & Burt, 1978). In fact, even complete removal of the ovaries tends to have only a negligible effect on a woman's sexual responsiveness. Instead, the sex hormones secreted by the adrenal glands appear to have a greater effect on the human female's arousal than those secreted by the ovaries. When the adrenal glands are surgically removed, a woman's sexual urge often drops appreciably. But even in this case, the effects of adrenal hormones are not clear-cut. Some women continue to be sexually responsive even after adrenal surgery—a finding that suggests that though hormones may influence a woman's sexual receptivity, they do not completely control it.

The influence of hormones on the human male's sexual responsiveness is also less pronounced than in other species. If the testes (which produce the hormone *testosterone*) are surgically removed from an adult male, a loss of sexual interest and responsiveness is not inevitable. Consider a study of over a hundred Scandinavian men whose testes were removed, either because of disease or as punishment for repeated sex crimes (Bremer, 1959). In a third of the men, sexual activity persisted for more than a year; in some, it continued for as long as ten years, though all eventually lost their ability to ejaculate during orgasm. Loss of the testes before adolescence, however, seems to have a more predictably negative effect. With some exceptions, without hormone replacement therapy, most castrated boys grow up to have little sexual interest or ability, and fail to develop secondary sex characteristics, such as facial hair and a deep-pitched voice (Money & Ehrhardt, 1972).

Hormones, of course, interact with the central nervous system, especially the hypothalamus. Recall that the hypothalamus stimulates the anterior pituitary gland to release hormones, which in turn stimulate both the *gonads* (the ovaries and testes) and the adrenal glands to secrete sex hormones. The sex hormones then travel through the bloodstream back to the hypothalamus, where they activate the neural networks involved in sexual arousal.

Sexually Arousing Stimuli

Hormones that reach the hypothalamus serve primarily to predispose human sexual responses. For full-fledged sexual arousal, sexual stimuli are needed. In humans a wide variety of visual and tactile sensations, from the sight of a nude body to the touch of someone's lips, are known to serve this purpose. But what about less obviously sexual stimuli, such as olfactory cues (those involving the sense of smell)? In many species, including some mammals, odors serve as powerful sexual signals (Carr & Caul, 1962; Michael & Keverne, 1968). Male dogs and monkeys, for example, are especially attracted to the scent of the female's vaginal secretions (Beach & Merari, 1970; Michael, Keverne, & Bonsall, 1971). In rats, the sexual odors of nursing females play a major role in arousing males when a sexually receptive female is near (Fillion & Blass, 1986). Some researchers think that humans, too, emit sexually arousing odors, though they are seldom consciously aware of them (Wiener, 1966). These scents may arise from the sweat glands and from secretions that accumulate in the genital regions (Comfort, 1971; Morris & Udry, 1978).

An intriguing question is why people develop sexual responsiveness to some stimuli but not to others. Do they learn to find certain sights, scents, and actions arousing, or are they born with those tendencies? As with most other sources of human behavior, the causes of sexual motivation are both varied and complex. Biological processes that occur before a child is born may influence adult sexual behavior. But from birth on, social learning, family dynamics, and other life experiences also play a role.

Human Sexual Responses

It is one thing to study the stimuli people find sexually arousing and quite another to study sexual acts themselves. For many years, psychologists considered this subject far too private for scientific investigation. Then, in the late 1950s, William Masters and Virginia Johnson sparked a revolution in the study of human sexuality. Masters and Johnson were the first scientists to conduct extensive laboratory observations of what actually happens in the human body during sexual activity. Using cameras and other devices to record internal and external responses, they studied nearly 700 male and female volunteers engaged in intercourse, masturbation, and other sexual behaviors. In all, the research team directly observed more than 10,000 sexual orgasms. A detailed summary of their findings was published in their landmark book *Human Sexual Response* (1966).

The Sexual Response Cycle

Masters and Johnson found that men and women respond quite similarly during sex. Both experience the same four physiological stages, called the **sexual response cycle** (see Figure 11-2). In the first stage, the **excitement phase,** breathing, heart rate, and muscular tension increase as arousal begins. Blood rushes into the genital organs, causing erection of the penis in a man and swelling of the clitoris in a woman. The lining of the vaginal walls becomes lubricated as drops of moisture, resembling perspiration, begin to form on it. The nipples of the woman—and sometimes of the man—become erect.

During the **plateau stage,** arousal heightens, further increasing breathing, heart rate, and muscle tension. A man's penis achieves maximum erection, and the glans, or head, turns a purplish color. Drops of fluid, which can contain especially active sperm, are often secreted from the opening of the penis. The testes increase in size and pull up tightly against the scrotum. In women, the vagina lubricates further to facilitate insertion of the penis. The inner two-thirds of the vagina balloon into a sac to receive semen, and the outer third decreases in diameter to put pressure on the penis. At the same time, a woman's clitoris retracts under its hood.

In the **orgasmic phase,** the muscles in the pelvic region and around the anus of both sexes undergo a series of contractions. In a woman the muscles of the vaginal walls and the uterus contract rhythmically, as do the muscles in and around the man's penis. Contraction of the penile muscles causes ejaculation, or the expulsion of semen, a milky white fluid that contains sperm. Though most of the ejaculate is expelled during the first few contractions, typically the contractions continue for a few more seconds. The

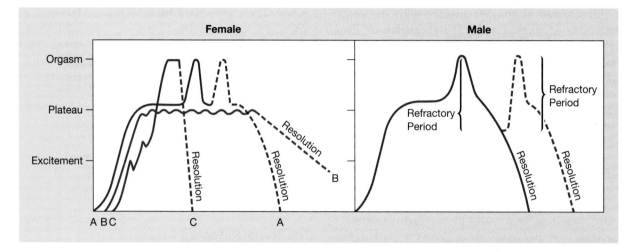

FIGURE 11-2   *The human sexual response cycle, first studied by Masters and Johnson. The four phases— excitement, plateau, orgasm, and resolution—are defined by physiological changes. In both sexes, excitement leads to a plateau that may be maintained for considerable periods without orgasm. The female may have one orgasm or several in succession (line A); may not achieve orgasm at all, and return relatively slowly to an unaroused state (line B); or, rarely, may have a single prolonged orgasm followed by rapid resolution (line C). The male has only one pattern of response after the plateau phase: he ejaculates quickly in orgasm, after which his arousal decreases rapidly. In the refractory period that follows ejaculation, he is incapable of another ejaculation. Males may repeat the orgasmic phase several times before returning to an unaroused state.*

woman's contractions may last longer, from ten to thirty seconds. Orgasm in a woman arises from penile stimulation of either the clitoris or the vaginal walls. Other muscles, particularly in the face and limbs, also contract involuntarily. In both sexes, blood pressure and heartbeat rise further, frequently reaching the level experienced by athletes at peak physical exertion. This state of extremely heightened arousal is accompanied by feelings of intense pleasure as muscle tension releases.

During the **resolution stage,** blood pressure, heart rate, and respiration gradually fall to normal. Men enter a *refractory period*, during which they are incapable of being stimulated to another orgasm for some time. Some women, in contrast, are capable of a series of multiple orgasms before passing into the resolution phase.

Although Masters and Johnson's model of the sexual response cycle is widely accepted, some aspects have been criticized. Some complain that because Masters and Johnson never fully described the methods they used to collect their data, their studies cannot be replicated precisely. Others question the universality of Masters and Johnson's stages, arguing that they may not apply equally well to all peo-

ple. More research needs to be done using standardized measurement techniques to resolve the issue of universality (Geer & Head, 1990).

Sexual Dysfunctions

Not only was Masters and Johnson's work important basic research, but it had applied significance as well, for it laid the foundation for understanding and treating sexual dysfunctions. A **sexual dysfunction** is any persistent or recurring problem that prevents a person from engaging in sexual relations or from reaching orgasm during sex.

There are several different kinds of sexual dysfunction. Men may suffer from **erectile failure,** or the inability to achieve or maintain an erection. In rare cases, the man has never been able to have an erection, a condition called **primary erectile failure.** More often, the man has problems maintaining an erection in some situations only, a condition called **secondary erectile failure.** For other sexually dysfunctional men, arousal is the problem; they acquire an erection easily enough, but ejaculate too soon. This **premature ejaculation** is the most common sexual complaint among male college students. Still other men have the opposite problem: they are unable to ejaculate during sex with a partner. This dysfunction is called **inhibited ejaculation.**

One of the sexual dysfunctions women suffer is **vaginismus,** involuntary muscle spasms that cause the vagina to shut tightly, so that penetration by a penis is extremely painful or even impossible. Other women engage in and often enjoy sexual intercourse, but do not experience orgasm. The term **primary orgasmic dysfunction** refers to cases in which the woman has never experienced an orgasm through any means. The term **secondary orgasmic dysfunction** refers to cases in which the woman sometimes experiences orgasms (through masturbation, for example), but not with her primary sexual partner or not during sexual intercourse.

When sexual difficulties are chronic and highly distressing, people may seek the help of a sex therapist. Masters and Johnson (1970) pioneered the development of sex therapy. In their approach, the couple is treated as a unit by a pair of sex therapists, one male and one female. The focus is on the sexual relationship, sexual education, and the reduction of sexual anxiety. To lessen the fear of failure, the couple is usually told not to engage in sexual intercourse at first. Instead, they are assigned "nondemanding" sensual exercises, such as massaging one another. Gradually, more sexual activities are introduced, and the couple is instructed in how to respond freely while giving each other pleasure. A diagnosis of sexual dysfunction should not be made hastily. Many people experience the problems just described at one time or another. Only when those problems are extremely persistent and upsetting should they be called *dysfunctions* (LoPiccolo & Stock, 1986).

The Mind's Role in Human Sexuality

The fact that the vast majority of sexual dysfunctions have no physiological basis, but instead are psychologically caused, attests to the powerful role of the mind in human sexuality. Similarly, the fact that people can become highly aroused through sexual fantasies attests to the mind's role in sexual behavior. In studies in which sexual arousal is measured while subjects merely think about erotic stimuli, researchers have found that the more explicit the erotic imagery, the more heightened the arousal (Dekker & Everaerd, 1989).

Studies also show that erotic imagery plays an important role in most people's daily sex lives. In a study of nearly a hundred men, a large majority reported imagining various sexual acts during both intercourse and masturbation. They also fantasized sexual scenes at least once daily, outside any overt sexual activity (Crewpault & Couture, 1980). Such mental images seem to heighten erotic arousal and increase the motivation to engage in sex. The same processes occur in women. The large majority of women fantasize sexually both during and outside the physical act (Crewpault et al., 1977; Hariton & Singer, 1974). Such erotic images often serve to enhance sexual responsiveness.

Because of the critical role of the mind in human sexuality, psychologists have proposed models of sexual arousal that emphasize cognitive processes. According to one of them, arousal begins when erotic cues trigger expectations of arousal (Barlow, 1986). If the person finds those expectations pleasant, he or she will focus more intently on the cues (noticing more details about them, for example). This increase in attention triggers physiological arousal, which helps to direct even more attention to the cues, thus heightening the physiological arousal—and so on, in a kind of feedback loop. Ultimately, if erotic cues are processed long enough, and arousal becomes sufficiently high, the person will seek some form of overt sexual activity.

The Three Dimensions of Emotion

Motivation is certainly influenced by (as well as an influence on) emotion. We are often motivated by "feelings" associated with situations or events. Emotions are so much a part of our daily existence, in fact, that we find it difficult to imagine life without them. Try to picture yourself standing in a line for two hours without annoyance, winning a $100,000 lottery without elation, or learning of a loved one's death without grief. Such a lack of emotion is almost inconceivable. Without the ability to feel rage, grief, joy, and love, we would hardly recognize ourselves as human.

Yet as familiar as emotion is to us, defining the term is not easy. Summarizing a vast body of research, David Watson and Lee Ann Clark (1994) have proposed that **emotion** has three central components. First, an emotion involves some type of expression, usually a facial expression; second, an emotion evokes consistent physiological changes, such as an increase in heart rate. Third, emotions are accompanied by a subjective state or feeling such as

Emotions often signal a person's internal state. Charles Rathbun (left), who was tried and convicted of murdering a former Los Angeles Raiders cheerleader, sat expressionless through much of his trial. Many observers interpreted his impassive mien as a sign of remorselessness.

fear, anxiety, or excitement. Though human emotions run the gamut from sorrow and despair, envy and hate, to joy and ecstasy, all have these three dimensions in common.

The Physiology of Emotion

When we are feeling frustrated or anxious, we say, "My nerves are on edge." When we are exhilarated we say, "What a rush!" These are not mere figures of speech. Rather, we are expressing a phenomenon psychologists have demonstrated time and again in the laboratory: strong emotions are associated with physiological arousal, specifically with changes in the peripheral nervous system.

The Peripheral Nervous System and Emotion

As we saw in Chapter 3, the peripheral nervous system consists of two main parts: the somatic (or voluntary) nervous system and the autonomic (or involuntary) nervous system. The somatic nervous system innervates the smooth muscles (including facial muscles), allowing us to interact with our physical and social environments. To understand how important the somatic nervous system is, try to imagine life without it. Would we have emotions without a somatic nervous system? Perhaps, but we would not be able to express them or act on them. At the very least, our emotions would lose their purpose.

The innervation of facial muscles is of particular interest to emotion researchers. Most of our smooth muscles are attached to the skeleton; they enable us to move around. But the facial muscles are attached to skin and connective tissue, not to bone. Their sole function is to move the skin on the face, producing changes in facial expression. As you will learn in later sections of this chapter, the face plays a fascinating part in the experience of emotion.

The autonomic nervous system regulates the body's internal environment and usually functions without conscious control. It is composed of two subsystems, the sympathetic and the parasympathetic, both of which connect to almost every muscle of the internal organs and also to every gland. The sympathetic and the parasympathetic systems have broadly opposite effects. In general, the sympathetic system dominates during emergencies or stress, promoting the expenditure of energy. It encourages the increased blood sugar levels, heart rate, and blood pressure needed to sustain physical activity and, at the same time, inhibits digestion. The parasympathetic system, in contrast, dominates during relaxation, promoting the conservation of energy. It works to decrease the heart rate and blood flow to the skeletal muscles, and also to promote digestion. Not surprisingly, most of the physiological changes associated with strong emotion, such as intense anger or fear, are caused by activation of the sympathetic nervous system. What happens, exactly, when the sympathetic nervous system is activated? Suppose it is 2 a.m. and you are going to get your car, which is parked on a deserted city street. Suddenly a man emerges from a dark alley. In this fear-arousing situation, the following physiological changes would occur:

1. *Vascular changes.* The blood vessels leading to your stomach and intestines would constrict, and digestion would virtually stop. At the same time, the vessels leading to your large skeletal muscles would expand, diverting the oxygen and nutrients carried in your blood to where they might be needed for fight or flight.

2. *Hormonal changes.* Your pancreas would secrete the hormone *glucagon,* which would stimulate your liver to release stored sugar into the bloodstream. The sugar would supply extra energy to your skeletal muscles, should they need it. In addition, your adrenal glands would secrete the hormone *epinephrine* (adrenaline), which would help sustain many of the other physiological changes brought about by

The sympathetic nervous system (SNS) dominates the body during emergencies like storms, floods, and other stressful situations, increasing blood sugar, heart rate, and blood pressure in order to sustain physical activity.

activation of your sympathetic nervous system.

3. *Respiratory changes.* Your breathing would become deeper and more rapid, and your *bronchioles* (the small air passages leading to your lungs) would expand. These changes would increase the supply of oxygen in your blood (the extra oxygen would be needed to burn the sugar being sent to your skeletal muscles).

4. *Circulatory changes.* Your heartbeat rate would increase, perhaps more than double, speeding the circulation of your blood and hastening the delivery of oxygen and nutrients to your skeletal muscles.

5. *Visual changes.* Your pupils would dilate, allowing your eyes to take in more light.

6. *Sweat gland changes.* Activity in your sweat glands would increase. The glands on the palms of your hands, in particular, would secrete moisture.

7. *Muscular changes.* The muscles just beneath the surface of your skin would contract, causing your hairs to stand on end. For our furry ancestors, the erection of body hair may have been part of a display of threat. We relatively hairless humans simply break out in "goose bumps" (Lang, Rice, & Sternbach, 1972). Your neck and shoulder muscles would also tense quickly, orienting your eyes and face toward the source of threat. And the muscles over your eyebrows would contract, pulling your brows together and pushing them out, so that they partially cover your eyes. This response, which is part of the expression of fear, may help to protect the eyes in a fight.

Once a threatening situation is over, other physiological changes take place. Suppose your would-be attacker turned out to be a police officer on patrol. Almost immediately, the opposing effects of the parasympathetic nervous system would begin to reassert themselves. Your heart rate, respiration, glandular secretions, blood flow, and muscular tension would all return to normal, and the bodily sensations associated with fear would subside. This cycle of physiological arousal—assertion of the sympathetic nervous system over muscles and glands, followed by a reassertion of the parasympathetic division—is a general cycle that is associated with most strong emotions.

Physiological Measures of Emotion

In extreme cases, such as the encounter with a stranger in a dark alley, we feel as if our senses have been turned up full blast. An observer can easily detect the emotions we are feeling. More often, however, the physiological changes that are associated with emotion are so slight that others do not notice. How can psychologists monitor and record the subtle activities of the peripheral nervous system?

The emotion researcher's primary tool is a machine called a **polygraph,** meaning literally "many pens." In a sense, a polygraph works like a radio. A

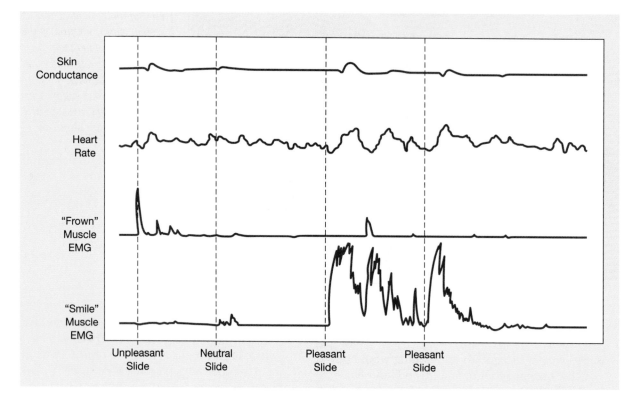

FIGURE 11-3   *Polygraphs detect changes in the sympathetic and parasympathetic nervous system. In most cases, the technician records the subject's heart rate, respiration, blood pressure, and changes in skin conductance, or electrodermal activity. Though polygraphs are often called "lie detectors," they actually measure changes in the nervous system that are associated with fear and anxiety. They are not reliable indicators of lying and, as a result, are not admitted as evidence in most legal settings.* (Courtesy of Randy J. Larsen.)

radio detects small electrical impulses in the air (radio waves), amplifies those signals, and transduces or converts them into the energy that drives a speaker, producing sound. Similarly, the polygraph detects small changes in the subject's nervous system, which it transduces into electrical signals that are recorded by pens resting on a moving roll of paper. Older polygraphs produced a strip chart, but modern polygraphs usually send the electrical signals to a computer (see Figure 11-3).

A polygraph can make a number of different physiological measurements simultaneously. One of the most widely used measures in emotion research is that of *electrodermal activity,* or EDA (formerly called a galvanic skin response, or GSR) (Fowles et al., 1981). When the autonomic nervous system is aroused, sweat glands in the palm of the hand begin releasing moisture. (Called the "sweaty palm syndrome," this

response is a frequent cause of embarrassment on first dates and job interviews.) Since water conducts electricity, researchers can pass a tiny current (too weak to be felt) across a subject's palm and detect the slightest change in conductance, thereby measuring autonomic nervous system activity.

Cardiovascular measures are also popular among emotion researchers (Cacioppo & Tassinary, 1990). The most common is the *electrocardiogram,* or EKG, in which electrodes attached to the subject's chest are used to measure changes in heart rate. (The "K" in EKG comes from the original German spelling of cardiogram.) Another sensor attached to the thumb may be used to measure the time a contraction pulse takes to travel from the heart to the thumb, and thus indicate how constricted or relaxed the subject's arteries are. A rubber tube (called a *pneumograph*) around the subject's chest records changes in the rate

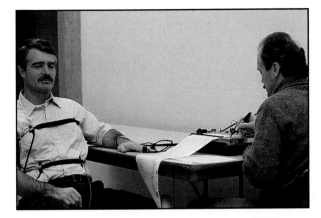

Polygraphs, or "lie detectors," do not actually detect lying; they measure changes in activity in the nervous system. Because many other factors besides lying can arouse the nervous system, including surprise, pain, and anxiety, polygraph tests are no longer considered admissible evidence in most legal settings.

and depth of breathing. Blood pressure is measured with the inflatable cuff, used routinely in physical examinations.

Emotion researchers have become increasingly interested in the muscles that produce facial expressions (Dimberg, 1990). As was noted earlier, the somatic nervous system controls the facial muscles. When those muscles contract, they give off small electrical potentials, on the order of a few microvolts (or millionths of a volt). The *electromyogram* (EMG) can pick up, and the polygraph amplify, changes in facial muscle action so small and fleeting that they do not produce any visible change in facial expression (Cacioppo et al., 1986). Finally, researchers who are interested in the brain's role in emotion (in addition to sympathetic nervous system activity) may use an *electroencephalogram* (EEG) to record brain activity.

Using the polygraphs, psychologists can investigate a wide range of questions. For example, polygraphs have been used to measure changes in phobic reactions. In the popular mind, however, the polygraph is associated with lie detector tests. Though the use of polygraphs in this context is widespread, it is often misunderstood. A million or more lie detector tests are given in the United States each year (Ekman, 1985). Until recently, the majority of them were given by private employers, from banks to fast-food outlets, to screen prospective em-

ployees and control internal crime. Federal law now prohibits the use of polygraphs in the private sector for preemployment screening, but not for examining those employees suspected of theft or other crimes.

Another common use of the lie detector is in criminal investigations, not only to assess the guilt or innocence of criminal suspects but to test the credibility of witnesses and victims. Although most states do not permit the results of a polygraph to be reported in a trial, some do if the defendant agrees. The federal government frequently uses lie detector tests both to screen applicants for jobs with access to classified material and to examine employees suspected of crimes like espionage or of "leaking" sensitive information to the press. Periodic random screening of current government employees with security clearance—the "dragnet" approach—is highly controversial. At this writing, government agencies could not require an employee to submit to a polygraph unless there is evidence the person may have violated a rule or law.

In a typical lie detector test, the subject is first asked a series of neutral control questions to establish a baseline: "Is your name John Doe?" "Do you live on Elm Street?" "Did you eat eggs for breakfast?" Questions that would indicate "guilty knowledge"—facts known only by the criminal—follow. But how accurate is this procedure? Unfortunately, polygraphs are not reliable indicators of lying. First, polygraphs do not detect lying; rather, they measure changes in a person's nervous system activity. Only if we assume that lying produces such changes can we infer that a polygraph identifies lies. But many other extraneous factors can cause physiological arousal, including surprise, pain, anxiety, joy, and novelty. Moreover, individuals vary widely in their physiological responses. Just as some people can lie with "a straight face," others can lie with cool palms and a steady heartbeat.

Most people think of lie detectors only in terms of their use in detecting guilt. Can these machines be used to detect innocence? Studies show that polygraphs are somewhat accurate in detecting guilt, but are not so reliable in detecting innocence. In other words, they tend to convict the innocent (Kleinmuntz & Szucko, 1984; see Saxe, Dougherty, & Cross, 1985, for a review). Unfortunately, an innocent person is likely to volunteer for a polygraph (whether in a criminal investigation or an employment setting) in the mistaken belief that he or she has nothing to lose and everything to gain. Despite these weaknesses, polygraphs are still widely used. If you look in the Yellow Pages of your telephone directory under "Lie Detection," you will find that most cities have at least one company, and often several, that provides these services.

The Brain and Emotion

Although the peripheral nervous system exhibits most clearly the physiological changes associated with emotion, it is coordinated by the brain. The hypothalamus and certain areas of the limbic system, in particular, are involved in a number of emotional reactions, including anger, aggression, and fear; so are general arousal centers in the brain (Panksepp, 1994; Pribram, 1981; Steriade et al., 1990; Steriade & Llinas, 1988). This relationship has been demonstrated by research in which different parts of an animal's brain were stimulated or surgically removed. Research with cats, for example, has shown that stimulation of particular areas of the hypothalamus can induce intense activation of the sympathetic nervous system, producing an emotional display that can be interpreted only as feline rage. The cat's pupils dilate; the fur on its back stands erect; the ears flatten, the back arches, and the cat unsheathes its claws, hissing and snarling intensely (Flynn et al., 1970). In contrast, surgical lesions in the amygdala produce extremely docile behavior. Researchers have found similar links between the amygdala and mood, especially certain types of depression (Schulkin, 1994).

In humans, exaggerated emotional behavior may accompany damage to certain areas of the limbic system. Such damage can take place before, during, or after birth. It can arise from a variety of causes, including brain disease, drug abuse, and trauma resulting from an accident, athletic injury, or gunshot wound. This chapter opened with the story of Todd Hall's role in the Ohio fireworks explosion of July 1996. The brain damage inflicted during Hall's skateboard accident (and his subsequent neurosurgery) contributed significantly to Hall's willingness to light the firecrackers that ignited the crowded store.

For many years, psychologists believed that the brain's control over emotion was exerted largely through the "primitive" structures of the hypothalamus and the amygdala. More recently, however, they have realized that the cerebral cortex is intimately involved in emotion. Evidence is accumulating that the cortex's role in emotion is asymmetrical: the left frontal cortex is associated with positive feelings, and the right frontal cortex with negative feelings (Heller, 1990). In laboratory experiments, when pleasant emotions are induced in subjects, the left hemisphere shows greater activation than the right; when unpleasant emotions are induced, the right hemisphere shows the greater activation of the two (Davidson et al., 1990). Other research has shown that individual differences in resting hemisphere activity predict readiness or predisposition toward positive or negative emotions. In one study (Davidson & Fox, 1989), ten-month-old infants who showed relatively greater right-hemisphere activation (a negative predisposition) during a quiet, baseline period were more likely to cry when they were later separated from their mothers. Conversely, infants who showed greater left-hemisphere activation (a positive predisposition) during the baseline period were less likely to cry.

In a similar study of adults (Tomarken, Davidson, & Henriques, 1990), researchers used an electroencephalogram (EEG) to measure hemispheric asymmetry under quiet, neutral conditions. They found no relationship between activity in right or left hemisphere activity and self-reported mood. Then they showed the subjects film clips designed to invoke pleasant emotions (a puppy playing with flowers, monkeys cavorting in a zoo) or negative emotions (a nurse training film showing an amputation and third-degree burns). Subjects whose EEGs suggested a predominance of right-hemisphere activity described more intense feelings of fear while watching the training film than subjects whose EEGs suggested predominance of left-hemisphere activity. Other studies have shown that depressed patients have a much higher level of activation in the front portion of the right hemisphere than people who are not depressed (Davidson, 1984).

Finally, emotion and physiological changes associated with it depend in part on brain chemistry. Depression, for instance, is known to be associated with reduced levels of the neurotransmitters norepinephrine and serotonin (see Chapter 3). Drugs that deplete norepinephrine and serotonin produce depression, while antidepressant drugs usually stimulate their secretion or prevent their reuptake (Ray, 1993). Other researchers have found links between depression and hormones (Schulkin, 1994).

Even without words, the couple in this picture is displaying powerful emotions. Notice the man's averted gaze and folded arms, and the woman's upturned palms, which suggest resignation.

What can we conclude about the relative contributions of the brain and the peripheral nervous system to emotion? Some years ago psychologist George W. Hohmann (1966), a paraplegic, interviewed twenty-five veterans whose spinal cords had been severed. He found that the nature and intensity of certain of their emotions, especially anger and fear, were significantly different from normal emotional reactions. In general, the higher the lesion on the spinal cord, the more extensive the disruption of sympathetic arousal, and the greater the change in emotional experience. The veterans still perceived the significance of emotional situations, and even displayed many of the behaviors associated with strong emotion, but the quality of their emotional experience was often altered; something was missing. As one man explained, "Sometimes I get angry when I see some injustice. I yell and cuss and raise hell, because if you don't do it sometimes I've learned people will take advantage of you. But it just doesn't have the heat it used to. It's a mental kind of anger." This research has often been cited as evidence that autonomic arousal and feedback are an essential part of emotional experience.

In a recent study (Chwalisz, Diener, & Gallagher, 1988), researchers compared university students with spinal-cord injuries, students with other problems that confined them to a wheelchair (such as a broken leg), and nonhandicapped students. They found that students with spinal-cord injuries experienced the full range of emotions: joy, love, sentimentality, anger,

sadness, and fear. All reported emotional highs and lows. But in general, the intensity of their emotional experiences was somewhat lower than that of other subjects. The researchers concluded that though feedback from the autonomic nervous system may amplify emotional experience, it is not essential. In their view, the essential organs of emotion are the brain and the face: "The excitation of particular brain pathways and accompanying facial expressions may be sufficient for emotional experience" (Chwalisz, Diener, & Gallagher, 1988, p. 821).

The Behavioral Expression of Emotion

Consider the photograph on the left. Though the man and woman are saying nothing, they are speaking volumes. The man's folded arms, the tilt of his head, his averted eyes—all suggest a stubborn indifference, even anger. The woman conveys resignation and despair through her upturned hands. Clearly, this is not a casual conversation; powerful emotions are being expressed.

Psychologists have wondered why people show their emotions in such recognizable patterns. Are these behavioral patterns the product of socialization, or are they part of our genetic heritage? The following section examines the evidence.

The Biological Basis of Emotional Expression

In his book *The Expression of the Emotions in Man and Animals* (1896), Charles Darwin argued that many patterns of nonverbal communication in humans are inherited. That is, they evolved because they had survival value. Darwin approached the topic of emotion from a functional perspective. "Why do emotional expressions exist?" he asked. His answer was that their primary function is to broadcast information about a person's internal state. By telling others how we feel, our emotions also tell them how we are likely to behave.

When we are enraged, for example, we, like other animals, commonly grimace and bare our teeth. In most cases a threat is sufficient. Advance warning enables others to take action by backing off, signaling deference or friendly intentions, and so on, to avoid violence. For social animals who live in groups, such as humans, this rapid communication of internal states is highly adaptive; much actual fighting is avoided. The human grimace may be left over from a time in our evolutionary past when we fought with our teeth—a weak form of preparatory

Photograph Judged						
Judgment	Happiness	Disgust	Surprise	Sadness	Anger	Fear
Culture	**Percent Who Agreed with Judgment**					
99 Americans	97	92	95	84	67	85
40 Brazilians	95	97	87	59	90	67
119 Chileans	95	92	93	88	94	68
168 Argentinians	98	92	95	78	90	54
29 Japanese	100	90	100	62	90	66

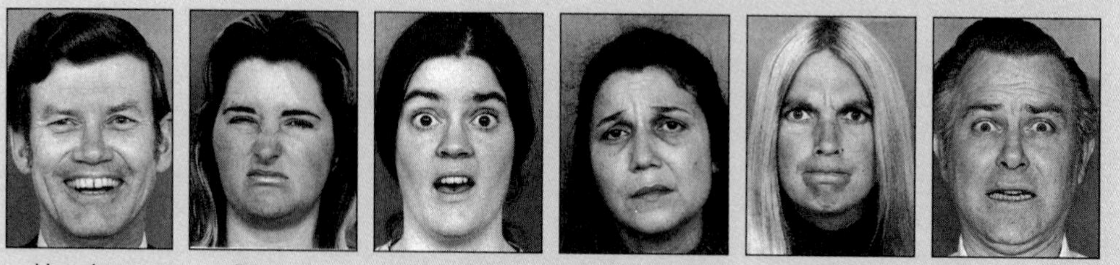

FIGURE 11-4 *The interpretation of facial expressions. According to Darwin, natural selection favors humans who can recognize and interpret facial expressions. Therefore, people from different cultures should interpret facial expressions in the same way. In one experiment, people from six different cultures were asked to identify the expressions in these photographs. The column totals how the percentage of subjects in each culture who agreed on the meaning of each expression. The results suggest that Darwin's hypothesis was correct: to some extent humans are genetically programmed to recognize and produce the emotions conveyed by certain facial expressions. (After Ekman et al., 1972.)*

action that had previously been adaptive. Although human aggression today seldom involves biting, the grimace still communicates that we are angry and might become aggressive in other ways. Our snarl is part of our species' biological equipment and a product of our evolution.

In showing how the expression of emotions is adaptive, Darwin extended the laws of natural selection from physical, biological characteristics to behavior patterns. If emotional expressions are a product of evolution, Darwin reasoned, they should be universal: people from remote places who do not understand one another's spoken language should nevertheless understand each other's expressive language. Darwin documented some cross-cultural similarities; later researchers have found extensive evidence for the universality of certain emotional expressions. In one study, people from different countries were asked to identify the emotions expressed in a series of photographs of faces, some of which are shown in Figure 11-4. Anger, fear, disgust, surprise,

sadness, and happiness were consistently recognized, regardless of the culture from which a person came. Even members of New Guinea tribes, who had had little contact with Westerners and their characteristic patterns of expression, were able to label these basic emotions (Ekman & Friesen, 1974). Other researchers have found that the facial expression of interest, shame, and contempt is virtually the same across cultures (Ekman & Friesen, 1986; Izard, 1971). Such findings support Darwin's view that certain characteristic patterns of emotional expression are at least in part genetically transmitted (Izard, 1984).

Emotion and the Tendency toward Action

Emotions predispose people to behave in specific ways. Happiness, for example, leads them to relax and recuperate after attaining some goal; sadness, to appeal for support from others; fear, to withdraw or flee; anger, to threaten or attack; and disgust, to get rid of some noxious object. Because emotions tend to exert some control over action, they serve as the motivational link between experience and behavior (Frijda, 1986; Frijda, Kuipers, & ter Schure, 1989). Emotions can create a state of readiness or unreadiness to interact with the environment—as when a person "freezes with fear."

"Motivational urges" are what distinguish emotions from mere feelings of pleasantness or unpleasantness. They also differentiate between different emotions. Consider fear and anger: both emotions are associated with high levels of unpleasantness. Both are accompanied by similar patterns of physiological arousal (a racing heart, sweaty palms). But these two emotions are linked with quite different action tendencies. Fear is associated with the tendency to withdraw, anger with the tendency to attack. Physiological arousal prepares the body to effectively carry out both these actions.

The Role of Learning in Emotional Expression

To say that certain expressions of emotion are prewired, and that emotions prepare us to act in a specific way (fight or flight), does not rule out learning. Culture dictates when the expression or suppression of an action tendency is appropriate. In Japan people are expected to smile and be polite, even when they are seething with rage. A Kiowa woman is supposed to scream and tear her face when her brother dies, regardless of whether she liked him (Tavris, 1982).

People of different cultures also vary in their use of certain nonverbal cues to express emotion. In Chinese literature, the expression "He scratched his ears and his cheeks" is supposed to indicate that a character is happy (Klineberg, 1938). In Western culture, that description might be interpreted as indicating that a character is anxious, even distraught. To test for cultural differences in nonverbal expression, researchers use the Profile of Nonverbal Sensitivity (PONS), which measures an individual's ability to decode nonverbal signals. After administering the test to more than 2,000 subjects from twenty nations, one group of researchers found that people from cultures similar to that of the United States, where the test was developed, performed best. Although all subjects did better on the test than they would have simply by guessing, the differences in their performance strongly suggest that some aspects of nonverbal expression are culturally learned (Hall et al., 1978).

Additional evidence for the role of learning in nonverbal expression is provided by the fact that men and women differ in their nonverbal display of emotion. When Ross Buck (1976) showed the same series of emotion-arousing pictures to a group of men and women, observers could guess the content of the pictures much more easily from the women's faces than from the men's. Though the men often reacted with increased heart rate and sweating palms, they kept their faces "masked." Significantly, this sex-based difference in emotional expressiveness is not found in preschool children. Although young children vary in their response to emotion-arousing pictures, their reactions are a function of personality, not gender. In the process of growing up, boys apparently learn to control certain aspects of their emotional expression.

Ekman and others (Ekman et al., 1982; Levenson, Ekman, & Friesen, 1990) have taken the study of facial expression a step further. They contend that movement of the facial muscles is closely tied to the autonomic nervous system, which controls heart rate, breathing, and other essential involuntary functions. Thus, adopting the facial expression that is characteristic of a certain emotion may trigger the related physiological changes. In a typical experiment, Ekman asked subjects to combine the following actions: raise the eyebrows, pull the eyebrows together, raise the upper eyelids, tighten the lower lids, drop the jaw, and stretch the lower lip wide. As the subjects did so, the researchers monitored their brain waves, heart rate, breathing rate, and skin temperature. Although subjects were not told that they were mimicking an expression of anger, they experienced the physiological effects associated with anger. Ekman conjectures that the contraction or relaxation of certain facial muscles triggers a specific response in the nervous system, which, in turn, produces mood-changing hormones (McDonald, 1985). Other researchers' work buttresses Ekman's notion that unique brain pathways control each major emotion (Davidson, 1984).

The Interpretation of Emotional Expressions

Our ability to interpret behavioral expressions of emotion is, like the unspoken communication itself, partly biological and partly learned. We appear to be "prepared" to pick up the meaning of certain faces and gestures (Dimberg, 1990; Dimberg & Ohman,

The interpretation of emotion involves both verbal and non-verbal cues. The comedian Richard Lewis, for example, usually dresses in black; throughout his routine he shakes his head in mock despair. These non-verbal cues contribute to the impression that Lewis is anxious and unhappy, the basis of his comedy.

1983). Presented with a novel situation or a new toy, infants check their mother's facial expression before deciding how to act (Lamb & Campos, 1982). If she looks happy or relaxed, the infant generally will approach; if she looks frightened, the infant will try to avoid the new situation or even flee.

In the course of socialization we learn which expressive behaviors to notice and which to ignore. Women are generally better at detecting emotional undercurrents than men, perhaps because girls are socialized to be more sensitive to the feelings of others (Ekman, 1982; Rosenthal et al., 1974). Whatever their skill at interpreting emotional expressions, however, people tend to trust nonverbal messages (Ekman, 1985; Ekman & Friesen, 1969; Mehrabian, 1972). When verbal and nonverbal information is

contradictory—if, for example, a person denies she is angry while repeatedly clenching and unclenching her fist—an observer will generally conclude that the nonverbal message is the true one. The assumption is that body language is relatively difficult to disguise.

Psychologists have shown that there may be some truth to this common assumption. In one experiment designed to test people's control over their nonverbal expression (Ekman & Friesen, 1969, 1974), subjects watched a film showing gory amputations and burns. They were then asked to conceal the true nature of the film in describing it to others. When observers could see only the speaker's head and face, they could not distinguish the subjects who were lying from members of a control group who were truthfully describing a pleasant film they had seen. But when given the opportunity to view the rest of the speaker's body, many of the observers could perceive the intended deception. Apparently the liars managed to mask their feelings with a pleasant smile, but showed their anxiety in body movements. Of course, whether or not the people we are trying to deceive do notice such nonverbal cues depends on a number of factors, including the strength of the emotions we are trying to conceal and how well our observers know us (Miller & Burgoon, 1982). Trained observers can usually (but not always) distinguish between a felt and a false smile.

Emotions as Subjective States or Traits

Besides inducing behaviors, emotions are also subjective internal states, which we commonly call "moods" and "feelings." Often we have difficulty translating these feelings into words. If we ourselves have difficulty describing our feelings, how then can psychologists develop models and measures of our subjective states?

Most contemporary researchers in this field view emotions in terms of opposing or bipolar states, such as relaxed versus anxious, or elated versus bored. Furthermore, most agree that the two most important dimensions of emotion are pleasant-to-unpleasant and high-to-low activation (Larsen & Diener, 1987). These two dimensions are the basis of the circular model of emotions, first popularized by James Russell (Russell, 1980; Russell et al., 1989) (see Figure 11-5). (In the scientific literature, this model is known as the *circumplex model of emotion.*)

In principle, all emotions can be located on the cir-

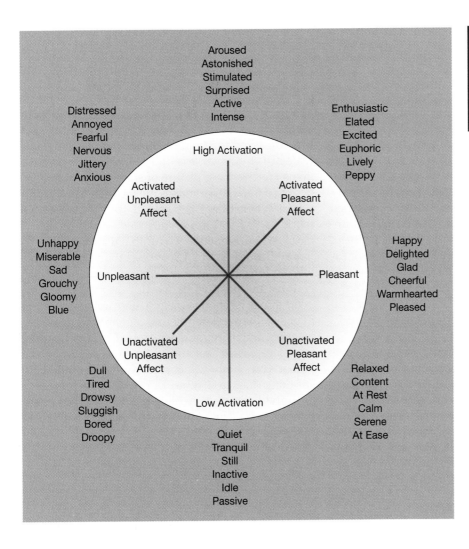

FIGURE 11-5   The circumplex model of emotions, showing typical adjectives that define the dimensions of emotional experience. (After Larsen & Diener, 1992.)

cle. Some are characterized by high or low degrees of activation, some by high or low degrees of pleasure, and others by various combinations of the two. Thus excitement is a pleasant state of moderate activation; nervousness is an unpleasant state of moderate activation. Relaxation is a pleasant state of low activation, and so on. Empirical studies show that most people conceive of emotions in terms of these two basic dimensions (Watson & Tellegen, 1985; Watson, Clark, & Tellegen, 1988).

Not all researchers agree with this approach, however. Some feel that a two-dimensional model glosses over important distinctions between emotions. For example, fear and anger are both characterized by highly activated unpleasant feelings, but they feel quite different to the person experiencing them. (They also lead to different action tendencies.)

For this reason, some researchers prefer models that identify specific emotional categories, such as anxiety, hostility, and depression (e.g., Zuckerman & Lubin, 1985).

Emotional states are transient and temporary; they come and go. Many people become anxious when called upon to make a public speech, for example. When the speech is over, they relax. But emotions can also be thought of as traits, that is, relatively stable and consistent ways in which people differ from one another (see Chapter 14). Some people are anxious most of the time, worry about little things, and seem unable to enjoy success or to relax. When the speech is over, they continue to fret. ("Are they applauding just to be polite? Will they ask me to speak again?") For such people, anxiety is more than an occasional experience; it is part of their enduring psychological makeup. This distinction between emotional *states* and *traits* is an important one. Everyone has experienced the state of anxiety, but not everyone possesses the trait of being anxious.

Some of the most interesting insights into emotional traits grew out of the (scientific) pursuit of happiness. What distinguishes people who are generally enthusiastic and cheerful from those who are chronically worried and blue? One answer is the frequency of positive as opposed to negative emotions. Everyone experiences emotional ups and downs. People who describe themselves, and are described by others, as happy report more pleasant than unpleasant emotions. In most studies, a majority of people put themselves in the happy category. For example, when asked to estimate the percentage of time in which they feel happy, unhappy, or neutral (so that the percentages add up to 100), college students typically report that they are happy about 70 percent of the time (Larsen et al., 1987).

When one looks at the intensity of happy emotions, however, a different picture emerges. Reports of extreme emotional highs—jubilance, rapture, bliss, euphoria—are relatively rare. Moreover, individuals who report great emotional peaks are not necessarily happy people. To the contrary, they also report deep emotional valleys. Upon reflection, this surprising finding makes sense. Suppose you are going to a college football game. You want to have a good time, so you get yourself "psyched up," you cheer a lot, and you get very involved in the game. If your team wins, you will be much happier than someone who is indifferent to the game. But if your team loses, you will be much unhappier than someone who is indifferent. Over the long run, then, happiness seems to depend on being able to sustain pleasant feelings (even at a low level, as in calm contentment), rather than intense moments of bliss (Diener, Sandvik, & Pavot, 1989).

Studies of happiness led researchers to the discovery of another emotional trait, *affect* (or emotional) *intensity* (Larsen & Diener, 1987). People who are high in this trait tend to experience their emotions quite strongly. They react intensely to both good and bad events in their lives—even to things other people might consider trivial, such as losing a pen or receiving a compliment. These people's emotions are also highly variable, with many mood swings. Conversely, people who are low on affect intensity tend to experience their emotions quite mildly. They take

everyday successes and frustrations in stride. Evidence for these two emotional patterns comes from records of subjects' daily moods reported over a period of eighty-four days. (See Figure 11-6.)

What is interesting about affect intensity is that it applies to both positive and negative emotions. In Randy Larsen's Affect Intensity Measure (AIM), subjects are asked to rate their emotional reactions on a scale of 1 (for never) to 6 (for always). Some sample items are "Seeing a picture of some violent car accident in a newspaper makes me feel sick to my stomach"; "When things are good I feel 'on top of the world'"; "When I'm nervous I get shaky all over"; and "When someone compliments me, I get so happy I could burst." Larsen has found that people who endorse the negative items on this measure also endorse the positive items. In other words, when good things happen to people who are high in affect intensity, they feel happier than people who are low in affect intensity; and when bad things happen, they feel worse. As the old adage suggests, the higher you climb, the harder you fall, emotionally speaking (Larsen, 1987).

Individuals who are high and low in affect intensity also experience emotions differently from others (Larsen & Diener, 1987). They experience happiness as exuberance, and are typically zestful and enthusiastic, whereas others experience happiness as contentment and serenity, and are typically calm and easygoing. Apparently, there are different styles of happiness. The "In Depth" section at the end of this chapter will discuss happiness in greater detail.

Theories of Emotion

So far in this chapter we have concentrated on the experience and consequences of emotion. In this section we will discuss theories of emotion. What is its purpose? What causes emotion? According to many older theories, emotions are maladaptive (e. g., Angier, 1927)—primitive physiological responses that interfere with logical, rational action. Thus, people become emotional when they are unable to cope, and their emotions compound the problem, further undermining their ability to cope. The idea that emotions are disruptive is part of our popular culture. We often dismiss someone by saying, "Don't mind her, she's just being emotional."

Most modern theories emphasize the functional aspects of emotions (Smith, 1989; Smith & Ellsworth,

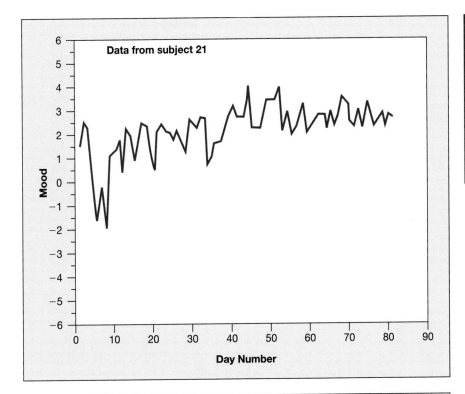

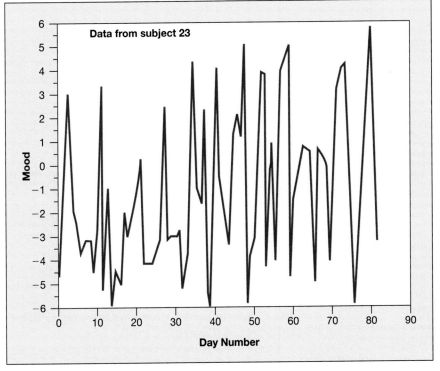

FIGURE 11-6 Daily mood reports by two subjects. The two subjects whose data are graphed here experienced similar events during the three months of the study. Yet subject 21 displayed a relatively stable mood, while subject 23's mood was much more variable. (After Larson & Diener, 1992.)

1985; Tomkins, 1980). According to this view, one function of emotions is to prepare and motivate us to deal with challenges in our environment. Anger, for example, prepares and motivates us to get rid of an obstacle or irritant; fear prepares and motivates us to avoid or escape danger. Thus, emotions act somewhat like instincts in animals, prompting a response to changes in the environment. But they are more flexible than instincts, allowing us to fine-tune our responses. When a wolf is threatened, it attacks; when a rabbit is threatened, it runs. But when humans are threatened, they may choose to flee or stand their ground, to fight or attempt to negotiate.

Emotions also serve as a signal to others. They reveal how we are feeling and thus how we are likely to behave. Children, especially young children, unwittingly signal when they are lying. They may avoid eye contact, shuffle their feet, or speak more softly. Other animals display emotions as well. When a strange wolf invades another wolf's territory, the home wolf snarls, letting the intruder know that it had better clear out or prepare to fight. Rather than being disruptive, such displays should be viewed as adaptive.

Emotion, then, serves a positive purpose. But what *causes* emotion? Modern theories of emotion can be divided into two broad categories: those that emphasize physiological factors and those that emphasize cognitive factors.

The Role of Physiological Arousal

Many early psychologists considered emotions too varied, too vague, too private and personal for scientific study. But William James (1890–1950) disagreed. For James, the key to understanding emotions was physiological arousal.

The James-Lange Theory

Common sense holds that emotions cause physiological arousal and motivate behavior. When we see a mysterious figure in a dark alley, we feel frightened, and our fear causes our hearts to pound and we run. In other words, environmental events trigger a psychological state—an emotion—which in turn gives rise to physiological response.

James turned this commonsense notion upside down:

> My theory, on the contrary, is that the bodily changes follow directly the perception of the exciting fact, and that our feeling of the same changes as they occur IS

the emotion . . . we feel sorry because we cry, angry because we strike, afraid because we tremble. . . .

James, 1890

According to James we do not act because we feel; rather, we feel because we act. Our perception of a certain stimulus (to James, an "exciting fact") triggers changes in the body, causing sensory messages to be sent to the brain and producing the actual experience of emotion.

James held that each emotional state is associated with a unique physiological pattern. Originally he proposed that feelings might arise from changes in the viscera (abdominal organs), skin, muscles, respiration, circulation, and even posture. Danish psychologist Carl Lange proposed a similar theory at about the same time as James. But whereas James saw emotion as a whole-body experience, Lange located it in the autonomic nervous system and the viscera. In his later writings, James embraced Lange's position (Izard, 1990a). The theory that emotions arise from the perception of bodily changes has since become known as the **James-Lange theory** (Lange & James, 1922).

The Cannon-Bard Theory

The James-Lange theory stimulated a great deal of research on emotion, much of it designed to disprove the theory. In 1927 Walter Cannon, a pioneer in the study of the autonomic nervous system, published a powerful critique. Cannon's main argument was that physiological changes are uniform across different emotional states. Both fear and rage, for example, are associated with a pounding heart, sweaty palms, tremor, and so on. If the James-Lange theory were correct—if emotion is the interpretation of bodily sensations—then each emotion would be characterized by a somewhat different set of physiological changes. But that was not the case, at least not according to the research techniques available to Cannon. Note that Cannon did not deny that physiological arousal played a role in emotion; rather, he argued that bodily changes were too generalized and diffuse to permit discrimination among different emotions (Blascovich, 1990).

Cannon also cited evidence that physiological arousal alone cannot induce emotion. In one study, Gregorio Maranyon (1924) produced physiological arousal artificially, by injecting several hundred subjects with the hormone epinephrine. When asked to report its effects, more than two-thirds of the subjects said they experienced only physical symptoms—rapid heartbeat, tightness in the throat. The remainder reported an emotional response of some kind, mostly what Maranyon called "as if" emotions ("I feel as if I were afraid" or "I feel as if I were happy"). These subjects' feelings, then, were similar to emotions but not identical to them.

Furthermore, Cannon noted, emotional responses are often quite rapid: we feel the car skidding out of control and experience immediate panic; we spot an old friend and feel instantaneous joy. Yet the viscera are relatively insensitive organs, with few nerve endings. How, Cannon asked, can the viscera be regarded as the source of sudden emotion?

In addition to pointing out the shortcomings of the James-Lange theory, Cannon (1927) and his associate L. L. Bard proposed a theory of their own. According to the **Cannon-Bard theory,** the part of the brain called the *thalamus* plays a key role in emotions. In an emotion-arousing situation stimuli from the senses are first passed to the thalamus, which acts as a relay station. The thalamus transmits the information to two parts of the body simultaneously: upward, to the cerebral cortex (resulting in the subjective experience of emotion), and downward, by way of the autonomic nervous system to the body's internal organs (resulting in physiological responses). Thus, bodily reactions occur with feelings of emotion; they do not produce emotions, as James believed. Finally, Cannon (1929) proposed a motivating function to emotion: preparing the body to deal with "emergency" situations, as in the urge toward "fight or flight."

Later researchers refined the Cannon-Bard theory. Anatomist James Papez (1937) pointed out the critical roles of the hypothalamus and parts of the limbic system. The hypothalamus, Papez argued, triggers physiological arousal, while the limbic system is intimately involved in the subjective experience of emotion. This basic view has been supported by many studies and is widely accepted today, along with the involvement of the cortex (Buck, 1985; Panksepp, 1982).

The Facial Feedback Hypothesis

For many years the case against the James-Lange theory appeared to be closed. Then, in the 1960s and 1970s, when researchers began to test Darwin's theory of the universality of facial expressions of emotion, they unearthed some ideas that psychologists had previously overlooked. "The free expres-

Extroverts appear to be predisposed toward the experience of pleasant emotions.

sion by outward signs of an emotion intensifies it," Darwin has written. "On the other hand, the repression, as far as this is possible, of all outward signs softens our emotions" (Darwin, 1872, p. 365). Eighteen years later, James (1890–1950) had made a similar observation: "Refuse to express a passion and it dies . . ." (1890, p. 463). Both believed that sensory feedback from the face could stimulate or inhibit emotion. Was it possible that James had the right idea but had looked for evidence in the wrong place (the viscera instead of the face)?

As often happens in science, a rereading of old sources led to new insights (Adelmann & Zajonc, 1989; Izard, 1990a). The **facial feedback hypothesis** holds that facial expressions play a key role in initiating, or at least modulating, the experience of emotion. According to this view, facial expressions are not merely the outward expression of emotion: they contribute to the feeling itself.

To test this hypothesis, researchers devised ways to get subjects to simulate emotional expressions without realizing it. In one experiment (Strack, Martin, &

Stepper, 1988), subjects were told they were participating in a study of their ability to use parts of their body to perform unusual tasks, as they might need to do if they were injured or handicapped. Some of the subjects were asked to hold a pen in their teeth, which can only be done by pulling the lips back, as in a smile. Other subjects were asked to hold a pen with their lips, which relaxes the cheek muscles and prevents smiling. While holding the pen in this way, they were asked to rate cartoons on a scale from 0 (not at all funny) to 9 (very funny). As the facial feedback hypothesis would predict, subjects who held the pen in their teeth (in a simulated smile) rated the cartoons as funnier than those who held the pen in their lips (in an inhibited smile). Other studies (reviewed in Adelmann & Zajonc, 1989; Izard, 1990b) have led to the same conclusion: the simple act of smiling or frowning can alter subjective emotional feelings.

The question of how facial feedback works has not been resolved, however. Some psychologists have proposed that sensory feedback from the skin and facial muscles has a direct impact on the brain centers responsible for the experience of emotion (Izard, 1971; Tomkins, 1962). Others have proposed that facial feedback is a matter of self-perception: when we feel ourselves clenching our teeth, we infer "I must be angry" (Buck, 1985; Laird, 1974, 1984). Still others see facial feedback as the result of classical conditioning, in which specific facial expressions have been repeatedly paired with specific emotions (Cacioppo et al., 1986). A new proposal suggests that when certain facial muscles are tightened or relaxed, they raise or lower the temperature of the blood flowing to the brain. That, in turn, influences activity in the brain centers that regulate emotion. Smiles cool the blood, causing pleasant feelings, while frowns heat the blood, causing unpleasant feelings (Zajonc, Murphy, & Inglehart, 1989). Only continued research will tell which, if any, of these explanations is correct.

Most contemporary psychologists accept the view that physiological arousal and facial expressions are an integral part of emotion (a weak version of the James-Lange theory and facial feedback hypothesis). But many do not accept the idea that physiological arousal and/or facial expression play a *causal* role in emotion (a strong version of the James-Lange theory and facial feedback hypothesis). According to these critics, neo-Jamesians have greatly improved our description of emotional experience,

but they have not explained where emotions come from. A racing heart may be an essential part of the experience of fear. But *why* does a person feel afraid in the first place?

The Role of Cognition

Neurologist Antonio Damasio has studied the relationship between cognition and emotion for over two decades. Because of the nature of his work (he is a neurologist who specializes in recovery from brain trauma) he is often consulted on cases involving brain damage from a stroke or motor vehicle accident. In cases involving extensive damage to the *prefrontal area of the cortex* (see Chapter 3), Damasio often sees changes in affect. As might be suspected, the nature of the impairment varies considerably from case to case, depending on the location and extent of the injury. Most of the cases, however, seem to share one important feature: though intellectual capabilities were not impaired, the patient had lost the ability to make sound choices. In many ways, Damasio's patients resembled Phineas Gage, whose case was discussed in Chapter 3. Gage's brain damage was extensive, but restricted largely to the prefrontal area of the cortex. After the injury, Gage changed drastically—his emotions became unpredictable, and his judgment impaired—even though his physician's diagnosis indicated little loss of intellectual ability.

Damasio describes one recent patient, Elliot, who was referred to him following the removal of a fast-growing tumor from his frontal cortex (Damasio, 1994). The surgery was successful in removing the tumor (and preventing its return), but the tumor had already damaged Elliot's prefrontal area. Following surgery, Elliot recovered well—initially. By the time he was referred to Damasio, however, he was living with one of his siblings because he could no longer hold a job. Intelligent and skilled prior to surgery, Elliot had not lost his intellectual abilities. Why had he lost his job?

Damasio administered a battery of intelligence, cognitive, and personality tests, all of which indicated that Elliot was "normal." In a final test, Damasio found a solution to the puzzle. He showed Elliot a series of emotional pictures—houses burning to the ground, a gruesome accident. After the test, Elliot remarked that though such sights *used* to evoke feelings in him—anger, despair, delight—now, he felt *nothing*.

Elliot showed excellent reasoning skills. Confronted with a choice in behavior, even something as trivial as what to order for dessert, he could list the reasons that should influence his decision: "Strawberry shortcake. . . . Strawberries cause me to break out in a rash. Banana pudding. . . . The last time I had banana pudding the bananas were rotten," and so forth. But after listing the options, Elliot would smile and say, "And after all this, I still wouldn't know what to do!" (See Damasio, 1994, p. 49.) He would then choose haphazardly, perhaps selecting strawberry shortcake, even though he "knew" he was allergic to strawberries.

Elliot's case demonstrates a remarkable and abnormal dissociation between intellect and affect. As Damasio points out, intellect without affect can be disastrous. Elliot would repeatedly select the wrong business venture or fail to attend his child's birthday party, not because he did not understand the options but because he was unable to grasp their emotional meaning. Humans, Damasio contends, cannot separate emotion from intellect, despite being urged to "think with our minds, not our hearts." Damasio (1994) suggests that "emotions and feelings may not be intruders in the bastion of reason at all; they may be enmeshed in its networks, for worse *and* for better" (p. xii).

Cases like this one prompted theorists to question some of their assumptions. The James-Lange and the Cannon-Bard theories of emotion were both developed during the time when psychology was dominated by behaviorists. Therefore, they assumed that a specific environmental stimulus will always provoke the same emotional response. As the cognitive revolution swept through psychology in the 1950s and 1960s, researchers looked for other explanations for emotion. In some cases, cognitivists argued, emotions arise from the *interpretation* of events, not the events themselves.

Schachter and Singer's Theory of Cognitive Arousal

Stanley Schachter and Jerome Singer (1962) were pioneers in the study of emotion and cognition. In a sense, they provided a bridge from earlier physiological theories of emotion to contemporary cognitive theory. Schachter and Singer accepted James's view that physiological arousal plays a primary role in emotion. They also accepted Cannon's view that arousal is general and diffuse.

How, then, do we *know* what we are feeling?

Schachter and Singer hypothesized that in order to explain their feelings, people search their surroundings for a reasonable cause. When people are asked to describe their emotions, for instance, they typically begin with a descriptive term—excited, angry, frightened, peaceful—and then immediately launch into an explanation. "I just got a job in summer stock theater" (excited). "They broke into my car—again" (angry). "My mother has to have an operation" (frightened). Depending on the available environmental cues, they might decide that the same state of arousal is joy, love, jealousy, or even hate. This tendency to label a general state of physiological arousal as a specific emotion is referred to as the **cognitive arousal interpretation** (Schachter, 1964).

To test this hypothesis, Schachter and Singer injected subjects with epinephrine, under the pretext of testing the effects of "vitamins" on vision. Some of the subjects were correctly informed about the side effects of epinephrine (heart palpitations, hand tremors, and the like); some were deliberately misinformed (they were told the shot might cause itching or headaches). Still others were told the shot would have no side effects (the ignorant condition). A control group received saline injections, which do not have side effects. Schachter and Singer predicted that the misinformed and ignorant subjects, lacking an adequate explanation for their aroused state, would search the environment for an explanation.

After the injections, subjects were asked to fill out a questionnaire while they waited with another person for the "vision test." The other person was actually a confederate in the experiment. In some cases the accomplice acted very happy and frivolous, throwing paper airplanes, laughing, and playing with a hula hoop. In other cases the accomplice grew increasingly sullen and irritable, complained about the questionnaire, and finally tore it up and stormed out of the room. Meanwhile, the researchers watched through a one-way mirror.

The results of this experiment gave some support to Schachter and Singer's theory. The misinformed and ignorant subjects, who had no logical explanation for their aroused state, did tend to adopt the accomplice's mood. Many of those who waited with the euphoric accomplice reported feeling "good or happy." Informed and control subjects were less likely to share the confederate's mood.

Critics were quick to point out flaws both in the experiment and in Schachter and Singer's conclusions

(Kemper, 1978; Plutchik & Ax, 1966; Zimbardo et al., 1974). One common criticism was that Schachter and Singer seemed to conclude that a single, undifferentiated state of arousal leads to a wide array of emotions, an implausible explanation. In fact, researchers have begun to identify emotion-specific patterns of activity in the autonomic nervous system (e. g., Levenson, Ekman, & Friesen, 1990). James may have been right after all.

A second criticism was that Schachter and Singer assumed that their subjects' behavior and self-reported moods were based solely on the cues provided by their confederate. By implication, a cognitive interpretation of arousal must be based on a rapid and uncritical assimilation of information in the immediate environment. But the subjects' responses might have reflected an event that had happened earlier that day; prior experiences with injections or tests; memories that were cued by the experimenter who gave the shot, the confederate, or even the waiting room; or a general predisposition to enjoy or fear new situations.

To be fair, Schachter and Singer never intended this experiment to become the sole basis for a theory of emotion. Nevertheless, their notion of cognitive arousal filled a void. Though the idea that emotions are nothing more than feelings (implied by the James-Lange theory) struck many psychologists as false, the theory dominated emotion research for almost two decades. Then, in the 1980s, researchers began to look more closely at the role of cognition.

Cognitive Appraisal and Emotion

For Schachter, Singer, and their followers, cognition provided the missing link between physiological arousal and emotion. For many contemporary psychologists, cognition plays the central, causal role in emotion. Richard Lazarus (1993), a leading proponent of **cognitive appraisal theory,** calls emotions "organized psychophysiological reactions to good news and bad news about ongoing relationships with the environment" (pp. 13–14). In this view, people are continually searching the environment for meaning, looking for cues not only on how to act but also on how to feel (Smith & Ellsworth, 1985). Emotions arise when a situation or encounter has personal meaning for them, and so might be helpful or harmful to their current well-being or long-term goals.

Cognitive appraisal, then, is more than simple information gathering; it involves a judgment process.

Emotions are closely related to physiological reactions. In his book "Anatomy of an Illness," Norman Cousins recounted his battle against cancer, and how emotional factors—especially laughter—contributed to his recovery.

The information that someone has threatened or insulted us, by itself, does not cause emotion. If the threat comes from a child who is playing with make-believe guns, we do not feel fear; if an insult comes from a friend with whom we have a long-standing joking relationship, we are unlikely to feel anger. But if an offense is committed by someone we consider extremely powerful and capable of causing us harm, our response will likely be fear. Emotions, in other words, are the result not of the objective situation in which we find ourselves but of our appraisal of that situation in relation to our needs, wants, and resources.

Lazarus distinguishes between two levels of cognitive appraisal. In a **primary appraisal,** we assess whether what is happening is relevant to our personal well-being, or how it might affect us. In **secondary appraisal,** we evaluate our options and resources, or how we might respond to the problem.

Cognitive theorists believe that we make these appraisals in terms of a limited number of dimensions (Smith & Ellsworth, 1985), including:

- *Attention.* Does this require my full attention, or can I safely ignore or avoid it?
- *Novelty.* Does this meet or violate my expectations? Should I examine it more closely, or walk away?
- *Certainty.* Do I know what will happen, or is the outcome unpredictable?
- *Control.* Can I cope with this situation myself, or is it controlled by others or by forces beyond anyone's control (such as an earthquake)?
- *Pleasantness.* Is this agreeable and satisfying? Will it help me to achieve my positive goals (and avoid negative outcomes)?
- *Perceived obstacle.* Is someone or something standing in my way?
- *Responsibility and legitimacy.* Who set this chain of events in motion? Is the outcome deserved or undeserved?
- *Anticipated effort.* Does this require action, or can I relax or withdraw?

Analyzing emotions in terms of these dimensions can help psychologists to understand not only the nature of emotions but the relationships among them. For instance, the appraisal that someone else is causing an unpleasant situation leads to anger; that one has only oneself to blame, to guilt; and that no one can be blamed, to sadness.

In an investigation of this model, Craig Smith and Phoebe Ellsworth (1985) found that students associated anger with receiving an unfair grade, having personal property stolen, and, in one case, having wine poured over one's head in a restaurant. Students felt guilty about stealing, lying, spreading gossip about a friend, and failing to meet an obligation.

Several linked sadness to the death of a loved one; one mentioned being sad when she learned that her parents were getting divorced "because I didn't want it, I knew it had to be, and yet I didn't want it" (Smith & Ellsworth, 1985, p. 834).

In sum, cognitive appraisal theorists see emotions as functional. Specific appraisals lead to specific emotions, and they in turn motivate appropriate actions. Thus anger motivates us to remove an irritant or obstacle; guilt motivates us to adhere more closely to our personal standards and societal norms; and sadness motivates us to seek comfort. Each emotion is also accompanied by a distinct pattern of physiological arousal, which presumably prepares us to cope with the problem, and an identifiable facial expression, which communicates our intentions to others (Smith, 1989).

An Integration of Theories of Emotion

Emotion is a complex and largely subjective experience. Though there are physiological correlates to subjective emotional states, physiology alone does not explain emotion. Consider two athletes who are competing against each other. Both show the same physiological responses: increased heart rate, increased perspiration and breathing, huge increases in adrenaline, and the like. Why does one athlete experience intense anxiety, while the other experiences exhilaration? The answer to such questions must address both the physiological and the psychological aspects of the situation. Certainly temperament and other genetic factors will come into play. And the two athletes are likely to have different learning histories: perhaps one has typically failed in these contests, while the other has been more successful. Motivation and emotions are at the core of the human experience. Complex behaviors seldom have simple explanations, and these are no exception.

In Depth

What Makes People Happy?

PSYCHOLOGIST MICHAEL FORDYCE reports, "When I ask people, 'What's the most important thing in life?' about half of them immediately say, 'Happiness'" (in Swanbrow, 1989). Each person has his or her personal definition of happiness. But most would agree that happiness is an enduring, positive emotional state that includes satisfaction with one's life and self as well as active pleasures and accomplishments (Warr, 1978). The real question is how one achieves this state. Aristotle wrote that happiness is attained "by living the virtuous life." French philosopher Jean-Jacques Rousseau recommended "a good bank account, a good cook, and a good digestion." Probing deeper, William James, the founder of American psychology, defined happiness as the ratio of one's accomplishments to one's aspirations:

$$\text{Happiness} = \frac{\text{accomplishments}}{\text{aspirations}}$$

According to James, the closer we come to achieving our goals, the happier we will be. By implication, there are two routes to happiness: working harder to achieve success and limiting what we try to accomplish, that is, "lowering one's sights." In the years since James declared happiness a subject worthy of scientific study, psychologists have done much work on the questions of what makes people happy.

Initial Studies

Suppose a researcher asked you, "How happy or satisfied are you with your life?" **Social comparison theory**—one of the earliest and most enduring theories of happiness—holds that you would answer by looking at the people around you and comparing your life to theirs. If you thought you were doing better than most, you would probably say you were happy. If you thought you were not doing as well as others, you would probably say you were unhappy. Simply put, happiness equals "keeping up with the Joneses" or, more accurately, keeping one step *ahead* of the Joneses.

Empirical research has often supported the social comparison theory of happiness. One of the first pieces of evidence in its favor came from a survey of soldiers during the 1940s (Merton & Kitt, 1950). The survey raised a number of paradoxes. For example, soldiers who lacked a high school diploma were much less likely to be promoted than soldiers with a high school education or better. Yet the men with less education were generally more satisfied with the army's promotion policies than their better-educated counterparts. The reason for the difference in attitude apparently had to do with each group's sources of comparison. Compared to their peers in the civilian world, the better educated soldiers were doing quite poorly, but the less-educated soldiers were doing quite well. As a result, the well-educated were dissatisfied, while the less-educated were reasonably content.

Such findings suggest that if we could only change peoples' sources of comparison, we might be able to change their level of happiness. Advertisers, in fact, regularly attempt to do this. By bombarding us with pictures of people whose possessions are far more elegant than our own, advertisers try to induce us to feel discontented with our possessions (and to buy new ones) (Brickman, 1978). The reverse, of course, might also be attempted. If unfavorable sources of comparison are eliminated, people may become more satisfied with their lives. For instance, Cuban president Fidel Castro may have raised the Cuban people's happiness considerably just by eliminating the rich American tourists who used to flock to Cuba each year (Brickman & Campbell, 1971). This ability to change people's perceived happiness simply by changing the sources of social comparison available to them has been demonstrated experimentally. In one study, Milwaukee residents who read vivid descriptions of how terrible life was in their city at the turn of the century reported more satisfaction with their current circumstances than residents who read a glowing description of Milwaukee's earlier years (Dermer, Cohen, & Anderson, 1978).

Outside the laboratory, the sources of comparison available to us are seldom so tightly controlled. As a result, people may choose which groups to compare themselves to. Research suggests that when given such a choice, people are often strongly motivated to enhance their feeling of well-being by comparing themselves with less fortunate others (Wills, 1981). This tendency has been clearly demonstrated in interviews with cancer patients, who had every reason to think of themselves as worse off than almost everyone else. Remarkably, however, even these victims of the dread disease found ways to think of themselves as relatively lucky (Taylor, Wood, & Lichtman, 1983). Women who had had a malignant tumor removed from a breast compared themselves with less fortunate women who had undergone mastectomies (removal of the entire breast). The mastectomy patients, in turn, focused on others who were worse off than themselves—those whose cancer was spreading despite surgery, or those whose amputations had been more disfiguring (the loss of an arm or leg, for instance). Thus people make not only upward social comparisons ("keeping up with the Joneses") but downward social comparisons as well.

Social comparison is only one of the measures people use to evaluate their lives. They may also use the past as a standard (Smith, Diener, & Wedell, 1989): "Am I better off today than I was last year?" For example, the poet T. S. Eliot suffered through a long and miserable first marriage (Ackroyd, 1984). When he married for a second time in the last decade of his life, he felt rejuvenated. Comparing his new marital life to his past, he considered himself extraordinarily happy. People may also apply different standards to different parts of their lives. Eliot was more successful than most poets of his generation, in terms of both recognition and income (social comparison). He admitted to being happy with his "fame and fortune," even during his wretchedly unhappy first marriage. Thus Eliot used social comparison to judge his professional life, and past self-comparisons in judging his marital life.

Criticisms, Alternatives, and Further Research

Most contemporary researchers consider social comparison an important element of happiness (e.g., Emmons & Diener, 1985; Schwarz & Strack, 1990), but not the only one. A major flaw in social comparison theory is its failure to explain why a person who is extremely fortunate in relation to others can still be unhappy. One study has shown, for instance, that winners of a million-dollar state lottery report no more satisfaction in life than those less fortunate financially (Brickman et al., 1978). If happiness depends on social comparison alone, how could that be? Clearly, some other factors must be involved.

Adaptation theory suggests that change is one of those factors ((Brickman & Campbell, 1971; Helson, 1964). When something highly positive happens, we quickly adapt to our new level of fortune, accepting it as an integral part of our lives. As a result, simple things that once gave us pleasure tend to lose some of their appeal, at least in the short run, because they seem so much less exciting than our recent windfall. This phenomenon is called the *contrast effect.* In the long run, the pleasure we once derived from the sudden windfall tends to erode. What at first seemed a thrilling stroke of fortune gradually loses its luster and becomes part of the status quo. This phenomenon is called the *habituation effect.*

In contrast, unpleasant emotions endure so long as the conditions that are producing them continue. While we adapt quickly to comfort, we never get used to continuing humiliation or harassment. Nico Frijda (1988) offers an intriguing evolutionary explanation for this paradox. The function of emotion is to alert us to conditions requiring action. As such it is part of our evolutionary history, necessary for survival. When alertness and action are no longer required—when we experience satisfaction—our emotions "switch off." But that does not mean that we are doomed to chronic unhappiness. In Frijda's words, "Enduring happiness seems possible, [but] it does not come naturally, by itself. It takes effort" (p. 354).

To test adaptation theory, Philip Brickman and Dan Coates (1978) interviewed twenty-two winners in the Illinois state lottery and twenty-two other nonwinners with similar backgrounds, who had never experienced a financial windfall. Brickman and Coates found that as predicted, the lottery winners described themselves as no more happy than the nonwinners. They also tended to derive less satisfaction from such simple pleasures as watching television and eating a good breakfast. Apparently, winning a lottery is not nearly so rich a source of happiness as we might expect. Although winners may initially compare themselves with others, thinking how lucky they are, the contrast and habituation effects may eventually lessen their overall pleasure.

Some people might interpret these findings in an optimistic light: great wealth, fame and power, and all the fabulous things we will probably never acquire would not make us very happy anyway. But a pessimistic interpretation is also possible. These same findings can be used to argue that the pursuit of happiness is a kind of pleasure-seeking treadmill, in which today's great joys tend to overshadow simpler pleasures, only to become lackluster themselves with the passage of time. According to this perspective, happiness cannot be permanent unless our circumstances are constantly improving—an unlikely occurrence.

Many psychologists take issue with this pessimistic outlook, however. They point out that in surveys, a sizable number of people report being "very happy," and those who are happy tend to stay that way over long periods (Andrews & Withey, 1976; Gurin, Veroff, & Feld, 1960; Palmore & Kivett, 1977). What could account for these chronically happy people, if we assume that relatively few of them enjoy constantly improving life circumstances? One possibility is that certain of their personality traits (or combinations of traits) foster happiness, an explanation proposed by psychologists Paul Costa and Robert McCrae (1980, 1986). In a correlational study of personality traits and subjective well-being, these researchers found that extroverted traits (sociability, warmth, involvement with other people) are strongly associated with positive emotions, while neurotic traits (a tendency to worry, to be irritable and anxious) are strongly associated with negative emotions. A follow-up study showed that these personality traits were predictive of relative happiness ten years later. Thus a person's overall potential for happiness may be thought of as the sum of two personality dimensions. One who is high in extroversion and low in neuroticism has the greatest potential for happiness, while one who is high in neuroticism and low in extroversion has the greatest potential for unhappiness.

The weakness of Costa and McCrae's theory is that it is based on correlational studies, and therefore cannot determine cause and effect. Perhaps extroverts and neurotics create or choose different lifestyles, and those different life-styles—not the personality traits per se—are responsible for the general happiness or unhappiness of the two groups. Are extroverts predisposed to enjoy life, or are they happy because they lead active social lives and their sociability promotes good moods? Likewise, are neurotics predisposed toward unpleasant emotions, or are they unhappy because their emotional instability fosters difficult life situations, situations that make them unhappy?

To answer these questions, Randy Larsen and Timothy Ketelaar (1989, 1991) conducted a series of laboratory experiments using college students as subjects. On the basis of standard personality tests, they identified the students as extroverted or introverted, neurotic or stable. Then the researchers exposed the students to mood-induction procedures and asked them to fill out mood reports. Larsen and Ketelaar found that extroverts responded strongly to positive mood induction (such as imagining that they had won a $50,000 lottery) but modestly to negative mood induction. The neurotics responded strongly to negative mood induction (imagining they had been expelled from college under embarrassing circumstances) but modestly to positive mood induction. These results support a personality-based theory of happiness. That is, extroverts appear to be predisposed to experience high levels of pleasant emotions, while neurotics appear to be predisposed to experience high levels of unpleasant emotions. This conclusion is supported in a recent study by William Pavot and his colleagues (Pavot, Diener, & Fujita, 1990), which found that extroverts are happier than introverts even when they are not in social situations.

Research on personality and happiness has also exposed a common misunderstanding. Happiness and unhappiness are generally seen as opposite sides of the same emotional coin. That is, the more happiness we experience, the less unhappiness we will suffer. But research suggests that happiness and unhappiness are distinct feelings that rise and fall independently (Swanbrow, 1989). The extroverts in Larsen and Ketelaar's study experienced strong positive emotions, but average (not low) negative emotions. Likewise, the neurotics had experienced strong negative emotions, but average (not low) positive emotions. Thus, though extroverted traits contribute to enjoyment and satisfaction, they do not inoculate a person against unpleasant experiences. And while neurotic traits contribute to anxiety and distress, they do not diminish the capacity to enjoy pleasant experiences. By implication, personality traits do not dictate happiness or unhappiness; other factors must be involved.

Another possible factor in happiness is specific life circumstances. Intuitively, most of us believe that wealth, youth, and prestige contribute greatly to happiness. After all, the rich don't have to worry about how they will pay next month's bills. They can go skiing or sailing, to the opera or the Superbowl, more often than people of average or low income.

When misfortune strikes, they have the resources to cope (the best medical care, legal advice, and so on). Moreover, the rich enjoy more power and respect than the average person.

Does money lead to happiness? Brickman and Coates, in the study of lottery winners mentioned earlier, found that the euphoria of "striking it rich" wore off quickly. To test such findings, Ed Diener and his colleagues (Diener, Horowitz, & Emmons, 1985) studied the very wealthy. They selected subjects from *Forbes* magazine's list of the 400 wealthiest Americans. The average net worth of the subjects in their sample was $125 million or more, and most had annual incomes of over $10 million. Diener matched rich subjects with control subjects from the same geographic area (their average net worth was $120,000, their mean family income, $36,000). He asked both groups to fill out a questionnaire designed to measure satisfaction in life. He found that the superrich were slightly happier than the nonwealthy control subjects. The rich said they were happy 77 percent of the time, the control group, 62 percent of the time. But 37 percent of the wealthy subjects reported being less happy than the average nonwealthy control subjects, while 47 percent of the nonwealthy subjects reported being much happier than the average multimillionaire. Though great wealth may contribute to happiness, it is certainly not a guarantee.

In a review of the literature, Diener (1984) found that other life circumstances—including age, gender, education, religion, and health—have surprisingly little relationship to subjective well-being. The single most relevant life circumstance is a satisfying marriage and family life (Campbell, Converse, & Rogers, 1976; Glenn & Weaver, 1981). Diener has also found that most people consider themselves happy (Diener & Diener, 1996; Myers & Diener, 1995). Well over 80 percent of those he surveyed reported positive levels of "subjective well-being." Significantly, his findings span many different socioeconomic levels, as well as almost 90 percent of the forty-three countries surveyed.

Most recently, research in behavioral genetics has indicated that heredity plays a substantial role in happiness, or subjective well-being. In a study of several thousand middle-aged twins, Lykken & Tellegen (1996) found that the genetic component (technically, the heritability) of happiness approaches 80 percent! Furthermore, they found few other reliable contributing factors. Somewhat tongue in cheek, Lykken and Tellegen concluded that since genetic factors contribute so much to happiness (and few other factors seemed to), the "individual differences in human happiness—how one feels at the moment and also how one feels on average over time—are primarily a matter of chance" (p. 189).

Patterns and Conclusions

Can we generalize about what makes people happy? How can people bring more happiness into their lives? Researcher Michael Fordyce (1988; see Swanbrow, 1989) has translated the results of empirical and theoretical studies into a practical program. Happiness is within reach, he believes, but it requires work. Fordyce has outlined eight steps to happiness:

1. Spend time with your loved ones. Of all the characteristics and circumstances that happy people share, loving relationships stand out.

2. Seek challenging, meaningful work. If love is the first priority, work is the second; happy people work hard and enjoy what they do. If your current job or college major is not rewarding, then consider switching to one that is.

3. Be helpful to others. Doing good enhances self-esteem and relieves stress.

4. Make time for activities that you enjoy. Most people waste a lot of time doing things that leave them feeling empty or bored, like watching TV. Decide what makes you happy—whether it is gardening, reading, or fixing the kitchen sink—and do it.

5. Keep fit—run, bike, swim, play a sport, dance. No one knows exactly why aerobic exercise increases subjective well-being, but there is abundant evidence that it does.

6. Be organized but flexible. Planning ahead is important (especially if you include plans for fun), but your life should not be so tightly scheduled that you cannot spontaneously try something different. People who seek new experiences are happier than people who stick to the "tried and true."

7. Think positively. If you expect good things to happen, you generally will get what you are looking for (and vice versa).

8. Keep things in perspective. Everyone has emotional highs and lows, but try to stay on an even keel as much as possible.

SUMMARY

1. **Motivation** is what gives impetus to our behavior by arousing, sustaining, and directing it toward the attainment of goals.

2. One motivational factor is **instinct,** an innate force found in all members of a species that directs behavior in predictable ways when the right eliciting stimulus is present. **Evolutionary psychology** is a more contemporary approach to the study of innate factors, attempting to explain motivators in terms of their adaptive significance.

3. Sigmund Freud proposed that people have two basic instincts: one is the urge toward life, procreation, and self-preservation, which includes the sexual drive; the other is the urge toward death and self-destruction, which is often turned outward as aggression against others. Because people's ways of satisfying these impulses may conflict with society's moral standards, the impulses are often blocked from consciousness.

4. In the 1930s and 1940s, behaviorist Clark Hull and others developed **drive-reduction theories** of motivation. They saw biological needs (for food, water, relief from pain, and so forth) as the basic motivators of action. These needs gave rise to **primary drives.** By adding the concept of **secondary drives** (drives learned through association with a primary drive and its reduction), drive-reduction theories could account for a large number of behaviors.

5. Drive-reduction theories cannot explain certain behaviors that seemed to involve **intrinsic motivation,** however. Nor could they account for actions that seemed to be as much the product of incentives as they are of drives. Recognizing the need for a more cognitive approach to motivation, psychologists began to develop expectancy-value models.

6. Psychologist Donald Hebb, among others, has proposed that there is an **optimum level of arousal** for effective behavior, which organisms try to maintain. This theory can help explain why both sensory deprivation and sensory overload hinder performance on complex cognitive tasks.

7. No single theory has been able to explain all facets of motivation. Therefore, most psychologists recognize that motivators often have a biological (or genetic) component, can be shaped by experiences, and in some cases involve unconscious processes.

8. Sexual activity is strongly influenced by hormones, especially estrogen (primarily secreted by the ovaries) and testosterone (primarily secreted by the testes). But sexually arousing stimuli are also needed to activate sexual responses. In humans the **sexual response cycle** has four distinct phases: **excitement, plateau, orgasm,** and **resolution.** Cognition plays a crucial role in interpreting sexual signals and in directing sexual behavior toward appropriate goals.

9. **Emotions** are largely involuntary responses involving visceral changes, and visible expressive (especially facial) changes. They are accompanied by subjective states or feelings. Many older theories viewed emotions as primitive and disruptive, but most modern theories consider emotions functional and adaptive.

10. One of the defining features of emotion is physiological arousal. Numerous studies have shown that strong emotions are associated with activation of the peripheral nervous system; such changes can be measured with the **polygraph.**

11. The brain coordinates the activities of the peripheral nervous system. A number of emotional responses involve the limbic system, particularly the hypothalamus. More recent research shows that the cerebral cortex is also involved in emotional experience.

12. Behavioral expression is also an integral part of emotion: often our face and posture say more about what we are feeling than the words we use. Darwin believed that many patterns of nonverbal communication are the product of evolution and served the adaptive function of alerting others to our state of mind and how we are likely to act. Recent studies show that many facial expressions are the same across cultures and are universally recognized. But which emotions we express freely or attempt to conceal, and how well we read emo-

tional expressions, is largely the result of cultural learning.

13. Emotions are also subjective states, what we call "moods" and "feelings." The circle of emotions model holds that emotions vary along two primary dimensions: pleasant-to-unpleasant and high-to-low activation. Many contemporary researchers are interested not only in emotional states, but also in emotional traits. Individuals differ from each other in the frequency and the intensity of their emotions.

14. Theories of emotions can be divided into two broad groups. The first emphasize physiological arousal. The **James-Lange theory** proposes that our perception of bodily changes is itself the emotion, and that each emotional state is signaled by a unique physiological pattern. However, physiological arousal may be too vague, diffuse, and slow to cause emotions. One alternative, the **Cannon-Bard theory,** proposes that sensory information is sent first to the thalamus, where it is simultaneously routed to both the cerebral cortex (triggering the subjective experience) and the autonomic nervous system (causing physiological changes). Research on **facial feedback** suggests that physiological changes in the face may initiate, or at least modulate, the experience of emotion.

15. The second group of theories emphasizes the role of cognition in emotion. Schachter and Singer's **theory of cognitive arousal,** which held that we interpret physiological arousal by reading cues in our environment, attracted both support and criticism. A more contemporary view, **cognitive appraisal,** holds that emotions arise from how we appraise events in our environment in relation to our short- and long-term goals and our abilities and resources for coping. The question of whether cognitions are essential to emotions has not been resolved, however.

SUGGESTED READINGS

Damasio, A. R. (1994). *Descartes' error: Emotion, reason, and the human brain.* New York: G. P. Putnam. A fascinating look at the complex link between emotion and cognition; Damasio presents a convincing cases that regardless of our attempts to make rational decisions, reason may always be influenced by emotional involvement.

Ekman, P. (1985). *Telling lies: Clues to deceit in the marketplace, politics, and marriage.* New York: Norton. Written for the popular audience, a summary of the author's many years of research on facial expressions. Through many examples and illustrations, the author instructs the reader in how to distinguish felt from false emotions through facial expressions. There is also an excellent chapter on lie detection through polygraph techniques.

Geen, R. G. (1995). *Human motivation: A social psychological approach.* San Diego: Brooks-Cole. An easy-to-read introduction to motivation; especially useful as a adjunct to more traditional approaches based on Hullian theory.

Kavanaugh, R. D., Zimmerberg, B., & Fein, S. (1996). *Emotion: Interdisciplinary perspectives.* Hillsdale, NJ: Erlbaum. An interesting collection of essays on emotion, from a number of different perspectives: neuroscience, social psychology, clinical psychology, and development.

Siegman, A. W., & Smith, T. W. (Eds.) (1994). *Anger, hostility, and the heart.* Hillsdale, NJ: Erlbaum. A recent look at the factors underlying coronary heart disease, anger, and "Type A" personality.

CHAPTER 12

|Health Psychology

Thomas and John met through friends nine years ago. For the last eight years, they have been monogamous, same-sex partners. Five-and-a-half years ago, Thomas tested positive for the human immunodeficiency virus (HIV), the virus that causes AIDS. Though he cannot be certain, Thomas believes he was infected through sexual contact with a previous partner, one with whom he had a brief relationship nearly ten years ago. John was infected through his contact with Thomas, before either knew Thomas was HIV-positive.

Like many who are HIV-positive, Thomas showed few symptoms for several years. Three years ago, though, the disease progressed, and soon Thomas was diagnosed with AIDS. With his immune system weakened, he became ill more frequently; minor respiratory infections—the kind that he used to recover from quickly—now became serious. Six months ago one such infection led to pneumonia, nearly killing him.

After this last illness Thomas was no longer able to care for himself, and John became his primary caregiver. In addition to the psychological distress of watching his partner suffer, John found himself physically exhausted. He rarely slept more than four or five hours a night, usually in one- or two-hour intervals. Because he no longer had time to cook, he began eating less, losing more than 20 pounds in the last six months.

When Thomas passed away, John sank into a deep depression. Although he no longer had to care for his sick partner, he could not become interested in the things he used to enjoy. Paradoxically, though he found it difficult to sleep at night, he also found it difficult to get out of bed in the morning. He seldom went out with friends, continued to lose weight, and even contemplated suicide. Nine months following Thomas's funeral, John found himself unable to shake a nagging winter cough. Several weeks later he visited his doctor and heard the news he dreaded, yet somehow expected: he, too, had developed full-blown AIDS. He died just a few months later.

The case of Thomas and John illustrates the complex relationship between psychological factors, stress, and illness. As you will learn in this chapter, AIDS has become what many consider to be the most significant health problem of our time. Recently, however, psychologists have begun identifying a number of *psychological* factors that influence the progression of AIDS. For example, in cases where both partners are infected, the stress associated with caring for a loved one with AIDS—as John did in this example—can significantly alter the progression of AIDS in the caregiver (Folkman et al., 1996; Kemeny & Dean, 1995; Kemeny et al., 1994, 1995). Furthermore, the depression and suicidal thoughts experienced by John are not uncommon; those, too, are associated with reduced life expectancy (Schneider et al., 1991).

These studies reflect the **biopsychosocial approach** to health and health care. Traditionally, our society has viewed illness and injury as strictly medical problems. According to the **biomedical model,** sickness is the result of a biological malfunction that can be explained and treated without reference to the victim's psychological state or social situation. In this view the mind and body are thought to be two separate entities. Illness is a "technical" matter, best treated by trained medical practitioners. If a person is sick, he or she requires medical attention; if not, he or she is presumed to be healthy. But the biopsychosocial model holds that social, psychological, and biological factors interact to affect one's health. In this model, the mind and body work together, and health and illness are seen as a continuum rather than an either/or condition. Good health is viewed as the result of the active management of one's habits and life-style. While the biomedical approach focuses on containing illness, then, the biopsychosocial approach seeks to promote health.

For instance, when treating a man in his forties who has suffered a heart attack, physicians have traditionally emphasized continuing drug treatment, along with frequent monitoring of the condition. But today, many doctors, influenced by the biopsychosocial approach, would also emphasize the patient's life-style. Does he smoke? Drink? Eat properly? Exercise? A smoking cessation program, nutritional counseling, and a controlled exercise program might be recommended. The biopsychosocial practitioner would also be concerned about the man's personal life. A high-powered executive who works fourteen-hour days, six days a week, might be urged to re-order his priorities in order to spend more time with his family and relaxing hobbies.

The biopsychosocial model is at the heart of the growing field of **health psychology:** the subfield of psychology that is dedicated to promoting good health and health care. One of the aims of re-

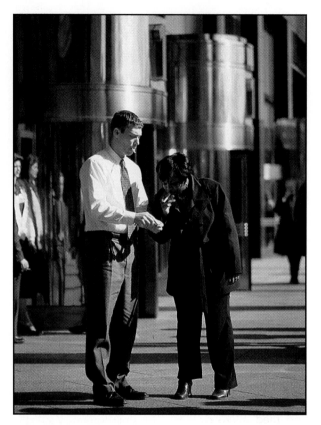

Some health problems, such as smoking, drinking, and overeating, are considered disorders of life-style, *because they can be traced to behavior patterns.*

searchers in this field is to investigate the psychological and social factors that influence the prevention and treatment of illness, such as personal habits, stress levels, and personality traits. A second aim is to warn people about risky behaviors and develop programs to promote healthier habits. Finally, health psychologists try to understand and improve the health-care system itself.

In this chapter we will look at the relationship between psychological factors and health. The first section will examine sexual behavior and weight control, factors related to life-style. Next, we'll study how the body reacts to stress, and how some kinds of stress lead to health problems. The third section will discuss various ways in which people can minimize the psychological consequences of stress. Finally, the "In Depth" section of this chapter explores anorexia nervosa, the most prevalent of all eating disorders.

This family is enjoying a balanced diet. As the effect of life-style factors such as diet has gained recognition, psychologists have begun to stress health promotion, or the process of enabling people to modify their life-styles in order to improve their health.

Life-Style and Health

Before the twentieth century, the major causes of death in the United States were acute infectious diseases such as influenza, tuberculosis, and pneumonia. Thanks to innovations in public health (improved sanitation, purified water, pasteurized milk) and medical technology (vaccinations and antibiotics), these diseases are far less common and less deadly than they once were. Instead, the major causes of disability and death today are such chronic, often incurable disorders as cardiovascular disease, cancer, diabetes, strokes, and automobile accidents. These health problems have been called diseases or *disorders of life-style*, because they often can be traced to patterns of behavior, including smoking, overeating, alcohol consumption, or failure to use safety devices such as seatbelts and motorcycle helmets. Tobacco consumption is a prime example of a life-style problem. Smoking accounts for approximately 125,000 deaths from cancer, and another 170,000 deaths from cardiovascular disease, in the United States each year (American Cancer Society, 1989). It is also linked to chronic bronchitis, emphysema, death and injury in fires, and pregnancy problems (Centers for Disease Control, 1989). AIDS and drug abuse also fall into the life-style category. Furthermore, disorders such as cardiovascular disease, cancer, and strokes can have a major impact on life-style. Although some can be controlled, most cannot be cured, and their victims often live with them for many years.

As the role of life-style factors in disease has gained recognition, more and more attention has been paid to *health promotion*, or the process of enabling people to gain some control over their health and improve it. Eating a balanced diet, cutting down on cholesterol and fat intake, exercising regularly, developing good preventive health behaviors (such as regular medical checkups)—and avoiding behaviors that compromise health (such as smoking, taking drugs, and drinking to excess)—all are practices associated with the promotion of health.

Beliefs, Attitudes, and Health

A walk into any grocery store reveals dozens of products labeled "low fat," "no cholesterol," and "only 300 calories." Health clubs and exercise gear (especially athletic shoes) are big business. Almost every public facility has no-smoking areas. On the surface, Americans appear to be extremely health-conscious—but appearances can be deceiving.

Consider breast cancer. One in every eleven American women will develop breast cancer at some point in her lifetime. Yet little more than a third of women practice breast self-examination, and many do not use the right method (American Cancer Society, 1989). Why don't more women take this simple step to safeguard their health? Research shows that four beliefs influence preventive health behaviors: (1) how severe the threat is perceived to be, (2) how vulnerable a person feels, (3) beliefs about whether one can act to reduce the threat of disease (self-

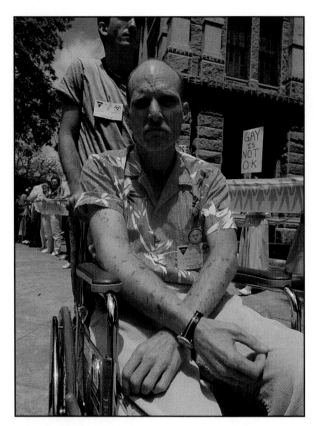

Acquired immune deficiency syndrome (AIDS), an incurable disease caused by the human immunodeficiency virus (HIV), attacks and weakens the immune system, leaving the victim vulnerable to other illnesses. According to recent estimates, as many as 8% of Americans may be HIV-positive.

efficacy), and (4) beliefs about whether one's actions can overcome the threat (response efficacy) (Bandura, 1986; Janz & Becker, 1984; Rogers, 1984). Most women know that breast cancer is serious, though they may not know how common it is. Young women may see breast cancer as a disease that afflicts older women, and so postpone preventive measures. Older women may practice self-examination once or twice, but conclude they can't detect changes anyway. Finally, women may worry about what will happen if they do find a lump. Many would prefer not knowing to facing a possibly incurable problem (Gallup Organization, 1979). In the abstract at least, some women may feel they would "rather die" than have a breast removed.

One of the jobs of health psychologists is to disseminate accurate information. For instance, young

women should know that while breast cancer strikes more often after age forty-five, the age of onset is decreasing and more and more young women are affected. Statistics on successful treatment need to be publicized: when breast cancer is detected early, a woman has an 85 to 90 percent chance of being cured (American Cancer Society, 1989). Furthermore, in many cases a *mastectomy* (removal of the entire breast plus adjacent muscle tissue) is not necessary; cure rates for *lumpectomies* (removing only the cancerous lump and some surrounding tissue) are just as high. Finally, health practitioners should give women explicit instructions and practice in self-examination and send regular reminders (like those dentists mail).

Sexual Behavior and Health

In Chapter 11 we saw that sexual drives are strong and powerful motivators of sexual human behavior. Not surprisingly, these drives often produce risky sexual behavior that can lead to serious health problems. *Sexually transmitted diseases (STDs)* like syphilis and gonorrhea have affected virtually every society, and until relatively recently, they were a leading cause of death in adults. In fact, one of the earliest psychological disorders to be approached from a physical (medical) perspective was *general paresis*, a dementia (degeneration of the brain) caused by syphilis infection.

In recent years, no STD has captured more public attention than *acquired immune deficiency syndrome (AIDS)*, an incurable disease caused by the *human immunodeficiency virus (HIV)*. For some time following diagnosis the virus may produce no symptoms in the infected person, who is referred to as "HIV-positive." For example, former Los Angeles Lakers basketball star Earvin "Magic" Johnson was diagnosed as HIV-positive in 1991 but, as of this writing, has shown no symptoms of AIDS. Furthermore, as a result of medication and other interventions, the length of time between an HIV-positive diagnosis and fully developed AIDS has increased steadily— up to fifteen years in some cases. With such a long inactive period, many researchers now consider AIDS to be similar to diabetes or other chronic diseases, rather than a rapidly progressing terminal illness. Even so, about half die within three years of diagnosis; ten years after diagnosis that number is greater than 90 percent (Centers for Disease Control, 1996).

As the name implies, the virus attacks and weakens the immune system, leaving the victim vulnerable to other illnesses, such as pneumonia and a rare type of cancer known as *Kaposi's sarcoma*. These symptoms, and the presence of other indicators in the blood, indicate a diagnosis of AIDS. According to recent estimates, perhaps as many as 8 percent of the U.S. population is currently HIV-positive (U.S. Dept. of Health & Human Services, 1995).

AIDS is spread through blood, and contact with infected blood is necessary for transmission. Between 1994 and 1996, the most common source of exposure for males was sexual contact with other males, accounting for 53 percent of all cases. The second most common source was IV drug use; about 25 percent became infected through the sharing of needles with another user who was infected with the virus. For females, the most common source of infection was heterosexual contact, which was responsible for 40 percent of infections in females. For females under twenty-five, that proportion was even greater—more than 50 percent were infected through heterosexual contact. The second most likely source, responsible for about a third of the infections, was IV drug use. Since females are often influenced by different biological and sociological factors (especially in the United States), the experiences of women with AIDS may present unanticipated difficulties (Ickovics & Rodin, 1992).

To date, relatively few cases of AIDS have been reported among adolescents and college-age adults—a fact that may erroneously reinforce young people's belief that they are not at risk. But recall that the HIV virus may lie dormant for many years. Many of those who are exposed to it in adolescence may not show symptoms until they reach their mid- to late twenties and, as a result, may unknowingly pass it along. According to the Centers for Disease Control, American adolescents continue to engage in risky sexual behavior. One-fourth of sexually active adolescents failed to use a reliable method of contraception the last time they had intercourse; about half failed to use a condom, increasing their chances of contracting sexually transmitted diseases like AIDS (Centers for Disease Control, 1995).

Diet, Nutrition, and Weight Control

Americans are obsessed with weight, yet they display remarkably inconsistent attitudes and behaviors. For exaple, fashion models are generally considered to represent some kind of "ideal," even though many health experts would consider them too thin. Only 100 calories a day—about the caloric value of a handful of peanuts—can thoretically add 100 pounds to one's body weight in just ten years.

The mechanisms underlying food intake and body weight regulation are complex and not yet fully understood. Clearly, however, many health problems involve food, diet, and eating. This section will examine three different food-related problems: obesity, anorexia nervosa, and bulimia. The "In Depth" section at the end of this chapter will look more closely at anorexia, one of the greatest health risks for young women and one that has become more common in recent years.

Obesity

Obesity may be defined as an excess of body weight. The simplest formulas for normal body weight are based on easily measured body dimensions like height and frame size. Such formulas are simplistic, though, because they are incapable of distinguishing between an athlete who is a muscular 210 pounds and a fatty "couch potato" of the same height and weight. Tables 12-1 and 12-2 present two different methods for determining obesity. Note that charts like those in Table 12-2 should be used only as general guidelines, not strict rules.

According to the U.S. Department of Health and Human Services, one-third of all adults are overweight (USDHHS, 1995), and half of all Americans are obese by mid-life (Brody, 1986). One explanation for the tendency toward obesity is that some people respond strongly to external cues to eat; that is, they are susceptible to the sight, smell, and taste of food. Psychologist Stanley Schachter proposed this theory some twenty years ago. Schachter's ideas about eating and obesity grew out of his theory of human emotion, discussed in Chapter 11. Recall that Schachter argued that emotion has both cognitive and physiological components. Hunger, he reasoned, might also have a dual origin, including both thoughts about eating (is it time for a meal? does the food look tempting?) and the internal changes associated with hunger (stomach contractions and changes in blood chemistry). Schachter proposed that individuals differ in their sensitivity to these internal and external cues. Those who are highly sensitive to external eating cues are apt to overeat, and eventually to become obese (Schachter, 1971).

TABLE 12-1   The Body/Mass Index
Bray (1992) offers these guidelines for interpreting BMI: A number of different weight guidelines have been proposed. One of the simplest is produced by the Metropolitan Life Insurance company (see Table 12-2). A newer, more sensitive measure, the body/mass index (BMI), has been proposed as an alternative, and is considered by some to provide a better measure for judging obesity (see Bray, 1992). BMI is computed using the following formula:[*][†]

$$\frac{Body/mass/index}{(BMI)} = \frac{body\ weight\ (kg)}{[height\ (m)]^2}$$

BMI Range	Obesity/Health Risk
20–25	Not obese, no risk
25–30	Low risk
30–35	Moderate risk
35–40	High risk
Above 40	Very high risk

Williamson (1993) uses slightly higher cutoffs to define obesity:
- For males BMI must exceed 27.8.
- For females BMI must exceed 27.3.

[*]To convert height to meters, divide height (in inches) by 39.37

[†]To convert weight to kilograms, multiply weight (in pounds) by 0.454

While Schachter's theory has generated a great deal of research, not all psychologists agree with it. Psychologist Richard Nisbett has argued that obesity may be related to a **setpoint** for fat, that is, a fat level that the brain is "set" to consider normal. Setpoints seem to vary from one person to the next. Some people, Nisbett argues, have a setpoint for fat that is far above average. As a result, their bodies are constantly telling them they are hungry and need to eat. A high setpoint for fat may be caused partly by a large number of fat cells, which may in turn be caused either by genetics or by overeating (Bennett & Gurin, 1982; Knittle & Hirsch, 1968). The fact is, once someone has acquired a great many fat cells, he or she can never be rid of them. Even after extreme weight loss, fat cells do not disappear; they merely shrink in size. A large number of fat cells, all clamoring to be fed, could conceivably produce the chronic state of hunger Nisbett posits.

Setpoints are a double-edged sword. They allow one's weight to remain relatively constant, despite fluctuations in the number of calories consumed and burned. But should one's caloric intake suddenly drop—as would happen on a diet—the setpoints would tend to keep one's weight level relatively constant despite attempts to reduce it. What is more, once a diet is discontinued and a person returns to a "normal" eating pattern, body weight is likely to increase. In fact, in one study, 95 percent of those who had lost weight on heavily marketed "fad" diets regained *all* of their lost weight within one year (Haney, 1983). Even those in medically supervised crash diets are likely to regain weight; nearly 75 percent regain all (or most) of what they lose.

Does obesity have a genetic component? As one might suspect, it does. Identical twins are more similar in body weight than fraternal twins, who share on average only half their genes. This finding holds even among identical twins who were raised apart (Stunkard et al., 1990). Similarly, parents and their

Genetic factors contribute to obesity: parents and their biological children are more alike in weight than adoptive parents and their adopted children.

TABLE 12-2   *Comparison of the BMI to the Metropolitan Life Insurance Charts*
The final column displays the maximum weight in the "acceptable" category, using standards adapted from Bray
(1992) and Williamson (1993).

| | | Metropolitan Life Insurance Charts | | | | | | Body Mass Index (BMI) | |
| | | Men | | | Women | | | Max Weight "Acceptable" | |
Ft	In	Small Frame	Medium Frame	Large Frame	Small Frame	Medium Frame	Large Frame	Men BMI = 27	Women BMI = 26.5
4	10	—	—	—	102–111	109–121	118–131	129	127
4	11	—	—	—	103–113	111–123	120–134	134	131
5	0	—	—	—	104–115	113–126	122–137	138	136
5	1	—	—	—	106–118	115–129	125–140	143	140
5	2	128–134	131–134	138–150	108–121	118–132	128–144	147	145
5	3	130–136	133–136	140–153	111–124	121–135	131–147	152	149
5	4	132–138	135–138	142–156	114–127	124–138	134–151	157	154
5	5	134–140	137–140	144–160	117–130	127–141	137–155	162	159
5	6	136–142	139–142	146–164	120–133	130–144	140–159	167	164
5	7	138–145	142–145	149–168	123–136	133–147	143–163	172	169
5	8	140–148	145–148	152–172	126–139	136–150	146–167	177	174
5	9	142–151	148–151	155–176	129–142	139–153	149–170	183	179
5	10	144–154	151–154	158–180	132–145	142–156	152–173	188	185
5	11	146–157	154–157	161–184	135–148	145–159	155–176	193	190
6	0	149–160	157–160	164–188	138–151	148–162	158–179	199	195
6	1	152–164	160–164	168–192	—	—	—	204	201
6	2	155–168	164–168	172–197	—	—	—	210	206
6	3	158–172	167–172	176–202	—	—	—	216	212
6	4	162–176	172–176	181–207	—	—	—	222	218

Range	Description*
Within 20% of standard	Not obese
20%–40% above standard	Mildly obese
41%–100% above standard	Moderately obese
More than 100% above standard	Severely obese

*Definitions of obesity taken from Berkow, 1987.

biological children are more alike in weight than adoptive parents and their adopted children (Foch & McLearn, 1980). Researchers have found that animals can be bred for a propensity toward fatness simply by mating the fattest in each generation (Bray & York, 1971).

What weight-related factors are passed on through genes? One possibility, a certain **metabolic rate**—that is, the rate at which food energy is burned away—was suggested by a study of male identical twins (Bouchard et al., 1990). Twelve pairs of identical twins were housed together in a closed-off section of a dormitory, where their diet and exercise were carefully controlled. Each of the men received an extra 1,000 calories a day above the level he needed to maintain a stable weight. The overeating, which continued six days a week for a total of twelve weeks, involved enough excess calories to produce 21 extra pounds of fat. But the subjects did not all gain 21 pounds; instead their weight gains ranged from 9 to 29 pounds. Furthermore, in each pair of twins, both twins gained close to the same amount of weight, as if each had inherited a tendency to burn calories at a certain rate.

Anorexia Nervosa

Some people become so obsessed with the subject of weight control that they literally starve themselves to death in an attempt to shed pounds. This condition, known as **anorexia nervosa,** is far more prevalent in women than in men. About 95 percent of anorexics are female—most of them teenagers and young adults. These women have lost at least a quarter of their weight—some as much as two-thirds—and so tend to look like walking skeletons.

Despite their emaciated appearance, the anorexics' body image is so distorted that they insist they are too fat and must drastically restrict their diets (Bemis, 1978; Bruch, 1973, 1980). These women maintain a remarkably high energy level, often exercising for hours a day. The "In Depth" section at the end of this chapter examines anorexia in more detail.

Bulimia

About half of all anorexics suffer from another eating disorder called **bulimia,** which is characterized by episodes of "bingeing" and "purging." On a typical binge of just a few hours, the average bulimic may consume thousands of calories. In some cases, caloric intake has been measured at *20,000* calories in a single sitting (Schlesier-Stropp, 1984). Often, bulimics eat everything available—a loaf of bread, a jar of peanut butter, a half-gallon of ice cream, a barrel of fried chicken, several bags of cookies, a quart of potato salad—before the compulsive eating stops. Afterward, most bulimics either fast to avoid weight gain or purge their systems by vomiting or taking laxatives. Not surprisingly, bulimics have a love-hate relationship with food. They tend to derive psychological comfort from eating and to use food as their major self-reward (Lehman & Rodin, 1989), but they also feel guilty after eating many foods (Ruggiero et al., 1988).

Although bulimia is often found in anorexics, most bulimics are of average or even above-average weight. Virtually all, however, have strongly internalized the value our culture places on being thin. Most are highly dissatisfied with their own weight, thinking they are too heavy even if they are not (Ruderman & Grace, 1988; Williamson et al., 1988). They are preoccupied not only with their weight but also with how others perceive them in general, what psychologists call their "social self" (Striegel-Moore, Silberstein, & Rodin, 1993). This dissatisfaction with themselves helps to explain why bulimia usually begins after a period of stringent dieting. Some authorities think that the hunger caused by dieting may exacerbate a tendency toward bingeing (Polivy & Herman, 1985; Smead, 1988). Social learning may also play a part in the onset of bulimia. College women living in large-group housing (where they can observe the eating patterns of many other women) have a bulimia rate more than twice as high as that of other college women (Drewnowski, Hopkins, & Kessler, 1988).

Change in Health Habits: The Cognitive-Behavioral Approach

A person's behavior is the result of both external events—such as rewards, praise, and other reinforcements—and internal events, including how one thinks about one's own actions. The cognitive-behavioral approach to changing health habits is based on the observation that modifying behavior without modifying the attitudes and beliefs people hold about their behavior is rarely successful. For example, most smokers want to quit, but self-doubt interferes with their motivation. They tell themselves, "I'll never be able to give up smoking" or "I've tried before and failed," and so they postpone a decision to quit. In cognitive-behavioral therapy, both the unhealthy habit and the beliefs that accompany it are targets for change. Initially, the impetus for cognitive-behavioral change may come from a therapist, a physician, or a formal group program. But ultimately the client must carry out the behavior change.

A Multimodal Program

The most successful programs for habit change use a broad spectrum of learning techniques, an approach sometimes called a *multimodal* program. A typical multimodal program might begin with *self-observation* and *self-monitoring*, in which the client keeps a detailed record of the target behavior. An obese man who needs to lose weight, for example, would keep a diary of when he ate, what he ate, and what else was happening at the time, including how he felt. This record helps the therapist and client to identify the thoughts, feelings, or circumstances that elicit unwanted behavior, as well as the dimensions of the problem. (Frequently people do not realize how often or how much they eat or smoke.)

The second step might be to remove the stimuli that trigger the undesirable behavior. A smoker would be advised to remove all ashtrays from his office and apartment; an obese client, to clear the refrigerator and cupboards of unhealthy high-fat food. The goal of such *stimulus control* is to eliminate unthinking, reflexive behaviors, making unhealthy behaviors more difficult to indulge in.

Next, the therapist would help the client to change the patterns of *self-reinforcement* that are maintaining the unhealthy habit. Drawing on the principles of operant conditioning, the smoker might set up a schedule of rewards for each day lived without cigarettes: a movie for the first day, a new CD for the second, dinner with a friend for the third, and so on. Some people find that they cannot stop a behavior all at once, going "cold turkey." In those cases, the therapist would use the principles of *shaping* to draw up a schedule of rewards based on cutting back from twenty to fifteen cigarettes, then to ten, five, and finally none. The goal of self-reinforcement is to change the consequences of a behavior, so that gradually, not smoking (or snacking or drinking) becomes associated with rewards rather than with punishment.

Another behavioral technique that is used to change habits is **contingency contracting.** A person makes a contract with another individual detailing the rewards or punishments that are contingent on succeeding or failing to make a behavior change. In one actual case a black woman who was attempting to control her use of amphetamines made a contingency contract with her therapist authorizing payment of $50 to the Ku Klux Klan each time she abused the drug. The contract was extremely successful (Thoresen & Mahoney, 1974).

The therapist might also help the client to correct self-defeating thought patterns through *cognitive restructuring*. People who are giving up old habits often feel as if they are losing a close friend. The therapist helps the client to reverse this cognitive pattern by focusing on gains rather than losses. Thus the

smoker might be taught to remind himself "When I don't smoke, my meals taste better, I can run without getting winded, and my children are proud of me." Deep down, clients may believe that they cannot change. Thus the dieter who sneaks one candy bar in the afternoon may say to herself "I'm a hopeless case" and pick up a gallon of ice cream and an apple pie on the way home. The therapist would teach her to tell herself instead "I've been doing great; I can run extra laps tomorrow at the gym; think what my old friends will say when I've lost 10 pounds."

Finally, the therapist may use skills training to help the client deal more effectively with the situations that evoke the unwanted behavior. A client may have begun drinking to excess because he or she felt anxious in social situations, stressed at work, or alone and lonely. Depending on the problem, the therapist might work on developing the client's social skills, finding healthier ways for the client to relax after work (such as exercise or a hobby), or getting the client back into circulation socially. The great advantage of the multimodal approach is that it allows the therapist to tailor a program to the client's needs and problems.

One of the more widely recognized organizations for promoting health-related behavioral change is Alcoholics Anonymous (AA). AA was founded in the 1930s by two alcoholics known in AA literature as "Dr. Bob" (a real physician) and "Bill W." (AA meetings are sometimes called gatherings of "Friends of Bill W.") One recent study indicates that nearly 10 percent of all American adults have attended an AA or AA-related meeting (Room & Greenfield, 1993). Interestingly, of those who have sought help for alcohol abuse, females (about 80 percent) are considerably more likely to have attended AA than males (about 60 percent) (Weisner, Greenfield, & Room, 1995).

Unlike some programs that are designed to monitor and control drinking (Baer et al., 1989; Land & Marlatt, 1978), AA promotes complete abstinence. Its program combines cognitive/behavioral interventions with spiritual principles. One of the hallmark guidelines is that alcoholics should attempt to remain sober "one day at a time," a goal that stresses immediate intervention and prevention. AA members are also encouraged to admit to their alcoholism (a cognitive intervention), attend regular meetings (a behavioral intervention), and phone other alcoholics when they feel the urge to drink (a combination of both). AA appears to be effective for many alcoholics (see Emrick, 1987), though its anonymous nature makes evaluating the long-term effectiveness of its program difficult.

Relapse Prevention

Once an unhealthy habit such as smoking or drinking has been broken, the next step is to prevent a relapse once the program ends. The relapse rate for addictive disorders such as alcoholism, smoking, drug abuse, and overeating runs from 50 to 90 percent (Brownell et al., 1986). People may relapse because their bodies never fully adjust to abstinence, because they are under stress, because they have suddenly been exposed to stimuli that evoke old associations (such as meeting an old "drinking buddy"), or simply because over time their motivation has faded and their vigilance worn down.

Anyone who has tried to give up smoking knows how easy it is to slip back into the habit. A review of studies of people who have tried to quit smoking on their own found that quitting is often a cyclical process (Cohen et al., 1989). Over the course of a lifetime, many smokers move from smoking to abstinence and back to smoking again. Among smokers who succeeded in quitting for six months, researchers found a median relapse rate of 24 percent. Heavy smokers had higher relapse rates than light smokers. In general, smoking cessation programs seem to be less successful than quitting on one's own: most have relapse rates of about 70 percent (Glasgow & Lichtenstein, 1987; Schwartz, 1987). One reason for these results may be that studies do not take into account the cyclical pattern of quitting; another, that hard-core smokers are the most likely to seek help from cessation programs.

To date, no one has found a solution to the relapse problem. Neither "booster sessions" (periodic checkup meetings with a therapist or group), contingency management (requiring substantial deposits to be forfeited if a person relapses), nor lifelong treatment has shown a particularly high rate of success. The problem with these strategies may be that they imply the individual cannot control his or her own behavior. The most promising technique seems to be building protection against relapse into the initial program. Clients are encouraged to anticipate situations that might encourage a relapse (romantic problems, job stress, or returning to a favorite bar) and to work out strategies for coping in advance. They are also taught to think of single transgressions ("bum-

Constant exposure to minor stresses like traffic jams can induce both physiological responses, like increased blood pressure, and psychological responses, like irritability.

ming" one cigarette, "pigging out" at a celebration) as simple missteps rather than signs of a lack of willpower. As was pointed out earlier, *self-efficacy* (a feeling that one can do something) and *response efficacy* (a feeling that one knows how to deal with a problem) are important to healthy behavior.

Thus far, most of the health-related problems discussed in this chapter have involved behavioral patterns that are more or less "voluntary." As we have seen throughout this book, there is ample evidence that obesity, alcoholism, drug abuse, and even smoking have a strong genetic component (Plomin, DeFries, & McClearn, 1990). Of course, that does not mean that some people are "predestined" to lead unhealthy lives, but rather that they are genetically more vulnerable than others and so more likely to become addicted. Even so, behaviors such as drinking, smoking, overeating, or taking drugs are typically a matter of choice. One thing that none of us chooses,

TABLE 12-3   The Stages of Selye's General Adaptation Model of Stress

Stage	Response	Physiological Reaction
Stage 1. *alarm*	Organism "mobilizes" to defend against threat	Increased sympathetic nervous system (SNS) responses (increases in heart rate, blood pressure, respiration; slowing of digestion)
Stage 2. *resistance*	"Fight-or-flight" reaction: organism responds to threat, e.g., physical attack, escape, and so on	Continued high levels of SNS activity
Stage 3. *exhaustion*	Organism begins weakening and can no longer sustain fight-or-flight response	SNS activity gradually diminishes, replaced with antagonistic PNS (peripheral nervous system) activity, (decreased heart rate, blood pressure, respiration, etc.)

but all of us experience, is stress. In the sections that follow we will look at what causes stress, how it affects our health, and how we can cope with it.

Stress

You have to catch a train and you can't find your keys. Your car won't start. It's Friday, your first exam is Monday, and you haven't begun writing a forty-page term paper due the same day. You were turned down for a student loan and you don't know whether you will be able to earn enough over the summer for next semester's tuition, much less how you will pay this month's phone bill. You receive the news that a close friend has been diagnosed with cancer.

Everyone experiences stress, ranging from minor irritations to major traumas. Intuitively we recognize that stress has both physiological and psychological components. Under stress our palms sweat, our hearts race, our neck and shoulder muscles tense, our heads ache, and our stomachs churn (physiological components). We may also have difficulty concentrating, get angry over little things, and tend to dwell on unpleasant thoughts, however much we try to avoid them (psychological components).

The earliest theoretical models of stress focused on physiological reactions. One model held that when an organism perceives a threat, the *sympathetic nervous system* and endocrine system become aroused to enable the organism to attack the invader or flee. This arousal was called the **fight-or-flight response** (Cannon, 1932). Later, Hans Selye (1956) pro-

posed a somewhat different model. His **general adaptation syndrome** had three phases, shown in Table 12-3. In the *alarm stage,* the organism mobilizes to meet a threat, a process that is directed by the adrenal glands, which promote sympathetic nervous system activity (breathing rate increases, heart rate and blood pressure increase, blood is directed to the muscles, digestion slows, and so on—see Chapter 3). In the second stage, *resistance,* the organism tries to come to terms with the threat—through confrontation, for example. The third stage, *exhaustion,* occurs if the organism depletes its physiological resources in the process of trying to overcome a threat. Thus repeated or prolonged exposure to stress causes wear and tear on the body. According to Selye, the response to a stressful event is nonspecific; regardless of the cause of stress, an organism will respond with the same physiological pattern.

Selye's work was important for several reasons. First of all, it showed that stress reactions are not necessarily maladaptive. In fact, they are entirely appropriate in many situations: a threat from a predator, an insufficient food supply, and so on. In these situations, stress reactions *help* an organism survive. Selye's model also offered a general theory of stress reaction that was applicable to a wide variety of events, and it provided a framework that included physiological and environmental factors. Finally, the general adaptation syndrome underscored the problems of ongoing stress. Although mobilization and resistance (stages 1 and 2) are vital, they cannot be sustained. Long-term stress eventually leads to exhaustion (stage 3) and may therefore be particularly harmful.

The major criticism of Selye's model is that it virtually ignored psychological factors. Because not all people respond to potentially threatening events in the same way, the *psychological view* defines **stress** as that which a person appraises as harmful, threatening, or challenging (Lazarus & Folkman, 1984; Lazarus & Launier, 1978). This definition takes into account wide variations in the experience of stress, although it also implies a more negative, maladaptive aspect of "stress" than Selye's. Clearly, some events (the loss of a loved one, or prolonged unemployment) are more stressful than others (losing a sweater, waiting in a long line). Moreover, individuals differ in the way they respond to similar events. Some people panic at the very thought of a deadline; others do their best when working under pressure. Some people thrive on parties: they love the crowd, the noise, and the excitement of meeting new people. Others find walking into a room full of strangers and attempting to strike up a conversation excruciating. While some people are terrified of heights, others are passionate about mountain climbing. Some people recover fairly rapidly from divorce, feeling they are stronger and happier as a result; others remain hurt, angry, and socially and emotionally disoriented for years (Wallerstein & Blakeslee, 1989). In short, what some people find stressful, others find benign and even beneficial or exciting.

One determinant of whether or not we feel stress depends on how we evaluate or appraise a situation. A classic study illustrated the importance of appraisal in the experience of stress (Speisman et al., 1964). College students viewed a graphic film depicting tribal initiation rites, including genital surgery. Before seeing the film, the students were assigned to one of four experimental conditions. One group heard a dry anthropological description of the rites. The second group listened to a lecture that emphasized the excitement of the initiates rather than the pain they experienced. A third group was given a detailed description of the pain and trauma the initiates underwent. The fourth group received no preparation. Measures of autonomic arousal (heart rate and skin conductance) as well as self-reports suggested that the first two groups—who were prepared to see the rites as a meaningful, even religious experience for participants—experienced far less stress than the second two groups, who focused on the initiates' pain.

In real-life situations, appraisal involves two steps (Lazarus, 1990): whether we judge the event or situation as a threat to our well-being (*primary appraisal*) and whether we believe we have the resources to cope with it (*secondary appraisal*). The level of stress we experience depends on the balance between the two. When we perceive the threat as mild and our ability to cope as high, stress will be minimal. But when we perceive the threat as severe and our ability to cope as weak, stress will be substantial.

Much has been written in the popular press about the negative effects of stress on health. What are the facts? Psychologists have approached this issue from different angles. Some have investigated the impact of stress on the body. Others have focused on major life events and the question of what kinds of events are most likely to compromise health. Still others are concerned with individual differences in the experience of stress. The sections that follow will examine each of these approaches.

Stress and the Immune System

> The 27-year-old army captain who commanded the ceremonial troops at the funeral of President Kennedy . . . died 10 days later.
>
> A 39-year-old pair of twins who had been inseparable died within weeks of each other; no cause of death was mentioned.
>
> A 64-year-old woman who was said never to have recovered from the death of her son in an auto accident 14 years earlier died 4 days after her husband was murdered in a holdup.

(Adapted from Engel, 1971, p. 774)

For psychologists, cases of *sudden death syndrome* provide dramatic evidence that stress can be dangerous to one's health. But what exactly is the relationship between stress and illness? How does stress affect the body? Research has begun to establish a connection between stress and the immune system. Indeed, a new field—**psychoneuroimmunology**—has developed to examine how psychological factors alter the immune system and ultimately increase the risk of immune system–related diseases, such as AIDS, cancer, arthritis, infections, and allergies.

The **immune system** guards the body against foreign invaders (called *antigens*). The primary tasks of the immune system are, first, to detect and identify antigens and, second, to neutralize them and remove them from the body. The cells that handle these tasks are produced in the lymph organs and bone marrow, and are known collectively as *lymphocytes*. When bacteria invade the body, *B-lymphocytes* coat them or neutralize their toxin. This activity attracts *macrophages* ("big eater cells"), which ingest and destroy them. When viruses, cancer cells, fungi, or parasites appear in the body, other cells spring into action. *T-lymphocytes* attack these invaders directly, breaking down their cell membranes. *Natural killer* (*NK*) cells attack cells already infected by a virus and secrete *interferon*, which inhibits viral reproduction in uninfected cells. (T-lymphocytes and NK cells are also responsible for the body's rejection of organ and tissue transplants.)

The term **immunocompetence** refers to how well the immune system is operating. Researchers assess immunocompetence by measuring the levels of lymphocytes and antibodies present in a person's blood or saliva and testing whether they are active by exposing them to natural and artificial "toxins" in the laboratory.

A growing body of research suggests that even commonplace stressors can suppress the immune system. Academic stress is a prime example. In a study of forty second-year medical students, researchers tested immune functioning six weeks before finals and again during final exams. The levels of lymphocytes, how active and responsive they were, and even the amount of interferon secreted by NK cells were all significantly lower during exams (Glaser et al., 1985, 1986). The implication was clear: academic stress compromises immunity, making students more vulnerable to illness.

Immunosuppression has been linked to a wide range of stressful conditions, including problems in interpersonal relationships. Researchers have found lowered immunity and higher rates of illness in women who have recently lost a spouse (Irwin et al., 1987), couples who have recently separated or divorced (Kiecolt-Glaser et al., 1987), and unhappily married couples. That is not to say that everyone whose marriage is disrupted suffers increased vulnerability and poor health. Men who initiate divorce show better immune functioning than those who have divorce thrust upon them (Kiecolt-Glaser et al., 1988).

One of the most difficult interpersonal roles appears to be caring for a family member or friend who is suffering from a long-term illness, such as AIDS or Alzheimer's disease (Folkman, Chesney, & Christopher-Richards, 1994; Kiecolt-Glaser et al., 1987). The chronic stress of being a caregiver significantly lowers one's immunocompetence, compared to people of the same age and general health status (including nutrition, caffeine consumption, alcohol use, and amount of sleep). The case of Thomas and John, whose story opened this chapter, provided a clear illustration of the interaction between illness, stress, and immune system functioning (see also Taylor et al., 1993).

Both acute and long-term stress can lower resistance to disease. The *Apollo* astronauts experienced sharp declines in immune functioning following splashdown (Fischer et al., 1972). And people who lived near the Three Mile Island nuclear power plant after the accident there showed lower resistance as well (McKinnon et al., 1989). Daily hassles and even anticipated stress can affect the immune system (Kemeny et al., 1989; Moss, Moss, & Peterson, 1989).

To summarize, there is strong evidence of a connection between stress and lowered immune system function. A question for ongoing research is whether stress affects the immune system directly, by causing wear and tear on the system, or indirectly, as a result of depression, negative mood, poorer health habits, and other side effects of stress.

Stress and Life Events

While the research we have been describing deals with the consequences of stress, other studies have looked at the origins of stress. What events or types of events are most likely to lead to stress? Although the most negative events in our lives—the death of a loved one, divorce, getting fired—cause the most stress, even happy events—getting married, having a baby, being promoted, or going on vacation—may cause stress. Two early stress researchers, Thomas Holmes and Richard Rahe (1967), found that any life change, whether positive or negative, is stressful and can have a negative impact. According to Holmes and Rahe, changes in external circumstances force us to adapt by giving up old habits and establishing new patterns.

To assess the impact of life changes, Holmes and Rahe developed the **Social Readjustment Rating Scale (SRRS)**, a list of forty-three items that were determined through extensive testing to require people to make the most changes in their lives (see Table 12-4). Each item carries a point value that reflects the amount of adaptation required. The death of a spouse, for example, disrupts virtually every aspect of one's life, so it carries the highest number of points (100). Retirement demands fewer adjustments, and so it is given a lower rating (45 points). A minor violation of the law is irritating but does not force a person to alter his or her life-style significantly, and so it carries

TABLE 12-4   *The Holmes and Rahe (1967) Social Readjustment Rating Scale (SRRS)*

Life Event	Mean Value
Death of a spouse	100
Divorce	73
Marital separation	65
Jail term	63
Death of a close family member	63
Personal illness or injury	53
Marriage	50
Fired at work	47
Marital reconciliation	45
Retirement	45
Change in health of family member	44
Pregnancy	40
Sex difficulties	39
Gain of new family member	39
Business readjustment	39
Change in financial state	38
Death of a close friend	37
Change to different line of work	36
Change in number of arguments with spouse	35
Large mortgage*	31
Foreclosure of mortgage or loan	30
Change in responsibilities at work	29
Child leaving home	29
Trouble with in-laws	29
Outstanding personal achievement	28
Wife beginning or stopping work	26
Beginning or ending school	26
Change in living conditions	25
Revision of personal habits	24
Trouble with boss	23
Change in work hours or conditions	20
Change in residence	20
Change in schools	20
Change in recreation	19
Change in church activities	19
Change in social activities	18
Small mortgage*	17
Change in sleeping habits	16
Change in number of family gatherings	15
Change in eating habits	15
Vacation	13
Christmas	12
Minor violations of the law	11

*Holmes and Rahe used $10,000 when the scale was developed in 1967. A comparable modern figure would be closer to $100,000.

Score	Description	Percentage Experiencing Illness in Year Following Events (Holmes & Masuda, 1974)
300+	Major	79%
200–299	Moderate	51%
150–199	Mild	37%

Scale based on Holmes & Rahe, 1967.

the lowest rating (11 points). Using this scale, a researcher asks individuals to check off every event that has occurred in a given time period (usually the preceding year). The researcher then totals the points. According to Holmes and Rahe, people who score 300 or more are at high risk for illness and injury. For example, in a study of college football players, they found that 50 percent of those who were identified as high risk were injured that season, compared to 25 percent of those at medium risk and 9 percent of those at low risk (Holmes & Masuda, 1974).

Other researchers have found that this approach to assessing life stress is only moderately successful in predicting subsequent mental or physical health. One problem is that some of the items on the scale are ambiguous. For example, "personal illness" could mean anything from a cold to a heart attack. Second, people can experience the same events quite differently. One person may experience retirement as liberating, another as disheartening. Third, the SRRS does not consider the context of specific life events. Surely, losing a job will be more stressful for someone who has just bought a new house and taken out a large mortgage than for someone with modest expenses and substantial savings. Another problem is that the scale is retrospective; it does not assess a person's current state. Someone who is under considerable stress at the time he or she fills out the questionnaire might recall an earlier illness as being more severe than it actually was, for example.

Because of such problems, many stress researchers have abandoned the use of simple rating scales like the SRRS. Instead, most try to obtain information about the context in which an event occurred, as well as how the individual reacted to the event in question. Life events researchers are also increasingly interested in identifying the features of particular life events that make them more stressful, such as how predictable or controllable they are (Wortman et al., in press). Even so, the main point of Holmes and Rahe's research—that social readjustment of *any* kind may lead to stress and potentially to stress-related health problems—is widely accepted by contemporary psychologists.

Chronic Stress and Daily Hassles

Increasingly, researchers are studying the impact of chronic stress on mental and physical health. Is continuing, unremitting strain, with no end in sight, more stressful than a single episode of acute strain? Chronic stress might affect people both directly, exhausting their resources for coping, and indirectly, making coping with other life events or even daily hassles more difficult.

For many people, like the spouses of soldiers who fought in the Persian Gulf War, chronic stress (waiting and wondering) is worse than acute stress (knowing their husbands are in combat). Some research supports this view (Brown & Harris, 1978; Eckenrode, 1984; Pearlin & Schooler, 1978; see also House, 1981, 1987). But in most cases separating the effects of acute stress from chronic stress is difficult (Kessler et al., 1985). For example, the loss of a job (a single event) has multiple, often long-lasting repercussions (struggling to pay bills, looking for a new job, finding ways to fill one's time, depending on a spouse). Moreover, determining from subjective self-reports whether a person is under constant or intermittent stress (a mixture of good days and bad days) is difficult. If a person were tested on a "bad day," he or she might report more anguish and strain than if tested on a "good day." Work is under way to develop better measures of chronic stress (such as inventories of a "typical week").

Other researchers have focused on the health impact of daily hassles—getting stuck in traffic jams, waiting in line, being behind in household chores. Everyone experiences such minor frustrations. Can these irritants pile up to the point where one's health suffers as a result? Using scales to measure the severity of daily hassles, researchers in several studies have tied the presence of such stresses directly to declines in physical health (Delongis et al., 1982; Holahan, Holahan, & Belk, 1984). Indeed, some psychologists hold

Elderly nursing home residents who were told they were responsible for the way their rooms were arranged and how they spend their time showed greater improvement in health than residents who were told that the staff was responsible.

that daily hassles may be more stressful and harmful to one's health than major misfortunes (Fleming et al., 1987). Others, however, wonder whether subjects' reports of constant annoyances reflect a preexisting state of psychological distress (Dohrenwend et al., 1984; Monroe, 1983). In other words, feeling "hassled" might be the symptom rather than the cause of mental and perhaps physical health problems.

Controllable versus Uncontrollable Stress

The wives of soldiers serving in the Persian Gulf faced not only *chronic* stress but *uncontrollable* stress. They had no say in whether allied troops would engage Iraqi forces, when the war would begin, or how it would be conducted. Many studies have suggested that uncontrollable stress is more harmful than controllable stress. For example, one team of researchers (Suls & Mullens, 1981) asked people to list which life events on the Holmes and Rahe scale they considered controllable. They found that the rate of illness was significantly higher among people who had experienced uncontrollable life events (such as death, injury, or mandatory retirement) than among those who had experienced controllable events (such as divorce, moving, or career changes). Another study (Baum & Valins, 1977) compared college students who had been randomly assigned to small suites on short corridors to students assigned to rooms on long, crowded corridors (where by necessity they were constantly bumping into people). Researchers found the latter group to be less well

adapted on a variety of measures. Apparently, the "crowded" students felt they had no control over their social interactions.

People who must live in institutions—prisons, mental hospitals, military barracks, and nursing homes—often feel stripped of control. Studies of elderly residents of nursing homes illustrate how a small increase in control can improve their health. In one (Langer & Rodin, 1976), residents were divided into two groups who were roughly equal in health status and socioeconomic background. In a meeting with the nursing home administrator, the first group was reminded of the many options available to them. It was up to them, they were told, to decide how to arrange their rooms, spend their time, and use the home's facilities. If they wanted to make changes, they could speak to the staff, who would be happy to oblige. "[I]t's your life and you can make of it whatever you want," the administrator concluded. Each patient was then given a potted plant and told it was "yours to keep and take care of as you'd like" (pp. 193–194).

The second group also met with the home administrator, but the tone of the meeting was subtly different. These residents were told they were "permitted" to use all the home's facilities; that the staff had tried to "make your rooms nice for you"; and that if they had any complaints or suggestions, "Let us know how best we can help you." The administrator emphasized, "We feel that it's *our responsibility* to make this a home you can be proud of and happy in . . ." (p. 194, emphasis added). Like the first group, these residents also received plants, but were told "the nurses will water them and care for them for you." Thus, while the first group was encouraged to take control of their lives, the second group was encouraged to depend on the nurses.

The results of these simple interventions were dramatic. In the first three weeks after the meeting, both nurses and residents reported that members of the first group were significantly happier, more active, and more assertive than those in the second group. In a follow-up study done eighteen months later (Rodin & Langer, 1977), the researchers found that members of the first group had made significant improvements in health compared to the second group. Moreover, the death rates in the two groups were different: seven of the forty-seven residents in the first group had died (15 percent), compared to thirteen of forty-four members of the second group (30 percent) and an overall death rate of 25 percent for the nursing home as a whole. These statistics should be treated with caution. All of the subjects were elderly, and all had health problems serious enough to require institutionalization, so it is impossible to say how many would have died with or without these simple interventions. But at least one other study found similar improvements when elderly patients were given more control over their lives (Schulz, 1976). As a result of these studies, attitudes toward and treatment of nursing home residents have changed significantly (Hall, 1984).

Posttraumatic Stress

Some researchers have concentrated on delayed reactions to stress, especially to traumatic events. **Posttraumatic stress disorder (PTSD),** first identified among combat veterans, is commonly known as "battle fatigue" or "shell shock." PTSD may also occur in victims of rape, kidnapping (including hostage taking), natural disasters, and confinement to concentration camps. People who have been exposed to these traumatic experiences sometimes suffer psychological side effects and poor health for months or even years afterward. Symptoms include hyperalertness, sleep disturbance, guilt over having survived when others did not, memory loss, and emotional distance (difficulty in establishing and maintaining close relationships) (Frye & Stockton, 1982). Some psychologists estimate that as many as 50 percent of combat veterans suffer from PTSD;

among Vietnam veterans the proportion may have been higher. This disorder is discussed more fully in Chapter 15.

In sum, evidence exists that both major traumas and minor irritations can affect one's health. But the relationship between stress and illness is not strong (Kessler et al., 1985). The fact is, most people do not become ill after experiencing stress. That fact has encouraged health psychologists to investigate the possibility that some people are more vulnerable to stress than others.

Stress and Individual Differences: Optimism versus Pessimism

Why do some people experience more stress and stress-related illness than others? For that matter, why do individuals react to the same event in different ways? Some people are frazzled or "charged up" most of the time, while others remain cool and collected under the most adverse circumstances. Some recover quickly from loss, disappointment, and even illness and injury, while others suffer for months and even years. To explain these differences, researchers have looked for personality traits that might make a person more or less vulnerable to stress.

One dimension of personality that has been linked to stress and the likelihood of illness is optimism versus pessimism. In an interesting study (Scheier & Carver, 1985), students were asked at the beginning of the semester to fill out a questionnaire designed to measure their tendency toward optimism or pessimism. They were asked to answer "true" or "false" in response to items, like the following (cited in Taylor, 1991, p. 240):

1. In uncertain times, I usually expect the best.
2. If something can go wrong for me, it will.
3. I always look on the bright side of things.
4. I'm always optimistic about my future.
5. I hardly ever expect things to go my way.
6. Things never work out the way I want them to.
7. I'm a believer in the idea that "every cloud has a silver lining."
8. I rarely count on good things happening to me.

At the end of the semester, students who had scored high in optimism reported fewer physical symptoms like headaches and upset stomachs than students

When companies "downsize," mid-career employees are often forced to look for new employment. Some respond to the stress with constructive activity, a problem-directed *coping strategy. These job seekers are learning new job skills.*

who had scored lower on the scale. In another study of college students, pessimists reported almost twice as many infectious diseases, and visited a physician twice as often, as optimists (Peterson, Seligman, & Vaillant, 1988). In a recent review, Scheier and Carver (1992) concluded that optimistic individuals tend to display better physical and psychological adaptation to stress.

The difference between pessimists and optimists may be largely a matter of attribution. Pessimists tend to blame themselves for negative events ("It's my fault") and overgeneralize ("It will never end," "This ruins everything"), so that even a minor setback threatens their ability to cope. Optimists, in contrast, tend to attribute negative events to external circumstances, which they assume are temporary and limited ("It wasn't my fault," "It won't happen again," "It's not the end of the world"). They are confident that good things will happen to them, and that they will be able to manage whatever problems present themselves.

Evidence has been accumulating that pessimism increases stress and vulnerability to illness. In a longitudinal study (Peterson, Seligman, & Vaillant, 1988), researchers analyzed interviews with Harvard graduates from the classes of 1939 to 1944, conducted when the graduates were twenty-five years old. The researchers were particularly interested in the subjects' interpretations of negative events in their lives. For instance, they asked subjects about their experiences in World War II: what combat was

like, how well they got along with superiors, and whether they felt they had dealt successfully with their difficulties. The researchers coded each response as optimistic or pessimistic. A typical optimistic response was "My career in the Army has been checkered but, on the whole, characteristic of the Army," reflective of a man who took the ups and downs of his military career in stride. A typical pessimistic response was "I cannot seem to decide firmly on a career. . . . This may be my unwillingness to face reality," indicative of a man who dwelled on the negative and blamed himself. The subjects of this study are now in their late seventies and have had physical checkups every five years. Beginning at about age forty-five, those who had been pessimists at age twenty-five began to show significantly poorer health than those rated as optimists—a pattern that continued as they entered old age. (Indeed, the pessimist just quoted died before age fifty-five.) By implication, pessimism can have lifelong negative effects.

Other studies have focused on the effects of optimism versus pessimism on recovery from illness. One followed thirty-four women who had had a recurrence of breast cancer over five years (Levy et al., 1989). The pessimists died sooner than the optimists, regardless of the severity of the disease. Another study followed patients who had had coronary artery bypass surgery (Scheier et al., 1989). Researchers found that optimists recovered more quickly than pessimists, left the hospital earlier, returned to normal activities sooner, and reported a higher quality of life six months later. By implication, optimism is good medicine.

Not all health psychologists are convinced of "the power of positive thinking," however. Some point out that while a little optimism can be healthy, too much can be maladaptive (Baumeister & Scher, 1988; Perloff, 1987; Weinstein, 1980, 1982). These psychologists argue that unrealistic optimism can cause people to deny problems like physical illnesses that require early treatment until it is too late to cope with them, or to assume they can maintain control in uncontrollable situations, such as gambling or abusing drugs. Other psychologists (e.g., Scheier, Weintraub, & Carver, 1986) argue that the opposite is true. In their view, pessimists are more likely than optimists to engage in maladaptive behavior (by denying stressful events and dwelling on their negative emotions, rather than dealing with a problem), whereas optimists are more likely to adopt successful coping strategies (focusing on the positive aspects of a stressful situation, seeking social support, and attacking the problem directly). This issue remains controversial.

What is more, some psychologists are beginning to question one of the basic assumptions of this research. While most researchers investigating optimism and pessimism have conceptualized the two factors as polar opposites, recent research indicates that might not be the case (Chang, 1997; Chang, D'Zurilla, & Maydeu-Olivares, 1994). Instead, these two dimensions may be independent or at least partly independent of each other (Marshall et al., 1992; Mroczek et al., 1993). Being optimistic, according to these new studies, involves more than simply *not* being pessimistic. For example, in one study (Chang, 1996), Asian-Americans were found to be generally more pessimistic than other Americans, but *not* less optimistic. These findings suggest not only that optimism and pessimism may be somewhat independent of each other but that they are significantly influenced by culture.

One problem with viewing optimism as a protection against stress and illness is that it can lead to "blaming the victim." For example, a woman who suffers a recurrence of breast cancer may blame herself (and be blamed by others) for worrying about her illness and not taking a more positive "I can lick this" attitude. The idea that individuals can ward off or conquer serious illness through sheer willpower is based on a misreading of the scientific literature (or a reading of too many popular sources that misrepresent the facts). No health psychologist would argue that optimism can "prevent" or "cure" cancer or any other illness. Rather, some health psychologists believe that other things being equal, optimists may be less likely to develop cancer and more likely to recover from or live for a longer time with the disease than pessimists. Yet, in life, "other things" (genetic vulnerability, exposure to environmental toxins, life-style, and many other factors associated with cancer) are rarely equal. Though scientists attempt to reduce the influence of "other things" on research findings by studying people with similar backgrounds, life-styles, and diseases, they can never eliminate their effects entirely. That is why the results of such research are reported in terms of probabilities rather than cause and effect. Unfortunately, this distinction is often lost when scientific findings are reported in the popular media and passed on through word of mouth.

Finally, like many personality traits, optimism and pessimism appear to have a strong genetic component. Using data obtained from twin and adoption studies, Robert Plomin and his colleagues found significant genetic influences on optimism and pessimism (Plomin et al., 1992). Furthermore, those differences were associated with differences in mental health: in general, optimists displayed fewer negative symptoms than pessimists. Although these data, like all behavioral genetic data, do not *prove* that individual differences are genetic in origin, they do indicate that a person's outlook may be relatively stable, making long-term change on their part difficult (remember that genetic influences remain consistent throughout one's life).

Stress and Illness: A Model

What can we conclude about the connection between stress and illness? A review of the evidence suggests that there is a relationship between the two, but it is not a simple one. Rather, stress affects health in a variety of ways. The first is the *direct route:* stress may produce physiological and psychological changes that contribute to the development of illness. For example, it can lower immunity, making a person more vulnerable to colds, the flu, and other diseases. But not everyone who is under stress gets sick, suggesting that other preexisting and/or intervening variables also come into play.

One such preexisting variable is *personality*. People who rate high on hostility or pessimism, for example, may be more vulnerable to stress, and thus more prone to illness and injury. A third possibility is that stress increases a person's vulnerability to illness by *altering his or her behavior*. For example, under the stress of exam week, students are more likely to sleep less, smoke more, eat poorly, and engage in other behaviors that can compromise their health. Fourth, stress may promote *"illness behavior."* That is, people who are under stress are more likely to treat fatigue, insomnia, anxiety, and depression as symptoms of illness and to seek medical care as a result (Gortmaker, Eckenrode, & Gore, 1982). Playing the sick role (staying home in bed) also allows a person to avoid the stressful situation and to elicit concern and sympathy from others. Finally, these different factors may interact. The experience of stress, psychological vulnerability, or poor behavior alone might not be enough to cause illness, but a combination of those factors might.

Coping with Stress

According to the federal Centers for Disease Control, fewer than 30 percent of adults with AIDS live more than three years after the disease has been diagnosed. Victims of AIDS are constantly reminded of these odds. They watch their friends die, and live not knowing which infection will attack their weakened immune systems next (Navarro, 1991). A more stressful situation is difficult to imagine. Listen to how some AIDS patients cope:

> In the beginning, AIDS made me feel like a poisoned dart, like I was a diseased person and I had no self-esteem and no self-confidence. That's what I have been really working on, is to get the self-confidence and self-esteem back.

(Reed, 1989)

> Even if something happens next week, if I'm diagnosed with a lymphoma, it's better for me to live my life as if I'm going to live another 20 years.

(Navarro, 1991)

> I made a list of all the other diseases I would rather not have than AIDS. Lou Gehrig's disease, being in a wheelchair; rheumatoid arthritis, when you are in knots and in terrible pain. So I said, you've got to get some perspective on this, and where you are on the Great Nasty Disease List.

(Reed, 1989)

Faced with an apparently hopeless situation—in effect, a death sentence—some AIDS patients undoubtedly give up. But many others strive to lead normal and productive lives and to live as long and as well as they can. In other words, they cope. "I don't know anybody who survives this by accident," said one AIDS patient. "You have to make a conscious decision" (Navarro, 1991).

Coping is the process of managing internal and external demands that are taxing or even overwhelming (Lazarus, 1993; Lazarus & Folkman, 1984). Coping with stress takes two main forms: *problem-directed coping*, or attempts to do something constructive about the stressful situation, and *emotion-focused coping*, or efforts to regulate the emotional consequences of the situation (Lazarus & Folkman, 1984; Pearlin & Schooler, 1978). Often the two work together. For example, a couple having marital difficulties might see a marriage counselor to help sort out their differences and develop better ways of communicating (problem solving). At the same time they might strive to set aside feelings of anger and hurt, and to think about the good times they have had together (emotion-focused coping).

Coping Strategies

Researchers who study different strategies for dealing with stressful situations often use the Ways of Coping Questionnaire. Subjects are first asked to list important events or experiences in their lives and to rate them on a scale from 1 for "extremely stressful" to 5 for "not stressful." They are then asked to indicate the thoughts and actions they have used to deal with those stressful events. In one study (Folkman et al., 1986), married couples were interviewed once a week for a period of six months. After indicating their most stressful experiences, they completed the Ways of Coping Questionnaire. Researchers suggested that the specific coping methods subjects used could be grouped into eight distinct strategies.

Consider how you might use these eight strategies to manage the stress of being fired from a job. One strategy is *confrontational coping*, or standing your ground and fighting for what you want. Thus you might demand to know why you were fired and try to convince your boss to reverse the decision. A second strategy is to *seek social support*, turning to others for comfort and advice on how to handle the situation. A third strategy, *planful problem solving*, involves devising a plan of action to deal with the situ-

| TABLE 12-5   Different Strategies for Coping with Stressful Events |

Problem-Directed Coping Strategies	
Confrontational coping	Forcefully standing one's ground; refusing to change and attempting to change other person's belief
Social support	Relying on friends and family for advice and encouragement
Planful problem solving	Looking at options in detached, objective manner; considering multiple possibilities before taking action

Emotion-Directed Coping Strategies	
Self-control	Reacting stoically, without displays of emotion; "keeping a stiff upper lip"
Distancing	Withdrawal, detachment; attempting to downplay or discount stressful event(s)
Reappraisal	Attempting to view situation from a different perspective; trying to "look for the silver lining"
Accept responsibility	Acknowledging personal role in event; trying to learn from mistakes
Escape/avoidance	Refusing to accept changes by avoiding situations; sometimes escape/avoidance leads to substance abuse

ation. Thus, you might read the want ads, visit an employment agency, and send your résumé to prospective employers. All these strategies are examples of problem-directed coping.

At the same time, you might attempt to deal with your feelings about being fired. One emotion-focused strategy is *self-control*, "keeping your chin up" and not letting your feelings show. Another is *distancing*, telling yourself, "I'm not going to let this get to me." To take your mind off the problem, you might try to immerse yourself in other activities. A third emotion-focused strategy is *positive reappraisal*, or "looking for the silver lining." For example, you might reappraise getting fired as the impetus you needed to look for a more interesting and rewarding job. Alternatively, you might *accept responsibility*, acknowledging that you brought the experience on yourself ("I was late all the time; I didn't try as hard as I could have; I antagonized the boss"). Finally, you might choose *escape/avoidance*, engaging in wishful thinking ("Maybe my boss will change her mind") or escape through drugs, drinking, or overeating. These coping styles are summarized in Table 12-5.

Avoidance versus Confrontation

A number of researchers have compared people who cope with stress by minimizing or avoiding it to those who use more confrontational or vigilant strategies, such as gathering information and taking action (Holahan & Moos, 1987). In general, research shows that confrontation is a more successful strategy than avoidance. Individuals who deal with a problem directly not only are more likely to solve the problem but are better prepared (emotionally and otherwise) to handle stress in the future. Indeed, some research suggests that chronic avoidance of problems places people at risk for added stress and perhaps for related health problems (Felton, Revenson, & Hinrichsen, 1984; Quinn, Fontana, & Reznikoff, 1987). For example, Cole and associates (1996) found that (HIV-negative) gay men who actively concealed their homosexual identity were more likely to display health-related problems.

To illustrate, assume you have gone to your physician with what you think is a minor complaint. Your doctor is concerned about more serious problems, however, and orders a series of tests. At this stage, focusing on the risks of serious illness, reading everything you can about your symptoms, and demanding that your physician tell you "the worst-case scenario" (a confrontational strategy) will only add to your stress. However, if the tests reveal that you do have a serious health problem—say, diabetes—avoidance becomes a dangerous strategy. In this case, vigilance (taking insulin shots, following the prescribed diet, learning as much as you can about your disease) is far more adaptive.

The same principles apply to situations that are not health-threatening. For example, in a romantic relationship, vigilance may translate into unwarranted jealousy (confronting your girlfriend when you see her having lunch or merely talking with another man, constantly demanding to know where she has been and with whom) that can undermine a relationship. However, if your girlfriend seems cool and distant much of the time and constantly makes excuses for not being able to see you, avoidance (pretending nothing has changed) becomes maladaptive. She may have a problem she is embarrassed to discuss with you, you may have done something to offend her, or she may be losing interest. In any of these cases, you are better off knowing and taking action, whether that means changing your behavior or facing the fact that the relationship is over. In short, vigilance and avoidance both have their uses, but too much or too little of either can be maladaptive.

In many cases, a combination of coping strategies is most successful (Collins, Taylor, & Skokan, 1990). If your dog disappears, for example, you might cope best by both minimizing the stress (telling yourself he is just lost, someone probably took him in, and you'll get him back) and confronting the problem (calling the ASPCA lost and found, putting up posters in pet shops, etc.).

Emotional Venting

Psychologist James Pennebaker and his colleagues have explored the value of venting emotions, or *catharsis* (from the Greek, "to cleanse"), on long-term health. They asked some college students to write about stressful events (including their feelings about college), while others were asked to write about trivial subjects. They found that venting emotions increased stress in the short term, but produced long-term benefits, including fewer visits to the health center (Berry & Pennebaker, 1993; Pennebaker, 1993; Pennebaker, Colder, & Sharp, 1990). Pennebaker and

his colleagues found that the inhibition of emotional expression following stressful or traumatic events— "keeping a stiff upper lip"—increases the risk for a variety of health problems (Berry & Pennebaker, 1993; Pennebaker, 1995).

A related study qualified these results. Researchers assigned a task to a group of sixty undergraduates (Greenberg & Stone, 1990), who had been divided into three groups: those who had previously disclosed traumatic events, those who were disclosing them for the first time, and those who wrote about trivial topics. Researchers found that those who had previously disclosed the traumatic events in their lives exhibited far greater stress and more negative moods than members of the other two groups. (They found no differences in health among the three groups, measured in terms of visits to the health center and self-reports.) Researchers hypothesized that confiding in others about stressful events may intensify rather than reduce the negative emotions associated with a traumatic experience.

Though reliving a painful experience over and over may delay the process of recovery, most researchers have found that venting one's emotions has clear benefits. Talking with others can provide useful information about how to cope; it can also reassure people that they are not alone, that others have faced the same problems and feelings (Lazarus, 1966; Wortman & Dunkel-Schetter, 1979). It can also help people to organize their thoughts and perhaps to find meaning in the experience (Meichenbaum, 1977; Silver & Wortman, 1980). The next section describes more fully the support others can provide in times of stress.

Reliance on Social Support

How people manage stress depends not only on their internal resources but on their external resources—their social support systems. Social support is the knowledge that one is loved, cared for, valued, and included in a network of mutual concern (Cobb, 1976). This kind of information can help to mute the effects of stress and reduce the risk of illness. Sources of support can include friends, spouses, lovers, children, church members, club members, or even a devoted pet. The sense of support itself is more important than who provides it.

The various forms of social support fall into three categories: tangible assistance, information, and emotional support (House, 1981; Schaefer, Coyne, &

How well people manage stress depends not only on their internal resources, but on their external resources. In addition to family members and co-workers, a person's social support system often includes a place of worship.

Lazarus, 1981). Tangible assistance can take the form of a gift of money to tide a person over bad times or the meals provided to families during time of bereavement. Information includes ideas on specific actions to take to overcome a stressful situation. Perhaps most valuable of all is the emotional support of family and friends, which reassures the individual under stress that others care. Research has shown that social support can effectively reduce distress (Cohen & Wills, 1985) as well as lower the likelihood of illness, speed recovery from illness, and reduce the risk of death from serious disease (House, Umberson, & Landis, 1988; Kulik & Mahler, 1989). In one classic study, researchers asked 7,000 adults living in California about their social and community ties and then tracked their mortality rates over a nine-year period (Berkman & Syme, 1979). They found that those people who reported few social and community ties were more likely to die than people who claimed to have many ties. Women who had access to a social support system lived an average of 2.8 years longer, and men an average of 2.3 years longer, than those with few social contacts. Support from others also appears to encourage better health habits. People with high levels of social support are more likely to follow medication recommendations and to use health services (Umberson, 1987).

A social support system does not need to be extensive to be beneficial. Most important is having at least one confidante to whom one can turn. In fact, in some cases, advice or support from too many people

may actually increase stress. Sometimes people who are trying to be helpful may even provide the wrong kind of support. Imagine, for example, that you are trying to decide which graduate school to attend. In an effort to help, relatives may offer facts and opinions about the schools, but their information may conflict, making your decision process even more confusing and stressful. You might do better just to accept their emotional support in the form of reassurances that you will make the right decision (Dakof & Taylor, 1990).

Attempts at emotional support can also go awry when friends are trying to comfort those who are bereaved. One study found that 60 percent of those who were coping with the loss of a spouse or child reported others had said or done something unhelpful (Wortman & Lehman, 1985). The four tactics most commonly identified as unhelpful were giving advice ("You can always have another child"), encouraging recovery ("A trip would do you a world of good"), minimizing the loss or forcing cheerfulness ("It's a good thing you have other children"), and identifying with the feelings of the bereaved ("I know just how you feel"). Tactics that were judged helpful included "just being there," providing an opportunity to discuss feelings, and expressing concern.

Another study has attempted to identify the kinds of support that help or hinder attempts to quit smoking (Cohen & Lichtenstein, 1989). More than 200 subjects who wanted to quit smoking were surveyed after their quit dates to determine the frequency of both positive and negative support received from a partner or someone else close. Among the positive behaviors listed in the questionnaire were "compliment you on not smoking," "tell you to stick with it," and "express confidence in your ability to quit." Negative behaviors included "comment that the house smells of smoke," "refuse to let you smoke in the house," and "talk you out of smoking a cigarette." The researchers found that success in quitting was associated not with the frequency of these behaviors but with the ratio of positive to negative behaviors. In every follow-up (one month, three months, six months, and twelve months), the greater the proportion of positive to negative behaviors a subject reported receiving, the greater the subject's rate of abstinence from smoking.

Stress Management Training

People who cannot reduce stress either through their own efforts or with the support of others may benefit from learning the techniques of stress management. Workshops in stress management are increasingly common in the workplace, where stress-related disorders are estimated to account for as much as $17 billion a year in lost productivity (Adams, 1978). Stress management programs are also directed at people who suffer from or are at risk for stress-related illness or disorders, such as headaches, alcohol abuse, obesity, cardiovascular disease, and hypertension. Increasing numbers of college administrators are making stress management programs available to students. Some of these programs make use of the cognitive-behavioral approach introduced earlier in this chapter.

Cognitive-Behavioral Techniques

Many students find the first semester of college very stressful. Suddenly they find themselves in a noisy dormitory full of strangers. Making friends, getting used to communal bathrooms and kitchens, and adapting to a roommate's quirks and habits can be difficult. Often, college courses are far more demanding than high school classes; a former A student may see her first C or even D. Furthermore, college students receive few daily or weekly homework assignments; instead, they receive reading lists and due dates for papers and exams, but are otherwise left on their own. When they realize no one is checking to see that they are keeping up with their studies, many students begin to feel overwhelmed.

The basic goal of stress management programs for college is to help students learn to cope with their new environment before they drop out or flunk out. Most programs include three stages. The first is *education*. The counselor begins by assuring students that many young people find college stressful (they are not alone). He explains what stress is, emphasizing that it depends more on how people appraise a situation and their ability to cope with it than on the situation itself. He talks about how stress can affect one's psychological and physical health, as well as one's academic performance and social behavior. Next, he trains students to recognize the symptoms of stress (overeating, sleep problems, palpitations) and to keep a record of situations that cause them as well as their efforts to cope. He also urges them to listen to their inner thoughts, to recognize (and record) negative self-talk ("I always get tongue-tied when the professor calls on me," "I'll never be able to write a forty-page term paper").

The next stage is *training*, which might include instruction in time management (establishing priorities, setting specific times for work and play, breaking large assignments down into small steps, and taking periodic breaks to stretch and relax); in social skills (such as assertiveness, or confronting those who are causing the stress); in good health habits (regular meals and exercise); and in relaxation techniques. In this stage, students learn to establish realistic goals, use positive self-talk, and reward themselves for reaching their goals. The high school science whiz who was devastated by a C on her first chemistry quiz might aim for a C+ on the next quiz and a B on her midterm. Whenever she begins to feel discouraged, she will remind herself that the reason she got into the premed program was that she showed high potential in high school. A student who is terrified about being called on in a particular class might first observe students who seem comfortable in class and later write down questions he would like to ask and rehearse them in private. When he succeeds in asking three questions, he rewards himself with a movie. In addition to these "homework" assignments, students might role-play with one another. For example, a student whose roommate borrows his things without asking might practice confronting the roommate with another student, who tries to make the conversation as difficult as possible.

The third stage in a cognitive-behavioral program is *practice*. Students apply the skills they have been

In biofeedback, a patient receives information on a physiological function, such as heart rate, that is normally outside his or her conscious awareness. The aim of this stress management technique is to train the patient to recognize, monitor, and control stress-related physiological functions.

rehearsing to real-life situations and report back to the group on their experiences. Ideally, this three-stage program enables students to "inoculate" themselves against stress (Meichenbaum & Deffenbacher, 1988).

Biofeedback

In the 1970s, a new technology for managing stress took the health professions and popular press by storm. **Biofeedback** is a specialized procedure for monitoring and controlling the physiological aspects of stress (and pain). This technique involves giving the individual feedback on a body function that is normally outside conscious awareness so that the individual can be trained to recognize and control it. For example, a patient might be connected to a machine that translates heart rate into a tone, so that one can hear how fast or slowly one's heart is beating. Through trial and error the patient gradually learns to control what was previously an automatic response. For example, a patient might find that shutting out all sound and concentrating on breathing slowly helps to reduce his or her heart rate.

At one time, biofeedback was recommended for the treatment of hypertension, chronic pain, muscle-contraction headaches, and migraines, as well as general stress. But this initial flurry of enthusiasm faded when careful research found mixed success. Biofeedback may help some people to overcome some problems, especially in combination with other types of therapy, but other techniques that are

much less costly and easier to implement are just as effective (Turk, Meichenbaum, & Berman, 1979). One of the simplest and most successful of those techniques is relaxation training.

Relaxation Techniques

Relaxation is the counterpoint to stress. When relaxed, the body is in a state of low arousal, which means it is less apt to react to stress. Through relaxation techniques one can learn to shift the body into this pleasant state of low arousal, thus reducing the abnormal tension associated with stress. Relaxation techniques are considered effective treatments for insomnia, hypertension, tension headaches, anxiety disorders, and general autonomic arousal.

One such technique involves the progressive relaxation of the body's muscle groups (Everly, 1989). The idea is that since stress and anxiety are related to muscle tension (the contraction of muscle fibers), reducing muscle tension can lessen feelings of stress and anxiety. Starting usually in the lower body and progressing up to the facial muscles, the subject systematically tenses and relaxes selected muscles until the whole body is relaxed. Continual practice allows the subject to become accustomed to feelings of repose and to develop a more relaxed attitude.

Another relaxation technique is controlled breathing. Because states of relaxation are associated with deep, long breaths, relaxation can be induced by intentionally creating such a breathing pattern. To begin, one takes a long, cleansing breath, exhaling

Relaxation techniques like yoga can be an effective treatment for health problems such as insomnia, hypertension, and anxiety.

through the mouth. Eventually, deep breaths lasting as long as ten seconds replace short, shallow breaths. This technique seems to have some effect in controlling stress-related pain, such as headache or facial pain (Turk, Meichenbaum, & Berman, 1979; Weisenberg, 1977).

Practiced regularly, relaxation techniques appear to improve the functioning of the immune system. In one study, first-year medical students were assigned to either a relaxation group or a comparison group (Kiecolt-Glaser et al., 1984). Those in the experimental condition attended five to ten relaxation sessions that took place in the month before their exams. At the time of the exams, both groups showed signs of decreased functioning in their immune systems (fewer T-cells and lower killer cell counts). But members of the relaxation group reported less anxiety, and those who had practiced relaxation more frequently (ten sessions) had higher T-cell counts than those who had practiced less frequently (five sessions).

In another study, forty-five elderly residents of an independent-living facility were assigned to one of three groups: one that received relaxation training, one that received social contact, and a control group (Kiecolt-Glaser et al., 1985). Members of the first two groups were seen three times a week for one month. At the end of the month, the relaxation group showed significant increases in killer cell activity and other signs of improved functioning of the immune system, as well as significant decreases in self-

rated distress. A follow-up study done one month after the relaxation training ended found no significant effects, suggesting the importance of regular, long-term practice of relaxation techniques.

Exercise

Stress prepares the body for "fight or flight," increasing the blood supply to the heart, tensing the muscles, and so on. Stifling the physical expression of this response—getting "revved up" without releasing the resulting tension—may increase the risk of stress-related disorders. Exercise is a healthful way to jettison tension and its negative effects. Indeed, exercise has been called "nature's own prescription" for stress.

In terms of physical fitness, the best kind of exercise is *aerobic*. Swimming, walking, running, skiing, cycling, dancing, jumping rope—any activity that demands increased oxygen intake will give the cardiovascular system a workout. Such exercise should consist of coordinated rhythmic movements performed for their own sake, not to "win" or prove a point. To be maximally effective, aerobic exercise must be consistent. Healthy adults should exercise briskly and continuously at least three times a week for at least fifteen minutes at a time. Each session should consist of warm-up, exercise, and cool-down periods.

Numerous studies have found that regular exercise improves cardiovascular fitness, endurance, muscle tone and strength, flexibility, and optimal

Regular exercise is one of the most effective stress management techniques. It improves one's mood and sense of well-being and reduces anxiety, depression, and tension.

weight; helps to control hypertension (high blood pressure) and cholesterol levels; and increases tolerance of stress. For example, in one study of adolescents, researchers found that subjects who exercised regularly experienced less stress and fewer illnesses in the face of negative life events than those who did not (Brown & Seigel, 1988).

Exercise can also improve one's mood and general sense of well-being, as well as reduce anxiety, depression, and tension—though perhaps not as much as popular articles imply. People who are committed to a regular exercise program tend to have a more positive self-image, greater self-esteem, and a higher sense of self-efficacy than those who exercise sporadically or not at all (Rodin & Plante, 1989). What researchers do not know is whether exercise affects one's psychological well-being directly, through some biochemical process as yet unidentified, or indirectly—because people often exercise with friends and enjoy the sociability, because they feel they are accomplishing something, or simply because they believe that exercise will improve their mood (Hughes, 1984; Hughes, Casal, & Leon, 1986).

Though physical fitness has reached the level almost of a fad in our culture, long-term commitment to exercise is less widespread. Whether or not one exercises seems to depend on whether or not people see themselves as athletic, or the type of person who exercises (Kendzierski, 1990); the convenience of exercise facilities (Dishman, 1982); and habit (Valois, Desharnais, & Godin, 1988). The first three to six months of an exercise program appear to be critical. People who exercise continually for three to six months are more likely than others to keep it up, though before six months, even regular exercisers may give up.

While more and more adults plunged into exercise routines in the 1980s, their children became less active, fatter, weaker, and slower. A ten-year study of more than 12,000 boys and girls in grades one through twelve found that in 1990 only 32 percent could satisfactorily complete physical fitness tests of strength, flexibility, and muscular and cardiovascular endurance, compared to 43 percent a decade earlier (*The New York Times,* May 24, 1990, p. B14). Television and cutbacks in physical education programs seem to be taking their toll on the health and fitness of American youth.

The importance of an exercise program in promoting good health underscores the point that health is an active achievement. Protection from illness and injury is not a matter of "luck of the draw" or a question of "medical potluck." As this chapter has emphasized, people can play an active role in establishing healthy habits and learning to cope with stressful conditions. They can eat regular nourishing meals, refrain from smoking and drinking to excess, and abusing drugs, develop positive yet realistic attitudes, exercise routinely, and, occasionally, just slow down and relax.

In Depth

Anorexia Nervosa

OF ALL THE health-related disorders with psychological origins, one of the most striking is anorexia. Though the incidence of anorexia appears to have increased in recent years, the first documented cases occurred more than three centuries ago (Brannon & Feist, 1997). Sir William Gull, a nineteenth-century British physician, was among the first to study the problem systematically (Gull, 1874, reported in Brannon & Feist, 1997). Like contemporary researchers, Gull believed the condition to be psychological in origin, and so named it *anorexia nervosa* (literally, "not eating due to nervous causes").

As has been mentioned, anorexia is puzzling for many reasons. First, even those anorexics on the verge of starvation view themselves as overweight (Bruch, 1973, 1982). (Bulimics generally do not display this irrational belief; instead, they usually express disapproval of their eating patterns.) Second, anorexics display many symptoms of starvation, such as *amenorrhea*, or cessation of normal menstrual cycles, but they usually display those symptoms *before* they begin to diet. Third, the vast majority of anorexics (between 90 and 95 percent) are female (Garfinkel & Garner, 1982). Finally, while the disorder is still relatively rare—current estimates are that between 1 and 2 percent of all American females suffer from anorexia, and that females between fifteen and twenty are at highest risk (Hsu, 1990)—it is quite resistant to treatment. In one study of hospitalized female anorexics (Goldner & Birmingham, 1994), 86 percent (twenty-five out of twenty-nine) gained weight during their hospital stay. Some months after they were discharged from the hospital, however, two out of twenty-seven of the original patients (less than 10 percent) were eating normally and maintaining an acceptable weight; almost half (twelve out of twenty-seven) required further hospitalization (Pertshuk, 1977; see also Goldner & Birmingham, 1994).

Initial Studies

Various explanations have been proposed for anorexia. One of the most influential was developed by Hilde Bruch (Bruch, 1973; for a more current version, see also Bruch, 1980, 1985), who believed that anorexia was triggered by the anxiety associated with sexual maturation and perhaps even pregnancy. Consistent with Bruch's theory, the incidence of anorexia is highest among women in the years immediately following puberty and adolescence, from about age fifteen to twenty. Furthermore, the weight loss associated with anorexia usually reduces the size of the breasts and hips, giving anorexics a much younger appearance commonly associated with sexual immaturity. Recall that ovulation and menstruation also cease with the onset of this disorder. Regardless of whether ambivalence and anxiety about sex are the primary cause, the symptoms certainly produce that effect. Anorexics are usually considered unattractive and sexually undesirable; even if they engage in sexual intercourse, they run almost no risk of pregnancy.

The little research that has been conducted on males who suffer from anorexia indicates they have sexually related difficulties as well. Herzog and colleagues (1984) found the incidence of homosexual orientation in male anorexics to be about 25 percent—considerably higher than the rate in the general population. Most of the other subjects in the study reported little or no interest in sex, as well as anxiety and doubts about their sexuality.

Criticisms, Alternatives, and Further Research

Almost immediately after Bruch proposed her theory, alternative theories were advanced. One influential model, offered more as a refinement of rather than an alternative to Bruch's model, was developed by Minuchin (1974; Minuchin, Rosman, & Baker, 1978). According to Minuchin, whose views are derived from an interpersonal or family-systems perspective (see Chapter 15), the families of anorexics tend to have similar characteristics (see also Pike & Rodin, 1991). For example, the families he studied tended to be overprotective and inflexible and to display a superficial "closeness" rather than genuine warmth and concern for one another. In these families the onset of anorexia tends to draw attention away from other chronic family difficulties, serving as a kind of lightning rod for the family's anger and frustration. According to Minuchin, for drawing the family's attention away from deeper problems, the anorexic is subtly reinforced. During the course of treatment, Minuchin works with the entire family. His rate of success (over 80 percent, as reported in Minuchin, Rosman, & Baker, 1978) has been far better than that of many other therapists.

Other theorists emphasize the role of social and cultural factors in anorexia. As was pointed out earlier in the chapter, American society tends to promote a thin body as the feminine "ideal." Williamson and colleagues (1990) report that during the past few decades, the women shown in magazine advertisements have become increasingly thin, roughly corresponding to the increase in the incidence of anorexia. Anorexia is much less common in cultures that do not encourage extreme thinness in women, such as the Chinese (Lee & Chiu, 1989), Jamaican (Smith & Cogswell, 1994), or African-American cultures (Dolan, 1991). In recent years, Japan has seen a cultural shift toward thinness in women, and the rate of anorexia among Japanese women has increased (Pate et al., 1992).

Finally, many researchers believe that biological factors play a significant role in anorexia. For example, Gwirtsman and Gerner (1981) found that anorexics often show disturbances in neurotransmit-ter function similar to those seen among patients suffering from depressive disorders. Because the hypothalamus is known to regulate hunger and eating, some researchers suspect that hypothalamic abnormalities may be involved in anorexia (e.g., Fava et al., 1989). The cerebrospinal fluid of anorexics contains abnormally high levels of neurochemicals known to be involved in hunger and appetite; these abnormalities disappear after a normal weight is achieved (Leibowitz, 1991).

Patterns and Conclusions

The recent increases in the incidence of anorexia have fueled research efforts. Not surprisingly, researchers have been unable to identify a single cause of the disorder. Instead, a number of factors appear to be involved—family environment, sexually related fears and anxieties, cultural expectations, and neurochemical disturbances. Because so many factors play a role in developing and maintaining anorexia, a single intervention to treat—much less "cure"—the disorder is unlikely. However, new therapeutic techniques are constantly being introduced, and successful intervention is more common today than it was twenty years ago. Until the underlying causes of anorexia are better understood, however, the disorder will remain something of an enigma.

SUMMARY

1. The idea that social, psychological, and biological factors can interact to affect our health is known as the **biopsychosocial model.** This model departs from the traditional view of illness as a purely biological malfunction—the **biomedical model.** The biopsychosocial model focuses on how the mind and body influence each other and how we can actively achieve health by developing healthy habits and life-styles.

2. The field of **health psychology** refers to the contributions that psychology can make to maintaining health, preventing illness, and improving health care and policy. Health psychol-ogists are active in health promotion, enabling people to increase control over their health and improve it.

3. One way of promoting health is to publicize accurate information to correct people's misperceptions and to acquaint them with health facts about their life-styles. Some life-style factors impact sexual behavior and can have profound health consequences. The most serious of the sexually transmitted diseases is acquired immunodeficiency disorder, or AIDS. AIDS is caused by the human immunodeficiency virus (HIV) and is transmitted through contact with infected blood. HIV can be transmitted through

the sharing of infected needles (and, less frequently, through other forms of blood-to-blood contact), but it is most commonly spread through unprotected sexual intercourse. In males, the most common mode of transmission is same-sex contact, though infection through heterosexual contact also occurs. In females, especially younger females, heterosexual contact is a common source of exposure.

4. Life-style factors also influence diet, nutrition, and weight control. **Obesity** results when caloric intake consistently exceeds energy expenditure. Obesity has genetic, cognitive, and social causes. One influential theory proposes that weight is regulated through a **setpoint** for fat, which is determined by the nervous system.

5. Some people become so obsessed with being thin that they literally starve themselves, a condition called **anorexia nervosa.** Most anorexics are teenage girls. Some suffer from another eating disorder called **bulimia,** which involves periodic bingeing, in which many thousands of calories may be consumed. This is followed by purging, often through self-induced vomiting or taking laxatives.

6. Knowing that behavior is risky does not necessarily cause people to change. For this reason health psychologists are also involved in designing programs to help people change their health habits through cognitive-behavioral techniques (such as self-monitoring, stimulus control, and self-reinforcement) and also to prevent relapse.

7. Although not everyone engages in unhealthy behavior, all experience **stress.** Early accounts of stress focused on physiological reactions: the **fight-or-flight response,** in which an organism is aroused to either attack a threatening invader or flee, and the **general adaptation syndrome,** which describes three phases of mobilizing and responding to stress. The latter account holds that prolonged or repeated exposure to stress will cause wear and tear on the system. But neither hypothesis takes psychological factors into account. Today there is increasing recognition that our responses to stress vary, depending on the person and the stressful event. Thus the psychological view defines stress as that which an individual appraises as harmful, threatening, or challenging.

8. A number of studies in the field of **psychoneuroimmunology** suggest that the experience of stress can affect our **immunocompetence,** the measure of how well the immune system protects our bodies from illness. Lowered immunity has been found in people experiencing a wide range of stressful conditions, from unhappy marriages to daily hassles.

9. Some researchers seeking to find the link between stress and illness have focused on major life events, such as the death of a spouse, divorce, or retirement. Other researchers have tried to identify the types of events that lead to stress and illness. There is some evidence that the cumulative effects of chronic stress, or even daily hassles, take a toll on health. Research also shows that uncontrollable situations are usually more stressful than controllable ones. However, it is important to remember that most people do not become ill after experiencing stress.

10. Sometimes intense, traumatic events lead to delayed stress reactions. Soldiers, victims of crimes such as rape or kidnapping, and others may display **posttraumatic stress disorder (PTSD),** characterized by anxiety, depression, sleeplessness, and other cognitive and emotional difficulties.

11. Still other researchers have investigated the reasons why some individuals are more vulnerable to stress and illness than others. This research focuses on personality traits. Pessimism (a tendency to see problems as global and insolvable and to blame oneself) may increase our propensity for illness in times of stress. In general, optimists have been found to have better health over their lifetime, and to recovery more quickly from illness, than pessimists.

12. The process of **coping** with stress, managing the external and internal demands that are appraised as taxing, takes two forms: problem-solving efforts, geared to direct and constructive action, and emotion-focused efforts, putting the emphasis on regulating the emotional consequences of a stressful event. Within these two categories are many distinct coping strategies. Vigilant strategies seem to be more

successful than avoidant ones, and venting emotions appears to promote health more than keeping them bottled up.

13. How we manage stress depends a great deal on our social support system, the people around us who let us know they love and care for us. Having social ties makes us more able to cope with stress and its effects, although the number of ties seems to be less important than the closeness of those ties. Social support takes three general forms: tangible assistance, information, and emotional support.

14. Techniques in stress management are directed at those who suffer from, or are at risk for, stress-related illnesses and disorders. Programs in stress management may include cognitive-behavioral techniques, **biofeedback** (the process of monitoring bodily functions and learning to control them), relaxation techniques, and aerobic exercise.

SUGGESTED READINGS

Brannon, L., & Feist, J. (1997). *Health psychology: An introduction to behavior and health* (2nd ed.). Belmont, CA: Wadsworth. One of the best introductory books on the topic of health psychology.

King, B. M. (1996). *Human sexuality today* (2nd ed.). Upper Saddle River, NJ: Prentice-Hall. A recent, readable introduction to sexuality, including a good section on sexually transmitted diseases.

Pryor, J. B., & Reeder, G. D. (Eds.) (1993). *The social psychology of HIV infection.* Hillsdale, NJ: Lawrence Erlbaum. An advanced, edited volume containing chapters by several highly regarded researchers in sexuality, health, and social psychology.

Shapiro, A. P. (1996). *Hypertension and stress: A unified concept.* Hillsdale, NJ: Lawrence Erlbaum. A recent work summarizing the current research on stress and cardiovascular functioning, including discussion of life-style and personality factors.

Taylor, S. E. (1989). *Positive illusions.* New York: Basic Books. In this book, Taylor presents research illustrating that illusions may be important in maintaining physical and mental health. This view is intriguing because it runs counter to the popular belief that distorted perceptions of reality are a sign of mental illness. Taylor shows that in many situations, such distortions are adaptive and necessary.

Cousins, N. (1979). *Anatomy of an illness as perceived by the patient: Reflections on healing and regeneration.* New York: Norton.

Sacks, O. (1984). *A leg to stand on.* New York: Summit Books. Two marvelous firsthand accounts of battles against illness and injury. Cousins discusses his recovery and how he found laughter (including *Three Stooges* films!) to be an invaluable aid to recovery. Sacks discusses recovery from injury rather than illness, but his explorations of the depression, boredom, and fear involved in his lengthy convalescence make for compelling reading.

Theories of Personality

Suppose you were asked to write a letter describing yourself to a total stranger. What would you say about yourself? How could you paint an accurate self-portrait in words? You might begin with a few simple facts (I am a man or woman; I am a student; I am a member of a certain ethnic group). Then you would describe your personal traits—your ways of responding to various situations. Are you thick-skinned or sensitive? Outgoing or shy? Aggressive or timid? Emotional or restrained? Try to list at least five or six traits that you think describe you quite well. Now answer this question: Do you think these traits will still describe you in ten or twenty years? Most people answer with a qualified yes. Although they recognize that ways of thinking and acting can and do change, they think of themselves as having certain fundamental features that will endure across the years. These features together form one's personality. More formally defined, **personality** consists of all the relatively stable and distinctive styles of thought, behavior, and emotional response that characterize a person's adaptations to surrounding circumstances (Maddi, 1976; Mischel, 1976).

Psychologists who study personality seek the answers to certain key questions. The first concerns the origins of differences among people. When several people encounter the same situation, why don't they all react alike? Why are some people terrified at the prospect of speaking in public, while others enjoy it? Why do some people enjoy dangerous activities like skydiving or bungee jumping, while others prefer to spend their leisure time reading or playing chess? Clearly, people have different personalities, but why do their differences develop? As you will see later in this chapter, psychologists have given a variety of answers. Some have stressed the influence of early life experiences and childhood conflicts, some the influence of people's biological makeup, while still others have stressed the influence of learning. Many factors undoubtedly play a role in shaping the traits people display.

Another major question that personality theorists ask concerns the consistency of people's individual differences. This question can be expressed in two different ways. The first concerns a person's personality across different situations. Do shyness, friendliness, and other traits persist in all a person's activities,

Why do some people enjoy bungee jumping, while others prefer to spend their leisure time playing chess? Psychologists who study personality seek the answers to such questions.

or do people often let the situation determine their response? For instance, might a student be scrupulously honest in handling a campus club's funds but be willing to cheat on an exam if given the opportunity? Or would the student's honesty cause him or her to behave with integrity in both these situations? The question of the stability of personality traits can

also be studied in terms of behavior throughout the life span. Is someone who is friendly and outgoing at age twenty likely to be friendly and outgoing at age seventy? Or are the traits that make up one's personality likely to change with age?

Psychologists have come up with different answers to such questions. Some have concentrated on specific traits, such as honesty and shyness, asking how each person's traits can best be measured and described. Others have stressed factors that integrate personality, such as self-concept. Still others have emphasized internal feelings (anxiety, conflict, self-fulfillment) that seem to be associated with various personality makeups. These diverse perspectives are what make the field of personality so challenging—and so frustrating. As you study personality, you may find that several different theories presented in this chapter seem persuasive. While no single theory of personality is able to account for all the facts, each theory contains elements that have been supported by research. As a result, you should think of the theories you are about to encounter as complementary rather than competing. Each sheds valuable light on certain, but not all, aspects of the subject. Together, they paint a rich portrait of why individuals behave as they do.

In this chapter we will be discussing five major perspectives in personality. The first is the **psychoanalytic approach,** which began with Sigmund Freud. This school of theories emphasizes childhood experiences as critically important in shaping adult personality. It also stresses the role of the unconscious in motivating human actions. The second perspective is based on the concept of enduring traits. Rather than probing for hidden motives, **trait theories** hold that human personality can be described in terms of observable, measurable characteristics or traits (aggression, friendliness, emotional stability, and so on). Individual differences in personality are the result of different combinations of traits of varying strengths. The third perspective, the **social cognitive approach,** is based on the principles of learning and information processing. Social cognitive theories focus on the different ways in which individuals interpret events, and how their interpretations shape the ways in which they cope with the problems of everyday life. The fourth perspective, the **humanistic approach,** emphasizes the human potential for growth, creativity, and spontaneity. Those who take this approach reject both the Freudian preoccupation with irrational and sometimes destructive instincts and the social cognitive emphasis on rational interpretation. And finally, the fifth perspective, the **evolutionary/biological approach** focuses on behavior patterns that may result from physiology, genetic inheritance, and adaptive pressures that may have existed in our evolutionary past. As you will see, despite the widely varying emphases of these perspectives, they offer valuable insights into the questions of why people behave as they do and why individuals differ from one another.

Psychoanalytic Theories

Psychoanalytic theories of personality are rooted in the work of Sigmund Freud (see Chapters 1 and 9). Although some of these theories have expanded and modified Freud's concepts, most have two themes in common. First, all are concerned with powerful but largely unconscious motivations believed to exist in every human being. Second, most maintain that human personality is governed by conflict between opposing motives, anxiety over unacceptable motives, and defense mechanisms that develop to prevent the anxiety from becoming too great.

Basic Concepts of Freudian Theory

Freud is rightfully considered the single most important theorist in the field of personality. His ideas have had a profound impact not only on psychology but on twentieth-century art, literature, and philosophy. Some of his concepts, such as the "Freudian slip," are known by people who have never opened a psychology text. Because of his enormous influence, we will discuss his theory in some detail.

The Unconscious

As has been stated elsewhere in this book, one of Freud's most important contributions to psychology was the unconscious—his realization that events we no longer consciously remember may still influence our behavior. The concept of the unconscious was a major breakthrough. Before Freud, psychologists were concerned primarily with people's conscious thoughts and feelings (though some, like Helmholtz, discussed certain aspects of unconscious influences). Freud, however, likened the mind to an enormous iceberg, of which consciousness is only the small exposed tip. The massive structure that lies beneath the surface he compared to the unconscious. To Freud, the unconscious was both a vast reservoir of instinctual drives and a storehouse of all the thoughts and

Freud believed that even seemingly purposeless acts like doodling can provide insight into the hidden world of the unconscious.

wishes that are concealed from conscious awareness because they cause psychological conflict. In fact, he maintained that the unconscious is *the* major motivating force behind human behavior. According to Freud, much of what we say and do is either an effort to find some socially acceptable way of expressing unconscious impulses or an effort to keep those impulses from being expressed.

One provocative aspect of Freud's view is that even seemingly trivial words and actions often have deeper meanings. Accidents, forgetfulness, mislaying of objects, mispronunciations, and attempts at making jokes were to Freud signs of unconscious drives, wishes, and conflicts. The well-known "Freudian slip" is one example of the hidden meaning behind our words and actions. Even the most seemingly purposeless acts—doodling, twirling a button or lock of hair, humming a tune to oneself—had a deeper significance. To Freud, each afforded a glimpse into the dark, murky world of the unconscious.

A number of experiments on subliminal stimulation have demonstrated the existence of unconscious mental activity (Geisler, 1986; Silverman, 1976, 1982). Undergraduates were asked to study a passage presented on a screen. Before the passage appeared, one of several subliminal messages was flashed on the screen too quickly to be registered consciously. In some cases the message was designed to be reassuring (for example, "Mommy and I are one"); in others it was upsetting ("I am losing Mommy"). A group of control subjects were shown an emotionally neutral message ("People are walking"). Subjects who were shown the reassuring message remembered considerably more of the passage they studied than the control subjects and even more than the subjects who were shown the upsetting subliminal message. Evidently the emotionally charged messages influenced subjects' behavior, even though they were not consciously aware of it. Hardaway (1990) reviewed fifty-six studies of the effects of unconscious stimulation using the "Mommy and I are one" phrase. He found that the subliminal effect, though modest, is very real. Studies in many different laboratories, using many different subject samples, have found that the phrase affects subjects' emotional state without their conscious awareness.

Recall the "In Depth" section from Chapter 5, on dissociations between behavior and consciousness. Many of the behaviors discussed in that section could be considered products of the unconscious. In fact, Loftus and Klinger (1992) have concluded that the existence of unconscious processes is now beyond question. What is not known is how sophisticated—Loftus and Klinger use the term *smart*—the unconscious is. Most contemporary theories of personality have incorporated a "dumb" unconscious that influences behavior in the relatively unsophisticated ways discussed in Chapters 5 and 7. Should the unconscious prove to be more sophisticated, most contemporary personality theories would need to be extensively revised. As yet, however, researchers have found virtually no evidence supporting a "smart" unconscious.

Structure of the Human Psyche

Freud divided the human psyche into three separate but interacting elements: the *id*, the *ego*, and the *superego*. As you read about these elements, do not make the mistake of viewing them as three distinct entities, locked in perpetual combat. Freud used these terms to refer to strong psychological forces, not physical locations in the brain. Rather than attempting to study these forces directly, Freud inferred their existence from the ways in which people behave.

Freud described the **id** as a reservoir of psychic energy, arising from the need for food, water, warmth, sexual gratification, avoidance of pain, and so forth. Freud believed that these biological drives power and direct all human behavior. An unconscious force with no link to objective reality, the id seeks one thing only: the discharge of tension arising from biological drives. Its exclusive devotion to gratification—without regard for logic or reason, reality or morality—is called the **pleasure principle.** In short, the id is like a demanding, impulsive, selfish child: it seeks only its own pleasure, has no inhibitions, and cannot abide frustration or deprivation of any kind.

Though the id seeks satisfaction of bodily needs, it has no way of determining which means of doing so are safe and which are dangerous. That task falls to the ego. According to Freud, the **ego** begins to develop soon after birth, but does not become apparent until the age of about six months. Its primary role is to serve as mediator between the id and reality (Freud, 1920/1975, 1932). Unlike the id, most of the ego is conscious. And whereas the id operates according to the pleasure principle, the ego operates according to the **reality principle.** Taking into account past experiences, it seeks the best time to obtain the most pleasure with the least pain or damage to the self. The ego cannot banish the id entirely. Instead, like a patient parent, it seeks to restrain, divert, and protect the id.

In addition to regulating the id's impulses, the ego must also contend with the **superego,** the part of personality that represents the ideals and moral standards of society, as conveyed to the child by his or her parents. The superego is roughly equivalent to what we call a *conscience*. Like the id, the superego is oblivious to reality. It does not consider what is realistic or possible, nor does it distinguish between desires and actions. It constantly commands that sexual and aggressive urges be stifled, and pleasure be postponed, in the pursuit of lofty ideals of moral perfection. It backs these commands with rewards for "good" behavior (feelings of pride and self-esteem) and threats of severe punishment for even thinking of "bad" behavior (feelings of guilt and inferiority). The superego can be a harsh, punitive taskmaster that does not take either the individual's capabilities or the limitations of a situation into account. It is never quite satisfied.

The ego then must perform a delicate balancing act. Somehow it must satisfy both the pleasure-seeking demands of the id and the equally powerful perfection-seeking commands of the superego. You may have seen cartoons in which a character debates whether or not to do something forbidden like stealing a piece of candy, for example. A devil (representing the id) sits on one shoulder, an angel (representing the superego) on the other. The devil whispers, "Take the candy!" while the angel whispers, "Thou shalt not steal." The ego must contend not only with these two opposing forces but with the constraints of reality: perhaps the store manager is watching or a security camera silently records the scene.

Anxiety and Defense Mechanisms

How can the ego balance the conflicting goals of the id and the superego, as well as the constant demands of reality? This question brings us to Freud's ideas about anxiety and defense mechanisms. According to Freud, when the ego is losing its struggle to reconcile the demands of the id, the superego, and reality, a person experiences a state of psychic distress called **anxiety.** Anxiety is the inner struggle that arises when the ego realizes that the expression of an id impulse will lead to some kind of harm, and/or that the superego is making an impossible demand. It serves as an alarm signal alerting the ego to the need to resolve the conflict. To do so, the ego resorts to a **defense mechanism,** a mental strategy that blocks the harmful id impulse while reducing anxiety.

The most basic defense mechanism is **repression,** pushing an unacceptable id impulse back into the unconscious. In effect, the ego is reasoning, "What I don't know—or what I can't remember—can't hurt me." But according to Freud's psychoanalytic theory, the impulse is not in fact forgotten but remains active in the unconscious, influencing the person's thoughts and behavior. Individuals who frequently repress their impulses often report that they are not feeling anxious, when physiological measures clearly indicate they are (their hearts are pounding, their palms sweating, and their muscles tensing). These people are not lying about their feelings; rather they have shut them out of consciousness.

In several recent studies (Davis, 1987; Davis & Schwartz, 1987; Hansen & Hansen, 1988), questionnaires were used to identify potential "repressors" (who rarely report experiencing anxiety or other negative emotions) and "nonrepressors" (who experience high or low levels of anxiety). Subjects were then asked to recall times in their childhood when they felt angry, embarrassed, sad, or afraid. The repressors reported fewer negative emotional memories than the nonrepressors, implying that they had successfully banished many anxiety-provoking experiences from consciousness. On the other hand, perhaps the repressors really *did* experience fewer negative events in childhood than the nonrepressors. Yet in other research (e. g. Davis, 1987), repressors remember fewer negatives than nonrepressors in learning new information about themselves, suggesting that they do indeed deliberately banish some memories from consciousness.

Howard Shevrin and his colleagues have conducted pioneering studies on the role of unconscious processes in repression. Shevrin (1988, 1990) attempted to study unconscious processing as it occurs, by presenting emotionally charged words at levels below those required for conscious detection and recording the brain's electrical activity in response. In these studies, clients with a psychological disorder, usually a phobia, were interviewed by clinicians, who later selected words they believed reflected an unconscious conflict the client was struggling with. For example, an interview with one client suggested that he had long-standing problems with aggressive sexual impulses toward women. Words selected from this client's interview included *beating up* and *screaming.* Shevrin found that when words like these were presented subliminally, they were recognized earlier by the brain than control words with no special meaning. But when they were presented supraliminally—that is, *above* the threshold for consciousness awareness—they were recognized later than control words. These results suggest that there is indeed a selective inhibitory process that screens out threatening stimuli first, as psychodynamic theory predicts.

Repression is both a defense mechanism in its own right and the aim of all other defense mechanisms. For no matter what the specific strategy for coping with anxiety may be, the ultimate aim is to make sure that "forbidden" thoughts and feelings stay out of consciousness. One of the other defense mechanisms Freud identified was **denial,** or the refusal to acknowledge a threat. For example, a student who is afraid that she might not be accepted into medical school might deny that she wants to become a physician, telling herself and others that the

Freudian theory suggests that those who vehemently oppose certain behaviors, like the anti-gay protesters shown here, may be exhibiting reaction formation, *a defense mechanism in which the anxiety-producing impulse or feeling is replaced by its direct opposite.*

only reason she is taking the MCAT is to please her parents. By convincing herself that she does not care, she protects herself from the fear of failure.

Another defense mechanism, **regression,** involves a return to behaviors characteristic of an earlier stage in life. A middle-aged man who is having difficulties with his wife, for example, may resort to taking long afternoon naps on weekends, just as he did as a small child.

In **reaction formation,** still another defense strategy, the anxiety-producing impulse or feeling is replaced by its direct opposite. A person who is strongly attracted to pornography, for instance, may vehemently insist that all sexually explicit material is filthy and disgusting. Thus, many of those who lead crusades against pornography—those who "protest too much"—may in reality be displaying their attraction to it.

Projection is the attribution of one's own objec-tionable impulses to others. A man who has had many extramarital affairs, for example, may accuse his wife of being unfaithful, attributing his own shortcomings to her. Similarly, a woman who is apprehensive about an upcoming marriage may accuse her fiancé of being unwilling to commit.

Displacement is the transfer of unacceptable feelings from their appropriate target to a much "safer" one. A familiar example is the man who is constantly belittled by his boss, and so vents his anger on his secretary, a store clerk, or his children—anyone who is unlikely or unable to retaliate. Thus in some cases wife beating and child abuse may be forms of displaced aggression.

In one type of displacement, **sublimation,** forbidden impulses are redirected toward the pursuit of socially desirable goals. Freud argued in *Civilization and Its Discontents* (1930) that civilized society itself came about through such rechanneling of primitive drives. And in *Leonardo Da Vinci: A Psychosexual Study of Infantile Reminiscence,* Freud suggested that da Vinci's urge to paint Madonnas was a sublimated expression of his longing for reunion with his mother, from whom he had been separated at an early age.

Rationalization, a defense with which we are all familiar, occurs when one attempts to explain failure or shortcoming in nonthreatening ways. The familiar fable in which a bunch of grapes hangs just out of reach of a fox demonstrates rationalization. After several unsuccessful attempts to reach the grapes, the fox gives up, reasoning that the grapes were probably sour anyway. Similarly, a high school student who fails to gain admission to a prestigious university may respond by thinking that the university is overrated.

Defense mechanisms are common and often useful ways of coping with life's unpleasant experiences. When we are in anxiety-arousing situations, they prevent us from making the situation worse by worrying. Short-term use of denial or other defense mechanisms may also be helpful in getting people through an initial crisis period, thus buying them time to formulate a more effective coping strategy (Hamburg & Adams, 1967). For example, one study found that victims of heart attack who denied the severity of their condition were less depressed and anxious, and resumed normal activities more rapidly, than those who were more "realistic" (Stern, Pascale, & McLoone, 1976).

Defense mechanisms become harmful, though, when they are carried to an extreme. Freud saw the

In some cases, Freud believed, forbidden impulses are redirected toward the pursuit of socially desirable goals—a defense mechanism known as sublimation. Freud taught that da Vinci's paintings of the Madonna were a sublimated expression of his longing for reunion with his mother, from whom he had been separated at an early age.

hallmarks of a healthy adulthood as the ability to love and work, to be sociable and productive. When defense mechanisms become the primary way of coping with problems, interfering with abilities, they are counterproductive. For example, a person who constantly projects his or her weaknesses onto others may have difficulty keeping friends. And a person who habitually defends against the fear of failure by practicing denial may miss opportunities for more creative and rewarding work.

Stages of Psychosexual Development

As we saw in Chapters 1 and 9, Freud developed one of the first extensive theories about the influence of early life experiences on the adult personality. He argued that at each stage in a child's life, the drive for pleasure centers around a particular area of the body: first the mouth, then the anus, and finally the genitals. All these id urges Freud loosely labeled "sexual," to emphasize that the earlier strivings for sensual pleasure emanate from the same reservoir of psychic energy as the later striving for genital sex. He believed that adult personality is shaped by the way in which the conflicts between these early sexual urges and the requirements imposed by society (weaning, toilet training, prohibitions against masturbation, and so forth) are resolved. Failure to resolve any of these conflicts can result in a **fixation,** in which the person becomes "stuck" in that particular psychological battle, repeating the conflict in symbolic ways. To understand these ideas let us consider each of Freud's five stages of psychosexual development more fully. Freud believed that during the first year of life—the **oral stage**—a child's sexual pleasure focuses on the mouth. Since sucking is the only way for a baby to obtain food, this activity is an important aspect of the child's life. But Freud argued that to a baby, the significance of sucking goes far beyond the satisfaction of hunger; it is a source of intense pleasure in its own right. Thus babies suck, lick, bite, and chew virtually anything they can get into the mouth. Fixation at the oral stage can occur for a variety of reasons. For example, when babies repeatedly experience anxiety over whether food will be given or withheld, they may learn that they are totally dependent on others—a lesson that may produce a passive, overly dependent, and unenterprising adult.

The next stage of development, the **anal stage,** occurs during the second year of life, when children begin to develop voluntary control over their bowel movements. As a result, they derive great sensual pleasure from holding in and expelling the feces. But no sooner are these pleasures discovered than the demands of toilet training are imposed. According to Freud, toilet training is a crucial event, because it is the first large-scale conflict between the child's id impulses and society's rules. If this conflict is not resolved satisfactorily, fixation may occur. For example, children who undergo strict, punitive toilet training may repress the urge to defecate in a free and enjoyable manner. Repeated repression of the urge may produce an *anal-retentive* personality characterized by a preoccupation with orderliness and neatness in the adult.

The third stage of development, the **phallic stage,** spans the years from about three to five or six. During this time the child's erotic pleasure is focused on

According to Freud, toilet training is a crucial event, because it is the first serious conflict between the child's id impulses and society's dictates.

masturbation—self-manipulation of the genitals. Freud thought of the phallic stage as particularly important to a person's psychological development because it is the period when the *Oedipus conflict* occurs. This conflict, which involves an intense desire to receive the affection of the opposite-sex parent by taking the place of the same-sex parent, Freud saw as explicitly sexual. He argued that "when the little boy shows the most open sexual curiosity about his mother, wants to sleep with her at night, or even attempts physical acts of seduction, the erotic nature of his attachment to her is established without a doubt" (Freud, 1935, p. 342). Plagued by conflict—drawn toward the parent of the opposite sex but fearful of being punished by the jealous same-sex parent—the child fears retribution for these incestuous longings.

The healthiest resolution of this conflict, according to Freud, is for the child to recognize that he or she can never physically possess the opposite-sex parent. So instead, the child will try to become like the person who does enjoy that privilege, striving to adopt the attitudes, behaviors, and moral values of the same-sex parent. This striving to be like the same-sex parent is a form of defense. By becoming like the powerful person who poses a potential threat, the child feels less likely to become the victim of punishment. Freud considered identification with the same-sex parent to be crucial to the development of the child's conscience, or superego.

Following the phallic stage, children move into a fourth stage of psychosexual development called **latency.** From the age of five or six until the onset of puberty, sexual impulses seem to become less important while the child is busy learning a range of social and cognitive skills. Finally, during adolescence, sexual feelings reemerge and the **genital stage,** which focuses on the pleasures of sexual intercourse, begins. Feelings of dependency and Oedipal strivings that were not resolved earlier may resurface during this time. In fact, Freud maintained that the turmoil of adolescence may arise partly from such conflicts. With their successful resolution at this stage, however, a person becomes capable of forming deep and mature love relationships and of assuming a place in the world as a fully independent adult.

Freud considered the ability to form relationships and to be productive—not necessarily happiness—to be the hallmarks of adequate personality development. Mature adults do not live without conflict and anxiety; life constantly provides challenges and threats to which they must adjust. Even if everything goes well during childhood, then, a happy adulthood is not guaranteed. In fact, Freud believed that sometimes the best hope for therapy is to turn a patient's misery into common, everyday unhappiness. Freud would consider only those adults who consistently experience problems with relationships, or who are unable to function in a productive way, to be neurotic. A person who is merely unhappy is not necessarily the victim of abnormal personality development.

Freud's theory of the psycho*sexual* development of personality both shocked and titillated his Victorian contemporaries. His suggestion that innocent young children were capable of powerful sexual thoughts and behaviors was considered perverse. However, such an evaluation of Freudian theory is simplistic. Freud was not attempting to uncover the "sins" of childhood but rather to emphasize that all human beings are born with innate biological drives. Human sexuality, he reasoned, does not suddenly emerge out of nowhere when a person reaches puberty. Erotic impulses are present all through childhood, though they take different forms at different ages. (Contemporary psychologists have also criticized Freud's emphasis on sexuality, but for different reasons, as we will see in the next section.)

Neo-Freudian Theories

In spite of—or perhaps because of—the controversy over his ideas, Freud attracted many followers. People from all over Europe and the United States flocked to Vienna to study with him, ushering in the psychoanalytic movement. Like Freud himself, some of these students were highly creative thinkers. Not surprisingly, many began to expand and modify Freud's original ideas. These theories, derived from Freud's original comcepts, are often referred to as *neo-Freudian.*

Three trends in particular stand out in neo-Freudian thinking. First, neo-Freudians have tended to emphasize the role of the ego and to minimize the importance of the id. Freud viewed the ego merely as the id's dutiful servant, trying to satisfy the id's instincts without neglecting reality or causing the superego remorse. Neo-Freudians saw the ego as an important force in its own right, capable of creativity, rational planning, and the formation of satisfying goals. Second, neo-Freudians have emphasized the importance of social interaction in personality development. Instead of seeing a person's nature as solely the outcome of conflicts over the id's impulses, they saw it as much more the product of a child's relationships with significant others. Finally, these later theorists extended the period of critical developmental stages. While Freud believed that psychosexual development stopped in puberty, some later theorists have argued that personality continues to develop throughout the life span; others have placed greater emphasis on infancy.

Of all the theories derived from orthodox Freudian concepts during Freud's lifetime, the most influential (and the most distressing to Freud) were proposed by two of his closest colleagues, Carl Jung (1875–1961) and Alfred Adler (1870–1937). Jung disagreed with Freud on two important points. First, Jung held that the unconscious holds not only the *individual's* repressed urges and desires (as Freud taught) but the collective memories of the entire human race. The

Devil's Postpile National Monument. Jung believed that the unconcsious contains archetypes—collective memories of the entire human race—the symbols of which recur in myths, art, and even nature.

same symbols, or *archetypes,* Jung argued, recur in myths and fables, religion and art, and dreams, no matter the culture or times that produced them. Second, whereas Freud saw personality development as a process of resolving childhood conflicts, Jung saw personality development as a lifelong process of striving to reconcile opposing urges (such as introversion and extroversion, or "feminine" passivity and "masculine" assertiveness).

Adler's main difference with Freud concerned the primary source of psychic energy. Adler believed that the great motivation in human life is not the striving for satisfaction of sexual urges but rather the striving upward toward "superiority" (Adler, 1930). By superiority Adler did not mean social distinction or prominence; he meant instead an inner quest for self-perfection. All children, he proposed, are born with a deep sense of inferiority because of their small size, physical weakness, and lack of knowledge and power compared to adults. Coining the widely used term **inferiority complex,** Adler (1931) argued that the way parents interact with their children has a crucial effect on the children's ability to overcome their feelings of inferiority, and so achieve competency later in life. Thus, Adler saw personality as being heavily influenced by the quality of early social relationships.

Other psychoanalytic thinkers have elaborated Adler's view of the self as the product of social relationships. Like Freud, psychoanalyst Karen Horney (1885–1952) thought the adult personality is largely shaped by childhood experiences. But like Adler, she focused on social relationships, especially with parents, rather than on the resolution of id-related conflicts (Horney, 1945). In particular, Horney argued, in cases in which parents' behavior toward a child is indifferent, disparaging, and erratic, the child feels helpless and insecure—a feeling Horney called **basic anxiety.** Deep resentment toward the parents, or **basic hostility,** accompanies basic anxiety. This hostility cannot be expressed directly, because the child needs and fears the parents and strongly wants their love. So it is repressed, producing feelings of unworthiness and anxiety.

This childhood conflict causes the disturbed child, and later the neurotic adult, to adopt one of three modes of social interaction: moving toward others, moving against others, or moving away from others. Someone who moves toward others becomes compliant, always anxious to please in order to gain affection and approval. The person who moves against others is attempting to find security through domination. The person who moves away from others is trying to find security by becoming aloof and withdrawing, refusing to allow close relationships. Clearly, all of these self-protective strategies give rise to many interpersonal problems.

Another of Freud's students, Erik H. Erikson, agreed with Freud that a person's basic personality is established in early childhood; however, Erikson maintained that childhood conflicts are primarily psycho*social* rather than psycho*sexual* in origin (see Chapter 10 for a more thorough discussion of this model). For example, Erikson saw the anal stage not as a conflict over the pleasure of holding in or letting go of feces, but as a conflict between cooperating with or distressing parents. For the first time the child can wield power, cooperating with or battling against the parent. The resolution of these early "power struggles," Erikson believed, is critical. If

they are successfully resolved, the child may develop a sense of autonomy; if not, the child will suffer feelings of shame and doubt. Erikson agreed with Freud's concept of "fixation"—that if a conflict is not adequately resolved in one stage of development, elements of that conflict may carry over into later stages. But whereas Freud held that personality is more or less determined in childhood, Erikson held that every stage in life presents new psychosocial challenges, up to and including old age. The challenge of adolescence is to develop an identity (versus role confusion); of young adulthood, to develop intimacy (versus isolation); of middle age, to develop generativity (versus stagnation); and of old age, to develop integrity (versus doubt). Thus Erikson offered a theory of adult development, a subject not found in Freud's writings.

In addition to emphasizing social relationships and lifelong development, many neo-Freudians have forged a new view of the ego. One of these **ego psychologists,** Heinz Hartmann (1939), argued that the ego develops independently of the id with its own autonomous functions. The ego, Hartmann wrote, does not just mediate conflicts between the id and the superego, or between the id and reality. Instead, the ego operates in its own "conflict-free" domain, which includes cognitive processes such as memory, perception, and learning. This view of the ego has brought the psychodynamic perspective closer to the mainstream of contemporary psychology, in which cognitive processes are given a great deal of attention.

A merging of Hartmann's focus on the ego with the emphasis on social relationships can be seen in a modern approach called **object relations theory** (Klein, 1967; Winnicott, 1965). In this phrase, the term *object* refers to the people to whom an infant becomes attached, especially the mother. Object relations theory emphasizes the importance of early attachments to the development of the child's ego, self-image, and later interpersonal relationships. In this view, personality development is the product of a person's striving to relate to others in emotionally satisfying ways.

One influential object relations theorist was Margaret Mahler. Mahler's major contribution was to chart the process by which infants separate themselves psychologically from their mothers—a process she called *separation-individuation* (Mahler, 1968; Mahler, Pine, & Bergman, 1975). Mahler felt that this process would determine the child's psychological future, for the features of the crucial relationship with the mother would be repeated in later intimate relations. Thus, if the mother hurried the separation process or tried to resist it, the child's personality development would be disturbed.

Like Mahler, Heinz Kohut, another contemporary neo-Freudian, was interested primarily in the psychological consequences of early parent-child relations. Kohut proposed that the development of the *self*, or core of the personality, depends on two essential supports: confirmation of the child's sense of vigor and "greatness," and a sense of calmness and control—the feeling that everything will ultimately come out right (Kohut, 1978). Parents encourage these psychological outlooks through their daily behavior. When they acknowledge and praise the child's small successes, or reassure the upset child, they are building the foundations of a strong, self-confident ego. Conversely, when parents fail to provide these supports, personality problems are apt to develop.

Evaluating Psychoanalytic Approaches

Like all controversial ideas, psychoanalytic theories of personality face strong and persuasive criticism. One serious charge is that supporting data have not been collected and analyzed in a rigorous, scientific way. Like Freud, most psychoanalytic theorists have relied almost exclusively on case studies. Because psychoanalytic sessions are private, there is no way of checking what was actually said. The analyst may influence what patients recall by showing more interest in some topics than in others. And in reporting on therapy sessions, the analyst may selectively recall statements that confirmed certain hypotheses and overlook others.

In addition, the sample on which psychoanalytic theory is based is small and atypical—namely, individuals undergoing psychoanalysis. Freud himself reported only twelve cases in detail; most were emotionally disturbed upper-class women. Freud also relied heavily on his own self-analysis. Contemporary theories are also based on atypical samples. Today, most individuals who seek psychoanalysis are usually young or middle-aged, white, above average in intelligence, and relatively affluent. A large proportion of them work in the mental health field. Such a select group cannot buttress a sweeping, universal theory of personality.

A more serious charge is that many Freudian concepts are untestable: they are defined in such a way that they can be neither proved nor disproved. Precisely what behaviors must a little boy engage in to be considered embroiled in an Oedipus conflict? Are signs of strong attachment to the mother enough, or must the boy's words and actions have explicitly sexual overtones? Some of Freud's concepts are defined in ways that allow virtually any behavior to be seen as evidence in their support. If a person acts in a blatantly sexual or aggressive manner, for instance, he or she can be said to be expressing an unbridled id instinct. But if the same person acts in the opposite manner, he or she may also be said to be driven by the id impulse—only this time the impulse is surfacing as a reaction formation. In fact, many different actions can be interpreted as forms of compromise between a particular id impulse and the demands of conscience or reality. Frederick Crews, one of Freud's most outspoken critics, writes:

> Once [Freud] had forsaken laboratory work for the care and understanding of neurotics, [he] neither thought nor acted like a scientist; he sincerely but obtusely mistook his loyalty to materialistic reductionism [a tendency to explain behavior using a relatively small number of simple processes, like repression] for methodological rigor. In fact, it was just the opposite, an inducement to dogmatic persistence in folly.

(Crews, 1996, p. 67)

Finally, Freud's writings show a strong gender bias. According to Freud (1925/1976), when little girls first notice that they lack a penis, they "feel themselves heavily handicapped . . . and envy the boy's possession of it" (p. 327). This discovery, Freud wrote, is the beginning of a long slide into inferiority. Because a girl lacks a large and visible external genital organ, Freud reasoned, she cannot experience as intense an Oedipus conflict as a boy, who often comes to fear that his father will punish his Oedipal longings by cutting off his penis. This terrible dread, called **castration anxiety,** is so powerful that it propels the boy toward identification with his father and the development of a strong superego. Because a girl feels that she has already been castrated, Freud theorized, she has less motivation to identify with her mother and to develop a strong superego. As a result, she feels less pressure to achieve and is less likely to condemn herself for violations of moral standards.

Karen Horney was the first psychoanalyst to publicly oppose Freud's notion of penis envy. In 1926 she argued that Freud, lacking exposure to women in other societies and to women in his own society who did not have serious psychological problems, was in a poor position to know what normal, healthy girls think. According to Horney (1967), it is not girls who see themselves as "castrated" but boys who perceive girls as deficient—in part to compensate for their envy of a female's capacity to give birth. A more general criticism of Freud's treatment of women is that he used males as the standard or prototype of all human personality development. As a result, he not only overlooked female experiences and perspectives, but implied that females should strive to be like males.

Despite these strong criticisms of Freud's thinking, its influence on twentieth-century thought has been profound. Though few contemporary psychologists adhere to a strict interpretation of Freudian theory, psychologists and laypeople alike use the concepts of anxiety, repression, and defense mechanisms. Freud was among the first theorists to recognize the enduring impact of early childhood experiences and the role of unconscious influences on behavior. In addition, psychoanalytic theory offers one of the most detailed and explicit explanations of personality development. Though Freud may not have been a rigorous scientist, he was a keen observer of human behavior. The enormous originality of his thinking, his perseverance in the face of severe criticism, the comprehensiveness of his theory, and even the controversy his work continues to inspire have earned him a place of honor in the history of psychological thought.

Trait Theories

Psychoanalytic theory focuses on the development of personality; trait theory is concerned with the basic *components* of personality. What are the fundamental elements, the building blocks, of personality? An analogy can be drawn between the structure of personality and that of color. The human eye can perceive an almost infinite array of colors. Yet every possible color, from chartreuse to vermilion, is simply a combination of the three primary colors: red, blue, and yellow. Likewise, human beings exhibit an almost unlimited variety of personalities. Yet perhaps each is simply a combination of a few primary personality traits. Discovering what these primary characteristics are is a major objective of trait theory.

A **trait** may be defined as "any relatively endur-

ing way in which one individual differs from another" (Guilford, 1959). This definition highlights three assumptions that underlie trait theory. First, *personality traits are relatively stable over time.* Thus a person who is shy at parties at age twenty is likely still to be shy at parties five, ten, even twenty years later. A good deal of evidence supports this view (Block, 1971; Block & Block, 1979, 1980; Costa & McCrae, 1986; Thomas, Chess, & Birch, 1970). For instance, when James Conley (1985) compared the personality traits of several hundred adults at three different times in their lives, he discovered that extroversion, neuroticism, and impulse control barely changed over a forty-five-year period.

The second assumption that underlies trait theory is that *personality traits are consistent over situations.* A person who is domineering at work is likely to be domineering at home, at parties, in stores, and in other settings. To be sure, certain situations call for behavior that is out of character: even the most sociable, talkative person will be quiet during a funeral service. Nevertheless, trait theorists assume that on average, people will act the same way in many different situations. This view, too, has been supported by research (Epstein, 1983). For example, Nancy Cantor and her colleagues (1985) found that college freshmen used consistent strategies to pursue varied goals, such as getting good grades and making friends. Some decided on a plan and followed through, working hard at their assignments and their social lives; others primed themselves by imagining worst-case scenarios, in class and at parties. But none used different strategies to achieve different goals.

The third assumption underlying trait theory is that regardless of the number of human traits that may ultimately be identified, *individual differences are the result of differences in the strength and combination of traits.* That is, the differences among us are largely a matter of degree. To return to the analogy of color, consider how television reproduces color. Most televisions have only three projector elements (blue, red, and green), yet they can reproduce all the colors in the visible spectrum by altering the *relative* amounts of light produced by the projector elements. Just as three projectors can be mixed to produce any color, so can a small number of traits produce a vast range of distinct personalities.

To some degree, trait theory matches our everyday experience. When we learn that John's hobby is racing motorcycles, we naturally assume that he seeks excitement in other ways and would not enjoy sedentary pastimes like stamp collecting or needlepoint (consistency). We can imagine John racing around the playground on a tricycle as a child (stability). And we are likely to contrast him with our supercautious friend, who will not board a plane until he has checked the weather reports and purchased life insurance (individual differences). Trait theorists have elaborated this commonsense approach to personality into a science.

Allport's Trait Approach

Gordon Allport was a pioneer in trait psychology. He wrote the first textbook on personality, published in 1937, and continued to develop and refine his ideas over almost four decades (Allport, 1961, 1966). Allport believed that the words people use to describe themselves and others provide a window on the human personality. One of his first steps was to comb an unabridged dictionary for words that are used to describe people (Allport & Odbert, 1936); he found almost 18,000! Even after Allport had eliminated words that are used to evaluate a person's character (such as *worthy* or *insignificant*) or to describe a temporary state (for example, *joyous* or *flustered*), 4,000 to 5,000 terms remained. Allport found that when people are asked to characterize an individual, they tend to use the same or similar words, and these words fall into certain general categories such as "honest," "gregarious," and "independent." He called these categories *central traits.*

Allport believed that traits unify and integrate a person's behavior by causing that person to approach different situations with similar goals or plans. A person who is highly competitive, for instance, will view a variety of situations as opportunities to "beat" other people—to show that he or she is superior in strength, intelligence, or talent. Allport acknowledged that situations do influence behavior, but he maintained that the way a person interprets situations depends on his or her inner disposition. Thus a person who is highly competitive will see a political discussion as an opportunity to discredit the other participants, whereas a person who is highly cooperative will see the same discussion as an opportunity to share information and arrive at a consensus. "The same fire that melts the butter hardens the egg," wrote Allport, meaning that different peo-

Tom Cruise and Jonathan Lipnicki in "Jerry Maguire." Much as actors tend to portray their characters with consistency throughout a play or film, people tend to display consistent personality traits across a variety of situations.

ple respond to the same situation in ways that reflect their differing traits.

Allport also believed that two people who possess the same trait often express that trait in different ways. For example, one ambitious person may strive to achieve in the business world; another, to become a social climber; and another, to win a marathon. Allport saw each individual as a unique personality, regardless of the general traits shared with others (see Funder, 1991, for a modern variant of Allport's personality theory). For this reason, he is sometimes referred to as an *idiographic* theorist—that is, a theorist whose primary focus is on the unique, idiosyncratic cluster of traits that distinguishes each person from all others. Allport maintained that individuals can be understood only partially through standardized testing based on group norms. In-depth case studies are necessary to do justice to the uniqueness of each human being.

In contrast to idiographic theorists, *nomothetic* theorists search for general, all-encompassing laws of personality. One such theorist is Raymond Cattell.

Cattell's Research Approach

Raymond Cattell earned a bachelor's degree in chemistry before turning to psychology in his graduate studies. His background in chemistry played an important role in his approach to the study of personality. Cattell firmly believed that psychology could become as exact and rigorous a science as chemistry: that it should be possible to identify the basic elements of personality, classify them in a kind of periodic table, and express the general laws that govern their interaction. In six decades of research, he has never abandoned this conviction. "The clinician [or idiographic theorist]," Cattell (1959) wrote, "has his heart in the right place, but perhaps we might say that he remains a little fuzzy in the head" (p. 45).

Like Allport, Cattell believed that the vocabulary people use to describe themselves and others provides essential clues to the structure of personality. The problem was to identify the few basic or primary traits that underlie the huge array of descriptive adjectives. Cattell found a solution in **factor analysis**, a mathematical technique similar to a correlation (see Chapter 2). In this approach, individuals are given various tests and their responses compared to all other responses. Analysts look for similarities among the responses.

Factor analysis produces "clusters" of related items—items that are correlated with one another but are generally *not* correlated with the items in other clusters. The researcher then examines the items in a single cluster more closely, looking for similarities among them. Suppose, for example, that researchers find that scores on math tests are correlated with grades in chemistry: people who score high on math tests usually (but not always) do well in chemistry, and vice versa. They find that scores are less strongly correlated with history grades and have little relationship to English grades. Grades in English, however, are highly correlated with grades in history. Analyzing these two clusters, researchers might conclude that two distinct underlying factors are at work: mathematical ability and verbal ability. This, in a nutshell, is how Cattell approached personality traits.

Cattell believed that if there are basic elements of personality, he should be able to find them using many different measures. He applied factor analysis to subjective peer ratings (people's descriptions of one another) in order to identify basic underlying traits. Then he used the results to devise questionnaires, which he administered to thousands of people of different ages and backgrounds. Cattell also used several hundred "objective tests" to explore how traits might be expressed. For example, is the tendency to be assertive associated with quick reflexes?

Cattell concluded that personality is composed of sixteen primary or source traits, which he described

TABLE 13-1   *Cattell's Sixteen Personality Traits*

1. Reserved	Outgoing
2. Less intelligent	More intelligent
3. Stable, ego strength	Emotionality/neuroticism
4. Humble	Assertive
5. Sober	Happy-go-lucky
6. Expedient	Conscientious
7. Shy	Venturesome
8. Tough-minded	Tender-minded
9. Trusting	Suspicious
10. Practical	Imaginative
11. Forthright	Shrewd
12. Placid	Apprehensive
13. Conservative	Experimenting
14. Group-dependent	Self-sufficient
15. Undisciplined	Controlled
16. Relaxed	Tense

Pervin, 1987, p. 306. (© 1987. Used by permission of John Wiley & Sons.)

in terms of opposing tendencies (see Table 13-1). Virtually all trait theorists credit Cattell with introducing and refining the quantitative approach to the study of personality. But many feel that his table of personality elements is too complex and includes too many "surface" (as opposed to underlying "source") traits. One such critic is Hans Eysenck.

Eysenck's Dimensions of Personality

Like Cattell, Hans Eysenck relied heavily on standardized tests and statistical tools for assessing and comparing personalities. But Eysenck (1970) concluded that personality can be reduced to just a few essential dimensions. One was *neuroticism versus emotional stability,* the degree to which people have control over their feelings. At one extreme of this dimension is the highly neurotic person—anxious, moody, touchy, restless, quick to fly out of control. At the other extreme is the highly stable person—calm, even-tempered, reliable, almost never falling to pieces. A second major dimension Eysenck called *extroversion versus introversion,* or the extent to which people are socially outgoing or socially withdrawn. At one extreme are those who are active, gregarious, impulsive, and thrill-seeking. At the other, those who are passive, quiet, cautious, and reserved. The third dimension Eysenck called *psychoticism* or, as

	Yes	No
1. Do you usually take the initiative in making new friends?	____	____
2. Do ideas run through your head so that you cannot sleep?	____	____
3. Are you inclined to keep in the background on social occasions?	____	____
4. Are you inclined to be moody?	____	____
5. Do you very much like good food?	____	____
6. When you get annoyed do you need someone friendly to talk to about it?	____	____
7. Do you usually keep "yourself to yourself" except with very close friends?	____	____
8. Do you often make up your mind too late?	____	____

FIGURE 13-1   *Sample items from the Eysenck Personality Inventory. The odd-numbered items measure extroversion versus introversion; the even-numbered items, neuroticism versus emotional stability. (A third dimension, psychoticism, is not represented here.)*

psychologists in the United States put it, "psychopathology": a lack of feeling for others, a tough manner of interacting with them, and a tendency to defy social conventions. Figure 13-1 lists some of the items from a questionnaire Eysenck developed.

Like all personality theorists, Eysenck explored individual differences. Some of these differences, he thought, have a biological basis. Consider extroversion-introversion. Eysenck hypothesized that people who are extroverted have a naturally low level of arousal in their brain. As a result, they seek out stimulating social situations to raise their arousal levels to the optimum. The introvert, in contrast, has a naturally high level of arousal in the brain and is easily overstimulated. So the introvert seeks out situations that minimize social contact, thus preventing overarousal of the sensitive nervous system.

To test these hypotheses, Eysenck and his colleagues compared introverts and extroverts, looking for physiological differences between the two types. They found that introverts take longer to fall asleep and are more sensitive to pain than extroverts, which suggests that their brains are more alert than those of others. They also found that alcohol, which lowers cortical arousal, causes introverts to behave more like extroverts. When *extroverts* take amphetamines, which *increase* cortical arousal, they become more like introverts.

More recent experiments have confirmed and refined Eysenck's biologically based hypothesis. These studies show that introverts and extroverts differ not in their resting or baseline levels of arousal but in their response to stimulation (Stelmack, 1990). They also show striking differences in the tendency toward sensation seeking. As Eysenck suggested, extroverts are more likely to participate in sensation-seeking activities, even when they are children (Patton, 1994; Zuckerman, 1994b). Studies of identical twins add further evidence that Eysenck's speculations may be correct. That is, inherited biological factors do seem to make a major contribution to individual differences in the extroversion-introversion dimension of personality (Eysenck, 1991; Shields, 1976).

The extroversion-introversion dimension has interesting implications for college students. When trying to study, extroverts have been found to prefer more background noise and social opportunities than introverts. They are also inclined to take more study breaks than their introverted peers (Campbell & Hawley, 1982). These differences in study habits may be related to the fact that introverts usually do better in school than extroverts, particularly in higher-level subjects (Pervin, 1984). The introvert's preference for studying in quiet places, with few interruptions, may be more conducive to academic achievement. Introverts also have a tendency to be more thorough and careful than extroverts, which could contribute to their scholastic success (Wilson, 1978). Whatever the causes, extroverts are more likely to drop out of college for academic reasons than introverts.

Emerging Consensus: The "Big Five" Dimensions of Personality

For decades, trait theorists have debated whether personality is composed of a large number of traits (Guilford, 1987, proposed as many as 150) or a small number (Eysenck's 3). In recent years, however, a consensus has emerged (Digman, 1990; McCrae, 1989). Both new research and a reanalysis of older studies indicate that people of different ages, different walks of life, and even different cultures repeatedly and consistently refer to five major dimensions of personality, often called the "Big Five":

- *Extroversion.* Socially active, assertive, outgoing, talkative, fun-loving—the opposite of shy
- *Neuroticism.* Emotionally unstable, anxious, worried, fearful, distressed, irritable, hypersensitive—the opposite of well-adjusted
- *Agreeableness.* Helpful, cooperative, friendly, caring, nurturant—the opposite of hostile and self-centered
- *Conscientiousness.* Achievement-oriented, dependable, responsible, prudent, hardworking, self-controlled—the opposite of impulsive
- *Openness to experience.* Curious, imaginative, creative, original, intellectually adventuresome, flexible—the opposite of rigid

Many psychologists regard the development of this model as a major scientific breakthrough. It provides a framework for understanding and integrating the large body of research on personality traits as well as broad dimensions with which to characterize the major ways in which people differ from one another. Measures of these dimensions have proved both reliable and valid (Digman, 1990). The model has been supported by studies using vastly different experimental techniques and has been found in a number of different cultures. For example, Paunonen and colleagues (1992) discovered similar five-factor personality structures in Canada, Finland, Poland, and Germany, using both standard personality inventories (which rely heavily on verbal self-reports) and nonverbal personality instruments.

Evaluation of Trait Theories

According to Robert McCrae and Paul Costa (1994), two of the most influential contemporary personality theorists, the past two decades of research on personality traits have produced remarkably consistent findings. They have summarized four main points:

1. In general, personality traits change somewhat during development, reaching final adult levels at age thirty. (In fact, personality is relatively stable by age twenty.) After age thirty, changes in personality are minor and subtle.

2. Individual differences in personality are also stable after age thirty, even over intervals as long as thirty years.

3. Long-term stability is seen in all five of the major dimensions of personality.

4. Whatever generalizations that can be made about personality hold for almost everyone, regardless of ethnicity, gender, and intelligence. Those who suffer from dementia and/or some kinds of psychiatric disorders are an important exception to this generalization.

Despite reasonably wide acceptance of trait theory, especially the "Big Five" model, some psychologists remain critical of the approach. Most trait models lack a theory of development; personality is seen as essentially static. Even if one accepts the "Big Five" model, then, important questions remain. Why does an individual develop one set of traits instead of another? Can traits change? Trait theory is largely silent on these questions. Because it does not deal with the issues of development and growth, this approach is the only theory of personality that does not include a strategy for therapy, such as psychoanalysis.

Another criticism of the trait approach is that it relies too heavily on simple mathematical analysis of massive amounts of data (Church, 1994; Church & Burke, 1994). Statistics can create a false impression of objectivity and scientific precision. And factor analysis, the statistical tool most often used to evaluate trait theories, has its drawbacks. While the technique can identify clusters of traits, it does not explain *why* certain traits are related. The *labels* given to dimensions like extroversion and neuroticism are supplied by the researchers, which means they are subject to bias. Furthermore, some kinds of factor analysis are used to confirm preexisting theories. In part, Cattell found sixteen traits, and Eysenck three, because that is what they expected to find. Their expectations, in turn, influence the methods of analysis they chose.

Council (1993) has taken this criticism one step further. He points out that many of the studies on personality—over 60 percent, by his estimate—are based on self-reported questionnaires administered to college students in group settings. Typically, the decision to use students as subjects is not made because researchers are particularly interested in college students but because students are easily accessible and willing to participate. Even ignoring the problem of generalizing from this pool of subjects to the general population (see Chapter 2), Council points out that the very act of completing a personality inventory may influence subjects' later responses—a particularly powerful example of demand characteristics.

Walter Mischel (1968) and others have argued that trait theories greatly exaggerate the consistency of human behavior. Casual observation reveals that on occasion, the most agreeable person may turn disagreeable. Someone who is assertive, even domineering, in the office may be shy and hesitant in social situations. A good deal of research supports this notion of the inconsistency of human nature. For example, in a classic study of honesty (Hartshorne & May, 1928), children were exposed to a range of temptations. Researchers found little correlation in the way an individual child behaved in different situations. A child who lied to save face in an interview might pass up an opportunity to steal money, while a child who cheated on a test might later admit the misdeed. More recently, Mischel and his colleagues (e.g., Shoda, Mischel, & Wright, 1994) have suggested that we may want to see ourselves and others as consistent because consistency in personality allows us to predict what will happen in a given situation. Yet personality traits may not predict what a specific person will do in a specific situation. Rather, they may indicate only an average tendency to behave in certain ways over many situations.

Perhaps the most serious criticism of trait theories is that they are based on circular reasoning. Why does Jane go to so many parties? Because she is extroverted. How do we know she is extroverted? Because she goes to so many parties. Put another way, trait theories tend to confuse description with explanation, a common problem in psychology. The label "extrovert" may be an accurate description, but by itself it does not explain why Jane behaves the way she does.

Social Cognitive Theories

While psychoanalytic and trait theories focus on the stable underlying structure of personality, social cognitive theories emphasize the active, conscious aspects of personality. For social cognitive theorists, the key to our behavior lies in our thoughts—specifically, the way we think about ourselves and our experiences.

Consider how two different men behave at a party. Tom has always been anxious and withdrawn around women, convinced that if they get to know him, they will consider him unattractive and boring. As a result of his outlook, when he is introduced to a woman at a party, he feels shy and uncomfortable. After a few minutes of awkward conversation the woman excuses herself, confirming his belief that he is not attractive. The other man, Larry, is confident and outgoing; he sees an introduction to an attractive woman as an opportunity. Because of his attitude, he is relaxed and friendly when they are introduced. She accepts his invitation to dinner the next night, confirming his belief that he is likable. If she were to decline, Larry would likely believe whatever reason she gave (rather than assuming that she was making a polite excuse). And if she were more direct and said flatly that she was not interested in him, he would likely conclude that there was something wrong with her, not him.

The cognitive approach to personality is rooted in the work of Julian Rotter (1954) and George Kelly (1955), who reasoned that individuals may interpret the same event quite differently based on different memories, beliefs, and expectations. Their personal interpretations of the event affect the way they behave, and the way they behave affects their experience of the event. This pattern of interpretation, behavior, and experience becomes a self-perpetuating loop, so that a person's behavior and personality tend to shape each other. In Chapter 16 we will examine a psychological treatment called *cognitive restructuring,* which attempts to break the vicious circle by modifying patients' expectations and interpretations of events.

The Role of Observational Learning

One form of social cognitive theory stresses **observational learning,** or the process of acquiring complex patterns of behavior by watching other people (see Chapter 6). Through observational learning we acquire cognitive representations of others' behavior

Social cognitive theory stresses observational learning, *the process of acquiring complex patterns of behavior by watching others. These Amish children have come to watch an adult bid at an auction.*

patterns, which may then serve as models for our own behavior. Social cognitive theorists assert that many of our habitual ways of responding—our personality styles—have been influenced by observational learning.

Consider what is being learned in the following incident:

> Jim, age five, found a dead rat, picked it up by the tail, and brought it over to Rita, also age five, waving it in front of her, and evidently hoping to frighten her. Rita showed interest in the rat and wanted to touch it, much to Jim's apparent disappointment. He then took the rat to Dorothy, age seven, who reacted with apparent disgust and fear and ran away from Jim toward Rita, screaming. When Jim pursued Dorothy, Rita also ran away from Jim and the rat and began to scream. Later, when Jim showed up with his rat, Rita ran and showed fear even though Dorothy was not around any more.

(Corsini, 1977, pp. 422–423)

In this encounter, Rita has learned through observation not only overt acts (running and screaming at the sight of a dead rat) but several related cognitions. She seems to have learned that dead animals are dirty and disgusting. From the fact that Dorothy ran to her rather than to a boy for support, she may also have learned that girls, in particular, fear dead animals and, furthermore, that girls should stick together when boys do nasty things. While at first Rita may have imitated Dorothy to win the older girl's approval, she quickly incorporated fear of dead animals into her idea of how girls should behave and began to act on that fear on her own. In short, people do not respond to events in mechanical, passive ways. Instead, they filter events through their own past experiences and develop their expectations accordingly. Thus social cognitive theorists stress that our behavior is shaped not only by the events but by our expectations—including our expectations of reward or ridicule. Rather than being stable, like a personality trait or a Freudian fixation, our expectations are malleable. We continually revise them through observational learning.

According to Albert Bandura (1977a, 1982, 1986), one of the most important products of past experience and observational learning is an estimate of our own capabilities. In Bandura's terms, when people believe they are capable of dealing effectively with a situation, they possess a sense of **self-efficacy.** Self-efficacy is important to personality development because it greatly affects whether or not a person will even try to behave in a certain manner. If a little girl is convinced, for instance, that she cannot touch a dead rat, she is likely to avoid dead animals; such squeamishness may become one of her characteristics. In Chapter 16 we will see how instilling a sense of self-efficacy may help people to overcome a variety of maladaptive behaviors, from acute shyness to irrational fears.

Other Social Cognitive Theories

In recent years social cognitive theorists have turned to the question of how and why expectations (or, more generally, personality styles) are maintained over time. Nancy Cantor (1990) has identified three basic elements of personality that distinguish one individual from another: schemas, tasks, and strategies. **Schemas,** as we have noted, are organized sets of knowledge about particular domains of life, including the self. A schema functions as a personalized cognitive filter, coloring the way we perceive events, what we pay attention to and remember, and how we feel about ourselves and others. For example, a woman with a "shyness schema" will view the slightest misstep in a social situation as a disaster, quickly recalling the many social blunders she has made in the past and perceiving other people as everything she is not—outgoing, charming, totally at ease. Equally important, she will not process the information that no one else has noticed she pronounced a name incorrectly, that other people feel awkward and ill at ease too, and that many times people have chosen to speak to her at parties. Her shyness schema filters out this positive social feedback.

Tasks are the goals we set for ourselves, the ideals for which we strive. Everyone is faced with a wide array of culturally prescribed goals and biologically based demands. From these we choose a small selection that are personally important to us. In so doing we may overlook social realities in favor of dreams, failing to consider "alternative possibilities for the self in the future" (Cantor, 1990, p. 737). For example, a college student may focus exclusively on the task of making friends, neglecting alternative tasks such as getting good grades and maintaining family relationships.

Strategies are the specific techniques or procedures people use to work on their life tasks. Depending on their schemas and tasks and the context in which they find themselves, people might adopt a strategy of looking on the bright side or expecting the worst, of acting helpless or taking risks. These strategies are a combination of thoughts, feelings, and actions—a coordinated program of anticipation, planning, effort, and self-monitoring.

One study of strategies involved the task of making new friends in college (Langston & Cantor, 1989). Most of the students saw making friends as an important task, but only a minority perceived the task as extremely difficult. These "social pessimists" were competent in other areas but harbored extreme self-doubt about their social capabilities. They adopted a self-protective strategy in social situations, taking their cues from other people. For example, instead of seeking other people out, they waited for people to come to them. In getting acquainted they asked questions, but rarely volunteered information about themselves. When they did speak out it was to endorse what other people were saying, not to express themselves. Their other-directed stance may have helped these students to avoid social anxiety, but at a

high cost. The study suggests that the more they looked to others for social guidance, the more inadequate they felt. Always on the alert for rejection, they rarely enjoyed social encounters. Moreover, their self-protective strategy probably cost them friends: people who always "hold back" and "play it safe" are not much fun. In their junior year these students were much more likely than others to express dissatisfaction with their social lives.

Where some social cognitive theorists stress strategies, others emphasize **self-schemas,** or organized sets of knowledge about the self that guide the perception and interpretation of information in social situations. Like other schemas, the self-schema acts as a filter, letting in some information and blocking out other data. In a series of experiments on self-schemas, Hazel Markus (1977) asked subjects to rate themselves on an independent-dependent scale. Then she divided them into three groups: Independents, Dependents, and Aschematics (who did not show a clear tendency one way or the other). Markus found that the Independents were quicker than the Dependents or the Aschematics to recognize words that described independence (*adventurous, self-confident*), wrote more detailed descriptions of past actions that demonstrated independence, predicted more than others that they would behave in a similar manner in future situations, and rejected information suggesting that they were not independent.

More recently, Markus and others have been investigating the notion that each of us has not one but several self-schemas (Markus & Nurius, 1986). These possible selves include the type of person we think we might become, the type of person we would like to become, and the type of person we are afraid of becoming. Markus believes that each of these schemas acts as a framework for interpreting information about the self. In interpreting past events and planning future actions, we consider all our self-schemas, striving toward our ideal selves and away from our undesired selves.

Evaluation of Social Cognitive Theories

In recent years, social cognitive theories have become increasingly popular and influential (see Srull & Wyer, 1994; Wyer & Srull, 1989). Nevertheless, their usefulness as a comprehensive theory of personality is limited. Though social cognitive theorists assume that the ways we think about ourselves (schemas) determine our actions, it is just as plausible to assume the reverse—that behavior determines schemas. In other words, we may form our self-images in the same way we develop images of others: by observing what we do and inferring our general characteristics from specific actions.

Second, social cognitive theory tends to neglect the emotions. It portrays human beings almost as information-processing robots, calculating the best strategy to achieve a given task. Too little attention is paid in this theory to the passionate and spontaneous aspects of human behavior—joy, love, hate, envy, anger, and sorrow.

Third, the social cognitive approach tends to be quite narrow. Whereas other theories of personality seek consistency over a variety of situations, social cognitive theory focuses on responses to specific situations. Why, for example, does John race motorcycles? A social cognitive theorist might answer that he has developed an expectation that the sport will earn him status in the eyes of friends, or that taking risks is part of his self-schema. But these answers do not provide a coherent picture of John as a whole person. Is risk taking central to John's personality? Does he take risks in other situations? How do his behaviors in various settings relate to one another? Social cognitive theorists have not addressed these questions.

Despite these drawbacks, the social cognitive approach has added to the study of personality by focusing on life as it is lived in ordinary, everyday settings. While trait theories place little emphasis on environmental factors, social cognitive theory in general, and Cantor's work in particular, stresses the importance of the environment, emphasizing the problems and tasks of everyday life. The manner in which people attack these problems, their strategies for attaining goals, and the outcomes that are important to them are in effect their personalities.

| Humanistic Theories

The humanistic approach to personality is based on two main assumptions. The first is that because subjective experiences are in many ways unique, we can understand another's personality only by trying to see the world through that person's eyes. The second is that people are free to become what they want—to fulfill themselves—carving out their own destinies and writing their own histories. At the heart of the humanistic approach is a strong belief in self-determination and individual potential.

The humanistic view contrasts sharply with earlier perspectives on personality, especially psychoanalytic theory, which holds that our actions are molded largely by forces beyond our control. We will examine the theories of two highly influential members of the humanistic school, Carl Rogers and Abraham Maslow, as well as the newer psychobiographical approach of a contemporary humanistic theorist, Don McAdams.

Rogers' Theory of the Self

Carl Rogers (1902–1987), a clinical psychologist, developed his theory of personality from observations he made while practicing psychotherapy. Rogers noticed that his *clients* (a term he preferred to *patients*, because it does not imply illness) repeatedly expressed an organized set of perceptions, feelings, and attitudes about themselves, making statements such as "I haven't been acting like myself; it doesn't seem like me" and "I don't have any emotional responses to situations; I'm worried about myself." Such comments suggested to Rogers that the *self*—the body of perceptions we think of as "I" or "me"—is a vital part of human experience. Furthermore, Rogers found that most people are constantly struggling to become their "real" selves. Rogers concluded that the overriding human motivation is a desire to become all that one truly is meant to be—to fulfill one's capabilities and achieve one's total potential. This powerful, lifelong motive Rogers called a striving toward **self-actualization** (Rogers, 1970, 1971).

Rogers believed that self-actualization is often thwarted by a narrow and restricting self-concept. His clients seemed to have learned during childhood that in order to obtain the regard of others, they had to feel and act in ways that distorted or submerged who they really were. In short, to be accepted by parents, relatives, or peers they had to deny certain feelings and inclinations. Rogers saw this denial or distortion of feelings as the result of **conditional positive regard,** by which he meant that love and praise are often withheld until a child conforms to parental or social standards. If a boy dislikes rough-and-tumble play, for instance, he may be admonished not to be a "sissy." Or if he enjoys long, solitary walks in the woods, he may be cautioned not to be a "loner." Contact sports and group activities, though, may be rewarded with smiles and compliments. According to Rogers, children incorporate into the self these so-called **conditions of worth**—strong ideas about which thoughts and behaviors will bring positive regard, and so are desirable and "good." At the same time, they suppress, distort, or deny those feelings and experiences that prevent positive regard, even though they are genuine and would be intrinsically satisfying.

Rogers saw two possible outcomes from these early life experiences. When the conditions of worth a person learns are few and reasonable, the self will usually be flexible enough to allow a wide range of feelings and behaviors. Rogers described such people as **fully functioning:** they are open, undefensive, realistic, creative, and self-determining, and have an underlying confidence in themselves. If conditions of worth are severely restrictive, however, prohibiting many thoughts and actions in which the person would otherwise engage, self-actualization will be blocked. These people are anxious, fearful, defensive, conforming, and unrealistic in the demands they place on themselves. They feel manipulated rather than free.

Like Freud's psychoanalytic theory, Rogers' theory of personality was shaped by those he counseled. Like Freud, Rogers treated people who were experiencing difficulty in their lives. But while Freud believed that psychological problems were produced primarily by internal, largely unconscious conflicts, Rogers was much more optimistic. He believed that those who sought psychotherapy had formed unreasonable conditions of self-worth, and their irrational beliefs were blocking their progress toward self-actualization. He maintained that all humans always have the potential to break free from beliefs and feelings that hamper their growth. Rogers' view has been supported by some research (Epstein, 1979). When college students were asked to describe the life experience that had the most positive impact on their self-concept, many mentioned a situation in which they had at first been *negatively* evaluated by others. Rogers would not have been the least surprised at this paradoxical finding. To him it would have suggested that these students had been oppressed by unreasonable conditions of worth but had managed to assert their true selves in order to function more fully. Thus a young woman whose career choice is greeted negatively by parents and friends may be forced to reconsider her goals and values—an act that eventually strengthens her career commitment, her sense of self-reliance and self-worth.

Though Rogers' humanistic approach has certainly influenced personality theory, it has had an even greater impact in clinical settings. Many psychologists, even those who do not describe themselves as humanistic, have adopted elements of Rogers' psychotherapeutic techniques. We will examine the humanistic approach to therapy in Chapter 16.

Maslow's Self-Actualized Person

Like Carl Rogers, psychologist Abraham Maslow (1908–1970) began with the assumption that people are free to shape their own lives, and they are motivated by a desire to achieve self-actualization. According to Maslow, a self-actualized person finds fulfillment in doing the best that he or she is capable of, not in competition with others but in an effort to become "the best me I can be" (Maslow, 1971a, 1971b). Maslow criticized traditional psychoanalysts for their pessimistic conceptions of the human personality. Why cannot psychology, he asked, take account of gaiety, exuberance, love, and expressive art to the same extent as misery, conflict, shame, hostility, and habit (Maslow, 1966, 1968)? Maslow deliberately set out to create what he called a "third force" in psychology—one that would offer an appealing alternative to psychoanalysis and cognitive theory.

One of Maslow's key concepts is the **hierarchy of needs,** illustrated in Figure 13-2. Maslow believed that all humans face a series of needs, and that basic needs must be met before a person can fulfill higher-level needs. At the bottom of Maslow's hierarchy are **fundamental needs:** those associated with physical needs, such as thirst and hunger, and those related to obtaining a safe and secure environment. Above these, Maslow placed a set of **psychological needs,** including both the need to develop a sense of belonging and the need to achieve competence, recognition, and high self-esteem. Once all the fundamental and psychological needs have been met, a person can begin to fulfill the need for self-actualization. That includes not just excelling at one's lifework, but devoting oneself to higher social goals, such as bringing about justice or stopping cruelty and exploitation. According to Maslow, the self-actualized person does not seek fame and glory, or universal love and approval. Instead, he or she finds peace and contentment in the inner satisfaction that comes with being the best that one can be (Landsman, 1974; Maslow, 1971a).

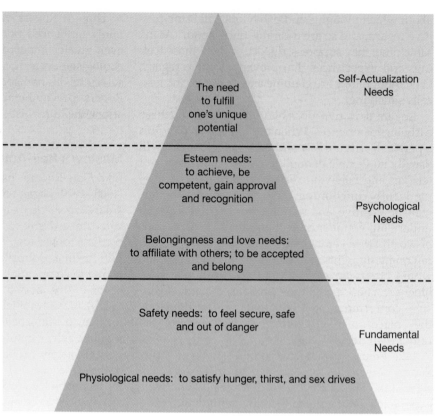

FIGURE 13-2 Maslow's hierarchy of needs. According to Maslow, fundamental needs must be satisfied before psychological needs can be addressed. Only after other needs are met can a person strive toward self-actualization. (Eysenck, 1970.)

Self-Actualization Needs

The need to fulfill one's unique potential

Esteem needs: to achieve, be competent, gain approval and recognition

Psychological Needs

Belongingness and love needs: to affiliate with others; to be accepted and belong

Safety needs: to feel secure, safe and out of danger

Fundamental Needs

Physiological needs: to satisfy hunger, thirst, and sex drives

Unlike Rogers and many other personality theorists, Maslow derived his concepts of personality largely from his studies of healthy, creative people who made full use of their talents and capabilities. They included some historical figures—Abraham Lincoln, Henry David Thoreau, Ludwig van Beethoven, Eleanor Roosevelt, and Albert Einstein—as well as some of Maslow's own friends (Maslow, 1954). Table 13-2 lists the distinguishing personality traits of these people.

Maslow's critics have noted that some self-actualized people do not seem to have fulfilled their needs in the hierarchical sequence Maslow predicted. Many writers and artists, for example, have created their masterpieces despite miserable childhoods, insecurity, social rejection, and poverty. To Maslow, however, these people are the exceptions who prove just how strong the drive toward self-fulfillment can be.

McAdams' Theory of Psychobiography

Don McAdams' (1988a, 1988b) theory of psychobiography combines elements of humanistic theory with concepts adapted from Erikson's theory of psy-

chosocial development. To McAdams, the key issue in the study of personality is *identity*. He argues that individuals construct their own identities through the stories they tell about themselves. "[T]he main thesis of my work," McAdams (1988b) writes, "[is]: *Identity is a life story*—an internalized narrative integration of past, present, and anticipated future which provides lives with a sense of unity and purpose." In other words, people try to make sense of their lives by envisioning them as narratives with key scenes and a clear plot that leads to an appropriate ending. Thus, rather than self-actualization, McAdams proposes that all human beings have what might be called a *drive for self-coherence*.

According to McAdams, the construction of a life story begins in adolescence, when the young person asks, " Who was I? Who am I now? Who will I become in the future?" Adolescents answer these questions by selectively remembering (or even rewriting) scenes from their past in order to explain how they became the people they are. But the adolescent's life story is often grandiose, a personal fable that depicts the teenager as totally unique (Elkind, 1981). In young adulthood the life story becomes both more

Former President Jimmy Carter, shown here working for the charitable organization Habitat for Humanity, exemplifies Maslow's self-actualized person: one who finds fulfillment in doing the best he or she is capable of, in a noncompetitive way.

realistic and more complex. The young adult begins to realize that his or her story contains a number of distinct characters who are roughly equivalent to what Markus called "possible selves." One of the tasks of young adulthood is to reconcile these different selves and arrive at a more integrated self-image. Another is to reconcile the conflicting drives for love (intimacy, communion, cooperation, merger) and glory (power, mastery, control, and separation). In middle adulthood, people become aware of their mortality. This awareness calls up feelings of what Erikson called "generativity": a desire to leave a legacy to future generations—to invest in people, relationships, and work that will outlive the self. Thus at each of these stages the life story is revised and rewritten to meet current needs.

McAdams argues that if identity is a life story, then identities (or personalities) can be analyzed in much the same way as works of literature. The per-

sonality theorist's job, then, is to collect autobiographies; to analyze these in terms of their themes, settings, scenes, characters, and plot; and to classify or catalog them. Ultimately, it is to discover how one individual's life story is at once like all other stories, like some other stories, and like no other story (Kluckhohn & Murray, 1953).

Recently, psychologists in very different fields have stressed the importance of life stories. Developmental psychologist Kathryn Nelson (1993), for example, considers the ability to describe one's life in narrative form a precondition to the development of autobiographical memory. According to Nelson, childhood amnesia occurs partly because young children lack this ability (see Chapters 7 and 9). David Pillemer, a contemporary memory researcher, also stresses the importance of narratives, suggesting that distortions in autobiographical memory (specifically, in flashbulb memories) result from the tendency to reinterpret personal memories so that they "make sense" (Pillemer, 1991). While neither Nelson nor Pillemer discusses the direct effects of autobiography on personality, their work underscores the powerful human tendency to understand our lives as narrative.

Evaluation of the Humanistic Approach

The humanistic approach has attracted many followers—and many critics. One common complaint is that humanistic theories are oversimplified: all human behavior is explained in terms of a single overriding principle—self-actualization, self-fulfillment, or identity. Humanistic theorists do not attempt to explain where such drives come from; they simply assume that they exist. Nor do they deal with the possibility that people vary in their need for self-actualization. The drive for self-fulfillment may explain some aspects of personality and behavior, but surely not all of them.

Another common criticism is that humanistic theories are unscientific. Maslow, for example, first identified individuals he considered to be self-actualized, then searched for those characteristics they had in common. While that approach can identify personality traits that are *correlated* with self-actualization, it cannot determine the cause of self-actualization. Had Maslow gone on to test whether the presence of certain characteristics predicted that an individual would become self-actualized—which he did not do—his conclusions might be considered scientifically valid. Carl Rogers did record his therapeutic

| TABLE 13-2   *Characteristics of Self-Actualized Persons*

They are realistically oriented.

They identify with humankind.

They accept themselves, other people, and the natural world for what they are.

Their intimate relationships with a few specially loved people tend to be profound and deeply emotional rather than superficial.

They have a great deal of spontaneity.

They are problem-centered rather than self-centered.

Their values and attitudes are democratic.

They have an air of detachment and a need for privacy.

They do not confuse means with ends.

They are autonomous and independent.

Their sense of humor is philosophical rather than stereotyped.

They have a great fund of creativeness.

Their appreciation of people and things is fresh rather than hostile.

Most of them have had profound mystical or spiritual experiences, although not necessarily religious in character.

They resist conformity to the culture.

They transcend the environment rather than just cope with it.

Source: Maslow, 1954.

sessions and submit the records to quantitative analysis, but his explanations of the results were difficult to prove or disprove, as he himself admitted (Rogers, 1985). For example, Rogers never offered a clear definition of a fully functioning person. In fact, he maintained that behaviors that constitute progress and maturity for one person might indicate stagnation and immaturity for another. McAdams, of course, walks a fine line between scientific analysis and literary criticism.

Furthermore, neither Rogers nor Maslow offered an explicit description of personality development. Are there predictable changes in the way people think, act, and feel over the course of their lives? Is there a pattern of change that can be charted and analyzed? Rogers and Maslow did not say. McAdams, however, has begun to repair this hiatus in the theory by adapting and refining concepts from Erikson's theory of psychosocial development.

Finally, the humanistic approach has been widely criticized as romantic and naive. To many, the theory presents an idealized picture of human nature, focusing on its positive, rational, and caring side and the potential for growth while ignoring its negative, irrational, and aggressive side and the potential for self-destruction. The humanistic belief that one can apply the scientific method to subjective experience strikes others as unrealistic.

And though humanistic theory assigns great importance to the *possibility* of change, past behavior, as Recurring Theme 1 states, is an excellent predictor of future behavior. The fact is that profound changes in personality are the exception, not the rule.

 **THEME** The Best Predictor of Future Behavior Is Past Behavior

The primary appeal of the humanistic approach is its recognition of human freedom and creativity, concepts that are conspicuously lacking in other theories—particularly the psychoanalytic approach, with its emphasis on the darker side of human nature. Both Rogers and Maslow questioned Freud's notion that adaptation to the demands of society is necessary to healthy development. From their viewpoint, excessive adaptation produces a conforming, unimaginative, inhibited, and unfulfilled personality. Although some degree of accommodation is essential, these theorists stressed the importance of transcending—going beyond—social conventions. Likewise, McAdams questioned the mechanical aspects of the social cognitive approach, arguing that people's schemas are closer to literature and mythology than to computer programs. These are important additions to the study of personality.

Biological Approaches

In the second century A.D., the Roman physician Galen proposed that personality is determined by the relative amounts of certain fluids in the body. Galen held that there were four main bodily fluids, or *humors* (phlegm, black bile, blood, and yellow bile), directly related to four main personality characteristics (phlegmatic, melancholic, sanguine, and choleric). For example, an excess of phlegm produced a phlegmatic or apathetic character, one lacking in emotion. An excess of black bile produced a melancholic character—generally sad and anxious. Galen thought he could change an individual's personality by correcting the imbalance in bodily fluids through a bathing and dietary regimen. Although few people today believe Galen's theory, it is noteworthy as one of the first truly biological theories of personality.

Modern scientists have developed sophisticated theoretical models and precise research techniques for evaluating the relationship between biology and personality (Buss, 1990, 1991; Nisbett, 1991). Biological views of personality can be divided into three basic categories: evolutionary, behavioral genetic, and psychophysiological approaches.

The Evolutionary Approach

At least since Freud, personality theorists have been concerned with defining human nature—with identifying the core human motives and basic psychological mechanisms found in all (or most) members of our species (Buss, 1990). Thus Freud proposed that human behavior is motivated by two basic instincts, sex and aggression; that the human psyche is divided into three parts, the id, the ego, and the superego; and that all human beings go through the same stages of psychosexual development—the oral, anal, phallic, latency, and genital phases. Likewise, Maslow argued that human behavior is driven by the need to fill basic biological needs and ultimately to achieve self-actualization. And contemporary trait theorists have identified five basic elements of the personality.

From an evolutionary perspective, these attempts at pinning down human nature are largely speculative. Psychologists who have adopted an evolutionary perspective argue that to understand the human mind, one must consider the adaptive tasks human beings faced over the eons. In Chapter 3 we discussed the evolution of the structures and functions of the brain. Recall that Lieberman (1991) referred to the brain as "miserly opportunistic," meaning that newer brain structures merely *add to, rather than replace,* existing ones. The same principle applies to personality traits. That is, we cannot evaluate traits solely on their usefulness to modern society; rather, we must examine their adaptive value over time. In this view, human nature consists of behavioral strategies that evolved among our ancient ancestors in response to the twin problems of survival and reproduction.

Evolutionary theorists measure adaptation in terms of "reproductive success." Individuals who possess traits that give them an advantage in acquiring resources, ensuring their own safety, and attracting mates can produce more offspring than individuals who do not possess those traits. Their offspring inherit those traits and so enjoy greater reproductive success in the next generation. Thus their adaptive traits are passed on to future generations. Just as our upright human posture and opposable thumbs are the product of natural selection, so too are our behavioral tendencies.

Evolutionary approaches to personality are often misconstrued as postulating human "instincts"—rigid behavioral tendencies that are uninfluenced by the environment. As DeKay and Buss (1992) point out, that is simply untrue; current theories recognize that evolutionary factors may influence behavior at different levels. At one level, the *historical context,* humans faced the pressure of natural selection over thousand of generations. In modern society, for instance, a violent and explosive temper is considered maladaptive; those prone to violent outbursts are likely to find themselves in legal difficulties. However, the same tendency may have been advantageous to our ancestors, allowing them greater access to resources like food and increasing their chance of reproducing.

At another level, the *ontogenetic context,* developmental experiences may predispose individuals to certain kinds of behavior. For example, Buss (1991) points out that the presence or absence of a father during childhood appears to influence a child's later

Recent research has shown that children who are raised with a father are more likely to engage in monogamous sexual relationships later in life.

reproductive behavior. Children who are raised without a father tend to be more promiscuous, while those who are raised with a father are more likely to engage in monogamous sexual relationships. (See Buss, 1991, for a thorough discussion of this complex argument.) In this case, evolutionary tendencies do not prescribe certain behaviors; rather, they confer an increased ability to react to certain aspects of the environment. Genetic predispositions to diseases like schizophrenia or alcoholism may operate in this way. Though a child of an alcoholic will not necessarily become an alcoholic, her genetic history makes her more vulnerable to the addictive properties of alcohol *under certain environmental conditions.*

Finally, evolutionary psychologists recognize the ability of *immediate situational inputs* to modify behavior. Just as a callous will form if skin is subjected to repeated irritation, so some adaptive psychological mechanisms will be activated if the environment presents certain repeated cues. For example, males and females respond differently to jealousy-provoking situations, such as threats to monogamy. According to DeKay and Buss (1992), the two sexes respond differently because each faces different potential threats. Males face the problem of paternal uncertainty: in most cases, they cannot be *certain* they are the fathers of children born to their partners. Females, on the other hand, face the risks of reduced commitment from their partners: the loss of important resources like protection or food and water. Based on this reasoning, signs of a partner's sexual infidelity should

produce jealousy in males because the infidelity increases the likelihood of an illegitimate child. Jealousy in females would more likely be triggered by signs of "emotional" infidelity in a partner, because in itself a male's sexual infidelity does not directly threaten a child's well-being.

To test this hypothesis, DeKay and Buss presented males and females with the following question:

> What would upset or distress you more: (a) imagining your mate having sexual intercourse with someone else, or (b) imagining your mate forming a deep emotional attachment to someone else?
>
> (DeKay & Buss, 1992, p. 188).

Eighty-five percent of the women in the study said they would be more upset by the second thought, while 60 percent of the males said they found the first thought more distressing. Physiological measures (e.g., increased heart rate) confirmed these self-reports.

The Behavioral Genetic Approach

We have seen that a theory of personality must explain the stability of personality throughout the life span; the consistency of personality traits in many different situations; and the tremendous individual differences in personality. Not surprisingly, some psychologists have looked for genetic determinants of these phenomena. Genetic factors would remain constant throughout a person's life, of course, and would persist in many different situations. And variability, as we saw in Chapter 1, is a fundamental Darwinian principle. Therefore, genetics could—at least in principle—address all three of these principles of personality development.

Using techniques such as those described in Chapter 2, behavioral geneticists have provided evidence that many personality traits do indeed have strong genetic influences. While the evolutionary approach focuses on the universal aspects of human behavior, the behavioral genetic approach seeks to explain individual variations. To answer the question, "Where does personality come from?" behavioral geneticists must examine three possible sources of variation: genetic contributions (the traits or dispositions individuals inherit from their parents); shared environmental influences (the parents, schools, neighborhood, and other environmental influences siblings share), and nonshared influences (those environmental influences that are unique to the individual, such as a childhood illness or friends).

Researchers have found strong genetic components for most personality traits (Bouchard & McGue, 1990; Bouchard et al., 1990; Plomin, DeFries, & McClearn, 1990). The Big Five factors, for example, usually display heritabilities between 30 and 60 percent (Zuckerman, 1995). (Recall that heritability scores provide an estimate of the proportion of the difference between subjects that can be attributed to genetic factors.) Though these estimates are quite high, they still indicate that between 40 and 70 percent of personality differences are attributable to factors *other* than genetics. Thus current behavioral genetic research suggests that personality results from the combination of, or the interaction of, those traits individuals inherit from their parents and their unique life histories.

Like the findings of evolutionary psychology, those of behavioral genetics are often misinterpreted as suggesting that humans are automatons—slaves to their genetic endowment. In reality, behavioral geneticists recognize the powerful effects of environment, particularly the interaction between genetic and environmental factors (see Plomin & Neiderhiser, 1992). But genetic factors can also *shape* experiences. For example, someone who is shy and reserved is likely to seek an environment that minimizes social interaction. That environment is in turn likely to reinforce the person's shyness. To paraphrase Sandra Scarr (1992), a leading developmental psychologist, people make their own environments.

Evaluation of Biological Approaches

Most psychologists accept the position that personality differences have some biological basis. After all, even newborns display tremendous differences in temperament, and in many ways adult personalities reflect those differences (Kagan & Snidman, 1992). Despite their general acceptance, however, the evolutionary and genetic approaches have received criticism—some of it justified, but some of it derived from incorrect interpretations.

The most substantive criticism of the evolutionary and genetic approaches is that they involve circular reasoning. If a trait or characteristic is found in all or most people, it must be adaptive. How do we know it is adaptive? Because it is widespread. Indeed, much evolutionary theorizing simply fills in the gaps in this circle. Because some evidence for natural selection lies in the very distant past, proving or disproving evolutionary explanations of personality traits is all but impossible.

Evolutionary and genetic explanations have also been criticized because they minimize the role of the environment and because they seem to propose a type of fatalistic determinism. While these criticisms may have been valid in the past, they certainly are not true of modern evolutionary and genetic theories. Because they are so frequently heard, however, we will look more closely at them.

On the surface, both evolutionary and genetic theories of personality appear to stress the importance of genetic factors at the expense of environmental factors. Critics have correctly pointed out that environmental factors account for between 40 and 70 percent of the variability in behavior—often more than genetic factors. Does this mean that behavioral geneticists are ignoring powerful environmental influences? Absolutely not, according to Plomin and Neiderhiser (1992). Modern genetics theorists acknowledge the importance of environment, especially the *interaction* between genetics and environment, which they call "context." However, as Plomin and Neiderhiser point out, one's genetic predispositions help *shape* the environment: "Genetic influence seems most likely to occur to the extent that individuals actively select, modify, and create the environment they experience" (p. 162).

Finally, critics contend that evolutionary psychology is rigidly deterministic, removing any possibility of "choice" in human behavior: in fact, critics say, it suggests that people should not be held accountable for their actions. A husband who is unfaithful to his wife, for instance, might justify his behavior by saying, "I can't help it. I'm male, and my genes made me do it." This interpretation is *not* consistent with evolutionary psychology, however. Certainly evolutionary and genetic factors *influence* behavior, but with very few exceptions, they do not *determine* it. In almost every case, genetic influences interact with environmental influences.

In sum, most psychologists welcome the "reunion" of biology and psychology. For decades personality and physiological psychologists have gone their separate ways, barely talking to one another. They pursued different questions, employed different research methods, and spoke different technological and conceptual languages. New efforts to bring the two groups together can only be seen as a step forward for the field of psychology as a whole.

Integrating Different Approaches to Personality

Of all the theories of personality we have described, which one is right? In a sense, they all are. The human personality is extremely complex and can therefore be viewed from several different perspectives. Each of the theories covered in this chapter represents a unique perspective on human nature, each with its own strengths and weaknesses. Most psychologists take an eclectic approach to personality, accepting the strong points of each theory—those that seem most useful in understanding, predicting, and explaining human behavior.

The overriding concerns of all personality theorists are, "Why do people behave as they do? Why do individuals differ from one another?" Because of their common interests, personality theorists of all persuasions tend to share several concepts. One is the idea of conflict, first introduced to psychology by Sigmund Freud. According to Freud, conflict is inherent in the human psyche. The best we can hope for is an uneasy balance among competing forces. Although other psychoanalytic theorists have been less pessimistic than Freud was in his views of the inevitability and persistence of conflict, they also have incorporated the concept in their work. Carl

Rogers referred to conflict when he argued that clashes between a person's true inclinations and the values of others can produce denial and distortion of reality.

A second shared concept in personality research is the importance of external influences on thought and behavior. This idea can be seen in the work of Alfred Adler and Karen Horney, who stressed that the social environment has a crucial impact on early childhood development. Carl Rogers recognized the importance of social influences when he argued that a person's self-concept is shaped partly by conditions of worth imposed by others.

Another shared concept, the continuity and consistency of personality, was first emphasized by Freud, who took the extreme view that personality is formed exclusively by the resolution of childhood conflicts and is thus highly resistant to change in adulthood. Trait theorists stress continuity and consistency in their efforts to identify and measure relatively enduring elements of personality. And the striving for consistency plays a key role in McAdams' theory of psychobiography.

Finally, the shared concept of self-fulfillment can be seen in the writings of Alfred Adler, who viewed life as a kind of striving for self-perfection. The concept is developed more fully in the humanistic approaches of Carl Rogers and Abraham Maslow, in which the striving to realize one's potential becomes the overriding human motivation.

In conclusion, though personality theorists often differ sharply in their views, sometimes engaging in heated debate over seemingly irreconcilable ideas, a broader look shows that all touch in different ways on many of the same points. Contemporary psychologists see human personality as an immensely complex subject influenced by a host of factors, yet still susceptible to scientific study (Mischel, 1981). Humans are at once shaped by their past experiences and their present conditions; at the same time, they have an enormous impact on the people and events around them. Sometimes they are driven by motivations that seem to arise from unconscious needs and conflicts. But they are also quite capable of resolving those conflicts creatively and of using their impressive cognitive powers to set their own agendas and to fulfill their own goals.

In Depth

Personality and Health: Are Some People More "Illness-Prone"?

IN MAY 1983, psychologist Logan Wright was told that he would have to undergo coronary bypass surgery. Wright was shocked. In a decade of annual physicals, he had always had good blood-pressure readings and low cholesterol levels. He did not smoke, was not overweight, and led an active life, exercising regularly. "Why me?" Wright asked. As a result of his experience, Wright was drawn into research on the link between personality and health. One of the first health problems he studied was *coronary heart disease* (CHD), among the deadliest of diseases that affect Americans, accounting for over half of all mortalities. Wright knew that people with high blood pressure, high levels of serum cholesterol, and a nicotine habit were six times as likely as others to develop CHD. Even so, those physiological risk factors accounted for only a small proportion (about 14 percent) of heart disease cases. Identifying other risk factors for CHD had become a major goal for medical researchers (Dembroski & Costa, 1987). As a psychologist, Wright had heard of the Type A personality, but he had never given the idea much thought. "Bypass surgery," he later wrote, "has a way of getting one's attention" (Wright, 1988, p. 2).

Initial Studies. In the 1950s two cardiologists, Meyer Friedman and Ray Rosenman, noticed that many of their patients possessed similar personality traits: they were high-powered, ambitious, competitive "workaholics" who seemed unable to slow down and relax. Friedman and Rosenman (1974) defined this **Type A personality** as "an action-emotion complex that can be observed in any person who is aggressively involved in a chronic, incessant struggle to achieve more and more in less and less time, and if required to do so, against the opposing efforts of other things or other persons" (p. 37). Could Type A personality characteristics play a role in CHD?

Rosenman (1978) developed a structured interview procedure to identify the Type A behavior pattern. Subjects were asked twenty-five questions about how they would respond to situations likely to provoke Type A behavior, such as waiting in a long line or working with a slow partner. Interviewers who administered the survey also attempted to elicit Type A behavior from respondents—for example, by speaking slowly and hesitantly. Scores were based both on the subjects' answers and on their behavior during the interview.

Using the results of the Structured Interview, Friedman, Rosenman, and their colleagues divided a group of 3,000 subjects into Type A and Type B groups (**Type B personality** was defined as the absence of Type A traits). They then followed the two groups over eight and a half years (Rosenman et al., 1975). They found that Type A subjects were twice as likely as Type B subjects to develop some form of CHD. The results of this impressive study attracted widespread attention, in both the medical community and the mass media. At a 1978 conference sponsored by the National Heart, Lung, and Blood Institute, a panel of scientists announced that the risks of a Type A personality were equal to or greater than the risks of high blood pressure, high cholesterol levels, or smoking.

A Type A personality is a high-powered, ambitious, competitve workaholic who seems unable to slow down and relax.

Criticisms, Alternatives, and Further Research. No sooner had scientists embraced the link between a Type A personality and CHD than contradictory evidence began to appear. At least seven major studies (reviewed in Dembroski & MacDougall, 1985, and Matthews, 1986) failed to find a significant link between the two. Attempts to create other measures of a Type A personality also failed. Some critics (O'Rourke, et al., 1986; Shekelle et al., 1985) argued that the Type A personality raises the risk of CHD only among middle- and upper-class white men, not among blacks or blue-collar working men, who are all at high risk. Nor did a Type A personality appear to predict CHD among women (Eaker & Castelli, 1988). Others found that the Structured Interview overpredicted the risk for CHD. In a random sample, 70 percent of adult males and 85 to 90 percent of top executives and senior military officers tested positive for Type A personality—many more than could be expected to develop CHD (Dembroski & Costa, 1987).

Gradually a consensus began to build that the original concept of the Type A behavior pattern did not describe a single personality type or a unified syndrome, but rather a cluster of distinct traits, including impatience, workaholism, striving for achievements, and generalized hostility. Researchers now believe that the critical factor that predisposes a Type A personality to health risks is hostility (Booth-Kewley & Friedman, 1987; Friedman, 1992; Miller et al., 1991; Smith, 1992). In this context, *hostility* is defined as a tendency to become angry, irritable, and resentful in response to everyday frustrations, and/or a tendency to be antagonistic, rude, surly, critical, and uncooperative in everyday interactions (Dembroski & Costa, 1987). Much current research indicates that hostility is a major factor in CHD, if not the only predictor (Dembroski & Williams, in press; Wright, 1988).

Indeed, one reason Friedman and Rosenman found a strong correlation between Type A personality and CHD was that their Structured Interview focused on hostility, while other measures gave more weight to other traits, such as the pressure to achieve and involvement in one's work. Specifically, the Structured Interview included three overlapping measures of hostility. One was the content of the subject's response. Subjects scored high in hostility if they admitted to becoming angry in a variety of goal-blocking situations, such as getting stuck behind a slow-moving automobile, waiting to be seated in a restaurant, waiting in line, and waiting for someone who was late. Logan Wright, a self-confessed Type A, argues that time urgency is a major factor in hostility, because people who feel pressed for time become angry when others slow them down. In his view, time urgency is not a symptom of hostility but a frequent cause.

The second measure of hostility included in the Structured Interview was the intensity of the subject's response. Subjects who scored high in hostility reported not just that they became irritated when they had to wait in line, but that they became infuriated. Their interviews were filled with profanity, emotion-laden words like *hate,* and negative generalizations (for example, calling all coworkers *lazy*). These subjects often shouted or hissed their answers rather than speaking in a normal voice.

The third measure of hostility included in the Structured Interview was the subject's style of interaction with the interviewer. Subjects who scored high in hostility tended to be disagreeable and uncooperative. They acted arrogant ("What is that supposed to mean?"), bored ("Aren't we finished yet?"), argumentative ("How would you answer that?"), or condescending (calling a female interviewer "Honey" or "Toots"). Interviews were tape-recorded, and all three measures factored into the overall score.

Patterns and Conclusions. The emerging picture of personality and health is now even more comprehensive than Friedman and Rosenman first envisioned (see Friedman, Hawley, & Tucker, 1994). For example, Friedman has gone beyond risk factors to identify what he calls the "self-healing personality" (Friedman, 1991; Friedman, Hawley, & Tucker, 1994):

> A brief, nontechnical way to describe a self-healing personality is in terms of enthusiasm. Self-healing, emotionally-balanced people are alert, responsive, and energetic, although they may be calm and conscientious. They are curious, secure, and constructive—people one likes to be around. . . . [They are] spontaneous and creative, are good problem solvers, have close relationships to other people, and have a playful sense of humor. . . . [and] they develop a sense of humor that is philosophical rather than hostile.

Friedman, Hawley, & Tucker, 1994, p. 40

Friedman and his colleagues (1994) have drawn

four conclusions regarding the link between personality and health. First, those with chronic illnesses are likely to be depressed and hostile. Second, recovery from life-threatening illness and surgery is to some extent influenced by the psychological makeup of the patient. Third, certain aspects of personality that appear as early as childhood are related to longevity. Finally, the *hostile Type A* personality is related to increased risk for disease. One of the major challenges of the future is to incorporate these psychological "risk factors" into health care.

SUMMARY

1. **Personality** consists of all the relatively stable and distinctive styles of thought, behavior, and emotional responses that characterize a person's adaptations to surrounding circumstances.

2. The **psychoanalytic approach** to personality stresses the importance of childhood experience in shaping the adult personality and focuses on the role of the unconscious in motivating human actions. Central to all psychoanalytic theories are the concepts of conflict between opposing motives, anxiety over unacceptable motives, and defense mechanisms to prevent anxiety from becoming too great.

3. Sigmund Freud, the founder of the psychoanalytic perspective, originated the concept of the unconscious which he considered the motivating force behind all human behavior. Freud saw the human psyche as divided into three separate but interacting elements: the id, the ego, and the superego. The **id**, part of the unconscious, seeks only the satisfaction of bodily needs, and is therefore said to operate on the **pleasure principle**. The **ego**, which serves as a mediator between the id and reality, is largely concerned with personal safety, and thus is said to act according to the **reality principle**. The **superego**, which represents the moral standards of society, is equivalent to what we call the "conscience. "

4. When the demands of the three conflicting forces in the human psyche cannot be met, people experience **anxiety**, and turn to **defense mechanisms** in an attempt to reduce it. One defense mechanism is **repression**—pushing unacceptable id impulses into the unconscious. Others are **denial, regression, reaction formation, projection, displacement,** and **sublimation**.

5. According to Freud, the child goes through five stages of psychosexual development: the **oral, anal, phallic, latency,** and **genital stages**. Each stage is characterized by conflict between the id and society. Presumably, the resolution of these conflicts shapes the adult personality. A person who fails to resolve any of these conflicts may become fixated, locked in a psychological struggle that is expressed symbolically throughout the life span.

6. Important psychoanalytic theorists besides Freud include Carl Jung, Alfred Adler, Karen Horney, Margaret Mahler, and Heinz Kohut. These neo-Freudian psychoanalysts have paid less attention to the id and more to the ego, the seat of creativity, planning, and the formation of self-fulfilling goals. They have also come to see personality development less as the result of conflicts over id impulses and more as the product of a child's relationships with significant others.

7. Another approach to personality is called **trait theory**. A **trait** is any relatively enduring way in which one individual differs from another. Trait theorists focus on these various attributes to explain the consistency in human behavior. One of the earliest trait theorists, Gordon Allport, adopted an idiographic approach, relying heavily on case studies. Raymond Cattell used sophisticated statistical analyses to identify sixteen source traits. Hans Eysenck believed that there were only three major traits, which were rooted in biology and could be tested experimentally. In recent years, trait theorists have agreed on five major personality traits, collective known as the "Big Five" extroversion/introversion, neuroticism/lack of

neuroticism, agreeableness/hostility, conscientiousness/impulsivity, and openness to experience/rigidity.

8. **Social cognitive approaches** to personality hold that differences among individuals are largely the result of differences in the way people think about themselves and others. Some theorists in this school emphasize **observational learning**; others are concerned with how cognitive personality structures are maintained over time. Nancy Cantor identified three cognitive mechanisms involved in the development of personality: **schemas**, **tasks**, and **strategies**. Hazel Markus has investigated **self-schemas** and the concept of possible selves.

9. The **humanistic approach** to personality development stresses human potential and the individual's unique perception of the world. Psychologist Carl Rogers saw each person as being engaged in a lifelong striving for **self-actualization**. Many people are thwarted in that goal, he found, because in order to receive approval from others, they must deny their true selves and conform to others' **conditions of worth.** Psychologist Abraham Maslow proposed a **hierarchy of needs**, with self-actualization at the top of the hierarchy; but more basic needs must be fulfilled before one can realize one's potential. More recently, Don McAdams has proposed that individuals actively construct their identities by "writing" life stories that explain how they got to be who they are.

10. **Biological approaches** to personality are based on the theory that common behavioral patterns may be the result of genetic and evolutionary forces. Thus, personality traits may to some degree be genetically determined. Some personality traits may result from differences in physiological functioning.

11. While psychologists take many different approaches to describing and explaining human personality, all touch on at least some of the following four basic themes: inner conflict, the influence of the environment, continuity and consistency of personality traits, and the drive for self-fulfillment. Most personality psychologists take an eclectic approach, incorporating what they consider to be the strongest points of various theories.

12. The announcement in 1974 that a cluster of traits labeled **Type A personality** places individuals at high risk for coronary heart disease (CHD) was premature. However, ongoing research using a structured interview has shown that one trait, hostility, does predict susceptibility to CHD. Important questions for future research are, "What is the origin of this trait? And how does it damage the cardiovascular system?"

SUGGESTED READINGS

Allen, B. P. (1997). *Personality theories: Development, growth, and diversity* (2nd ed.). Needham Heights, MA: Allyn & Bacon. A good introduction to personality theory.

Buss, D., & Cantor, N. (1989). *Personality psychology: Recent trends and emerging directions.* New York: Springer-Verlag. Not an introductory text but a collection of chapters by active, contemporary personality psychologists, expressing their views of important and emerging issues in personality psychology.

Gay, P. (1989). *Freud: A life for our time.* New York: Anchor Books. A remarkably thorough biography of Sigmund Freud. Contemporary Freudian theory is much easier to comprehend after learning the circumstances of Freud's fascinating and unusual life.

Hjelle, L. A., & Ziegler, D. J. (1992). *Personality theories: Basic assumptions, research and applications* (3rd ed.). New York: McGraw-Hill. An introductory look at personality, with particular attention to the sometimes hidden assumptions of each theoretical viewpoint.

Horney, K. (1973). *Feminine psychology.* Harold Kelman (Ed.). New York: Norton. A paperback edition of the classic discussion of the forces that influence the development and expression of personality in women.

Psychological Assessment and Individual Differences

 Suppose a large international company has been having problems selecting and retaining employees. The company has been hiring applicants on the basis of their educational backgrounds, references from previous employers, and personal interviews. Though these hiring criteria seem reasonable, newly hired employees fail to thrive in their jobs,

and later leave the company. Nor do the hiring criteria identify those new employees who will be successful and those who will not. Many who have good educational backgrounds and gave good interviews later struggle to adjust to their jobs, while others with marginal academic credentials and unimpressive interviews perform well.

To identify those applicants who are most

likely to succeed, the corporation hires several consultants. One provides the following recommendation:

> If [the corporation] were to use only intelligence tests, and select the highest scoring applicant for each job, results would be predictable regardless of the job, and the overall performance from the employees selected would be maximized.

Another consultant makes this recommendation:

> Conventional intelligence tests . . . provide a fairly creditable, although certainly incomplete, prediction of such performance, as well as of performance in job training. But their prediction of *performance on the job* [emphasis added] is weaker, and their prediction of roughly 5% to 10% of the variance of job performance leaves plenty of room for other kinds of predictors.

While the corporation in this example is fictitious, the two "recommendations" are not. The first is taken from an influential—and controversial—article by Malcom Ree and James Earles (1992). Shortly after the article was published, five rebuttals and/or commentaries were published in the same journal. The second "recommendation," which was taken from one of those rebuttals, was written by two widely respected intelligence researchers, Robert Sternberg and Richard Wagner (1993). Two of the five other commentaries supported Sternberg and Wagner's position (Calfee, 1993; McClelland, 1993), while two others supported Ree and Earles' position (Jensen, 1993; Schmidt & Hunter, 1993; see also a follow-up commentary by Ree Earles, 1993).

Which of the two "recommendations" was correct? Does intelligence predict job success? Certainly it does to some extent, but exactly to *what* extent is still being debated. More important, this controversy has implications far beyond the domain of job performance. The *real* debate concerns the nature of intelligence in general: is "intelligence" best understood as a *single* broad factor that influences many different cognitive tasks, or is it a *collection* of different abilities that function more or less independently? We will return to this question later in the chapter.

Americans are among the most extensively tested people in the world (National Academy of Sciences, 1982). In the United States, tests are used in industry, hospitals and clinics, the military, and schools. Mental health professionals use tests to evaluate cases, assess disabilities, diagnose psychological problems, and decide on treatments (Piotrowski & Keller, 1989). In the public schools alone, more than 250 million standardized tests are given each year to measure academic abilities, perceptual and motor skills, emotional and social characteristics, and vocational interests (Bersoff, 1980). Medical schools require you to take the Medical College Admissions Test, law schools the Law School Aptitude Test, and graduate schools the Graduate Record Examinations. Graduates of professional schools must take additional tests to be certified in their fields. Poor performance at any point in this extensive testing process can seriously jeopardize a career.

Psychologists stress both the virtues of tests and their inherent limitations. On the one hand, tests can indicate whether or not someone has mastered a body of information. They can also help to diagnose a less-than-obvious problem, such as identifying a child who is so far ahead of his class that he has lost interest in school. On the other hand, tests must be used with caution. Many written tests place so much emphasis on language ability that some people, such as dyslexics, have difficulty demonstrating what they really know. Tests may also overlook certain factors that are often important to success, such as creativity, motivation, and a willingness to cooperate with others.

At several points in this chapter we will look in more detail at the pros and cons of testing. But first we will consider what is involved in constructing and evaluating a good test: What characteristics must a test have to be an accurate measurement device? We will then turn to some specific types of tests that psychologists have developed, including intelligence, personality, vocational, and job screening tests. Finally, we discuss some of the ethical issues that surround testing.

Constructing and Evaluating Tests

A newspaper ad seeks camp counselors to tutor emotionally disturbed children in math. You are a math major with a minor in psychology, so the job appears to be perfect for you. When you apply, you and other applicants are asked to take two tests, one to assess your knowledge of math and the other your emotional maturity.

Is this a good way to select camp counselors? Is such a procedure fair to the applicants, as well as in the best interest of the children who will be tutored? The answer depends a great deal on how the tests were constructed and evaluated. A good test must be properly standardized, reliable, and valid.

Standardization

The process of **standardization** involves the development of uniform procedures for giving and scoring a test. Ideally, all people who take a test are subject to identical conditions—the same directions, the same materials, the same time limits. If one person were given only fifteen minutes to take a test, while another had half an hour, the administration of the test would not be standardized. Without standardized conditions different scores might reflect only differences in the testing conditions.

Standardization also involves the establishment of **norms**, or standards of performance, for a test. Norms are established by administering the test to a large group of people that is representative of those for whom the test is intended and then determining the distribution of their scores. Subsequent scores are interpreted based on this distribution. It is essential that the group used to establish the norms is representative of all those who will be tested; otherwise test scores may seem misleadingly high or low. For instance, if the test a college sophomore takes to determine her math ability was standardized on a group of junior high school students, her score would probably be deceptively high. Similarly, if an intelligence test was normed on privileged, upper-middle-class youngsters, the IQ achieved by a child from a very poor family might be misleadingly low. To avoid this problem, many tests are developed with separate norms for people of different ages, ethnic backgrounds, and social classes.

Standardizing tests can be a time-consuming and costly process. As a result, some tests (like the ones you may have taken as part of your college application process) are in continuous standardization. Ac-

Almost every student has taken some kind of standardized exam. One important criterion for such tests is that they have predictive validity—that is, that they can be used to predict a student's future performance.

tual scores are determined by performance on a subset of items, not the entire set; the remaining items are used to standardize items for upcoming editions of the test. By comparing performance on the newer items to that on older, more established items, researchers refine the tests, discarding or revising those items that fail to meet representative norms. In tracking performance on these items over a number of years, they can also document rising or declining scores for the nation as a whole.

Reliability

A test is considered **reliable** if it consistently yields the same results. If the same person scores high on a test on one occasion and low on another shortly after, the test is not reliable. Assuming that the trait being tested is relatively stable, wide fluctuations in performance indicate that the score is heavily influenced by factors *other* than the trait being tested.

Researchers have developed several procedures for measuring reliability. In one, known as a **test-retest** procedure, a test is given to the same people twice. If individuals obtain similar scores on each occasion, the test may be considered reliable. One problem with the test-retest procedure is the possibility that on the second administration, subjects will simply recall the answers they gave the first time around. To avoid this problem, the test can be given in two separate but equivalent forms. Or the test items can be randomly divided into two halves, and the scores on the two halves correlated—a procedure called the

split-halves method. If the test is reliable, the correlation coefficient should be about +.90, indicating a strong positive relationship. This measure of reliability is sometimes called **internal consistency.** A test is considered internally consistent if a person responds much the same way to items that measure the same ability.

Of course, few tests are ever totally reliable. People may perform differently on different occasions for any number of reasons. You may feel alert one day and drowsy another, ill one week and healthy the next. These unwanted sources of variation are hard to eliminate. A good test, however, is designed to make sure that nothing about the test itself—how it is given or scored—contributes to inconsistencies in individual performance.

Validity

Measures of reliability assure psychologists that they have established reasonably consistent tests that will not be distorted by influences within their power to control. One other aspect of test evaluation remains to be addressed, however. Does a test really measure what it is supposed to measure? In other words, is it **valid**? In the case of job screening tests, for example, have applicants who have been selected on the basis of those tests done well in the job? A math aptitude test may identify those who are skilled at math rather than those who are skilled at teaching. If so, that test is not valid for screening prospective math tutors.

Validity can be assessed in several ways. One, **criterion validity,** is important for tests of a specific trait or ability. To assess criterion validity, test validators determine the correlation between a score on the test and some other yardstick of the factor the test presumably measures. For example, a psychologist might validate a paper-and-pencil test of depression by comparing scores obtained on that test with the judgments of trained clinicians. Similarly, on-the-job performance might be used to validate the results of a job screening test. The measure against which the test scores are compared is called the *criterion*, hence the term *criterion validity.*

Sometimes an investigator is interested less in whether test scores correlate with currently available criteria than in whether they predict future performance. What types of student are likely to be successful in college? Which job applicants are likely to make an important contribution to the company? If test results can help to answer such questions, the tests are said to have **predictive validity.** Many years of research are required to demonstrate predictive validity. The developers of the Scholastic Aptitude Test (SAT), for example, have invested a great deal of time and effort in establishing that test's predictive validity regarding college grades.

The subject of test validity will come up again in connection with the current controversy over IQ testing. To discuss such matters, however, we must know more about intelligence tests. We will begin by exploring what intelligence is and how it is defined. We will see that a researcher's definition of intelligence greatly affects how it is measured.

Measuring Intelligence

We are all quick to size up others in terms of their intelligence. When you start a new class, for instance, you probably categorize your classmates mentally as smart, not so smart, and somewhere in between. But how, exactly, do you make those assessments? Just what abilities constitute intelligence?

What Is Intelligence?

One group of researchers has tried to define **intelligence** by asking hundreds of people to list the behaviors that characterize it (Sternberg et al., 1981). They found much agreement between the answers of ordinary people and those of psychologists who specialize in the subject. Many of the behaviors

listed fell into two categories: problem-solving abilities ("sees all aspects of a problem," "poses problems in an optimal way," "gets to the heart of problems," "makes good decisions") and verbal abilities ("has a good vocabulary," "reads with high comprehension," "is verbally fluent," "converses easily," "is well read"). The researchers concluded that a definition of intelligence should include both these abilities. Consequently, we may define intelligence as the capacity to acquire and retain knowledge, and to understand concepts and relationships—capacities an intelligent person would use effectively in solving problems and communicating.

But this definition leaves unanswered some important questions about intelligence. For example, how many basic cognitive abilities does the concept of intelligence encompass? Is intelligence more than just problem-solving and verbal ability? Does some single general factor underlie all the cognitive skills? To answer these questions researchers have used a statistical technique called **factor analysis.**

"General Abilities" (g) *Approaches*

Chapter 13 discussed some theories of personality that have been developed through the technique of factor analysis. A similar approach can be taken to the topic of intelligence. Assuming that intelligence has various components that may be referred to as **factors,** researchers try to identify those factors by administering different types of mental tests and correlating the scores. They then determine which groups of scores tend to cluster together. That is, they identify groups of tests on which subjects tend to perform similarly. Next, they make educated guesses on what underlying factors may explain the clusters. For instance, if strong positive correlations exist between scores on tests of vocabulary, sentence completion, and paragraph comprehension, researchers might hypothesize that all three scores reflect the underlying factor of verbal ability.

Different researchers have drawn different conclusions about the factors that may be involved in intelligence. One of the most important and controversial questions involves the very nature of intelligence. Is there one overriding general factor—one measured by every item on an intelligence test? An early proponent of this view was British educational psychologist Charles Spearman (1927), whose factor analyses suggested that scores on a wide variety of mental tests are to some extent related. That is, many people who score high on tests of verbal ability also do fairly well on tests of mathematical reasoning, of spatial-perceptual skills, and so forth. Spearman concluded that a general intelligence factor, which he called the **g factor** (g stands for "general") accounted for the positive correlations. Spearman's influence can be seen in contemporary IQ tests that yield a single score indicative of general intelligence.

Several decades later psychologist Raymond Cattell (1971) proposed that there are actually two g factors, g f (for *fluid intelligence*) and gc (for *crystallized intelligence*). Fluid intelligence includes the ability to think creatively, to reason abstractly, to make inferences from data, and to understand relationships. It can be measured by analogy problems and problems in classification. According to Cattell, fluid intelligence is strongly influenced by heredity—a finding that has been supported by other research (Schaie, 1983, 1989; Schaie et al., 1992). Crystallized intelligence, in contrast, includes what a person learns and retains from experience, so it is strongly influenced by the environment. Tests of vocabulary size and general information can be used to measure crystallized intelligence. Since the tasks on IQ tests demand the use of both fluid and crystallized intelligence, a person's IQ can be said to be affected by both heredity and environment.

In a project known as the Seattle Longitudinal Study, K. Warner Schaie and his colleagues followed a group of about 5,000 adults living in the Seattle area for over four decades. The study—one of the largest, most extensive of its kind—produced results that are generally consistent with Cattell's dichotomy (see Schaie, 1993). Schaie found that fluid intelligence tends to decline at an earlier age than crystallized intelligence (though both show a rapid decline starting in the late seventies) (Schaie, 1988, 1990; see also Horn, 1982). Shimamura and colleagues (1995) found that those who are more "cognitively active" generally displayed smaller age-related declines in cognitive abilities.

Recently, another form of the "g factor" hypothesis has been proposed, based primarily on the work of Arthur Jensen and his colleagues (Jensen, 1992, 1993; Reed & Jensen, 1991, 1992; see also Eysenck, 1987, and Fry & Hale, 1996). Jensen and his associates have shown a strong correlation between reaction time on fairly easy information-processing tasks and traditional measures of g. (Simple reaction tests, such as those requiring a button press in response to

Retired news broadcaster Walter Cronkite testifying before Congress in 1991. While fluid intelligence may peak when in a person's 30s, crystallized intelligence continues to increase throughout the life span.

the onset of a signal, correlate weakly, if at all, with measures of g. Those tasks apparently tap sensorimotor rather than cognitive abilities.) Jensen (1993b) has proposed that this correlation reflects three neurologically based components of intelligence: rate of neural transmission (which he calls "nerve conduction velocity"), coordinated activity among clusters of neurons (called "oscillation"), and the duration of activity in the neural clusters. However, he cautions that his results are based on tests that measure general cognitive factors (g), which do *not* necessarily equal intelligence: "We should not use the overextended word *intelligence* in the present context because correlations between RT [reaction time] and scores on psychometric tests reflect only the tests' g factor, that is, the general factor common to all measures of complex cognitive performance. . . . So we are really talking about RT-g correlation" (Jensen, 1993b, p. 53).

I *Table 14-1   Thurstone's Seven Primary Mental Abilities*

Ability	Measure
Verbal comprehension	Test of vocabulary
Verbal fluency	Test that requires listing in a limited time as many words as possible that start with a given letter
Inductive reasoning	Tests of analogies and number series
Spatial visualization	Tests requiring mental rotation of pictures of objects
Number	Tests of computation and simple mathematical problem solving
Memory	Tests of pictures and word recall
Perceptual speed	Tests that require finding small differences in pictures

Alternatives to g-Factor Approaches

While *g*-factor approaches to intelligence have proved useful in many respects, others who study intelligence have taken very different perspectives. Some have used factor-analytic techniques similar to those just described, but have arrived at a different conclusion: that intelligence is best captured by a *series* of abilities, not a single factor (*g*). This approach derives from the work of American psychologist Louis Thurstone (1938). Other researchers view intelligence in more traditional information-processing terms. This approach is best characterized by the work of contemporary psychologists Robert Sternberg (1985, 1990) and Howard Gardner (1983).

Recall that factor analysis produces clusters of related items, but does not tell researchers why those items are related. Nor does factor analysis always indicate clearly how *many* factors may be involved in a trait. As a result, some researchers believe that a single factor (*g*) model of intelligence is too simplistic. Using scores from fifty-six different cognitive tests, Thurstone (1938) suggested that there are seven major intelligence factors, each of which is relatively independent of the others (see Table 14-1). Thurstone's influence can be seen in modern IQ tests, which produce not one but several scores, each for a different mental ability.

Other researchers have reached similar conclusions. A few have concluded that the seven abilities Thurstone identified are inadequate. After a massive factor analysis, J. P. Guilford (1982) proposed no fewer than 150 separate cognitive abilities. Most researchers who support multifactor models, however, believe that seven are sufficient (Gardner, 1983); some suggest fewer (Gustaffson, 1984; Horn, 1994).

For many years, factor analysis dominated research into human intelligence. But then, as the cognitive perspective gained influence, researchers began to look more closely at how people think and reason. They wanted to know what goes on in the mind when a person is solving a problem or performing some other cognitive task. This subject became the focus of researchers who took an **information-processing view of intelligence.**

One leader in the field, Robert Sternberg (1982, 1985, 1990, 1994; Sternberg & Wagner, 1986), has tried to identify the mental operations that are involved in answering questions on intelligence tests. Chief among them are the operations involved in planning a strategy for answering, monitoring its appropriateness, and evaluating the quality of the solution. Sternberg has found that a good test taker spends more time than a poor one in analyzing and understanding a problem before trying to solve it. This finding contradicts the commonsense assumption that someone who is good at taking tests works quickly. Apparently, correct answers do not just leap into the minds of people who score high on intelligence tests. Sternberg has suggested that psychologists try to develop intelligence tests that measure the mental operations that underlie "intelligent" thinking. Such tests would be quite different from the intelligence tests now in use, all of which are essentially based on the factor-analysis concept of intelligence.

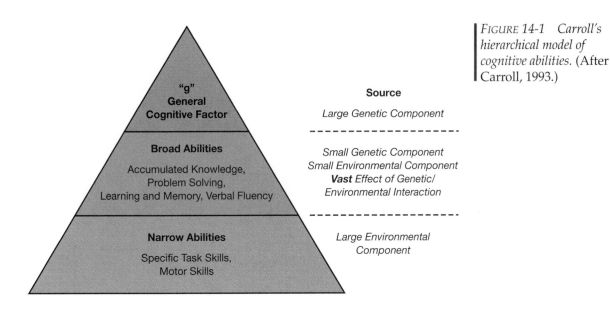

FIGURE 14-1 Carroll's hierarchical model of cognitive abilities. (After Carroll, 1993.)

Reconciliation of Different Views of Intelligence

We have seen several different approaches to intelligence. One emphasizes the importance of a single, largely inherited component; others emphasize environmental, developmental, and educational factors. Which view is correct? The answer, as is so often the case, appears to be that intelligence involves *both* inherited and environmental differences.

One way to combine these seemingly disparate views has been suggested by noted psychologist John B. Carroll (1992, 1993). Carroll, who began his work in this area over fifty years ago, refrains from using the word *intelligence,* preferring instead the term *cognitive abilities.* He recently identified over 450 studies on individual differences in cognitive abilities published over a sixty-year period (1927–1987). Carroll grouped all these observations into a single sample representing over 130,000 people who varied widely in their age, occupation, ability, education, and so forth.

The factor-analytic techniques Carroll used on this combined sample suggest the three-tiered hierarchical model shown in Figure 14-1. The "apex" of the hierarchy is the general factor *g*. The second level in the model includes "broad abilities" like learning and memory, while the final level includes "narrow abilities"—specific skills acquired in response to different environmental demands.

In describing *g*, the factor at the top of the model, Carroll states that it has a substantial genetic component (at least 50 percent). The *g* factor is consistent across tasks and over the life span, and it is resistant to outside influences like training or family environment. The "narrow abilities" at the bottom of the model Carroll sees as being acquired in response to environmental demands. For example, the ability to drive a car with a manual transmission (a "stick shift") would be considered a specific ability. Though individuals no doubt vary widely in this ability, the greatest source of the differences is likely to be *practice* rather than some genetic predisposition.

In a review of Carroll's work, Sternberg (1994) found the second tier in the model, "broad abilities," to be the most interesting. Broad abilities include learning and memory, verbal fluency, perceptual abilities, and fluid and crystallized intelligence. (Note that Carroll treats fluid and crystallized intelligence somewhat differently from Cattell, who believed that genetic influence was stronger in fluid than in crystallized intelligence. Carroll considers genetic influence similar for both.) According to Carroll, broad abilities do have a genetic component, though it is generally weaker and more easily modified than the genetic influence on *g*. While *g* may be largely genetic in origin, and specific abilities largely environmental, "broad abilities" appear to be influenced by the *interaction* of heredity and environment. Thus cognitive abilities with modest genetic influences may develop only in a rich environment. Conversely, a positive genetic influence can be negated by a poor environment.

Researchers have not yet had time to evaluate the significance of Carroll's approach to cognitive abilities. Shortly after his work was published, an-

Environmental differences are important determiners of intellectual behavior. A child raised in the environment shown at left is likely to outperform a child raised in the environment shown at right.

other massive work on intelligence, *The Bell Curve,* by Richard Herrnstein and Charles Murray (1994), was published. Herrnstein and Murray, argued that psychologists have ignored the importance of intelligence in everyday life and have understated the degree to which intelligence is genetically determined. The firestorm of controversy triggered by *The Bell Curve* is the subject of the In Depth segment at the end of this chapter.

The Early History of Intelligence Testing

The idea of intelligence testing originated with the English scientist Francis Galton (1822–1911). The youngest of seven children, Galton was born into a distinguished family descended from the eminent physician and poet Erasmus Darwin (Fancier, 1985); the brilliant naturalist Charles Darwin was his second cousin. Galton's precocious childhood raised academic expectations that he never fulfilled. Puzzled by his lack of distinction at boarding school and later Cambridge, he concluded that he simply lacked the ability to achieve intellectual brilliance. So Galton quit his academic career and became an explorer and geographer. In the course of his travels, he made a study of ethnic diversity in psychological characteristics.

In 1859 Charles Darwin published his theory of evolution in his book *On the Origin of Species.* Although Darwin wrote about the evolution of physical traits, Galton believed that psychological traits (such as intelligence and moral character) were also genetically inherited, and so were capable of evolving. This idea prompted him to take up the cause of

eugenics, an attempt to improve the human species through selective breeding. Since Galton believed that superior ability could be passed from eminent parents to their children, he needed a way to identify young adults who were destined to become eminent. So he tried to devise a test to predict eminence in later life. High-scoring men and women could then be encouraged to marry one another and produce potentially eminent children.

Galton's test consisted of measures of reaction time, sensory acuity, physical energy, and head size, all of which he thought indicated differences in brain efficiency and thus native intelligence. In a London museum he set up a laboratory where he tested thousands of people, carefully recording the results. Galton hoped the government would eventually compile a register (a "golden book of natural nobility") of all the highly intelligent and marriageable people in the country. But the results of Galton's testing were disappointing. High scores failed to correlate with more accepted indicators of intelligence or with actual accomplishments.

Though Galton's testing procedures were flawed and his theory questionable, he established the concept of the intelligence test, an idea that subsequent researchers took further. Alfred Binet (1857–1911), a gifted and versatile French psychologist, was the first to develop a valid intelligence test. Binet's research on the measurement of children's intelligence, the work for which he is best known today, came at the end of a career that included degrees in both law and medicine and the writing of plays, psychological treatises, and books on hypnosis, zoology, and chess (Miller, 1962).

Binet's work departed markedly from prevailing methods of measuring intelligence. Like Galton, most psychologists at the time thought that people with high intelligence were likely to have keen motor and perceptual skills. After all, they reasoned, we come to learn everything we know by moving in and perceiving the world. So they set about testing people's ability to estimate the passage of time, the efficiency of their hand-eye coordination, and their speed at finger tapping. Binet conducted these perceptual-motor tests on his two young daughters; he found that when they paid close attention to the tasks, they could duplicate the performance of adults. He concluded that the tests must not be good measures of adult intellectual abilities. Perhaps intelligence could be assessed by examining the far more complex processes of memory, mental imagery, comprehension, and judgment (Kail & Pellegrino, 1985).

Binet and his assistants spent many hours administering various kinds of tests to a large number of schoolchildren. They found that cognitive tests did in fact work better than tests of motor skills in differentiating students who were successful in the classroom from those who were not. They also found that performance varied partly as a function of age. An average seven-year-old, for instance, would perform just the same as a slow learner who was considerably older, while a very bright seven-year-old would match the performance of an older child of average ability. Binet reasoned that children whose performance surpassed that of others their age must be mentally older—more intelligent—than their peers.

By the early twentieth century, the French educational system had taken a turn that would put Binet's research to use. The Minister of Public Instruction for the Paris schools wanted to develop a test that could differentiate between normally intelligent children and those who required special help. If educators had such information, he reasoned, all children could be educated according to their abilities and needs. Misdiagnosis of subnormal intelligence could also be better avoided—a goal that was very important to Binet. So in 1905, in collaboration with psychiatrist Theodore Simon, Binet introduced the world's first standardized intelligence test, thirty items arranged in order of increasing difficulty.

Originally, Binet defined as *retarded* any child whose score was two years or more below the average for all children of that age. One problem with that definition, however, was that children aged twelve who were two years behind their age group were considered just as retarded as children aged six who were two years behind their peers. Yet intuitively the six-year-olds would seem to be more retarded because the two-year disparity between them and their peers is larger in proportion to the children's total age. A German psychologist, William Stern (1914), suggested a solution: instead of using the absolute difference between mental age and chronological age, testers should use the ratio between the two ages. This idea resulted in the **intelligence quotient,** or **IQ,** which is computed by dividing a child's mental age (the average age of those who obtain that child's score) by the child's chronological age, and multiplying by 100 to eliminate the decimal point. If, for example, a child has a mental age of 12 and a chronological age of 10, his or her IQ would be 12/10 (100), or 120.

Binet did not regard a child's score on his test as a fixed measure of intelligence (Fancier, 1985; Kamin, 1974). For one thing, the construction of the test was subject to error; it was not a perfect measurement device. In addition, Binet believed that few people ever reach the upper limits of their intelligence, so improvement would always be possible through education and experience. But this enlightened and cautious view has not always been shared by the educators who have used Binet's tests.

One of those who considered IQ to be a fixed measure of innate intelligence was Lewis Terman, a professor at Stanford University (Baron, 1985). Terman was responsible for bringing Binet's test to America in a revised form known as the **Stanford-Binet** (Terman, 1916). He made the scoring of the test more exact and added some new items, but in other respects it closely resembled Binet's test. Terman's version, now in its fourth edition, is still widely used today.

An enthusiastic believer in eugenics, Terman regarded his test as particularly useful in diagnosing borderline mental "defectives," so that they could be discouraged from having children and passing on their defective genes. He believed that doing so would eliminate "an enormous amount of crime, pauperism, and industrial inefficiency" (quoted in Kamin, 1974, p. 392). Such views, shared by many other psychologists in the early part of this century, prompted a number of state legislatures to adopt sterilization laws, to prevent the "feeble-minded" from reproducing.

During World War I the U.S. government called on psychologists to administer intelligence tests to almost 2 million army recruits. The tremendous amount of data they obtained encouraged a great many studies. Perhaps the most controversial was conducted by Carl Brigham (1923), who focused on the IQs of immigrant draftees. Because Brigham found that those draftees who had been born in Slavic and Latin countries performed much worse than those born in Scandinavian and English-speaking countries, he concluded that some ethnic groups were intellectually inferior to others. This assumption helped to sway Congress in severely restricting immigration from southern and eastern Europe. Unfortunately, Brigham had not taken into account how long each group of immigrants had lived in America. Those recruits born in southern and eastern Europe were generally more recent arrivals than those born in northern Europe—a fact that surely would have affected their relative performance on an American IQ test. Brigham did not retract his conclusion until 1930, by which time the new immigration act had been in force for six years (Kamin, 1974).

Thus the early years of intelligence testing were filled with incidents in which IQ scores were misinterpreted or misapplied. Six decades later, psychologists are still concerned about the potential abuses of IQ testing, a topic we will return to shortly. First, however, we will look at the tests themselves.

Contemporary Intelligence Tests

Intelligence tests may be given in one of two ways. Some are administered in one-on-one fashion, often by a psychologist or a psychological assistant. Others are given to large groups of people at the same time. While individual tests may be more sensitive measures, they are considerably more expensive to administer than group tests.

Individual Tests

Intelligence tests that are administered individually allow subjects to answer orally and to work on performance tasks (to manipulate objects) that are difficult to administer in groups. Two individual intelligence tests that are widely used today are the current version of the Stanford-Binet test and the intelligence scales developed by David Wechsler.

The Stanford-Binet Test The fourth edition of the Stanford-Binet Intelligence Scale (Thorndike, Hagen, & Sattler, 1985) is designed to assess the intelligence of children and adults aged two to twenty-four. The Stanford-Binet contains a number of subtests, some of verbal ability and some of performance skills, that

Besides tests of verbal ability, the Stanford-Binet has non-verbal components, including a "block-design" test in which subjects are asked to reproduce a geometric pattern with colored blocks.

are grouped together by age level. The performance subtests include activities such as completing a drawing, reproducing a geometric pattern with colored blocks, and assembling an object.

Because the Stanford-Binet was originally designed for school-age children, the development of an adult version created a scoring problem. After early adolescence the pace of improvement on the test items slows. Thus, if the formula of mental age divided by chronological age were to be applied to young adults, their IQs would decrease as they grew older. To solve this problem, researchers assigned a score of 100 to the mean or average performance at any given age. Then they used standard deviation as a yardstick for measuring how much better or worse than average a particular score was. Recall from Chapter 2 that the standard deviation indicates the average extent to which all scores in a given distribution vary from the mean. In the case of intelligence tests like the Stanford-Binet, the standard deviation is about 15. Consequently, a person who scores 1 standard deviation above the mean would receive an intelligence score of 115; someone who scores 1 standard deviation below the mean would receive an intelligence score of 85. Such scores are often referred to as IQs, even though they technically are not quotients. They are more accurately thought of as standard-deviation-from-the-mean scores. Psychologists prefer the term *standard score*.

The Wechsler Scales The most frequently used of the individual intelligence tests are the Wechsler scales. These scales are among the most reliable and

General Information
1. How many wings does a bird have?
2. How many nickels make a dime?
3. What is steam made of?
4. Who wrote "Paradise Lost"?
5. What is pepper?

General Comprehension
1. What should you do if you see someone forget his book when he leaves his seat in a restaurant?
2. What is the advantage of keeping money in a bank?
3. Why is copper often used in electrical wires?

Arithmetic
1. Sam had three pieces of candy and Joe gave him four more. How many pieces of candy did Sam have altogether?
2. Three men divided eighteen golf balls equally among themselves. How many golf balls did each man receive?
3. If two apples cost 15¢, what will be the cost of a dozen apples?

Similarities
1. In what way are a lion and a tiger alike?
2. In what way are a saw and a hammer alike?
3. In what way are an hour and a week alike?
4. In what way are a circle and a triangle alike?

Vocabulary
"What is a puzzle?"
"What does 'addition' mean?"

FIGURE 14-2   *Sample items similar to those of the Wechsler scales. Examples have been drawn from each of the verbal subtests.*

valid tests used in clinical assessment (Parker, Hanson, & Hunsley, 1988). They include the Wechsler Adult Intelligence Scale (WAIS-R); the Wechsler Intelligence Scale for Children (WISC-III), used for ages six to sixteen; and the Wechsler Preschool and Primary Scale of Intelligence (WPPSI-R), used for ages four to six (Wechsler, 1949, 1955, 1967, 1974, 1981, 1989). Each of these tests has been revised and updated; hence the initial *R* in the names.

Like the Stanford-Binet, the Wechsler scales are divided into verbal and performance testing, each with various subtests. Figure 14-2 lists items similar to those on the Wechsler scales.

The performance subtests include picture arrangement (putting pictures in a sequence that tells a story); picture completion (identifying the missing part in a drawing); object assembly (constructing an object from various pieces, much like putting together a jigsaw puzzle); and coding (matching digits with symbols they were previously paired with).

The **Wechsler scales** differ from the Stanford-Binet test in several ways. First, they include more

performance tasks, and so are less biased toward verbal skills than the Stanford-Binet. Second, the Wechsler scales yield separate scores for the various subtests, which are then combined into separate IQs for verbal and performance abilities (the Stanford-Binet yields a single IQ score). The scoring procedure for the WISC-R is summarized in Figure 14-3.

Group Tests   Most group tests of intelligence are paper-and-pencil measures. Because there is no person-to-person interaction, the role of the test administrator is greatly simplified. The convenience and the economy of group tests have led to their use in schools, employment offices, and many other mass testing situations. One of the primary purposes of group tests is to classify large numbers of people. For example, the U.S. military uses group tests to assess the general intelligence and special abilities of its recruits in order to channel them into appropriate jobs.

Despite their convenience, group tests have disadvantages. Putting subjects at ease and maintaining their interest is difficult. Examiners are also unlikely to detect illness, fatigue, anxiety, or other variables

FIGURE 14-3 Sample summary page from the WISC-III manual. The subtests on the scale are listed in the section marked "C." The scaled scores from that section are then added to produce the verbal, performance, and full scale scores in Section D. The scores are also shown graphically: Part E displays the subtest scores, Part F the IQ scores. (D. Wechsler, 1991.)

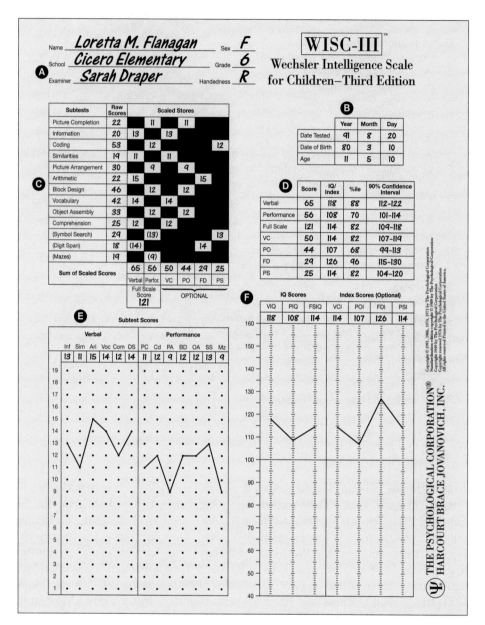

that may hinder test performance. As a result, most experts suggest that when important decisions are being made about people, scores on group tests should be supplemented by individual testing or by information obtained from other sources (Anastasi, 1976; Baumeister, 1987).

College admissions officers generally heed this advice in considering scores on the group test many college-bound students take: the **Scholastic Aptitude Test,** or **SAT.** Although the SAT is designed to measure aptitude for college, not IQ, it does measure

some of the abilities that are often included on IQ tests. Studies show that college admissions staffs consider SAT scores along with several other pieces of information, including high school grades, letters of recommendation, and personal interviews. One survey found that only 2 percent of all colleges considered aptitude scores the most important factor in an admissions choice (Hargadon, 1981).

This finding has not prevented critics from attacking the SAT, however. What is it about the SAT that some people find so objectionable? In a harsh attack,

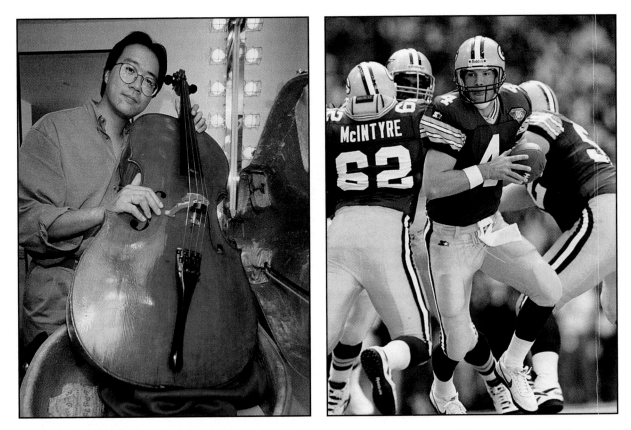

According to the psychologist Howard Gardner, there are seven different types of intelligence, most of which are not gauged by traditional IQ tests. The cellist Yo-Yo Ma (left) would probably score high on Gardner's tests of musical ability, *while the Green Bay Packers quarterback Brett Favre (right) would score high on tests of* bodily ability.

Allan Nairn and his associates (1980), in cooperation with Ralph Nader's consumer advocacy group, charged that the SAT discriminates against minorities. Success on the test, he argued, is more a product of an upper-middle-class background than a reflection of scholastic aptitude. Nairn claimed too that the SAT is not a good predictor of success in college—a criticism that others have raised. One recent study concluded that SAT scores add little or nothing over high school records as the basis for college admissions (Crouse & Trusheim, 1988).

Some knowledgeable statisticians have challenged these highly negative views (Kaplan, 1982; Linn, 1982). The correlation between SAT verbal and math scores and freshman grade-point averages is in the range of +.40, far from insignificant. Moreover, there is little convincing evidence that the SAT is unfairly biased against minorities. The predictive validity of the test is quite consistent across income and ethnic groups (Linn, 1982). In fact, use of the SAT

may actually raise the proportion of low-income students who enter selective colleges, because the test gives those who attend academically inferior high schools the chance to demonstrate superior aptitude compared to more privileged college applicants (ETS, 1980; Kaplan, 1982).

When high school grades and SAT scores are used together to predict performance in college, their combined power surpasses that of either yardstick alone (Kaplan, 1982; Linn, 1982). This finding makes sense. Two methods of measurement, neither of which is perfect, are bound to produce better judgments than one alone. The SAT also provides a way of demonstrating the scholastic potential of those whose high school grades may be misleadingly low.

New Directions in Intelligence Testing

One of today's most prominent researchers in intelligence testing, Howard Gardner, argues that traditional IQ tests tell only part of the story. After

Those who score below 70 on the Stanford-Binet Test, like these men, are classified as mentally retarded. While some are able to live and work independently, most require a sheltered work environment with constant supervision.

observing the different ways intelligence is defined in different cultures, Gardner has suggested that it has seven different components, most of which are not gauged at all by traditional IQ tests (Gardner, 1986; Gardner & Hatch, 1989). Such tests measure, at best, only three components: language ability, mathematical-logical reasoning, and spatial-perceptual skills. The other four components in Gardner's theory are musical ability (the ability to perceive and create rhythmic patterns), bodily ability (the ability possessed by a prima ballerina or a skilled mime), intrapersonal ability (the ability to understand oneself), and interpersonal ability (the ability to understand others). To get a full picture of a person's cognitive capacities, Gardner says, we need to measure all these skills.

Psychologist Robert Sternberg also believes that psychologists must try to broaden what intelligence

tests measure (Sternberg, 1984, 1988). Sternberg lists a number of capacities that are part of what is generally meant by intelligence, but are not included on standard IQ tests. One is the ability to adapt to novel or unexpected situations—quickly finding a way to an important appointment when the car breaks down, for instance (Sternberg & Gastel, 1989). Another is the capacity to generate sudden insights when solving problems, such as suddenly seeing a link between the current problem and one that has been solved before. A third is the ability to learn in context, not just from direct instruction (for example, figuring out the meaning of an unfamiliar word from the sentence in which it is embedded). A fourth is the capacity to perform different tasks at once, as when someone carries on a complicated conversation while continuing to repair a broken toy (Hawkins et al., 1979; Lansman & Hunt, 1980). If these capacities are part of what is generally meant by intelligence, why not include them in IQ tests? Sternberg asks.

Extremes of Human Intelligence

When large numbers of people take IQ tests, their scores form close to normal distributions. That is, when plotted on a line graph, the scores produce the characteristic bell-shaped curve described in Chapter 2. Such a curve is shown in Figure 14-4. Note that about 68 percent of all scores fall somewhere between the mean (100) and 1 standard deviation (15 points) to either side of it. That range of scores, 85 to 115, is generally considered the "normal" range. Moving 1 more standard deviation to either side of the mean encompasses all the scores between 70 and 130. More than 95 percent of a large sample population falls within this range. Most of those who score between 70 and 85 are considered low normal, while most of those who score between 115 and 130 are considered high normal.

Beyond the 70 to 130 range lie the scores of a small number of people of exceptionally low or exceptionally high intelligence. That small fraction of the population is the subject to which we turn next.

The Mentally Retarded

A person whose general intelligence has from childhood been significantly below average, and who consistently has difficulty functioning in everyday settings, is usually classified as **mentally retarded** (Grossman, 1983). Different levels of retardation have traditionally been associated with certain

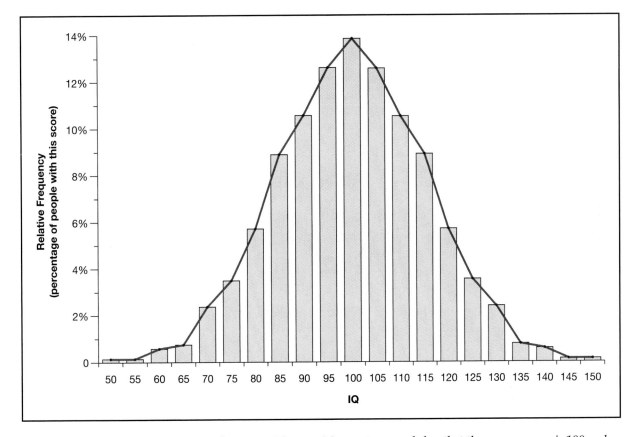

FIGURE 14-4   *Normal distribution of scores on IQ tests. Most tests are scaled so that the average score is 100 and the standard deviation is 15.*

ranges of scores on standardized IQ tests. Those who score between 70 and 50 on the Stanford-Binet have traditionally been classified as *mildly retarded*; those who score between 49 and 35, as *moderately retarded*; those who score between 34 and 20, as *severely retarded*; and those who score below 20, as *profoundly retarded*. These IQ ranges should not be viewed rigidly, however. A person's ability to function in everyday life is important. For instance, children whose test scores suggest moderate retardation, but who show some everyday skills (the ability to communicate, interact socially, and feed, clean, and dress themselves), are more appropriately classified as mildly retarded. Table 14-2 lists the levels of everyday functioning associated with the different levels of mental retardation.

The stigma of being retarded has led educators to plead for greater care in evaluating children who appear to have below-normal intelligence. In the past, children from non-English-speaking families, emo-

tionally disturbed children, and children with hearing and vision problems were sometimes mistakenly classified as retarded on the basis of a single intelligence test poorly chosen or administered. Federal law now prohibits school officials from assigning children to special classes for the mentally retarded on the basis of IQ alone. Children must be tested for normal hearing, vision, and health; and their linguistic and cultural backgrounds must be considered, as well as their ability to function in everyday life. Children should be classified as retarded only if they exhibit both a low IQ and deficiencies in everyday skills, and only if those problems cannot be explained by linguistic or cultural barriers, physical handicaps, emotional disturbances, or ill health.

The Mentally Gifted

In our culture the genius is often expected to be a misfit—someone who has trouble coping in a world beyond test tubes and books, who is eccentric,

TABLE 14-2 *Characteristics of Mentally Retarded Children*

Area of Functioning	Mild	Moderate	Severe and Profound
Self-help skills	Feeds and dresses self and cares for own toilet needs	Has difficulties and requires training but can learn adequate self-help skills	No skills to partial skills, but some can care for personal needs on a limited basis
Speech and communication	Receptive and expressive language is adequate; understands communication	Receptive and expressive language is adequate; has speech problems	Receptive language is limited to good; expressive language is limited to poor
Academics	Optimal learning environment, third to sixth grade	Very few academic skills; first or second grade is maximal	No academic skills
Social skills	Has friends; can learn to adjust quickly	Capable of making friends but has difficulty in many social situations	Not capable of having real friends; no social interactions
Vocational adjustment	Can hold a job; competitive to semicompetitive; primarily unskilled work	Sheltered work environment; usually needs constant supervision	Generally no employment; may be in an activity center; usually needs constant care
Adult living	Usually marries, has children; needs to help during stress	Usually does not marry or have children; dependent	No marriage or children; always dependent on others

Van Osdol & Shane, 1977, p. 68.

socially awkward, or physically frail. But this is, in fact, a false stereotype of the **mentally gifted**.

In the early part of this century, Lewis Terman launched a landmark study of 1,500 gifted children (Terman, 1916). His subjects, aged three to nineteen at the start of the study, all had IQs over 135. As Terman followed their development, his findings disproved most of the common myths about unusually intelligent children (Oden, 1968; Terman & Oden, 1947). Not only were gifted children generally superior to their peers in health, social adjustment, and achievement, but they maintained their relative superiority as they moved through adulthood. They far exceeded persons with average IQs in educational attainment, occupational level, and income, and their adult health and emotional adjustment were well above average. As a group they suffered fewer divorces, fewer cases of alcoholism, less trou-

ble with the law, and even fewer premature deaths than people with lower IQs. Other studies have also indicated that gifted children typically are well-adjusted and have fewer behavior problems than their less gifted peers (Horowitz & O'Brien, 1986).

Do these findings mean that high intelligence is a key to personal happiness and success? Not necessarily. Psychologists note that most of Terman's subjects were nominated for inclusion in the study by their teachers. This selection process could easily have produced a bias in favor of bright children who were especially well-adjusted, socially skilled, and motivated. We have no way of knowing whether other high-IQ children turned out to be equally successful.

Some other factors shared by the high-IQ subjects could also have been responsible for their positive outcomes (McClelland, 1973). For instance, Terman's sample consisted heavily of middle- and upper-middle-class whites, a privileged group. Perhaps the results show largely that the privileged have more opportunities than other people, and so do better in life. Interestingly, the 100 most successful men in the sample (as measured by job status and income) were more likely to have had a professional father with a college education than the 100 least successful men. The most successful men also tended to come from more intellectually stimulating home environments, where initiative and achievement were stressed. Perhaps another critical factor in their success, then, was early encouragement by parents.

Today's rapidly accelerated academic programs for gifted children do not seem to have any negative social or emotional effects (e. g., Fox & Washington, 1985; Stanley, 1983). That is not to say that some very gifted children (with IQs over 180) do not sometimes have adjustment problems. But those problems often spring more from atypical social relations (with parents as well as peers) than from academic acceleration per se (Janos & Robinson, 1985). A puzzle to those who study giftedness is why, in a time of greatly expanded educational and occupational opportunities, gifted women still achieve and earn less than gifted men. One answer is that many gifted women still adhere to traditional gender roles, a choice that can lower their expectations of success in traditionally male careers and channel them into traditionally female occupations that do not fully use their talents (Eccles, 1985). Furthermore, *others*—especially those in supervisory roles—may expect women to embrace traditional gender roles. In spite of the enhanced opportunities available to them, women in contemporary Western society still suffer the effects of sex discrimination. If these influences are to be counteracted, parents, educators, and counselors must encourage gifted girls from an early age to broaden their horizons and consider all the career options open to them.

Variations in Intelligence Explained

Why do some people have IQs of 180, while others have "normal" intelligence, and still others are mentally retarded? In other words, what is the cause of individual differences in intelligence? The answer to this question, as is almost always the case in psychology, lies in two sets of factors, hereditary and environmental. The models of intelligence described earlier in this chapter acknowledge both factors, of

Because people actively create their own environments, heritability can increase over the lifespan. Someone who is shy—an attribute with a strong genetic influence—may prefer to sit at home, quietly reading a book, rather than go to a crowded party. Such a choice would likely inhibit the development of social skills, making the person even less likely to attend parties in the future.

course. In general, though, *g*-factor models tend to attribute a greater emphasis to genetic than to environmental factors.

Behavioral geneticists try to answer this question using the techniques described in Chapter 2. By comparing certain kinds of individuals (twins, adopted siblings), they can estimate the heritability (h^2) of IQ, that is, the proportion of the variation in intelligence that can be attributed to genetic differences. Recall that they can also estimate the influence of being raised in a certain family (shared environmental influence, or E_S) and the influence of unique experiences independent of family (nonshared environmental influences, or E_{NS}).

In most studies of individual differences and IQ, heritability estimates are both significant and reliable, averaging about .5 (Bouchard & McGue, 1981; Chipuer, Rovine, & Plomin, 1990; Plomin, DeFries, & McClearn, 1990). Interestingly, several recent studies (Bouchard, Lykken, McGue, Segal, & Tellegen, 1990; Pedersen et al., 1985; Pedersen et al., 1992; Tambs, Sundet, & Magnus, 1984) suggest that the role of genetic influences *increases* during the life span. For those older than fifty, heritability is typically about 80 percent, even among *twins who have been reared apart* (Bouchard et al., 1990). This may seem puzzling: shouldn't twins who have been reared apart—presumably, they were exposed to quite different environments—be *less* similar the longer they have been separated? To borrow a phrase from Pedersen and colleagues (1992), "It would be reasonable to assume that heritability decreases during early development as experiences accumulate or that environmental influence becomes increasingly important later in life, with the accumulation of wounds from 'life's slings and arrows of outrageous fortune'" (p. 346). In fact, however, heritability increases over the life span (Plomin, 1986).

The key to understanding this seeming paradox also underscores the difficulty associated with separating genetic from environmental causes. In Chapter 13 we discussed the fact that humans actively *create* their own environments. For example, someone who is shy (shyness is known to have a strong genetic component; see Kagan & Snidman, 1992; Kagan, Snidman, & Arcus, 1992) may decide to sit home quietly reading a book or completing a crossword puzzle rather than go to a crowded party. This avoidance of social gatherings would likely inhibit the development of social skills, making the person even less likely to attend parties in the future. Thus the experience of staying home alone is greatly influenced by shyness, which has a strong genetic component. In a type of "positive feedback" loop, genetic tendencies influence behavior, and the behavior reinforces those genetic tendencies.

The life experiences of twins who were separated at birth are therefore much more similar than they appear to be. The twins' similar genetic makeup will predispose them to select certain similar environments, which in turn will shape their future choices. Over time, the twins will continue to select similar environments, increasing the similarity of their behavior and inflating their heritability estimates as they age.

What about the role of experience? Certainly, experience is important in the shaping of intelligence, especially Carroll's "broad abilities" (see p. 471). More will be said on this subject in the In Depth section at the end of this chapter.

Assessing Personality

Though psychological testing began with the goal of measuring human intelligence, soon psychologists were developing personality tests. A number of uses have been found for such tests. Clinicians and social workers use them to gain insight into people's social and emotional problems, so as to diagnose and treat them. School psychologists, industrial psychologists, and vocational counselors use them to help people select suitable careers. And researchers who are interested in personality use them to investigate some of the concepts and theories of personality.

The method psychologists choose to assess personality often depends on their theoretical approach. Those who see personality as a set of fairly stable traits tend to select personality tests that have been developed to measure such characteristics. Most of these tests rely on **self-reports,** in which a person answers a series of questions about personal behavior, thoughts, feelings, and attitudes. The questionnaires are easy to score, and they tend to produce consistent assessments. As a result, they are often referred to as *objective tests* of personality.

Other theorists who believe that personality is shaped by unconscious conflicts (such as psychoanalytic theorists) tend to favor techniques that allow a person's underlying motives and feelings to be tested indirectly. One example of this kind of method is a **projective test** (Elias, 1989), in which the person being tested is shown ambiguous pictures and asked to describe them. Presumably subjects "project" some of their internal struggles and conflicts into their descriptions of the pictures. In the following section we will look more closely at the two types of personality test.

Self-Report Tests

One obvious way to assess personality is to ask people what they feel and how they usually act. Do you feel awkward in most social situations? Do you often say things you immediately regret? Do you think most people can be trusted? Psychologists who developed the self-report test believe that people's answers to such questions yield valid psychological profiles.

How do psychologists come up with the items on a self-report test? There are several approaches. Usually the test developers begin with a thorough and clear definition of the trait they want to measure, including all the elements they think it is composed of (McAdams, 1990). Suppose we want to develop a test of conscientiousness, a trait that was defined in Chapter 13 as involving an orientation toward achievement, dependability, carefulness, hard work, perseverance, self-control, and a sense of responsibility. We could write test items that tapped all the various aspects of conscientiousness included in this definition.

For instance, we could write items such as, "I always make sure I finish the projects I start"; "If someone gives me a job to do, I feel an obligation to do it well"; "I am very careful and meticulous in most of the things I do." To identify people who tend to answer "yes" to everything they are asked, we could also include some contrary items, such as "I see nothing wrong with cutting a few corners to get a job done" or "When I lose interest in a task, I just put it aside and do something else." We could also include some items on elements closely related to those involved in conscientiousness—honesty and selflessness, for instance. Finally, we might throw in a few items that do not directly address a person's traits, but which may turn out to be good indicators nonetheless. "I would enjoy a career as a scientist" would be one possibility, since people who are not conscientious might not be interested in the exacting work that scientists do.

To decide which items we should keep in the final version of the test, we would first administer the test to a large number of people. Then, using factor-analytic techniques, we would analyze the answers to each of the items, to see how they relate to the overall scores. Those items that contributed only negligibly to the total score could be eliminated. Finally, we would have to validate our test by making sure it does in fact measure what people generally consider to be conscientiousness. We could do that by seeing how closely the test scores correlate with conscientiousness ratings made by people who know the test takers well. Or we might conduct a laboratory experiment in which we gave the test takers a chance to behave in a conscientious manner. If we find that those who scored high on the test are the most conscientious in the experiment, then we have some evidence that our test is indeed valid.

The Minnesota Multiphasic Personality Inventory

The **Minnesota Multiphasic Personality Inventory (MMPI)** is a widely used self-report test. In fact, in outpatient mental health facilities it is the most widely used assessment test of any kind (Newmark, 1996). The test yields scores on each of the ten clinical scales listed in Table 14-3.

The MMPI was originally developed to aid in the diagnosis of psychiatric patients. The test contained 550 questions, all of which could be answered true or false. The items were first given to those who suffered from various psychological disorders—schizophrenia, depression, paranoia, hypochondria, and so forth—as well as to a group of psychologically healthy people. Items that discriminated between the groups were incorporated into the test.

While responses to a single question were not very useful, researchers observed certain *patterns* of responses in those who suffered from some psychological disorders. For instance, of the original pool of test items, fifty-three were found to discriminate sharply between depressed and healthy people. Later, a few more items were added to sharpen the discrimination between the severely depressed and those with other psychiatric conditions (Winters et al., 1985). The result was the *D*, or *depression*, scale of the MMPI, a highly sensitive indicator not only of major depression but of less severe downswings in mood.

Though it was quite useful, the original MMPI did have some problems. First, the group that was used to define a normal or average profile was not representative of the general population. All the individuals used to develop the norms were white residents of Minnesota, most of them semiskilled workers or farmers with no more than an eighth-grade education. Second, many of the items were outdated (such as, "Horses that don't pull should be beaten or kicked") or offensive to some respondents because of objectionable content (for example, some items dealt with sexist attitudes, bowel and bladder functions, and religious beliefs).

The Revised Minnesota Multiphasic Personality Inventory

In 1989, after several years of work, a revised and updated form of the MMPI was published (Butcher et al., 1989). The MMPI-2 contains 567 items; to keep the research on the original MMPI applicable to the MMPI-2, the scientists who worked on the revision changed the ten clinical scales as little as possible

| TABLE 14-3   *Scales of the MMPI-R*

Clinical Scales	
1. Hypochondriasis (Hs)	Items selected to discriminate people who persist in worrying about their bodily functions despite strong evidence that they have no physical illness
2. Depression (D)	Items selected to discriminate people who are pessimistic about the future, feel hopeless or worthless, are slow in thought and action, and think a lot about death and suicide
3. Hysteria (H)	Items selected to discriminate people who use physical symptoms to solve difficult problems or avoid mature responsibilities, particularly under severe psychological stress
4. Psychopathic deviate (Pd)	Items selected to discriminate people who show a pronounced disregard for social customs and mores, an inability to profit from punishing experiences, and emotional shallowness with others, particularly in sex and love
5. Masculinity-femininity (Mf)	Items selected to discriminate men who prefer homosexual relations to heterosexual ones, either overtly or covertly because of inhibitions or conflicts; women tend to score low on the scale, but the scale cannot be interpreted as simply upside down for women
6. Paranoia (Pa)	Items selected to discriminate people who have delusions about how influential and how victimized they are or how much attention is paid to them by other people
7. Psychasthenia (Pt)	Items selected to discriminate people with obsessive thoughts, compulsive actions, extreme fear or guilt feelings, insecurity, and high anxiety
8. Schizophrenia (Sc)	Items selected to discriminate people who are constrained, cold, aloof, apathetic, and inaccessible to others and who may have delusions or hallucinations
9. Mania (Ma)	Items selected to discriminate people who are physically overactive and emotionally excited and have rapid flights of disconnected, fragmentary ideas; the activities may lead to accomplishment but more frequently are inefficient and unproductive
10. Social introversion (Si)	Items selected to discriminate people who are withdrawn from social contacts and responsibilities and display little real interest in people

Based on Dahlstrom, Welsh, & Dahlstrom, 1972.

(see Table 14-3). Three validity scales, designed to determine whether the test taker is responding honestly to the test, were also retained.

One such validity scale, the *Lie scale,* is designed to identify people who are faking their responses in order to appear better than they really are. For example, a person who answers "yes" to statements such as "I always tell the truth" would score high on such a scale, since most people tell a lie occasionally. A second validity scale, the *F scale,* is designed to

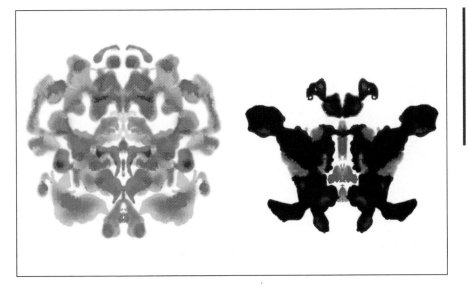

identify people who are deliberately trying to portray themselves as disturbed. Such people typically answer "true" to statements that would seem to indicate pathology (for example, "I see things, animals, or people around me that most people do not see") but which in fact are typically not endorsed by the truly disturbed. The *K scale* is similar to the Lie scale, except that the items are more subtle (for example, "At times I feel like swearing"). Many false responses to such statements suggest that the respondent is being less than frank and is trying to conceal his or her distress.

Several new scales were developed for the MMPI-2, including a *Post-Traumatic Stress Disorder* scale, a *Gender Role* scale, a *Shyness* scale, and scales designed to measure anger, cynicism, Type A behavior patterns, health concerns, and family problems. Although research continues on the MMPI-2, many clinicians regard it as a substantial improvement over the MMPI. Thus far the test has been widely adopted and has generated considerable enthusiasm.

Projective Tests

Projective tests assess the way people respond to and interpret ambiguous stimuli, such as inkblots and pictures of people in which their motives and feelings are unclear. Those who are being tested are asked to describe what they see in these materials. Presumably, in doing so, they project their unconscious feelings and conflicts onto the materials. Thus, someone who repeatedly sees peering eyes

and threatening figures in abstract blots of ink may be projecting the fears and suspicions typical of paranoia.

The Rorschach Inkblot Test

Perhaps the best-known projective test for clinical diagnosis is the one developed in 1921 by Hermann Rorschach (1884–1922), a Swiss psychiatrist. In the **Rorschach Inkblot Test,** people look at ten inkblots (such as those shown in Figure 14-5) and report what they see in each one. The examiner notes not only what a person says, but how the person says it— quickly or cautiously, with what kind of emotion, and so forth. After all ten cards have been presented, the examiner shows them a second time and asks the person why he or she gave each answer. If in one blot the subject saw two elephant heads, for instance, the examiner would ask what part of the blot suggested that particular image.

The Rorschach is scored by considering what part or parts of the inkblot a person focused on; whether the shape, color, or some other aspect of it was significant; what kind of objects or activities the person saw; and how common or uncommon the person's responses were. Traditionally, certain answers on the Rorschach are assumed to indicate certain personality traits. For instance, if a person often focuses on the entire inkblot (not just a part of it), that person is assumed to be good at abstract, conceptual thought. Many responses to the shape of an inkblot supposedly suggests dispassionate thinking, while many

In projective tests like the TAT, a subject is shown a series of pictures of ambiguous social encounters and is asked to tell a story about each picture. The hope is that the subject will project her own feelings onto the characters in the picture.

responses to color suggests strong emotion and impulsiveness (McAdams, 1990). A skilled Rorschach examiner also interprets the overall pattern of answers a person gives, to get a general picture of what that person is like. Consider a man who saw in one inkblot two headless people with arms touching, who might be women with bad figures; in another, some women trying to lift weights; and in a third, Count Dracula ready to suck a woman's blood and strangle her. The overall pattern of these responses suggested to the examiner a man who was in conflict over his sexual orientation. While he seemed to want contact with a nurturing mother figure, he also seemed very angry and hostile toward women (Pervin, 1989).

Historically, the value of the Rorschach as a personality test has been questionable. Some say that people's answers are too easily influenced by transitory thoughts and feelings; others, that the scoring procedures for the test are not well standardized. Still others complain that the Rorschach is not a good tool for diagnosing specific psychiatric disorders, that it simply helps clinicians identify general themes involved in people's psychological problems (Feshbach & Weiner, 1982; Korchin & Schuldberg, 1981).

In 1969 John Exner, a noted psychologist, initiated an extensive study of the Rorschach test that culminated in a more objective and comprehensive scoring system (Exner, 1974). Exner later expanded and revised his scoring system, which now fills three

separate volumes (Exner, 1991, 1993; Exner & Weiner, 1994). Exner's system provides guidelines for scoring that increase the likelihood that different psychologists will "see" the same things in a response. More important, it provides consistent guidelines for the *interpretation* of responses. Largely because of Exner's system, use of the Rorschach is now much more common than it was several decades before.

Recently, Wood, Nezworski, and Stejskal (1996a) have identified some potentially serious problems in Exner's scoring system. The most serious revolves around the data Exner used to develop, evaluate, and revise his system. Most of Exner's data have not been subjected to a rigorous "peer review" process: according to Wood and his colleagues, less than 20 percent have been published in peer-reviewed journals. Responding to Wood and his associates, Exner (1996) has defended his procedures, taking exception to the implication that "the unpublished works are, in some way, mediocre in quality or may be flawed in design or analysis" (p. 12). Wood and colleagues (1996b) responded that they had implied no such thing:

> In fact, we have no way of knowing whether the unpublished works are mediocre or flawed, *for the simple reason that we have been unable to examine them* (p. 16) [emphasis added].

Should Exner's Comprehensive Scoring System be abandoned? Not necessarily. The system is elegant and thorough, a vast improvement over earlier scoring schemes. While many psychologists continue to use Exner's system, some are likely to remain skeptical, at least until more extensive studies have been conducted and the results published.

The Thematic Apperception Test

The **Thematic Apperception Test (TAT),** developed by Henry Murray in 1935, is another projective test that is widely used in both clinical work and studies of motivation (Newman, 1996). The TAT consists of a series of pictures of ambiguous social encounters. Usually, the person being tested is shown as many as twenty of the pictures, chosen for their appropriateness to his or her age and sex. The person tells a story about each picture, including what led up to the scene, what the characters are thinking and feeling, and how the scene ends. Figure 14-6 shows a picture similar to those used in the TAT.

Vocational tests may be used either to help people select appropriate careers or to help companies choose the best applicants for a job.

In analyzing a subject's TAT responses, the examiner first determines the character, usually the story's central figure, on whom the subject has apparently projected aspects of him- or herself. Other characters in the story are thought to reflect traits of people who are important in the subject's life. Murray originally suggested that responses be analyzed for both the subject's psychological needs (including the needs for achievement, affiliation, nurturance, aggression, dependency, power, and sex) and the environmental factors that might be helping or hindering fulfillment of those needs. For instance, if the central character in several of a person's stories is striving hard for success, but is constantly thwarted by the lack of social connections, the examiner presumes a need for achievement and a concern over obstacles related to social status.

Like the Rorschach, the TAT has been criticized as too open-ended and too reliant on the examiner's interpretive skill. Nonetheless, the test continues to be used in a variety of clinical and research contexts to assess underlying motivations that respondents may not be able to express directly. In one study, for example, the TAT was used to assess respondents' feelings of ambivalence toward their same-sex siblings (Bedford, 1989). In another investigation, it was used to study attitudes toward death among the offspring of Holocaust survivors (Schneider, 1988). The TAT is also used in research to test aspects of psychodynamic theory. For example, it is used to examine whether individuals with certain personality disorders show disordered orientations toward interper-

sonal relationships, such as a preconception that others are malevolent or an incapacity to invest in relationships with others (Westen et al., 1990).

Vocational Tests

In addition to tests of intelligence and personality, psychologists have developed a number of tests that are designed either to help people select appropriate careers or to help companies choose the best applicants for a job. *Interest tests,* as their name implies, are designed to suggest careers that are consistent with a person's interests. *Screening tests* are usually given by employers and are intended to identify the applicants best suited for a particular job.

Interest Tests

Identifying your interests can help you find a career in which you are likely to succeed and find personal satisfaction. But why do you need a formal test to identify your interests? Aren't you aware of your interests already? Not necessarily. Many people never deliberately analyze their interests; even if they do, they may not know how those interests relate to the requirements of various jobs. A young woman who is very interested in science, for example, may think

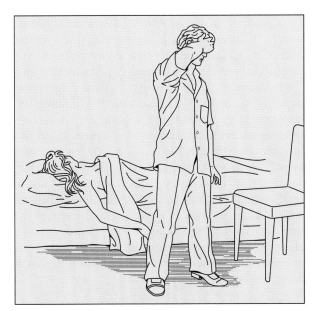

Figure 14-6   Card similar to those used in the TAT. The person being tested is asked to provide a story based on the illustration on the card. (After Alloy, Acocella, & Bootzin, 1995, p. 135.)

she wants to be a doctor. But if she has no interest in dealing with sick people, she is overlooking an important part of a physician's work. Interest tests can help to avoid such oversights by matching the full range of a person's interests with the demands of different types of jobs.

The **Strong-Campbell Interest Inventory (SCII),** developed in the 1920s by E. K. Strong, Jr., consists of 325 items, most of which list particular occupations, school subjects, amusements, activities (repairing a clock, giving a speech, raising money for charity), and people with whom one might associate (old people, people who like to live dangerously). The test taker marks each of these items *like, indifferent,* or *dislike.* Other items include a choice between pairs of activities ("Would you prefer to deal with things or to deal with people?") and simple self-descriptions to be marked *yes* or *no* ("I make friends easily"; "I am always on time with my work").

The subject's answers generate scores on three major scales. One is the *Occupational Scale,* which tells how similar a person's answers are to those of successful people in specific occupations (psychologist, architect, advertising executive, musician, army officer, and so on). A woman may find, for instance, that her answers are very similar to those given by a group of engineers but very dissimilar to those given by a group of social workers. Dissimilar answers, which are believed to be more revealing than similar ones, can be used to eliminate career options, in this case, social worker. The Strong-Campbell also has a *Basic Interest Scale,* which lists twenty-three vocational areas, including agriculture, the military, science, art, sales, writing, and teaching. The test taker receives a score showing his or her degree of interest in each area. Finally, the test has a *General Occupational Themes Scale,* based on six adjectives (realistic, conventional, enterprising, social, artistic, and investigative) that describe general styles of thinking and acting. The test taker is rated as high, medium, or low on each of those styles. Occupations are also classified according to this scale, so the test taker can gain insight into which occupations seem to match his or her behavioral style.

Screening Tests

Most companies evaluate job applicants through personal interviews, a method they say they prefer because they want to get to know applicants. When evaluated scientifically, however, interviews do not serve employers well. Most studies have found that choices made on the basis of interviews alone are at best random and at worst unfairly biased toward certain applicants (Tenopyr, 1981). What can psychologists do to make the selection process more successful?

Many companies now evaluate job applicants through *screening tests,* which are designed to identify those applicants who are likely to perform well on the job. Recall the scenario described in the opening to this chapter: a hypothetical company is looking for a test that can be used to select the best applicants for a job. The second consultant advised using task-specific *aptitude tests,* or tests designed to measure a person's potential to perform a specific task. For example, companies that are seeking factory workers to assemble tiny electronic components often give applicants a manual dexterity test. Other corporations use personality tests to match candidates with specific jobs. To enter an executive training program, for example, a person may have to rank exceptionally high in assertiveness and tolerance for stress, and moderately high in social conformity.

Used appropriately, screening tests can be helpful, but companies must be cautious in their use. Employers must demonstrate that the tasks measured by a test are relevant to the job. They must also demonstrate that a screening test is not unfairly biased against certain groups (for example, those who are older or who belong to certain ethnic groups). We will discuss this potentially serious shortcoming of tests in the next section.

The Ethics of Testing

Because standardized tests are used so extensively in the United States, psychologists, government officials, and the general public are concerned about the ethical standards for testing. The American Psychological Association has issued several documents on the subject, legislators have enacted laws, and some corporations have voluntarily tightened their policies regarding employee screening. *Standards,* a volume compiled by a Joint Committee on Testing Standards (AERA, APA, NCME, 1985), has established guidelines for a wide range of testing activities, from developing tests to interpreting them (Jones & Appelbaum, 1989). What are some of the ethical issues people are most concerned about?

One concern is that the people who use tests choose, administer, and evaluate them properly (London & Bray, 1980). Tests must be used only for appropriate purposes—that is, purposes for which they have been demonstrated to be valid. Tests must also be fair to members of all the social groups that take them; no test that discriminates unfairly should ever be used. Furthermore, those who use tests must be aware of their limitations. At best test scores can provide only a good estimate of the trait or skill they are designed to measure. Therefore important decisions about a person should never be made solely on the basis of one test score. Finally, someone who does poorly on a test should at least be given the chance to retake it.

Another ethical issue in testing is the disclosure of test results. Who should have access to test scores? Only the test takers themselves, unless they agree otherwise? In general, most ethics committees stress the test taker's right to confidentiality. Test scores should not be released to outside parties without subjects' prior knowledge, and often their express consent (London & Bray, 1980). Whether test takers have a right to see exactly how a test was scored is a related question that has been highly controversial. Developers of tests often argue that if both questions and answers are disclosed to those people who have taken a test, new test items must constantly be generated to avoid cheating on future tests, and the quality of the items may suffer. Though that may be true, public opinion has generally sided with the test taker's right to know. In 1980, for example, the New York State legislature passed a law requiring that the questions and answers to college entrance exams be made available to those who have taken the tests. This legislation reflects the growing belief that tests should be administered for the benefit of all—those who take the tests as well as those who use them.

The Bell Curve: Are There Racial Differences in IQ?

A PRESUMED RELATIONSHIP between intelligence and race preceded—and, in some sense, initiated—the formal study of intelligence. Recall Francis Galton's early attempts at developing intelligence tests and his belief in *eugenics,* a misguided attempt to "improve" the human race through selective breeding. Alfred Binet's earliest tests, much to his consternation, were also used to substantiate prevailing views of the intellectual superiority of whites. And in studies of World War I draftees, Carl Brigham reported that eastern European immigrants scored consistently lower on intelligence tests than members of other ethnic groups. As we have seen, Brigham failed to recognize that many of those immigrants were newly arrived in the United States. Since intelligence tests of that time were heavily influenced by linguistic and cultural knowledge, they discriminated against immigrants who had not yet acquired that knowledge. Fortunately, these blatant misuses of intelligence testing became less common in the middle part of the twentieth century. Yet the idea that race and intelligence are related has persisted in other ways.

Initial Studies. In 1969 Arthur Jensen, an educational psychologist, was asked to write an article for the *Harvard Educational Review* on why compensatory education programs for minority groups had so far produced disappointing results. A number of years earlier Jensen had attended a lecture by an eminent English psychologist, Sir Cyril Burt, who specialized in studying the causes of variations in intelligence. Burt's data on fifty-three pairs of twins who had been raised apart suggested that among the white population in England, individual differences in IQ were heavily influenced by heredity. Estimated **heritability factors** consistently topped .80 in these studies. Jensen reasoned that if variations in IQ within a white population were so heavily genetic in origin, perhaps *average* differences in IQ between whites and blacks were also. "It seems a not unreasonable hypothesis," Jensen wrote, "that genetic factors are strongly implicated in the average Negro–white intelligence difference" (Jensen, 1969, p. 82).

The ink was barely dry on Jensen's article before the news media began to print highly simplified and sometimes inaccurate versions. A piece in *Newsweek* (March 31, 1969) titled "Born Dumb?" summed up Jensen's theory as the belief that black intelligence is fixed at birth at a level far below that of whites, implying that no amount of compensatory schooling would ever make any difference. Though Jensen had never made that statement, nearly every popular article on his work drew that conclusion (Cronbach, 1975). The political climate of the time contributed to public outrage against Jensen. The civil rights movement was in full swing; just a year earlier, Martin Luther King, Jr., had been assassinated. Racial riots were erupting in cities across the country. Angry students who saw Jensen's theory as racist disrupted his speeches and classes. Jensen received so many threats of violence that the University of California had to hire bodyguards to protect him (Fancier, 1985).

Unlike many of his predecessors, Jensen's approach to the debate was decidedly scientific. He was trying to reconcile two facts that are now acknowledged without dispute (see Patterson, 1995). First, whites score consistently higher than blacks on traditional tests of intelligence; most scholars acknowledge the difference to be about 1 standard deviation, or 15 points, on tests like the WAIS-R (see Humphreys, 1992). Second, heritability estimates of intelligence hover consistently around .5. Though many possible explanations of this result do not rely on purely genetic differences between the races (see Sternberg, 1995), genetic differences *could* exist, and as Jensen pointed out, psychologists should consider all the alternatives.

Then, just as the debate was quieting, stunning new evidence suggested that some of Cyril Burt's published findings may have been fabricated. Leon Kamin (1974, 1986), an American psychologist, and Oliver Gillie, a reporter for the *London Sunday Times,* had discovered peculiarities in some of Burt's data. Identical correlations between twins' IQ scores (to three decimal places) kept showing up, regardless of how many new sets of twins Burt added to his sample. The odds against this happening even once are

Are racial differences in academic achievement caused by genetic or environmental factors? Corla Hawkins, founder of the Recovering the Gifted Child Academy in Chicago, thinks the environment is important. She recommends high academic expectations, a strict ethical code, and no tolerance for excuses. Although her local school district has a dropout rate of over 50 percent, more than 95% of the students who attend Hawkins's Academy for four years finish high school.

many millions to one, but in Burt's research it happened twenty times (Gillie, 1977). In addition, Kamin and Gillie could not locate two of Burt's alleged collaborators, who Burt said had collected much of the data. Had those collaborators really existed, or had Burt "invented" them to bolster his arguments? Leslie Hearnshaw, a biographer hired by Burt's sister, found other suggestions of fraud. For example, Burt had apparently written articles supporting his analyses and published them under fictitious names in a scholarly journal he controlled. Such fraud is probably the worst sin a scientist can commit, for it threatens to destroy the very foundations of science (Aronson, 1975, p. 115).

More recent reviews of Burt's work have been less damning (Fletcher, 1991; Loynson, 1989). While some inconsistencies, even outright errors, undoubtedly plagued Burt's work, the evidence of deliberate and widespread fraud may have been overstated. One scholar (Green, 1992) wrote:

> Burt may have been overly sure of himself, and to many he seemed arrogant and high-handed. He may have remained too long as editor of "his" journal. None of this is commendable, but neither could it be called unethical. . . . Burt's main mistake lay in not recognizing that standards had changed, in not seeing that time had passed his data by, in not letting go.

(Green, 1992, p. 331)

Criticisms, Alternatives, and Further Research. Even before the scandal over Burt's work broke, Jensen's critics had amassed powerful arguments against him. They correctly stressed that Jensen had made an unwarranted leap in logic when he suggested that heritability factors related to variations within groups might identify the *cause* of variations between groups. In fact, the causes of differences *within groups* do not necessarily say anything about the causes of differences *between groups*.

Consider a simple example. Suppose you have two groups of 100 seeds each, group A and group B. Genetically, the individual seeds in each group are equally diverse. You plant group A in fertile soil, with plenty of sunlight and water, and group B in poor soil, with little light or moisture. Six months later you measure the height of the resulting plants. To what should you attribute any differences among them? Because all the plants within each group were exposed to exactly the same conditions, you can attribute any differences within a group almost entirely to heredity. But what about the differences *between* the two groups? Should they also be attributed largely to heredity? Obviously not. Despite high heritability factors *within each group*, the evironmental differences *between each group* probably greatly influenced the differences in their growth.

Blacks and whites, Jensen's critics point out, also experience significant differences in their environments. A far higher proportion of blacks than whites live in poverty, receiving poorer prenatal care, nutrition, and medical services as a result, and suffering increased exposure to pollutants and toxins that can hinder development. The higher risk of lead poisoning poor black children face is an enormously important environmental difference from the middle-class white environment. Young children who live in substandard housing can easily ingest lead-contaminated paint particles, a toxin that can significantly lower their IQ scores into young adulthood (Needleman et al., 1990).

The debate over intelligence and race has intensified in the past few years, fueled by the publication of *The Bell Curve,* a best-selling, highly controversial examination of intelligence and class structure by Richard J. Herrnstein and Charles Murray (1994). Herrnstein and Murray used the National Longitudinal Survey of Youth (NLSY), an extensive database of more than 12,000 young people who have been followed since 1979. Using regression techniques, they found evidence that *intelligence* is one of the most powerful predictors of academic, financial, and social success. Furthermore, they found that levels of intelligence (and therefore later success) are stratified by race: blacks are disproportionately represented at the bottom end of the distribution. Pretending these differences do not exist, Herrnstein and Murray (1994) asserted, would be foolish and irresponsible:

> In trying to think through what is happening and why and in trying to understand thereby what ought to be done, the nation's social scientists and journalists and politicians seek explanations. They examine changes in the economy, changes in the demographics, changes in the culture. They propose solutions founded on better education, on more and better jobs, on specific social interventions. But they ignore an underlying element that has shaped the changes: human intelligence—the way it varies within the American population and its crucially changing role in our destinies during the last half of the twentieth century. To try to come to grips with the nation's problems without understanding the role of intelligence is to see through a glass darkly indeed, to grope with symptoms instead of causes, to stumble into supposed remedies that have no chance of working.

(pp. xxii–xxiii)

The reaction to *The Bell Curve* was predictably fierce and swift. Steven J. Gould, the noted anthropologist, Darwinian scholar, and author of *The Mismeasure of Man* (1981), one of the more eloquent indictments of intelligence testing, wrote:

> The Bell Curve . . . contains no new arguments and presents no compelling data to support its anachronistic social Darwinism, so I can only conclude that its success in winning attention must reflect the depressing temper of our time—a historical moment of unprecedented ungenerosity, when a mood for slashing social programs can be powerfully abetted by an argument that beneficiaries cannot be helped, owing to inborn cognitive limits expressed as low IQ scores.

(Gould, 1995, p. 11).

Howard Gardner, author of the multifactor theory of intelligence, pointed out another problem in *The Bell Curve*'s analysis. Herrnstein and Murray adopted a *g*-factor approach, (correctly) pointing out that the heritability estimates for *g* are typically about .5. However, that does *not* necessarily indicate that "intelligence is fifty percent genetics." Rather, it means that parents and their children produce similar scores on *certain parts of IQ tests.* Furthermore, while IQ and some societal outcomes *are* correlated, the size of the correlation is modest, accounting for about .20 of all variability. Since the heritability of IQ scores is about .5, the actual genetic contribution to *socioeconomic status* is about .10 (.50 of the correlation of .20):

> One's ultimate niche in society is overwhelmingly determined by non-IQ factors, ranging from initial social class to luck. And since close to half of one's IQ is due to factors other than heredity [the heritability of *g* is about .5], well over 90% of one's fate does not lie in one's genes.

(Gardner, 1995, p. 27).

Patterns and Conclusions

The question of possible racial differences in intelligence is likely to remain controversial for some time. The implications extend far beyond psychology, in fact, to the very heart of modern existence. Some psychologists agree with the position adopted by Herrnstein and Murray, which could be summarized as follows: "We cannot pretend the differences don't exist simply because they make us uncomfortable." Others, like Sternberg, strongly disagree:

One could read this book as scapegoating . . . people with low IQs. These people are portrayed as causing many of the ills society is currently experiencing. It is not clear, though, whether they are really the problem, or whether the problem is in society's treatment of them. ₊. . We must be careful about scapegoating because it is inherently unfair. . . . It is for this reason that we need to be concerned at least as much by the attention this book is receiving as about what it says. We will then realize that *The Bell Curve* tolls not just for society's unfortunates, but for us all.

(Sternberg, 1995b, pp. 260–261).

SUMMARY

1. **Standardization** involves developing uniform procedures for giving and scoring a test, as well as establishing **norms,** or standards of performance, against which people's scores on the test can be evaluated. A good test must be both **reliable** and **valid,** meaning that it must consistently yield the same results and measure what it is intended to measure.

2. **Intelligence** involves the capacities to acquire and retain knowledge and to understand concepts and relationships, capacities that an intelligent person uses effectively when solving problems and communicating. One technique used to study intelligence is **factor analysis,** in which researchers try to identify different components of intelligence by seeing which scores on mental tests tend to cluster together. Some psychologists who use this approach argue for the existence of *g,* a general intelligence factor that underlies intelligence. Others question the existence of a general intelligence factor, arguing instead that intelligence is a collection of relatively independent abilities, what is called the **information-processing view.** Most contemporary researchers believe intelligence to be a combination of general and specific abilities.

3. The first valid test of intelligence was developed by Alfred Binet, a French psychologist, in collaboration with psychiatrist Theodore Simon. This test measured the **intelligence quotient** or **IQ,** a ratio of a child's mental age to his or her chronological age. Lewis Terman, a professor at Stanford University, brought Binet's test to America in a revised version called the **Stanford-Binet.** Another set of widely used tests are the **Wechsler scales,** developed by David Wechsler. In addition to these individual tests of intelligence (those given to only one person at a time), there are also group tests, paper-and-pencil measures that many people can take at once. One group test that measures some of the abilities often assessed by IQ tests is the **Scholastic Aptitude Test (SAT).** Although they are often criticized, SAT scores are reasonably good predictors of grades in college.

4. At one extreme of human intelligence are the **mentally retarded,** whose IQs are significantly below average and who have difficulty functioning independently in everyday life. In evaluating mental retardation today, educators are careful to take into account factors such as vision and hearing, language skills, and cultural background, which can sometimes deceptively lower a person's IQ. At the other extreme of human intelligence are the **mentally gifted,** who, contrary to popular stereotypes, are not awkward, eccentric, and frail. But it is not clear whether the success and good adjustment of high-IQ people should be attributed solely to their cognitive abilities. Other factors, particularly family background and motivation, also contribute to the tendency to excel.

5. A **heritability factor** is an estimate of the contribution heredity (genetics) makes to the individual differences we observe in a trait like intelligence. Current estimates are that about 50 percent of the individual variability in IQ scores is due to genetic factors. This leaves an equally large influence from environment. Behavioral geneticists separate environmental factors related to the home environment (called shared environmental influence, or E_S) from those related to unique experiences (nonshared environmental influences, or E_{NS}).

6. Psychologists have developed a number of tests to assess personality. **Self-report tests,** such as the **Minnesota Multiphasic Personality Inventory-Revised (MMPI-R),** are associated with the trait approach to personality. These tests assume that valid personality profiles can be obtained by asking people straightforward questions about themselves. **Projective tests,** such as the **Rorschach Inkblot Test** and the **Thematic Apperception Test (TAT),** are related to the psychoanalytic perspective because they assume that people project unconscious conflicts and needs into their interpretations of ambiguous test material.

7. Vocational tests have been developed to help people select appropriate careers for themselves (interest tests) and to help companies choose the best applicants for a job (screening tests). The **Strong-Campbell Interest Inventory (SCII),** one of the most widely used interest tests, measures people's interests and relates them to various occupations.

8. People have become increasingly concerned about the ethical standards that apply to testing.

Among the issues raised are the uses to which tests are put and the people to whom test results are disclosed. Several organizations are attempting to set guidelines in these and other areas.

9. The role of genetic factors in intelligence, especially as they relate to racial differences, is among the most controversial of all issues in psychology. Though racial differences in IQ have been observed by a number of researchers throughout the past century, Arthur Jensen was among the first contemporary psychologists to examine the problem. Although Jensen generated considerable debate, the recent publication of *The Bell Curve,* by Richard J. Herrnstein and Charles Murray, has intensified the controversy. Herrnstein and Murray argue that racial differences in intelligence—leading to disparity in many socioeconomic factors—can no longer be ignored. Others contend that racial differences in intelligence are small and are overwhelmed by even greater differences in environment.

SUGGESTED READINGS

Aiken, L. R. (1997). *Psychological testing and assessment* (9th ed.). Needham Heights, MA: Allyn & Bacon. A good introduction to basic concepts of testing and measurement in psychology.

Fletcher, R. (1991). *Science, ideology, and the media: The Cyril Burt scandal.* New Brunswick, NJ: Transaction Publishers; Joynson, R. B. (1989). *The Burt affair.* London: Routledge. Two books on the Burt scandal, written from quite different perspectives.

Fraser, S. (Ed.) (1995). *The bell curve wars.* New York: Basic Books. A collection of essays on and critiques of *The Bell Curve,* written for nontechnical readers by some of the most esteemed researchers in the field (Sternberg, Gould, Gardner, for example).

Gould, S. J. (1981). *The mismeasure of man.* New York: Norton. The history of misguided attempts to measure intelligence, written by a gifted science writer.

Herrnstein, R. J., & Murray, C. (1994). *The bell curve: Intelligence and class struggle in American life.* New York: The Free Press. An impressively researched summary of the role of intelligence in American society; it has caused an almost unprecedented response from the psychological community.

Mogdil, S., & Mogdil, C. (Eds.) (1987). *Arthur Jensen: Consensus and controversy.* New York: Falmer. A collection of thoughtful, provocative essays based on the controversial writings of Jensen.

Newmark, C. S. (1996). *Major psychological assessment instruments* (2nd ed.). Needham Heights, MA: Allyn & Bacon. An advanced text covering only the most frequently used assessment instruments.

Sternberg, R. J. (1990). *Metaphors of mind: Conceptions of the nature of intelligence.* New York: Guilford Press. One of the best reviews of intelligence research, as well as a clear exposition of information-processing approaches.

CHAPTER 15

Psychological Disorders

A twenty-four-year-old man, armed with a .44-caliber revolver, cruises a New York City neighborhood late at night, looking for "pretty girls" to shoot. When he is finally captured by police after a year-long search, he has killed six people and wounded seven others. He says that "demons" drove him to commit these crimes.

A middle-aged businessman—fed up with his stressful job, his hour-long commute, and the demands of his suburban life-style—packs a small bag and flees to the mountains, where he settles in an abandoned cabin, determined to live in isolation.

A young woman who showed great academic promise in high school begins to have difficulty with her studies in college. She believes that she is constantly behind in her work and will not be able to catch up, no matter how hard she tries. She feels lonely and becomes increasingly depressed and withdrawn.

A widely acclaimed young pianist, winner of many awards, begins to suffer inexplicable attacks of "nerves" whenever he has to play before an audience. This anxiety becomes increasingly intense and develops into waves of panic. Eventually the very thought of performing in public becomes so terrifying that the pianist's career is jeopardized.

How many of these people have a psychological disorder? Do all of them need psychiatric help? How would trained professionals diagnose their condition? And what kinds of therapy might be recommended? These are questions we will be addressing in this chapter and the next, which deal with psychological disorders and their treatment. We begin this chapter by exploring how psychologists define psychological disorders. We then examine some major perspectives on the causes of disorders and investigate how disorders are currently classified. Finally, we describe the symptoms of some major psychological disorders, as well as the insights current theories and research provide.

Definition of Psychological Disorders

Psychologists and psychiatrists define psychological disorders by evaluating behavior according to certain criteria. One criterion is violation of widely accepted social expectations. A woman who walks around her neighborhood in summer wearing a heavy coat and screaming insults at strangers would, by this measure, be considered disordered. She is violating social expectations regarding dress and polite behavior. Her actions are also statistically rare—another criterion for defining a disorder.

But deviation from statistical norms and violation of social expectations are not always

Chapter Outline

Colin Fergu___n (left) was tried for murder in the December __ 1993, shooting rampage on a Long Island Rail Road c___muter train in which six people were killed and 1S injured. Though his attorneys recommended an insanity plea, he refused. He was found guilty of murder in February 1995 and sentenced to life imprisonment.

Many of those who are homeless suffer from some kind of psychological disorder, most often schizophrenia or substance-related disorders like alcoholism.

enough to identify a psychological disorder, for the statistically rare and socially unexpected can vary with time and place. For instance, worshiping ancestral ghosts is not common in the United States, where it violates

social norms, so in that society it would be considered symptomatic of a disorder. In other societies, however, ancestor worship is widespread, and the person who practices it in no way seems odd. Should a psychological disorder depend so much on where a person lives? Many psychologists feel that in general, it should not.

Nor should a definition of a psychological disorder fail to take into account that some unusual behaviors have positive outcomes. What about the divorced father of thirty years ago who wanted custody of his young children? At the time, his behavior was both statistically rare and opposed to social expectations, but few people then or now would consider him disordered. The same could be said about people throughout history who have pursued unconventional but worthwhile goals. Much of society's vitality comes from those who venture beyond the norms, striking out in new directions. To label all

such actions disorders would be to discourage many valuable innovations. Labeling all such actions disorders would also force us to say that people are disordered when they defy social norms because of moral convictions. Consider citizens of Nazi Germany who actively resisted their government's efforts to exterminate Jews. Although they were few in number and violated social expectations, they were certainly not people whom we would call disordered.

A way around these problems is to add to the definition of a psychological disorder some widely accepted standards of what is psychologically "unhealthy." These standards would include persistent emotional pain and suffering, behavior that is disturbing to others, failure to perform ordinary day-to-day activities, and irrationality or frequent failure to exercise self-control. The example of the man who believed demons urged him to kill fits several of these standards. His thoughts and actions were irrational, lacked any semblance of self-restraint, and were highly disturbing to everyone but himself. Similarly, the young pianist who was so terrified he could no longer perform in public was causing himself enormous emotional pain and distress, and was unable to carry out his normal activities. Thus, according to prevailing standards of mental health, both these people would, for different reasons, be considered to have a psychological disorder.

Of course, any standard of mental health we use has its limitations. Likewise, by themselves, emotional pain and suffering are insufficient to indicate a psychological disorder. The person who goes through life with little anxiety and upset is not necessarily well-adjusted. There are times when great emotional distress is the expected reaction, as when a parent experiences the death of a child. The person who remains indifferent in such a situation can hardly be considered normal. In fact, a lack of emotional responsiveness and concern for other people is one symptom of some serious psychological disorders. Even a mild lack of distress is not *necessarily* healthy. Some psychologists believe that humans cannot grow and reach their full potential without sometimes taking steps that prove upsetting. From this perspective, painful choices are an essential part of achieving self-fulfillment. Other prevailing standards of mental health are subject to similar limitations when used alone.

Thus, no single definition of a psychological disorder is adequate. Psychologists need to apply several yardsticks before labeling a behavior disordered. The more criteria that can be applied to a given way of thinking and acting, the more the use of the label *disorder* is justified. Together, statistical rarity, violation of social norms, and contradiction of popular standards of mental health can help us to distinguish the psychologically normal from the psychologically disordered behavior. Even so, there is no universally accepted dividing line between the normal and the abnormal. Mental health is best viewed as a continuum. At the extreme ends of that continuum, normality and abnormality are easy to distinguish. In the middle range, however, one condition shades gradually into another, making diagnosis more difficult.

Perspectives on Psychological Disorders

Over the years, many theories have been proposed to explain psychological disorders. The idea that madness results from possession by devils dates back to ancient times. Archaeologists have found skulls of Stone Age people with surgical holes chipped in them—perhaps to let out the evil spirits. Exorcism of demons by prayers, potions, and often physical torture was fairly common during the Middle Ages. Such practices demonstrate that people's views about the causes of abnormal behavior often determine how the mentally disturbed are treated.

In the following sections we will review some cur-

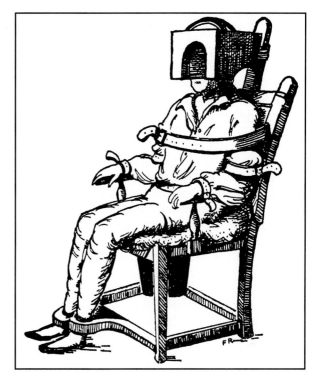

Early psychiatric interventions, such as this nineteenth-century "tranquilizer chair," appear cruel and brutal by contemporary standards.

rent perspectives on the causes of psychological disorders. We will see how theories about causes help to suggest treatments. Of course, prevailing theories and widely used treatments need not be related. Today, for instance, biological factors (such as biochemical imbalances) are considered a major cause of schizophrenia, but drugs that affect those imbalances are not the only treatment for the disorder. Schizophrenia is also treated with therapies that focus on improving communications in the family, even though faulty communication is not the major cause of the disorder. With this in mind, let us turn to the various perspectives on psychological disorders.

The Biological Perspective

Physicians in ancient Greece were among the first to identify a set of strange symptoms that occurred mainly in women. The patient would suffer headaches and dizzy spells, accompanied by inexplicable aches and pains. Suddenly, part of the body might become paralyzed; just as suddenly the patient might go blind or lose her voice. The Greeks named this condition *hysteria* because they believed it was caused by the effects of a wandering uterus (the Greek word for uterus is *hystera*). To the Greeks, the uterus was a separate living organism that could roam about the body, wreaking havoc wherever it went. Although the theory of a wandering uterus seems silly to us today, it shows that for thousands of years people have wondered if abnormal behavior might be caused by some biological dysfunction.

The **biological perspective** gained strength in the late nineteenth century, when researchers discovered that some baffling mental disorders could be traced to specific diseases of the brain. The most dramatic of these discoveries was the finding that **general paresis**—an irreversible deterioration of all mental and physical processes—is in fact the final stage of the venereal disease *syphilis* (the stage at which the syphilitic microorganisms deeply penetrate the brain and other body organs). Following this discovery, optimism ran high that medical science would someday conquer all mental and emotional disorders.

Today biological researchers are using modern technology to explore the brains of mentally disturbed people. They believe that abnormalities in the workings of chemicals in the brain called *neurotransmitters* (see Chapter 3) may contribute to many psychological disorders. For example, overactivity of the neurotransmitter dopamine, perhaps caused by an overabundance of certain dopamine receptors in the brain, has been linked to the bizarre symptoms of schizophrenia (Wong et al., 1986). As yet, however, biological researchers have not found organic causes for most mental disorders. That is not to say that such causes do not exist. With further advances in technology, scientists may find more biological factors underlying abnormal behavior.

Psychological Perspectives

Despite the fact that the biological perspective has been an influential one, few people believe that all mental and emotional disorders are strictly biological in origin. A large number of mental health professionals place great emphasis on psychological factors, such as emotional conflict, inappropriate learning, and self-defeating thought processes. In this chapter we will examine three psychological perspectives: the psychoanalytic, learning, and cognitive behavioral perspectives. Because they overlap with theories of personality discussed in Chapter 13, we will summarize them only briefly here.

As we learned in Chapter 13, Sigmund Freud, the founder of the **psychoanalytic approach,** believed that the human psyche consists of three interacting forces: the *id* (a pool of biological urges), the *ego* (which mediates between the id and reality), and the *superego* (which represents society's moral standards). In Freud's view, abnormal behavior is caused by the ego's inability to manage the conflict between the opposing demands of the id and the superego. Especially important to Freud was a failure to manage the conflict between the id's sexual impulses during childhood and society's sexual morality. Although later psychoanalytic thinkers have tended to place less emphasis on the id's sexual urges, they too believe that how people resolve emotional conflicts during childhood affects their thoughts and behavior for the rest of their lives. Through **psychoanalysis,** a psychoanalyst probes a person's current thoughts and feelings for clues to unconscious conflicts—hoping that the patient will gain critical insight into the roots of problems, insight that might ultimately improve the patient's psychological health. We will examine the process of psychoanalysis in Chapter 16.

In sharp contrast to psychoanalytic thinkers, proponents of the **learning perspective** argue that most mental and emotional disorders arise not from unresolved psychic conflicts but rather from inadequate or inappropriate learning. Learning theorists believe that people acquire abnormal behaviors through the various kinds of learning discussed in Chapter 6. Therapies based on this perspective are designed to undo past lessons that have instilled inappropriate behaviors and to provide new lessons that will foster more desirable responses.

The earliest therapies based on learning theories were not particularly concerned with what a person thought, so long as that person's undesirable responses were reduced. But today, many psychologists recognize the importance of thought, or cognition, in shaping behavior. Those who take a **cognitive perspective** on abnormal behavior say that the quality of one's internal dialogue—accepting or berating oneself, building oneself up or tearing oneself down—has a profound effect on a person's mental health. Consider a student who fails a difficult exam, decides that he does not have the brains for college, becomes depressed, and drops out. To stop his self-defeating actions, he must first stop attributing his failure to a lack of ability. Cogni-

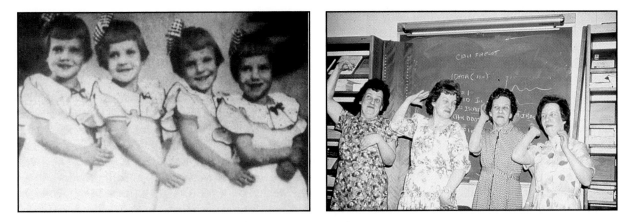

Schizophrenia, like many psychological disorders, has a powerful genetic component. All four of the Genain quadruplets, shown as children (left), were diagnosed with schizophrenia as adults (right).

tive therapies focus specifically on changing such negative cognitions to help people break free of maladaptive behaviors.

Other Perspectives

Two other perspectives on psychological disorders consider the social world in which a disturbed person lives. According to the **interpersonal,** or **family-systems perspective,** psychological disorders arise partly from a person's network of social relationships. One of the most crucial of those networks, especially to a young child, is the family. In fact, this perspective developed from the experiences of child psychotherapists, who found that they often had to extend their search for causes, as well as their efforts at treatment, to parents and siblings of their young clients.

Psychologists who take a **sociocultural perspective** find that the roots of mental disturbance often lie in social ills such as poverty, poor nutrition, inadequate housing, crime, and discrimination. The primary evidence in support of this view is the generally higher rate of serious mental disorders (such as schizophrenia and alcoholism) among the lowest socioeconomic classes. This pattern may stem from higher levels of stress among the poor, less effective strategies for coping with stress, and a greater reluctance to seek treatment for psychological problems.

Perspectives Combined

The various perspectives on psychological disorders are not mutually exclusive. Often the richest insights into the causes of a disorder arise from a combina-

tion of several viewpoints. Today many clinicians are trying to develop an integrated model of abnormal behavior—one that incorporates elements from numerous theoretical approaches (Liem, 1980).

One such model, very popular in recent years, is the **diathesis–stress model.** According to this approach, for various reasons, a given individual may have a predisposition, or diathesis, to develop a certain mental disorder. Whether or not the disorder actually develops depends on the environmental stresses the person experiences. This model suggests that preventive treatment can be targeted at people who are at risk for developing a given disorder, as a result of their genetic makeup or other factors.

Throughout this book we have discussed the contributions of behavioral genetics, stressing that genetic influences almost always interact with environmental factors, as they do in the diathesis–stress model. Many psychological disorders have genetic components; in some (such as alcoholism and depression) genetic influences are quite strong. Even so, many people with a genetic predisposition toward a certain disorder will not experience symptoms unless certain factors are present in the environment.

Classification of Psychological Disorders

Classifying psychological disorders involves identifying sets of symptoms that tend to occur together. Each set of symptoms forms a *syndrome.* Thus, when we talk about schizophrenia, mania, or depression, we are talking about syndromes that clinicians have classified on the basis of their observations.

Why bother classifying psychological disorders? What purposes does it serve? First, a classification system gives mental health professionals a shorthand way of communicating among themselves. When a diagnosis of bipolar disorder is made, for instance, a single term summarizes the patient's major symptoms. Second, a classification system helps to suggest effective treatments. By grouping together people with the same symptoms, clinicians can identify the kinds of treatments that work best for that particular group. This knowledge can then be applied to other cases of the same disorder. Third, a classification system enables the pooling of research data on abnormal behaviors. Without such a system, researchers would have no way of knowing when they were studying the same or different disorders. Finally, a classification system aids in making predictions. It can provide information about the likelihood of a given disorder, which people are most susceptible to it, and how the condition is likely to progress.

Today, the classification system on which virtually all mental health care professionals rely is the *Diagnostic and Statistical Manual of Mental Disorders, fourth edition (DSM-IV)*, published by the American Psychiatric Association in 1994. *DSM-IV* contains a detailed list of the major mental disorders and their symptoms. Because such classification systems are based on professionals' judgments, they tend to change over time. For example, in the first two editions of *DSM*, homosexuality was considered a disorder, but in 1973 the American Psychiatric Association voted to strike that category from the manual. *DSM-III* (published in 1980) included only a category called "ego-dystonic homosexuality," which applied exclusively to homosexuals who were disturbed by their sexual orientation. In 1987, when *DSM-III* was revised *(DSM-III-R)*, all mention of homosexuality as a diagnostic category was removed, a practice that has been continued in *DSM-IV*.

DSM-IV recommends a thorough approach to the evaluation of psychiatric disorders based on an assessment in terms of five dimensions, or "axes." Axis I lists the clinical syndromes, that is, the problems that lead people to seek psychotherapy. Most serious disorders, such as major depression and schizophrenia, are found on Axis I. Axis II lists "background" problems that may contribute to the person's psychopathology. Such problems that are typically long-standing include maladaptive personality traits (for example, compulsiveness and overdependency) as well as developmental problems (language difficulties, for instance). Axis III covers physical illnesses or conditions that may be related to the psychological symptoms. Axis IV specifies the level of stress in the person's life, for stress is often linked directly to psychological problems. Finally, Axis V represents the highest level of functioning the client has shown in the last year—at work, at home, with friends, and in leisure activities. This level of functioning is often a good indication of the person's chances for recovery.

Although the American Psychiatric Association has worked hard to produce the most useful diagnostic manual possible, there are those who criticize the attempt to classify mental disorders. These critics charge that diagnostic labels obscure individual differences. One schizophrenic is not identical with every other schizophrenic, nor is one depressed person exactly like all others. In trying to fit every psychiatric patient into some category, psychologists may inadvertently lose valuable information (Mirowsky & Ross, 1989). And, say these critics, applying diagnostic labels to patients can affect not only their self-perceptions but how others perceive them (Rosenhan, 1973). When people are labeled *schizophrenic*, for instance, other people expect odd behavior from them and may interpret *any* unusual action as a sign of mental illness. Given such problems, some critics have suggested that psychiatric categories be eliminated altogether.

Most psychologists do not agree with this position. They believe that some diagnosis of mental disorders is essential if knowledge about them is to expand (Swartz, Carroll, & Blazer, 1989; Tweed & George, 1989). How, they ask, are they to investigate the effectiveness of treatments for schizophrenia, depression, alcoholism, and so forth, without diagnostic labels? Without those labels, they would be hard-pressed even to identify a sample population to study. Supporters of psychiatric classification also point out that the *DSM-IV* system has reasonably good reliability, meaning that there is substantial agreement among clinicians as to what is and is not an instance of a particular disorder. However, the system has greater reliability in the diagnosis of some disorders, such as mental disorders and substance use disorders, than of others, such as personality disorders. Whether *DSM-IV* is valid—that is,

Panic disorder can be so severe that the victim never goes anywhere—a disorder known as agoraphobia.

whether it accurately classifies what it intends to classify—is more of an issue. But even if the current system has some problems with validity, most psychologists do not want to discard it entirely, feeling that the benefits of classification far outweigh the drawbacks.

The rest of this chapter explores some of the major disorders listed in *DSM-IV.* As you read about these disorders, you may be tempted to conclude that some of them apply to people you know, perhaps even yourself. Be cautious in making such amateur diagnoses. It is quite common for normal people to suffer mild, temporary versions of the syndromes described in this chapter. In such cases, professional help is not usually needed. Only when symptoms become severe and persistent—when they interfere with ordinary life, causing significant distress—is professional help essential.

Anxiety Disorders

Anxiety disorders, as the name suggests, are characterized by anxiety—emotional distress that is caused by feelings of vulnerability, apprehension, or fear. Some people try to cope with these feelings through ritualized behaviors that may reduce the anxiety slightly, though never completely. Others try to avoid situations that trigger the anxiety—a strategy that can interfere greatly with normal life. We will examine five anxiety disorders, beginning with panic disorder.

Panic Disorder

Mr. Wright, a man of 35, was referred to the hospital because of a "dizzy turn" which he had experienced during his work as a laborer. He had had similar attacks in the past but, with each one, the associated feelings of panic became more acute. . . .
[Later] he began to complain of pressure in the front of his head and uncontrollable trembling and palpitations. He became more and more dependent on his wife and would go nowhere without her. . . .This meant of course that he had to give up work.

(McCulloch & Prins, 1975, p. 54).

Like Mr. Wright, people who suffer **panic disorder** experience sudden, inexplicable attacks of intense fear that may last for a number of minutes, sometimes even for hours. Victims may have difficulty breathing; feel nauseated, numb, or dizzy; sweat, tremble, or choke for no reason; suffer chest pains, heart palpitations, hot or cold flashes, and an overwhelming terror of dying or going crazy. Such *panic attacks* occur in approximately 3.5 percent of all Americans during their lives; they are more prevalent in women than men (Kessler et al., 1994). Panic disorder can be so intense that the victim never goes anywhere, a condition known as **agoraphobia.** Agoraphobics have an intense fear of being trapped in places from which they cannot escape quickly or without embarrassment, or where they could not get help in the event of a panic attack, such as on a bus, train, or car. Panic disorder may also be accompanied by depression (Breier, Charney, & Heninger, 1986).

One of the defining characteristics of panic disorder is a sense of inescapable doom. In fact, those who suffer from panic disorder often arrive at emergency rooms, thinking they are suffering from a heart attack (Kaplan & Sadock, 1991). These "catastrophic thoughts" are central to panic disorder, distinguishing it from other anxiety disorders (Clark et al., 1988). At one time panic attacks were thought to have no precipitating event. More recently, however, experts have begun to suspect that most panic attacks are triggered by an event, perhaps a relatively benign experience such as exercise (Craske, 1991).

Of all the anxiety disorders, panic disorder appears most likely to be genetically influenced (Crowe, 1991). In a study of Norwegian twins, Torgersen (1983) found that the disorder is more commonly shared by monozygotic (identical) twins than by dizygotic (fraternal) twins. Other evidence also suggests that biological factors are involved. Those who suffer from panic disorder often display lower than normal levels of the neurotransmitters serotonin and norepinephrine, the same transmitters that are implicated in depression (Butler, O'Halloran, & Leonard, 1992).

One of the most influential approaches to panic disorder over the past decade has focused on the disorder's cognitive components (Clark et al., 1988). According to this perspective, panic disorder is a reaction to *misperceived threats*. In other words, stimuli that most of us would disregard—like shortness of breath after exercising, or the sight of a fast-approaching car in the rearview mirror—are misinterpreted by those with panic disorder as genuine threats. Rather than attributing the shortness of breath to exercise, the panic disordered person mistakenly interprets it as signaling the onset of a heart attack. The anxiety brought on by the perceived "heart attack" is likely to stimulate the person's sympathetic nervous system, inducing even more rapid breathing and shortness of breath. The recognition of the cognitive component of panic disorder has led to a treatment, one that will be described in the next chapter.

Phobic Disorders

An irrational fear that is focused on some specific object or situation (other than the fear of having a panic attack) is called a **phobia** from the Greek word for "fear." Sometimes people fear humiliating themselves in public. For instance, some are terrified of losing their voice when speaking in front of others.

Such groundless fears are called *social phobias*. Phobias that involve nonsocial fears are called *specific phobias*. For example, some phobics are terrified of enclosed places (claustrophobia), others of heights (acrophobia), still others of particular animals (dogs, insects, snakes, mice). Table 15-1 lists some additional phobias.

Phobias are among the more common anxiety disorders. Up to 11 percent of the population is affected by specific phobias, twice as many women as men. Social phobias are somewhat more common, affecting about 13 percent of the population at some time in their lives. The incidence of social phobias, unlike that of many other anxiety disorders, is roughly equivalent for men and women (Kessler et al., 1994). Ironically, most phobics know that their fears are unreasonable and excessive, yet they are unable to overcome them. They try as best they can to avoid the feared stimulus, though that is sometimes difficult. The following case is fairly typical.

> The client was a 30-year-old male who reported intense fear of crossing bridges and of heights. The fear had begun 3 years earlier when he was driving over a large suspension bridge while feeling anxious due to marital and career conflicts. Looking over the side he had experienced intense waves of fear. From that time onward his fear of bridges had become progressively more severe. At first, only bridges similar to the original were involved, but slowly the fear generalized to all bridges. Concurrently, he developed a fear of heights. Just before he came for treatment, he had been forced to dine with his employer in a restaurant atop a 52-story building. He had developed nausea and diarrhea and had been unable to eat. [Subsequently, he] decided to seek treatment.

(Hurley, 1976, p. 295).

Several explanations for phobias have been proposed. Freudians have argued that a phobia develops as a defense mechanism against some unacceptable id impulse. The ego, struggling to control the impulse, displaces the anxiety produced by the impulse onto some symbolically related object or event. Thus, a man with a bridge phobia may be defending against a suicidal urge to jump off high places. Learning theorists, in contrast, believe that many phobias are caused by a combination of classical and operant conditioning. A boy who has been bitten by a dog may come to fear dogs, because he associates them with the fear-arousing stimulus of a painful bite: this is an instance of classical conditioning. The boy may then learn to reduce his fear by avoiding

TABLE 15-1   Common Phobias

Phobia	Feared Object or Situation
Acrophobia	High places
Claustrophobia	Enclosed places
Ergasiophobia	Work
Gamophobia	Marriage
Haphephobia	Being touched
Hematophobia	Blood
Monophobia	Being alone
Ocholophobia	Crowds
Xenophobia	Strangers

dogs as much as possible—an operantly conditioned response that is maintained by its reinforcing consequences (the reduction of anxiety).

But what about phobias that arise in the absence of any real harm? Most people with snake phobias, for instance, have never been bitten by a snake. Some psychologists believe that the human brain may be *prepared* to learn the fear of certain stimuli, such as dogs or snakes, probably because those animals resemble ancient predators (Seligman, 1971). Significantly, establishing a conditioned arousal to the sight of snakes previously paired with electric shock is much easier than establishing conditioned arousal to the sight of a human face. So perhaps a propensity toward certain types of phobias is partly innate (Davey, 1995). But observational learning may also play a role in the acquisition of phobias (Bandura, 1986). A girl who repeatedly hears her mother expressing a fear of heights may imitate that response.

Generalized Anxiety Disorder

Less common than phobias is **generalized anxiety,** a state of persistent apprehension without good cause. Generalized anxiety disorder affects about 5 percent of the population, occurring twice as often in females than males (Rapee & Barlow, 1991). People who have this disorder worry constantly, for no apparent reason. They may fear that something terrible is going to happen to their children, even though their children are not in any danger. They may worry that they will be unable to pay their bills, even though they have money in the bank. When asked why they worry in these ways, they are unable to give rational answers. The worries are simply there, plaguing them all the time.

Symptoms of tension often accompany generalized anxiety disorder. Victims may be so preoccupied with their worries that they cannot concentrate on anything else, becoming forgetful and disorganized (Barlow et al., 1986; Rapee & Barlow, 1993). They may also be irritable and tired, with sore, aching muscles, especially of the shoulders and neck. Yet they often have trouble sleeping at night. Dizziness, nausea, excessive sweating, shortness of breath, heart palpitations, dryness of mouth, and difficulty swallowing are other common complaints. All are signs of a body under prolonged stress.

According to the psychoanalytic perspective, generalized anxiety disorder arises from an unconscious conflict between sexual or aggressive id impulses and the ego's fear that those impulses will be punished. This unconscious conflict leads to chronic worry and tension, a condition Freud called *free-floating anxiety*. The cognitive perspective provides a very different explanation that focuses on an inability to control negative life events. Research shows that when people feel powerless to eliminate a painful stimulus, they tend to become very upset and give up trying to cope—a phenomenon originally called *learned helplessness* (Seligman, 1975). In time such people may develop a chronic feeling of helplessness accompanied by persistent anxiety and tension. The "In Depth" section in this chapter will explore the links between helplessness, hopelessness, anxiety, and depression.

Obsessive-Compulsive Disorder

An **obsession** is an unwanted thought or image that keeps intruding into consciousness, despite a person's efforts to dismiss it. The most common obsessions are recurring thoughts of violence (such as killing a loved one), contamination (dwelling on the possibility of infection), and doubt (wondering whether the stove was turned off before you left for vacation, for instance).

A **compulsion** is a repetitive behavior a person feels compelled to engage in despite the fact that it is senseless or excessive. Obsessions and compulsions are often closely related; that is, obsessive thinking can lead to compulsive behavior. The person who is obsessed with the thought of germs and so cleans everything repeatedly, and the person who is plagued by doubt about having locked the doors and so checks them over and over, are exhibiting obsessive-compulsive behavior. A compulsion, of course, need not always be caused by an obsession. Compulsive people are simply following rigid rules of their own making:

> Mr. B was unmarried, aged 45, and had a 30-year history of obsessive-compulsive problems. . . . [His] basic problem was a compulsion to be slow, meticulous, and ritualistic, especially when dressing, washing, shaving, cleaning his teeth and combing his hair. . . . For instance, cleaning his teeth involved 192 slow meticulous brush strokes for each application of toothpaste and for each rinse. . . . Bathing would take him up to three hours with half an hour spent in rinsing the bath before filling it and half an hour rinsing the bath afterwards. Every action was performed in a slow meticulous manner reminiscent of the care taken by a bomb disposal expert.
>
> (Hodgson & Rachman, 1976, p.29)

Similarly, obsessions need not produce compulsions. For instance, a young man may find that each time he is attracted to a woman, he becomes obsessed with the question of whether to call her for a date. If he calls and is rejected, he will be devastated; if he does not call, he will have no chance at all. Seeing one side of the issue and then the other, he is never able to come to a decision. Over and over he ruminates on the pros and cons, exhausting himself with his perpetual uncertainty.

Psychologists have offered several theories to account for obsessions and compulsions, which in mild form are fairly common. In the psychoanalytic view, both are seen as symptoms of underlying psychological conflict. For instance, compulsive hand washing would be interpreted as a combination of fixation and reaction formation, in which the ego defends itself against the anal desire to be messy and destructive. In the learning view, in contrast, compulsions are seen as negative reinforcers that reduce anxiety. That is, when anxious people discover that some behavior, such as washing their hands, reduces their anxiety, that response is strengthened. The relief, of course, is only temporary, so the behavior must be repeated over and over. The reduction of anxiety cannot account for obsessions, however, for obsessive thinking typically raises anxiety. Some learning theorists argue that obsessions can arise

when a person experiences a disturbing thought—the kind of thought all of us have occasionally (Rachman & Hodgson, 1980). While a normal person would probably dismiss such a thought, an obsessive might become extremely concerned, making an active effort to inhibit such thoughts in the future. But, in fact, the effort to inhibit them may actually magnify them, causing them to intrude into consciousness more, thus raising the person's anxiety (Wegner et al., 1987).

Finally, the biological perspective suggests that abnormalities in the brain may contribute to obsessions and compulsions. Significantly, identical twins are more likely to develop obsessive-compulsive disorders than nonidentical twins. Identical twins may inherit a tendency toward emotional overarousal, which then triggers an anxiety disorder when combined with unusual life stress (Turner, Beidel, & Nathan, 1985). Alternatively, obsessive-compulsives may suffer from overactivity in certain parts of the brain involved in filtering out irrelevant stimuli and persisting at tasks (Baxter et al., 1987). Some of the drugs recently introduced to treat depression have been effective in compulsive disorder. The antidepressants that are effective are the ones that work almost exclusively on the neurotransmitter *serotonin*, which has been implicated in other anxiety disorders (Barr et al., 1992).

Posttraumatic Stress Disorder

> One [Vietnam] veteran had warned his close friend, the squad medic, not to go near a crying baby lying in a village road until they had checked the area. In his haste to help the child, the medic raced forward and "was blown to bits" along with the child, who had been booby-trapped. The veteran came into treatment three years later . . . because he was made fearful and anxious by his eight-month-old daughter's crying. He had been unable to pick her up or hold her since her birth despite his conscious wish to "be a good father."
>
> (Haley, 1978, p. 263).

This man was diagnosed as having **posttraumatic stress disorder,** a state of anxiety, depression, and psychological "numbing" that follows exposure to severe trauma, such as war, rape, the violent death of a loved one, or a catastrophic natural disaster. The onset of posttraumatic stress disorder may be immediate or delayed, as in this veteran's case. Victims complain of tension, insomnia, and difficulty concentrating, plus a feeling that they are remote from others and that life has lost its meaning. Involuntary mental "flashbacks" are also typical, often accompanied by recurrent nightmares in which the trauma is relived. Situations that trigger the recollection of the trauma, such as hearing a baby cry, can intensify the symptoms. Posttraumatic stress disorder can be extremely persistent. Studies of survivors of Nazi concentration camps and soldiers returning from war show that many suffer symptoms twenty, thirty, or even forty years later (Kluznik et al., 1986). Dutch soldiers who fought in the Resistance against the Nazis were still exhibiting symptoms forty years after the war (Hovens et al., 1992).

Women who have been raped experience unusually severe trauma. Soon after an attack many display symptoms of posttraumatic stress, including high anxiety, stomach pains, headaches, jumpiness, insomnia, and other signs of tension. Barbara Rothbaum and her colleagues (Rothbaum et al., 1992) studied almost 100 rape victims, looking for such symptoms. Unlike many researchers, Rothbaum was able to study subjects *prospectively;* that is, they first interviewed victims shortly after the rape had occurred (less than two weeks on average) and then continued to interview them on a weekly basis. Thus they established a reliable "baseline" against which to evaluate victims' progress and were able to isolate factors related to the victims' recovery. One month after the rape, about two-thirds of those studied by Rothbaum and her colleagues were suffering from posttraumatic stress syndrome. Three months after the attack, more than half the victims still showed symptoms.

What factors are related to the persistence of this syndrome? Clearly, one factor is the severity of the trauma (Foy et al., 1987; Foy, Carroll, & Donahoe, 1992). However, other factors have been identified as well, including the *victims'* characteristics. As is the case with many psychological disorders, those who are relatively poorly adjusted before the trauma have a greater likelihood of developing posttraumatic stress disorder (McFarlane, 1988, 1989). In addition, the victims' "coping styles"—the way in which they understand and deal with the trauma—are important. Those whose reactions are primarily emotional (such as denial, wishful thinking, or "emotional venting") were more likely to develop the syndrome than those who examine the events more analytically, identifying those problems with which they need help (Mikulincer & Solomon, 1988).

Severe psychological trauma, such as rape, war, or the violent death of a loved one, can produce posttraumatic stress disorder, a state of anxiety, depression, and psychological numbing.

In the case of rape, Rothbaum and her colleagues (1992) found little evidence of spontaneous recovery after the first few months; they suggest that any victim who is still suffering symptoms two months after an attack should seek professional help.

The one common factor in *all* anxiety disorders is an irrational perception of threat. Everyone reacts to dangerous and threatening stimuli. What differentiates those with anxiety disorders is the *kind* of stimuli they perceive as threatening. Anxiety disorder patients are likely to misperceive relatively neutral stimuli as threatening and to respond accordingly. This common characteristic has led to several successful cognitive therapies designed to change the way patients view triggering stimuli. Cognitive techniques of therapy will be covered in Chapter 16.

Somatoform Disorders

The distinguishing characteristic of a **somatoform disorder** is the presence of one or more symptoms of a physical dysfunction for which there is no identifiable organic cause. Patients may complain of stomach pains when doctors can find nothing to explain the problem. There is strong indication that such symptoms are related to psychological conflict. (Somatoform disorders are *not* the same as psychosomatic illnesses, which are real physical problems, like ulcers, that have a psychological component, stress.) The person with a somatoform disorder is not pretending to be ill. These people have no sense whatsoever that their minds could be creating their symptoms; to them, the symptoms are absolutely real. Of the several types of somatoform disorders, we will discuss two: hypochondriasis and conversion disorder.

Hypochondriasis

People who suffer from **hypochondriasis** are persistently fearful that they have contracted some terrible, often fatal disease. The hypochondriac spends much of life scrutinizing bodily functions for signs of serious illness. Minor aches, pains, bumps, and bruises that are impossible to avoid are immediately taken as signs of some dreaded malady in its early stages. Thus, simple headaches are interpreted as symptoms of a brain tumor; an occasional cough, as a sign of lung cancer. When medical tests reveal that the hypochondriac's fears are groundless, the person's anxiety does not end. The typical hypochondriac refuses to accept a doctor's reassurance, insisting that the doctor has simply failed to recognize the illness. Many hypochondriacs go from doctor to doctor complaining of the same minor ailments, always receiving the same reassurances, yet never finding relief from their irrational fears.

Little is known about the causes of hypochondriasis. One hypothesis is that for some hypochondriacs, reports of physical symptoms may be substitutes for the expression of emotional pain. An aching shoulder, for example, may be easier to talk about than the pain of a son's failure to call home. Alternatively, the attention a hypochondriac gets from doctors, and perhaps from family and friends, may reinforce the person's chronic fears.

We have seen that anxiety disorders can be understood as a response to stimuli that are misperceived as threats. A similar explanation has been offered for somatoform disorders (Barsky, 1992). According to this view, hypochondriacs exaggerate normal bodily sensations, interpreting them as indications of serious illness.

Conversion Disorder

People who suffer from a **conversion disorder** manifest what appears to be a genuine physical dysfunction: they suddenly become blind, deaf, or paralyzed, or lose sensation in a part of the body usually during a stressful situation. Yet there is no organic basis for their condition; it is purely psychological in origin. Conversion disorder was fairly common at the turn of the century, but today it is rare. One exception is the relatively high incidence of the disorder among combat soldiers during wartime. Interestingly, conversion symptoms often disappear as suddenly as they appear. Many "miracle" cures, in which the paralyzed suddenly leave their wheelchairs or the deaf suddenly hear, may involve conversion disorders.

Conversion disorders reduce anxiety in those who suffer them, preventing them from engaging in some activity that causes them distress. The student who fears she will fail a crucial exam becomes blind and can no longer study. The soldier who has had a brush with death develops paralysis in his arm and can no longer fire a rifle. The anxiety-reducing role of these ailments is further suggested by the calm manner in which many people with conversion disorder accept their disabilities.

Several theories have been offered to explain the symptoms of conversion disorder. Freud argued that they are defenses against forbidden urges. For instance, guilt over an urge to strike one's parents might result in paralysis of the arm. Learning theorists stress the rewards of conversion symptoms: they enable people to reduce anxiety and escape onerous duties, while at the same time gaining sympathy from others. Family-systems theorists have broadened the search for causes by asking whether a conversion disorder serves some useful role within the family. Consider the case of a woman who developed conversion blindness when her husband retired (Haley, 1973). Her condition helped him to cope with the transition from a demanding job to a less active role at home. That is, caring for his wife and running the household made him feel useful. When his wife began to recover, he became depressed, getting better only after she suffered a relapse. According to the interpersonal or family-systems perspective, then, conversion disorder may be a way of helping other family members to function. The victim, however, pays a high price for such assistance.

Finally, some theorists emphasize the role society and culture play in the expression of psychological discomfort. These theorists point out that psychological discomfort is often expressed differently in different cultures. For example, fainting was considered "socially acceptable" in Victorian times. Victorian women, faced with difficult or threatening situations, often fainted. In contemporary Western society fainting is no longer considered an acceptable response to psychological stress; therefore it is seldom seen (Goldberg & Bridges, 1988).

Dissociative Disorders

The **dissociative disorders** affect a person's psychological rather than physical functioning. Personal memory or identity is disturbed in such a way that part of the self is split off, or dissociated. Dissociative disorders include dissociative amnesia, dissociative fugue, and dissociative identity disorder.

Dissociative Amnesia

Dissociative amnesia is the partial or total forgetting of past experiences after some stressful event. Unlike amnesia that has an organic basis, dissociative amnesia is caused strictly by psychological trauma. For instance, a man who saw his child killed by a hit-and-run driver may be unable to remember anything from the time of the accident until several days later. Less commonly, the man may remember bits and pieces of the blacked-out period. For example, he might recall sitting in the hospital waiting room and the thick black mustache one of the doctors wore. Least common of all is the type of dissociative amnesia in which a person's whole life is blacked out following a trauma. Interestingly, even in cases of extensive memory loss, the person always remembers something from the past. A woman may not recognize her family, for instance, but she may remember how to knit. Because dissociative amnesia is related to severe trauma, it is usually quite rare, except in wartime and during natural disasters.

Dissociative Fugue

Dissociative fugue (from the Latin word for "flight") is another relatively rare disorder. Victims walk away from their homes and their identities for a period of hours, days, months, or even years. In some cases, the person takes up an entirely new life. Recovered fugue victims usually recall nothing of what happened during the fugue state. The following case is fairly typical:

> A young married woman, chronically unhappy and in conflict over her marriage, occasionally wandered from her home in the daytime and got lost, much as unhappy little children do. She would suddenly "come to" far from home, and with no memory of having left it.

(Cameron, 1963, p. 339)

In an exceedingly rare form of dissociation called dissociative identity disorder (or sometimes multiple-personality disorder), a person, usually female, evolves two or more separate and independent personalities. This woman was diagnosed with four distinct personalities.

Dissociative Identity Disorder

A more extreme form of dissociation is **dissociative identity disorder** (sometimes called **multiple-personality disorder,** the term used prior to *DSM-IV*). In this disorder, a person (more often a female) evolves two or more separate personalities, each well defined. Often the personalities contrast sharply. In the film *The Three Faces of Eve,* for example, one character expressed both "good girl" personality (Eve White) and a naughty, uninhibited personality (Eve Black). The transition from one personality to another is usually rapid, often a matter of seconds. Suddenly the person's voice and facial expressions change and another personality emerges. Occasionally, someone with this disorder may harbor as many as ten distinctive personalities.

The personalities exhibited in this disorder generally take on very different patterns; for example, different personalities might be dominated by different emotional states (happy, angry, aggressive, impulsive, and the like) or be centered around different areas of functioning (such as work or family). Most patients have at least one personality who is a child; a majority have at least one personality of the opposite sex (Loewenstein & Ross, 1992). Typically, the personality that approaches a therapist for treatment has little or no knowledge of the other personalities. Instead, the individual is troubled by gaps in time about which he or she has no recollection. Friends may have reported that the person has been behaving oddly (for instance, a normally demure woman may have been seen swearing at a cab driver or drinking heavily in a bar). While the person cannot recall doing such things, he or she may have noticed strange signs of the personality. A nonsmoker, for example, may discover cigarette butts in a living room ashtray. Interestingly, the other personalities may know of one another to varying degrees. Sometimes they think of one another as friends, sometimes as adversaries.

Dissociative identity disorder should not be confused with schizophrenia. Contrary to conventional wisdom, schizophrenics do not display multiple personalities. Traditionally, dissociative identity disorder has been considered rare, but recent reports suggest that it may be more common than was once thought. The first signs of dissociative identity disorder tend to appear in childhood, though they usually do not come to a therapist's attention until adulthood.

Almost all cases of dissociative identity disorder involve those who were once victims of severe abuse, often sexual abuse, during childhood. (Most victims of childhood abuse do *not* suffer from dissociative identity disorder, however.) Kihlstrom, Glisky, and Angluno (1994) report that those who are fantasy-prone, hypnotizable, and suggestible are at greater risk for this disorder than others.

The memory impairments that are seen in dissociative disorders are consistent with Tulving's (1985) three-level theory of memory (see Chapter 7). Tulving proposed that *procedural* memories involving "how to" knowledge are the most basic of all memories. Procedural memories can be formed and expressed without conscious awareness. *Semantic* memories, or memories for facts and knowledge, involve an awareness that does not have a "personal" component. *Episodic* memories, such as the personal memory of high school graduation or a wedding, demand both conscious awareness *and* some kind of personal reference. Characteristically, dissociative amnesia involves the loss of only episodic memory. Amnesiacs cannot remember their names or where they live, but their semantic and procedural memories remain intact. They know whose picture is on the penny (a semantic memory) and how to operate a telephone (a procedural memory) (Kihlstrom, Tataryn, & Hoyt, 1993).

Mood Disorders

Most of the time, the moods we feel are related to what is happening in our lives. We become elated if we win a lottery, dejected if we fail an exam. Sometimes, however, we feel marvelous or miserable for no apparent reason. People with **mood disorders** have much the same experience, but their moods are more intense, and they tend to last longer. As a result, their emotions distort their entire outlook on life, greatly interfering with their normal functioning. Mental health professionals have identified two major types of mood disorder: **depressive disorders,** in which a sad, discouraged mood is the major symptom; and **bipolar disorder,** which involves periods of both depression and excessive elation.

Depressive Disorders

Like many psychological disorders, depressive disorders can be categorized according to the course and severity of symptoms. *DSM-IV* distinguishes between major depression—acute episodes of intense sadness—and dysthymia, a longer-lasting but usually less intense sadness.

Major Depressive Disorder

Major depressive disorder (sometimes called simply *major depression*) is a condition characterized by one or more episodes of deep sadness and despair, each of which persists virtually all day for a period of at least two weeks. People with major depression describe themselves as down, discouraged, and hopeless. They lose interest in formerly pleasurable activities; many say they do not care about anything anymore.

People with major depression display a number of other symptoms, several of which must be present before the diagnosis is made. One is a significant *loss of energy.* That is, many people with major depression feel perpetually tired; even the slightest exertion exhausts them. In keeping with their chronic fatigue, depressed people frequently display a *slowing down of behavior:* posture may become stooped, movements labored, and speech filled with pauses. The opposite may also occur, however: the depressed person may become *agitated,* pacing, wringing his hands, and rubbing his clothing. Depressives also tend to have *difficulty thinking.* They cannot concentrate or remember well and have great trouble making decisions. Frequently an *eating disturbance* (loss of appetite or marked overeating) is involved as well as *problems in sleeping* (insomnia or a tendency to sleep for hours on end). Many depressives also suffer an *exaggerated sense of worthlessness.* They see no virtue in themselves and tend to greatly magnify their failures. Such feelings can lead to a final symptom of depression, *recurring thoughts of death and suicide.*

Of course, many people experience some of these symptoms when they are "low" or "blue." But for a person with major depression, the symptoms are far more intense (Eastwood et al., 1985). Those with major depression may also fail to "bounce back" quickly. The disorder lasts an average of three to six months, depending on its severity (Coryell et al., 1994). Relapses are common, occurring in about 50 percent of all patients within two years after recovery (Shea et al., 1992). Those who have had several such episodes, who are under unusual stress, and who lack emotional support from their families are especially prone to a relapse (Belsher & Costello, 1988). One woman described the spiral downward into a major depression this way:

> I began not to be able to manage as far as doing the kinds of things that I really had always been able to do easily, such as cook, wash, take care of the children, play games, that kind of thing. . . . I think one of the most frightening aspects at the beginning was that time went so slowly. It would seem sometimes that at least an hour had gone by and I would look at my watch and it would only have been three minutes. And I began not to be able to concentrate. . . . I couldn't even read any more. And if awakened early . . . I sometimes would lie in bed two hours trying to make myself get up because I just couldn't put my feet on the floor. Then when I did, I just felt that I couldn't get dressed. And then, whatever the next step was, I felt I couldn't do that.

> (From "Depression: The Shadowed Valley," from the series *The Thin Edge,* Copyright © 1975 by the Educational Broadcasting Corporation.)

Dysthymic Disorder

While major depression is characterized by acute episodes of sadness that last for several months and then go away, another form of depression, **dysthymic disorder** (or just **dysthymia**), endures for years at a time. The diagnosis of dysthymia is made if depression persists for at least two years without periods of remission lasting more than two months. The most common form of dysthymia involves an early onset. The person suffers lifelong negative moods either persistently or interrupted by periods

of normal mood lasting a few days or weeks at a time. Dysthymia is a particularly severe form of depressive disorder (Klein et al., 1988). It sometimes occurs among people who also experience periodic episodes of major depression. The prognosis for people who suffer from both disorders is especially poor (Keller et al., 1982).

Depression and Suicide

The despair of depression and its relatively long duration can lead some depressed people to attempt suicide. In one study of depressed patients, 10 percent made at least one suicide attempt within a year (Shapiro & Keller, 1981). Nearly 30,000 suicides a year are recorded in the United States, and the actual number is probably closer to 100,000. Suicide is the second most common cause of death, surpassed only by accidents, for those Americans aged fifteen to twenty-four (Harvard Medical School, 1986; National Center for Health Statistics, 1988). Although three times more men kill themselves than women, three times more women than men attempt suicide. Men, apparently, choose more lethal methods, such as shooting or hanging, than women, who tend to use sleeping pills (Garland & Zigler, 1993; Holden, 1986).

Many common beliefs about suicide are nothing more than myths. For example, there is little truth to the widespread notion that people who attempt suicide are not serious about killing themselves, but are instead "crying for help." The lifetime risk of suicide among those with mood disorders is nearly 20 percent (Goodwin & Jamison, 1990). About 40 percent of the people who do commit suicide have made another attempt or threat (Maris, 1992); the more attempts, the greater the likelihood of succeeding (Goldstein et al., 1991). There is also no truth to the belief that those who talk about committing suicide seldom do it—that those most likely to commit suicide are the "silent type." In a recent study, more than half of the seventy-one suicide victims had clearly communicated their suicidal intent within the three months prior to their death (Isometa et al., 1994). The message is clear: those who threaten suicide *must* be taken seriously.

What are the signs of an impending suicide attempt? The two most powerful predictors of suicide attempts (and actual suicide) are life stressors and hopelessness. Stressful life events include financial or marital difficulties, illness, and divorce (Rich

The despair of depression provokes some people to attempt suicide. In one study, researchers estimated that 10 percent of those who suffer from depression make at least one suicide attempt a year.

et al., 1991). Hopelessness, the cognitive factor most often associated with depression (Weishaar & Beck, 1992), was found to be the best predictor of suicide in a ten-year follow-up study of people who had been hospitalized for depression (Beck et al., 1985). Ironically, it is when depression begins to lift that people may find the energy and resolve to carry out a suicidal wish (Shneidman, 1973). Table 15-2 displays some of the most important factors that contribute to the decision to end one's life. The "In Depth" section of Chapter 16 examines the topic of suicide more closely.

Depression Explained

Because depression occurs so frequently, it has been called the common cold of mental illness. In total, an estimated 70 percent of women and over 40 percent of men will experience some form of depression before age sixty-five (McGuffin, Bebbington, & Katz, 1989). The incidence of depression has been rising over the past century, and the disorder has been appearing at an increasingly early age (Blazer et al., 1994; Klerman et al., 1985). Since depression is so widespread, we will devote more space to its causes than to the causes of other disorders.

The Psychoanalytic Perspective

Psychoanalytic thinkers have offered several explanations for depression. One that was first proposed by Karl Abraham (1911/1948, 1916/1948), a student of Freud's, and elaborated later by Freud (1917) holds that depression arises from feelings of anger toward a parent or other attachment figure who has died or otherwise abandoned the person. Turned inward, this anger produces guilt and self-loathing, which then bring about depression.

Has research supported the psychoanalytic theory of depression? Although a link between depression and unexpressed anger often does exist, there is little evidence that it originates in the way Freud thought. Many contemporary researchers believe that a second psychoanalytic theory is more promising (Stricker, 1983). According to this view, depression is a reaction to the loss of something deeply valued by a person whose need to be taken care of as an infant was not adequately met (through neglect or the death of a parent, for instance). Such people become fixated on the issue of dependency and the need for love. Later in life, when something valued is taken from them, they feel unbearably vulnerable and are plunged into deep depression.

Indeed, depressed people are more likely than others to have experienced the death of a parent during childhood (Barnes & Prosen, 1985; Nietzel & Harris, 1990). But more recent evidence suggests that the actual *loss* of a parent is not necessary; instead, poor parenting may predispose people to depression (Kendler et al., 1992, 1993). Specifically, depression seems to be more common in those whose parents were overly protective toward them while displaying little genuine care—a pattern that is sometimes called *affectionless control* (Blatt & Homann, 1992;

| TABLE 15-2   *Suicide Risk Factors* |

Risk Factor	Description
Pain	A sense of unbearable psychological pain, directly related to thwarted psychological needs
Self-denigration	A traumtized self-image that cannot tolerate intense psychological pain
Constriction	A narrowing of the thoughts and an unrealistic narrowing of the world and life's actions
Isolation	Feelings of loss of support and desertion, especially from those closest
Hopelessness	A powerful, overwhelming sense that the situation cannot get any better, and that one is helpless to change things
Egression	A deliberate, conscious decision that suicide is the *only* (or at least the best possible) solution to the unbearable pain

Source: Based on Shneidman, 1992, as cited in Alloy, Acocella, & Bootzin, 1995.

Parker, 1992). Moreover, depressive episodes are often triggered by critical losses in a person's life— divorce, the death of a loved one, being fired from a job, and so forth (Paykel & Cooper, 1992). Evidence also suggests that people who are very dependent on others are particularly prone to become depressed over lost interpersonal relationships (Hammen et al., 1985). They seem especially sensitive to rejection or abandonment, and so they readily become depressed when those events occur.

The Learning Perspective

Learning theorists have offered several theories of depression. Peter Lewinsohn (1974) has argued that depression can arise when a person's behavior no longer elicits the rewards it once did. The loss of rewards is often related to some change in the person's social environment—perhaps the death of a loved one, perhaps the loss of or retirement from a job. Suddenly the person is placed in a new situation in which he or she no longer receives the love and approval of others. Without those rewards, the person gives up trying, becoming depressed and withdrawn. That only worsens the problem, for withdrawing from others virtually guarantees that the person will experience few pleasures, and so the depression deepens. Forced into social situations (made to go to a party, for instance), depressed people usually lack the motivation and skill to interact

with others and enjoy themselves. In Lewinsohn's view, they must be helped to become involved in rewarding social activities, so that the negative cycle that maintains their depression can be broken.

The Cognitive Perspective

While Lewinsohn focused on the depressed person's behavior and the failure to achieve rewards, cognitive theorists focus on the negative ways in which depressed people think about themselves and their lives. Two of the most influential cognitive theorists are Aaron Beck and Martin Seligman, whose theory is the subject of this chapter's "In Depth" section.

Beck (1974, 1985) argues that depressed people harbor negative schemas about themselves, the world, and the future ("I'm unlikable; nothing ever goes right; tomorrow will be just as bad as today"). They also tend to confirm their negative schemas by concentrating on irrelevant information, taking small details out of context, overgeneralizing from single incidents, and minimizing the importance of positive events. Consider one depressed patient's assessment of her therapist's behavior. If the therapist arrived late, she heaped blame on herself ("He doesn't want to see me; I'm too hopeless"). If the therapist arrived early, she blamed herself ("I'm so sick he has to rush to the office"). Such distorted thinking, Beck believes, is a major factor in causing and maintaining depression. To lift depression, Beck argues, therapists must help people to break free from such negative outlooks and ways of reasoning.

The Biological Perspective

Some of the factors that underlie mood disorders are undoubtedly biological. For example, concordance rates can be used to estimate the magnitude of genetic influence on a behavior. Concordance rates are computed across pairs of individuals who are genetically rated—twins, siblings, or parent/child, for example. If one member of the pair develops a disorder, the concordance rate indicates the probability that the second member will develop the same disorder. Studies of depression show that monozygotic twins have a much higher concordance rate for depression (40 percent) than dizygotic twins (11 percent) (Allen, 1976). In a more recent study of monozygotic and dizygotic twins, Kendler and associates (1992) estimated that nearly half the difference in the rates of depression in the two groups could be attributed entirely to genetic factors. Consistent with most other behavioral genetics studies, these researchers found that a shared environment (that is, a family environment) had no consistent effect on depression rates. Another group of researchers examined the relatives of two groups of adoptees: those who developed mood disorders as adults and those who did not. Depression was eight times more common in the biological parents of adoptees who suffered from depression (Wender et al., 1986).

Though these results clearly demonstrate the importance of inherited factors in depression, they do not identify the biological mechanism that is involved. For a number of years, researchers have suspected that depression may be related to imbalances in the neurotransmitters *norepinephrine* and *serotonin.* The earliest supporting evidence of this theory came from a drug that was once used to treat those who suffer from tuberculosis, called *iproniazid.* Ironically, the drug had no effect on tuberculosis itself, but it did brighten patients' mood. This discovery helped researchers to develop a number of new **antidepressants.** At about the same time, doctors discovered that *reserpine,* a drug that is used to reduce hypertension (high blood pressure), could also be used to calm highly agitated behavior in seriously disturbed mental patients. Unfortunately, about 15 percent of the time it had an unwanted side effect: serious depression, sometimes to the point of suicide (Lemieux, Davignon, & Genest, 1965).

What effects could these various drugs have on the brain? Researchers found that the new antidepressants (called *tricyclics* and *MAO inhibitors*) increased the levels of norepinephrine and serotonin in the brain. Reserpine, in contrast, had the *opposite* effect on those neurotransmitters, reducing their levels in the brain. Researchers suspect that depression might arise when norepinephrine and serotonin levels dropped below some critical points.

Unfortunately, the answer was not that simple. Although most depressed patients were found to have low serotonin levels, many did not appear to have chronically low levels of norepinephrine (McNeal & Cimbolic, 1986; Muscettola et al., 1984). Even more puzzling was the so-called *therapeutic lag* of most antidepressants; though most of them alter neurotransmitter levels within a few hours, they do not begin to relieve symptoms for several weeks. Depression may not be the result of too little serotonin and norepinephrine in the brain, but of subtle changes in the way neurons in the brain respond to those transmitters.

Many researchers have begun to suspect that in addition to neurotransmitters, hormones may be implicated in depression. Many of the classic depressive symptoms—changes in appetite, levels of arousal, and sexual interest, for instance—are regulated by the hypothalamus and related neural structures (Holsboer, 1992). Furthermore, one of the more common side effects of abnormal hormonal activity is depression. One intriguing possibility is that depression may result from disturbances in normal biological rhythms (Ehlers, Frank, & Kupfer, 1988).

One form of depression, **seasonal affective disorder (SAD),** is known to occur in response to a relative lack of sunlight, most often in the winter. Significantly, the higher the latitude at which people live, the more frequent, long-lasting, and severe the condition (the higher the latitude, the fewer the hours of sunlight during the winter months). When people who suffer from winter depression travel south in the winter (where the days are longer), their depressive symptoms improve. When they travel north in the winter (where the days are shorter), their depressive symptoms worsen (Rosenthal et al., 1986). These findings have led to the use of artificial light as a form of treatment for wintertime depression (Hellekson, Kline, & Rosenthal, 1986; Lewy et al., 1987). In most cases, those who suffer from SAD show marked improvement in response to *light ther-*

Seasonal affective disorder (SAD) is a type of depression brought on by a relative lack of sunlight. It occurs most often in the winter, in northern countries like Finland.

apy, or exposure to bright artificial sunlight for several hours each day, typically during the predawn or evening hours (Oren & Rosenthal, 1992). Some research suggests that timely light therapy can even prevent a full-blown depressive episode (Meesters et al., 1993).

A complete understanding of the biological factors involved in depression will no doubt incorporate disturbances in serotonin, norepinephrine, and hormonal functioning. In Chapter 16 we will look more closely at some of the pharmacological treatments for depression that provide additional clues to the puzzle.

The Interpersonal or Family-Systems Perspective

Though biological factors seem to play a role in producing and maintaining the symptoms of depression, the way in which others respond to a depressed person may also be implicated. According to the interpersonal perspective, depression is not a disorder that arises solely within a person; it has its origin in interpersonal relationships as well. When someone begins to manifest depressive symptoms (sadness, tiredness, apathy), others may react negatively (Coyne, 1976a, 1976b). Though they may try at first to reassure the person and offer some support, their concern is not always genuine. Frequently, they show their true feelings in rejection and avoidance. The depressed person, of course, perceives these negative reactions and responds with deepening despair—which only heightens the reaction of others, who withdraw all the more. A vicious cycle of despondence and rejection develops.

In an interesting experiment designed to test the theory that others are often hostile and rejecting toward depressed people, forty-five normal subjects spoke by telephone to either a depressed or nondepressed person. Those who spoke to a depressed person reported feeling more depressed themselves following the conversation, and they reported increased hostility as well. What is more, they expressed much less willingness than the other subjects to talk with the same person again (Coyne, 1976a). These findings contrast sharply with the cognitive view that the depressed person's negative perceptions are largely a distortion of reality. Apparently, depressed people often do live in a world in which others respond to them negatively—a factor that could easily contribute to their disturbance and perhaps perpetuate a disorder that arose for other reasons.

What exactly does a depressed person do to elicit negative reactions from others? J. C. Coyne (1990) finds no clear answer: "Precisely what depressed people do that leads them to evoke such [negative and rejecting] responses, to be less liked, and to be negatively evaluated remains elusive" (p. 40). Furthermore, in many cases the cause-and-effect relationship between depression and others' negative reactions is not known (Segrin & Abramson, 1994). Joiner, Alfanao, and Metalsky (1992) recently examined the interactions between depressed college students and their roommates. They found that depressed students were more likely to seek reassurance from their roommates, as would be predicted by the interpersonal theory. Their seeking reassurance increased rejection only when it was excessive, however, and only in those cases in which the person seeking reassurance had low self-esteem. Surprisingly, rejection occurred only among *male* roommates; females did not become more rejecting of depressed roommates. This study illustrates the interwoven nature of cause and effect in depression. Who is more likely to seek reassurance? Those with low self-esteem. Why are people with low self-esteem depressed? In part because of the negative reactions they elicit from those around them. Why do people respond to them in negative ways? Because they are always seeking reassurance. . . .

Perspectives Combined

In sum, depression probably has many causes, any number of which can work together to produce depressive symptoms (Akiskal, 1979; Akiskal & McKinney, 1973, 1975; Kendler et al., 1993). One case might be triggered by biological changes and then made worse by negative thinking and negative social reactions. Another might begin with some distressing life event, which sets in motion both a negative outlook and a physiological reaction that intensifies the problem. Because the roots of depression are many and complex, the disorder is best understood from a combination of perspectives.

Manic-Depressive (Bipolar) Disorders

Because depressive disorders usually involve emotional swings in a single direction only—down—they are often called *unipolar* disorders. That is, a depressed person's mood generally cycles between depression and a normal state. In some disorders, though, the depressive mood alternates with periods of extreme elation. Historically, this type of pattern has been called *manic-depression,* but *DSM-IV* refers to it as *bipolar* disorder (in extreme cases) or cyclothymic disorder (in less extreme cases).

Bipolar Disorder

In 5 to 10 percent of mood disorders, depressive symptoms are only half the problem. **Mania,** a condition that is characterized by one or more periods of exaggerated elation, complicates these cases. When depression is combined with mania, the resulting syndrome is known as *bipolar disorder.* Bipolar disorder affects about 1 to 1.5 percent of the population (Kessler et al., 1994). Some few individuals experience mania without depression, but these cases are quite rare.

Besides exaggerated elation, the emotional high of manic episodes is sometimes mixed with intense *irritability*—especially when others try to restrain the manic person. Another common symptom is *hyperactivity.* The manic may plunge headlong into a string of ambitious projects—composing music, writing film scripts, designing a new missile to be sold to the Pentagon—even though he or she has never shown any talent at those tasks. This hyperactive behavior is related to a *decreased need for sleep;* many manics carry on their feverish activities with only a few hours' rest each night. Typically, the manic also displays *constant talkativeness,* speaking rapidly, loudly, and endlessly. Manics are often impossible to interrupt. In part, their speech may reflect "racing" thoughts, a sensation that is referred to clinically as a *flight of ideas.* Another common symptom of mania is great *distractibility:* in conversation, the manic leaps from topic to topic. Many manics also have enormously *inflated self-esteem.* They are convinced that they are brilliant, irresistibly attractive, and superior to everyone else. This greatly distorted self-image is undoubtedly related to a final symptom of mania: *irrational, reckless behavior.* Many manics go on extravagant buying sprees, invest the family savings in foolhardy business ventures, or commit sexual indiscretions, all without the slightest awareness that their behavior could have disastrous results.

You might think that from the manic's viewpoint, mania is an exhilarating experience—a feeling of being invincible, all-powerful, and all-wise. In milder forms of the disorder, that is precisely how the manic feels. The problem, however, is that mania often escalates to such feverish heights that the manic is totally and frighteningly out of control. Here is how one woman described the terrible transition from relatively mild mania (called *hypomania*) to much more severe symptoms:

> [Hypomania] At first when I'm high it's tremendous . . . ideas are fast . . . like shooting stars you follow 'til brighter ones appear . . . all shyness disappears, the right words and gestures are suddenly all there . . . uninteresting people, things become intensely interest-

ing. Sensuality is pervasive, the desire to seduce and be seduced is irresistible. Your marrow is infused with unbelievable feelings of ease, power, well-being, omnipotence, euphoria . . . you can do anything. . . . But somewhere this changes. . . . [Mania] The fast ideas become too fast and there are far too many . . . overwhelming confusion replaces clarity . . . you stop keeping up with it—memory goes. Infectious humor ceases to amuse—your friends become frightened . . . everything is now against the grain . . . you are irritable, angry, frightened, uncontrollable and trapped in the blackest caves of the mind—caves you never knew were there. It will never end.

(Goldstein, Baker, & Jamison, 1980)

Not surprisingly, during a full-blown manic episode, the manic is severely impaired both on the job and in social relationships. Sometimes hospitalization is necessary to prevent the manic from harming him- or herself or others.

Bipolar disorder can take several forms. In some cases, either the mania or the depression predominates; that is, many episodes of depression are interspersed with just a few of mania, or vice versa. Less frequently, the mania and depression alternate regularly. In rare cases, the disorder is *rapid-cycling:* moods switch regularly on a twenty-four- or forty-eight-hour cycle, suggesting that the disorder may be linked to the person's physiological rhythms (Bunney et al., 1972; Jenner et al., 1967; Mendels, 1970). (Such a connection is consistent with Ehler's hypothesis regarding mood disorders and biological rhythms, which was discussed in the previous section [Ehlers, Frank, & Kupfer, 1988].) Often the periods of mood disturbance are relatively short and are separated by intervals of normal functioning. However, in some cases—particularly those that involve rapid cycling—the prognosis for recovery is poor (Bauer et al., 1994).

Clinicians have found that the depression suffered by people with bipolar disorder differs from *unipolar* depression—major depression without manic episodes. Bipolar depression usually starts earlier in life than unipolar depression and is more likely to run in families. A drug called lithium carbonate is more effective in treating depression in those suffering from bipolar disorder than in those with unipolar depression. And while unipolar depression is more common in females, bipolar disorder is found equally as often in males as in females, suggesting that the two forms of depression may have different causes.

Cyclothymia

Just as unipolar depression has a chronic but milder form (*dysthymia*), so bipolar disorder has a chronic but milder form, called **cyclothymia.** In cyclothymia, a person has numerous episodes of both hypomania and depression over at least a two-year period. Though the depressive episodes are not severe enough to be labeled major depressions, they are nonetheless disturbing. Some periods of normal mood may separate the abnormal, but these never last more than two months. Overall, the person seems to be on an endless treadmill of upswings and downswings in mood.

Bipolar Disorders Explained

Though the exact cause(s) of bipolar disorder are not yet known, biological factors are strongly implicated: genetic relatives of those with bipolar disorder are at risk of developing the disorder themselves (McGuffin & Katz, 1989). One possibility is that an inherited biochemical defect is involved (Alloy, Acocella, & Booitzin, 1996). The brains of manic-depressives may "overcorrect" for emotional highs and lows by producing too much of the chemicals that normally neutralize extreme mood (Wehr, Sack, & Rosenthal, 1987). Like depression, though, bipolar disorder almost certainly involves complex interactions between genetic, neurochemical, cognitive, and developmental factors (Whybrow, Akisal, & McKinney, 1984).

Schizophrenia

Though **schizophrenia** affects only 1 to 2 percent of the general population (Reiger et al., 1988), it accounts for half of all cases committed to mental hospitals (Kaplan & Sadock, 1991; Taube & Rednick, 1973; von Korff et al., 1985). Schizophrenia is 1.5 times as likely to develop in men than women (Iacono & Beiser, 1992a, 1992b). A severe disorder with bizarre symptoms, in its acute phase, it prevents its victims from functioning normally, either at work or in their social lives. Schizophrenia is highly resistant to treatment; even with drug therapy, little more than a third of schizophrenics recover (Stephens, 1978).

The following case illustrates the active phase of schizophrenia:

Six months before his admission Arnold began to scream while at work with no apparent provocation, turned off all the machinery, and continually interfered with the work of others. When his supervisor reprimanded him, Arnold told him to go to hell, and was fired. He claimed that he could see his mother's body floating in the air. . . . Four months before his admission he broke in the door of his home with an ax and threatened the members of his family. He was arrested for this, but released soon thereafter. On the day before his admission he threatened to burn the house, and then broke into his father's room and said, "You have got to kill me or I will kill you. Tonight the time is up." Faced with this choice his father had Arnold arrested again. The next morning Arnold told the police, "I see a whole bunch of dead people sitting here now. They run about my cell at night like crazy men, pulling me around. I hear them whispering to me." He was then committed to the local state hospital.

On admission he was quiet and indifferent to his commitment. His conversation and behavior were childish and marked by foolish and inappropriate laughter. At first he thought it was "awful to be among so many crazy people" but shortly thereafter he realized that it was quite a joke, and laughed heartily about his fate. He felt that the attendants were going to kill him, but laughed foolishly while telling of his fears. . . . He experienced a series of vivid hallucinations, including feeling a man's claws on his throat, although he did not see or hear the man, feeling electricity jar him, seeing ghosts haunting him, seeing blue shadows going around and red shadows going up and down through the air, and seeing wingless female spirits flying through the air.

(Zax & Stricker, 1963, p. 101–102)

Arnold's disorganized thoughts and bizarre behaviors are typical of the *active phase* of the disorder. The active phase is usually preceded by a period of progressively deteriorating behavior, during which the person's actions become more and more peculiar. Following the active phase, a schizophrenic usually enters a residual phase, when the symptoms weaken. Generally, each residual phase is followed by another active episode. Arnold's case is fairly typical in that his first symptoms appeared in early adulthood. Although the disorder may also begin in middle or later life, it is more likely to start during or soon after adolescence.

Symptoms of Schizophrenia

The name *schizophrenia,* coined by Swiss psychiatrist Eugen Bleuler (1911), comes from the Greek words *schizein,* meaning "split," and *phren,* meaning "mind." Bleuler referred not to a splitting of the personality into several parts, as in dissociative identity disorder, but to a breaking of the connections among various psychological functions. A schizophrenic's emotions, for example, may be split from his perceptions so that they are totally inappropriate to the situation.

DSM-IV lists a number of disturbances in thought, emotion, perception, and behavior, most of which must be present for at least six months in order to support a diagnosis of schizophrenia. Prominent among these are *disturbances in the content of thought,* especially **delusions**—irrational beliefs that are held despite overwhelming evidence to the contrary. Schizophrenic delusions may take several forms. People who suffer delusions of grandeur may believe that they are some famous person, such as Napoleon or Jesus Christ. Delusions of persecution involve the belief that others—often extraterrestrial beings or secret agents—are plotting against the schizophrenic, controlling his thoughts and actions. Schizophrenics often contend that their thoughts are being stolen or broadcast aloud, or that "foreign" thoughts are being inserted into their heads.

Schizophrenics also suffer from *disturbances in the form of thought.* For instance, their thoughts tend to be very loosely related; they leap from one idea to another even though the two ideas may be only vaguely connected. As a result, their speech is disjointed and is sometimes referred to as a "word salad." Here is one example:

I have just looked up "simplicity" and the dictionary says "sim—one, plicare—to fold, one fold." I told Dr. H. that I dreamed he returned to me the story I sent him which he had folded six times when I had folded it once making it double. Jesus said that the sheep he called would make one fold. I thought at the time that the Latin for six is sex, and that the number of the Beast is 666. Is sex then beastly? I think I will leave you to puzzle out the difference between 6 and 666 and 6 fold in substitution of one fold; for the number of the Beast is a mystery.

(Mayer-Gross, Slater, & Roth, 1969, p. 267)

Note how the speaker moves from a fold in a piece of paper to a sheepfold, from the number 6 to the Latin word for six (*sex*), and from there to the nature of sexual intercourse. Such rambling associations, of course, are not characteristic of normal speech.

Schizophrenic speech is abnormal, too, in its poverty of content. A schizophrenic can talk for a long time and say almost nothing, speaking in vague abstractions or dwelling on tiny details that require

A picture drawn by a schizophrenic patient. In addition to thought disorders, schizophrenics of manifest hallucinations and other disturbances of perception.

many words but convey little information. Schizophrenic speech may also contain many clichéd phrases, monotonous repetitions, nonsense words, and words thrown in simply because they rhyme.

In addition to thought disorders, schizophrenics manifest *disturbances of perception.* They report auditory, visual, olfactory, and sometimes tactile hallucinations. Arnold's visions of ghosts and spirits, and his feeling of being choked or jolted by electricity, are quite characteristic. Often, too, schizophrenics hear voices commenting on their actions, repeating their thoughts aloud, or telling them what to do.

Disturbances of emotion are also typical of schizophrenia. A schizophrenic's emotional responses are either inappropriate or peculiarly blunted. The person may laugh on hearing of a favorite relative's death, become angry on receiving a gift, or show no emotion at all on either occasion. At the same time, schizophrenics have difficulty reading others' emotions (Corrigan & Green, 1993; Feinberg et al., 1986). Even when someone is obviously sad, annoyed, surprised, or frightened, a schizophrenic may hardly notice.

Another schizophrenic symptom is *disturbance in the sense of self.* Schizophrenics are often deeply perplexed about who they are and the meaning of their existence. Those who think that other people's thoughts are being inserted into their heads may become confused about the boundary between the self and others. Most schizophrenics also suffer *disturbances in volition,* that is, in their ability to initiate plans and carry out goal-directed activities. They appear to lack interest and motivation, and often seem unable to follow a course of action to its logical conclusion.

Not surprisingly, schizophrenics suffer from *disturbances in interpersonal relationships.* They tend to become immersed in their own inner world and to avoid involvement with others. Some even act as if other people do not exist: others with the opposite tendency press themselves on people, oblivious to the discomfort their excessive closeness causes.

TABLE 15-3   *Symptoms of Four Subtypes of Schizophrenia*

Subtype	Symptoms
Disorganized (hebephrenic) schizophrenia	Most severe disintegration of personality. Most common symptoms are frequent or constant incoherent speech and odd affect, such as laughing or crying at inappropriate times. Disorganized hallucinations and delusions are present.
Catatonic schizophrenia	Characterized either by excessive, sometimes violent, motor activity or by a mute, unmoving, stuporous state. Some catatonic schizophrenics alternate between these two extremes, but often one or the other behavior pattern predominates.
Paranoid schizophrenia	Characterized by delusions of persecution, grandeur, or both. Paranoid schizophrenics trust no one and are constantly watchful, convinced that others are plotting against them. They may seek to retaliate against supposed tormentors.
Undifferentiated schizophrenia	Characterized by hallucinations, delusions, and incoherence without meeting the criteria for the other types or showing symptoms characteristic of more than one type.

Finally, schizophrenics suffer too from *disturbances in motor behavior.* Some behave in a bizarre fashion, banging their heads against a wall. More often their behavior is simply inappropriate or extremely repetitive. One may spend hours rubbing his forehead or slapping his leg; another may sit all day on a couch, tracing the pattern in the fabric with her finger. Some schizophrenics are motionless, remaining in one position for hours at a time and responding neither to people nor to things, a condition known as **catatonic stupor.**

Subtypes of Schizophrenia

Not all schizophrenics are alike. There are several subtypes of the disorder, each with a different set of symptoms. Table 15-3 describes four of the subtypes listed in *DSM-IV.* The first three were proposed many years ago by German psychiatrist Emil Kraepelin. The difference between catatonic schizophrenia and the others is great, both behaviorally and in terms of treatment.

A newer classification system divides schizophrenics into three categories: those with *positive or active symptoms* (behavioral excesses such as hallucinations, delusions, and bizarre actions, like head banging); those with *negative or passive symptoms* (behavioral deficits such as social withdrawal, lack of interest in pleasurable activities, lack of emotional response, and lack of movement); and those with *mixed symptoms,* some negative and some positive (Andreasen & Olsen, 1982). Researchers suspect that each of these three subtypes may have a different biological cause.

Schizophrenia Explained

Schizophrenia remains one of the most puzzling of all mental disorders. Insights into its causes have come very slowly. In the following sections we will examine the most prominent perspectives on the disorder.

The Biological Perspective

Studies of schizophrenics have consistently shown that this disorder runs in families. That is, genetic relatives of schizophrenics are more likely to develop the condition than people from families that are free of schizophrenia (Gottesman, 1991; Gottesman, McGuffin, & Farmer, 1987). Furthermore, the incidence of schizophrenia is directly related to the amount of genetic overlap. Figure 15-1 displays the concordance rates for schizophrenia among relatives.

Of course, concordance rates could be high because of shared environmental factors. As we have

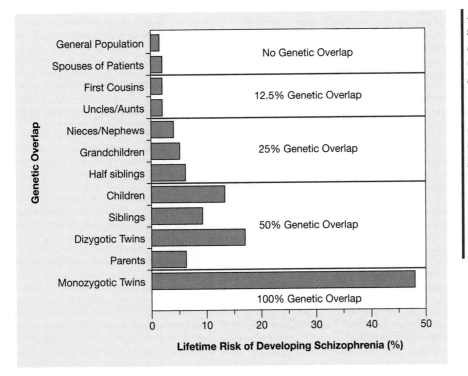

FIGURE 15-1 *Incidence of schizophrenia among biological relatives (concordance rates). A hypothetical lifetime risk of 100 percent would mean that if one member of a biologically related pair were schizophrenic, the other person would be also. Note that the concordance rate for identical twins is far higher than that for fraternal twins.* (After Gottesman, 1990. Used by permission of John Wiley & Sons, Inc.)

seen before, twin studies can help to separate genetic and environmental influences. A review of twin studies shows that the concordance rate for schizophrenia among monozygotic twins is three to five times higher than that for dizygotic twins (Gottesman & Shields, 1976, 1982). Adoption studies provide additional evidence of the importance of genetic factors. In a massive Danish study involving over 5,000 adopted children (Rosenthal et al., 1968), those children whose biological parents had been diagnosed as schizophrenic were found to be nearly twice as likely to develop schizophrenia as adopted children whose biological parents had no history of the disorder. In a related study using the same data (Kety, 1988; Kety et al., 1994), researchers were able to identify thirty-three adoptees who developed schizophrenia (researchers called these *index* cases) and match them with a group of adoptees who were not schizophrenic (the *control* cases). Biological relatives of the index cases were found twice as likely to develop schizophrenia as biological relatives of the control cases. This later study also found that *adoptive* relatives of the index cases were no more likely to develop schizophrenia than adoptive relatives of the control cases. These studies make clear the importance of genetic factors in schizophrenia.

In searching for the biological mechanisms that underlie schizophrenia, researchers have examined the role of neurotransmitters (Valenstein, 1978). Several lines of evidence point to the involvement of the transmitter dopamine. For example, phenothiazines—drugs that are highly effective in reducing certain symptoms of schizophrenia—block the uptake of the neurotransmitter dopamine at its receptor sites in the brain (Creese, Burt, & Snyder, 1975). In addition, drugs that are known to increase dopamine levels, such as amphetamine and cocaine, can induce schizophrenic-like symptoms at high doses. Recall the story from John C. Flynn's book *Cocaine* (1991) that opened Chapter 5: "Helen," a young woman who had been brought to the hospital in a frenzy, was experiencing delusions, hallucinations, and other symptoms of what appeared to be an acute schizophrenic episode—except that her symptoms were brought on by a toxic reaction to cocaine. Other drugs, mostly stimulants like amphetamine, have been known to induce similar reactions. If amphetamine or cocaine is administered to a schizophrenic, the symptoms of the disorder become more intense almost immediately.

Since many dopamine receptors are located in the *limbic forebrain,* an area that is intimately involved in attention and emotion, overactivity in those receptors could produce schizophrenic symptoms. But exactly what might be entailed in such overactivity is not known. One theory is that schizophrenics have an excess of dopamine; another is that their dopamine receptors are unusually sensitive; and a third is that schizophrenics have an abnormally large number of dopamine receptors (Lee & Seeman, 1977; Meltzer & Stahl, 1976; Wong et al., 1986). Though these theories are appealing, some studies have failed to support them, nor have researchers yet found a single abnormal trait related to dopamine activity that is shared by all schizophrenics (*Schizophrenia Bulletin*, 1982).

Some investigators suspect that what is labeled a single disorder—schizophrenia—may in fact be several disorders, each with its own causes. Recall the distinction between two classes of schizophrenic symptoms: positive or active symptoms, like hallucinations and delusions, and negative or passive symptoms, like blunted emotions and social withdrawal (Andreasen & Olsen, 1982). The positive symptoms of schizophrenia may be linked to dopamine, for they respond quite well to phenothiazines (Andreasen, 1989; Haracz, 1982). The negative symptoms, which typically do not respond to phenothiazines, may be unrelated to dopamine levels. They may be tied instead to structural damage in the brain.

For instance, many schizophrenics who do not improve with drug therapy have been found to have enlarged cerebral ventricles (fluid-filled brain regions), which suggests that their brain tissue has atrophied (Brown et al., 1986). The more enlarged the cerebral ventricles, the more social isolation and other passive symptoms patients tend to show (Andreasen et al., 1982). At the same time, schizophrenics with passive symptoms often have smaller frontal lobes than normal people, as well as signs of degenerated neurons, especially in the cerebral cortex (Andreasen et al., 1986; Benes, 1986). Recently, some researchers have found links between schizophrenia and prenatal brain trauma (Bilder et al., 1994; Bogerts, 1993). Postmortem investigations show that neuronal connections that are usually made in the second trimester (the fourth to sixth months of pregnancy) are disrupted or incomplete in schizophrenics (Akbarina, Bunney, et al., 1993; Akbarina, Vinuela et al., 1993).

Finally, many of the disturbances that are seen in schizophrenics may have a cognitive basis—specifically problems of attention. The positive symptoms of schizophrenia (delusions, hallucinations) appear to be related to overattention (Perry & Braff, 1994). Bombarded by input they cannot screen out, schizophrenics are unable to distinguish between important and unimportant stimuli. The negative symptoms of schizophrenia, on the other hand, appear to be the product of underattention (Braff, 1993). Though most people react physiologically when their environment changes (with a change in heart rate or respiration, for example), those with negative symptoms do not display such "orienting responses." Apparently ability to attend to the world is impaired. As might be expected, those with diminished attentiveness tend to become withdrawn and unresponsive.

Much more research needs to be done before psychologists can draw firm conclusions about the biological causes of schizophrenia. Today investigators are pursuing several leads. In addition to studying dopamine activity, scientists are exploring the involvement of other neurotransmitters, including serotonin, norepinephrine, and some of the neuropeptides. Some researchers continue to explore structural defects in the brains of schizophrenics, while others are looking into the possibility that a virus infection, a toxin, or a deficiency in the immune system might be involved in the disorder (Mednick et al., 1988; Schmeck, 1986). When the mystery of schizophrenia is finally solved, it will probably be found that many biochemical and structural factors contribute to its varied symptoms.

Though biological factors play a major role in schizophrenia, environmental factors contribute as well. If schizophrenia were entirely a matter of biological inheritance, the second in a pair of identical twins would always develop the disorder if the first twin did. That does not always happen, however. The second twin is affected only 40 to 50 percent of the time, suggesting that environmental influences the twins do not always share may be involved.

The Interpersonal or Family-Systems Perspective

Some psychologists think that maladaptive ways of interacting with family members may trigger schizophrenic breakdowns. Studies show that the highest relapse rates and the severest recurring symptoms are often found among discharged schizophrenics who

TABLE 15-4   *Statements by Relatives of Schizophrenics Showing High and Low Expressed Emotion*

Degree of Expressed Emotion	Examples
High expressed emotion	
Note the intrusiveness and negative tone of the feelings they express toward the patient:	"I always say, 'why don't you pick up a book, do a crossword or something like that to keep your mind off it.' *That's* even too much trouble."
	"I've tried to jolly him out of it and pestered him into doing things."
	"He went round the garden 90 times, in the door, back out the door. I said 'Have a chair, sit out in the sun.' Well, he nearly bit my head off."
Low expressed emotion	
Note their low-key acceptance of the patient's behavior:	"I know it's better for her to be on her own, to get away from me and try to do things on her own."
	"Whatever she does suits me."
	"I just tend to let it go because I know that when she wants to speak she will speak."

Source: Hooley, 1985.

have returned home to be cared for by their families. In these cases, the family may aggravate the disorder. But what aspects of family life might be involved?

One factor seems to be high **expressed emotion**—that is, an emotionally charged atmosphere characterized by an overbearing attitude, hostility, and criticism (Hooley, 1985; Miklowitz et al., 1989). (See Table 15-4 for a comparison of the statements made by family members who were judged high or low in expressed emotion.) One study compared the long-term outcome of schizophrenics who came from families with a history of high expressed emotion (Miklowitz et al., 1989). Nine months after they had been discharged from their psychiatric facility, those from families high in expressed emotion were three to four times as likely to have suffered a schizophrenic relapse. Fortunately, the relatives of schizophrenics can often be taught to lower their levels of expressed emotion (Falloon, 1988), a tactic that substantially reduces relapse rates (Leff et al., 1982). Relapse rates can also be reduced by instructing patients to spend less time with family members who are high in expressed emotion.

Perspectives Combined: The Diathesis–Stress Model

Apparently, many factors, both biological and environmental, can increase a person's risk of developing schizophrenia. Though genetic factors certainly contribute, behavioral geneticists emphasize the *interaction* between genetic and environmental factors. The *diathesis–stress model* summarizes this interaction. A person may have a biological predisposition toward schizophrenia, which is most likely genetic in origin: that is the diathesis side of the model. The role played by life stresses, such as a troubled family environment or the hardships of poverty, forms the other side of the model. Thus, in a person with a strong biological predisposition toward schizophrenia, comparatively few life stresses might be needed to trigger the disorder. In a person with a weak biological predisposition, many external pressures would probably be needed to provoke schizophrenic symptoms. A person with no biological predisposition would probably never develop the disorder (Gottesman & Shields, 1982).

A study of adopted children supports the diathesis–stress model (Tienari, 1991). Youngsters who

Like many people with antisocial personality disorder, the killer Ted Bundy had a history of violent and antisocial acts that began in his childhood. He displayed no guilt or remorse for his actions.

were born to schizophrenic mothers (and so were apt to become schizophrenic themselves) showed more signs of mental illness if they were raised in a troubled adoptive family. In contrast, among children born to nonschizophrenic mothers, growing up in a maladjusted adoptive family was unrelated to poor mental health. Often, then, both a genetic predisposition (a diathesis) and a stressful environment are needed for schizophrenic symptoms to surface (Gottesman & Bertelsen, 1989). Since stress is what ultimately pushes many genetically vulnerable people over the edge, improving the ability to cope with stress may be one of the best defenses against schizophrenic breakdown (Zubin & Spring, 1977).

Finally, genetic and environmental factors are not independent; in many cases, genetic predispositions serve to *create* a person's environment. (Recall the discussion of Plomin and Neiderhiser's work, 1992, in Chapter 13.) For example, many of the destructive patterns in the families of schizophrenics may have begun *in response* to the genetically influenced behavior of the schizophrenic in the family. Once initi-

ated, the family's negative criticism exacerbates the schizophrenic's symptoms, and a vicious cycle develops. The high relapse rates of schizophrenics who return to such toxic family environments (Miklowitz et al., 1989)—and the fact that those rates can be lowered by helping families to lower the levels of expressed emotion (Leff et al., 1982)—show the importance of environmental factors in this disorder.

Personality Disorders

Personality disorders are defined in *DSM-IV* as "an enduring pattern of inner experience and behavior that deviates markedly from the expectations of the individual's culture, is pervasive and inflexible, has an onset in adolescence or early adulthood, is stable over time, and leads to distress or impairment" (American Psychiatric Association, 1994, p. 629). Often the disturbed person does not even recognize that there is a problem. The person's maladaptive behaviors are so deeply ingrained that they are accepted by others as familiar traits. Their acceptance provides no incentive for the person to change, for personality disorders typically cause more distress to others than to the people who have them. Table 15-5 lists ten personality disorders and their primary symptoms. We will look at three: antisocial personality disorder (the most serious and extensively studied), narcissistic personality disorder, and borderline personality disorder.

Antisocial Personality Disorder

The **antisocial personality,** or **sociopath,** has a history of antisocial acts beginning in childhood or adolescence and continuing into adulthood. These people act on impulse without considering others, with no guilt or remorse. They seem to lack a conscience as well as many normal emotions. From 3 to 5 percent of American males and 1 percent of American females have this disorder (Kessler et al., 1994).

Though signs of an antisocial personality become apparent before the age of fifteen, the condition is not diagnosed as an antisocial disorder until age eighteen. In individuals younger than eighteen, it is referred to as conduct disorder. These youngsters have serious behavior problems, including truancy, running away from home, fighting, cruelty, destruction of property, stealing, and habitual lying. The problems continue in adulthood, revealing themselves in impulsiveness, recklessness, blatant disregard for the truth, excessive irritability and aggres-

| TABLE 15-5   *Symptoms of Personality Disorders* |

Disorder	Symptoms
Paranoid personality disorder	Pervasive and long-standing suspiciousness and mistrust of people; hypersensitivity and difficulty in getting along with others
Schizotypal personality disorder	Eccentricities of thinking, perception, communication, and behavior, not severe enough to be schizophrenic
Schizoid personality disorder	Social withdrawal and lack of normal emotional relationships with others
Avoidant personality disorder	Hypersensitivity to rejection and unwillingness to enter into relationships; social withdrawal despite a desire for interaction; low self-esteem
Dependent personality disorder	Failure to assume responsibility for major areas of one's life; reliance on others to make important decisions; lack of self-esteem
Borderline personality disorder	Instability in behavior, mood, and self-image
Histrionic personality disorder	Overly reactive behavior; exaggerated expressions of emotion seemingly "performed" for an audience
Narcissistic personality disorder	Grandiose sense of self-importance; preoccupation with fantasies of unlimited success; exhibitionistic need for constant admiration
Obsessive-compulsive personality disorder	Preoccupation with rules, order, organization, efficiency, and detail; rigidity and inability to express warm emotions or take pleasure in normally pleasurable activities
Antisocial personality disorder	Chronic and continuous behavior that violates the rights of others; inability to form attachments or (often) to succeed in an occupation; onset before age fifteen

Source: Alloy, Acocella, & Bootzin, 1996, pp. 259–266.

sion, repeated violations of the law, irresponsible parenting, the inability to hold a steady job, failure to honor financial obligations, and an incapacity for normal friendship or love. Remember that personality disorders are usually problems *of degree,* however. While many people are impulsive, that trait alone would not warrant a diagnosis of antisocial personality disorder (see Patton, 1994).

Psychologists have debated the causes of antisocial personality disorder. Psychoanalysts believe that sociopaths are the product of rejecting parents. If there is no love between parent and child, the child is unlikely to adopt the parents' moral values, and so to develop a conscience. Studies provide some support for this explanation: a lack of parental affection is a recurring theme in the histories of people with antisocial personality disorder (McCord & McCord, 1964). So are a lack of parental supervision and discipline, conflict between parents, and a father who is antisocial (McCord, 1979; Robins, 1966). The last factor—an antisocial father—suggests that antisocial tendencies may be both learned and inherited (Cloninger & Gottesman, 1987). Children could learn antisocial behavior by observing a father's irresponsible actions. Their misconduct might then be reinforced when it gains them attention they cannot get in other ways.

Biological theorists have proposed that sociopaths may be born with certain physiological traits that predispose them to develop an antisocial

The character Jennifer Jason Leigh played in the movie "Single White Female" was a classic example of borderline personality disorder. Such individuals are moody, unstable, and have intense and stormy relationships.

behavior pattern. Among these is a chronic under-arousal of the autonomic nervous system, which is greatly involved in emotional responses (Hare, 1970). This could explain why sociopaths seek to gratify their impulses at all costs, behave recklessly, and commit crimes for thrills—presumably to boost their arousal levels. At the same time, chronic under-arousal could explain why sociopaths are unresponsive to certain kinds of punishment (electric shock, for example) that would upset normal people (Lykken, 1957; Schachter & Latané, 1964). Because sociopaths seek to compensate for underarousal, they may view punishment positively. However, recent research by Newman and his colleagues suggests a cognitively based explanation: those with antisocial personality disorder may focus on rewards rather than punishments (Newman, Konnon, & Patterson, 1992; Patterson & Newman, 1993). These researchers found that sociopaths were just as likely to fear punishment but were less likely to pay attention to aversive events.

Narcissistic Personality Disorder

People with **narcissistic personality disorder** have an overblown sense of their own importance and tend to describe themselves in grandiose terms. They crave the attention and admiration of others and are constantly trying to impress. Yet underneath their self-aggrandizement lies a very fragile sense of self-esteem. These people greatly fear failure and are highly sensitive to criticism. Always envious of those who seem smarter, more handsome, or more successful than themselves, they cannot empathize with others' feelings and tend to exploit friendships for their own ends.

Some psychologists believe that this disorder develops when parents fail to give children the love, respect, and empathy they need. Personal shortcomings make such children feel vulnerable, and they seek unending approval from others (Benjamin, 1987; Kohut, 1978). This theory, however, has not been confirmed. Narcissistic personality disorder seems to be increasing in incidence in our society.

Borderline Personality Disorder

The principal feature of **borderline personality disorder** is an instability of self-image, interpersonal relations, and mood. These people are highly uncertain about who they are, what their values and goals are, and who their friends ought to be. When they do form relationships, they are usually intense and stormy, with great highs and lows. One day the friend or lover is idealized and pursued, the next day, scorned and rejected. Yet if someone threatens to abandon the person with borderline personality disorder, that person will make frantic efforts to keep the relationship intact.

The moods of a person with borderline personality disorder are also erratic, changing rapidly from normal to very depressed, irritable, or anxious, and then back again. Often the person complains of a chronic feeling of emptiness and boredom, which may explain the self-destructive impulses such as spending sprees, sexual indiscretions, or drug binges these people engage in. Psychologists do not yet know what causes a borderline personality disorder to develop. The condition does tend to run in families and is more prevalent among women than men (Baron et al., 1985; McGlashan, 1983).

Substance-Related Disorders

A psychoactive substance is any chemical that can alter a person's thoughts, moods, perceptions, and behaviors. This definition includes a wide variety of recreational drugs, many of which were discussed in Chapter 5: alcohol, marijuana, LSD, cocaine, and amphetamines. The discussion in this chapter is restricted to alcohol, which is the most frequently used (by well over 100 million people) *and* most fre-

Symptoms of alcoholism include solitary drinking, social withdrawal or isolation, and repeated failure to limit the amount of alcohol consumed.

quently abused (by as many as 13 million) substance in American society (Kaplan & Sadock, 1991). We will discuss only those situations in which continuing use of alcohol leads to problems—that is, in which "use" becomes "abuse."

Alcohol Dependence and Abuse

The use of alcohol to modify mood and behavior is widely considered appropriate and normal in our society. A great many people have a few drinks at a party or while relaxing with friends or family after a busy day. But for millions of Americans, alcohol consumption has expanded far beyond moderate recreational use. These people suffer from alcohol dependence and abuse, the most widespread of **substance-related disorders** in the United States.

Alcohol dependence involves an inability to limit drinking, even if one desires to do so. Alcohol-dependent people are often aware that drinking is causing them serious problems in their work and social lives, yet they feel powerless to change their drinking habits. Frequently they are intoxicated or "hung over" when they are expected to fulfill some major obligation, such as going to work, showing up for an exam, or taking care of their children. They also tend to develop a tolerance for the drug, so that they need more and more of it to achieve the same high. Refraining from alcohol may cause withdrawal symptoms (trembling, sweating, anxiety, and, in severe cases, hallucinations). Alcohol-dependent people are commonly called *alcoholics*. **Alcohol abusers,**

in contrast, are people who are not (or not *yet*) alcoholics, but for whom alcohol is causing problems. The college student who binges on alcohol every few weekends, to the point of missing classes the following Monday mornings, but who has no other troubles related to the drug, would be diagnosed an alcohol abuser.

About 13 percent of Americans will have a problem with drinking at some point in their lives (Robins et al., 1984). Currently, between 10 and 15 million people in the United States meet the definition of alcohol dependence or alcohol abuse (Kaplan & Sadock, 1991). Perhaps as many as 35 million others are experiencing the negative effects of these problem drinkers' behavior. One Gallup poll indicated that fully a third of all American families have experienced difficulties related to alcohol use (Saxe et al., 1983). Although alcohol dependence is more common among adult males, it is on the rise among women and teenagers (Becker & Kronus, 1977; Hansen, 1993).

Alcoholism takes a staggering toll economically, medically, and socially. The United States loses as much as $120 billion annually as a result of alcohol dependence, a large proportion of which stems from the sharp decline in the alcoholic's productivity on the job. An estimated 40 percent of all hospital beds are filled with people suffering from alcohol-related illnesses; direct medical treatment and social support services for these disorders cost an estimated $20 billion each year (Rice et al., 1990, cited in Alloy,

Acocella, & Bootzin, 1996). Prolonged alcoholism can cause irreparable liver damage, brain dysfunction, and cardiovascular disease. Not surprisingly, the life expectancy of an alcoholic is ten to twelve years shorter than that of the average person. Alcoholism is also frequently implicated in a long list of legal and social problems. An estimated half of all traffic accidents, two-fifths of all family court cases, a third of all suicides, and sizable proportions of assaults, rapes, and murders involve the use of alcohol (Eckardt et al., 1981; NIAAA, 1982). Yet the vast majority of problem drinkers—an estimated 85 percent—receive no treatment.

Alcoholism Explained.

What causes alcoholism? Some psychoanalysts have theorized that it arises in those who as babies have developed a conflict over the need for oral gratification. As infants they were uncertain whether food would be given or withheld, so they came to be abnormally dependent and highly anxious. As adults, these people may reveal their fixation in "oral behaviors" like drinking. Interestingly, alcoholics tend to be heavier smokers than nonalcoholics; smoking may be another way of gratifying oral needs (Maletzky & Klotter, 1974). Psychoanalytic thinkers have also suggested that heavy alcohol use may be a way of combating low self-esteem and acquiring an illusion of mastery and power. The aggressiveness of some intoxicated alcoholics may express their quest for self-importance and control. But the psychoanalytic prediction that alcoholics have similar personalities before the onset of the disorder has not necessarily been supported (Saxe et al., 1983). Many kinds of people fall prey to alcoholism, a finding that suggests causes other than personality traits.

Learning theorists argue that the causes of alcoholism lie in the rewards of drinking, especially the reduction in tension that alcohol consumption can bring. According to this view, many people begin drinking to alleviate stress. At first their cares and worries do lessen, so their drinking behavior is reinforced. But the more they drink, the greater the likelihood that their problems will worsen. Excessive drinking creates additional troubles at home and on the job. Because people often drink alone, when they have no companions to distract them from their worries and cares, they may dwell on their problems even more than usual, making them seem worse (Steele & Josephs, 1988; Steele, Southwick, & Pagano,

1986). The additional stress the behavior pattern creates leads to even heavier drinking, and a vicious cycle begins.

Several lines of evidence seem to support the tension-reduction theory. For example, the more stresses there are in a given community (high crime rate, high divorce rate, low income, poor housing), the more widespread alcoholism is likely to be (Linsky et al., 1985). Similarly, people who have recovered from alcoholism often have relapses when they encounter very stressful events (Marlatt & George, 1988). A need to reduce tension may encourage them to begin drinking again.

Tests of the tension-reduction theory have not always supported it, however. While subjects under stress do sometimes drink more than nonstressed subjects, at other times they drink the same amount or even significantly less (Higgins & Marlatt, 1973, 1975; Holroyd, 1978; Marlatt, Kosturn, & Lang, 1975). In one study, for instance, students were led to believe they had done well or poorly on a difficult test and then were given a chance to drink (Volpicelli et al., 1982). Those who thought they had done well (the low-stress subjects) actually drank more than those who thought they had done poorly (the high-stress subjects). In this instance, relief from tension, rather than tension itself, seemed to foster drinking. Such findings have led to the theory that the desire to drink may be related to a drop in the level of endorphins, neurotransmitters that reduce pain and elevate mood in the brain (Volpicelli, 1987). During stress, the body responds by boosting endorphin levels; after stress, endorphin levels drop. Drinking at that point may be a way of compensating for endorphin reduction, for alcohol seems to stimulate the endorphin receptors.

Psychologists have proposed other biological theories to explain why people drink to excess. One is that some people inherit a neurological defect that alcohol helps to correct (Tarter et al., 1985). This idea is supported by the finding that alcohol consumption reverses certain abnormal neurological symptoms in men at high risk for becoming alcoholics (Hegedus et al., 1984; Schuckit, 1987). People who are at high risk for alcoholism may also have inherited a tolerance for the drug: they may be able to drink more than others without experiencing ill effects (Schuckit & Gold, 1988). Such a tolerance would allow them to consume the large amounts of alcohol necessary to become an alcoholic.

Alcoholism clearly has a genetic component. The concordance rate for male monozygotic twins is nearly twice that for dizygotic twins—55 to 28 percent (Hrubec & Omenn, 1981). More recent research (McGue, Pickens, & Svikis, 1992) found even higher concordance rates in male twins: 77 percent for monozygotic twins and 54 percent for dizygotic twins. However, the concordance rates for women were considerably lower (about 40 percent). Curiously, in females, there was no significant difference in the concordance rates for monozygotic (39 percent) and dizygotic (41 percent) twins. This finding may illustrate how important the *interaction* between heredity and environment can be. Regardless of one's genetic makeup, a person cannot become an alcoholic *unless he or she drinks alcohol.* Genetic factors would more accurately be described as "predisposing" an individual toward alcoholism.

Although the biological factors involved in alcoholism have not been identified, researchers believe that some genetic influences may encourage alcoholism, especially in males born to parents with a history of continual drinking and antisocial behavior. These boys run a much higher risk than normal of becoming alcoholics, even when they are adopted into families in which alcohol is not abused. Those who do become alcoholics seem to develop a form of the disorder with a very strong genetic component. There is probably another form of alcoholism that is more heavily influenced by environmental factors (Cloninger et al., 1985). Because of the diversity of contributing causes, clinicians today use many approaches to treating alcoholism. We will say more about them in the next chapter.

In Depth

Hopelessness, Helplessness, and Depression

EARLIER IN THIS chapter you were introduced to Martin Seligman's theory of *learned helplessness*. When people feel powerless to eliminate a painful stimulus, they often become upset, hopeless, and give up trying to cope—classic symptoms of depression. Seligman's theory has been extremely influential during the past twenty-five years. Though it has since been revised and modified, learned helplessness remains one of the most compelling theoretical accounts of depression.

Initial Studies. Seligman's research began with some unusual experiments on dogs (Seligman, Maier, & Geer, 1968). He exposed one group of dogs to a long series of electric shocks, from which they could not escape. Later, when the same dogs were placed in another situation, in which they could escape shocks by jumping to one side, they tended not to do so. Instead, most lay down motionless, passively enduring as many shocks as the experimenter chose to give. A second group of dogs that had not received any shocks behaved differently. Animals in this second group invariably managed to jump in order to escape the pain. Moreover, the two groups of dogs differed markedly in their postexperimental behavior. Those in the first group displayed symptoms of depression—lethargy, inactivity, loss of appetite—while those in the second group did not.

Seligman concluded that the differences between the groups stemmed from what they had learned. Animals in the first group had learned that they were helpless to control the shocks and so continued to act helplessly in the second stage of the experiment, when the shocks were controllable. Such "learned helplessness," Seligman speculated, could be an important cause of depression in humans. When people are unable to influence a situation that is important to them, they may not only give up trying to change that situation but become depressed as well, showing little initiative in new situations.

Criticisms, Alternatives, and Further Research. Seligman's original theory and research generated much controversy. Critics charged that learned helplessness alone cannot explain the many variations in cases of depression. Why do some depressed people constantly blame themselves, while others do so much less often? Why are some depressive episodes so severe and prolonged, while others are much shorter and milder?

As a result of these and other criticisms, Seligman and his colleagues modified their original theory (Abramson et al., 1978). Uncontrollable outcomes alone do not determine the nature and magnitude of human depression, they argued; the way a person explains those outcomes also plays a crucial part. Consider three types of people. The first attributes undesirable outcomes to temporary external causes. Such people may feel dejected for a time, but because they do not reproach themselves, their chances for bouncing back are good. The second type of person attributes undesirable outcomes to personal inadequacies. Such people will probably experience depression accompanied by guilt and self-blame. The third type of person not only attributes negative outcomes to personal shortcomings but sees those shortcomings as enduring traits. Such people will probably experience the severest form of depression, because they see themselves as inadequate and prone to failure and rejection.

To gather support for this revised theory, Seligman and his colleagues developed a questionnaire that assesses how people explain negative life events. Using this questionnaire, they have found that many depressed people do attribute negative experiences to inborn traits, while nondepressed people generally do not. Moreover, this mode of thought often precedes depression; it is not always the result of an emotionally dejected state. In one study, researchers found that a tendency to attribute negative events to oneself could be used to predict subsequent bouts of depression, even though some subjects were not yet depressed when their explanatory style was assessed (Zullow & Seligman, 1985). Seligman's theory is similar to Beck's (1974, 1985) in that both suggest that negatively distorted thinking can cause depression. (See p. 513 for a discussion of Beck's theories.)

Not all psychologists agree with this perspective, however. Some point to findings which suggest that depressed people's thinking may not be as distorted as Seligman and Beck believe (Coyne & Gotlib, 1983). Compared with other people, those who are depressed are indeed more apt to feel that they cannot control negative outcomes, as Seligman contends. But Seligman may be wrong in assuming that is so because depressed people imagine they have less control than they actually do. Research shows that the depressed are sometimes more realistic in estimating their degree of control over outcomes than nondepressed people (Alloy & Abramson, 1979). Similarly, depressed people rate themselves as having poorer social skills than other people; they do seem to have the negative self-schemas Beck says they do. But are those schemas distortions of reality, as Beck suggests? Perhaps not, for unbiased observers agree with the low social-skill ratings depressed people give themselves (Lewinsohn et al., 1980). Thus, when depressed people view themselves and their experiences negatively, they may be making fairly accurate assessments. If depressed people's lives are going badly, and their own actions and lack of effort are involved (Coyne & Gotlib, 1983), is their view of the world really distorted?

Seligman responds that it may not matter how realistic or unrealistic the views of depressed people are. If, for whatever reason, people think that their own enduring faults cause their negative experiences, that style of thinking is apt to bring on intense and long-lasting dejection. The evidence on this assumption is mixed. In one study, several hundred college students who were taking an introductory psychology course were assessed for their style of explaining negative events (Metalsky et al., 1987). Shortly thereafter they received their grades on the midterm exam. Most of those who did poorly on the exam became depressed, regardless of how they explained their low scores. A negative way of thinking, then, was not the major cause of their depression. Those students who stayed depressed for longer than a few days were prone to blame their own enduring faults, however. Apparently, when people with a negative outlook experience an upsetting event, they respond with more intense and prolonged dejection than others.

Critics of the theory of learned helplessness are not satisfied, though. Some question whether a tendency to blame oneself for negative outcomes typically precedes depression, as Seligman has suggested. Although some studies have supported Seligman's contention, others have not. In one study, for example, patients were assessed at two different times: first while in the midst of a major depression, and later when they were ready to be discharged from the hospital (Hamilton & Abramson, 1983). During the first assessment, many manifested a negative style of thinking (blaming negative outcomes on their own shortcomings). But in the second assessment, that tendency disappeared. These findings call into question Seligman's hypothesis that a negative attributional style promotes depression. More likely, one's attributional style interacts with one's mood, each influencing the other. If so, attributional style may be considered a contributor to depression, but not its major cause.

Such findings have encouraged another revision of learned helplessness theory known as the *hopelessness theory* (Abramson, Metalsky, & Alloy, 1989). According to hopelessness theory, a negative style of thinking is just one of several cognitive tendencies that make a person vulnerable to depression. Another is the tendency to cast oneself in a negative light, that is, to form the negative self-schemas Aaron Beck studied. A third is the tendency to assume that negative experiences will have severe consequences—that they are capable of virtually crippling a person's life. Finally, and perhaps most importantly, those suffering depression believe that their lack of control will persist, and they abandon hope for the future.

Current research on the hopelessness theory has generally been positive. For example, Spirito and his colleagues found that hopelessness is the single best predictor of suicide, greatest risk single best predictor of suicide, especially in adolescents (Spirito et al., 1989a; Spirito, Overholser, & Stark, 1989).

Patterns and Conclusions. If psychologists are to fully understand the causes of depression, they cannot ignore cognitive factors. Today researchers are examining many different styles of thinking to discover which are related to severe mood disturbances. For instance, when women experience sadness, they often ruminate about it more than men do, which may only serve to intensify and prolong the mood. Men, in contrast, are more inclined to shake off negative feelings by getting involved in some physical activity, such as sports. This positive response could help explain why only half as many men as women suffer from depression (Nolen-Hoeksema, 1987). Of course, such theories have not yet been proved. New studies are needed, especially longitudinal studies, to pinpoint the various cognitive factors involved in depression (Downey, Silver, & Wortman, 1991). Psychologists must also try to determine how various cognitive factors interact with one another, and with other significant forces, to bring on serious depression.

SUMMARY

1. Various criteria can be used to assess the abnormality of any behavior. Among them are deviation from statistical norms, nonconformity with social values, and behavior that is considered psychologically "unhealthy" according to generally accepted standards—for example, persistent emotional suffering, behavior that is disturbing to others, and an inability to perform daily activities.

2. According to the **biological perspective,** abnormal behavior is caused by physical dysfunction; according to various psychological perspectives, it is caused by personal experience, including emotional conflict (prominent in the **psychoanalytic approach**), inappropriate learning (central to the **learning perspective**), and maladaptive thinking (the focus of the **cognitive perspective**). Some perspectives on abnormality look beyond the individual for the cause of abnormal behavior. In the **interpersonal** or **family-systems perspective,** abnormal behavior is seen as the product of the important relationships in a person's life; in the **sociocultural perspective,** mental disturbance is seen as rooted in social ills such as poverty.

3. Today, the most widely used system for classifying mental disorders is the *Diagnostic and Statistical Manual of Mental Disorders,* fourth edition *(DSM-IV),* published by the American Psychiatric Association. Although such systems have their critics, without them, treatment of the mentally disturbed would be difficult.

4. **Anxiety disorders** are characterized by emotional distress arising from feelings of vulnerability, apprehension, or fear. In **panic disorder,** a person suffers from sudden, inexplicable attacks of intense fear. In **phobic disorders,** one particular stimulus, such as dogs or high places, arouses intense fear. In **generalized anxiety disorder,** a person is constantly in a state of apprehension provoked by groundless worries. In **obsessive-compulsive disorder,** senseless, unwanted thoughts (obsessions) keep intruding into a person's consciousness. To reduce anxiety, the person may feel compelled to perform some behavior over and over (a compulsion). **Posttraumatic stress disorder** is a state of anxiety, depression, and psychological numbing that follows exposure to a severe trauma, such as warfare, rape, or a catastrophic natural disaster.

5. A **somatoform disorder** is characterized by some physical ailment that has no organic cause. In hypochondriasis, a person is persistently fearful of having contracted some terrible disease, despite doctors' reassurances to the contrary. In **conversion disorder,** psychological distress produces what appears to be a genuine physical dysfunction (paralysis or blindness, for instance) even though no organic cause can be found.

6. **Dissociative disorders** involve a splitting off (dissociation) of a part of one's personality, so that memory or identity is disturbed. Victims of **dissociative amnesia** forget all or part of their past histories, while victims of **dissociative fugue** flee their identities for a time. Victims of **multiple-personality disorder** develop two or more distinct personalities, which may contrast sharply.

7. **Mood disorders** can be divided into two classes: **depressive disorders** (in which a sad, discouraged mood is the major symptom) and **bipolar disorders** (which involve periods of both depression and excessive elation, called **mania**). One type of depressive disorder, called **major depression,** is characterized by acute episodes of deep despondency and despair. A

milder, more chronic form of depression is called **dysthymia.** In **seasonal affective disorder,** mood disturbances are related to changes in the seasons.

8. **Schizophrenia** is characterized by severe disorders of thought (such as delusions and disjointed thinking), of perception (especially hallucinations), and of emotion (inappropriate or blunted feelings). Severe disturbances are also seen in the sense of self, in volition (difficulty in initiating and carrying out plans), in interpersonal relationships (avoidance of others or overintrusiveness), and in motor behavior (extremely repetitive actions or no movement at all). Schizophrenics cannot cope with most of the ordinary demands of life.

9. **Personality disorders** are deeply ingrained maladaptive behavior patterns that are often more distressing to others than to the people who have them. The most serious, **antisocial personality disorder,** is characterized by a history of impulsive, irresponsible behaviors and total disregard for others. People with **narcissistic personality disorder** have an overblown sense of their own importance and are constantly trying to gain others' attention and admiration. People with **borderline personality disorder** are highly unstable in their self-image, interpersonal relations, and mood.

10. **Substance-related disorders** involve an inability to refrain from the use of a psychoactive drug, even though its use is causing serious social, occupational, or medical problems. In the United States, the most common substance-related disorders are **alcohol dependence** and **alcohol abuse.**

SUGGESTED READINGS

Alloy, L. B., Acocella, J., & Bootzin, R. R. (1996). *Abnormal psychology: Current perspectives* (7th ed.). New York: McGraw-Hill. A comprehensive textbook that describes the principal psychological disorders and the major perspectives on them.

Gottesman, I. I. (1991). *Schizophrenia genesis: The origins of madness.* New York: Freeman. The author reviews current research on schizophrenia, with a focus on the genetic and environmental factors implicated in its onset and course. He discusses the issues and controversies associated with diagnosis of the disorder as well as ethical issues pertaining to genetic counseling and national policies.

Maris, R. W., Berman, A. L., Maltsberger, J. T., & Yufit, R. I. (Eds.) (1990). *Assessment and prediction of suicide.* New York: Guilford Press. A comprehensive survey of suicide, with particular emphasis on the identification of those at greatest risk.

Prochaska, J. O. (1984). *Systems of psychotherapy: A transtheoretical analysis* (2nd ed.). Homewood, IL: Dorsey Press. This book describes one case (an obsessive-compulsive woman) through twelve different theoretical approaches. It is interesting, vivid, and engaging.

Seligman, M. E. P. (1991). *Learned optimism.* New York: Knopf. This lively and engaging book blends science with practical advice on how people can modify pessimistic ways of thinking that can hold them back and detract from their quality of life.

Spitzer, R. L., Skodol, A. E., Gibbon, M., & Williams, J. B. W. (1986). *A psychiatrist's casebook.* New York: Warner Books. This collection of case studies gives examples of most major psychological disorders. The discussion of each case includes diagnostic criteria and recommended forms of therapy.

Styron, W. (1990). *Darkness visible: A great writer's battle with depression.* New York: Random House. In this book, the author provides a moving account of the agonies he experienced in his struggle to overcome depression.

Sutker, P. B. & Adams, H. E. (Eds.) (1993). *Comprehensive handbook of psychopathology* (2nd ed.). New York: Plenum Press. An advanced text dealing with psychological disorders, written by leading researchers in each area. The chapter on dissociative disorders written by Kihlstrom, Tataryn, and Hoyt is particularly noteworthy.

Psychological Treatments

Jeff is a 37-year-old mechanical engineer for an automotive corporation in Detroit. He has loved cars for as long as he can remember. In addition to his work, he spends his spare time restoring classic automobiles. In recent years he has won several awards for his projects and has been elected to serve as vice president of the local automobile club. He rarely misses a club meeting and never misses an auto show.

This description of Jeff was written several months before his behavior changed markedly. Soon after, Jeff

missed several auto shows and stopped working on the restoration of his 1956 Corvette, of which he had been particularly proud. He even quit reading his automobile magazines. Jeff's performance at work began to suffer, too. He had always been a model employee and had recently earned a promotion to project manager. Now, deadlines passed as his work went unfinished, and he called in sick as often as he dared. Those who worked for Jeff had noticed these changes, and some had even requested to be transferred out of his division.

Jeff had always been a wonderful father, reading

stories and playing with his children for hours each evening. After the change in his behavior he did almost nothing with them, or with anyone else. At first he spent his evenings staring blankly at the television. After a while he moved to the garage, where he just sat around doing nothing. There, Jeff began to wonder if his family might be better off without him. An obvious suicide, he thought, would be tough on them. Better to walk in front of a bus or to drive his car—though not his prized car—into a bridge support. Though these thoughts of death had once disturbed him, eventually they began to have a calming effect.

One evening Bill, a buddy from the auto club, phoned to say he had missed Jeff at recent meetings and shows. Though they spoke only briefly, Bill detected a sad, almost hopeless tone in Jeff's voice. He asked Jeff if everything was OK, if he might like to talk to someone. After a brief delay, Jeff asked Bill if he could remember the name of his friend who worked at the University Psychology Department—the one who worked in the clinic.

Five minutes later the phone rang again, and the caller introduced himself as "Bill's friend from the clinic." The two men spoke briefly, and the therapist asked Jeff to meet him at the University hospital in 20 minutes. He then asked to speak to Jeff's wife. Explaining why he had called, he told her that Jeff needed to go to the hospital, perhaps for a few days. And, he mentioned, she, not Jeff, should drive there.

Once he had arrived at the hospital, Jeff was given several questionnaires, including the Beck Depression Inventory (Beck et al., 1961), a commonly used diagnostic test for depression. Jeff's scores on those tests indicated severe depression. The therapist asked Jeff to describe the events of the past few months, leading up to the thoughts of suicide he had mentioned on the phone. Jeff's mood had been more or less steady during recent weeks. He seldom cried, but felt hopeless and dejected most of the time. He had lost interest in his family, his job, his cars. His appetite and sexual desire had decreased greatly. Despite feeling tired and listless, Jeff slept poorly, if at all. Like many people, he had felt down and discouraged in the past, but never anything like this. He could remember no family member ever displaying such symptoms, either—though he knew no one in his family would have admitted to it.

The therapist then consulted with a staff psychiatrist, who confirmed his initial diagnosis of *major depressive disorder* (see Chapter 15). In spite of Jeff's suicidal thoughts, they did not consider him to be in immediate danger of suicide. They started him on the drug fluoxetine (Prozac), a commonly used antidepressant medication. The psychiatrist would monitor his use of the drug, and the therapist would meet with Jeff once a week to explore factors that might be contributing to his depression.

During the first few sessions with Jeff, the therapist gathered information about his depression, his interpersonal relations, and his personal history. He noted that Jeff's depressive symptoms had arisen shortly after his promotion to project manager, when Jeff found himself dealing with difficult disagreements within his group. Jeff thought he was incapable of resolving such problems. "Some people can manage," Jeff said, "and some can't. I can't." At about the same time Jeff had been elected vice president of his auto club. Though he had looked forward to the challenge, he soon found himself facing the same problems that plagued him at work. He was responsible for settling personality conflicts, but did not have the authority to do anything really constructive.

Three weeks after beginning therapy, Jeff reported feeling much less depressed. He no longer had any thoughts of suicide. He was sleeping better, and his appetite and sexual desires had returned. At that point, Jeff's therapist proposed a "therapy contract" that would establish the goals, methods, and duration of Jeff's treatment. They two men agreed to meet weekly for four months, at which point therapy would be terminated. Jeff would work on three issues: his managerial role at work, his interpersonal relationships at home, and his perceptions of what behavior was and was not appropriate in various interpersonal situations.

At the end of the four-month therapy period, Jeff no longer exhibited any depressive symptoms. He was able to solve many of the work-related problems he had previously thought impossible and was once again enjoying time with his family and his hobbies. Jeff's long-term prognosis was also good. His depressive episode had followed a stressful life event (his job change), a common occurrence, and he had no family or personal history of depression. He had responded well to medication and had taken action to remedy the problems that had led to his feelings of helplessness.

(Adapted from Vitkus, 1996, p. 69–84)

For many people, **psychotherapy** is synonymous with psychology. However, as you learned in Chapter 2, *changing* behavior is not a goal of the *scientific* study of psychology. Instead, it is an application of psychological principles, in much the same way in which medicine is an application of the principles of anatomy, physiology, and pathology. Even so, many people are drawn to psychology by a desire to help those in need. As you read through the descriptions of psychological disorders included in the preceding chapter, you may have found yourself trying to think of ways to treat the disorders.

Clinical psychologists (and other psychotherapists) employ a wide range of therapeutic techniques. For example, cognitively based therapies often involve *cognitive restructuring*, or a change in the way in which a person perceives events. These interventions often rely on a reexamination and reinterpretation of previously experienced events. Someone who suffers from depression might recall being fired from a job, an experience that reinforced her feeling of incompetence and worthlessness. A therapist might then encourage her to think of the same event in a different way. Perhaps she was fired because her company was downsizing, or perhaps her supervisor had made a poor decision. By giving a troubled person alternative ways in which to view events—and by recognizing that one's beliefs and memories are somewhat malleable—the therapist can provide meaningful assistance.

Not all disorders respond to cognitive interventions, however. Some of the more serious disorders (those involving breaks with reality, like schizophrenia) appear to be *qualitatively different* from normal functioning. They do not respond well to therapies that are designed to point out the irrational aspects of thought and behavior. For example, treating schizophrenics simply by telling them to ignore the voices they are hearing in their heads is usually not successful.

In this chapter we will explore some of the many available treatments for psychological disorders, including psychoanalytic therapies, humanistic therapies, behavior and cognitive-behavior therapies, family-systems therapies, and other group approaches to treatment. We will also examine various biological treatments, all of which attempt to alter the physiological workings of the brain. These treatments include psychosurgery, electroconvulsive shock therapy, and the use of psychoactive drugs. As you read, keep in mind three important principles. First, no single type of therapy is likely to be successful in treating all disorders. Second, in many situations a *combination* of approaches is more successful than any one approach alone. In the case that opened this chapter, Jeff's therapy involved the combination of a biologically based intervention (antidepressant medication) and cognitive restructuring. Finally, keep in mind that the behavioral change associated with psychotherapy can be difficult to ef-

TABLE 16-1   Mental Health Professionals

Title of Professional	Typical Training and Requirements
Clinical psychologists	Doctorates in psychology who have been trained in psychological treatments and interventions
Psychiatrists	Physicians (M.D.s) who have been clinically trained in diagnosing and treating mental illness
Psychoanalysts	Professionals (usually psychiatrists) with advanced training in psychoanalysis, which includes being psychoanalyzed oneself
Counseling psychologists	Those with a Ph.D. in counseling psychology; these therapists are trained to treat relatively mild problems of social and emotional adjustment
Licensed counselors	Varies from state to state, but typically requires (at least) a master's degree in psychology or related field (such as social work, educational psychology, or gerontology), a lengthy supervised iternship (usually twelve months), and successful passing of a licensing exam
Psychotherapists	Similar to licensed counselor
Psychiatric social workers	Those with a master's degree in social work who handle cases involving people with psychiatric disorders

fect. Recidivism rates among substance abusers, for example, often run as high as 75 percent.

Psychotherapies

Anyone who has ever tried to calm a distraught person or bolster a friend who is feeling depressed has used techniques that are akin to those of psychotherapy. But the professional therapist supplements intuitions about how to minister to someone who is in pain with methods that have been clinically tested. Psychotherapy is a series of interactions between someone who has been professionally trained in alleviating psychological problems and a client who is suffering from such a problem. The psychotherapist seeks to change undesirable ways of thinking, feeling, and acting, and to improve the troubled person's ability to handle stress. Psychotherapy is offered by a variety of mental health professionals (see Table 16-1).

In recent years the field of psychotherapy has expanded and diversified. Freudian psychoanalysis, which once dominated the field, now coexists with newer therapeutic approaches, especially behavior and cognitive-behavior therapies, humanistic thera-

pies, and family therapies. Each of these approaches has spawned a host of specific treatments, so that today more than a hundred different types of treatment exist. As it has expanded, psychotherapy also has gained increased public acceptance, to the point that most of the stigma once attached to it has disappeared.

Knowing the difference between the various forms of treatment that are available is very valuable. Some treatments are more effective than others in overcoming particular kinds of problems. For instance, certain types of behavior therapy are very quick and effective in curing bed-wetting in school-age children. Unfortunately, most people who seek help for psychological disorders do not know that different approaches to treatment exist. Understanding the difference between treatments can save time and effort, as well as the disappointment of undergoing a therapy that is not really suited to one's needs.

Contemporary therapists do not adhere rigidly to only one form of treatment. Most are to some extent eclectic: they use a variety of approaches and techniques, depending on their clients' problems and needs. Thus, some behavioral psychologists integrate

Freud's couch, an important tool in psychoanalysis. Freud believed that a reclined posture helped to loosen conscious restraints on the unconscious.

elements of psychoanalytic theory into their treatments, while some family therapists use behavioral strategies. We will discuss eclecticism in the treatment of psychological disorders later in this chapter.

Psychoanalytic Therapies

The oldest form of psychotherapy that is practiced today is Freudian **psychoanalysis.** For a variety of reasons, few contemporary therapists still follow Freud's method faithfully. Traditional psychoanalysis is a long and expensive process, one most people cannot afford. Consequently, many psychoanalytically oriented therapists, though they still strive for insight into their clients' unconscious conflicts and motives, have substantially shortened the amount of time they expect clients to be in analysis. Freud's influence on the treatment of disorders has been enormous, however. We will therefore examine traditional Freudian psychoanalysis in some detail before describing the more modern approaches that have developed from it.

Freudian Psychoanalysis

According to Freud, the major purpose of psychoanalysis is to make people aware of the unconscious motives and conflicts that influence their behavior. Freud's experience in treating patients led him to conclude that the source of most disorders is the anxiety that arises when unconscious and unacceptable id impulses threaten to break into a person's conscious awareness. To deal with this threat, a person resorts to

defense mechanisms, especially *repression*—the pushing back of shameful thoughts and desires into the unconscious. (See Chapter 13 for a discussion of defense mechanisms.) But while id impulses can be hidden temporarily, they cannot be banished entirely. As a result, the ego must constantly work to keep them from surfacing. Freud believed that the best treatment for psychological disorders was to bring the forbidden thoughts and desires into consciousness, so that the patient could finally confront them. The thoughts and desires can then be "worked through," or explored rationally, to facilitate a healthy understanding of their implications. According to Freud, this process should gradually reduce anxiety, freeing psychic energy for more constructive purposes.

Freud and his followers developed several techniques to draw troublesome urges and feelings out of the unconscious and into conscious awareness. One was **free association,** in which the patient lies on a couch—a posture that helps to loosen conscious restraints—and says whatever comes to mind. The patient is told that no thought is to be willfully censored; no logical structure is imposed on the flow of ideas. The therapist listens, rarely interrupting. In time, clues to the patient's unconscious thoughts begin to surface.

A second technique Freud developed to uncover clues to the unconscious was **dream analysis.** Freud believed that during sleep, restraints on the unconscious were loosened. He therefore considered dreams the "royal road to the unconscious." Even in sleep, however, the ego censors the unconscious, so that forbidden thoughts appear only in symbolic form. Thus, every dream has both **manifest content** (a plot or story line) and **latent content** (symbolic meaning) that expose unconscious conflicts. Recall the dream of the woman who had just had a baby, described in Chapter 5. The woman dreamed that she had given birth to two boys and that one had died (the manifest content). The symbolic meaning (latent content) of that dream might be that the woman felt ambivalent toward her new child, whom she both wanted and did not want.

Free association is sometimes used to help clients gain insight into the hidden meanings of their dreams. Here is an example of how the process works:

> "Well," she said, "this is what I dreamed. . . . I was in what appeared to be a ballroom or a dance hall, but I knew it was really a hospital. A man came up to me and told me to undress, take all my clothes off. He was going to give me a gynecological examination. I did as I was told but I was very frightened. While I was undressing, I noticed that he was doing something to a woman at the other end of the room. She was sitting or lying in a funny kind of contraption with all kinds of levers and gears and pulleys attached to it. I knew that I was supposed to be next, that I would have to sit in that thing while he examined me. Suddenly he called my name and I found myself running to him. The chair or table—whatever it was—was now empty, and he told me to get on it. I refused and began to cry. It started to rain—great big drops of rain. He pushed me to the floor and spread my legs for the examination. I turned over on my stomach and began to scream. I woke myself up screaming."
>
> Following the recital Laura lay quietly on the couch, her eyes closed, her arms crossed over her bosom.
>
> "Well," she said after a brief, expectant silence, "what does it mean?"
>
> "Laura," I admonished, "you know better than that. Associate, and we'll find out."
>
> "The first thing I think of is Ben," she began. "He's an intern at University, you know. I guess that's the doctor in the dream—or maybe it was you. Anyhow, whoever it was, I wouldn't let them examine me."
>
> "Why not?"
>
> "I've always been afraid of doctors . . . afraid they might hurt me."
>
> "How will they hurt you?"
>
> "I don't know. By jabbing me with a needle, I guess. . . . "
>
> "What about gynecological examinations?"

> "I've never had one. I can't even bear to think of someone poking around inside me." Again silence; then, "Oh," she said, "I see it now. It's sex I'm afraid of. The doctor in the dream is Ben. He wants me to have intercourse, but it scares me and I turn away from him. That's true. . . . "
>
> "But why, Laura?"
>
> "I don't know," she cried, "I don't know. Tell me."
>
> "I think the dream tells you," I said.
>
> "The dream I just told you?"
>
> "Yes. . . . There's a part of it you haven't considered. What comes to your mind when you think of the other woman in the dream, the woman the doctor was examining before you?"
>
> "The contraption she was sitting in," Laura exclaimed. "It was like a—wheel chair—my mother's wheel chair! Is that right?"
>
> "Very likely," I said.
>
> "But why would he be examining her? What would that mean?"
>
> "Well, think of what that examination signified for you."
>
> "Sex," she said. "Intercourse—that's what it means. So that's what it is—that's what it means! Intercourse put my mother in the wheel chair. It paralyzed her. And I'm afraid that's what it will do to me. So I avoid it—because I'm scared it will do the same thing to me. . . . "

(Lindner, 1954, p 93–95)

In fact, the mother's paralysis was totally unrelated to sex. But Laura had unconsciously connected her mother's condition with the muffled cries and moans that as a child she had heard through the walls during her parents' lovemaking.

Naturally, the conscious confrontation of thoughts like these is not pleasant. As patients near the exposure of particularly painful thoughts and feelings, they may show signs of **resistance,** or attempts to block their treatment. They may avoid talking about certain topics, pause frequently, or report that their minds have gone blank. They may even launch into lengthy monologues about irrelevant subjects, such as world politics. The therapist's interpretation of such resistance is an important part of the treatment, for it helps patients to see their unconscious motives at work.

As psychoanalysis progresses, patients may transfer to the therapist the emotions they felt toward people who were important to them in their childhood, particularly their parents. Thus, the therapist may become the target of dependency, hostility, or whatever other feelings lie at the core of the person's problem. Throughout this process of **transference,** the therapist tries to serve as a "blank screen" onto which the patient can *project* conflicts. With the therapist's help, the patient can then begin to acknowledge distorted perceptions, ultimately putting them into perspective. An analysis of transference, in fact, is considered the key to the full understanding and resolution of the patient's unconscious conflicts.

Other Psychoanalytic Treatments

Even as Freud was formulating psychoanalytic theory, some of his early associates, like Carl Jung and Alfred Adler, were modifying it. These former disciples developed variations on Freud's therapeutic techniques that later psychoanalysts carried further. Unlike Freud, who maintained that all psychic energy originates in the id, some post-Freudian theorists have argued that the ego possesses substantial energy of its own. As therapists, they have tried to help their clients to strengthen their egos and develop firm, well-integrated, autonomous identities. Erik Erikson and Heinz Hartmann, whose ideas were discussed in Chapter 13, were both ego psychologists. Other post-Freudians have stressed the importance of a person's style of relating to others. In their view, faulty relationships with others do not merely contribute to psychological problems; they are the defining feature of all psychological disturbances. This theme can be seen in the writings of Karen Horney, whose work was discussed in Chapter 13. Finally, still another approach, *object relations theory,* merges the focus on the ego with Horney's emphasis on social relationships (Klein, 1967; Kohut, 1971). This approach stresses the importance of a child's early attachments to the development of the person's sense of self as well as to subsequent interpersonal relationships.

Because few clients can afford intensive, long-term psychoanalysis, most psychoanalytic therapists today do not practice traditional Freudian psychoanalysis. "Neo-Freudians," ego psychologists, and object relations theorists have all made a major effort to develop briefer forms of psychoanalytic therapy that may last no longer than thirty to fifty sessions. Freud's general approach remains: the therapist still seeks to uncover unconscious motives, break down defenses, and deal with clients' resistance. But some of the classic Freudian techniques are missing. The couch has been dispensed with; most clients now talk face to face with the therapist, who advises, interprets, and directs rather than remaining silent. Moreover, modern psychoanalytic therapists tend to place more emphasis on present problems and relationships than Freud did.

Evaluation of Long-Term Psychoanalytic Treatment

Among psychotherapists today, there are few issues as controversial as whether classical psychoanalytic therapy is effective. Psychoanalysis has many proponents, among them many "graduates" of analysis who believe their lives have been bettered by the process. A wealth of case studies report enormous gains in self-knowledge and emotional awareness among those who have undergone analysis. The treatment appears to be most appropriate for anxiety disorders; those with severe psychopathologies, such as schizophrenia, generally do not do well in analysis. And because psychoanalysis is based on talk and insight, it is most effective with the articulate and well-educated (Luborsky & Spence, 1978).

In fact, critics have charged that traditional psychoanalysis is geared toward "YAVIS" clients—those who are *y*oung, *a*ttractive, *v*erbal, *i*ntelligent, and successful. As a group, these people are less in need of help than the disadvantaged. Given the duration of the treatment and the expense, critics question its value as a general treatment. They point as well to a lack of carefully controlled scientific studies that might demonstrate the effectiveness of long-term psychoanalysis (Bower, 1991). Of course, systematic research on traditional psychoanalysis would be extremely difficult to conduct, given the practical obstacles involved in launching a controlled study that spans several years (Garfield & Bergin, 1986).

In recent years, considerable research has been done on the efficacy of brief psychoanalytic therapy, often called *psychodynamic* or *dynamic* psychotherapy (Koss et al., 1986). Psychodynamic therapy has been shown to be effective for a wide variety of specific problems, including posttraumatic stress disorder, grief, and personality disorders (Goldfried, Greenberg, & Marmar, 1990). Psychoanalytic therapy also appears to be effective in dealing with interpersonal conflicts. The more accurate the therapist's interpretation of the conflict, the more likely the client is to show improvement (Crits-Christoph, Cooper, & Luborsky, 1988; Luborsky, Crits-Christoph, & Mellon, 1986; Piper et al., 1993).

Rogers believed that therapists could convey unconditional positive regard—a liking for the client that is not conditional on the client behaving in a certain way—through empathetic listening.

Humanistic Therapies

Like psychoanalytic therapies, **humanistic therapies** are based on the belief that psychological problems can be treated by giving people insight into needs and motives they may not be aware of. But humanistic therapists flatly reject the determinism that is implicit in psychoanalysis. Freud viewed troubled people as victims of childhood conflicts over which they had little control. A major tenet of humanism, in contrast, is freedom of choice. Humanistic therapists maintain that a person is ultimately free to choose whoever he or she becomes. The goal is to liberate the client's innate tendency toward growth and self-actualization. There are many different kinds of humanistic treatment. We will discuss two: Carl Rogers' client-centered therapy and gestalt therapy.

Rogers' Client-Centered Therapy

The best known of the humanistic treatments is Carl Rogers' **client-centered therapy,** in which the therapist helps clients to clarify their true feelings and come to value who they really are. A central assumption of client-centered therapy is that people develop psychological problems because others impose on them unreasonable **conditions of worth.** That is to say, parents, peers, and spouses withhold respect and affection until a person acts in ways that conform to their expectations—even though that kind of behavior may be out of keeping with the person's true self. Thus, a sensitive teenager may have to deny his sensitivity and behave aggressively in order to gain approval from his peers. The result is profound unhappiness and a stifling of self-actualization.

To free the person from unreasonable conditions of worth, the client-centered therapist establishes a warm and accepting environment, never disapproving of what the client does or says. This unqualified support for the client Rogers called **unconditional positive regard** (a liking for the client that is not conditional on the client behaving in a certain way). The therapist also strives to show *accurate empathy* for the client's feelings by "mirroring" them. *Mirroring* does not mean parroting what the client says, but rather restating the client's feelings in a genuine attempt to adopt the client's perspective. When the therapist shows that she understands and accepts the client's point of view, the client is able to express his emotions more freely.

The following excerpt from a client-centered therapy session illustrates Rogers' technique. The client in this case is a college student who is plagued by feelings of inferiority:

Client: Well, it happened again yesterday. I got back that exam in American Lit.
Therapist: I see.
Client: Just like before. I got an A all right—me and eight others. But on the third question the instructor wrote a comment that I could have been a little clearer or else could have given more detail. The same old crap. I got an A all right, but it's pretty damn clear that I'm like a machine that can generate correct answers without ever understanding. That's it. I memorize, but there's no spark, no creativity. Boy! . . .

Therapist: Even though you got an A you are not satisfied.
Client: That's right. Never satisfied. I could get 42 A-pluses and never feel good. I hate myself . . .

(Phares, 1979)

The therapist's mirroring of the young man's dissatisfaction with his performance conveys an understanding of the client's feelings and encourages him to elaborate on them. Notice especially how the therapist accepts the client's unhappiness with his grade. He does not try to dissuade the client from his viewpoint, nor does he express disapproval. This nonjudgmental attitude is considered vital if the client is to break free of unreasonable conditions of worth.

Mirroring a client's feelings, called **primary empathy,** is only the first step in client-centered therapy. The ultimate goal is to bring the client to a new, more productive view of the self. To do so, the therapist gradually begins to suggest what might be causing the client's problems, while still showing an understanding of the client's point of view. This technique is called **advanced empathy.** For the young man with feelings of inferiority, advanced empathy would involve helping him to see how others have imposed on him unreasonable conditions of worth, which in turn have made him feel inadequate. The therapist begins to do so right after the young man states that he hates himself for his lack of potential:

Therapist: Yeah. I guess you really felt people put you down because of this lack of potential?
Client: Boy, did they! Especially my folks. They never really said so, but I could tell from the way they acted. . . .
Therapist: And this made you feel sort of worthless? . . .
Client: That's right.

(Phares, 1979)

When these new insights are fully established, the client should be able to shed his need to become the "perfect son." Instead, he should be able to develop pride in his accomplishments and acquire a sense that he is indeed a capable person. Advanced empathy is of central importance to client-centered therapy, for without a new perspective on their lives, troubled people cannot overcome their negative feelings.

Gestalt Therapy

Frederick (Fritz) Perls, who developed the therapeutic approach called **gestalt therapy,** was originally trained as a psychoanalyst. From his Freudian training, Perls derived the belief that psychological problems arise from unresolved, repressed conflicts—conflicts that must be uncovered and somehow worked through. But Perls saw past conflicts as important only when they bear on a person's present life. Like other humanistic therapists, Perls believed that people must take responsibility for their own feelings and actions. He saw people as ultimately free to decide whether past conflicts should be allowed to hamper current relationships.

Perls adopted the German term *Gestalt,* meaning "whole," to suggest his aim of fostering a well-integrated or psychologically whole personality. He strove to help his clients shed their old defenses, release their pent-up feelings, and increase their self-awareness, in order to open up their blocked potential for growth. Perls emphasized getting in touch with one's feelings, expressing them honestly, and accepting responsibility for them. To accomplish these goals, he and other gestalt therapists have used a variety of techniques. Clients were encouraged to use the first person singular (*I, me, mine*) and the active voice (*I am, I do, I feel*) to show that they took responsibility for their feelings and actions. For example, the client should say, "I am angry" rather than demand "Don't you think I have a right to be annoyed?" (Levitsky & Perls, 1970). Sometimes clients were asked to assume responsibility explicitly, adding an emphatic "and I take responsibility for that" after expressing some truth about themselves.

Other gestalt exercises were designed to heighten the client's awareness of important psychological conflicts. They might be asked to voice a conversation between opposing parts of the self. The ambitious, competitive side of the self, for example, might argue with the side that lacks confidence, each side expressing itself forcefully. Perls hoped that out of such role-playing dialogues, an integration of opposing forces might emerge, one that was psychologically healthier than the two competing forces. The client might also be asked to engage in an imaginary dialogue with some emotionally significant person, the aim being to take care of "unfinished business"—to bring closure to unresolved issues. The following excerpt from a gestalt therapy session illustrates several of Perls' strategies:

Therapist: Tom, what are you experiencing now?
Patient: Anger.
Therapist: Where do you feel this anger?
Patient: [indicating chest] Here, and [indicating hands] here.

Therapist: Just stay with the feeling, and let it increase. And you may get more in touch with it if you breathe deeply, in your abdomen, and let a sound come out when you exhale. . . .
Patient: [breathing abdominally] Ooooh! ooooh! ooooh!
Therapist: What is that experience?
Patient: Anger, resentment.
Therapist: Will you address that resentment to somebody?
Patient: Mother, I resent you...everything about you.
Therapist: Specify your resentment.
Patient: I . . . I resent you for making me dependent on you.
Therapist: Tom, how is your voice?
Patient: It's . . . it's a whine.
Therapist: Will you own your voice? Take responsibility?
Patient: I . . . I'm whining. . . . I'm whining.
Therapist: Do that. Whine to your mother, and experience yourself doing that.
Patient: [whining voice; reaching out with hands] Mother . . . Please . . . please let me go . . . please turn me loose.

(Phares, 1979, p. 374)

This approach, with its emphasis on the expression of pent-up feelings, has had considerable influence on other therapies, particularly group therapies. It has attracted many adherents, possibly because modern society discourages the expression of intense feelings in most contexts. Research in support of gestalt therapy is beginning to be published (Johnson & Greenberg, 1985).

Evaluation of Humanistic Therapies

Not coincidentally, humanistic therapy was most popular during the 1960s, when its basic tenets like intrinsic self-worth were consistent with prevailing social and political sentiments. Today, a strictly humanistic approach to therapy is less common, though many therapists have adopted the humanistic principles of empathy and support. In general, humanistic psychologists have not felt the need to validate their approaches with experimental evidence, although some recent studies suggest that the approach can be successful, at least with *some* kinds of difficulties and *some* kinds of clients. One study found that the degree of warmth and empathy expressed by the therapist is related to a successful therapeutic outcome (Beutler, Machado, & Neufeldt, 1994; Orlinsky, Grawe, & Parks, 1994). Like psychodynamic approaches, however, the humanistic approach works best with "YAVIS" clients, and it is often long and expensive.

Behavior and Cognitive-Behavior Therapies

Behavior therapies involve the application of experimentally derived principles of learning in an attempt to change maladaptive thoughts, feelings, and behaviors. At first, behavior therapy was based primarily on the principles of classical and operant conditioning. But in recent years behavior therapists have diversified their approaches to include the principles of observational, social, and cognitive learning. One of the most important developments in behavior therapy was the integration of the cognitive point of view. Generally, practitioners of cognitive-behavior therapy try to change their clients' thought processes in order to change their feelings and behavior (Dryden & Golden, 1986).

Despite this diversity in practice, behavior and cognitive-behavior therapies share a number of features. All are based on the assumption that the same learning principles that govern normal behavior, such as modeling and conditioning, are responsible as well for abnormal behavior. No deep probing of unconscious conflicts is thought necessary to the treatment of psychological disorders, then. Instead, the therapist focuses on the problems the client reports and on how new learning can be used to alleviate those problems. Changing maladaptive thoughts and feelings is central to these treatments. Both behavior and cognitive-behavior therapists take a client's cognitions at face value, rather than as defenses against unconscious urges. They also participate actively in the therapeutic process, asking direct questions and giving explicit advice and instructions rather than listening to clients recalling their childhood experiences, describing their dreams, and free-associating (Sloane et al., 1975). Behavior and cognitive-behavior therapists also focus more on the factors that are maintaining a client's problem, and less on the past factors that may originally have created it.

Behavior and cognitive-behavior therapies are believed to be effective largely because of their step-by-step approach, which enables clients to gain a sense of self-efficacy and mastery over the situation (Bandura, 1977a). With each step in the treatment, the person learns "I can do that" and thus acquires the confidence that is needed to try the next step in the process. Not only are these repeated successes intrinsically rewarding, but they reinforce clients' expectations of success, encouraging perseverance.

Systematic desensitization, a technique based on the principle that anxiety and relaxation are incompatible, involves controlled exposure to a feared stimulus. Here an airline pilot talks with patients seeking to overcome their fear of flying.

In the following sections we will explore a number of behavior and cognitive-behavior therapies. First we will cover some treatments based on the principles of classical and operant conditioning. Then we will examine some newer approaches based on modeling and cognitive learning principles.

Therapies Based on Classical and Operant Conditioning

In Chapter 6 we discussed two broad types of learning: *classical conditioning*, in which one stimulus (such as food) is paired with another stimulus (such as the ringing of a bell); and *operant conditioning*, in which behaviors are associated with certain outcomes (reinforcers and punishers). Many behavioral techniques are based on these two types of learning, from exposure-based treatments and aversion conditioning to time out and token economies.

Exposure-Based Treatments Classical conditioning involves the repeated pairing of a neutral stimulus with another stimulus that evokes some involuntary response. Gradually, the formerly neutral stimulus comes to elicit that same response as the one it has been paired with. In John B. Watson's experiment with little Albert, a frightening noise was repeatedly paired with the sight of a laboratory rat, until eventually the rat alone came to frighten the boy. In most cases, a classically conditioned response will extinguish if the conditioned stimulus is not paired with the unconditioned stimulus at least occasionally. But in some cases like little Albert's, the

conditioned stimulus may be so terrifying that the person has difficulty "unlearning" the association. To deal with such deeply ingrained fears, behavior therapist Joseph Wolpe (1958, 1973, 1976) developed the technique called systematic desensitization.

Systematic desensitization involves controlled exposure to a feared stimulus. The technique is based on the principle that anxiety and relaxation are incompatible. If a person can be taught to relax when confronting a fear, he or she will learn to overcome the anxiety. Systematic desensitization is effective in treating anxiety disorders such as agoraphobia, obsessive-compulsive disorder, and phobias (Barlow, 1988; Barlow & Cerny, 1988).

Suppose, for instance, that a client is anxious about flying in airplanes. The therapist begins by asking the person to describe what part of the experience of flying is most frightening. She then asks what part is slightly less frightening, what part only moderately frightening, and so on. The therapist then arranges these situations in a hierarchy, from most frightening to least frightening. For example:

Most Fearful
1. Experiencing midair turbulence
2. Taking off
3. Taxiing down the runway
4. Boarding the plane
5. Waiting to get on the plane

6. Riding to the airport in a car
7. Buying an airline ticket

Least Fearful

Next the therapist teaches the client the technique of deep muscle relaxation. Then she asks the person to imagine the least frightening scene on the list while remaining relaxed. When the client can do so, they repeat the procedure with the next lowest item on the list. Eventually, the client learns to imagine the most frightening scene without becoming afraid. This procedure enables the client to be more confident in confronting the feared situation in real life. Often, however, the best results are obtained through real-life desensitization. For instance, after imagining midair turbulence while remaining relaxed, the person with a fear of flying would take a flight on a plane, perhaps with the therapist. The therapist would help the client to remain relaxed through the flight, allowing him to confront the phobia firsthand, and in doing so to overcome it.

One of the best-known applications of exposure treatment is Barlow's program for women with agoraphobia (a fear of crowds, public places, and open spaces). The treatment involves group meetings with agoraphobics and their spouses, usually on a weekly basis. At the meetings, the women are encouraged to make gradual forays away from home, and their spouses are taught to support them in the efforts. Sixty to seventy percent of agoraphobics show marked improvement following this treatment (Barlow & Waddell, 1985).

Another exposure-based treatment, **flooding,** involves intense, rapid exposure to fearful stimuli. For example, someone who fears snakes might be locked in a room containing several harmless snakes. Theoretically, the fear (the CS) will *extinguish* with repeated exposure, since the exposure does not bring actual harm. Because such exposure can be extremely unpleasant until habituation is reached, however, therapists' rapport with the patient is crucial. Recent research has shown that flooding tends to produce more rapid therapeutic change than systematic desensitization, though obviously it is much more difficult for clients to tolerate. For flooding to be successful the person must not be allowed to escape the fearful stimulus, even if he is experiencing great anxiety. If the therapist were to allow the person to escape, the experience would *reinforce* the

phobia. (Exiting the room reduces anxiety, *negatively reinforcing* the avoidance or escape behavior.)

Aversion Conditioning   Another therapeutic technique that is derived from conditioning principles is **aversion conditioning.** In this approach, the problem behavior, or cues related to it, is paired repeatedly with an aversive stimulus (electric shock, for instance, or a drug that induces vomiting). The aversive stimulus serves as a punishment that suppresses the unwanted behavior. At the same time, just by being in the presence of cues associated with the problem behavior, the person acquires a negative emotional or physiological reaction (fear, nausea). This involuntary negative reaction, which is classically conditioned, further deters the person from engaging in the undesired behavior.

To understand aversion conditioning more fully, consider its use in the treatment of alcoholism (Nathan, 1976b). If the look, taste, and smell of alcohol are repeatedly paired with a drug that causes vomiting, they will eventually evoke intense feelings of nausea and revulsion. The drug is usually given immediately before a drink or is mixed with it, so that the two stimuli occur almost simultaneously. After a sufficient number of pairings, the person will be unable to stomach the beverage at least temporarily. Other problem behaviors that have been treated with aversion therapy include smoking, overeating, self-mutilation in autistic children, and various sexual deviances, such as exhibitionism.

Because there is debate over how long the learned avoidance response lasts, aversion conditioning is seldom used alone. Indeed, one study found that the new response may extinguish quickly, and old behaviors reemerge (Wilson, 1987). Most of the behaviors that are treated in this way (such as alcohol abuse) have an extensive, varied learning history, including many occasions in which the behavior was *reinforced.* To be effective, aversion conditioning must overcome past learning, a difficult task. For this reason, aversion conditioning is more effective in modifying behaviors acquired relatively recently (Barker, 1997).

By itself, aversion conditioning does not replace unwanted behaviors. For this reason, it is almost always used with more positive forms of treatment (Mahoney & Arnkoff, 1978). An alcoholic person undergoing aversion conditioning would receive instructions on how to drink appropriately, how to refuse a drink, and so forth. Even so, controversy surrounds the use of aversion conditioning. Should therapists inflict pain and discomfort on people, even with their consent? This ethical question has made aversion conditioning a treatment of last resort.

Time Out A less controversial way of suppressing an unwanted behavior is to withdraw rewards whenever the behavior occurs, a procedure involved in the form of contingency management known as **time out.** Children who persist in doing something that is dangerous to themselves or to others, or whose behavior is in some other way intolerable, may be disciplined in this way. The technique involves following the undesirable behavior with a period of isolation from positive reinforcement. Gradually, the unwanted response should extinguish, and time out can be replaced with positive reinforcement to encourage desirable behavior.

Though time out is reminiscent of the old-fashioned remedy of sending misbehaving children to their rooms, it is more effective than most parent-imposed exiles. The therapist sets clear rules on when time out will be administered (when the child throws a tantrum or bites someone, for instance). The child is informed of the rules, and they are strictly enforced. The place to which the child is sent for time out, though not frightening, contains no rewards: there are no toys, books, or tapes there, none of the pleasant distractions usually found in a child's room. The amount of time a child spends in time out is also carefully regulated. Usually a timer is set; when the buzzer sounds, time out is over, as long as the child has cooperated with the procedure. Generally, a time-out session is quite brief; a minute for every year of age is a common rule of thumb. Finally, the adult who imposes time out does so dispassionately, not with annoyance, because some children find any kind of attention—even anger—reinforcing.

The last requirement makes time out a difficult procedure for many parents to use. When a child who has been placed in time out begins to scream loudly, or starts to kick or throw things, parents may lose their patience and speak harshly to the child. The child, having successfully manipulated the parents, is then apt to continue resisting. Experts recommend that resistance on the part of the child should be met calmly with extra minutes in time out or, if that does not work, with the addition of a backup consequence, such as the removal of a favorite toy or privilege. In all cases, the consequences should be imposed calmly, and the child should know the rules beforehand.

Many parents also have difficulty applying time out consistently, because the problem behavior often occurs at inconvenient times. For instance, the child who kicks his brother when he and his siblings are late for school may be let off "just this once," so as not to miss the school bus. In this situation, the child is learning to time his misbehavior in order to avoid negative consequences. Finally, some parents abandon time out prematurely, because their child's misbehavior seems to be getting worse. Their perception is often correct. An operant response that has previously been rewarded typically intensifies when the reward is suddenly withdrawn. Parents must stay with the time-out procedure until the unwanted behavior extinguishes.

Token Economies Other therapies based on *contingency management* involve systematic rewards for desirable behaviors. One example is the **token economy,** developed more than twenty years ago (Ayllon & Azrin, 1968). In this procedure, specific behaviors immediately earn a person "tokens" (poker chips or slips of paper) that can be exchanged for rewards (candy, magazines, television privileges). Token economies have been used successfully in many settings: classrooms, residential programs for juvenile offenders, institutions for the mentally retarded, hospital wards for schizophrenics, to name just a few (Fixsen, Phillips, & Wolf, 1976; Kazdin, 1977). One recent study combined a token economy with individual behavior therapy for the treatment of cocaine dependence (Higgins et al., 1994). As part of the treatment program, each person was required to have a urine test several times a week. Half of those being treated were simply told the test results; the others were given a voucher that could be used to buy merchandise in local stores every time a urine test came back negative. During the first three months of treatment, the monetary value of the voucher increased with each consecutive negative test. During the next three months, the vouchers were replaced with state lottery tickets. Researchers found that those who received vouchers (and later lottery tickets) were significantly more likely to complete the six-month treatment program (75 percent completed the program, compared with 44 percent of the other subjects). Those who received rewards also abstained significantly longer from cocaine.

What happens when people leave the setting in which a token economy was used? Do they gradually revert back to their old behaviors? Not if the contingency management program has been care-

TABLE 16-2 A Treatment for Insomnia Based on Stimulus Control

1. Lie down intending to go to sleep *only* when you are sleepy.
2. Do not use your bed for anything except sleep; that is, do not read, watch television, eat, or worry in bed. Sexual activity is the only exception.
3. If you find yourself unable to fall asleep, get up and go into another room. Stay up as long as you wish and then return to the bedroom to sleep. Although we do not want you to watch the clock, we want you to get out of bed if you do not fall asleep immediately. Remember, the goal is to associate your bed with going to sleep *quickly*! If you are in bed more than about ten minutes without falling asleep and have not gotten up, you have not followed this instruction.
4. If you still cannot fall asleep, repeat Step 3. Do this as often as necessary throughout the night.
5. Set your alarm and get up at the same time every morning, regardless of how much sleep you got during the night. This will help your body acquire a consistent sleep rhythm.
6. Do not nap during the day.

Source: From Bootzin, Epstein, & Wood, 1991.

fully planned. First, therapists can select target behaviors (those to be rewarded) that are either reinforcing in themselves (such as interaction with others) or reinforced by social approval (such as improved personal hygiene). Second, as patients acquire the desired behaviors, therapists can gradually substitute social approval for tokens in rewarding patients. This strategy brings the reward structure closer to that found in the "outside" world. Third, arrangements can often be made to continue systematic reinforcement outside an institution (for instance, by training family members to reward target behaviors). And fourth, people can be taught to provide their own reinforcement (such as treating themselves to a movie as a reward for looking for a job). These tactics seem to be effective. Compared with traditional hospital care, institutional programs that systematically reward positive behaviors not only increase patients' likelihood of being discharged but decrease their chances of being admitted again (Kazdin & Wilson, 1978).

Stimulus Control Another successful approach based on behavioral theory focuses on rearranging the environment—the cues that are often associated with problem behaviors. In **stimulus control,** the association between the environment and the desired response is achieved by eliminating all other options. A dieter who removes all snacks from the house except fruits and vegetables is exercising stimulus control.

A more extensive example of this technique can be seen in the treatment for insomnia devised by Bootzin, Epstein, and Wood (1991). Many insomniacs use their beds for activities other than sleeping: reading, watching television, and so on. Bootzin and associates emphasize that the bed must be reestablished as a cue associated only with sleeping. Table 16-2 shows the instructions insomniacs receive. These stimulus control techniques are considered the most effective known treatment for insomnia (Lacks & Morin, 1992).

Though behavioral therapies are not effective in treating all disorders, they have proved quite effective for some. Behavioral therapies have been quite successful in the treatment of anxiety disorders (especially phobias) (Emmelkamp, 1994). As might be expected, they have also been implemented successfully in the treatment of disorders involving "excessive" behaviors, such as obesity (Brownell & Wadden, 1992) and alcohol dependence (Nathan, Marlatt, & Loberg, 1978). Behavioral treatments for depression are generally just as effective as cognitively based approaches (Agency for Health Care Policy and Research, 1993).

Therapies Based on Modeling

Although therapies based on contingency management are widely used, rewards and punishments are not always necessary to learn. Often people learn through *observation*, without overt rewards or punishments. When people shape their own behavior on the basis of what others do, they are said to be acquiring new behaviors through **modeling.** Of course, they are far more likely to imitate behavior that they see rewarded than behavior that they see punished.

Modeling has been successfully put to use for therapeutic purposes, particularly in the treatment of phobias. Sometimes the client merely watches another person interacting with the feared object (either live or on film). For instance, Albert Bandura and his coworkers have had much success in eliminating dog phobias in children by having phobic youngsters observe as a fearful child approaches a dog, then pets it, and finally plays with it (Bandura, Grusec, & Menlove, 1967). In a variation of this technique, called **participant modeling,** the therapist first models the feared activity for the client, then guides the client through a series of gradual steps that culminate in the modeled behavior. In one study, for example, Bandura and others led people with snake phobias from first thinking about snakes to looking at a snake in a cage, approaching the snake, touching it through the wire walls of the cage, and finally holding it (Bandura, Blanchard, & Ritter, 1969). The researchers found that participant modeling was more effective in ridding people of their fear than either symbolic modeling (watching a model on film) or systematic desensitization. Other research has yielded similar results (Rimm & Mahoney, 1969; Thase & Moss, 1976).

Phobias are not the only disorders for which modeling techniques are used. Even severe disorders like schizophrenia have been eased by such treatments. In one study, researchers asked chronic schizophrenics to pretend that they were in various social situations and to act as people in those situations should (Bellack, Hersen, & Turner, 1976). At first the schizophrenics performed very poorly; they did not seem to know what feelings or behaviors were appropriate. But when a therapist modeled the appropriate responses, and praised them for their successes, all the patients did much better. Apparently, even people with severe psychological disorders can improve their social skills through modeling (Wallace & Liberman, 1985).

Therapies Based on Cognitive Restructuring

In therapies based on classical and operant conditioning, and even in some of those based on modeling, the main emphasis has traditionally been on changing overt behavior. In fact, when behavior therapy began, practitioners virtually ignored people's thoughts and feelings. In recent years thinking on this subject has changed, however. Psychologists now recognize that the way in which people interpret events, perceive themselves, and judge their own abilities is central to their mental health. Specifically, people with behavior problems may be caught in an insidious web of negative, self-defeating thoughts. Like maladaptive behaviors, such thoughts are learned and can thus be replaced with more appropriate thoughts. Therapies that stress the teaching of new, healthier ways of thinking—that is, the restructuring of negative cognitions—are called **cognitive-behavior therapies.**

Perhaps the oldest cognitive-behavior treatment is **rational-emotive therapy (RET),** developed by Albert Ellis (1962). Ellis argues that thousands of people lead unhappy lives because of irrational beliefs that color their interpretations of events. Thus, failure itself is not psychologically damaging, but rather failure screened through the irrational belief that one must excel at everything. Similarly, rejection itself does not cause depression, but rather rejection filtered through the irrational belief that one must be loved by everyone. Ellis's strategy is to make people aware of the irrationality of views and to help them replace problematic outlooks with more realistic ones. In particular, he focuses on changing the maladaptive statements people make to themselves ("I can't do anything right!" thought to oneself whenever something goes wrong; or "Everyone must think I'm boring!" muttered under one's breath when a new acquaintance turns away at a party). Rational-emotive therapy has proved effective in reducing anxiety in stressful situations and may also be useful in treating excessive anger and depression (Haaga & Davison, 1989).

Somewhat similar in approach is Donald Meichenbaum's **self-instructional training** (Meichenbaum, 1977). Meichenbaum teaches clients how to think rational and positive thoughts in stressful situations, instead of plunging into old, self-defeating internal monologues. For instance, a student who always becomes nervous when taking exams is apt to think this way:

> I'm so nervous, I'm afraid I'll forget the most important material. The teacher will read this test and think I'm an idiot. If I get a D on this test, I'll have to get a B on the final just to get a C for the course. I know everybody here studied more than I did, which will shoot the curve way up. If I don't get an A in this course, I may as well forget about graduate school. . . .

Of course, this thought pattern makes the student even more nervous, and even less likely to do well

TABLE 16-3   *Examples of Statements That Individuals Rehearsed to Manage the Anger They Anticipated before, during and after a Confrontation*

Preparing for a Provocation

This could be a rough situation, but I know how to deal with it.

I can work out a plan to handle this. Easy does it.

Remember, stick to the issues and don't take it personally.

There won't be any need for an argument. I know what to do.

Impact and Confrontation

As long as I keep my cool, *I'm* in control of the situation.

You don't need to prove yourself. Don't make more out of this than you have to.

There is no point in getting mad. Think of what you have to do.

Look for the positives and don't jump to conclusions.

Coping with Arousal

Muscles are getting tight. Relax and slow things down.

Time to take a deep breath. Let's take the issue point by point.

My anger is a signal of what I need to do. Time for problem-solving.

He probably wants me to get angry, but I'm going to deal with it constructively.

Subsequent Reflection
a. Conflict Unresolved

Forget about the aggravation. Thinking about it only makes you upset.

Try to shake it off. Don't let it interfere with your job.

Remember relaxation. It's a lot better than anger.

Don't take it personally. It's probably not so serious.

b. Conflict Resolved

I handled that one pretty well. That's doing a good job!

I could have gotten more upset than it was worth.

My pride can get me into trouble, but I'm doing better at this all the time.

I actually got through that without getting angry.

Source: Reprinted by permission of Dr. Ray Novaco, University of California, Irvine.

on the exam. Meichenbaum's remedy for this anxious student would be a new, more positive internal monologue:

> I'm going to take slow, deep breaths and keep myself calm. All I have to do is be calm and take my time. . . . Just consider the questions one by one. I spent a fair amount of time studying for this test and I'm going to take each question in turn and be calm while I'm thinking about the answer. I'm an intelligent, competent person, and that fact is not altered by whatever grade I get on this test.

Meichenbaum's approach has been particularly useful in helping people to control their anger. Table 16-3 reproduces some other internal monologues his clients have used.

Self-instructional training, or training in problem-solving skills, has been gaining in popularity recently (D'Zurilla, 1986). This type of training focuses on general coping skills that can be applied to a variety of problem situations (e.g., giving a speech or meeting new people) as well as to situations that require increased self-control (cutting back on excessive smoking, drinking, or eating, for example). Over the past decade, research demonstrated the effectiveness of this treatment in dealing with a wide variety of stressful situations and life circumstances (Goldfried, Greenberg, & Marmar, 1990).

Another treatment that focuses on restructuring negative thoughts is Aaron Beck's **cognitive therapy.** Like Ellis, Beck holds that emotional problems are caused primarily by irrational thoughts, or schemas. His approach has been successful in the treatment of panic disorder (Michelcon & Marchione, 1991), substance abuse, and even some personality disorders (Beck et al., 1990). Beck is best known for his work in treating depression (Beck, 1976, 1985; Beck, Kovacs, & Weissman, 1979). He argues that the disorder is rooted in three types of negative thought:

(1) persistent self-devaluation, (2) negative interpretations of events, and (3) a pessimistic outlook on the future (Beck, Kovacs, & Weissman, 1979). In Beck's view, when people interpret trivial setbacks as substantial, read disparagement into innocuous comments made by others, and criticize themselves harshly for events they cannot possibly control, they become vulnerable to depression.

To change such cognitions, Beck questions clients in such a way that they discover the irrationality of their thinking. This approach makes the therapist and client partners in the effort to uncover the maladaptive nature of the patient's thoughts. Beck also encourages unconvinced clients to test the validity of their negative assumptions and in doing so to prove them wrong. In the following exchange, Beck helps a client who is clinging to a failed marriage to work through the implications logically:

Therapist: Why do you want to end your life?
Patient: Without Raymond, I'm nothing. . . . I can't be happy without Raymond. . . . But I can't save our marriage.
Therapist: What has your marriage been like?
Patient: It's been miserable from the very beginning. . . . Raymond has always been unfaithful. . . . I have hardly seen him in the past five years.
Therapist: You say that you can't be happy without Raymond. . . . Have you found yourself happy when you are with Raymond?
Patient: No, we fight all the time and I feel worse.
Therapist: You say you are nothing without Raymond. Before you met Raymond, did you feel you were nothing?
Patient: No, I felt I was somebody.
Therapist: If you were somebody before you knew Raymond, why do you need him to be somebody now?
Patient: [Puzzled] Hmmm. . . .
Therapist: If you were free of the marriage, do you think that men might be interested in you—knowing that you were available?
Patient: I guess that maybe they would be.
Therapist: Is it possible that you might find a man who would be more constant than Raymond?
Patient: I don't know. . . . I guess it's possible. . . .
Therapist: Then what have you actually lost if you break up the marriage?
Patient: I don't know.
Therapist: Is it possible that you'll get along better if you end the marriage?
Patient: There is no guarantee of that.
Therapist: Do you have a real marriage?
Patient: I guess not.

Therapist: If you don't have a real marriage, what do you actually lose if you decide to end the marriage?
Patient: [Long pause] Nothing, I guess.

(Beck, 1976, p. 289–291)

Research has shown that Beck is correct about the negative schemas of depressed people. The depressed do typically devalue themselves; the more self-inadequacies they perceive, the more persistent their depression tends to be (Dent & Teasdale, 1988). The depressed also interpret events more negatively than others, just as Beck contends. In one study, depressed college students were more apt than nondepressed students to inflate the importance of a test they were told they had done poorly on (Wenzlaff & Grozier, 1988). These students seemed inclined to see things as worse than they really were.

Research also suggests that Beck's method of treating negative schemas is effective. For instance, one recent meta-analysis found that cognitive therapy has been at least as successful as drug treatment in treating depression (Dobson, 1989)—a finding that was confirmed by subsequent research (Hollon & Beck, 1994). In fact, in the latter study cognitive therapy was found to be *superior* to drug treatment in reducing the likelihood of further depressive episodes. Not all researchers agree with this conclusion, however, especially the idea that Beck's approach is superior to drug treatment for relatively severe depression (Elkin et al., 1989). In fact, the relative efficacy of cognitive and pharmacological (drug) treatments for depression remains controversial (we will return to this issue later in the chapter).

How exactly does cognitive therapy help to lift depression? Do new, more rational ways of thinking bring an improvement in mood, or does an elevated mood help a person to think more positively? No one is sure. Interestingly, although depressed people who undergo cognitive therapy end up thinking more positively, so do those who undergo drug treatment (Hollon & Beck, 1986; Rush et al., 1982). Perhaps cognitive change is a mediator of all therapeutic improvement in depression, by whatever means.

One of the most important new trends in the development of treatments for anxiety disorders is the combination of cognitive restructuring with exposure and relaxation training. In Chapter 15 we saw that many of the anxiety-related disorders (as well as the somatoform disorders) involve the misinterpre-

Family-systems therapies is based on the recognition that people have psychological problems not in isolation, but within a wider context—the most important of which is the family.

tation of a relatively innocuous stimulus as threatening. Viewed in this way, anxiety disorders do not stem from inappropriate *reactions* to threatening stimuli. Rather, the reactions are "normal," *but they are mistakenly directed at harmless stimuli.* Thus, panic attacks can be treated by helping sufferers to label situations appropriately.

This is exactly the approach adopted by David Clark and his colleagues to treat panic disorder (Clark, 1988; Clark, Salkovskis, & Chalkley, 1985). Clark's cognitive treatment has three components. First, the therapist identifies patients' negative interpretations. Next, the therapist suggests other, noncatastrophic interpretations of those events. Finally, the therapist guides the patient in recognizing and validating the new interpretations. For example, a person who is prone to panic attacks may be accustomed to labeling increases in heart rate or respiration as fear. At the beginning of treatment, the therapist asks the client to hyperventilate. When the client begins to experience the sensations of hyperventilation (dizziness, increase in heart rate), the therapist shows the client how to *control* this reaction by taking slow, shallow breaths. Finally, when the client begins to experience symptoms that have triggered panic attacks in the past, the therapist teaches the client to react by breathing shallowly. This combination of attacking symptoms directly (by slowing respiration) and intervening cognitively (by learning to recognize symptoms and reinterpret them) has proved very successful: success rates exceed 90 per-

cent in some cases (Clark, 1991, cited in Alloy, Acocella, & Bootzin, 1996).

Family-Systems Therapies

Family-systems therapies grew out of the recognition that people have psychological problems not in isolation, but within a wider social context. One of the most important social contexts in most people's lives, of course, is the family. Not only may relations within the family contribute to the onset of a psychological problem, but they may help to maintain that problem once it has developed. Changing maladaptive patterns of interaction within families has therefore become an important focus of treatment. Family-systems therapists view the family as an organized system, with each person playing specific roles in relation to the others. Sometimes the family consists of a married (or cohabiting) couple; at other times, a couple and their children, or perhaps even other relatives, such as the couple's parents. Whoever seems to be involved in the maladaptive behavior patterns is included in the treatment.

Treating an entire family to alleviate one member's psychological problems has been tried with a variety of disorders, including childhood conduct disorder, anorexia, schizophrenia, depression, alcoholism, and agoraphobia (Falloon et al., 1982, 1985; Haley, 1980; Jacobsen et al., 1989). Overall, the approach seems to be quite effective when compared with both individual forms of treatment and control groups (Hazelrigg, Cooper, & Borduin, 1987). There are no set procedures involved in family-systems treatment; different therapists take different approaches. We will examine five of the most common.

Strategic Approaches

The strategic approach focuses on getting family members to perform various tasks aimed at improving faulty communications in the family. Unfortunately, simply explaining to family members that they are not communicating well is often not helpful. Patterns of interaction tend to be deeply entrenched and highly resistant to change. In fact, direct attempts to change an unwanted behavior may only trigger resistance, intensifying the problem. How, then, can a family therapist intervene successfully?

A frequently used strategy is called **paradoxical intention.** In one form of this strategy, the therapist requests that a person with negative symptoms go right on displaying those symptoms, perhaps even more forcefully than before. This paradoxical request is often presented as a necessary first step in gaining control over the problem ("If you can learn to turn the symptoms on, you can learn to turn them off"). Or the therapist may "reframe" the behavior in positive terms ("Your angry outbursts show that you are really in touch with your feelings and able to express yourself freely; go ahead and give vent to your anger some more"). But the real reason for this tactic is to place the person with the negative symptoms in a bind (Stanton, 1981).

Imagine a family that has sought treatment because of a teenage daughter's delinquent behavior (Haley, 1980). During the first session the daughter becomes so disruptive that no real interaction is possible. The family therapist then *praises* her for expressing her feelings so openly and freely, and instructs her to do so again, as loudly as she can. Suddenly the girl is placed in a position in which her uncooperative behavior no longer has the desired effect. If her behavior is disruptive, she is following the therapist's directives and cooperates with the treatment. If she quiets down and behaves normally, she is showing improvement and allowing the session to proceed. The confusion that results from this psychological dilemma can bring new insight into family relationships and promote more positive communication among family members.

Structural Family Therapy

In another family-systems approach, **structural family therapy,** the therapist studies roles family members adopt (Minuchin, 1974; Minuchin & Fishman, 1981). According to Minuchin, members of a family assume roles much as actors in a play. Each role is defined in part by its relationship to the other roles in the play. For example, if one family member adopts a "helpless victim" role, then by definition others in the family become "caregivers," "protectors," or "heroes." If any one player in the family drama changes roles, all others may be forced to change as well.

Structural family therapy has been used successfully to teach the families of schizophrenics new and different ways to communicate. As we saw in Chapter 15, schizophrenic relapse is much more likely to occur in families with unhealthy patterns of interaction (Halford & Hayes, 1991). Family therapy is also frequently used in the treatment of eating disorders like *anorexia nervosa* (Minuchin, Rosman, & Baker, 1978). From a family-systems perspective, each member plays a role in maintaining (if not creating) an eating disorder. To achieve a successful long-term outcome, then, each family member must learn new ways of interacting, ways that do not revolve around the eating disorder.

How effective are strategic and structural family therapies? In one meta-analysis, they were found to be as effective as many other therapeutic procedures immediately after treatment, and even more effective than the others a month later. Apparently, paradoxical interventions have good long-term effects (Shoham-Salomon & Rosenthal, 1987). Results are especially good when the therapist uses paradoxical intervention to reframe the client's negative behavior in a positive way. Changing the meaning of negative behaviors seems to erode their foundations.

Behavioral Approaches

In another approach to family-systems therapy, the stress is on teaching family members to encourage and reinforce positive interactions. Consider the behavioral approach to a troubled marriage. The therapist assumes that the more positive interactions the two partners experience, the more satisfied they will be with their relationship (Wood & Jacobson, 1985). One way to increase the couple's positive interactions is to institute "caring days" (Stuart, 1976). One day the husband agrees to concentrate on pleasing his wife, expecting nothing in return. On another day, the wife agrees to please her husband, again with no expectation of an immediate payback. If the positive feelings created by these reciprocal caring behaviors are reinforcing, then in time the couple will begin to care for each other in a more natural way. The same is true of the inevitable conflicts that occur in marriage. Couples who are taught these interaction skills are better able to solve their problems in constructive ways (Alexander, Holtzworth-Munroe, & Jameson, 1994).

The behavioral approach to family therapy has a reasonably good record of success (Shadish et al., 1993). In marital therapy, about half the couples who complete this type of treatment improve their relationships to the point that they are no longer considered distressed (Baucom & Epstein, 1990). Studies also show that family therapy generally produces better outcomes than individual psychotherapy in the treatment of marital discord and depression (Beach, Whisman, & O'Leary, 1994). However, couples who have been treated with behavior therapy alone typically complain that their marriage is only satisfactory, rather than exceptionally good (O'Leary & Smith, 1991). That is why in recent years, behavioral family therapy has expanded to include cognitive restructuring.

Cognitive Restructuring

Research suggests that treating the cognitive component of a behavior can significantly enhance the effectiveness of the behavioral approach (Baucom, 1985; Baucom & Lester, 1986). For some family therapists, a technique called *cognitive restructuring* has become the primary focus of treatment. Cognitive restructuring involves teaching family members how to change the negative ways of thinking that are giving rise to their problems. For instance, a wife who assumes that "men are only interested in sex" may judge her husband's motives unfairly, causing conflict in their marriage. Similarly, a husband who believes that caring for home and family is strictly a woman's job will probably expect too much of a wife who works outside the home. Helping people to adopt more realistic assumptions and standards is one way to reduce family tension and strife (Jordan & McCormick, 1987).

Another way to reduce domestic tension is to help family members understand the causes of one another's behavior. Troubled families often assume that a family member's actions are the result of undesirable personality traits rather than situational pressures (Fincham, Beach, & Nelson, 1987; Fincham & Bradbury, 1988). For instance, the parents of a three-year-old who frequently has tantrums might con-clude that he is high-strung and temperamental by nature, instead of searching for inadvertent rewards that might be reinforcing his behavior. Helping these parents to understand the real causes of the tantrums would be a first step toward solving their problem.

The Psychoanalytic Approach

Family therapists with a psychoanalytic orientation search for unconscious wishes, fears, and conflicts rooted in a person's early relationships, especially with parents. The theory is that those early relationships may be having a negative effect on current family relations. For instance, a man whose need for maternal love was not fully met as a child may seek excessive mothering from his wife, whom he unconsciously identifies with his mother. Such hidden motives must be uncovered so that they can be rationally analyzed and eventually modified (Nichols & Schwartz, 1991; Wachtel & Wachtel, 1986). Family members usually are seen together, so the therapist can observe the way they interact.

One recent study found the psychoanalytic approach to family therapy to be more effective than behavior therapy in reducing marital conflict over the long run (Snyder, Willis, & Grady-Fletcher, 1991). Of twenty-six couples who completed behavior therapy, ten divorced in the first four years following treatment, compared with only one of twenty-nine couples who completed psychoanalytic therapy. Moreover, those psychoanalytically treated couples who remained married reported less conflict than behaviorally treated couples who remained married. These results have not yet been replicated by other researchers, however. Perhaps if the behavioral treatments studied were to include specific training in communication skills, as well as cognitive restructuring, long-term results would be better.

Other Group Therapies

Family-systems therapy is only one kind of group approach to the treatment of psychological disorders. Any therapy that is applied to an interacting group of people is a **group therapy.** In fact, therapeutic groups often consist of people who are initially strangers to one another. They are treated together because people who face similar problems often benefit from one another as well as from a therapist. From one another they learn that their problems are not unique—that there are others who understand and can provide emotional support. And by listening to the advice directed toward other

> *Group therapy can be beneficial; by interacting with people who face similar problems, patients learn that their problems are not unique.*

group members, they can learn how to handle their own problems. Group therapy is particularly useful in treating interpersonal problems, for it offers opportunities for people to work toward building more effective relationships. Group therapy is also economical: since the therapist's time is devoted to several clients at once, they can be treated at a lower fee.

Each of the individual therapies discussed in this chapter has produced one or more forms of group therapy. Thus, there are psychoanalytic therapy groups, behavior and cognitive-behavior therapy groups, and humanistic (especially gestalt) therapy groups. Other kinds of group therapy draw their approaches from several theoretical schools of thought. The following sections focus on two popular types of group therapy: behavior and cognitive-behavior therapy groups and self-help groups.

Behavior and Cognitive-Behavior Therapy Groups

In behavior and cognitive-behavior therapy groups, experimentally derived principles of learning are applied to maladaptive thoughts, feelings, or behaviors shared by all members of the group. People with a specific phobia (toward dogs or flying), social anxiety (speaking in public), or problem behavior (eating or smoking) might choose a therapy group with a behavioral orientation. Those who feel they need training in social skills might also choose this approach.

Consider behaviorally oriented social-skills groups. Many people lack confidence in interviews or in making conversation with people they don't know well. In a behavior therapy group, they can practice those skills with others who share their deficiency. Although the therapist models appropriate behavior, points out mistakes, gives constructive advice, and praises successes, group members also perform those roles for one another—ideally, in a way that is understanding and supportive. For example, in a group dedicated to training people in self-assertiveness, the therapist would present the group members with hypothetical situations in which a person must make a point in a persuasive way. Group members then act out those situations asserting themselves in appropriate ways (without generating anxiety or offense). In the process, they comment on each other's performances and make constructive suggestions. Group members also discuss their efforts to be assertive in real-life situations, often role-playing to learn how they might have performed better.

Studies suggest that this form of treatment can be quite successful for certain kinds of problems (Bednar & Kaul, 1994; Rose, 1986). For instance, group therapy focusing on social skills has been successful with schizophrenic patients who are preparing to leave institutional settings (Bellack et al., 1990; Benton & Schroeder, 1990).

Self-Help Groups

A fast-growing phenomenon in recent years has been the **self-help group**—a group of people who share a particular problem and meet to discuss it

Alcoholics Anonymous members freely admit to and discuss their problems, offering one another encouragement and advice. This mutual understanding and support is the hallmark of the organization: members can call on one another for assistance at any hour of the day or night.

among themselves, without the active involvement of a professional therapist (Lieberman & Borman, 1979). The most familiar, and to some extent the inspiration for all such groups, is Alcoholics Anonymous (AA), established by two recovering alcoholics in 1935. AA members freely admit to and discuss their problem drinking, offering one another encouragement and advice on how to refrain from alcohol use and avoid an alcoholic relapse. Mutual understanding and support is the hallmark of the organization: members can call on one another for assistance at any hour of the day or night. Many other problems lend themselves to a similar kind of treatment. Self-help groups have been formed by widows, single parents, cancer patients, overeaters, smokers, drug addicts, and former mental patients, to name just a few.

There is evidence that self-help groups can be very effective (e.g., Emerick, 1987; Spiegel, Bloom, & Yalom, 1981), probably resulting from a number of factors (Dunkel-Schetter & Wortman, 1987). One is the shared experiences and feelings among members of the group. Because members of self-help groups have all been through the same trials, they can understand each other's problems and reach out in ways outsiders may find difficult. Members of self-help groups can also model their behavior after that of other members who are coping effectively and can also exchange practical information with one another. For example, former alcoholics can discuss how to cope with the social pressure to drink; cancer patients can discuss what they should tell their children or coworkers. Members of self-help groups can

learn as well that what they are feeling is normal for people in their situation. Widows, for instance, can learn from one another that it is normal for a woman to feel angry at a spouse for "abandoning" her. Finally, self-help groups offer a sense of companionship and belonging: members no longer feel alone in coping with their troubles.

Of course, not all problems are alleviated by self-help groups. In one study of parents who had experienced the sudden loss of a child, neither participation in a self-help group nor professional psychotherapy brought improvement in members' mental health or social functioning (Videka-Sherman & Lieberman, 1985). Apparently, some losses are so overwhelming even the support of sympathetic others is not enough to ease the pain.

Eclectic Therapies

Combining different types of psychotherapy to improve the effectiveness of treatment is becoming increasingly common among mental health professionals. In the mid-1980s some 30 to 40 percent of clinicians reported that they took an eclectic approach to treatment (Norcross, 1986); today that percentage is probably higher. **Eclectic therapists** believe that an openness to different approaches allows them to tailor a treatment program to the needs of each patient.

Even approaches that seem very different in their underlying assumptions about psychological disorders can be successfully combined. Consider the combination of behavior therapy and psychoanalytic therapy. Behavior therapies focus on overt behavior and current thoughts and feelings; psychoanalytic therapy focuses on deeper, unconscious conflicts rooted in childhood experience. Yet these two approaches to treatment are no longer considered mutually exclusive. A number of prominent psychotherapists have explored ways in which the two therapies can be integrated to enrich the overall treatment program (Messer & Arkowitz, 1984; Wachtel, 1977, 1982).

Consider the case of Joe M., who has gone to a psychoanalyst complaining of problems in dealing with women (Davison & Neale, 1990). Joe thinks women take advantage of him because they see him as weak and unassertive. He is suspicious of friendly overtures from women, whom he considers condescending and manipulative. Analysis reveals a deeply repressed anger toward his mother, who mistreated his father when Joe was a child. Joe has developed his meek and deferential behavior toward women as a defense against his anger. But meekness encourages women to take advantage of him—confirming his belief that they are domineering and hurtful.

After psychoanalytic therapy has helped Joe to gain insight into the causes of his problem with women, behavioral techniques can help him to alter his maladaptive thoughts and behaviors. For example, the therapist might use assertiveness training to help Joe interact more confidently with women. Once Joe begins to see that every encounter with a woman need not leave him feeling "pushed around," his negative expectations of women will begin to diminish. Or the therapist could use gestalt techniques to help Joe express his pent-up anger toward his mother. If Joe is having marital troubles because of his negative attitudes, he and his wife might be treated together, as a family. The point is that no approach to treatment should be disregarded if it seems likely to alleviate a problem. And in some cases psychotherapies should be combined with biological treatments.

Biological Treatments

Many psychological disorders are associated with changes in the delicate chemical balance of the brain. Some neurotransmitters may be in short supply, while others may be too abundant. Some receptors may be underactive, others overactive. One group of psychologists believes that the best way to treat psychological disorders is by influencing these chemical

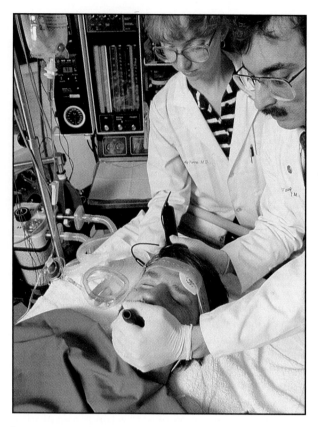

Electroconvulsive therapy (ECT), sometimes called shock treatment, has proven extremely effective in the treatment of severe depression. Psychologists do not know exactly how it works.

changes. The light therapy that is used to treat seasonal affective disorder, discussed in Chapter 15, is an example of such a treatment. In this section we will examine three other biological treatments: psychosurgery, electroconvulsive shock therapy, and psychoactive drug therapy. All work by affecting the brain's intricate neural systems.

Psychosurgery

Psychosurgery, the most extreme of the biological treatments, is a high-risk surgical procedure with irreversible effects. (Recall from Chapters 3 and 7 that H. M. suffered devastating memory impairments as a result of the psychosurgery performed to mitigate his epilepsy.) Psychosurgery was first attempted in 1935 when Egas Moniz and Almeida Lima performed a procedure known as a *prefrontal lobotomy* by inserting a surgical instrument between the frontal lobes and thalamus, and rotating it to destroy tissue. Moniz and Lima expected the break in the communication between the two brain areas to reduce the impact of disturbing stimuli on chronically agitated or violent patients. Over the next twenty years, as other methods of psychosurgery were developed, thousands of mental patients may have been operated on in this way. Though some severely disturbed patients were helped by the procedure, many were left in a lethargic state or became childlike in their behavior. Still others died on the operating table.

Today, the psychosurgical techniques of the 1940s and 1950s have been abandoned in favor of microsurgery, in which very small amounts of brain tissue in precise locations are destroyed (Valenstein, 1973, 1980). In the United States, fewer than a hundred such operations are performed each year, and only after all other treatment options have been exhausted (Donnelly, 1985). In cases of severe depression or intractable obsessive-compulsive disorder, psychosurgery is sometimes effective as a treatment of last resort (Bridges & Bartlett, 1977; Mindus & Jenicke, 1992; Tippin & Henn, 1982). It may also help to reduce manic episodes in people with severe and chronic bipolar disorder (Lovett & Shaw, 1987; Poynton, Bridges, & Bartlett, 1988; Sachdev, Smith, & Matheson, 1990). To protect the rights and the welfare of the patient, however, psychosurgery must be used only under the most stringent safeguards.

Electroconvulsive Therapy

Electroconvulsive therapy (ECT), commonly called "shock treatment," has proved extremely effective in the treatment of cases of severe depression that fail to respond to drug therapy (Abrams, 1992). ECT is particularly useful in treating depression that has been triggered by physiological change rather than by some negative event in a person's life (NIMH, 1985; Scovern & Kilmann, 1980). It is most effective when depression has persisted for less than two years, that is, when the problem is not exceptionally long-term and chronic (Black, Winokur, & Nasarallah, 1989). Although psychologists do not know exactly how, ECT appears to cause a net increase in the brain's norepinephrine level (Lerer, Weiner, & Belmaker, 1986).

Each year an estimated 30,000 to 50,000 Americans receive ECT (Beck & Cowley, 1990). Over a pe-

riod of several weeks, they undergo a series of brief electric shocks of approximately 70 to 130 volts—enough to induce a convulsion that is similar to an epileptic seizure. The convulsion, not the electrical current, produces the therapeutic effect. Because patients are first given a sedative and a muscle relaxant to prevent injury from involuntary movements, they experience very little discomfort. They awake with no memory of the treatment shortly after the shock is given. Some patients experience more extensive memory loss than others, but the side effect is usually only temporary. In some cases, however, memory impairment can last for years—a major reason for caution in the use of shock treatment. Because this method works more quickly than most antidepressants, it is sometimes used to treat suicidal patients.

One alternative to shock therapy is treatment with a combination of antidepressants and lithium (Barry, 1989). Together the two drugs can sometimes lift depression more quickly than ECT.

Drug Therapies

Psychoactive drugs, most of which were introduced over the past few decades, are now the most common form of biological treatment for anxiety, schizophrenia, depression, mania, and other psychological disorders. One benefit of **drug therapy** is that it is available to all, not just those who have the time and money for extended analysis. Drugs have also proved useful in cases in which no other therapy has worked. Before the introduction of antipsychotic drugs, some schizophrenics spent virtually their whole lives confined to mental hospitals. Today, with drug therapy, many can live successfully in the care of their families or even on their own. In the following sections we will discuss some of the drugs that have brought about this revolution in treatment.

Antianxiety Drugs

Antianxiety drugs, commonly known as minor tranquilizers, sedate; that is, they produce a general calming effect. Some, such as Halcion, tend to induce drowsiness and so are sometimes prescribed as *hypnotics,* or "sleeping pills." (Long-term use of hypnotics like Halcion can be counterproductive, however—see Chapter 5.) Since anxiety, tension, and difficulty sleeping are common complaints, these drugs are widely used. Family doctors often prescribe them for people who are having trouble coping during difficult periods in their lives. These drugs are also frequently administered prior to surgery, before general anesthesia.

There are three kinds of antianxiety drugs: *barbiturates, propanediols,* and *benzodiazepines.* The barbiturates have long been used as sleeping medications; years ago, before alternatives were developed, they were also used to ease stress and tension. But a barbiturate overdose can be deadly, particularly if it is mixed with alcohol. Consequently, many doctors switched to prescribing propanediols like Miltown and Equanil when they were introduced in the 1950s. The propanediols soothe anxiety by reducing muscle tension. More recently benzodiazepines—like Valium, Librium, Xanax, and Klonopin—have become available. These antianxiety drugs reduce anxiety without seriously impairing a person's alertness and concentration. Benzodiazepines work by enhancing activity of the neurotransmitter *GABA,* which in turn inhibits certain neurons, dampening the excitement of the central nervous system (Bender, 1990). Because benzodiazepines bind to specific receptors in the brain, some neurotransmitter that is similar to benzodiazepines in chemical structure must have essentially the same calming effect.

In the mid-1970s, the benzodiazepine Valium was the most widely prescribed drug of any kind in the United States. Though sales have dropped since then, it is still used every day by millions of Americans. Critics charge that many people take Valium to avoid dealing with stress in their lives. Questions have also been raised about the long-term effectiveness of the drug. Nevertheless, Valium remains the most widely prescribed of the tranquilizers.

Two high-potency benzodiazepines, Xanax and Klonopin, are widely used to alleviate the sudden, inexplicable attacks of intense fear brought on by panic disorder. Klonopin has some advantages over Xanax, in that its effects are longer and it is easier to withdraw from when treatment has been discontinued. Both have produced very positive results in many who suffer from panic disorder (Tesar, 1990). Of course, like all drugs, Xanax and Klonopin can have negative side effects, so their use must be monitored closely. They can also be dangerous—even fatal—when combined with other depressants, especially alcohol.

One of two antidepressants, either Anafranil or Prozac, is used to treat obsessive-compulsive disor-

der. In up to two-thirds of those who take Anafranil, recurring negative thoughts are significantly reduced, and the accompanying anxiety lessens. When combined with behavior therapy, compulsive-ritualistic behaviors can also be alleviated (Rasmussen & Eisen, 1989). These drugs work primarily by enhancing the action of the neurotransmitter *serotonin,* suggesting that a serotonin dysfunction may be involved in many cases of obsessive-compulsive disorder (Bender, 1990). Prozac also works primarily by boosting serotonin activity (Levine et al., 1989).

Mood-Regulating Drugs

Antidepressants were discovered by accident in 1952, when doctors who were treating tuberculosis patients with a drug called Iproniazid noticed an elevation in the patients' mood (see Chapter 15). Recall that Iproniazid is an *MAO inhibitor*—a drug that stops the action of the enzyme monoamine oxidase that breaks down the neurotransmitters norepinephrine and serotonin, halting their action. Thus, an MAO inhibitor enhances the activity of norepinephrine and serotonin. Pharmaceutical companies have developed a number of MAO inhibitors that have proved effective in reducing depression, including Marplan, Nardil, and Parnate. They have also developed a class of antidepressants called *tricyclics,* because of their three-ringed molecular structure. Tricyclics like Elavil and Tofranil work by blocking the reuptake of norepinephrine and serotonin into the neurons, where they are normally stored, thus increasing the action of those neurotransmitters. Unfortunately, MAO inhibitors and tricyclics can have negative side effects, some of which are serious, including a dry mouth, dizziness, blurred vision, and unwanted weight gain. MAO inhibitors can also cause a dangerous rise in blood pressure if a patient does not follow dietary restrictions.

A second generation of antidepressants—including Paxil, Zoloft, and Prozac—has recently been introduced. Most of these drugs have fewer negative side effects than the tricyclics and MAO inhibitors. Prozac, in fact, has been so effective in this regard that it is now the nation's most prescribed antidepressant (Mandos, Clary, & Schweizer, 1990). These antidepressants block the reuptake of serotonin without disturbing norepinephrine levels (which is why they are often referred to as "select serotonin reuptake inhibitors," or SSRIs). Because they are less toxic in overdose than older antidepressants, doctors can prescribe SSRIs without con-

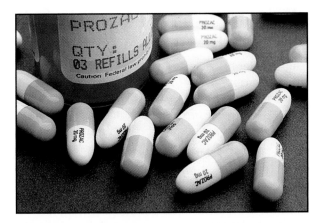

Prozac is probably the most commercially successful psychoactive drug since the introduction of Valium. It alleviates the symptoms of depression by selectively inhibiting the reuptake of the neurotransmitter serotonin.

stantly monitoring the patient's blood levels. The drugs do have side effects, however, including headache, nausea, insomnia, nervousness, and weight loss. Nevertheless, many patients find the side effects are easier to endure than depression. Prozac is probably the most commercially successful psychoactive drug since the introduction of Valium nearly forty years ago (Kramer, 1993). While it appears to be very useful in treating depression with minimal side effects, its long-term effects have not yet been determined.

Scientists have also discovered that **lithium,** a metallic substance found in water, can be used to treat bipolar disorder (alternating episodes of mania and depression). A lithium maintenance program can substantially reduce the frequency and severity of abnormal mood swings without diminishing a person's capacity for normal emotional response (Prien et al., 1984). Apparently, lithium allows the body to regulate its emotional ups and downs normally (Shou, 1988; Siever & Davis, 1985). Like other psychiatric drugs, however, lithium can have negative side effects, including upset stomach, hand tremors, and increased urination. If blood levels become too high, however, it can have an adverse effect on the thyroid gland and kidneys and can even cause death (Lydiard & Gelenberg, 1982). For this reason, patients who take the drug must have their dosage carefully monitored. Lithium can also be toxic to an unborn fetus, especially during the first three months of fetal develop-

ment (Cohen, Rosenbaum, & Heller, 1988). Consequently, doctors do not prescribe lithium for pregnant women, unless an untreated bipolar disorder would put the woman and her baby at even greater risk.

Antipsychotic Drugs

The most popular **antipsychotic drugs** (sometimes called *neuroleptics*) are the phenothiazines, which include Thorazine and Stelazine, two drugs widely used in the treatment of schizophrenia. Though antipsychotics help to alleviate *active* symptoms of psychosis—including extreme agitation, bizarre behavior, hallucinations, and delusions—they are not effective in treating *passive* symptoms like social withdrawal, emotional unresponsiveness, and lack of interest in pleasurable activities. In fact, drug treatment may even exacerbate these passive symptoms, because some of the side effects of antipsychotics, like sluggishness and lethargy, mimic those symptoms (Diamond, 1985). Partly as a result of this problem, antipsychotic drugs are generally combined with psychotherapies aimed at improving the patient's social interactions, as well as aspects of the family environment that may encourage a relapse.

To reduce the risk of relapse, antipsychotic drugs must be continued through the residual phase of schizophrenia, when psychotic symptoms lessen. Because an antipsychotic drug maintenance program can continue for years, the drugs' negative side effects are extremely important. Chronic apathy and lack of interest in life can become psychologically numbing. In one patient's words:

> On Thorazine everything's a bore. Not a bore, exactly. Boredom implies impatience. You can read comic books and *Reader's Digest* forever. You can tolerate talking to jerks forever. Babble, babble, babble. The weather is dull, the flowers are dull, nothing's very impressive. Musak, Bach, Beatles, Lolly and the Yum-Yums, Rolling Stones. It doesn't make any difference. . . . What the drug is supposed to do is keep away hallucinations. What I think it does is just fog up your mind so badly you don't notice the hallucinations or much else.

(Vonnegut, 1975, p. 196–197)

Antipsychotic drugs can also have negative physical effects. Often they produce a *pseudoparkinsonism,* a cluster of symptoms similar to those of Parkinson's disease, including uncontrollable hand tremors, stiffened muscles, a shuffling gait, and drooling.

Worse symptoms may continue for up to a year after drug therapy has been stopped. Some patients also experience dizziness, fainting, nausea, diarrhea, blurred vision, heightened sensitivity to sunlight, and other various physical ailments. Most serious is an often irreversible condition called **tardive dyskinesia,** which may develop in patients who take these drugs for prolonged periods or in high doses. Symptoms include grotesque movements of the face—grimaces, lip smacking, cheek puffing, and protrusions of the tongue. Some victims, acutely embarrassed by these uncontrollable behaviors, avoid all contact with other people, becoming social isolates (Widroe & Heisler, 1976). Tardive dyskinesia plagues at least 10 to 20 percent of patients who take antipsychotic drugs and at least 40 percent of elderly patients who have taken these drugs for years (Task Force on Tardive Dyskinesia, 1980).

Not surprisingly, when schizophrenics leave a hospital setting, they often stop antipsychotics in order to avoid the negative side effects. Because such patients still need the drugs to prevent a relapse, finding ways to reduce the unwanted side effects of antipsychotic drugs is especially important. Doctors try to prescribe the lowest possible dose necessary to control psychotic symptoms. They also carefully monitor patients' reactions to medication and may try several different antipsychotics to find the one that is least aversive to a particular person.

A relatively new antipsychotic drug, Clozaril, does not produce the involuntary movements other antipsychotics can cause. Clozaril has been highly effective in treating cases of schizophrenia that are resistant to other drug treatments (Bablenis, Weber, & Wagner, 1989). This drug can be highly toxic in overdose, however, so its use is restricted (Benecke, Conrad, & Klingelhofer, 1988). Clozaril probably has fewer side effects than other antipsychotics because its effects on the brain are more selective. Recall from Chapter 15 that schizophrenia seems to be caused partly by overactivity of the neurotransmitter dopamine. While most antipsychotics block the dopamine receptors in several parts of the brain (both in the limbic system, where bizarre thoughts and emotions originate, and in the basal ganglia of the forebrain, where normal body movements are regulated), Clozaril affects the limbic system alone (Baldessarini, 1985; Weintraub & Evans, 1989). Scientists hope that other less toxic antipsychotics will soon be developed.

The Effectiveness of Psychological Treatments

This chapter has detailed numerous studies suggesting that various forms of psychological treatment are effective. Are some more helpful than others in treating certain kinds of disorders? Do some produce faster or more long-lasting results, for instance? And what about the overall effectiveness of available treatments? Do psychotherapy or psychoactive drugs produce more improvement than could occur with just the passage of time alone?

These are difficult questions to answer. Many of the studies that have been conducted to evaluate the effectiveness of various treatments for psychological disorders have produced conflicting results. To summarize the results of a large number of studies, researchers often turn to meta-analysis, a technique discussed in Chapter 2. Using meta-analysis, one group of researchers found that the average person who has undergone psychotherapy is better off than 80 percent of those who remain untreated (Smith & Glass, 1977; Smith, Glass, & Miller, 1981). Many other meta-analyses have found that treating a psychological disorder brings about significantly more improvement than simply depending on the passage of time.

In recent years researchers have broadened their efforts to evaluate the effectiveness of treatment to include not just whether treatment is generally effective but which particular treatments are best for certain disorders (Goldfried, Greenberg, & Marmar, 1990). They do so mainly by conducting studies in which clients with a certain disorder are randomly assigned to various forms of treatment or to a no-treatment control group. In one such study, conducted by the National Institute of Mental Health (NIMH), researchers investigated the effectiveness of three different treatments for depression: Beck's cognitive therapy, a psychodynamic treatment that focuses on current problems and interpersonal relationships, and a tricyclic antidepressant drug treatment (Elkin et al., 1989; Imber et al., 1990). After sixteen weeks, researchers found no significant differences in the effectiveness of the three forms of treatment. They did find some evidence that the psychodynamic treatment and the drug therapy were more effective than a control condition in which clients were treated with a placebo. For people suffering from a relatively severe form of depression, however, the drug treatment seemed to work faster and more effectively than either of the other two therapies.

As neuroscientific knowledge has progressed, more and often more effective drug treatments have been devised. Some psychologists welcome these advances, because they have increased the options available for treatment. Indeed, the effectiveness of new drugs like Prozac has forced "a rethinking of fundamental assumptions in psychiatry" (Barondes, 1994). But others fear that drug treatments work primarily on the *symptoms* of psychological problems, not on the problems themselves. They argue that long-term use of drugs like Valium is counterproductive, since it essentially postpones examination of the root causes of anxiety.

Which is more effective, then, drug therapy or psychotherapy? The answer depends on the form and severity of the disturbance. Some disorders, like schizophrenia, respond best to drug therapy. Others, like anxiety disorders, respond best over the long-term to conventional psychotherapy. However, most comparisons of the two approaches have focused on their use in treating depression, and the evidence there is decidedly mixed. A recent large-scale review of the research on depression came to the following conclusions (Agency for Health Care Policy and Research, 1993):

- Drug therapy produced marked improvement in about half of all cases.
- Drug treatment is most appropriate for those patients with severe depressive symptoms, especially those prone to recurring bouts of depression and those with family histories of depression.
- Psychotherapy (in particular the cognitive, behavioral, and interpersonal approaches) is effective in treating mild to moderate cases of depression.
- A combination of treatments is effective in treating those with severe depression and those who do not respond to either drug treatment or psychotherapy alone.

Though the debate over the relative effectiveness of various treatments is not likely to end soon, a growing number of mental health professionals is acknowledging that in many cases, a combination of drug therapy and psychotherapy is most effective.

In Depth

Treating Suicidal People

Dear Jim:
I've just emptied 40 capsules and put the powder in a glass of water. I'm about to take it. I'm scared and I want to talk to someone but I just don't have anybody to talk to. I feel like I'm completely alone and nobody cares. I know our breakup was my fault, but it hurts so bad. Nothing I do seems to turn out right, but nothing. My whole life has fallen apart.

I've thought about all of the trite phrases about how it will get brighter tomorrow and how suicide is copping out and really isn't a solution, and maybe it isn't, but I hurt so bad. I just want it to stop. I feel like my back is up against the wall and there is no other way out.

Dear Daddy:
Please don't grieve for me or feel that you did something wrong, you didn't. I'll leave this life loving you and remembering the world's greatest father.

I'm sorry to cause you more heartache, but the reason I can't live anymore is because I'm afraid. Afraid of facing my life alone without love. No one ever knew how alone I am. No one ever stood by me when I needed help. No one brushed away the tears. I cried for "help" and no one heard.

These suicide notes, left by college students, tell of the deep despair and anguish that can prompt people to take their own lives. Suicide is the second most common cause of death among those aged fifteen to nineteen (Gould et al., 1992); only accidents claim more lives. (In addition, some auto accidents—perhaps as many as 15 percent—are really suicides.) Astonishingly, nearly 10 percent of all high school students have attempted suicide, and some have made multiple attempts (Andrews & Lewinsohn, 1992). The factors most closely linked to suicide in teenagers—pregnancy, family difficulties or distress, substance abuse, and delinquency—have prompted some researchers to suggest that suicide might be prevented more effectively by attacking those social problems (Garland & Zigler, 1993). Nor are college students immune: on American college campuses over 10,000 students attempt suicide each year; many succeed (National Center for Health Statistics, 1988). The risk of suicide is even greater—just under 20 percent—among those with a history of mood disorders (usually depression) (Goodwin & Jamison, 1990).

Why do some people conclude that death is preferable to life? How can such people be helped to get through a crisis without acting on their suicidal thoughts? The answers to these questions are so important that we will explore them in depth.

Initial Studies. The earliest studies of suicide concentrated on the social-psychological factors correlated with self-destruction. In the late nineteenth century, French sociologist Émile Durkheim conducted extensive research of this type (Durkheim, 1897–1951). He found that Protestants committed suicide three times more often than Catholics, and Catholics more often than Jews. Single people killed themselves more often than married people, who in turn had a higher suicide rate than those married with children.

Durkheim wondered what could cause these patterns. He hypothesized that suicide is more likely among those with few social ties, or very weak social ties. Jews, he reasoned, were a more closely knit group than Catholics, and Catholics were a more closely knit group than Protestants. Similarly, married couples, especially those with children, had more social ties than single people. In short, the more socially isolated a person is, the greater that person's vulnerability to suicide. Modern research lends support to this view. Being single, widowed, divorced, or separated; living alone; being childless; and lacking emotional support from others—all place a person at higher-than-average risk for suicide (Hawton, 1987; Hoyer & Lund, 1993). Both suicide notes presented at the beginning of this section express a sense of social isolation.

Durkheim's research also revealed that the suicide rate increases during times of rapid economic change. He hypothesized that sudden, dramatic disruptions in people's lives were highly disorienting, making people more vulnerable to suicide. Contemporary research supports this aspect of Durkheim's theory as well. People who have suffered sudden reversals in health or economic status have a higher-than-average incidence of suicide (Brown & Sheran, 1972; Hawton, 1987; Whitlock, 1986).

Vigil for the singer Kurt Cobain, who committed suicide in 1994. Some who commit suicide may see death as a release from an anguish they can no longer endure. Cobain's chronic substance abuse made him highly vulnerable.

Another factor that increases a person's risk for suicide is an interpersonal loss of some kind, such as the death of a loved one or the breakup of a marriage (Bunch, 1972). Among high school and college students, breaking up with a girlfriend or boyfriend is a common precipitating factor (Rich et al., 1991; Westefeld & Furr, 1987). Sigmund Freud theorized that when we lose someone we both love and hate—some of whose traits we have unconsciously incorporated into ourselves—we may direct repressed hostility toward that person inward, sometimes to the point of self-destruction. This view of suicide is difficult to prove or disprove. One pioneering analysis of suicide notes revealed that people who kill themselves do not usually express outright hostility toward either a loved one or themselves (Tuckman, Kleiner, & Lavell, 1959). That fact alone does not discredit Freud's theory, however, for if anger and hostility have been repressed, they are not apt to be stated directly in a suicide note. However, they might be stated indirectly. The suicide letter to "Daddy" at the start of this section implies a deep and poignant disappointment in the father, who apparently was not present when his daughter needed him. The implied disappointment is mixed ambivalently with expressions of love.

More recently, E. Shneidman (1969, 1992) has proposed that people who kill themselves see death as a release from an anguish they can no longer endure. The suicide letter to "Jim" at the start of this section expresses such anguish well. Indeed, researchers have found that the anguish of depression is one of the most important factors that increase a person's risk of suicide. About half of all those who kill themselves suffer from depression. Especially important is the sense of hopelessness that often accompanies depression. The correlation between suicidal wishes and measures of hopelessness is stronger than that between suicidal wishes and measures of any other symptom of depression (Beck, 1967). Hopelessness is also a better predictor of who will ultimately commit suicide than either the overall level of depression or the degree to which a person thinks about suicide (Beck et al., 1985; Weishaar & Beck, 1992). Interestingly, a longitudinal study of people with either severe depression or bipolar disorder suggests that anxiety-related symptoms—such as excessive worrying, severe insomnia, and lack of concentration—may be even more predictive of suicide than hopelessness (Fawcett et al., 1990).

Finally, in Shneidman's view, people who kill themselves have often so narrowed their perceived range of solutions to their problems that they can see "no other way out." (The letter to Jim is a good example of this kind of thinking.) Other researchers have found that many suicide victims do indeed exhibit impaired problem-solving abilities, including inflexibility and "tunnel vision," in coping with challenges and dilemmas (Linehan et al., 1987; Patsiokas, Clum, & Luscomb, 1979; Schotte & Clum, 1987). Table 16-4 summarizes the social-psychological risk factors for suicide, which are additive: the more of them that apply to a person, the greater the chance that he or she will commit suicide.

I TABLE 16-4 *Risk Factors Associated with Suicide*

Risk Factor*	Examples
Social isolation	Living alone; single, widowed, divorced; weak ties to relatives and friends
Recent interpersonal loss	Death of a loved one; end of an important relationship
Sudden economic downturn	Unemployment; bankruptcy
Ill health	Especially chronic illness
Psychiatric condition	Depression; schizophrenia; personality disorder; alcoholism or other drug abuse
Anxiety-related symptoms	Excessive worrying, severe insomnia, panic attacks, lack of concentration
Impaired problem solving	Tunnel vision; inflexible thinking; previous suicide attempt
Gender	Females 3 to 1 (attempted suicide); males 3 to 1 (completed suicide)
Others	Sense of hopelessness; communication of a wish to die to others; family history of suicide or attempted suicide

*See also Table 15-2.

The list of social-psychological risk factors for suicide suggests a form of treatment: reducing or eliminating those factors that can be changed. For instance, a therapist might reduce impaired problem-solving ability in a suicidal patient by helping that person to imagine solutions other than dying. Shneidman, who has relied heavily on this tactic in his own practice, reports that though suicidal patients may not immediately accept an alternative solution, the act of making a list of potential solutions can open their minds to other options, and thus weaken their suicidal leanings (Shneidman, 1987). Aaron Beck has used a similar tactic, but has taken it one step further. Not only does he ask suicidal patients to consider other solutions to their problems, but he encourages them to rehearse how they might carry out those solutions (Beck et al., 1979; Rush & Beck, 1978).

Beck also tries to reduce the suicidal sense of hopelessness by pointing to evidence to the contrary—occasions when goals have been reached and problems have been solved. By helping his patients to see that a totally hopeless view is irrational, he makes death seem to be a less desirable option.

Deep despair and hopelessness are also frequently treated with antidepressants. The rapid treatment of anxiety symptoms through the use of antianxiety drugs may substantially reduce suicide rates among those with severe depression or bipolar disorder (Fawcett et al., 1990). If drugs are ineffective, deeply depressed or dangerously suicidal people may be given shock treatments (electroconvulsive therapy).

Finally, staying involved with a suicidal patient is important in overcoming the social isolation that can raise the risk of suicide (Himmelhoch, 1987). For this reason clinicians usually schedule frequent therapy sessions, remain accessible to patients by phone, and may even hospitalize a patient so that he is not left alone. If a patient is not hospitalized, relatives or friends may be enlisted to monitor the person's psychological state and "be there" when needed. This tactic strengthens the patient's social network. Finally, continued contact with a therapist after the crisis is over can help to reduce the risk of a recurrence of a suicidal episode (Allebock & Allgulander, 1990).

Criticisms, Alternatives, and Further Research. Despite the effectiveness of treatment in helping specific individuals, the overall suicide rate has not been reduced. In fact, the rate of suicide in the general population—about 12 in every 100,000 people—has remained level for the last forty years. What explains this finding?

One answer to this question is that many of those who need help the most—those who are strongly suicidal and have formulated a plan to kill themselves—are not getting it (Diekstra, 1989). Once a person has decided that suicide is the "only answer," his thinking is usually too impaired to consider seeking treatment. Moreover, relatives and friends often misread the signs of impending suicide and do not insist on treatment until it is too late. Add the fact that some of the factors encouraging suicide may be increasing (social isolation, disruptive life changes), and it is not surprising that the suicide rate stays constant despite the development of effective treatments.

Some psychologists contend that there are other explanations for the stable suicide rate. They say that current treatments focus mainly on reducing those social-psychological factors that have long been related to suicide. But those factors alone, they argue, cannot identify those who will actually commit suicide. Those people considered to be at high risk do not always kill themselves, and some of those who seem to be at relatively low risk do kill themselves. What is needed, these critics say, is a better marker of who is truly suicidal.

That marker may turn out to be a biochemical one. Recent research has shown that people who die of suicide have significantly reduced levels of the neurotransmitter *serotonin* in certain parts of their brains compared to people of a similar age and background who died of other causes (Mann et al., 1992; Nordström & Asberg, 1992; Stanley & Stanley, 1990). Moreover, reduced serotonin levels are found in suicide victims regardless of their psychiatric diagnosis (depression, schizophrenia, personality disorder, alcoholism, drug abuse). Interestingly, serotonin levels fluctuate during the year and are at their lowest during the spring—the time of year when the suicide rate is highest (Brewerton, 1989).

These findings have important implications for treatment (Stanley & Stanley, 1989). They suggest that suicidal tendencies should not be treated as just a symptom of some other disorder, primarily depression. Instead, they may be more accurately treated as symptoms of a separate disorder with a strong biological component, one that can occur simultaneously with a number of other psychiatric conditions. Drugs that are known to enhance serotonin levels, especially Prozac, may help to reduce the risk of suicide, though that has yet to be demonstrated.

That is not to say that the social-psychological factors involved in suicide should be ignored, nor should the other disorders that often accompany it be deemphasized. Rather, in thinking of suicide as a separate and distinct problem, psychologists may be better able to develop treatments to prevent it. While the psychotherapeutic part of the treatment can probably remain much the same, drug treatments should probably focus on specifically rectifying the depletion of serotonin (rather than serotonin *and* norepinephrine, as most current drug treatments do).

Patterns and Conclusions. Therapists are often successful in preventing suicide and may in the future be even more effective (Liberman & Eckman, 1981; Patsiokas & Clum, 1985). Suicidal people *can* be helped to see other ways of dealing with their problems. Does that mean they should be compelled to accept professional help? Surprisingly, not all clinicians think so, at least not in every case. Thomas Szasz believes that no one, even someone who is suicidal, should be forced to accept treatment that he or she does not want. According to Szasz, people have a right to end their own lives if that is what they truly wish to do (Szasz, 1986).

Most other clinicians disagree strongly with Szasz's position, however. They argue that suicidal people do not have a right to inflict a lifetime of sorrow on the loved ones they leave behind (Holmes, 1987). They also point out that the suicidal person's ability to think rationally is greatly reduced by mental illness (Clum, 1987). How can we fail to intervene when their thinking is so impaired? Significantly, many formerly suicidal people who have been forced into treatment later say they are glad that others stepped in during their crises (Mather, 1987). Suicide victims, in other words, are often ambivalent about dying and long for someone to help them. (Both letters at the start of this section expressed this common view.) From this perspective, it is imperative that we know how to identify suicidal people and that we assist them in getting professional help. With over half a million attempted suicides a year in the United States, each of us may someday know (or even be close to) a suicidal person.

SUMMARY

1. **Psychotherapy** is a systematic series of interactions between a person who is trained in alleviating psychological problems and another who is suffering from them. These interactions are structured by both theories and scientific findings as to why such disturbances occur.

2. In Freudian **psychoanalysis,** the goal is to bring unconscious conflicts into consciousness, where they can be worked through and resolved. Various techniques are used to accomplish this aim, among them **free association** and **dream analysis.** Newer psychoanalytic treatments differ from Freudian psychoanalysis in several ways. For instance, the newer approaches are briefer, with the therapist taking a more active role in advising and directing the client.

3. **Humanistic therapies** are a diverse group of treatments that aim at liberating a person's innate tendencies toward self-actualization and growth. Carl Rogers' **client-centered therapy** tries to free people from the unreasonable **conditions of worth** imposed by others. The therapist creates a warm and empathic environment in which the client can come to understand and to value the true self. **Gestalt therapy,** another humanistic treatment, emphasizes the need to release pent-up emotions and to take responsibility for one's actions.

4. **Behavior** and **cognitive-behavior therapies** involve applying experimentally derived principles of learning to change maladaptive thoughts, feelings, and behaviors. Some of the techniques used (including **systematic desensitization, aversion conditioning, time out,** and **token economies**) are based on principles of classical and operant conditioning. Others (such as **participant modeling** to treat phobias) are based on principles of modeling and observational learning. Still others [including **rational-emotive therapy (RET), self-instructional training,** and Beck's **cognitive therapy**] are based on cognitive learning principles.

5. **Family-systems therapies** treat psychological problems by trying to change maladaptive patterns of interaction within a person's family. Family-systems therapies often involve all the members of a family, not just those who are displaying the unwanted symptoms. Different family therapists take different approaches, including a strategic approach (which focuses heavily on changing faulty family communications), a behavioral approach, a cognitive restructuring approach, and a psychoanalytic orientation.

6. Family therapy is just one form of treatment in which more than one client may be involved. In recent decades other **group therapies** have become widely used. Among those currently most popular are behavior and cognitive-behavior therapy groups and **self-help groups** like Alcoholics Anonymous.

7. Many contemporary psychotherapists use more than one approach to treating psychological disorders. These therapists are to some extent **eclectic,** combining different kinds of approaches and methods depending on the particular problems and needs of the client.

8. Biological treatments attempt to alleviate psychological disorders by altering the delicate balance of the brain's neural systems. One contemporary biological treatment is **psychosurgery,** a treatment of last resort. It involves destroying small amounts of brain tissue in very precise locations in order to relieve chronic and severe symptoms. Another biological treatment, **electroconvulsive therapy (ECT),** uses electric current to induce a brief convulsion similar to an epileptic seizure. For reasons still unknown, this brief convulsion can relieve severe depression.

9. A third category of biological treatment is **drug therapy. Antianxiety drugs** are widely used by people who are having trouble coping with situational stress. **Antidepressant drugs,** especially in combination with psychotherapy, are quite effective in combating depression. **Lithium** works well in controlling abnormal mood swings, from mania to depression, without diminishing a person's capacity for normal emotional responses. Finally, **antipsychotic drugs** are widely used in the treatment of schizophrenia.

10. Numerous studies have shown that treatment

for a psychological disorder brings about significantly more improvement than just letting "time" do the healing. In recent years researchers have broadened their efforts to evaluate the effectiveness of treatments for psychological disorders by exploring which particular treatments are best for which disorders.

11. Ideas about the causes of a psychological problem can suggest forms of treatment for it. For instance, identification of social-psychological factors that increase the risk of suicide (such as social isolation, impaired problem-solving ability, and a sense of hopelessness) has given rise to therapies that try to reduce these factors. Examples are strengthening a person's social network to overcome social isolation, pointing out alternative solutions to improve problem solving, and demonstrating the irrationality of negative thinking to combat hopelessness. These approaches to treatment may be made even more effective if they are combined with drugs that counteract the reduced levels of serotonin that suicide victims have been found to have.

SUGGESTED READINGS

Beck, A. T., & Emery, G. (1985). *Anxiety disorders and phobias: A cognitive perspective.* New York: Basic Books. The authors discuss how the principles of cognitive therapy may be successfully applied to anxiety disorders such as panic disorder, agoraphobia, social anxiety, and phobias. They also present a broad overview of the components of cognitive therapy.

Bender, K. J. (1990). *Psychiatric medications.* Newbury Park, CA: Sage. This book provides information on the use of medication for psychological problems. It describes when medications are indicated, the mechanisms of drug actions, side effects, dosage levels, and generic and brand names.

Ivey, A. E., Ivey, M. B., & Simek-Morgan, L. (1997). *Counseling and psychotherapy: A multicultural perspective* (4th ed). Needham Heights, MA: Allyn & Bacon. The most recent edition of a solid introduction to psychotherapy and counseling, written from a multicultural framework.

Kramer, P. D. (1993). *Listening to Prozac.* New York: Viking. Written for a mass market audience, Kramer (a psychiatrist in private practice) discusses the impact of Prozac on those he treats. Kramer thoughtfully wrestles with some difficult issues associated with those who use Prozac to feel "better," though they may not meet normal diagnostic criteria for depression.

Sacks, O. (1987). *Awakenings.* New York: HarperCollins. Sacks describes his work with patients suffering from a severe neurological disorder. With the use of the drug L-DOPA, these patients, previously considered hopeless cases, experienced radical, although temporary, changes. Robin Williams starred in a movie of the same name, based on actual events.

Vitkus, J. (1996). *Casebook in abnormal psychology.* New York: McGraw-Hill. A well-written, engaging collection of nineteen clinical cases, using a variety of different theoretical approaches. Each case provides an extensive discussion of the issues involved, as well as an honest appraisal of the long-term prognosis for improvement. Unlike many books of this type, it also contains an extensive, up-to-date reference list.

Wolpe, J. (1990). *The practice of behavior therapy.* New York: Pergamon. A recent description of current behaviorally oriented approaches to therapy, from one of the leading scholars in the area.

Yalom, I. D. (1989). *Love's executioner, and other tales of psychotherapy.* New York: Basic Books. Includes ten fascinating vignettes, each focusing on therapy with a different client. Readers will discover what therapy is like and how it affects the therapist as well as the client.

CHAPTER 17

Social Psychology I: Attitudes and Social Cognition

A riot has broken out in a maximum-security prison. Inmates have gained control of one of the cell blocks and have gone on a rampage of destruction to protest overcrowding. How will the authorities react? Will they quell the rebellion brutally, without concern for how many inmates are injured? Or will they take a more restrained approach?

To answer these questions, you might want to know more about the personalities of the prison guards and the warden. Are they harsh and callous, punitive and quick to anger, or are they more humane, even tempered, and

After only six days, the psychologist Phillip Zimbardo terminated his "mock prison" study—not because it was a failure, but because students' behavior had become frighteningly real. Research in social psychology has demonstrated that behavior is the result not simply of our personalities, but of the social situations in which we find ourselves.

rational? As much as you may want to know such information before predicting how the incident will end, social psychological research has shown that such personal characteristics may not matter at all. Indeed, in some situations a person's dispositions are quite unrelated to his behavior (Ross & Nisbett, 1991). What matters far more than the guards' personal qualities are the social circumstances in which they find themselves.

This central tenet of social psychology was dramatically illustrated in a classic study of the effects of prison life on people's behavior. In the basement of a university building, Philip Zimbardo and his colleagues (Zimbardo et al., 1972; Zimbardo, Haney, & Banks, 1973) created a mock prison. Over the summer session, student volunteers were given extensive personality tests; only those judged to be mature and emotionally stable were invited to participate in the study. Half were randomly assigned the role of prisoner, half the role of guard. Then the study began. Six days later, however, Zimbardo was forced to call it off because the students' behavior had become too frighteningly real. Those who were acting as guards were using their power harshly and arbitrarily. Those who were acting as prisoners either had been reduced to servile robots or had developed symptoms of severe anxiety. These perfectly normal college students, assigned to their roles by the flip of a coin, appeared to have become the people their social circumstances told them they ought to be.

This is one fascinating aspect of social psychology: how people think, feel, and act is not simply the result of their personalities and predispositions, but is shaped to a very large degree by the social situations in which they find themselves. What others around us are doing, thinking, and feeling, and how they structure our environment, has a marked impact on our thoughts, emotions, and behavior. Social psychologists investigate these powerful situational forces, seeking to understand how we are influenced by the presence and actions of others, whether actual, imagined, or implied (Allport, 1985).

The subject of social psychology is so broad that we will devote two chapters to it. This chapter explores how people and the social environments they create often shape our innermost thoughts and feelings. We will discuss social influences on our attitudes, our impressions of others, our explanations for their behavior. We will also consider how we come to love or hate other people. In Chapter 19 we will examine how social forces influence our behavior. We will examine pressures to conform to group norms, to obey those in authority, to adhere to social roles, and to follow the lead of others under a variety of circumstances. As both these chapters will show, human thoughts, feelings, and actions do not originate solely from within; they are products too of the social situations in which we find ourselves.

| Attitudes

People have attitudes toward just about everyone and everything, from O. J. Simpson to Prince Charles, from chocolate ice cream to nuclear reactors. An **attitude** is a disposition to respond favorably or unfavorably toward some person, thing, event, place, idea, or situation (often called an **attitude object**) (Chaiken & Stangor, 1987; Zanna & Rempel, 1988). Attitudes, in other words, are the

thoughts and feelings that encourage us to act as if we like or dislike something. Sometimes people dismiss attitudes as unimportant by saying, "That's just your opinion." But attitudes can be a matter of life or death (Flora, Maibach, & Maccoby, 1989). Your attitudes toward diet and exercise, drinking and smoking, using seatbelts and engaging in safe sex affect how long and how well you are apt to live.

Cognition, Emotion, and Behavior

Psychologists often describe attitudes as having three components: what we think or believe about something (the *cognitive* component), how we feel about it (the *emotional* component), and how we act toward it (the *behavioral* component). Sometimes these three components are consistent with one another. For instance, if people think that the death penalty serves as a deterrent to murder (the cognitive component), and they become angry when they hear that a murderer has been granted parole (the emotional component), they are likely to vote for a political candidate who supports capital punishment (the behavioral component).

The three components of an attitude are not always consistent, however (Breckler, 1983, 1984). For example, although more than 90 percent of Americans know that smoking causes lung cancer and heart disease (the cognitive component), about 30 percent of them still smoke (the behavioral component) (Shopland & Brown, 1987). Some of them even smoke despite negative feelings toward cigarette use (the emotional component). Similarly, although most teenagers in the United States believe that contraceptives can guard against unwanted pregnancies, roughly a third of American teens who are sexually active do not use contraceptives (Flora, Maibach, & Maccoby, 1989). These are not isolated examples. The correlation between the cognitive and emotional components of an attitude and a person's behavior is surprisingly weak. Knowing what someone thinks and feels about an issue, then, does not enable us to accurately predict how that person will act (Kraus, 1995; Wicker, 1969).

Why are people's thoughts and feelings sometimes at odds with their behavior? Why, if they know something is dangerous, do they sometimes do it anyway? One reason is that although attitudes can exert a strong influence on behavior, so can many other powerful forces (Cooper & Croyle, 1984; Fishbein & Ajzen, 1975). Those forces include social

Attitudes such as those being displayed at this abortion-rights rally have three components: a cognitive *component (what a person thinks about something), an* emotional *component (how a person feels about it), and a* behavioral *component (how a person acts).*

norms and values, as well as specific circumstances that pressure people to act in particular ways. Consider the pressure placed on teenagers *not* to use contraceptives. Acquiring contraceptives can be an embarrassing task for an adolescent, to say nothing of the fear that parents will find out. Teenage girls also worry that having contraceptives may make them seem promiscuous to boys. For their part, boys are often concerned that in fumbling for a condom, they will show their sexual inexperience. Both sexes may be too embarrassed to discuss contraception with a partner. The result of these converging social pressures is a good deal of unprotected sex and unwanted pregnancy.

Notice in this case how different sets of beliefs and feelings are related to a single behavior (using contraceptives). A girl may have positive feelings about avoiding pregnancy, but negative feelings about appearing to be promiscuous. A boy may be fearful of fathering a child, but may very much want to appear experienced. Thus, behavior that at first glance seems inconsistent with a person's beliefs and feelings may actually be consistent with the full range of a person's opinions. To increase the accuracy with which behavior can be predicted from opinions, researchers try to solicit beliefs and feelings that are specifically related to the behavior of interest (Ajzen & Fishbein, 1980). For instance, to accurately predict contraceptive use among teenagers, asking "Do you favor contraception?" would be too general. Rather, researchers might ask, "Do you favor using contraceptives, despite the inconvenience and embarrassment they may cause you and the potential effect on how others view you?"

Furthermore, only opinions that are clearly and strongly held predict behavior. Weak or vague opinions seldom predict how someone will behave in a given situation. In contrast, someone who knows exactly how she thinks and feels about an issue, and whose thoughts and feelings on the issue are uppermost in her mind, is very apt to act in ways consistent with her views (Fazio, 1990, 1995).

In one study, students at the University of Minnesota were questioned about their beliefs and feelings toward affirmative action in employment (Snyder & Swann, 1978). Two weeks later the students were invited to serve as jurors on a sex-discrimination case. Only those who were first asked to take a few minutes to think about their views on affirmative action delivered verdicts that were consistent with the opinions they had expressed earlier. Apparently, being reminded of their opinions prompted them to reach verdicts that were consistent with those opinions.

Social psychologists have tried to identify the factors that strengthen and clarify beliefs, so that they are more apt to influence behavior. One of those factors is the personal relevance of an issue (Sivacek & Crano, 1982). Consider the study in which college students read a statement that advocated a new policy at their campus—either a parking fee or a mandatory senior exam (Leippe & Elkin, 1987).

Advertising like this is an example of persuasive communication.

Some were told that the policy might be enacted the following year (in other words, it had high personal relevance); others were told that it would not be implemented for six years (it had low personal relevance). The students were asked to express their thoughts and feelings about the policy, then were given time to think the matter over more fully. Those for whom the policy had personal relevance thought more about the issue than the other students—an investment of time that probably made their opinions clearer, stronger, and more salient. Later those students were over three times more likely than others to act on their opinions, by writing to the school administration to voice their views.

Knowledge about an issue is another factor that seems to promote behavior that is consistent with beliefs and feelings. In one study, for example, those college students who were the most knowledgeable about conservation were also the most likely to act on their stated feelings when given the chance to sign a petition and participate in a recycling project

(Kallgren & Wood, 1986). Knowledgeability probably enhances the clarity and strength of beliefs and feelings, just as personal relevance does. The more knowledgeable a person is about a topic, the clearer his opinions and the stronger his feelings, pro or con. Thus the more likely he is to act in ways that match his views. When knowledge has been gained from firsthand experience, it is even more apt to influence behavior (Fazio & Zanna, 1981). For instance, if a teenager has had a great deal of firsthand experience with smokers, her beliefs and feelings about smoking will be better predictors of whether or not she will start to smoke (Sherman et al., 1982).

In an exhaustive review of the literature (called a *meta-analysis;* see Chapter 16), Kraus (1995) identified a number of factors that predicted attitude-behavior consistency. He found that attitudes are better predictors of behavior when they are:

- Stable over time
- Held with a high degree of certainty
- Consistent with the person's affect (emotional reaction) toward a behavior
- Formed as a result of direct experience
- Easily remembered

Persuasive Communications and Attitude Change

Every year U.S. advertisers spend more than $50 billion to change consumers' attitudes. Political candidates spend another half a billion dollars yearly (McGuire, 1985), and countless public interest groups weigh in with their messages. The Surgeon General warns that smoking is hazardous to our health; environmental groups exhort consumers to recycle cans and bottles; the National Safety Council urges motorists to buckle up. Even everyday conversations are filled with attempts to change attitudes. Shultz (1992) estimates that, in the United States, the average adult is exposed to as many as 1,500 persuasive messages a day.

What factors lead people to change their attitudes? Psychologists are interested in both the conditions under which people may be persuaded to change their attitudes and the conditions under which they resist attitude change. One perspective on these important issues is the **persuasive communications** approach. During World War II, the War Department asked psychologist Carl Hovland and his colleagues to help in the design of persuasive messages, to be used in training and morale boosting. After the war, Hovland continued his work at Yale University (Hovland, Lumsdaine, & Sheffield, 1949; Hovland et al., 1957), trying to identify the characteristics of a persuasive message—one that people will attend to, comprehend, remember, and act on. He found that the source and content of the message, as well as the characteristics of the audience, were particularly important.

The Source of the Message

A message is often more persuasive if it comes from an expert source, that is, someone who knows a lot about the topic (Hass, 1981; Kelman & Hovland, 1953). Especially when a listener is not closely involved in an issue, he may be willing to accept an expert's opinion without much further thought (Chaiken, 1980).

A message is also more persuasive if it comes from someone who seems honest and sincere (McGuire, 1985). Such trustworthiness is partly inspired by the absence of ulterior motives (McGinnies & Ward, 1980), which is the reason TV commercials sometimes use the "hidden camera" technique. If a shopper candidly praises a detergent's cleaning power, unaware that she is being filmed, viewers are more likely to believe what she says.

Another factor that influences the persuasiveness of a message is the attractiveness of the source. In general, those who are perceived as attractive are more persuasive than those who are not (Chaiken, 1980; Dion & Stein, 1978; Pallack, Murroni, & Koch, 1983). Communicators who are similar to the target audience are also more effective at changing attitudes (Van Knippenberg & Wilke, 1992). For example, speakers who are racially similar to the intended audience are generally more effective than those who are not (Wilder, 1990).

Body language plays a part in communicating honestly, and thus in persuading an audience. For instance, eye contact is important to credibility. When someone looks you right in the eye, you are more likely to believe the person. For this reason, politicians often read from a Teleprompter mounted directly on a camera. Other gestures are perceived as deceitful—for example, averting the eyes, smiling constantly and nodding the head, and biting the lips nervously—and therefore tend to lower a speaker's credibility (Feldman, Devin-Sheehan, & Allen, 1978; Kraut, 1978).

Recent evidence also indicates that some factors that influence persuasiveness are cultural. For example, to Americans, a rapid rate of speech is indicative of power and competence; as a result, rapid speakers are more persuasive to them than slow speakers. Korean audiences, however, are not influenced by rapid rates of speech (Peng, Zebrowitz, & Lee, 1993; Smith & Shaffer, 1991).

The Content of the Message

The message itself, not just the person who delivers it and the mode of delivery, has an effect on a communication's persuasiveness. For instance, would ignoring an opponent's arguments, as if to indicate that they are not worth your time and attention, be a good idea? Social psychologists have found that failing to respond to charges is generally ill-advised. Acknowledging and countering an opponent's claims is usually wiser, especially if those views are well known or controversial (Hass & Linder, 1972). Countering the opposition is even more important when listeners are well educated and knowledgeable about a topic and tend to be against your position (Hovland, Lumsdaine, & Sheffield, 1949). Increasingly, advertisers are recognizing this principle. Twenty years ago, most carefully avoided mentioning competing products, but today many address the competition head-on (McGuire, 1985).

What about fear appeals—the kind of message meant to warn people about dangerous or unhealthy behaviors (such as failing to use seatbelts, engaging in unsafe sex, smoking, drinking and driving, or abusing drugs). Though many people believe such appeals are persuasive, the results of a classic experiment show that they are not necessarily helpful. Researchers showed subjects one of three presentations on oral hygiene. The low-fear appeal simply stated that failure to brush one's teeth can lead to tooth decay and gum disease. The mild-fear appeal illustrated those conditions with pictures of mild infection and decay, while the high-fear appeal showed hideously rotted teeth and diseased gums, which could lead, the message warned, to kidney damage, paralysis, and blindness. Contrary to the researchers' expectations, the appeal that aroused the most fear was the least effective in changing behavior.

Why wasn't the high-fear appeal more effective? One reason is that fear promotes attitude change only up to a point; after that point, it interferes with attention and learning. In one study, people who were highly anxious about getting cancer proved much poorer at attending to an article explaining how regular checkups can help to detect cancer in its early stages (Jepson & Chaiken, 1986, 1990). They were also less likely to be persuaded by the article's message. Apparently, when people are very frightened, they either "turn off" to messages about the frightening subject or become so nervous that they cannot pay attention well (Baron et al., 1994; Witte, 1992).

Another reason why fear appeals can sometimes be ineffective is that fear alone may not be persuasive enough to change behavior. People need concrete, personalized information about the risks of a dangerous behavior in order to change. The more personal the appeal, the more likely people are to be persuaded (Weinstein, 1989). Thus, a description of one man's struggle with lung cancer would probably be more persuasive on the dangers of smoking than gory pictures of diseased lungs or statistics on the death rate from lung cancer. People must also know what steps to take to avoid the feared outcome, and they must believe that they are capable of taking those steps (Leventhal & Nerenz, 1983; Rogers & Mewborn, 1976). This point was illustrated by a study of the efforts made to get a group of eighth graders to stop smoking (Evans, 1980). Researchers found that messages about the dangers of smoking were seldom enough to change the teens' behavior; they needed specific information on how to resist peer pressure to smoke, because peer pressure played a critical role in maintaining their behavior.

The Audience Receiving the Message

Certain characteristics of the *audience* can influence the persuasiveness of a message. For example, Rhodes and Wood (1992) found that audiences who score low on tests of intelligence or self-esteem are more easily persuaded than others. The mood of an audience can also influence its susceptibility to a message. Indirect forms of communication (in which persuasive information is introduced peripherally rather than as the main point) are more successful with audiences that are in a positive mood (Mackie & Worth, 1990; Petty et al., 1993). Finally, individuals who are high "self-monitors"—who desire the attention and approval of others—are particularly susceptible to messages that they believe promote a desirable self-image (DeBono, 1987; DeBono & Packer, 1991). For example, people who want to be

considered muscular and athletic would be more likely to respond to an advertisement for a treadmill that stresses how much better the person will look after using the treadmill.

Summary of Research on Persuasive Communications

Over decades, researchers have collected a great quantity of information about those characteristics of persuasive appeals that tend to promote attitude change. None of those characteristics is influential all the time. Sometimes an expert source can prompt people to change their opinions; at other times an expert source has little or no effect. In some situations persuasive appeals foster enduring attitude change; in others attitude change is short-lived and superficial. How can these differences in influence be explained?

Richard Petty and John Cacioppo (1981) have proposed a unifying theory of persuasion. They argue that there are two mental routes through which persuasive communications can affect attitude change. One is the *route of systematic analysis*, which involves attending to central aspects of the message (such as the accuracy of the information and the logic of the argument), thinking about them carefully, and weighing their merits in order to come to a sound conclusion. Persuasion through systematic analysis tends to produce very strong and enduring attitude change.

People do not always analyze a persuasive appeal carefully, however. They may not care about the issue enough to waste much time and effort thinking about it. Or they may not be sufficiently knowledgeable about a subject to evaluate the content of the message. At times, the amount of information they would need to consider may seem overwhelming. In such cases people tend to use the *heuristic route*, which is based on shortcut, rule-of-thumb strategies for processing information. Just as people use heuristics to make other kinds of judgments (see Chapter 8), they use them to judge the worth of persuasive appeals. When you think to yourself, "That person's an expert, so she's probably right" or "Everyone else here agrees with that view, so it's probably valid," you are using heuristics based on peripheral cues that can be processed very easily and quickly. Not surprisingly, attitudes that are formed through the heuristic route are often rather weak and changeable.

Political advisors work hard to present candidates for office in a positive, upbeat way, in the hope that voters will respond to their appeal via peripheral routes. The approach can be very effective. Bill Clinton's positive, smiling image won handily over Bob Dole's negative, dour image.

This two-route theory of persuasion helps to explain some interesting findings. For example, when people are not motivated to analyze a message systematically, even a poorly argued appeal can often persuade them, as long as peripheral cues encourage attitude change (Zimbardo & Leippe, 1991). That is why campaign strategists spend so much time working on the peripheral cues surrounding their candidates' messages. They are hoping that the audience will use the heuristic route and respond to peripheral cues such as physical attractiveness or an upbeat tone. Often, that is exactly what happens. In all but one of the ten presidential elections from 1948 to 1984, the candidate with the more optimistic tone won (Zullow et al., 1988). Perhaps we live in an era when the complexity of the issues makes systematic analysis of them too overwhelming a task for many voters. Or perhaps modern campaigns provide little more than peripheral cues. In any case, persuasion through the heuristic route is widespread in our so-

ciety. That is not to say that heuristics cannot be valuable tools; but too much reliance on them can lead to flawed judgments.

Cognitive Consistency and Attitude Change

Another approach to attitude change involves the concept of **cognitive consistency**—keeping various cognitions in relative agreement with one another. Several cognitive consistency theories of attitude change have been proposed. All are based on the idea that a perceived inconsistency among cognitions makes people feel uncomfortable and motivates them to reduce the inconsistency.

The Theory of Cognitive Dissonance

One of the most influential perspectives on cognitive consistency is cognitive dissonance theory, proposed more than forty years ago by Leon Festinger (1957). **Cognitive dissonance** is the unpleasant state of tension that develops when people are aware of entertaining two inconsistent thoughts simultaneously. If you tell yourself you want to save money, but then go out and spend $50 on compact disks; if you claim to be concerned about the environment, but don't make an effort to recycle anything; if you say you are in love, but often think of other people when you are with the loved one, you are experiencing cognitive dissonance. This state of mind occurs most often when the cognitive component of an attitude clashes with a behavior. According to Festinger, the disparity produces a state of extreme discomfort. The dissonance can be reduced and the tension relieved in one of two ways: changing the behavior, or changing the beliefs.

Consider the president of a company that manufactures cigarettes. If he believes himself to be a moral person, and believes as well that smoking causes heart disease and cancer, he will probably experience cognitive dissonance. "I am a kind, well-intentioned person, yet by manufacturing cigarettes I am contributing to the premature death of thousands of people," he will reason. To reduce the dissonance, this man is unlikely to convince himself that he is uncaring and ruthless, nor is he likely to give up his job. Instead, he will probably modify his thoughts concerning the dangers of cigarettes or the effects of his producing them. He might minimize the link between smoking and fatal illness ("Most of those studies were done when cigarettes contained more tar and nicotine than they do now"). Or he might add positive thoughts to counterbalance his negative thoughts about smoking ("Cigarettes may create health problems, but they also reduce stress and make life more enjoyable"). Or he might attempt to downplay the importance of the dissonance-arousing behavior ("If smokers didn't buy my cigarettes, they'd just buy someone else's").

Researchers have created cognitive dissonance in the laboratory by prompting people to behave in ways that are inconsistent with their opinions. Suppose a person is paid a great deal of money to say something he or she does not believe, while another person is paid very little to do so. Which one would you expect to experience cognitive dissonance, and what would be the result? In a classic experiment (Festinger & Carlsmith, 1959), subjects were asked to perform an exceedingly boring task: either turning the pegs on a pegboard a quarter turn each, and then repeating the procedure many times, or lining up

spools in a tray, dumping them out, and lining them up again. When each subject finished, the experimenter confided that he was actually investigating the effects of preconceptions on performance. Would the subject tell the next subject that the study had been fun and exciting? The researcher offered some of the subjects $1 to tell this lie and others $20. (A third group, the control group, merely did the task and were not asked to lie.) All the subjects complied with the researcher's request. When each subject was asked to evaluate the experimental task, those who had been paid $20 to tell the lie (and those who had not had to lie at all) rated the job as boring—which by objective standards it certainly was. But those who had been paid only $1 to tell the lie rated the experimental task as fairly enjoyable!

Why did these $1 subjects rate a boring task as enjoyable? According to cognitive dissonance theory, saying something one does not believe causes psychological discomfort, unless one has adequate justification for the lie, like a large fee—and $20 was a substantial sum in 1959. But the subjects who received only $1 were unable to justify the lie to themselves. As a result, they experienced cognitive dissonance and responded by convincing themselves that the task had not been so boring after all. This method of reducing dissonance is similar to the Freudian defense mechanism of rationalization (see Chapter 13). Suppose a child auditions for a play, hoping to get the lead role. If the child is not selected, his desire to play the role will conflict with his failure to be selected, introducing cognitive dissonance. To reduce the dissonance, the child may change his attitude about acting: "Acting is stupid. I didn't want to be in that dumb old play anyway!" Freud would call this process *rationalization*, while Festinger would call it dissonance reduction. In both cases, the attitude change is precipitated by the inconsistency between the initial attitude (wanting to be in the play) and the outcome (failing to be selected).

These results have direct practical applications. They suggest that the *greater* the reward for engaging in a disliked behavior, the *less* likely that attitudes will change to justify that behavior. For instance, when a girl who dislikes schoolwork is offered $10 for a good report card, she may decide that she is working for the money and continue to dislike studying. If she is offered only $1, however, she may experience cognitive dissonance and resolve it by convincing herself that studying isn't really so bad. The same logic can be applied to the use of punishment. To convince a preschooler not to play with the stereo set, threatening severe punishment is probably the wrong approach. The threat may temporarily reduce the unwanted behavior, but it probably will not produce lasting attitude change. A better tactic would be to make only a mild threat. In that case the child will have less justification for avoiding the stereo, and so will be more apt to decide that playing with it is not that much fun after all. The validity of this approach has been demonstrated in several experiments (Carlsmith, 1963; Freedman, 1965). Preschoolers who are told that they will be severely punished for playing with a very attractive toy are more likely to play with that toy when left alone with it later than children who are threatened with only mild punishment.

Despite the evidence that supports the theory of cognitive dissonance, it has been criticized (Chapanis & Chapanis, 1964; Rosenberg, 1965). Some have argued that the findings can be explained in other ways. One alternative explanation is *impression-management theory* (Baumeister, 1982), which holds that the subjects in cognitive dissonance studies change their attitudes or behavior not because cognitive inconsistency makes them feel uncomfortable, but simply because they wish to make a good impression on the experimenter—a form of the *demand characteristic* that is discussed in Chapter 2. For example, subjects in the boring-task experiment might have said the task was interesting because they didn't want the experimenter to think they would lie for only a dollar. Another alternative explanation, *self-affirmation theory* (Steele, 1988; Steele, Spencer, & Lynch, 1993), holds that those who convinced themselves that the boring task was really fun were trying to avoid the damaged self-image that would result from knowing that they had deliberately lied to another person.

These criticisms of and alternatives to traditional cognitive dissonance theory have inspired researchers to conduct more sophisticated studies. Many of those studies have shown that cognitive dissonance occurs under more restricted circumstances than originally believed. For instance, we now know that cognitive dissonance arises only when behavior is voluntary and when the subject feels responsible for it (Collins & Hoyt, 1972). It also requires negative consequences of some kind, either for oneself or for others. In short, by itself, cognitive inconsistency is not sufficient to foster cognitive dis-

sonance (Scher & Cooper, 1989). Some researchers have even questioned whether cognitive inconsistency is a necessary ingredient in the arousal of cognitive dissonance (Cooper & Fazio, 1989). They suggest that the guilt or remorse people feel when they are responsible for some negative outcome often fosters attitude change (Scher & Cooper, 1989). Future research may help psychologists to better understand the process involved in cognitive dissonance.

Bem's Self-Perception Theory

Another problem with dissonance theory has been the difficulty of measuring the psychological tension that dissonance presumably creates. How do some psychologists know that such a state of tension arises? Couldn't attitude change be produced without such inner conflict? Daryl Bem (1967) is one researcher who thinks that it could be, and often is.

Bem's **self-perception theory** is based on the idea that we come to know others' attitudes through inference. For instance, if we observe shoppers buying a certain brand of coffee and that brand is not on sale, we are likely to conclude that they must like the way that brand of coffee tastes. If, however, we observe shoppers eagerly buying the same product in a television commercial, we are not likely to make the same inference. The paid actors in the commercial have an ulterior motive that ordinary shoppers do not. Both behavior and the situation are therefore relevant to an assessment of the opinions of others. Bem goes on to suggest that we often use the same strategy to assess our own attitudes. At times, he says, we are not very sure of our own opinions. As a result, we must look to our behavior and the circumstances surrounding it to "know" how we feel.

Suppose, for instance, that someone asks you if you like lamb stew—a question to which most people do not have a ready answer, because they don't eat lamb stew very often. You might think to yourself: "I ate a large serving of lamb stew a few weeks ago, even though I wasn't very hungry. I guess I must like lamb stew." Bem argues that the subjects who received $1 in the boring-task experiment may also have been unsure of their opinions. If so, they would probably have asked themselves, "What must my attitude toward this task be if, for only a dollar, I was willing to tell another person it was fun? I guess my feelings must be somewhat positive." Notice how in this explanation, there is no feeling of psychological discomfort that fosters attitude change, as proposed by cognitive dissonance theory. Instead, people who are faced with an ambiguous situation infer their attitudes by examining their own behavior as well as the surrounding circumstances. They do so dispassionately, just as they do when inferring the feelings of others.

How valid is Bem's reinterpretation of cognitive dissonance studies? Research suggests that it may not always be accurate. When attitudes and behavior are inconsistent, people often do experience an uncomfortable state of arousal, as predicted by dissonance theory (Croyle & Cooper, 1983). In such situations, the theory of cognitive dissonance is probably a better explanation of attitude change than Bem's.

But Bem's self-perception theory nicely explains other attitude changes that cognitive dissonance theory cannot explain. For instance, when people are rewarded for doing something they like to do (that is, for doing something that is consistent with their feelings), their interest in the activity may actually decline (Deci & Ryan, 1980; Ross & Fletcher, 1985). Consider one experiment in which nursery school children who enjoyed drawing with felt-tip pens were told that they would be given a special prize for using those pens to draw a picture. The children complied, but a week later their interest in felt-tip pens had decreased markedly. The same drop in interest did not occur among children who had been asked to draw a picture for no reward (Lepper, Greene, & Nisbett, 1973). Why should we lose interest in something that gives us pleasure just because we are rewarded for it? According to Bem, the reasoning is as follows: "If I'm being rewarded for doing X, maybe I'm only doing it for the reward. Maybe I don't really like X that much after all."

This intriguing application of self-perception theory has stimulated research into ways to maximize people's intrinsic motivation (Lepper & Greene, 1978). Apparently, the effect of rewards depends on the meaning people attach to them (Ross & Fletcher, 1985). If rewards are given as an acknowledgment of competence, they can actually increase intrinsic motivation, by making people feel good about their abilities (Ross & Fletcher, 1985). Thus praise, a verbal acknowledgment of good work, often enhances interest in a task (Johnson et al., 1978). In contrast, when a reward is viewed as the primary reason for doing something, one's intrinsic motivation is apt to suffer (Deci & Ryan, 1985). In such cases, people may convince themselves that they do not really like something as much as they thought, because the reward they received suggests another explanation (they were paid to do it).

Many theories of attitude change imply that changes in a person's attitude may influence later behavior. Bem's theory suggests that the reverse may be true as well: changes in one's behavior may influence later attitudes. Thus people who are put in a situation in which they must behave differently from the way they usually would—for example, a shy person who is made to act more outgoing—may modify their self-perceptions. In later situations, the modified self-perception can modify future behavior (Schlenker, Dlugolecki, & Doherty, 1994; Tice, 1992). In one study, for instance, people read a description of a man and then described him to another person (Higgins & Rohles, 1978). When told that the other person liked the man they were about to describe, they painted a favorable portrait of him; and when told that the other person disliked the man, they described him negatively. Most of us, it seems, are audience pleasers: we automatically (even unconsciously) slant what we say in keeping with what others want to hear. How did the subjects in this study rate the man they had described when they were later asked their own opinions of him? Because they lacked good reason for slanting their descriptions, they convinced themselves that what they said must have been what they really felt. That is, those who had spoken favorably about the man said that they did indeed like him, while those who had spoken unfavorably of him said that they disliked him. Apparently, in some situations, "saying is believing." This approach—changing a person's behavior in order to change his thought—is similar to many of the behaviorally oriented treatment techniques discussed in Chapter 16.

This finding has important implications. Just by getting people to act in a certain way (without too much external pressure), we may be able to convince them that they feel good about what they are doing. Thus, to convince school-age children to take a positive attitude toward members of another race, lecturing them on the "Golden Rule" and the value of brotherly love may not be the most effective approach. Rather, getting them to act in helpful, cooperative ways in interracial groups may be more successful. Since people tend to like those they are friendly to, interracial cooperation should help to foster positive feelings among the races (Cook, 1985).

Social Cognition

When Sherlock Holmes first met Dr. Watson, he knew in an instant that Watson had just come from Afghanistan. Watson was astonished. How could Holmes, a stranger, know where he had been? To Holmes the answer was simple. He knew Watson was a doctor, and his military bearing made him an army physician. A tanned and haggard face suggested recent service in a hot, sunny climate, and an injured left arm (Watson held his arm stiffly) implied a battle wound. Since the British were fighting in Afghanistan at the time, Watson had most likely just returned from there.

Few of us are as clever as Sherlock Holmes at deducing information from a few simple clues. But all of us engage in a good deal of detective work in our efforts to try to understand people. This process of making sense of other people and ourselves is called **social cognition** (Fiske & Taylor, 1991). In the following sections we will take a look at two aspects of social cognition: how we form impressions of other people, and how we attribute causes to their behavior.

Forming Social Impressions

Suppose a new tenant moves into the apartment next door to yours. He is about twenty, very big and brawny, probably a student. His hair is cut short in a military style, his nose large, his forehead narrow, and his eyes close-set. As you watch him carry a set of barbells up the front steps, you decide he is definitely a "jock." So you ignore him, except for a curt "Hi" when you meet by chance in the hall. Six months later, you are astounded to learn that your new neighbor, a philosophy major, has been elected to Phi Beta Kappa.

All of us constantly size up strangers on the basis of scanty information. What is surprising, however, are some of the factors that influence those impressions. For instance, the traits we perceive first often count the most, a tendency that is called the **primacy effect.** In one classic study, subjects were presented with one or both of the two paragraphs shown in Figure 17-1, which describe a young man named Jim (Luchins, 1957). Those who read only paragraph A saw Jim as extroverted and friendly. Those who read only paragraph B saw him as introverted and shy. If subjects were asked to read *both* paragraphs, the order of their presentation usually governed subjects' impressions. Most of those who read the "extroverted" paragraph first perceived Jim as basically outgoing, while most of those who read the "intro-

"*Good Lord, Holmes! How did you come to know I'd seafood for lunch?*"

Though they may not be as systematic as Sherlock Holmes, social cognition theory suggests that most people do engage in some kind of "detective work" when trying to make sense of their own and other people's behavior.

verted" paragraph first saw him as essentially a loner.

Why does initial information often dominate our impression of a person? One reason is a simple shift in attention (Belmore, 1987; Zanna & Hamilton, 1977). When you first meet someone, you are curious about the person. Later, once you feel you have gotten some answers, your attention may flag, and you stop acquiring new information. This failure to attend to additional information is especially likely when you do not have the time or motivation to probe beneath the surface (Kruglanski & Freund, 1983). Another reason for the primacy effect is the fact that initial information can influence the way in which additional information is interpreted (Higgins & Bargh, 1987). Bits of data that do not fit a first impression may simply be discounted as atypical. For instance, if you have decided that Jim is basically

FIGURE 17-1 The powerful effects of first impressions. Read the description of Jim in paragraph A. What impressions do you have of him? Now read paragraph B. Does your impression of Jim change? How would your impression of him change if you read the two descriptions in reverse order? (Luchins, 1957.)

A Jim left the house to get some stationery. He walked out into the sun-filled street with two of his friends, basking in the sun as he walked. Jim entered the stationery store, which was full of people. Jim talked with an acquaintance while he waited for the clerk to catch his eye. On his way out, he stopped to chat with a school friend who was just coming into the store. Leaving the store, he walked toward school. On his way out he met the girl to whom he had been introduced the night before. They talked for a short while, and then Jim left for school.

B After school Jim left the classroom alone. Leaving the school, he started on his long walk home. The street was brilliantly filled with sunshine. Jim walked down the street on the shady side. Coming down the street toward him, he saw the pretty girl whom he had met on the previous evening. Jim crossed the street and entered a candy store. The store was crowded with students, and he noticed a few familiar faces. Jim waited quietly until the counter-man caught his eye and then gave his order. Taking his drink, he sat down at a side table. When he had finished his drink he went home.

friendly, you may assume that he just has something on his mind if you later see him avoiding other people.

The Influence of Schemas

This last explanation of the primacy effect suggests the importance of *schemas,* or integrated sets of cognitions about objects, people, or events that are used to help interpret new information. There are several different kinds of schemas that relate to people. A **person schema** is a set of logically integrated ideas about what a particular person is like, which is used to help us interpret the meaning of that person's behavior. For instance, if you think a particular person is a liar, an opportunist, and a cheat, you would probably decide he is trying to steal something if you saw him looking through your CD collection. A **self-schema,** in contrast, is an integrated set of cognitions about you yourself (Markus & Wurf, 1987), which may be similar or dissimilar to the way other people

view you. Yet another kind of schema, the **social stereotype,** is a set of beliefs about the way members of a particular group think and act. Such beliefs are often widely shared, but are not substantiated.

Why do we develop schemas about people? Part of the reason probably has to do with our limited information-processing capabilities, which force us to find ways to screen the many pieces of information we receive about anyone. So, we fall back on schemas, focusing on some facts and largely ignoring others. The strategy allows us to avoid becoming so overwhelmed by information that we can make no decision, solution, or judgment. Not surprisingly, we tend to rely on schemas most when we have the least time to spend (Gibbons & Kassin, 1987).

But though schemas save cognitive effort, they also pose some risks. When the information we gather about someone is sketchy, we tend to fill in missing details based on our schemas, even though those schemas may not be applicable (Bower, Black,

While schemas *are often useful in interpreting new information, they may also be a hindrance. Vivian Malone (left), one of the first black students to enroll at the University of Alabama, repeatedly encountered individuals with firmly held but inaccurate racial schemas, or stereotypes.*

& Turner, 1979; Cantor & Mischel, 1977). That is precisely what happened in the example of the muscular new neighbor, who was assumed to be unintelligent based on his looks. The schema was used to fill in the details, which turned out to be inapplicable.

Just as a schema can affect the characteristics we attribute to a person, it can also affect what we remember about him or her (Markus & Zajonc, 1985). In one study, for instance, subjects watched a film of a woman and her husband having dinner (Cohen, 1981). Later, those who were told that the woman was a waitress tended to recall that she drank beer and owned a TV set (traits that are consistent with a waitress schema); those who were told the woman was a librarian tended to recall that she wore glasses and listened to classical music (traits that are consistent with a librarian schema).

Confronted with an example that does not match one of our schemas (such as a librarian who attends rock concerts), we are not apt to change our schema to accommodate the new information. Schemas, particularly those we have held a long while, are often highly resistant to change (Fiske & Neuberg, 1990; Higgins & Bargh, 1987). In an intensive study, people with firmly held schemas regarding the value of capital punishment were asked to evaluate two studies on the subject, one that supported their view and another that opposed it (Lord et al., 1979). Despite the fact that one of the studies presented disconfirming data, the subjects' existing schemas became even more firmly

entrenched. Apparently, subjects searched for flaws in the study that opposed their schema, but accepted at face value the study that supported their view. This study clearly shows the power of schemas. By filtering information through a schema, we can see even contradictory data as being supportive of our views.

The tendency to seek out information that confirms our existing schemas has been called **confirmatory hypothesis testing** (Higgins & Bargh, 1987). A schema is essentially a hypothesis that we test by comparing it with real-life observations. The problem is, we "stack the deck" in favor of our own schemas, by attending to supporting information and ignoring contradictory data (or skewing it to make it seem less problematic). The result is a reinforcement of our existing schemas, making them even more resistant to change.

But though schemas tend to be resistant to change, they are not immutable. We do sometimes revise our schemas, especially when we are exposed repeatedly to contradictory evidence (Weber & Crocker, 1983). Consider again the example of the muscular new neighbor. If you were to hear classical music coming from his apartment on one occasion, you might dismiss it ("Maybe someone else is staying there"). But if you were to hear him play classical music almost every night, see him often in the library, and notice that he subscribes to intellectual publications and appreciates foreign films, you might begin to reconsider your schema. So it is with schemas about whole categories of people, such as racial stereotypes. We tend to dismiss one person who does not fit the stereotype as "the exception that proves the rule," but meeting a number of people who do not conform to our expectations has more of an impact.

The Effects of Priming

You are home alone, watching a murder mystery on TV. You hear a stair creak, a window rattle. When the dog barks, you jump up and run to the front door to make sure it is locked. The stair has always creaked, the window has always rattled, and your dog is a notorious loudmouth. But the movie has "primed" you to pay attention to these noises and reinterpret them as signs of an intruder. Such **priming** involves the unconscious activation of a schema, which then encourages ideas associated with that schema to flow readily into mind (Fiske & Taylor, 1991). In this case, the movie has activated your "murder mystery" schema, which includes the ideas of strange noises and dogs barking warnings in the night.

 **THEME** **A Large Proportion of Behavior Is Controlled by Unconscious Activity** People can also be primed to perceive a new acquaintance in a certain way if a particular schema has been activated before they meet the person (Higgins & Bargh, 1987; Wyer & Srull, 1986). In one study, for instance, some subjects were shown a list of positive traits (such as "brave" and "persistent") and others a list of negative traits (such as "foolish" and "stubborn") (Higgins, Rholes, & Jones, 1977). Then, in a supposedly unrelated test of reading comprehension, they learned about Donald, a man who enjoyed shooting rapids, drove in a demolition derby, and was planning to learn to skydive. Those who had been primed with positive traits generally saw Donald as adventurous and liked him; those who had been primed with negative traits generally saw him as reckless, someone to avoid. Apparently, people can be primed to form favorable or unfavorable impressions of others, even though they may not be aware of it. Even if priming words are presented so briefly that people say they cannot read them, the priming process still takes place unconsciously (Erdley & D'Agostino, 1988). Interestingly, priming can affect a person's judgments and actions up to a week afterward (Sinclair, Mark, & Shotland, 1987); with so much time in which to exert its influence, it has ample opportunity to color social perceptions.

Moods and emotions can also prime our reactions to others. For instance, if you are elated about having finished your last exam of the semester (and you think you did well), you will be primed to have a good time at a party and to like virtually everyone you meet. If, on the other hand, you go to the party after a fight with your girlfriend or boyfriend (whom you suspect of seeing someone else), you will be primed to see others in a hostile light.

In sum, priming is a "behind the scenes" type of influence (Bargh, 1989). Usually we are completely unaware that a previously activated schema is affecting how we think and act (Chaiken, Liberman, & Eagly, 1989; Gilbert, 1989). Suddenly we make an association, and because that association comes to mind so readily, it fosters false confidence that our thinking must be right. That is not to say that we cannot resist the effects of priming, however. With deliberate effort we can reject prime-activated schemas and examine hard evidence instead (Bargh, 1989). For example, if you are highly motivated to be accurate in your judgment about a person (if a great deal is at stake), you will probably look beyond a prime-activated schema. The same is true if you know you will be held accountable for the judgment you make (Fiske & Taylor, 1991). Since—by definition—priming occurs outside of conscious awareness, however, discounting its influence completely is difficult.

Self-Fulfilling Prophecies

We have seen that in forming impressions of people we sometimes make incorrect assumptions based on schemas. Then, despite contradictory information, we often cling to those incorrect assumptions. That in itself is unfortunate, but consider an additional effect of incorrect impressions. Mistaking someone as aloof, you may respond in a standoffish way yourself—causing that person to behave coolly toward you, thus "confirming" your impressions. Through your own behavior, in other words, you may encourage the very aloofness you expected. Your once erroneous belief becoming a reality is referred to as a **self-fulfilling prophecy.**

Self-fulfilling prophecies have been demonstrated in a number of provocative experiments (e. g., Miller & Turnbull, 1986; Rosenthal, 1966). In one, college men and women were asked to "get to know one another" through ten-minute phone conversations (Snyder, Tanke, & Berscheid, 1977). The men were given profiles of their future "phonemates," which included photographs. Some of the photographs showed an extremely attractive woman; others, an unattractive woman. In fact, the photographs were of completely different women. The men responded as expected. Those who thought they were talking to an attractive woman were friendlier, funnier, and sexier than those who thought they were talking to an unattractive woman. More important, the women responded in kind. Those who had been cast as attractive were judged by unbiased listeners to be poised and outgoing, while those who had been cast as homely were judged to be awkward and withdrawn. Apparently, each woman took her cue from her partner's behavior, becoming the person he expected her to be. A substantial amount of research on self-fulfilling prophecies suggests that such effects are common (Fiske & Taylor, 1991).

Attributing Causes to Others' Behavior

Our evaluations of other people certainly do not end with the formation of first impressions. Even when we know another person quite well, we often want to find out why that person is acting in a certain way. If we can attribute an action to some enduring cause (a stable personality trait, for instance), we add some predictability to our social world. We gain confidence that under similar conditions, this particular person will act much the same way again. Fritz Heider (1944, 1958), the first psychologist to study **causal attribution**—how people attribute causes to behavior—believed that all of us are constantly searching for relatively stable factors underlying other people's actions. Our ability to find such factors makes our social environment seem less random and chaotic.

The problem is that attributing causes to behavior is not always easy. Often we must decide among several plausible explanations. When a student tells a professor how much he likes her organic chemistry course, does he really mean what he is saying, or is he trying to wheedle a favorable recommendation for medical school? This kind of ambiguity may even arise when we are assessing our own motives, as we saw earlier with regard to Daryl Bem's views. Bem's work, in fact, helped to focus social psychologists' attention on the general process of making causal inferences.

In studying how people attribute causes to behavior, researchers have raised two main questions. First, what information do we look to in drawing causal inferences? And second, what kinds of errors

do we typically make as we go about this process? In the following sections we will explore some answers to both of these intriguing questions.

The Process of Causal Inference

There are two influential theories of how people infer the cause of others' behavior. One, proposed by Jones and Davis (1965), focuses on the kinds of behavior people attend to when they make causal attributions. Not all behaviors are equally informative, Jones and Davis argue. Some are so common, so socially expected, that they reveal very little about a person. If, for example, a political candidate smiles broadly while shaking hundreds of hands, do you immediately assume he is genuinely warm and friendly? Probably not, because those behaviors are widely expected of people seeking public office. Behavior that is in some way unexpected provides more insight into a person's nature.

Another influential theory of how people make causal attributions was suggested by Harold Kelley (1967, 1971). Kelley's theory is not incompatible with Jones and Davis's; it simply focuses on different aspects of the attribution process. He argues that when we infer the cause of a behavior, we tend to compare a person's present actions with past actions, as well as with how others act in similar circumstances.

Suppose a friend drags you to her dorm party. Soon after you arrive, a classmate named Harry walks over to you and starts "coming on." Why is he behaving this way? Is it something about Harry? (Maybe he's perpetually "on the make.") Something about you? ("Am I especially attractive tonight?") Or something about the situation? ("Maybe Harry's had too much to drink.")

To find out, Kelley says, you would first consider a factor he calls *consistency*. Has Harry behaved this way in other settings? If so, you have some evidence that Harry is the kind of guy who is always coming on to women. Next, to confirm this theory, you might consider the factor Kelley calls *consensus*, by comparing Harry's behavior to that of other men. Do most other men behave the way Harry does? If so, you may conclude that Harry is just being one of the pack. If not, you have added reason to believe that a special personality trait prompts Harry to act as he does. Finally, you may consider the issue of *distinctiveness*. Is Harry's attention directed exclusively toward you? What if several friends tell you that Harry has used the same line with them ("I've been wanting to meet you ever since I first saw you")? In that case, you are very apt to decide that Harry is perpetually "on the make," and therefore a man you should avoid.

Like Jones and Davis's view of how people attribute causes to behavior, Kelley's view has also been confirmed by research (Hazelwood & Olson, 1986; Hewstone & Jaspers, 1987; McArthur, 1972). Notice that both these theories assume that people infer the causes of behavior in highly logical ways. They screen available evidence, eliminate that which is questionable, and conduct further tests to prove or disprove their hypotheses. In this respect, they behave much like amateur scientists.

Attribution Biases

As amateur psychologists, most people have limitations. Despite frequent successes at attributing causes to others' behavior, they also make attribution errors. Those errors are seldom haphazard; most people are prone to very systematic attribution biases (Nisbett & Ross, 1980; Ross & Nisbett, 1991). We will discuss three of them.

The Fundamental Attribution Error Probably the most common attribution error is the tendency to see others' behavior as being caused by their personalities (sometimes called *dispositional factors*) rather than external forces (*situational factors*). If you observe a woman behaving rudely, you will be much more inclined to infer that she is rude by nature than that she is caught in unusual circumstances. This tendency is so powerful that it can cause you to overlook even strong situational pressures. For example, even when people know that an essay writer has been assigned to take a certain point of view, they assume that the essay reflects the writer's true opinions (Gilbert & Jones, 1986). And even though we know an actor is playing a role, we often attribute a character's personality characteristics to the actor. This tendency to attribute others' behavior to their inner dispositions is so pervasive that it has been called the **fundamental attribution error** (Ross, 1977).

Why do we make this mistake so often? One reason may be that our attention is usually drawn to whatever is most salient—that is, to whatever is most distinctive in relation to its surroundings, and therefore tends to stand out (Bargh, 1984; Fiske & Taylor, 1991). An overt behavior can be seen, but many situational factors are invisible. When we are wondering about the causes of a behavior, then, we tend to focus on the person who is doing the acting or, more specifically, on that person's nature. This quick, automatic kind of attribution occurs without much thought.

Of course, we are capable of looking deeper for causes. Some psychologists have argued that causal attribution can be a two-step process (Gilbert, 1989; Gilbert et al., 1992). First, we almost always make a quick attribution that assigns the cause to the person. For instance, an instructor who notices a student yawning will probably assume at first glance that the student is bored and poorly motivated. But then we may think again, reconsidering the hasty judgment. For instance, the instructor may adjust her initial judgment in light of what she knows about the situation. ("He told me he's working evenings; his paper is due today; maybe he was up all night.") Because the second step requires a higher order of reasoning and deliberate, conscious effort, it is not always taken, particularly if a person is busy or distracted, as is the case in many social situations (Gilbert, Pelham, & Krull, 1988). The instructor who noticed the student yawning was also proceeding with her lecture, registering a raised hand in the back of the room, keeping an eye on the clock, reaching for the chalk, and wondering if her husband would remember to pick up dessert for the dinner party they were giving that night. Such cognitive "busyness" may help to encourage fundamental attribution errors. When people have time to assess circumstances more fully, they are less likely to make such mistakes.

Krull (1993; see also Krull & Erickson, 1995) has proposed a variation of this attribution process. Rather than assuming that first attributions are always dispositional, Krull suggests that we make the *easiest* attribution first. In most cases, the easiest attribution *is* dispositional—but not always. For example, if we see people coming out of a movie theater laughing and patting each other on the back, the easiest attribution is situational. We don't assume they are happy by disposition but that they saw a funny movie (a situational attribution). After making the initial attribution, we consider the other possibility, but only if we have the time and motivation to do so.

We are less likely to make a fundamental attribution error when we know we are going to be held accountable for our judgments and decisions, and when something we want or need depends on the

	Friend	Self
Aggressive	_____	_____
Introverted	_____	_____
Thoughtful	_____	_____
Warm	_____	_____
Outgoing	_____	_____
Hard driving	_____	_____
Ambitious	_____	_____
Friendly	_____	_____
	Total _____	Total _____

Rating Scale

−2   Definitely does not describe
−1   Usually does not describe
 0   Sometimes describes, sometimes not
+1   Usually describes
+2   Definitely describes

FIGURE 17-2   *The actor-observer bias. Use this scale to evaluate the characteristics of a friend. Then use the same scale to evaluate yourself. Total the scores in both columns. Then total the scores a second time, ignoring the pluses and minuses. Most people find that in the second set of totals, their own scores are higher than their friend's. This exercise demonstrates the tendency to attribute our own behavior to stable, internal causes, and others' behavior to less stable, external causes.* (Fiske & Taylor, 1984.)

person whose behavior we are seeking to explain (Neuberg, 1989; Tetlock, 1989). In those cases, responsibility and self-interest prod us into taking the second cognitive step.

The Actor-Observer Bias   In thinking about our *own* behavior, we tend to avoid the fundamental attribution error. Instead, we look to situational causes rather than personality factors (Jones & Nisbett, 1971). Thus, there may be marked differences in the way actors and observers explain the same behavior. To the observer, a behavior seems to arise from the actor's disposition; to the actor, from the surrounding circumstances. This common difference in attribution style, called the **actor-observer bias,** may be caused by differences in knowledge. An actor has extensive knowledge of his or her own behavior, and how it has varied in different situations. An observer, in contrast, has seen the actor in far fewer circumstances, and so is apt to think of the current behavior as typical.

Sometimes this bias can cause interpersonal conflict (Kelley, 1979), as when parents attribute a son's poor grades to his laziness (a dispositional factor), while the son may blame a heavy course load (a situational cause). An awareness of the actor-observer

bias can help both parties in a conflict to be more sensitive to each other's point of view. If you think you are immune to the actor-observer bias, take the test in Figure 17-2. You will probably feel that your friend's behavior is more stable than your own, as reflected in the higher score you give your friend. That is because you attribute your friend's behavior largely to a stable disposition, while you see your own behavior as depending more on the situation.

The Self-Serving Bias   In some circumstances actors are strongly motivated to attribute causes to themselves rather than to the situation. When the outcome of a behavior is favorable, people are usually quick to claim personal responsibility. Only when an outcome is unfavorable are people more apt to pin the blame on circumstances. For instance, students often say that they "earned" an A in one course but "were given" a D in another. This tendency to take credit for successes and find situational excuses for failure has been aptly called the **self-serving bias.** To give another example, when students do well on an exam, they usually credit themselves ("I always knew I was intelligent"); when they do poorly, they usually fault someone or something else ("The instructor doesn't like me";

"The questions were full of tricks") (Whitley & Frieze, 1985). Similarly, in competitive games, winners usually attribute the results to skill, while losers attribute them to luck (Stephan et al., 1979). Likewise, people also tend to overestimate their own contribution when a joint effort succeeds. For example, each coauthor of a successful publication usually thinks that he or she put in the most work (Ross & Sicoly, 1979).

One way to make the self-serving bias especially convincing is to publicly announce before you attempt an activity that you are handicapped by negative circumstances. To protect your self-esteem, that is, you claim to be starting out at a disadvantage. You won't play well in the tennis match because your knee is injured. You're bound to do poorly on your final exam because you didn't have much time to study. Stephan Berglas and Edward Jones (1978) have called this tactic *self-handicapping.* The self-handicap provides an alibi for poor performance and makes good performance seem all the more likely to be the result of extraordinary personal ability (Baumgardner, 1991; Shepperd & Arkin, 1991; Turner & Pratkinis, 1993).

In some cases people may actively sabotage their own performance—by not preparing as much or not trying as hard as they might have, or by starting slowly, so as not to create great expectations (Baumgardner & Brownlee, 1987). In a recent experiment, Guerin (1994) examined drivers' assessments of their own ability. He found that most considered themselves to be "above average" drivers, even if they had been in an accident. Even tennis champion Martina Navratilova has admitted to self-handicapping. After losing to some young players, she confessed that she had been afraid to play her best for fear that if she lost, she would have to attribute the cause to herself. "I was scared to find out if they could beat me when I'm playing my best," she said, "because if they can, then I am finished" (Frankel & Snyder, 1987).

Psychologists are divided on the question of whether such strategies are adaptive or maladaptive. Some think that self-serving attributions and self-handicapping protect our self-esteem, insulating us from anxiety in competitive situations and helping us to avoid depression when our performance is not good (Snyder & Higgins, 1988; Taylor, 1989; Taylor & Brown, 1988). Others argue that such strategies backfire in the long run (Nisbett & Ross,

1980). Though self-handicapping may protect us from losing face, it can also "protect" us from doing our best. If we don't really try hard or create obstacles that can serve as excuses, we will never know how well we might have done.

A self-serving bias can also lead to unrealistic optimism. For example, Taylor and colleagues (1992) examined high-risk sexual behavior in men. They found that those who were sexually active actually *discounted* their risk of contracting AIDS in relation to those who were not sexually active. Thus, the self-serving bias may actually *increase* the likelihood of engaging in risky behavior—"It won't happen to me, because I'm not like all the rest."

Attraction, Friendship, and Love

Forming impressions and attributing causes to behavior are processes that apply to everyone we meet. Liking and loving, in contrast, are selective. Few people become our close friends, and fewer still spark that special, intense feeling we call romantic love. Forming friendships and falling in love are among life's most enriching experiences. What light can psychologists shed on friendship and love?

What Promotes Attraction?

You have accepted a job in a city halfway across the country. You are excited about the new career opportunity, but a little worried about your social life. How will you make friends? Will you meet "Mr. or Ms. Right"? Social psychology cannot tell you whether you will find the love of your life in Cleveland, but it can tell you what factors will tend to attract you to other people.

Physical Attractiveness

Although most people end up with romantic partners who are roughly equal to themselves in attractiveness, physical beauty is still a social magnet that draws us to other people and encourages us to like them. This fact was demonstrated in a classic experiment (Walster et al., 1966). Over 700 college freshmen attended a dance with computer-matched dates supposedly chosen for them on the basis of shared interests. Each person was first assessed for physical attractiveness, intelligence, and personality traits, but dates were in fact assigned completely at random. After the dance researchers asked participants to rate their dates. They found that the only factor

Attractive individuals like Cindy Crawford and George Clooney are usually perceived favorably. People associate beauty with many positive traits, like sensitivity, kindness, and intelligence, but with only a few negative traits, like vanity.

that consistently influenced a date's rating was physical attractiveness; intelligence and personality mattered hardly at all. If you are thinking that looks may count a lot at first, but other factors become important later, you are being too idealistic. In another study, students were paired at random for a series of five dates; over time the importance to them of physical attractiveness actually increased (Mathes, 1975).

What is it about beautiful people that so attracts us to them? There is a tendency to associate beauty with a host of positive traits (sensitivity, kindness, intelligence, conversational ability, strength, poise, sociability, good health, sexual responsiveness) and only a relatively few negative characteristics (vanity and conceit, for example) (Cunningham, 1986; Dion, Berscheid, & Walster, 1972; Eagly et al., 1991; Hatfield & Sprecher, 1986). Moreover, not only do we attribute many desirable traits to beautiful people, but we also think highly of those who associate with the

beautiful (Sigall & Landy, 1973). If a man is dating a very beautiful woman, we assume he must be special; after all, she could have any man she wanted. One reason for our pursuit of beautiful people, then, may be that associating with them enhances our social status.

If our pursuit of beauty were solely an effort to enhance our social status, however, physical attractiveness would be as important in the choice of a same-sex friend as it is in the choice of a mate—but it isn't (Feingold, 1988, 1990, 1991). Undoubtedly, many people gravitate to beautiful mates because they find them sexually arousing. Interestingly, men are more attracted to beautiful mates than women. For women, the economic status of a man they are romantically involved with is equally, if not more, important (Buss, 1988), though the importance of economic status tends to vary across cultures (Sprecher et al., 1994).

Proximity and Exposure

Another important ingredient in interpersonal attraction is proximity, or nearness. People are most apt to like, and even to marry, someone who lives near them, sits near them in class, or works near them at the office. In a classic study of this effect, researchers surveyed married couples in a student housing complex (Festinger, Schachter, & Back, 1950). The closer to each other people lived, the more likely they were to become friends. Moreover, couples who were assigned apartments near busy areas (by the mailboxes, for example) tended to be more popular than those assigned to more secluded places.

These results were undoubtedly related to the frequency with which the people involved saw one another. Apparently, just repeated exposure to another person can create positive feelings (Bornstein, Rappoport, Kerpel, & Katz, 1989; Hoorens & Nuttin, 1993; Hoorens et al., 1990). Consider an experiment in which students were told they were participating in a study on taste (Saegert, Swap, & Zajonc, 1973). Shuttled in and out of small cubicles, they tasted and rated different liquids, in the process encountering a number of other people whom they were not permitted to speak with. Later, the subjects tended to express the greatest liking for those people they had encountered most often.

Why do people tend to like those they see repeatedly? One possible explanation is that as we become more familiar with a person, that person grows more predictable and less threatening. Though we may never come to love another person solely through repeated exposure, we may at least learn to feel comfortable in that person's presence. This feeling of comfortable familiarity is a basis on which friendship can be built.

Similarity

Folk wisdom holds both that "birds of a feather flock together" and that "opposites attract." Which cliché is right? More often the first, research shows. We tend to like people who are similar to us—in age, ethnic background, level of education, socioeconomic status, values and attitudes, personality traits, even habits like cigarette smoking and physical characteristics like height and weight (Buss, 1985). Furthermore, judgments about similarities are often made fairly quickly (Sprecher & Duck, 1994).

Why like attracts like is not exactly clear. One possibility is that similar people enjoy each other's company because they confirm each other's values and opinions (Arrowood & Short, 1973; Sanders, 1982). Obviously, being with someone who constantly criticizes our taste, disagrees with our ideas, and challenges our beliefs is not much fun. Similarity also paves the way for shared activities, whether discussing Plato or going bowling, and shared activities are another foundation on which to build a friendship.

Perceptions of Mutual Liking

Finally, we are attracted to people who seem to like us in return. Spending time with people who reciprocate our feelings sets the stage for positive interactions, on which a friendship can be formed. In one study, for instance, college students who were led to believe that another person liked them disclosed more about themselves to that person, spoke to him or her in a more pleasant way, and disagreed with the person less often (Curtis & Miller, 1986). Those behaviors, in turn, encouraged similar responses from the other person, who came to develop a liking for the other person.

Conversely, when we think another person does not like us, we are not likely to pursue a friendship. That is unfortunate when the other person is not really unfriendly, just shy. For many shy people, expectations that social interactions will be unpleasant are confirmed because of their behavior (Jones & Carpenter, 1986; Leary, 1983). Awkward and inhibited in social situations, they tend to be passive and unresponsive. Others may interpret their behaviors as a rejection and reciprocate with aloofness or avoidance. This self-fulfilling prophecy can be broken, however. One group of researchers found that shy people can gain increased social confidence and skill by following a simple social script: "Find out as much as you can about another person" (Leary, Kowalski, & Bergen, 1988).

Three Types of Love

Love is an intense positive feeling toward another person—the strongest positive feeling we can experience (Liebowitz, 1983). Although being in love sometimes puts us on an emotional roller coaster, most people would not trade the experience for anything. In the In Depth section of this chapter we will take a look at why people fall in love and what makes their love last over a lifetime.

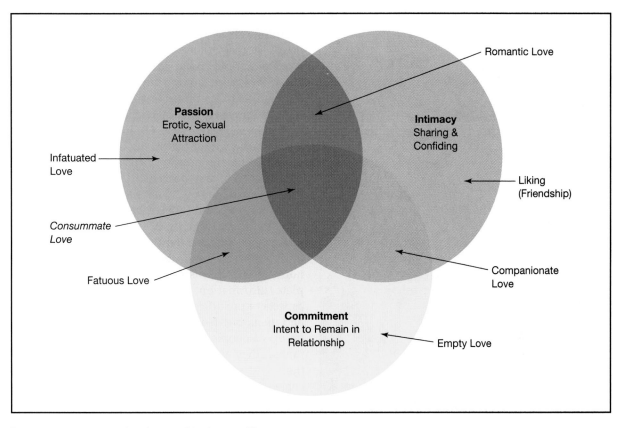

❙ *FIGURE 17-3   Sternberg's triarchic theory of love.*

Just as differences exist in all kinds of human relationships, there are different types of love relationships. Psychologist Robert Sternberg (1986) has identified three components of loving: *intimacy* (the feeling of closeness and connectedness that allows two people to confide in one another); *passion* (the drive to be physically united); and *commitment* (the decision to be and stay together). Best friends have a relationship that is based on intimacy and commitment but not passion—a relationship Sternberg calls **companionate love** (see Figure 17-3). Passion without intimacy or commitment produces "infatuated love," a torrid but shallow and short-lived affair. Commitment without passion or intimacy yields "empty love," typified by the marriage in which the two partners have grown distant but have elected to stay together. **Consummate love**—which combines intimacy, passion, and commitment—is in Sternberg's view the most difficult type of relationship to achieve and maintain. Two other researchers (Hendrick & Hendrick, 1993), have proposed a model

similar to Sternberg's, in which the three components are identified as *eros* (passion), *ludus* (game playing), and *storge* (friendship).

Romantic love may pass through stages, much as people themselves pass through developmental stages. According to this view, a romantic love based on strong physical attraction often develops first. This **passionate love** is characterized by emotional highs and lows. The lovers vacillate between feelings of tenderness and desire, joy and despair, anxiety and relief, trust and jealousy, feeling that they cannot live without each other. Their passionate love may at first lack intimacy and commitment, resembling the infatuated love in Sternberg's model. But if intimacy and commitment develop over time, the relationship blossoms into consummate love. Passion is difficult to sustain indefinitely, however. Gradually, as the relationship ages, passion fades, leaving the intimacy and commitment of companionate love—the warm, affectionate bond between two people deeply committed to each other. In this stage, lovers feel at home

The psychologist Robert Sternberg has proposed that love has three major components: intimacy (a feeling of closeness); passion (the drive to be physically united); and commitment (a willingness to be and stay together).

with each other; they are partners who share their thoughts, feelings, and lives (Hatfield, 1988). An alternative view holds that passionate love and companionate love usually have different origins and that most couples experience one or the other, but not both.

The Psychology of Prejudice

In the summer of 1989, four black teenagers answered an ad for a used car. The owner lived in Bensonhurst, a mostly white, mostly Italian working-class section of Brooklyn, New York. On the same night, a young white woman in Bensonhurst was celebrating her eighteenth birthday. She had told a former boyfriend that she had invited many of her black and Hispanic friends. Soon after the four black teenagers exited the subway, they were confronted by a mob of some forty

white youths, wielding baseball bats and a gun and shouting "They're here. They're here. Blacks are here." Moments later, one of the black teenagers—sixteen-year-old Yusuf Hawkins—lay dead in the street, shot twice through the chest. Later, when black leaders organized protest marches through the community, they were met by residents brandishing watermelons and shouting racial slurs. Hardly anyone in Bensonhurst would talk to the detectives who were investigating the murder. "Yusuf Hawkins died of racism in the first degree," declared New York's Mayor David Dinkins. "That's a crime far more common than most of us have been willing to admit" (*New York Times*, May 18, 1990, p. B3).

Racism is just one form of social **prejudice,** an inflexible negative attitude toward members of a minority group that is based on erroneous or incomplete information. This definition stresses three aspects of prejudice. First, prejudice involves hostile and negative feelings, usually toward an entire group of people. Second, those feelings are unwarranted; they are based on faulty or partial information. And third, prejudice is peculiarly resistant to change, even in the face of strong contradictory evidence. Because social prejudices are so widespread and can cause so much harm to their targets, studying and understanding them is critically important.

The cognitive component of social prejudice is a **stereotype,** that is, a preconceived idea of what members of a particular group are like. Social stereotypes are essentially group schemas. To some extent they are an inevitable part of trying to understand and simplify our complex world, but unfortunately, they can become so ingrained that we accept them without question. Thus, we may assume that anyone who possesses a certain trait (femaleness, for example) necessarily possesses a whole range of other traits stereotypically associated with the first (docility, emotionalism, lack of managerial skills). As a result, stereotypes blind us to individual differences. Even favorable stereotypes are unjust, because they ignore each person's uniqueness. Of course, the stereotypes involved in social prejudice are by definition unfavorable, which is why they support and help to maintain a dislike of the target group. When negative stereotypes are used to justify **discrimination,** the behavioral expression of prejudice, they can easily become abusive. For instance, the stereotype of blacks as less intelligent than whites has been used to justify denying blacks equal opportunity for education and employment.

Although anti-Semitic acts may seem to be a recent phenomenon, racially motivated violence has plagued society for centuries, both in Europe and the United States.

Racism—an inflexible negative attitude toward members of a minority group that is based on incorrect or incomplete information—is one form of social prejudice.

A number of factors contribute to stereotyping. For example, in looking at developmental trends in gender-based stereotypes, Biernat (1991) found that younger children were significantly more likely than older children to rely on stereotypes. Because stereotyped thinking requires little cognitive effort (Macrae et al., 1994), people are more likely to rely on stereotypes when they are busy or distracted (Gilbert & Hixon, 1991), or emotionally aroused (Bodenhausen, Kramer, & Susser, 1994; Stroessner & Mackie, 1993). In fact, Bodenhausen (1990) found there is a circadian rhythm of discriminatory thinking: people are more likely to stereotype when they are tired! Members of small, powerless groups are also likely to stereotype others (Fiske, 1993).

How can people maintain stereotypes in the face of so much evidence that they are overgeneralizations? The answer lies partly in the way human memory works. Remember from the discussion of schemas earlier in this chapter that people filter new information through their existing knowledge and beliefs. That is, we often reinterpret or ignore anything that does not meet our expectations. Furthermore, anything that does confirm our expectations usually makes a strong impression on us. Memory is also a constructive process. In reconstructing our memories, we often rely on schemas; if those schemas contain stereotypes, they are likely to influence our retrieval.

THEME 4 Cognition and Thought Are Dynamic, Active Processes, Best Considered Reconstructive, Not Reproductive

Finally, recall the tendency of humans to look for confirmation through confirmatory hypothesis testing (see p. 581). Rather than looking for reasons to discard our stereotypes, we look instead for evidence that *confirms* them.

Two of the most widespread prejudices are **racism** (prejudice directed toward members of certain racial groups) and **sexism** (prejudice directed toward one sex, almost always women). Although racism and sexism have much in common, they are distinctive enough to be considered separately.

Racism

The murder in Bensonhurst described at the beginning of this section was part of a rising wave of racial hate crimes that took the United States by surprise in the late 1980s. Relatively rare in the 1970s and early 1980s, racially motivated attacks have since become more common. Racial and ethnic violence also flared in the Soviet Union and Eastern Europe, where riots between Azerbaijanis and Armenians, Czechs and Slovaks, Romanians and Hungarians killed scores in 1989 and 1990, and anti-Semitic attacks rose. Though such fighting may appear to be a recent phenomenon, racially motivated violence has plagued society for centuries, in both Europe and the United States.

The Dynamics of Contemporary Racism

Polls consistently show that the majority of white Americans support racial equality—up to a point (National Research Council, 1989). For example, nearly all whites believe that blacks and other racial and ethnic minorities should have equal opportunity in education, employment, and housing. But far fewer support programs designed to promote racial equality, such as affirmative action, school busing, and open-housing laws. Similarly, most whites endorse racial integration, but when certain boundaries are crossed—when racial contact is too frequent or too close, or when too many people are involved—they back off. For example, although most white Americans would not think twice about sitting next to a black person on a bus, they might feel uncomfortable dancing with a black person or going to a restaurant in which nearly all patrons are black. A significant minority of whites still holds extremely negative stereotypes about members of other races and seeks to maintain strict social distance. Thus, half of whites disapprove of interracial marriage, a third do not want blacks in the neighborhood, and 20 percent would not send their children to an integrated school (David & Gaertner, 1986).

Many psychologists believe that the overt racism of the past has been replaced by a new form of disguised racism (Katz & Hass, 1988; Kinder & Sears, 1981). According to this view, many white Americans are ambivalent toward blacks. They believe in racial equality and are sympathetic toward blacks because of their past and present hardships. But at the same time, they suspect blacks of violating traditional American values such as self-reliance, discipline, and hard work. They see blacks as largely responsible for their own problems because of a lack of ambition, a failure to take advantage of opportunities, criminal behavior, drug and alcohol abuse, and a high rate of out-of-wedlock childbearing. Of course, the majority of whites are not willing to admit to these views; in fact, many bend over backward to appear to be nonracist. But their prejudices are revealed in subtle ways.

In one study, for instance, white students examined lists of positive and negative adjectives, such as *clean* and *ambitious* versus *stupid* and *lazy* (David et al., 1986). Each adjective was paired with the word *whites* or *blacks*. The students were to press a button if they thought the two words went together. Although the students did not express racial stereotypes overtly, their responses were subtly suggestive of them. They were quicker to press the button when presented with a positive adjective paired with the word *whites* than when presented with a positive adjective paired with the word *blacks*. Deep inside themselves, these students may have harbored schemas that were less favorable toward blacks than toward whites.

How do whites handle conflict between their egalitarian values and nagging negative feelings toward blacks? One way to resolve the cognitive dissonance is to maintain their social distance (David & Gaertner, 1986). By avoiding blacks they can avoid confronting their racial prejudices. Another way to handle the conflict is to express racial prejudices only when doing so can be justified in nonracial terms. This second tactic was demonstrated in a study in which white college students were asked to give electric shocks to another student as part of what was described as a biofeedback study (Rogers & Prentice-Dunn, 1981). (Actually, the recipients of the shocks were accomplices in the experiment, and the electrical current was never turned on.) Significantly, when a black accomplice insulted the person who was supposedly delivering the shocks, that person usually delivered more intense shocks than when a white accomplice behaved the same way. In a situation in which their hostility was provoked, white students apparently took the opportunity to express their racial animosities.

Racism Explained

Psychologists have offered many theories to explain racism. Some have argued that certain personality traits may incline people toward racial bigotry. Research into this topic began at the University of California's Berkeley campus (Adorno et al., 1950), where investigators identified the characteristics of an **authoritarian personality**: rigid adherence to conventional values, a preference for strong, antidemocratic leaders, and a fear and hatred of almost anyone who is different from oneself. The researchers found that many people with this personality type had experienced harsh discipline as children, from parents who frequently withdrew their love, making the children feel insecure. Very dependent on their parents, these children were also very angry at them. Afraid to express their feelings, they became angry, fearful adults who displaced their repressed hostilities toward their parents onto a much "safer" target: members of minority groups, who were powerless to retaliate.

As interesting as this psychoanalytic theory of racial prejudice is, social psychologists do not believe it can fully explain racism. Racial bigotry and hatred are far too widespread to be caused by aberrant personality development alone. For instance, although many South Africans who supported apartheid most strongly had authoritarian traits, many others did not (van Staden, 1987). Clearly, social situational factors must foster racial prejudice as well. Social psychologists have devoted a great deal of effort to identifying what these factors are. (Don't allow yourself to fall victim to the fundamental attribution error, the tendency to explain others' behavior, especially negative behavior, in terms of personality factors.)

One social psychological theory holds that prejudice arises when different groups are in strong competition with each other. A classic study conducted some forty years ago supports this view (Sherif & Sherif, 1953). Twelve-year-old boys attending summer camp were assigned to one of two groups, the Red Devils or the Bulldogs. After a period of friendly cooperation between the groups, the researchers began to pit them against each other in a series of intensely competitive games. The result was a great deal of intergroup hostility. Apparently, fierce competition can indeed promote prejudice.

Frustration over losing something that is highly valued (such as a desirable prize or the self-esteem of winning) can help to explain the link between competition and prejudice. When people are frustrated by adverse conditions they cannot change, they often vent their anger and aggression on the most readily available scapegoat. This tendency has been demonstrated experimentally (Miller & Bugelski, 1948). Researchers measured subjects' attitudes toward various minority groups, then placed them in a frustrating situation: they denied them the chance to see an interesting movie, requiring instead that they complete a long series of difficult tests. When they were asked again to express their attitudes toward the same minorities, most subjects showed significant increases in prejudice. No such increases were found among control subjects who had not experienced frustration.

But competition and frustration over losing something that is valued cannot be the only situational factors that promote racial prejudice. Members of the same racial group also compete, sometimes causing each other frustration, yet their hatred tends to be directed outward toward other races. What prompts this tendency to vent one's hostilities on "outsiders"? One answer lies in the different way people perceive **in-groups** (those groups with which they identify) and **out-groups** (those groups to which they do not belong), which can produce an "us versus them" mentality (Ostrom & Sedikides, 1992). People tend to see in-groups as collections of varied individuals, partly because they have had much experience with many different members of those groups. For example, Judd, Ryan, and Park, (1991) looked at three distinct groups: sorority members, business majors, and engineering students. Members of all three groups viewed their *own* group as diverse and the other two groups as alike.

The human tendency to view members of an in-group as diverse individuals biases our attributions. If one member of an in-group angers another, his behavior is likely to be explained as the exception ("That guy is just a bad apple") rather than the rule. But because an out-group is seen as homogeneous, if an in-group member encounters an out-group member he doesn't like, he tends to generalize to all members of the group. In this way, group stereotypes are formed (see Brown & Wootton-Millward, 1993).

Finally, people may simply learn racial prejudice as a cultural norm that is passed on from generation to generation. As such, racism is taught to children by their elders, in the same way as any other widely shared attitude. In keeping with this view, children's racial attitudes do tend to match those of their parents (Ashmore & Del Boca, 1976). Children, for their part, may internalize prevailing racial biases, because in doing so they are rewarded with the approval of others or with self-approval for thinking as they believe a person "ought" to think. And the natural tendency to avoid those they have been taught to dislike creates a social distance that furthers racial fears and suspicions.

Ways to Combat Racism

How can racial prejudice be reduced? Somehow people must look beyond their racial stereotypes and stop seeing in people of other races only what

Although Americans may not consider themselves to be sexist, many important social and political roles are still predominantly the preserve of males. Since Nancy Kassebaum, the former Senator from Kansas, retired from the Senate in 1996, women have made up less than 10% of that body.

they expect to see. Somehow they must assimilate new information that disconfirms their stereotypes, so that eventually they will discard those stereotypes in favor of more positive schemas (Devine, 1989). Simply increasing contact among the races may not be enough to accomplish this goal (Fiske & Neuberg, 1990). Because stereotypes are so resistant to change, only under certain conditions will interracial contact help to reduce prejudice (Stuart, 1979).

One of those conditions is equal status. If whites encounter blacks only in low-status roles such as porter, janitor, and domestic servant, traditional stereotypes will probably persist. But when members of different races find themselves similar in status, background, and values, traditional stereotypes are more likely to break down. Enabling people to get to know one another well also helps, as do norms that prescribe friendliness and courtesy. Simply living next door to a minority family may not reduce prejudice, unless the two families become involved with one another. Similarly, if the belief that neighbors should act "neighborly" overrides all others, prejudice may decline. Several studies have found that encouraging cooperation between different subgroups often reduces racial stereotyping (Gaertner et al., 1993; Gaertner et al., 1990; Gaertner et al., 1989).

The effects of cooperation were also seen in a study of children in newly integrated fifth- and sixth-grade classrooms (Aronson & Osherow, 1980). Psy-

chologists set up special interracial study groups in which each child contributed part of the lesson. Consequently, all the children had to cooperate with each other to pass their exams. The results were dramatic. Within about a week, most of the children had abandoned the old racial put-downs in favor of much more positive interactions. Equally good results occurred in a more recent study in which highly prejudiced white women were paid to work with a black confederate on an "important project" (Cook, 1985). The cooperative interactions continued two hours a day for three weeks. At the end of the study, the white women were much less prejudiced than they had been before; furthermore, the drop in their prejudice endured for months. In contrast, a control group of women who were equally high in prejudice showed no such decline in their negative racial attitudes. Apparently, then, the right circumstances can help people to overcome racial prejudices.

Some new research by Fletcher Blanchard (1991) suggests that people who are antiracist and are willing to speak up about their convictions can help to establish the sort of climate that will discourage acts of racism. In 1989 at Smith College, anonymous notes containing statements of racial hatred were sent to four black students. Several months later, the ugly incident became the focus of Blanchard's study. A young woman who said she was conducting an opinion poll for her psychology class approached 144 Smith College students individually as they were walking across campus. Each time, a second student who was actually a confederate of the researcher stopped and was asked to participate. When both students were asked how they felt the college should respond to the notes, the confederate always answered first. If she condemned racism with an answer like "Whoever wrote those notes should be expelled," the other student reacted similarly. But if she condoned racism—for example, by suggesting that the students must have done something to deserve the notes—the other student was less likely to condemn the notes and sometimes even expressed approval of them. This study emphasizes the importance of an aggressive policy against racist acts.

Sexism

Throughout recorded history, women have been viewed as weak and inferior to men. Both the Bible and the Koran (the sacred book of the Muslim religion) are filled with references to men's moral and intellectual preeminence. When God banished Adam and Eve from the Garden of Eden, he did so for Eve's supposed moral weakness and disobedience. Even men of the eighteenth-century Enlightenment, who advocated sweeping social reforms, were unwilling to view women as equals. Females "must be trained to . . . master their own caprices," wrote the French philosopher Rousseau, "and to submit themselves to the will of others." This strong prejudice against women continued for generations.

Today in the United States, a nation that is considered progressive, women continue to carry out tasks such as shopping, cooking, and housekeeping, despite the fact that most also hold full-time jobs outside the home (Rochschild, 1989). Even in families in which the husband and wife are both professionals, the wife assumes more responsibility for household tasks, doing the lion's share of child rearing (Biernat & Wortman, 1991). Moreover, in the paid-job market, men continue to hold most of the high-status, high-paying jobs. This so-called "glass ceiling" prevents women managers and executives from advancing beyond a certain point in their organizations' structure. As a result of the Civil Rights Act of 1991, a 21-member Glass Ceiling Commission was appointed by the President and Congressional leaders and chaired by the Secretary of Labor. After several years of investigation, this commission found improvement in some areas—for example, the number of males and females entering professional jobs is almost equal. However, males still dominate management: while women constitute nearly 40 percent of the labor force, they hold less than 17 percent of the managerial positons, and only six percent of executive-level leadership (U.S. Department of Labor, 1991). The inequality was even greater for non-Caucasians (Cornell University School for Industrial and Labor Relations, 1996).

Despite the lack of any concrete evidence that women are less capable leaders than men (Spence et al., 1985), many employers simply refuse to consider women for high-status positions traditionally filled by men. In one study, for instance, researchers sent fictional résumés to real employers (Glick et al., 1988). The applicant, a recent college graduate, was named either Kate or Ken Norris. According to their résumés, Kate or Ken had experience working in a sporting goods store and on a grounds-maintenance crew, as well as serving as captain of a basketball team. The employers were asked if they would consider the applicant for the position of sales manager at a machinery company (a traditionally "male" job). Most said they would interview Ken but not Kate, even though the two had identical backgrounds.

In other parts of the world, the economic position of women is far worse than in the United States. Although women constitute one-half the world's population, they contribute two-thirds of the total working hours, earn one-tenth of the total income, and own only one-hundredth of all the property. What could possibly justify such unequal treatment?

Sex Stereotypes

The answer to this question lies in widespread stereotypes of women. Even though the behavioral differences between the two sexes are very small, most people believe they are substantial. For instance, when asked to describe the personality of the "average" man, people tend to say he is active, aggressive, independent, dominant, competitive, ambitious, and a good decision maker—all the traits associated with competency (Romer & Cherry, 1980). Men "take charge" and "get things done"; they are considered "natural" leaders. The "average" woman, in contrast, is seen in much the opposite way. She is believed to be passive, unaggressive, uncompetitive, dependent, submissive, low in ambition, and a generally poor decision maker—in short, a "natural" subordinate. Despite changes in men's and women's roles over recent decades, these sex stereotypes survive (Martin, 1987).

Sex stereotypes begin to influence parents and their children at birth. The parents of newborn girls describe their babies as smaller, softer, weaker, more delicate, and more fine-featured than the parents of newborn boys (Rubin, Provenzano, & Luria, 1974; Spence, Deaux, & Helmreich, 1985). Though the differences are more perceived than real, most parents soon begin to act on the stereotypes (see Chapter 10). Without being aware of it, they teach their children a host of traditional assumptions about what boys and girls are like.

Gender differentiation occurs at every stage of development and in virtually every setting and activity. Consider the example of computers. Computer literacy will be essential for tomorrow's workers, yet the majority of computer and video games are designed with boys in mind. In school, computer programming is usually treated as a branch of math, which parents and teachers alike tend to see as a male preserve (Chipman et al., 1985). When forty-three educators were asked to design a computer program to teach grammar to seventh graders, they used questions and examples that appealed to boys, even though thirty-four of the educators were themselves female (Huff & Cooper, 1987). This trend may be changing, however; for example, one toy manufacturer recently released an interactive CD-ROM based on the popular doll Barbie, intended primarily for young females.

Why Sex Stereotypes Endure

Why do sex stereotypes endure in a society that claims to adhere to egalitarian values and has even passed laws against sex discrimination? Earlier in this chapter we noted that even when evidence contradicts stereotypes, people will use the evidence to confirm the stereotypes. Take the case of a woman who rises to a position of influence in a firm. Because others at her level are primarily men, her "femaleness" is very salient. When other people want to explain her behavior, this salient feature is often the first thing they think of. Thus, if the woman is perceptive enough to foresee some critical problem, her male colleagues may attribute her insight to "woman's intuition." If she delays in making a decision for valid reasons, they may interpret her behavior as feminine indecisiveness. In these ways the men confirm their stereotyped views, and the stereotypes endure despite the woman's demonstrated capabilities in a high-level job.

Sex stereotypes also endure because social situations often encourage people to act in ways that are consistent with those stereotypes. For example, women have been found to eat less when they are with men, apparently because eating a lot is considered unfeminine, and women think that men like "femininity" (Gilbert, Waldroop, & Deutsch, 1981; Mori, Chaiken, & Pliner, 1987). Significantly, the more attractive the man she is with, the less a woman will eat! This finding suggests that people

shape the gender roles they play to suit their social situations. A woman who is submissive and coy on a date is perfectly capable of adopting a "take-charge" approach when organizing a group of children for an outing. Similarly, a man who acts "macho" with his football buddies can be "sweet" and gentle when he visits his elderly grandmother. The problem is, because of the way men's and women's work has traditionally been divided, the two sexes typically find themselves in roles that call for gender-stereotyped behaviors (Eagly, 1987). In our society, for instance, the construction and finance industries are dominated by men, while women are more apt to provide services as nurses, teachers, waitresses, mothers, and homemakers. Thus, men are often called on to wield physical or economic power, while women are expected to show patience and concern for others. Over time we come to believe that the actors are truly "living" their parts—that men are dominant and women are caring "by nature." This cycle, of course, is self-perpetuating. We place people in certain roles, they behave accordingly, and then we take their behavior as evidence that their roles are "right" for them. As a result, we steer future generations into the same roles, and the pattern repeats itself.

Recent evidence suggests that some gender stereotypes are based largely on real differences between men and women. For example, women are often considered more sensitive and less aggressive than men, an attribution generally supported by research. As a result, some aspects of the stereotyping of women lead to favorable evaluations in some ways, in that they are perceived as more understanding, kind, and helpful (Eagly, Mladinic, & Otto, 1991; Haddock & Zanna, 1994). In fact, Swim (1994) found that students' stereotypes of traits such as restlessness, nonverbal sensitivity, and aggressiveness were equal to or sometimes *underestimated* actual gender differences.

In Depth

What Helps Love to Last?

The power of a glance has been so much abused in love stories that it has come to be disbelieved in. Few people dare now to say that two beings have fallen in love because they looked at each other. Yet it is in this way that love begins, and in this way only. The rest is only the rest, and comes afterwards. Nothing is more real than those great shocks which two souls give each other in exchanging this spark.

(Victor Hugo, *Les Miserables*)

Though the idea of a romantic thunderbolt sounds appealing, for many men and women, falling in love is a slower process. In one survey of more than 200 engaged college students, only 8 percent of the men and 5 percent of the women reported feeling a strong physical attraction for their partners within the first day or two after they had met—a far cry from the cliché of love at first sight. For most of these couples, mutual love had developed slowly over several months (Rubin, 1973).

Regardless of whether love grows from one passionate glance or takes its time, what makes it last? Because we know from earlier chapters that maintaining close, satisfying relationships can influence not only our happiness but our mental and physical health, we will pursue this question in depth.

Initial Studies. When two people begin dating, friends pull out their crystal balls, declaring: "They're perfect for each other!" or "It will never work." Social psychologists too try to predict whether love will last, but their predictions are based on research. Typically, they first interview and test couples when they begin dating. They then recontact them later and compare those who have broken up with those who have stayed together. In this way, social psychologists have identified a number of factors that improve the chances that a love relationship will last.

The more alike two romantic partners are, the more apt they are to stay together. Relationships in which the partners are well matched for age, intelligence, educational plans, physical attractiveness, and so forth, have a better than average chance of surviving (Hill, Rubin, & Peplau, 1976). Closeness is

also important: couples who stay together tend to spend a lot of time together, to engage in many shared activities, and to consider each other when making everyday plans and decisions (Berg & McQuinn, 1986; Berscheid, Snyder, & Omoto, 1989). For such couples, the enjoyment of being together tends to increase over time.

Personality factors seem to matter as well. Certain traits can affect how people behave toward a romantic partner, how they perceive themselves and are perceived by that person, and how satisfied their partners are with the relationship. Among the traits most important to maintaining a relationship is empathy (a feeling of compassion and sympathy for the other person). Women even more than men want a partner who is a good listener and able to talk about feelings (Davis & Oathout, 1987).

Criticisms, Alternatives, and Further Research. The first studies on what makes love endure focused exclusively on what partners were like at the time they first met. In contrast, Phillip Shaver and Cindy Hazan have focused on a person's attachment style, which is formed during infancy. According to these investigators, people who experience loving and dependable relationships during infancy and childhood tend to have schemas about love and commitment that serve as solid foundations for stable marriages. That is, they strongly believe that the style of attachment a person develops in infancy often affects that person's love relationships throughout life.

Shaver and Hazan gathered evidence for this view by asking adults to fill out a questionnaire about themselves, their love lives, and their childhoods (Shaver & Hazan, 1985, 1987; Shaver, Hazan & Bradshaw, 1988). (A sample question is shown in Figure 17-4.)

They found that adults' styles of romantic love closely paralleled the three attachment patterns seen in human infants: secure attachment (characterized by trust in the parent's availability), anxious-avoidant attachment (characterized by avoidance of the parent when the child is upset and associated

In some respect, adult styles of romantic love parallel the three attachment patterns seen in human infants, secure attachment, anxious-avoidant attachment, *and* anxious-ambivalent attachment. *Secure adults, like secure infants, generally trust the people they love, find becoming close to someone else relatively easy, and rarely worry about being abandoned.*

with a parent who is hostile or indifferent), and anxious-ambivalent attachment (characterized by ambivalence toward the parent in stressful situations and associated with a parent whose caregiving is inconsistent). Secure adults, like secure infants, generally trusted the people they loved and viewed themselves as worthy of being loved. They found becoming close to someone else relatively easy and rarely worried about being abandoned. Most described their parents as caring and responsive. In contrast, avoidant adults feared closeness and were very distrustful of others. Many claimed not to believe in romantic love or the need for it, as if they were trying to compensate for deep insecurities. Many reported that their parents had been cold and rejecting. Finally, ambivalent adults were preoccupied with finding "real" love, but were painfully unable to do so. They were constantly falling in and out of love and were prone to emotional extremes and self-doubts. Often they described their parents in both positive and negative terms, suggesting they had received inconsistent parenting. Interestingly, research evidence suggests that once a person develops a certain style of attachment to others, that style tends to endure.

How could the attachment patterns of infancy affect the love relationships of adults? John Bowlby (1969, 1973, 1980) suggests that babies develop an "inner working model" or schema of the self and others. Though this model is not fixed for life, it can become a self-fulfilling prophecy. A person who expects rejec-

tion, for instance, may behave so defensively—becoming jealous and distrustful at every step—that rejection becomes more likely.

Another factor that affects the longevity of a relationship is the way in which partners attribute causes to each other's behavior (Bradbury & Fincham, 1990). Happy couples tend to attribute each other's positive actions to enduring dispositions, while excusing negative actions on the basis of extenuating circumstances. Unhappy couples, in contrast, tend to attribute negative actions to enduring dispositions, and positive actions to temporary situations (Holtzworth-Munroe & Jacobson, 1985). Thus, if a wife spends too much money on a new outfit, her husband will tend to attribute it to personal irresponsibility, rather than to the situational demands of an important job interview. And if the husband offers to take his wife out to dinner, the wife may conclude that he feels guilty rather than that he is being thoughtful. Clearly, this pattern of attribution can ruin a relationship. No matter how hard one person tries to please the other, the other person usually fails to see the effort as an act of love.

What about disagreements and arguments between couples: can't they ruin a relationship too? Surprisingly, no, as long as the partners do not become stubborn or defensive. In fact, open expression of feelings during conflict between lovers or spouses may even be good for the relationship (Gottman & Krokoff, 1989). For instance, a wife's satisfaction with her marriage tends to increase if she expresses

Question: Which of the following best describes your feelings?

A. I find it relatively easy to get close to others and am comfortable depending on them and having them depend on me. I don't often worry about being abandoned or about someone getting too close to me.

B. I am somewhat uncomfortable being close to others; I find it difficult to trust them completely, difficult to allow myself to depend on them. I am nervous when anyone gets too close, and often, love partners want me to be more intimate than I feel comfortable being.

C. I find that others are reluctant to get as close as I would like. I often worry that my partner doesn't really love me or won't want to stay with me. I want to merge completely with another person, and this desire sometimes scares people away.

The first type of attachment style is described "secure," the second as "avoidant," and the third as "anxious/ambivalent."

FIGURE 17-4   Sample item from Shaver and Hazan's attachment style questionnaire. (Shaver et al., 1988.)

anger during arguments with her husband. But when the wife becomes sad or fearful, and the husband whiney or withdrawn, marital satisfaction tends to drop. Apparently, keeping the peace by remaining silent takes a greater toll on a relationship than letting emotions out. When negative feelings are harbored, they tend to fester and grow.

Patterns and Conclusions. At present, most of the research on love relationships focuses on how people's expectations and assumptions about a partner's behavior will influence the course of the relationship. Unlike earlier studies on similarity and attraction, more recent research has important implications for ways in which relationships can be improved. As we saw in Chapter 16, those forms of marital therapy that attempt to change the couple's underlying assumptions and expectations are especially promising. Of course, styles of attachment that were formed at an early age may be very difficult to change. But people can be helped by discovering how their behavior toward a lover may have been shaped by the treatment they received from parents or other adults many years before.

SUMMARY

1. Social psychologists believe that the presence and behavior of other people strongly influence how we think and act. One area they investigate is **attitudes**—dispositions to respond favorably or unfavorably toward some person, thing, event, place, idea, or situation. How attitudes can be changed is a topic that has generated much research. One approach has been to study **persuasive communications,** messages deliberately intended to change attitudes. Some messages are more persuasive than others because of differences in such things as their content and source. Sometimes people carefully analyze central aspects of a message before deciding to accept or reject it. Other times they take a shortcut (heuristic) route to persuasion and focus on peripheral factors such as how much applause the speaker is getting. Persuasion through the heuristic route is more likely when people lack the time, knowledge, or motivation to consider an issue closely.

2. Another approach to studying attitude change involves the concept of **cognitive consistency,** the tendency to seek compatibility among our various thoughts and behaviors. When such compatibility is lacking, people can experience psychological discomfort, or **cognitive dissonance,** which they then try to reduce, by changing either attitudes or behavior. One alternative to cognitive dissonance theory is **self-perception theory.** It holds that in situations of potential cognitive inconsistency, we are often unsure what our true attitudes are. In such cases we simply infer nondissonance-arousing attitudes by interpreting our own behavior in light of the circumstances that surround it.

3. The process of trying to make sense of other people is called **social cognition.** One aspect of social cognition is forming impressions of others. Often we do this on the basis of very little information. Traits that we perceive first often count the most, called the **primacy effect.** One explanation of the primacy effect is that initial information is used to form a schema of what someone is like. This schema is then used to screen additional information, and so new in-

formation tends to be skewed to match the original view. Sometimes we are so sure that the schemas we have formed of people are right that we act toward them in ways that make them confirm those schemas, thus creating **self-fulfilling prophecies.**

4. **Priming** occurs when someone encounters stimuli that activate a certain schema, and the schema is then used to interpret (sometimes unfairly) new, unrelated information. Priming is an unconscious form of influence. Usually, we are completely unaware that a previously activated schema is affecting what we think and do.

5. People often try to figure out the causes of others' behavior, a process called forming **causal attribution.** Jones and Davis argue that behavior that is in some way unexpected provides the greatest insight into a person's nature. Kelley believed that we can sometimes attribute the cause even of ambiguous behavior if we have time to analyze the nature of the behavior carefully. Kelley considered three factors particularly important in attribution: consistency, the tendency for behaviors to be repeated; consensus, the degree to which others display the same behaviors; and distinctiveness, the likelihood that a certain behavior was restricted to an isolated incident.

6. Frequently we make errors in causal attributions. The **fundamental attribution error** refers to the tendency when interpreting others' behavior to give too much weight to personality factors and not enough to situational ones. We do not usually do this when assessing our own behavior, however. When we are the actor (as opposed to the observer), we are much more likely to consider the situation when making causal inferences. This is called the **actor-observer bias.** One exception is the inclination to take personal credit for things that go well, called the **self-serving bias.**

7. Social psychologists have also studied interpersonal attraction, friendship, and love. They have found that people are drawn to each other for a variety of reasons, including physical attractiveness; proximity and repeated exposure;

perceptions of mutual liking; and similarities in attitudes, habits, and backgrounds. Similarity between two people can also help to make a love relationship last. So can certain personality traits, such as empathy for others, a "forgiving" way of attributing causes to a loved one's behavior (seeing extenuating circumstances for undesirable actions), and a generally secure, trusting style of relating to other people. This last factor may be heavily influenced by experiences in infancy.

8. People are also capable of forming social **prejudices,** inflexible, negative attitudes toward members of a minority group based on erroneous or incomplete information. The cognitive components of social prejudices are social **stereotypes,** preconceived ideas about what members of minority groups are like. Stereotypes are often used to justify **discrimination,** the behavioral expression of prejudice.

9. **Racism** is prejudice toward members of racial groups other than one's own. Often the overt racism of the past is being replaced by a new form of disguised racism. People bend over backward to appear nonracist, but their prejudices are revealed in subtle ways. Causes of lingering racism may include **authoritarian personality** traits, strong intergroup competition (which may also involve frustration), perceptions of **in-groups** and **out-groups,** the self-esteem derived from devaluating out-groups, and the tendency of racial prejudice to be learned as a cultural norm. Psychologists have found that one of the best ways to combat racism is to encourage participation in cooperative activities with someone of another race.

10. **Sexism,** or prejudice toward one sex (almost always women), has existed throughout recorded history. Even today in democratic nations, people hold negative stereotypes about women. Children learn these stereotypes from their parents and other adults, from their peers, and from the mass media. The stereotypes endure partly because those who hold them tend to focus on confirming information and ignore contradictory evidence (or discount it as exceptions). Gender stereotypes also survive because social traditions often place men and women in roles where sex-typed behaviors are more likely. Observers then make the fundamental attribution error: they assume that the behaviors they see are caused by the "inner natures" of the two sexes, rather than by situational forces.

SUGGESTED READINGS

Aronson, E. (1984). *The social animal* (4th ed.). New York: Freeman. This book, which won an American Psychological Association National Media award, is an engaging, easy-to-read introduction to social psychology.

Fiske, S., & Taylor, S. (1991). *Social cognition.* New York: McGraw-Hill. A scholarly yet readable discussion of major topics in the field of social cognition, including attribution, schemas, and social inferences.

Hatfield, E., & Specher, S. (1986). *Mirror, mirror . . . The importance of looks in everyday life.* New York: SUNY Press. In this excellent, popular book, social psychologists describe and analyze the importance attributed to physical attractiveness.

Ross, L., & Nisbett, R. E. (1991). *The person and the situation.* New York: McGraw-Hill. An excellent, brief introduction to the field of social psychology. Citing many examples across cultures and history, the authors explain how powerful social forces interact with our personal psyches to shape our beliefs, our behavior, and our lives.

Zimbardo, P., & Leippe, R. (1991). *Attitudes and attitude change.* New York: McGraw-Hill. This book combines a discussion of classic research with contemporary findings to provide an engaging overview of the field of attitude change.

Social Psychology II: Social Influence, Aggression, and Altruism

On March 16, 1968, three platoons of U.S. soldiers known collectively as Charlie Company swept into the South Vietnamese village of My Lai, killing several hundred women,

children, and aged men. Though the fleeing villagers offered no resistance, the soldiers set fire to their huts, drove them into open areas, and began shooting at them. Most of the soldiers joined in the shooting; of those who did

Were soldiers in Vietnam cruel and without conscience? More likely, they were ordinary people responding to extraordinary circumstances.

not fire, not one attempted to stop the slaughter. Instead, they stood by as bodies piled up in ditches and the village burned to the ground. Later, some of the men reported that they had followed orders from their leader, Lieutenant William Calley. Others said they had simply done what the others did.

When reports of the massacre reached the United States, most citizens were outraged. How could the soldiers—normal, decent "all-American boys"—have committed such an atrocity? The investigation that followed revealed that the soldiers of Charlie Company had sustained heavy casualties since their arrival in Vietnam a month earlier. Frightened by the danger of entering My Lai, which they thought to be an enemy stronghold, and eager for revenge for the loss of their comrades, the soldiers apparently shot without thinking.

The My Lai massacre, one of the darkest moments in the long and controversial Vietnam war, was a disturbing illustration of the influence of a group on individual behavior. The men of Charlie Company probably were not

Steven Spielberg's film "Schindler's List" was a moving reminder of the unspeakable horrors of the Holocaust. One of the unsettling implications of social psychological research is that we, too, might behave similarly in such a situation.

cruel and without conscience, as many people thought at the time (another instance of the fundamental attribution error discussed in Chapter 17). More likely they were ordinary people responding to extraordinary circumstances. In fact, chances are good that you would have responded to those circumstances in much the same way yourself. This chapter examines some of the powerful social forces that can sometimes make people behave in unexpected ways.

While Chapter 17 focused primarily on how social circumstances shape people's attitudes, perceptions, and feelings, this chapter focuses mainly on how social situations influence the way people act. It begins with two behavioral patterns of major concern to social psychologists: conformity and obedience. Provocative findings on both these behaviors explain much about the events at My Lai. The next section examines the ways in which groups can influence individual behaviors, including problem solving and decision making. The two concluding sections on aggression and altruism illustrate how the social forces that influence people can be harnessed for both good and ill.

Going Along with Others

Steven Spielberg's recent film *Schindler's List* was a moving reminder of the unspeakable horrors of the Holocaust, the deliberate extermination of millions

of Jews during World War II. Could all the Germans who not only tacitly acquiesced in this crime but actively carried it out have been cruel and sadistic? As in the case of the My Lai massacre, the answer is "no." Some social forces are so powerful that average people can be swept into supporting a view they do not really believe in or committing an act they would otherwise consider morally indefensible. That fact does not excuse their actions, of course, but it illustrates the importance of social influences on individual behavior. One of the unsettling implications of social psychological research is that we, too, might behave similarly in such a situation. In this section we will investigate three behaviors that are heavily influenced by social pressure: conformity, obedience, and compliance.

Conforming to Prevailing Norms

Conformity is the tendency to alter one's opinions or actions so that they will correspond with those of others because of either implicit or explicit social pressure (Kiesler & Kiesler, 1969). The extreme conformity manifested by soldiers at My Lai occurred under the fear, stress, and confusion of battle. As one soldier put it, "I looked around and saw everyone shooting. I didn't know what to do, so I started shooting" (*Time*, Dec. 5, 1969). Although the consequences of conformity are seldom as devastating as those of My Lai, essentially the same psychological process underlies many of the choices people make every day. Have you ever found yourself ridiculing

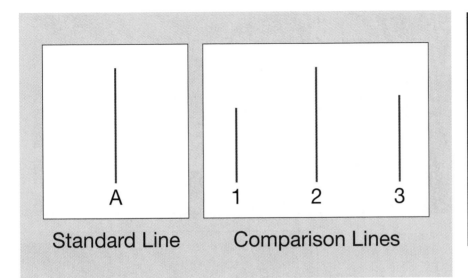

Standard Line   Comparison Lines

FIGURE 18-1   Stimulus from a single trial in Asch's experiment. The subject must state which of the comparison lines he or she judges to be the same length as the standard line. The discrimination is easy to make: control subjects (those who made the judgments without any group pressure) chose line 2 as the correct one more than 99 percent of the time. (After Asch, 1951.)

an acquaintance because others you admire were doing so? Note that when you conform to their behavior, you are not necessarily convinced that what you are doing is right; you may even feel that your actions are wrong. But you feel that others expect or demand you to go along with them.

Just how powerful and extensive is the tendency to conform? To find out, social psychologist Solomon Asch (1951) devised a classic series of experiments. If you had been a subject in one of Asch's studies, you and seven other students would have reported to a classroom for an experiment on visual judgment. The experimenter would have displayed two large white cards like the ones shown in Figure 18-1. One card would carry a single vertical line, which would serve as a standard. The other card would carry three vertical lines of different lengths. You would be asked to determine which of the three lines is the same length as the standard line.

The experiment would open uneventfully. The subjects would give their answers in the order in which they are seated, your place being next to last. On the first trial, everyone would choose the correct line. On the second trial, the choice would be unanimous. Because the judgments are easy, you would settle in for what you expect to be a rather boring experiment. But on the third trial, something strange would happen. The first person would say that line 1 matches the standard, even though line 2 is obviously the correct choice. The second person would unhesitatingly agree, as would the third, fourth, fifth,

and sixth subjects. Then it would be your turn, and you would be faced with a dilemma. Though your own eyes tell you unmistakably that line 2 is the correct response, six other people have confidently selected line 1. What would you do? Stand alone as a minority of one, or go along with the majority?

A surprising number of Asch's subjects went along with the majority's choice of an incorrect answer. The other participants in the studies were of course confederates of the experimenter. Asch's experiment included twelve such "critical" trials, in which the majority agreed on an obviously wrong answer, interspersed among many other trials in which other participants chose the correct line. Of a total of fifty subjects, about a third gave conforming responses to the critical trials; two-thirds gave independent responses. Roughly 70 percent of the subjects conformed at least once. Twenty-five percent always answered independently, and 5 percent always conformed. Though independent responses prevailed, the amount of conformity was significant, considering how easy the task was. A comparison group that gave its answers privately, in writing, made very few errors.

Types of Conformity

The conformity of the subjects in Asch's experiment can be described as an outward yielding to a group consensus; inwardly, subjects retained their own opinions (Kelman, 1958, 1961). The major motivation for this type of conformity is a fear of negative

(A)

(B)

(C)

(D)

The pressure to conform affects all ages and social groups. Notice the similar styles of clothing worn by gang members (A), sorority girls (B), middle school students (C), and engineers (D).

consequences—in this case, an appearance of foolishness for deviating from the majority view. Comments made by Asch's subjects in postexperiment interviews show that many realized their answers had been wrong but did not want to appear to be "misfits" or to stick out from the crowd. One subject noted, "If I'd been first I probably would have responded differently" (Asch, 1956, p. 31)—his way of saying that he knew perfectly well what the correct answers were, but he was unable to contradict the group. Such findings are relevant to the My Lai incident, discussed earlier. The soldiers of Charlie Company knew that their actions violated guidelines they had learned during their training, but that knowledge did not prevent them from killing the villagers. Even when conformity will produce extremely negative consequences, then, the tendency to conform is strong.

As might be expected, those who provide answers that they "know" are incorrect often experience cognitive dissonance, because they are behaving in a way that is inconsistent with their attitudes and beliefs. Some (like those in Asch's experiment quoted above) try to reduce the dissonance by emphasizing the external pressures. Others change their attitudes or reconstruct the facts in such a way that they do not appear to have conformed mindlessly (Buehler & Griffin, 1994; Griffin & Buehler, 1994). Later, when they are asked about their old attitudes, they tend to reconstruct them differently, so as to deemphasize their conformity.

In addition to an outward yielding to avoid negative consequences, conformity can involve **identification**—the tendency to go along with others because we admire and wish to be like them (Kelman, 1958, 1961). A young German soldier who treated Jewish prisoners cruelly because he wanted to emulate older officers would have been conforming through identification. Conformity can also involve **internalization,** or the acceptance of others' views and actions as ap-

just 5 percent (Asch, 1956). Another factor that influences conformity is previous exposure to dissenters. In one experiment, subjects observed the behavior of a lone dissenter in a study of color discrimination. In a subsequent experiment, the same subjects exhibited independence in deviating from a unanimously incorrect choice 76 percent of the time. In contrast, subjects who had not witnessed the dissenter's behavior conformed 70 percent of the time (Nemeth & Chiles, 1988).

Anonymity also appears to reduce conformity. When people are allowed to sit in private compartments and indicate their answers by pressing a button, they conform much less frequently (Deutsch & Gerard, 1955). Personal traits, too, influence the tendency to conform. Those who are high in self-doubt conform significantly more often than those who are self-confident (Campbell, Tesser, & Fairey, 1986). A lower status than other group members, generally low self-esteem, and the knowledge that one will have to interact with other members of a group in the future can all predispose a person to conform (Aronson & Osherow, 1980; Dittes & Kelley, 1956; Raven & French, 1958).

Dissent and Its Consequences

What are the consequences of not going along with the group? In Hitler's Germany, those who opposed, resisted, or interfered with Hitler's policy of persecuting the Jews could lose their lives. But Asch's nonconforming subjects did not live in Nazi Germany. Were they really made to feel so psychologically uncomfortable?

Research shows that the negative outcomes of nonconformity are often greater than people think. The nonconformist is usually ostracized, in both subtle and not-so-subtle ways. When conventionally and unconventionally dressed college students asked shoppers in a supermarket to change a dime for two nickels, the unconventional-looking students were much more likely to be refused (Raymond & Unger, 1972). The desire to stay in the good graces of fans may even explain the behavior of referees during professional basketball games. In one recent basketball season, referees for the Los Angeles Lakers called fewer fouls on star players when the team was playing at home (2.4 fouls per game) than when they were away (3.1 fouls per game). Other players were called for the same number of fouls at home and away (Lehman & Reifman, 1987).

Even NBA referees are subject to social pressure. In a recent season, referees at Los Angeles Lakers games called fewer fouls on the team at home than away.

propriate and right. A young soldier who not only mimics his superiors' actions but actually believes their cruelty is justified would be conforming because of internalized prejudices. Identifying the source of conformity can help to predict how enduring the behavior will be. For instance, the person who is merely complying to avoid negative consequences will probably stop if the threat of negative consequences is lifted. In contrast, the person who is conforming because of internalized values is much more likely to continue conforming, even when there is no external pressure to do so.

Factors That Influence Conformity

Several factors have been found to influence how much a subject will conform during an experiment. One is the extent of agreement among participants in the experiment. Asch found that when just one confederate out of six gave the correct answer, the subjects' conforming responses dropped dramatically, to

(A)

(B)

While obedience is sometimes essential, in some situations it can be a terribly destructive behavior. In April 1993, the charismatic cult leader David Koresh (A) ordered members of the Branch Davidian religious compound in Waco, Texas, to set the compound afire. Nearly a hundred people perished in the blaze (B).

Despite the negative consequences, some people with a strong need for self-expression will take the opportunity to dissent in social situations. Such expressions of individuality are most likely to occur when they involve a new solution to a problem, rather than simple disagreement with the majority's findings (Santee & Maslach, 1982). In that case, dissent can take some creative forms. In one study of conformity, those who were found to be "creative dissenters" showed certain common characteristics: high self-esteem, low anxiety in social situations, and a willingness to stand out in a crowd (Maslach, Stapp, & Santee, 1985). On average, men were more likely than women to dissent, perhaps because they equated competence with "standing out." Women, on the other hand, tended to associate competence with cooperation and agreement. For them, a con-

forming response may have been a more positive way of expressing themselves than dissent (Santee & Jackson, 1982).

Although the consequences of conformity can be brutal, as My Lai and Nazi Germany showed, conformity also has a positive side (Zimbardo & Leippe, 1991). Recently, more and more Eastern Europeans took to the streets to protest repressive Communist regimes; the social pressure to join in won over many fence straddlers. Finally a "critical mass" was reached, and protesters were able to topple the hated rulers. Conformity, then, can encourage people to perform socially responsible acts as well as to fulfill the need to be liked and accepted. As one social psychologist has noted, "The person who refused to accept anyone's word of advice on any topic whatsoever would probably make just as big a botch of life . . . as the person who always conformed" (Collins, 1970, p. 21).

Obeying Orders: Doing the Unthinkable

Obedience—following the specific commands of a person in authority—differs from conformity in that it is a response to explicit instructions rather than implicit social pressure. Sometimes obedience serves a constructive purpose. Society could not function if most people disobeyed the laws requiring them to pay taxes or stop at traffic lights. But at other times, obedience can be a terribly destructive behavior. In April 1993, a group of nearly 100 members of the Branch Davidian religious cult were killed in a raging fire in a heavily armed compound located outside Waco, Texas. Following the orders of their charismatic leader David Koresh, the Branch Davidians apparently set the fire themselves and prevented others from fleeing the burning building.

What causes such blind obedience? This question was the focus of experiments performed by social psychologist Stanley Milgram (1963, 1965). Milgram's research has shown that many "average" people—people who think they could never participate in brutality—will inflict severe pain on fellow human beings if an authority figure tells them to do so.

The Milgram Studies

Milgram's subjects were men of different ages and occupations who had answered a request for volunteers for a study on learning at Yale University (Milgram, 1963). On arriving at the laboratory, each man was introduced to his supposed cosubject, a mild-mannered, likable man of about fifty who was actually a confederate in the experiment. The two were asked to draw lots to determine who would be the "teacher" and who would be the "learner." Actually, the drawing was rigged so that the real subject would always become the teacher.

The experimenter, a stern man in a gray laboratory coat, then explained the purpose and procedure of the study. The experiment, he said, was designed to investigate the effects of punishment on learning. The teacher was to read a list of word pairs to the learner, who was supposed to memorize them. Then the teacher was to test the learner. Since the teacher and the learner would occupy separate rooms, the learner was to indicate his responses by pressing a button on a panel before him. Doing so would activate a corresponding light on the teacher's control panel.

Every time the learner made a mistake, the teacher was to punish him by administering an electric shock from an authentic-looking shock generator. The generator carried thirty clearly marked switches ranging from 15 to 450 volts. Labels under the switches indicated the intensity of the shock, beginning with slight shock and progressing through moderate, strong, very strong, intense, extremely intense, and severe (also marked "Danger"), ending with a label ominously marked "XXX." With each additional mistake the learner made, the teacher was to increase the voltage by one level, or 15 volts.

Everyone then proceeded to the room where the learner would sit. The teacher watched as the learner was strapped into a chair and an electrode (presumably connected to the shock generator) attached to his wrist. The teacher and the experimenter then went to the generator room, where the teacher was given a "sample shock" of 45 volts from a concealed battery. The generator itself was harmless—incapable of producing anything but buzzing and clicking sounds. For the teacher, however, the sample shock "proved" the machine's authenticity.

The learning trials were now ready to begin. The experimental plan called for the learner to make many mistakes, requiring the teacher to administer increasingly severe shocks. If the teacher proceeded up to 300 volts (the highest level in the "intense" shock range), the learner would pound on the wall in protest. At 315 volts ("extremely intense" shock) the learner would pound loudly once more and then fall silent. After that, no lights would flash on the teacher's panel in answer to his questions. If the teacher asked the experimenter how to proceed,

the experimenter would instruct him to treat the lack of a response as an incorrect answer and to raise the voltage. If at any point the teacher asked to stop the procedure, the experimenter would tell him to continue using a number of standardized commands, ranging from a stern "Please go on" to an emphatic "You have no choice, you *must* go on." If the teacher refused to obey, the experiment would end.

How far do you think most subjects went in delivering what they believed to be painful and increasingly dangerous electric shocks to a defenseless victim? When Milgram posed this question to a group of psychology majors, they confidently predicted that few if any would go beyond the "very strong" shock level; that is, they would never reach the point at which the learner had to pound on the wall for release. A group of psychiatrists offered a similar opinion: only 4 percent of the subjects would continue to shock the learner when he failed to respond at 315 volts, and less than 1 percent would administer the highest possible shock. In fact, most people would agree with such predictions—which is why the true results of the experiment were truly disturbing. Out of a total of forty subjects, twenty-six, or 65 percent, obeyed the experimenter all the way to the very highest voltage level (see Figure 18-2).

These men were not sadists. In fact, most showed signs of severe emotional strain and psychological conflict during the experiment. They trembled, stuttered, groaned, perspired heavily, bit their lips, laughed nervously, and dug their fingernails into their palms. They frequently asked if they might stop. But when the experimenter told them to continue, they obeyed. As one observer who watched the proceedings through a one-way mirror related:

> I observed a mature and initially poised businessman enter the laboratory smiling and confident. Within 20 minutes he was reduced to a twitching, stuttering wreck, who was rapidly approaching a point of nervous collapse. He constantly pulled on his earlobe and twisted his hands. At one point he pushed his fist into his forehead and muttered: "Oh God, let's stop it." And yet he continued to respond to every word of the experimenter and obeyed to the end.

(Quoted in Milgram, 1963, p. 377)

Furthermore, Milgram's sample was not at all unrepresentative. His advertisement did not by chance attract an unusual number of men who were incapable of defying authority. Milgram's results have been replicated many times in about half a dozen

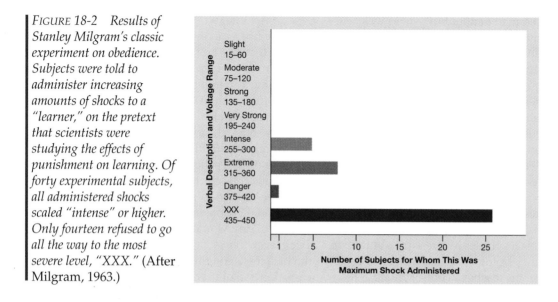

FIGURE 18-2   Results of Stanley Milgram's classic experiment on obedience. Subjects were told to administer increasing amounts of shocks to a "learner," on the pretext that scientists were studying the effects of punishment on learning. Of forty experimental subjects, all administered shocks scaled "intense" or higher. Only fourteen refused to go all the way to the most severe level, "XXX." (After Milgram, 1963.)

different countries, using women as well as men as subjects. Very reliably, roughly two-thirds of all subjects obey the experimenter to the end (Manell, 1971; Milgram, 1974).

To find out what factors might lessen such an extraordinary degree of obedience, Milgram (1965, 1974) designed a series of follow-up experiments. He discovered that as auditory, visual, and physical contact with the victim increased, the maximum shock subjects would deliver decreased (see Figure 18-3). Obedience also dropped sharply when the experimenter left the room and gave his orders by telephone. Only 22 percent of subjects obeyed to the end when the experimenter was not present. Disobeying an authority was also easier when others modeled defiance. After subjects observed two coteachers refusing to proceed, only 10 percent obeyed to the end. Apparently, when the illusion of unanimity is broken, most people stop cooperating in an activity that is clearly wrong. This finding stresses the importance of speaking out against an observed injustice. Not only may protests help the victim in such cases, but they may prompt others to resist as well (Hollander, 1975).

The Ethics of the Milgram Studies

Milgram's experiment provoked an explosive controversy over the ethics of his procedures. Critics charged that without forewarning and prior permission, Milgram had knowingly exposed subjects to enormous stress and may have caused them long-term psychological harm (Baumrind, 1964). Indeed, subjects who followed the experimenter's com-

mands to the very end learned a disturbing fact about themselves: they were willing to obey an authority figure, even if that meant performing a callous and inhumane act. Might not some subjects have found this revelation difficult to live with? At the very least, might not it have injured their self-concepts? According to Bem's self-perception theory, discussed in Chapter 17, people who observe themselves acting cruelly in the absence of sufficient external pressure may conclude that they are less sensitive than they had assumed. And might not participation in Milgram's experiments have reduced subjects' trust in legitimate authority?

Milgram flatly denied that his procedures had caused any lasting harm (Milgram, 1964, 1968, 1974). He pointed out that all his sessions had ended with a thorough debriefing in which the experimenter explained that no shocks had been given and reassured subjects that their behavior had been normal. As a result, Milgram argued, no subject left the laboratory in a state of anxiety. Moreover, follow-up questionnaires indicated that most of the subjects (84 percent) were glad to have participated in Milgram's research, because they had learned something important about human behavior. And as for damaging the subjects' trust in legitimate authority, Milgram argued that skepticism toward authorities who require us to act cruelly is valuable.

The Meaning of the Milgram Studies

Like Asch's study, Milgram's experiments yielded important information about human behavior. The

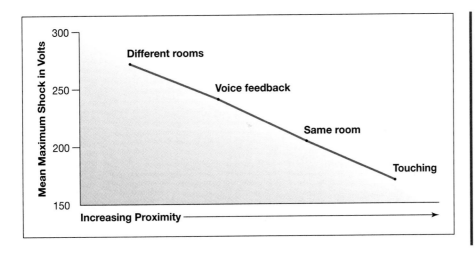

FIGURE 18-3   *Results of Milgram's experiments on obedience as a function of proximity. This graph of the results of some of Milgram's studies of obedience shows that the closer the subject was to the victim, the less shock he was willing to administer, despite the experimenter's demands that he continue. That is, as proximity increased, compliance decreased.* (After Milgram, 1974.)

human moral sense appears to be vulnerable to external pressure, in that the influence of others can override strongly held convictions. The cruelty exhibited by the subjects in Milgram's experiment resulted from greater social pressure than was exerted on subjects in Asch's studies of conformity. Milgram's subjects did not set out to be cruel, but they did respond to the power of the experimenter's commands, which were apparently more influential than the victims' pleas for release. In other words, obedience took precedence over the desire to avoid doing harm.

A more recent experiment shows that obedience is still a relevant social phenomenon. Two Dutch psychologists devised an experiment that called for subjects to disrupt an employment test being administered to a job applicant, ultimately causing the applicant to fail the test (Meeus & Raaijmakers, 1986, 1987). The subjects were told that the experiment was a test of the effects of stress on the job applicants, but in fact the experimenters were interested in how far the subjects would go in following orders. The subjects were asked to send the applicant fifteen derogatory computerized messages in an attempt to make the applicant progressively more tense and irritable. Despite finding the task very disagreeable, 90 percent of the subjects complied, justifying their actions by transferring their responsibility to the experimenters. The lessons of Milgram's studies and subsequent experiments on obedience like this one should teach us to be wary of authority figures (including political leaders) and alert us to the potential for destructiveness that lies within. As Milgram warned in explaining the fundamental lesson of his study, "Ordinary people, simply doing their jobs, and without any particular hostility on their part, can become agents in a terrible destructive process" (Milgram, 1974, p. 6).

Creating Compliance: Common Techniques

Have you ever said "yes" to a sales pitch when you did not really want the product? Have you agreed to join a committee and then a moment later regretted your response? If so, you have experienced **compliance**—the act of assent to an explicit request from someone who does not hold authority over you. Why do people comply, even against their own better judgment? Psychologists have found that the answer lies largely in the way they are approached: certain techniques can sway even those who "know better." Social psychologists have studied these techniques by observing those who make their living by getting others to comply with their requests including fund-raisers, car salespersons, and con artists of various kinds. One psychologist even took an automobile sales training course to get a firsthand look at the techniques (Cialdini, 1988).

One such compliance technique relies on the **foot-in-the-door phenomenon.** It involves first making a very small request that almost anyone would be sure to comply with (the foot in the door, so to speak), then making a much bigger request. Salespeople have found that people who go along with the first request tend to comply with the second one, too. In one study of this technique, a researcher telephoned housewives, ostensibly as part of a consumer survey (Freedman & Fraser, 1966). The women who agreed to talk with the researcher were asked eight simple

Some salespeople use the low-ball phenomenon. When a customer is ready to sign a sales contract, the salesperson eliminates the price advantage, claiming that the manager has disallowed the deal because the price was so low, the dealer would lose money.

questions about the soaps they used. Three days later, the researcher called the same women and asked if a team of half a dozen men could come to their homes to count and classify all their household products. The same intrusive request was also made of another group of women who had not complied with first survey. Researchers found that the women who had first agreed to the small request were two times more likely than the other women to agree to the second request. Other researchers have conducted studies that confirm these findings, even among young children (Dillard, Hunter, & Burgoon, 1984; Eisenberger, Cotterell, & Marvel, 1987; see Dillard, 1991, for a review).

What explains this tendency? Perhaps once people have agreed to one request, their attitudes toward agreement change, and they come to perceive themselves as people who cooperate with others or who are committed to what they have begun (Dejong & Musilli, 1982; Freedman & Fraser, 1966). Advertisers seek to induce such attitudes in consumers through the offers they send potential customers. By making a small request, such as asking a potential buyer to scratch a card or to place a token on an order blank, they hope ultimately to commit the consumer to purchasing the product.

Robert Cialdini and his colleagues (1975) tried reversing the foot-in-the-door phenomenon by first asking for a big favor and then following with a more realistic request. In one study, for instance, some subjects were asked to escort disadvantaged

children on a two-hour trip to the zoo. Only 32 percent agreed. Other subjects were first asked to make a two-year commitment to counsel delinquent youth. All refused, but when they were later asked if they could escort children on a two-hour trip to the zoo, nearly 56 percent agreed. This approach has been called the **door-in-the-face technique,** because the person who is asked to do the favor seems at first to be slamming the door in the requester's face. The technique apparently works because most people feel obligated to make mutual concessions. If the requester accepts the first rejection without argument, the person then feels obligated to agree to the second request.

A third compliance technique is based on the **low-ball phenomenon,** which is reportedly used by new-car salespeople. The salesperson first talks a customer into buying a car at a very good price. When the customer is ready to sign the sales contract, the salesperson eliminates the price advantage, typically saying that "the boss" has disallowed the deal because "we'd be losing money." Those who work in the automobile sales business claim that more customers will buy the car under these circumstances, even though the price has risen, than if the actual price is divulged at the beginning.

Cialdini and his colleagues (1978) demonstrated the low-ball phenomenon in a series of experiments. In one study, college students were invited to participate in an experiment on thought processes. Of those who were first told that the experiment was to be held at an inconveniently early hour (7 a.m.), only 24 percent agreed to participate and later showed up for the appointment. But more than twice that number (53 percent) showed up after agreeing to participate first and then being told the time of the appointment. Apparently, once people have made a commitment, many feel compelled to go through with it even when key conditions change.

In the **that's-not-all technique,** a person is first offered a product or service at a certain price. Before being given a chance to reply, the seller then demands "How much would you pay? Don't answer yet! There is even more!" and either lowers the price or adds additional merchandise. Though the seller had planned to make the apparent concession all along, the buyer is not supposed to know that. The idea behind this technique is that one concession deserves another—and who can resist a bargain? In a study of the technique, Jerry Burger (1986) set up a booth at a fair at which he sold cupcakes. The first customers were told that the cupcakes cost 75 cents; later customers were given a price of $1, but before they could reply, Burger "reduced" the price to 75 cents. Sales increased dramatically as a result of the technique.

The techniques of creating compliance are not always as harmless as these examples suggest. The same technique of escalating commitment was used to devastating effect in Milgram's experiments on obedience. Not many subjects would have administered the most severe shock on the first learning trial, but by starting with mild shocks and gradually strengthening the subjects' commitment, the experimenter brought about complete obedience in many. Torturers have been trained using the same step-by-step approach (Haritos-Fatouros, 1988).

The Social Significance of Groups

What constitutes a group? Do passengers on a bus make a group? How about two people who regularly play tennis together? In social psychological terms, the first example would not qualify as a group, but the second would. To be a **group,** a collection of two or more people must meet three criteria (McGrath, 1984; Shaw, 1976). First, they must interact regularly in fairly structured and predictable ways. Second, they must share one or more specific goals aimed at satisfying certain mutual needs. And finally, they must identify themselves as part of a whole, sharing to some extent a common fate.

Groups can influence human behavior in countless ways; in this chapter we will focus on just a few. First, we will look at how the roles people play in groups can cause them to think and act in ways they might never imagine themselves capable of. Second, we will examine how merely being in a group or in the presence of a group can affect the quality of people's performance and decision making. Finally, we will take a look at the conditions that permit minorities within a group to exercise a powerful influence over the majority.

The Effect of Roles on Thought and Behavior

Psychologists have noticed that people often seem to "fit" the roles they play. The clergyman, for instance, is often paternal; the drill sergeant, demanding; the bureaucrat, inflexible; the college professor, intellectual. But though people may seem to fall into roles that suit their inner nature, that is not always the case; often the role shapes the person. No better illustration of this fact exists than a study conducted by psychologist Philip Zimbardo and his colleagues (Zimbardo et al., 1972, 1973).

Zimbardo set out to examine how the roles of prison inmate and guard affect how the people who play those roles behave. As was described in Chapter 17, he set up a "mock" prison in the basement of a building at Stanford University. More than seventy-five young men, mostly college students on summer vacation, volunteered to participate in the paid two-week simulation of prison life. Of those, Zimbardo selected twenty-one for their emotional stability and maturity. He randomly assigned ten to the role of prisoner and eleven to the role of guard, giving the guards no other instructions than to maintain "law and order."

To make the simulation as authentic as possible, prisoners were "arrested" at their homes and "booked" at the Palo Alto police station. They were then taken to the so-called Stanford County Prison, where they were issued uniforms and ushered into sparsely furnished cells. The first day passed without incident, but on the second day the prisoners staged a revolt. The episode marked a critical turning point in the participants' behavior. After quelling the rebellion by threatening the prisoners with billy clubs and spraying them with fire extinguishers, the guards began to exercise their power harshly and arbitrarily. They created petty rules and demanded that the prisoners follow them to the letter. They ordered the inmates to perform meaningless, exhausting, degrading chores, and repeatedly ridiculed and demeaned them. The prisoners' reactions were equally disturbing. Five developed such severe symptoms of anxiety that they had to be released from the study. The other five were reduced to the status of servile robots. After just six days, Zimbardo was forced to abandon the research; the mock prison had become too real.

How can such alarming behavior be explained? Because the participants had been screened for emotional stability, Zimbardo could be reasonably sure they had not been psychologically disturbed when the study began. And each person had been randomly assigned to his role, so at the start there had been no consistent personality differences between the two groups. Zimbardo concluded that the outcome must have been caused by the power of the prison roles. The demands of being an inmate or a guard had become so dominant that the subjects' personalities had changed temporarily. As one ex-prisoner told an interviewer: "I began to feel that I was losing my identity. The person I call [subject's real name] . . . was distant from me, was remote, until finally I wasn't that. I was 416—I was really my number." If a normal, well-adjusted young man can be thus transformed by the part he is playing in a psychological study, then real-life roles are likely to exert an enormous influence on us.

Zimbardo admits that his study created an ethical dilemma similar to the one raised by Milgram's research on obedience. In an effort to avoid any long-term harm to his subjects, Zimbardo "debriefed" them extensively at the end of the project, encouraging them to vent their feelings. Subsequent questionnaires, interviews, and group reunions suggest that the subjects did recover reasonably well from the experience. Zimbardo argues that although the emotional price paid for his research was indeed high, the information he gained was very valuable (Zimbardo et al., 1972). Certainly it provided dramatic evidence that a prison environment can be socially destructive, regardless of the prior personalities of the inmates. Zimbardo has made a great effort to communicate his findings to a wide audience, including prison administrators and inmates, legislators and other government officials, and the general public. In this way he hopes to make the experiment socially worthwhile (Zimbardo, 1975).

Group Effects on Problem Solving and Performance

Clearly, roles shape our actions. What effect, if any, do groups have on our performance and problem-solving abilities? Does working in a group or in the presence of others help us to produce a better product, or do people usually do their best when working alone?

Social Facilitation

One of the earliest experiments in social psychology showed that people perform simple motor tasks more quickly when they compete with one another than when they race the clock (Triplett, 1898). Several decades later, psychologist Floyd Allport arrived at a similar finding concerning simple cognitive tasks. When solving multiplication problems or generating word associations, people performed better in the presence of four or five others, even though each worked independently (Allport, 1920, 1924). Allport called the tendency for people's performance to improve in the presence of others **social facilitation.** Even lower animals show this effect at times. For instance, in one experiment, ants worked harder at digging tunnels (they moved more dirt) when working in groups of two or three than when working alone (Chen, 1937).

But the findings on social facilitation have not been consistent. People who are trying to learn complex mazes usually do better when they are alone. And in experiments with birds, performance on certain tasks seemed to be inhibited by the presence of other birds. How can these contradictory findings be reconciled?

Psychologist Robert Zajonc (1965, 1966) proposed that many of the contradictions could be eliminated by assuming that the presence of others increases a person's motivation or drive. Studies had already demonstrated that when drive increases, subjects fall back on their most well-learned, "automatic" responses—their so-called dominant responses. To this Zajonc added the observation that dominant responses sometimes facilitate, but at other times hinder, the performance of a task. Specifically, when a person is confronted with very familiar tasks (such as simple arithmetic) to which the solutions are well known, an increase in drive should improve the subject's performance, because the correct responses are dominant responses. In contrast, when people are faced with difficult tasks that they have not yet mastered (such as solving a complex maze), an increase in drive should hinder performance, because dominant responses are usually inappropriate in such situations. Subsequent research has tended to support Zajonc's model of social facilitation (Guerin, 1986; Schmitt et al., 1986).

Social facilitation is also mediated by the perceived importance of the observer. For example, Seta (1982) found that performance is best when the observer is considered to be slightly superior to the person performing the activity. But if the actor is unconcerned about the observer's appraisal, the observer's presence diminishes the actor's performance, apparently because the observer's presence is distracting (Baron, 1986; Sanders, Baron, & Moore, 1978; Seta & Seta, 1992). Performance may actually be enhanced by the *attention* rather than the mere presence of others. For example, Worringham and Messick (1983) found that runners sped up if a woman in the stands faced the running track, but not if she faced away from the track.

What are the practical implications of the effects of social facilitation? People who are very familiar with and skillful at the tasks they are performing—professional athletes, musicians, or actors, for example—are likely to do better in front of an audience than when they are alone. Beginning pianists and actors, however, are likely to become rattled by the presence of others. They may revert to older, more familiar—but also less skillful—patterns, and so perform more poorly than they would have alone. In one study that supported this prediction, four confederates closely observed various college students as they played pool. The results bore out Zajonc's theory. When good players were shooting before an audience of four, their accuracy increased from 71 to 80 percent; when poor players were watched, their accuracy fell from 36 to 25 percent (Michaels et al., 1982).

Psychologists are still trying to determine just why the presence of others causes an increase in drive. One theory is that we simply become more alert and aroused when other people are present, especially if they are strangers (Guerin, 1986). Another possibility is that the presence of others arouses apprehension about being evaluated, which heightens drive. Recall that male runners increased their speed only when a female observer was facing them (Worringham & Messick, 1983). The self-consciousness associated with being evaluated may interfere with

behaviors that are best performed without thinking, however, such as throwing free throws in a basketball game (Mullen & Baumeister, 1987). Finally, drive may increase out of a desire to overcome the distractions that others create (Baron, 1986). On easy tasks, we may compensate for those distractions by trying harder, possibly improving our performance. But on difficult tasks, distractions may make the work even harder to perform. Which explanation is most plausible? That depends on the situation; in some situations all three may have some validity.

Social Loafing

Would you perform better as part of a group than as an individual? After all, you would have the benefit of a team effort and the comfort of not being scrutinized individually. But in fact, these factors often have the opposite effect: most people tend to slack off when they are part of a group, a behavior that is known as **social loafing.** Thinking back on group projects you have participated in, no doubt you will recall some team members who contributed very little, or less than they were capable of (you might even point to yourself). In many ways, social loafing is the mirror image of social facilitation. Social facilitation improves performance because it spotlights individual effort; in social loafing, performance deteriorates because it is not measured individually.

Social loafing was discovered in experiments conducted in the 1880s by a French agricultural engineer, Max Ringelmann. He found that on simple tasks that call for collective effort, such as pulling a rope or pushing a cart, individual output declined (as measured against a solitary effort) (Ringelmann, 1913). Nearly 100 years later, Bibb Latané and his colleagues, who coined the term *social loafing*, obtained similar results (Latané, Williams, & Harkins, 1979). They blindfolded college students and equipped them with earphones that gave off a staticlike noise. Then they asked the students to yell as loudly as they could. Some students were asked to do so alone, while others were part of a group or thought they were in a group (but were in fact alone). The subjects who were actually alone yelled louder than those in the other two groups.

More than four dozen studies that have replicated these results show that loafing increases as the size of the group increases (Jackson & Williams, 1988). The apprehension over being evaluated that increases drive in individual efforts does not seem to

Most people tend to slack off when they are part of a group, a phenomenon known as social loafing. Would the members of this crew team work harder if they were alone?

have the same effect in group efforts. Instead, when individuals can get lost in the crowd, they do not feel accountable for their contributions, and so lose their concern about being evaluated. One way to control social loafing, then, might be to make people more aware of their own performance, perhaps by setting some standard or norm or by comparing them with others in the group (Harkins & Szymanski, 1987, 1988, 1989). Another way might be to have someone evaluate individual efforts, much as a coach does in going over the videotape of a game. Other conditions that can minimize social loafing include being engaged in a challenging or involving task (Brickner et al., 1986), believing that one's teammates are working hard as well (Zaccaro, 1984), feeling committed to the group, and being rewarded for the group's success (Hackman, 1986). A recent meta-analysis by Karau and Williams (1993) confirmed many of these findings: they reported that in a number of studies, subjects loafed less if they believed a task was challenging, appealing, or involving.

Group Decision Making

Pressure to conform is especially powerful in small, close-knit groups (Blake & Mouton, 1979). When a small, cohesive group becomes so concerned with maintaining unanimity that its members can no longer appraise alternatives realistically, it has fallen victim to a phenomenon that social psychologist Irving Janis (1982, 1985) calls **groupthink.** A classic case

of groupthink occurred during John F. Kennedy's presidency, preceding what has come to be known as the Bay of Pigs fiasco. In the early part of 1961, Kennedy and his inner circle of foreign policy advisers decided unanimously to mount an invasion of Cuba using Cuban exiles trained by the Central Intelligence Agency. Foreseeing an easy victory, the group underestimated the size, strength, and loyalty of Cuban troops, and overestimated the morale of the invaders. Within three days of their landing at the Bay of Pigs, 1,200 of the exiles had been captured and some 200 killed. "How," Kennedy asked after the fiasco was over, "could we have been so stupid?"

Another disastrous case of groupthink was the decision-making process that sent the space shuttle *Challenger* on its fatal journey in January 1986 (Magnuson, 1986). Engineers at the companies that had manufactured the rocket boosters and the orbiter had warned company managers and NASA officials of the danger of launching in below-freezing temperatures. But NASA officials pressed the managers to authorize the much-delayed launch. Overruling the engineers, the managers agreed to go ahead. In fact, the NASA executive who made the final decision to launch was never told of the engineers' objections. A more detailed investigation of the *Challenger* disaster (Moorhead, Ference, & Neck, 1991) has since confirmed the role of groupthink.

Janis maintains that in both situations, poor decision making arose from some powerful conditions within the groups. First, both groups were highly cohesive. In such groups, Janis argues, members often feel a strong compulsion to avoid disrupting the group's unity and the positive feelings it creates. As a result, they tend to convince themselves that anyone who remains silent during policy talks must be in complete accord with the rest of the group—an assumption that Janis calls the *illusion of unanimity.* That, of course, may not be the case, but once the illusion of unanimity has been established, it tends to stifle divergent thinking.

Strong cohesiveness can impair group decisions in another way. The close camaraderie that often arises within such groups can create feelings of euphoria and an *illusion of invulnerability.* That is, close-knit groups sometimes come to believe that they will always be successful, no matter what the odds. As one member of Kennedy's inner circle recalled: "It seemed that, with John Kennedy leading us and with all the talent he had assembled, nothing could stop us" (quoted in Janis, 1982, p. 35).

These negative tendencies do not occur in *all* close-knit groups, however. Only those that meet other conditions are likely to fall prey to groupthink. According to Janis, a highly cohesive group that is insulated from other decision-making bodies, lacks established procedures for searching out and appraising various options, and is headed by a strong-minded and respected leader is most susceptible to groupthink. Stress generated by the difficulty of a decision or by time pressure (Callaway, Marriott, & Esser, 1985), as in the case of the *Challenger* launch, may also contribute to groupthink. At least one researcher, however, finds structural conditions (the nature of the group) to be far more predictive of groupthink than situational conditions, such as time pressure (McCauley, 1989).

How can close-knit groups avoid succumbing to groupthink? Janis has offered several suggestions (Janis, 1982; Janis & Mann, 1977). His prescriptions go beyond just avoiding conditions that are conducive to groupthink and actually establish the norm for a no-holds-barred critical debate (McCauley, 1989). First, the group leader should acquaint the group with the consequences of groupthink and encourage members to express any doubts without fear of disapproval. In discussions, the leader should be careful to maintain an impartial stance while others air their views. Members should be encouraged to consider all the alternatives and evaluate them critically. Dividing members into sub-

When a small, cohesive group becomes overly concerned with maintaining unanimity, groupthink can result. The decision to go ahead with the final launch of the Challenger *was a disastrous case of groupthink.*

groups, each of which is to consider the issues independently, can increase the range of options generated by the group as a whole. In addition, at every meeting, at least one member should adopt the role of "devil's advocate," challenging the majority's preferences. Outside experts with differing views should be invited to address the group, and members should be encouraged to discuss their deliberations with colleagues whose opinions they value.

Finally, listing all the advantages and disadvantages of each alternative can provide a helpful perspective (Janis, 1972). In a study in which subjects were asked to list the reasons why they might be wrong in their decisions and were then given a chance to make corrections, the effect of overconfidence decreased significantly (Koriat, Lichtenstein, & Fischoff, 1980). An application of this finding might be to hold a "second chance" meeting once a decision has been reached, that so any lingering doubts can be aired. In a similar tactic, called *anticipated regret* (Janis & Mann, 1977), group members are asked to imagine how their decision might be viewed in the future: will they be likely to regret it?

Minority Influence on Groups

Group influence does not always flow from the group to the individual. At many crucial points in history, one person or a minority of people have influenced the larger group. Think of what Galileo or Martin Luther or Martin Luther King, Jr., accomplished, despite belonging to a distinct minority. Ralph Waldo Emerson attributed great power to minorities: "If the single man plant himself indomitably on his instincts, and there abide, the huge world will come round to him."

The secret of minority influence is expressed in Emerson's sentiment. To prevail, *the minority view must be indomitable and abiding.* In one study a minority of subjects who consistently identified blue slides as green sometimes won over members of the majority. But if the minority wavered, occasionally calling a third of the blue slides blue, virtually no member of the majority agreed with their wrong judgments (Moscovici, 1985; Moscovici, Lage, & Naffrechoux, 1969). A minority that is highly visible and can create conflict in the group also tends to be influential, because those qualities focus attention on the minority's position (Moscovici & Mugny, 1983). Once the members of a majority begin to consider other positions, the norm of conformity has been broken, and convincing people to change their views is easier.

Majorities and minorities influence people in different ways (Moscovici & Personnaz, 1980). People tend to simply conform to a majority view out of intimidation or fear of rejection, but a minority view piques their interest. Because they are not so concerned about rejection in considering a minority view, they can think more deeply about the issue. Their reconsideration can produce real attitude change on their part, rather than just outward compliance. Finally, minority views seem to influence decision making by encouraging divergent thinking (Baker & Petty, 1994; Legrenzi et al., 1991).

Charlan Nemeth (1979, 1992) holds that the differences between majority and minority influence extend to the way groups process information. The intimidating majority view produces superficial processing, in which group members focus on the majority position without considering other aspects of the issue. Minorities, on the other hand, stimulate the kind of deep thinking that results in creative and novel solutions. Studies of group problem solving show that while majorities elicit greater compliance, minorities do induce people to devise original and accurate solutions to problems (Nemeth & Kwan, 1986; Nemeth & Wachtler, 1983). A study on jury deliberation also showed that minorities stimulate decisions of high quality (Cowan et al., 1984). Nemeth's intriguing ideas are the subject of increasing attention by researchers (Chaiken & Stangor, 1987).

Though the force of a minority's conviction can have a stunning impact on a group—whether it is a jury or an entire society—there is often a price to be paid for such courage. When Nemeth (1979) planted a minority of two on a simulated jury, they were invariably disliked, though they often got the majority to rethink their positions. Other experiments have shown that going against the majority can be a painful experience (Levine, 1989).

Aggression

Each year millions of Americans become the victims of violent crime—murder, rape, robbery, and aggravated assault (Langan & Innes, 1985). The greatest number of these crimes occurred in families, through child abuse or neglect, spousal abuse, and other forms of domestic violence (Straus, Gelles, & Steinmetz, 1980; Widom, 1989). Such crimes are easily identified as acts of aggression, but what about a person with AIDS or HIV who deliberately does not practice safe sex? And would incessantly nagging and criticizing a spouse or child be counted as an act of aggression? What about throwing a tennis racket? Giving a boxing opponent a black eye? Committing suicide? Though all involve some sort of emotional, often violent outburst, the last three would not fit the definition of **aggression:** behavior that is directed toward intentionally injuring another person who does not wish to be hurt (Baron, 1977; Baron & Richardson, 1992; Krebs & Miller, 1985). Keep in mind that the injury can be psychological as well as physical.

Not all acts of aggression are contemptible. Sometimes we must be aggressive in standing up for what we think is right or in protecting ourselves or others. In wartime, aggression is rewarded with medals of honor. But the kind of aggression we are concerned with here is hostile behavior that is excessive and unprovoked. What factors make people overly aggressive?

Almost always, aggression is the product of both *dispositional* (personality) and *situational* (environmental) factors. In the sections that follow, we will see that biological dispositions, social learning, and emotional states—especially frustration—all help to account for the disturbingly high level of aggression in our society today.

Biological Influences on Aggression

Freud (1930–1963) believed that aggression was part of human nature—"an innate, independent, instinctual disposition" (p. 102). Aggressive energy, he argued, builds up within people, demanding some form of release, called **catharsis.** The release of aggressive energy can be direct, as when we shout in anger or hit someone. But it can also be vicarious, as when we cheer the contestants in a boxing match. In either case, Freud believed, such cathartic behaviors temporarily reduce the aggressive drive.

Building on Freud's theory that aggression is innate, researchers in the field of **sociobiology** have examined the biological factors that underlie social behavior in all animal species, including human beings (Wilson, 1975, 1978). Sociobiologists believe that some human behavioral inclinations—such as the tendency to respond aggressively when we are threatened—may be a direct outgrowth of the way the human brain and nervous system are structured. As such, those inclinations are part of our genetic inheritance, retained through natural selection because they helped our ancestors to survive.

Nobel-prize-winning ethologist Konrad Lorenz has described this evolutionary process in some detail. Lorenz argues that all animals have a "fighting instinct" that is directed toward members of their own species (Lorenz, 1974). This instinct, he maintains, has great survival value. For example, aggressive contests over mates ensure that the strongest males will father the most offspring, thus improving the species as a whole. But Lorenz believes that violence has become a problem for humans, because unlike many animal species, our ancestors never evolved an innate inhibition against killing members of their own species. Instead, they developed artificial means of aggression (spears, guns, bombs) faster than they could develop a natural inhibition toward aggression against their own kind. In effect, cultural invention has outpaced biological evolution. At the same time, modern civilization demands that humans suppress their aggressive urges. Lorenz believes that if expression of the fighting instinct is repeatedly prohibited in any animal, aggressive impulses build up and may eventually be discharged in particularly vicious ways. Thus he explained the periodic outbreaks of extreme violence that plague even modern civilization.

Aggression, then, appears to be a universal biological trait. If so, how can we explain the great differences among people in their display of aggressiveness? Some aspects of aggression appear to be genetically influenced. People who behave aggressively as children tend to develop into aggressive adults. The behavior is fairly consistent even if it is expressed in different ways at different ages. That is, a child who repeatedly bites other children at age five may get into repeated fistfights at age ten and use a weapon at age twenty—yet another example of Recurring Theme 1.

THEME The Best Predictor of Future Behavior Is Past Behavior

Since aggression differs *between individuals* but is consistent *within individuals*, behavioral geneticists suspected a strong genetic component to the behavior. Studies of aggressiveness in twins found correlations of about .40 for identical twins (who share the same genetic makeup) but only .04 for fraternal twins, who share about half of their genes (Rushton et al., 1986). While such evidence suggests to some social scientists that there is a major genetic component to aggression (Plomin et al., 1991; Tellegen et al., 1988; Wilson & Herrnstein, 1985), others remain unconvinced (Kamin, 1986).

Are sex differences in aggression attributable to biological effects? Common sense suggests that males are generally more aggressive than females, but appearances can be deceiving. For example, while males are more likely to display physical aggression, the two sexes differ little in the display of verbal aggression (Deluty, 1985; Eagly & Steffen, 1986). Furthermore, females are more likely than males to display indirect aggression (Bjorkqvist, Lagerspetz, & Kaukiainen, 1992; Bjorkqvist & Niemela, 1992; Bjorkqvist, Osterman, & Kaukiainen, 1992). Finally, a recent meta-analysis suggests that situational factors may be more important than was previously thought (Bettencourt & Miller, 1996). If males and females are equally provoked, females are just as likely to respond aggressively as males. Males are more likely than females to behave aggressively at least in part because they are more likely to put themselves into provocative situations.

The Influences of Social Learning on Aggression

Most social scientists agree that aggressive behavior can be *learned.* Research has shown that even in lower animals, many responses once considered purely "instinctive" are actually learned responses. For instance, young cats do not hunt rats solely through instinct; they learn the behavior by watching older cats (Kuo, 1930). In humans, of course, the influence of learning is even more extensive, which is why social learning theories of aggression have generated so much interest. These theories by no means invalidate the inborn component of aggression; they merely add to our knowledge of the way in which aggressive behavior is expressed.

According to social learning theories, people learn how to injure others through exposure to violent models and positive reinforcement for aggression (Bandura, 1977c). The power of models to elicit aggressive behavior was demonstrated in a classic experiment (Bandura, Ross, & Ross, 1961) in which nursery school students observed one of two adults: one adult ignored a 5-foot inflated "Bobo" doll while playing quietly with a Tinkertoy set; the other abused the doll. The adult's attack on the doll was unlike anything a normal preschooler would do spontaneously. He punched the doll in the face, beat it over the head with a mallet, tossed it angrily in the air, and kicked it about the room, punctuating his assaults with cries of "Sock him in the nose!" . . . "Kick him!" . . . "Pow!" Later, when the children were given access to a Bobo doll under mildly frustrating conditions, those who had been exposed to the violent model behaved much more aggressively than those who had been exposed to the subdued model. Furthermore, the children who had witnessed the violent model's behavior tended to imitate it: they punched, hammered, tossed, and yelled, right down to the final kick and last emphatic "Pow!"

Exposure to aggressive models, then, appears both to reduce inhibitions against aggression and to suggest specific aggressive acts. Indeed, Bandura has written that one way models may instigate aggression is to indicate, implicitly or explicitly, that such behavior is appropriate, desirable, or permissible (Bandura, 1977c). But the influence of a *non*aggressive model should not be underestimated. Observing such a model provides another option for action and may serve to strengthen a person's resistance to aggression. An angry person who observes someone acting calmly and reasonably is likely to cool off rather than strike out (Baron, 1983).

What factors affect the degree to which a person is likely to imitate aggression? One important influence is the presence of rewards or punishments. In a

The psychologist Albert Bandura found that children who had witnessed a model playing aggressively with an inflatable doll tended to imitate the model's behavior. They punched, hammered, and kicked the doll, and even mimicked the model's shouts of "Pow!"

follow-up study, Bandura (1965) found that children are much less likely to imitate a model who is punished for aggression. The inhibiting effect of punishment, however, is complex (see Chapter 6). Generally, several conditions must be met for the fear of punishment to work (Baron, 1983):

- Alternative ways of obtaining what the aggressive individual wants must be available.
- The punishment must be perceived as quick and certain.
- The individual must not be extremely angry and must believe that the punisher has the right to deliver punishment.

Unfortunately, as soon as the threat of punishment is removed, a person may reenact observed aggression—especially if the potential rewards for doing so are great. Research shows that most aggression is extremely rewarding. In one study nearly 80 percent of children's physical and verbal assaults produced highly positive results for the aggressor (Patterson, Littman, & Bricker, 1967). Sometimes those rewards were tangible (such as obtaining a desirable toy), at other times they were social (winning the admiration of peers), and in still other instances they were internal (boosting the child's sense of power). At times an aggressor received all three types of rewards.

One of the most controversial issues surrounding the social learning of aggression is the effect of violence seen on television, a topic that was explored in depth in Chapter 2. Eight out of ten TV programs contain violence (Gerbner et al., 1986), and children watch an average of thirty hours of television each week (Tangney & Feshbach, 1988). That constitutes a rather heavy dose of violent modeling. Defenders of television programming argue that for the most part, exposure to TV violence has a positive effect, providing viewers with catharsis—a release of pent-up hostility. But others argue that violence on TV has a far more negative influence, providing viewers with models of destructive behavior. Young children, critics charge, are especially likely to imitate the violent behavior of TV heroes, whose aggressive acts are usually rewarded. Reviewing the existing literature, Wood, Wong, and Chachere (1991) found that for both children and adolescents, exposure to televised violence enhanced aggression in interactions with strangers, classmates, and friends. Both lab and field studies showed the effect, though the effect was somewhat larger in lab studies.

Although findings regarding the impact of TV violence have not always agreed, most studies to date show that its role is a negative one. Clearly, people who witness aggressive acts on television sometimes imitate them shortly thereafter (Baron, 1977; Liebert, Neale, & Davidson, 1973; Parke et al., 1977). Some correlation studies indicate that while TV violence does not necessarily trigger direct imitation, it does raise the general level of aggressive behavior. For instance, heavily publicized prizefights tend to be followed by significantly higher levels of homicide in the general population (Phillips, 1983, 1986). What is perhaps most disturbing is that TV violence has a desensitizing effect: the more people see of it, the more they become inured to it. The result is that people become more accepting of aggressive behavior and less likely to be upset by it (Cline, Croft, & Courrier, 1973; Thomas, 1982). We will see the consequences of that desensitization later in the "In Depth" discussion of violence against women.

Frustration and Aggression

Social learning theories provide great insight into how people acquire aggressive behaviors and how their performance of those behaviors is shaped by rewards and punishments. But they do not address the relationship between a person's emotional state and the amount of aggression he or she shows. For instance, many highly aggressive acts seem to occur after intense or prolonged frustration. Is there a link between frustration and aggression?

Many years ago, psychologist John Dollard and his colleagues took the extreme position that "aggression is always a consequence of frustration" and, moreover, that "frustration always leads to some form of aggression" (Dollard et al., 1939, p. 1). **Frustration** may be defined as unanticipated interference with any goal-directed behavior. Thus, when people are thwarted in their attempt to obtain food or shelter, sex or sleep, love or recognition, they become aggressive. That is not to say that frustrated people immediately lash out at the cause of their frustration. An aggressive response, Dollard argued, can be delayed, disguised, transferred to other people and objects (displaced), or otherwise deflected from its immediate and logical goal. Nevertheless, in Dollard's view, frustration always leads to some kind of behavior that is aimed at releasing aggressive urges.

Critics were quick to question Dollard's **frustration-aggression hypothesis.** Aggression, they claimed, is only one of many possible reactions to frustration. For example, some people withdraw when their efforts are thwarted; others simply work harder to achieve their goal. Other critics have found that contrary to Dollard's theory, frustration is not the only cause of anger and aggression. In interviews about real-life experience with anger, people report becoming angry for a variety of reasons, including injury to their pride or self-esteem and violation of accepted social norms by others (Averill, 1982, 1983). Finally, some critics maintained that frustration produces aggression only when the frustrated person feels her goal has been interfered with unjustifiably or feels personally affronted (Averill, 1982; Dodge, 1986; Weiner, 1985).

In reviewing studies of frustration and aggression, Leonard Berkowitz (1989) found Dollard's core proposition valid when modified to state that aggression is generated only to the extent that frustration is perceived as unpleasant. Frustration is an aversive event; the more negative feeling it produces, the more likely it is to instigate aggression. Furthermore, Berkowitz proposed that any kind of negative feeling—sadness or depression, hostility or irritability—can produce anger and aggressive behavior (Finman & Berkowitz, 1989).

Altruism

One year after a band of teenage boys brutally beat and raped a jogger in New York's Central Park, several young men made the headlines for a very different reason: they had risked their lives to rescue five young children locked in a burning car. Though none of the youths knew the children, they responded without hesitation to their distress, despite warnings from bystanders that the car might blow up at any moment. Such heroism is an extreme form of **altruism,** or unselfish concern for others. But altruistic behavior is actually quite common. Some people make their living, in fact, by helping others. Firefighters and emergency medical workers routinely risk their lives to ensure others' safety. Other people require no reward to tutor schoolchildren, assist in hospitals, visit AIDS patients, take meals to the elderly, and donate blood. What causes them to do so?

Some psychologists think that human beings are genetically programmed to help one another, in other words, that they have altruistic instincts (Dawkins, 1975; Wilson, 1975). In twin studies, genetic correlations have been found for both altruism as well as aggressiveness (Rushton et al., 1986). However, most social scientists reject the notion that altruism is strongly influenced by heredity. Such an explanation seems to them insufficient to explain the great observed variations in altruistic behavior. Instead, they suspect that both learning and situational pressures must play a part in this behavior. Specifically, they have sought to discover what conditions might encourage or inhibit the helping response in humans.

Influences on Bystander Intervention

In the summer of 1990, a six-year-old Italian girl became a symbol of shame for her nation. Vanessa Moretti and her father were on their way to the beach when her father suffered a fatal heart attack while driving through a tunnel. Before dying, he managed to pull the car over to the side of the road. Vanessa got out of the car to seek help, but was repeatedly knocked over by gusts of wind from the speeding cars. For the next half hour, bleeding and in tears, she stumbled along more than a mile of open highway. Hundreds of cars passed by before a motorist pulled over and came to her aid. It was the start of the summer holidays in Italy, and as one newspaper noted, "along the happy road of vacation there were no scheduled stops for attending to the pain of others" (C. Haberman, *New York Times,* July 19, 1990, p. 1).

Years earlier another highly publicized case of bystander apathy became the catalyst for research into why people do or do not help others. At about 3 a.m. in a middle-class neighborhood in Queens, a borough of New York City, a young woman named Kitty Genovese was savagely attacked outside her apartment building as she arrived home from work. As the victim screamed for help, at least thirty-eight neighbors looked out their windows, but not one came to her aid. The attack continued for more than thirty minutes before Kitty Genovese died of multiple stab wounds.

The Genovese murder caused a sensation in the press. How could people be so apathetic, so indifferent to another's pain? Many saw the incident as a classic illustration of urban callousness, of city dwellers' reluctance to "get involved." Yet an investigation revealed that the witnesses to Kitty Genovese's murder had been far from indifferent. The neighbors did not close their blinds and go back to bed; they stood and watched, transfixed, "unable to act but unwilling to turn away" (Latané & Darley, 1976, pp. 309–310). What prevented these people from acting? Research on *bystander intervention* indicates that a number of powerful social forces operate in any emergency situation, and some of them strongly inhibit helping.

Factors That Inhibit Helping

John Darley and Bibb Latané, who studied bystander intervention extensively, found that the act of aiding the victim in an emergency is the result of many events and choices, all of which are less likely to occur in the presence of others (Darley & Latané, 1968). First, the bystander must notice that something is wrong: the emergency must intrude into his or her private thoughts. The problem is that most people feel that watching others closely, especially strangers, is poor manners. So in a crowd, people tend to tune out sights and sounds and stare straight ahead, decreasing the likelihood that they will even notice the signs of a potential emergency.

Having noticed the signs of an emergency, a bystander must determine whether or not it is serious enough to warrant intervention. The decision is often far from easy, for most of the signs that suggest an emergency are ambiguous. Cries for help from the next apartment might be genuine, or they might be coming from a TV. Because we are afraid of appearing foolish, most of us think twice before rushing to the rescue. So we adopt an air of calm indifference, while looking around to see how others will react. Since everyone else may be trying to appear indifferent as well, each bystander may be taken in by the others' nonchalance and led—or misled—to define the situation as a nonemergency (Latané, Nida, & Wilson, 1981).

But even if bystanders notice an event and label it an emergency, the presence of others may decrease their tendency to intervene. Being in a group tends to dilute one's sense of personal responsibility, to suggest that others have just as much obligation to respond. As a result, everyone hesitates, wondering who should step forward, until it is too late. Such a diffusion of responsibility may have contributed to Kitty Genovese's murder. Onlookers may have reasoned that someone else had already summoned help.

To test whether a diffusion of responsibility does indeed occur during emergencies, Darley and Latané (1968) staged an incident. College students who had volunteered to participate in a discussion about the personal problems caused by life in a high-pressure urban environment were ushered into private rooms containing earphones and a microphone. They learned that their talk would take place over an intercom system, to preserve their anonymity, and that the experimenter would not be listening in. Each subject was led to believe that one, two, or five other people were participating in the discussion. In fact, all the voices except the subjects' were prerecorded.

The first speaker, in the course of talking about the pressures of living in New York City, acknowledged that he suffered nervous seizures under severe stress. When it was his turn to speak again, he began to stutter and fumble for words, simulating the onset of a seizure. Within a few minutes he was choking and pleading for help. As Darley and Latané had predicted, the larger the perceived group of subjects who overheard his distress (and therefore the greater the potential diffusion of responsibility), the less likely a subject was to summon help. Of those who thought they were alone, 85 percent reported the speaker's plight. Only 62 percent of those who thought there was one other bystander did so, and only 31 percent of those who thought there were four other bystanders. Thus, the tendency for feelings of personal responsibility to decline as a group grows larger seemed quite strong.

Furthermore, the phenomenon of *bystander apathy* may not be apathy at all. In the experiment just de-

When the signs of an emergency are unambiguous, as in this November 1996 crash of an Ethiopian airliner, bystanders are more likely to assist victims.

scribed, those who failed to report the seizure were anything but indifferent. Many showed signs of extreme anxiety as they considered what to do. Their failure to intervene seemed not so much a decision against responding as a state of indecision. The typical bystander to an emergency, Darley and Latané argued, is "an anguished individual in genuine doubt, concerned to do the right thing but compelled to make complex decisions under pressure of stress and fear. His reactions are shaped by the actions of others—and all too frequently by their inaction" (Darley & Latané, 1968, p. 300).

Factors That Encourage Helping

Though Darley and Latané's findings are pessimistic about the prospects of victims receiving help when numerous bystanders are present, the social forces they describe are not the only ones that operate in an emergency. When the signs of an emergency are unambiguous and observers can tell whether or not help has been summoned, a victim may be *more* rather than less likely to receive aid from a sizable group (Solomon, Solomon, & Stone, 1978).

This possibility was demonstrated in an emergency that was staged repeatedly on a subway train in New York City (Piliavin, Rodin, & Piliavin, 1969). In 70 percent of the trials, bystanders immediately came to the aid of a young man who suddenly collapsed onto the floor. Help was offered more quickly when seven or more people were present than when only one, two, or three people occupied the car. Perhaps when helping is clearly the "right" reaction, a larger group increases the pressure to conform to the ethical norm.

Influences on Other Helping Behaviors

Besides bystander intervention in emergencies, social psychologists have studied other forms of helping, such as giving to charities or doing favors. Their research has shown that many factors can boost or inhibit helping responses. We will explore just a few.

Mood and Level of Stress

People who feel good are very likely to do good. Thus many charity drives are mounted just before Christmas, on the idea that people are more generous when they are in a holiday mood. Social psychologists have confirmed this tendency in experimental situations. For example, Alice Isen and Paula Levin (1972) induced positive moods in subjects by leaving change in the coin return of a public telephone. They then watched to see whether those who found the money would help a confederate who had dropped a pile of papers just outside the phone booth. As might be expected, those who had found the money were more likely to offer assistance than control subjects who had found no money. Even a mood raiser as simple as sunny skies and pleasant weather can increase a person's tendency to help others (Cunningham, 1979). There are several possible explanations for the "good mood" effect. First, people may want to continue in a good frame of mind, a desire that is supported by positive behavior. A good mood also evokes positive thoughts, which may lead to good deeds (Carlson, Charlin, & Miller, 1988). Research has shown that helping is more likely when the rewards associated with doing so are salient (Cunningham et al., 1990). The more obvious the rewards, the more people tend to help. Finally, people are more likely to help others when they perceive them as good and deserving of help (Forgas & Bower, 1987; Isen, 1987).

What about negative mood states: does being in a bad mood *inhibit* helping? On the contrary; under certain circumstances, people are increasingly likely to help others when they are feeling unhappy (Carlson & Miller, 1987). According to the **negative state relief model,** many people seek relief from negative moods by doing something positive that will lift their spirits (Cialdini, Darby, & Vincent, 1973), suggesting that the motivation for helping is primarily self-serving (Cialdini et al., 1987). However, many psychologists are skeptical about the role of negative state relief in altruism (see Miller & Carlson, 1990).

Empathic Concern

We have seen that helping is at least partly a matter of egotism: we help others because it makes us feel good. But aren't we ever motivated by genuine *unselfish* concern for others? Psychologist C. Daniel Batson thinks we are (Batson, 1987). He bases his theory on the existence of **empathy,** or the experience of another's emotional condition as one's own. According to Batson, to the extent that we empathize with one another, we will engage in altruistic helping.

Batson devised a number of experiments in which he stimulated empathic concern in subjects and then tried to sort out their motives for helping. Were the subjects interested primarily in reducing their own distress, or in reducing another's distress? The key factor in these experiments was the difficulty of escaping from a helping situation. Batson theorized that people who were high in empathic concern would help others even when it was easy to escape from the situation, in other words, when a means of relieving their own distress was available.

If you were to participate in one of these experiments, you would report to a laboratory to take part in an investigation of task performance under unpleasant conditions. You would be introduced to a fellow subject (actually a confederate of the experimenter), and the two of you would draw lots to see who would perform a task while receiving random shocks and who would observe. The drawing would be rigged so that you would be assigned to the role of the observer. While watching the confederate on closed-circuit TV, you would note that she was becoming increasingly uncomfortable and would listen as she described a traumatic experience with an electric fence she had had as a child. The experimenter would hesitate and ask if you would be willing to take her place.

1. Movies in which good triumphs over evil are unrealistic.
2. Students almost always deserve the grades they receive in school.
3. Although evil men may hold political power for awhile, in the general course of history good wins out.

FIGURE 18-4 *Sample items from the Just-World Scale. The scale is composed of two types of statements: those like item 1, with which people who believe in a just world tend to disagree; and those like items 2 and 3, with which people who believe in a just world tend to agree.* (Rubin & Peplau, 1973, p. 79.)

Your reaction at this point would depend on how Batson had varied the conditions of the experiment, that is, whether you were told at the outset that the woman held personal values and interests close to your own or ones that were quite different. Batson reasoned that if you thought the confederate was like yourself, you would feel more empathy for her than if you thought her different. Batson also varied the conditions of escape. You might have been told that you could leave after only two trials (the easy-escape condition), or you might have agreed to stay for all ten trials, and either volunteer to take some shocks yourself or continue to watch the subject suffer (the difficult-escape condition). If the experimenter asked you to trade places with the woman after two trials, how do you think you would react?

The results of Batson's experiment (Batson et al., 1981) closely matched his predictions. An overwhelming percentage of subjects who were high in empathy acted to help the confederate, whether escape was easy or difficult. When escape was difficult, even a majority of those who were low in empathy offered to trade places. Only those who measured low in empathy and were offered an easy escape were unlikely to trade places with the confederate. Batson concluded that true altruistic behavior does exist.

Critics of Batson's hypothesis have offered other reasons why subjects might have helped in these sit-

uations. They might have been motivated by a desire to avoid social disapproval (Archer, 1984), or they might have wanted to lift their own mood—a response that would be consistent with the negative relief model (Schaller & Cialdini, 1988). Batson did consider whether empathic individuals might have been tending to their own internal needs, such as the need to feel pride or to avoid shame or guilt. But he tested those possibilities in another series of experiments and rejected them in favor of his *empathy-altruism hypothesis* (Batson et al., 1988). Batson also tested the possibility of negative mood relief and found that model wanting (Batson et al., 1989). His conclusions—and their increasing acceptance among social psychologists—are important: they indicate that human behavior is not inevitably selfish.

Belief in a Just World

Another factor that contributes to altruism is belief in a *just world*—the conviction that in the long run, wrongdoing will be punished and good deeds be rewarded (see Figure 18-4). Research suggests that this belief is common among both children and adults (Lerner, Miller, & Holmes, 1976).

Psychologist Melvin Lerner has theorized that people with a strong belief in a just world may be motivated to try to restore justice when they see innocent people suffer. They may also perform altruistic acts, in anticipation of receiving some reward for their kindness. In one series of experiments, Zuckerman (1975) found that when students were asked two days before a final exam to help a person with research, or to serve as a reader for the blind, those students who were strong believers in a just world were more likely than others to comply with the request. According to Zuckerman, the students may have reasoned that if they did something kind for another person, they would be repaid with success on their exam. Significantly, when final exams were five months away, these strong believers were no more likely than others to perform a favor.

Belief in a just world, however, is a two-edged sword (Lerner, 1974); sometimes it prompts people to derogate victims of misfortune. Suppose you saw people suffering through no fault of their own. Suppose further that there was nothing that could be done to right the injustice. If you strongly believed that life was fair, such misfortune would be highly upsetting to you. To deal with this challenge to your belief system, you might come to see the victims in a

Primates have demonstrated altruistic behavior, especially toward their offspring. But according to sociobiologists, the motivation for this apparently selfless behavior may be selfish. Ensuring the safety of one's offspring increases the likelihood that the parent's genes, which the offspring carry, will be passed on to future generations.

negative light, enabling you to conclude that they *deserve* to suffer. Studies provide some evidence that people do reason in this way. Subjects in experiments will derogate the personal qualities of a fellow subject who has been assigned to receive painful electric shocks, even if the assignment was clearly random (Lerner, 1970; Lerner & Matthews, 1967; Lerner & Simmons, 1966). Outside the laboratory, people have been known to blame, derogate, and shun victims of violent crime and those who suffer psychological disorders (Farina et al., 1971; Symonds, 1975). For example, a person who has been raped or mugged may be censured by friends ("You should have known better than to walk alone in that neighborhood").

Sociobiological Factors

As we saw in Chapters 1, 2, and 11, sociobiologists attempt to understand the motivation for behavior by looking at the *adaptive significance* of inherited tendencies (Barash, 1982; Dawkins, 1976, 1986, 1996; Wilson, 1975). At first glance, altruistic behavior would seem to be *counterproductive;* acting altruistically involves risks, including the risk of injury or even death. Furthermore, while altruism increases the likelihood that the one being helped will survive and reproduce (the ultimate evolutionary goal), it *decreases* the likelihood that the helper will survive.

Genetic tendencies toward altruism, then, should not be favored by natural selection.

But Richard Dawkins, one of the world's foremost Darwinian scholars, proposed a mechanism through which altruistic behavior would be favored by natural selection. In his book *The Selfish Gene,* Dawkins pointed out that the "goal" of an organism is not necessarily to survive and reproduce, but to *pass the organism's genes on to future generations.* Obviously, the most likely way for an organism to do so would be to reproduce. However, according to Dawkins, there are other ways to pass along one's genes—specifically, by ensuring the safety of one's offspring, which allows *them* to survive and reproduce. (Remember that children share 50 percent of their genetic material with each biological parent.) From an evolutionary perspective, it may be more advantageous for an adult to risk his own life to save the life of a child. If the offspring survives and reproduces, the parent's genes *will* be passed on.

Several lines of evidence support such a theory. First, altruistic behavior is more common in species that have relatively few offspring, like primates. In these species, children are "expensive," in the sense that they require considerable resources to raise and are difficult to "replace." Among species that produce many offspring, like insects, altruism is less common. According to sociobiologists, that is because their offspring are relatively plentiful and therefore more easily "replaced." The parent's genetic investment is minimal.

Second, cases of child abuse, including infanticide (the killing of children), are much more common in blended families. In these cases, violence against the children is usually perpetrated by the stepparent rather than the biological parent (Archer, 1991; Dailey & Wilson, 1991; see also Dawkins, 1976). According to sociobiologists, that is exactly what should be expected. The stepparent has no genetic investment in the spouse's children, so any innate tendencies toward altruistic behavior would not apply to them.

Situational Factors

You may have wondered why no mention has yet been made of the effect of inner dispositions on altruism. Surely a primary reason for either altruistic or selfish acts must be a person's underlying character traits? Yet research shows that this is not the case. The "good Samaritan" is often more the product of circumstance than of inner disposition (another example of the fundamental attribution error). In fact, very few personality traits have been found to be consistently related to altruistic behavior. In one study that compared people who had intervened to stop a crime with people who had not, the researchers could not distinguish the helpers from the nonhelpers using tests of "humanitarianism" and "social responsibility" (Huston et al., 1981). What mattered instead was whether a person felt competent to deal with the crime. Thus, the challenges of a particular incident can overpower the tendency to act on one's "nature."

A similar study used seminary students as subjects—just the type of people who might be expected to act as "good Samaritans" (Darley & Batson, 1973). The students were asked to participate in an experi-ment in another building. Half were told that they were late and that everyone was waiting for them to arrive in order to start the experiment; half were told that they were early and could take their time in going to the other building. En route, each student encountered a man slumped in a doorway. How many of the students stopped to help him? Of the early students, 63 percent stopped; of the late students, only 10 percent. We can assume that the two groups did not differ significantly in inner disposition. But they did differ in situational factors. Apparently, being in a hurry can prevent people from following the inclination to help. That, in fact, is the central message of social psychology: the way people act is shaped to a large extent by the social situations in which they find themselves.

Pornography and Its Relationship to Rape

THE FACTS ARE startling:

According to FBI statistics, about 100,000 rapes are reported to the police every year (Federal Bureau of Investigation, 1991). Some estimate that since most rapes go unreported, the number may be as much as fifteen times higher than that.

(Koss, 1993)

In one survey, more than 27 percent of female college students reported an experience that met the legal definition of rape (or attempted rape). More than half of the women had experienced some form of sexual victimization, ranging from unwanted fondling to rape. In the same survey, 7.7 percent of the males reported perpetrating such an act.

(Koss, Gidycz, & Wisniewski, 1987)

A random survey of female residents of Charleston County, South Carolina, found that close to 15 percent had experienced one or more attempted or completed sexual assaults; 5 percent had been raped.

(Kilpatrick et al., 1985)

In the fall of 1996, amidst allegations of sexual harassment of new female recruits by drill sergeants, the U. S. Army set up a harassment hotline. While Army officials expected only a few complaints, by February 1997, more than 1,100 criminal probes had been conducted.

(*Time* magazine, Feb. 27, 1997, p. 46)

The attackers in these crimes are not likely to be lurking strangers. Sexual violence is so pervasive that it must take place within the everyday interactions of "normal" men and women (Johnson, 1980). In fact, rape is most likely to occur within a close relationship—a fact that may explain why so many rapes go unreported. In fact, only 2 percent of women who are victims of so-called date or acquaintance rapes report the crime (Koss et al., 1988). Many social scientists are convinced that rape is actually "rooted in the dominant norms of our culture" (Miller & Moran, 1989). It is the dark side of a socialization process that cultivates a dominant and aggressive male sexuality and a submissive, passive female sexuality.

Various studies have shown the extent to which normal males are willing to engage in sexual coercion. In one survey, 12 percent of male college students acknowledged that they had used strong physical force or violence in an attempt to engage in a sex act against a partner's will (Sigelman et al., 1984). In another survey, 15 percent of college men reported having forced intercourse at least once; personality and attitude tests revealed that they had particularly negative feelings toward women (Rapaport & Burkhart, 1984). In other surveys, 35 percent of the college male respondents admitted that they might rape a woman, if they were absolutely sure they would not be caught (Malamuth, 1981; Stille et al., 1987). Typically these men are aggressive toward women both in the laboratory and on dates.

Men are particularly likely to be aggressive toward women if they watch pornography frequently (Malamuth, 1984, 1989). Does that mean that pornography causes rape? To illuminate this issue, we will take an in-depth look at research on the effects of pornography.

Initial Studies. **Pornography** is material that is designed to sexually arouse its viewers or readers. The sexual revolution that began in the 1960s has changed what is portrayed in pornographic magazines and films. "Ordinary" sex is no longer considered taboo, so pornographers have gone to more extreme lengths to titillate readers and viewers. The new trend in pornography involves the inclusion of violence against women as an integral part of sex—including rape, torture, beating, and bondage. In response to this trend, feminists have raised questions about the impact of viewing such material (Lerman, 1978–1979).

Since most pornography is directed toward heterosexual males, learning how such material affects their attitudes toward women is particularly important. Certain relationships are clear. First, any type of arousal increases the likelihood of anger and aggression (Zillman, 1983); for heterosexual males, sexual arousal automatically focuses the anger on women. Many studies have shown that men who are aroused by pornographic material tend to be aggressive toward women. Edward Donnerstein and a colleague

While "mainstream" pornography may desensitize those who view it, pornography that incorporates violence against women (including rape, torture, and bondage) is particularly disturbing. Not only do such films generate high arousal in males; they induce aggressive behavior directed specifically at women.

(Donnerstein & Barrett, 1978) designed an experiment in which male subjects were first angered by either a male or a female confederate and were then shown a nonviolent pornographic film. After seeing the film, subjects took part in a "learning" experiment in which they had an opportunity to deliver shocks to the confederate who had angered them. The men who had seen the film were more aggressive toward the confederate than control subjects who had seen a neutral film; they were equally aggressive toward male and female confederates.

But what if the social restraints on male aggression against females were loosened by repeated opportunities to retaliate against the confederate? Would the male subjects be more aggressive toward the female confederate than toward the male? Donnerstein and John Hallam (1979) constructed another experiment in which they gave subjects two chances to show their aggression after seeing the pornographic film. As expected, on the second opportunity to retaliate, subjects were more aggressive toward the female confederate than toward the male. In sum, pornographic material does arouse aggression in males, and that aggression is *gender-specific*— that is, directed against women—when social restraints on male-to-female aggression are reduced.

What effect does long-term exposure to pornographic material have on arousal and aggression? In one experiment, Dolf Zillmann and Jennings Bryant (1984) showed thirty-six X-rated films to one group

of male and female college students, over a course of six weeks. They showed eighteen of the films to another group, and no film or neutral films to a control group. The results were somewhat surprising. The more pornographic films the students saw, the less aroused they became, and the *less* aggressive they were. In fact, those students who had seen thirty-six X-rated films responded even less aggressively in response to provocation than students in the control group. Habituation to pornography apparently decreases its power to arouse, which may reduce aggression.

Does that mean that we should inoculate males against aggression toward women by showing them pornography? An additional result of the experiment would argue that we should not. Three weeks after showing the last film, Zillmann and Bryant examined the students' *attitudes*. When asked their opinion of a rape trial, both males and females who had seen the pornographic films recommended lighter sentences for the rapist than the control subjects; they also expressed less support for the women's liberation movement. Male students who had seen the films showed more callous attitudes toward women than males in the control group. Thus, while aggressive behavior may have decreased as a consequence of the repeated exposure to pornography, the attitudes that normally restrain aggression were diminished. Furthermore, subjects were not *aware* of the change in their attitudes. Thus, becoming desensitized to pornography may open the door to later acts of aggression (Thomas, 1982).

The results of research on **violent pornography**— material that combines sexual explicitness with violence—are even more disturbing. Typically, films that combine sex and violence show a woman being attacked by a rapist, fighting him off at first but then becoming aroused and begging for more. Not only do such films generate high arousal, but they elicit aggressive thoughts that are specifically directed toward women. In several studies, men who watched violent pornography increased their aggression toward women, while their level of aggression toward men remained about the same as it had been after watching nonviolent pornography (Donnerstein, Linz, & Penrod, 1987; Linz, Donnerstein, & Penrod, 1987).

Researchers are specifically interested in knowing whether such movies perpetuate men's belief in the **rape myth**—the idea that women mean "yes" when they say "no," and in fact are secretly wishing for rape. Men who subscribe to the rape myth are likely to see nothing wrong with inappropriate sexual behavior, such as forcing a kiss on an unwilling woman (Margolin, Miller, & Moran, 1989).

Two investigators studied the effect of violent pornographic films on male attitudes (Malamuth & Check, 1981). They arranged for some college students to see two commercial films, *Swept Away* and *The Getaway*, that showed women being sexually aroused by an assailant. A control group of students watched two movies without sexual content. Several days later, all the students filled out a questionnaire that measured their attitudes about violence toward women and beliefs about rape. Those male students who had seen the sexually violent films were found to be more tolerant of rape, and more likely to agree that women enjoyed rape, than the control group.

A similar study (Malamuth & Check, 1985) revealed that false beliefs about rape were likely to increase as a result of watching movies with sexually violent content—especially among men who had already expressed aggressive attitudes toward women. Former Surgeon General C. Everett Koop, in commenting on his report on pornography and public health (Mulvey & Haugaard, 1986), put the matter this way:

> Impressionable men—many of them still in adolescence—see this material and get the impression that women like to be hurt, to be humiliated, to be forced to do things they do not want to do, or to appear to be forced to do things they really do want to do. It is a false and vicious stereotype that leads to much pain and even death for victimized women.
>
> (Koop, 1987, p. 945)

The Attorney General's Commission on Pornography (1986), concluding that many forms of pornography produce antisocial effects that are expressed in the form of increased violence against women, has recommended legal action, including stricter enforcement of existing obscenity laws and consideration of additional legal measures.

Criticisms, Alternatives, and Further Research. Some social scientists challenge the conclusions and recommendations of public commissions on pornography. Daniel Linz and his colleagues have argued that getting rid of pornography will not solve the problem of violence against women (Linz, Donnerstein, & Penrod, 1987), because violence against women permeates material that is not sexually explicit or "pornographic." Consider again the Malamuth and Check experiment; the males who behaved aggressively toward women in the study had watched commercially successful R-rated films containing nonexplicit scenes of sexual violence. Another researcher who has analyzed the content of videos has found more examples of forced sex or overt aggression in nonpornographic videos than in X-rated videos (Palys, 1986). And an analysis of detective magazines found that the covers of 76 percent showed domination of women; 38 percent showed women in bondage (Dietz et al., 1986). The pervasiveness of portrayals of violence against women in our culture led Linz and his colleagues (1987) to question the appropriateness of singling out pornographic material for legal action.

Patterns and Conclusions. The point Linz and his colleagues sought to make was that perpetuation of the rape myth and of sexual violence is not exclusively the fault of legally obscene materials. The mass media are saturated with scenes of violence against women; to legislate against all of them would be impractical, as well as potentially harmful to the rights of free expression. Rather, they recommended educating the public to combat negative images of women, thus helping people to make wiser choices and become more critical consumers of the media. Thus, those who write and produce TV shows, screenplays, books, and magazine articles should recognize the dangers of conveying messages of sexual violence; and the public should be aware that the rape myth grossly distorts women's reactions to rape. In fact, more and more researchers are concluding that negative attitudes toward women, more than any brief arousal from pornographic material, are what really motivate sexual aggression against women (Demare, Briere, & Lips, 1988; Malamuth, Check, & Briere, 1986). The danger of violent pornography is in its power to perpetuate those negative attitudes. Ultimately, the public needs to be disabused of the rape myth and convinced that sexually violent images demean not only those who are portrayed but those who watch them (Donnerstein, Linz, & Penrod, 1987).

SUMMARY

1. Social pressure often induces conformity, a shifting of our opinions or actions to correspond with those of other people. In some cases of conformity we may outwardly yield to a group consensus while inwardly retaining our own opinions. In other situations, the conformity is more extreme: we actually embrace new values through **identification** or **internalization.**

2. Research on **obedience**—following the explicit instructions of a person in authority—has shown that many of us are willing to obey orders even when our actions might harm other people. Although this research remains controversial, Milgram's basic finding that people are susceptible to destructive obedience has not been refuted.

3. Another form of going along with others is **compliance**—the act of acceding to an explicit request from someone who does not hold any particular authority. Common techniques used to obtain compliance include the **foot-in-the-door phenomenon,** the **door-in-the-face technique,** the **low-ball phenomenon,** and the **that's-not-all technique.**

4. A **group** is a collection of two or more people who interact regularly, share specific goals, and identify themselves as part of a whole. The role we play within a group can be very powerful in changing our behavior, as Zimbardo's mock prison study showed.

5. Being among others may enhance our ability to perform some tasks, an effect known as **social facilitation.** But if our effort in a group is anonymous and we rely too much on the contribution of others, we may tend to slack off, a behavior known as **social loafing.** Pressures to conform are particularly powerful in small, close-knit groups, where we may fall victim to **groupthink,** a mode of decision making characterized by suppression of alternative views and distorted appraisals of reality. Occasionally, a minority can change the views of a majority in a group, but only when the minority view is unwavering and highly visible.

6. Excessive interpersonal **aggression** is a fundamental problem among human beings. Freud and Lorenz have argued that our aggressive drives are innate. Freud believed that aggressive drives demand some form of release, or **catharsis;** Lorenz maintains that the "fighting instinct" has survival value. **Sociobiology** suggests that biological factors such as the structure of the human brain and nervous system may contribute to aggression.

7. Social learning theorists have shown that aggression can be learned from violent models and positive reinforcement of aggressive behavior. **Frustration,** or unanticipated interference with goal-directed behavior, can also play a role in promoting aggression. According to Dollard's **frustration-aggression hypothesis,** aggression in some form is always a consequence of frustration. Critics, however, maintain that aggression is only one of many possible reactions to frustration and that sources other than frustration can cause anger and aggression. Berkowitz modifies Dollard's hypothesis to state that frustrations generate aggression only to the extent they are felt as unpleasant.

8. Whether we display **altruism,** unselfish concern for others, depends on many factors, including the nature of the event demanding our response, the number of other people present, our emotional state at the time, the amount of stress present, the degree to which the situation seems just or unjust, and our beliefs. Altruistic behavior seems to depend more on external circumstances than on inner dispositions.

9. **Violent pornography,** material that combines sexual explicitness with violence, is highly arousing and elicits negative emotions and aggressive thoughts directed specifically toward women. Because sexually violent material is increasingly common in movies, books, and magazines that are not considered pornographic under the obscenity laws, relying on legal action may not solve the problem of violence against women. For that reason some psychologists think the only solution is to educate the public to become more critical consumers of the mass media.

SUGGESTED READINGS

Aronson, E. (1988). *The social animal* (5th ed.). New York: Freeman. This book, which won an American Psychological Association National Media Award, is an engaging, easy-to-read introduction to the topics central to social psychology.

Baron, R. A., & Richardson, D. R. (1992). *Human aggression* (2nd ed.). New York: Plenum. This very readable introduction to research on aggression discusses social, environmental, and individual determinants of aggression and techniques for controlling or preventing aggression.

Hunt, M. (1990). *The compassionate beast: What science is discovering about the humane side of mankind.* New York: Morrow. Hunt, a science writer, draws from new research in social psychology to clarify such mysteries as why Kitty Genovese was murdered and why people risked their lives during World War II by hiding Jews from the Nazis.

Kelman, H. C., & Hamilton, V. L. (1989). *Crimes and obedience: Toward a social psychology of authority and responsibility.* New Haven, CT: Yale University Press. A social psychologist and a sociologist analyze the My Lai massacre, Watergate, and the Iran-Contra affair, presenting a major analysis of the rationale behind illegal acts ordered by authority.

Milgram, S. (1974). *Obedience to authority: An experimental view.* New York: Harper & Row. Though first published more than twenty years ago, it remains the definitive work on obedience. Milgram discusses the important issues as he describes a series of eighteen of his obedience experiments, searching for an explanation of destructive obedience.

Spielberg, S. (1994). *Schindler's list* (movie). Spielberg's masterpiece portraying the Holocaust and the horrific atrocities carried out against the Jews in Nazi Germany. Even if you have previously seen the movie, you may wish to watch it again after learning of some of the social psychological factors contributing to the violence (and/or apathy) of German soldiers in the concentration camps.

GLOSSARY

accommodation   According to Piaget, a mental process that involves altering old ways of thinking to incorporate new knowledge and information.   **9**

acetylcholine   A neurotransmitter found in various parts of the peripheral nervous system, in the spinal cord, and in specific regions of the brain. It plays an important role in learning and memory, and has been implicated in Alzheimer's disease.   **3**

action potential   An abrupt change in a cell's polarity that temporarily makes the cell's interior positive and the cell's exterior negative. This change travels the length of a neuronal axon.   **3**

activation-synthesis hypothesis   Proposed by J. A. Hobson, a theory of sleep and dreaming in which the often strange quality of dreams is thought to be caused by the brain trying to make sense of and impose order on random, meaningless neural activity.   **5**

actor-observer bias   The tendency to attribute one's own behavior to environmental causes, rather than to some enduring personality trait.   **17**

advanced empathy   A later stage in client-centered therapy in which the therapist gradually begins to suggest what might be causing the client's problems, while still showing a deep understanding of the client's point of view.   **16**

afferent pathways   Nerve pathways leading toward the central nervous system.   **3**

age-thirty crisis   A time when people in their early thirties sometimes feel that any unsatisfactory aspect of their lives must be rectified immediately; otherwise, it will be too late to do so.   **10**

aggression   Behavior that is directed toward intentionally injuring another person who does not wish to be hurt.   **18**

agoraphobia   An intense fear of being in places that are hard to escape from quickly or without embarrassment, or where help would not be readily available.   **15**

alcohol abusers   People who are not alcoholic (alcohol-dependent) but who do have a drinking problem.   **15**

alcohol dependence   Any problem involving alcohol; psychological and physical addiction to alcohol.   **15**

algorithm   A precisely stated set of rules for solving problems of a particular kind.   **8**

alpha waves   Moderately slow brain waves that occur when a person relaxes with eyes closed.   **5**

altruism   Unselfish concern for others.   **18**

amplitude   A measure of light intensity as determined by the variation between the "peak" and "trough" of the light wave. For sound waves, the intensity as measured by the distance of the wave's peaks and valleys from a baseline of zero; amplitude determines loudness.   **4**

amygdala   One of the three interrelated structures of the limbic system; the others are the septum and hippocampus.   **3**

anal stage   According to Freud, the second psychosexual stage (occurring during the second year of life), during which bowel control is accomplished and pleasure focused on the function of elimination.   **13**

anorexia nervosa   A condition in which a person becomes so obsessed with the subject of weight control that she (it is usually a teenage girl) literally starves herself to death in an attempt to shed pounds.   **12**

anterograde amnesia   A form of amnesia that affects memory only for new events and information, *not* for things stored in the past.   **7**

antianxiety drugs   Commonly known as minor tranquilizers, they sedate, that is, produce a calming effect.   **16**

antidepressant drugs   Mood-regulating drugs effective in treating certain types of depression.   **15, 16**

antipsychotic drugs   Any major tranquilizer used to alleviate extreme agitation and hyperactivity in psychotic patients.   **16**

antisocial personality (sociopath)   A person with a history of antisocial acts beginning in childhood or adolescence and continuing into adulthood. These people act on impulse without considering others, with no guilt or remorse.   **15**

anxiety   According to Freud, a state of psychic distress that results when the ego is losing its struggle to reconcile the demands of the id, the superego, and reality.   **13**

anxiety disorders   A group of mental disorders characterized by feelings of vulnerability, apprehension, or fear.   **15**

anxious attachment   The type of bond between infant and caregiver characterized by the expectation that the caregiver will be inaccessible at times and somewhat unresponsive and ineffective.   **10**

assimilation According to Piaget, a mental process that involves the incorporation of new information into old ways of thinking and behaving. **9**

associative learning Learning that certain events are connected with one another. **6**

attitude A disposition to respond favorably or unfavorably toward a person, thing, event, place, idea, or situation. **17**

attitude object The target of an attitude; that person, thing, event, idea, or situation that we have a disposition to evaluate in a particular way. **17**

auditory canal The passageway that extends from the opening of the outer ear to the eardrum. **4**

auditory nerve The nerve that carries neural impulses, triggered by movement of hair cells, to the brain stem. From there the impulses ascend through the thalamus to the auditory cortex, where the perception of sound begins. **4**

authoritarian A parenting style, identified by Diana Baumrind, characterized by harsh controlling behavior, lack of responsiveness to a child's wishes, and inflexible thinking. **10**

authoritarian personality An individual characterized by rigid adherence to conventional values, a preference for strong, antidemocratic leaders, and a fear and hatred of almost anyone who is different from oneself. **17**

authoritative A parenting style, identified by Diana Baumrind, characterized by responsiveness, coupled with firmness in setting limits, and flexibility in thinking. **10**

autobiographical memories Personal, individual memories that pertain to one's own life. **7**

automatic encoding Memory encoding that happens effortlessly. **7**

autonomic nervous system The division of the peripheral nervous system that controls the internal muscles (blood vessels, heart, intestines) and the glands. **3**

availability heuristic An approach people use to judge odds involving the assessment of the probability of an uncertain event to occur according to the ease with which past examples come to mind. **8**

aversive conditioning A therapeutic technique that attempts to reduce the frequency of deviant behavior by pairing an aversive stimulus with the undesired behavior. **6, 16**

avoidance learning A cause-and-effect relationship whereby learning takes place through avoiding the stimulus. It can be established through negative reinforcement. **6**

axon The long extension of a neuron that usually transmits impulses away from the cell body. **3**

Babinski reflex A baby's response to stroking on the bottom of the foot; when the foot is stroked, the toes fan out. **9**

backward conditioning Presenting the unconditioned stimulus before the conditioned stimulus, thereby reversing the usual order. **6**

backward search A heuristic in which a person begins at the end (or resolution) of a problem and then works backward in order to discover the steps involved. **8**

basal ganglia An area in the forebrain that coordinates fine motor activity. **3**

basic anxiety According to Karen Horney, the helplessness and insecurity a child feels when parents' behavior is indifferent, disparaging, and erratic. **13**

basic hostility According to Karen Horney, a child's feeling of deep resentment toward parents who arouse the child's basic anxiety. **13**

basilar membrane An elastic membrane in the inner ear that helps transmit sound waves to the auditory nerve. **4**

behavior modification The conscious use of operant conditioning principles to change human behavior. **6**

behavior therapies The application of experimentally derived principles of learning in an attempt to change maladaptive thoughts, feelings, and behaviors. **16**

behavioral genetics The study of the relative contributions of environmental and heredity factors to differences in human thought and behavior. **2**

behaviorist perspective The view that explains behavior by asserting that environmental stimuli shape and control an individual's actions. **1**

beta waves Rapid or high-frequency brain waves common when a person is fully awake and alert. **5**

bi-directional influence The mutual effects of parent and child on each other, as each responds to the other. **10**

binocular disparity The difference between the retinal images of the two eyes. **4**

biofeedback A specialized procedure for monitoring and controlling the physiological aspects of stress (and pain). **12**

biological perspective A view of social and personality development as guided by inherited biological tendencies. **10, 15**

biomedical model The traditional view of illness as the result of a biological malfunction that can be explained and treated without reference to the victim's psychological state or social situation. **12**

biopsychosocial approach A multi-approach view of illness suggesting that treatment requires consideration of the biological, psychological, and social causes. It is the basis for the field of health psychology.   **12**

bipolar cells   Cells in the eye that are stimulated by rods or cones and in turn stimulate ganglion cells.   **4**

bipolar disorder   A mood disorder that involves periods of both depression and excessive elation.   **15**

borderline personality disorder   A personality disorder characterized by an instability of self-image, interpersonal relations, and mood.   **15**

bounded rationality   The theory of problem solving proposed by Nobel-prize-winning psychologist Herbert Simon. According to him, we search for a solution until we have found one that will work, even if it isn't the best possible solution; in other words, we behave rationally, within certain constraints.   **8**

bulimia   An eating disorder that involves periodic bingeing alternating with purging to avoid gaining weight.   **12**

Cannon-Bard theory   The view developed by Walter Cannon and L. L. Bard that the basis of emotion lies in the central nervous system, specifically in the thalamus.   **11**

case study   Intensive investigation and in-depth analysis of a single individual.   **2**

castration anxiety   According to Freud, the fear a young boy experiences that his father will punish him for his Oedipal longings by cutting off his penis.   **13**

catatonic stupor   Characteristic of some schizophrenics, the victims are motionless, remaining in one position for hours at a time and responding neither to people nor to things.   **15**

catharsis   The release of aggressive energy.   **18**

causal attribution   How people attribute causes to behavior.   **17**

cell body   Region of the neuron that contains the cell nucleus and all other life-sustaining systems of the cell.   **3**

central nervous system (CNS)   The ultimate control center of all human behavior, consisting of the brain and the spinal cord.   **3**

central tendency   A middle value (such as a mean, median, or mode) of a set of scores.   **2**

cerebellum   Located to the rear of the pons, it coordinates voluntary movement of the skeletal muscles and regulates physical balance.   **3**

cerebral cortex   The covering that surrounds the entire outer surface of the brain. Much of the "higher-order" processing occurs here, relating to learning, speech, reasoning, and memory.   **3**

cerebral hemispheres   Also the forebrain. The two large structures lying above the brain's central core that are involved in learning, speech, reasoning, and memory.   **3**

childhood amnesia   Our lack of conscious memories from infancy.   **9**

chromosomes   Thread-shaped structures within the cell nucleus that carry the organism's genes.   **2**

chunking   Perceiving related items as a larger unit or cluster; used to increase the capacity of normal short-term memory.   **7**

ciliary muscles   Muscles in the eye that change the shape of the lens for focus.   **4**

circadian rhythms   Naturally occurring daily cycles of the body.   **5**

circadian theory   The theory that sleep is not a time to restore lost energy but rather is an adaptive response to night and day; in other words, humans sleep at night because they are not well adapted to living in the dark environment.   **5**

classical conditioning   A process of learning discovered by Ivan Pavlov in which a conditioned stimulus (CS) repeatedly presented with an unconditional stimulus (US) that normally evokes an involuntary response develops into a learned or conditioned response even in the absence of the CS.   **6**

classically conditioned response   The behavior that results when a neural stimulus is repeatedly paired with another stimulus that evokes an involuntary response, such as emotions or physical reflexes.   **6**

client-centered therapy   Carl Rogers' humanistic treatment in which the therapist helps clients to clarify their true feelings and come to value who they really are.   **16**

clinical psychologists   Practitioners in the subfield of psychology that deals with the diagnosis and treatment of psychological disorders.   **1**

cochlea   The spiral-shaped part of the inner ear containing the receptors for hearing.   **4**

cochlear implant   A surgical procedure in which microelectrodes are surgically positioned at various points along the cochlea. This procedure is designed to help people with neural deafness.   **4**

cognitive appraisal theory   The view proposed by Richard Lazarus that people are continually searching the environment for meaning, looking for cues not only on how to act but also on how to feel. Emotions arise from how we appraise events in our environment in relation to our short- and long-term goals and our abilities and resources for coping.   **11**

cognitive arousal interpretation   A theory developed by Stanley Schacter and Jerome Singer which holds that we explain our feelings by searching our surroundings for a reasonable cue.   **11**

cognitive consistency   The tendency of people to keep their various cognitions in relative agreement with one another.   **17**

cognitive development   The changes associated with the "thinking" components of behavior.   **9**

cognitive developmental perspective   A view of social and personality development based on the idea that a child's understanding of the world changes with age.   **10**

cognitive dissonance   The unpleasant state of tension that develops when people are aware of entertaining two inconsistent thoughts simultaneously.   **17**

cognitive learning   Learning that involves the formation of concepts, schemas, theories, and other mental abstractions.   **6**

cognitive perspective   The view that the quality of one's internal dialogue—accepting or berating oneself, building oneself up or tearing oneself down—has a profound effect on a person's mental health.   **15**

cognitive psychology   An approach to understanding personality that emphasizes mental processes, or cognitions, and addresses topics like memory, language, thought, problem solving, and decision making.   **1**

cognitive therapy   A variation of cognitive restructuring therapy developed by Aaron Beck in which patients are questioned in such a way that they themselves discover the irrationality of their thoughts.   **16**

cognitive-behavior therapies   Therapies that stress the teaching of new, healthier ways of thinking, that is, the restructuring of negative cognitions.   **16**

companionate love   According to Robert Sternberg, a relationship (like best friends) that is based on intimacy and commitment but not love.   **17**

compliance   The act of assenting to an explicit request from someone who does not hold authority over you.   **18**

comprehension   The process of determining the meaning of a string of words and morphemes.   **8**

compulsion   A repetitive behavior a person feels compelled to engage in despite the fact that it is senseless or excessive.   **15**

concepts   Mental constructions involved in grouping together and classifying objects and events based on common features.   **8**

conceptually driven processing   Knowledge stored in the brain that influences what we hear, see, and feel.   **4**

concrete operations   Logical operations that involve reversible transformations of concrete objects and events.   **9**

concrete-operational period   The second stage of Piaget's theory of intellectual growth (which usually consists of the elementary school years), during which a child begins to think logically—but only in regard to concrete objects.   **9**

conditional positive regard   According to Carl Rogers, the withholding of love and praise from a child unless he or she conforms to parental and social standards.   **13**

conditioned operant response   Results from a learned association between a particular action and a desired consequence.   **6**

conditioned response (CR)   A response to a previously neutral stimulus learned through association in the process of conditioning.   **6**

conditioned stimulus (CS)   The stimulus that elicits a new response as a result of the conditioning process.   **6**

conditions of worth   Carl Rogers' term for the strong ideals children hold about which thoughts and behaviors will bring positive regard and so are desirable and "good."   **13, 16**

conduction deafness   Malfunctions of the outer or middle ear that impair the ear's ability to mechanically amplify sound waves, for example, wax buildup in the ear canal.   **4**

cones   Receptor cells in the retina that are sensitive to color and that are used primarily for daytime or high-light-intensity vision.   **4**

confirmatory hypothesis testing   The tendency to seek out information that confirms our existing schemes.   **17**

consciousness   An active awareness of the many thoughts, images, perceptions, and emotions that occupy one's mind at any given time.   **5**

conservation   The recognition that certain features of an object remain the same (are conserved) despite changes in other features.   **9**

constituent   A group of words that make sense when placed together.   **8**

consummate love   According to Robert Sternberg, the kind of love that combines intimacy, passion, and commitment—the most difficult type of relationship to achieve and maintain.   **17**

contiguity   In operant conditioning, the temporal relationship between the conditioned stimulus and the unconditioned stimulus. In general, the closer the timing between the conditioned stimulus and the unconditioned stimulus, the stronger the associative relationship between them.   **6**

contingency   In operant conditioning, the likelihood that the conditioned stimulus signals the unconditioned stimulus, which can usually be expressed in terms of a probability.   **6**

contingency contracting   A behavioral technique used in therapy whereby a person makes a contract with another individual detailing the rewards or punishments that are contingent on succeeding or failing to make a behavior change.   **12**

contingency management   An operant-conditioning therapy that seeks to increase desirable behaviors by reinforcement and to decrease undesirable ones by punishment or withdrawal of rewards.   **6**

continuity   A gestalt principle of organization proposing that items will be perceived as belonging together if they appear to form a single, continuous grouping.   **4**

continuous reinforcement   Providing reinforcement each time the subject exhibits the desired behavior.   **6**

contralateral control   A basic principle of brain organization where the motor cortex of the right hemisphere controls movement on the left side of the body and the left hemisphere controls right-side movement.   **3**

control group   In an experiment, subjects who experience all the same conditions as experimental subjects *except* the key factor that is being evaluated.   **2**

conventional level   According to Kohlberg, the stage in moral development during which a child adheres to rules to win the approval of others, and is inclined to follow the dictates of established authority.   **10**

conversion disorder   The loss of a sensory or motor function without organic impairment, usually following some traumatic event.   **15**

coping   The process of managing internal and external demands that are taxing or even overwhelming.   **12**

cornea   The tough, transparent, curved outer covering of the front of the eyeball that admits light into the interior of the eye.   **4**

correlation coefficient   A numerical value that indicates the strength and direction of the relationship between two variables.   **2**

correlational designs   Research studies used to find out the extent to which two variables are related when a true experiment is not feasible.   **2**

counseling psychologists   Professionals trained to help individuals deal with mild problems of social and emotional adjustment.   **1**

counterconditioning   The reduction or elimination of a classically conditioned response. See **systematic desensitization.**   **6**

criterion validity   The type of validity a test has if a person's score on it can be correlated with some other yardstick of what is being measured.   **14**

cutaneous   Refers to the senses responsible for sensations of the skin.   **4**

cyclothymia   A chronic but milder form of bipolar disorder (manic-depression).   **15**

data-driven processing   Information flowing from our sense organs to the brain.   **4**

deep processing (elaborative rehearsal)   The mental activity that facilitates the transfer of information from short-term to long-term memory storage by emphasizing the meaning of the stimulus.   **7**

defense mechanism   According to Freud, a mental strategy that blocks the harmful id impulse while reducing anxiety.   **13**

delta sleep   The deepest stage of sleep when delta waves occupy more than 5O percent of a sleeper's EEG.   **5**

delta waves   Very slow brain waves that predominate during deep sleep.   **5**

delusions   Irrational beliefs that are held despite overwhelming evidence to the contrary.   **15**

demand characteristics   In an experiment, any clues felt by the subjects about the responses they think the researcher wants them to make.   **2**

dendrites   The short, branched extensions of a neuron that usually carry neural impulses toward the cell body.   **3**

denial   According to Freud, a defense mechanism that involves a refusal to acknowledge some threat.   **13**

dependent variable   A factor that is expected to change when the independent variable is manipulated.   **2**

depolarized   Decreased electrical imbalance associated with the resting state.   **3**

depressants   Drugs that suppress central nervous system activity, causing feelings of relaxation or reduced anxiety.   **5**

depressive disorders   A mood disorder in which a sad, discouraged mood is the major symptom.   **15**

depth perception   The ability to see the world in three dimensions and tell how far away an object is.   **4**

descriptive statistics   Statistical methods used to summarize a vast amount of data in forms that are brief and easy to understand.   **2**

developmental psychologists   Researchers who try to describe and explain the systematic changes that occur throughout the life cycle.   **1**

developmental psychology   The study of progressive changes in human traits and abilities that occur throughout the life span.   **9**

dialectic operations stage   According to Klaus Riegel, the highest stage of intellectual functioning, whereby mature thinkers debate a deep moral, religious, or philosophical issue. **9**

diathesis–stress model A theory that the interaction of factors such as biological predisposition combined with life stress may cause schizophrenia. **15**

dichotic listening A technique, developed by E. C. Cherry, involving the simultaneous input of different information into each ear; used to study the "cocktail party phenomenon." **7**

dichromats People who are partially color-blind because of the lack or loss of one of the three forms of iodopsin normally found in the cones. **4**

direct perspective A theory of perception that sensory data presented to the eye are passed to the brain, which automatically structures the data into a meaningful whole. **4**

direct tests Tests that require conscious awareness, like recall and recognition. **7**

discrimination The behavioral expression of prejudice. **17**

discrimination training A procedure used to teach an animal to respond only to a specific stimulus by presenting similar stimuli that will not elicit a reward. **6**

discriminative stimulus The stimulus that elicits the reward in discrimination training. **6**

dispersion The degree of scatter among the individual numbers of a set of numbers. **2**

displacement According to Freud, a defense mechanism that involves the transfer of unacceptable feelings from their appropriate target to a much "safer" one. **13**

dissociation A split in consciousness whereby certain thoughts, feelings, and behaviors operate independently from others; one theory of what happens in hypnosis. **5**

dissociative amnesia The partial or total forgetting of past experiences after some stressful event. **15**

dissociative disorders Psychological disorders that involve the splitting off of a part of the personality so that personal memory or identity is disturbed. **15**

dissociative fugue A psychological disorder in which the victims walk away from their homes and their identities for a period of hours, days, months, or even years. **15**

dissociative identity disorder (multiple-personality disorder) A psychological disorder in which a person (more often a female) evolves two or more separate personalities, each well defined. **15**

divergent thinking The ability to generate many different answers to a question. **8**

door-in-the-face technique A compliance strategy in which a smaller counter request is made in response to a refusal to a larger request. **18**

dopamine A monoamine (neurotransmitter) found in the limbic system, cerebellum, and basal ganglia of the brain. It plays a critical role in thought disorders and movement disorders. **3**

double-blind technique A procedure in which neither the experimenter nor the subjects know who has been assigned to the experimental group or who is acting as a control. **2**

dream analysis A psychoanalytic technique in which the hidden meaning of a dream can be brought to light, and unconscious wishes, fantasies, and conflicts can be explored. **16**

drive-reduction theory A theory of motivation developed by behaviorist Clark Hull and others stating that biological needs are the basic motivator of action. **11**

drug therapy The treatment of psychological disorders through the administration of drugs. **16**

dysthymic disorder (dysthymia) A chronic form of depression that lasts for years at a time. **15**

eardrum A thin membrane between the outer and inner ear that responds to changes in air pressure by vibrating, thus amplifying sound. **4**

eclectic therapists Psychotherapists who believe that an openness to different approaches allows them to tailor a treatment program to the needs of each patient. **16**

ecological validity The issue concerning research methods suggesting that conditions in a laboratory experiment may not always mirror those in real-life settings. **2**

educational psychologists Researchers who are concerned with all aspects of the learning process. **1**

effector cells Cells specialized for contracting muscles and for stimulating glandular secretions. **3**

efferent pathways Nerve pathways leading away from the central nervous system. **3**

effortful encoding A deliberate attempt to store something into memory. **7**

ego According to Freud, the part of the psyche that mediates transactions between the external environment and the demands of the id and the superego. The ego operates on the reality principle. **13**

ego psychologists Psychologists who consider themselves Freudians but who elaborate on Freud's theory, emphasizing ego functions. **13**

egocentric Among young children, the belief that everyone views the world from the same perspective as the child. **9**

electroconvulsive therapy (ECT) Commonly called "shock treatment," it has proved extremely effective in the treatment of cases of severe depression that fail to respond to drug therapy.   **16**

electroencephalogram (EEG)   Tracings of brain-wave patterns made by an electroencephalograph.   **5**

emotion   A reaction pattern that includes physiological changes, expressive behaviors, and states of feeling, arising involuntarily in response to a challenging situation.   **11**

empathy   The experience of another's emotional condition as one's own.   **18**

empiricist view   A theory of perceptual development, linked to the indirect perspective, which holds that perceptual processes are learned from sensory experience.   **4**

encoding   The process through which sensory information is converted into a form that can be remembered.   **7**

encoding specificity   A phenomenon whereby memory is best when the conditions during retrieval match the conditions during encoding.   **7**

endorphins   Neurotransmitters found throughout the brain, but especially in the limbic system. They modulate pain and pleasure, and regulate eating and drinking.   **3**

environment   The external surroundings in which a person lives.   **2**

episodic memory   The recollection of events an individual has personally experienced.   **7**

equilibration   According to Piaget, the mental process by which development is achieved by attempting to reach a balance between assimilation and accommodation.   **9**

erectile failure   A sexual dysfunction that occurs in men characterized by the inability to achieve or maintain an erection.   **11**

escape learning   A cause-and-effect relationship whereby learning is achieved through escaping the stimulus. It can be established through negative reinforcement.   **6**

evolutionary psychology   A field of psychology that focuses on the genetic bases of a wide range of animal and human social behaviors—including aggression, cooperation, competition, sex roles, and altruism—especially toward those who share one's genes.   **11**

evolutionary/biological approach   A perspective on personality that focuses on behavior patterns that may result from physiology, genetic inheritance, and adaptive pressures that may have existed in our evolutionary past.   **13**

excitatory potentials   Inputs that cause the inside of the cell to become less negative.   **3**

excitement phase   The first stage of Masters and Johnson's sexual response cycle, characterized by increased breathing, heart rate, and muscular tension in both men and women.   **11**

exemplars   Multiple examples of concepts we might be exposed to. Whereas prototypes are abstract entities, exemplars are more directly related to actual experiences.   **8**

experimental group   In an experiment, those subjects experiencing the experimental condition.   **2**

experimental psychology   The approach to psychology in which psychologists use experimentation to gather data on the basic processes shared by many animal species, such as sensation, perception, learning, memory, problem solving, communication, emotion, and motivation.   **1**

experiments   Research methods used to identify (and test) cause-and-effect relationships.   **2**

explicit memory   Memory that refers to conscious awareness.   **7**

expressed emotion   The amount of criticism and hostility directed toward schizophrenics by other people, especially from within families.   **15**

extinction   The slow weakening and eventual disappearance of a conditioned response.   **6**

facial feedback hypothesis   The view that facial expressions play a key role in initiating, or at least modulating, the experience of emotion.   **11**

factor analysis   A mathematical technique similar to a correlation whereby individuals are given various tests and their responses compared to all other responses to find similarities.   **13, 14**

factors   Basic abilities; the components of intelligence.   **14**

family-systems therapies   Psychotherapy that stresses the importance of altering family roles and patterns of communication that maintain maladaptive behavior.   **16**

Fechner's law   A law stating that as the intensity of a stimulus increases, larger and larger increases in intensity are required to produce subjectively equivalent changes.   **4**

fetal alcohol syndrome   A group of defects including mental retardation, deficient growth, and defects of the skull, face, and brain that tend to occur in the infants of women who consume large amounts of alcohol during pregnancy.   **5**

fight-or-flight response   A physiological reaction to stress in which an organism is aroused either to attack a threatening invader or to flee.   **12**

fixation   According to psychoanalytic theory, a state of arrested development whereby an individual becomes stuck in a particular psychological battle, repeating the conflict in symbolic ways.   **13**

fixed-interval (FI) schedule A partial reinforcement schedule in which a reward is given for the first correct response after a certain time interval. **6**

fixed-ratio (FR) schedule A partial reinforcement schedule in which a reward is given after a specified number of responses. **6**

flashbulb memories Memories of extraordinary events, such as the assassination of John F. Kennedy or the explosion of the space shuttle *Challenger*. **7**

flooding In behavior therapies, an exposure-based treatment involving intense, rapid exposure to fearful stimuli. **16**

foot-in-the-door phenomenon A tendency to comply with a larger request if a person has previously agreed to a smaller one. **18**

forebrain Also the cerebral hemispheres. The two large structures lying above the brain's central core that are involved in learning, speech, reasoning, and memory. **3**

forgetting function Hermann Ebbinghaus's pattern of forgetting, characterized by two distinct features: forgetting is initially very rapid (within an hour, savings have fallen to 50 percent), but the rate eventually levels off (even after a month's delay, savings are about 25 percent). **7**

form perception The ability to detect unified patterns in a mass of sensory data. **4**

formal operations stage Piaget's term for the cognitive changes in adolescence marking the onset of adultlike thinking, characterized by the ability to think hypothetically and in abstract terms. **9**

formal-operational period The last stage of Piaget's theory of intellectual growth (from adolescence through adulthood), during which a person learns to think simultaneously about many systems of operations and to think hypothetically. **9**

forward conditioning Presenting the conditioned stimulus slightly before the unconditioned stimulus in order to create the perception of a contingency. **6**

fovea A pitlike depression near the center of the retina, densely packed with cones but no rods, that provides a person's sharpest, most detailed vision. **4**

free association A psychoanalytic technique for exploring the unconscious through a patient's unrestrained expression of thoughts that occur spontaneously. **16**

frequency A measure of the timing between light waves, calculated by counting how many waves occur in a given unit of time. For sound waves, the number of compression-rarefaction cycles that occur per second; the frequency of a sound wave corresponds to the pitch one hears. **4**

frequency theory A theory of pitch arguing that the basilar membrane vibrates in exactly the same frequency pattern as the original sound wave. Thus pitch is determined by the frequency per second of neural impulses sent to the brain. **4**

frontal lobes The portion of each cerebral hemisphere that is concerned with the regulation of voluntary movements. **3**

frustration An unanticipated interference with any goal-directed behavior. **18**

frustration-aggression hypothesis John Dollard's view that aggression is always a consequence of frustration and that frustration always leads to some form of aggression. **18**

fully functioning Carl Rogers' term for people who are open, undefensive, realistic, creative, and self-determining, and have an underlying confidence in themselves. **13**

functional fixedness The tendency to overlook novel uses for things. **8**

functionalism The view, influenced by Darwin's theories and expounded chiefly by William James, that psychological processes have adaptive functions that allow the human species to survive and that these processes are more important to investigate than the mind's structure. **1**

fundamental attribution error The tendency to attribute others' behavior to their inner dispositions rather than to situational factors. **17**

fundamental needs In Abraham Maslow's hierarchy, those needs associated with physical requirements, such as satisfying thirst and hunger, and those related to obtaining a safe environment. **13**

***g* factor** Charles Spearman's term for general intellectual ability. **14**

gamma-amino butyric acid (GABA) The most prevalent inhibitory neurotransmitter, it is found in parts of the brain involving emotion and anxiety. **3**

ganglion cells Nerve tissue cells of the eye that form the fibers of the optic nerve. **4**

gate-control theory A theory asserting that the sensation of pain depends on the balance of activity between large- and small-diameter nerve fibers within the spinal cord. **4**

gender roles Patterns of behavior generally associated with masculinity or femininity. **10**

general adaptation syndrome According to Hans Selye, the set of physiological responses that are evoked by all unusually demanding stresses, pleasurable as well as painful, on the body. **12**

general paresis An irreversible deterioration of all mental and physical processes. It is the final stage of syphilis. **15**

generalization gradient The decreasing tendency to generalize a conditioned response as the resemblance between a new stimulus and a conditioned one declines. **6**

generalized anxiety   A state of persistent apprehension without good cause.   **15**

generativity   According to Erik Erikson's theory of social and personality development, the challenge of learning how to reach out and become concerned with the well-being of future generations.   **10**

genital stage   According to Freud, the fifth psychosexual stage (occurring from puberty on), during which the sexual focus shifts from autoeroticism to sexual intercourse.   **13**

gestalt   A meaningful pattern that the brain constructs from sensory information.   **4**

gestalt therapy   A therapeutic approach developed by Frederick Perls that emphasizes the present and attempts to make a client *whole* by ridding him or her of defenses, increasing awareness, and releasing pent-up feelings.   **16**

glia   Cells that hold neurons in place, carry nutrients to them, repair and protect them, and aid in the propagation of impulses.   **3**

graded potentials   Changes in electrical potential of dendrites in proportion to the amount of stimulation being received.   **3**

grasping reflex   The tendency of a baby to grasp a person's finger if you place it on one of the baby's hands.   **9**

group   A collection of two or more people who interact regularly in fairly structured and predictable ways, share one or more specific goals, and identify themselves as part of a whole, sharing to some extent a common fate.   **18**

group therapy   Any therapy that is applied to an interacting group of people.   **16**

groupthink   A phenomenon that occurs when a small, cohesive group becomes so concerned with maintaining unanimity that its

members can no longer appraise alternatives realistically.   **18**

hair cells   Cells containing hairlike projections that are receptors for hearing in the inner ear.   **4**

hallucinogens   Drugs that produce hallucinations and impaired thinking.   **5**

Hawthorne effect   The phenomenon in which subjects behave in unusual ways simply because they are part of a scientific study.   **2**

health psychologists   Researchers who study the relationships between mind and body as they try to identify and treat the psychological factors related to disease.   **1**

health psychology   A subfield of psychology that is dedicated to promoting good health and health care.   **12**

heredity   The inherited set of developmental instructions that make us who we are, instructions that are transmitted to us by the genes we are born with.   **2**

heritability   Genetic factors that contribute to the individual differences in people who belong to the same population.   **2, 14**

heuristic   A rule-of-thumb problem-solving strategy.   **8**

hierarchy of needs   Abraham Maslow's concept that all humans face a series of needs in life, and that needs at more basic levels must be met before the person can go on to fulfill higher-level needs.   **13**

hindbrain   An area in the brain's central core consisting of the medulla, the pons, the reticular formation, and the cerebellum.   **3**

hippocampus   One of the three interrelated structures of the limbic system; the others are the septum and the amygdala.   **3**

human information-processing (HIP) model   A model of cognition that suggests the mind takes in information serially (one task at

a time) and in discrete stages, much like a computer.   **1**

humanistic approach   A perspective on personality that emphasizes the human potential for growth, creativity, and spontaneity. It stresses the importance of an individual's subjective experience of the world.   **13**

humanistic psychology   An approach to understanding personality that emphasizes the striving for self-fulfillment and growth as the prime motivators of behavior.   **1**

humanistic therapies   Treatment based on the belief that psychological problems can be treated by giving people insight into needs and motives they may not be aware of.   **16**

hyperpolarization   An increase in the electrical imbalance associated with the resting state.   **3**

hypnotic susceptibility   The measurable trait used to classify how easily a person can be hypnotized.   **5**

hypochondriasis   A psychological disorder in which people are persistently fearful that they have contracted some terrible, often fatal disease despite reassurance from doctors that no physical illness exists.   **15**

hypothalamus   A structure located below the thalamus that regulates the body's internal environment and acts to maintain balance within the body.   **3**

hypothesis   A proposition or idea that one sets out to test.   **2**

id   According to Freud, the impulsive and unconscious part of the psyche that operates through the pleasure principle toward the gratification of instinctual drives.   **13**

identification   The tendency to go along with others because we admire and wish to be like them.   **18**

immune system   The body's "surveillance system," which guards against foreign invaders (called *antigens*). **12**

immunocompetence The measure of how well the immune system protects the body from illness. **12**

implicit memory Memory without conscious awareness. **7**

in-groups Those groups with which one identifies. **17**

incus One of a set of three tiny, interconnected bones in the middle ear that transmit sound from the eardrum to the cochlea. **4**

independent variable A factor that an experimenter deliberately manipulates. **2**

indirect perspective A theory of perception that all we process directly are sensory cues about the environment. To make sense of those cues we must supplement them with additional information stored in memory. **4**

indirect tests Tests that do not require conscious awareness, such as those involving word fragments that subjects are asked to complete. 7

industrial and organizational psychologists Researchers who study all aspects of the relationship between people and their workplace. **1**

inferiority complex Alfred Adler's theory that all children are born with a deep sense of inferiority because of their small size, physical weakness, and lack of knowledge and power in the adult world. **13**

information-processing model of memory A theory that divides memory into three types: sensory, short-term, and long-term. **7**

information-processing view of intelligence An approach to studying intelligence that looks closely at *how* people think and reason intelligently. **14**

inhibited ejaculation A sexual dysfunction characterized by a man's

inability to ejaculate during sex with a partner. **11**

inhibitory potentials Inputs that cause the inside of the cell to become more negative. **3**

insomnia Difficulty falling asleep or staying asleep all night. **5**

instinct An innate force found in all members of a species that directs behavior in predictable ways in the presence of the right eliciting stimulus. **11**

instinctive drift A reversion to a genetically based behavior that competes with a learned behavior. **6**

intelligence The capacity to acquire and retain knowledge and to understand concepts and relationships. **14**

intelligence quotient (IQ) A measure of mental development computed by dividing a child's mental age (the average age of those who obtain that child's score) by the child's chronological age, and multiplying by 100 to eliminate the decimal point. **14**

internal consistency The characteristic of a test that yields the same responses from people to items that measure the same thing. **14**

internalization The acceptance of others' views and actions as appropriate and right. **10, 18**

interpersonal (family-systems) perspective The view that psychological disorders arise partly from a person's network of social relationships, especially the family. **15**

intrinsic motivation The internal satisfaction of acting competently that explains behavior; those things that are rewarding "in and of themselves." **11**

intrinsic reinforcement and punishment Those self-reactions such as self-esteem and self-reproach that affect a person's learning and behavior. **6**

iodopsin A light-sensitive chemical pigment found in the retina's cone cells. **4**

ions Electrically charged particles. **3**

iris A ring of pigmented tissue that gives the eye its color. It expands and contracts the pupil to control the amount of light that enters the eye. **4**

James-Lange theory The view of William James and Carl Lange that the perception of stimuli in the environment triggers bodily changes that produce the actual experience of emotion. **11**

just noticeable difference From Weber's law, formulated by Gustav Fechner, the minimum difference between two stimuli that can be accurately perceived. **4**

kinesthetic Refers to the senses responsible for detecting the movement of the body, especially the limbs. **4**

Korsakoff's syndrome An acute condition of the memory caused by excess alcohol whereby the person can remember almost nothing about events that occurred since the disorder set in. **5**

latency According to Freud, the fourth psychosexual stage (occurring from age five or six until the start of puberty), during which sexual impulses are repressed while the child learns social and cognitive skills. **13**

latent content In psychoanalysis, the symbolic meanings of dreams that expose unconscious wishes. **5, 16**

law of effect Thorndike's theory that responses that lead to satisfying consequences will be strengthened and are likely to be repeated, whereas responses that lead to unsatisfying consequences will be weakened and are unlikely to occur again. **6**

learned motives Secondary drives, learned through association with the reduction of primary drives.   **11**

learning   A relatively permanent change in observable behavior potential that results from experience with the environment.   **6**

learning perspective   The view that most mental and emotional disorders arise not from unresolved psychic conflicts (as Freud proposed) but rather from inadequate or inappropriate learning.   **15**

lens   A transparent, elastic structure that allows the eye to adjust its focus in accordance with an object's distance.   **4**

limbic system   The innermost borders of the cerebral hemispheres that are involved in emotion, motivation, and sexual and feeding behavior.   **3**

linear perspective   A monocular depth cue; the impression of depth created by the convergence of parallel lines as they recede into the distance.   **4**

linguistic relativity hypothesis   Benjamin Lee Whorf's notion that language heavily influences thought.   **8**

lithium   A drug used to treat bipolar disorder (alternating episodes of mania and depression).   **16**

long-term memory   The storage of information for an indefinite period of time to be used over and over again.   **7**

low-ball phenomenon   A compliance technique based on the idea that a person's decision to perform a certain act often holds even if that action becomes more costly. **18**

major depressive disorder   A condition characterized by one or more episodes of deep sadness and despair, each of which persists virtually all day for a period of at least two weeks.   **15**

malleus   One of a set of three tiny, interconnected bones in the middle

ear that transmit sound from the eardrum to the cochlea.   **4**

mania   A condition that is characterized by one or more periods of exaggerated elation. When depression is combined with mania, the resulting syndrome is known as **bipolar disorder.**   **15**

manifest content   In psychoanalysis, the plot or story line of a dream.   **5, 16**

mean   The arithmetic average of a set of numbers.   **2**

means-end analysis   A heuristic that involves comparing one's current position to the desired state (the "end") and then trying to find a way to attain the end (the "means").   **8**

median   The number that falls in the exact middle of a distribution of numbers arranged from highest to lowest.   **2**

meditation   The focusing of attention on a single stimulus, thus restricting sensory input and producing an altered state of consciousness.   **5**

medulla   The part of the hindbrain that controls autonomic activities, such as circulation and breathing, and is also involved in chewing, salivation, and facial movements.   **3**

memory skill hypothesis   Ericsson's theory that memory is characterized by three properties: meaningful and redundant encoding, rich and highly associated retrieval cues stored with items, and increased performance through tremendous practice.   **7**

menarche   The start of the menstrual cycle.   **10**

mental set   The inclination to apply an old or inappropriate perspective to a new situation.   **8**

mentally gifted   A person whose general intelligence has from childhood been significantly above average.   **14**

mentally retarded   A person whose general intelligence has from childhood been significantly below average, and who consistently has difficulty functioning in everyday settings.   **14**

metabolic rate   The rate at which food energy is burned away.   **12**

metacognition   The ability to monitor one's own thoughts.   **9**

method of loci   A mnemonic device for organizing material when storing it in long-term memory. It involves associating the items to be remembered with a series of places, or loci, already firmly fixed in memory.   **7**

midbrain   A small area in the brain's central core above the hindbrain containing centers for visual and auditory reflexes.   **3**

Minnesota Multiphasic Personality Inventory (MMPI)   A self-report personality test designed to provide a detailed list of a subject's personality traits based on his or her answers to a series of over 550 statements.   **14**

misinformation acceptance   The unconscious adoption of untruths into one's memory after the fact.   **7**

mode   The number or score that is most frequently obtained in a distribution.   **2**

modeling   The process by which someone learns a new behavior by observing other people perform that behavior.   **16**

monoamines   Neurotransmitters such as dopamine, norepinephrine, and serotonin that play critical roles in emotion, movement, learning, and memory.   **3**

monochromats   People whose cones contain only one form of iodopsin and who thus see shades of gray.   **4**

monocular depth cues   Perceptual cues that augment depth perception and are potentially available to one eye only.   **4**

mood disorders People with mood disorders can feel intensely marvelous or miserable for long periods of time and for no apparent reason. As a result, their emotions come to distort their entire outlook and interfere greatly with their normal lives. **15**

mood-congruent recall A bias in retrieving memories where a positive mood may act to screen out negative thoughts and situations, and vice versa. **7**

mood-dependent memory Memory that is easier to retrieve when the person is in the psychological state in which the information was originally stored. **7**

Moro reflex A startle response that occurs in reaction to an intense, sudden movement or noise. **9**

morphemes The combining of phonemes into meaningful units of speech that cannot be subdivided without losing their meaning. **8**

motion parallax A monocular depth cue; the differences in the relative movement of retinal images that occur when we change position. **4**

motivation That which gives impetus to behavior by arousing, sustaining, and directing it toward the attainment of goals. **11**

multiple memory systems Endel Tulving's theory that memory is composed of a hierarchy of systems consisting of procedural memories (the most basic), semantic memory (relying on verbal abilities), and episodic memory (relating to specific episodes in the past). **7**

myelin sheath The fatty, whitish substance around an axon. **3**

narcissistic personality disorder A personality disorder characterized by an overblown sense of one's own importance. **15**

narcolepsy A condition in which a wide-awake person loses muscle control and lapses into sleep. **5**

nativism A theory that language acquisition is controlled by the genetically programmed development of certain neural circuits in the brain. **9**

nativist view A theory of perceptual development, linked to the direct perspective, which holds that perceptual processes are accounted for partly by learning and partly by the ways in which sensory systems work. **4**

natural concepts Categories used in daily thought to classify objects. They are believed to be encoded through prototypes, not a list of defining features. **8**

naturalistic observation The study of subjects in a natural setting without interference or distraction from the investigator. **2**

negative punishment A punishment that involves the removal of some desired stimulus. **6**

negative reinforcement Reinforcement that strengthens a response because the response removes some painful or unpleasant stimulus or enables the individual to avoid it. **6**

negative state relief model A model of behavior holding that we seek relief from negative moods by doing something positive, something that will lift our spirits. **18**

nerve deafness A hearing disorder resulting from damage to the basilar membrane and hair cells. **4**

nerves Bundles of neurons that transmit messages by electrochemical impulses from one part of the body to another. **3**

neuroscience An approach to understanding personality that explains thoughts, feelings, and behaviors in terms of the workings of the brain and nervous system. **1**

neuroscientists Psychologists who study how basic processes are controlled by the nervous system, of

which the brain is the central part. **1**

neurotransmitters Chemical substances that diffuse across synapses and activate receptor sites on adjacent cells. **3**

nodes of Ranvier Gaps in the myelin sheath of an axon that help speed the action potential impulses. **3**

non-REM sleep All the stages of sleep, collectively, when rapid eye movement (REM) is absent. **5**

nonshared environmental influences The effects of unique experiences of each individual. **2**

norepinephrine A monoamine (neurotransmitter) found in the limbic system and frontal cortex of the brain. It plays a role in arousal and mood. **3**

normal curve A line graph of a distribution having a bell-shaped curve. **2**

normal distribution A statistical distribution showing a normal curve. **2**

norms Standards of performance for a test. **14**

obedience Following the specific commands of a person in authority. **18**

obesity An excess of body weight. **12**

object permanence The ability to represent objects "in the head"—to know that things exist even when they cannot be physically sensed. **9**

object relations theory An approach to the ego that emphasizes the importance of early attachments to the development of the child's ego, the child's feelings about the self, and later interpersonal relationships. **13**

observational learning The process of learning how to act by watching the behavior of others. **6, 13**

obsession   An unwanted thought or image that keeps intruding into consciousness, despite a person's efforts to dismiss it.   **15**

occipital lobes   A rear portion of each cerebral hemisphere that is concerned with the reception and analysis of visual information.   **3**

Oedipus conflict   According to Freud, the tendency of children to see themselves as rivals of the same-sex parent for the affection of the parent of the opposite sex. When resolved, the conflict leads to adoption of the values of the same-sex parent.   **10**

olfaction   The sense of smell.   **4**

operant conditioning   Learning to either make or withhold a particular response because of its consequences.   **6**

opiates   Narcotics such as morphine and heroin that mimic the action of endorphins, thus modulating pain and pleasure.   **3**

opponent-process theory   Proposed by Ewald Hering, the theory of color vision stating that there are four primary colors which, when linked in complementary pairs in the brain, form "opponent" systems. One opponent system contains cells that are stimulated by red and inhibited by green, and others that are stimulated by green and inhibited by red. In a second opponent system, yellow and blue similarly act in opposition to each other. A third opponent system is achromatic and enables the perception of brightness.   **4**

optic nerve   The nerve that carries visual information from the eye to the brain.   **4**

optimal arousal theory   The view that humans are motivated to maintain a comfortable level of arousal. If they are understimulated, they act to increase their arousal. If overstimulated, they act to bring their level of arousal down.   **11**

oral stage   According to Freud, the first psychosexual stage (occurring during the first year of life) in which sexual pleasure is focused on the mouth's activities.   **13**

orgasmic phase   The third stage of Masters and Johnson's sexual response cycle, characterized by strong muscle contractions, rise in blood pressure and heartbeat, and extremely heightened arousal accompanied by feelings of intense pleasure as muscle tension is released.   **11**

out-groups   Those groups to which one does not belong.   **17**

oval window   A membrane between the middle ear and the inner ear that transmits sound to the cochlea.   **4**

overextension   The phenomenon that occurs when a young child uses a word to describe many similar things. For example, the word *dada* is used in reference to every male person the child encounters.   **9**

overregularization   The tendency of preschoolers to overextend a grammatical rule to instances where it does not apply.   **9**

Pacinian corpuscles   Receptors deep under the skin surface sensitive to pressure within muscles and internal organs.   **4**

panic disorder   An anxiety disorder in which the sufferer experiences sudden, inexplicable attacks of intense fear that last for minutes or even hours.   **15**

papillae   The bumpy, hill-like projections on the top surface of the tongue that contain the taste buds.   **4**

paradoxical intention   A technique used in family therapy in which the therapist demands that a person with negative symptoms continue to display or even intensify those symptoms, as a first step in gaining control over the problem.   **16**

parasympathetic nervous system   The division of the autonomic nervous system that dominates under conditions of relaxation and tends to conserve the body's energy.   **3**

parietal lobes   A portion of the cerebral hemisphere, behind the frontal lobes on the opposite side of the cortex's central fissure, concerned with skin senses and the sense of body position.   **3**

partial overlap   The illusion, created when one object partially covers another, that the covered object is farther away.   **4**

partial reinforcement   Reinforcing a desired behavior only part of the time.   **6**

participant modeling   A therapeutic technique in which the therapist serves as a model by performing activities feared by the patient and then guiding the patient through a series of steps culminating in the same activity.   **16**

passionate love   According to Robert Sternberg, a romantic love, based on strong physical attraction and characterized by emotional highs and lows.   **17**

Pavlovian conditioning   See **classical conditioning.**   **6**

peg word method   A mnemonic device that involves associating items to be learned with appropriate key words that are easily visualized.   **7**

perception   The process in which the brain interprets sensations, giving them order and meaning.   **4**

perceptual constancy   The tendency of the brain to perceive objects with stable properties even though the visual images received are constantly changing.   **4**

perceptual illusions   Perceptions that differ from the true characteristics of objects.   **4**

perceptual set   A frame of mind that "sets" or readies a person to perceive stimuli in a certain way.   **4**

peripheral nervous system (PNS)
The branch of the nervous system that conveys signals from the body's sensory receptors to the central nervous system and transmits messages back to the muscles and glands.   **3**

permissive   A parenting style, identified by Diana Baumrind, characterized by responsiveness, coupled, however, with a failure to set firm limits or to require age-appropriate behavior.   **10**

person schema   A set of logically integrated ideas about what a particular person is like, which is used to help us interpret the meaning of the person's behavior.   **17**

personality   All the relatively stable and distinctive styles of thought, behavior, and emotional response that characterize a person's adaptations to surrounding circumstances.   **13**

personality development   The emergence of the distinctive styles of thought, feeling, and behavior that make each human being a unique individual.   **10**

personality disorders   Deep-seated maladaptive patterns of relating to others that cause distress either to the victim, those around the victim, or both.   **15**

personality psychology   The branch of psychology concerned with describing and explaining individual differences in behavior.   **1**

persuasive communications   A message consciously intended to persuade or to promote attitude change.   **17**

phallic stage   According to Freud, the third psychosexual stage (occurring from about the third to the fifth or sixth year of life), during which a child struggles with identification with the same-sex parent.   **13**

phobia   An irrational fear that is focused on some specific object or situation.   **15**

phonemes   The smallest units of sound in a language.   **8**

photons   Subatomic particles of light radiation.   **4**

pinna   The projection of skin-covered cartilage visible on the outside of the head, through which sound enters the outer ear.   **4**

pituitary gland   A small endocrine gland at the base of the brain that controls a wide range of bodily functions and that has been called the "master gland."   **3**

place theory   Proposed by Hermann von Helmholtz, a theory about how the brain distinguishes among tones of different pitches. It argues that each pitch we hear depends on the area of the basilar membrane that vibrates most in response to a given sound wave.   **4**

plateau stage   The second stage of Masters and Johnson's sexual response cycle, characterized by heightened arousal.   **11**

pleasure principle   According to Freud, the principle of mental functioning of the id whereby physical tensions are reduced by gratification of instinctual drives without regard to logic, reality, or morality.   **13**

polygraph   Often called a lie detector, this instrument monitors the physiological changes (blood pressure, heart rate, and the like) that accompany emotion.   **11**

pons   The structure of the brain that transmits information about body movement from the higher brain centers and spinal cord to the cerebellum, and is vital in integrating movements between the right and left sides of the brain.   **3**

pornography   Material that is designed to sexually arouse its viewers or readers.   **18**

positive punishment   A punishment that involves an unpleasant stimulus following a behavior.   **6**

positive reinforcement   The strengthening of a conditioned re-sponse because the response is followed by a positive or pleasant stimulus.   **6**

postconventional level   According to Kohlberg, the final stage in moral development during which a person recognizes that universal ethical principles can transcend specific societal laws. Failure to adhere to these principles brings self-condemnation.   **10**

postreinforcement pause   In a fixed-interval reinforcement schedule, the period of time immediately following reinforcement, when relatively few responses are made.   **6**

posttraumatic stress disorder (PTSD)   A state of anxiety, depression, and psychological "numbing" following exposure to severe trauma.   **12, 15**

pragmatics   The field that studies the implicit understandings people have about how language should be used in different social contexts.   **8, 9**

preconventional level   According to Kohlberg, the early stage in moral development during which a child adheres to the rules of society because he or she fears the consequences of breaking them.   **10**

predictive validity   The type of validity a test has if results can be correlated with people's future performance.   **14**

prejudice   An inflexible negative attitude toward members of a minority group that is based on erroneous or incomplete information.   **17**

premature ejaculation   A common sexual complaint characterized by ejaculation before both partners are mutually satisfied.   **11**

preoperational period   The second stage of Piaget's theory of intellectual growth (from age two through six), during which a child understands complex events but cannot use mental operations or coordinate thoughts into logical systems. **9**

prepared learning Learning for which an organism is biologically predisposed. **6**

primacy effect The principle that information perceived first tends to outweigh later information; this explains the strength of first impressions. **17**

primary appraisal The first level of Lazarus's cognitive appraisal, where we assess whether what is happening is relevant to our personal well-being, or how it might affect us. **11**

primary drives The most fundamental drives—the ones arising from needs that are built into our physiological systems. **11**

primary empathy The first step in client-centered therapy during which the therapist mirrors a client's feelings. **16**

primary erectile failure A sexual dysfunction in which the man has never been able to have an erection. **11**

primary orgasmic dysfunction A sexual dysfunction in which the woman has never experienced an orgasm. **11**

primary reinforcer In operant conditioning experiments, the reward that establishes and maintains the conditioned response. **6**

priming The unconscious activation of a schema, which then encourages ideas associated with that schema to come readily to mind. **17**

procedural memories Learned associations between stimuli and responses that allow a person to easily perform motor skills. **7**

projection According to Freud, a defense mechanism that involves the unknown attribution of one's own objectionable impulses to other people. **13**

projective test A personality test in which a person is shown ambigu-

ous pictures and asked to describe them. **14**

propositions The smallest "idea units" in a sentence. **8**

proprioceptive Refers to the senses responsible for awareness of body and limb position. **4**

prototype An example that best illustrates a concept; the means by which natural concepts are thought to be encoded in memory. **8**

proximity The principle of gestalt psychology that stimuli close together tend to be seen as a group. **4**

psychiatrist A medical doctor who specializes in the diagnosis and treatment of mental disorders. **1**

psychoactive Refers to a drug that interacts with the central nervous system to alter a person's mood, perception, mode of thinking, and behavior. **5**

psychoanalysis Freudian psychotherapy that probes a person's current thoughts and feelings for clues to unconscious conflicts. **1, 15, 16**

psychoanalyst Usually a psychiatrist (although sometimes a layperson or psychologist) who has had advanced training in psychoanalysis and who has been psychoanalyzed as part of that training. **1**

psychoanalytic theory (psychosexual approach) A view of social and personality development initiated by Freud that emphasizes childhood experiences as critically important in shaping adult personality. **1, 10, 13, 15**

psychological needs In Abraham Maslow's hierarchy, all higher-level needs, including both the need to develop a sense of belonging and the need to achieve competence, recognition, and high self-esteem. **13**

psychology The scientific study of behavior, both external observable action and internal thought. **1**

psychoneuroimmunology A subfield of psychology that examines how psychological factors alter the immune system and ultimately increase the risk of immune system–related diseases such as AIDS, cancer, arthritis, infections, and allergies. **12**

psychopharmacology The study of the link between drugs and behavior. **1**

psychosocial theory Erik Erikson's view of social and personality development that emphasizes eight developmental challenges and two possible outcomes for each. **10**

psychosurgery A high-risk surgical procedure with irreversible effects. It is the most extreme of the biological treatments. **16**

psychotherapy A systematic series of interactions between a person who is trained in alleviating psychological problems and another who is suffering from them. **16**

punishment A stimulus that decreases the frequency of a response. **6**

pupil The opening in the center of the eye through which light enters and travels to the retina. **4**

racism Prejudice directed toward members of certain racial groups. **17**

random sampling A technique in which every member of the population has an equal chance of being included. **2**

range The difference between the highest and lowest scores of a set of scores. **2**

rape myth The idea that women mean "yes" when they say "no," and in fact secretly wish to be raped. **18**

rapid eye movement (REM) sleep A stage of sleep when a person experiences rapid eye movement. Vivid dreaming appears to take place primarily during episodes of REM sleep. **5**

rational-emotive therapy (RET)
Albert Ellis's cognitive-behavior treatment. It seeks to replace irrational, problem-provoking outlooks with more realistic ones. **16**

rationalization According to Freud, a defense mechanism whereby one attempts to explain failure or shortcomings in nonthreatening ways. **13**

reaction formation According to Freud, a defense mechanism that involves the replacement of an anxiety-producing impulse or feeling with its direct opposite. **13**

reaction range The range of social and developmental possibilities that depend on the person's experiences. **10**

reality principle According to Freud, the operating principle of the ego based on the need for gratification of instinctual drives to be curbed by the realistic demands of the environment. Gratification is thereby modified or delayed to ensure the safety of the individual. **13**

recall The retrieval of specific pieces of information from long-term memory, usually guided by cues. **7**

receptor cells Cells embedded in the sense organs that are sensitive to various types of stimulation from the environment. **3**

recognition Realizing that a particular stimulus was encountered previously and matches something stored in long-term memory. **7**

recuperative theory The theory that sleep is a time for the body to repair and recover from the day's activities. **5**

regression According to Freud, a defense mechanism that involves a return to behaviors characteristic of an earlier stage in life; a special type of correlational technique that uses the relationship between variables to make specific predictions. **2, 13**

rehearsal The conscious repetition of information in an effort to retain it in short-term memory, usually involving speech. **7**

reinforcement (reward) A stimulus that increases the frequency of a response. **6**

relative closeness A monocular depth cue; objects that are closer to the horizon are generally seen as more distant. **4**

relative size A monocular depth cue; of two objects thought to be the same size, the one that casts the smaller retinal image is perceived to be farther away. **4**

reliable (reliability) Refers to a test that consistently yields the same results. Reliability is an essential criterion in determining the value of a test. **14**

REM rebound Compensation for lost REM sleep on one night by more REM sleep the next night. **5**

replication Reconstruction of the basic features of a study to see if the results are similar. **2**

representational thought The ability to represent objects mentally when they are no longer physically present. **9**

representative sample A sample in which important subgroups are represented according to their incidence in the population as a whole. **2**

representativeness heuristic A heuristic by which given information is matched with a stereotype. **8**

repression The psychological defense mechanism, first described by Freud, by which people push unacceptable, anxiety-provoking thoughts and impulses into the unconscious to avoid confronting them directly.
7, 11, 13

resistance In psychoanalysis, attempts by the patient to block treatment. **16**

resolution stage The final stage of Masters and Johnson's sexual response cycle, characterized by the gradual reduction of heart rate, blood pressure, and muscle tension as the body returns to normal. **11**

resting potential The electrical imbalance that occurs across the cell membrane when a cell is polarized; in this state, the nerve cell membrane is negatively charged inside and positively charged outside. **3**

reticular formation Clusters of neurons and nerve fibers that extend from the spinal cord to the thalamus, acting as a sentry system to arouse the forebrain and also affecting the sleep-waking cycle. **3**

retina The light-sensitive inner surface of the eyeball. The retina is a predominantly neural structure consisting of several layers, including a layer of rods and cones. **4**

retrieval The process of finding stored memories and making them available for use. **7**

retrieval cues Bits of information that are related to items stored in long-term memory. **7**

retrograde A form of amnesia that involves a memory loss for only a segment of the past, not for the recollection of new events. **7**

rhodopsin The deep red pigment in the rods of the eye. **4**

rods Long, thin receptor cells in the periphery of the retina that are sensitive to light of low intensity and that function in dim light and nighttime vision. **4**

rooting reflex The tendency of a baby to turn toward any object that gently touches its cheek. **9**

Rorschach Inkblot Test A projective psychological test in which people look at ten inkblots and report what they see in each. The responses are evaluated for their emotional expression, their focus, and their recurring patterns. **14**

sample A selected segment of the available data that is representative of the whole. **2**

scalloping In a fixed-interval reinforcement schedule, a scalloped pattern on a graph made by a cumulative record. It indicates a high rate of response just before reinforcement and a pause in responding immediately after. **6**

scanning hypothesis Proposed by William Dement, the theory that rapid eye movements accompanying dreams may be due to the dreamer "watching" the activity in the dream. **5**

schedules of reinforcement The way in which rewards are given for appropriate behavior. **6**

schemes Mental representations of objects and events against which incoming data can be compared and interpreted. **1, 4, 7, 13**

schizophrenia A severe mental disorder characterized by disturbances in thought, emotion, perception, and behavior. **15**

Scholastic Aptitude Test (SAT) A verbal and mathematical test developed by the College Entrance Examination Board and designed to measure "aptitude for college studies." **14**

school psychologists Practitioners who apply psychological knowledge in the areas of learning difficulties and behavior problems among elementary and secondary school students. **1**

scientific theories Attempts to go beyond a single case or experiment, and provide a larger explanation that applies to many situations. **1**

seasonal affective disorder (SAD) A mood disorder related to changes in the seasons. It occurs in response to a relative lack of sunlight, most often in the winter. **15**

secondary appraisal The second level of Lazarus's cognitive appraisal where we evaluate our options and resources, or how we might respond to the problem. **11**

secondary drives Drives learned through association with the reduction of primary drives. **11**

secondary erectile failure A condition in which the man has problems maintaining an erection in some situations. **11**

secondary orgasmic dysfunction A condition in which the woman may sometimes experience orgasm, but not with her primary sexual partner or during intercourse. **11**

secondary reinforcer In operant conditioning experiments, a stimulus that does not satisfy an inherent biological need but has acquired reinforcing properties through association with primary reinforcers. **6**

secondary sexual characteristics The physical features of gender identity not directly involved with reproduction, such as the development of pubic hair, changes in voice, etc. **10**

secure attachment The type of bond between infant and caregiver characterized by the expectation that the caregiver will be available and responsive. **10**

selective attention The brain's ability to screen out some information entering a particular sensory channel and focus primarily on only one aspect of information entering the same channel. **7**

self-actualization According to Carl Rogers, the striving for the fulfillment of one's own capabilities and potential. **1, 13**

self-efficacy The feeling people have of being able to deal effectively with a situation. **13**

self-fulfilling prophecy The phenomenon whereby investigators' expectations influence their findings. **2, 17**

self-help group A group of people who share a particular problem and meet to discuss it among themselves, without the active involvement of a professional therapist. **16**

self-instructional training Donald Meichenbaum's cognitive-behavior treatment in which he teaches clients how to think rational and positive thoughts in stressful situations, instead of plunging into old, self-defeating internal monologues. **16**

self-perception theory Daryl Bem's theory that people infer their attitudes by observing their own behavior and the circumstances surrounding it, much as they infer the attitudes of others. **17**

self-reports A method of measuring variables by recording and tallying the responses of subjects about their behavior, thoughts, feelings, and attitudes. **14**

self-schemas Organized sets of knowledge about the self that guide the perception and interpretation of information in social situations. **13, 17**

self-serving bias The tendency of an individual to take credit for successes and find situational excuses for failures. **17**

semantic The aspects of language that have to do with comprehension and expression of meaning. **8**

semantic memory Mental representation of objects, states, and qualities in a person's world. **7**

sensation The process in which the stimulation of receptor cells in various parts of the body sends nerve impulses to the brain. **4**

sensorimotor period The first stage of Piaget's theory of intellectual growth (from birth to about two years), during which an infant learns through perceiving sensations and physical actions. **9**

sensory adaptation The reduced ability of a sensory system to provide information after prolonged, constant stimulation. **4**

sensory memory The momentary lingering of sensory information after a stimulus has been removed. **7**

sensory threshold The minimum stimulus needed to produce a detectable sensation. **4**

septum One of three interrelated structures of the limbic system; the others are the hippocampus and amygdala. **3**

serotonin A monoamine (neurotransmitter) found in the thalamus and brain stem. It is suspected to have an important influence on arousal-related activities such as sleep. **3**

setpoint The level of fat that the brain considers normal. When body fat goes significantly above setpoint, loss of appetite sets in; when body fat falls significantly below it, hunger takes over. **12**

sexism Prejudice directed toward one sex, almost always women. **17**

sexual dysfunction Any persistent or recurring problem that prevents a person from engaging in sexual relations or from reaching orgasm during sex. **11**

sexual response cycle The sequence of four physiological stages of human sexual response identified by Masters and Johnson. **11**

shallow processing (maintenance rehearsal) The mental activity that is inattentive and rote, concerned only with superficial features of a stimulus without consideration of the *meaning* of the stimulus; this information can be maintained only in short-term memory. **7**

shaping A method developed by B. F. Skinner in which an animal is systematically reinforced for displaying closer and closer approxi-

mations of the desired response. **6**

shared environmental influences The effects of family environment, which are common to all members of the household. **2**

short-term memory The conscious awareness of what you are actively thinking about at any particular moment. **7**

similarity A gestalt principle of organization proposing that objects will be perceived as groups if they are similar in shape, color, texture, and the like. **4**

simultaneous conditioning Presenting the conditioned stimulus at the same time as the unconditioned stimulus. **6**

single-blind technique A procedure in which the experimenter knows who is in the experimental group and who is in the control group but the subjects do not. **2**

Skinner box A small compartment that provides a controlled setting in which an animal may be trained to perform a specific behavior for a reward. **6**

sleep apnea A biological factor in insomnia; when muscles of the throat relax and shut off air passages, repeated shortages of oxygen cause the sleeper to awake and gasp for air. **5**

social cognition The process of making sense of other people and ourselves. **17**

social cognitive approach A perspective on personality that is based on the principles of learning and information processing. It focuses on the different ways in which individuals interpret events and on how these interpretations shape their styles of coping with the problems of everyday life. **13**

social comparison theory One of the earliest and most enduring theories of happiness, it holds that to determine whether you are satisfied with your life, you look at the

people around you and compare your life to theirs. **11**

social development The ways in which a person's interactions and relationships with others change as that person grows older. **10**

social facilitation The tendency for people's performance to improve in the presence of others. **18**

social learning perspective A view of social and personality development that emphasizes the role of the external environment in shaping behavior. **10**

social learning theory The belief of cognitive psychologists that a great deal of learning is accomplished by observation of other people's behavior, often in the absence of reinforcement. **6**

social loafing The tendency for people to slack off when they are part of a group. **18**

social psychologists Researchers who study how environmental factors, especially the presence of others, influence individual perception, belief, motivation, and behavior. **1**

Social Readjustment Rating Scale (SRRS) A table developed by Thomas Holmes and Richard Rahe consisting of forty-three common life events, ranking their stress value according to the degree of adjustment required. **12**

social smile One aspect of infant behavior, triggered by the sight of the human face, by which the infant enhances its prospects for survival by attracting the attention of the caregiver. **10**

social stereotype A set of beliefs about the way members of a particular group think and act. **17**

socialization Learning the expectations and values of one's society. **10**

sociobiology The systematic study of the biological basis of all social behavior. **11, 18**

sociocultural perspective   The view that the roots of mental disturbance often lie in social ills such as poverty, poor nutrition, inadequate housing, crime, and discrimination.   **15**

somatic   Refers to those senses responsible for sensations of the skin, detecting the movement in the body (especially the limbs), and awareness of body and limb position.   **4**

somatic nervous system   The division of the peripheral nervous system that controls the skeletal muscles.   **3**

somatoform disorder   The presence of one or more symptoms of a physical dysfunction for which there is no identifiable organic cause.   **15**

split-halves   A procedure for randomly dividing a test into two halves, and comparing subjects and scores on both halves to measure the test's reliability.   **14**

spontaneous recovery   The temporary reappearance of an extinguished response when an organism is returned to the original learning situation.   **6**

standard deviation   A measure of variability showing average extent to which all the numbers in a particular set vary from the mean.   **2**

standardization   The process of developing uniform procedures for giving and scoring a test.   **14**

Stanford-Binet test   The Stanford University revision of Binet's test. It is currently employed, usually with children, to judge intelligence by verbal and performance tests grouped according to the subjects' age levels.   **14**

stapes   One of a set of three tiny, interconnected bones in the middle ear that transmit sound from the eardrum to the cochlea.   **4**

stereotype   A preconceived idea of what members of a particular group are like.   **17**

stimulants   Drugs that produce physiological and mental arousal by stimulating the central nervous system.   **5**

stimulus   Any form of energy to which an organism is capable of responding.   **4**

stimulus control   A behavioral therapy technique that focuses on rearranging the environment—the cues that are often associated with problem behaviors. The association between the environment and the desired response is achieved by eliminating all other options.   **6, 16**

stimulus discrimination   The process of learning to make a particular response only to a particular stimulus.   **6**

stimulus generalization   The performance of a learned response in the presence of a similar stimulus.   **6**

storage   The way in which information is kept in memory for later use.   **7**

strategies   Specific techniques or procedures people use to work on their life tasks.   **13**

stress   That which a person appraises as harmful, threatening, or challenging.   **12**

Strong-Campbell Interest Inventory (SCII)   A test designed to measure a subject's pattern of interests in order to aid in occupational choices.   **14**

structural family therapy   A family-systems therapy developed by Minuchin that involves role playing to teach the families of schizophrenics new and different ways to communicate.   **16**

structuralism   Developed by Wilhelm Wundt, the study of how the basic units of human consciousness form the organization, or structure, of the mind.   **1**

subgoal analysis   A heuristic by which a problem is analyzed into a

set of manageable smaller problems.   **8**

sublimation   According to Freud, a defense mechanism whereby forbidden impulses are redirected toward the pursuit of socially desirable goals.   **11, 13**

subliminal perception   The brain's ability to register a stimulus presented so briefly or weakly that it cannot be consciously perceived.   **4**

substance-related disorders   Psychological disturbances resulting from abuse of drugs or alcohol.   **15**

sucking reflex   The reflex that helps the baby to begin nursing. When an object is placed in the baby's mouth, the baby automatically begins to suck.   **9**

superego   According to Freud, that part of the personality that represents the ideals and moral standards of society, as conveyed to the child by his or her parents.   **10, 13**

superstitious behavior   Behavior that is strengthened or weakened because by chance it happens to precede reinforcement or punishment.   **6**

surveys   Attempts to estimate the opinions, characteristics, or behaviors of a particular population by investigation of a representative sample.   **2**

sympathetic nervous system   The division of the autonomic nervous system that mobilizes the body's resources in an emergency or stress situation.   **3**

synapse   The area surrounding a synaptic cleft, including the tip of the axon on one side and the receiving cell's membrane on the other.   **3**

synaptic cleft   The tiny gap that separates neuronal axons from adjacent cells.   **3**

synaptic transmission   The passing of information from one neuron to another.   **3**

syntactic   The rules of a language that determine the allowable combinations of words, phrases, and sentences.   **8**

systematic desensitization   A technique in behavioral therapy for reducing anxiety or removing phobias by pairing muscle relaxation with the presentation of potentially threatening objects or situations in hierarchical order, from least to most feared.   **6, 16**

tardive dyskinesia   Uncontrollable physical behaviors, including grotesque facial movements, that are an apparently irreversible side effect of prolonged use of antipsychotic drugs.   **16**

tasks   Goals we set for ourselves, the ideals for which we strive.   **13**

telegraphic speech   The tendency of very young children to construct short sentences made up entirely of nouns and action verbs, without articles, conjunctions, or modifiers, for example, "car go."   **9**

temperament   A relatively stable behavioral disposition that can be seen in an individual's behavior.   **10**

temporal lobes   The area of each cerebral hemisphere that is concerned with hearing and visual processing.   **3**

test-retest   A procedure for administering a test to the same people on more than one occasion to measure its reliability.   **14**

texture gradients   An influence on depth perception in which highly textured near objects appear coarser, and more distant ones appear finer.   **4**

thalamus   A structure above the midbrain that relays information from the sensory organs to the cerebral cortex.   **3**

that's-not-all technique   A compliance strategy in which a small, usually preplanned concession is made to "sweeten" the deal.   **18**

Thematic Apperception Test (TAT)   A projective psychological test in which a subject's responses to a series of cards with ambiguous scenes are analyzed on an individual basis.   **14**

time out   An operant-conditioning therapy technique that involves following undesirable behavior with a period of time away from positive reinforcement.   **16**

tip-of-the-tongue phenomenon   The experience of feeling as though something is stored somewhere in one's memory but cannot be located quickly.   **7**

token economies   Structured environments in which objects such as poker chips are used as rewards that may be exchanged by patients for desired activities or objects; a technique used in operant-conditioning therapy.   **6, 16**

trace conditioning   Presenting the conditioned stimulus before the unconditioned stimulus, but with a somewhat longer delay than in forward conditioning, thus reducing contiguity.   **6**

trait   According to J. P. Guilford, any relatively enduring way in which one individual differs from another.   **13**

trait theories   A perspective on personality that organizes human behavior according to characteristics, or traits, that distinguish a person and can be objectively measured.   **13**

transference   In psychoanalysis, the transfer to the analyst of feelings of love and hostility that were originally directed toward a client's parents or other authority figure.   **16**

trichromatic   The theory of color vision that only three different types of color receptors in the eye (blue, green, and red) are necessary for detecting every color on the visible spectrum.   **4**

Type A personality   A label for people who display an excessive competitive drive, aggressiveness, hostility, and impatience, and are prone to heart disease.   **13**

Type B personality   A label for people who are calmer and more relaxed than Type A personalities and also less susceptible to heart disease.   **13**

unconditional positive regard   In Carl Rogers' humanistic treatment, acceptance and support that a therapist would give to a client regardless of what he or she said or did.   **16**

unconditioned response (UR)   A response elicited by an unconditioned stimulus without any form of learning.   **6**

unconditioned stimulus (US)   A stimulus that elicits an unconditioned response without any form of learning.   **6**

underextension   The phenomenon that occurs when a young child uses a general term in a very limited situation. For example, the word *dog is* used to describe the family pet but not the neighbor's dog.   **9**

utility   The value one places on potential outcomes in a decision-making situation.   **8**

vaginismus   A sexual dysfunction of women characterized by involuntary muscle spasms that cause the vagina to shut tightly so that penetration by a penis is extremely painful or impossible.   **11**

valid (validity)   An essential criterion in determining the value of a test. A test is valid if it measures what it is supposed to measure.   **14**

variable-interval (VI) schedule   An unpredictable and irregular partial reinforcement schedule in which there is no perceived relationship between the time elapsed and the frequency of rewards.   **6**

variable-ratio (VR) schedule An unpredictable and irregular partial reinforcement schedule in which there is no perceived relationship between the number of responses and the number of rewards.   **6**

variables   Factors capable of change.   **2**

vicarious reinforcement and punishment   Environmental consequences following the behavior of others that affect how an observer will behave.   **6**

violent pornography   Material that combines sexual explicitness with violence.   **18**

volley principle   A theory that explains why people can hear high-frequency sound. It is based on the assumption that the frequency of neural firing that the brain detects is determined not by the rate of firing of single neurons but rather by groups of neurons.   **4**

wavelength   A measure of the physical distance between the crest of one light wave and the crest of the next.   **4**

Weber's law   Formulated by Gustav Fechner, a law stating that the amount by which a stimulus must be increased to produce a "just noticeable difference" in sensation is always a constant proportion of the initial stimulus intensity.   **4**

Wechsler scales   The Wechsler Adult Intelligence Scale (WAIS), the Wechsler Intelligence Scale for Children (WISC), and the Wechsler Preschool and Primary Scale of Intelligence (WPPSI). Along with the Stanford-Binet, these are the most frequently used individual intelligence tests. They differ from the Stanford-Binet in several ways, primarily in yielding not a single IQ score but separate scores for each subtest.   **14**

Yerkes-Dodson law   A law of motivation stating that performance is best when stimulation or arousal is intermediate, not too high or too low.   **11**

REFERENCES

Aanstoos, C. M. (1991). Experimental psychology and the challenge of real life. *American Psychologist, 46,* 77–78.

Aber, J. L., & Allen, J. P. (1987). Effects of maltreatment on young children's socioemotional development: An attachment theory perspective. *Developmental Psychology, 23*(3), 406–414.

Abraham, K. (1911/1948). *Notes on psychoanalytic investigation and treatment of manic-depressive insanity and allied conditions* (D. Bryan & A. Strachey, Trans.). London: Hogarth Press.

Abraham, K. (1916/1948). *The first pregenital stage of the libido* (D. Bryan & A. Strachey, Trans.). London: Hogarth Press.

Abrams, R. (1992). *Electroconvulsive therapy* (2nd ed.). New York: Oxford University Press.

Abramson, L. Y., Metalsky, G. I., & Alloy, L. B. (1989). The hopelessness theory of depression: A metatheoretical analysis with implications for psychopathology research. *Psychological Review, 96,* 358–372.

Ackroyd, P. (1984). *T.S. Eliot: A life.* New York: Simon & Schuster.

Acredolo, L. P., & Hake, J. L. (1982). Infant perception. In B. B. Wolman (Ed.), *Handbook of developmental psychology.* Englewood Cliffs, NJ: Erlbaum.

Adair, J. G. (1984). The Hawthorne effect: A reconsideration of the methodological artifact. *Journal of Applied Psychology, 69,* 334–345.

Adams, D. B., Gold, A. R., & Burt, A. D. (1978). Rise in female-initiated sexual activity at ovulation and its suppression by oral contraceptives. *New England Journal of Medicine, 299,* 1145–1150.

Adams, J. D. (1978). Improving stress management: An action-research based OD intervention. In W. W. Burke (Ed.), *The cutting edge.* La Jolla, CA: University Associates.

Adams, J. L. (1976). *Conceptual blockbusting: A pleasurable guide to better problem solving.* San Francisco: San Francisco Book Co.

Adams, M. J. (1990). *Beginning to read: Thinking and learning about print.* Cambridge, MA: MIT Press.

Adams, M. J. (1994). The progress of the whole-language debate. *Educational Psychologist, 29,* 217–222.

Adams, M. J., & Bruck, M. (1995). Resolving the "Great Debate." *American-Educator, 19,* 7–20.

Adelmann, P. K., & Zajonc, R. B. (1989). Facial efference and the experience of emotion. In M. R. Rosenzweig & L. W. Porter (Eds.), *Annual Review of Psychology* (Vol. 40, pp. 249–280). Palo Alto, CA: Annual Reviews, Inc.

Adler, A. (1930). Individual psychology. In C. A. Murchison (Ed.), *Psychologies of 1930* (pp. 395–405). Worcester, MA: Clark University Press.

Adorno, T. W., Frenkel-Brunswick, E., Levinson, D. J., & Sanford, R. N. (1950). *The authoritarian personality.* New York: Harper & Row.

Agency for Health Care Policy and Research. (1993). *Depression in primary care: Treatment of major depression* (DHHS, AHCPR Publication No. 93:0551). Rockville, MD: Author.

Aiken, L. R. (1997). *Psychological testing and assessment* (9th ed.). Needham Heights, MA: Allyn & Bacon.

Ainsworth, M. (1989). Attachments beyond infancy. *American Psychologist, 44,* 709–716.

Ainsworth, M., Bleher, M., Waters, E., & Wall, S. (1978). *Patterns of attachment.* Hillsdale, NJ: Erlbaum.

Ajzen, I., & Fishbein, M. (1980). *Understanding attitudes and predicting social behavior.* Englewood Cliffs, NJ: Prentice Hall.

Akabas, M. H., Dodd, J., & Al-Awqati, Q. (1988). A bitter substance induces a rise in intercellular calcium in a subpopulation of rat taste cells. *Science, 242,* 1047–1050.

Akbarina, S., Bunney, W. E. J., Potkin, S. G., Wigal, S. B., Hagman, J. O., Sandman, C. A., & Jones, E. G. (1993). Altered distribution of nicotinamide-adenine dinucleotide phosphate-diaphorase neurons in frontal lobes of schizophrenics implies anomalous cortical development. *Archives of General Psychiatry, 50,* 169–177.

Akbarina, S., Vinuela, A., Kim, J. J, Potkin, S. G., Bunney, W. E. J., & Jones, E. G. (1993). Distorted distribution of nicotinamide-adenine dinucleotide phosphate-diaphorase neurons in temporal lobes of schizophrenics implies anomalous cortical development. *Archives of General Psychiatry, 50,* 178–187.

Akiskal, H. S. (1979). A biobehavioral approach to depression. In R. A. Depue (Ed.), *The psychobiology of the depressive disorders.* New York: Academic Press.

Akiskal, H. S., & McKinney, W. T., Jr. (1973). Depressive disorders: Toward a unified hypothesis. *Science, 182,* 20–29.

Akiskal, H. S., & McKinney, W. T., Jr. (1975). Overview of recent research in depression. *Archives of General Psychiatry, 32,* 285–305.

Alarcon, M., & DeFries, J. C. (1997). Reading performance and general cognitive ability in twins with reading difficulties and control pairs. *Personality and Individual Differences, 22,* 793–803.

Alba, J. W., & Hasher, L. (1983). Is memory schematic? *Psychological Bulletin, 93,* 203–231.

Albin, R. L., Young, A. B., & Penney, J. B. (1989). The functional anatomy of basal ganglia disorders. *Trends in Neuroscience, 12,* 366–375.

Alexander, J. F., Holtzworth-Munroe, J. F., & Jameson, P. (1994). The process and outcome of marital and family therapy: Research review and evaluation. In A. E. Bergin & S. L. Garfield (Eds.), *Handbook of psychotherapy and behavior change* (4th ed., pp. 595–630). New York: Wiley.

Alford, B. A., & Beck, A. T. (1997). *The integrative power of cognitive therapy.* New York: Guilford Press.

Allebeck, P., & Allgulander, C. (1990). Psychiatric diagnoses as predictors of suicide: A comparison of diagnoses at conscription and in psychiatric care in a cohort of 50 465 young men. *British Journal of Psychiatry, 159,* 339–344.

Allen, B. P. (1997). *Personality theories: Development, growth, and diversity* (2nd ed.). Needham Heights, MA: Allyn & Bacon.

Allen, L., Cipielewski, J., & Stanovich, K. E. (1992). Multiple indicators of children's reading habits and attitudes: Construct validity and cognitive correlates. *Journal of Educational Psychology, 84,* 489–503.

Allen, M. G. (1976). Twin studies of affective illness. *Archives of General Psychiatry, 27,* 1476–1478.

Alloy, L. B., & Abramson, L. Y. (1979). Judgment of contingency in depressed and nondepressed: Sadder

but wiser? *Journal of Experimental Psychology: General, 108,* 441–485.

Alloy, L. B., Acocella, J., & Bootzin, R. R. (1996). *Abnormal psychology: Current perspectives* (7th ed.). New York: McGraw-Hill.

Allport, F. H. (1920). The influence of the group upon association and thought. *Journal of Experimental Psychology, 3,* 159–182.

Allport, F. H. (1924). *Social psychology.* Boston: Houghton Mifflin.

Allport, G. W. (1961). *Pattern and growth in personality.* New York: Holt, Rinehart & Winston.

Allport, G. W. (1966). Traits revisited. *American Psychologist, 21,* 1–10.

Allport, G. W. (1985). Attitudes. In C. Murchison (Ed.), *Handbook of social psychology.* Worcester, MA: Clark University Press.

Allport, G. W., & Odbert, H. S. (1936). Trait-names: A psycho-texical study. *Psychological Monographs, 47* (Whole No. 211).

Allport, G. W., & Postman, L. J. (1947). *The psychology of rumor.* New York: Holt.

Ambuel, B. (1995). Adolescents, unintended pregnancy, and abortion: The struggle for a compassionate social policy. *Current Directions in Psychological Science, 4,* 1–5.

American Cancer Society. (1989). *Cancer facts and figures—1989.* Atlanta: Author.

American Psychiatric Association. (1994). *Diagnostic and statistical manual of mental disorders* (4th ed.). Washington, DC: Author.

American Psychological Association. (1990). Ethical principles of psychologists. *American Psychologist, 45,* 390–395.

American Psychological Association. (1994/1995). *Graduate study in psychology and associated fields.* Washington, DC: American Psychological Association.

American Psychological Association, Ethics Committee. (1988). Trends

in ethics cases, common pitfalls, and published resources. *American Psychologist, 43,* 564–572.

Amible, T. M. (1983). *The social psychology of creativity.* New York: Springer-Verlag.

Amoore, J. E., Johnston, J. W., Jr., & Rubin, M. (1964). The stereochemical theory of odor. *Scientific American, 210,* 42–49.

Anand, B. K., Chhina, G. S., & Singh, B. (1961). Some aspects of electroencephalographic studies in yogis. *Electroencephalography and Clinical Neurophysiology, 13,* 452–456.

Anastasi, A. (1976). *Psychological testing* (4th ed.). New York: Macmillan.

Anderson, C. A., & DeNeve, K. M. (1992). Temperature, aggression, and the negative affect escape model. *Psychological Bulletin, 111,* 347–351.

Anderson, C. A., Deuser, W. E., & DeNeve, K. M. (1995). Hot temperatures, hostile affect, hostile cognition, and arousal: Tests of a general model of affective aggression. *Personality and Social Psychology Bulletin, 21,* 434–448.

Anderson, J. R. (1995). *Learning and memory: An integrated approach.* New York: Wiley.

Anderson, R. C., & Prichert, J. W. (1978). Recall of previously unrecallable information following a shift in perspective. *Journal of Verbal Learning and Verbal Behavior, 17,* 1–12.

Andreasen, N. C. (1989). Neural mechanisms of negative symptoms. *British Journal of Psychiatry, 155,* 93–98.

Andreasen, N. C., Nasrallah, H. A., Dunn, V., Olson, S. C., Grove, W. M., Ehrhardt, J. C., Coffman, J. A., & Crossett, J. H. (1986). Structural abnormalities in the frontal system in schizophrenia: A magnetic resonance imaging study. *Archives of General Psychiatry, 43,* 136–144.

Andreasen, N. C., & Olsen, S. (1982). Negative versus positive schizophrenia: Definition and validation. *Archives of General Psychiatry, 39,* 789–794.

Andrews, E. A., & Braveman, N. S. (1975). The combined effects of dosage level and interstimulus interval on the formation of one-trial poison-based aversions in rats. *Animal Learning and Behavior, 3,* 287–289.

Andrews, F. M., & Withey, S. B. (1976). *Social indicators of well-being: Americans' perceptions of life quality.* New York: Plenum Press.

Andrews, J. A., & Lewinsohn, P. M. (1992). Suicidal attempts among older adolescents: Prevalence and co-occurrence with psychiatric disorders. *Journal of the American Academy of Child and Adolescent Psychiatry, 31,* 655–662.

Angier, R. P. (1927). The conflict theory of emotion. *American Journal of Psychology, 39,* 390–401.

Archer, J. (1991). Human sociobiology: Basic concepts and limitations. *Journal of Social Issues, 47,* 11–26.

Archer, R. L. (1984). The farmer and the cowman should be friends: An attempt at reconciliation. *Psychological Journal of Personality and Social Psychology, 46,* 709–711.

Arkowitz, H., & Messer, S. B. (Eds.). (1984). *Psychoanalytic therapy and behavior therapy: Is integration possible?* New York: Plenum Press.

Armstrong, R. H. (1965, March). *Gastric secretion during sleep and dreaming.* Paper presented at the Association for the Psychophysiological Study of Sleep, Washington, DC.

Arndt, J., Greenberg, J., Pyszczynski, T., & Solomon, S. (1997). Subliminal exposure to death-related stimuli increases defense for the cultural worldview. *Psychological Science, 8,* 379–385.

Aronfreed, J. (1969). The concept of internalization. In D. A. Goslin (Ed.), *Handbook of socialization theory and research.* Chicago: Rand McNally.

Aronson, E. (1988). *The social animal* (5th ed.). New York: Freeman.

Aronson, E., & Osherow, N. (1980). Cooperation, prosocial behavior, and academic performance: Experiments in the desegregated classroom. In L. Bickman (Ed.), *Applied Social Psychology Annual* (Vol. 1, p. 19). Beverly Hills, CA: Sage.

Arrowood, J., & Short, J. A. (1973). Agreement, attraction, and self-esteem. *Canadian Journal of Behavioral Science, 5,* 242–252.

Asch, S. E. (1951). Effects of group pressure upon the modification and distortion of judgments. In H. S. Guetzkow (Ed.), *Groups, leadership, and man: Research in human relations.* Pittsburgh: Carnegie University Press.

Asch, S. E. (1956). Studies of independence and conformity: A minority of one against a unanimous majority. *Psychological Monographs, 70(9)* (Whole No. 416).

Ashmore, R. D., & Del Boca, F. K. (1976). Psychological approaches to understanding intergroup conflicts. In P. A. Katz (Ed.), *Towards the elimination of racism.* Elmsford, NY: Pergamon Press.

Aslin, R. N., Pisoni, D. B., & Jusczyk, P. W. (1983). Auditory development and speech perception in infancy. In P. Mussen (Ed.), *Handbook of child psychology* (Vol. 2). New York: Wiley.

Aspinwall, L. G., & Taylor, S. E. (1997). A stitch in time: Self-regulation and proactive coping. *Psychological Bulletin, 121,* 417–436.

Atkinson, R. C., & Shiffrin, R. M. (1968). Human memory: A proposed system and its control. In K. W. Spence & J. T. Spence (Eds.), *The psychology of learning and motivation* (Vol. 2). New York: Academic Press.

Atkinson, R. C., & Shiffrin, R. M. (1971). The control of short-term memory. *Scientific American, 225,* 82–90.

Ault, R. L. (1983). *Children's cognitive development* (2nd ed.). Oxford: Oxford University Press.

Averill, J. R. (1982). *Anger and aggression: An essay on emotion.* New York: Springer-Verlag.

Averill, J. R. (1983). Studies on anger and aggression: Implications for theories of emotion. *American Psychologist, 38,* 1145–1160.

Axelrod, S., & Apsche, J. (Eds.). (1983). *The effects of punishment on human behavior.* New York: Academic Press.

Ayllon, T., & Azrin, N. H. (1968). *The token economy: A motivational system for therapy and rehabilitation.* New York: Appleton-Century-Crofts.

Bablenis, E., Weber, S. S., & Wagner, R. L. (1989). Clozapine: A novel antipsychotic agent. *DICP: The Annals of Pharmacotherapy, 23,* 109–115.

Baddeley, A. (1990). *Human memory: Theory and practice* (2nd ed.). Needham Heights, MA: Allyn & Bacon.

Baddeley, A. (1994). *Your memory: A user's guide* (2nd ed.). New York: Penguin Press.

Baer, J. D., Kivlahan, D. R., Fromme, K., & Marlatt, G. A. (1989). Secondary prevention of alcohol abuse with college student populations: A skills-training approach. In G. Howard (Ed.), *Issues in alcohol use and misuse by young adults.* Notre Dame, IN: Notre Dame University Press.

Bahrick, H. P. (1984). Semantic memory content in permastore: Fifty years of memory for Spanish learned in school. *Journal of Experimental Psychology: General, 113,* 1–37.

Bahrick, H. P., Bahrick, P. O., & Wittlinger, R. (1975). Fifty years of memory for names and faces: A cross-sectional approach. *Journal of Experimental Psychology: General, 104,* 54–75.

Bahrick, H. P., & Phelps, E. (1987). Retention of Spanish vocabulary over eight years. *Journal of Experimental Psychology: General, 13,* 344–349.

Baillargeon, R. (1987). Object permanence in 3- and 4-month-old infants. *Developmental Psychology, 23,* 655–664.

Baillargeon, R. (1994). How do infants learn about the physical world? *Current Directions in Psychological Science, 3,* 133–139.

Baillargeon, R., Kotovsky, L., & Needham, A. (1995). The acquisition of physical knowledge in infancy. In G. Lewis, D. Premack, & D. Sperber (Eds.), *Causal understanding in cognition and culture.* New York: Oxford University Press.

Baillargeon, R., Spelke, E., & Wasserman, S. (1985). Object permanence in five-month-old infants. *Cognition, 20,* 191–208.

Baird, J. C., Wagner, M., & Fuld, K. (1990). A simple but powerful theory of the moon illusion. *Journal of Experimental Psychology: Human Perception and Performance, 16,* 675–677.

Baker, L., & Brown, A. L. (1984). Metacognitive skills in reading. In R. Barr, M. Kamil, & P. Mosenthal (Eds.), *Handbook of reading research.* New York: Longman.

Baker, S. M., & Petty, R. E. (1994). Majority and minority influence: Source-position imbalance as a determinant of message scrutiny. *Journal of Personality and Social Psychology, 67,* 5–19.

Baldessarini, R. J. (1985). Drugs and the treatment of psychiatric disorders. In A. G. Gilma, L. S. Goodma, T. W. Rall, & F. Murad (Eds.), *The pharmacological basis of therapeutics* (7th ed., pp. 387–445). New York: Macmillan.

Balentine, J., & Hagman, J. (1997). More on melatonin. *Journal of the American Academy of Child and Adolescent Psychiatry, 36,* 1013.

Baltes, P. B., & Schaie, K. W. (1974). Aging and IQ: The myth of the twilight years. *Psychology Today, 7,* 35–40.

Banaji, M. R., & Crowder, R. G. (1989). The bankruptcy of everyday memory. *American Psychologist, 44,* 1185–1193.

Banaji, M. R., & Crowder, R. G. (1991). Some everyday thoughts on ecologically valid methods. *American Psychologist, 46,* 78–79.

Bandura, A. (1965). Influence of models' reinforcement contingencies on the acquisition of imitative responses. *Journal of Personality and Social Psychology, 1,* 589–595.

Bandura, A. (1977b). *Social learning theory.* Englewood Cliffs, NJ: Prentice Hall.

Bandura, A. (1982). Self-efficacy mechanism in human agency. *American Psychologist, 37,* 122–147.

Bandura, A. (1986). *Social foundations of thought and action: A social cognitive theory.* Englewood Cliffs, NJ: Prentice Hall.

Bandura, A., Blanchard, E. B., & Ritter, B. (1969). Relative efficacy of desensitization and modeling approaches for inducing behavioral, affective, and attitudinal changes. *Journal of Personality and Social Psychology, 13,* 173–199.

Bandura, A., Grusec, J. E., & Menlove, F. L. (1967). Vicarious extinction of avoidance behavior. *Journal of Personality and Social Psychology, 5,* 16–23.

Bandura, A., Ross, D., & Ross, S. (1961). Transmission of aggression through imitation of aggressive models. *Journal of Abnormal and Social Psychology, 63,* 575–582.

Banks, M. S., & Salapatek, P. (1983). Infant visual perception. In M. M. Haith & J. Campos (Eds.), *Handbook of child psychology: Infancy and developmental psychology* (Vol. 2, pp. 435–571). New York: Wiley.

Barash, D. (1982). *Sociobiology and behavior* (2nd ed.). New York: Elsevier.

Bargh, J. A. (1989). Conditional automaticity: Varieties of automatic influence in social perception and cognition. In J. S. Uleman & J. A. Bargh (Eds.), *Unintended thought* (pp. 3–51). New York: Guilford.

Barker, L. M. (Ed.). (1982). *The psychobiology of human food selection.* Westport, CT: Avi.

Barker, L. M. (1994). *Learning and behavior.* New York: Macmillan.

Barker, L. M. (1997). *Learning and behavior* (2nd ed.). New York: Prentice Hall.

Barker, L. M., Best, M. R., & Domjan, M. (Eds.). (1977). *Learning mechanisms in food selection.* Waco, TX: Baylor University Press.

Barker, L. M., & Weaver, C. A., III. (1991). Conditioning flavor preferences in rats: Dissecting the "medicine effect." *Learning and Motivation, 22,* 311–328.

Barlow, D. H. (1986). Causes of sexual dysfunction: The role of anxiety and cognitive interference. *Journal of Counseling and Clinical Psychology, 54,* 140–148.

Barlow, D. H. (1988). *Anxiety and its disorders.* New York: Guilford.

Barlow, D. H., Blanchard, E. B., Vermilyea, J. A., Vermilyea, B. B., & DiNardo, P. A. (1986). Generalized anxiety and generalized anxiety disorder: Description and reconceptualization. *American Journal of Psychiatry, 143,* 40–44.

Barlow, D. H., & Cerny, J. A. (1988). *Psychological treatment of panic.* New York: Guilford.

Barlow, D. H., & Waddell, M. T. (1985). Agoraphobia. In D. H.

Barlow (Ed.), *Clinical handbook of psychological disorders*. New York: Guilford.

Barlow, H. B., & Mollon, J. D. (Eds.). (1982). *The senses*. Cambridge: Cambridge University Press.

Barnes, G. E., & Prosen, H. (1985). Parental death and depression. *Journal of Abnormal Psychology, 94*, 64–69.

Baron, J. (1985). *Rationality and intelligence*. Cambridge, England: Cambridge University Press Press.

Baron, R. A. (1977). *Human aggression*. New York: Plenum Press.

Baron, R. A. (1983). The control of human aggression: An optimistic perspective. *Journal of Social and Clinical Psychology, 1*, 97–119.

Baron, R. A., Logan, H., Lily, J., Inman, M., & Brennan, M. (1994). Negative emotion and message processing. *Journal of Experimental Social Psychology, 30*, 181–201.

Baron, R. A., & Richardson, D. R. (1992). *Human agression* (2nd ed.). New York: Plenum Press.

Baron, R. S. (1986). Distraction-conflict theory: Progress and problems. In L. Berkowitz (Ed.), *Advances in experimental social psychology*. Orlando, FL: Academic Press.

Barondes, S. H. (1994). Thinking about Prozac. *Science, 263*, 1102–1103.

Barr, L. C., Goodman, W. K., Price, L. H., McDougle, C. J., & Charney, D. S. (1992). The serotonin hypothesis of obsessive compulsive disorder: implications of pharmacological challenge studies. *Journal of Clinical Psychiatry, 53*, 17–28.

Barsky, A. J. (1992). Amplification, somatization, and the somatoform disorders. *Psychosomatics, 33*, 28–34.

Bartlett, F. C. (1932). *Remembering: A study in experimental and social psychology*. London: Cambridge University Press.

Bartoshuk, L. M. (1988). Taste. In R. C. Atkinson, R. J. Hernstein, L. Gardner, & R. D. Luce (Eds.), *Stevens' handbook of experimental psychology* (2nd ed., pp. 461–502). New York: Wiley.

Bass, E., & Davis, L. (1988). *The courage to heal: A guide to women survivors of child sexual abuse*. New York: Harper & Row.

Bates, J. E. (1987). Temperament in infancy. In J. D. Osofsky (Ed.), *Handbook of infant development* (2nd ed., pp. 1101–1149). New York: Wiley.

Batson, C. D. (1987). Prosocial motivation: Is it ever truly altruistic? In L. Berkowitz (Ed.), *Advances in experimental personality* (Vol. 20). San Diego: Academic Press.

Batson, C. D., Batson, J. G., Griffitt, C. A., Barrientos, S., Brandt, J. R., Sprengelmeyer, P., & Bayly, M. J. (1989). Negative-state relief and the empathy-altruism hypothesis. *Journal of Personality and Social Psychology, 56*, 922–933.

Batson, C. D., Duncan, B. D., Ackerman, P., Buckley, T., & Birch, K. (1981). Is empathic emotion a source of altruistic motivation? *Journal of Personality and Social Psychology, 40*, 290–302.

Batson, C. D., Dyck, J. L., Brandt, J. R., Batson, J. G., Powell, A. L., McMaster, M. R., & Griffitt, C. (1988). Five studies testing two new egoistic alternatives to the empathy-altruism hypothesis. *Journal of Personality and Social Psychology, 55*, 52–57.

Baucom, D. H., & Lester, G. W. (1986). The usefulness of cognitive restructuring as an adjunct to behavioral marital therapy. *Behavior Therapy, 17*, 385–403.

Bauer, M. C., Calabrese, J., Dunner, D. L., Post, R., Whybrow, P. C., Gyulai, L., Tay, L. K., Younkin, S. R., Bynum, D., Lavori, P., & Price, R. A. (1994). Multisite data reanalysis of the validity of rapid-cycling

as a course modifier for bipolar disorder in DSM-IV. *American Journal of Psychiatry, 151*, 47.

Baum, A., & Valins, S. (1977). *Architecture and social behavior: Psychological studies of social density*. Hillsdale, NJ: Erlbaum.

Baumeister, A. A. (1987). Mental retardation: Some conceptions and dilemmas. *American Psychologist, 42*, 796–800.

Baumeister, R. F. (1982). A self-presentational view of social phenomena. *Psychological Bulletin, 91*, 3–26.

Baumeister, R. F., & Scher, S. J. (1988). Self-defeating behavior patterns among normal individuals: Review and analysis of common self-destructive tendencies. *Psychological Bulletin, 104*, 3–22.

Baumgardner, A. H. (1991). Claiming depressive symptoms as a self-handicap: A protective self-presentation strategy. *Basic and Applied Social Psychology, 12*, 97–113.

Baumgardner, A. H., & Brownlee, E. A. (1987). Strategic failure in social interaction: Evidence for expectancy disconfirmation process. *Journal of Personality and Social Psychology, 52*, 525–535.

Baumrind, D. (1964). Some thoughts on the ethics of research: After reading Milgram's "Behavioral study of obedience." *American Psychologist, 19*, 421–423.

Baumrind, D. (1967). Child care practices anteceding three patterns of preschool behavior. *Genetic Psychology Monographs, 75*, 43–88.

Baumrind, D. (1984, March). *Family socialization and development competence project*. Paper presented at the Program in Social Ecology, Irvine, CA.

Baxter, L. R., Phelps, M. E., Mazziotta, J. C., Guze, B. H., Schwartz, J. M., & Selin, C. E. (1987). Local cerebral glucose metabolic rates in obsessive-compulsive disorder: A comparison with rates in unipolar depression and normal controls.

Archives of General Psychiatry, 44, 211–218.

Beach, F., & Merari, A. (1970). Coital behavior in dogs: V. Effects of estrogen and progesterone on mating and other forms of social behavior in the bitch. *Journal of Comparative and Physiological Psychology Monograph, 70*(Pt. 2), 1–22.

Beach, L. R., Campbell, F. L., & Townes, B. D. (1979). Subjective utility and the prediction of birth-planning decisions. *Organizational Behavior and Human Performance, 24,* 18–28.

Beach, S. R. H., Whisman, M. A., & O'Leary, K. D. (1994). Marital therapy for depression: Theoretical foundation, current status, and future directions. *Behavior Therapy, 25,* 345–371.

Beck, A. T. (1967). *Depression: Clinical, experimental and theoretical aspects.* New York: Hoeber.

Beck, A. T. (1974). The development of depression: A cognitive model. In R. J. Friedman & M. M. Katz (Eds.), *The psychology of depression: Contemporary theory and research.* Washington, DC: WinstonWiley.

Beck, A. T. (1976). *Cognitive therapy and the emotional disorders.* New York: International Universities Press.

Beck, A. T. (1985). Cognitive models of depression. *Journal of Cognitive Therapy, 1,* 5–37.

Beck, A. T. (1997). Cognitive therapy: Reflections. In J. K. Zeig (Ed.), *The evolution of psychotherapy: The third conference* (pp. 55–64). New York: Brunner/Mazel.

Beck, A. T., & Emery, G. (1985). *Anxiety disorders and phobias: A cognitive perspective.* New York: Basic Books.

Beck, A. T., Freeman, A., Pretzer, J., Davis, D., Fleming, B., Ottaviani, R., Beck, J., Simon, K. M., Padesky, C., Meyer, J., & Trexler, L. (1990). *Cognitive therapy of personality disorders.* New York: Guilford.

Beck, A. T., Hollon, S. D., Young, J. E., Bedrosian, R. C., & Budenz, D. (1985). Treatment of depression with cognitive therapy and amitriptyline. *Archives of General Psychiatry, 42,* 142–148.

Beck, A. T., Kovacs, M., & Weissman, A. (1979). Assessment of suicidal intention: The scale for suicide ideation. *Journal of Clinical and Consultant Psychology, 47,* 243–252.

Beck, A. T., Rush, A. J., Shaw, B. F., & Emery, G. (1979). *Cognitive therapy of depression.* New York: Guilford.

Beck, A. T., Steer, R. A., Kovacs, M., & Garrison, B. (1985). Hopelessness and eventual suicide: A ten-year prospective study of patients hospitalized with suicide. *American Journal of Psychiatry, 142,* 559–563.

Beck, A. T., Ward, C. H., Mendelson, M., Mock, J. E., & Erbaugh, J. (1961). An inventory for measuring depression. *Archives of General Psychiatry, 4,* 53–63.

Beck, M., & Cowley, G. (1990, March 26). Beyond lobotomies. *Newsweek, 44.*

Becker, C., & Kronus, S. (1977). Sex and drinking patterns: An old relationship revisited in a new way. *Social Problems, 24,* 482–497.

Becker, H. C., Diaz Granados, J. L., & Weathersby, R. T. (1997). Repeated ethanol withdrawal experience increases the severity and duration of subsequent withdrawal seizures in mice. *Alcohol, 14,* 319–326.

Bedford, V. H. (1989). Ambivalence in adult sibling relationships. *Journal of Family Issues, 10,* 211–224.

Bednar, R. L., & Kaul, T. (1994). Experiential group research. In A. E. Bergin & S. L. Garfield (Eds.), *Handbook of psychotherapy and behavior change* (4th ed., pp. 630–663). New York: Wiley.

Begg, I. M., Needham, D. R., & Bookbinder, M. (1993). Do backward messages unconsciously affect listeners? No. *Canadian Journal of Experimental Psychology, 47,* 1–14.

Bekesy, G. von (1959). Synchronism of neural discharges and their demultiplication in pitch perception on the skin and in learning. *Journal of the Acoustical Society of America, 31,* 338–349.

Bellack, A. S., Hersen, M., & Turner, S. M. (1976). Generalization effects of social skills training in chronic schizophrenics: An experimental analysis. *Behaviour Research and Therapy, 14,* 391–398.

Bellack, A. S., Morrison, R. L., Wixted, J. T., & Mueser, K. T. (1990). An analysis of social competence in schizophrenia. *British Journal of Psychiatry, 56,* 809–818.

Belli, R. F. (1989). Influences of misleading postevent information: Misinformation interference and acceptance. *Journal of Experimental Psychology: General, 118,* 72–85.

Bellugi, U. (1964). *The emergence of inflections and negative systems in the speech of two children.* Paper presented at the New England Psychological Association, Boston.

Bellugi, U. (1970). Learning the language. *Psychlogy Today, 4,* 32–35ff.

Bellugi, U., Poizner, H., & Klima, E. S. (1989). Language, modality and the brain. *Trends in Neurosciences, 12,* 380–388.

Belmore, S. M. (1987). Determinants of attention during impression formation. *Journal of Experimental Psychology: Learning, Memory, and Cognition, 13,* 480–489.

Belsher, G., & Costello, C. G. (1988). Relapse after recovery from unipolar depression: A critical review. *Psychlogical Bulletin, 104,* 84–96.

Belsky, J. (1988). The effects of infant day care reconsidered. *Early Childhood Quarterly, 3,* 235–272.

Belsky, J., & Cassidy, J. (1994). Attachment: Theory and evidence. In M. Rutter & D. Hay (Eds.), *Development through life: A handbook for clinicians* (pp. 373–402). Oxford, England: Blackwell.

Belsky, J., Fish, M., & Isabella, R. (1991). Continuity and discontinuity in infant negative and positive emotionality: Family antecedents and attachment consequences. *Developmental Psychology, 27,* 421–431.

Belsky, J., & Isabella, R. (1988). Maternal, infant, and social-contextual determinants of attachment security. In J. Belsky & T. Nezworski (Eds.), *Clinical implications of attachment* (pp. 41–94). Hillsdale, NJ: Erlbaum.

Bem, D. (1967). Self-perception: An alternative interpretation of cognitive dissonance phenomena. *Psychological Review, 74,* 183–200.

Bemis, K. M. (1978). Current approaches to the etiology and treatment of anorexia nervosa. *Psychological Bulletin, 85,* 593–617.

Bender, K. J. (1990). *Psychiatric medications: A guide for mental health professionals.* Newbury Park, CA: Sage.

Benecke, R., Conrad, B., & Klingel-hofer, J. (1988). Successful treatment of tardive and spontaneous dyskinesia with corticosteroids. *European Neurology, 28,* 146–149.

Benedict, H. (1979). Early lexical development: Comprehension and production. *Journal of Child Language, 6,* 183–200.

Benjamin, L. S. (1987). The use of the SASB dimensional model to develop treatment plans for personality disorders I: Narcissism. *Journal of Personality Disorders, 1,* 43–70.

Bennett, W., & Gurin, J. (1982). *The dieter's dilemma.* New York: Basic Books.

Benton, M. K., & Schroeder, H. E. (1990). Social skills training with schizophrenics: A meta-analytic evaluation. *Journal of Consulting and Clinical Psychology, 58,* 741–747.

Berg, J. H., & McQuinn, R. D. (1986). Attraction and exchange in continuing and noncontinuing relationships. *Journal of Personality and Social Psychology, 50,* 942–952.

Berglas, S., & Jones, E. E. (1978). Drug choice as a self-handicapping strategy in response to noncontingent success. *Journal of Personality and Social Psychology, 36,* 405–417.

Berkman, L. F., & Syme, S. L. (1979). Social networks, host resistance, and mortality: A nine-year follow-up study of Alameda County residents. *American Journal of Epidemiology, 109,* 186–204.

Berkow, R. (Ed.). (1989). *The Merck manual.* Rahway, NJ: Merck Sharp & Dohme Research Laboratories.

Berkowitz, L. (1989). Frustration-aggression hypothesis: Examination and reformulation. *Psychological Bulletin, 106,* 59–73.

Berlin, B., & Kay, P. (1969). *Basic color terms: Their universality and evolution.* Berkeley: University of California Press.

Berlyne, D. E. (1950). Novelty and curiosity as determinants of exploratory behaviour. *British Journal of Psychology, 41,* 68–80.

Bernard, L. L. (1924). *Instinct.* New York: Holt.

Bernstein, I. L. (1978). Learned taste aversions in children receiving chemotherapy. *Science, 200,* 1302–1303.

Bernstein, I. L. (1985). Learned food aversions in the progression of cancer and its treatment. *Annals of the New York Academy of Sciences, 443,* 365–380.

Bernstein, I. L. (1986). Food aversion learning: A role in cancer anorexia. *Nutrition and Behavior, 3,* 117–127.

Bernstein, I. L., Webster, M. M., & Bernstein, I. D. (1982). Food aversions in children receiving chemotherapy for cancer. *Cancer, 50,* 2961–2963.

Berridge, K. C., & Robinson, T. E. (1995). The mind of an addicted brain: Neural sensitization of wanting versus liking. *Current Directions in Psychological Science, 4,* 71–76.

Berry, D. S., & Pennebaker, J. W. (1993). Nonverbal and verbal emotional expression and health. *Psychotherapy and Psychosomatics, 59,* 11–19.

Berscheid, E., Snyder, M., & Omoto, A. M. (1989). The Relationship Closeness Inventory. *Journal of Personality and Social Psychology, 57,* 792–807.

Bersoff, D. N. (1980). P. v. Riles : Legal perspective. *School Psychology Review, 9,* 112–122.

Best, M. R. (1995, April). *Of rats and tastes. Presidential address.* Paper presented at the 40th annual meeting of the Southwestern Psychological Association, San Antonio, TX.

Best, M. R., & Meachum, C. L. (1986). The effects of stimulus preexposure on taste mediated environmental conditioning: Potentiation and overshadowing. *Animal Learning and Behavior, 14,* 1–5.

Bettencourt, B. A., & Miller, N. (1996). Gender differences in aggression as a function of provocation: A meta-analysis. *Psychological Bulletin, 119,* 422–447.

Beutler, L. E., Machado, P. P. P., & Neufeldt, S. A. (1994). Therapist variables. In A. E. Bergin & S. L. Garfield (Eds.), *Handbook of psychotherapy and behavior changes* (4th ed., pp. 229–269). New York: Wiley.

Bevan, W. (1964). Subliminal stimulation: A pervasive problem for psychology. *Psychological Bulletin, 61,* 89–99.

Biederman, I., Glass, A. L., & Stacy, E. W., Jr. (1973). Searching for objects in real-world scenes. *Journal of Experimental Psychology, 97,* 22–27.

Biederman, I., Mezzanotte, R. J., & Rabinowitz, J. C. (1982). Scene perception: Detecting and judging objects undergoing relational violations. *Cognitive Psychology, 14,* 143–177.

Biederman, I., Mezzanotte, R. J., Rabinowitz, J. C., Francolini, C. M., & Plude, D. (1981). Detecting the unexpected in photointerpretation. *Human Factors, 23*, 153–164.

Biederman, I., Rabinowitz, J. C., Glass, A. L., & Stacy, E. W., Jr. (1974). On the information extracted from a glance at a scene. *Journal of Experimental Psychology, 103*, 597–600.

Biernat, M., & Wortman, C. B. (1991). Sharing of home responsibilities between professionally employed women and their husbands. *Journal of Personality and Social Psychology, 60*, 844–860.

Bilder, R. M., Wu, H., Bogerts, B., Degreef, G., Ashtari, M., Alvir, J. M., Snyder, P. J., & Lieberman, J. A. (1994). Absence of regional hemispheric volume asymmetries in first-episode schizophrenia. *American Journal of Psychiatry, 151*, 1437–1447.

Birren, E., Schaie, K. W., Abeles, R. P., Gatz, M., & Salthouse, T. (1996). *Handbook of the psychology of aging* (4th ed.). San Diego: Academic Press.

Bjorkqvist, K., Lagerspetz, K. M. J., & Kaukiainen, A. (1992). Do girls manipulate and boys fight? Developmental trends regarding direct and indirect aggression. *Aggressive Behavior, 18*, 117–127.

Bjorkqvist, K., & Niemela, P. (Eds.). (1992). *New trends in the study of female aggression.* San Diego, CA: Harcourt Brace Jovanovich.

Bjorkqvist, K., Osterman, K., & Kaukiainen, A. (1992). The development of direct and indirect aggressive strategies in males and females. In K. Bjorkqvist & P. Niemela (Eds.), *Of mice and women: Aspects of female aggression* (pp. 51–64). San Diego: Harcourt Brace Jovanovich.

Black, D. W., Winokur, G., & Nasarallah, A. (1989). Illness duration and acute response in major depression. *Counseling Therapy, 5*, 338–343.

Blake, R. R., & Mouton, J. (1979). Intergroup problem solving in organizations: From theory to practice. In W. Austin & S. Worchel (Eds.), *The social psychology of intergroup relations.* Monterey, CA: Brooks/Cole.

Blanchard, F. A., Crandall, C. S., Brigham, J. C., & Vaughn, L. A. (1994). Condemning and condoning racism: A social context approach to interracial settings. *Journal of Applied Psychology, 79*, 993–997.

Blanchard, F. A., Lilly, T., & Vaughn, L. A. (1991). Reducing the expression of racial prejudice. *Psychological Science, 2*, 101–105.

Blanchard, M., & Main, M. (1979). Avoidance of the attachment figure and social-emotional adjustment in day-care infants. *Developmental Psychology, 15*, 445–446.

Blaney, P. H. (1986). Affect and memory: A review. *Psychological Bulletin, 99*, 229–246.

Blascovich, J. (1990). Individual differences in physiological arousal and perception of arousal: Missing links in Jamesian notions of arousal-based behavior. *Personality and Social Psychology Bulletin, 16*, 665–675.

Blatt, S. J., & Homann, E. (1992). Parent-child interaction in the etiology of dependent and self-critical depression. *Clinical Psychology Review, 12*, 47–91.

Blazer, D. G., Kessler, R. C., McGonagle, K. A., & Swartz, M. S. (1994). The prevalence and distribution of major depression in a national community sample: The national comorbidity survey. *American Journal of Psychiatry, 151*, 979–986.

Blehar, M. C. (1974). Anxious attachment and defensive reactions associated with day care. *Child Development, 45*, 683–692.

Bleuler, E. (1911/1950). *Dementia praecox or the group of schizophrenias* (J. Sinkin, Trans.). New York: International Universities Press.

Block, J. (1971). *Lives through time.* Berkeley, CA: Bancroft Books.

Block, J., & Block, J. (1980). The role of ego-control and ego resiliency in the organization of behavior. In W. A. Collins (Ed.), *The Minnesota Symposium on Child Psychology.* Hillsdale, NJ: Erlbaum.

Bloom, L. M. (1970). *Language development: Form and function in emerging grammars.* Cambridge, MA: MIT Press.

Blume, E. S. (1990). *Secret survivors: Uncovering incest and its after effects in women.* New York: Ballantine.

Bodenhausen, G. V. (1990). Stereotypes as judgmental heuristics: Evidence of circadian variations in discrimination. *Psychological Science, 1*, 319–322.

Bodenhausen, G. V., Kramer, G. P., & Susser, K. (1994). Happiness and stereotypic thinking in social judgment. *Journal of Personality and Social Psychology, 66*, 621–632.

Bogerts, B. (1993). Recent advances in the neuropathology of schizophrenia. *Schizophrenia Bulletin, 19*, 431–445.

Booth-Kewley, S., & Friedman, H. S. (1987). Psychological predictors of heart disease: A quantitative review. *Psychological Bulletin, 101*, 343–362.

Bootzin, R. R. (1997). Examining the theory and clinical usage of writing about emotional experiences. *Psychological Science, 8*, 167–169.

Bootzin, R. R., Epstein, D., & Wood, J. M. (1991). Stimulus control instructions. In P. Hauri (Ed.), *Case studies in insomnia.* New York: Plenum Press.

Bornstein, R. F. (1989). Exposure and affect: Overview and meta-analysis of research, 1968–1987. *Psychological Bulletin, 106*, 265–289.

Bornstein, R. F., & D'Agostino, P. R. (1992). Stimulus recognition and the mere exposure effect. *Journal of Personality and Social Psychology, 63,* 545–552.

Bouchard, C., Tremblay, A., Despres, J. P., Nadeau, A., Lupien, P. J., Theriault, G., Dussault, J., Moorjani, S., Pinault, S., & Fournier, G. (1990). The response to long-term over-feeding in identical twins. *New England Journal of Medicine, 322,* 1477–1482.

Bouchard, T. J., Jr. (1993). Genetic and environmental influences on adult personality: Evaluating the evidence. In J. Hettema & I. J. Deary (Eds.), *Foundations of personality.* Dordrecht, the Netherlands: Kluwer Academic.

Bouchard, T. J., Jr., & McGue, M. (1981). Familial studies in intelligence: A review. *Science, 210,* 139–149.

Bouchard, T. J., Jr. ,& McGue, M. (1990). Genetic and rearing environmental influences on adult personality: An analysis of adolescent twins reared apart. *Journal of Personality, 58,* 263–292.

Bower, B. (1991). Science and clinical tradition clash amid new insights into depression. *Science News, 139,* 56–57.

Bower, G. H. (1972). A selective review of organizational factors in memory. In E. Tulving & W. Donaldson (Eds.), *Organization of memory.* New York: Academic Press.

Bower, G. H., Black, J., & Turner, T. (1979). Scripts in text comprehension and memory. *Cognitive Psychology, 11,* 177–220.

Bower, G. H., & Mayer, J. D. (1985). Failure to replicate mood-dependent retrieval. *Bulletin of the Psychonomic Society, 23,* 39–42.

Bower, G. H., Monteiro, K. P., & Gilligan, S. G. (1978). Emotional mood as a context of learning and recall. *Journal of Verbal Learning and Verbal Behavior, 17,* 573–585.

Bower, T. G. R. (1989). *The rational infant.* San Francisco: Freeman.

Bowers, K. S. (1983). *Hypnosis for the seriously curious.* New York: Norton.

Bowlby, J. (1969). *Attachment and loss* (Vol. 1). New York: Basic Books.

Bowlby, J. (1973). Separation, anxiety, and anger. In J. Bowlby (Ed.), *Attachment and Loss* (Vol. 2). New York: Basic Books.

Bowlby, J. (1982). *Attachment and loss* (2nd ed.). New York: Basic Books.

Boynton, R. M. (1988). Color vision. *Annual Review of Psychology, 39,* 69–100.

Bradbard, M. R., Martin, C. L., Endsley, R. C., & Halverson, C. F. (1986). Influence of sex stereotypes on children's exploration and memory: A competence versus performance distinction. *Developmental Psychology, 22,* 481–486.

Bradbury, T. N., & Fincham, F. D. (1990). Attributions in marriage: Review and critique. *Psychological Bulletin, 107,* 3–33.

Bradshaw, J. (1990). *Homecoming.* New York: Bantam Books.

Bradshaw, J. (1992, August). Incest: When you wonder if it happened to you. *Lear's, 5,* 49.

Braff, D. L. (1993). Information processing and attention dysfunctions in schizophrenia. *Schizophrenia Bulletin, 19,* 233–259.

Brainerd, C. J. (1978). The stage question in cognitive-developmental theory. *Behavioral and Brain Sciences, 1,* 173–213.

Brannon, L., & Feist, J. (1997). *Health psychology: An introduction to behavior and health.* Pacific Groves, CA: Brooks/Cole.

Bransford, J. D., & Johnson, M. K. (1972). Contextual prerequisites for understanding: Some investigations of comprehension and recall. *Journal of Verbal Learning and Verbal Behavior, 11,* 717–726.

Bransford, J. D., & Stein, B. S. (1984). *The ideal problem solver: A guide for improving thinking, learning, and creativity.* New York: W. H. Freeman.

Bray, G. A. (1992). Psychophysiology of obesity. *American Journal of Clinical Nutrition, 55,* 488–494.

Brazelton, T. B. (1983). *Infants and mothers: Differences in development* (2nd ed.). New York: Dell.

Breckler, S. J. (1983). *Validation of affect, behavior and cognition distinct components of attitudes.* (Unpublished dissertation). Columbus: Ohio State University.

Breckler, S. J. (1984). Empirical validation of affect, behavior, and cognition as distinct components of attitudes. *Journal of Personality and Social Psychology, 47,* 1191–1205.

Breier, A., Charney, D. S., & Heninger, G. R. (1986). Agoraphobia with panic attacks. *Archives of General Psychiatry, 43,* 1029–1036.

Breland, K., & Breland, M. (1961). The misbehavior of organisms. *American Psychologist, 61,* 681–684.

Bremer, J. (1959). *Asexualisation: A follow-up study of 244 cases.* New York: Macmillan.

Brewer, W. F., & Nakamura, G. V. (1984). The nature and functions of schemas. In R. S. Wyer & T. K. Srull (Eds.), *Handbook of social cognition* (Vol. 1, pp. 119–160). Hillsdale, NJ: Erlbaum.

Brewerton, T. D. (1989). Seasonal variation of serotonin function in humans: Research and clinical implications. *Annals of Clinical Psychiatry, I,* 153–164.

Brickman, P. (1978). *Happiness: Can we make it last?* (Unpublished manuscript): Northwestern University.

Brickman, P., & Campbell, D. T. (1971). Hedonic relativism and planning the good society. In M. H. Appley (Ed.), *Adaptation level theory.* New York: Academic Press.

Brickner, M. A., Harkins, S. G., & Ostrom, T. M. (1986). Effect of personal involvement: Thought-provoking implications for social loafing. *Journal of Personality and Social Psychology, 51*, 763–769.

Bridges, P. K., & Bartlett, J. R. (1977). Psychosurgery: Yesterday and today. *British Journal of Psychiatry, 131*, 249–260.

Brigham, C. C. (1923). *A study of American intelligence.* Princeton, NJ: Princeton University Press.

Brody, J. (1986, February 14). Federal panel issues warning of obesity peril. *The Oregonian*, p. A1.

Brody, L. R., Zelazo, P. R., & Chaika, H. (1984). Habituation-dishabituation to speech in the neonate. *Developmental Psychology, 20*, 114–119.

Bromley, S. M., & Doty, R. L. (1995). Odor recognition memory is better under bilateral than unilateral test conditions. *Cortex, 31*, 25–40.

Brooks-Gunn, J., & Furstenberg, F. F. (1989). Adolescent sexual behavior. *American Psychologist, 44*, 249–257.

Brown, A. L., & Kane, M. J. (1988). Preschool children can learn to transfer: Learning to learn and learning from example. *Cognitive Psychology, 20*, 493–523.

Brown, G. M. (1994). Light, melatonin, and the sleep-wake cycle. *Journal of Psychiatry and Neuroscience, 19*, 345–353.

Brown, G. W., & Harris, T. (1978). *Social origins of depression: A study of psychiatric disorders in women.* New York: Free Press.

Brown, J. A. (1958). Some tests of the decay theory of immediate memory. *Quarterly Journal of Experimental Psychology, 10*, 12–21.

Brown, J. D., & Seigel, J. M. (1988). Exercise as a buffer of life stress: A prospective study of adolescent health. *Health Psychology, 57*, 1103–1110.

Brown, R. (1973). *A first language: The early stages.* Cambridge, MA : Harvard University Press.

Brown, R., & Bellugi, U. (1964). Three processes in the child's acquisition of syntax. *Harvard Educational Review, 34*, 133–151.

Brown, R., Cazden, C., Bellugi, U., & Klima, U. (1968). The child's grammar from I to III. In J. P. Hill (Ed.), *Minnesota Symposium on Child Development* (Vol. 2, pp. 28–73). Minneapolis: University of Minnesota Press.

Brown, R., Colter, N., Corsellis, J. A., Crow, T. J., Frith, C. D., Jagoe, R., Johnstone, E. C., & Marsh, L. (1986). Postmortem evidence of structural brain changes in schizophrenia: Differences in brain weight, temporal horn area, and parahippocampal gyrus compared with affective disorder. *Archives of General Psychiatry, 43*, 36–42.

Brown, R., & Kulik, J. (1977). Flashbulb memories. *Cognition, 5*, 73–99.

Brown, R., & McNeill, D. (1966). The "tip of the tongue" phenomenon. *Journal of Verbal Learning and Verbal Behavior, 5*, 325–337.

Brown, R., & Wootton-Millward, L. (1993). Perceptions of group homogeneity during group formation and change. *Social Cognition, 11*, 126–149.

Brown, T. R., & Sheran, T. J. (1972). Suicide prediction: A review. *Life-Threatening Behavior, 2*, 67–98.

Brownell, K. D., Marlatt, G. A., Lichtenstein, E., & Wilson, G. T. (1986). Understanding and preventing relapse. *American Psychologist, 41*, 765–782.

Brownell, K. D., & Wadden, T. A. (1992). Etiology and treatment of obesity: Understanding a serious, prevalent, and refractory disorder. *Journal of Consulting and Clinical Psychology, 60*, 505–517.

Bruch, H. (1973). *Eating disorders: Obesity, anorexia nervosa, and the person within.* New York: Basic Books.

Bruch, H. (1980). *The golden cage: The enigma of anorexia nervosa.* New York: Random House.

Bruch, H. (1982). Anorexia nervosa: Therapy and theory. *American Journal of Psychiatry, 139*, 1531–1538.

Bruch, H. (1985). Four decades of eating disorders. In D. M. Gardner & P. E. Garfinkel (Eds.), *Handbook of psychotherapy for anorexia and bulimia.* New York: Guilford.

Bruck, M., Cavanagh, P., & Ceci, S. (1991). Fortysomething: Recognizing faces at one's 25th reunion. *Memory and Cognition, 19*, 221–228.

Bruck, M., & Ceci, S. J. (1997). The suggestibility of young children. *Current Directions in Psychological Science, 3*, 75–78.

Bruner, J. S., Goodnow, J. J., & Austin, G. A. (1956). *A study of thinking.* New York: Wiley.

Brunner, D. P., Dijk, D. J., Tobler, I., & Borbély, A. A. (1990). Effects of partial sleep deprivation on sleep stages and EEG power spectra: Evidence for non-REM and REM homeostasis. *Electroencephalography and Clinical Neurophysiology, 75*, 492–499.

Brunnquell, D., Crichton, L., & Egeland, B. (1981). Maternal personality and attitude in disturbances of child rearing. *American Journal of Orthopsychiatry, 51*, 680–691.

Bryan, J. H. (1975). Children's cooperation and helping behaviors. In E. M. Hetherington (Ed.), *Review of child development research* (Vol. 5). Chicago: University of Chicago Press.

Buck, R. (1976). A test of nonverbal receiving ability: Preliminary studies. *Human Communication Research, 2*, 162–171.

Buck, R. (1985). Prime theory: An integrated view of motivation and emotion. *Psychological Review, 92*, 389–413.

Buckley, K. W. (1989). *Mechanical man: John Broadus Watson and the beginnings of behaviorism.* New York: Guilford.

Buehler, R., & Griffin, D. (1994). Change of meaning effects in conformity and dissent: Observing construal processes over time. *Jour-*

nal of Personality and Social Psychology, 67, 984–996.

Bunch, J. (1972). Recent bereavement in relation to suicide. Journal of Psychosomatic Research, 16, 361–366.

Bunney, W. E., Jr., Murphy, D. L., Goodwin, F. K., & Borge, G. F. (1972). The "switch process" in manicdepressive illness: A systematic study of sequential behavior changes. Archives of General Psychiatry, 27, 295–302.

Burger, J. M. (1986). Increasing compliance by improving the deal: The that's-not-all technique. Journal of Personality and Social Psychology, 51, 277–283.

Busby, P. A., Tong, Y. C., & Clark, G. M. (1993). The perception of temporal modulations by cochlear implant patients. Journal of the Acoustical Society of America, 94, 124–131.

Buss, D., & Cantor, N. (Eds.). (1989). Personality psychology: Recent trends and emerging directions. New York: Springer-Verlag.

Buss, D. M. (1985). Human mate selection. American Scientist, 73, 47–51.

Buss, D. M. (1988). Love acts: The evolutionary biology of love. In R. J. Sternberg & M. L. Barnes (Eds.), The psychology of love (pp. 100–118). New Haven: Yale University Press.

Buss, D. M. (1990). Toward a biologically informed psychology of personality. Journal of Personality, 58, 1–16.

Buss, D. M. (1991). Evolutionary personality psychology. Annual Review of Psychology, 42, 459–491.

Buss, D. M. (1994). The strategies of human mating. American Scientist, 82, 238–249.

Buss, D. M., Larsen, R. J., Westen, D., & Semmelroth, J. (1992). Sex differences in jealousy: Evolution, physiology, and psychology. Psychological Science, 3, 251–255.

Butcher, J. N., Dahlstrom, W. G., Graham, J. R., Tellegen, A., &

Kaemmer, B. (1989). Manual for Restandardized Minnesota Multiphasic Personality Inventory: MMPI-2. Minneapolis: University of Minnesota Press.

Butcher, J. N., & Rouse, S. V. (1996). Personality: Individual differences and clinical assessment. Annual Review of Psychology, 47, 87–111.

Butler, J., O'Halloran, A., & Leonard, B. E. (1992). The Galway study of panic disorder: II. Changes in some peripheral markers of noradrenergic and serotonergic function in DSM-IIIR panic disorder. Journal of Affective Disorders, 26, 89–100.

Cacioppo, J. T., Petty, R. E., Losch, M. E., & Kim, H. S. (1986). Electromyographic activity over facial muscle regions can differentiate the valence and intensity of affective reactions. Journal of Personality and Social Psychology, 50, 260–268.

Cacioppo, J. T., & Tassinary, L. (1990). Principles of psychophysiology: Physical, social, and inferential elements. Cambridge, England: Cambridge University Press.

Cain, W. S. (1988). Olfaction. In R. C. Atkinson, R. J. Hernstein, L. Gardner, & R. D. Luce (Eds.), Stevens' handbook of experimental psychology (2nd ed., pp. 409–460). New York: Wiley.

Calfee, R. (1993). Paper, pencil, potential, and performance. Current Directions in Psychological Science, 2, 6–7.

Callaway, M. R., Marriott, R. G., & Esser, J. K. (1985). Effects of dominance on group decision making: Toward a stress-reduction explanation of groupthink. Journal of Personality and Social Psychology, 49, 949–952.

Camara, K. A., & Resnick, G. (1988). Interparental conflict and cooperation: Factors moderating children's post-divorce adjustment. In E. M. Hetherington & J. D. Arasteh (Eds.), Impact of divorce, single parenting, and stepparenting on children

(pp. 169–195). Hillsdale, NJ: Erlbaum.

Cameron, N. (1963). Personality development and psychopathology. Boston: Houghton Mifflin.

Campbell, A., Converse, P. E., & Rogers, W. L. (1976). The quality of American life: Perceptions, evaluations and satisfactions. New York: Russell Sage Foundation.

Campbell, J. B., & Hawley, C. W. (1982). Study habits and Eysenck's theory of extroversion-introversion. Journal of Research in Personality, 16, 139–146.

Campbell, J. D., Tesser, A., & Fairey, P. J. (1986). Conformity and attention to the stimulus: Some temporal and contextual dynamics. Journal of Personality and Social Psychology, 51, 315–324.

Campos, J. J., Barrett, K., Lamb, M., Goldsmith, H., Stenberg, C., Haith, M. M., & Campos, J. (1983). Socioemotional development. In P. Mussen (Ed.), Handbook of child psychology: Infancy and developmental psychology (4th ed., pp. 783–915). New York: Wiley.

Canestrari, R. E., Jr. (1963). Paced and self-paced learning in young and elderly adults. Journal of Gerontology, 18, 165–168.

Cannell, C. G., & Kahn, R. L. (1968). Interviewing. In G. Lindzey & E. Aronson (Eds.), Handbook of social psychology: Research methods (Vol. 2). Reading, MA: Addison-Wesley.

Cannon, W. B. (1927). The James-Lange theory of emotions: A critical examination as an alternative theory. American Journal of Psychology, 39, 106–124.

Cannon, W. B. (1929). Bodily changes in pain, hunger, fear, and rage. New York: Appleton-Century.

Cannon, W. B. (1932). The wisdom of the body. New York: Norton.

Cantor, N. (1990a). From thought to behavior: "Having" and "doing" in the study of personality and cognition. *American Psychologist, 45*, 735–750.

Cantor, N. (1990b). Social psychology and sociobiology: What can we leave to evolution? [Special Issue: Symposium on sociobiology.] *Motivation and Emotion, 14*, 245–254.

Cantor, N., & Mischel, W. (1977). Traits as prototypes: Effects on recognition memory. *Journal of Personality and Social Psychology, 35*, 38–48.

Caporael, L. R., & Brewer, M. B. (1995). Hierarchical evolutionary theory: There is an alternative, and it's not creationism. *Psychological Inquiry, 6*, 31–34.

Carlsmith, J. M., & Gross, A. (1969). Some effects of guilt on compliance. *Journal of Personality and Social Psychology, 11*, 232–240.

Carlson, M., Charlin, V., & Miller, N. (1988). Positive mood and helping behavior: A test of six hypotheses. *Journal of Personality and Social Psychology, 55*, 211–229.

Carlson, M., & Miller, N. (1987). Explanation of the relation between negative mood and helping. *Psychological Bulletin, 102*, 91–108.

Carlson, N. R. (1992). *Foundations of biological psychology.* Boston: Allyn & Bacon.

Carmichael, L., Hogan, H. P., & Walter, A. A. (1932). An experimental study of the effect of language on the reproduction of visually perceived form. *Journal of Experimental Psychology, 15*, 73–86.

Carr, W. J., & Caul, W. F. (1962). The effect of castration in rats upon the dissemination of sex odors. *Animal Behavior, 10*, 20–27.

Carroll, J. B. (1992). Cognitive abilities: The state of the art. *Psychological Science, 3*, 266–270.

Carroll, J. B. (1993). *Human cognitive abilities.* New York: Cambridge University Press.

Cartwright, R. D. (1979). The nature and function of repetitive dreams:

A survey of speculation. *Psychiatry, 42*, 131–137.

Case, R. (1985). *Intellectual development: Birth to adulthood.* New York: Academic Press.

Cattell, R. B. (1959). Anxiety, extroversion, and other second order personality factors in children. *Journal of Personality, 27*, 464–476.

Cattell, R. B. (1971). *Abilities: Their structure, growth, and action.* Boston: Houghton Mifflin.

Ceci, S. J., & Bruck, M. (1993). Suggestibility of the child witness: A historical review and synthesis. *Psychological Bulletin, 113*, 403–439.

Ceci, S. J., Huffman, M. L. C., & Smith, E. (1994). Repeatedly thinking about a non-event: Source misattributions among preschoolers [Special Issue: The recovered memory/false memory debate.] *Consciousness and Cognition: An International Journal, 3*, 388–407.

Ceci, S. J., & Liker, J. K. (1986). A day at the races: A study of IQ, expertise, and cognitive complexity. *Journal of Experimental Psychology: General, 115*, 255–266.

Ceci, S. J., Loftus, E. F., Leichtman, M. D., & Bruck, M. (1994). The possible role of source misattributions in the creation of false beliefs among preschoolers [Special Issue: Hypnosis and delayed recall: I]. *International Journal of Clinical and Experimental Hypnosis, 42*, 304–320.

Centers for Disease Control. (1989). *Surgeon General's report on smoking: Reducing health consequences of smoking: 25 years of progress.* Washington, DC: U.S. Government Printing Office.

Centers for Disease Control. (1995). *Highlights of a new report from the National Center for Health Statistics.* Atlanta: Author.

Chaiken, S. (1980). Heuristic versus systematic information processing and the use of source versus message cues in persuasion. *Journal of*

Personality and Social Psychology, 39, 752–766.

Chaiken, S., Liberman, A., & Eagly, A. H. (1989). Heuristic and systematic information processing within and beyond the persuasion context. In J. S. Uleman & J. A. Bargh (Eds.), *Unintended thought* (pp. 212–251). New York: Guilford.

Chaiken, S., & Stangor, C. (1987). Attitudes and attitude change. *Annual Review of Psychology, 38*, 575–630.

Chang, E. C. (1996). Cultural differences in optimism, pessimism, and coping: Predictors of subsequent adjustment in Asian–American and Caucasian Americans. *Journal of Counseling Psychology, 43*, 113–123.

Chang, E. C. (1997). Distinguishing between optimism and pessimism: A second look at the optimism-neuroticism hypothesis. In R. R. Hoffman, M. F. Sherrik, & J. S. Warm (Eds.), *Psychology beyond the threshold.* Washington: American Psychological Association.

Chang, E. C., D'Zurilla, T. J., & Maydeu-Olivares, A. (1994). Assessing the dimensions of optimism and pessimism using a multimeasure approach. *Cognitive Therapy and Research, 18*, 143–160.

Chapanis, N. P., & Chapanis, A. C. (1964). Cognitive dissonance: Five years later. *Psychological Bulletin, 61*, 1–22.

Charlesworth, W. R., & Dzur, C. (1987). Gender comparisons of preschoolers' behavior and resource utilization in group problem-solving. *Child Development, 58*, 191–200.

Chase, M. H., & Morales, F. R. (1983). Subthreshold excitatory activity and motoneuron discharge during REM periods of active sleep. *Science, 221*, 1195–1198.

Chase, W. G., & Simon, H. A. (1973a). The mind's eye in chess. In W. G. Chase (Ed.), *Visual information processing.* New York: Academic Press.

Chase, W. G., & Simon, H. A. (1973b). Perception in chess. *Cognitive Psychology, 4,* 55–81.

Chassin, L., & Sherman, S. (1985, April). *Adolescents' changing relationships with parents and peers: A cohort sequential study.* Paper presented at the Society for Research in Child Development, Toronto.

Chen, S. C. (1937). Social modification of the activity of ants in nest-building. *Physiological Zoology, 10,* 420–436.

Cherry, E. C. (1953). Some experiments on the recognition of speech with one and two ears. *Journal of the Acoustical Society of America, 25,* 975–979.

Cheseman, J., & Merikle, P. M. (1985). Word recognition and consciousness. In D. Besner, T. G. Waller, & G. E. MacKinnon (Eds.), *Reading research: Advances in theory and practice* (Vol. 5). New York: Academic Press.

Chi, M. T. H. (1978). Knowledge structures and memory development. In R. S. Siegler (Ed.), *Children's thinking: What develops?* Hillsdale, NJ: Erlbaum.

Chi, M. T. H., & Ceci, S. J. (1986). The restructuring of knowledge in memory development. In H. W. Reese & L. P. Lipsitt (Eds.), *Advances in child development and behavior* (Vol. 22, pp. 1–42). Orlando: Academic Press.

Chi, M. T. H., Glaser, R., & Reese, E. (1982). Expertise in problem solving. In R. J. Sternberg (Ed.), *Advances in the psychology of human intelligence* (Vol. 1, pp. 7–76). Hillside, NJ: Lawrence Erlbaum.

Children's Defense Fund. (1987). *A children's defense budget, FY 1988: An analysis of our nation's investment in children.* Washington, DC: Author.

Chipuer, H. M., Rovine, M. J., & Plomin, R. (1990). LISREL model-ing: Genetic and environmental influence of intelligence revisited. *Intelligence, 14,* 11–29.

Chomsky, N. (1957a). Review of Skinner's "Verbal Behavior." *Language, 35,* 26–58.

Chomsky, N. (1957b). *Syntactic structures.* The Hague, Netherlands: Mouton.

Chomsky, N. (1972). *Language and mind* (Vol. 9). New York: Harcourt Brace Jovanovich.

Chomsky, N. (1979). *Language and responsibility.* New York: Pantheon.

Church, A. T. (1994). Relating the Tellegen and five-factor models of personality structure. *Journal of Personality and Social Psychology, 67,* 898–909.

Church, A. T., & Burke, P. J. (1994). Exploratory and confirmatory tests of the big five and Tellegen's three- and four-dimensional scale. *Journal of Personality and Social Psychology, 66,* 93–114.

Chwalisz, K., Diener, E., & Gallagher, D. (1988). Autonomic arousal feedback and emotional experience: Evidence from the spinal cord injured. *Journal of Personality and Social Psychology, 54,* 820–828.

Cialdini, R. B., Cacioppo, J. T., Bassett, R., & Miller, J. A. (1978). Low-ball procedure for producing compliance: Commitment then cost. *Journal of Personality and Social Psychology, 36,* 463–476.

Cialdini, R. B., Darby, B. L., & Vincent, J. E. (1973). Transgressional altruism: A case for hedonism. *Journal of Personality and Social Psychology, 9,* 502–516.

Cialdini, R. B., Schaller, M., Houlihan, D., Arps, K., Fultz, J., & Beaman, A. L. (1987). Empathy-based helping: Is it selflessly or selfishly motivated? *Journal of Personality and Social Psychology, 52,* 749–758.

Cialdini, R. B., Vincent, J. E., Lewis, S. K., Catalan, J., Wheeler, D., & Darby, L. (1975). Reciprocal conces-sions procedure for inducing compliance: The door-in-theface technique. *Journal of Personality and Social Psychology, 31,* 206–215.

Clark, D. M., Salkovskis, P. M., & Chalkley, A. J. (1985). Respiratory control as a treatment for panic attacks. *Journal of Behavior Therapy and Experimental Psychiatry, 16,* 23–30.

Clark, D. M., Salkovskis, P. M., Gelder, M., Koehler, C., Martin, M., Anastasiades, P., Hackmann, A., Middleton, H., & Jeavons, A. (1988). Tests of a cognitive theory of panic. In I. Hand & H. V. Wittchen (Eds.), *Panic and phobias.* Berlin: Springer-Verlag.

Clark, E., Flavell, J. H., & Markman, E. (1983). Meanings and concepts. In P. Mussen (Ed.), *Handbook of child psychology: Cognitive Development.* (4th ed.) New York: Wiley.

Clarke-Stewart, A. (1982). *Day care.* Cambridge, MA: Harvard University Press.

Clarke-Stewart, A., Fein, G., Haith, M. M., & Campos, J. (1983). Early childhood programs. In P. Mussen (Ed.), *Handbook of child psychology: Infancy and developmental psychobiology* (4th ed., pp. 917–1000). New York: Wiley.

Clarke-Stewart, A., Thompson, W., & Lepore, S. (1989, April). *Manipulating children's interpretations through interrogation.* Paper presented at the Society for Research in Child Development, Kansas City, MO.

Cline, V. B., Croft, R. G., & Courrier, S. (1973). Desensitization of children to television violence. *Journal of Personality and Social Psychology, 27,* 360–365.

Cloninger, C. R., & Gottesman, I. I. (1987). Genetic and environmental factors in antisocial behavior disorders. In S. Mednick, T. Moffitt, & S. Strack (Eds.), *The causes of crime: New biological approaches.* Cambridge, England: Cambridge University Press.

Clum, G. A. (1987). Abandon the suicidal? A reply to Szasz. *American Psychologist, 42*, 883–885.

Cobb, S. (1976). Social support as a moderator of life stress. *Psychosomatic Medicine, 38*, 300–314.

Cohen, F., Kearney, K. A., Zegans, L. S., Kemeny, M. E., Neuhaus, J. M., & Stites, D. P. (1989). *Acute stressors, chronic stressors, and immunity and the role of optimism as a moderator* (Unpublished manuscript).

Cohen, L. (1996, April). *Infants are dumber than we think.* Paper presented at the Annual Meeting of the Southwestern Psychological Association, Houston.

Cohen, L., Rosenbaum, J. F., & Heller, V. (1988). Prescribing lithium for pregnant women. *American Journal of Psychiatry, 145*, 772–773.

Cohen, L. J. (1981). Can human irrationality be experimentally demonstrated? *Behavior and Brain Science, 4*, 317–331.

Cohen, N. J., McCloskey, M., & Wible, C. G. (1988). There is still no case for a flashbulb-memory mechanism: Reply to Schmidt and Bohannon. *Journal of Experimental Psychology: General, 117*, 336–338.

Cohen, S., & Lichtenstein, E. (1990). Partner behaviors that support quitting smoking. *Journal of Consulting and Clinical Psychology, 58*, 304–309.

Cohen, S., & Wills, T. A. (1985). Stress, social support, and the buffering hypothesis. *Psychological Bulletin, 98*, 310–357.

Cohn, T. E., & Lasley, D. J. (1986). Visual sensitivity. *Annual Review of Psychology, 37*, 495–521.

Cole, S. W., Kemeny, M. E., & Taylor, S. E. (1997). Social identity and physical health: Accelerated HIV progression in rejection-sensitive gay men. *Journal of Personality and Social Psychology, 72*, 320–335.

Cole, S. W., Kemeny, M. E., Taylor, S. E., & Visscher, B. R. (1996). Elevated physical health risk among gay men who conceal their homosexual identity. *Health Psychology, 15*, 243–251.

Collias, N. E. (1956). The analysis of socialization in sheep and goats. *Ecology, 37*, 228–239.

Collins, B. E. (1970). *Social psychology.* Reading, MA: Addison-Wesley.

Collins, B. E., & Hoyt, M. F. (1972). Personal responsibility-for-consequences: An integration and extension of the forced compliance literature. *Journal of Experimental Social Psychology, 8*, 558–593.

Collins, R. L., & Marlatt, G. A. (1981). Social modeling as a determinant of drinking behavior: Implications for prevention and treatment. *Addictive Behaviors, 6*, 233–239.

Collins, R. L., Taylor, S. E., & Skokan, L. A. (1990). A better world or a shattered vision? Changes in perspectives following victimization. *Social Cognition, 8*, 263–285.

Coltheart, M. (1989). Cognition and its disorders. *Science, 246*, 827–828.

Comfort, A. (1971). Likelihood of human pheromones. *Nature, 230*, 432–433.

Committee, A. P. A. E. (1988). Trends in ethics cases, common pitfalls, and published resources. *American Psychologist, 43*, 564–572.

Condry, J., & Condry, S. (1976). Sex differences: A study of the eye of the beholder. *Child Development, 47*, 812–819.

Conger, J. (1977). *Adolescence and youth: Psychological development in a changing world.* New York: Harper & Row.

Conley, J. J. (1985). Longitudinal stability of personality traits: A multi-trait-multimethod-multioccasion analysis. *Journal of Personality and Social Psychology, 49*, 1266–1282.

Cook, N. M. (1989). The applicability of verbal mnemonics for different populations: A review. *Applied Psychology, 3*, 322–334.

Cook, S. W. (1985). Experimenting on social issues: The case of school desegregation. *American Psychologist, 40*, 452–460.

Cooper, J., & Croyle, T. (1984). Attitudes and attitude change. *Annual Review of Psychology, 35*, 395–426.

Cooper, J., & Fazio, R. H. (1989). Research traditions, analysis, and synthesis: Building a faulty case around misinterpreted theory. *Personality and Social Psychology Bulletin, 15*, 519–529.

Corina, D. P., Vaid, J., & Bellugi, U. (1992). The linguistic basis of left hemisphere specialization. *Science, 255*, 1258–1260.

Corrigan, P. W., & Green, M. F. (1993). Schizophrenic patients' sensitivity to social cues: The role of abstraction. *American Journal of Psychiatry, 150*, 589–594.

Coryell, W., Akiskal, H. S., Leon, A. C., Winokur, G., Maser, J. D., Mueller, T. I., & Keller, M. B. (1994). The time course of nonchronic major depressive disorder: Uniformity across episodes and samples. *Archives of General Psychiatry, 51*, 405–410.

Costa, P. T., & McCrae, R. R. (1980). Still stable after all these years: Personality as a key to some issues in adulthood and old age. In P. B. Baltes & J. O. G. Brim (Eds.), *Lifespan development and behavior.* New York: Academic Press.

Costa, P. T., & McCrae, R. R. (1986). Personality stability and its implications for clinical psychology. *Clinical Psychology, 6*, 407–423.

Council, J. R. (1993). Context effects in personality research. *Current Directions in Psychological Science, 2*, 31–34.

Cousins, N. (1979). *Anatomy of an illness as perceived by the patient: Reflections on healing and regeneration.* New York: Norton.

Cowan, W. M., Fawcett, J. W., Dennis, D. M., & Stanfield, B. B. (1984).

Regressive events in neurogenesis. *Science, 225,* 1258–1265.

Coyne, J. (1976a). Depression and the response of others. *Journal of Abnormal Psychology, 85,* 186–193.

Coyne, J. (1976b). Toward an interactional description of depression. *Psychiatry, 39,* 14–27.

Coyne, J. C. (1990). Interpersonal processes in depression. In G. I. Keitner (Ed.), *Depression and families* (pp. 31–54). Washington: American Psychiatric Press.

Coyne, J. C., & Gotlib, I. H. (1983). The role of cognition in depression: A critical appraisal. *Psychological Bulletin, 94,* 472–505.

Craik, F. I. M., & Byrd, M. (1982). Aging and cognitive deficits: The role of attentional resources. In F. I. M. Craik & S. E. Trehub (Eds.), *Advances in the study of communication and affect: Aging and cognitive processes* (Vol. 8, pp. 191–211). New York: Plenum Press.

Craik, F. I. M., & Lockhart, R. S. (1972). Levels of processing: A framework for memory research. *Journal of Verbal Learning and Verbal Behavior, 11,* 671–684.

Craik, F. I. M., & Simon, E. (1980). Age differences in memory: The roles of attention and depth of processing. In L. W. Poon, J. L. Fozard, L. S. Cermak, D. Arenberg, & L. W. Thompson (Eds.), *New directions in memory and aging.* Hillsdale, NJ: Erlbaum.

Craik, F. I. M., & Tulving, E. (1975). Depth of processing and retention of words in episodic memory. *Journal of Experimental Psychology: General, 104,* 268–294.

Craske, M. G. (1991). Phobic fear and panic attacks: The same emotional states triggered by different cues? *Clinical Psychology Review, 11,* 599–620.

Crawford, H. J. (1985). *Cognitive flexibility, dissociation, and hypnosis.* Presidential address presented to the meeting of the Hypnosis Division of the APA, Los Angeles.

Creese, I., Burt, D. R., & Snyder, S. H. (1975). Brain's dopamine receptor—labeling with [dopamine-H3/43] and [H3/421 operidol-H3/43]. *Psychopharmacology Communications, 1,* 663–673.

Crewpault, C., Abraham, G., Porto, R., & Couture, M. (1977). Erotic imagery in women. In R. Gemme & C. C. Wheeler (Eds.), *Progress in Sexology* (pp. 267–283). New York: Plenum Press.

Crewpault, C., & Couture, M. (1980). Men's erotic fantasies. *Archives of Sexual Behavior, 9,* 565–582.

Crews, F. (1996). The verdict on Freud. *Psychological Science, 7,* 63–68.

Crick, F. (1994). *The astonishing hypothesis.* New York: Simon & Schuster.

Crits-Christoph, P., Cooper, A., & Luborsky, L. (1988). The accuracy of therapists' interpretations and the outcome of dynamic psychotherapy. *Journal of Consulting and Clinical Psychology, 56,* 490–495.

Crockenberg, S. (1986). *Maternal anger and the behavior of two-year-old children.* Paper presented at the International Conference on Infant Studies, Beverly Hills.

Cronbach, L. J. (1975). Five decades of public controversy over mental testing. *American Psychologist, 30,* 1–14.

Crouse, J., & Trusheim, D. (1988). *The case against the SAT.* Chicago: University of Chicago Press.

Crowe, R. R. (1991). Genetic studies of anxiety disorders. In M. T. Tsuang, K. S. Kendler, & M. T. Lyons (Eds.), *Genetic issues in psychosocial epidemiology* (pp. 175–190). New Brunswick, NJ: Rutgers University Press.

Croyle, R. T., & Cooper, J. (1983). Dissonance arousal: Physiological evidence. *Journal of Personality and Social Psychology, 45,* 782–791.

Csikszentmihalyi, M. (1996). *Creativity: Flow and the psychology of discovery and invention.* New York: HarperCollins.

Cummings, E. M. (1980). Caregiver stability and day care. *Developmental Psychology, 16,* 31–37.

Cunningham, M. R. (1979). Weather, mood, and helping behavior: Quasi-experiments with the Sunshine Samaritan. *Journal of Personality and Social Psychology, 37,* 1947–1956.

Cunningham, M. R. (1986). Measuring the physical in physical attractiveness: Quasi-experiments on the sociobiology of female facial beauty. *Journal of Personality and Social Psychology, 50,* 925–935.

Cunningham, M. R., Shaffer, D. R., Barbee, A. P., Wolff, P. L., & Kelley, D. J. (1990). Separate processes in the relation of elation and depression to helping: Social versus personal concerns. *Journal of Experimental Social Psychology, 26,* 13–33.

Curtis, R. C., & Miller, K. (1986). Believing another likes or dislikes you: Behaviors making the beliefs come true. *Journal of Personality and social Psychology, 51,* 284–290.

Curtiss, S. (1977). *Genie: A psycholinguistic study of a modern-day "wild Child."* New York: Academic Press.

Cytowic, R. E. (1993). *The man who tasted shapes: A bizarre medical mystery offers revolutionary insights into emotions, reasoning, and consciousness.* New York: Putman.

Czeisler, C. A., Moore-Ede, M. C., & Coleman, R. M. (1982). Rotating shift work schedules that disrupt sleep are improved by applying circadian principles. *Science, 217,* 460–463.

Dakof, G. A., & Taylor, S. E. (1990). Victims' perceptions of social support: What is helpful from whom? *Journal of Personality and Social Psychology, 58,* 80–89.

Damasio, A. R. (1994). *Descartes' error: Emotion, reason, and the human brain*. New York: Putnam.

Damon, W. (1977). *The social world of the child*. San Francisco: Jossey-Bass.

Damon, W. (1983). *Social and personality development*. New York: Norton.

Damon, W., & Hart, D. (1982). The development of self-understanding from childhood to adolescence. *Child Development, 53*, 841–864.

Darley, J. M., & Batson, C. D. (1973). From Jerusalem to Jericho: A study of situational and dispositional variables in helping behavior. *Journal of Personality and Social Psychology, 27*, 100–119.

Darley, J. M., & Latané, B. (1968). Bystander intervention in emergencies: Diffusion of responsibility. *Journal of Personality and Social Psychology, 8*, 377–383.

Daro, D. (1988). *Confronting child abuse: Research for effective program design*. New York: Free Press.

Darwin, C. (1859). *On the origin of species by means of natural selection, or the preservation of favoured races in the struggle for life*. London: John Murray.

Darwin, C. (1896). *The expression of the emotions in man and animals*. London: John Murray.

Datan, N., Rodeheaver, D., & Hughes, F. (1987). Adult development and aging. *Annual Review of Psychology, 38*, 153–180.

Davey, G. C. L. (1995). Preparedness and phobias: Specific evolved associations or a generalized expectancy bias? *Behavioral and Brain Sciences, 18*, 289–325.

Davidson, R. (1984). *Emotion, cognition, and behavior*. New York: Cambridge University Press.

Davidson, R. J., Ekman, P., Saron, C. D., Senulis, J., & Friesen, W. (1990). Approach/withdrawal and cerebral asymmetry: Emotional expression and brain physiology I. *Journal of Personality and Social Psychology, 58*, 330–341.

Davidson, R. J., & Fox, N. A. (1989). Frontal brain asymmetry predicts infants' response to maternal separation. *Journal of Abnormal Psychology, 98*, 127–131.

Davies, H. T., Crombie, I. K, & Macrae, W. A. (1993). Polarised views on treating neurogenic pain. *Pain, 54*, 341–346.

Davis, L. (1990). *The courage to heal workbook: For women and men survivors of child sexual abuse*. New York: HarperCollins.

Davis, M. H., & Oathout, H. A. (1987). Maintenance of satisfaction in romantic relationships: Empathy and relational competence. *Journal of Personality and Social Psychology, 53*, 397–410.

Davis, P. J. (1987). Repression and the inaccessibility of affective memories. *Journal of Personality and Social Psychology, 53*, 585–593.

Davis, P. J., & Schwartz, G. E. (1987). Repression and the inaccessibility of affective memories. *Journal of Personality and Social Psychology, 52*, 155–162.

Davison, G. C., & Neale, J. M. (1990). *Abnormal psychology* (5th ed.). New York: Wiley.

Daw, N. W. (1968). Colour-coded ganglion cells in the goldfish retina: Extension of their receptive fields by means of new stimuli. *Journal of Physiology [London], 197*, 567–592.

Dawes, R. M. (1988). *Rational choice in an uncertain world*. San Diego: Harcourt Brace Jovanovich.

Dawkins, R. (1976). *The selfish gene*. London: Oxford University Press.

Dawkins, R. (1986). *The blind watchmaker*. London: Longman.

Dawkins, R. (1996). *Climbing Mount Improbable*. London: Viking.

DeBono, K. G. (1987). Investigating the social-adjustive and value-expressive functions of attitudes: Implications for persuasion processes. *Journal of Personality and Social Psychology, 52*, 279–287.

DeBono, K. G., & Packer, M. (1991). The effects of advertising appeal on perception of product quality. *Personality and Social Psychology Bulletin, 17*, 194–200.

DeCasper, A. J., & Spence, M. J. (1986). Prenatal maternal speech influences newborn's perception of speech sounds. *Infant Behavior and Development, 9*, 133–150.

Deci, E. L., & Ryan, R. M. (1980). The empirical exploration of intrinsic motivational processes. In L. Berkowitz (Ed.), *Advances in experimental social psychology* (Vol. 13, p. 18). New York: Academic Press.

De Groot, A. D. (1965). *Thought and choice in chess*. The Hague, Netherlands: Mouton.

Deguchi, H., Fujita, T., & Sato, M. (1988). Reinforcement control of observational learning in young children: A behavioral analysis of modeling. *Journal of Experimental Child Psychology, 46*, 362–371.

DeJong, W., & Musilli, L. (1982). External pressure to comply: Handicapped versus nonhandicapped requesters and the foot-in-the-door phenomenon. *Personality and Social Psychology Bulletin, 8*, 522–527.

DeKay, W. T., & Buss, D. M. (1992). Human nature, individual differences, and the importance of context: Perspectives from evolutionary psychology. *Current Directions in Psychological Science, 1*, 184–189.

Dekker, J., & Everaerd, W. (1989). Psychological determinants of sexual arousal: A review. *Behavioral Research Therapy, 27*, 353–364.

DeLoache, J. S., & Todd, C. M. (1988). Young children's use of spatial categorization as a mnemonic strategy. *Journal of Experimental Child Psychology, 46*, 1–20.

DeLongis, A., Coyne, J. C., Dakof, G., Folkman, S., & Lazarus, R. S. (1982). Relationship of daily hassles, uplifts, and major life events to health status. *Health Psychology, 1,* 119–136.

Deluty, R. H. (1985). Consistency of assertive, aggressive, and submissive behavior for children. *Journal of Personality and Social Psychology, 49,* 1054–1065.

Demare, D., Briere, J., & Lips, H. M. (1988). Violent pornography and selfreported likelihood of sexual aggression. *Journal of Research in Personality, 22,* 140–153.

Dembroski, T. M., & Costa, P. T., Jr. (1987). Coronary prone behavior: Components of the Type A pattern and hostility. *Journal of Personality, 55,* 211–235.

Dembroski, T. M., & MacDougall, J. M. (1985). Beyond global Type A: Relationships of paralinguistic attributes, hostility, and anger-in to coronary heart disease. In T. Field, P. McAbe, & N. Schneiderman (Eds.), *Stress and coping* (pp. 223–242). Hillsdale, NJ: Erlbaum.

Dembroski, T. M., & Williams, R. B. (1989). Definition and assessment of coronary-prone behavior. In N. Schneiderman, P. Kaufman, & S. M. Weiss (Eds.), *Handbook of research methods in cardiovascular behavioral medicine.* New York: Plenum Press.

Dement, W. C. (1960). Dream deprivation. *Science, 132,* 1420–1422.

Dement, W. C. (1976). *Some must watch while some must sleep: Exploring the world of sleep.* New York: Norton.

Dement, W. C., & Kleitman, N. (1957). The relation of eye movement during sleep to dream activity: An objective method for the study of dreaming. *Journal of Experimental Psychology, 53,* 543–553.

Dennett, D. (1991). *Consciousness explained.* New York: Little, Brown.

Dent, J., & Teasdale, J. D. (1988). Negative cognition and the persistence of depression. *Journal of Abnormal Psychology, 97,* 29–34.

Denton, G. G. (1971). *The influence of visual pattern on perceived speed.* Crowthorne, England: Road Research Library.

Depression: The shadowed valley. (1975). In *The thin edge* [television series]. New York: Educational Broadcasting Corporation.

Dermer, M., Cohen, S. J., & Anderson, E. A. (1978). *Evaluative aspects of life as a function of vicarious exposure to hedonic extremes.* Unpublished manuscript, University of Wisconsin, Milwaukee.

Deutsch, M., & Gerard, H. B. (1955). A study of normative and informational influences on social judgment. *Journal of Abnormal and Social Psychology, 51,* 629–636.

DeValois, R. L., & DeValois, K. (1975). Neural coding of color. In E. C. Carterette & M. P. Friedman (Eds.), *Handbook of perception* (pp. 117–166). New York: Academic Press.

Devine, P. G. (1989). Stereotypes and prejudice: Their automatic and controlled components. *Journal of Personality and Social Psychology, 56,* 5–18.

deVries, M. W., & Peeters, F. P. M. L. (1997). Melatonin as a therapeutic agent in the treatment of sleep disturbance in depression. *Journal of Nervous and Mental Disease, 185,* 201–202.

Diamond, R. (1985). Drugs and quality of life: The patient's point of view. *Journal of Clinical Psychiatry, 46,* 29–35.

Diaz Granados, J. L., Greene, P. L., & Amsel, A. (1993). Mitigating effects of combined prenatal and postnatal exposure to ethanol on learned persistence in the weanling rat: A replication under high-peak conditions. *Behavioral Neuroscience, 107,* 1059–1066.

Diekstra, R. F. W. (1989). Suicidal behavior in adolescents and young adults: The international picture. *Crisis, 10,* 16–35.

Diener, E. (1984). Subjective well-being. *Psychological Bulletin, 95,* 542–575.

Diener, E., & Diener, C. (1996). Most people are happy. *Psychological Science, 7,* 180–185.

Diener, E., Horowitz, J., & Emmons, R. A. (1985). Happiness of the very wealthy. *Social Indicators Research, 16,* 263–274.

Diener, E., Sandvik, E., & Pavot, W. (1989). Happiness is the frequency, not intensity, of positive versus negative affect. In F. Strack, M. Argyle, & N. Schwarz (Eds.), *The Social Psychology of subjective well-being.* Oxford, England: Pergamon Press.

Dietz, P. E., & Evans, B. (1982). Pornographic imagery and prevalence of paraphilia. *American Journal of Psychiatry, 139,* 1493–1495.

Digman, J. M. (1990). Personality structure: Emergence of the five-factor model. *Annual Review of Psychology, 41,* 417–440.

Dillard, J. P. (1991). The current status of research on sequential-request compliance techniques. *Personality and Social Psychology Bulletin, 17,* 283–288.

Dillard, J. P., Hunter, J. E., & Burgoon, M. (1984). Sequential-request persuasive statements: Meta-analysis of foot-in-the-door and door-in-the-face. *Human Communication Research, 10,* 461–488.

Dimberg, U. (1990). Facial electromyography and emotional reactions. *Psychophysiology, 27,* 481–494.

Dimberg, U., & Ohman, A. (1983). The effect of directional facial cues on electrodermal conditioning to facial stimuli. *Psychophysiology, 20,* 160–167.

Dinan, T. G., & Barry, S. (1989). A comparison of electroconvulsive therapy with a combined lithium and tricyclic combination among depressed tricyclic nonresponders. *Acta Psychiatrica Scandinavica, 80,* 97–100.

Dion, K., Berscheid, E., & Walster, E. (1972). What is beautiful is good. *Journal of Personality and Social Psychology, 24*, 285–290.

Dion, K. K., & Stein, S. (1978). Physical attractiveness and interpersonal influence. *Journal of Experimental Social Psychology, 14*, 97–109.

Dishman, R. K. (1982). Compliance/adherence in health related exercise. *Health Psychology, 1*, 237–267.

Dittes, J., & Kelley, I. (1956). Effects of different conditions of acceptance upon conformity to group norms. *Journal of Abnormal and Social Psychology, 53*, 100–107.

Dixon, N. F. (1971). *Subliminal perception: The nature of a controversy.* London: McGraw-Hill.

Dobson, K. S. (1989). A meta-analysis of the efficacy of cognitive therapy for depression. *Journal of Counseling and Clinical Psychology, 57*, 414–419.

Dodge, K. A. (1986). Social information processing variables in the development of aggression and altruism in children. In C. Zahn-Waxler, E. M. Cummings, & R. Iannoti (Eds.), *Altruism and aggression: Biological and social origins.* Cambridge, England: Cambridge University Press.

Dohrenwend, B. S., Dohrenwend, B. P., Dodson, M., & Shrout, P. E. (1984). Symptoms, hassles, social supports, and life events: Problem of confounded measures. *Journal of Abnormal Psychology, 93*, 222–230.

Dolan, B. (1991). Cross-cultural aspects of anorexia nervosa and bulimia: A review. *International Journal of Eating Disorders, 10*, 67–79.

Dollard, J., Doob, L. W., Miller, N. E., Mowrer, O. H., & Sears, R. R. (1939). *Frustration and Aggression.* New Haven: Yale University Press.

Donaldson, M. (1988). Children's reasoning. In K. Richardson & S. Sheldon (Eds.), *Cognitive development to adolescence: A reader.* Hove, England: Erlbaum.

Donnelly, J. (1985). Psychosurgery. In H. I. Kaplan & B. J. Sadock (Eds.), *Comprehensive textbook of psychiatry* (4th ed., p. 1563). Baltimore: Williams & Williams.

Donnerstein, E., & Barrett, G. (1978). The effects of erotic stimuli on male aggression towards females. *Journal of Personality and Social Psychology, 36*, 180–188.

Donnerstein, E., & Hallam, J. (1978). Facilitating effects of erotica on aggression against women. *Journal of Personality and Social Psychology, 36*, 1270–1277.

Donnerstein, E., Linz, D., & Penrod, S. (1987). *The question of pornography.* New York: Free Press.

Dormen, L., & Edidin, P. (1989). Original spin. *Psychology Today*, 47–52.

Downey, G., Silver, R., & Wortman, C. B. (1990). Reconsidering the attribution-adjustment relation following a major negative event: Coping with the loss of a child. *Journal of Personality and Social Psychology, 59*, 925–940.

Drewnowski, A., Hopkins, S. A., & Kessler, R. C. (1988). The prevalence of bulimia nervosa in the U.S. college student population. *American Journal of Public Health, 78*, 1322–1325.

Drummey, A. B., & Newcombe, N. (1995). Remembering versus knowing the past: Children's explicit and implicit memories for pictures. *Journal of Experimental Child Psychology, 59*, 549–565.

Dryden, W., & Golden, W. L. (Eds.). (1986). *Cognitive behavioral approaches to psychotherapy.* London: Harper & Row.

Duncker, K. (1945). *On problem-solving* (L. S. Lees, Trans.). (Vol. Whole no. 58).

Dunkel-Schetter, C., & Wortman, C. B. (1982). The interpersonal dynamics of cancer: Problems in social relationships and their impact on the patient. In H. Freedman (Ed.), *Interpersonal issues in health care* (pp. 69–100, 117). New York: Academic Press.

Dunn, J. (1988). Mothers and siblings: Connections between three family relationships. In R. Hinde & J. Stevenson-Hinde (Eds.), *Towards understanding families.* Cambridge, England: Cambridge University Press.

Dunn, J. (1997). Lessons from the study of bidirectional effects. *Journal of Social and Personal Relationships, 14*, 565–573.

Dunn, J., & Plomin, R. (1990). *Separate lives: Why siblings are so different.* New York: Basic Books.

Dunn, J., Stocker, C., & Plomin, R. (1991). Nonshared experiences within the family: Correlates of behavioral problems in middle childhood. *Annual Progress in Child Psychiatry and Child Development*, 27–44.

Durkheim, E. (1897/1951). *Suicide: A study of sociology* (J. A. Spaulding & G. Simpson, Trans.). New York: Free Press.

Dusek, D., & Girdano, D. (1980). *Drugs: A factual account.* Reading, MA: Addison-Wesley.

Dutta, R., Schulenberg, E., & Lair, T. J. (1986, April). *The effect of job characteristics on cognitive abilities and intellectual flexibility.* Paper presented at the meetings of the Eastern Psychological Association, New York.

Dweck, C. S., & Leggett, E. L. (1988). A social-cognitive approach to motivation and personality. *Psychological Review, 95*, 256–273.

Dworetsky, J. P., & Davis, N. J. (1989). *Human development: A lifespan approach.* St. Paul, MN: West.

D'Zurilla, T. J. (1986). *Problem solving therapy.* New York: Springer-Verlag.

Eagly, A. H. (1987). *Sex differences in social behavior: A social role interpretation.* Hillsdale, NJ: Erlbaum.

Eagly, A. H., Ashmore, R. D., Makhijani, M. G., & Longo, L. C. (1991). What is beautiful is good, but: A meta-analytic review of research on the physical attractiveness stereotype. *Psychological Bulletin, 110*, 109–128.

Eagly, A. H., Mladinic, A., & Otto, S. (1991). Are women evaluated more favorably than men? *Psychology of Women Quarterly, 15*, 203–216.

Eagly, A. H., & Steffen, V. J. (1986). Gender and aggressive behavior: A meta-analytic review of the social psychology literature. *Psychological Bulletin, 100*, 309–330.

Eaker, E. D., & Castelli, W. P. (1988). Type A behavior and coronary heart disease in women: Fourteen-year incidence from the Framingham Study. In B. K. Houston & C. R. Snyder (Eds.), *Type A behavior pattern: Research, theory, and intervention* (pp. 83–97). New York: Wiley.

Eastwood, M. R., Whitton, J. L., Kramer, P. M., & Peter, A. M. (1985). Infradian rhythms: A comparison of affective disorders and normal persons. *Archives of General Psychiatry, 42*, 297–299.

Eccles, J. S. (1985). Why doesn't Jane run? Sex differences in educational and occupational patterns. In F. D. Horowitz & M. O'Brien (Eds.), *The gifted and talented: Developmental perspectives*. Washington, DC: American Psychological Association.

Eckardt, M. J., Hartford, T. C., & Kaelber, C. T. (1981). Health hazards associated with alcohol consumption. *Journal of the American Medical Association, 246*, 648–666.

Eckenrode, J. (1984). Impact of chronic and acute stressors on daily reports of mood. *Journal of Personality and Social Psychology, 46*, 907–918.

Educational Testing Service. (1980). *Test scores and family income*. Princeton, NJ: Author.

Edwards, B. (1979). *Drawing on the right side of the brain*. Los Angeles: J.P. Tarcher.

Egeland, B. (1991, February). Paper presented at the American Association for the Advancement of Science, Washington, DC.

Ehlers, C. L., Frank, E., & Kupfer, D. J. (1988). Social zeitbars and biological rhythms: A unified approach to understanding the etiology of depression. *Archives of General Psychiatry, 45*, 948–952.

Eibl-Eibesfeldt, I. (1970). *Ethology: The biology of behavior* (E. Klinghammer, Trans.). New York: Holt, Rinehart & Winston.

Eich, E., Macaulay, D., Schwartz, A., Ho, K., & Ritov, I. (1997). Memory, amnesia, and dissociative identity disorder. *Psychological Science, 8*, 417–422.

Eichorn, D., Hunt, J., & Honzik, M. P. (1981). Experience, personality, and IQ: Adolescence to middle age. In D. Eichorn, J. Clausen, N. Haan, M. Honzik, & P. Mussen (Eds.), *Present and past in middle life*. New York: Academic Press.

Eimas, P. D., Siqueland, E. R., Jusczyk, P., & Vigorito, J. (1971). Speech perception in infants. *Science, 171*, 303–306.

Eisdorfer, C., Axelrod, S., & Wilkie, F. (1963). Stimulus exposure time as a factor in serial learning in an aged sample. *Journal of Abnormal and Social Psychology, 67*, 594–600.

Eisenberger, R., Cotterell, N., & Marvel, J. (1987). Reciprocation ideology. *Journal of Personality and Social Psychology, 53*, 743–750.

Ekman, P. (1982). *Emotion in the human face* (2nd ed.). New York: Cambridge University Press.

Ekman, P. (1985). *Telling lies: Clues to deceit in the marketplace, marriage, and politics*. New York: Norton.

Ekman, P., & Friesen, W. V. (1969). The repertoire of nonverbal behavior categories, origins, usage, and coding. *Semiotica, 1*, 49–98.

Ekman, P., & Friesen, W. V. (1974). Detecting deception from body or face. *Journal of Personality and Social Psychology, 29*, 288–295.

Ekman, P., & Friesen, W. V. (1986). A new pan-cultural facial expression of emotion. *Motivation and Emotion, 10*, 159–169.

Elias, J. Z. (1989). The changing American scene in the use of projective techniques: An overview. *British Journal of Projective Psychology, 34*(2), 31–39.

Elkin, I., Shea, M. T., Watkins, J. T., Imber, S. D., Sotsky, S. M., Collins, J. F., Glass, D. R., Pilkonis, P. A., Leber, W. R., Docherty, J. P., Fiester, S. J., & Parloff, M. B. (1989). National institute of mental health treatment of depression collaborative research program. *Archives of General Psychiatry, 46*, 971–982.

Elkind, D. (1961). Children's discovery of the conservation of mass, weight, and volume: Piaget replications studies II. *Journal of Genetic Psychology, 98*, 37–46.

Elkind, D. (1981). *Children and adolescents: Interpretive essays on Jean Piaget*. New York: Oxford University Press.

Emerick, C. D. (1987). Alcoholics anonymous: Affiliation processes and effectiveness as treatment. *Alcoholism: Clinical and Experimental Research, 11*, 416–423.

Emmelkamp, P. M. G. (1994). Behavior therapy with adults. In A. E. Bergin & S. L. Garfield (Eds.), *Handbook of psychotherapy and behavior change* (4th ed., pp. 379–427). New York: Wiley.

Emmons, R. A., & Diener, E. (1985). Factors predicting satisfaction judgments: A comparative examination. *Social Indicators Research, 16*, 157–167.

Empson, J. F. F. (1990). *Sleep and dreaming*. Winchester, MA: Faber & Faber.

Endler, N. S., Rushton, J. P., & Roediger, H. L., III. (1978). Productivity and scholarly impact (citations) of British, Canadian, and U.S.

Departments of Psychology (1975). *American Psychologist, 33,* 1064–1082.

Engel, G. L. (1975). The death of a twin: Mourning and anniversary reactions: Fragments of 10 years of self-analysis. *International Journal of Psycho Analysis, 56*(1), 23–40.

Engel, G. L. (1995). Is grief a disease? A challenge for medical research. In A. M. Eward, J. E. Dimsdale, B. T. Engel, D. R. Lipsitt, D. Oken, J. D. Sapira, D. Shapiro, & H. Weiner (Eds.), *Toward an integrated medicine: Classics from "Psychosomatic Medicine," 1959–1979* (pp. 1–8). Washington, DC: American Psychiatric Press.

Engen, T., Lipsitt, L. P., & Kaye, H. (1963). Olfactory responses and adaptation in the human neonate. *Journal of Comparative and Physiological Psychology, 56,* 73–77.

English, C. J., Maclaren, W. M., Court-Brown, C., Hughes, S. P., Porter, R. W., Wallace, W. A., Graves, R. J., Pethick, A. J., & Soutar, C. A. (1995). Relations between upper limb soft tissue disorders and repetitive movements at work. *American Journal of Industrial Medicine, 27,* 75–90.

Epstein, S. (1979). The ecological study of emotions in humans. In K. Blankstein (Ed.), *Advances in the study of communication and affect.* New York: Plenum Press.

Epstein, S. (1983). Aggregation and beyond: Some basic issues on the prediction of behavior. *Journal of Personality, 51,* 360–392.

Erber, J. T., Herman, J., & Botwinick, J. (1980). The effects of encoding instructions on recall and recognition memory. *Experimental Aging Research, 6,* 341–348.

Erdelyi, M. H. (1992). Psychodynamics and the unconscious. *American Psychologist, 47,* 784–787.

Erdelyi, M. H. (1994). Hypnotic hypermnesia: The empty set of hypermnesia. [Special Issue: Hypnosis and delayed recall.]

International Journal of Clinical and Experimental Hypnosis, 42, 379–390.

Erdley, C. A., & D'Agostino, P. R. (1988). Cognitive and affective components of automatic priming effects. *Journal of Personality and Social Psychology, 54,* 741–747.

Erickson, R. P. (1984). On the neural bases of behavior. *American Scientist, 72,* 233–241.

Ericsson, A. E. (1985). Memory skill. *Canadian Journal of Psychology, 39,* 188–231.

Ericsson, A. E., & Chase, W. G. (1985). Exceptional memory. *American Scientist, 70,* 607–615.

Ericsson, K. A., Chase, W. G., & Faloon, S. (1980). Acquisition of a memory skill. *Science, 208,* 1181–1182.

Ericsson, K. A., & Polson, P. G. (1988). An experimental analysis of the mechanisms of a memory skill. *Journal of Experimental Psychology: Learning, Memory, and Cognition, 14,* 305–316.

Ericsson, K. A., & Simon, H. A. (1980). Verbal reports as data. *Psychological Review, 87,* 255–261.

Erikson, E. H. (1950). *Childhood and society.* New York: W. W. Norton.

Ernst, E. (1994). Is acupuncture effective for pain control? *Journal of Pain and Symptom Management, 9,* 72–74.

Ervin, S. (1964). Imitation and structural change in children's language. In E. H. Lenneberg (Ed.), *New Directions in the study of language.* Cambridge, MA: MIT Press.

Evans, J. S. B. T. (1982). On statistical intuitions and inferential rules: A discussion of Kahneman and Tversky. *Cognition, 12,* 319–323.

Evans, R. (1980). Behavioral medicine: A new applied challenge to social psychologists. In L. Bickman (Ed.), *Applied social psychology annual* (Vol. 1). Beverly Hills: Sage.

Everly, G. S., Jr. (1989). *A clinical guide to the treatment of the human stress response.* New York: Plenum Press.

Eward, A. M., Dimsdale, J. E., Engel, B. T., Lipsitt, D. R., Oken, D., Sapira, J. D., Shapiro, D., & Weiner, H. (Eds.). (1995). *Toward an integrated medicine: Classics from "Psychosomatic Medicine," 1959–1979.* Washington, DC: American Psychiatric Press.

Exner, J. E., Jr. (1969). *The Rorschach systems.* New York: Grune & Stratton.

Exner, J. E., Jr. (1974). *The Rorschach: A comprehensive scoring system.* (Vol. 1). New York: Wiley.

Exner, J. E., Jr. (1991). *The Rorschach: A comprehensive scoring system: Vol. 2. Interpretation* (2nd ed.). New York: Wiley.

Exner, J. E., Jr. (1993). *The Rorschach: A comprehensive scoring system: Vol. 1. Basic Foundations* (3rd ed.). New York: Wiley.

Exner, J. E., Jr. (1996). A comment on "The comprehensive scoring system for the Rorschach: A critical examination." *Psychological Science, 7,* 11–13.

Exner, J. E., Jr., & Weiner, I. B. (1994). *The Rorschach: A comprehensive scoring system: Vol. 3. Assessment of children and adolescents* (2nd ed.). New York: Wiley.

Eysenck, H. J. (1970). *The structure of human personality.* London: Methuen.

Eysenck, H. J. (1991). Dimensions of personality: The biosocial approach to personality. In J. Strelau & A. Angleitner (Eds.), *Explorations in temperament* (pp. 87–103). London: Plenum Press.

Eysenck, H. J. (1987). Intelligence and reaction time: The contributions of Arthur Jensen. In S. Mogdil & C. Mogdil (Eds.), *Arthur Jensen: Consensus and controversy.* New York: Falmer.

Fackelman, K. (1993). Marijuana and the brain. *Science News, 143,* 88–89.

Falloon, I. R. (1988). Behavioral family management in coping with functional psychosis: Principles, practice, and recent developments. *International Journal of Mental Health, 17*(1), 35–47.

Falloon, I. R., Boyd, J. L., McGill, C. W., Razani, J., Moss, H. B., & Gilderman, A. N. (1982). Family management in the prevention of exacerbation of schizophrenia: A controlled study. *New England Journal of Medicine, 306,* 1437–1440.

Falloon, I. R., Boyd, J. L., McGill, C. W., Williamson, M., Razani, J., Moss, H. B., Gilderman, A. N., & Simpson, G. M. (1985). Family management in the prevention of morbidity of schizophrenia. *Archives of General Psychiatry, 42,* 887–896.

Fancier, R. E. (1985). *The intelligence men: Makers of the IQ controversy.* New York: Norton.

Farina, A., Gliha, D., Boudreau, L. A., Allen, J. G., & Sherman, M. (1971). Mental illness and the impact of believing others know about it. *Journal of Abnormal Psychology, 77,* 1–5.

Fava, M., Copeland, P., Schweiger, U., & Herzog, D. (1989). Neurochemical abnormalities in anorexia nervosa and bulimia nervosa. *American Journal of Psychiatry, 146,* 963–971.

Fawcett, J. (1990). *Before it's too late: What to do when someone you know attempts suicide.* West Point, PA: American Association of Suicidology, prepared in cooperation with Merck, Sharp and Dohme Health Information Services.

Fazio, R. H. (1990). Multiple processes by which attitudes guide behavior: The MODE model as an integrative framework. In M. P. Zanna (Ed.), *Advances in experimental social psychology* (Vol. 23, pp. 75–109). New York: Academic Press.

Fazio, R. H. (1995). Attitudes as object-evaluation associations: Determinants, consequences, and correlates of attitude accessibility.

In R. E. Petty & J. A. Krosnick (Eds.), *Attitude strength: Antecedents and consequences.* Hillsdale, NJ: Erlbaum.

Fazio, R. H., & Zanna, M. P. (1981). Direct experience and attitude-behavior consistency. In L. Berkowitz (Ed.), *Advances in experimental social psychology* (Vol. 14, pp. 161–202). New York: Academic Press.

Fechner, G. T. (1860). *Elemente der psychophysik [Elements of Psychophysics].* Leipzig: Breitkopf & Hartel.

Federal Bureau of Investigation. (1991). *Uniform crime reports.* Washington, DC: U.S. Dept. of Justice.

Feinberg, I., & Fein, G. (1982). Computer-detected patterns of electroencephalographic delta activity during and after extended sleep. *Science, 215,* 1131–1133.

Feinberg, T. E., Rifkin, A., Schaffer, C., & Walker, E. (1986). Facial discrimination and emotional recognition in schizophrenia and affective disorders. *Archives of General Psychiatry, 43,* 276–279.

Feingold, A. (1988). Cognitive gender differences are disappearing. *American Psychologist, 43*(2), 95–103.

Feingold, A. (1990). Gender differences in effects of physical attractiveness on romantic attraction: A comparison across five research paradigms. *Journal of Personality and Social Psychology, 59,* 981–993.

Feingold, A. (1991). Sex differences in the effects of similarity and physical attractiveness on opposite-sex attraction. *Basic and Applied Social Psychology, 12,* 357–367.

Feingold, B. F. (1975). *Why your child is hyperactive.* New York: Random House.

Feldman, R. S., Devin-Sheehan, L., & Allen, V. L. (1978). Nonverbal clues as indicators of verbal dissembling. *American Educational Research Journal, 15,* 217–231.

Felton, B. J., Revenson, T. A., & Hinrichsen, G. A. (1984). Stress and

coping in the explanation of psychological adjustment among chronically ill adults. *Social Science and Medicine, 18,* 889–898.

Fendrich, R., Wessinger, C. M., & Gazzaniga, M. S. (1992). Residual vision in scotoma: Implications for blindsight. *Science, 258,* 1489–1491.

Fernald, A., & Kuhl, P. (1987). Acoustic determinants of infant preferences for motherese speech. *Infant Behavior and Development, 10,* 279–293.

Festinger, L. (1957). *A theory of cognitive dissonance.* Stanford, CA: Stanford University Press.

Festinger, L., & Carlsmith, J. M. (1959). Cognitive consequences of forced compliance. *Journal of Abnormal and Social Psychology, 58,* 203–210.

Festinger, L., Schachter, S., & Back, K. (1950). *Social pressures in informal groups: A study of human factors in housing.* New York: Harper & Row.

Field, T. M., Woodson, R., Greenberg, R., & Cohen, D. (1982). Discrimination and imitation of facial expressions by neonates. *Science, 218,* 179–181.

Figley, C. R. (1989). *Helping traumatized families.* San Francisco: Jossey-Bass.

Fillion, T. J., & Blass, E. M. (1986). Infantile experience with suckling odors determines adult sexual behavior in male rats. *Science, 231,* 729–731.

Fincham, F. D., Beach, S., & Nelson, G. (1987). Attribution processes in distressed and nondistressed couples: Causal and responsibility attributions for spouse and behavior. *Cognitive Therapy and Research, 11,* 71–86.

Fincham, F. D., & Bradbury, T. (1988). The impact of attributions in marriage: Empirical and conceptual foundations. *British Journal of Clinical Psychology, 27,* 77–90.

Finman, R., & Berkowitz, L. (1989). Some factors influencing the effect of depressed mood on anger and overt hostility toward another. *Journal of Research in Personality, 23,* 70–84.

Fischer, C. L., Daniels, J. C., Levin, S. L., Kimzey, S. L., Cobb, E. K., & Ritzman, W. E. (1972). Effects of the spaceflight environment on man's immune system: II. Lymphocyte counts and reactivity. *Aerospace Medicine, 43,* 1122–1125.

Fishbein, M., & Ajzen, I. (1975). *Belief, attitude, intention, and behavior: An introduction to theory and research.* Reading, MA: Addison-Wesley.

Fiske, S. (1993). Controlling other people: The impact of power on stereotyping. *American Psychologist, 48,* 621–628.

Fiske, S., & Taylor, S. (1984). *Social cognition.* New York: Random House.

Fiske, S., & Taylor, S. (1991). *Social cognition.* New York: McGraw-Hill.

Fivush, R., Hudson, J., & Nelson, K. (1984). Children's long-term memory for a novel event. *Merrill-Palmer Quarterly, 30,* 303–316.

Fixsen, D. L., Phillips, E. A., & Wolf, M. M. (1976). The teaching-family model of group home treatment. In W. E. Craighead, A. E. Kazdin, & M. J. Mahoney (Eds.), *Behavior modification: Principles, issues, and applications.* Boston: Houghton Mifflin.

Flannigan, O. (1992). *Consciousness reconsidered.* Cambridge, MA: MIT Press.

Flavell, J. H. (1986). Development of children's knowledge about the appearance-reality distinction: Distinguished Scientific Contributions Award Address. *American Psychologist, 41,* 418–425.

Flavell, J. H., Miller, P. H., & Miller, S. A. (1993). *Cognitive development.* Englewood Cliffs, NJ: Prentice Hall.

Flavell, J. H., Shipstead, S. G., & Croft, K. (1978). Young children's knowledge about visual perception: Hiding objects from others. *Child Development, 49,* 1208–1211.

Fleming, I., Baum, A., Davidson, L. M., Rectanus, E., & McArdle, S. (1987). Chronic stress as a factor in physiologic reactivity to challenge. *Health Psychology, 6,* 221–237.

Fletcher, R. (1991). *Science, ideology, and the media: The Cyril Burt scandal.* New Brunswick, NJ: Transaction.

Flora, J. A., Maibach, E. W., & Maccoby, N. (1989). The role of the media across four levels of health promotion intervention. *Annual Review of Public Health, 10,* 181–201.

Flynn, J. C. (1991). *Cocaine.* New York: Birch Lane Press.

Flynn, J. P., Vanegas, H., Foote, W., & Edwards, S. (1970). Neural mechanisms involved in a cat's attack on a rat. In R. E. Whalen (Ed.), *Neural control of behavior* (pp. 135–173). New York: Academic Press.

Folkard, S., Arendt, J., & Clark, M. (1993). Can melatonin improve shift-workers' tolerance of the night shift? Some preliminary findings. *Chronobiology International, 10,* 315–320.

Folkman, S. (1997). Introduction to the special section: Use of bereavement narratives to predict well-being in gay men whose partner died of AIDS—Four theoretical perspectives. *Journal of Personality and Social Psychology, 72,* 851–854.

Folkman, S., Chesney, M., Collette, L., & Boccellari, A. (1996). Postbereavement depressive mood and its prebereavement predictors in HIV+ and HIV− gay men. *Journal of Personality and Social Psychology, 70,* 336–348.

Folkman, S., Chesney, M. A., & Christopher-Richards, A. Cooke (1994). Stress and coping in caregiving partners of men with AIDS. *Psychiatric Clinics of North America, 17,* 35–53.

Folkman, S., Lazarus, R. S., Dunkel-Schetter, C., DeLongis, A., & Gruen, R. J. (1986). Dynamics of a stressful encounter: Cognitive appraisal, coping, and encounter outcomes. *Journal of Personality and Social Psychology, 50,* 992–1003.

Folkman, S., Moskowitz, J. T., Ozer, E. M., & Park, C. L. (1997). Positive meaningful events and coping in the context of HIV/AIDS. In B. H. Gottlieb (Ed.), *Coping with chronic stress. The Plenum series on stress and coping* (pp. 293–314). New York: Plenum Press.

Fordyce, M. W. (1988). A review of results on the happiness measures: A 60 second index of happiness and mental health. *Social Indicators Research, 20,* 355–381.

Forehand, R., Long, N., & Brody, G. (1988). Divorce and marital conflict: Relationship to adolescent competence and adjustment in early adolescence. In E. M. Hetherington & J. D. Arasteh (Eds.), *Impact of divorce, single parenting, and stepparenting on children* (pp. 155–167). Hillsdale, NJ: Erlbaum.

Forgas, J. P., & Bower, G. H. (1987). Mood effects on person-perception judgments. *Journal of Personality and Social Psychology, 53,* 53–60.

Foulkes, D. (1964). Theories of dream formation and recent studies of sleep consciousness. *Psychological Bulletin, 62,* 236–247.

Fowles, D. C., Christie, M. J., Edelberg, R., Grings, W. W., Lykken, D. T., & Venables, P. H. (1981). Public recommendations for electrodermal measurements. Committee Report. *Psychophysiology, 232–239.*

Fox, L. H., & Washington, J. (1985). Programs for the gifted and talented: Past, present, and future. In F. D. Horowitz & M. O'Brien (Eds.), *The gifted and talented: Developmental perspectives* (pp. 197–221). Washington, DC: American Psychological Association.

Fox, N. A., Kimmerly, N. L., & Schafer, W. D. (1991). Attachment to mother/attachment to father: A meta-analysis. *Child Development, 61,* 832–837.

Foy, D. W., Carroll, E. M., & Donahoe, C. P. (1987). Etiological factors in the development of PTSD in clinical samples of combat veterans. *Journal of Clinical Psychology, 43,* 17–27.

Foy, D. W., Resnick, H. S., Sipprelle, R. C., & Carroll, E. M. (1987). Premilitary, military, and postmilitary factors in the development of combat-related posttraumatic stress disorder. *Behavior Therapist, 10,* 3–9.

Fraser, S. (Ed.). (1995). *The bell curve wars.* New York: Basic Books.

Freedman, J. L. (1965). Long-term behavioral effects of cognitive dissonance. *Journal of Experimental Social Psychology, 1,* 145–155.

Freedman, J. L., & Fraser, S. C. (1966). Compliance without pressure: The foot-in-the-door technique. *Journal of Personality and Social Psychology, 4,* 195–202.

Freud, S. (1900). *The interpretation of dreams* (J. Strachey, Trans.). New York: Avon.

Freud, S. (1917). Mourning and melancholia. In E. Jones (Ed.), *Collected papers* (pp. 152–170). London: Hogarth Press/Institute of Psycho-Analysis.

Freud, S. (1920/1975). *Beyond the pleasure principle* (J. Strachey, Trans.). New York: W. W. Norton.

Freud, S. (1923). *The ego and the id.* London: Hogarth Press.

Freud, S. (1925/1976). *Some physical consequences of the anatomical distinction between the sexes* (J. Strachey, Trans.). (Vol. 19). New York: W. W. Norton.

Freud, S. (1930/1963). *Civilization and its discontents* (J. Strachey, Trans.). New York: W. W. Norton.

Freud, S. (1935). *A general introduction to psychoanalysis.* New York: Washington Square Press.

Frey, D., & Gaertner, D. (1986). Helping and the avoidance of inappropriate interracial behavior: A strategy that perpetuates a non-prejudiced self-image. *Journal of Personality and Social Psychology, 50,* 1083–1090.

Friedman, H. S. (1991). *The self-healing personality: Why some people achieve health and others succumb to illness.* New York: Henry Holt.

Friedman, H. S. (1992). *Hostility, coping, and health.* Washington, DC: American Psychological Association.

Friedman, H. S., Hawley, P. H., & Tucker, J. S. (1994). Personality, health, and longevity. *Current Directions in Psychological Science, 3,* 37–41.

Friedman, M., & Rosenman, R. H. (1974). *Type A behavior and your heart.* New York: Knopf.

Fries, J. F., & Crapo, L. M. (1981). *Vitality and aging: Implications of the rectangular curve.* San Francisco: W. H. Freeman.

Frijda, N. H. (1986). *The emotions.* New York: Cambridge University Press.

Frijda, N. H. (1988). The laws of emotion. *American Psychologist, 43,* 349–358.

Frijda, N. H., Kuipers, P., & ter Schure, E. (1989). Relations among emotion, appraisal, and emotion action tendencies. *Journal of Personality and Social Psychology, 57,* 212–228.

Fry, A. F., & Hale, S. (1996). Processing speed, working memory, and fluid intelligence: Evidence for a developmental cascade. *Psychological Science, 7,* 237–241.

Fryauf-Bertschy, H., Tyler, R. S., Kelsay, D. M., & Gantz, B. J. (1992). Performance over time of congenitally deaf and postlingually deafened children using a multichannel cochlear implant. *Journal of Speech and Hearing Research, 35,* 913–920.

Frye, J. S., & Stockton, R. A. (1982). Discriminant analysis of posttraumatic stress disorder among a group of Viet Nam veterans. *American Journal of Psychiatry, 139,* 52–56.

Funder, D. C. (1991). Global traits: A neo-Allportian approach to personality. *Psychological Science, 2,* 31–39.

Furstenberg, F. F. (1988). Child care after divorce and remarriage. In E. M. Hetherington & J. D. Arasteh (Eds.), *Impact of divorce, single parenting, and stepparenting on children* (pp. 245–261). Hillsdale, NJ: Erlbaum.

Gaertner, S. L., Dovidio, J. F., Anastasio, P. A., Bachman, B. A., & Rust, M. C. (1993). The common ingroup identity model: Recategorization and the reduction of intergroup bias. In W. Stroebe & M. Hewstone (Eds.), *European Review of Social Psychology* (Vol. 4). London: Wiley.

Gaertner, S. L., Mann, J., Murrell, A., & Dovidio, J. F. (1989). Reducing intergroup bias: The benefits of recategorization. *Journal of Personality and Social Psychology, 57,* 239–249.

Gaertner, S. L., Mann, J. A., Dovidio, J. F., Murrell, J. A., & Pomare, M. (1990). How does cooperation reduce intergroup bias? *Journal of Personality and Social Psychology, 59,* 692–704.

Garbarino, J., & Garbarino, A. (1986). *Emotional maltreatment of children.* Chicago: National Commission for Prevention of Child Abuse.

Garcia, J., Hankins, W. G., & Rusiniak, K. W. (1974). Behavioral regulation of the *milieu interne* in man and rat. *Science, 185,* 824–831.

Garcia, J., Kimeldorf, D. J., & Hunt, E. L. (1961). The use of ionizing radiation as a motivating stimulus. *Psychological Review, 68,* 383.

Garcia, J., Kimeldorf, D. J., Hunt, E. L., & Davies, B. P. (1956). Food and water consumption of rats during exposure to gamma radiation. *Radiation Research, 4*, 33–41.

Garcia, J., & Koelling, R. A. (1966). Relation of cue to consequence in avoidance learning. *Psychonometric Science, 4*, 123–124.

Gardner, B. T., & Gardner, R. A. (1972). Two-way communication with an infant chimpanzee. In A. M. Schrier & F. Stollnitz (Eds.), *Behavior of nonhuman primates* (Vol. 4). New York: Academic Press.

Gardner, H. (1983). *Frames of mind: The theory of multiple intelligences.* New York: Basic Books.

Gardner, H. (1985). *The mind's new science.* New York: Basic Books.

Gardner, H. (1993). *Creating minds.* New York: Basic Books.

Gardner, H. (1995). Cracking open the IQ box. In S. Fraser (Ed.), *The bell curve wars* (pp. 23–35). New York: Basic Books.

Gardner, H., Hatch, T., & Torff, B. (1997). A third perspective: The symbol systems approach. In R. J. Sternberg & E. L. Grigorenko (Eds.), *Intelligence, heredity, and environment* (pp. 243–268). New York: Cambridge University Press.

Gardner, H., Torff, B., & Hatch, T. (1996). The age of innocence reconsidered: Preserving the best of the progressive traditions in psychology and education. In N. T. David & R. Olson (Eds.), *The handbook of education and human development: New models of learning, teaching and schooling* (pp. 28–55). Oxford, England: Blackwell.

Garfield, S. L., & Bergin, A. E. (Eds.). (1986). *Handbook of psychotherapy and behavior change* (3rd ed.). New York: Wiley.

Garfinkle, P. E., & Garner, D. M. (1982). *Anorexia nervosa: A multidimensional perspective.* New York: Brunner.

Garland, A. F., & Zigler, E. (1993). Adolescent suicide prevention: Current research and social policy implications. *American Psychologist, 48*, 169–182.

Gay, P. (1989). *Freud: A life for our time.* New York: Anchor Books/Doubleday.

Gazzaniga, M. S., Fendrich, R., & Wessinger, C. M. (1994). Blindsight reconsidered. *Current Directions in Psychological Science, 3*, 93–96.

Geen, R. G. (1995). *Human motivation: A social psychological approach.* San Diego: Brooks/Cole.

Geer, J. H., & Head, S. (1990). The sexual response system. In J. T. Cacioppo & L. G. Tassinary (Eds.), *Principles of psychophysiology: Physical, social, and inferential elements.* Cambridge, England: Cambridge University Press.

Geers, A. E., & Moog, J. S. (1992). The Central Institute for the Deaf cochlear implant study: A progress report [Special Issue: Cochlear implants]. *Journal of Speech, Language, Pathology, and Audiology, 16*, 129–140.

Geisler, C. (1986). Repression: A psychoanalytic perspective revisited. *Psychoanalysis and Contemporary Thought, 8*, 253–298.

Geldard, F. A. (1972). *The human senses* (2nd ed.). New York: Wiley.

Gelman, D. (1989, August 14). Dreams on the couch. *Newsweek*, 45–47.

Gelman, R. (1972). Logical capacity of very young children: Number invariance rules. *Child Development, 43*, 75–90.

Gerbner, G., & Gross, L. (1976). Living with television: The violence profile. *Journal of Communications, 26*, 172–199.

Gerbner, G., Gross, L., Morgan, M., & Signorielli, N. (1986). Living with television: The dynamics of the cultivation process. In J. Bryant & D. Zillman (Eds.), *Perspectives on Media Effects.* Hillsdale, NJ: Erlbaum.

Geschwind, N. (1979). Specialization of the human brain. *Scientific American, 241*, 180–199.

Ghiselin, B. (1952). *The creative process.* Berkeley: University of California Press.

Gianoulakis, C. (1993). Endogenous opioids and excessive alcohol consumption. *Journal of Psychiatry and Neuroscience, 18*, 148–156.

Gibbons, F. X., & Kassin, S. M. (1987). Information consistency and perceptual set: Overcoming the mental retardation "schema." *Journal of Applied Social Psychology, 17*, 810–827.

Gibbs, J., & Schnell, S. (1986, April). *Moral development versus socialization: A critique of the controversy.* Paper presented at the Society for Research in Child Development, Toronto.

Gibbs, R. W. (1992a). *The poetics of mind: Figurative thought, language, and understanding.* New York: Cambridge University Press.

Gibbs, R. W. (1992b). What do idioms really mean? *Journal of Memory and Language, 31*, 485–506.

Gibbs, R. W., & Kearney, L. R. (1994). When parting is such sweet sorrow: The comprehension and appreciation of oxymora. *Journal of Psycholinguistic Research, 23*, 75–89.

Gibson, J. J. (1950). *The perception of the visual world.* Boston: Houghton Mifflin.

Gibson, J. J. (1966). *The senses considered as perceptual systems.* Boston: Houghton Mifflin.

Gibson, J. J. (1979). *The ecological approach to visual perception.* Boston: Houghton Mifflin.

Gick, M. L., & Holyoak, K. J. (1980). Analogical problem solving. *Cognitive Psychology, 12*, 306–355.

Gigerenzer, G., Hell, W., & Blank, H. (1988). Presentation and content: The use of base rates as a continuous variable. *Journal of Experimental Psychology: Human Perception and Performance, 14*, 513–525.

Gilbert, D. T. (1989). Thinking lightly about others: Automatic components of the social inference process. In J. S. Uleman & J. A. Bargh (Eds.), *Unintended thought* (pp. 189–211). New York: Guilford.

Gilbert, D. T., & Hixon, J. G. (1991). The trouble of thinking: Application of stereotypic beliefs. *Journal of Personality and Social Psychology, 60,* 509–517.

Gilbert, D. T., & Jones, E. E. (1986). Perceiver-induced constraint: Interpretations of self-generated reality. *Journal of Personality and Social Psychology, 50,* 269–280.

Gilbert, D. T., McNulty, S. E., Giuliano, T. A., & Benson, J. E. (1992). Blurry words and fuzzy deeds: The attribution of obscure behavior. *Journal of Personality and Social Psychology, 62,* 18–25.

Gilbert, D. T., Pelham, B., & Krull, D. (1988). On cognitive busyness: When person perceivers meet persons perceived. *Journal of Personality and Social Psychology, 54,* 733–740.

Gilbert, L. A., Waldroop, J. A., & Deutsch, C. J. (1981). Masculine and feminine stereotypes and adjustment: A reanalysis. *Psychology of Women Quarterly, 5,* 790–794.

Gilger, J. W. (1995). Behavioral genetics: Concepts for research and practice in language development and disorders. *Journal of Speech and Hearing Research, 38,* 1126–1142.

Gilligan, C. (1977). In a different voice: Women's conceptions of self and of morality. *Harvard Educational Review, 47,* 481–517.

Gilligan, C. (1982). *In a different voice: Psychological theory and women's development.* Cambridge, MA: Harvard University Press.

Gilligan, C. (1989). *Mapping the moral domain.* Cambridge, MA: Harvard University Press.

Gilligan, S. G., & Bower, G. H. (1984). Cognitive consequences of emotional arousal. In C. Izard, J. Kagan, & R. Zajonc (Eds.), *Emotions, cognitions, and behavior.* New York: Cambridge University Press.

Gillovich, T., Vallone, R., & Tversky, A. (1985). The hot hand in basketball: On the misperception of random sequences. *Cognitive Psychology, 17,* 295–314.

Glaser, R., Kiecolt-Glaser, J. K., Stout, J. C., Tarr, K. L., Speicher, C. E., & Holliday, J. E. (1985). Stress-related impairments in cellular immunity. *Psychiatry Research, 16,* 233–239.

Glaser, R., Rice, J., Speicher, C. E., Stout, J. C., & Kiecolt-Glaser, J. K. (1986). Stress depresses interferon production by leukocytes concomitant with a decrease in natural killer cell activity. *Behavioral Neuroscience, 100,* 675–678.

Glasgow, R. E., & Lichtenstein, E. (1987). Long-term effects of behavioral smoking cessation interventions. *Behavior Therapy, 18,* 297–324.

Glenn, N. D., & Weaver, C. N. (1981). The contribution of marital happiness to global happiness. *Journal of Marriage and the Family, 43,* 161–168.

Glick, P., Zion, C., & Nelson, C. (1988). What mediates sex discrimination in hiring decisions? *Journal of Personality and Social Psychology, 55,* 178–186.

Goldberg, D. P., & Bridges, K. (1988). Somatic presentations of psychiatric illness in primary care settings. *Journal of Psychosomatic Research, 32,* 137–144.

Goldfried, M. R., Greenberg, L. S., & Marmar, C. (1990). Individual psychotherapy: Process and outcome. *Annual Review of Psychology, 41,* 659-688.

Goldner, E. M., & Birmingham, C. L. (1994). Anorexia nervosa: Methods of treatment. In L. Alexander-Mott & D. M. Lumsden (Eds.), *Understanding eating disorders: Anorexia nervosa, bulimia nervosa, and obesity* (pp. 135–158). Washington, DC: Taylor & Francis.

Goldsmith, H., & Campos, J. J. (1990). The structure of temperamental fear and pleasure in infants: A psychometric perspective. *Child Development, 61,* 1944–1964.

Goldstein, E. B. (1996). *Sensation and perception.* Pacific Grove, CA: Brooks/Cole.

Goldstein, M. J., Baker, B. L., & Jamison, K. R. (1980). *Abnormal psychology: Experiences, origins and interventions.* Boston: Little, Brown.

Goldstein, R. B., Black, D. W., Nasrallah, A., & Winokur, G. (1991). The prediction of suicide: Sensitivity, specificity, and predictive value of a multivariate model applied to suicide among 1906 patients with affective disorders. *Archives of General Psychiatry, 48,* 418–422.

Goleman, D. (1977). *The varieties of the meditative experience.* New York: Dutton.

Goodall, J. (1988). Interview on "The Mind: Language" [television program]. PBS: Nova.

Goodwin, F. K., & Jamison, K. R. (1990). *Manic-depressive illness.* New York: Oxford University Press.

Gortmaker, S. L., Eckenrode, J., & Gore, S. (1982). Stress and the utilization of health services: A time series and crosssectional analysis. *Journal of Health and Social Behavior, 23,* 25–38.

Gottesman, I. (1978). Schizophrenia and genetics: Where are we? Are you sure? In L. C. Wynne, R. L. Cromwell, & S. Matthysse (Eds.), *The nature of achizophrenia: New approaches to research and treatment.* New York: Wiley.

Gottesman, I., (1991). *Schizophrenia genesis: The origins of madness.* New York: Freeman.

Gottesman, I., & Bertelsen, A. (1989). Confirming unexpressed genotypes for schizophrenia. *Archives of General Psychiatry, 46,* 867–872.

Gottesman, I., McGuffin, P., & Farmer, A. E. (1987). Clinical genetics as clues to the "real" genetics of schizophrenia. *Schizophrenia Bulletin, 13,* 23–47.

Gottesman, I., & Shields, J. (1976). A critical review of recent adoption, twin and family studies of schizophrenia: Behavioral genetics perspectives. *Schizophrenia Bulletin, 2*(3), 360–398.

Gottesman, I., & Shields, J. (1982). *Schizophrenia: The epigenic puzzle.* New York: Cambridge University Press.

Gottesman, I., Shields, J., & Meehl, P. (1982). *Schizophrenia and genetics: A twin study vantage point.* New York: Academic Press.

Gottman, J. M., & Krokoff, L. (1989). Marital interaction and satisfaction: A longitudinal view. *Journal of Consulting and Clinical Psychology, 57,* 47–52.

Gould, J. L. (1986). The biology of learning. *Annual Review of Psychology, 37,* 163–192.

Gould, M. S., Shaffer, D., Fisher, P., Kleinman, M., & Morishima, A. (1992). The clinical prediction of adolescent suicide. In R. W. Maris, A. L. Berman, J. T. Maltsberger, & R. I. Yufit (Eds.), *Assessment and prediction of suicide* (pp. 130–143). New York: Guilford.

Gould, R. L. (1972). The phases of adult life: A study in developmental psychology. *American Journal of Psychiatry, 129,* 521–531.

Gould, R. L. (1978). *Transformations.* New York: Simon & Schuster.

Gould, S. J. (1981). *The mismeasure of man.* New York: W. W. Norton.

Gould, S. J. (1995). Curveball. In S. Fraser (Ed.), *The bell curve wars.* New York: Basic Books.

Grant, G. M., Salcedo, V., Hynan, L. S., & Frisch, M. B. (1995). Effectiveness of quality of life therapy for depression. *Psychological Reports, 76*(3, Pt 2), 1203–1208.

Greco, C., Rovee-Collier, C., Hayne, H., Griesler, P., & Earley, L. (1986). Ontogeny of early event memory: I. Forgetting and retrieval by 2- and 3-month olds. *Infant Behavior and Development, 9,* 441–460.

Green, B. F. (1992). Exposé or smear? The Burt affair. *Psychological Science, 3,* 328–331.

Green, D. M., & Swets, J. A. (1966). *Signal detection theory and psychophysics.* New York: Wiley.

Greenberg, M. A., & Stone, A. A. (1990). Writing about disclosed versus undisclosed traumas: Health and mood effects. *Health Psychology, 9,* 114–115.

Greene, P. L., Diaz Granados, J. L., & Amsel, A. (1992). Blood ethanol concentration from early postnatal exposure: Effects on memory-based learning and hippocampal neuroanatomy in infant and adult rats. *Behavioral Neuroscience, 106*(1), 51–61.

Greene, P. L., Diaz Granados, J. L., & Amsel, A. (1994). Postnatal high-peak blood ethanol concentration and external cue-based discrimination learning and reversal in the preweanling rat: Comparison with memory-based discrimination learning. *Behavioral Neuroscience, 108,* 333–339.

Gregory, R. L. (1970). *The intelligent eye.* New York: McGraw-Hill.

Gribbin, K., Schaie, K. W., & Parham, I. A. (1980). Complexity of life style and maintenance of intellectual abilities. *Journal of Social Issues, 36,* 47–61.

Griffin, D., & Buehler, R. (1994). Role of construal processes in conformity and dissent. *Journal of Personality and Social Psychology, 65,* 657–669.

Grossman, H. J. (1983). *Classification in mental retardation.* Washington, DC: American Association of Mental Deficiency.

Groves, P. M., & Rebec, G. V. (1992). *Introduction to biological psychology.* Dubuque, IA: Wm. C. Brown.

Gruber, H. (1981). *Darwin on man* (2nd ed.). Chicago: University of Chicago Press.

Guerin, B. (1986). Mere presence effects on humans: A review. *Journal of Personality and Social Psychology, 22,* 38–77.

Guerin, B. (1994). What do people think about the risks of driving? Implications for traffic safety interventions. *Journal of Applied Social Psychology, 24,* 994–1021.

Guilford, J. P. (1959). *Personality.* New York: McGraw-Hill.

Guilford, J. P. (1967). *The nature of human intelligence.* New York: McGraw-Hill.

Guilford, J. P. (1982). Cognitive psychology's ambiguity: Some suggested remedies. *Psychological Review, 89,* 48.

Gurin, G., Veroff, J., & Feld, S. (1960). *Americans view their mental health: A Nationwide interview survey.* New York: Basic Books.

Gustaffson, J. E. (1984). A unifying model for the structure of intellectual abilities. *Intelligence, 8,* 179–203.

Gwirtsman, H., & Gerner, R. (1981). Neurochemical abnormalities in anorexia nervosa: Similarities to affective disorders. *Biological Psychiatry, 16,* 991–995.

Haaga, D. A., & Davisson, G. C. (1989). Outcome studies of rational-emotive therapy. In M. E. Bernard & R. DiGiuseppe (Eds.), *Inside rational-emotive therapy.* New York: Academic Press.

Hackman, J. R. (1986). The design of work teams. In J. Lorsch (Ed.), *Handbook of organizational behavior.* Englewood Cliffs, NJ: Prentice Hall.

Haddock, G., & Zanna, M. P. (1994). Preferring "housewives" to "feminists." *Psychology of Women Quarterly, 18,* 25–52.

Haley, J. (1973). *Uncommon therapy*. New York: W. W. Norton.

Haley, J. (1980). *Leaving home: The therapy of disturbed young people*. New York: McGraw-Hill.

Haley, S. A. (1978). Treatment implications of post-combat stress response syndromes for mental health professionals. In C. R. Figley (Ed.), *Stress disorders among Vietnam veterans*. New York: Brunner/Mazel.

Halford, W. K., & Hayes, R. (1991). Psychological rehabilitation of chronic schizophrenic patients: Recent findings on social skills training and family psycho-education. *Clinical Psychology Review, 11*, 23–44.

Hall, C. S., & Van de Castle, R. L. (1966). *The content analysis of dreams*. New York: Appleton-Century-Crofts.

Hall, J. A., Rosenthal, R., Archer, D., Di Matteo, M. R., & Rogers, P. L. (1978, May). Decoding wordless messages. *Human Nature*, 68–75.

Hamburg, D. A., & Adams, J. E. (1967). A perspective on coping behavior: Seeking and utilizing information in major transitions. *Archives of General Psychiatry, 17*, 277–284.

Hamilton, E. W., & Abramson, L. Y. (1983). Cognitive patterns and major depressive disorder: A longitudinal study in a hospital setting. *Journal of Abnormal Psychology, 92*, 173–184.

Hammen, C., Marks, T., Mayol, A., & de Mayo, R. (1985). Depressive selfschemas, life stress, and vulnerability to depression. *Journal of Abnormal Psychology, 94*, 308–319.

Haney, D. (1983, November). Girth control. *The Oregonian*, p. B1.

Hansen, R. D., & Hansen, C. H. (1988). Repression of emotionally tagged memories: The architecture of less complex emotions. *Journal of Personality and Social Psychology, 55*, 811–818.

Hansen, W. B. (1993). School-based alcohol prevention programs. *Alcohol, Health and Research World, 17*, 54–60.

Haracz, J. H. (1982). The dopamine hypothesis: An overview of studies with schizophrenic patients. *Schizophrenia Bulletin, 8*, 438–469.

Hardaway, R. A. (1990). Subliminally activated symbiotic fantasies: Facts and artifacts. *Psychological Bulletin, 107*, 177–195.

Hare, R. D. (1970). *Psychopathy: Theory and research*. New York: Wiley.

Hargadon, F. (1981). Tests and college admissions. *American Psychologist, 36*, 1112–1119.

Hariton, E. B., & Singer, J. L. (1974). Women's fantasies during sexual intercourse: Normative and theoretical implications. *Journal of Consulting and Clinical Psychology, 42*, 313–322.

Haritos-Fatouros, M. (1988). The official torturer: A learning model for obedience to the authority of violence. *Journal of Applied Social Psychology, 18*, 1107–1120.

Harkins, S. G., & Szymanski, K. (1987). Social loafing and social facilitation: New wine in old bottles. In C. Hendrick (Ed.), *Group processes and intergroup relations: Review of personality and social psychology* (Vol. 9). Newbury Park, CA: Sage.

Harkins, S. G., & Szymanski, K. (1988). Social loafing and self-evaluation with an objective standard. *Journal of Experimental Social Psychology, 24*, 354–365.

Harkins, S. G., & Szymanski, K. (1989). Social loafing and group evaluation. *Journal of Personality and Social Psychology, 56*, 934–941.

Harkness, S. (1980). The cultural context of child development. In C. M. Super & S. Harkness (Eds.), *New directions for child development: Anthropological perspectives on child development* (Vol. 8, pp. 7–13). San Francisco: Jossey-Bass.

Harlow, H. F. (1953). Mice, monkeys, men, and motives. *Psychological Review, 60*, 23–32.

Harlow, H. F. (1958). The nature of love. *American Psychologist, 13*, 673–685.

Harlow, H. F., & Harlow, M. K. (1966). Learning to love. *American Scientist, 54*, 244–272.

Harlow, H. F., & Harlow, M. K. (1969). Effects of various mother-infant relationships on rhesus monkey behaviors. In B. M. Foss (Ed.), *Determinants of infant behavior* (Vol. 4, pp. 15–36). London: Methuen.

Harris, L., & Associates. (1986). *American teens speak: Sex, myths, TV, and birth control: The planned parenthood poll*. New York: Planned Parenthood Federation of America.

Hartmann, H. (1939). *Ego psychology and the problem of adaptation*. New York: International Universities Press.

Hartshorne, H., & May, M. A. (1928). *Studies in the nature of character (1): Studies in deceit*. New York: Macmillan.

Harvard Medical School. (1986). Suicide—Part II. *Mental Health Letter, 2*(8), 1–4.

Hasher, L., & Zacks, R. T. (1984). Automatic processing of fundamental information: The case of frequency occurrence. *American Psychologist, 39*, 1372–1388.

Hass, R. G. (1981). Effects of source characteristics on cognitive responses in persuasion. In R. E. Petty, T. M. Ostrom, & T. C. Brock (Eds.), *Cognitive responses in persuasion*. Hillsdale, NJ: Erlbaum.

Hass, R. G., & Linder, D. E. (1972). Counterargument availability and the effects of message structure on persuasion. *Journal of Personality and Social Psychology, 23*, 219–233.

Hatch, T. C., & Gardner, H. (1986). From testing intelligence to assessing competencies: A pluralistic view of intellect. *Roeper Review, 8*(3), 147–150.

Hatfield, E. (1988). Passionate and companionate love. In R. J. Sternberg & M. I. Bargas (Eds.), *The psychology of love.* New Haven, CT: Yale University Press.

Hatfield, E., & Sprecher, S. (1986). *Mirror, mirror: The importance of looks in everyday life.* New York: SUNY Press.

Hauri, P. (1982). *The sleep disorders* (2nd ed.). Kalamazoo, MI: Upjohn Corp.

Hawton, K. (1987). Assessment of suicide risk. *British Journal of Psychiatry, 150,* 145–153.

Hayes, K. J., & Hayes, C. (1951). The intellectual development of a home-raised chimpanzee. *Proceedings of the American Philosophical Society, 95,* 105–109.

Hazelrigg, M. D., Cooper, H. M., & Borduin, C. M. (1987). Evaluating the effectiveness of family therapies: An integrative review and analysis. *Psychological Bulletin, 101,* 428–442.

Hazelwood, J. D., & Olson, J. M. (1986). Covariation information, causal questioning, and interpersonal behavior. *Journal of Experimental Social Psychology, 22,* 276–291.

Hebb, D. (1955). Drives and the CNS. *Psychological Review, 62,* 243–253.

Hefner, R. S., & Hefner, H. E. (1983). Hearing in large and small dogs: Absolute thresholds and size of the tympanic membrane. *Behavioral Neuroscience, 97,* 310–318.

Hegedus, A. M. (1984). Neuropsychiatric characteristics associated with primary biliary cirrhosis. *International Journal of Psychiatry in Medicine, 14,* 303–314.

Heider, F. (1944). Social perception and phenomenal causality. *Psychological Review, 51,* 358–374.

Heider, F. (1958). *The psychology of in-* *terpersonal relations.* New York: Wiley.

Heimann, M. (1989). Neonatal imitation, gaze aversion, and mother-infant interaction. *Infant Behavior and Development, 12,* 495–505.

Hellekson, C. J., Kline, J. A., & Rosenthal, N. E. (1986). Phototherapy for seasonal affective disorder in Alaska. *American Journal of Psychiatry, 143,* 1035–1037.

Heller, W. (1990). The neuropsychology of emotion: Developmental patterns and implications for psychopathology. In N. L. Stein, B. Leventhal, & T. Trabasso (Eds.), *Psychological and biological approaches to emotion* (pp. 167–211). Hillsdale, NJ: Erlbaum.

Hellige, J. B., Bloch, M. I., & Taylor, A. K. (1988). Multitask investigation of individual differences in hemispheric asymmetry. *Journal of Experimental Psychology: Human Perception and Performance, 14,* 176–187.

Helson, H. (1964). *Adaptation-level theory.* New York: Harper & Row.

Helweg-Larsen, M., & Collins, B. E. (1997). A social psychological perspective on the role of knowledge about AIDS in AIDS prevention. *Current Directions in Psychological Science, 3,* 23–26.

Hendrick, C., & Hendrick, S. (1993). *Romantic love.* Newbury Park, CA: Sage.

Herman, L. M., Morrel-Samuels, P., & Pack, A. A. (1990). Bottlenosed dolphin and human recognition of veridical and degraded video displays of an artificial gestural language. *Journal of Experimental Psychology: General, 119,* 215–230.

Herman, L. M., Richards, D. G., & Wolz, J. P. (1984). Comprehension of sentences by bottlenosed dolphins. *Cognition, 16,* 129–219.

Herrnstein, R. J., & Murray, C. (1994). *The bell curve: Intelligence and class struggle in American life.* New York: Free Press.

Hertsens, T. (1995). *HeadRoom: The manual.* Bozeman, MT: HeadRoom Corporation.

Herzog, D. B., Norman, D. K., Gordon, C., & Pepose, M. (1984). Sexual conflict and eating disorders in 27 males. *American Journal of Psychiatry, 141,* 989–990.

Hetherington, E. M. (1988). Parents, children, and siblings six years after divorce. In R. Hinde & J. S. Hinde (Eds.), *Relations between relationships within families.* Oxford: Oxford University Press.

Hetherington, E. M. (1989). Coping with family transitions: Winners, losers, and survivors. *Child Development, 60,* 1–14.

Hewstone, M., & Jaspers, J. (1987). Covariation and causal attribution: A logical model of the intuitive analysis of variance. *Journal of Personality and Social Psychology, 53,* 663–672.

Higbee, K. L. (1988). Practical aspects of mnemonics. In M. M. Gruenberg, P. E. Morris, & R. N. Sykes (Eds.), *Practical aspects of memory: Current research and issues* (Vol. 2, pp. 409–414). New York: Wiley.

Higgins, E. T., & Bargh, J. A. (1987). Social cognition and social perception. *Annual Review of Psychology, 38,* 369–425.

Higgins, E. T., Rohles, W. S., & Jones, C. R. (1977). Category accessibility and impression formation. *Journal of Experimental Social Psychology, 13,* 141–154.

Higgins, R. L., & Marlatt, G. A. (1973). Effects of anxiety arousal on the consumption of alcohol by alcoholics and social drinkers. *Journal of Consulting and Clinical Psychology, 41,* 426–433.

Higgins, R. L., & Marlatt, G. A. (1975). Fear of interpersonal evaluation as a determinant of alcohol consumption in male social drinkers. *Journal of Abnormal Psychology, 84,* 644–651.

Higgins, S. T., Budney, A. J., Bickel, W. K., Foerg, F. E., Donham, R., & Badger, G. J. (1994). Incentives improve outcome in outpatient behavioral treatment of cocaine dependence. *Archives of General Psychiatry, 51*, 568–576.

Hilgard, E. R. (1965). *Hypnotic susceptibility*. New York: Harcourt Brace Jovanovich.

Hilgard, E. R. (1973). A neodissociation interpretation of pain reduction in hypnosis. *Psychological Review, 80*, 396–411.

Hilgard, E. R. (1975). Hypnosis. *Annual Review of Psychology, 26*, 19–44.

Hilgard, E. R., Leary, D. E., & McGuire, G. R. (1991). The history of psychology: A survey and critical assessment. In M. R. Rosenzweig & L. W. Porter (Eds.), *Annual review of psychology* (Vol. 42, pp. 79–107). Palo Alto: Annual Reviews, Inc.

Hilgard, E. R. I. E. (1994). Neodissociation theory. In S. J. Lynn & J. W. Rhue (Eds.), *Dissociation: Clinical and theoretical perspectives* (pp. 32–51). New York: Guilford Press.

Hilgard, J. R. (1970). *Personality and hypnosis: A study of imaginative involvement*. Chicago: University of Chicago Press.

Hilgard, J. R. (1974). Imaginative involvement: Some characteristics of the highly hypnotizable and the nonhypnotizable. *International Journal of Clinical and Experimental Hypnosis, 22*, 128–156.

Hill, C. T., Rubin, Z., & Peplau, L. A. (1976). Breakups before marriage: The end of 103 affairs. *Journal of Social Issues, 32*, 147–168.

Hill, W. F. (1985). *Learning: A survey of psychological interpretations* (4th ed.). New York: Harper & Row.

Hilts, P. (1995). *Memory's ghost: The nature of memory and the strange tale of Mr. M.* New York: Simon & Schuster.

Himmelhoch, J. M. (1987). Lest treatment abet suicide. *Journal of Clinical Psychiatry, 48*, 44–54.

Hix, M., Ebner, D., Stanford, M., & Pantle, M., (1994). The Rorschach and personality classifications of the California Psychological Inventory. *Perceptual and Motor Skills, 78*, 142.

Hjelle, L. A., & Ziegler, D. J. (1992). *Personality theories: Basic assumptions, research and applications* (3rd ed.). New York: McGraw-Hill.

Hobson, J. A. (1989). *Sleep.* New York: Scientific American Library.

Hock, E., & Schirtzinger, M. B. (1992). Maternal separation anxiety: Its developmental course and relation to maternal mental health. *Developmental Psychology, 63*, 93–102.

Hodgson, R., & Rachman, S. (1976). The modification of compulsive behavior. In H. J. Eysenck (Ed.), *Case Studies in Behaviour Therapy*. Boston: Routledge & Kegan Paul.

Hoffman, M. L. (1976). Empathy, role-taking, guilt, and development of altruistic motives. In T. Lickona (Ed.), *Moral development and behavior: Theory, research and social issues*. New York: Holt, Rinehart & Winston.

Hoffman, M. L., & Saltzstein, H. D. (1967). Parent discipline and the child's moral development. *Journal of Personality and Social Psychology, 5*, 45–57.

Hogan, R. (1975). Theoretical egocentrism and the problem of compliance. *American Psychologist, 30*, 533–540.

Hogarth, R. (1981). Beyond discrete biases: Functional and dysfunctional aspects of judgmental heuristics. *Psychology Bulletin, 90*, 197.

Hohmann, G. W. (1966). Some effects of spinal cord lesions on experienced emotional feelings. *Psychophysiology, 3*, 143–156.

Holahan, C. J., & Moos, R. H. (1987). Personal and contextual determinants of coping strategies. *Journal of Personality and Social Psychology, 52*, 946–955.

Holahan, C. K., Holahan, C. J., & Belk, S. S. (1984). Adjustment in aging: The roles of life stress, hassles, and self-efficacy. *Health Psychology, 3*, 315–328.

Holden, C. (1986). Researchers grapple with problems of updating classic psychological tests. *Science, 233*, 1249–1251.

Holden, C. (1989). Universities fight animal activists. *Science, 243*, 17–19.

Hollander, E. P. (1975). Independence, conformity, and civil liberties: Some implications from social psychological research. *Journal of Social Issues, 31*, 55–67.

Hollon, S. D., & Beck, A. T. (1986). Cognitive and cognitive-behavioral therapies. In S. L. Garfield & A. E. Bergin (Eds.), *Handbook of psychotherapy and behavior change* (3rd ed.). New York: Wiley.

Hollon, S. D., & Beck, A. T. (1994). Cognitive and cognitive-behavioral therapies. In A. E. Bergin & S. L. Garfield (Eds.), *Handbook of psychotherapy and behavior change* (4th ed., pp. 428–466). New York: Wiley.

Holmes, C. B. (1987). Comment on Szasz's view of suicide prevention. *American Psychologist, 42*, 881–882.

Holmes, T. H., & Masuda, M. (1974). Life change and illness susceptibility. In B. S. Dohrenwend & B. P. Dohrenwend (Eds.), *Stressful life events: Their nature and effects.* New York: Wiley.

Holmes, T. H., & Rahe, R. H. (1967). The social readjustment rating scale. *Journal of Psychosomatic Research, 11*, 213–218.

Holroyd, K. A. (1978). Effects of social anxiety and social evaluation on beer consumption and social interaction. *Journal of Studies on Alcohol, 39*, 737–744.

Holsboer, F. (1992). The hypothalamic-pituitary-adrenocortical system. In E. S. Paykel (Ed.), *Handbook of affective disorders* (2nd ed., pp. 267–288). New York: Guilford Press.

Holstein, C. B. (1976). Irreversible, stepwise sequence in the development of moral judgment: A longitudinal study of males and females. *Child Development, 47*, 31–61.

Holtzworth-Munroe, A., & Jacobson, N. S. (1985). Causal attribution of married couples: When do they search for causes? What do they conclude when they do? *Journal of Personality and Social Psychology, 48*, 1398–1412.

Holyoak, K. J. (1984). Analogical thinking and human intelligence. In R. J. Sternberg (Ed.), *Advances in the psychology of human intelligence* (pp. 199–230). Hillsdale, NJ: Erlbaum.

Hood, K. E. (1995). Social psychology and sociobiology: Which is the metatheory? *Psychological Inquiry, 6*, 54–56.

Hooley, J. M. (1985). Expressed emotion: A review of the critical literature. *Annual Review of Psychology, 5*, 119–139.

Hoon, P. W., Bruce, K., & Kinchloe, B. (1982). Does the menstrual cycle play a role in sexual arousal? *Psychophysiology, 19*, 21–26.

Hoorens, V., & Nuttin, J. M. (1993). Overvaluation of own attributes: Mere ownership or subjective frequency? *Social Cognition, 11*, 177–200.

Hoorens, V., Nuttin, J. M., Herman, I. E., & Pavakanum, U. (1990). Mastery pleasure versus mere ownership: A quasi-experimental cross-cultural and cross-alphabetical test of the name letter effect. *European Journal of Social Psychology, 20*, 181–205.

Horn, J. L. (1982). The aging of human abilities. In B. B. Wolman (Ed.), *Handbook of developmental psychology*. Englewood Cliffs, NJ: Prentice Hall.

Horn, J. L. (1994). Theory of fluid and crystallized intelligence. In R. J. Sternberg (Ed.), *Encyclopedia of human intelligence*. New York: Macmillan.

Horney, K. (1945). *Our inner conflicts*. New York: W. W. Norton.

Horney, K. (1967). *Feminine psychology*. New York: W. W. Norton.

Horney, K. (1973). *Feminine psychology*. New York: W. W. Norton.

Horowitz, F. D., & O'Brien, M. (1986). Gifted and talented children: State of knowledge and directions for research. *American Psychologist, 41*, 1147–1152.

Horrigan, J. P., & Barnhill, L. J. (1997). More on melatonin. *Journal of the American Academy of Child and Adolescent Psychiatry, 36*, 1014.

Hothersall, D. (1984). *History of psychology*. New York: Random House.

House, J. S. (1981). *Work stress and social support*. Reading, MA: Addison-Wesley.

House, J. S. (1987). Chronic stress and chronic disease in life and work: Conceptual and methodological issues. *Work and Stress, 1*, 129–140.

House, J. S., Umberson, D., & Landis, K. R. (1988). Structures and processes of social support. *American Review of Sociology, 14*, 293–318.

Hovens, J. E., Falger, P. R. J., Op den Velde, W., Schouten, E. G. W., de Groen, J. H. M., & van Duijn, H. (1992). Occurrence of current post traumatic stress disorder among Dutch World War II resistance veterans according to the SCID. *Journal of Anxiety Disorders, 6*, 147–157.

Hovland, C. I., Janis, I. J., & Kelley, H. H. (1953). *Communication and persuasion*. New Haven, CT: Yale University Press.

Hovland, C. I., Lumsdaine, A. A., & Sheffield, F. D. (1949). *Studies in social psychology in World War II. Vol. 3. Experiments in Mass Communication*. Princeton, NJ: Princeton University Press.

Howard, D. (1983). *Cognitive psychology: Memory, language and thought* (Vol. 9). New York: Macmillan.

Howe, M. L., & Courage, M. L. (1993). On resolving the enigma of infantile amnesia. *Psychological Bulletin, 113*, 305–326.

Howes, C. (1990). Can the age of entry into child care and the quality of child care predict adjustment in kindergarten? *Developmental Psychology, 26*, 292–303.

Howes, C., & Eldredge, R. (1985). Responses of abused, neglected, and nonmaltreated children to the behaviors of their peers. *Journal of Applied Developmental Psychology, 6*, 261–270.

Howes, C., & Rubenstein, J. L. (1981). *Determinants of toddler experience in day care: Social-affective style of age of entry and quality of setting*. Unpublished manuscript, University of California at Los Angeles.

Hoyer, G., & Lund, E. (1993). Suicide among women related to number of children in marriage. *Archives of General Psychiatry, 50*, 134–137.

Hrubec, Z., Floderus-Myrhed, B., deFaire, U., & Sarna, S. (1984). Familial factors in mortality with control of epidemiological covariables: Swedish twins born 1886–1925. Fourth International Congress on Twin Studies (1983, London, England). *Acta Geneticae Medicae et Gemellologiae Twin Research, 33*, 403–412.

Hsu, L. K. G. (1990). *Eating disorders*. New York: Guilford Press.

Hubel, D. H. (1995). *Eye, brain, and vision*. New York: Scientific American Books.

Hubel, D. H., & Wiesel, T. N. (1959). Receptive fields of single neurons in the cat's striate cortex. *Journal of Physiology, 148,* 574–591.

Hubel, D. H., & Wiesel, T. N. (1979). Brain mechanisms of vision. *Scientific American, 241,* 150–162.

Hudspeth, A. J. (1985). The cellular basis of hearing: The biophysics of hair cells. *Science, 230,* 745–752.

Huff, C., & Cooper, J. (1987). Sex bias in educational software: The effects of designers' stereotypes on the software they design. *Journal of Applied Social Psychology, 17,* 519–532.

Hughes, J. R. (1984). Psychological effects of habitual aerobic exercise: A critical review. *Preventive Medicine, 13,* 66–78.

Hughes, J. R., Casal, D. C., & Leon, A. S. (1986). Psychological effects of exercise: A randomized cross-over trial. *Journal of Psychosomatic Research, 30,* 355–360.

Hull, C. L. (1943). *Principles of behavior.* New York: Appleton.

Hultsch, D. F., Hertzog, C., & Dixon, R. A. (1987). Age differences in metamemory: Resolving the inconsistencies. *Canadian Journal of Psychology, 41,* 193–208.

Humphreys, L. G. (1992). Commentary: What both critics and users of ability tests need to know. *Psychological Science, 3,* 271–274.

Hunt, M. (1990). *The compassionate beast: What science is discovering about the humane side of mankind.* New York: Morrow.

Hurley, A. D. (1976). Unsystematic desensitization using pleasurable images to inhibit anxiety. *Journal of Behavior Therapy and Experimental Psychiatry, 7,* 295.

Hurvich, L. M., & Jameson, D. (1957). An opponent-process theory of color vision. *Psychological Review, 64,* 384–404.

Huston, T. L., Ruggiero, M., Conner, R., & Geis, G. (1981). Bystander intervention into crime: A study based on naturally occurring episodes. *Social Psychology Quarterly, 44,* 14–23.

Huttenlocher, J., & Presson, C. C. (1979). The coding and transformation of spatial information. *Cognitive Psychology, 11,* 375–394.

Hyman, I. E., Jr., & Loftus, E. F. (1997). Some people recover memories of childhood trauma that never really happened. In P. S. Appelbaum, L. A. Uyehara, & M. R. Elin (Eds.), *Trauma and memory: Clinical and legal controversies* (pp. 3–24). New York: Oxford University Press.

Hyman, I. E., & Rubin, D. C. (1990). Memorabeatlia: A naturalistic study of long-term memory. *Memory & Cognition, 18,* 205–214.

Iacono, W. G., & Beiser, M. (1992a). Are males more likely than females to develop schizophrenia? *American Journal of Psychiatry, 149,* 1070–1074.

Iacono, W. G., & Beiser, M. (1992b). Where are the women in the first episode studies of schizophrenia? *Schizophrenia Bulletin, 18,* 471–480.

Iacono, W. G., & Lykken, D. T. (1997). The validity of the lie detector: Two surveys of scientific opinion. *Journal of Applied Psychology, 82,* 426–433.

Ickovics, J. R., & Rodin, J. (1992). Women and AIDS in the United States: Epidemiology, natural history, and mediating mechanisms. *Health Psychology, 11,* 1–16.

Imber, S., Pilkonis, P., Sotsky, S., & Elkin, I. (1990). Mode-specific effects among three treatments for depression. *Journal of Consulting and Clinical Psychology, 58,* 352–359.

Imperato-McGinley, J., Peterson, R. E., Gautier, T., & Sturla, E. (1979). Androgens and the evolution of male gender identity among male pseudo-hermaphrodites with 5-reductase deficiency. *New England Journal of Medicine, 300,* 1233–1270.

Irwin, M., Daniels, M., Smith, T. L., Bloom, E., & Weiner, H. (1987). Impaired natural killer cell activity during bereavement. *Brain, Behavior, and Immunity, 1,* 98–104.

Isen, A. M. (1987). Positive affect, cognitive processes, and social behavior. In L. Berkowitz (Ed.), *Advances in experimental social psychology* (Vol. 20, pp. 203–253). New York: Academic Press.

Isen, A. M., & Levin, P. F. (1972). Effect of feeling good on helping: Cookies and kindness. *Journal of Personality and Social Psychology, 21,* 384–388.

Isometsa, E. T., Henriksson, M. E., Aro, H. M., Heikkinen, M. E., Kuoppasalmi, K. l., & Lonnqvist, J. K. (1994). Suicide in major depression. *American Journal of Psychiatry, 151,* 530–536.

Ivey, A. E., Ivey, M. B., & Simek-Morgan, L. (1997). *Counseling and psychotherapy: A multicultural perspective* (4th ed.). Needham Heights, MA: Allyn & Bacon.

Izard, C. E. (1971). *The face of emotion.* New York: Appleton-Century-Crofts.

Izard, C. E. (1984). Emotion-cognition relationships and other human development. In C. E. Izard, J. Kagan, & R. B. Zajonc (Eds.), *Emotion, cognitions and behavior.* New York: Cambridge University Press.

Izard, C. E. (1990a). Facial expressions and the regulation of emotions. *Journal of Personality and Social Psychology, 58,* 487–498.

Izard, C. E. (1990b). The substrates and functions of emotion feelings: William James and current emotion theory. *Personality and Social Psychology Bulletin, 16,* 626–635.

Jackson, J. M., & Williams, K. D. (1988). *Social loafing: A review and theoretical analysis.* Unpublished manuscript, Fordham University.

Jacoby, L. L., & Kelley, C. (1992). A process-dissociation framework for investigating unconscious influences: Freudian slips, projective tests, subliminal perception, and signal detection theory. *Current Directions in Psychological Science, 1*, 174–179.

James, B. (1991). *The baseball book 1991*. New York: Villard Press.

James, W. (1890/1950). *The principles of psychology*. New York: Dover.

Jameson, D., & Hurvich, L. (1989). Essay concerning color constancy. *Annual Review of Psychology, 40*, 1–22.

Janis, I. L. (1972). *Victims of groupthink: A psychological study of foreign policy decisions and fiascoes*. Boston: Houghton Mifflin.

Janis, I. L. (1982). Counteracting the adverse effects of concurrence-seeking in policy-planning groups: Theory and research perspectives. In H. Brandstatter & J. Davis (Eds.), *Group Decision Making (European Monographs in Social Psychology* (Vol. 25) New York: Academic Press.

Janis, I. L. (1985). Sources of error in strategic decision making. In J. M. Pennings (Ed.), *Organizational strategy and change*. San Francisco: Jossey-Bass.

Janis, I. L., & Mann, L. (1977). *Decision making: A psychological analysis of conflict, choice, and commitment*. New York: Free Press.

Janos, P. M., & Robinson, N. M. (1985). Psychosocial development in intellectually gifted children. In F. D. Horowitz & M. O'Brien (Eds.), *The gifted and talented: Developmental perspectives* (pp. 149–195). Washington, DC: American Psychological Association.

Janz, N. K., & Becker, M. H. (1984). The health belief model: A decade later. *Health Education Quarterly, 11*, 1–47.

Jarvik, L. F. (1975). Thoughts on the psychobiology of aging. *American Psychologist, 30*, 576–583.

Jastreboff, P. J. (1990). Phantom auditory perception (tinnitus): Mecha-

nisms of generation and perception. *Neuroscience Research, 8*, 221–254.

Jenner, F. A., Gjessing, L. R., Cox, J. R., Davies-Jones, A., & Hullin, R. P. (1967). A manic-depressive psychotic with a 48-hour cycle. *British Journal of Psychiatry, 113*, 859–910.

Jensen, A. R. (1969). How much can we boost IQ and scholastic achievement? *Harvard Educational Review, 39*, 1–123.

Jensen, A. R. (1992). Commentary: Vehicles of *g. Psychological Science, 3*, 275–278.

Jensen, A. R. (1993a). Test validity: *g* versus "tacit knowledge." *Current Directions in Psychological Science, 2*, 9–10.

Jensen, A. R. (1993b). Why is reaction time correlated with psychometric *g? Current Directions in Psychological Science, 2*, 53–56.

Jepson, C., & Chaiken, S. (1986). *The effect of anxiety on the systematic processing of persuasive communications*. Paper presented at the American Psychological Association, Washington, DC.

Jepson, C., & Chaiken, S. (1990). Chronic issue-specific fear inhibits systematic processing of persuasive communications. *Journal of Social Behavior and Personality, 5*, 61–84.

Johansson, G., & Vallbo, A. B. (1983). Tactile sensory coding in the glabrous skin of the human hand. *Trends in Neuroscience, 6*, 27–32.

Johnson, A. G. (1980). On the prevalence of rape in the United States. *Journal of Women in Culture and Society, 6*, 136–146.

Johnson, S. M., & Greenberg, L. S. (1985). Differential effects of experiential and problem-solving interventions in resolving mental conflict. *Journal of Consulting and Clinical Psychology, 53*, 175–184.

Joiner, T. E., Jr., Alfano, M. S., & Metalsky, G. l. (1992). When depres-

sion breeds contempt: Reassurance seeking, self-esteem, and rejection of depressed college students by their roommates. *Journal of Abnormal Psychology, 101*, 165–173.

Jones, E. E., & Davis, K. E. (1965). From acts to dispositions: The attribution process in person perception. In L. Berkowitz (Ed.), *Advances in experimental social psychology* (Vol. 2, pp. 219–266). New York: Academic Press.

Jones, E. E., & Nisbett, R. E. (1971). *The actor and observer: Perceptions of the causes of behavior*. New York: General Learning Press.

Jones, G. V. (1988). Analyzing memory blocks. In M. M. Gruenberg, P. E. Morris, & R. N. Sykes (Eds.), *Practical aspects of memory: Current research and issues* (Vol. 1, pp. 215–220). New York: Wiley.

Jones, L. V., & Appelbaum, M. I. (1989). Psychometric methods. *Annual Review of Psychology, 40*, 23–43.

Jones, W. H., & Carpenter, B. N. (1986). Shyness, social behavior, and relationships. In W. H. Jones, J. M. Cheek, & S. R. Briggs (Eds.), *Shyness: Perspectives on research and treatment* (pp. 227–238). New York: Plenum Press.

Jordan, T. J., & McCormick, N. B. (1987, April). *The role of sex beliefs in intimate relationships*. Paper presented at the annual meeting of the American Association of Sex Educators, Counselors, and Therapists, New York.

Jouvet, M. (1967). The stages of sleep. *Scientific American, 216*, 62–72.

Joynson, R. B. (1989). *The Burt affair*. London: Routledge.

Judd, C. M., Ryan, C. S., & Park, B. (1991). Accuracy in the judgment of in-group and out-group variability. *Journal of Personality and Social Psychology, 61*, 366–379.

Julien, R. M. (1981). *A primer of drug action* (3rd ed.). San Francisco: Freeman.

Julien, R. M. (1995). *A primer of drug action* (7th ed.). San Francisco: Freeman.

Jusczyk, P. W., Pisoni, D. B., & Mullennix, J. (1993). Some consequences of stimulus variability on speech processing by 2-month-old infants; recognition of the sound patterns in their own names. *Cognition, 43,* 253–291.

Kagan, J. (1984). *The nature of the child.* New York: Basic Books.

Kagan, J. (1995). *Galen's prophecy: Temperament in human nature.* New York: Basic Books.

Kagan, J., Kearsley, R. B., & Zelazo, P. R. (1978). *Infancy: Its place in human development.* Cambridge, MA: Harvard University Press.

Kagan, J., Reznik, J. S., & Snidman, N. (1988). Biological bases of childhood shyness. *Science, 240,* 167–171.

Kagan, J., & Snidman, N. (1992). Infant predictors of inhibited and uninhibited profiles. *Psychological Science, 2,* 40–44.

Kail, R. (1990). *The development of memory in children.* New York: W. H. Freeman.

Kail, R., & Cavanaugh, J. C. (1996). *Human development.* Pacific Grove, CA: Brooks/Cole.

Kail, R., & Pellegrino, J. W. (1985). *Human intelligence: Perspectives and prospects.* New York: W. H. Freeman.

Kalat, J. W. (1992). *Biological psychology.* Belmont, CA: Wadsworth.

Kalat, J. W., & Rozin, P. (1971). Role of interference in taste-aversion learning. *Journal of Comparative and Physiological Psychology, 77,* 53–58.

Kales, A., Hoedemaker, F., Jacobson, A., & Lichtenstein, E. (1964). Dream deprivation: An experimental reappraisal. *Nature, 204,* 1337–1338.

Kallgren, C. A., & Wood, W. (1986). Access to attitude-relevant information in memory as a determinant of attitude-behavior consistency. *Journal of Experimental Social Psychology, 22,* 328–338.

Kamin, L. J. (1974). The science and politics of IQ. *Social Research, 41,* 387–425.

Kamin, L. J. (1986). Is there crime in the genes? The answer may depend on who chooses what evidence. *Scientific American, 254*(2), 22–27.

Kandel, E. R., Schwartz, J. H., & Jessell, T. M. (1991). *Principles of neural science.* Norwalk, CT: Appleton & Lange.

Kandel, E. R., Schwartz, J. H., & Jessell, T. M. (1995). *Essentials of neural science and behavior* (2nd ed.). Norwalk, CT: Appleton-Lange.

Kangas, J., & Bradway, K. (1974). Intelligence at middle age: A thirty-eight-year follow-up. *Developmental Psychology, 5,* 333–337.

Kantowitz, B. H., Roediger, H. L., III, & Elmes, D. G. (1994). *Experimental psychology: Understanding psychological research* (5th ed.). Minneapolis: West.

Kaplan, H. l., & Sadock, B. J. (1991). *Synopsis of psychiatry: Behavioral sciences, clinical psychiatry* (6th ed.). Baltimore: Williams & Wilkins.

Kaplan, J. (1988). The use of animals in research. *Science, 243,* 839–940.

Kaplan, R. M. (1982). Nader's raid on the testing industry: Is it in the best interest of the consumer? *American Psychologist, 37,* 15–23.

Karau, S. J., & Williams, K. D. (1993). Social loafing: A meta-analytic review and theoretical integration. *Journal of Personality and Social Psychology, 65,* 681–706.

Karp, D. A. (1988). A decade of reminders: Changing age consciousness between fifty and sixty years old. *Gerontologist, 28,* 727–738.

Kasamatsu, A., & Hirai, T. (1966). An electroencephalographic study on the Zen meditation. *Zayen Folia Psychiatrica et Neurologica Japonica, 20,* 315–366.

Katz, H., & Beilin, H. (1976). A test of Bryant's claims concerning the young child's understanding of quantitative invariance. *Child Development, 47,* 877–880.

Katz, I., & Hass, R. G. (1988). Racial ambivalence and American value conflict: Correlational and priming studies of dual cognitive structures. *Journal of Personality and Social Psychology, 55,* 893–905.

Katz, J. (1992). Psychophysiological contributions to phantom limbs. *Canadian Journal of Psychiatry, 37,* 282–298.

Kavanaugh, R. D., Zimmerberg, B., & Fein, S. (1996). *Emotion: Interdisciplinary perspectives.* Hillsdale, NJ: Erlbaum.

Kaye, K., & Marcus, J. (1978). Imitation over a series of trials without feedback: Age six months. *Infant Behavior and Development, 1,* 141–155.

Kazdin, A. E. (1977). *The token economy: A review and evaluation.* New York: Plenum Press.

Kazdin, A. E., & Wilson, G. T. (1978). *Evaluation of behavior therapy: Issues, evidence, and research strategies.* Cambridge, MA: Ballenger.

Keating, D. P. (1980). Thinking processes in adolescence. In J. Adelson (Ed.), *Handbook of adolescent psychology.* New York: Wiley.

Keating, D. P. (1988). Byrnes' reformulation of Piaget's formal operations. *Developmental Review, 8,* 376–384.

Keller, M. B., Shapiro, R. W., Lavori, P. W., & Wolfe, N. (1982). Recovery in major depressive disorder: Analysis with the life table and regression models. *Archives of General Psychiatry, 35,* 905–910.

Kelley, H. H. (1967). Attribution theory in social psychology. In D. Levine (Ed.), *Nebraska Symposium of Motivation* (pp. 192–238). Lincoln: University of Nebraska Press.

Kelley, H. H. (1971). *Attribution in social interaction*. Morristown, NJ: General Learning Press.

Kelley, H. H. (1979). *Personal relationships*. Hillsdale, NJ: Erlbaum.

Kelling, S. T., & Halpern, B. P. (1983). Taste flashes: Reaction times, intensity, and quality. *Science, 219,* 412–414.

Kelly, D. D. (1981). Somatic sensory system: 4. Central representations of pain and analgesia. In E. R. Kandel & J. H. Schwartz (Eds.), *Principles of neural science* (2nd ed.). New York: Elsevier.

Kelly, G. (1955). *The psychology of personal constructs*. New York: W. W. Norton.

Kelman, H. C. (1958). Compliance, identification, and internalization: Three processes of attitude change. *Journal of Conflict Resolution, 2,* 51–60.

Kelman, H. C. (1961). Processes of opinion change. *Public Opinion Quarterly, 25,* 57–78.

Kelman, H. C., & Hamilton, V. L. (1989). *Crimes and obedience: Toward a social psychology of authority and responsibility*. New Haven, CT: Yale University Press.

Kelman, H. C., & Hovland, C. I. (1953). "Reinstatement" of the communicator in delayed measurement of opinion change. *Journal of Abnormal and Social Psychology, 48,* 327–335.

Kemeny, M. E., Cohen, R., Zegans, L. S., & Conant, M. A. (1989). Psychological and immunological predictors of genital herpes recurrence. *Psychosomatic Medicine, 51,* 195–208.

Kemeny, M. E., & Dean, L. (1995). Effects of AIDS-related bereavement on HIV progression among New York City gay men. *AIDS Education and Prevention, 7*(Suppl), 36–47.

Kemeny, M. E., Weiner, H., Duran, R., & Taylor, S. E. (1995). Immune system changes after the death of a partner in HIV-positive gay men. *Psychosomatic Medicine, 57,* 547–554.

Kemeny, M. E., Weiner, H., Taylor, S. E., & Schneider, S. (1994). Repeated bereavement, depressed mood, and immune parameters in HIV seropositive and seronegative gay men. *Health Psychology, 13,* 14–24.

Kemp, S., & George, R. N. (1992). Masking of tinnitus induced by sound. *Journal of Speech and Hearing Research, 35,* 1169–1179.

Kemper, T. D. (1978). *A social interaction theory of emotions*. New York: Wiley.

Kendler, K. S., Kessler, R. C., Neale, M. C., Heath, A. C., & Eaves, L. J. (1993). The prediction of major depression in women: Toward an integrated etiologic model. *American Journal of Psychiatry, 150,* 1139–1148.

Kendler, K. S., Neale, M. C., Heath, A. C., & Kessler, R. C. (1994). A twin-family study of alcoholism in women. *American Journal of Psychiatry, 151,* 707–715.

Kendler, K. S., Neale, M. C., Kessler, R. C., Heath, A. C., & Eaves, L. J. (1992). Childhood parental loss and adult psychopathology in women: A twin study perspective. *Archives of General Psychiatry, 49,* 109–116.

Kendler, K. S., Neale, M. C., Kessler, R. C., Heath, A. C., & Eaves, L. J. (1993). A longitudinal twin study of 1-year prevalence of major depression in women. *Archives of General Psychiatry, 50,* 843–852.

Kendzierski, D. (1990). Exercise self-schemata: Cognitive and behavioral correlates. *Health Psychology, 9,* 69–82.

Kennell, J. H., Jerauld, R., Wolfe, H., Chesler, D., Kreger, N. C., McAlpine, W., Steffa, M., & Klaus, M. H. (1974). Maternal behavior one year after early and extended post-partum contact. *Developmental Medicine and Child Neurology, 16,* 172–179.

Kessler, R. C., McGonagle, K. A., Zhao, S., Nelson, C. B., Hughes, M., Eshleman, S., Wittchen, H. U., & Kendler, K. S. (1994). Lifetime and 12-month prevalence of DSM-III-R psychiatric disorders in the United States: Results from the National Comorbidity Study. *Archives of General Psychiatry, 51,* 8–19.

Kety, S. (1988). Schizophrenic illness in the families of schizophrenic adoptees: Findings from the Danish national sample. *Schizophrenia Bulletin, 14,* 217–222.

Kety, S. S., Wender, P. H., Jacobson, B., Ingraham, L. J., Jansson, L., Faber, B., & Kinney, D. K. (1994). Mental illness of the biological and adoptive relatives of schizophrenic adoptees: Replication of the Copenhagen study in the rest of Denmark. *Archives of General Psychiatry, 51,* 442–445.

Kiecolt-Glaser, J. K., Garner, W., Speicher, C., Penn, G. M., Holliday, J., & Glaser, R. (1984). Psychosocial modifiers of immunocompetence in medical students. *Psychosomatic Medicine, 46,* 7–14.

Kiecolt-Glaser, J. K., Glaser, R., Shuttleworth, E., Dyer, C. S., Ogrocki, P., & Speicher, C. E. (1987). Chronic stress and immunity in family caregivers of Alzheimer's disease victims. *Psychosomatic Medicine, 49,* 523–535.

Kiecolt-Glaser, J. K., Glaser, R., Williger, D., Stout, J., Messick, G., Sheppard, S., Ricker, D., Romisher, S. C., Briner, W., Bonnell, G., & Donnerberg, R. (1985). Psychosocial enhancement of immunocompetence in a geriatric population. *Health Psychology, 4,* 25–41.

Kiecolt-Glaser, J. K., Kennedy, S., Malkoff, S., Fisher, L., Speicher, C. E., & Glaser, R. (1988). Marital discord and immunity in males. *Psychosomatic Medicine, 50,* 213–229.

Kiesler, C. A., & Kiesler, S. B. (1969). *Conformity*. Reading, MA: Addison-Wesley.

Kihlstrom, J. F. (1984). Conscious, subconscious, unconscious: A cognitive perspective. In K. S. Bowers & D. Meichenbaum (Eds.), *The unconscious reconsidered* (pp. 149–211). New York: Wiley.

Kihlstrom, J. F. (1985). Hypnosis. *Annual Review of Psychology, 36*, 385–418.

Kihlstrom, J. F. (1987). The cognitive unconscious. *Science, 237*, 1445–1452.

Kihlstrom, J. F. (1992). Dissociation and dissociations: A comment on consciousness and cognition. *Consciousness and Cognition, 1*, 47–53.

Kihlstrom, J. F. (1993). The continuum of consciousness [Claremont Conference on Consciousness and Cognition]. *Consciousness and Cognition, 2*, 334–354.

Kihlstrom, J. F., Glisky, M. L., & Angiulo, M. J. (1994). Dissociative tendencies and dissociative disorders. *Journal of Abnormal Psychology, 103*, 117–124.

Kihlstrom, J. F., Schacter, D. L., Cork, R. C., Hurt, C. A., & Behr, S. E. (1990). Implicit and explicit memory following surgical anesthesia. *Psychological Science, 1*, 303–306.

Kihlstrom, J. F., Tataryn, D. J., & Hoyt, I. P. (1993). Dissociative disorders. In P. B. Sutker & H. E. Adams (Eds.), *Comprehensive handbook of psychopathology* (2nd ed.). New York: Plenum Press.

Kilpatrick, D. G., Best, C. L., Veronen, L. J., Amick, A. E., Villeponteaux, L. A., & Ruff, G. A. (1985). Mental health correlates of criminal victimization: A random community survey. *Journal of Consulting and Clinical Psychology, 53*, 866–873.

Kinder, D. R., & Sears, D. O. (1981). Prejudice and politics: Symbolic racism versus racial threats to the good life. *Journal of Personality and Social Psychology, 40*, 414–431.

King, B. M. (1996). *Human sexuality today* (2nd ed.). Upper Saddle River, NJ: Prentice Hall.

Kinsbourne, M. (1982). Hemispheric specialization and the growth of human understanding. *American Psychologist, 37*, 411–420.

Kintsch, W. (1974). *The representation of meaning in memory*. Hillsdale, NJ: Erlbaum.

Kintsch, W., & Kennan, J. (1974). The psychological reality of text bases. In W. Kintsch (Ed.), *The representation of meaning in memory*. Hillsdale, NJ: Erlbaum.

Kirk, R. E. (1990). *Statistics: An introduction* (3rd ed.). Fort Worth: Harcourt Brace.

Klaus, M. H., Jerauld, R., Kreger, N. C., McAlpine, W., Steffa, M., & Kennell, J. H. (1972). Maternal attachment: Importance of the first post-partum days. *New England Journal of Medicine, 286*, 460–463.

Klaus, M. H., & Kennell, J. H. (1976). *Maternal-infant bonding*. St. Louis: C.V. Mosby.

Klawans, H. L. (1990). *Newton's madness: Further tales of clinical neurology*. New York: Harper & Row.

Klein, D. N., Clark, D. C., Dansky, L., & Margolis, E. T. (1988). Dysthymia in the offspring of parents with primary unipolar affective disorder. *Journal of Abnormal Psychology, 97*, 265–274.

Klein, G. S. (1967). Peremptory ideation: Structure and force in motivated ideas. In R. Jessor & S. Feshback (Eds.), *Cognition, personality, and clinical psychology* (p. 17). San Francisco: Jossey-Bass.

Klein, S. B. (1991). *Learning principles and applications* (2nd ed.). New York: McGraw-Hill.

Kleinmuntz, B., & Szucko, J. J. (1984). A field study of the fallibility of polygraph lie detectors. *Nature, 308*, 449–450.

Klerman, G. L., Lavori, P. W., Rice, J., Reich, T., Endicott, J., Reason, N. C.,

Keller, M. B., & Hirshfield, R. M. A. (1985). Birth cohort trends in rates of major depressive disorder among relatives of patients with affective disorder. *Archives of General Psychiatry, 42*, 689–693.

Kliegl, R., Smith, J., & Baltes, P. B. (1989). Testing-the-limits and the study of adult age differences in cognitive plasticity of a mnemonic skill. *Developmental Psychology, 25*, 247–256.

Klineberg, O. (1938). Emotional expression in Chinese literature. *Journal of Abnormal and Social Psychology, 33*, 517–520.

Kluckhohn, C., & Murray, H. A. (1953). Personality formation: The determinants. In C. Kluckhohn, H. A. Murray, & D. M. Schneider (Eds.), *Personality in nature, society, and culture* (pp. 53–67). New York: Knopf.

Kluznik, J. C., Speed, N., Van Valkenburg, C., & Magraw, R. (1986). Forty year follow-up of United States prisoners of war. *American Journal of Psychiatry, 143*(11), 1443–1446.

Knittle, J. L., & Hirsch, J. (1968). Effect of early nutrition on the development of rat epididymal fat pads: Cellularity and metabolism. *Journal of Clinical Investigation, 47*, 2091.

Kobasigawa, A. (1974). Utilization of retrieval cues by children in recall. *Child Development, 45*, 127–134.

Kohlberg, L. (1963). The development of children's orientation toward a moral order: 1. Sequence in the development of moral thought. *Vita Humana, 6*, 11–33.

Kohlberg, L. (1969). Stage and sequence: The cognitive-developmental approach to socialization. In D. A. Goslin (Ed.), *Handbook of socialization and research* (pp. 347–480). Chicago: Rand McNally.

Kohut, H. (1971). *The analysis of the self*. New York: International Universities Press.

Kohut, H. (1978). *The search for self.* New York: International Universities Press.

Kohut, H., & Wolfe, E. S. (1978). The disorders of self and their treatment: An outline. *International Journal of Psychoanalysis, 59,* 413–425.

Kolata, G. (1984). Studying in the womb. *Science, 225,* 302–303.

Kolb, B., & Whishaw, I. Q. (1990). *Fundamentals of human neuropsychology* (3rd ed.). New York: W. H. Freeman.

Kolb, B., & Whishaw, I. Q. (1996). *Fundamentals of human neuropsychology* (4th ed.). New York: W. H. Freeman.

Kolodny, R. C., Masters, W. C., Kolodner, R. M., & Toro, G. (1974). Depression of plasma testosterone levels after chronic intensive marahuana use. *New England Journal of Medicine, 290,* 872–874.

Koop, C. E. (1987). Report of the Surgeon General's Workshop on Pornography and Public Health. *American Psychologist, 42,* 944–945.

Korchin, S. J., & Schuldberg, D. (1981). The future of clinical assessment. *American Psychologist, 36,* 1147–1158.

Koriat, A., Lichtenstein, S., & Fischoff, B. (1980). Reasons for confidence. *Journal of Experimental Psychology: Human Learning and Memory, 6,* 107–118.

Koshland, D. E. (1989). Animal rights and animal wrongs. *Science, 243,* 1253.

Koss, M. P. (1993). Rape: Scope, impact, interventions, and public policy responses. *American Psychologist, 48,* 1062–1069.

Koss, M. P., & Butcher, J. N. (1986). Research on brief psychotherapy. In S. L. Garfield & A. E. Bergin (Eds.), *Handbook of psychotherapy and behavior change* (3rd ed.). New York: Wiley.

Koss, M. P., Dinero, T. E., Seibel, A. C., & Cox, S. L. (1988). Stranger and acquaintance rape: Are there differences in the victim's experience? *Psychology of Women Quarterly, 12,* 1–24.

Koss, M. P., Gidycz, C. A., & Wisniewski, N. (1987). The scope of rape: Incidence and prevalence of sexual aggression and victimization in a national sample of higher education students. *Journal of Consulting and Clinical Psychology, 55,* 162–170.

Kotre, J., & Hall, E. (1990). *Seasons of life: Our dramatic journey from birth to death.* Boston: Little, Brown.

Kramer, P. D. (1993). *Listening to Prozac.* New York: Viking.

Krane, E. J., & Heller, L. B. (1995). The prevalence of phantom sensation and pain in pediatric amputees. *Journal of Pain and Symptom Management, 10,* 21–29.

Krass, J., Kinoshita, S., & McConkey, K. M. (1989). Hypnotic memory and confident reporting. *Applied Cognitive Psychology, 3,* 35–51.

Kraus, S. J. (1995). Attitudes and the prediction of behavior: A meta-analysis of the empirical literature. *Personality and Social Psychology Bulletin, 21,* 58–75.

Kraut, R. E. (1978). Verbal and nonverbal cues in the perception of lying. *Journal of Personality and Social Psychology, 36,* 380–391.

Krebs, D. L., & Miller, D. T. (1985). Altruism and aggression. In G. Lindsey & E. Aronson (Eds.), *Handbook of social psychology* (3rd ed.). Reading, MA: Addison-Wesley.

Kroll, N. E. A., Schepeler, E. M., & Angin, K. T. (1986). Bizarre imagery: The misremembered mnemonic. *Journal of Experimental Psychology: Learning, Memory, and Cognition, 12*(1), 42–53.

Kruglanski, A. W., & Freund, T. (1983). The freezing and unfreezing of lay inferences: Effects on impressional primacy, ethnic stereotyping, and numerical anchoring. *Journal of Experimental and Social Psychology, 19,* 448–468.

Krull, D. S. (1993). Does the grist change the mill? The effect of the perceiver's inferential goal on the process of social inference. *Personality and Social Psychology Bulletin, 19,* 340–348.

Krull, D. S., & Erickson, D. J. (1995). Inferential hopscotch: How people draw social inferences from behavior. *Current Directions in Psychological Science, 4,* 35–38.

Kuczaj, S. (1982). *Language development: Syntax and semantics* (Vol. 1). Hillsdale, NJ: Erlbaum.

Kuhl, P. K. (1987). Perception of speech and sound in early infancy. In P. Salapatek & L. B. Cohen (Eds.), *Handbook of infant perception* (Vol. 2). New York: Academic Press.

Kuhn, D., Langer, J., Kohlberg, L., & Haan, N. S. (1977). The development of formal operations in logical and moral judgment. *Genetic Psychology Monographs, 95L,* 97–188.

Kulik, J. A., & Mahler, H. I. M. (1989). Social support and recovery from surgery. *Health Psychology, 8,* 221–238.

Kunst-Wilson, W., & Zajonc, R. (1980). Affective discrimination of stimuli that cannot be recognized. *Science, 207,* 557–558.

Kuo, Z. Y. (1930). The genesis of the cat's responses to the rat. *Journal of Comparative Psychology, 11,* 1–35.

Kurtines, W., & Grief, E. B. (1974). The development of moral thought: Review and evaluation of Kohlberg's approach. *Psychological Bulletin, 81,* 453–470.

Labov, W., & Fanshel, D. (1977). *Therapeutic discourse: Psychotherapy as conversation.* New York: Academic Press.

Lacks, P., & Morin, C. M. (1992). Recent advances in the assessment and treatment of insomnia. *Journal of Counseling and Clinical Psychology, 60,* 586–594.

Ladwig, G. B., & Anderson, M. D. (1989). Substance abuse in women: Relationships between chemical dependency of women and past reports of physical and sexual abuse. *International Journal of Addictions, 24,* 739–754.

Laird, J. D. (1974). Self-attribution of emotion: The effects of expressive behavior on the quality of emotional experience. *Journal of Personality and Social Psychology, 29,* 475–486.

Laird, J. D. (1984). The real role of facial response in the experience of emotion: A reply to Tourangeau and Ellsworth, and others. *Journal of Personality and Social Psychology, 47,* 909–917.

Lamb, M. (1987). The emergent American father. In M. L. Lamb (Ed.), *The father's role: Cross-cultural perspectives* (pp. 3–25). Hillsdale, NJ: Erlbaum.

Lamb, M. E., & Campos, J. (1982). *Development in infancy.* New York: Random House.

Lamb, M. E., & Hwang, C. P. (1982). Maternal attachment and mother-neonate bonding: A critical review. In M. E. Lamb & A. L. Brown (Eds.), *Advances in developmental psychology* (pp. 1–39). Hillsdale, NJ: Erlbaum.

Lamb, R. J., Preston, K. L., W, S. C., Meisch, R. A., Davis, F., Katz, J. L., Henningfeld, J. E., & Goldberg, S. R. (1991). The reinforcing and subjective effects of morphine in post-addicts: A dose-response study. *Journal of Pharmacology and Experimental Therapeutics, 259,* 1165–1173.

Lancet, D. (1984). Molecular view of olfactory reception. *Trends in Neurosciences, 7,* 35–36.

Landsman, T. (1974). The humanizer. *American Journal of Orthopsychiatry, 44,* 345–352.

Lang, P. J., Rice, D. G., & Sternbach, R. A. (1972). The psychophysiology of emotion. In N. S. Greenfield & R. A. Sternbach (Eds.), *Handbook of Psychophysiology.* New York: Holt, Rinehart & Winston.

Langan, P. A., & Innes, C. A. (1985). *The risk of violent crime* (Bureau of Justice Statistics Special Report No. NCJ-97119). Washington, DC: U.S. Government Printing Office.

Lange, C. G., & James, W. (1922). *The emotions* (I. A. Haupt, Trans.). Baltimore: Williams & Wilkins.

Langer, E. J. (1989). *Mindfulness.* Reading, MA: Addison-Wesley.

Langer, E. J., & Rodin, J. (1976). The effects of choice and enhanced personal responsibility for the aged: A field experiment in an institutional setting. *Journal of Personality and Social Psychology, 34,* 191–198.

Langer, E. J., Rodin, J., Beck, P., Weinman, C., & Spitzer, L. (1979). Environmental determinants of memory improvement in late adulthood. *Journal of Personality and Social Psychology, 37,* 2003–2013.

Langston, C. A., & Cantor, N. (1989). Social anxiety and social constraint: When making friends is hard. *Journal of Personality and Social Psychology, 56,* 649–661.

Lansman, M., Donaldon, G., Hunt, E., & Yantis, S. (1982). Ability factors and cognitive processes. *Intelligence, 6,* 347–386.

Larsen, R. J. (1987). The stability of mood variability: A spectral analytic approach to daily mood assessments. *Journal of Personality and Social Psychology, 52,* 1195–1204.

Larsen, R. J., & Diener, E. (1985). An evaluation of subjective well-being measures. *Social Indicators Research, 17,* 1–18.

Larsen, R. J., & Diener, E. (1987). Affect intensity as an individual difference characteristic: A review. *Journal of Research in Personality, 21,* 1–39.

Larsen, R. J., & Ketelaar, T. (1989). Extraversion, neuroticism and susceptibility to positive and negative mood induction procedures. *Journal of Personality and Individual Differences, 10,* 1221–1228.

Larsen, R. J., & Ketelaar, T. (1991). Personality and susceptibility to positive and negative emotional states. *Journal of Personality and Social Psychology, 61,* 132–140.

Larsson, M., & Backman, L. (1993). Semantic activation and episodic odor recognition in young and older adults. *Psychology and Aging, 8,* 582–588.

Latané, B., & Darley, J. M. (1968). Group inhibition of bystander intervention in emergencies. *Journal of Personality and Social Psychology, 10,* 215–221.

Latané, B., & Darley, J. M. (1976). *Help in a crisis: Bystander response to an emergency.* Morristown, NJ: General Learning Press.

Latané, B., Nida, S. A., & Wilson, D. W. (1981). The effects of group size on helping behavior. In J. P. Rushton & R. M. Sorrentino (Eds.), *Altruism and helping behavior: Social, personality, and developmental perspectives.* Hillsdale, NJ: Erlbaum.

Latané, B., Williams, K., & Harkins, S. (1979). Many hands make light the work: The causes and consequences of social loafing. *Journal of Personality and Social Psychology, 37,* 822–832.

Lazarus, R. (1966). *Psychological stress and the coping process.* New York: McGraw-Hill.

Lazarus, R. S. (1990). Constructs of the mind in adaptation. In N. L. Stein, B. Leventhal, & T. Trabasso (Eds.), *Psychological and biological approaches to emotion* (pp. 3–20). Hillsdale, NJ: Erlbaum.

Lazarus, R. S. (1993). From psychological stress to the emotions: A history of changing outlooks. *Annual Review of Psychology, 44,* 1–21.

Lazarus, R. S., & Folkman, S. (1984). *Stress, appraisal, and coping.* New York: Springer-Verlag.

Lazarus, R. S., & Launier, R. (1978). Stress-related transactions between person and environment. In L. A. Pervin & M. Lewis (Eds.), *Internal and external determinants of behavior.* New York: Plenum Press..

Leahy, T. H. (1994). *A history of modern psychology* (2nd ed.). Englewood Cliffs, NJ: Prentice Hall.

Leary, M. R. (1983). *Understanding social anxiety: Social, personality, and clinical perspectives.* Beverly Hills: Sage.

Leary, M. R., Kowalski, R. M., & Bergen, D. J. (1988). Interpersonal information acquisition and confidence in first encounters. *Personality and Social Psychology Bulletin, 14,* 68–77.

Lee, S., & Chiu, H. F. (1989). Anorexia nervosa in Hong Kong—Why not more in Chinese? *British Journal of Psychiatry, 154,* 683–688.

Lee, T., & Seeman, P. (1977). *Dopamine receptors in normal and schizophrenic human brains* (Vol. 3, p. 443). Bethesda, MD: Society for Neuroscience.

Leff, J., Kuipers, L., Berkowitz, R., Eberlein-Vries, R., & Sturgeon, D. (1982). A controlled trial of social intervention in the families of schizophrenic patients. *British Journal of Psychiatry, 141,* 121–134.

Lefrancois, G. R. (1982). *Psychological theories and human learning* (2nd ed.). Monterey, CA: Brooks/Cole.

Legrenzi, P., Butera, F., Mugny, G., & Perez, J. (1991). Majority and minority influence in inductive reasoning: A preliminary study. *European Journal of Social Psychology, 21,* 359–363.

Lehman, A. K., & Rodin, J. (1989). Styles of self-nurturance and disordered eating. *Journal of Consulting and Clinical Psychology, 57,* 117–122.

Lehman, D. R., & Reifman, A. (1987). Spectator influence on basketball officiating. *Journal of Social Psychology, 127,* 673–675.

Leibowitz, S. F. (1991). Brain neuropeptide Y: An integrator of endocrine, metabolic, and behavioral progress. *Brain Research Bulletin, 27,* 333–337.

Leichtman, M. D., Ceci, S. J., & Morse, M. B. (1997). The nature and development of children's event memory. In P. S. Appelbaum, L. A. Uyehara, & M. R. Elin (Eds.), *Trauma and memory: Clinical and legal controversies* (pp. 158–187). New York: Oxford University Press.

Leippe, M. R., & Elkin, R. A. (1987). When motives clash: Issue involvement and response involvement as determinants of persuasion. *Journal of Personality and Social Psychology, 52,* 269–278.

Lemieux, G., Davignon, A., & Genest, J. (1965). Depressive states during Rauwolfia therapy for arterial hypertension. *Canadian Medical Association Journal, 74,* 522–526.

Lenneberg, E. (1967). On explaining language. *Science, 164,* 635–643.

Lepper, M. R., & Greene, D. (Eds.). (1978). *The hidden cost of reward.* Hillsdale, NJ: Erlbaum.

Lepper, M. R., Greene, D., & Nisbett, R. E. (1973). Undermining children's intrinsic interest with extrinsic reward: A test of the "overjustification" hypothesis. *Journal of Personality and Social Psychology, 28,* 129–137.

Lerer, B., Weiner, R. D., & Belmaker, R. H. (1986). *ECT: Basic mechanisms.* Washington, DC: American Psychiatric Press.

Lerman, L. (1978–1979). Preface to violent pornography: Degradation of women versus right of free speech. *New York University Review of Law and Social Change, 8*(2), 181–189.

Lerner, M. J. (1970). The desire for justice and reaction to victims. In J. R. Macaulay & L. Berkowitz (Eds.), *Altruism and helping behavior.* New York: Academic Press.

Lerner, M. J. (1974). Social psychology of justice and interpersonal attraction. In T. Huston (Ed.), *Foundations of interpersonal attraction.* New York: Academic Press.

Lerner, M. J., & Matthews, G. (1967). Reactions to suffering of others under conditions of indirect responsibility. *Journal of Personality and Social Psychology, 5,* 319–325.

Lerner, M. J., Miller, D. T., & Holmes, J. (1976). Deserving and the emergence of forms of justice. In L. Berkowitz & E. Walster (Eds.), *Advances in experimental social psychology.* New York: Academic Press.

Lerner, M. J., & Simmons, C. H. (1966). Observer's reaction to the "innocent victim": Compassion or rejection? *Journal of Personality and Social Psychology, 4,* 203–210.

Levenson, R. W., Ekman, P., & Friesen, W. V. (1990). Voluntary facial action generates emotion-specific autonomous nervous system activity. *Psychophysiology, 27,* 363–382.

Leventhal, H., & Nerenz, D. R. (1983). A model for stress research with some implications for the control of stress disorders. In D. Meichenbaum & M. E. Jaremko (Eds.), *Stress reduction and prevention.* New York: Plenum Press.

Levine, J. M. (1989). Reaction to opinion deviance in small groups. In P. Paulus (Ed.), *Psychology of group influence: New perspectives.* Hillsdale, NJ: Erlbaum.

Levine, M. (1988). *Effective problem-solving.* Englewood Cliffs, NJ: Prentice Hall.

Levine, R., Hoffman, J. S., Knepple, E. D., & Kenin, M. (1989). Long-term fluoxetine treatment of a large number of obsessive compulsive patients. *Journal of Clinical Psychopharmacology, 9,* 281–283.

Levinson, D. J., with Darrow, C. N., Klein, E. B., Levinson, M. H., &

McKee, B. (1978). *The seasons of a man's life*. New York: Knopf.

Levinson, S. C. (1983). *Pragmatics* (Vol. 9). New York: Cambridge University Press.

Levitsky, A., & Perls, F. S. (1970). The rules and games of gestalt therapy. In J. Fagan & I. L. Sheperd (Eds.), *Gestalt therapy now*. Palo Alto, CA: Science and Behavior Books.

Levy, J. (1985, May). Right brain, left brain: Fact and fiction. *Psychology Today*, 38–44.

Levy, S. M., Herberman, R. B., Lee, J. K., Lippman, M. E., & d'Angelo, T. (1989). Breast conservation versus mastectomy: Distress sequelae as a function of choice. *Journal of Clinical Oncology, 7*, 367–375.

Lewinsohn, P. H. (1974). A behavioral approach to depression. In R. J. Friedman & M. M. Katz (Eds.), *The psychology of depression: Contemporary theory and research*. Washington, DC: Winston-Wiley.

Lewinsohn, P. M., Mischel, W., Chaplin, W., & Barton, R. (1980). Social competence and depression: The role of illusionary self-perceptions. *Journal of Abnormal Psychology, 89*, 203–212.

Lewy, A. J., Sack, R. I., & Miller, L. S. (1987). Antidepressant and circadian phase-shifting effects of light. *Science, 235*, 352–354.

Liberman, A. M., & Mattingly, I. G. (1989). A specialization for speech perception. *Science, 243*, 489–494.

Liberman, R. P., & Eckman, T. (1981). Behavior therapy vs. insight-oriented therapy for repeated suicide attempters. *Archives of General Psychiatry, 38*, 1126–1130.

Lieberman, M. A., & Borman, L. (1979). *Self-help groups for coping with crisis*. San Francisco: Jossey-Bass.

Lieberman, P. (1991). *Uniquely human: The evolution of speech, thought, and selfless behavior*. Cambridge, MA: Harvard University Press.

Liebert, R. M., Neale, J. M., & Davidson, E. S. (1973). *The early window: Effects of television on children and youth*. Elmsford, NY: Pergamon Press.

Liem, J. H. (1980). Family studies schizophrenia: An update and commentary. In S. J. Keith & L. R. Mosher (Eds.), *Special report: Schizophrenia* (pp. 82–108). Washington, DC: U.S. Government Printing Office.

Lindner, R. (1954). *The fifty-minute hour*. New York: Holt, Rinehart & Winston.

Linehan, M. M., Camper, P., Chiles, J. A., Strosahal, K., & Shearin, E. S. (1987). Interpersonal problem solving and parasuicide. *Cognitive Therapy and Research, 11*, 1–12.

Lingenfelser, T., Kaschel, R., Weber, A., & Zaiser-Kaschel, H. (1994). Young hospital doctors after night duty: Their task-specific cognitive status and emotional condition. *Medical Education, 28*, 566–572.

Linn, R. L. (1982). Admissions testing on trial. *American Psychologist, 37*, 279–291.

Linsky, A. S., Straus, M. A., & Colby, J. P. (1985). Stressful events, stressful conditions and alcohol problems in the United States: A partial test of Bales's theory. *Journal of Studies on Alcohol, 46*, 72–80.

Linz, D., Donnerstein, E., & Penrod, S. (1987). The findings and recommendations of the Attorney General's Commission on Pornography: Do the psychological "facts" fit the political fury? *American Psychologist, 42*, 946–953.

Livingston, M. S. (1988). Art, illusion, and the visual system. *Scientific American, 258*, 78–85.

Livingston, M. S., & Hubel, D. H. (1987). Psychophysical evidence for separate channels for the perception of form, color, movement, and depth. *Journal of Neuroscience, 7*, 3416–3468.

Lobaugh, N. J., Wigal, T., Greene, P. L., & Diaz Granados, J. L. (1991). Effects of prenatal ethanol exposure on learned persistence and hippocampal neuroanatomy in infant, weanling and adult rats. *Behavioural Brain Research, 44*(1), 81–86.

Loeb, G. E. (1985). The functional replacement of the ear. *Scientific American, 253*, 104–111.

Loewenstein, R. J., & Ross, D. R. (1992). Multiple personality and psychoanalysis: An introduction. *Psychoanalytic Inquiry, 12*, 3–48.

Loftus, E. F. (1975). Leading questions and the eyewitness report. *Cognitive Psychology, 7*, 560–572.

Loftus, E. F. (1993). Desperately seeking memories of the first few years of childhood: The reality of early memories. *Journal of Experimental Psychology: General, 122*, 274–277.

Loftus, E. F. (1997a). Memory for a past that never was. *Current Directions in Psychological Science, 3*, 60–64.

Loftus, E. F. (1997b). Repressed memory accusations: Devastated families and devastated patients. *Applied Cognitive Psychology, 11*(1), 25–30.

Loftus, E. F., Garry, M., Brown, S. W., & Rader, M. (1994). Near-natal memories, past-life memories, and other memory myths. *American Journal of Clinical Hypnosis, 36*, 176–179.

Loftus, E. F., Garry, M., & Feldman, J. (1994). Forgetting sexual trauma: What does it mean when 38% forget? *Journal of Consulting and Clinical Psychology, 62*, 1177–1181.

Loftus, E. F., & Greene, E. (1980). Warning: Even memory for faces may be contagious. *Law and Human Behavior, 4*, 323–334.

Loftus, E. F., & Hoffman, H. G. (1989). Misinformation and memory: The creation of new memories. *Journal of Experimental*

Psychology: General, 118(1), 100–104.

Loftus, E. F., & Ketchum, K. (1994). *The myth of repressed memory: False memories and allegations of sexual abuse.* New York: St. Martin's Press.

Loftus, E. F., & Klinger, M. R. (1992). Is the conscious smart or dumb? *American Psychologist, 47,* 761–765.

Loftus, E. F., Levidow, B., & Duensing, S. (1991). Who remembers best? Individual differences in memory for events that occurred in a science museum. *Applied Cognitive Psychology, 6,* 93–107.

Loftus, E. F., & Loftus, G. R. (1980). On the permanence of stored information in the human brain. *American Psychology, 35,* 409–420.

Loftus, E. F., Miller, D. G., & Burns, H. J. (1978). Semantic integration of verbal information into a visual memory. *Journal of Experimental Psychology, 4,* 19–31.

Loftus, E. F., & Palmer, J. C. (1974). Reconstruction of automobile destruction: An example of the interaction between language and memory. *Journal of Verbal Learning and Verbal Behavior, 13,* 585–589.

Loftus, E. F., & Pickerel, J. E. (1995). The formation of false memories. *Psychiatric Annals, 25,* 720–725.

Logue, A. W. (1979). Taste aversion and the generality of the laws of learning. *Psychological Bulletin, 86,* 276–296.

London, M., & Bray, D. W. (1980). Ethical issues in testing and evaluation for personnel decisions. *American Psychologist, 35,* 890–901.

Lopes, L. L. (1989, January 15). *The rhetoric of irrationality.* Paper presented at the meeting of the American Association for the Advancement of Science, San Francisco.

LoPiccolo, J., & Stock, W. E. (1986). Treatment of sexual dysfunction. *Journal of Consulting Psychology, 54,* 158–167.

Lorenz, K. (1937). The companion in the bird's world. *Auk, 54,* 245–273.

Lorenz, K. (1950). The comparative methods in studying innate behavior patterns. *Symposia of the Society for Experimental Biology, 4,* 221–268.

Lorenz, K. (1974). *The eight deadly sins of civilized man* (Marjorie Kerr-Wilson, Trans.). New York: Harcourt Brace Jovanovich.

Lovell, J., & Kluger, J. (1994). *Lost moon: The perilous voyage of Apollo 13.* Boston: Houghton Mifflin.

Lovett, L. M., & Shaw, D. M. (1987). Outcome in bipolar affective disorder after stereotactic tractotomy. *British Journal of Psychiatry, 151,* 113–116.

Luborsky, L., Crits-Christoph, P., & Mellon, J. (1986). Advent of objective measures of the transference concept. *Journal of Consulting and Clinical Psychology, 54,* 39–47.

Luborsky, L., & Spence, D. P. (1978). Quantitative research on psychoanalytic therapy. In S. L. Garfield & A. E. Bergin (Eds.), *Handbook of psychotherapy and behavior change: An empirical analysis* (2nd ed.). New York: Wiley.

Luce, R. D., & Krumhansl, C. L. (1988). Measurement, scaling, and psychophysics. In R. C. Atkinson, R. J. Hernstein, L. Gardner, & R. D. Luce (Eds.), *Stevens' handbook of experimental psychology* (2nd ed., Vol. 1, pp. 3–74). New York: Wiley.

Luchins, A. S. (1957). Primacy-recency in impression formation. In C. I. Hovland (Ed.), *The order of presentation in persuasion* (pp. 33–61). New Haven, CT: Yale University Press.

Luria, A. R. (1968/1987). *The Mind of a Mnemonist* (Lynn Solotaroff, Trans.). New York: Basic Books.

Luria, Z., & Herzog, E. (1985, April). *Gender segregation across and within settings.* Paper presented at the Society for Research in Child Development, Toronto.

Lydiard, R. B., & Gelenberg, A. J.

(1982). Hazards and adverse effects of lithium. *Annual Review of Medicine, 33,* 327–344.

Lykken, D. T. (1957). A study of anxiety in the sociopathic personality. *Journal of Abnormal and Social Psychology, 55,* 6–10.

Lykken, D. T. (1997). Incompetent parenting: Its causes and cures. *Child Psychiatry and Human Development, 27,* 129–137.

Lykken, D. T., & Tellegen, A. (1996). Happiness is a stochastic phenomenon. *Psychological Science, 7,* 186–189.

Lynn, S. J., Lock, T. G., Myers, B., & Payne, D. G. (1997). Recalling the unrecallable: Should hypnosis be used to recover memories in psychotherapies? *Current Directions in Psychological Science, 3,* 79–83.

Lynn, S. J., & Rhue, J. W. (1988). Fantasy proneness: Hypnosis, developmental antecedents, and psychopathology. *American Psychologist, 43*(1), 35–44.

Maccoby, E. E. (1988). Gender as a social category. *Developmental Psychology, 24,* 755–765.

Maccoby, E. E., & Jacklin, C. N. (1974). *The psychology of sex differences.* Stanford, CA: Stanford University Press.

Maccoby, E. E., & Jacklin, C. N. (1987). Gender segregation in childhood. In H. Reese (Ed.), *Advances in child behavior and development* (Vol. 20). Orlando: Academic Press.

Macfarlane, A. (1977). *The psychology of childbirth.* Cambridge, MA: Harvard University Press.

Mackie, D. M., & Worth, L. T. (1990). "Feeling good, but not thinking straight": The impact of positive mood on persuasion. In J. T. Forgas (Ed.), *Affect and social judgments* (pp. 201–220). Oxford: Pergamon Press.

MacNichol, E. F., Jr.. (1964). Three-pigment color vision. *Scientific American, 211,* 48–56.

Macrae, C. N., Bodenhausen, G. V., & Milne, A. B., Jetten, J. (1994). Out of mind but back in sight: Stereotypes on the rebound. *Journal of Personality and Social Psychology, 67,* 808–817.

Maddi, S. (1976). *Personality theories: A comparative analysis* (3rd ed.). Homewood, IL: Dorsey Press.

Madsen, K. B. (1959). *Theories of motivation: A comparative study of modern theories of motivation.* Copenhagen: Munksgaard.

Magnuson, E. (1986, March 10). "A serious deficiency": The Rogers Commission faults NASA's "flawed" decision-making process. *Time,* 40–42.

Mahler, M. S. (1968). *On human symbiosis and the vicissitudes of individuation: Infantile psychosis.* New York: International Universities Press.

Mahler, M. S., Pine, F., & Bergman, A. (1975). *The psychological birth of the human infant.* New York: Basic Books.

Mahoney, M. J., & Arnkoff, D. (1978). Cognitive and self-control therapies. In S. L. Garfield & A. E. Bergin (Eds.), *Handbook of psychotherapy and behavior change: An empirical analysis* (2nd ed.). New York: Wiley.

Maier, N. R. F. (1931). Reasoning in humans. *Journal of Comparative Psychology, 12,* 181–194.

Main, M., & George, C. (1985). Responses of abused and disadvantaged toddlers to distress in age-mates: A study in the day-care setting. *Developmental Psychology, 21,* 407–412.

Maki, R., & Berry, S. L. (1984). Metacomprehension of text material. *Journal of Experimental Psychology: Learning, Memory, and Cognition, 10,* 663–679.

Maki, R., & Serra, M. (1992). The basis of test predictions for test material. *Journal of Experimental Psychology: Learning, Memory, and Cognition, 18,* 116–126.

Malamuth, N. M. (1981). Rape fantasies as a function of exposure to violent sexual stimuli. *Archives of Sexual Behavior, 10,* 33–47.

Malamuth, N. M. (1984). Aggression against women: Cultural and individual causes. In N. M. Malamuth & E. Donnerstein (Eds.), *Pornography and sexual aggression.* Orlando, FL: Academic Press.

Malamuth, N. M. (1989). The attraction to sexual aggression scale: Part one. *Journal of Sex Research, 26,* 26–49.

Malamuth, N. M., & Check, J. V. P. (1981). The effects of mass media exposure on acceptance of violence against women: A field experiment. *Journal of Research in Personality, 15,* 436–446.

Malamuth, N. M., & Check, J. V. P. (1985). The effects of aggressive pornography on beliefs in rape myths: Individual differences. *Journal of Research in Personality, 19,* 299–320.

Malamuth, N. M., Check, J. V. P., & Brier, J. (1986). Sexual arousal in response to aggression: Ideological, aggressive, and sexual correlates. *Journal of Personality and Social Psychology, 50,* 330–350.

Maletzky, B. M., & Klotter, J. (1974). Smoking and alcoholism. *American Journal of Psychiatry, 131*(4), 445–447.

Malotki, E. (1983). *Hopi time: A linguistic analysis of temporal concepts in the Hopi language.* Berlin: Mouton.

Maltz, D. N., & Borker, R. A. (1983). A cultural approach to male-female miscommunication. In J. A. Gumperz (Ed.), *Language and social identity* (pp. 195–216). New York: Cambridge University Press.

Mandel, D. R., Jusczyk, P. W., & Pisoni, D. B. (1995). Infants' recognition of the sound patterns in their own names. *Psychological Science, 6,* 314–317.

Mandos, L., Clary, C., & Schweizer, E. (1990). Prescribing practices for fluoxetine: A brief survey. *Journal of Clinical Psychopharmacology, 10,* 74–75.

Manke, B., & Plomin, R. (1997). Adolescent familial interactions: A genetic extension of the Social Relations Model. *Journal of Social and Personal Relationships, 14,* 505–522.

Mann, J. J., McBride, A., Brown, R. P., Linnoila, M., Leon, A. C., DeMeo, M., Mieczkowski, T., Myers, J. E., & Stanley, M. (1992). Relationship between central and peripheral serotonin indexes in depressed and suicidal psychiatric inpatients. *Archives of General Psychiatry, 49,* 442–446.

Maranyon, G. (1924). Contribution à l'étude de l'action emotive de l'adrenaline. *Revue Française d'Endocrinologie, 2,* 301–325.

Maratsos, M., Flavell, J. H., & Markman, E. (1983). Some current issues in the study of the acquisition of grammar. In P. Mussen (Ed.), *Handbook of child psychology: Cognitive development* (4th ed., pp. 707–786). New York: Wiley.

Marcel, A. (1983). Conscious and unconscious perception: An approach to the relation between phenomenal experience and perceptual process. *Cognitive Psychology, 15,* 238–300.

Margolin, L., Miller, M., & Moran, P. (1989). When a kiss is not just a kiss: Relating violations of consent in kissing to rape myth acceptance. *Sex Roles, 20,* 231–243.

Maris, R. W. (1992). The relation of nonfatal suicide attempts to completed suicides. In R. W. Maris, A. L. Berman, J. T. Maltsberger, & R. l. Yufit (Eds.), *Assessment and prediction of suicide* (pp. 362–380). New York: Guilford.

Maris, R. W., Berman, A. L., Maltsberger, J. T., & Yufit, R. I. (Eds.). (1990). *Assessment and prediction of suicide.* New York: Guilford.

Markman, E. (1977). Realizing that you don't understand: A preliminary investigation. *Child Development, 48*, 986–992.

Markus, H. (1977). Self-schemata and processing information about the self. *Journal of Personality and Social Psychology, 35*(2), 63–78.

Markus, H., & Nurius, P. (1987). Possible selves. *American Psychologist, 41*(9), 954–969.

Markus, H., & Zajonc, R. B. (1985). The cognitive perspective in social psychology. In G. Lindsey & E. Aronson (Eds.), *Handbook of social psychology* (3rd ed.). Reading, MA: Addison-Wesley.

Marlatt, G. A., & George, W. H. (1988). Relapse prevention and the maintenance of optimal health. In S. Shumaker, E. Schron, & J. K. Ockene (Eds.), *The adoption and maintenance of behaviors for optimal health*. New York: Springer-Verlag.

Marlatt, G. A., Kosturn, C. F., & Lang, A. R. (1975). Provocation to anger and opportunity for retaliation as determinants of alcohol consumption in social drinkers. *Journal of Abnormal Psychology, 84*, 652–659.

Marlatt, G. A., & Nathan, P. E. (Eds.). (1978). *Behavioral approaches to alcoholism*. New Brunswick, NJ: Rutgers Center for Alcohol Studies.

Marshall, G. N., Wortman, C. B., Kusulas, J. W., Hervig, L. K., & Vickers, R. R., Jr. (1992). Distinguishing optimism from pessimism: Relations to fundamental dimensions of mood and personality. *Journal of Personality and Social Psychology, 62*, 1067–1074.

Martin, C. L., & Halverson, C. F., Jr. (1981). A schematic processing model of sex typing and stereotyping in children. *Child Development, 52*, 1119–1134.

Martin, G., & Pear, J. (1983). *Behavior modification: What it is and how it works* (2nd ed.). Englewood Cliffs, NJ: Prentice Hall.

Martin, L. (1986). Eskimo words for snow: A case study in the genesis and decay of an anthropological example. *American Psychologists, 88*, 418–423.

Maslach, C., Stapp, J., & Santee, R. T. (1985). Individuation: Conceptual analysis and assessment. *Journal of Personality and Social Psychology, 49*, 729–738.

Maslow, A. H. (1954). *Motivation and personality*. New York: Harper & Row.

Maslow, A. H. (1966). *The psychology of science: A reconnaissance*. New York: Harper & Row.

Maslow, A. H. (1968). *Toward a psychology of being* (2nd ed.). New York: Van Nostrand Reinhold.

Maslow, A. H. (1971a). *The farther reaches of the human mind*. New York: Viking.

Maslow, A. H. (1971b). Some basic propositions of a growth and self-actualization psychology. In S. Maddi (Ed.), *Perspectives on personality*. Boston: Little, Brown.

Masten, A. S. (1986, August). *The patterns of adaptation to stress in middle childhood*. Paper presented at the American Psychological Association, Washington, DC.

Masters, J. C., Burish, T. G., Hollon, S. D., & Rimin, D. C. (1987). *Behavior therapy: Techniques and empirical findings*. San Diego: Harcourt Brace Jovanovich.

Masters, W. H., & Johnson, V. E. (1966). *Human sexual response*. Boston: Little, Brown.

Masters, W. H., & Johnson, V. E. (1970). *Human sexual inadequacy*. Boston: Little, Brown.

Mather, D. B. (1987). The case against preventing suicide prevention: Comments on Szasz. *American Psychologist, 42*, 882–883.

Mathes, E. W. (1975). The effects of physical attractiveness and anxiety on heterosexual attraction over a series of five encounters. *Journal of Marriage and Family, 37*, 769–773.

Mayer, R. E. (1983). *Thinking, problem solving, cognition*. New York: W. H. Freeman.

Mayer-Gross, W., Slater, E., & Roth, M. (1969). *Clinical psychiatry*. Baltimore: Williams & Wilkins.

McAdams, D. P. (1988a). Biography, narrative, and lives: An introduction. *Journal of Personality, 56*(1), 1–18.

McAdams, D. P. (1988b). *Power, intimacy, and the life story: Personological inquiries into identity*. New York: Guilford.

McAdams, D. P. (1990). *The person: An introduction to personality psychology*. San Diego: Harcourt Brace Jovanovich.

McArthur, L. A. (1972). The how and what of why: Some determinants and consequences of causal attribution. *Journal of Personality and Social Psychology, 22*, 171–193.

McBurney, D. H., & Collings, V. B. (1984). *Introduction to sensation/perception* (2nd ed.). Englewood Cliffs, NJ: Prentice Hall.

McCarthy, R. A., & Warrington, E. K. (1990). *Cognitive neuropsychology: A clinical introduction*. San Diego: Academic Press.

McCartney, K., Scarr, S., Phillips, D., Grajek, S., & Schwarz, J. C. (1982). Environmental differences among day care centers and their effect on children's development. In E. F. Zigler & E. W. Gordon (Eds.), *Day care: Scientific and social policy issues*. Boston: Auburn House.

McCauley, C. (1989). The nature of social influence in groupthink: Compliance and internalization. *Journal of Personality and Social Psychology, 57*, 250–260.

McClearn, G. E., Johansson, B., Berg, S., & Pedersen, N. L., (1997). Substantial genetic influence on cognitive abilities in twins 80 or more years old. *Science, 276*(58), 1560–1563.

McClelland, D. C. (1973). Testing for competence rather than for "intelligence." *American Psychologist, 28,* 1–14.

McClelland, D. C. (1993). Intelligence is not the best predictor of job performance. *Current Directions in Psychological Science, 2,* 5–6.

McCloskey, M., Wible, C., & Cohen, N. (1988). Is there a special flashbulb memory mechanism? *Journal of Experimental Psychology: General, 117,* 171–181.

McCord, W. (1979). Some child-rearing antecedents of criminal behavior in adult men. *Journal of Personality and Social Psychology, 37,* 1477–1486.

McCord, W., & McCord, J. (1964). *The psychopath: An essay on the criminal mind.* New York: Van Nostrand Reinhold.

McCrae, R. R. (1989). Why I advocate the five factor model: Joint factor analyses of the NEO-PI with other instruments. In D. M. Buss & N. Cantor (Eds.), *Personality psychology: Recent trends and emerging directions* (pp. 237–245). New York: Springer-Verlag.

McCrae, R. R., & Costa, P. T., Jr. (1984). *Emerging lives, enduring dispositions: Personality in adulthood.* Boston: Little, Brown.

McCrae, R. R., & Costa, P. T., Jr.. (1988). Recalled parent-child relations and adult personality. *Journal of Personality, 56*(2), 417–434.

McCrae, R. R., & Costa, P. T., Jr. (1994). The stability of personality: Observations and evaluations. *Current Directions in Psychological Science, 3,* 173–175.

McCulloch, J. W., & Prins, H. A. (1975). *Signs of stress.* London: Collins.

McFarlane, A. C. (1988). The aetiology of post-traumatic stress disorders following a natural disaster. *British Journal of Psychiatry, 152,* 116–121.

McFarlane, A. C. (1989). The aetiology of post-traumatic morbidity: Predisposing, precipitating, and perpetuating factors. *British Journal of Psychiatry, 154,* 221–228.

McGinnies, E., & Ward, C. D. (1980). Better liked than right: Trustworthiness and expertise as factors in credibility. *Personality and Social Psychology Bulletin, 6,* 467–472.

McGrath, J. E. (1984). *Groups: Interaction and performance.* Englewood Cliffs, NJ: Prentice-Hall.

McGue, M., Pickens, R. W., & Svikis, D. S. (1992). Sex and age effects on the inheritance of alcohol problems: A twin study. *Journal of Abnormal Psychology, 101,* 3–17.

McGuffin, P., Bebbington, P., & Katz, R. (1989). The Camberwell Collaborative Depression Study: III. Depression and adversity in the relatives of depressed controls: Reply. *British Journal of Psychiatry, 154,* 565.

McGuire, W. J. (1985). Attitudes and attitude change. In G. Lindsey & E. Aronson (Eds.), *Handbook of social psychology* (3rd ed., pp. 233–346). Reading, MA: Addison-Wesley.

McKean, K. (1985, April). Of two minds: Selling the right brain. *Discover,* 34–40.

McKinnon, W., Weisse, C. S., Reynolds, C. P., Bowles, C. A., & Baum, A. (1989). Chronic stress, leukocyte subpopulations, and humoral response to latent viruses. *Health Psychology, 8,* 389–402.

McLean, P. O. (1982). On the origins and progressive evolution of the triune brain. In E. Armstrong & D. Falk (Eds.), *Primate brain evolution.* New York: Plenum Press.

McNeal, E. T., & Cimbolic, P. (1986). Antidepressants and biochemical theories of depression. *Psychological Bulletin, 99,* 361–374.

McNeill, D. (1966). Developmental psycholinguistics. In F. L. Smith & G. A. Miller (Eds.), *The genesis of language: A psycholinguistic approach.* Cambridge, MA: MIT Press.

Mead, M. (1935). *Sex and temperament in three primitive societies.* New York: Morrow.

Medin, D., & Ross, M. W. (1989). *Cognition* (2nd ed.). New York: Holt, Rinehart & Winston.

Medin, D. L., & Smith, E. E. (1984). Concepts and concept formation. *Annual Review of Psychology, 35,* 113–138.

Mednick, S. A., Machon, R., Huttunen, M. O., & Bonett, D. (1988). Fetal viral infection and adult schizophrenia. *Archives of General Psychiatry, 45,* 189–192.

Meesters, Y., Jansen, J. H. C., Beersma, D. G. M., Bouhuys, A. L., & van den Hoofdakker, R. H. (1993). Early light treatment can prevent an emerging winter depression from developing into full-blown depression. *Journal of Affective Disorders, 29,* 41–47.

Meeus, W. H. J., & Raaijmakers, Q. A. W. (1986). Administrative obedience: Carrying out orders to use psychological-administrative violence. *European Journal of Social Psychology, 16,* 311–324.

Meeus, W. H. J., & Raaijmakers, Q. A. W. (1987). Administrative obedience as a social phenomenon. In W. Doise & S. Moscovici (Eds.), *Current Issues in European Social Psychology* (Vol. 2, pp. 183–230). Cambridge, England: Cambridge University Press.

Mehrabian, A. (1972). *Nonverbal communication.* Hawthorne, NY: Aldine-Atherton.

Meichenbaum, D. H. (1977). *Cognitive behavior modification: An integrative approach.* New York: Plenum Press.

Meichenbaum, D. H., & Deffenbacher, J. L. (1988). Stress inoculation training. *Counseling Psychologist, 16*(1), 69–90.

Melton, G., & Gray, J. (1988). Ethical dilemmas in AIDS research: Individual privacy and public health. *American Psychologist, 43,* 60–64.

Meltzer, H. Y., & Stahl, S. M. (1976). Dopamine hypothesis of schizophrenia—Review. *Schizophrenia Bulletin, 2,* 19–76.

Meltzoff, A. N., & Moore, M. K. (1977). Imitation of facial and manual gestures by human neonates. *Science, 198,* 75–78.

Meltzoff, A. N., & Moore, M. K. (1983). Newborn infants imitate adult facial gestures. *Child Development, 54,* 702–709.

Melzack, R. (1992). Phantom limbs. *Scientific American, 266,* 121–126.

Melzack, R., & Wall, P. D. (1988). *The challenge of pain.* New York: Penguin.

Mendels, J. (1970). *Concepts of depression.* New York: Wiley.

Mendelson, J. H. (1987). Marijuana. In H. Y. Metzler (Ed.), *Pharmacology: Third generation of progress* (pp. 1565–1571). New York: Raner.

Merikle, P. M. (1988). Subliminal auditory messages: An evaluation. *Psychology and Marketing, 5,* 355–372.

Merton, R. K., & Kitt, A. S. (1950). Contributions to the theory of reference group behavior. In R. K. Merton & P. F. Lazarsfeld (Eds.), *Continuities in social research: Studies in the scope and method of "the American soldier."* New York: Free Press.

Mervis, C. B., Catlin, J., & Rosch, E. (1976). Relationships among goodness of example, category norms, and word frequency. *Bulletin of the Psychonomic Society, 7,* 283–284.

Metalsky, G. I., Haberstadt, L. J., & Abramson, L. Y. (1987). Vulnerability and invulnerability to depressive mood reactions: Toward a more powerful test of the diathesis-stress and causal mediation components of the reformulated theory of depression. *Journal of Personality and Social Psychology, 52,* 386–393.

Michael, R. P., & Keverne, E. B. (1968). Pheromones in the communication of sexual status in primates. *Nature, 218,* 746–749.

Michael, R. P., Keverne, E. B., & Bonsall, R. W. (1971). Pheromones: Isolation of male sex attractants from a female primate. *Science, 172,* 964–966.

Michaels, J. W., Blommel, J. M., Brocata, R. M., Linkous, R. A., & Rowe, J. S. (1982). Social facilitation and inhibition in a natural setting. *Replications in Social Psychology, 2,* 21–24.

Michelson, L. K., & Marchione, K. (1991). Behavioral, cognitive, and pharmacological treatments of panic disorder with agoraphobia: Critique and synthesis. *Journal of Consulting and Clinical Psychology, 59,* 100–114.

Miers, M. L. (1985). Current NIH perspectives on misconduct in science. *American Psychologist, 40,* 831–835.

Miklowitz, D. J., Velligan, D. I., Goldstein, M. J., Nuechterlein, K. H., & Giltin, M. J. (1989). Communication deviance in families of schizophrenic and manic patients. *Journal of Abnormal Psychology, 100,* 163–173.

Mikulincer, M., & Solomon, Z. (1988). Attributional styles and combat-related posttraumatic stress disorder. *Journal of Abnormal Psychology, 97,* 308–313.

Milgram, S. (1963). Behavioral study of obedience. *Journal of Abnormal and Social Psychology, 67,* 371–378.

Milgram, S. (1964). Issues in the study of obedience: A reply to Baumrind. *American Psychologist, 19,* 848–852.

Milgram, S. (1965). Some conditions of obedience and disobedience to authority. In I. D. Steiner & M. Fishbein (Eds.), *Current studies in social psychology* (pp. 243–262). New York: Holt, Rinehart & Winston.

Milgram, S. (1968). Some conditions of obedience and disobedience to

authority. *Human Relations, 18,* 56–76.

Milgram, S. (1974). *Obedience to authority.* New York: Harper & Row.

Miller, D. T., & Turnbull, W. (1986). Expectancies and interpersonal processes. In M. R. Rosenzweig & L. W. Porter (Eds.), *Annual review of psychology* (Vol. 37, pp. 233–256). Palo Alto, CA: Annual Review.

Miller, G. A. (1956). The magical number seven, plus or minus two: Some limits on our capacity for processing information. *Psychological Review, 63,* 81–97.

Miller, G. A. (1962). *Psychology.* New York: Harper & Row.

Miller, G. A. (1981). *Language and speech.* New York: W. H. Freeman.

Miller, G. A., & Glucksberg, S. (1988). Psycholinguistic aspects of pragmatics and semantics. In R. C. Atkinson & R. J. Hernstein (Eds.), *Stevens' handbook of experimental psychology* (Vol. 2, pp. 417–472). New York: Wiley.

Miller, G. R., & Burgoon, J. K. (1982). Factors affecting assessments of witness credibility. In N. L. Kerr & R. M. Bray (Eds.), *The psychology of the courtroom.* New York: Academic Press.

Miller, I. J., Jr., & Bartoshuk, L. M. (1991). Taste perception, taste bud distribution, and spatial relationships. In T. V. Getchell, R. L. Doty, L. M. Bartoshuk, & J. B. Snow (Eds.), *Smell and taste in health and disease* (pp. 175–204). New York: Raven Press.

Miller, N., & Carlson, M. (1990). Valid theory-testing meta-analyses further question the negative state relief model of helping. *Psychological Bulletin, 107,* 215–225.

Miller, N. E. (1985). The value of behavioral research on animals. *American Psychologist, 40,* 423–440.

Miller, N. E., & Bugelski, R. (1948). Minor studies of aggression: 2. The influence of frustrations imposed by the ingroup on attitudes expressed toward outgroups. *Journal of Psychology, 25*, 437–452.

Miller, S. A. (1976). Nonverbal assessment of conservation of number. *Child Development, 47*, 722–728.

Miller, T. Q., Turner, C. W., Tindale, R. S., Posvac, E. J., & Dugoni, B. L. (1991). Reasons for the trend toward null findings in research on Type A behavior. *Psychological Bulletin, 110*, 469–485.

Miller, W. (1975). Psychological deficit in depression. *Psychological Bulletin, 82*, 238–260.

Milner, B. (1966). Amnesia following operation on the temporal lobe. In C. Whitey & O. Zangwell (Eds.), *Amnesia*. London: Butterworth.

Milner, B. (1976). CNS maturation and language acquisition. In H. Whitaker & H. A. Whitaker (Eds.), *Studies of neurolinguistics* (Vol. 1). New York: Academic Press.

Milner, B., & Petrides, M. (1984). Behavioral effects of frontal lobe lesions in man. *Human Neurobiology, 4*, 403–407.

Mindus, P., & Jenicke, M.A. (1992). Neurosurgical treatment of malignant obsessive compulsive disorder. *Psychiatric Clinics of North America, 15*, 921–938.

Minuchin, S. (1974). *Families and family therapy techniques*. Cambridge, MA: Harvard University Press.

Minuchin, S., & Fishman, H. C. (1981). *Family therapy techniques*. Cambridge, MA: Harvard University Press.

Minuchin, S., Rosman, B. L., & Baker, L. (1978). *Psychosomatic families: Anorexia nervosa in context*. Cambridge, MA: Harvard University Press.

Mirowsky, J., & Ross, C. E. (1989). Psychiatric diagnosis as reified measurement. *Journal of Health and Social Behavior, 30*, 11–25.

Mischel, W. (1968). *Personality and assessment*. New York: Wiley.

Mischel, W. (1981). *Introduction to personality* (3rd ed.). New York: Holt, Rinehart & Winston.

Mishkin, M., & Appenzeller, T. (1987). The anatomy of memory. *Scientific American, 256*, 80–89.

Mitchell, D. C. (1989). How many memory systems are there? Evidence from aging. *Journal of Experimental Psychology: Learning, Memory, and Cognition, 15*, 31–49.

Miyake, K., & Zuckerman, M. (1993). Beyond personality impressions: Effects of physical and vocal attractiveness on false consensus, social comparison, affiliation, and assumed and perceived similarity. *Journal of Personality, 61*, 411–437.

Mogdil, S., & Mogdil, C. (Eds.). (1987). *Arthur Jensen: Consensus and controversy*. New York: Falmer.

Mollon, J. D. (1982). Color vision. *Annual Review of Psychology, 33*, 41–85.

Money, J., & Ehrhardt, A. A. (1972). *Man and woman, boy and girl*. Baltimore: Johns Hopkins University Press.

Monge, R., & Hultsch, D. (1971). Paired associate learning as a function of adult age and the length of anticipation and inspection intervals. *Journal of Gerontology, 26*, 157–162.

Monnier, M., Boehmer, A., & Scholer, A. (1976). Early habituation, dishabituation, and generalization induced in visual center by color stimuli. *Vision Research, 16*, 1497–1504.

Monnier, M., Dudler, L, Gaechter, R. M., P. F, Tobler, H. J., & Schönenberger, G. A. (1975). The delta-sleep inducing peptide (DSIP): comparative properties of the original and the synthetic non-peptide. *Experientia, 33*, 548–552.

Monroe, S. M. (1983). Major and minor life events as predictors of psychological distress: Further issues and findings. *Journal of Behavioral Medicine, 6*, 189–205.

Moorcroft, W. H. (1993). *Sleep, dreaming, and sleep disorders: An introduction* (2nd ed.). Landham, MD: University Press of America.

Moore, T. E. (1982). Subliminal advertising: What you see is what you get. *Journal of Marketing, 46*, 38–47.

Moore, T. E. (1988). The case against subliminal manipulation. *Psychology and Marketing, 5*, 297–316.

Moore, T. E. (1995). Subliminal self-help auditory tapes: An empirical test of perceptual consequences. *Canadian Journal of Behavioural Science, 27*, 9–20.

Moorhead, G., Ference, R., & Neck, C. P. (1991). Group decision fiascoes continue: Space shuttle *Challenger* and a revised groupthink framework. *Human Relations, 44*, 539–550.

Mori, D., Chaiken, S., & Pliner, P. (1987). "Eating lightly" and the self-presentation of femininity. *Journal of Personality and Social Psychology, 53*, 693–702.

Morris, N. M., & Udry, J. R. (1978). Pheromonal influences on human sexual behavior: An experimental search. *Journal of Biosocial Science, 10*, 147–157.

Morrongiello, B. A., Fenwick, K. D., & Chance, G. (1990). Sound localization acuity in very young infants. *Developmental Psychology, 26*, 75–84.

Morse, R. C., & Stoller, D. (1982, September). The hidden message that breaks habits. *Science Digest, 28*.

Moscovici, S. (1985). Social influence and conformity. In G. Lindsey & E. Aronson (Eds.), *Handbook of social psychology* (3rd ed., p. 19). Reading, MA: Addison-Wesley.

Moscovici, S., Lage, S., & Naffrechoux, M. (1969). Influence of a consistent minority on the responses of a majority in a color perception task. *Sociometry, 32*, 365–380.

Moscovici, S., & Mugny, G. (1983). Minority influence. In P. Paulus (Ed.), *Basic group process*. New York: Springer-Verlag.

Moscovici, S., & Personnaz, B. (1980). Studies in social influence vs. minority influence and conversion behavior in a perceptual look. *Journal of Experimental Social Psychology, 16*, 270–283.

Moskowitz, D. S., Schwarz, J. C., & Corsini, D. A. (1977). Initiating day care at three years of age: Effects on attachment. *Child Development, 48*, 1271–1276.

Moss, H. A. (1967). Sex, age, and state as determinants of mother-infant interaction. *Merrill-Palmer Quarterly of Behavior and Development, 13*, 19–36.

Moss, R. B., Moss, H. B., & Peterson, R. (1989). Microstress, mood, and natural killer-cell activity. *Psychosomatics, 30*, 279–283.

Mowbray, C. T. (1988). Post-traumatic therapy for children who are victims of violence. In F. M. Ochberg (Ed.), *Posttraumatic therapy and victims of violence* (pp. 196–212). New York: Brunner/Mazel.

Mowrer, O., & Mowrer, W. (1930). Enuresis: A method for its study and treatment. *American Journal of Orthopsychiatry, 8*, 436–459.

Mroczek, D. K., Spiro, A., Aldwin, C. M., Ozer, D. J., & Bossé, R. (1993). Construct validation of optimism and pessimism in older men: Findings from the normative aging study. *Health Psychology, 12*, 406–409.

Mullen, B., & Baumeister, R. F. (1987). Group effects on self–attention and performance: Social loafing, social facilitation, and social impairment. In C. Hendrick (Ed.), *Group processes and intergroup relations: Review of personality and social psychology* (Vol. 9). Newbury Park, CA: Sage.

Mulvey, E. P., & Haugaard, J. L. (1986). *Surgeon General's workshop on pornography and public health* (Report). Washington, DC: U.S. Department of Health and Human Services, Office of the Surgeon General.

Munger, K., & Harris, S. J. (1989). Effects of an observer on handwashing in a public restroom. *Perceptual and Motor Skills, 69*, 733–734.

Murray, H. A. (1959). Vicissitudes of creativity. In H. H. Anderson (Ed.), *Creativity and its cultivation*. New York: Harper & Row.

Muscettola, G., Potter, W. Z., Pickar, D., & Goodwin, F. K. (1984). Urinary 3methoxy-4-hydroxyphenyl-glycol and major affective disorders. *Archives of General Psychiatry, 41*, 337–342.

Mussen, P., Honzik, M., & Eichorn, D. (1982). Early adult antecedents of life satisfaction at age 70. *Journal of Gerontology, 37*, 315–322.

Muter, P. (1980). Very rapid forgetting. *Memory and Cognition, 8*, 174–179.

Myers, D. G., & Diener, E. (1995). Who is happy? *Psychological Science, 6*, 10–19.

Myers, D. G., & Ridl, J. (1979, August). Can we all be better than average? *Psychology Today, 7*, 89–98.

Nairn, A., & Associates. (1980). *The reign of ETS: The corporation that makes up minds*. Washington, DC: Nader.

Nathan, P. E. (1976a). The gate control theory of pain. *Brain, 99*, 123–158.

Nathan, P. E. (1976b). Alcoholism. In H. Leitenberg (Ed.), *Handbook of behavior modification and behavior therapy*. Englewood Cliffs, NJ: Prentice Hall.

Nathan, P. E., Marlatt, G. A., & Loberg, T. (Eds.). (1978). *Alcoholism: New directions in behavioral research and treatment*. New York: Plenum Press.

Nathans, J. (1989). The genes for color vision. *Scientific American, 260*, 42–49.

National Academy of Sciences. (Ed.). (1982). *Ability testing: Uses, consequences, and controversies*. Washington, DC: National Academy Press.

National Center for Health Statistics. (1988). *Advance report of final mortality statistics* (Monthly Vital Statistics Report). Washington, DC: U.S. Dept. of Health and Human Services.

National Institute of Alcohol Abuse and Alcoholism (NIAAA). (1982). *Alcohol and health monograph No. 1*. Washington, DC: U.S. Department of Health and Human Services.

National Institute of Mental Health (NIMH). (1985). *Mental health, United States*. Washington, DC: U.S. Government Printing Office.

Natsoulas, T. (1983). Concepts of consciousness. *Journal of Mind and Behavior, 4*, 13–59.

Navarro, M. (1991, March 4). Life salvaged, now savored: Living longer with AIDS. *New York Times*, pp. A1, B6.

Needleman, H. L., Schell, M. A., Bellinger, D., Leviton, A., & Allred, E. N. (1990). The long-term effects of exposure to low doses of lead in children: An 11 year follow-up report. *New England Journal of Medicine, 322*(2), 85–88.

Neisser, U. (1982). *Memory observed: Remembering in natural contexts*. San Francisco: Freeman.

Neisser, U. (1987). From direct perception to conceptual structure. In U. Neisser (Ed.), *Concepts and conceptual development*. Cambridge, England: Cambridge University Press.

Neisser, U. (1991). A case of misplaced nostalgia. *American Psychologist, 46*, 34–36.

Neisser, U., & Harsh, N. (1992). Phantom flashbulbs: False recollections of hearing the news about the *Challenger*. In E. Winograd & U. Neisser (Eds.) *Affect and accuracy in recall: Studies of "flashbulb memory"* (pp. 9-31.) New York: Cambridge University Press.

Nelson, K. (1973). Structure and strategy in learning to talk. *Monographs of the Society for Research in Child Development, 38.*

Nelson, K. (1977). Facilitating children's syntax acquisition. *Developmental Psychology, 13,* 101–107.

Nelson, K. (1981). Individual differences in language development: Implications for development and language. *Developmental Psychology, 17,* 170–187.

Nelson, K. (1993). The psychological and social origin of autobiographical memory. *Psychological Science, 4,* 7–14.

Nemeth, C. (1979). The role of an active minority in intergroup relations. In W. G. Austin & S. Worchel (Eds.), *The social psychology of intergroup relations.* Monterey, CA: Brooks/Cole.

Nemeth, C. (1992). Minority dissent as a stimulant to group performance. In S. Worchel, W. Wood, & J. A. Simpson (Eds.), *Group processes and productivity.* Newbury Park, CA: Sage.

Nemeth, C. J., & Kwan, J. L. (1987). Minority influence, divergent thinking and detection of correct solutions. *Journal of Applied Social Psychology, 17,* 788–799.

Nemeth, C. J., & Wachtler, J. (1983). Creative problem solving as a result of majority vs minority influence. *European Journal of Social Psychology, 13,* 45–55.

Neuberg, S. L. (1989). The goal of forming accurate impressions during social interactions: Attenuating the impact of negative expectancies. *Journal of Personality and Social Psychology, 56,* 374–386.

Neugarten, B. L. (1976). Adaptation and the life cycle. *Counseling Psychologist, 6,* 16–20.

Newberger, C., Melnicoe, L., & Newberger, E. (1986). The American family in crisis: Implications for children. *Current Problems in Pediatrics, 16,* 674–721.

Newell, A., & Simon, H. A. (1972). *Human problem solving* (Vol. 8). Englewood Cliffs, NJ: Prentice Hall.

Newman, J. P., Konnon, D. S., & Patterson, C. M. (1992). Delay of gratification in psychopathic and nonpsychopathic offenders. *Journal of Abnormal Psychology, 101,* 630–636.

Newmark, C. S. (1996). *Major psychological assessment instruments* (2nd ed.). Needham Heights, MA: Allyn & Bacon.

Nichols, M. P., & Schwartz, R. C. (1991). *Family therapy: Concepts and methods* (2nd ed.). Boston: Allyn & Bacon.

Nickerson, R. S., & Adams, M. J. (1982). Long-term memory for a common object. In U. Neisser (Ed.), *Memory observed* (pp. 163–175). San Francisco: Freeman.

Nietzel, M. T., & Harris, M. J. (1990). Relationship of dependency and achievement/autonomy to depression. *Clinical Psychology Review, 10,* 279–297.

Nisbett, R. E. (1991). Evolutionary psychology, biology, and cultural evolution. *Motivation and Emotion, 14,* 255–263.

Nisbett, R. E., Fong, G. T., Lehman, D. R., & Cheng, P. W. (1987). Teaching reasoning. *Science, 238,* 625–631.

Nisbett, R. E., & Ross, L. (1980). *Human inference: Strategies and shortcomings of social judgment.* Englewood Cliffs, NJ: Prentice Hall.

Nisbett, R. E., & Wilson, T. (1977). Telling more than we know. *Psychological Review, 84,* 231–259.

Nolen-Hoeksema, S. (1987). Sex differences in unipolar depression: Evidence and theory. *Psychological Bulletin, 101,* 259–282.

Norcross, J. C. (1986). *Handbook of eclectic psychotherapy.* New York: Brunner/Mazel.

Nordstrom, P., & Asberg, M. (1992). Suicide risk and serotonin. *International Clinical Psychopharmacology, 6,* 12–21.

Nova. (1995). *Secrets of the "wild child"* [television program]. PBS: Nova.

O'Brien, D. F. (1982). The chemistry of vision. *Science, 218,* 916–966.

Oden, M. H. (1968). The fulfillment of promise: Forty-year follow-up of Terman gifted group. *Genetic Psychology Monographs, 7,* 3–93.

Olds, J., & Milner, P. (1954). Positive reinforcement produced by electrical stimulation of septal area and other regions of the rat brain. *Journal of Comparative and Physiological Psychology, 47,* 419–427.

O'Leary, K. D., & Smith, D. A. (1991). Marital interactions. *Annual Review of Psychology, 42,* 191–212.

Oren, D. A., & Rosenthal, N. E. (1992). Seasonal affective disorders. In E. S. Paykel (Ed.), *Handbook of affective disorders* (2nd ed., pp. 551–568). New York: Guilford.

Orlinsky, D. E., Grawe, K., & Parks, B. K. (1994). Process and outcome in psychotherapy. In A. E. Bergin & S. L. Garfield (Eds.), *Handbook of psychotherapy and behavior change* (4th ed., pp. 270–376). New York: Wiley.

Orne, M. T. (1962). On the social psychology of the psychological experiment: With particular reference to demand characteristics and their implications. *American Psychologist, 17,* 776–783.

Orne, M. T., & Evans, F. J. (1965). Social control in the psychological experiment: Antisocial behavior and hypnosis. *Journal of Personality and Social Psychology, 1,* 189–200.

Ornstein, R. (1977). *The psychology of consciousness* (2nd ed.). New York: Harcourt Brace Jovanovich.

O'Rourke, K. (1986). *Medical ethics: Common ground for understanding.* St. Louis, MO: Catholic Health Association of the U.S.

Oster, M. I. (1994). Psychological preparation for labor and delivery using hypnosis. *American Journal of Clinical Hypnosis, 37,* 12–17.

Ostrom, T. M., & Sedikides, C. (1992). Out-group homogeneity effects in natural and minimal groups. *Psychological Bulletin, 112,* 536–552.

Pallack, S. R., Murroni, E., & Koch, J. (1983). Communicator attractiveness and expertise, emotional versus rational appeals, and persuasion: A heuristic versus systematic processing interpretation. *Social Cognition, 2,* 122–141.

Palmore, E., & Kivett, V. (1977). Change in life satisfaction: A longitudinal study of persons aged 46–70. *Journal of Gerontology, 32,* 311–316.

Palys, T. S. (1986). Testing the common wisdom: The social content of video pornography. *Canadian Psychology, 27,* 22–35.

Panksepp, J. (1982). Toward a general psychobiological theory of emotions. *Behavioral and Brain Sciences, 5,* 407–467.

Panksepp, J. (1994). Subjectivity may have evolved in the brain as a simple value-coding process that promotes the learning of new behaviors. In P. Ekman & R. J. Davidson (Eds.), *The nature of emotion* (pp. 313–315). New York: Oxford University Press.

Pantle, M. L., Ebner, D. L., & Hynan, L. S. (1994). The Rorschach and the assessment of impulsivity. *Journal of Clinical Psychology, 50*(4), 633–638.

Papez, J. W. (1937). A proposed mechanism of emotion. *Archives of Neurology and Psychiatry, 38,* 725–743.

Papouseuk, H. (1969). Individual variability in learned responses in human infants. In R. J. Robinson (Ed.), *Brain and early behavior: Development in the fetus and infant* (pp. 251–266). London: Academic Press.

Park, C. L., & Folkman, S. (1997). Stability and change in psychosocial resources during caregiving and bereavement in partners of men with AIDS. *Journal of Personality, 65,* 421–447.

Parke, R. D., Berkowitz, L., Leyens, J. P., West, S. G., & Sebastian, R. J. (1977). Some effects of violent and nonviolent movies on the behavior of juvenile delinquents. In L. Berkowitz (Ed.), *Advances in experimental social psychology* (Vol. 10, pp. 135–172). New York: Academic Press.

Parker, G. (1992). Early environment. In E. S. Paykel (Ed.), *Handbook of affective disorders* (2nd ed., pp. 171–184). New York: Guilford.

Parker, K. C. H., Hanson, R. K., & Hunsley, J. (1988). MMPI, Rorschach, and WAIS: A meta-analytic comparison of reliability, stability, and validity. *Psychological Bulletin, 103,* 367–373.

Pate, J. E., Pumariega, A. J., Hester, C., & Garner, D. M. (1992). Cross-cultural patterns in eating disorders: A review. *Journal of American Academy of Child and Adolescent Psychiatry, 31,* 802–809.

Patsiokas, A., & Clum, G. A. (1985). Effects of psychotherapeutic strategies in the treatment of suicide attempters. *Psychotherapy: Theory, Research, and Practice, 22,* 281–290.

Patsiokas, A., Clum, G., & Luscomb, R. (1979). Cognitive characteristics of suicide attempters. *Journal of Consulting and Clinical Psychology, 47,* 478–484.

Patterson, C. M., & Newman, J. P. (1993). Reflectivity and learning from aversive events: Toward a psychological mechanism for learning the syndromes of inhibition. *Psychological Review, 100,* 716–736.

Patterson, D. R., Burns, G. L., Everett, J., J, , & Marvin, J. A. (1992). Hypnosis for the treatment of burn pain. *Journal of Consulting and Clinical Psychology, 5,* 713–171.

Patterson, G. R., Littman, R. A., & Bricker, W. (1967). Assertive behavior in children: A step toward a theory of aggression. *Monographs of the Society for Research in Child Development, 32.*

Patterson, O. (1995). For whom the bell curves. In S. Fraser (Ed.), *The bell curve wars* (pp. 187–213). New York: Basic Books.

Patton, J. H. (1994). Sensation seeking. In V. S. Ramachandran (Ed.), *The encyclopedia of human behavior.* San Diego: Academic Press.

Paunonen, S. V., Jackson, D. N., Trzebinski, J., & Forsterling, F. (1992). Personality structures across cultures: A multimethod evaluation. *Journal of Personality and Social Psychology, 62,* 447–456.

Pavlov, I. P. (1927). *Conditioned reflexes* (G. V. Anrep, Trans.). London: Oxford University Press.

Pavot, W., Diener, E., & Fujita, F. (1990). Extroversion and happiness. *Journal of Personality and Individual Differences, 11,* 1299–1306.

Paykel, E. S., & Cooper, Z. (1992). Life events and social stress. In E. S. Paykel (Ed.), *Handbook of affective disorders* (2nd ed., pp. 149–170). New York: Guilford.

Pearlin, L. I., & Schooler, C. (1978). The structure of coping. *Journal of Health and Social Behavior, 19,* 2–21.

Pedersen, N. L., McClearn, G. E., Plomin, R., & Friberg, L. (1985). Separated fraternal twins: Resemblance for cognitive abilities. *Behavioral Genetics, 15,* 407–419.

Pedersen, N. L., Plomin, R., Nesselroade, J. R., & McClearn, G. E. (1992). A quantitative genetic analysis of cognitive abilities during the second half of the lifespan. *Psychological Science, 3,* 346–353.

Peng, Y., Zebrowitz, L. A., & Lee, H. K. (1993). The impact of cultural background and cross-cultural experience on impressions of American and Korean male speakers. *Journal of Cross-Cultural Psychology, 24,* 203–220.

Pennebaker, J. W. (1993). Putting stress into words: Health, linguistic, and therapeutic implications. *Behaviour Research and Therapy, 31,* 539–548.

Pennebaker, J. W. (Ed.). (1995). *Emotion, disclosure, and health.* Washington, DC: American Psychological Association.

Pennebaker, J. W. (1997). Writing about emotional experiences as a therapeutic process. *Psychological Science, 8,* 162–166.

Pennebaker, J. W., Colder, M., & Sharp, L. K. (1990). Accelerating the coping process. *Journal of Personality and Social Psychology, 58,* 528–537.

Pennebaker, J. W., Mayne, T. J., & Francis, M. E. (1997). Linguistic predictors of adaptive bereavement. *Journal of Personality and Social Psychology, 72*(4), 863–871.

Pennebaker, J. W., & Memon, A. (1997). "Recovered memories in context: Thoughts and elaborations on Bowers and Farvolden (1996)": Correction. *Psychological Bulletin, 121*(2), 191.

Penrose, R. (1994). *Shadows of the mind: A search for the missing science of consciousness.* Oxford: Oxford University Press.

Perlmutter, M. (1983). Learning and memory through adulthood. In M. W. Riley, B. B. Hess, & K. Bond (Eds.), *Aging in society: Selected reviews of research.* Hillsdale, NJ: Erlbaum.

Perlmutter, M., & Mitchell, D. B. (1982). The appearance and disappearance of age differences in adult memory. In F. Craik & S. Trehub (Eds.), *Aging and cognitive processes.* New York: Plenum Press.

Perloff, L. S. (1987). Social comparison and illusions of invulnerability. In C. R. Snyder & C. R. Ford (Eds.),

Coping with negative life events: Clinical and social psychological perspectives. New York: Plenum Press.

Perry, W., & Braff, D. L. (1994). Information-processing deficits and thought disorder in schizophrenia. *American Journal of Psychiatry, 151,* 363–367.

Pertshuk, M. J. (1977). Behavior therapy: Extended follow-up. In R. A. Vigersky (Ed.), *Anorexia nervosa.* New York: Raven Press.

Pervin, L. A. (1984). *Personality: Theory, assessment, and research* (4th ed.). New York: Wiley.

Pervin, L. A. (1989). *Personality: Theory and research* (5th ed.). New York: Wiley.

Petersen, A. C. (1989). *Developmental transitions and adolescent mental health.* Paper presented at the American Psychological Association, New Orleans.

Peterson, C., Seligman, M. E. P., & Vaillant, G. E. (1988). Pessimistic explanatory style is a risk factor for physical illness: A thirty-five-year longitudinal study. *Journal of Personality and Social Psychology, 55,* 23–27.

Peterson, L. (1994). Child injury and abuse-neglect: Common etiologies, challenges, and courses towards prevention. *Current Directions in Psychological Science, 3,* 116–120.

Peterson, L. R., & Peterson, M. (1959). Short-term retention of individual verbal items. *Journal of Experimental Psychology, 58,* 193–198.

Petrill, S. A., Plomin, R., McLearn, G. E., & Smith, D. L. (1997). No association between general cognitive ability and the A1 allele of the D2 dopamine receptor gene. *Behavior Genetics, 27*(1), 29–31.

Petty, R. E., & Cacioppo, J. T. (1981). *Attitudes and persuasion: Classic and contemporary approaches.* Dubuque, IA: William C. Brown.

Petty, R. E., Schumann, D. W., Richman, S. A., & Strathman, A. J.

(1993). Positive mood and persuasion: Different roles for affect under high and low elaboration conditions. *Journal of Personality and Social Psychology, 64,* 5–20.

Phares, E. J. (1979). *Clinical psychology: Concepts, methods, and profession.* Homewood, IL: Dorsey Press.

Phillips, D. P. (1983). The impact of mass media violence on U.S. homicides. *American Sociological Review, 48,* 560–568.

Phillips, D. P. (1986). Natural experiments on the effects of mass media violence on fatal aggression: Strength and weaknesses of a new approach. In L. Berkowitz (Ed.), *Advances in experimental social psychology* (Vol. 19, pp. 207–250). New York: Academic Press.

Phillips, S., with King, S., & Du Bois, L. (1978). Spontaneous activities of female versus male newborns. *Child Development, 49,* 590–597.

Piaget, J. (1930/1969). *The child's conception of physical causality.* Totowa, NJ: Littlefield, Adams.

Piaget, J., & Inhelder, B. (1956). *The child's conception of space.* London: Routledge & Kegan Paul.

Piaget, J., & Inhelder, B. (1969). *The Psychology of the child.* New York: Basic Books.

Pike, K. M., & Rodin, J. (1991). Mothers, daughters, and disordered eating. *Journal of Abnormal Psychology, 100,* 198–204.

Piliavin, I. M., Rodin, J., & Piliavin, J. A. (1969). Good Samaritanism: An underground phenomenon? *Journal of Personality and Social Psychology, 13,* 289–299.

Piliavin, J. A., & Piliavin, I. M. (1972). Effect of blood on reactions to a victim. *Journal of Personal and Social Psychology, 23,* 353–361.

Pillemer, D. (1993). Remembering personal circumstances: A functional analysis. In E. Winograd & U. Neisser (Eds.), *Affect and accuracy in recall: Studies of "flashbulb* memory" (pp. 121–137). New York: Cambridge University Press.

Pinel, J. P. J. (1992). *Biopsychology*. Needham Heights, MA: Allyn & Bacon.

Pinel, J. P. J. (1996). *Biopsychology* (3rd ed.). Needham Heights, MA: Allyn & Bacon.

Pines, M. (1982, February). Baby, you're incredible. *Psychology Today,* 48–53.

Pinker, S. (1994). *The language instinct.* New York: William Morrow.

Piotrowski, C., & Keller, J. W. (1989). Psychological testing in outpatient mental health facilities: A national study. *Professional Psychology: Research and Practice, 20,* 423–425.

Piper, W. E., Joyce, A. S, McCallum, M., & Azim, H. F. A. (1993). Concentration and concentration of transference interpretations in short-term psychotherapy. *Journal of Consulting and Clinical Psychology, 61,* 586–595.

Plomin, R. (1986). *Development, genetics, and psychology.* Hillsdale, NJ: Erlbaum.

Plomin, R. (1989). Environment and genes: Determinants of behavior. *American Psychologist, 44,* 105–111.

Plomin, R. (1990). *Nature and nurture: An introduction to human behavioral genetics.* Pacific Grove, CA: Brooks/Cole.

Plomin, R., DeFries, J. C., & McClearn, G. E. (1990). *Behavioral genetics: A primer* (2nd ed.). New York: Freeman.

Plomin, R., Fulker, D. W., Corley, R., & DeFries, J. C. (1997). Nature, nurture, and cognitive development from 1 to 16 years: A parent-offspring adoption study. *Psychological Science, 8,* 442–447.

Plomin, R., & Neiderhiser, J. M. (1992). Genetics and experience. *Current Directions in Psychological Science, 1,* 160–163.

Plomin, R., Scheier, M. F., Bergeman, C. S., Pedersen, N. K., Nesselroad,

J. R., & McClearn, G. E. (1992). Optimism, pessimism, and mental health: A twin/adoption study. *Personality and Individual Differences, 13,* 921–930.

Plug, C., & Ross, H. E. (1994). The natural moon illusion: A multifactor angular account. *Perception, 23,* 321–333.

Plunkett, J. W., Klein, T., & Meisels, S. J. (1988). The relationship of preterm infant-mother attachment to stranger sociability at three years. *Infant Behavior and Development, 11,* 83–96.

Plutchik, R., & Ax, A. F. (1966). A critique of "Determinants of Emotional State" by Schachter and Singer. *Psychophysiology, 4,* 79–82.

Polivy, J., & Herman, C. P. (1985). Dieting and binging: A causal analysis. *American Psychologist, 40,* 193–201.

Poon, L. W. (Ed.) (1986). *Handbook for clinical memory assessment of older adults.* Washington, DC: American Psychological Association.

Portnoy, F., & Simmons, C. (1978). Day care and attachment. *Child Development, 49,* 239–242.

Posner, M. I. (1973). *Cognition: An introduction.* Glenview, IL: Scott, Foresman.

Power-Smith, P., & Turkington, D. (1993). Fluoxetine in phantom limb pain. *British Journal of Psychiatry, 163,* 105–106.

Poynton, A., Bridges, P. K., & Bartlett, J. R. (1988). Resistant bipolar affective disorder treated by stereotactic subcaudate tractotomy. *British Journal of Psychiatry, 152,* 354–358.

Prechtl, R. R. (1982). Regressions and transformations during neurological development. In T. G. Bever (Ed.), *Regression in mental development: Basic phenomena and theories* (pp. 103–116). Hillsdale, NJ: Erlbaum.

Premack, D. (1971a). Language in the chimpanzee? *Science, 172,* 808–822.

Premack, D. (1971b). On the assessment of language competence in the chimpanzee. In A. M. Schrier & F. Stollnitz (Eds.), *Behavior of nonhuman primates* (pp. 185–228). New York: Academic Press.

Premack, D. (1976). Language and intelligence in ape and man. *American Scientist, 64,* 674–683.

Premack, D. (1986). *Gavagai! or the future history of the animal language controversy.* Cambridge, MA: MIT Press.

Pribram, K. H. (1981). Emotions. In S. B. Filskov & T. J. Boll (Eds.), *Handbook of clinical neuropsychology.* New York: Wiley.

Prien, R. F., Kupfer, D. J., Mansky, P. A., Small, J. G., Tuason, V. B., Voss, C. B., & Johnson, W. E. (1984). Drug therapy in the prevention of recurrences in unipolar and bipolar affective disorders. *Archives of General Psychiatry, 41,* 1096–1104.

Prochaska, J. O. (1984). *Systems of psychotherapy: A transtheoretical analysis* (2nd ed.). Homewood, IL: Dorsey Press.

Pryor, J. B., & Reeder, G. D. (Eds.). (1993). *The social psychology of HIV infection.* Hillsdale, NJ: Erlbaum.

Pullum, G. K. (1991). *The great Eskimo vocabulary hoax and other irreverent essays on the study of language.* Chicago: Chicago University Press.

Putnam, F. W. (1989). *Diagnosis and treatment of multiple personality disorder.* New Tork: Guilford.

Quinn, M. E., Fontana, A. F., & Reznikoff, M. (1987). Psychological distress in reaction to lung cancer as a function of spousal support and coping strategy. *Journal of Psychosocial Oncology, 4,* 79–90.

Rabinowitz, F. M. (1987). An analysis of the maturation/learning controversy. *Canadian Psychology, 28,* 322–337.

Rachman, S. J., & Hodgson, R. J. (1980). *Obsessions and compulsions.* Englewood Cliffs, NJ: Prentice Hall.

Radke-Yarrow, M., & Zahn-Waxler, C. (1984). Roots, motives, and patterns in children's prosocial behavior. In E. Staub, D. Bar-Tal, J. Karylowski, & J. Reykowski (Eds.), *Development and maintenance of prosocial behavior.* New York: Plenum Press.

Raichle, M. E. (1994). Images of the human mind. *Neuropsychopharmacology, 10*(3, Suppl Pt 1), 28S–33S.

Ramachandran, V. S. (1988). Perceiving shape from shading. *Scientific American, 259,* 76–83.

Rapaport, K., & Burkhart, B. R. (1984). Personality and attitudinal characteristics of sexually coercive college males. *Journal of Abnormal Psychology, 93,* 216–221.

Rapee, R. M., & Barlow, D. H. (1991). *Chronic anxiety: Generalized anxiety disorder and mixed anxiety-depression.* New York: Guilford.

Rapee, R. M., & Barlow, D. H. (1993). Generalized anxiety disorder, panic disorder, and the phobias. In P. B. Sutker & H. E. Adams (Eds.), *Comprehensive handbook of psychopathology* (2nd ed., pp. 109–127). New York: Plenum Press.

Ratcliff, R., & McKoon, G. (1978). Priming in item recognition: Evidence for the propositional structure of sentences. *Journal of Verbal Learning and Verbal Behavior, 17,* 403–417.

Raven, B. H., & French, J. (1958). Legitimate power, coercive power, and observability in social influence. *Sociometry, 21,* 83–97.

Ray, O. S. (1993). *Drugs, society and human behavior.* St. Louis: Mosby YearBook.

Raymond, B. J., & Unger, R. K. (1972). "The apparel oft proclaims the man": Cooperation with deviant and conventional youths. *Journal of Social Psychology, 87,* 75–82.

Reason, J., & Mycielska, K. (1982). *Absent minded? The psychology of mental lapses and everyday errors.*

Englewood Cliffs, NJ: Prentice Hall.

Ree, M. J., & Earles, J. A. (1992). Intelligence is the best predictor of job performance. *Current Directions in Psychological Science, 1,* 86–89.

Ree, M. J., & Earles, J. A. (1993). g is to psychology what carbon is to chemistry: A reply to Sternberg, Wagner, McClelland, Calfee. *Current Directions in Psychological Science, 2,* 11–12.

Reed, C. F., & Krupinski, E. A. (1992). The target in the celestial (moon) illusion. *Journal of Experimental Psychology: Human Perception and Performance, 18,* 247–256.

Reed, G. M. (1989). *Stress, coping, and psychological adaptation in a sample of gay and bisexual men with AIDS.* Unpublished doctoral dissertation, University of California, Los Angeles.

Reed, S. K. (1987). A structure-mapping model for word problems. *Journal of Experimental Psychology; Learning, Memory, and Cognition, 13,* 124–139.

Reed, T. E., & Jensen, A. R. (1992). Conduction velocity in a brain nerve pathway of normal adults correlates with intelligence. *Intelligence, 16,* 259–272.

Reedy, M. N., Birren, J. E., & Schaie, K. W. (1981). Age and sex differences in satisfying love relationships. *Human Development, 24,* 52–66.

Reese, W. H., & Rodeheaver, D. (1985). Problem-solving and complex decision-making. In J. E. Birren & K. W. Schaie (Eds.), *Handbook of the psychology of aging* (2nd ed.). New York: Van Nostrand Reinhold.

Reeves, R. (1983, December). George Gallup's nation of numbers. *Esquire,* 91–96.

Reiger, D. A., Boyd, J. H., Burke, J. D., Jr., Rae, D. S., Myers, J. K., Kramer, M., Robins, L. N., George, L. K., Karno, M., & Locke, B. Z. (1988).

One-month prevalence of mental disorders in the United States. *Archives of General Psychiatry, 45,* 977–986.

Reinisch, J., & Beasley, R. (1980). *The Kinsey Institute new report on sex.* New York: St. Martin's Press.

Reinke, B. J. (1985). Psychosocial changes as a function of chronological age. *Human Development, 28,* 266–269.

Renken, B., Egeland, B., Marvinney, D., Mangelsdorf, S., & Sroufe, L. A. (1989). Early antecedents of aggression and passive-withdrawal in elementary school. *Journal of Personality, 57,* 257–282.

Rescorla, R. A. (1988). Pavlovian conditioning: It's not what you think it is. *American Psychologist, 43,* 151–160.

Rhodes, N., & Wood, W. (1992). Self-esteem and intelligence affect influenceability: The mediating role of message reception. *Psychological Bulletin, 111,* 156–171.

Rice, F. P. (1995). *Human development: A life-span approach* (2nd ed.). Englewood Cliffs, NJ: Prentice Hall.

Rice, M. L. (1989). Children's language acquisition. *American Psychologist, 44*(2), 149–156.

Rich, C. L., Warsradt, M. D., Nemiroff, R. A., Fowler, R. C., & Young, D. (1991). Suicide, stressors, and the life cycle. *American Journal of Psychiatry, 148,* 534–537.

Rimm, D. C., & Mahoney, M. J. (1969). The application of reinforcement and participant modeling procedures in the treatment of snake-phobic behavior. *Behavior Research and Therapy, 7,* 369–376.

Ringelmann, M. (1913). Research on animate sources of power: The world of man. *Annales de l'Institut National Agronomique, 2*(12), 1–40.

Roberts, P., & Newton, P. M. (1987). Levinsonian studies of women's adult development. *Psychology and Aging, 2,* 154–163.

Robertson, J. M., & Tanguay, P. E. (1997). Case study: The use of melatonin in a boy with refractory bipolar disorder. *Journal of the American Academy of Child and Adolescent Psychiatry, 36,* 822–825.

Robins, L. N. (1966). *Deviant children grow up.* Baltimore: Williams & Wilkins.

Robins, L. N., Helzer, J. E., Weissman, M. M., Orvaschel, H., Gruenberg, E., Burke, J. D., & Reiger, D. A. (1984). Lifetime prevalence of specific psychiatric disorders in three sites. *Archives of General Psychiatry, 41,* 942–949.

Rock, I. (1984). *The logic of perception.* Cambridge, MA: MIT Press.

Rock, I. (Ed.). (1990). *The perceptual world: Readings from* Scientific American. San Francisco: Freeman.

Rodin, J., & Langer, E. J. (1977). Longterm effects of a control-relevant intervention with the institutionalized aged. *Journal of Personality and Social Psychology, 35,* 897–902.

Rodin, J., & Plante, T. (1989). The psychological effects of exercise. In R. S. Williams & A. Wallace (Eds.), *Biological effects of physical activity* (pp. 127–137). Champaign, IL: Human Kinetics.

Roe, A. (1946). The personality of artists. *Educational Psychology Measuremen, 6,* 401–408.

Roe, A. (1953). *The making of a scientist.* New York: Dodd, Mead.

Roediger, H. L., III. (1990). Implicit memory: Retention without remembering. *American Psychologist, 45,* 1043–1056.

Roediger, H. L., III. (1991). They read an article? A comment on the everyday memory controversy. *American Psychologist, 46,* 37–40.

Rogers, C. R. (1970). *On becoming a person: A therapist's view of psychotherapy* (2nd ed.). Boston: Houghton Mifflin.

Rogers, C. R. (1971). A theory of personality. In S. Maddi (Ed.), *Perspectives on Personality.* Boston: Little, Brown.

Rogers, C. R. (1985). Toward a more human science of the person. *Journal of Humanistic Psychology, 25,* 7–24.

Rogers, R. W., & Mewborn, C. R. (1976). Fear appeals and attitude change: Effects of a threat's noxiousness, probability of occurrence, and the efficacy of coping responses. *Journal of Personality and Social Psychology, 34,* 54–61.

Rogers, R. W., & Prentice-Dunn, S. (1981). Deindividuation and anger-mediated interracial aggression: Unmasking regressive racism. *Journal of Personality and Social Psychology, 41,* 63–73.

Rogers, W. (1984). Changing health-related attitudes and behavior: The role of preventive health psychology. In J. H. Harve, E. Maddux, R. P. McGlynn, & C. D. Stoltenberg (Eds.), *Social perception in clinical and counseling psychology* (Vol. 2, pp. 91–112). Lubbock: Texas Technical University Press.

Romer, N., & Cherry, D. (1980). Ethnic and social class differences in children's sex-role concepts. *Sex Roles, 6,* 246–263.

Room, R., & Greenfield, T. (1993). Alcoholics Anonymous, other 12-step movements and psychotherapy in the US population, 1990. *Addiction, 88,* 555–562.

Rosch, E. (1973). On the internal structures of perceptual and semantic categories. In T. E. Moore (Ed.), *Cognitive development and the acquisition of language.* New York: Academic Press.

Rosch, E. (1978). Principles of categorization. In E. Rosch & B. B. Lloyd (Eds.), *Cognition and categorization.* New York: Wiley.

Rosch, E., & Mervis, C. B. (1975). Family resemblances: Studies in the internal structure of categories. *Cognitive Psychology, 7,* 573–605.

Rose, S. D. (1986). Group methods. In F. H. Kanfer & A. P. Goldstein (Eds.), *Helping people change: A textbook of methods.* Elmsford, NY: Pergamon Press.

Rosenberg, M. J. (1965). When dissonance fails: On eliminating evaluation apprehension from attitude measurement. *Journal of Personality and Social Psychology, 1,* 28–42.

Rosengard, C., & Folkman, S. (1997). Suicidal ideation, bereavement, HIV serostatus and psychosocial variables in partners of men with AIDS. *AIDS Care, 9,* 373–384.

Rosenhan, D. L. (1973). On being sane in insane places. *Science, 179,* 250–258.

Rosenman, R. H. (1978). The interview method of assessment of the coronary-prone behavior pattern. In T. M. Dembroski, S. M. Weiss, J. L. Shields, S. G. Haynes, & M. Feinleib (Eds.), *Coronary-prone behavior* (pp. 55–70). New York: Springer-Verlag.

Rosenman, R. H., Brand, R. J., Jenkins, C. D, Friedman, M., Straus, R., & Wurm, M. (1975). Coronary heart disease in the Western Collaborative Group Study: Final follow-up experience of 8½ years. *Journal of the American Medical Association, 233,* 872–877.

Rosenthal, D., Wender, P. H., Kety, S. S., Schulsinger, F., Weiner, J., & Ostergaard, L. (1968). Schizophrenics' off-spring reared in adoptive homes. In D. Rosenthal & S. S. Kety (Eds.), *The transmission of schizophrenia.* Oxford, England: Pergamon Press.

Rosenthal, N. E., Carpenter, C. J., James, S. P., Parry, B. L., Rogers, S. L. B., & Wehr, T. A. (1986). Seasonal affective disorder in children and adolescents. *American Journal of Psychiatry, 143,* 356–358.

Rosenthal, R. (1966). *Experimenter effects in behavioral research.* New York: Appleton-Century-Crofts.

Rosenthal, R., Archer, D., Di Matteo, M. R., Koivumaki, J. H., & Rogers, P. L. (1974, September). Body talk and tone of voice: The language without words. *Psychology Today*, 64–68.

Rosnow, R. L., & Rosenthal, R. (1989). Statistical procedures and the justification of knowledge in psychological science. *American Psychologist, 44*, 1276–1284.

Rosnow, R. L., & Rosenthal, R. (1996). *Beginning behavioral research: A conceptual primer* (2nd ed.). Englewood Cliffs, NJ: Prentice Hall.

Ross, A. (1981). *Child behavior therapy*. New York: Wiley.

Ross, B. H., & Spalding, T. L. (1994). Concepts and categories. In R. J. Sternberg (Ed.), *Handbook of perception: Thinking and problem solving*. New York: Academic Press.

Ross, D. F., Dunning, D., Toglia, M. P., & Ceci, S. J. (1990). The child in the eyes of the jury: Assessing mock jurors' perceptions of the child witness. *Law and Human Behavior, 14*, 5–23.

Ross, L. (1977). The intuitive psychologist and his shortcomings: Distortions in the attribution process. In L. Berkowitz (Ed.), *Advances in experimental social psychology*. New York: Academic Press.

Ross, L., & Nisbett, R. E. (1991). *The person and the situation: Perspectives of social psychology*. New York: McGraw-Hill.

Ross, M., & Fletcher, G. J. O. (1985). Attribution and social perception. In G. Lindsey & E. Aronson (Eds.), *Handbook of Social psychology* (3rd ed., pp. 73–122). Reading, MA: Addison-Wesley.

Ross, M., & Sicoly, F. (1979). Egocentric biases in availability and attribution. *Journal of Personality and Social Psychology, 37*, 322–336.

Rothbart, M. K. (1986). Longitudinal observation of infant temperament. *Developmental Psychology, 22*, 356–365.

Rothbaum, B. O., Foa, E. B., Riggs, D. S., Murdock, T., & Walsh, W. (1992). A prospective examination of post-traumatic stress disorder in rape victims. *Journal of Traumatic Stress, 5*, 455–475.

Rotter, J. (1954). *Social learning and clinical psychology*. Englewood Cliffs, NJ: Prentice Hall.

Rovee-Collier, C. (1990). *Infant memory*. Paper presented at the Annual Meeting of the American Psychological Association, Boston.

Rubin, D. (1986). *Autobiographical memory*. New York: Cambridge University Press.

Rubin, D., & Schulkind, M. D. (1997). Distribution of autobiographical memories across the lifespan. *Memory and Cognition, 26*, 859–866.

Rubin, J. L., Provenzano, F. J., & Luria, Z. (1974). The eye of the beholder: Parents on sex of newborns. *American Journal of Orthopsychiatry, 44*, 512–519.

Rubin, Z. (1973). Liking and loving: Patterns of attraction in dating relationships. In T. L. Huston (Ed.), *Foundations of interpersonal attraction*. New York: Academic Press.

Rubinstein, J., & Slife, B. D. (1992). *Taking sides: Views on controversial psychological issues* (7th ed.). Guilford, CT: Dushkin.

Ruderman, A. J., & Grace, P. S. (1988). Bulimics and restrained eaters: A personality comparison. *Addictive Behavior, 13*, 359–368.

Ruggiero, L., Williamson, D., Davis, C. J., Schlundt, D. G., & Carey, M. P. (1988). Forbidden food survey: Measure of bulimics' anticipated emotional reactions to specific foods. *Addictive Behaviors, 13*, 267–274.

Rumbaugh, D. M., Gill, T. V., & von Glaserfeld, E. C. (1963). Reading and sentence completion by a chimpanzee. *Science, 182*, 731–733.

Ruscher, J. B., & Fiske, S. T. (1990). Interpersonal competition can cause individuating processes. *Journal of Personality and Social Psychology, 58*, 832–843.

Rush, A. J., & Beck, A. T. (1978). Cognitive therapy of depression and suicide. *American Journal of psychotherapy, 32*, 201–219.

Rush, A. J., Beck, A. T., Kovacs, M., Weisenberger, J., & Hollon, S. D. (1982). Comparison of the effects of cognitive therapy on hopelessness and selfconcept. *American Journal of Psychiatry, 139*, 862–866.

Rushton, J. P., Rulker, D. W., Neale, M. C., Nias, D. K. B., & Eysenck, H. J. (1986). Altruism and aggression: The heritability of individual differences. *Journal of Personality and Social Psychology, 50*, 1192–1198.

Russell, J. A. (1980). A circumplex model of affect. *Journal of Personality and Social Psychology, 39*, 1161–1178.

Russell, J. A., Lewicks, M., & Niit, T. (1980). A cross-cultural study of a circumplex model of affect. *Journal of Personality and Social Psychology, 57*, 848–856.

Russo, J. E., Krieser, G., & Miyashita, S. (1975). An effective display of unit price information. *Journal of Marketing, 39*, 11–19.

Rutter, M. (1987). Psychosocial resilience and protective mechanisms. *American Journal of Orthopsychiatry, 57*, 316–331.

Rutter, M., Dunn, J., Plomin, R., & Simonoff, E., (1997). Integrating nature and nurture: Implications of person-environment correlations and interactions for developmental psychopathology. *Development and Psychopathology, 9*, 335–364.

Rymer, R. (1993). *Genie: Escape from a silent childhood*. New York: Viking Penguin.

Sachdev, P., Smith, J. S., & Matheson, J. (1990). Is psychosurgery antimanic? *Biological Psychiatry, 27*, 363–371.

Sacks, O. (1984). *A leg to stand on*. New York: Summitt.

Sacks, O. (1989). *Seeing voices: A journey into the world of the deaf.* New York: Harper Perennial.

Sacks, O. (1990). *Awakenings.* New York: HarperCollins. (First published 1973).

Saegert, S., Swap, W. C., & Zajonc, R. B. (1973). Exposure, context, and interpersonal attraction. *Journal of Personality and Social Psychology, 25,* 234–242.

Saffran, J. R., Newport, E. L., Aslin, R. N., Tunick, R. A., & Barrueco, S. (1997). Incidental language learning: Listening (and learning) out of the corner of your ear. *Psychological Science, 8,* 101–106.

Sampson, E. E. (1978). Scientific paradigms and social values: Wanted—a scientific revolution. *Journal of Personality and Social Psychology, 36,* 1332–1343.

Sampson, H. (1965). Deprivation of dreaming sleep by two methods. *Archives of General Psychiatry, 13,* 79–86.

Sanders, G. S. (1982). Social comparison as a basis for evaluating others. *Journal of Research in Personality, 16,* 21–31.

Sanders, G. S., Baron, R. S., & Moore, D. L. (1978). Distraction and social comparison as mediators of social facilitation effects. *Journal of Personality and Social Psychology, 14,* 291–303.

Santee, R. T., & Jackson, S. E. (1982). Sex differences in the evaluative implications of conformity and dissent. *Social Psychology Quarterly, 45,* 121–125.

Santrock, J. W. (1996). *Life-span development.* Madison, WI: Brown & Benchmark.

Santrock, J. W., & Bartlett, J. (1986). *Developmental psychology: A life-cycle perspective.* Dubuque, IA: W.C. Brown.

Saudino, K. J., Pedersen, N. L., Lichtenstein, P., & McClearn, G. E. (1997). Can personality explain genetic influences on life events? *Journal of Personality and Social Psychology, 72,* 196–206.

Saudino, K. J., & Plomin, R. (1997). Cognitive and temperamental mediators of genetic contributions to the home environment during infancy. *Merrill Palmer Quarterly, 43,* 1–23.

Savage-Rumbaugh, E. S., Pate, J. L., Lawson, J., Smith, S. T., & Rosenbaum, S. (1983). Can a chimpanzee make a statement? *Journal of Experimental Psychology: General, 112,* 457–492.

Savage-Rumbaugh, E. S., Romski, M. A., Sevcik, R., & Pate, J. L. (1983). Assessing symbol usage versus symbol competency. *Journal of Experimental Psychology: General, 112,* 508–512.

Savage-Rumbaugh, S., McDonald, K., Sevcik, R. A., Hopkins, W. D., & Rubert, E. (1986). Spontaneous symbol acquisition and communicative use by pygmy chimps *(Pan paniscus). Journal of Experimental Psychology: General, 115,* 211–235.

Saxe, L., Dougherty, D., & Cross, T. (1985). The validity of polygraph testing: Scientific analysis and public controversy. *American Psychologist, 40,* 355–366.

Saxe, L., Dougherty, D., Esty, K., & Fine, M. (1983). *Health technology case study 22: The effectiveness and costs of alcoholism treatment.* Washington, DC: Office of Technology Assessment.

Scarr, S. (1984a). *Mother care/other care.* New York: Basic Books.

Scarr, S. (1984b, May). What's a parent to do? *Psychology Today,* 58–63.

Scarr, S. (1992). Developmental theories for the 1990s: Development and individual differences. *Child Development, 63,* 1–19.

Scarr, S., & Deater-Deckard, K. (1997). Family effects on individual differences in development. In S. S. Luthar, J. A. Burack, D. Cicchetti, & J. R. Weisz (Eds.), *Developmental*

psychopathology: Perspectives on adjustment, risk, and disorder (pp. 115–136). New York: Cambridge University Press.

Scarr, S., & McCartney, K. (1983). How people make their own environment: A theory of genotype/environment effects. *Child Development, 54,* 424–435.

Scarr, S., Phillips, D., & McCartney, K. (1989). Working mothers and their families. *American Psychologist, 44,* 1402–1409.

Scarr, S., Phillips, D., & McCartney, K. (1990). Facts, fantasies, and the future of child care in the United States. *Psychological Science, 1,* 26–35.

Scarr, S., Phillips, D., McCartney, K., & Abbott-Shim, M. (1993). Quality of child care as an aspect of family and child care policy in the United States. *Pediatrics, 91,* 182–188.

Schachter, S. (1959). *The psychology of affiliation.* Stanford, CA: Stanford University Press.

Schachter, S. (1964). The interaction of cognitive and physiological determinants of emotional state. In L. Berkowitz (Ed.), *Advances in experimental social psychology* (pp. 48–81). New York: Academic Press.

Schachter, S. (1971). Some extraordinary facts about obese humans and rats. *American Psychologist, 26,* 129–144.

Schachter, S., & Singer, J. E. (1962). Cognitive, social and physiological determinants of emotional state. *Psychological Review, 69,* 379–399.

Schacter, D. (1996). *Searching for memory: The brain, the mind, and the past.* New York: Basic Books.

Schacter, D. L. (1997). False recognition and the brain. *Current Directions in Psychological Science, 3,* 65–69.

Schacter, D. L., Curran, T., Galluccio, L., Milberg, W. P., & Bates, J. (1996). False recognition and the right frontal lobe: A case study. *Neuropsychologia, 34,* 793–808.

Schaefer, C., Coyne, J. C., & Lazarus, R. S. (1981). The health-related functions of social support. *Journal of Behavioral Medicine, 4,* 381–406.

Schaie, K. W. (1984). The Seattle longitudinal: A 21 year exploration in the development of psychometric intelligence. In K. W. Schaie (Ed.), *Longitudinal studies of adult psychological development.* New York: Guilford.

Schaie, K. W. (1988). Internal validity threats in studies of adult cognitive development. In M. L. Howe & C. J. Brainard (Eds.), *Cognitive development in adulthood: Progress in cognitive development research.* New York: Academic Press.

Schaie, K. W. (1989). The hazards of cognitive aging. *Gerontologist, 29,* 484–493.

Schaie, K. W. (1990a). Intellectual development in adulthood. In J. E. Birren & K. W. Schaie (Eds.), *Handbook of the psychology of aging.* New York: Academic Press.

Schaie, K. W. (1990b). The optimization of cognitive functioning in old age: Predictions based on cohort-sequential and longitudinal data. In P. B. Baltes & M. M. Baltes (Eds.), *Longitudinal research and the study of successful (optimal) aging.* Cambridge, England: Cambridge University Press.

Schaie, K. W. (1993). The Seattle Longitudinal Studies of adult intelligence. *Current Directions in Psychological Science, 2,* 171–174.

Schaie, K. W., Plomin, R., Willis, S. L., Gruber-Baldini, A., & Dutta, R. (1992). Intellectual development in adulthood. In J. E. Birren & K. W. Schaie (Eds.), *Handbook of the Psychology of Aging.* New York: Academic Press.

Schaie, K. W., & Willis, S. (1986). Can decline in intellectual functioning be reversed? *Developmental Psychology, 22,* 223–232.

Schaller, M., & Cialdini, R. B. (1988). The economics of empathic helping: Support for a mood management motive. *Journal of Experimental Social Psychology, 24,* 163–181.

Scheier, M. F., & Carver, C. S. (1985). Optimism, coping, and health: Assessment and implications of generalized outcome expectancies. *Health Psychology, 4,* 219–247.

Scheier, M. F., & Carver, C. S. (1992). Effects of optimism on psychological and physical well-being: Theoretical overview and empirical update. *Cognitive Therapy and Research, 16,* 201–228.

Scheier, M. F., Weintraub, J. K., & Carver, C. S. (1986). Coping with stress: Divergent strategies of optimists and pessimists. *Journal of Personality and Social Psychology, 51,* 1257–1264.

Scheir, M. F., Matthews, K. A., Owens, J., Magovern, G. J., Sr, Lefevre, R. C., Abbott, R. A., & Carver, C. S. (1989). Dispositional optimism and recovery from coronary artery bypass surgery: The beneficial effects on physical and psychological well-being. *Journal of Personality and Social Psychology, 57,* 1024–1040.

Scher, S. J., & Cooper, J. (1989). Motivational basis of dissonance: The singular role of behavior consequences. *Journal of Personality and Social Psychology, 56,* 899–906.

Schlenker, B. R., Dlugolecki, D. W., & Doherty, K. (1994). The impact of self-presentation on self-appraisals and behavior: The power of public commitment. *Personality and Social Psychology Bulletin, 20,* 20–33.

Schlesier-Stropp, B. (1984). Bulimia: A review of the literature. *Psychological Review, 95,* 247–257.

Schmeck, H. M., Jr. (1984, March 27). Implant brings sound to deaf and spurs debate over its use. *New York Times,* p. C1A.

Schmeck, H. M., Jr. (1986, March 18). Schizophrenia focus shifts to dramatic changes in brain. *New York Times,* pp. C1, C3.

Schmidt, F. L., & Hunter, J. E. (1993). Tacit knowledge, practical intelligence, general mental ability, and job knowledge. *Current Directions in Psychological Science, 2,* 8–9.

Schmitt, B. H., Gilovich, T., Goore, N., & Joseph, L. (1986). Mere exposure and social facilitation: One more time. *Journal of Experimental Social Psychology, 22,* 242–248.

Schneider, S. (1988). Attitudes toward death in adolescent offspring of Holocaust survivors: A comparison of Israeli and American adolescents. *Adolescence, 23,* 703–710.

Schneider, S. G., Taylor, S. E., Hammen, C., & Kemeny, M. E. (1991). Factors influencing suicide intent in gay and bisexual suicide ideators: Differing models for men with and without human immunodeficiency virus. *Journal of Personality and Social Psychology, 61,* 776–788.

Schneider, W., Korkel, J., & Weinert, F. E. (1988). Domain-specific knowledge and memory performance: A comparison of high- and low-aptitude children. *Journal of Educational Psychology, 81,* 306–312.

Schneider-Helmert, D. (1985). Clinical evaluation of SDIP. In A. Wauguier, J. M. Monti, & M. Radulovacki (Eds.), *Sleep, neurotransmitters, and neuromodulators* (pp. 279–291). New York: Raven.

Schneider-Rosen, K., & Cicchetti, D. (1984). The relationship between affect and cognition in maltreated infants: Quality of attachment and the development of visual self-recognition. *Child Development, 55,* 648–658.

Schönenberger, G. A., & Graf, M. V. (1985). Effects of DSIP and DSIP-P on different biorhythmic parameters. In A. Wauguier, J. M. Gaillard, J. M. Monti, & M. Radulovacki (Eds.), *Sleep: Neurotransmitters and neuromodulators.* New York: Raven Press.

Schotte, D., & Clum, G. A. (1987). Problem-solving skills in suicidal psychiatric patients. *Journal of Consulting and Clinical Psychology, 55,* 49–54.

Schuckit, M. A., Gold, E., & Risch, S. C. (1988). Serum prolactin levels in sons of alcoholics and control subjects. *American Journal of Psychiatry, 144,* 584–589.

Schuckit, M. A., Risch, S. C., & Gold, E. O. (1988). Alcohol consumption, ACTH level, and family history of alcoholism. *American Journal of Psychiatry, 145,* 1391–1395.

Schulkin, J. (1994). Melancholic depression and the hormones of adversity: A role for the amygdala. *Current Directions in Psychological Science, 3,* 41–44.

Schulz, R. (1976). Effects of control and predictability on the physical well-being of the institutionalized aged. *Journal of Personality and Social Psychology, 33,* 563–573.

Schusterman, R. J., & Gisner, R. (1989). Please parse the sentence: Animal cognition in the procrustean bed of linguistics. *Psychological Record, 39,* 3–18.

Schwartz, B. (1989). *Psychology of learning and behavior* (3rd ed.). New York: Norton.

Schwartz, J. L. (1987). *Review and evaluation of smoking cessation methods: The United States and Canada* (NIH Publication No. 87-2940). Washington, DC: U.S. Department of Health and Human Services.

Schwartz, R. G., & Leonard, L. B. (1984). Words, objects, and actions in early lexical acquisition. *Journal of Speech and Hearing Research, 27,* 119–127.

Schwarz, N., & Strack, F. (1990). Evaluating one's life: A judgmental model of subjective well-being. In F. Strack, M. Argyle, & N. Schwarz (Eds.), *The social psychology of well-being.* Oxford: Pergamon Press.

Scovern, A. W., & Kilmann, P. R. (1980). Status of electroconvulsive therapy: Review of the outcome literature. *Psychological Bulletin, 87,* 260–303.

Sears, R. R. (1977). Sources of life satisfaction of the Terman gifted men. *American Psychologist, 32,* 119–128.

Sedlack, A. (1989, April). *National incidence of child abuse and neglect.* Paper presented at the Society for Research in Child Development, Kansas City.

Segrin, C., & Abramson, L. Y. (1994). Negative reactions to depressive behaviors: A communication theories analysis. *Journal of Abnormal Psychology, 103,* 655–668.

Sekula, L. K., Lucke, J. F., Heist, E. K., & Czambel, R. K. (1997). Neuroendocrine aspects of primary endogenous depression XV: Mathematical modeling of nocturnal melatonin secretion in major depressives and normal controls. *Psychiatry Research, 69,* 143–153.

Sekuler, R., & Blake, R. (1994). *Perception* (3rd ed.). New York: McGraw-Hill.

Seligman, M. E. P. (1971). Phobias and preparedness. *Behavior Therapy, 2,* 307–320.

Seligman, M. E. P. (1975). *Helplessness: On depression, development, and death.* San Francisco: Freeman.

Seligman, M. E. P. (1991). *Learned optimism.* New York: Knopf.

Seligman, M. E. P., Maier, S. F., & Geer, J. (1968). The alleviation of learned helplessness in the dog. *Journal of Abnormal Psychology, 78,* 256–262.

Selman, R. L. (1976). Toward a structural analysis of developing interpersonal relations concepts. In A. Pick (Ed.), *Minnesota symposia on child psychology* (Vol. 10). Minneapolis: University of Minnesota.

Selman, R. L., & Byrne, D. (1974). A structural-developmental analysis of levels of role-taking in middle childhood. *Child Development, 45,* 803–806.

Selye, H. (1956). *The stress of life.* New York: McGraw-Hill.

Senden, M. v. (1960). *Space and sight: The perception of space and shape in the congenitally blind before and after operation* (P. Heath, Trans.). New York: Free Press.

Seta, C. E., & Seta, J. J. (1992). Increments and decrements in mean arterial pressure levels as a function of audience composition: An averaging and summation analysis. *Personality and Social Psychology Bulletin, 18,* 173–181.

Seta, J. J. (1982). The impact of comparison processes on coactors' task performance. *Journal of Personality and Social Psychology, 42,* 281–291.

Shadish, W. R., Montgomery, L. M., Wilson, P., Wilson, R. R., Bright, L., & Okwumabua, T. (1993). Effects of family and marital psychotherapies: A meta-analysis. *Journal of Consulting and Clinical Psychology, 61,* 992–1002.

Shafii, M., MacMillan, D. R., Key, M. P., & Kaufman, N. (1997). Case study: Melatonin in severe obesity. *Journal of the American Academy of Child and Adolescent Psychiatry, 36,* 412–416.

Shallop, J. K., Arndt, P. L., & Turnacliff, K. A. (1992). Expanded indications for cochlear implantation: Perceptual results in seven adults with residual hearing [Special Issue: Cochlear implants]. *Journal of Speech, Language, Pathology, and Audiology, 16,* 141–148.

Shapiro, A. P. (1996). *Hypertension and stress: A unified concept.* Hillsdale, NJ: Erlbaum.

Shapiro, R. W., & Keller, M. B. (1981). Initial six-month follow-up of patients with major depressive disorder: A preliminary report from the NIMII Collaborative Study of the Psychobiology of Depression. *Journal of Affective Disorders, 3,* 205–220.

Shatz, M., & Gelman, R. (1973). The development of communication skills: Modifications in the speech of young children as a function of listener. *Monographs of the Society for Research in Child Development, 38*, 1–37.

Shaver, J. P., & Strong, W. (1976). *Facing value decisions: Rationale-building for teachers.* Belmont, CA: Wadsworth.

Shaver, P., & Hazan, C. (1985). Incompatibility loneliness, and "limerence." In W. Ickes (Ed.), *Compatibility and incompatibility in relationships* (pp. 163–184). New York: Springer-Verlag.

Shaver, P., Hazan, C., & Bradshaw, D. (1988). Love as attachment: The integration of three behavioral systems. In R. J. Sternberg & M. L. Barnes (Eds.), *The psychology of love.* New Haven, CT: Yale University Press.

Shaw, M. E. (1976). *Group dynamics: The psychology of small group behavior* (2nd ed.). New York: McGraw-Hill.

Shea, M. T., Elkin, I., Imber, S. D., Sotsky, S. M., Watkins, J. T., Collins, J. F., Pilkonis, P. A., Beckham, E., Glass, D. R., Dolan, R. T., & Parloff, M. B. (1992). Course of depressive symptoms over follow-up. *Archives of General Psychiatry, 49*, 782–787.

Sheehy, G. (1976). *Passages: Predictable crises of adult life.* New York: Dutton.

Sheingold, K., & Tenney, Y. J. (1982). Memory for a salient childhood event. In U. Neisser (Ed.), *Memory observed* (pp. 201–212). San Francisco: W. H. Freeman.

Shekelle, R. B., Hulley, S. B., Neaton, J. D., Billings, J. H., Borhani, N. O., Gerace, T. A., Jacobs, D. R., Lasser, N. C., Mittelmark, M. B., & Stamber, J. (1985). The MRFIT behavior pattern study: II. Type A behavior and incidence of coronary heart disease. *American Journal of Epidemiology, 122*, 559–570.

Shepperd, J. A., & Arkin, R. M. (1991). Behavioral other-enhancement: Strategically obscuring the link between performance and evaluation. *Journal of Personality and Social Psychology, 60*, 79–88.

Sherif, M., & Sherif, C. W. (1953). *Groups in harmony and tension.* New York: Harper & Row.

Sherman, R. A., Griffin, V. D., Evans, C. B., & Grana, A. S. (1993). Temporal relationships between changes in phantom limb pain intensity and changes in surface electromyogram of the residual limb. *International Journal of Psychophysiology, 13*, 71–77.

Sherman, S. J., & Corty, E. (1984). Cognitive heuristics. In R. S. Wyer & T. K. Srull (Eds.), *Handbook of social cognition* (Vol. 1, pp. 189–286). Hillsdale, NJ: Erlbaum.

Sherman, S. J., Presson, C. C., Chassin, L., Bensenberg, M., Corty, E., & Olshavsky, R. W. (1982). Smoking intentions in adolescents. *Personality and Social Psychology Bulletin, 8*, 376–383.

Shevrin, H. (1988). Unconscious conflict: A convergent psychodynamic and electrophysiological approach. In M. Horowitz (Ed.), *Psychodynamics and Cognition* (pp. 117–167). Chicago: University of Chicago Press.

Shevrin, H. (1990). Subliminal perception and repression. In J. L. Singer (Ed.), *Repression and dissociation: Implications for personality theory, psychopathology, and health* (pp. 103–119). Chicago: University of Chicago Press.

Shields, J. (1976). Heredity and environment. In H. J. Eysenck & G. D. Wilson (Eds.), *A textbook of human psychology.* Baltimore: University Park Press.

Shimamura, A. P., Berry, J. M., Mangels, J. A., Rusting, C. L., & Jurica, P. J. (1995). Memory and cognitive abilities in university professors. *Psychological Science, 6*, 271–277.

Shneidman, E. S. (1973). *Deaths of man.* New York: Quadrangle.

Shneidman, E. S. (1976). A psycho-logical theory of suicide. *Psychiatric Annals, 6*, 51–66.

Shneidman, E. S. (1987). A psychological approach to suicide. In G. R. VandenBos & B. K. Bryant (Eds.), *Cataclysms, crises, and catastrophes: Psychology in action.* Washington, DC: American Psychological Association.

Shneidman, E. S. (1992). A conspectus of the suicidal scenario. In R. W. Maris, A. L. Berman, J. T. Maltsberger, & R. I. Yufit (Eds.), *Assessment and prediction of suicide* (pp. 50–64). New York: Guilford.

Shobe, K. K., & Kihlstrom, J. F. (1997). Is traumatic memory special? *Current Directions in Psychological Science, 3*, 70–74.

Shoda, T., Mischel, W., & Wright, J. C. (1994). Intraindividual stability in the organizing and patterning of behavior: Incorporating psychological situations into the idiographic analysis of personality. *Journal of Personality and Social Psychology, 67*, 674–687.

Shoham-Salomon, V., & Rosenthal, R. (1987). Paradoxical interventions: A meta-analysis. *Journal of Consulting and Clinical Psychology, 55*, 22–28.

Shopland, D. R., & Brown, C. (1987). Toward the 1990 objectives for smoking: Measuring the progress with 1985 NHIS data. *Public Health Reports, 102*, 68–73.

Shou, M. (1988). Lithium treatment of manic depressive illness. *Journal of the American Medical Association, 259*, 1834–1836.

Shreve, A. (1982, November 21). Careers and the lure of motherhood. *New York Times Magazine,* pp. 38–42.

Sieber, J. E., & Stanley, B. (1988). Ethical and professional dimensions of socially Sensitive Research. *American Psychologist, 43*, 49–55.

Siegal, M. (1987). Are sons and daughters treated more differently by fathers than by mothers? *Developmental Review, 7*, 183–209.

Siegler, R. S. (1986). *Children's thinking* (2nd ed.). Englewood Cliffs, NJ: Prentice Hall.

Siegman, A. W., & Smith, T. W. (Eds.). (1994). *Anger, hostility, and the heart.* Hillsdale, NJ: Erlbaum.

Siever, L. J., & Davis, K. L. (1985). Overview: Toward dysregulation hypothesis of depression. *American Journal of Psychiatry, 142,* 10–17.

Sigall, H., & Landy, D. (1973). Radiating beauty: The effects of having a physically attractive partner on person perception. *Journal of Personality and Social Psychology, 28,* 218–224.

Silver, R. L., & Wortman, C. B. (1980). Coping with undesirable life events. In J. Garber & M. E. P. Seligman (Eds.), *Human helplessness: Theory and applications* (pp. 279–375). New York: Academic Press.

Silverman, L. H. (1976). The further use of the subliminal psychodynamic activation method for the experimental study of the clinical theory of psychoanalysis: On the specificity of the relationship between symptoms and unconscious conflicts. *Psychotherapy: Theory, Research, and Practice, 13*(1), 2–16.

Silverman, L. H. (1982). A comment on two subliminal psychodynamic activation studies. *Journal of Abnormal Psychology, 91*(2), 126–130.

Simmons, F. B., Epley, J. M., Lummis, R. C., Guttman, N., Frishkopf, L. S., Harmon, L. D., & Zwicker, E. (1965). Auditory nerve: Electrical stimulation in man. *Science, 148,* 104–106.

Simon, H., & Gilmartin, K. (1973). A simulation of memory for chess positions. *Cognitive Psychology, 5,* 29–46.

Simon, H. A. (1957). *Administrative behavior.* Towata, NJ: Littlefield, Adams.

Simonton, D. K. (1988). *Scientific genius: A psychology of science.* New York: Cambridge University Press.

Simonton, D. K. (1989, February 6). The surprising nature of scientific genius. *The Scientist.*

Simpson, E. L. (1974). Moral development research: A case study of scientific cultural bias. *Human Development, 17,* 81–106.

Sinclair, R. C., Mark, M. M., & Shotland, R. L. (1987). Construct accessibility and generalizability across response categories. *Personality and Social Psychology Bulletin, 13,* 239–252.

Singh, D. (1993). Adaptive significance of female physical attractiveness: Role of waist-to-hip ratio. *Journal of Personality and Social Psychology, 65,* 293–307.

Singh, D. (1994). Is thin really beautiful and good? Relationship between waist-to-hip ratio (WHR) and female attractiveness. *Personality and Individual Differences, 16,* 123–132.

Singh, D., & Luis, S. (1995). Ethnic and gender consensus for the effect of waist-to-hip ratio on judgment of women's attractiveness. *Human Nature, 6,* 51–65.

Sivacek, J., & Crano, W. D. (1982). Vested interest as a moderator of attitude-behavior consistency. *Journal of Personality and Social Psychology, 43,* 210–221.

Skinner, B. F. (1938). *The behavior of organisms: An experimental analysis* (Vol. 6). New York: Appleton-Century-Crofts.

Skinner, B. F. (1953). *Science and human behavior.* New York: Macmillan.

Skinner, B. F. (1957). *Verbal behavior.* Engelwood Cliffs, NJ: Prentice Hall.

Skinner, B. F. (1971). *Beyond freedom and dignity.* New York: Knopf.

Sloane, R. B., Staples, F. R., Cristal, A. H., Yorkston, W. J., & Whipple, K. (1975). *Psychotherapy vs behavior therapy.* Cambridge, MA: Harvard University Press.

Slobin, D. I. (1972, July). Children and language: They learn the same way all around the world. *Psychology Today,* 71–74ff.

Slobin, D. I. (1973). Cognitive prerequisites for the development of grammar. In C. A. Ferguson & D. I. Slobin (Eds.), *Studies of child language development.* New York: Holt, Rinehart & Winston.

Slobin, D. I. (1982). Universal and particular in the acquisition of language. In L. Gleitman & E. Wanner (Eds.), *Language acquisition: The state of the art.* New York: Cambridge University Press.

Sloman, S. A., Hayman, C. A. G., Ohta, N., Law, J., & Tulving, E. (1988). Forgetting in primed fragment completion. *Journal of Experimental Psychology: Learning, Memory and Cognition, 17,* 234–244.

Slovic, P., Fischhoff, B., & Lichtenstein, S. (1976). Cognitive processes and societal risk taking. *Oregon Research Institute Monograph, 15.*

Slovic, P., Fischhoff, B., & Lichtenstein, S. (1980, June). Risky assumptions. *Psychology Today,* 44–48.

Smead, V. S. (1988). Trying too hard: A correlate of eating related difficulties. *Addictive Behaviors, 13,* 307–310.

Smith, C. A. (1989). Dimensions of appraisal and physiological response in emotion. *Journal of Personality and Social Psychology, 56,* 339–353.

Smith, C. A., & Ellsworth, P. C. (1985). Patterns of cognitive appraisal in emotion. *Journal of Personality and Social Psychology, 48,* 813–838.

Smith, D. E., & Cogswell, C. (1994). A cross-cultural perspective on adolescent girls' body perception. *Perception and Motor Skills, 78,* 744–746.

Smith, D. S., Collins, M., Kreisberg, J. P., & Volpicelli, J. R. (1987). Screening for problem drinking in college freshmen. [Special Issue: Students, alcohol, and college health]. *Journal of American College Health, 36*, 89–94.

Smith, E. E., & Medin, D. L. (1981). *Categories and concepts.* Cambridge, MA: Harvard University Press.

Smith, K. H., & Rogers, M. (1994). Effectiveness of subliminal messages in television commercials: Two experiments. *Journal of Applied Psychology, 79*, 866–874.

Smith, M. L., & Glass, G. V. (1977). Meta-analysis of psychotherapy outcome studies. *American Psychologist, 32*, 752–760.

Smith, M. L., Glass, G. V., & Miller, R. L. (1981). *The benefits of psychotherapy.* Baltimore: Johns Hopkins University Press.

Smith, P. K., & Daglish, L. (1977). Sex differences in parent and infant behavior in the home. *Child Development, 48*, 1250–1254.

Smith, R. H., Diener, E., & Wedell, D. H. (1989). Intrapersonal and social comparison determinants of happiness: A range-frequency analysis. *Journal of Personality and Social Psychology, 56*, 317–325.

Smith, S. M., & Shaffer, D. R. (1991). Celebrity and cajolery: Rapid speech may promote or inhibit persuasion through its impact on message elaboration. *Personality and Social Psychology Bulletin, 17*, 663–669.

Smith, T. W. (1992). Hostility and health. *Health Psychology, 11*, 139–150.

Smith, T. W., & Brown, P. C. (1991). Cynical hostility, attempts to exert social control, and cardiovascular reactivity in married couples. *Journal of Behavioral Medicine, 14*, 581–592.

Smolak, L. (1986). *Infancy.* Englewood Cliffs, NJ: Prentice Hall.

Snyder, C. R., & Higgins, R. L. (1988). Excuses: Their effective role in the negotiation of reality. *Psychological Bulletin, 104*, 23–35.

Snyder, D. K., Willis, R. M., & Grady-Fletcher, A. (1991). Long-term effectiveness of behavioral and insight-oriented marital therapy. *Journal of Consulting and Clinical Psychology, 59*, 138–141.

Snyder, F. (1970). The phenomenology of dreaming. In L. Madow & L. H. Snow (Eds.), *The psychodynamic implications of the physiological studies on dreams.* Springfield, IL: Charles C Thomas.

Snyder, M., & Swann, W. B., Jr. (1978). Behavioral confirmation in social interaction: From social perception to social reality. *Journal of Personality and Social Psychology, 36*, 1202–1212.

Snyder, M., Tanke, E. D., & Berscheid, E. (1977). Social perception and interpersonal behavior: On the self-fulfilling nature of social stereotypes. *Journal of Personality and Social Psychology, 35*, 656–666.

Snyder, M. L., & Frankel, A. (1989). Making things harder for yourself: Pride and joy. In R. C. Curtis (Ed.), *Self-defeating behaviors: Experimental research, clinical impressions, and practical implications.* New York: Plenum Press.

Solomon, L. Z., Solomon, H., & Stone, R. (1978). Helping as a function of number of bystanders and ambiguity of emergency. *Personality and Social Psychology Bulletin, 4*, 318–321.

Solso, R. (1988). *Cognitive psychology.* Needham Heights, MA: Allyn & Bacon.

Solso, R. (1996). *Cognitive psychology* (4th ed.). Needham Heights, MA: Allyn & Bacon.

Spanos, N. P., Mondoux, T. J., & Burgess, C. A. (1995). Comparison of multi-component hypnotic and non-hypnotic treatments for smoking. [Special Issue: To the memory of Nicholas Spanos]. *Contemporary Hypnosis, 12*, 12–19.

Spearman, C. (1927). *The abilities of man.* New York: Macmillan.

Speisman, J., Lazarus, R. S., Mordkoff, A., & Davidson, L. (1964). Experimental reduction of stress based on ego defense theory. *Journal of Abnormal and Social Psychology, 68*, 367–380.

Spence, J. T., Deaux, K., & Helmreich, R. L. (1985). Sex roles in contemporary American society. In G. Lindsey & E. Aronson (Eds.), *Handbook of social psychology* (3rd ed.). Reading, MA: Addison-Wesley.

Spencer, J., G, D., Yaden, S., & Lal, H. (1988). Behavioral and physiological detection of classically-conditioned blood pressure reduction. *Psychopharmacology, 95*, 25–28.

Sperling, G. (1960). The information available in brief visual presentation. *Psychological Monographs, 74* (Whole No. 498).

Sperry, R. W. (1982). Some effects of disconnecting the cerebral hemispheres. *Science, 217*, 1223–1226.

Spiegel, D., Bloom, J., & Yalom, I. (1981). Group support for patients with metastatic cancer. *Archives of General Psychiatry, 38*, 527–533.

Spiegel, D., Frischholz, F. J., Fleiss, J. L., & Spiegel, H. (1993). Predictors of smoking abstinence following a single-session restructuring intervention with self-hypnosis. *American Journal of Psychiatry, 150*, 1090–1097.

Spirito, A., Brown, L., Overholser, J., & Fritz, G. (1989a). Attempted suicide in adolescents: A review and critique of the literature. *Clinical Psychology Review, 9*, 335–363.

Spirito, A., Brown, L., Overholser, J., & Fritz, G. (1989b). Common problems and coping strategies: II. Findings with adolescent suicide attempters. *Journal of Abnormal Child Psychology, 17*, 213–221.

Spitzer, R. L., Skodol, A. E., Gibbon, M., & Williams, J. B. W. (1986). *A psychiatrist's casebook.* New York: Warner Books.

Sprecher, S., Aron, A., Hatfield, E., Cortese, A., Potapova, E., & Levitskaya, A. (1994). Love: American style, Russian style, and Japanese style. *Personal Relationships, 1*, 349–369.

Springer, S. P., & Deutsch, G. (1985). *Left brain, right brain* (rev. ed.). New York: W. H. Freeman.

Springer, S. P., & Deutsch, G. (1989). *Left brain, right brain* (3rd ed.). San Francisco: W. H. Freeman.

Sprinthall, N., & Collins, W. A. (1984). *Adolescent psychology*. New York: Addison-Wesley.

Squire, L. R. (1986). Mechanisms of memory. *Science, 232,* 1612–1619.

Squire, L. R. (1987). *Memory and brain*. New York: Oxford University Press.

Squire, L. R. (1992). Memory and the hippocampus: A synthesis from findings with rats, monkeys, and humans. *Psychological Review, 99,* 195–231.

Squire, L. R., Haist, F., & Shimamura, A. P. (1989). The neurology of memory: Quantitative assessment of retrograde amnesia in two groups of amnesic patients. *Journal of Neuroscience, 9,* 828–839.

Sroufe, L. A. (1988). The role of infant-caregiver attachment in development. In J. Belsky & T. Nezworski (Eds.), *Clinical implications of attachment* (pp. 18–40). Hillsdale, NJ: Erlbaum.

Sroufe, L. A., Fox, N., & Pancake, V. (1983). Attachment and dependency in developmental perspective. *Child Development, 54,* 1615–1627.

Srull, T. K., & Wyer, R. S. (1994). *Handbook of social cognition: Vol. 1. Basic processes. Vol. 2. Applications* (2nd ed.). Hillsdale, NJ: Erlbaum.

Staddon, J. E. R., & Ettinger, R. H. (1989). *Learning: An introduction to the principles of adaptive behavior*. San Diego: Harcourt Brace Jovanovich.

Stanley, J. C. (1983, February). Education in the fast lane: Methodological problems of evaluating its effects. *Evaluation News,* 28–46.

Stanley, M., & Stanley, B. (1989). Biochemical studies in suicide victims: Current findings and future implications. *Suicide and Life-Threatening Behavior, 19,* 30–42.

Stanley, M., & Stanley, B. (1990). Postmortem evidence for serotonin's role in suicide. *Journal of Clinical Psychiatry, 51,* 22–28.

Stanovich, K. E., & Cunningham, A. E. (1992). Studying the consequences of literacy within a literate society: The cognitive correlates of print exposure. *Memory and Cognition, 20,* 51–68.

Stanovich, K. E., & Cunningham, A. E. (1993). Where does knowledge come from? Specific associations between print exposure and information acquisition. *Journal of Educational Psychology, 85,* 211–229.

Stanton, M. D. (1981). Strategic approaches to family therapy. In A. Gurman & D. P. Kniskern (Eds.), *Handbook of family therapy* (pp. 361–390). New York: Brunner/Mazel.

Steblay, N. M., & Bothwell, R. K. (1994). Evidence for hypnotically refreshed testimony: The view from the laboratory. *Law and Human Behavior, 18,* 635–651.

Steele, C. M., Southwick, L., & Pagano, R. (1986). Drinking your troubles away: The role of activity in mediating alcohol's reduction of psychological stress. *Journal of Abnormal Psychology, 95,* 173–180.

Steele, C. M., Spencer, S. J., & Lynch, M. (1993). Self-image resilience and dissonance: The role of affirmational resources. *Journal of Personality and Social Psychology, 64,* 885–896.

Stein, M. I. (1956). A transactional approach to creativity. In C. W. Taylor (Ed.), *The 1955 University of Utah Research Conference on the Identification of Creative Scientific Talent*. Salt Lake City: University of Utah Press.

Stein, N., Folkman, S., Trabasso, T., & Richards, T. A. (1997). Appraisal and goal processes as predictors of psychological well-being in bereaved caregivers. *Journal of Personality and Social Psychology, 72,* 872–884.

Steinberg, L. (1986). Latchkey children and susceptibility to peer pressure: An ecological analysis. *Developmental Psychology, 22,* 433–439.

Steinberg, L., & Belsky, J. (1990). *Infancy, childhood, and adolescence: Development in context*. New York: McGraw-Hill.

Stelmack, R. M. (1990). Biological bases of extroversion: Psychophysiological evidence. *Journal of Personality, 58*(1), 293–311.

Stephan, C., Burnam, M. A., & Aronson, E. (1979). Attributions for success and failure after cooperation, competition, or team competition. *European Journal of Social Psychology, 9,* 109–114.

Stephens, J. H. (1978). Long-term prognosis and followup in schizophrenia. *Schizophrenia Bulletin, 4,* 25–46.

Steriade, M., Gloor, P., Llinas, R. R., Lose de Silve, F. H., & Mesulam, M. M. (1990). Basic mechanisms of cerebral rhythmic activities. *Electroencephalography and Clinical Neurophysiology, 76,* 481–508.

Steriade, M., & Llinas, R. R. (1988). The functional states of the thalamus and the associated neuronal interplay. *Physiology Reviews, 68,* 649–742.

Stern, M. J., Pascale, L., & McLoone, J. B. (1976). Psychosocial adaptation following an acute myocardial infarction. *Journal of Chronic Diseases, 29,* 513–526.

Stern, W. (1912). *Psychologische Methoden der Intelligenz-Prüfung*. Leipzig: Barth.

Sternberg, R. J. (1984). *Beyond IQ: A triarchic theory of human intelligence*. New York: Cambridge University Press.

Sternberg, R. J. (1986). A triangular theory of love. *Psychological Review, 93,* 119–135.

Sternberg, R. J. (1988). Mental self-government: A theory of intellectual styles and their development. *Human Development, 31*, 197–224.

Sternberg, R. J. (1990). *Metaphors of mind: Conceptions of the nature of intelligence.* New York: Guilford.

Sternberg, R. J. (1994). 468 factor-analyzed data sets: What they tell us and don't tell us about human intelligence. *Psychological Science, 5*, 63–65.

Sternberg, R. J. (1995a). *Cognitive psychology.* Fort Worth: Harcourt Brace.

Sternberg, R. J. (1995b). For whom the bell curves: A review of "The Bell Curve." *Psychological Science, 6*, 257–261.

Sternberg, R. J. (1996). *Cognitive psychology.* Fort Worth: Harcourt Brace.

Sternberg, R. J., Conway, B. E., Ketron, J. L., & Berstein, M. (1981). Peoples' conceptions of intelligence. *Journal of Personality and Social Psychology, 41*, 37–55.

Sternberg, R. J., & Davidson, J. E. (1982, June). The mind of the puzzler. *Psychology Today*, 37–44.

Sternberg, R. J., & Davidson, J. E. (Eds.). (1986). *Conceptions of giftedness.* New York: Cambridge University Press.

Sternberg, R. J., & Gastel, J. (1989). Coping with novelty in human intelligence: An empirical investigation. *Intelligence, 13*, 187–197.

Sternberg, R. J., & Lubart, T. I. (1991). An investment theory in creativity and its development. *Human Development, 34*, 1–31.

Sternberg, R. J., & Wagner, R. K. (1993). The *g*-ocentric view of intelligence and job performance is wrong. *Current Directions in Psychological Science, 2*, 1–4.

Stevens, C. F. (1991). New recruit to the magnificent seven. *Current Biology, 1*, 20–22.

Stocker, C., Dunn, J., & Plomin, R. (1989). Sibling relationships: Links with child temperament, maternal behavior, and family structure. *Child Development, 60*, 715–727.

Stone, M. H. (1990). Incest in the borderline patient. In R. P. Kluft (Ed.), *Incest-related syndromes of adult psychopathology* (pp. 183–204). New York: Plenum Press.

Strachey, J. (Ed.). (1957). *The standard edition of the complete psychological works of Sigmund Freud* (Vol. 14). London: Hogarth Press.

Strack, F., Martin, L. L., & Stepper, S. (1988). Inhibiting and facilitating conditions of the human smile: A nonobtrusive test of the facial feedback hypothesis. *Journal of Personality and Social Psychology, 54*, 768–777.

Straus, M. A., Gelles, R. J., & Steinmetz, S. K. (1980). *Behind closed doors: Violence in the American family.* Garden City, NY: Anchor Books.

Stricker, G. (1983). Some issues in psychodynamic treatment of the depressed patient. *Professional Psychology: Research and Practice, 14*, 209–217.

Strickland, B. R. (1987). On the threshold of the second century of psychology. *American Psychologist, 42*, 1055–1056.

Striegel-Moore, R. H., Silberstein, L. R., & Rodin, J. (1993). The social self in bulimia nervosa: Public self-consciousness, social anxiety, and perceived fraudulence. *Journal of Abnormal Psychology, 102*, 297–303.

Stroessner, S. J., & Mackie, D. M. (1993). Affect and perceived group variability: Implications for stereotyping and prejudice. In D. M. Mackie & D. L. Hamilton (Eds.), *Affect, cognition, and stereotyping: Interactive processes in group perception.* San Diego: Academic Press.

Stroop, J. R. (1935). Studies of interference in serial verbal reactions. *Journal of Experimental Psychology, 18*, 643–662.

Stuart, R. B. (1976). An operant interpersonal program for couples. In D. H. L. Olson (Ed.), *Treating relationships.* Lake Mills, IA: Graphic.

Stuart, S., Wright, J. H., Thase, M. E., & Beck, A. T. (1997). Cognitive therapy with inpatients. *General Hospital Psychiatry, 19*(1), 42–50.

Stunkard, A. J., Harris, J. R., Pedersen, N. L., & McClearn, G. E. (1990). The body-mass index of twins who have been reared apart. *New England Journal of Medicine, 322*, 1483–1487.

Styron, W. (1990). *Darkness visible: A great writer's battle with depression.* New York: Random House.

Suedfeld, P., & Pennebaker, J. W. (1997). Health outcomes and cognitive aspects of recalled negative life events. *Psychosomatic Medicine, 59*(2), 172–177.

Suls, J., & Mullen, B. (1981). Life events, perceived control and illness: The role of uncertainty. *Journal of Human Stress, 7*(2), 30–34.

Sutker, P. B., & Adams, H. E. (Eds.). (1993). *Comprehensive handbook of psychopathology* (2nd ed.). New York: Plenum Press.

Swanbrow, D. (1989, August). The paradox of happiness. *Psychology Today*, 37–39.

Swann, W. B., Jr. (1997). The trouble with change: Self-verification and the allegiance to the self. *Psychological Science, 8*, 177–179.

Swanson, J., & Kinsbourne, M. (1980). Artificial color and hyperactive children. In R. M. Knights & D. J. Bakker (Eds.), *Treatment of hyperactive and learning disabled children.* Baltimore: University Park Press.

Swartz, M., Carroll, B., & Blazer, D. (1989). In response to "Psychiatric Diagnosis as Reified Measurement." *Journal of Health and Social Behavior, 30*, 33–34.

Swets, J. A. (1961). Is there a sensory threshold? *Science, 134*, 168–177.

Swets, J. A., Tanner, W. P., Jr., & Birdsall, T. G. (1961). Decision processes in perception. *Psychological Review, 68*, 301–340.

Swim, J. K., Aikin, W. S., & Hunter, B. A. (1995). Sexism and racism: Old-fashioned and modern prejudices. *Journal of Personality and Social Psychology, 68*, 199–214.

Symonds, M. (1975). Victims of violence: Psychological effects and aftereffects. *American Journal of Psychoanalysis, 35*, 19–26.

Szasz, T. (1986). The case against suicide prevention. *American Psychologist, 41*, 806–812.

Tambs, K., Sundet, J. M., & Magnus, P. (1984). Heritability analysis of the WAIS subtests. *Intelligence, 8*, 283–293.

Tangney, J. P., & Feshbach, S. (1988). Children's television viewing frequency: Individual differences and demographic correlates. *Personality and Social Psychology Bulletin, 14*, 145–148.

Tanner, J. M. (1982). *Growth at adolescence* (2nd ed.). Oxford: Scientific.

Tarter, R. E., Alterman, A. L., & Edwards, K. L. (1985). Vulnerability to alcoholism in men: A behaviorgenetic perspective. *Journal of Studies on Alcohol, 46*, 329–356.

Task Force on Tardive Dyskinesia. (1980). *American Psychiatric Association Task Force Report* (No. 18, p. 44). Washington, DC: American Psychiatric Association Press.

Taube, C. A., & Rednick, R. (1973). *Utilization of mental health resources by persons diagnosed with schizophrenia* (DHEW Publication). Rockville, MD: National Institute of Mental Health.

Tavassoli, N. T., & Shultz, C. J. (1995). Program involvement: Are moderate levels best for ad memory and attitude toward the ad? *Journal of Advertising Research, 35*, 61–72.

Tavris, C. (1982). *Anger: The misunderstood emotion.* New York: Simon & Schuster.

Tavris, C. (1987, September 27). Old age is not what it used to be. *New York Times Magazine,* pp. 24–25.

Taylor, S., & Thompson, S. (1981). *Stalking the elusive "vividness" effect.* Unpublished manuscript, University of California at Los Angeles.

Taylor, S. E. (1989). *Positive illusions: Creative self-deception and the healthy mind.* New York: Basic Books.

Taylor, S. E. (1991). *Health psychology* (2nd ed.). New York: McGraw-Hill.

Taylor, S. E., & Brown, J. D. (1988). Illusion and well-being: A social psychological perspective on mental health. *Psychological Bulletin, 103*, 193–210.

Taylor, S. E., Kemeny, M. E., Aspinwall, L. G., Schneider, S. G., Rodriguez, R., & Herbert, M. (1992). Optimism, coping, psychological distress, and high-risk sexual behavior among men at risk for acquired immunodeficiency syndrome (AIDS). *Journal of Personality and Social Psychology, 63*, 460–473.

Taylor, S. E., Kemeny, M. E., Schneider, S. G., & Aspinwall, L. G. (1993). Coping with the threat of AIDS. In J. B. Pryor & G. D. Reeder (Eds.), *The social psychology of HIV infection.* Hillsdale, NJ: Erlbaum.

Taylor, S. E., Repetti, R. L., & Seeman, T. (1997). Health psychology: What is an unhealthy environment and how does it get under the skin? *Annual Review of Psychology, 48*, 411–447.

Taylor, S. E., Wood, J. V., & Lichtman, R. R. (1983). It could be worse: Selective evaluation as a response to victimization. *Journal of Social Issues, 39*, 19–40.

Teasdale, J. D., & Fogarty, F. J. (1979). Differential effects of induced mood on retrieval of pleasant and unpleasant events from episodic memory. *Journal of Abnormal Psychology, 88*, 248–257.

Teghtsoonian, R. (1971). On the exponents in Stevens' law and the constant in Ekman's law. *Psychological Review, 78*, 7180.

Tellegen, A., Lykken, D. T., Bouchard, T. J., Wilcox, K. J., Segal, N. L., & Rich, S. (1988,). *Personality similarity in twins reared apart and together.* Paper presented at the Journal of Personality and Social Psychology.

Tenopyr, M. L. (1981). The realities of employment testing. *American Psychology, 36*, 1120–1127.

Terman, L. M. (1916). *The measurement of intelligence.* Boston: Houghton Mifflin.

Terman, L. M., & Oden, M. H. (1959). *Genetic studies of genius: The gifted group at midlife* (Vol. 4). Stanford, CA: Stanford University Press.

Terrace, H. S. (1979, September). How Nim Chimpsky changed my mind. *Psychology Today,* 65–76.

Tesar, G. E. (1990). High-potency benzodiazepines for short-term management of panic disorder: The U.S. experience. *Journal of Clinical Psychiatry,* 4–10.

Tetlock, P. E., & Boettger, R. (1989). Accountability: A social magnifier of the dilution effect. *Journal of Personality and Social Psychology, 57*, 388–398.

Thase, M. E., & Moss, M. K. (1976). The relative efficacy of covert modeling procedures and guided participant modeling on the reduction of avoidance behavior. *Journal of Behavior Therapy and Experimental Psychiatry, 7*, 7–12.

Thomas, A., Chess, S., & Birch, H. (1970). The origin of personality. *Scientific American, 223*, 102–109.

Thomas, M. H. (1982). Physiological arousal, exposure to a relatively lengthy aggressive film, and aggressive behavior. *Journal of Research in Personality, 16*, 72–81.

Thompson, C., & Cowan, T. (1986). Flashbulb memories: A nicer interpretation of a Neisser recollection. *Cognition, 2*, 199–200.

Thompson, L. A. (1997a). Behavioral genetics and the classification of mental retardation. In J. William & E. MacLean (Eds.), *Ellis' handbook of mental deficiency, psychological theory and research* (3rd ed., pp. 99–114). Mahwah, NJ: Erlbaum.

Thompson, L. A., Detterman, D. K., & Plomin, R. (1991). Associations between cognitive abilities and scholastic achievement: Genetic overlap but environmental differences. *Psychological Science, 2,* 158–165.

Thompson, M. (1997, February 27). Sergeants at odds. *Time,* 46.

Thompson, R. F. (1985). *The brain: An introduction to neuroscience* (Vol. 5). New York: W. H. Freeman.

Thompson, R. F. (1986). The neurobiology of learning and memory. *Science, 233,* 941–947.

Thompson, R. F. (1988). Brain substrates of learning and memory. In T. Boll & B. K. Bryant (Eds.), *Clinical neuropsychology and brain function: Research, measurement and practice* (pp. 61–83). Washington, DC: American Psychological Association.

Thompson, R. F. (1989). Neural circuit for classical conditioning of the eyelid closure response. In J. H. Byrne & W. O. Berry (Eds.), *Neural models of plasticity.* San Diego: Academic Press.

Thoresen, C. E., & Mahoney, M. J. (1974). *Behavioral self-control.* New York: Holt.

Thorndike, E. L. (1898). Animal intelligence. *Psychological Review Monograph, 2.*

Thorndike, E. L. (1932). *The fundamentals of learning.* New York: Teachers College.

Thorndike, R. L., Hagen, E. P., & Sattler, J. M. (1986). *Stanford-Binet intelligence scale* (4th ed.). Chicago: Riverside.

Thorne, B. (1986). Boys and girls together, but mostly apart: Gender arrangements in elementary schools. In W. W. Hartup & Z.

Rubin (Eds.), *Relationships and development.* Hillsdale, NJ: Erlbaum.

Thurstone, L. L. (1938). *Primary mental abilities.* Chicago: University of Chicago Press.

Tice, D. M. (1992). Self-concept change and self-presentation: The looking glass self is also a magnifying glass. *Journal of Personality and Social Psychology, 63,* 435–451.

Tienari, P., Sorri, A., Lahti, I., Naarala, M. N., Wahlberg, E., Moring, J., Pohjola, J., & Wynne, L. C. (1987). Genetic and psychosocial factors in schizophrenia: The Finnish adoptive family study. *Schizophrenia Bulletin, 13,* 477–484.

Till, R. E., Mross, E. F., & Kintsch, W. (1988). Time course of priming for associate and inference words in a discourse context. *Memory and Cognition, 16,* 283–298.

Tilles, D., Goldenheim, P., Johnson, D. C., Mendelson, J. H., Mello, N. K., & Hales, C. A. (1986). Marijuana smoking as a cause of reduction in single-breath carbon-monoxide diffusing capabilities. *American Journal of Medicine, 80,* 601–606.

Tippin, J., & Henn, F. A. (1982). Modified leucotomy in the treatment of intractable obsessive neurosis. *American Journal of Psychiatry, 139,* 1601–1603.

Tomarken, A. J., Davidson, R. J., & Henriques, J. B. (1990). Resting and frontal brain asymmetry predicts affective responses to films. *Journal of Personality and Social Psychology, 59*(4), 791–801.

Tomkins, S. S. (1962). *Affect, imagery, consciousness: Vol. 2. The negative affects.* New York: Springer-Verlag.

Tonkova-Yampol'skaya, R. V. (1973). Development of speech intonation in infants during the first two years of life. In C. A. Ferguson & D. I. Slobin (Eds.), *Studies of child language development* (pp. 128–138). New York: Holt, Rinehart & Winston.

Torgersen, S. (1983). Genetic factors in anxiety disorders. *Archives of General Psychiatry, 43,* 502–505.

Trask, C. H., & Cree, E. M. (1962). Oximeter studies on patients with chronic obstructive emphysema, awake and during sleep. *New England Journal of Medicine, 266,* 639–642.

Treadway, M., & McCloskey, M. (1989). Effects of racial stereotypes on eyewitness performance: Implications of the real and rumoured Allport and Postman studies. *Applied Cognitive Psychology, 3,* 53–63.

Trehub, S. E., Schneider, B. A., Thorpe, L. A., & Judge, P. (1991). Observational measures of auditory sensitivity in early infancy. *Developmental Psychology, 27,* 40–49.

Trickett, P. K., & Putnam, F. W. (1993). Impact of child sexual abuse on females: Toward a developmental, psychobiological integration. *Psychological Science, 4,* 81–87.

Triplett, N. (1898). The dynamogenic factors in pacemaking and competition. *American Journal of Psychology, 9,* 507–533.

Tuckman, J., Kleiner, R. J., & Lavell, M. (1959). Emotional content of suicide notes. *American Journal of Psychiatry, 116,* 59–63.

Tulving, E. (1985). How many memory systems are there? *American Psychologist, 40,* 385–398.

Tulving, E. (1989). Remembering and knowing the past. *American Scientist, 77,* 361–367.

Tulving, E. (1991). Memory research is not a zero-sum game. *American Psychologist, 46,* 41–42.

Tulving, E. (1993). What is episodic memory? *Current Directions in Psychological Science, 2,* 67–70.

Tulving, E., Hayman, C., & McDonald, C. (1991). Long-lasting perceptual and semantic priming in amnesia: A case experiment. *Journal of Experimental Psychology:*

Learning, Memory, and Cognition, 17, 595–617.

Tulving, E., Schacter, D. L., & Stark, H. (1982). Priming effects in word fragment completion are independent of recognition memory. *Journal of Experimental Psychology: Human Learning and Memory, 8*, 336–342.

Tulving, E., & Thompson, D. (1973). Encoding specificity and retrieval processes in episodic memory. *Psychological Review, 80*, 352–373.

Turk, D. C., Meichenbaum, D. H., & Berman, W. H. (1979). Application of biofeedback for the regulation of pain: A critical review. *Psychological Bulletin, 86*, 1322–1338.

Turner, M. E., & Pratkinis, A. R. (1993). Effects of preferential and meritorious selection on performance: An examination of intuitive and self-handicapping perspectives. *Personality and Social Psychology Bulletin, 19*, 47–58.

Turner, S. M., Beidel, D. C., & Nathan, R. S. (1985). Biological factors in obsessive-compulsive disorders. *Psychological Bulletin, 97*, 430–450.

Tversky, A., & Kahneman, D. (1971). Belief in the law of small numbers. *Psychological Bulletin, 76*, 105–110.

Tversky, A., & Kahneman, D. (1973). Availability: A heuristic for judging frequency and probability. *Cognitive Psychology, 5*, 207–232.

Tversky, A., & Kahneman, D. (1981). The framing of decisions and the psychology of choice. *Science, 211*, 453–458.

Tversky, A., & Kahneman, D. (1993). Belief in the law of small numbers. In G. Keren & C. Lewis (Eds.), *A handbook for data analysis in the behavioral sciences: Methodological issues* (pp. 341–349). Hillsdale, NJ: Erlbaum.

Tweed, D. L., & George, L. K. (1989). A more balanced perspective on "Psychiatric Diagnosis as Reified

Measurement." *Journal of Health and Social Behavior, 30*, 35–37.

Ulett, G. A. (1992). 3000 years of acupuncture: From metaphysics to neurophysiology. *Integrative Psychiatry, 8*, 91–100.

Ullman, M. (1962). Dreaming, lifestyle, and physiology: A comment on Adler's view of the dream. *Journal of Individual Psychology, 18*, 18–25.

Umberson, D. (1987). Family status and health behaviors: Social control as a dimension of social integration. *Journal of Health and Social Behavior, 28*, 306–319.

Underwood, G. (1994). Subliminal perception on TV. *Nature, 370*, 103.

U.S. Attorney General. (1986). *Final report of the Attorney General's Commission on Pornography* (Pub. No. 027-000-01259-1). Washington, DC: U.S. Government Printing Office.

U.S. Bureau of the Census. (1982). *Statistical abstract of the United States: 1982–1983* (Vol. 103). Washington, DC: U.S. Government Printing Office.

U.S. Department of Health, Education, and Welfare. (1978). *Alcohol and health*. Washington, DC: Author.

U.S. Dept. of Health Human Services. (1995). *Demographic information*. Washington, DC: Author.

Usher, J. A., & Neisser, U. (1993). Childhood amnesia and the beginning of memory for four early life events. *Journal of Experimental Psychology: General, 122*, 155–165.

Vaillant, G. (1977). *Adaption to life*. Boston: Little, Brown.

Valenstein, E. S. (1973). *Brain control: A critical examination of brain stimulation and psychosurgery*. New York: Wiley.

Valenstein, E. S. (1978, July). Science fiction, fantasy and the brain. *Psychology Today*, 28–39.

Valenstein, E. S. (1980). *The psychosurgery debate*. San Francisco: W. H. Freeman.

Valois, P., Desharnais, R., & Godin, C. (1988). A comparison of the Fishbein and Ajzen and the Triandis attitudinal models for the prediction of exercise intention and behavior. *Journal of Behavioral Medicine, 11*, 459–472.

Van Knippenberg, D., & Wilke, H. (1992). Prototypicality of arguments and conformity to ingroup norms. *European Journal of Social Psychology, 22*, 141–155.

Vandell, D. L., & Corasaniti, M. A. (1990). Child care and the family: Complex contributors to child development. *New Directions for Child Development, 49*, 23–37.

VanStaden, F. J. (1987). White South Africans' attitudes toward the desegregation of public amenities. *Journal of Social Psychology, 127*, 163–173.

Vaughn, B. E., Gove, F. L., & Egeland, B. (1980). The relationship between out-of-home care and the quality of infant mother attachment in an economically disadvantaged population. *Child Development, 51*, 1203–1214.

Videka-Sherman, L., & Lieberman, M. (1985). The effects of self-help and psychotherapy intervention on child loss: The limits of recovery. *American Journal of Othropsychiatry, 55*, 70–82.

Vitkus, J. (1996). *Casebook in abnormal psychology*. New York: McGraw-Hill.

Voderholzer, U., Laakmann, G., Becker, U., & Haag, C., (1997). Circadian profiles of melatonin in melancholic depressed patients and healthy subjects in relation to cortisol secretion and sleep. *Psychiatry Research, 71*(3), 151–161.

Volle, R. L., & Koelle, G. B. (1975). Ganglionic stimulation and blocking agents. In L. S. Goodman & A. Gillman (Eds.), *The pharmacological basis of therapeutics*. New York: Macmillan.

Volpicelli, J. R. (1987). Uncontrollable events and alcohol drinking [Special Issue: Psychology and addiction]. *British Journal of Addiction, 82,* 381–392.

Volpicelli, J. R., Tiven, J., & Kimmel, S. C. (1982). The relationship between tension reduction and ethanol consumption in rats. *Physiological Psychology, 10*(1), 114–116.

Von Korff, M., Nestadt, G., Romanoski, A., Anthony, J., Eaton, W., Merchant, A., Chahal, R., Kramer, M., Folstein, M., & Gruenberg, E. (1985). Prevalence of treated and untreated *DSM-III* schizophrenia: Results of a two-stage community survey. *Journal of Nervous and Mental Disease, 173,* 577–581.

Vonnegut, M. (1975). *The Eden Express.* New York: Praeger.

Wachtel, E. F., & Wachtel, P. L. (1986). *Family dynamics in individual psychotherapy: A guide to clinical strategies.* New York: Guilford.

Wachtel, P. (1977). *Psychoanalysis and behavior therapy.* New York: Basic Books.

Wachtel, P. L. (1982). Vicious circles: The self and the rhetoric of emerging and unfolding. *Contemporary Psychoanalysis, 18,* 259–273.

Waldhauser, F., Saletu, B., & Trinchard, L. I. (1990). Sleep laboratory investigations on hypnotic properties of melatonin. *Psychopharmacology, 100,* 222–226.

Wallace, C. J., & Liberman, R. P. (1985). Social skills training for patients with schizophrenia: A controlled clinical trial. *Psychiatry Research, 15,* 239–247.

Wallace, R. K., & Benson, H. (1972). The physiology of meditation. *Scientific American, 226,* 84–90.

Wallach, H., & Slaughter, V. (1988). The role of memory in perceiving subjective contours. *Perception and Psychophysics, 43,* 101–106.

Waller, N. G., Kojetin, B. A., Bouchard, T. J., & Lykken, D. T. (1990). Genetic and environmental influences on religious interests, attitudes, and values: A study of twins reared apart and together. *Psychological Science, 1,* 138–142.

Wallerstein, J. S., & Blakeslee, S. (1989). *Second chances: Men, women, and children a decade after divorce.* New York: Ticknor & Fields.

Walster, E., Aronson, V., Abrahams, D., & Rottman, L. (1966). Importance of physical attractiveness in dating behavior. *Journal of Personality and Social Psychology, 4,* 508–516.

Warr, P. (1978). Study of psychological well-being. *British Journal of Psychology, 69,* 111–121.

Warrington, E. K., & Weiskrantz, L. (1970). Amnesic syndrome: Consolidation or retrieval? *Nature, 228,* 629–630.

Warrington, E. K., & Weiskrantz, L. (1982). Amnesia: A disconnection syndrome. *Neuropsychologia, 20,* 233–249.

Wason, P., & Johnson-Laird, P. N. (1972). *Psychology of reasoning: Structure and content.* Cambridge, MA: Harvard University Press.

Waters, E., Wippman, J., & Sroufe, L. A. (1979). Attachment, positive affect, and competence in the peer group: Two studies in construct validation. *Child Development, 50,* 821–829.

Watson, D., & Clark, L. A. (1994). Emotions, moods, traits, and temperaments: Conceptual distinctions and empirical findings. In P. Ekman & R. J. Davidson (Eds.), *The nature of emotion* (pp. 89–93). New York: Oxford University Press.

Watson, D., Clark, L. A., & Tellegen, A. (1988). Development and validation of brief measures of positive and negative affect: The PANAS Scales. *Journal of Personality and Social Psychology, 54,* 1063–1070.

Watson, D., & Tellegen, A. (1985). Toward a consensual structure of mood. *Psychological Bulletin, 98,* 219–235.

Watson, J. B. (1924). *Behaviorism.* New York: People's Institute.

Watson, J. B. (1928). *Psychological care of the infant and child.* New York: Norton.

Watson, J. B., & Rayner, R. (1920). Conditioned emotional reactions. *Journal of Experimental Psychology, 3,* 1–14.

Watson, J. S. (1972). Smiling, cooing, and "the game." *Merrill-Palmer Quarterly of Behavior and Development, 18,* 323–339.

Wattenmaker, W. D., Dewey, G. I., Murphy, T. D., & Medin, D. L. (1986). Linear separability and concept learning: Context, relational properties, and concept naturalness. *Cognitive Psychology, 18,* 158–194.

Weaver, C. A., III. (1993). Do you need a "flash" to form a flashbulb memory? *Journal of Experimental Psychology: General, 122,* 39–46.

Weaver, C. A., III. (1994). Reading. In V. S. Ramachandran (Ed.), *The encyclopedia of human behavior* (pp. 1–8). San Diego: Academic Press.

Weaver, C. A., III. (1995). The search for "special mechanisms" in memory: Flashbulbs, flashbacks, and other not-so-bright ideas. *False Memory Syndrome Newsletter, 4,* 16–22.

Weaver, C. A., III, & Bryant, D. S. (1995). Monitoring of comprehension: The role of text difficulty in metamemory for narrative and expository text. *Memory and Cognition, 23,* 12–22.

Weaver, C. A., III, Bryant, D. S., & Burns, K. D. (1995). Comprehension monitoring: Extensions of the Kintsch and van Dijk Model. In C. A. Weaver, III, S. Mannes, & C. R. Fletcher (Eds.), *Discourse comprehension: Essays in honor of Walter Kintsch.* Hillsdale, NJ: Erlbaum.

Weaver, C. A., III, & Kintsch, W. (1992). Enhancing students' comprehension of the conceptual structure of algebra word problems. *Journal of Educational Psychology, 84,* 419–428.

Weaver, C. A., III, Mannes, S., & Fletcher, C. R. (Eds.). (1995). *Discourse comprehension: Essays in honor of Walter Kintsch.* Hillsdale, NJ: Erlbaum.

Webb, W. B. (1975). *Sleep: The gentle tyrant.* Englewood Cliffs, NJ: Prentice Hall.

Weber, R., & Crocker, J. (1983). Cognitive processes in the revision of stereotypic beliefs. *Journal of Personality and Social Psychology, 45,* 961–977.

Wechsler, D. (1949). *Wechsler Intelligence Scale for Children.* New York: Psychological Corporation.

Wechsler, D. (1955). *Wechsler Adult Intelligence Scale Manual.* New York: Psychological Corporation.

Wechsler, D. (1967). *Wechsler Preschool and Primary Scale of Intelligence.* New York: Psychological Corporation.

Wechsler, D. (1974). *The measurement and appraisal of adult intelligence.* Baltimore: Williams & Wilkins.

Wechsler, D. (1981). *Manual for the Wechsler Adult Intelligence Scale-revised.* New York: Psychological Corporation.

Wechsler, D. (1991). *WISC-III manual.* San Antonio: Psychological Corporation (Harcourt Brace).

Wegman, M. E. (1986). Annual summary of vital statistics—1985. *Pediatrics, 79,* 817–827.

Wegner, D. M., Schneider, D. J., Carter, S. R., & White, T. L. (1987). Paradoxical effects of thought suppression. *Journal of Personality and Social Psychology, 53*(1), 513.

Wehr, T. A., Sack, D. A., & Rosenthal, N. E. (1987). Seasonal affective disorder with summer depression and winter hypomania. *American Journal of Psychiatry, 144,* 1602–1603.

Weiner, B. (1985). An attributional theory of achievement motivation and emotion. *Psychological Review, 92,* 548–573.

Weinstein, N. D. (1980). Unrealistic optimism about future life events. *Journal of Personality and Social Psychology, 39,* 806–820.

Weinstein, N. D. (1982). Unrealistic optimism about susceptibility to health problems. *Journal of Behavioral Medicine, 5,* 441–460.

Weinstein, N. D. (1989). Effects of personal experience on self-protective behavior. *Psychological Bulletin, 105*(1), 31–50.

Weinstein, S. (1968). Intensive and extensive aspects of tactile sensitivity as a function of body part, sex, and laterality. In D. R. Kenshalo (Ed.), *The skin senses.* Springfield, IL: Thomas.

Weintraub, M., & Evans, P. (1989). Clozapine: A neuroleptic agent for selected schizophrenics and patients with tardive dyskinesia. *Hospital Formulary, 24,* 16–27.

Weisberg, R. W. (1986). *Creativity: Genius and other myths.* New York: W. H. Freeman.

Weisenberg, M. (1977). Pain and pain control. *Psychological Bulletin, 84,* 1008–1044.

Weisenberg, T., & McBride, K. E. (1935). *Aphasia: A clinical and psychological study.* New York: Commonwealth Fund.

Weishaar, M. E., & Beck, A. T. (1992). Clinical and cognitive predictors of suicide. In R. W. Maris, A. L. Berman, J. T. Maltsberger, & R. I. Yufit (Eds.), *Assessment and prediction of suicide* (pp. 467–483). New York: Guilford.

Weiskrantz, L. (1986). *Blindsight: A case study and implications.* New York: Oxford University Press.

Weiskrantz, L. (1995). Blindsight: Not an island into itself. *Current Directions in Psychological Science, 4,* 146–151.

Weisner, C., Greenfield, T., & Room, R. (1995). Trends in the treatment of alcohol problems in the U. S. population. *American Journal of Public Health, 85,* 1979–1990, 1955–1960.

Weitzman, E. D. (1981). Sleep and its disorders. *Annual Review of Neurosciences, 4,* 381–417.

Wellman, H., Collins, J., & Glieberman, J. (1981). Understanding the combination of memory variables: Developing conceptions of memory limitations. *Child Development, 52,* 1313–1317.

Wellman, H. M. (1987). The early development of memory strategies. In F. Weinert & M. Perlmutter (Eds.), *Memory development: Universal changes and individual differences.* Hillsdale, NJ: Erlbaum.

Wender, P. H., Kety, S. S., Rosenthal, D., Schulsinger, F., Ortman, J., & Lunde, I. (1986). Psychiatric disorders in the biological and adaptive families of adaptive individuals with affective disorders. *Archives of General Psychiatry, 43,* 923–929.

Wenzlaff, R. M., & Grozier, S. A. (1988). Depression and the magnification of failure. *Journal of Abnormal Psychology, 97,* 90–93.

Werner, E. E. (1987). Vulnerability and resiliency in childhood at risk for delinquency: A longitudinal study from birth to young adulthood. In J. D. Burchard & S. M. Burchard (Eds.), *Prevention of delinquent behavior* (pp. 68–84). Beverly Hills: Sage.

Werner, E. E. (1995). Resilience in development. *Current Directions in Psychological Science, 4,* 81–85.

Werner, H., & Siqueland, E. R. (1978). Visual recognition memory in the preterm infant. *Infant Behavior and Development, 1,* 79–94.

Westefeld, J. S., & Furr, S. R. (1987). Suicide and depression among college students. *Professional Psychology: Research and Practice, 18,* 119–123.

Westen, D., Ludolph, P., Lerner, H., & Ruffins, S. (1990). Object relations in borderline adolescents. *Journal of* the American Academy of Child and Adolescent Psychiatry, 29, 338–348.

Wetzler, S. (1985). Mood state-dependent retrieval: A failure to replicate. Psychological Reports, 65, 759–765.

Wetzler, S. E., & Sweeney, J. A. (1986). Childhood amnesia: An empirical demonstration. In D. Rubin (Ed.), Autobiographical memory. New York: Cambridge University Press.

Wever, E. G., & Bray, C. W. (1937). The perception of low tones and the resonance-volley theory. Journal of Psychology, 3, 101–114.

Wever, R. A. (1979). The circadian systems of man. Andechs: Max-Planck-Institut für Verhaltensphysiologie.

White, R. W. (1959). Motivation reconsidered: The concept of competence. Psychological Review, 66, 297–333.

White, S. H., & Pillemer, D. B. (1979). Childhood amnesia and the development of a socially accessible memory system. In J. F. Kihlstrom & F. J. Evans (Eds.), Functional disorders of memory (pp. 29–73). Hillsdale, NJ: Erlbaum.

Whitley, B. E., Jr., & Frieze, I. H. (1985). Children's causal attributions for success or failure in achievement settings: A meta-analysis. Journal of Education Psychology, 77, 608–616.

Whitlock, F. A. (1986). Suicide and physical illness. In A. Roy (Ed.), Suicide. Baltimore: Williams & Wilkins.

Whorf, B. L. (1956). Science and linguistics. In J. B. Carroll (Ed.), Language, thought, and reality: Selected writings of Benjamin Lee Whorf (pp. 207–219). Cambridge, MA: MIT Press.

Whybrow, P. C., Akisal, H. S., & McKinney, W. T., Jr. (1984). Mood disorders: Toward a new psychobiology. New York: Plenum Press.

Wicker, A. W. (1969). Attitudes versus action: The relationship of verbal and overt behavioral responses to attitude objects. Journal of Social Issues, 25, 41–43.

Widom, C. S. (1989). Does violence beget violence? A critical examination of the literature. Psychological Bulletin, 106, 3–28.

Widom, C. S. (1991a). Avoidance of criminality in abused and neglected children. Psychiatry, 54, 162–174.

Widom, C. S. (1991b). Childhood victimization: Risk factor for delinquency. In M. E. Colten & S. Gore (Eds.), Adolescent stress: Causes and consequences. Social institutions and social change. (pp. 201–221). New York: Aldine de Gruyter.

Widroe, H. J., & Heisler, S. (1976). Treatment of tardive dyskinesia. Diseases of the Nervous System, 37, 162–164.

Wiener, H. (1966). External chemical messengers 1: Emission and reception in man. New York State Journal of Medicine, 66, 3153–3170.

Wilder, D. A. (1990). Some determinants of the persuasive power of in-groups and out-groups: Organization of information and attribution of independence. Journal of Personality and Social Psychology, 59, 1203–1213.

Williams, L. M. (1994a). Recall of childhood trauma: A prospective study of women's memories of child sexual abuse. Journal of Consulting and Clinical Psychology, 62, 1167–1176.

Williams, L. M. (1994b). What does it mean to forget child sexual abuse? A reply to Loftus, Garry, and Feldman (1994). Journal of Consulting and Clinical Psychology, 62, 1182–1186.

Williams, L. M. (1995). Recovered memories of abuse in women with documented child sexual victimization histories [Special Issue: Research on traumatic memory]. Journal of Traumatic Stress, 8, 649–673.

Williams, M. (1996, July 6). Associated Press, reprinted in Tribune-Herald, pp. 1.

Williamson, D. A., Davis, C. J., Goreczny, A. J., & Blouin, D. C. (1988). Body-image disturbances in bulimia nervosa: Influences of actual body size. Journal of Abnormal Psychology, 98, 87–99.

Williamson, D. F. (1993). Descriptive epidemiology of body weight and weight change in U.S. adults. Annals of Internal Medicine, 119, 646–649.

Williamson, D. F., Kahn, H. S., Remington, P. L., & Anda, R. F. (1990). The 10-year incidence of overweight and weight gain in US adults. Archives of Internal Medicine, 150, 665–672.

Wills, T. A. (1981). Downward comparison principles in social psychology. Psychological Bulletin, 90, 245–271.

Wilson, E. O. (1975). Sociobiology: The new synthesis. Cambridge, MA: Harvard University Press.

Wilson, E. O. (1978). On human nature. Cambridge, MA: Harvard University Press.

Wilson, E. O. (1996). In search of nature. Washington, DC: Island Press.

Wilson, G. (1978). Introversion/extroersion. In J. E. Exner (Ed.), Dimensions of personality (pp. 217–261). London & New York: Wiley.

Wilson, G. T. (1982). From experimental research to clinical practice: Behavior therapy as a case study. In R. M. Adams, N. J. Smelser, & D. J. Treiman (Eds.), Behavioral and social science research: A national resource (Part II). Washington, DC: National Academy Press.

Wilson, G. T. (1987). Chemical aversion conditioning as a treatment for alcoholism: A re-analysis. Behaviour Research and Therapy, 25, 503–516.

Winnicott, D. W. (1965). The family and individual development. London: Tavistock.

Winningham, R., Hyman, I. E., Jr., & Dinnel, D. (1996, November). *Flashbulb memories? Recollections of O. J. Simpson's acquittal.* Paper presented at the 37th Annual Meeting of the Psychonomic Society., Chicago.

Winograd, E., & Killinger, W. A. (1983). Relating age at encoding in early childhood to adult recall: Development of flashbulb memories. *Journal of Experimental Psychology: General, 112,* 413–422.

Winograd, E., & Soloway, R. (1986). On forgetting the location of things stored in special places. *Journal of Experimental Psychology: General, 115,* 366–372.

Winters, K. C., Newmark, C. S., Lumry, A. E., Leach, K., & Weintraub, S. (1985). MMPI code-types characteristic of *DSM-III* schizophrenics, depressives, and bipolars. *Journal of Clinical Psychology, 41,* 382–386.

Wise, R. A., & Rompre, P. P. (1989). Brain dopamine and reward. *Annual Review of Psychology, 40,* 191–225.

Witte, K. (1992). Putting the fear back into fear appeals: The extended parallel process model. *Communication Monographs, 59,* 329–349.

Wittgenstein, L. (1922/1963). *Tractatus logico-philosophicus.* New York: Humanities Press.

Wolff, P. H. (1969). The natural history of crying and other vocalizations in early infancy. In B. M. Foss (Ed.), *Determinants of infant behavior* (Vol. 4). London: Methuen.

Wolpe, J. (1958). *Psychotherapy by reciprocal inhibition.* Stanford, CA: Stanford University Press.

Wolpe, J. (1973). *The practice of behavior therapy* (2nd ed.). Elmsford, NY: Pergamon Press.

Wolpe, J. (1976). *Theme and variations: A behavior therapy casebook.* Elmsford, NY: Pergamon Press.

Wolpe, J. (1990). *The practice of behav-ior therapy.* New York: Pergamon Press.

Wong, D. F., Wagner, H. N., Jr., Tune, L. E., Dannals, R. F., Pearlson, G. D., Links, J. M., Tamminga, C. A., Broussolle, E. P., Ravert, H. A., Wilson, A. A., Toung, J. K. T., Malat, J., Williams, J. A., O'Tuama, L. A., Snyder, S. H., Kuhar, M. J., & Gjedde, A. (1986). Positron emission tomography reveals elevated D5/82 dopamine receptors in drug-naive schizophrenics. *Science, 234,* 1558–1563.

Wood, G. (1983). *Cognitive psychology: A skills approach.* Monterey, CA: Brooks/Cole.

Wood, J. M., Nezworski, M. T., & Stejskal, W. J. (1996a). The comprehensive scoring system for the Rorschach: A critical examination. *Psychological Science, 7,* 3–10.

Wood, J. M., Nezworski, M. T., & Stejskal, W. J. (1996b). Thinking critically about the comprehensive system for the Rorschach: A reply to Exner. *Psychological Science, 7,* 14–16.

Wood, L. F., & Jacobson, N. S. (1985). Marital distress. In D. H. Barlow (Ed.), *Clinical handbook of psychological disorders.* New York: Guilford.

Wood, W., Wong, F. Y., & Chachere, J. G. (1991). Effects of media violence on viewers' aggression in unconstrained social interactions. *Psychological Bulletin, 109,* 371–383.

Woods, P. J. (Ed.). (1988). *Is psychology for them? A guide to undergraduate advising.* Washington, DC: American Psychological Association.

Worringham, D. J., & Messick, D. M. (1983). Social facilitation of running: An unobtrusive study. *Journal of Social Psychology, 121,* 23–29.

Wortman, C. B., & Dunkel-Schetter, C. (1979). Interpersonal relationships and cancer: A theoretical analysis. *Journal of Social Issues, 35,* 120–154.

Wortman, C. B., & Lehman, D. R. (1985). Reactions to victims of life crises: Support attempts that fail. In I. G. Sarason & B. R. Sarason (Eds.), *Social support: Theory, research, and applications.* Dordrecht, Netherlands: Martinus Nijhoff.

Wortman, C. B., Silver, R. C., & Kessler, R. C. (1993). The meaning of loss and adjustment to bereavement. In M. S. Stroebe, W. Stroebe, & R. O. Hansson (Eds.), *Bereavement: A sourcebook of research and intervention.* London: Cambridge University Press.

Wright, L. (1988). The Type A behavior pattern and coronary heart disease. *American Psychologist, 43,* 2–14.

Wundt, W. (1904). *Principles of physiological psychology.* New York: Macmillan. (Original work published 1874).

Wyer, R. S., Jr., & Srull, T. K. (1986). Human cognition in its social context. *Psychological Review, 93,* 322–359.

Wyer, R. S., & Srull, T. K. (1989). *Memory and cognition in its social context.* Hillsdale, NJ: Erlbaum.

Yalom, I. D. (1989). *Love's executioner, and other tales of psychotherapy.* New York: Basic Books.

Yerkes, R. M., & Dodson, J. D. (1908). The relationship of strength of stimulus to the rapidity of habit formation. *Journal of Comparative Neurology and Psychology, 18,* 459–482.

Youngblade, L. M., & Belsky, J. (1989). Child maltreatment, infant-parent attachment, security, and dysfunctional peer relationships in toddlerhood. *Topics in Early Childhood Special Education, 9,* 1–15.

Yussan, S. R., & Berman, L. (1981). Memory predictions for recall and recognition in first, third, and fifth grade children. *Developmental Psychology, 17,* 224–229.

Zaccaro, S. J. (1984). Social loafing: The role of task attractiveness.

Personality and Social Psychology Bulletin, 10, 99–106.

Zajonc, R. B. (1965). Social facilitation. *Science, 149*, 269–274.

Zajonc, R. B. (1966). *Social psychology: An experimental approach.* Belmont, CA: Wadsworth.

Zajonc, R. B. (1968). Attitudinal effects of mere exposure. *Journal of Personality and Social Psychology Monograph Supplement, 9*, 1–27.

Zajonc, R. B., Murphy, S. T., & Inglehart, M. (1989). Feeling and facial efference: Implications of the vascular theory of emotion. *Psychological Review, 99*, 395–416.

Zanna, M. P., & Hamilton, D. L. (1977). Further evidence for meaning change in impression formation. *Journal of Experimental Social Psychology, 13*, 224–238.

Zanna, M. P., & Rempel, J. K. (1988). Attitudes: A new look at an old concept. In D. Bar-Tal & A. Kruglanski (Eds.), *The social psychology of knowledge.* New York: Cambridge University Press.

Zax, M., & Stricker, G. (1963). *Patterns of psychopathology.* New York: Macmillan.

Zeki, S. (1980). Representation of colours in the cerebral cortex. *Nature, 284*, 412–418.

Zigler, E., & Lang, M. E. (1991). *Child care choices: Balancing the needs of children, families, and society.* New York: Free Press.

Zigler, E., & Styfco, S. J. (1993). *Head Start and beyond: A national plan for extended childhood intervention.* New Haven, CT: Yale University Press.

Zilbergeld, B. (1983). *The shrinking of America: Myths of behavioral change.* Boston: Little, Brown.

Zill, N. (1988). Behavior, achievement, and health problems among children in stepfamilies: Findings from a national survey of child health. In E. M. Hetherington & J. D. Arasteh (Eds.), *Impact of divorce, single parenting, and stepparenting on children* (pp. 325–368). Hillsdale, NJ: Erlbaum.

Zillman, D. (1983). Arousal and aggression. In R. G. Geen & E. Donnerstein (Eds.), *Aggression: Theoretical and empirical review.* New York: Academic Press.

Zillman, D., & Bryant, J. (1984). Effects of massive exposure to pornography. In N. M. Malamuth & E. I. Donnerstein (Eds.), *Pornography and social aggression* (pp. 115–138). New York: Academic Press.

Zimbardo, P. G. (1975). Transforming experimental research into advocacy for social change. In M. Deutsch & H. Hornstein (Eds.), *Applying social psychology: Implications for research, practice, and training.* Hillsdale, NJ: Erlbaum.

Zimbardo, P. G., Anderson, S. M., & Kabat, L. G. (1981). Paranoia and deafness: An experimental investigation. *Science, 212*, 1529–1531.

Zimbardo, P. G., Haney, C., & Banks, W. C. (1973, April 18). A Pirandellian prison. *New York Times Magazine*, 38–60.

Zimbardo, P. G., Haney, C., Banks, W. C., & Jaffe, D. (1972). *The psychology of imprisonment: Privation, power, and pathology.* Unpublished paper, Stanford University.

Zimbardo, P. G., & Leippe, M. R. (1991). *The psychology of attitude change and social influence.* New York: McGraw-Hill.

Zimbardo, P. G., Petersen, S. M., & Kabat, L. G. (1981). Paranoia and deafness: An experimental investigation. *Science, 212*, 1529–1531.

Zola-Morgan, S., Squire, L., & Mishkin, M. (1982). The neuroanatomy of amnesia: Amygdala-hippocampus versus temporal stem. *Science, 218*, 1337–1339.

Zubin, J., & Spring, B. (1977). Vulnerability—a new view of schizophrenia. *Journal of Abnormal Psychology, 86*, 103–126.

Zuckerman, M. (1960). The effects of subliminal and supraliminal suggestions on verbal productivity. *Journal of Abnormal and Social Psychology, 60*, 404–411.

Zuckerman, M. (1975). Belief in a just world and altruistic behavior. *Journal of Personality and Social Psychology, 31*, 972–976.

Zuckerman, M. (1991). *Psychobiology of personality.* Cambridge, England: Cambridge University Press.

Zuckerman, M. (1994a). An alternative five factor model for personality: The big three, the big five, and the alternative five. In C. F. Halverson, G. A. Kohnstamm, & R. P. Martin (Eds.), *The developing structure of temperament and personality from infancy to adulthood* (pp. 53–68). Hillsdale, NJ: Erlbaum.

Zuckerman, M. (1994b). *Behavioral expressions and the biosocial bases of sensation seeking.* New York: Cambridge University Press.

Zuckerman, M. (1994c). Good and bad humors: Biochemical bases of personality and its disorders. *Psychological Science, 6*, 325–332.

Zuckerman, M., Kuhlman, D. M., Joireman, J., Teta, P., & Kraft, M. (1994). A comparison of three structural models for personality: The big three, the big five, and the alternative five. *Journal of Personality and Social Psychology, 65*, 757–768.

Zuckerman, M., & Lubin, B. (1985). *Manual for Multiple Affect Adjective Check List—Revised.* San Diego, CA: Educational and Industrial Testing Service.

Zullow, H. M., Oettingen, G., Peterson, C., & Seligman, M. E. P. (1988). Pessimistic explanatory style in the historical record. *American Psychologist, 43*, 673–682.

CREDITS

Photo Credits

Photo research by Elyse Rieder

p. 5: Court TV. p. 7: AP/Wide World. p. 8: AP/Wide World. p. 9: Courtesy Dr. Maggie Bruck, Dept. of Psychology, McGill University. p. 11: By courtesy of the National Portrait Gallery, London. p. 15: Archives of the History of American Psychology, University of Akron, Ohio. p. 16: Corbis-Bettmann. p. 17: Corbis-Bettmann. p. 19 (left): Corbis-Bettmann. p. 19 (right): Archives of the History of American Psychology, University of Akron, Ohio. p. 20: National Library of Medicine. p. 20: Courtesy of B. F. Skinner Foundation. p. 21: Corbis-Bettmann. p. 22: Courtesy Carl Rogers Memorial Library. p. 22: Corbis-Bettmann. p. 23: Corbis-Bettmann. p. 25: © Bob Kramer/Picture Cube. p. 29: © M. Greenlar/Image Works. p. 41: © Billy E. Barnes/Photo Edit. p. 46: © Jeff Greenberg/Picture Cube. p. 48 (left): Bentley-Kemp. p. 48 (right): © Gary A. Conner/Photo Edit. p. 49: © Jeff Greenberg/Picture Cube. p. 52: © M. Richards/Photo Edit. p. 56: © Ed Malitsky/Liaison International. p. 58: © T. K. Wanstal/Image Works. p. 64: Courtesy Stanley Milgram. p. 65: AT&T Archives. p. 67: © Stephen McBrady/Photo Edit. p. 69: © Peter Smith/Gamma-Liaison. p. 76: Warren Anatomical Museum, Harvard Medical School. p. 77: © Sovfoto. p. 79: © Petit Format/Science Source/Photo Researchers. p. 85: © John Allison/Peter Arnold. p. 87: Everett Collection. p. 88: © Leinwand/Monkmeyer. p. 89: © Gerard Vandystadt/Photo Researchers. p. 91 (left): © A. Glauberman/Photo Researchers. p. 91 (middle right): © Pat Lynch/Photo Researchers. p. 91: © A. Glauberman/Photo Researchers.

p. 93: © Frank Siteman/Stock, Boston. p. 95: © Image Works. p. 97: © Steve Gooch/The Daily Oklahoman/SABA. p. 98 (left): © A. Glauberman/Photo Researchers. p. 98 (right): © A. Glauberman/Photo Researchers. p. 108 (top): Corbis-Bettmann. p. 108 (bottom): Amos Nachoum/Liaison International. p. 109: © Photo Works. p. 111: © Joseph Nettis/Science Source/Photo Researchers. p. 118: © Yvonne Hemsey/Gamma Liaison. p. 121: The Fine Arts Museum of San Francisco, Museum purchase, William H. Noble Bequest Fund, 1979.48. p. 125 (all): p. 127: © Rogers/Monkmeyer. p. 134: © Phil McCarten/Photo Edit. p. 135: © Peter Menzel/Stock, Boston. p. 142: © Richard T. Nowitz/Photo Researchers. p. 143: (After Gregory, 1970). p. 147: © Photo Works. p. 157: © Rick Browne/Stock, Boston. p. 158: © Will & Deni McIntyre/Photo Researchers. p. 161: © Siteman/Monkmeyer. p. 163: © Allan Hobson/Science Source/Photo Researchers. p. 165: © Crosby/Gamma Liaison. p. 166: © M. Siluk/Image Works. p. 167: Freud Museum, London/Sigmund Freud Copyrights. p. 168: © Drew Crawford/Image Works. p. 169: © Paula A. Scully/Gamma Liaison. p. 173: © Eric Ilasenko/Gamma Liaison. p. 174: UPI/Bettmann. p. 174: © Cary Wolinsky/Stock, Boston. p. 176: © Lawrence Migdale/Photo Researchers. p. 190 (top): © George White Location Photography. p. 190 (bottom): © Network Pro/Image Works. p. 192: © Gamma Liaison. p. 194: © D. Young-Wolff/Photo Edit. p. 195 (left): © Shackman/Monkmeyer. p. 195 (right): © Bob Daemmrich/Stock, Boston. p. 198: © Science Source/Photo Researchers.

p. 203: © M. Granitsas/Image Works. p. 205: © John Chiasson/Gamma-Liaison. p. 208: © Fritz Hoffman/Image Works. p. 209: © Gerald Davis/Woodfin Camp. p. 218: AP/Wide World Photos. p. 221 (top): © Paul Stepan/Photo Researchers. p. 221 (bottom): © Kolvoord/Image Works. p. 224: © Mark Richards/Photo Edit. p. 226: © Warner Bros. p. 230: © Tom McCarthy/Photo Edit. p. 232: © John Coletti/Picture Cube. p. 239: Myung Chun/AP/Wide World Photos. p. 241: © Rhoda Sidney/Stock Boston. p. 248: © Esbin-Anderson/Image Works. p. 251: © Shahn Kermani Gamma-Liaison p. 258: Courtesy of NASA. p. 260: Michael Gilmartin. p. 266: © Jon Levy/Gamma-Liaison. p. 269: © Fujifotos/Image Works. p. 270: Frances M. Roberts. p. 271: Australian Consolidated Press Ltd. p. 274: Steve C. Wilson/AP/Wide World Photos. p. 275: © Sidney/Monkmeyer. p. 281 (top): © Jeff Greenberg/Photo Researchers. p. 281 (bottom): John Running. p. 281: © David Lissy/Picture Cube. p. 283: Elizabeth Pugh Language Researcher Center, Georgia State University. p. 294: AP/Wide World Photos. p. 296: Courtesy John Watson. p. 297: © Margaret Miller/Photo Researchers. p. 300: © E. Crews/Image Works. p. 302: © Goodman/Monkmeyer. p. 303: © Goodman/Monkmeyer. p. 307: © Dorothy Freeman/PhotoEdit. p. 311: © Forsyth/Monkmeyer. p. 312: © Ullmann/Monkmeyer. p. 314: © Bob Daemmrich/Image Works. p. 317: © Laura Dwight/PhotoEdit. p. 318: © Kopstein/Monkmeyer. p. 320: © Merrim/Monkmeyer. p. 323: © Yvonne Hemsey/Gamma-Liaison. p. 332: © Jeff Greenberg/Image Works.

Text and Line Art

p. 71: quotation from Banaji, M.R., & Crowder, R. C. (1989). The bankruptcy of everyday memory. *American Psychologist, 44,* 1185–1193. Copyright © 1989 by the American Psychological Association. Reprinted with permission of American Psychological Association. **Pp. 71-72:** quotation from Roediger, H.L. III (1991). They read an article? A comment on the everyday memory controversy. *American Psychologist, 46,* 37–40. Copyright © 1991 by the American Psychological Association. Reprinted with permission of American Psychological Association. / **p. 99 Fig. 3-13:** Penfield, W., & Rasmussen, T. (1978). *The cerebral cortex of man.* Copyright 1950 Macmillan Publishing Company; copyright renewed 1978 Theodore Rasmussen. Reprinted by permission of Simon & Schuster. **p. 102, Fig. 3-15:** Springer, S. P., & Deutsch, G. (1993). *Left Brain, Right Brain,* 4th edition. Reprinted by permission of W. H. Freeman & Co. **p. 103, Table 3-3:** Kolb, B., & Whishaw, I.Q. (1990). *Fundamentals of human neuropyschology,* 3rd edition, 373. Reprinted by permission of W. H. Freeman & Co. / **p. 109, Fig. 4-1:** Hefner, R. S., & Hefner, H. E. (1983). Hearing in large & small dogs: Absolute thresholds and size of the tympanic membrane. *Behavioral Neuroscience, 97,* 310–318. Copyright © 1983 by the American Psychological Association. Reprinted with permission of American Psychological Association and the author. **p. 113, Table 4-1:** Teghtsoonian, R. (1971). On the exponents in Stevens' Law and the constant in Ekman's Law. *Psychological Review, 78,* 71–80. Copyright © 1971 by the American Psychological Association. Reprinted with permission of American Psychological Association and the author. **pp. 128 & 133, Figs. 4-12 & 4-14:** Sekuler, R., & Blake, R. (1990). *Perception,* 297 & 395. Reprinted by permission of McGraw-Hill Publishing Company. **p. 133, Fig. 4-15:** Weinstein, S. (1968). Intensive and extensive aspects of tactile sensitivity as a function of body part, sex and laterality. In D. R. Kenshalo (ed.), *The Skin Senses.* Courtesy of Charles C. Thomas Publisher, Ltd., Springfield, IL. **p. 139, Fig. 4-20:** Wallace, H., & Slaughter, V. (1988). The role of memory in perceiving subjective contours. *Perception and Psychophysics, 43,*101–106. Reprinted by permission of Psychonomic Society, Inc. **p. 140, Fig. 4-23:** Sekuler, R., & Blake, R. (1990). *Perception,* 242. Reprinted by permission of McGraw-Hill Publishing Company. **p. 143, Fig. 4-27:** Gregory, R. L. (1970). *The Intelligent Eye.* Reprinted by permission of McGraw-Hill Publishing Company. **p. 145, Fig. 4-28:** Biederman, I., Mazzanotte, R. J., & Rabinowitz, J. C. (1982). Scene perception: Detecting and judging objects udnergoing relational violations. *Cognitive Psychology, 14,* 143–177. Reprinted by permission of John Wiley & Sons. / **p. 154:** quotation from Flynn, J. C. (1991). *Cocaine,* 1–6. New York: Birch Lane Press. Reprinted by permission of Carroll Publishing. **p. 158, Fig. 5-1:** Hauri, P. J. (1982). *The Sleep Disorders,* 2nd edition. Kalamazoo: Upjohn Corp. Reprinted by permission of Peter J. Hauri, Sleep Disorder Center, Mayo Clinic, Rochester, MN. **p. 170, Fig. 5-4:** *U. S. News & World Report* (1983). How alcohol affects driving a car. *U.S. News & World Report,* April, 4:74. Reprinted by permission of U.S. News & World Report. **p. 181:** Quotaton from Lieberman, P. (1991). *Uniquely human: The evolution of speech, thought, and selfless behavior.* Copyright © 1991 by the President and Fellows of Harvard College. Reprinted by permission of Harvard University Press, Cambridge, MA. / **p. 183:** quotation from Goodall, J. (1987). In *The Mind* (PBS TV series). Reprinted by permission of Dr. Jane Goodall, The Jane Goodall Institute. **p. 208, Table 6-1:** Barker, L.M. (1997). *Learning and behavior: Biological, psychological, and sociocultural perspectives,* 2nd edition, 322–326. Reprinted by permission of Prentice Hall, Inc. **p. 211, Fig. 6-14:** Garcia, J., & Koelling, R. A. (1996). Relation of cue to consequence in avoidance learning. *Psychonomic Science, 4,* 123-124. Reprinted by permission of Psychonomic Society, Inc., and the author. / **p. 222, Fig. 7-4:** Bahrick, H. P., & Phelps, E. (1987). Retention of Spanish vocabulary over eight years. *Journal of Experimental Psychology: General, 13,* 344–349. Reprinted by permission of the author. **p. 223, Fig. 7-5:** Atkinson, R. C., & Shriffin, R. M. (1968). Human memory: A proposed system and its control. In K. W. Spence & J. T. Spence (Eds.), *The psychology of learning and motivation* (Vol. 2). Reprinted by permission of Academic Press and the author. **p. 229, Fig. 7-10:** Nickerson, R. S., & Adams, M. J. (1982). Long-term memory for a common object. In U. Neisser (Ed.), *Memory Observed,* 163–175. Reprinted by permission of W.H. Freeman & Co. **p. 231, Fig. 7-11:** Stroop, J. R. (1935). Studies of interference in serial verbal reactions. *Journal of Experimental Psychology, 18,* 643–662. Copyright © 1935 by The American Psychological Association. Reprinted by permission. **p. 233, Table 7-1:** Loftus, E. F., & Palmer, J. C. (1974). Reconstruction of automobile destruction: An example of the interaction between language and memory. *Journal of verbal learning and verbal behavior, 13,* 585–589. Reprinted by permission of author. **p. 237, Fig. 7-14:** Tulving, E. (1985). How many memory systems are there? *American Psychologist, 40,* 385–398. Copyright © 1985 by The American Psychological Association. Reprinted by permission of author. **p. 240, Fig. 7-15:** Rubin, D. (1986). *Autobiographical memory.*

Reprinted by permission of Cambridge University Press. **p. 241:** quotation from Neisser, U., & Harsh, N. (1992). Phantom flashbulbs: False recollections of hearing the news about the *Challenger.* In E. Winograd & U. Neisser (Eds.), *Affect and accuracy in recall: Studies of "flashbulb memory,"* 9–31. Reprinted by permission of Cambridge University Press. **p. 242:** quotation from Bransford, J. D., & Johnson, M. K. (1972). Contextual prerequisites for understanding: Some investigations of comprehension and recall. *Journal of Verbal Learning & Verbal Behavior, 11,* 717–726. **p. 243, Fig. 7-16:** Allport, G. W., & Postman, L. J. (1947). *The Psychology of Rumor.* Reprinted by permission of Henry Holt & Company. **p. 246:** quotation from Luria, A. R. (1968). *Mind of a mnemonist.* Copyright © 1968 by President and Fellows of Harvard College. Reprinted by permission of Harvard University Press. **p. 247, Table 7-2:** Baddeley, A. (1982). *Your memory: A user's guide,* 2nd edition. Copyright © 1982 by Multimedia Publications (UK) Ltd. Reprinted by permission of Simon and Schuster. **p. 252, Table 7-3:** Weaver, C. A., III (1995). The search for special mechanisms in memory: Flashbulbs, flashbacks, and other not-so-bright ideas. *False Memory Syndrome Newsletter, 4,* 16–22. Reprinted by permission of False Memory Snydrome Foundation. / **p. 262, Fig. 8-3:** Matlin, M. M. (1983). *Perception.* Reprinted by permission of Allyn & Bacon. **p. 264, Fig. 8-6:** Solso, R. (1988). *Cognitive psychology,* 424. Reprinted by permission of Allyn & Bacon. **p. 265, Table 8-1:** Reed, S. K. (1987). A structure-mapping model for word problems. *Journal of Experimental Psychology: Learning, Memory, and Cognition, 13,* 124–139. Copyright © 1987 by The American Psychological Association. Reprinted by permission of American Psy-

chological Association and the author. **p. 268, Fig. 8-8:** Sternberg, R. J., & Davidson, J. E. (1982). The mind of the puzzler. *Psychology Today* (June), 37–44. Copyright © 1982 (Sussex Publishers, Inc.). Reprinted with permission of Psychology Today Magazine. **p. 269, Fig. 8-9:** Adams, J. L. (1976). *Conceptual blockbusting: A pleasurable guide to better problem solving.* Reprinted by permission of Addison Wesley Longman. **p. 269:** quotation from Csikszentmihalyi, M. (1996). *Creativity: Flow and the psychology of discovery and invention,* 99. Reprinted by permission of HarperCollins Publishers. **p. 284, Fig. 8-13:** Lieberman, P. (1991). *Uniquely human: The evolution of speech, thought, and selfless behavior.* Copyright © 1991 by the President and Fellows of Harvard College. Reprinted by permission of Harvard University Press. / **p. 299, Table 9-1:** Frankenburg, W. K., Dodds, J., Archer, P., et al. (1990). *Denver II Training Manual,* 44–46. Reprinted by permission of Denver Developmental Materials, Inc. and the author. **p. 305, Fig. 9-3:** Baillargeon, R. (1994). How do infants learn about the physical world? *Current Directions in Psychological Science, 3*(5), 133–140. Reprinted by permission of Cambridge University Press. **p. 306, Fig. 9-4:** Piaget, J., & Inhelder, B. (1956). *The child's conception of space.* Reprinted by permission of Routledge & Kegan Paul International, Ltd. **p. 310, Fig. 9-7:** Kail, R. (1990). *The development of memory in children,* 76. Reprinted by permission of Lawrence Erlbaum Associates, Inc. **p. 311:** quotation from Goodall, J. (1987). *The Mind* (PBS TV series). Reprinted by permission of Dr. Jane Goodall, The Jane Goodall Institute. **pp. 312 & 316:** quotation from Pinker, S. (1994). *The language instinct: The new science of language and the mind,* 40 & 18. Reprinted by permission

of Penguin Putnam, Inc. **p. 319, Fig. 9-9:** Kail, R. (1990). *The development of memory in children,* 47. Reprinted by permission of Lawrence Erlbaum Associates, Inc. / **pp. 330, 331, 332:** quotation from Brazelton, T.B. (1983). *Infants and mothers: Differences in development,* 2nd edition, 14–15, 24–26, 22. Copyright © 1969, 1983 by T. Berry Brazelton, M.D. Used by permission of Delacorte Press / Seymour Lawrence, a division of Bantam Doubleday Dell Publishing Group, Inc. **p. 348:** quotation from Kohlberg, L. (1969). Stage & sequence: The cognitive-developmental approach to socialization. In D. A. Goslin (Ed.), *Handbook of socialization & research,* 347–480. Reprinted by permission of D. A. Goslin. **p. 350:** quotation from Selman, R. L., & Byrne, D. (1974). A structural-developmental analysis of levels of role-taking in middle childhood. *Child Development, 45,* 803–806. Reprinted by permission of the University of Michigan. **p. 354, Fig. 10-1:** Levinson, D. J., with Darrow, C. N., Klein, E. B., Levinson, M. H., & Mckee, B. (1978). *The seasons of a man's life.* Reprinted by permission of Alfred A. Knopf, Inc. **p. 356:** quotation from McCrae, R. R., & Costa, P. T., Jr. (1994). The stability of personality: Observations and evaluations. *Current Directions in Psychological Science, 3,* 173–175. Reprinted by permission of Cambridge University Press. / **pp. 383 & 385, Figs. 11-5 & 11-6:** Larsen, R. J., & Diener, E. (1992). Promises and problems with the circumplex model of emotion. *Review of Personality and Social Psychology, 13.* Reprinted by permission of Sage Publications and the author. **p. 391:** quotation from Smith, C. A., & Ellis, P. C. (1985). Patterns of cognitive appraisal in emotion. *Journal of Personality and Social Psychology, 48,* 813–838. Copyright © 1985 by The American Psychological

Association. Reprinted by permission of American Psychological Association and the author. / **Table 12-1:** Bray, G. A. (1992). Pathophysiology of obesity: Guidelines to interpret "The Body-Mass Index." *American Journal of Clinical Nutrition, 55,* 488–494. Reprinted by permission of American Society for Clinical Nutrition and the author. **p. 412, Table 12-4:** Holmes, T. H., & Rahe, R. H. (1967). The social readjustment scale. *Journal of Psychomatic Research, 11,* 213–218. Reprinted with permission of Elsevier Science Inc. / **p. 441:** quotation from Crews, F. (1996). The verdict on Freud. *Psychological Science, 7,* 63–68. Reprinted by permission of Cambridge University Press. **p. 446:** quotation from McCrae, R. R., & Costa, P. T., Jr. (1994). The stability of personality: Observations and evaluations. *Current Directions in Psychological Science, 3,* 173–175. Reprinted by permission of Cambridge University Press. **p. 452, Fig. 13-2:** Eysenck, H. J. (1970). *The structure of human personality.* Reprinted by permission of Curtis Brown Group Ltd. and Sybil Eysenck, University of London, Personality Investigations, Publications & Services. **p. 460:** quotation from Friedman, H. S., Hawley, P. H., & Tucker, J. S. (1994). Personality, health, and longevity. *Current Directions in Psychological Science, 3,* 37–41. Reprinted by permission of Cambridge University Press. **p. 454, Table 13-2:** Maslow, A. H. (1954). *Motivation and Personality.* Reprinted with permission of HarperCollins Publishers. / **p. 465:** quotation from Sternberg, R. J., & Wagner, R. K. (1993). The G-ocentric view of intelligence and job performance is wrong. *Current Directions in Psychological Science, 2,* 1–4. Reprinted by permission of Cambridge University Press. **p. 471, Fig. 14-1:** Carroll, J. B. (1993). *Human cognitive abilities.* Reprinted by permission of Cambridge University Press. **p. 476, Fig. 14-3:**

Wechsler, D. (1991). *Manual for the Wechsler Intelligence Scale for Children: Third Edition,* 55. Copyright © 1991, 1974, 1971 by The Psychological Corporation. Reprinted by permission. All rights reserved. "Wechsler Intelligence Scale for Children" and "WISC-III" are registered trademarks of The Psychological Corporation. **p. 480, Table 14-2:** Van Osdol, W. R., & Shane, D. G. (1977). *An introduction to exceptional children,* 68. Reprinted by permission of The McGraw-Hill Companies. **p. 484, Table 14-3:** Dahlstrom, Welsh, & Dahlstrom (1972). *An MMPI handbook, Vol. I: Clinical interpretation, a revised edition.* Reprinted by permission of University of Minnesota Press. **p. 491:** quotation from Green, B. F. (1992). Exposé or smear: The Burt affair. *Psychological Science, 3,* 328–331. Reprinted by permission of Cambridge University Press. **p. 492:** quotation from Gould, S. J. (1995). curve ball. In S. Fraser (Ed.), *The bell curve wars,* 11. Reprinted by permission of Basic Books, a division of HarperCollins Publishers. **p. 492:** quotation from Herrnstein, R. J., & Murray, C. (1994). *The bell curve: Intelligence and class struggle in American life.* Reprinted by permission of The Free Press, a division of Simon & Schuster. **p. 493:** quotation from Sternberg, R. J. (1995). For whom the bell tolls. *Psychological Science, 6,* 260–261. Reprinted by permission of Cambridge University Press. / **p. 504:** quotation from Hurley, A. D. (1976). Unsystematic desensitization using pleasurable images to inhibit anxiety. *Journal of Behavior Therapy and Experimental Psychiatry, 7(3),* 295. Reprinted by permission from Elsevier Science Ltd., The Boulevard, Landford Lane, Kidlington OX5 1GB, UK. **p. 506:** quotation from Hodgson, R., & Rachman, S. (1976). The modification of compulsive behavior. In H. J. Eysenck (Ed.), *Case studies in behaviour thera-*

py. Reprinted by permission of Routledge & Kegan Paul Ltd. **p. 506:** quotation from Haley, S. A. (1978). Treatment implications of post-combat stress response syndromes for mental health professionals. In C. F. Figley (Ed.), *Stress disorders among Vietnam veterans.* Reprinted by permission of Taylor & Francis Publishers, Brunner / Mazel Inc. **p. 511:** quotation from Educational Broadcasting Corporation (1976). Depression: The shadowed valley. In *The thin edge.* Copyright © 1975 by the Educational Broadcasting Corp. **p. 513, Table 15-2:** Shneidman, E. S. (1992). A conspectus of the suicidal scenario. In R. W. Maris et al. (Eds.), *Assessment and prediction of suicide,* 50–64. Published by The Guilford Press. Reprinted by permission of the author. **Pp. 517-518:** quotation from Zax, M., & Stricker, G. (1963). *Patterns of psychopathology.* Reprinted by permission of Prentice-Hall, Inc., a division of Simon & Schuster. **p. 523, Table 15-4:** Hooley, J. M. (1985). Expressed emotion: A review of the critical literature. *Annual Review of Psychology, 5,* 119–139. Reprinted by permission. **p. 525, Table 15-5:** Alloy, L. B., Acocella, J., & Bootzin, R. (1996). *Abnormal psychology: Current perspectives.* Reprinted by permission of The McGraw-Hill Companies. / **pp. 534–536:** Vitkus, J. (1996). *Casebook in abnormal psychology,* 69–84. Reprinted by permission of The McGraw-Hill Companies. **p. 539:** quotation from Lindner, R. (1954). *The fifty-minute hour,* 93–95. Reprinted by permission of Harcourt Brace & Company. **pp. 541–543:** quotation from Phares, E. J. (1979). *Clinical psychology: Concepts, methods, and profession.* Copyright © 1992, 1988, 1984, 1979 The Dorsey Press. Reprinted by permission of Brooks / Cole Publishing Company, Pacific Grove, CA 93950, a division of International Thomson Publishing Co. **p. 547, Table 16-2:** Bootzin,

R. R., Epstein, D., & Wood, J. M. (1991). Stimulus control instructions. In P. Hauri (Ed.), *Case studies in insomnia*. Reprinted by permission of Plenum Publishing Corporation and author. **p. 550:** Beck, A. T. (1976). *Cognitive therapy and the emotional disorders*. Reprinted by permission of International Universities Press. / **p. 580, Fig. 17-1:** Luchins, A. S. (1957). Primacy-recency in impression formation. In C. I. Hovland (Ed.), *The order of presentation in persuasion*, 33–61. Reprinted by permission of Yale University Press. **p. 585, Fig. 17-2:** Fiske, S. T., & Taylor, S. E. (1984). *Social cognition*. Reprinted by permission of The McGraw-Hill Companies. **p. 599, Fig. 17-4:** Shaver, P., Hazan, C., & Bradshaw, D. (1988). Love as attachment. In R. J. Sternberg & M. L. Barnes (Eds.), *The psychology of love*. Reprinted by permission of Yale University Press. / **p. 605, Fig. 18-1:** Asch, S. E. (1951). Effects of group pressure upon the modification and distortion of judgments. In H. S. Guetzkow (Ed.), *Groups, leadership, and man: Research in human relations*. Published by Carnegie Mellon University Press, Pittsburgh. **pp. 609 & 610:** quotation and **Fig. 18-2** from Milgram, S. (1963). Behavioral study of obedience. *Journal of Abnormal and Social Psychology, 67,* 371–378. Reprinted by permission of Mrs. Alexandra Milgram. **p. 611, Fig. 18-3:** Milgram, S. (1974). *Obedience to authority*. New York: Harper & Row. Reprinted by permission of Mrs. Alexandra Milgram. **p. 628:** quotation from Koss, M. P., Gidycz, C. A., & Wisniewski, H. (1987). The scope of rape: incidence and prevalence of sexual aggression and victimization in a national sample of higher education students. *Journal of Consulting and Clinical Psychology, 55,* 162–170. Copyright © 1987 by The American Psychological Association. Reprinted by permission of American Psychological Association and the author.

NAME INDEX

SUBJECT INDEX